Fundamentals of Pharmaceutical and Biologics Regulations
Volume I

Foreword

Fundamentals of Pharmaceutical and Biologics Regulations is a compilation of history, pharmaceutical and biologics information from RAPS' regional publications:

- Fundamentals of US Regulatory Affairs, 11th Edition
- Fundamentals of Canadian Pharmaceutical and Biologics Regulations
- Fundamentals of EU Regulatory Affairs, Eighth Edition
- Fundamentals of International Regulatory Affairs, Fourth Edition

With each section written by regulatory professionals, for regulatory professionals, this book is an outstanding reference for individuals working in multinational pharmaceutical and biologics product development and marketing at all levels—from seasoned regulatory personnel who need to check facts or are dealing with a new product type to those new to the profession. It also provides a basis for those working in another field to gain an understanding of biopharmaceutical products and is ideal for students and academicians.

Fundamentals of Pharmaceutical and Biologics Regulations is a handy preparatory tool, along with professional experience, training and other resources, for those planning to sit for the Regulatory Affairs Certification (RAC) Drugs exam.

Pamela A. Jones
Senior Editor
Regulatory Affairs Professionals Society

Table of Contents

SECTION I: Fundamentals of US Pharmaceutical and Biologics Regulations

Chapter 1   History of Food, Drug and Cosmetic Laws 1
Updated by Meredith Brown-Tuttle, RAC, FRAPS

Chapter 2   Overview of Drug, Biologic, Device, Combination Product or Food Regulatory Pathways 13
Updated by Michael R. Hamrell, PhD, RQAP-GCP, CCRA, FACRP, RAC, FRAPS

Chapter 3   Clinical Trials: GCPs, Regulations and Compliance for Drugs, Biologics and Medical Devices 45
Updated by Monique Carter, MS, RAC and Samantha Zappia, MS, RAC

Chapter 4   Current Good Manufacturing Practices and Quality System Design 83
Updated by Joscelyn Bowersock, MS-RA, and Richard Vincins, CQP, MCQL, CBA, CQA, RAC

Chapter 5   Prescription Product Drug Submissions 99
By Shyamala Jayaraman, PhD, Lean Six Sigma Black Belt and Glen D. Park, PharmD, MSJ

Chapter 6   Postapproval Submissions and Compliance: Prescription Drugs and Biologics 121
Updated by Emily Rapp, RAC and Dar Rosario, MBA, RAC

Chapter 7   Generic Drug Submissions 141
Updated by Amrita Ghosh, RAC and Sharry Arora, MPharm

Chapter 8   Patents and Exclusivity 153
Updated by Kurt R. Karst, JD

Chapter 9   Over-the-Counter (Nonprescription) Drug Products 167
Updated by Valerie Ramsey, DRSc, MS, RAC

Chapter 10   Prescription Drug Labeling, Advertising and Promotion 177
Updated by Anu Gaur, PhD, MBA, MSRA, RAC

Chapter 11   Pharmacovigilance and Risk Management 191
Updated by Stacy Woeppel, MBA and Robert Falcone, PhD

Chapter 12   Biologics Submissions 205
Updated by Jocelyn Jennings, MS, RAC

Chapter 13   Biologics Compliance 233
Updated by Anne Marie Woodland, MS, RAC

Chapter 14   Biosimilars 245
Updated by Nathalie Innocent, MS, RAC and Jennifer Wilhelm, MSc, MBA, RAC

Chapter 15   Biologics Labeling, Advertising and Promotion 267
By Kathrin Schalper, PhD, RAC

Appendices

Glossary of Terms 279
Index of Laws and Guidances 303
Index by Subject 307

Figures

Figure 2-1.	Decision Tree for Drug and Device Development and Approval When FDA Premarket Review is Required	21
Figure 2-2.	CTD Organization	27
Figure 3-1.	Types of Pharmaceutical and Biologic Clinical Trials and Typical Pathway	54
Figure 3-2.	Types of Medical Device Clinical Trials and Typical Pathway	67
Figure 4-1.	Quality System Documentation Elements	85
Figure 4-2.	Design Control "V" Model Process Flow	86
Figure 5-1.	FDA IND Review Process	105
Figure 5-2.	Diagram of the ICH Common Technical Document (CTD)	111
Figure 5-3.	Timeline and Product Review Clock	114
Figure 6-1.	Summery of Reporting Categories for Postapproval Changes	126
Figure 6-2.	Example of a CMC Index	132
Figure 9-1.	Example of an OTC Drug Facts Label	174
Figure 14-1.	Number of Biosimilar INDs Received by CDER by Fiscal Yeara	249
Figure 14-2.	Number of Biosimilar Type 1–4 Meetings Held by CDER by Fiscal Yeara	249

Tables

Table 1-1.	Electronic Resources for US Laws and Regulations	3
Table 1-2.	Other Laws, Regulations and Guidelines	10
Table 2-1.	Title 21 CFR Parts	20
Table 2-2.	Key Questions in a Drug Development Program	23
Table 2-3.	IND Safety Reporting Timeframes	29
Table 2-4.	Summary of Device Classification System	36
Table 3-1.	Significant Legislation Relevant to Clinical Trials in the US	48
Table 3-2.	Comparison of 21 CFR and ISO-GCP Requirements for Protocol Deviations in Medical Device Clinical Trials	52
Table 3-3.	Comparison of 21 CFR and ISO GCP Requirements for Investigator Responsibilities in Medical Device Clinical Trials	73
Table 3-4.	Comparison of 21 CFR and ISO-GCP Requirements for Recordkeeping in Medical Device Clinical Trials	74
Table 3-5.	Comparison of 21 CFR and ISO-GCP Requirements for Device Accountability in Medical Device Clinical Trials	75
Table 8-1.	180-Day Exclusivity Forfeiture Snapshot	161
Table 8-2.	Differences Among Applications Submitted and Approved Under FD&C Act Section 505	162
Table 9-1.	OTC Monograph Therapeutic Category Subtopics Evaluated as Part of the OTC Review Process	170
Table 9-2.	Acne Drug Products: Benzoyl Peroxide	171
Table 9-3.	NDA vs. OTC Drug Monograph	172
Table 10-1.	PLR Format, Associated Regulations and Guidance Documents	182
Table 10-1.	PLR Format, Associated Regulations and Guidance Documents (cont'd.)	183
Table 11-1.	Safety Reporting Requirements for Drugs/Biologics	200
Table 11-2.	Safety Reporting Requirements for Medical Devices	201
Table 12-1.	Key Milestones in the Regulatory Oversight of Biologics	209
Table 12-2.	Applications Regulated by PHS Act	210
Table 12-3.	Applications Regulated by the FD&C Act	211
Table 12-4.	Biologics Controlled by CDER and CBER	212
Table 12-5.	Submissions With Specific Regulatory Mandated Timelines (e.g., SPAs) or FDA Established Timelines (e.g., Reviews of Proposed Pediatric Study Requests)	214
Table 12-6.	Safety-Related Submissions	216
Table 12-7.	IND Drug Development Submissions	218
Table 12-7.	IND Drug Development Submissions (cont'd.)	219
Table 12-8.	Other Submission Types	220
Table 12-9.	Key CMC Guidance for Biological Product Development	222
Table 12-9.	Key CMC Guidance for Biological Product Development (cont'd.)	223
Table 12-10.	NDA/BLA Standard and Priority Review Process (PDUFA VI)	226
Table 14-1.	BsUFA Fees Financial Year 2019a	248
Table 14-2.	Meetings Between FDA and Biosimilar Biological Product Sponsors	250
Table 14-3.	Comparison of Development Programs Between Chemical Drugs and Biological Products	254
Table 14-4.	FDA-Approved Biosimilars	259

SECTION II: Fundamentals of Canadian Pharmaceutical and Biologics Regulations

Chapter 1   Health Canada Organization and Its History of Regulating Health Products in Canada 1
Updated by Hetal Mokashi, MBA and Penny Wilks, ND, RAC

Chapter 2   Good Laboratory Practice for Nonclinical Laboratory Studies 11
Updated by Navneet Sekhon

Chapter 3   Clinical Trial Applications, Good Clinical Practices 19
By Mahdis Dorkalam, MSc, RHN, and Navneet Sekhon

Chapter 4   Good Manufacturing Practices and Establishment Licensing in Canada 29
By Bocar Guisse, MSc and Fraidianie Sévigné

Chapter 5   New Drug Submission Process 45
Updated by Susanne Picard and Janice Weiler

Chapter 6   Postmarketing and Other Activities 59
Updated by Janice Weiler and Danny Germain, RAC

Chapter 7   Health Product Vigilance and Risk Management 69
Updated by Christopher Antonio, Roshni Celeste, Jenna Griffiths, Carole Légaré, Marc Poitras, Tanya Ramsamy, Thanh Vu, Bruce Wozny and Raymond Yang

Chapter 8   An Overview of Pharmaceutical Intellectual Property Protection in Canada 79
By Junyi Chen, JD, PhD, Danny Germain, RAC, Gordon Jepson, MA, LLB, and Bhavesh Patel, CChem

Chapter 9   Abbreviated New Drug Submissions 95
Updated by Bhavesh Patel, CChem, Bocar Guisse, MSc and Fraidianie Sevigne

Chapter 10 Nonprescription Drugs 105
Updated by Kristin Willemsen

Chapter 11 Biologics Submission, Approval and Postmarketing 115
Updated by Marcia Sam and Mahdis Dorkalam, MSc, RHN

Chapter 12 Labelling, Advertising and Promotion: Prescription Pharmaceutical Drugs, Biologics and Radiopharmaceuticals 127
Updated by Marcia Sam, Veronica Yip and Sandra Alderdice

Chapter 13 electronic Common Technical Document (eCTD) 133
By Khaled Yahiaoui, MSc, RAC

Chapter 14 Product Lifecycle Management Guidance 143
by Ajay Babu Pazhayattil, Naheed Sayeed-Desta and Queenia Lee

Index 149

Figures

Figure 1-1.	Health Canada	2
Figure 1-2.	Branches with Responsibility for the Regulation of Healthcare Products	3
Figure 5-1.	Diagram of the NDS Submission and Approval Procedure	51
Figure 5-2.	Example Boxed Text for Product Approved Under the NOC/c Policy	52
Figure 6-1.	Form IV Patent List	64
Figure 13-1.	Structure of a Regulatory Transaction in eCTD Format	135
Figure 13-2.	End-to-End Process for Preparing and Filing Regulatory Transactions in eCTD Format	141

Tables

Table 1-1.	Timeline—Regulating Health Products in Canada	6
Table 2-1.	Examples of Studies and the Requirement for GLP Compliance	14
Table 3-1.	Contents of a CTA Submission Package	22
Table 3-2.	Quality Changes—Biologics and Radiopharmaceuticals	24
Table 3-3.	Quality Changes—Pharmaceuticals	25
Table 3-4.	Postapproval Requirements	27
Table 4-1.	Definitions for Terms in This Chapter	30
Table 4-2.	GMP Regulations Applicable to Licensable Activities	33
Table 5-1.	Presentation of Information in the Common Technical Document (CTD) Format	49
Table 5-2.	Target Review Times	53
Table 7-1.	Clinical Trial Definitions	71
Table 7-2.	Postapproval Stage Definitions	74
Table 9-1.	Target Review Times	102
Table 10-1.	NAPRA Scheduling Factors	110
Table 11-1.	Drug Substance (Biologics and Radiopharmaceuticals)	118
Table 11-2.	Drug Product (Biologics and Radiopharmaceuticals)	119
Table 11-3.	Sample Table of Contents for a Schedule D (Biological) Product Monograph (PM)	120
Table 11-4.	Summary of Requirements for Evaluation Groups	123
Table 13-1.	Localization of Main XML Files Within an eCTD Sequence	136
Table 13-2.	Canadian eCTD Envelope Elements	136
Table 13-3.	m2-m5 eCTD Attributes	137
Table 13-4.	Validation Rule Samples and Their Descriptions and Severities	137
Table 13-5.	Document Formats Health Canada Expects for Specific Documents	138
Table 13-6.	Lifecycle Management Table Template	138
Table 13-7.	Lifecycle Management Table Example with Three Regulatory Activities and Related Regulatory Transactions	139
Table 13-8.	Lifecycle Management of Specific Documents	140

SECTION III: Fundamentals of EU Pharmaceutical and Biologics Regulations

See Volume II of *Fundamentals of Pharmaceutical and Biologics Regulations*

SECTION IV: Fundamentals of International Pharmaceutical and Biologics Regulations

See Volume II of *Fundamentals of Pharmaceutical and Biologics Regulations*

SECTION I
Fundamentals of US Pharmaceutical and Biologics Regulations

Copyright © 2019 by the Regulatory Affairs Professionals Society.
All rights reserved.

ISBN: 978-1-947493-36-0
Every precaution is taken to ensure accuracy of content; however, the publisher cannot accept responsibility for the correctness of the information supplied.

RAPS Global Headquarters
5635 Fishers Lane
Suite 400
Rockville, MD 20852
USA

RAPS.org

Acknowledgements

The Regulatory Affairs Professionals Society thanks the following individuals for sharing their expertise with their colleagues.

Sharry Arora, MPharm
Regulatory Affairs Manager
Novartis

Jennifer G. Brown PhD, RAC
Associate Director, Toxicology
MacroGenics Inc.

Meredith Brown-Tuttle, RAC, FRAPS
CEO, Principal Consultant
Regulatorium

Joscelyn Bowersock, MS-RA
Quality and Regulatory Manager
Carolina BioOncology Institute

Monique Carter, MS, RAC
Director, Global Regulatory Affairs—Internal Medicine
Pfizer Inc.

Robert Falcone, PhD
US Regulatory Affairs Director
HRA-Pharma

Anu Gaur, PhD, MBA, MSRA, RAC
Adjunct Faculty
Regulatory Affairs Graduate Program
College of Professional Studies (CPS)
Northeastern University

Amrita Ghosh RAC
Regulatory Affairs Specialist

Michael R. Hamrell, PhD, RQAP-GCP, CCRA, FACRP, RAC, FRAPS
President
MORIAH Consultants

Nathalie Innocent, MS, RAC
Manager Regulatory Affairs
Pfizer

Shyamala C. Jayaraman, PhD, Lean Six Sigma Black Belt
Senior Director, Regulatory Affairs, CMC
AbbVie

Jocelyn Jennings, MS, RAC
Deputy Director, Regulatory Coordination
Grifols Therapeutics LLC

Kurt R. Karst, JD
Director
Hyman, Phelps & McNamara, PC

Thomas McNamara, MSE, RAC
Senior Sustaining Engineer
Exactech

Glen D. Park, PharmD, MSJ
Executive Director, Regulatory Affairs and Quality Assurance
SCYNEXIS Inc.

Valerie Ramsey, DRSc, MS, RAC
Director, Regulatory Affairs and Quality Assurance
Dr. Brandt Skincare/Cosmetic Dermatology LLC

Emily Rapp, RAC
Senior CMC Scientist
Cardinal Health Regulatory Sciences

Dar Rosario, MBA, RAC
Principal
Velocity Consulting

Kathrin Schalper, PhD, RAC
Strategic Development Advisor
Halloran Consulting Group Inc.

Kurt M. Stahl
Toxicologist
MacroGenics Inc.

Richard A. Vincins, CQP MCQI, CBA, CQA, RAC
VP Global Regulatory Affairs
Oriel STAT A MATRIX

Jennifer (JJ) Wilhelm, MSc, MBA, RAC
Associate Director, Regulatory Affairs
Merck Canada

Stacy Woeppel, MBA
Director, Global Regulatory Lead
Mallinckrodt Pharmaceuticals

Anne Marie Woodland, MS, RAC
SVP, Regulatory Affairs and Quality Assurance
Replimune Group Inc.

Samantha K. Zappia, MS, RAC (US)
Principal Consultant
SK Regulatory Solutions, LLC

Section I
Table of Contents

Chapter 1	History of Food, Drug and Cosmetic Laws 1	
	Updated by Meredith Brown-Tuttle, RAC, FRAPS	
Chapter 2	Overview of Drug, Biologic, Device, Combination Product or Food Regulatory Pathways 13	
	Updated by Michael R. Hamrell, PhD, RQAP-GCP, CCRA, FACRP, RAC, FRAPS	
Chapter 3	Clinical Trials: GCPs, Regulations and Compliance for Drugs, Biologics and Medical Devices 45	
	Updated by Monique Carter, MS, RAC and Samantha Zappia, MS, RAC	
Chapter 4	Current Good Manufacturing Practices and Quality System Design 83	
	Updated by Joscelyn Bowersock, MS-RA, and Richard Vincins, CQP, MCQL, CBA, CQA, RAC	
Chapter 5	Prescription Product Drug Submissions 99	
	By Shyamala Jayaraman, PhD, Lean Six Sigma Black Belt and Glen D. Park, PharmD, MSJ	
Chapter 6	Postapproval Submissions and Compliance: Prescription Drugs and Biologics 121	
	Updated by Emily Rapp, RAC and Dar Rosario, MBA, RAC	
Chapter 7	Generic Drug Submissions 141	
	Updated by Amrita Ghosh, RAC and Sharry Arora, MPharm	
Chapter 8	Patents and Exclusivity 153	
	Updated by Kurt R. Karst, JD	
Chapter 9	Over-the-Counter (Nonprescription) Drug Products 167	
	Updated by Valerie Ramsey, DRSc, MS, RAC	
Chapter 10	Prescription Drug Labeling, Advertising and Promotion 177	
	Updated by Anu Gaur, PhD, MBA, MSRA, RAC	
Chapter 11	Pharmacovigilance and Risk Management 191	
	Updated by Stacy Woeppel, MBA and Robert Falcone, PhD	
Chapter 12	Biologics Submissions 205	
	Updated by Jocelyn Jennings, MS, RAC	
Chapter 13	Biologics Compliance 233	
	Updated by Anne Marie Woodland, MS, RAC	
Chapter 14	Biosimilars 245	
	Updated by Nathalie Innocent, MS, RAC and Jennifer Wilhelm, MSc, MBA, RAC	
Chapter 15	Biologics Labeling, Advertising and Promotion 267	
	By Kathrin Schalper, PhD, RAC	

Appendices

Glossary of Terms 279
Index of Laws and Guidances 303
Index by Subject 307

Figures

Figure 2-1.	Decision Tree for Drug and Device Development and Approval When FDA Premarket Review is Required	21
Figure 2-2.	CTD Organization	27
Figure 3-1.	Types of Pharmaceutical and Biologic Clinical Trials and Typical Pathway	54
Figure 3-2.	Types of Medical Device Clinical Trials and Typical Pathway	67
Figure 4-1.	Quality System Documentation Elements	85
Figure 4-2.	Design Control "V" Model Process Flow	86
Figure 5-1.	FDA IND Review Process	105
Figure 5-2.	Diagram of the ICH Common Technical Document (CTD)	111
Figure 5-3.	Timeline and Product Review Clock	114
Figure 6-1.	Summery of Reporting Categories for Postapproval Changes	126
Figure 6-2.	Example of a CMC Index	132
Figure 9-1.	Example of an OTC Drug Facts Label	174
Figure 14-1.	Number of Biosimilar INDs Received by CDER by Fiscal Yeara	249
Figure 14-2.	Number of Biosimilar Type 1–4 Meetings Held by CDER by Fiscal Yeara	249

Tables

Table 1-1.	Electronic Resources for US Laws and Regulations	3
Table 1-2.	Other Laws, Regulations and Guidelines	10
Table 2-1.	Title 21 CFR Parts	20
Table 2-2.	Key Questions in a Drug Development Program	23
Table 2-3.	IND Safety Reporting Timeframes	29
Table 2-4.	Summary of Device Classification System	36
Table 3-1.	Significant Legislation Relevant to Clinical Trials in the US	48
Table 3-2.	Comparison of 21 CFR and ISO-GCP Requirements for Protocol Deviations in Medical Device Clinical Trials	52
Table 3-3.	Comparison of 21 CFR and ISO GCP Requirements for Investigator Responsibilities in Medical Device Clinical Trials	73
Table 3-4.	Comparison of 21 CFR and ISO-GCP Requirements for Recordkeeping in Medical Device Clinical Trials	74
Table 3-5.	Comparison of 21 CFR and ISO-GCP Requirements for Device Accountability in Medical Device Clinical Trials	75
Table 8-1.	180-Day Exclusivity Forfeiture Snapshot	161
Table 8-2.	Differences Among Applications Submitted and Approved Under FD&C Act Section 505	162
Table 9-1.	OTC Monograph Therapeutic Category Subtopics Evaluated as Part of the OTC Review Process	170
Table 9-2.	Acne Drug Products: Benzoyl Peroxide	171
Table 9-3.	NDA vs. OTC Drug Monograph	172
Table 10-1.	PLR Format, Associated Regulations and Guidance Documents	182
Table 10-1.	PLR Format, Associated Regulations and Guidance Documents (cont'd.)	183
Table 11-1.	Safety Reporting Requirements for Drugs/Biologics	200
Table 11-2.	Safety Reporting Requirements for Medical Devices	201
Table 12-1.	Key Milestones in the Regulatory Oversight of Biologics	209
Table 12-2.	Applications Regulated by PHS Act	210
Table 12-3.	Applications Regulated by the FD&C Act	211
Table 12-4.	Biologics Controlled by CDER and CBER	212
Table 12-5.	Submissions With Specific Regulatory Mandated Timelines (e.g., SPAs) or FDA Established Timelines (e.g., Reviews of Proposed Pediatric Study Requests)	214
Table 12-6.	Safety-Related Submissions	216
Table 12-7.	IND Drug Development Submissions	218
Table 12-7.	IND Drug Development Submissions (cont'd.)	219
Table 12-8.	Other Submission Types	220
Table 12-9.	Key CMC Guidance for Biological Product Development	222
Table 12-9.	Key CMC Guidance for Biological Product Development (cont'd.)	223
Table 12-10.	NDA/BLA Standard and Priority Review Process (PDUFA VI)	226
Table 14-1.	BsUFA Fees Financial Year 2019a	248
Table 14-2.	Meetings Between FDA and Biosimilar Biological Product Sponsors	250
Table 14-3.	Comparison of Development Programs Between Chemical Drugs and Biological Products	254
Table 14-4.	FDA-Approved Biosimilars	259

Chapter 1

History of Food, Drug and Cosmetic Laws

Updated by Meredith Brown-Tuttle, RAC, FRAPS

OBJECTIVES

- Review differences between laws, regulations, guidance documents and other legal instruments affecting food, drugs and devices.

- Provide document reference resources.

- Provide an overview of laws, regulations and regulatory agencies governing food and medical products marketed in the US.

- Discuss the historical context in which those laws and regulations were developed and enacted.

LAWS, REGULATIONS AND GUIDELINES COVERED IN THIS CHAPTER

- *Pure Food and Drug Act* of 1906

- *Federal Food, Drug, and Cosmetic Act* of 1938

- *Durham-Humphrey Amendment* of 1951

- *Color Additive Amendment* of 1960

- *Kefauver-Harris Amendments* of 1962

- *Drug Price Competition and Patent Term Restoration Act* of 1984 (*Hatch-Waxman Act*)

- *Medical Device Amendments* of 1976

- *Safe Medical Devices Act* of 1990

- *Orphan Drug Act* of 1983

- *Medical Devices Amendments* of 1992

- *Prescription Drug User Fee Act* of 1992

- *Food and Drug Administration Modernization Act* of 1997

- *Medical Device User Fee and Modernization Act* of 2002

- *Food and Drug Administration Amendments Act* of 2007

- *Food Safety Modernization Act* of 2011

- *Food and Drug Administration Safety and Innovation Act* of 2012

- *Drug Quality and Security Act* of 2013

- *Improving Regulatory Transparency for New Medical Therapies Act* of 2015

- *21st Century Cures Act* of 2016

- *Right to Try Act* of 2018

Regulatory Affairs Professionals Society

Introduction

To understand US governance of food and medical products, it is important to have some knowledge of the legal instruments impacting drug law, the manner in which drug regulation is developed and the historical context in which food and drug laws have been established. Shifts in the food and drug regulatory paradigm often are reactions to shifts in political philosophies, economic concerns and significant public health events. This chapter discusses the US legislative and regulatory process and introduces resources that can be used to reference legal instruments. It also describes events that led to the introduction of new laws, and subsequent changes, affecting food and medical product governance.

Laws, Regulations and Guidance

This Constitution, and the Laws of the United States which shall be made in Pursuance thereof; and all Treaties made, or which shall be made, under the Authority of the United States, shall be the supreme Law of the Land; and the Judges in every State shall be bound thereby, any Thing in the Constitution or Laws of any State to the Contrary notwithstanding—Article VI, Clause 2 of Constitution of the United States

Article VI, Clause 2 of the US Constitution, commonly known as the Supremacy Clause, declares the Constitution, laws made under the Constitution and treaties made under US authority constitute the supreme law of the land. Further, the Constitution delegates power to the federal government's legislative, executive and judicial branches. Together, the three branches respectively make, execute and evaluate laws that guide regulations for products under the US Food and Drug Administration's (FDA's) jurisdiction.

The Legislative Branch

Article I of the US Constitution grants all legislative powers to a bicameral Congress consisting of the House of Representatives and the Senate. Congress uses its authority to regulate interstate commerce and to legislate federal statutes on food and drugs. A federal statute begins as a bill or a joint resolution introduced by either chamber of Congress. Once a member or members of Congress introduce a bill, it undergoes scrutiny in subject matter committees and may undergo discussion at public hearings. Bills are subject to House and Senate votes. When a bill is approved and agreed to in identical forms by both chambers, it is presented to the president. If the president signs or does not veto the bill, it is enacted and assigned a public or private law number.[1] An enacted law is known as a *statute*.

A public law affects society as a whole; food and drugs are under the purview of public laws, e.g., the *Food, Drug, and Cosmetic Act* (*FD&C Act*). In contrast, a private law affects an individual or a small group. Public or private law numbers consist of two parts: the number of the Congress, and a number indicating the sequential order of the enacted law for that Congress. For example, the first public law (*TALENT Act* of 2017) of the 115th Congress is designated Public Law 115–1; the first private law of the 115th Congress to be enacted would be designated Private Law 115–1.

The first official publication of a statute is in the form of a "slip law." Slip laws are published separately as an unbound pamphlet and are available for reference on the official website for US federal legislative information (**Table 1-1**, Resource 1). The Office of the Federal Register, National Archives and Records Administration (NARA), prepares slip laws and adds marginal notes with explanatory information. The slip laws are compiled into a sequential volume of *United States Statutes at Large*, forming a permanent collection of all laws (and resolutions) enacted during each session of Congress. For example, the volume containing the laws from the first session of the 111th Congress is numbered 123 and contains Public Laws 111-1 to 111-137; and sequentially, the volume containing the laws from the second session of the 111th Congress is numbered 124. Statutes are referenced by the volume and page number; Public Law 111-1 is on page 3 of the 123rd volume and referenced as 123 Stat. 3. Volumes of the *United States Statutes at Large*, also prepared by the Office of the Federal Register, are available for reference on the website of the Government Publishing Office (**Table 1-1**, Resource 2).[2]

Statutes are published or "codified" in the *United States Code (U.S.C.)*, where they are organized by subject under 54 title headings. For example, Title 21 is comprised of many individual federal statutes on food and drugs. The *FD&C Act* is found in Sections 321 to 399h of Title 21. Reference to the code includes the title and the section, e.g., 21 U.S.C. 321. The code is prepared by the Law Revision Council of the House of Representatives and can be accessed in electronic format (**Table 1-1**, Resource 3). Each code section references the codified organic laws or statutes. Similarly, marginal notes in slip laws provide information on related code sections.[3]

The Executive Branch

The Constitution vests the power to execute the laws enacted by Congress in the president. The president is the administrative head of the executive branch, which includes 15 executive departments, independent establishments and government corporations. Under the executive branch, the mission to protect public health by ensuring the safety of food supply, drugs and cosmetics is assigned

History of Food, Drug and Cosmetic Laws

Table 1-1. Electronic Resources for US Laws and Regulations

	Resource	Website	Applicable Years
1	Slip Law: 　Public 　Private	www.congress.gov/public-laws/ www.congress.gov/private-laws/	1973 to Current 1973 to Current
2	Statutes at Large	www.gpo.gov/fdsys/browse/collection.action?collectionCode=STATUTE www.loc.gov/law/help/statutes-at-large/	1951 to 2012 1789 to 2011
3	US Code	http://uscode.house.gov/	1994 to Current
4	Comment on Regulations	www.regulations.gov	All
5	Unified Agenda	https://www.gsa.gov/policy-regulations/policy/federal-regulation-policy/unified-agenda-of-federal-regulatory-and-deregulatory-actions	1995 to 2016
6	*Federal Register*	www.federalregister.gov	1994 to Current
7	Code of Federal Regulations: 　Official 　Unofficial	www.gpo.gov/fdsys/browse/collectionCfr.action?collectionCode=CFR www.ecfr.gov	1996 to Current 2015 to Current
8	FDA Guidance Documents	www.fda.gov/RegulatoryInformation/Guidances/	All
9	Court Opinions	https://www.supremecourt.gov/opinions/opinions.aspx	1991 to 2018

to FDA, an agency within the Department of Health and Human Services (HHS).[4]

Executive agencies, such as FDA, are charged with implementing statutes through regulations. Regulations interpret laws and describe how they will be enforced. The process by which FDA proposes and establishes regulations is called rulemaking, governed by the *Administrative Procedure Act* of 1946 (*APA*, 60 Stat. 237). *APA* requires agencies to keep the public informed and gives the public the right to participate in the rulemaking process by commenting on proposed regulations (**Table 1-1**, Resource 4). The public's rights were extended further via procedural rules establishing a 60-day minimum public comment period for significant regulations. The enactment of the *Government in the Sunshine Act* of 1976 required advance notice of rulemaking meetings and that those meetings be open to the public. A regulatory agenda, known as the Unified Agenda, is published semi-annually and summarizes each agency's planned rulemaking activities for the following six months (**Table 1-1**, Resource 5).

New regulations or changes to existing regulations are announced in the *Federal Register* (**Table 1-1**, Resource 6). Register publications are referenced by the volume and the page number, e.g., 82 FR 9501. Similar to the US Code's codification of statutes, regulations published in the *Federal Register* periodically are presented in a compact, practical publication called the Code of Federal Regulations (CFR, **Table 1-1**, Resource 7). The CFR is organized into 50 titles that represent broad areas subject to federal regulation. Regulations for food and drugs are found in CFR Title 21. The CFR may be cited by title and section. For example, "21 CFR 10.3" refers to Title 21, Code of Federal Regulations, Part 10, Section 3.

In addition to regulations, administrative agencies may issue guidance. Guidance documents may be used to convey FDA's "current thinking" or enforcement priorities to establish regulatory principles or practices aligned with that thinking. Guidance does not have the force of law and is not legally binding. FDA follows the procedures required by its "Good Guidance Practices" regulation (21 CFR 10.115) to issue guidance. Guidance documents may be referenced on the FDA website (**Table 1-1**, Resource 8).

FDA continuously adjusts to the challenges of regulating products in a global economy. International laws and agreements play an increasing role in its activities to support its public health mission. Important international legal instruments include treaties and trade agreements. A *treaty* is a written agreement between sovereign states (or other international bodies) dictating terms binding the parties to the agreement and becoming international law once the agreement is signed and ratified. A *trade agreement* establishes terms between parties regarding tariffs and trade restrictions. The president has the authority to make treaties with other countries, with the Senate's concurrence. FDA, under the president's authority, monitors and negotiates international agreements, including inter-governmental agreements, some of which affect how the agency regulates products.

The Judicial Branch

US judicial power is vested in the Supreme Court, the intermediate Courts of Appeals (also known as circuit

Regulatory Affairs Professionals Society

courts or appellate courts) and the District Courts. Any law or regulation must withstand constitutional scrutiny.[5] The judicial branch decides the constitutionality of federal laws and reviews and enforces orders of many federal administrative bodies. Judiciary decisions set precedents that influence food and drug laws and regulations. Law based on these judicial opinions is known as case law, as opposed to legislative law based on statutes. *United States Reports* is the official record of the proceedings of the Supreme Court and is accessible from the court website (**Table 1-1**, Resource 9). A case in *US Reports* may be cited by the volume and page number. For example, 529 U.S. 61 references page 61 of volume 529.

During the past 100 years, judicial opinions significantly influenced food and drug regulations. Decisions on the executive authority to regulate false therapeutic claims, chemicals in the food supply, labeling, ability to prosecute responsible individuals of a corporation, drug efficacy and even the scope of what is considered a drug or device are some examples of the courts' influence on regulation.

The Supreme Court's decision on FDA's authority to regulate tobacco is one such example. In 1996, FDA issued a final rule that prohibited nicotine-containing cigarette and smokeless tobacco product sales to children and adolescents (61 FR 44396). FDA considered nicotine a drug, and cigarettes and smokeless tobacco were considered devices to deliver nicotine to the body (61 FR 44619). This was challenged in the District Court, the Court of Appeals and, ultimately, the Supreme Court. In *FDA v. Brown & Williamson Tobacco Corp.* (529 U.S. 120), the Supreme Court ruled Congress had not granted FDA authority to regulate tobacco products. In response, Congress enacted the *Family Smoking Prevention and Tobacco Control Act* (123 Stat. 1776), which established the Center for Tobacco Products within FDA and provided authority to regulate tobacco products' manufacture, distribution and marketing. The example of tobacco regulations demonstrates how judicial opinions have shaped food and drug regulations.

Understanding the Impact of Laws and Regulations on Food and Drugs

Interaction among the legislative, executive and judicial branches influences food and drug legislation. To demonstrate this influence, laws described in this chapter include a reference to the organic statute or US Code. Current regulations derived on the authority of the law also are referenced where relevant.

Early Food and Drug Legislation

The history of modern food and drug law began in the 20th century. During the 1800s, food and drugs were largely unregulated due to concerns about government interference with free market trade and the inability of individual states to control sales of products manufactured in other states. This lack of regulation led to the use of food preservation ingredients with toxic or unknown safety profiles, and also to unsanitary conditions in large-scale food processing plants. Public exposure of these conditions resulted in widespread outrage and a demand for legislation. In response to the demand, Congress passed the *Pure Food and Drug Act* in 1906 (34 Stat. 768).

Pure Food and Drug Act of 1906

In the early 1900s, concerns grew about the safety of chemicals added to food for preservation. In 1902, Harvey Wiley, the head of the Bureau of Chemistry, received federal funding to conduct studies on chemical substances used in food preservation. In the fall of 1902, he convened a group of 12 male subjects, known as the Poison Squad, to consume meals containing chemical substances with unknown health effects. In initial experiments, Borax (boric acid) was added to food in controlled settings; Wiley later extended his research to include salicylic acid, sulfuric acid, sodium benzoate and formaldehyde over the course of the five-year study.

Although the Poison Squad reported experiencing adverse effects after consuming various tested substances, results from the laboratory analyses of fecal matter, perspiration and respiration were inconclusive. Wiley, however, continued his long-time efforts to lobby for oversight of food additives and maintained his stance that consumption of these chemicals had cumulative effects. As Wiley conducted his Poison Squad studies, investigations of the meat industry precipitated further support for the need to regulate the food industry. The Poison Squad studies and Wiley's activism garnered public attention for the regulation of certain food additives, laying the groundwork for US food regulation.

In 1904, Upton Sinclair, an author and member of the Socialist Party, ventured into Chicago's meat-packing plants to investigate a strike undertaken by the meat packers' union. Sinclair later published a novel based on his experiences in Chicago. His 1906 book, *The Jungle*, was a disturbing tale detailing not only grave working conditions for meat packers (primarily immigrants from Poland and Lithuania), but also unsanitary conditions under which meat sold for human consumption was prepared and packaged. Sinclair's book gained national attention as a best-seller, which brought further support for food industry regulation.

In response to public pressure, President Theodore Roosevelt appointed a special commission to investigate Chicago's meat-packing plants. The commission's report led the president to write to Congress declaring a need for a new law enabling the federal government to inspect and supervise meat preparation.

On 30 June 1906, both the *Meat Inspection Act* (34 Stat. 1260) and the *Pure Food and Drug Act* (34 Stat. 768) were signed into law. The *Pure Food and Drug Act* prohibited misbranded and adulterated foods, drinks and drugs from entering interstate commerce. This act was the predecessor for the 1938 *FD&C Act*. It was enforced by the Bureau of Chemistry in the Department of Agriculture, which became the Food and Drug Administration in 1930.

Sherley Amendment

On 13 May 1908, the Bureau of Chemistry seized a shipment of drugs from a company in Kansas City, Missouri, which was intended for the District of Columbia. The shipment contained various packages of tablets and bottles to be used in combination to treat cancer. The bureau analyzed package labels and determined the contents to be misbranded according to the *Pure Food and Drug Act*. The company's owner, O.J. Johnson, was prosecuted and convicted in the Western District of Missouri on six counts of willingly and knowingly violating provisions of the act by, among other things, including false and misleading statements on the drugs' labeling for shipment into interstate commerce.

Johnson challenged his conviction, and in *United States v. Johnson* (1911; 221 U.S. 488), the Supreme Court issued a ruling against the government, finding the product's claims for effectiveness were not within the *Pure Food and Drug Act*'s scope.

In response to the ruling, Congress enacted the *Sherley Amendment* (1912; 37 Stat. 416), named for the legislation's sponsor, Representative Joseph Swagar Sherley of Kentucky. The amendment prohibited labeling medicines with false therapeutic claims intended to defraud the purchaser. The burden to prove intent to defraud remained with the government, providing easy mechanisms of defense; thus, for the next two decades, the government had little power to prosecute alleged violators of the *Pure Food and Drug Act* successfully until subsequent legislation removed this requirement.

FD&C Act

In 1933, shortly after Franklin Roosevelt was inaugurated, Walter Campbell, FDA's chief inspector, met with Roger Tugwell, assistant secretary of agriculture, to discuss shortcomings in food and drug regulation. Tugwell later introduced a bill to reform the 1906 act. The "Tugwell Bill" introduced significant changes to FDA authority and was met with opposition from industry. The bill's supporters spent the next few years altering the bill to get it to pass. During this time, a significant public health event occurred that signaled the need for greater controls.

In 1937, a chemist at a drug manufacturing company discovered sulfanilamide (a synthetic antibacterial drug originally manufactured as a tablet or injection to treat streptococcal infections) could be dissolved in diethylene glycol for oral administration as an elixir. Raspberry flavoring and red coloring were added to the product so the medication would be more appealing to children. Without undergoing safety testing, several hundred bottles of Elixir Sulfanilamide were distributed to pharmacies, and samples were sent to physician's offices.

In the fall of 1937, 71 adults and 34 children died after ingesting Elixir Sulfanilamide. The drug was recalled, and FDA inspected the drug maker; however, the agency had little authority to take action. An Oklahoma mother, whose daughter died nine days after taking Elixir Sulfanilamide, wrote a letter to President Roosevelt, which garnered significant public attention and galvanized the passage of pending legislation for drug regulation reform.

On 28 June 1938, President Roosevelt signed the *FD&C Act* (52 Stat. 1040) into law. This new law included the following significant changes: manufacturers were required to provide scientific proof new drugs were safe for their intended use before being placed on the market; cosmetics and medical devices were regulated for the first time; adding poisonous substances to foods was prohibited except where unavoidable or required in production; and FDA was given authority to bring federal court injunctions, in addition to product seizures and criminal prosecutions, for violations of the *FD&C Act*. The *FD&C Act* also repealed the *Pure Food and Drug Act* of 1906; as a result of the repeal, the *Sherley Amendment* also was removed (proof of intent to defraud no longer being required to stop false claims for drugs).

Expansion of FDA Authority and Amendments to the FD&C Act up to the 21st Century

The FD&C Act, as amended, may be referenced in the US Code at 21 U.S.C. 301 et seq.

Public Health Service Act of 1944

In 1944, President Roosevelt signed the *Public Health Service Act* (*PHS Act*, 58 Stat. 682) into law. The *PHS Act* did not amend the *FD&C Act*; however, it gave FDA authority over biological products such as vaccines and serums. The *PHS Act* includes provisions for licensing new biological products through an application process. Regulations for the application process are implemented in 21 CFR Parts 600–680. The *PHS Act*, as amended, may be referenced at 42 U.S.C. 201 et seq.

Durham-Humphrey Amendment

Signed into law in 1951, the *Durham-Humphrey Amendment* (65 Stat. 648) clarified what constituted a prescription drug versus an over-the-counter drug. A drug may be limited to dispensing with a prescription if it is not safe for use except under the supervision of a licensed practitioner. The amendment also required any habit-forming or potentially harmful drug to be dispensed under the supervision of a health practitioner as a prescription drug. In addition, such drugs must carry the statement "Caution: Federal law prohibits dispensing without prescription." The *Food and Drug Administration Modernization Act* of 1997 (*FDAMA*) repealed the prescription requirement for habit-forming drugs.

Food Additives Amendment

The *FD&C Act* established criteria for food to be considered adulterated, mislabeled or harmful; however, the onus remained on the agency to demonstrate a food product was "unsafe." The act also included a requirement for "truthful" food additive labeling.

In 1958, the *Food Additives Amendment* (72 Stat. 1784) was enacted to delineate substances added to food products generally recognized as safe (GRAS) and substances that may affect food characteristics that were not GRAS and required marketing approval. Marketing approval requires the manufacturer to prove a product is safe for human consumption.

Kefauver-Harris Amendment

In 1957, a pharmaceutical company in West Germany began marketing a patented drug containing thalidomide as its active ingredient to treat nausea and morning sickness in pregnant women. As a result of exposure to the drug in the womb, several thousand infants were born with physical defects or malformations. The most prevalent of these was phocomelia, a congenital disorder where long limbs do not form or are truncated.

By 1960, thalidomide was marketed in 46 countries, and the drug maker had submitted an application to market the drug in the US. The application was reviewed by FDA's Frances Kelsey who, despite pressures from the drug maker, would not grant approval due to concerns over the drug's safety profile. Kelsey requested additional evidence to demonstrate the drug was safe for pregnant women. While the application was pending in the US, an Australian obstetrician, William McBride, began to associate thalidomide with severe birth defects and, eventually, the German press began to report on the drug's harmful effects. By March 1962, the drug was banned in most countries where it previously had been sold.

Frances Kelsey was heralded by President John F. Kennedy and an American public that likely felt indebted to her for her role in diverting the damaging impact thalidomide caused in jurisdictions where the drug had been marketed. The tragedy surrounding thalidomide also motivated profound changes in drug approval requirements.

In the late 1950s, Senator Estes Kefauver held hearings on drug industry prices. Concerns had been raised about price gouging in the pharmaceutical industry, including the effect of unsubstantiated advertising claims on marketed drugs' integrity. Following the hearings, Senator Kefauver introduced a bill some considered to be sweeping reform. The bill focused on intellectual property issues in drug innovation and follow-on therapeutics. It also focused on efficacy claim standards and proposed granting FDA power to demand proof of efficacy—in the form of "adequate and well-controlled investigations"— before approving a new drug for the US market. The bill was met with industry opposition and was not supported by President Kennedy's administration, which introduced an alternate bill in 1962. Kefauver's proposed legislation stalled until the thalidomide incident highlighted the need for significant drug safety reforms. In response, Congress enacted a compromise version of the legislation in the *Kefauver-Harris Amendment* (also known as *Drug Amendments* of 1962, 76 Stat. 780) to address standards for both safety and efficacy that must be met before a drug may be marketed in the US.

Medical Device Amendments

In 1938, when the *FD&C Act* was approved, medical devices were simple instruments such as scalpels and stethoscopes. While premarket approval did not apply to devices for regulatory purposes, the law equated them to drugs in every other sense. In the post-World War II years, however, a technology boom resulted in an increase in medical device complexity and numbers, including products such as heart-lung machines and dialysis equipment. In 1970, the Cooper Commission determined more than 700 deaths and 10,000 injuries were associated with medical devices. Among those, 512 deaths and injuries were attributed to heart valves, 89 deaths and 186 injuries were tied to heart pacemakers and 10 deaths and 8,000 injuries were attributed to intrauterine devices. As a result of the Cooper Report, Congress passed the 1976 *Medical Device Amendments* (90 Stat. 539) to the *FD&C Act*. This legislation established three medical device classes, each requiring a different level of regulatory scrutiny, up to premarket approval. The three classes were based on the degree of control necessary to ensure devices were safe and effective. The amendments also made provisions for device listing, establishment registration and adherence to Good Manufacturing Practices. Medical device regulations based on the amendments are found in 21 CFR Parts 800898.

Orphan Drug Act of 1983

The 1983 *Orphan Drug Act* (96 Stat. 2049) originally defined the term *orphan drug* as "a drug for a disease or condition which is rare." In October 1984, the term "rare" was defined in an amendment as "any rare disease or condition which (a) affects less than 200,000 persons in the U.S. or (b) affects more than 200,000 persons in the U.S. but for which there is no reasonable expectation that the cost of developing and making available in the U.S. a drug for such disease or condition will be recovered from sales in the U.S. of such drug." The act guarantees an orphan product developer seven years of market exclusivity following FDA's approval. Incentives also include tax credits for clinical research undertaken by a sponsor to generate data required for marketing approval. Regulations for orphan drugs are found in 21 CFR 316.

Safe Medical Devices Act of 1990 and Medical Device Amendments of 1992

Under the *Safe Medical Devices Act* of 1990 (*SMDA*, 104 Stat. 4511), device user facilities must report device-related deaths to FDA and the manufacturer, if known. Device user facilities also must report device-related serious injuries to the manufacturer, or to FDA if the manufacturer is not known. In addition, *SMDA* required device user facilities to submit to FDA, on a semiannual basis, a summary of all reports submitted during that time period. The device user facility reporting section of *SMDA* became effective 28 November 1991.

SMDA defined a *medical device* as "any instrument, apparatus, or other article that is used to prevent, diagnose, mitigate, or treat a disease or to affect the structure or function of the body, with the exception of drugs." It instituted device tracking and postmarket surveillance requirements, and allowed FDA to temporarily suspend or withdraw approval of premarket approval applications. The rule provided civil penalties for violating an *FD&C Act* requirement relating to devices. The act amended the *FD&C* Act to create an incentive for developing *orphan* or *humanitarian use devices*, defined as devices for use in the treatment or diagnosis of diseases or conditions affecting fewer than 4,000 patients in the US annually. This number was raised to 8,000 patients in the *21st Century Cures Act* (*CCA*) (described later).

SMDA also gave FDA the authority to add preproduction design controls to the Current Good Manufacturing Practice (CGMP) regulation. This change resulted from findings that approximately 44% of quality problems resulting in voluntary recalls during a six-year period were due to design-related defects. Even more striking was the recognition that more than 90% of all software-related device failures resulted from design-related errors. To overcome the frequent design errors, FDA incorporated design controls in the Quality System Regulation (QSR) issued in 1996 (61 FR 52602). The QSR is found in 21 CFR 820.

The primary impact of the 1992 *Medical Device Amendments* (106 Stat. 238) was to clarify certain terms and establish a single reporting standard for device user facilities, manufacturers, importers and distributors.

Drug Price Competition and Patent Term Restoration Act of 1984

Because the new product approval process required submission of full safety and efficacy data, economic pressures caused by the lengthy review process led to the *Drug Price Competition and Patent Term Restoration Act* of 1984 (98 Stat. 1585), also known as the *Hatch-Waxman Act*. This law established a process for approving drugs based on comparison to an already approved product and provided exclusive marketing status for a period based on the length of the new drug's approval process or the branded drug patent status for generics.

This act included provisions for patent term extension, which gave certain patent holders the opportunity to extend patent terms by five years for human drug products, including antibiotics and biologics, medical devices, food additives and color additives. By giving inventors a portion of the patent term lost during federal regulatory review, Congress sought to restore some of the incentive for innovation to US domestic drug companies, as federal premarket approval requirements became more expensive and time-consuming. The *Hatch-Waxman Act* authorized Abbreviated New Drug Applications (ANDAs) for generic drugs and specifically provided that FDA could require only bioavailability studies for ANDAs.

Similar to the *Drug Price Competition and Patent Restoration Act*, the *Biologics Price Competition and Innovation Act* of 2010 (124 Stat. 804) amended the *PHS Act* for approval of a biosimilar product. A biosimilar product is approved based on its similarity to an FDA-approved biological product.

PDUFA, Reauthorizations and Expansion of User Fees

The *Prescription Drug User Fee Act* (*PDUFA I*, 106 Stat. 4491), first enacted in 1992, authorized FDA to collect user fees from companies submitting applications for certain human drug and biological products. In addition, companies were required to pay annual fees for each manufacturing establishment and each prescription drug product marketed. Previously, taxpayers paid for product reviews through congressional budgets. In this program, industry provides the funding in exchange for FDA's agreement to meet drug review performance goals, which emphasize timeliness.

The user fee concept under *PDUFA* later expanded to other product categories FDA regulates. In 2002, the *Medical Device User Fee and Modernization Act* (*MDUFMA*, 116 Stat. 1588) required medical device companies to pay fees to FDA. In 2012, the *Food and Drug Administration Safety and Innovation Act* (*FDASIA*, 126 Stat. 993) extended FDA's authority to collect user fees from the generic drug and biologics industries.

User fees are subject to reauthorization by Congress every five years. *PDUFA* was most recently reauthorized under the *FDA Reauthorization Act* of 2017(*FDARA)* as *PDUFA VI* (Fiscal 2018–22). *MDUFA II* was reauthorized under the *Food and Drug Administration Amendments Act* in 2007 and *MDUFA IV* has been authorized for Fiscal 1028-22.

FDAMA

FDAMA (111 Stat. 2296) provided additional authority for drug and biologic postmarketing studies' monitoring. It required FDA to issue regulations allowing clinical study sponsors to modify any investigational device or study protocol by submitting a "Notice of Change" five days after instituting such a change, where the change(s) did not affect study design or patient safety significantly. The law codified the expedited review policy for certain medical devices, amended and clarified *SMDA*'s humanitarian device provisions and allowed FDA to recognize other national or international standards. *FDAMA* also directed FDA to consider the least-burdensome means of establishing substantial equivalence for certain device marketing applications. The act repealed *SMDA* mandatory tracking requirements for some high-risk devices and, instead, established requirements and a process under which FDA may order device tracking.

Supply Chain Globalization and Amendments to the FD&C Act in the 21st Century

The advent of easy access to raw materials, goods, services and human resources through e-commerce has facilitated increasingly global food, drug and device supply chains, but not without challenges. FDA is tasked with monitoring manufacturers' compliance with programs to ensure the safety of products they place on the market. For example, tracking and tracing a drug product from its release point to its destination is important to protect against diversion, prevent counterfeit drugs from gaining market access and ensure product quality during transport. The ability to recall items quickly for product quality safety issues is another concern. Recalls can be challenging, particularly when a problem is due to materials sourced from complex networks of upstream suppliers. Global supply chain challenges have been the underlying factor in many recently enacted legislative changes.

Food Safety Modernization Act of 2011

Food-borne illnesses from contaminated food products significantly impact annual US healthcare costs. For example, Salmonella causes more hospitalizations and deaths than any other germ found in food. One challenging aspect of regulating food in the 21st century is the difficulty of establishing traceability in a highly technological and complex global food supply chain. To address the negative impact of contaminated foods on public health, US food supply safety legislation has focused on the need for federal regulators to shift priorities from contamination to prevention.

The *FDA Food Safety Modernization Act* (*FSMA*, 124 Stat. 3885), which became law on 4 January 2011, was noted by FDA as the most sweeping food safety reform in 70 years. The law gave FDA new enforcement authority designed to achieve higher compliance rates with prevention- and risk-based food safety standards, and new tools to respond to and contain problems. For the first time, FDA had a legislative mandate to require comprehensive, science-based preventive controls across the food supply chain. The law also gave FDA new tools to hold imported foods to the same standards as domestic foods, and directed the agency to build an integrated national food safety system in partnership with state and local authorities.

FDASIA

FDASIA became law on 9 July 2012 and took effect 1 October 2012. It was the first major FDA legislation since the *Food and Drug Administration Amendments Act* (121 Stat. 823) was enacted in 2007.

Under *FDASIA*, existing user fees were reauthorized, and FDA was given authority to collect user fees to fund reviews of generics and biosimilar biologics. While House negotiations regarding the legislation focused primarily on new user fee programs under Titles III and IV, *FDASIA* ushered in several other significant changes in 11 titles under the act, such as creating new programs to gain timely access to medicines, reporting requirements to avoid drug shortages and a new drug supply chain control requirement under Title VII. For example, under Title VII Section 711, quality manufacturing standards now include "managing the risk and establishing the safety of raw materials, materials used in the manufacturing of pharmaceuticals, and finished drug products." Thus, suppliers become part of the quality management system, and if a pharmaceutical company does not establish adequate controls over raw materials and components, its products may be deemed "adulterated."

FDASIA Title VIII created Generating Antibiotic Incentives Now (GAIN). GAIN provides incentives, such as fast-track, priority review and a five-year exclusivity extension for certain applications for the development of antibacterial and antifungal drugs that treat serious or life-threatening infections designated as qualified infectious disease product (QIDPs). This five-year exclusivity extension is added to any exclusivity for which the application qualifies upon approval. A product must apply for and receive a QIDP designation to receive these benefits.

Drug Quality and Security Act

The 2013 *Drug Quality and Security Act* (*DQSA*, 127 Stat. 587) contained two titles: Title I addressed pharmacy compounding and Title II addressed supply chain security. *DQSA* Title I, the *Compounding Quality Act*, is a legislative response to a fungal meningitis outbreak that began in 2012 when approximately 14,000 patients received doses from contaminated lots of methylprednisolone administered by epidural injection into the spine. The lots were packaged and marketed by a small compounding pharmacy in Framingham, Massachusetts. By 10 March 2013, 48 people had died and 720 were being treated for persistent fungal infections.

The outbreak sparked a congressional investigation into compounding pharmacy practices, which led to significant concerns over sterile drug processing under unsanitary conditions. *DQSA* added a new section, 503B, to the *FD&C Act*, creating a new entity category called an outsourcing facility. An outsourcing facility is distinct from a traditional pharmacy. It is granted certain exemptions from having to obtain drug approval and include adequate drug label directions under the *FD&C Act*, provided it meets certain other criteria, such as compliance with CGMPs. Outsourcing facilities are not required to obtain patient-specific prescriptions to sell compounded products, although they are restricted from wholesaling.

DQSA also amended the existing *FD&C Act* Section 503A, under which compounded human drug products may be exempt from certain act requirements, including CGMP compliance, adequate labeling directions for use and FDA approval prior to marketing, as long as certain conditions are met. One such condition is the requirement to obtain patient-specific prescriptions for compounded drugs.

The legislation also removed a provision under Section 503A concerning commercial speech regulation. Removing this provision was the result of a longstanding debate over the provision's severability and applicability after the Supreme Court ruled in *Thompson v. Western States Medical Center* (2002) that restricting certain commercial speech under Section 503A violated the First Amendment.

DQSA Title II, the *Drug Supply Chain Security Act*, mandated implementing an electronic track and trace system to identify and trace certain prescription drugs throughout the US supply chain.

Improving Regulatory Transparency for New Medical Therapies Act

During new drug or biologic product review, FDA may recommend controls under the *Controlled Substances Act* of 1970 (84 Stat. 1242) if it believes the product has abuse potential. With such a control recommendation, FDA provides the Drug Enforcement Administration (DEA) a scientific and medical evaluation with an appropriate schedule placement recommendation. DEA places a controlled substance in Schedule I, II, III, IV or V, depending on its potential for abuse, accepted medical use and psychological or physiological dependence severity. A DEA ruling identifies the new drug or biological product's schedule placement based on FDA recommendations.

The *Improving Regulatory Transparency for New Medical Therapies Act* of 2015 (129 Stat. 698) amended the *Controlled Substances Act* to require DEA to schedule a drug by issuing an interim final rule within 90 days of receiving a recommendation. In addition, the *FD&C Act* and the *PHS Act* were amended to indicate such a drug or biological product's date of approval is the later of the date when the interim rule controlling the product is issued or the date when the product application is approved.

21st Century Cures Act

In December 2016, Congress passed sweeping legislation to advance drug and device development. The *CCA* (Public Law 114-255) amends various *FD&C Act* and *PHS Act* sections to include provisions for:
- patient-focused drug development
- advancing new drug therapies
- modern trial design and evidence development
- patient access to therapies and information
- antimicrobial innovation and stewardship
- medical device innovations
- improving FDA scientific expertise and outreach
- medical countermeasures innovation
- vaccine access, certainty and innovation

This section describes some of the important *CCA* provisions.

CCA aims to improve patient-focused drug and device development by allowing the use of "patient experience data." Patient experience data include data collected by any persons (including patients, their family members and caregivers, patient advocacy organizations, disease research foundations, researchers and drug manufacturers). Such data are intended to provide information about patients' experiences with a disease or condition, including a therapy's impact and patient treatment preference. The act also directs FDA to issue one or more guidance documents on collecting and using patient experience data and to issue reports assessing such data's use in application approvals.

Table 1-2. Other Laws, Regulations and Guidelines

Federal Meat Inspection Act of 1906
Wheeler-Lea Act of 1938
Poultry Products Inspection Act of 1957
Fair Packaging and Labeling Act of 1967
Animal Drug Amendments of 1968
Poison Prevention Packaging Act of 1970
Egg Products Act of 1970
Infant Formula Act of 1980
Generic Animal Drug and Patent Term Restoration Act of 1988
Animal Medicinal Drug Use Clarification Act of 1994
Dietary Supplement Health and Education Act of 1994
Food Quality Protection Act of 1996
Animal Drug Availability Act of 1996
Minor Use and Minor Species Animal Health Act of 2001
Best Pharmaceuticals for Children Act of 2002
Animal Drug User Fee Act of 2003
Pharmaceutical CGMPs for the 21st Century (2004)
Dietary Supplement and Nonprescription Drug Consumer Protection Act of 2006
Food and Drug Administration Amendments Act of 2007
Family Smoking Prevention and Tobacco Control Act of 2009
Biologics Price Competition and Innovation Act of 2010
Sunscreen Innovation Act of 2014
Comprehensive Addiction and Recovery Act of 2016
21st Century Cures Act of 2016
FDA Reauthorization Act of 2017
Right to Try Act of 2018

CCA also directs FDA to establish a process for "qualification of drug development tools" to advance new drug therapies. A development tool may include a biomarker, a clinical outcome assessment or any other method, material or measure that aids drug development. Once qualified for a proposed context of use, a tool may be used by any person in such context for supporting the investigational use or approval of a drug or biological product.

Further, *CCA* aims to incorporate modern trial design and evidence development for new drugs and biological products. The act authorizes FDA, after consulting with stakeholders, to release a guidance on the use of complex adaptive and other novel trial designs. In addition, it directs FDA to evaluate the use of real-world evidence for: 1) approving a new indication of an already approved drug; and 2) satisfying postapproval study requirements.

Another *CCA* provision proposes harmonizing HHS human subject regulations and FDA human subject regulations by reducing regulatory duplication and allowing the use of a joint or shared review. *CCA* also authorizes the waiver or alteration of informed consent for clinical trials of drugs and devices that pose no more than minimal risk.

CCA aims to improve patient access to therapies and information. To improve patient access, the act allows a supplemental application under the *FD&C Act* and *PHS Act* to rely on a summary of clinical data that demonstrates a drug's safety and effectiveness with respect to a qualified indication. *CCA* also improves patient access to information by directing manufacturers or distributors of an investigational drug for serious diseases or conditions to make a policy available on evaluating and responding to requests for expanded access. The policy shall be made public and include procedures for requests. Another provision calls for accelerated FDA approval of regenerative advanced therapies. Finally, *CCA* amended *FD&C Act* Section 503(g) on combination products containing a drug, device or biologic. This amendment provides a sponsor the opportunity to meet with FDA early in combination product development for clarity on marketing approval requirements.

CCA also gives FDA authority to approve an antimicrobial drug for a limited population if the drug is intended to treat a serious or life-threatening infection.

To promote medical device innovations, *CCA* authorizes use of flexible approaches to expedite development and provide for priority review of breakthrough device technologies. For Humanitarian Device Exemptions, used for devices that treat or diagnose diseases or conditions in fewer than 4,000 individuals in US, the cap was increased to 8,000 individuals. Other changes include a pathway for standards recognition, ensuring adequate expertise in panels for device classification, allowing Institutional Review Board flexibility by not requiring a local board, least-burdensome device review, and cleaning and validation requirements for reusable devices. Significantly, the act identifies specific software categories that should not be regulated as devices. For example, software used for encouraging a healthy lifestyle, but unrelated to the diagnosis, cure, mitigation, prevention or treatment of a disease or condition, shall not be considered a device or regulated as a device.

Right to Try

On 30 May 2018, the *Right to Try Act* was passed. This law offers another way for patients diagnosed with life-threatening diseases or conditions, who have tried all approved treatment options and are unable to participate in a clinical trial, to access certain unapproved treatments (drugs, devices or biologics).[6]

Other Food- and Drug-Related Laws

More information about the laws enforced by FDA can be found at https://www.fda.gov/RegulatoryInformation/LawsEnforcedbyFDA/. While the discussion above covers many of the laws forming the basis of current regulations, many others also affect food, drugs and medical devices. **Table 1-2** lists some of these other laws.

Summary

Food and drug laws, which provide a framework for regulatory practices, are linked closely to the larger historical context of the times in which they were enacted. Many laws, such as the *FD&C Act*, the *Kefauver-Harris Amendments* and *DQSA*, were enacted in response to specific events calling attention to the need for additional authority or controls. Based on this history, it is likely that future events will further shape food and drug laws and regulations.

References

1. How Our Laws Are Made—Learn About the Legislative Process. Congress.gov website. https://www.congress.gov/resources/display/content/How+Our+Laws+Are+Made+-+Learn+About+the+Legislative+Process. Accessed 18 April 2019.
2. Ibid.
3. Ibid.
4. United States Government Manual, 2018 Edition. US Government Publishing Office website. https://www.usgovernmentmanual.gov/?AspxAutoDetectCookieSupport=1. Accessed 18 April 2019.
5. Court Roles and Structure. United States Courts website. http://www.uscourts.gov/about-federal-courts/court-role-and-structure. Accessed 18 April 2019.
6. *Right to Try*. FDA website. https://www.fda.gov/ForPatients/Other/ucm625115.htm. Accessed 18 April 2019.

Chapter 2

Overview of Drug, Biologic, Device, Combination Product or Food Regulatory Pathways

Updated by Michael R. Hamrell, PhD, RQAP-GCP, CCRA, FACRP, RAC, FRAPS

OBJECTIVES

❑ Give an overview of US federal regulations and processes related to developing and filing a drug, biologic, device, combination product or food marketing application

❑ Provide an overview of scientific questions and approaches to the development process

❑ Review a roadmap showing how novel products are developed to meet US federal regulations

LAWS, REGULATIONS AND GUIDELINES COVERED IN THIS CHAPTER

Federal Laws Passed by Congress
❑ Drug Importation Act (1848)

❑ Tea Importation Act (1897)

❑ Biologics Control Act (1902)

❑ Food and Drugs Act (1906)

❑ Meat Inspection Act (1906)

❑ Sherley Amendment (1912)

❑ Gould Amendment (1913)

❑ McNary-Mapes Amendment (1930)

❑ Food, Drug, and Cosmetic Act (FD&C Act) (1938)

❑ Insulin Amendment (1941)

❑ Public Health Service Act (PHS Act) (1944)

❑ Penicillin Amendment (1945)

❑ Miller Amendment (1948)

❑ Oleomargarine Act (1950)

❑ Durham-Humphrey Amendment (1951)

❑ Factory Inspection Amendment (1953)

❑ Miller Pesticide Amendment (1954)

❑ Food Additives Amendment (1958)

❑ Color Additives Amendment (1960)

❑ Federal Hazardous Substances Labeling Act (1960)

❑ Kefauver-Harris Drug Amendments (1962)

❑ Drug Abuse Control Amendments (1965)

❑ Child Protection Act (1966)

❑ Fair Packaging and Labeling Act (1966)

❑ Animal Drug Amendments (1968)

Regulatory Affairs Professionals Society

- Comprehensive Drug Abuse Prevention and Control Act (1970)
- Medical Device Amendments (1976)
- Vitamins and Minerals Amendments (1976)
- Orphan Drug Act (1983)
- Hatch-Waxman Act (1984)
- Drug Price Competition and Patent Term Restoration Act (1984)
- Child Vaccine Act (1986)
- FDA Act (1988)
- Prescription Drug Marketing Act (1988)
- Generic Animal Drug and Patent Term Restoration Act (1988)
- Nutrition Labeling and Education Act (1990)
- Safe Medical Devices Act (1990)
- Generic Drug Enforcement Act (1992)
- Prescription Drug User Fee Act (PDUFA) (1992)
- Dietary Supplement Health and Education Act (DSHEA) (1994)
- Food and Drug Administration Modernization Act (FDAMA) (1997)
- Drug Quality Act (2000)
- Best Pharmaceuticals for Children Act (2002)
- Public Health Security and Bioterrorism Preparedness and Response Act (2002)
- Medical Device User Fee and Modernization Act (MDUFMA) (2002)
- Medicare Prescription Drug Improvement and Modernization Act (2003)
- Animal Drug User Fee Act (ADUFA) (2003)
- Pediatric Research Equity Act (PREA) (2003)
- Project BioShield Act (2004)
- FDA Amendments Act (FDAAA) (2007)
- Family Smoking Prevention and Tobacco Control Act (2009)
- Patient Protection and Affordable Care Act (includes Biologics Price Competition and Innovation Act (BPCIA)) (2010)
- Food Safety and Modernization Act (FSMA) (2011)
- FDA Safety and Innovation Act (FDASIA) (January 2012)
- Generic Drug User Fee Amendments (GDUFA) (January 2012)
- Biosimilar User Fee Act (BsUFA) (2012)
- Pandemic and All-Hazards Preparedness Reauthorization Act (PAHPRA) (2013)
- Drug Quality and Security Act (2013)
- Sunscreen Innovation Act (2014)
- 21st Century Cures Act (2016)
- FDA Reauthorization Act of 2017 (FDARA)

Code of Federal Regulations (CFR) Title 21

- 21 CFR 3 Subpart A—Assignment of Agency Component for review of premarket applications
- 21 CFR 4 Regulation of Combination Products
- 21 CFR 10.30 Citizen Petition
- 21 CFR 11 Electronic Records; Electronic Signatures
- 21 CFR 50 Protection of Human Subjects
- 21 CFR 54 Financial Disclosure by Clinical Investigators
- 21 CFR 56 Institutional Review Boards

- 21 CFR 58 Good Laboratory Practice for Nonclinical Laboratory Studies
- 21 CFR 70–82 Color Additives
- 21 CFR 99 Dissemination of Information on Unapproved/New Uses for Marketed Drugs, Biologics, and Devices
- 21 CFR 190 Dietary Supplements (New Dietary Ingredient Notification)
- 21 CFR 190.6 Requirement for premarket notification
- 21 CFR 207 Requirements for Foreign and Domestic Establishment Registration and Listing For Human Drugs, Including Drugs That Are Regulated Under a Biologics License Application, and Animal Drugs, and The National Drug Code
- 21 CFR 210 Current Good Manufacturing Practice in Manufacturing, Processing, Packing, or Holding of Drugs; General
- 21 CFR 211 Current Good Manufacturing Practice for Finished Pharmaceuticals
- 21 CFR 310 New Drugs
- 21 CFR 312 Investigational New Drug Application
- 21 CFR 312.23 IND content and format
- 21 CFR 312.32 IND safety reports
- 21 CFR 312.38 Withdrawal of an IND
- 21 CFR 312.45 Inactive status
- 21 CFR 312.50 General responsibilities of sponsors
- 21 CFR 312.52 Transfer of obligations to a contract research organization
- 21 CFR 312.52 Selecting investigators and monitors
- 21 CFR 312.57 Recordkeeping and record retention
- 21 CFR 312.60 General responsibilities of investigators
- 21 CFR 312.80–88 Subpart E Drugs intended to treat life-threatening and severely debilitating illnesses
- 21 CFR 314 Applications for FDA Approval to Market a New Drug
- 21 CFR 314.50 Content and format of an NDA
- 21 CFR 314.54 Procedure for submission of a 505(b)(2) application requiring investigations for approval of a new indication for, or other change from, a listed drug
- 21 CFR 314.92 Drug products for which abbreviated applications may be submitted
- 21 CFR 314.93 Petition to request a change from a listed drug
- 21 CFR 314.500–560 Subpart H Accelerated approval of new drugs for serious or life-threatening illnesses
- 21 CFR 316 Orphan Drugs
- 21 CFR 328–358 OTC Monographs
- 21 CFR 330.11 NDA deviations from applicable monograph
- 21 CFR 807 Subpart E Premarket notification procedures
- 21 CFR 807 Establishment Registration and Device Listing for Manufacturers and Initial Importers of Devices
- 21 CFR 812 Investigational Device Exemptions
- 21 CFR 814 Premarket Approval of Medical Devices
- 21 CFR 814.100–126 Subpart H Humanitarian Use Devices
- 21 CFR 820 Quality System Regulation
- 21 CFR 822 Post Market Surveillance

Chapter 2

- 21 CFR 862–892 Medical Device Classifications
- 21 CFR 900 Mammography
- 21 CFR 1000 Radiological Health
- 21 CFR 1100 Tobacco Products
- 21 CFR 1200 Other
- 21 CFR 1270 Human Tissue

Guidance Documents

- *Guidance for Industry: 180-Day Exclusivity When Multiple ANDAs are Submitted on the Same Day* (July 2003)
- *Guidance for Industry: Product Development under the Animal Rule* (October 2015)
- *Guidance for Industry: Contents of a Complete Submission for the Evaluation of Proprietary Names* (April 2016)
- *Guidance for Industry: Food-Effect Bioavailability and Fed Bioequivalence Studies* (December 2002)
- *Draft Guidance for Industry: Bioavailability and Bioequivalence Studies Submitted in NDAs or INDs—General Considerations* (March 2014)
- *Guidance for Industry: Statistical Approaches to Establishing Bioequivalence* (January 2001)
- *Guidance for Industry: Bioequivalence Recommendations for Specific Products* (June 2010)
- *Draft Guidance for Industry: Formal Meetings between the FDA and Sponsors or Applicants of PDUFA Products* (March 2015, revision 2)
- *Guidance for Industry: End-of-Phase 2A Meetings* (September 2009)
- *Draft Guidance for Industry: Special Protocol Assessment* (May 2016, Revision 1)

- *Guidance for Industry: Expedited Programs for Serious Conditions—Drugs and Biologics* (May 2014)
- *Guidance for Industry M2 eCTD: Electronic Common Technical Document Specification* (April 2003)
- *Guidance for Industry: M3(R2) Nonclinical Safety Studies for the Conduct of Human Clinical Trials and Marketing Authorization for Pharmaceuticals* (January 2010)
- *Guidance for Industry: M3(R2) Nonclinical Safety Studies for the Conduct of Human Clinical Trials and Marketing Authorization for Pharmaceuticals Questions and Answers(R2)* (February 2013)
- *Guidance for Industry M4: Organization of the CTD* (August 2001)
- *Guidance for Industry M4Q: The CTD—Quality* (August 2001)
- *Guidance for Industry M4S: The CTD—Safety* (August 2001)
- *Guidance for Industry M4S: The CTD—Safety Appendices* (August 2001)
- *Guidance for Industry M4E: The CTD—Efficacy* (August 2001)
- *Guidance for Industry: E2F Development Safety Update Report* (August 2011)
- *Guidance for Industry: E7 Studies in Support of Special Populations: Geriatrics* (August 1994)
- *Guidance for Industry: E7 Studies in Support of Special Populations: Geriatrics—Questions and Answers* (February 2012)
- *Guidance for Industry: S1C(R2) Dose Selection for Carcinogenicity Studies* (September 2008)
- *Guidance for Industry: Estimating the Maximum Safe Starting Dose in Initial Clinical Trials for Therapeutics in Adult Healthy Volunteers* (July 2005)

- *Guidance for Industry: Immunotoxicology Evaluation of Investigational New Drugs* (October 2002)

- *Guidance for Industry: Nonclinical Safety Evaluation of Pediatric Drug Products* (February 2006)

- *Guidance for Industry: Single Dose Acute Toxicity Testing for Pharmaceuticals* (August 1996)

- *Guidance for Industry: Dissolution Testing of Immediate Release Solid Oral Dosage Forms* (August 1997)

- *Guidance for Industry: cGMP for Phase 1 Investigational Drugs* (July 2008)

- *Guidance for Industry: Analytical Procedures and Methods Validation for Drugs and Biologics* (July 2015)

- *Guidance for Industry: Collection of Race and Ethnicity Data in Clinical Trials* (October 2016)

- *Guidance for Industry: Exposure-Response Relationships—Study Design, Data Analysis, and Regulatory Applications* (May 2003)

- *Guidance for Industry: Drug-Induced Liver Injury: Premarketing Clinical Evaluation* (July 2009)

- *Draft Guidance for Industry: Drug Interaction Studies—Study Design, Data Analysis, Implications for Dosing and Labeling Recommendations* (February 2012)

- *Guidance for Industry: Pharmacokinetics in Patients with Impaired Hepatic Function: Study Design, Data Analysis, and Impact on Dosing and Labeling* (May 2003)

- *Draft Guidance for Industry: Pharmacokinetics in Patients with Impaired Renal Function: Study Design, Data Analysis, and Impact on Dosing and Labeling* (March 2010)

- *Draft Guidance for Industry: How to Comply with the Pediatric Research Equity Act* (September 2005)

- *Guidance for Industry and Investigators—Safety Reporting Requirements for INDs and BA/BE Studies* (December 2012)

- *Draft Guidance for Industry and Review Staff: Target Product Profile—A Strategic Development Process Tool* (March 2007)

- *Guidance for Industry: Guideline for the Format and Content of the Nonclinical Pharmacology/Toxicology Section of an Application* (February 1987)

- *Guidance for Industry: Reproductive and Developmental Toxicities—Integrating Study Results to Assess Concerns* (September 2011)

- *Guidance for Industry and Review Staff: Recommended Approaches to Integration of Genetic Toxicology Study Results* (January 2006)

- *Draft Guidance for Industry: Statistical Aspects of the Design, Analysis, and Interpretation of Chronic Rodent Carcinogenicity Studies of Pharmaceuticals* (May 2001)

- *Guideline for the Format and Content of the Clinical and Statistical Sections of an Application* (July 1988)

- *Guidance for Industry: Integrated Summary of Effectiveness* (October 2015)

- *Guidance for Industry: Premarketing Risk Assessment* (March 2005)

- *Guidance for Industry: Development and Use of Risk Minimization Action Plans* (March 2005)

- *Guidance for Industry: Good Pharmacovigilance Practices and Pharmacoepidemiologic Assessment* (March 2005)

- *Guidance for Industry: Submitting Separate Marketing Applications and Clinical Data for Purposes of Assessing User Fees* (December 2004)

- *Guidance for Industry: Standards for Securing the Drug Supply Chain—Standardized Numerical Identification for Prescription Drug Packages* (March 2010)

- *Guidance for Providing Regulatory Submissions in Electronic Format—Drug Establishment Registration and Drug Listing* (May 2009)

- *Providing Regulatory Submissions in Electronic Format—Certain Human Pharmaceutical Product Applications and Related Submissions Using the eCTD Specifications: Guidance for Industry* (May 2015)

- *Draft Guidance for Industry: Applications Covered by Section 505(b)(2)* (October 1999)

- *Guidance for Industry: Structure/Function Claims Small Entity Compliance Guide* (January 2002)

- *The New 510(k) Paradigm—Alternate Approaches to Demonstrating Substantial Equivalence in Premarket Notifications: Final Guidance* (March 1998)

- *MAPP 6020.5: Good Review Practice: OND Review Management of INDs and NDAs for Nonprescription Drug Products* (July 2007)

- *Guidance for Industry: How to Write a Request for Designation (RFD)* (April 2011)

- *Draft Guidance for Industry and FDA Staff: Classification of Products as Drugs and Devices and Additional Product Classification Issues* (June 2011)

- *Guidance for Industry and Food and Drug Administration Staff: Factors to Consider Regarding Benefit-Risk in Medical Device Product Availability, Compliance, and Enforcement Decisions* (December 2016)

- *Guidance for Industry: Nonclinical Safety Evaluation of Drug or Biologic Combinations* (March 2006)

- *Formal Meetings Between the FDA and Biosimilar Biological Product Sponsors or Applicants: Guidance for Industry* (November 2015)

- *Guidance for Industry: E2F Development Safety Update Report* (August 2011)

- *Draft Guidance for Industry: Special Protocol Assessment* (April 2018)

- *Draft Guidance for Industry Best Practices in Developing Proprietary Names for Drugs* (April 2016)

- *Selection of the Appropriate Package Type Terms and Recommendations for Labeling Injectable Medical Products Packaged in Multiple-Dose, Single-Dose, and Single-Patient-Use Containers for Human Use: Guidance for Industry* (October 2018)

- *Citizen Petitions and Petitions for Stay of Action Subject to Section 505(q) of the Federal Food, Drug, and Cosmetic Act: Guidance for Industry* (October 2018)

- *Questions and Answers on Biosimilar Development and the BPCI Act: Guidance for Industry* (December 2018)

- *Interpretation of the "Deemed to be a License" Provision of the Biologics Price Competition and Innovation Act of 2009: Guidance for Industry* (December 2009)

- *Data Integrity and Compliance with Current Good Manufacturing Practice: Guidance for Industry* (December 2018)

- *Clinical Trial Endpoints for the Approval of Cancer Drugs and Biologics: Guidance for Industry* (December 2018)

- *Testicular Toxicity: Evaluation During Drug Development: Guidance for Industry* (October 2018)

- *Clinical Trial Imaging Endpoint Process Standards: Guidance for Industry* (April 2018)

- *Draft Guidance for Industry: Formal Meetings Between the FDA and Sponsors or Applicants of PDUFA Products* (December 2017)

- *Expedited Programs for Regenerative Medicine Therapies for Serious Conditions: Guidance for Industry* (February 2019)

- *The Least Burdensome Provisions: Concept and Principles: Guidance for Industry and Food and Drug Administration Staff* (February 2019)

Introduction

Creating new drugs, biologics, medical devices, combination products and foods often requires a scientific process to gather evidence regarding the product's actual risks and benefits before release onto the US market.

The manufacturer (and others) must comply with US federal laws and regulations to market the new product legally. The legal frameworks and codified regulations have evolved over the past century in a reactive fashion as documented in the Code of Federal Regulations (CFR).

To encourage compliance with the laws and regulations, the US Food and Drug Administration (FDA) uses scientific review, inspections of manufacturing controls (including conformity to international and other manufacturing standards), advertising controls, laboratory product testing and postmarket pharmacovigilance activities.

Many groups, including FDA and the International Council for Harmonization (ICH), issue guidelines to assist regulatory professionals when interpreting and defining the processes needed to successfully develop drugs, biologics, medical devices, combination products and foods for the US market.

Although not enforceable as regulations, FDA guidance documents provide an understanding of the agency's current thinking on any given topic. FDA often issues new guidance documents as drafts available for public comment before finalization.

This chapter presents an overview of prescription drug, biologic, device, combination and food product development and approval processes in the US regulatory environment. Other chapters in this book provide details regarding many of the development and approval aspects touched on in this chapter. This chapter ties the various topics together to provide a development context and roadmap through the maze of regulations for the different product types.

Regulatory professionals should understand where regulations originate and how they are organized and updated to be sure the most current information is being considered. In trying to understand the legal process, the difference between a law and a regulation sometimes is misunderstood. To be clear, only Congress can enact laws (these are "acts" of Congress). A list of interesting federal laws passed by Congress from 1848 to 2018 is provided at the beginning of this chapter.

Federal executive departments and agencies like FDA write "regulations" to implement (or codify) the authority of laws and provide further details on how to meet the law's requirements. The US Code (USC) is the official compilation of codified laws by subject, while the Code of Federal Regulations (CFR) is the official compilation of all regulations. The CFR is updated annually, and the section for food and drugs (Title 21) usually is updated around 1 April each year. The US government also publishes a daily summary of all changes, updates and revisions to regulations on each business day in the *Federal Register*. The *Federal Register* tracks these changes as daily CFR updates. Thus, these two resources should be used together to find the latest version of a regulation. During the annual CFR update, all changes are incorporated into the latest CFR version.

The *Food, Drug, and Cosmetic Act* of 1938 (*FD&C Act*) and its many subsequent amendments constitute the basic US food and drug law. The current version of the *FD&C Act* can be found at: https://www.fda.gov/regulatoryinformation/lawsenforcedbyfda/federalfooddrugandcosmeticactfdcact/default.htm.

The CFR is divided into 50 titles or sections representing broad subject areas (e.g., Title 21 for "Food and Drugs" also includes medical devices). Each title is divided into chapters, which usually bear the name of the issuing agency (e.g., Title 21 has three chapters: Chapter I by FDA Department of Health and Human Services (HHS), Chapter II by the Drug Enforcement Administration (DEA) and Department of Justice (DOJ), and Chapter III by the Office of National Drug Control Policy. Each chapter is further subdivided into parts covering specific regulatory areas (e.g., Title 21 has 1,499 parts) (**Table 2-1**). Large parts may be subdivided into subparts, and these subparts may be further divided into sections. The US Government Publishing Office (GPO) offers a paper or electronic version of the CFR (e-CFR) with a convenient search engine (www.accessdata.fda.gov/scripts/cdrh/cfdocs/cfcfr/CFRSearch.cfm).

Although this chapter describes drug, biologic, device, combination product and food approval processes in the US, modern product development programs are becoming more and more globalized. Hence, in any development program, the regulatory professional should consider the impact of specific regulations in other parts of the world carefully.

This chapter touches on aspects of drug, biologic, device, combination product and food development programs to explain relationships among different technical regulatory areas. Unique development issues are covered in detail in other chapters, including current Good Manufacturing Practices (CGMPs), chemistry, manufacturing and controls (CMC) for drugs and biologics, and Quality System Regulations (QSR) for devices.

FDA Overview

FDA regulates foods, more than 150,000 marketed drugs and medical devices. FDA also regulates cosmetics, animal health products and tobacco products (advertising practices only). At any time, more than 5,000 investigational new drugs are under development in around 15,000 INDs, and Advisory Committees are critical to FDA success.[1] Organizationally, FDA is part of the Public Health Service (PHS) within the Health and Human Services Department (HHS). The PHS also oversees the Centers for Disease Control and Prevention (CDC) and the National Institutes of Health (NIH), among other agencies.

Chapter 2

Table 2-1. Title 21 CFR Parts

Parts	General Topics
1–99	General Administrative Issues and Protection of Human Subjects, including 70–82 Color Additives
100–199	Food for Human Consumption
200–299	Drugs, General (Labeling, CGMPs, Controlled Substances, etc.)
300–499	Drugs for Human Use
500–599	Drugs for Animal Use
600–680	Biologics
700–799	Cosmetics (not covered in this chapter)
800–899	Medical Devices
1000–1400	Miscellaneous topics, including 1270 Human Tissues Intended for Transplantation and 1271 Human Cells, Tissues and Tissue-Based Products

FDA distributes work for drug, biologic, device, combination product and food development primarily across three centers, including the Center for Drug Evaluation and Research (CDER), the Center for Biologics Evaluation and Research (CBER) and the Center for Food Safety and Applied Nutrition (CFSAN). Chapter 1 describes the primary centers and offices involved in drug and device development; pathways and guidance documents dating back to 1973 are available to increase development process transparency and to help move products through the process more rapidly.

FDA has a set of Compliance Program Guidance Manuals (CPGMs), basically standard operating procedures (SOPs for FDA) designed to instruct FDA personnel on how to conduct activities in compliance with the *FD&C Act*, which are available online (https://www.fda.gov/iceci/compliancemanuals/complianceprogrammanual/default.htm).

CDER also has a Manual of Policies and Procedures (MAPP) to document its internal policies and procedures. For example, MAPP 4000.2 "Developing and Issuing Guidance" and MAPP 4000.1"Developing and Issuing MAPPs for CDER" describe the guidance development process. All MAPPs can be accessed online (https://www.fda.gov/aboutfda/centersoffices/officeofmedicalproductsandtobacco/cder/manualofpoliciesprocedures/default.htm). Several MAPPs regarding agency review processes are useful in understanding how FDA staff will use information from sponsors to make regulatory decisions and can help sponsors prepare more reviewer-friendly documents.

CBER has a similar system, termed manuals of Standard Operating Procedures and Policies (SOPPs), also available online (https://www.fda.gov/biologicsbloodvaccines/guidancecomplianceregulatoryinformation/proceduressopps/default.htm).

A simple overview for situations requiring FDA premarket review is provided in **Figure 2-1**. This decision tree provides details about the regulations and the FDA center or office primarily responsible for a given product's development and approval. Some complexities, such as the distinction between drugs and biologics and the development of combination products, OTC drugs and foods or dietary supplements, are not highlighted in this figure, but are discussed in this chapter.

FDA Relationships and Meetings

The relationship between FDA and an investigational product sponsor can begin very early in the process (e.g., for a drug, even before the sponsor submits an Investigational New Drug (IND) application to test the product in humans) and may extend throughout the typical product development process (for drugs, these phases are often defined as Phases 1, 2 and 3) to a marketing application and on to postapproval commitments, safety surveillance and product lifecycle management.

Although sponsor meetings with FDA occurred prior to 1997, the reauthorization of the 1992 *Prescription Drug User Fee Act* in 1997 (*PDUFA II*) created a formal process for meetings, with established expectations and commitments from both parties. Processes for meeting requests and classifications are covered in *Draft Guidance for Industry: Formal Meetings Between the FDA and Sponsors or Applicants of PDUFA Products* (December 2017). This guidance clarifies how different meeting types with FDA are categorized as Type A, B or C and the associated timeline for each type.

Meetings can be requested at any time for any valid reason, but FDA will decide whether sufficient justification exists for a face-to-face meeting or a written response to questions and/or a teleconference would suffice. These FDA meeting request decisions usually are dictated by the development stage, product background, draft questions submitted in a written meeting request and whether the

Overview of Drug, Biologic, Device, Combination Product or Food Regulatory Pathways

Figure 2-1. Decision Tree for Drug and Device Development and Approval When FDA Premarket Review is Required

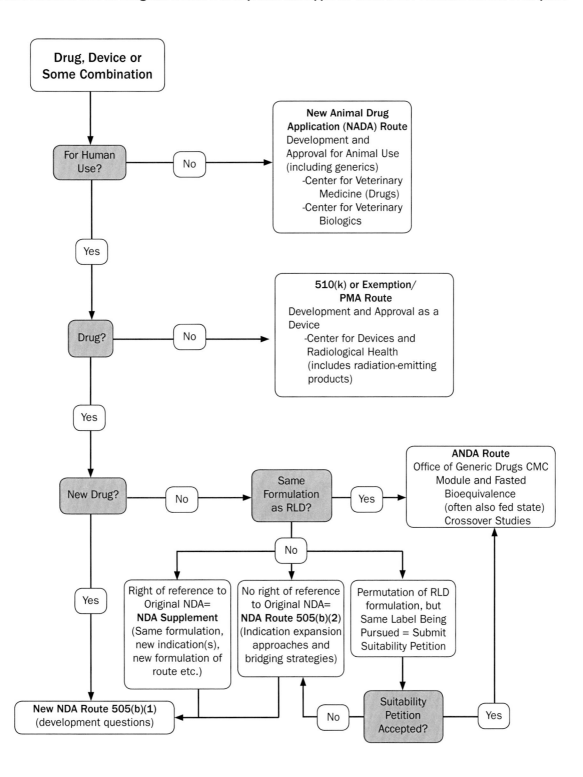

(ANDA, Abbreviated New Drug Application; CMC, Chemistry, Manufacturing, and Controls; NDA, New Drug Application; PMA, Premarket Approval; RLD, Reference Listed Drug (per Orange Book))

sponsor already had the meeting allotted for that development phase.

The most common meetings are the Pre-IND, End-of-Phase 2 (see *Guidance for Industry: End-of Phase 2A Meetings* (September 2009)) or Pre-NDA meetings. FDA often will allow an End-of-Phase 1 meeting for products granted expedited development, breakthrough or fast track designation.

For any meeting with FDA, clear and meaningful draft questions and a supporting pre-meeting package are highly recommended. The meeting package should not merely summarize what is known about a given drug (i.e., submission of only an Investigator's Brochure without any background and questions for FDA). Chapter 4 FDA Communications and Meetings provides more details on this topic.

The meeting request needs to meet FDA expectations, which sometimes vary slightly from one review division to the next. To succeed, it is important to learn—through experience or interaction—the relevant review division's approach to issues under its purview. The most effective interfaces between sponsors and FDA typically are formal meetings and Special Protocol Assessment (SPA) requests.

SPA

The SPA process is described in *Guidance for Industry: Special Protocol Assessment* (April 2018, Revision 1). Prior to 1997, FDA reviewed draft protocols on a case-by-case basis. The process often took several months and did not always address all the issues. *PDUFA II* established the SPA process where FDA agrees to evaluate certain protocols and related issues within 45 days of receipt to determine whether the SPA meets the scientific and regulatory requirements the sponsor identified (in the form of specific questions).

The *PDUFA* goals specify three main protocol types eligible for an SPA:
1. animal carcinogenicity protocols
2. final product stability protocols
3. human clinical trial protocols when the data will form the basis for an efficacy claim (i.e., for a Phase 3 or pivotal trial to be discussed at an End-of-Phase 2/Pre-Phase 3 meeting)

In addition, a SPA now can be used for:
- animal efficacy protocols for studies intended to provide primary evidence of effectiveness required for approval or licensure for products developed under the animal rule (animal rule efficacy protocols)
- protocols for any necessary clinical study or studies to prove biosimilarity and/or interchangeability

Although FDA generally adheres to the initial 45-day period, the agency may require several review/response cycles to ask and answer protocol-related questions before reaching a final understanding with the sponsor. If the FDA review division does not provide final agreement documentation, the sponsor should request written communication from FDA acknowledging the agreement.

Sponsors have several available avenues to help focus FDA attention on the drug development program and expedite marketing application approval. In addition to the traditional New Drug Application (NDA), sponsors may request Orphan Drug (for small/rare patient populations), Fast Track or Breakthrough Therapy (for drugs indicated for serious or life-threatening conditions), Qualified Infectious Disease Product (QIDP) (for antibiotic and antifungals only) and/or Priority Review designations (see 21 CFR 316 (Orphan) and *Guidance for Industry: Expedited Programs for Serious Conditions—Drugs and Biologics* (May 2014) for more information).

Sponsors also may seek accelerated NDA approval based on a surrogate endpoint or an effect on a clinical endpoint other than survival or irreversible morbidity (see 21 CFR 314.510, Subpart H Accelerated Approval of New Drugs for Serious or Life-threatening Illnesses). Confirmatory Phase 3 studies generally are required if FDA approves an NDA under Subpart H.

New Chemical Entities (NCEs) and the NDA (FD&C Act Section 505(b)(1))

Overview of FDA Approach to Drug Development and Approval

A "drug" is defined as a product used to diagnose, cure, mitigate, treat or prevent a disease or affecting a structure or function of the body (21 CFR 310.3), and a new drug is a:
- new use of a drug substance or component (e.g., active ingredient, excipient, carrier, coating, etc.)
- new use of a combination of approved drugs
- change in proportion of ingredients in a combination drug
- new intended use for the drug
- change in dosage, method or duration of administration or application

Thus, the following are subject to FDA approval:
1. a drug containing a novel chemical compound as its active ingredient (i.e., NCE)
2. a drug previously approved by FDA but now proposed for a new use or indication
3. a drug previously approved by FDA but in a different dosage form, route of administration or other key condition of use than that approved originally

Overview of Drug, Biologic, Device, Combination Product or Food Regulatory Pathways

Table 2-2. Key Questions in a Drug Development Program

In Vitro—Animals—Adults—Children		
Safety (Risk)	**Pharmacokinetics (PK)** (What the body does to the drug)	**Pharmacodynamics/Efficacy/Benefit** (What the drug does to the body)
How do you maximize the intellectual property aspect of the product?		
What is the known safety profile of other similar drugs and the class of drugs in general? For a new class of drugs or a new mechanism of action, safety in humans will not be known and will be associated with more risk.	Are competitor drugs with a less than ideal pharmacokinetic profile or route of administration on the market (e.g., substrates, inhibitors or inducers of more commonly used cytochrome P (CYP) 450 isoenzyme pathways)?	What endpoints have been accepted by FDA for other drugs developed to treat the target disease, or is this a first-in-class drug?
What safety profile would provide a competitive advantage?	What pharmacokinetic profile would provide a competitive advantage (including route of administration)?	What is the potential breadth of the target indication(s)?
What do you want to say about this product?		
What are the target organs/systems for toxicity?	What exposure profiles produce target organ/system effects?	What are the target organs/systems for pharmacological effects?
What toxicity is observed acutely versus chronically?	How is the time course of the effect related to the time-concentration curve of the parent drug and its metabolites?	What is the time course and duration of pharmacological/therapeutic effects?
Can the toxicities be monitored?	What are the potential or actual interactions with other drugs (especially those most commonly used by the target patient population)?	How do you measure the benefits?
Are the toxicities reversible?	What are the single-dose versus steady-state pharmacokinetics of the drug and its metabolites?	What happens to the therapeutic effects when you stop dosing?
What is the maximum tolerated dose, and what are risks of overdose?	Is the pharmacokinetic profile linear? If not, why not?	What is the minimal effective dose and duration of treatment?
What are the frequency and severity of safety findings, and what are the adverse events related to the new product?	How variable are drug concentrations (intra- and inter-subject)? These may be impacted by drug bioavailability or greater involvement of the more commonly used CYP isoenzyme systems.	How reproducible and clinically relevant are the pharmacodynamic and/or efficacy endpoints? These endpoint measures should be established, verified and validated.

The intake of any exogenous substance with pharmacological actions on the body presents some level of risk. Drug development consists of characterizing the drug's safety (i.e., the risk profile) and efficacy (i.e., the benefit profile) as it relates to the body's exposure to the drug (pharmacokinetic profile).

The most successful drugs are those with minimal risk and maximum benefit. The risk and benefit questions occurring during development are different for each product, based on such aspects as its formulation, chemical and physical characteristics, route of administration, target patient population, medical need, ability to monitor safety, ability to predict potential benefits from pharmacodynamic measures (surrogate endpoints) and the duration of treatment needed to demonstrate efficacy.

Table 2-2 lists some of the key questions FDA expects to be addressed as a drug is developed. Generally, due to risk, cost and time, evaluations are performed in the following order:
- *in vitro*
- live animals (juvenile if applicable, separated by species, smaller species first)
- adult humans (often in healthy subjects before patients)
- special subsets of the population (geriatrics, liver disease, kidney disease, etc.) as applicable
- pediatrics (if applicable)

As information is gained, new hypotheses may need to be tested; therefore, drug development is an iterative, dynamic process that requires effective communication among all the involved disciplines (i.e., clinical, nonclinical, manufacturing and regulatory). The company also will want to evaluate business risks (e.g., how to maximize

Regulatory Affairs Professionals Society

product market share and realize maximum return on investment with the least amount of risk).

PHS Act—Biologics and Biologics License Application (BLA)

Biological products, or biologics, are typically medical products made from natural sources (human, animal or microorganism) or containing large biological active macromolecules (like proteins) made by chemical processes. Like drugs, some biologics are intended to treat diseases and medical conditions, while other biologics are used to prevent or diagnose diseases. Examples of biological products include:
- vaccines
- blood and blood products for transfusion and/or manufacturing into other products
- allergenic extracts, which are used for both diagnosis and treatment (e.g., allergy shots)
- human cells and tissues used for transplantation (e.g., tendons, ligaments and bone)
- gene therapies
- cellular therapies
- tests to screen potential blood donors for infectious agents such as HIV

The BLA is a request for permission to introduce, or deliver for introduction, a biological product into interstate commerce (21 CFR 601.2). The BLA is regulated under 21 CFR 600–680 and is similar in content and structure to a New Drug Application (NDA) and submitted using the Common Technical Document (CTD) format.

The distinction between a drug and a biologic is based primarily on historic issues. After the St. Louis tetanus contamination, due to infected serum and other (smaller scale) occurrences of contaminated smallpox vaccine and diphtheria antitoxin, Congress passed the *Virus Serum and Toxin Act* (also known as the *Biologics Control Act*) in 1902. The act authorized the Hygienic Laboratory of the Public Health and Marine Hospital Service (which eventually became PHS) to issue regulations governing all aspects of vaccine, serum, toxin, antitoxin and similar product commercial production, with the objective of ensuring their safety, purity and potency.

In 1934, the Hygienic Laboratory (renamed NIH in 1930 by the *Ransdell Act*) issued a regulation indicating BLAs to manufacture new biologics would not be granted without evidence showing the products were effective. The *PHS Act* of 1944 reorganized PHS and gave NIH the authority to license, research and develop new biological products. Hence, one of the primary historic differences between biologics and drugs has been the inherent government research component of biologics, as opposed to emphasis on sponsor testing and regulation for drugs.[2] In addition, because biologics typically are derived from living organisms, immunogenicity issues and special requirements for specific nonclinical and clinical studies often distinguish them from small-molecule drugs.

In 1972, the Division of Biological Standards (part of NIH and, in turn, part of PHS) was transferred to FDA and eventually became CBER. Although the *PHS Act* established the BLA regulation, biologics are classified as drugs under the *FD&C Act*. Biologics require a BLA instead of an NDA, and new biological products require CBER safety and efficacy data review and approval prior to marketing. CBER focuses on therapeutic proteins, including vaccines and blood products. Also, as technology evolved, FDA shifted the review and approval of other, less complex, well characterized biological products, such as monoclonal antibodies, peptides and well-characterized proteins from CBER to CDER in 2003. Chapter 1 of 21 CFR summarizes the types of products now regulated by the two centers.

Generic Biologics and Biosimilars

The 2010 *Patient Protection and Affordable Care Act (Affordable Care Act)* amended the *PHS Act* to create an abbreviated licensure pathway for "biosimilar" or "interchangeable" biological products under the *Biologics Price Competition and Innovation Act* (*BPCI Act*). Biosimilar products may have minor differences in clinically inactive components but must not have any clinically meaningful differences in terms of safety and effectiveness from the reference product, which is a previously FDA-approved biological product already on the US market. An "interchangeable" biological product must meet additional standards to allow a practitioner to substitute the new biological for the reference product without the prescribing healthcare provider's intervention.

FDA requires licensed biosimilar and interchangeable biological products to meet the same rigorous safety and efficacy standards, which means patients and healthcare professionals will be able to rely on the biosimilar or interchangeable product's safety and effectiveness, just as they would the reference product. Chapter 27 provides a more detailed discussion of the biosimilar approval process.

User Fees—Biosimilar Investigational New Drug Applications (INDs)

The *FD&C Act*, as amended by the *Biosimilar User Fee Act* of 2012 (*BsUFA*), authorizes FDA to assess and collect fees for biosimilar biological products during the IND phase to support the enhanced development requirement for biosimilars (https://www.fda.gov/ForIndustry/UserFees/%20BiosimilarUserFeeActBsUFA/default.htm).

Orphan Drug Designation

The *Orphan Drug Act* of 1983 (21 CFR 316) provides incentives to develop necessary, and often life-saving, drugs for patients with rare diseases, but with minimal prospects for commercial return on investment. Congress has amended the act several times.

- The 1984 amendment redefined "rare disease or condition" as affecting fewer than 200,000 persons in the US at a given point or for which no reasonable expectation of recovering development costs through US sales are anticipated.
- The 1985 amendment extended the marketing exclusivity to all drugs and allowed federal grants for the clinical evaluation of orphan-designated drugs.
- The 1988 amendment required industry sponsors to apply for orphan designation prior to submitting a marketing application.
- The *Food and Drug Administration Modernization Act* of 1997 (*FDAMA*) included a provision exempting designated orphan product manufacturers from paying NDA user fees and allowing sponsors to seek waivers of annual postapproval establishment and product fees on a case-by-case, year-by-year basis.

The *Orphan Drug Act* provides a number of specific sponsor incentives:

- seven years of exclusive marketing rights for the designated indication once the drug receives FDA marketing approval
- a tax credit for up to 50% of qualified clinical research expenses incurred in developing a designated orphan product (This tax credit has a provision allowing the sponsor to carry the excess credit back one tax year if unable to use part or all of the credit because of tax liability limits, and then to carry forward any additional unused credit for up to 20 years after the year of the credit. This is important to start-up companies where profits are not available until the drug is on the market. The US Internal Revenue Service administers the tax credit provisions of the *Orphan Drug Act*.)
- eligibility for orphan drug grants

Details about the process to request orphan drug designation are at: https://www.fda.gov/forindustry/developingproductsforrarediseasesconditions/default.htm. The request must include:

- sponsor contact, drug names and sources
- description of rare disease or condition for which designation is being requested, with a medically plausible rationale for any patient subset approach
- drug description and scientific rationale for the indication for use among patients with the rare disease or condition
- summary of the drug's regulatory status and marketing history
- documentation showing the disease or condition affects fewer than 200,000 people in the US, or a rationale for why no reasonable expectation exists to recover the research and development costs through US sales for a drug to be administered to 200,000 or more persons per year

Once the request for designation has been received, the Office of Orphan Products Development (OOPD) will send a receipt letter; a formal response will take one to three months. Upon notification of orphan drug designation, the sponsor's name and the rare disease or condition will be entered into the searchable Orphan Drug Designations and Approvals database available online (https://www.accessdata.fda.gov/scripts/opdlisting/oopd/). As support for these products' development, FDA has harmonized the application form with the EMA, although the criteria and approval process are different. Once FDA grants an orphan drug designation, the designation can be revoked if the application is found to contain false data or if material data were omitted (e.g., if the disease actually had a higher prevalence than the sponsor reported). Notably, the designation cannot be revoked simply because the post-designation prevalence exceeds the original estimates.

The sponsor must provide annual updates including: a brief summary of any ongoing or completed nonclinical or clinical studies; a description of the investigational plan for the coming year; any anticipated difficulties in development, testing and marketing plans; and a brief discussion of any changes potentially affecting orphan drug status. Further details are covered in Chapter 35 Regulation of Products for Small Patient Populations.

Fast Track Designation

Fast track designation is described in *Guidance for Industry: Expedited Programs for Serious Conditions—Drugs and Biologics* (May 2014). In response to *FDAMA*, FDA better defined the fast track program in 1997 (21 CFR 312, Subpart E) to facilitate development and expedite review of new drugs intended to treat serious or life-threatening conditions with the potential to address significant, unmet medical needs. FDA has expanded the use of expedited programs to include products for regenerative medicines as well (Expedited Programs for Regenerative Medicine Therapies for Serious Conditions (February 2019)).

This guidance document defines a serious disease as: "a disease or condition associated with morbidity that has substantial impact on day-to-day functioning. Short-lived and self-limiting morbidity will usually not be sufficient, but the morbidity need not be irreversible if it is persistent or recurrent. Whether a disease or condition is serious is a matter of clinical judgment, based on its impact on such factors as survival, day-to-day functioning, or the likelihood that the disease, if left untreated, will progress from a less severe condition to a more serious one" (21 CFR 312.300(b)(1)).

In addition, "an unmet medical need" is defined as: "A condition whose treatment or diagnosis is not addressed adequately by available therapy. An unmet medical need includes an immediate need for a defined population (i.e., to treat a serious condition with no or limited treatment) or a longer-term need for society (e.g., to address the development of resistance to antibacterial drugs)."

A sponsor may request fast track designation at any point in the development process. When data become available to support the drug's potential to address unmet medical needs, the development plan should be designed to assess this potential and trigger a fast track designation application.

The agency will rely on available data summaries to determine whether the potential to address a serious, unmet medical need has been demonstrated and provide a designation response within 60 days. When emerging data no longer support fast track designation, or the designated drug development program is being pursued no longer, FDA may choose to send a letter notifying the sponsor the product has been reclassified.

The sponsor of a fast track development program product receives several benefits: eligibility for heightened interaction with FDA in sponsor meetings, greater probability of marketing application priority review (six months versus the standard 10 months) and submission of complete CTD modules as individual "reviewable units," known as a "rolling review" of the NDA or BLA. Note this rolling review is unique to fast track and breakthrough programs and needs to be specifically requested. The FDA review clock for the rolling NDA does not start until the marketing application submission is complete (i.e., once the last CTD module is submitted).

Breakthrough Therapy Designation

The 2012 *Food and Drug Administration Safety and Innovation Act* (*FDASIA*) expanded the accelerated approval pathway by defining a new "breakthrough therapy" designation to allow a sponsor increased FDA communication and attention above and beyond the fast track designation.

The breakthrough therapy goal is to expedite development and review of a potential new medicine if "intended, alone or in combination with one or more other drugs, to treat a serious or life-threatening disease or condition, and preliminary clinical evidence indicates that the drug may demonstrate substantial improvement over existing therapies on one or more clinically significant endpoints, such as substantial treatment effects observed early in clinical development."

A breakthrough therapy designation request should be submitted concurrently with, or as an amendment to, an IND. FDA will grant or deny determination no later than 60 days after submission receipt. For more information about designation content requirements, see *Guidance for Industry: Expedited Programs for Serious Conditions—Drugs and Biologics* (May 2014).

The following FDA resources are available to guide sponsors seeking this designation: frequently asked questions about breakthrough therapies (https://www.fda.gov/RegulatoryInformation/LawsEnforcedbyFDA/SignificantAmendmentstotheFDCAct/FDASIA/ucm341027.htm) and the *Fact Sheet: Breakthrough Therapies* (https://www.fda.gov/RegulatoryInformation/LawsEnforcedbyFDA/SignificantAmendmentstotheFDCAct/FDASIA/ucm329491.htm).

GAIN Act and QIDP Designation

FDASIA Title VIII, the *Generating Antibiotic Incentives Now Act* (*GAIN Act*), provides incentives for developing antibacterial and antifungal drugs for human use intended to treat serious and life-threatening infections. Under the *GAIN Act*, a drug may be designated as a QIDP, defined as "an antibacterial or antifungal drug for human use intended to treat serious or life-threatening infections, including those caused by an antibacterial or antifungal resistant pathogen, including novel or emerging infectious pathogens; or qualifying pathogen." A drug awarded QIDP designation is eligible for fast track designation and priority review, and the exclusivity period is extended by five years for a new prescription drug.

Rare Pediatric Disease and Tropical Diseases

FDAAA Section 1102 (2007) also authorized FDA to award priority review to sponsors of certain tropical disease product applications that meet the specified criteria. The law was designed to encourage development of new drug and biological products for prevention and treatment of certain tropical diseases affecting millions of people throughout the world. Because these diseases are found primarily in poor and developing countries,

Figure 2-2. CTD Organization

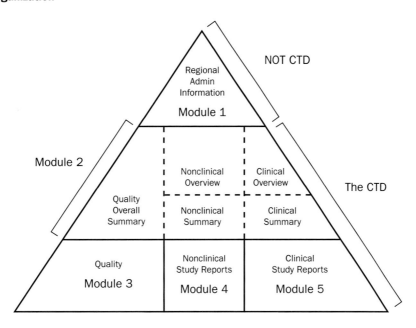

existing incentives have been insufficient to encourage such products' development. Although these tropical diseases generally are rare in the US, intercontinental jet transport, immigration, tourism and military operations are increasing the direct effect these diseases have on the health of Americans.

FDASIA Section 908 added section 529 to the *FD&C Act*. Under this section, FDA will award priority review to sponsors of certain rare pediatric disease product applications that meet the specified criteria. The law is intended to encourage development of new drugs to prevent and treat certain rare pediatric diseases. Although there are existing incentive programs to encourage the development and study of drugs for rare diseases, pediatric populations and unmet medical needs, Section 529 provides additional incentives.

Priority Review Vouchers

In addition to a variety of programs to expedite the development of products for serious and life-threatening diseases, FDA can award a voucher to a company for developing certain product types. This voucher can be used for a priority review of a subsequent NDA submission for a product that otherwise would not qualify. Since 2007, FDA has issued a number of special priority review vouchers that allow their recipients to expedite the review of any of their new drug products.[6] A company can obtain one of these vouchers for developing and gaining approval for a drug to treat a rare pediatric disease or a tropical disease, or for a product to be used as a medical countermeasure (*Tropical Disease Priority Review Vouchers:*

Guidance for Industry (October 2016) and *Rare Pediatric Disease Priority Review Vouchers: Draft Guidance for Industry* (November 2014)).

ICH

ICH was founded in 1990 by regulatory authorities from the EU, Japan and the US and pharmaceutical industry experts to discuss product registrations' scientific and technical aspects. This group's goal was to develop guidance to harmonize product registration requirements using technical guidelines to reduce or avoid duplicate testing during new drug research and development.

ICH's objectives include conserving human, animal and material resources and eliminating unnecessary delays in global development and availability of new medicines while safeguarding quality, safety, efficacy and protecting public health. ICH has issued numerous guidelines in four major categories:

- quality—topics relating to chemical and pharmaceutical quality assurance, including stability testing and impurity testing
- safety—topics relating to *in vitro* and *in vivo* nonclinical studies, including safety pharmacology, carcinogenicity testing, reproductive toxicology, anticancer nonclinical requirements, photosafety, chronic toxicology immunotoxicity and genotoxicity testing
- efficacy—topics relating to human subjects' clinical studies, including dose-response studies and GCPs

- multidisciplinary—topics covering cross-disciplinary issues or not uniquely fitting into one of the other categories, including the Medical Dictionary for Regulatory Activities (MedDRA), CTD and Electronic Standards for the Transfer of Regulatory Information (ESTRI)

Copies of guidelines and historic information about the four-step review and consensus processes are available at https://www.ich.org/products/guidelines.html.

Most ICH guidelines have been accepted by FDA and published in the *Federal Register* with statements indicating these ICH guidelines "reflect current agency thinking."

MedDRA is an accepted international medical terminology dictionary developed by ICH and is designed to support medical information classification, retrieval, presentation and communication throughout the drug and medical device regulatory cycle. *MedDRA* is particularly important in electronic adverse event report coding and transmissions and clinical trial data coding (ICH M1). Further details are available at http://www.meddra.org/.

CTD

The CTD includes five modules (see **Figure 2-2**) in a hierarchical structure, with the most detail at the base and higher-level summaries and integration above (see *Guidance for Industry M4: Organization of the CTD* (August 2001)). For electronic submissions, see *Guidance for Industry M2 eCTD: Electronic Common Technical Document Specification* (April 2003).

Module 1 is region-specific (US, EU, Japan) and, for US submissions, Module 1 contains FDA forms, draft labeling, Risk Evaluation and Mitigation Strategies (REMS), FDA correspondence (e.g., FDA meeting minutes) and patient information (e.g., Investigator's Brochure (IB) if the submission is focused on an IND).

Module 2 summarizes quality, nonclinical and clinical details and provides a concise context to integrate key benefit-risk data.

Module 3 details quality data (see *Guidance for Industry M4Q: The CTD—Quality* (August 2001)). The corresponding summary is in Module 2.3.

Module 4 includes nonclinical and safety data (see *Guidance for Industry M4S: The CTD—Safety* (August 2001) and *Guidance for Industry M4S: The CTD—Safety Appendices* (August 2001)). The corresponding summary is in Modules 2.4 Nonclinical Overview and 2.6 Nonclinical Written and Tabulated Summaries.

Module 5 contains clinical data (see *Guidance for Industry M4E: The CTD—Efficacy* (August 2001)), with summaries in Module 2.

Initial IND and IND Amendments

Before initiating a US clinical trial, other than bioequivalence studies to support an Abbreviated New Drug Application (ANDA), the sponsor must submit an IND including the required nonclinical, CMC and previous human experience data (if available) to FDA in a notice of claimed investigational exemption for a new drug (21 CFR 312). This IND application is not a request for approval; rather, it is a request for exemption from federal law to transport or distribute a drug across state lines in interstate commerce. Because in most cases the drug product must be shipped to investigative sites across state lines to be used in clinical trials, the sponsor must receive an exemption from this legal requirement.

After receiving the initial IND application, FDA will send the sponsor an email acknowledging the application's receipt. Since all submissions now must be electronic, sponsors need to request an IND number assignment prior to submission.

The email will indicate the proposed clinical trial cannot begin until 30 calendar days after IND receipt (unless contacted earlier). If the sponsor is not contacted by FDA within 30 days, the trial may begin. FDA approval to initiate clinical trials is federally mandated and implicit, i.e., the IND goes into effect. If FDA determines the proposed study is not reasonably safe for human subjects, it is required to inform the sponsor within 30 calendar days to not begin the clinical trial because the agency has placed the trial on "clinical hold."

Regardless of the IND decision, the sponsor should develop a relationship with the FDA project manager assigned to the submission, since many future agency interactions will be required during development before the product can reach the US market. The sponsor may want to learn more details about FDA's IND review.

For the initial IND (as for the initial NDA), FDA assigns a review team led by a regulatory project manager (RPM) that includes a medical reviewer, pharmacology/toxicology reviewer from the review division and a CMC reviewer from the Office of New Drug Quality Assessment (ONDQA). A clinical pharmacologist from the Office of Clinical Pharmacology and a statistician from the Office of Biostatistics also may be assigned.

The team generally will meet during the last week of the 30-day review period to decide, with the division director, whether the proposed study may proceed. In some cases, the RPM may contact the sponsor to request additional information or to propose the study may be initiated if certain modifications are made to its protocol. FDA typically will contact the sponsor by phone to discuss and issue a letter containing details of any requested modifications or supporting data.

Where previous clinical studies have not been conducted for an NCE, the initial IND is a major milestone because it summarizes the data required to move a drug from *in vitro* and animal testing into human clinical trials.

Although the initial IND's content and format are described in 21 CFR 312.23, INDs from commercial sponsors now must be filed electronically using the electronic CTD (eCTD) format. Paper IND submissions are allowed only for research INDs submitted by academic researchers. These INDs typically involve a single study that does not have a marketing application as the trial's endpoint.

IND Safety Reporting

If the IND is not withdrawn (21 CFR 312.38) or considered inactive (21 CFR 312.45), the active IND requires expedited IND safety reports for serious, unexpected adverse reactions (21 CFR 312.32). A Serious Adverse Event (SAE) is any untoward medical occurrence resulting in death or a life-threatening condition; requiring subject hospitalization or prolongation of existing hospitalization; resulting in persistent or significant disability or incapacity; or is a congenital anomaly or birth defect. IND safety report submission to FDA is time-sensitive; the day the sponsor is notified of the SAE is considered Day 1, and all reporting timeframes are tied to the date the sponsor became aware of the event (**Table 2-3**).

Guidance for Industry and Investigators—Safety Reporting Requirements for INDs and BA/BE Studies (December 2012) provides further details and covers SAE reporting requirements for bioavailability (BA) and bioequivalence (BE) studies as well.

IND Annual Reports

IND sponsors also are required to submit IND Annual Reports within 60 days of the anniversary date (i.e., the date the IND went into effect, per 21 CFR 312.33). The IND Annual Report focuses on clinical safety signals (especially any deaths or other SAEs or dropouts due to adverse events) or any new nonclinical safety findings and includes an outline of the coming year's development plan. *Guidance for Industry: E2F Development Safety Update Report* (August 2011) describes an approach for annual safety reporting, where the Developmental Safety Update Report (DSUR) is intended to replace the IND Annual Report with a comprehensive, harmonized safety summary representing a common standard for ICH regions.

FDA also requires clinical trials to be registered in NIH's Clinical Trials database (www.clinicaltrials.gov). The initiative began in 2001 with the posting of clinical studies for serious or life-threatening diseases and, under the 2007 *Food and Drug Administration Amendments Act* (*FDAAA*), the project was expanded to include all human, controlled clinical trials (i.e., other than Phase 1 studies and most BE studies). As of February 2019, almost 300,000 trials have been registered in virtually every country around the world, with more than 45% including sites outside the US. This database can be a good resource for clinical study information.

Table 2-3. IND Safety Reporting Timeframes

SAE Outcome	Deadline for Reporting
Fatal or life-threatening	Seven calendar days, by phone, email or facsimile, followed by a written report within eight additional calendar days
All other SAE outcomes	15 calendar days, in writing

NDA 505(b)(1)

General Considerations

Drugs gain approval for entry into the US market via the NDA (21 CFR 314). The culmination of a drug or biologic development program is preparing and submitting a marketing application (NDA or BLA). This is accomplished through studies either conducted by, or with a right of reference from, the sponsor (i.e., the 505(b)(1) approach) or by reference to FDA's safety and effectiveness findings for a previously approved product (i.e., the 505(b)(2) approach, sometimes referred to as the "paper NDA").

Sponsor and agency expectations should be aligned through frequent interactions during development, including a Pre-NDA meeting, usually held no later than three months prior to the target NDA filing date. The marketing application should contain sufficient data for FDA to decide whether the drug's benefits outweigh its risks in the context of the sponsor's proposed labeled use.

Labeling: Package Insert

In addition to study reports and summaries evaluating drug safety and efficacy, the draft labeling package insert, prescribing information or "label" is a primary NDA and BLA component. Labeling must be submitted to FDA in structured product label (SPL) format within an Extensible Markup Language (XML) backbone to meet FDA requirements. SPL is a model-derived standard adopted for exchange of FDA-regulated product information contained in the labeling, coded information from the labeling content (data elements) and a "wrapper" for electronic listing elements.

Most review divisions also will request a label content copy in Microsoft Word (and draft SPL format in the NDA) so they can use the track changes function to communicate with the sponsor during the label negotiation process. The label format should be confirmed in either the Pre-NDA meeting or with the FDA project manager prior to NDA filing. When agreement is reached on the labeling, the sponsor should submit a final copy of the

Chapter 2

label to FDA in SPL format. NDA labeling also must follow Physician Labeling Rule (PLR) format, which requires three parts: highlights (one page), contents and full prescribing information. The PLR format requires sponsors to identify and provide dates for recent major changes to the prescribing information, including the date of initial US approval for the active ingredient (www.fda.gov/Drugs/GuidanceComplianceRegulatoryInformation/LawsActsandRules/ucm084159.htm).

Electronic Submission
FDA eCTD format and electronic submission requirements are becoming more strict. Effective 5 May 2017, all NDAs, ANDAs, BLAs and master files had to be submitted electronically in eCTD format, and effective 5 May 2018, all commercial INDs were required to be submitted electronically in eCTD format. For further information, FDA maintains a useful Electronic Regulatory Submissions and Review website (www.fda.gov/Drugs/DevelopmentApprovalProcess/FormsSubmissionRequirements/ElectronicSubmissions/UCM085361) and a website discussing eCTD requirements (https://www.fda.gov/Drugs/DevelopmentApprovalProcess/FormsSubmissionRequirements/ElectronicSubmissions/ucm153574.htm).

REMS
Evaluating a product's risk potential is an important aspect of FDA drug approval. The sponsor must extrapolate and estimate risks from data derived from a few thousand patients exposed to the drug under relatively well-controlled conditions to millions of patients with much less oversight. FDA has a mandate to mitigate a drug's potential risks throughout development and marketing and has released three topical guidance documents to help with assessments on:
- premarketing risk
- development and use of risk minimization action plans
- Good Pharmacovigilance Practices and pharmacoepidemiologic risks

During development, FDA wants to know how a sponsor plans to mitigate a drug's actual and potential risks (RiskMAP) if a marketing application is approved and how risk would be monitored after approval. *FDAAA* gave FDA the authority to require a REMS plan from sponsors prior to approval. A REMS includes sponsor postapproval evaluations at 18 months, three years and seven years and may be as simple as including a Medication Guide with the package insert or as complex as developing a training program for patients and pharmacists (e.g., as Elements to Assure Safe Use (ETASU)).

Proprietary Name
The sponsor should request the review division to evaluate its proposed proprietary name(s) under the IND or as part of the initial NDA submission (see *Guidance for Industry: Contents of a Complete Submission for the Evaluation of Proprietary Names* (April 2016) and *Draft Guidance for Industry Best Practices in Developing Proprietary Names for Drugs* (April 2016)).

Although the guidance states this request should be submitted at the end of Phase 2 (with a 180-day review timeframe), FDA will give only tentative name approval until 90 days after the NDA has been accepted. The review division will forward the proprietary name request to the Office of Postmarketing Drug Risk Assessment, Division of Drug Risk Evaluation, which will perform the primary review in consultation with the Office of Prescription Drug Promotion (OPDP). FDA will accept or reject the proposed name. If a name is rejected, a sponsor can appeal or submit one or two additional names for review.

User Fees—Drugs and Biologics
Under the original *PDUFA* (and subsequent amendments), user fees are levied on each "human drug application," including applications for:
- approval of a new drug submitted under Section 505(b)(1)
- approval of a new drug submitted under Section 505(b)(2) for certain molecular entities or indications for use
- licensure of certain biological products submitted under *PHS Act* Section 351

User fees vary for original applications and are significantly higher if the application includes clinical data for safety and/or efficacy (other than BA/BE studies). The act also levies fees on supplements to human drug applications when they include clinical data. Original applications without clinical data, and supplements with clinical data, are assessed at approximately one-half the original application fee. Further details are provided in *Guidance for Industry: Submitting Separate Marketing Applications and Clinical Data for Purposes of Assessing User Fees* (December 2004).

The user fee for a full submission has increased every year and currently is more than $2.4 million for a full NDA with clinical data for FY 2019. FDA also levies annual program fees for each product presentation on the market to cover ongoing oversight activities. Further information on these fees can be found online (www.fda.gov/forindustry/userfees/default.htm).

Preapproval Inspection (PAI)

One of FDA's objectives in the NDA review process is to determine whether the manufacturing methods and controls used to maintain drug quality are adequate to preserve the drug's identity, strength, quality, stability and purity. In conjunction with this evaluation, FDA field inspectors conduct a CGMP Preapproval Inspection (PAI) of the drug product manufacturing site if it has not been inspected recently by FDA with a favorable outcome. A PAI can occur as early as 90 days after an NDA submission. An adequate PAI is required for NDA/BLA approval (CPGM 7346.832).

Peri-Approval Activities

A number of peri-approval activities should be included in the overall submission and approval plan. A safety update is required as an NDA amendment within 120 days of initial NDA submission. In addition, approximately one month prior to the FDA action date, the FDA RPM will contact the sponsor and begin label negotiations if approval is likely. At this time (if not submitted previously), the sponsor should submit a request for a National Drug Code (NDC) assignment (see *Guidance for Industry: Standards for Securing the Drug Supply Chain—Standardized Numerical Identification for Prescription Drug Packages* (March 2010)). The drug label, packaging artwork and labels and promotional material cannot be finalized until very near the approval date.

For some product approvals, FDA will seek the advice of one of its Advisory Committees prior to making a decision. FDA uses Advisory Committees to provide independent advice to guide the agency's regulatory decision making. This is especially important, as the complexity of benefit-risk decisions increases and gains more focus. Chapter 5 provides a detailed description of FDA Advisory Committees and the timing for FDA requesting such a meeting.

Establishment Listing

FDA requires establishments (e.g., manufacturers, repackers and relabelers), upon first engaging in the manufacture, preparation, propagation, compounding or processing of human drugs, veterinary drugs and biological products, with certain exceptions, to register their establishments and list information for all drugs and biological products in commercial distribution (See 21 CFR 207).

Registrants also are required to submit, on or before 31 December each year, updated establishment registration information. Form FDA 2656 is used for drug establishment registration (and the labeler code assignment), and Form FDA 2657 is used for drug product listing purposes. All submissions are to be electronic and in XML format, unless a waiver is granted (see *Guidance for Industry: Providing Regulatory Submissions in Electronic Format—Drug Establishment Registration and Drug Listing* (May 2009) and www.fda.gov/Drugs/GuidanceComplianceRegulatoryInformation/DrugRegistrationandListing/ucm531142.htm).

Patent Protection

The *Drug Price Competition and Patent Term Restoration Act* of 1984 *(Hatch-Waxman Act)* represented a compromise between the innovator pharmaceutical industry and the generic pharmaceutical industry. This act allowed innovator pharmaceutical companies to apply for up to five years of additional patent protection for new drugs to make up for time lost while their products were going through the development and regulatory review process.

The drug (animal or human), medical device, biologic, food or color additive must be the first commercial marketing or use of the product under the provision of the law for which regulatory review occurred. FDA assists the Patent and Trademark Office (PTO) in determining a product's eligibility for patent extension, but PTO ultimately is responsible for determining the patent extension period.

Similarly, up to three years of market exclusivity are granted for a change in an approved drug product where approval requires new clinical investigations other than BA/BE studies (e.g., new indication, strength, dosage form or route of administration). Further details on the patent term restoration program can be found online (www.fda.gov/Drugs/DevelopmentApprovalProcess/SmallBusinessAssistance/ucm069959.htm).

FDA also provides an incentive to conduct additional pediatric population drug studies by allowing six months of pediatric exclusivity in some cases (www.fda.gov/ScienceResearch/SpecialTopics/PediatricTherapeuticsResearch/ucm509709.htm).

NDA Amendments

Finally, an NDA amendment is submitted to change or add information to an unapproved NDA or NDA supplement. Other than the required 120-day safety update, sponsors should try to avoid initiating NDA amendments because they potentially will reset the review clock (especially if submitted in the final three months of the review period).

The 505(b)(2) "Paper" NDA
General Considerations

This approach allows applicants to use published literature and other published information to satisfy the requirements for full safety and efficacy reports. The 505(b)(2) NDA is a submission that shares characteristics of both traditional NDAs and ANDAs. About half of all new drugs approved in the US are submitted as 505(b)(2) NDAs.

As with a traditional 505(b)(1) NDA, a 505(b)(2) application is considered a complete application and is approved under *FD&C Act* Section 505(c). Like a 505(j) ANDA, the 505(b)(2) application references FDA safety and effectiveness findings for a previously approved product. Unlike the 505(j) ANDA for generics, both 505(b)(1) and 505(b)(2) NDA approvals offer potential patent and market exclusivity provisions.[3]

Regulations for 505(b)(2) applications are codified in 21 CFR 314.54, and additional information is provided in *Draft Guidance for Industry: Applications Covered by Section 505(b)(2)* (October 1999).

Bridging and Expansion Issues and Approaches
The most common 505(b)(2) applications are for:
- an NCE with studies conducted by other sponsors and published information pertinent to the application (e.g., a pro-drug or active metabolite of a previously approved drug)
- a change in dosage form or regimen (including route of administration), formulation and/or strength, including any changes not accepted by FDA in a Suitability Petition to the Office of Generic Drugs (OGD)
- a change in active ingredient (different salt, ester complex, chelate, etc.)
- a new combination product with previously approved active ingredients
- a change from a prescription indication to an over-the-counter (OTC) indication
- a change to an OTC monograph drug (e.g., new dosage form or indication not listed in monograph)
- an indication not previously approved for the active moiety

If the applicant is the original NDA holder or has the NDA holder's right of reference, the above changes become supplements to the original NDA ((505(b)(1)), as outlined in **Figure 2-2**.

The most commonly required 505(b)(2) application data provide a bridge between the data forming the basis for the referenced NDA's approval (agreed to by FDA in the approved drug product label) and the 505(b)(2) NDA label's different or additional claims. For active ingredient modifications, bridging focuses on impurity profiles and/or bioavailability and subsequent exposure changes. For drug product modifications, bridging looks at exposure profile differences. In both cases, a bridging toxicology program may be required, including multiple-dose toxicology studies (14–90 days), with toxicokinetics in appropriate species, as well as mutagenicity and genotoxicity studies. The bridging program generally should not be initiated until agreement is reached with FDA in a formal meeting.

Additional bridging studies usually are needed for clinical pharmacokinetics. The product should be at least as bioavailable as the reference listed drug (RLD) unless the drug has some other advantage, such as a smaller peak/trough exposure ratio, etc. Moreover, the proposed product's release pattern, although different, should be at least as favorable as the RLD release pattern.

A 505(b)(2) application may be granted three years of exclusivity if one or more clinical investigations, other than BA/BE studies, was essential to approval and conducted for or sponsored by the applicant. (If any clinical studies are required for the 505(b)(2) application, an IND application is required.) A 505(b)(2) application for a new molecular entity (NME) or NCE not previously approved also may be granted five years of exclusivity.

The Abbreviated NDA for 505(j) "Generics"
General Considerations
Partly in response to the thalidomide tragedy, Congress passed the *Kefauver-Harris Amendments* in 1962. These amendments required drug manufacturers to document and demonstrate both a drug's effectiveness and its safety prior to marketing. Previously, FDA focused only on safety under the original *FD&C Act. Kefauver-Harris* also gave FDA control over prescription drug advertising, established GMPs and created the IND requirement and the requirement for clinical trial subjects' informed consent.

In 1966, FDA contracted the National Academy of Sciences' National Research Council to conduct an evaluation of drugs approved 1938–62 to determine whether they met the new efficacy (and safety) demonstration requirements. The Drug Efficacy Study Implementation (DESI) program evaluated more than 3,000 separate products and 16,000 therapeutic claims. One of the DESI program's early results was developing the Abbreviated New Drug Application (ANDA). ANDAs were accepted for labeling changes for previously reviewed products determined not to be 'new drugs.' However, the 1962 Amendments only applied to generic versions of drugs approved prior to 1962. There was no provision for generics for drugs approved post-1962.

The *Hatch-Waxman Act* ushered in the modern era of generic drugs. It closed the gap by allowing a generic version of any drug approved by FDA (pre- or post-1962). This act expedited the availability of less-costly generic drugs by permitting FDA to approve abbreviated applications after the innovator drug's patent and exclusivity had expired. These are termed "abbreviated" NDAs because they are not required to include animal safety and clinical data to establish safety and effectiveness. For oral dosage forms, the generic drug must be bioequivalent to the innovator reference listed drug (RLD). Sponsors of such products as sterile injectables, otics and ophthalmics with a high solubility-high permeability rating (A/A rated) can obtain a waiver for *in vivo* bioequivalence testing from FDA.

To be bioequivalent, the generic drug product must deliver the same amount of active ingredient into a subject's bloodstream (within an FDA-specified range) over the same amount of time as the RLD. Specifically, a generic drug product is identical to the innovator drug product in dosage form, strength, route of administration, quality, performance characteristics and intended use. All approved products, both innovator and generic, are listed in FDA's Approved Drug Products with Therapeutic Equivalence Evaluations (*Orange Book*), accessible on FDA's website (www.accessdata.fda.gov/scripts/cder/ob/default.cfm).

The *Orange Book* identifies the RLD and the appropriate reference listed strength (RLS) of the approved product to be used as a reference. It also provides information on applicable patents, exclusivities and their expiration dates. A product approved under the ANDA process will have the same labeling as the RLD, except for minor allowed changes in wording. Nearly 80% of all drug prescriptions dispensed in the US are generic. The ANDA includes three primary components:
- CMC information
- bioequivalence data
- administrative information (e.g., labeling and patent certification information)

ANDA requirements for CMC information and manufacture under CGMPs do not differ significantly from NDA requirements.

An OGD initiative to streamline CMC review is to use a question-based review (QbR) format for ANDA Quality Overall Summary submission. The QbR questions and answers are placed in CTD Module 2. OGD also has developed a standard group of summary tables (Model Bioequivalence Data Summary Tables) consistent with the CTD format to ensure consistent and concise data are submitted in the applicable ANDA sections.

Clinical bioequivalence study design, conduct and analysis are covered in *Draft Guidance for Industry: Bioavailability and Bioequivalence Studies Submitted in NDAs or INDs—General Considerations* (March 2014) and *Draft Guidance for Industry: Bioanalytical Method Validation* (September 2013, Revision 1). *Guidance for Industry: Bioanalytical Method Validation* (May 2001) covers bioanalytical method validation requirements used to evaluate active ingredient blood concentrations, which also apply to drugs developed through the NDA route. OGD issued *Guidance for Industry: Bioequivalence Recommendations for Specific Products* in June 2010, which describes how and where OGD will release bioequivalence recommendations for specific products in the future.

Generally, two-way crossover studies of the generic product versus the RLD in the fasted state are performed (sometimes preceded by pilot studies to determine variability and group sizes). If the RLD label indicates a food effect, a second study in the fed state (using a standardized high-fat meal) typically is required. Additional studies may be needed to demonstrate bioequivalence of different strengths if the excipient-to-active pharmaceutical ingredient ratio in each generic drug dosage strength is not the same.

As defined by FDA, the generic is deemed bioequivalent to the RLD in any of the above studies if the 90% confidence interval for the population ratio geometric means between the two treatments, based on log-transformed data, is contained within the equivalence limits of 80%–125% for the area under the curve (AUC) and peak serum concentration (C_{max}). A common misinterpretation of this is generic drug active ingredient levels may vary from -20% to +25% compared to the innovator. In fact, those numbers relate to a derived statistical calculation and do not represent the actual difference in the amount of active ingredient in a patient's bloodstream, which generally is similar to the variation between different batches of the same innovator drug. A number of analyses published by FDA and others have demonstrated that, in order to meet the 90% confidence interval for the geometric means, the average real difference between the means was between 3–5%. This is consistent with same variation seen between two different lots of reference product when tested against each other.[4,5]

For the statistically minded, *Guidance for Industry— Statistical Approaches to Establishing Bioequivalence* (January 2001) describes how to conduct the above analysis. If bioequivalence studies are being conducted to support an ANDA, they do not have to be conducted under an IND unless the study will be conducted in patients instead of normal volunteers or involves a cytotoxic drug (oncology). They do need to be reviewed and approved (including informed consent) by an appropriate Institutional Review Board (IRB).

The ANDA also must contain one of the following patent certifications relative to the reference listed product (RLD) (21 CFR 314.94(a)(12)):
- No patent information has been filed (Paragraph I).
- The patent has expired (Paragraph II).
- The patent will expire on a specific date (Paragraph III), and the ANDA sponsor does not intend to market its product before that date.
- The patent is invalid or will not be infringed by the proposed drug product (Paragraph IV).

If the ANDA applicant certifies the patent is invalid or will not be infringed, Paragraph IV certifies the applicant is required to notify the NDA holder and patent owner. If the NDA holder brings an action for patent infringement within 45 days of this notification, FDA will not approve the ANDA for 30 months, or such shorter or longer period as a court may order, or until the date of a court decision (known as the 30-month stay).

Originally, the 180-day exclusivity for generic drugs applied only to the first company to submit an ANDA with a Paragraph IV certification. However, the current approach to 180-day exclusivity (described in *Guidance to Industry: 180-Day Exclusivity When Multiple ANDAs are Submitted on the Same Day* (July 2003)) is applicable to all cases in which multiple ANDA applicants submit Paragraph IV certifications challenging the same listed patent or patents on the same first day. This provides a shared incentive for multiple companies willing to challenge a listed patent and possibly defend a patent infringement suit.

Although generic development time is relatively short, ANDA review and approval times average approximately two years for several hundred applications each year, which clearly impacts the timeframe for moving generic products to the market. The *Generic Drug User Fee Amendments* of 2012 (*GDUFA*) was meant to address this lengthy timeframe. This suggests a proactive strategy of submitting ANDA applications well in advance of patent expiration. A company with an approved ANDA is subject to the same postapproval reporting requirements as an NDA holder (21 CFR 314.80 Postmarketing reporting of adverse drug experiences and 21 CFR 314.81 Field alert reports and annual reports). Many of the topics above are covered in more detail in Chapter 16 Generic Drug Submissions. OGD's website also is a good resource (www.fda.gov/AboutFDA/CentersOffices/OfficeofMedicalProductsandTobacco/CDER/ucm119100.htm).

Branded and Authorized Generics

"Branded" generics are approved in the same manner as all generics, but the ANDA applicant also applies for and receives a proprietary brand name under the same process as NDAs. A brand name allows the company to distinguish its generic from others when marketing activities are contemplated. Innovator companies also can offer a branded generic for their own products.

An "authorized generic" is a drug product with a licensing agreement between the innovator company and the generic drug manufacturer, allowing the innovator company to obtain revenue through the generic process by licensing a manufacturer to market the RLD as a generic using a different "trade dress" while continuing to market the innovator drug under the original proprietary name.

A list of authorized generics (updated quarterly), including the original NDA applicant name, is available on OGD's website (www.fda.gov/AboutFDA/CentersOffices/OfficeofMedicalProductsandTobacco/CDER/ucm119100.htm).

User Fees—Generic Drugs

GDUFA was designed to speed access to safe and effective generic drugs to the public and reduce industry costs and timeframes. The law requires industry to pay user fees to supplement generic drug application review and facility inspections. Additional resources enable the agency to reduce the backlog of pending applications, cut the average time required to review generic drug applications for safety and increase risk-based inspections. More information and current *GDUFA* fees are available at (http://www.fda.gov/ForIndustry/UserFees/GenericDrugUserFees/default.htm).

Dietary Supplements, New Dietary Ingredients and Claim Substantiation

A dietary supplement is a product taken by mouth that contains a "dietary ingredient" intended to supplement the diet. These dietary ingredients may be vitamins, minerals, herbs or other botanicals, amino acids or substances such as enzymes, organ tissues, glandulars and metabolites.

Until 1994, dietary supplements were subject to the regulatory requirements for foods. Congress passed the *Dietary Supplement Health and Education Act (DSHEA)* in 1994, which amended the *FD&C Act* to create a new dietary supplement safety and labeling regulatory structure under the food regulatory umbrella. *DSHEA* provisions define dietary supplements and dietary ingredients and describe the proper use of nutritional support statements. *DSHEA* also set forth new labeling requirements and required dietary supplement manufacturers to notify FDA of new dietary ingredients prior to marketing (21 CFR 190.6).

DSHEA authorized FDA to require CGMPs for dietary supplements. The *Final Rule on CGMP in Manufacturing, Packaging, Labeling, or Holding Operations for Dietary Supplements* established dietary supplement CGMPs for all domestic and foreign companies manufacturing, packaging, labeling or holding these supplements, including those involved with US testing, quality control, packaging and labeling and distribution. The dietary supplement CGMPs bear a stronger resemblance to drug CGMPs than to food CGMPs; however, dietary supplement and food CGMPs do not require the process validation mandated for drug CGMPs.

Like foods, dietary supplements do not require FDA premarket approval; however, the manufacturer must ensure each dietary supplement is safe before it is marketed. *DSHEA* places the burden on FDA to prove a marketed dietary supplement is unsafe prior to any action to remove it from the market. Because of this requirement and the fact FDA received numerous reports of safety concerns for a number of products, Congress passed the *Dietary Supplement and Nonprescription Drug Consumer Protection Act* in 2006, requiring the same adverse event reporting and recordkeeping for dietary supplements and nonprescription drugs as for prescription drugs.

New dietary ingredients, unlike dietary supplements, require notifications (NDINs) to be filed with FDA 75 days prior to marketing to demonstrate their safety. Food and color additives need FDA-approved petitions (e.g., food additive petition (FAP) or color additive petition (CAP)) prior to marketing.

Similar to those for marketing, dietary supplement claims are regulated by the Federal Trade Commission (FTC). Expressed or implied claims stating a dietary supplement will diagnose, mitigate, treat, cure or prevent a specific disease or class of diseases are not allowed. Examples of prohibited statements include: "protects against the development of cancer" or "reduces the pain and stiffness associated with arthritis."

FTC and FDA allow specific truthful, non-misleading claim types, for example: Qualified Health Claims, Structure Function Claims and Nutrient Content Claims. Examples of claims allowed under *DSHEA* include:
- claims of benefits related to nutrient deficiencies (if the disease prevalence in the US is disclosed)
- claims describing the role of the dietary supplement's effects on structure or function in humans (e.g., "calcium builds strong bones")
- claims describing the mechanism of effects on structure or function (e.g., "fiber maintains bowel regularity," "helps promote urinary health," "helps maintain cardiovascular function" or "promotes relaxation")
- general well-being claims

Further details can be found in *Guidance for Industry: Structure/Function Claims Small Entity Compliance Guide* (January 2002). Also, see Chapter 32 Dietary Supplements and Homeopathic Products.

Over-the-Counter (OTC) Drugs

An OTC product is a drug marketed for consumer use without the need for a healthcare professional's intervention. More than 80 OTC drug therapeutic categories and more than 100,000 OTC drug products are marketed in the US, encompassing approximately 800 active ingredients. OTC drug oversight is performed by CDER's Office of Nonprescription Drugs.

The distinction between prescription and nonprescription drugs dates back to the 1951 *Durham-Humphrey Amendment* to the *FD&C Act*. FDA applied the retrospective review principle of OTC drug active ingredients by expert panels starting in 1972. Initially, approximately 1,000 different moieties were reviewed. The agency published the OTC review results as a series of monographs in 21 CFR 328–358, specifying the active ingredient(s), formulation restrictions and labeling by therapeutic category for those drugs deemed appropriate for OTC use. However, 45 years later, the OTC review process still is not complete, and monographs that need revision and updating are lagging. A proposal is under consideration for an OTC drug user fee to provide additional resources to finish and modernize the process.

If the relevant monograph's standards are met, an OTC product does not require marketing preclearance. A 505(b)(2) NDA can be used to request OTC drug approval when the product deviates in any respect from a final monograph (21 CFR 330.11). A Citizen Petition (21 CFR 10.30) is an alternate route without a *PDUFA* user fee requirement.

"Prescription-to-OTC switch" refers to over-the-counter marketing of a former prescription drug product for the same indication, strength, dose, duration of use, dosage form, population and route of administration. An efficacy supplement to an approved prescription product NDA should be submitted if the sponsor plans to switch a drug product covered under an NDA to OTC status in its entirety, without a change in the previously approved dosage form or route of administration. A 505(b)(1) NDA should be submitted if the sponsor is proposing converting some, but not all, approved prescription indications to OTC marketing status. A 505(b)(1) or 505(b)(2) original NDA needs to be submitted if the sponsor plans to market a new product whose active substance, indication or dosage form has not been marketed previously (see CDER MAPP 6020.5 *Good Review Practice: OND Review Management of INDs and NDAs for Nonprescription Drug Products* (July 2007)).

FDA has approved the switch of a number of drugs from prescription to OTC status under NDAs:
- antidiarrheals (loperamide)
- topical antifungals (clotrimazole, terbinafine)
- antihistamines (clemastine fumarate, loratadine, fexofenadine, cetirizine)
- vaginal antifungals (clotrimazole, miconazole nitrate)
- analgesics (ketoprofen, naproxen sodium, ibuprofen)
- acid reducers (cimetidine, famotidine, ranitidine, omeprazole)
- hair growth treatments (minoxidil)
- smoking cessation drugs (nicotine polacrilex)
- weight reduction (orlistat)

In allowing these drugs to be sold OTC, FDA considered safety and effectiveness, benefit-risk ratio and whether clear and understandable labeling could be written to

Table 2-4. Summary of Device Classification System

Class	Required Controls			Exemptions	Examples
	General	Special	Premarket Approval		
I	X			**Exempt**=subject to limitations on exemptions covered under 21 CFR xxx.9, where xxx refers to Parts 862–892. Class I devices usually are exempt.	Elastic bandages, examination gloves, hand-held surgical instruments
II	X	X		**Nonexempt**=510(k) required for marketing	Powered wheelchairs, infusion pumps, surgical drapes
III	X	X	X	**Exempt**=if a pre-amendment device (i.e., on the market prior to passage of the *Medical Device Amendments* in 1976 or substantially equivalent to such a device) and PMAs have not been called for. If no PMA is required, a 510(k) will be the route to market	Heart valves, silicone gel-filled breast implants, implanted cerebellar stimulators

enable consumers to self-medicate safely. In 21 CFR 201.66, the agency established standardized OTC drug product labeling content and format. In addition, manufacturers commonly are required to conduct studies to determine whether consumers understand the proposed OTC labeling and can use the products in a safe and effective manner.

OTC product labeling requires use and safety information for consumers. With the introduction of the "Drug Facts" label regulation in 1999, the label information became more uniform and easier to read and understand. Patterned after the Nutrition Facts food label, the Drug Facts label uses simple language and an easy-to-read format to help people compare and select OTC medicines and follow dosage instructions. The following information must appear in the indicated order:
- active ingredients, including the amount in each dosage unit
- purpose
- uses (indications)
- specific warnings, including when the product should not be used under any circumstances and when it is appropriate to consult with a doctor or pharmacist; this section also describes possible side effects and substances or activities to avoid
- dosage instructions—when, how and how often to take the product
- inactive ingredients, to help consumers avoid ingredients that could cause an allergic reaction

More information is available on the OTC Drug Facts Label website (www.fda.gov/drugs/resourcesforyou/consumers/ucm143551.htm).

OTC guidance documents also can be found online (www.fda.gov/Drugs/GuidanceComplianceRegulatoryInformation/Guidances/ucm065013.htm).

See Chapter 18 Over-the-Counter Drugs for further details.

Medical Devices

Overview and Medical Device Classification

A "device" is defined by FDA as an instrument, apparatus, implement, machine, contrivance, implant, in vitro reagent or other similar or related article, including a component part or accessory:
- recognized in the official *National Formulary* or the *United States Pharmacopeia* or any supplement to them
- intended for use in the diagnosis of disease or other conditions, or in the cure, mitigation, treatment or prevention of disease in man or other animals
- intended to affect the structure or any function of the body of man or other animals, and not achieving any of its primary intended purposes through chemical action within or on the body of man or other animals and not dependent upon being metabolized for the achievement of any of its primary intended purposes

Devices were described and became subject to regulation first under the *FD&C Act* as a result of potential increasing hazards resulting from new, more-complicated devices being introduced in the 1960s and 1970s (e.g.,

pacemakers, kidney dialysis machines, replacement heart valves). Congress passed the *Medical Device Amendments* in 1976 and heralded the modern age of device regulation. These amendments:
- redefined medical devices to distinguish them from drugs and expanded the definition to include diagnostics for conditions other than disease
- established device safety and performance/effectiveness requirements
- established FDA premarket review
- established the medical device classification system
- created two routes to market (premarket notification and premarket approval) and established Investigational Device Exemptions (IDEs)

A second milestone in device regulation was passage of the *Safe Medical Devices Act* (*SMDA*) in 1990. This act extended adverse device incident reporting to user facilities, including hospitals, ambulatory surgical facilities and nursing homes. This was a landmark event because FDA never before had extended its jurisdiction so broadly. A user facility must report information regarding a death caused by a device to FDA and the manufacturer. A user facility also must report any information received about a serious injury or illness caused by a device to the manufacturer. In addition, a user facility must submit an annual summary of its reports to the agency. In addition, *SMDA*:
- required high-risk device tracking requirements
- defined substantial equivalence
- required 510(k) submitters to receive FDA clearance prior to marketing
- gave FDA the authority to regulate combination products
- defined the humanitarian device exemption
- gave FDA recall authority

These regulatory milestones gave rise to most of the modern regulatory components used by FDA's Center for Devices and Radiological Health (CDRH) to fulfill its responsibilities for regulating manufacturers, re-packagers, re-labelers and/or importers of medical devices sold in the US.

The medical device regulations vary depending on the device's intended use and indications for use, complexity, benefits and risks. FDA places medical devices into one of three regulatory classes to ensure their safety, performance and effectiveness. The classification is based on the type of control needed to manage the risk the device poses to the patient and/or user. Class I includes devices with the lowest risk, needing only general controls; Class II devices have moderate risk and require both general and special controls; Class III devices have the greatest risk and require premarket authorization (PMA).

FDA classification determines the required premarketing submission or application type (**Table 2-4**). General controls for all classes include:
- establishment registration with FDA under 21 CFR 807.20, e.g., manufacturers, distributors, re-packagers and re-labelers and foreign establishments
- listing medical devices with FDA
- manufacturing devices in accordance with 21 CFR 820 GMP regulations
- labeling devices in accordance with 21 CFR 801 or 809 labeling regulations
- submitting a premarket notification (510(k)) (unless exempt)) before marketing a device

Special controls may include special labeling requirements, mandatory performance standards and specific postmarket surveillance activities.

The Premarket Approval (PMA) application (21 CFR 814) is the required scientific review process to ensure Class III device safety and effectiveness before placing the device on the market. Class III devices are those for which insufficient information exists to ensure safety and effectiveness solely through general or special controls. These devices usually support or sustain human life, are of substantial importance in preventing impairment of human health or present a potential, unreasonable risk of illness or injury.

A PMA is the most stringent device marketing application. The applicant must receive FDA PMA application approval prior to marketing the device. Approval is based on FDA's determination that the PMA contains sufficient valid scientific evidence to ensure the device is safe and effective for its intended use(s). An approved PMA is, in effect, a license granting the applicant (or owner) permission to market the device.

The PMA application is similar in content and organization to a traditional (non-CTD format) NDA application, although it may require much less clinical data. FDA has observed problems with study designs, study conduct, data analyses, presentations and conclusions. Although FDA has 180 days to review the PMA, in reality, this usually takes longer, due to frequent Advisory Committee involvement.

CBER reviews marketing and investigational device submissions (510(k)s, PMAs and IDEs) for medical devices associated with blood collection and processing procedures, and some in vitro diagnostics if they employ biological technology to achieve their endpoint. Although these products are reviewed by CBER, the medical device laws and regulations still are applicable, and they are approved as medical devices.

FDA has established detailed classifications for approximately 1,700 different generic device types and grouped them into 16 medical specialties, referred to as "panels." Device classification can be obtained through the CFR or the CDRH database.

The first step in working on medical device regulatory submissions and documentation is to ensure a clear device definition is documented. Responses to the following questions will help to guide this effort:
- What will the device do (intended use)?
- For what clinical conditions or patient populations will the device be used (indications for use)?
- How does the device work (principles of operation)?
- What are the product features? For example, is the device: electronic versus mechanical, controlled by software or other mechanism, invasive or noninvasive, implanted or not, sterile versus nonsterile or disposable versus reusable (product characteristics)?
- What are the device's inherent benefits and risks (see *Guidance for Industry and FDA Staff: Factors to Consider Regarding Benefit-Risk in Medical Device Product Availability, Compliance and Enforcement*)?

Humanitarian Use Device (HUD) Classification

HUD classification is a device designation similar to orphan drug designation because it provides an incentive for developing devices to be used in the treatment or diagnosis of diseases affecting small populations. A Humanitarian Use Device (HUD) is intended to benefit patients by treating or diagnosing a disease or condition affecting or manifesting in fewer than 4,000 individuals in the US per year. A request for HUD designation under 21 CFR 814 Subpart H needs to be submitted to FDA. Once designated by FDA, the HUD device is eligible for a humanitarian device exemption (HDE). An HDE submission is similar in both form and content to a PMA but is exempt from PMA effectiveness requirements.

An approved HDE authorizes HUD marketing; however, an HUD may be used only in facilities with an established Insitutional Review Board (IRB) to supervise these devices' clinical use and only after the IRB has approved the device to treat or diagnose the specific disease. HUD labeling must state the device's classification and, although authorized by federal law, its effectiveness for the specific indication has not been demonstrated.

CDRH's website contains a number of useful, searchable databases, including one for device classifications, one for 510(k)s, a similar one for PMAs and one for registrations and listings. See Device Advice (www.fda.gov/MedicalDevices/DeviceRegulationandGuidance/default.htm) or the CDRH Learn site (www.fda.gov/MedicalDevices/ResourcesforYou/Industry/ucm126230.htm) for more information, including both visual and audio components. In addition, Chapters 21–24 are devoted to devices and provide more detailed information.

Premarket Notification 510(k) and Exemptions

A sponsor wishing to market a Class I or II device intended for human use in the US, for which a PMA is not required, must submit a 510(k) exemption to FDA unless the device is exempt from those requirements and does not exceed the limitations in the CFR device classification exemptions as detailed below.

FD&C Act Section 513(d)(2)(A) authorizes FDA to exempt certain generic Class I devices from 510(k) requirements, and the agency has exempted more than 800 generic types of Class I devices and 60 Class II devices from these requirements. Companies must document the exempt status and any limitations in 21 CFR 862–892, the CDRH Product Code Classification Database or subsequent *Federal Register* announcements on Class I or II exemptions. The 510(k) exemption has certain limitations, noted in each regulation chapter's Subsection 9.

FDA does not provide a 510(k) form; however, 21 CFR 807 Subpart E describes 510(k) submission requirements. This FDA premarket notification demonstrates the device is as safe and effective as (i.e., substantially equivalent to) a legally marketed predicate device not subject to PMA. A predicate device can be a:
- pre-amendment device (a device on the market prior to 1976 and still marketed)
- device reclassified from Class III to Class II or I
- device found to be substantially equivalent to a device in one of the above two categories

A device is substantially equivalent if, in comparison to a predicate, the device:
- has the same intended use and the same technological characteristics as the predicate

or
- has the same intended use as the predicate, with different technological characteristics, and the information submitted to FDA:
    o does not raise new questions of safety and effectiveness and
    o demonstrates the device is at least as safe and effective as the legally marketed device

A substantial equivalence claim does not mean the new device and the predicate device must be identical. Substantial equivalence is established with respect to intended use, design, energy used or delivered, materials, performance, safety, effectiveness, biocompatibility, standards and other applicable characteristics (e.g., sterility).

FDA determines substantial equivalence, usually within 90 days. If the device is determined to be substantially equivalent, it can be marketed in the US when the submitter receives a letter from the agency and complies with the general and special controls provisions as required. If FDA determines the device is not substantially equivalent (NSE), the applicant may:
- submit another 510(k) with new data
- request a Class I or II designation through the *de novo* process
- file a reclassification petition
- submit a PMA

FDASIA included the *Medical Device User Fee Amendments* of 2012 (*MDUFA III*), which introduced, in exchange for user application fees, new performance goals for FDA decision making regarding a variety of medical device submission types (such as whether or not to clear a premarket notification or 510(k) within 90 days of active FDA review for at least 90% of submissions accepted in Fiscal 2018).

A 510(k)'s content and complexity can vary significantly depending on the amount of information needed to establish substantial equivalence to the predicate. A typical 510(k) is between 15 and 100 pages. FDA has established three 510(k) sub-types: a traditional 510(k), described in 21 CFR 807; a special 510(k); and an abbreviated 510(k). The latter two are described in *The New 510(k) Paradigm—Alternate Approaches to Demonstrating Substantial Equivalence in Premarket Notifications: Final Guidance* (March 1998). There is also a Frequently Asked Questions companion guidance regarding these alternative pathways (October 1998).

De Novo Classification

FD&C Act Section 513(f)(2), also referred to as *de novo* classification or evaluation of automatic Class III Designation, was amended by *FDASIA* Section 607 and provides two options for *de novo* classification. First, within 30 days of receiving a not-substantially equivalent (NSE) determination notice in response to a 510(k) for a device not previously classified under the act, the sponsor may request FDA to make a risk-based classification of the device under Section 513(a)(1). Alternatively, any sponsor with a device having no legally marketed predicate or equivalent device may request FDA to make a risk-based classification of the device without first submitting a 510(k).

IDE and Premarket Approval (PMA) Process

An Investigational Device Exemption (IDE) under 21 CFR 812 allows an investigational device to be used in a clinical study (e.g., to collect safety and performance/ effectiveness data required to support a PMA application or 510(k) submission to FDA). Clinical studies are conducted most often to support a PMA (about 90% of PMAs require clinical data, while only about 30% of 510(k)s require clinical data to support the application). Investigational uses also include clinical evaluations of certain modifications or new intended uses of legally marketed devices. FDA now applies the expectation for the minimum amount of information necessary to adequately address a relevant regulatory question or issue through the most efficient manner at the right time. This least burdensome definition considers the type of information, different approaches to generating or providing information, and when during the total product lifecycle information should be generated or provided to FDA. This concept applies to all products that meet the statutory definition of a device, throughout the total product lifecycle (premarket and postmarket). This is defined in the recent guidance on the topic (*The Least Burdensome Provisions: Concept and Principles: Guidance for Industry and Food and Drug Administration Staff* (February 2019)).

All clinical evaluations of investigational devices, unless exempt, must have an approved IDE before the study is initiated. The IDE is similar in content and organization to an IND. The sponsor may begin unless the agency objects and written approval is obtained, usually within 30 days. This is different than drug INDs where the clinical trial may begin 30 days after receipt by FDA unless FDA objects. Clinical evaluation of devices not yet cleared for marketing requires:
- an IDE approved by FDA and an IRB, if the study involves a significant-risk device
- informed consent from all patients
- labeling for investigational use only
- study monitoring
- records and reports

An approved IDE permits a device to be shipped lawfully across state lines for the purpose of conducting investigations without complying with other *FD&C Act* requirements applying to devices in commercial distribution. While the device is under investigation with an IDE, sponsors need not submit a PMA or Premarket Notification 510(k), register their establishment or list the device. IDE sponsors also are exempt from many aspects of the Quality System Regulation (QSR), except the design control requirements.

Planning and conducting a clinical study can have a serious impact on a company's financial resources, especially in an industry of 15,000 device manufacturers, where half have fewer than 10 employees. For significant-risk devices, where trials can be relatively complex and expensive, following the types of industry-sponsored drug trial processes is advisable to protect the validity of the company's investment. This should include the use of clinical study protocols, informed consent forms meeting all FDA regulations (21 CFR 50) and using duly constituted IRBs (21 CFR 56), source documents, clinical study reports and well-written investigator agreements, including financial disclosure aspects (21 CFR 54) and requirements for compliance with the study protocol and all IDE responsibilities (Good Clinical Practices (GCPs)).

Sponsors always should consult all applicable FDA guidance documents, industry standards and recommended practices prior to starting an IDE trial and submitting regulatory documents to FDA. Numerous device-specific FDA guidance documents are available.

User Fees—Medical Devices

The *Medical Device User Fee and Modernization Act* of 2002 (*MDUFMA*) was enacted to provide FDA "with the resources necessary to better review medical devices, to enact needed regulatory reforms so that medical device manufacturers can bring their safe and effective devices to the American people at an earlier time, and to ensure that reprocessed medical devices are as safe and effective as original devices." Medical device companies pay fees to FDA when they register their establishments and list their devices with the agency, whenever they submit an application or a notification to market a new medical device in the US and for certain other types of submissions. For more information on fees, by type of application, device or establishment, see www.fda.gov/forindustry/userfees/medicaldeviceuserfee/default.htm.

Establishment Registration and Medical Device Listing

Establishments involved in producing and distributing medical devices intended for marketing or leasing (commercial distribution) in the US are required to register with FDA (establishment registration). Registration provides medical device manufacturing and importer locations to FDA. An establishment is defined as any place of business under one management at one physical location at which a device is manufactured, assembled or otherwise processed for commercial distribution. The "owner/operator" is defined as the corporation, subsidiary, affiliated company, partnership or proprietor directly responsible for the registered establishment's activities. The owner/operator is responsible for registering the establishment.

Establishment registration regulations are provided in 21 CFR 807, and all establishment registrations and listings must be submitted electronically using FDA's Unified Registration and Listing System (FURLS)/Device Registration and Listing Module (DRLM), unless a waiver has been granted. Congress also authorized FDA to implement a user fee for certain establishment registration types. Establishment registration is not an FDA approval of the establishment or its products. That is, establishment registration does not mean FDA has granted clearance or approval to market. Unless exempt, premarketing clearance or approval is required before a device can be placed into US commercial distribution.

Most medical device establishments required to register with FDA also must list their devices in commercial distribution (21 CFR 807), including those produced exclusively for export. This medical device listing is a means of keeping FDA advised of the device category(s) an establishment is manufacturing or marketing.

Combination Drug-Device and Drug-Drug Products

Combination products (i.e., drug-device, drug-biologic and device-biologic products, formally defined in 21 CFR 3.2(e)) have been regulated for decades. Prior to 1990, FDA regulated such products on a case-by-case basis. Generally, the sponsor and FDA negotiated an *ad hoc* regulatory approach without explicit statutory guidance. As combination products multiplied and increased in complexity, the *ad hoc* approach no longer was satisfactory, and Congress enacted the *SMDA*. This law required the agency to designate a center (CDER, CBER or CDRH) with primary jurisdiction based on the product's primary mode of action.

FDA issued inter-center agreements among the three centers in 1991; however, a number of problems still exist with this approach.

As part of *MDUFMA* in 2002, Congress established the Office of Combination Products (OCP) within FDA's Office of the Commissioner to ensure combination products' prompt assignment to the appropriate FDA center and to coordinate the development and approval processes.

A company may obtain a formal agency determination of a combination product's primary mode of action and assignment of the lead center for premarket review and regulation by submitting a Request for Designation (RFD). OCP will make a determination within 60 days of RFD receipt. *Guidance for Industry: How to Write a Request for Designation* (April 2011) and *Draft Guidance for Industry and FDA Staff: Classification of Products as Drugs and Devices & Additional Product Classification Issues* (June 2011) each provide more specifics. Chapter 34 Combination Products discusses additional details.

The *21st Century Cures Act* (*CCA*), enacted in December 2016 (P.L. 114-255), substantially amended *FD&C Act* Section 503(g). These amendments include enhancing clarity, predictability, efficiency and consistency of premarket regulatory expectations for combination products. It also enhances agency components and staff

to coordinate appropriately on premarket review of these products, and ensure agency thinking is aligned in conducting these reviews (*Principles of Premarket Pathways for Combination Products:*
Draft Guidance for Industry and FDA Staff (February 2019).

Summary

Drug, biologic, device, combination product and food development involve scientific processes in the context of objective and subjective interpretations of real and potential product risks and benefits. The scope, interpretation and application of US federal regulations to market a product in the US have evolved over the past century and are documented in the numerous laws and updates and in the CFR. FDA uses scientific review, standards, manufacturing and other inspections, advertising controls, conditional approvals, laboratory product testing and postmarketing pharmacovigilance activities to evaluate product safety and risk to the US consumer. Over the last 50 years, many FDA and ICH guidelines have been issued to assist in interpreting and defining the processes to develop drugs, biologics, devices, combination products and foods successfully for the US market.

A "drug" is defined as a product used in diagnosing, curing, mitigating, treating or preventing a disease or affecting a structure or function of the body. A "biologic" is defined as a substance derived from or made with the aid of living organisms or made of large macromolecules found in the body (i.e., proteins). Drug development consists of characterizing the safety profile (risk) and the efficacy profile and benefit as they relate to the body's exposure to the drug (the pharmacokinetic profile). The most successful drugs are those with minimal risk and maximum benefit.

The relationship between FDA and an investigational drug product sponsor can begin before the sponsor submits an IND and typically extends through the IND development process (often defined as Phases 1, 2 and 3) to the marketing application and postapproval commitments, safety surveillance and product lifecycle management. Meetings with FDA are important process components. Meetings can be requested at any time for any valid reason, but FDA will decide whether sufficient justification has been provided for a meeting (usually, the sponsor must submit the product background and draft questions in a written meeting request) or a written response to questions and/or teleconference would suffice.

A sponsor can submit a Special Protocol Assessment (SPA) request. Within 45 days of receipt, FDA will evaluate certain protocols and related issues to determine whether they meet scientific and regulatory requirements and provide the sponsor formal, written, binding feedback. Several different types of protocols are eligible for an SPA under the *PDUFA* goals—animal carcinogenicity protocols, final product stability protocols, clinical protocols for Phase 3 trials whose data will form the basis for an efficacy claim (i.e., a pivotal trial), some products under special pathways and products subject to the animal rule.

The *Orphan Drug Act* provides incentives for developing drugs necessary, and often life-saving, for patients with rare diseases (defined as a US prevalence of fewer than 200,000 patients) but with minimal prospects for commercial return on investment. The fast track, breakthrough therapy, qualified infectious disease, and rare tropical disease designation programs are designed to facilitate the development and expedite review of new drugs intended to treat serious or life-threatening conditions and demonstrate the potential to address unmet medical needs or for certain targeted conditions. A sponsor may request fast track or breakthrough therapy designation or most of the other designations at any point in the development process. A product designated as fast track or breakthrough therapy is eligible for heightened FDA interest in sponsor meetings, a greater probability of priority marketing application review and a piecemeal submission of portions (i.e., complete CTD modules) of a marketing application (i.e., "rolling NDA/BLA").

ICH was formed in 1990, composed originally of regulatory authorities and pharmaceutical industry experts from the EU, Japan and the US, to discuss scientific and technical product registration aspects. It recommends ways to achieve greater harmonization in interpreting and applying technical guidelines and product registration requirements to reduce or avoid duplicating testing during new drug research and development. The ICH process has resulted in numerous guidelines in four major categories—quality, safety, efficacy and multidisciplinary. Two important ICH accomplishments are the CTD format and *MedDRA*. The ICH program has undergone significant enhancement and growth and now includes regulatory authorities and industry experts from China, Korea, Brazil, Switzerland and other countries.

Before initiating a US clinical trial (other than bioequivalence studies to support an ANDA), the sponsor must submit nonclinical, CMC and previous human experience data (if applicable) to FDA in the form of an IND. The IND application requests permission to initiate clinical trials. It is not a request for approval; rather, it is a request for exemption from federal law requiring an approved NDA or BLA prior to transporting or distributing a drug in interstate commerce. For an NCE, the initial IND is a major milestone because the IND summarizes the data and moves a drug from *in vitro* and animal testing into human clinical trial evaluations. Sponsors may initiate their proposed clinical trials if they have not received any communication from FDA within 30 days of agency receipt of the initial IND application.

A drug or biologic development program culminates in preparing and submitting a marketing application (NDA or BLA). This is accomplished either through studies conducted by (or with a right of reference from) the sponsor (505(b)(1) approach) or by reference in part to the safety and effectiveness findings for a previously approved drug product (Section 505(b)(2) approach). Through frequent interactions with FDA during the development program, including a Pre-NDA meeting, sponsor and agency expectations should be aligned reasonably well. Items to be considered when preparing a marketing application include package inserts (labeling), electronic submissions, Risk Evaluation and Mitigation Strategies (REMS), proprietary names, user fees, preapproval inspections (PAIs), establishment listings, patent restoration, other peri-approval activities, NDA amendments and supplements.

The modern generic drug era was born with passage of the *Hatch-Waxman Act* in 1984. This act expedited the availability of less-costly generic drugs by permitting FDA to approve abbreviated applications after innovator drug patent expiration. These abbreviated applications generally are not required to include animal safety and clinical data to establish safety and effectiveness. Specifically, a generic drug product is identical to the innovator drug product in dosage form, strength, route of administration, quality, performance characteristics and intended use.

A dietary supplement is a "dietary ingredient" taken by mouth and intended to supplement the diet. The *Dietary Supplement and Health Education Act* (*DSHEA*) created a regulatory framework for dietary supplement safety and labeling under the regulatory umbrella of foods. *DSHEA* provisions define dietary supplements and dietary ingredients and describe the proper use of nutritional support statements. *DSHEA* also defines labeling requirements and requires dietary supplement manufacturers to use GMPs and notify FDA of new dietary ingredients prior to marketing.

Dietary supplements do not require FDA premarket approval; however, all serious adverse events must be reported to the agency. The manufacturer is responsible for ensuring a dietary supplement is safe before US marketing. *DSHEA* places the burden on FDA to prove a marketed dietary supplement is unsafe (including CGMP noncompliance) prior to any action to remove the product from the market.

An over-the-counter (OTC) product is a drug product marketed for consumer use without healthcare provider intervention. CDER's Office of Nonprescription Drugs oversees OTC drugs. In allowing drugs to be sold OTC, FDA considers safety and effectiveness, benefit-risk ratio and whether clear and understandable labeling can be written to enable consumers to safely self-medicate.

A "device" is defined as an instrument, apparatus, implement, machine, contrivance, implant, in vitro reagent or other similar or related article, including a component part or accessory that meets a number of conditions. FDA places medical devices into one of three regulatory classes based on the level of control necessary to ensure their safety and effectiveness. Classification depends on the device's intended use and indications for use, and the risk it poses to the patient and/or user. Class I includes devices with the lowest risk, and Class III are those with the greatest risk.

The class determines the type of device premarketing submission or application required. A sponsor wishing to market a Class I, II or III device intended for human use, for which a PMA is not required, must submit a 510(k) exemption to FDA unless the device is exempt from those requirements and does not exceed the CFR device classification exemption limitations. A 510(k)'s content and complexity can vary significantly depending on the amount of information needed to establish substantial equivalence to the proposed predicate.

Class III devices are those for which insufficient information exists to ensure safety and effectiveness solely through general or special controls. They usually support or sustain human life, are of substantial importance in preventing human health impairment or present a potential, unreasonable risk of illness or injury. Premarket approval is the required scientific review process to ensure Class III devices' safety and effectiveness data are sufficient. An IDE allows the investigational device to be used in a clinical study to collect safety and effectiveness data required to support a PMA application or a Premarket Notification (510(k)) submission.

Combination products are defined as drug-device, drug-biologic and device-biologic products. As part of *MDUFMA*, Congress established OCP to ensure prompt combination product assignment to FDA centers and oversee the development and approval request processes. By submitting an RFD, a company may obtain a formal agency combination product primary mode of action determination and lead center assignment for the product's premarket review and regulation.

References

1. Advisory Committees: Critical to the FDA's Product Review Process. FDA website. https://www.fda.gov/drugs/resourcesforyou/consumers/ucm143538.htm. Accessed 17 March 2019.
2. Bren L. The Road to the Biologic Revolution—Highlights of 100 Years of Biologics Regulation. FDA Consumer Magazine, January–February 2006. http://www.fda.gov/AboutFDA/WhatWeDo/History/FOrgsHistory/CBER/ucm135758.htm. Accessed 17 March 2019.
3. Nadler HL, DeGraft-Johnson D. Demystifying FDA's 505(b)(2) Drug Registration Process. October 2009. DJA Global Pharmaceuticals website. Available online at http://www.djaglobal-pharma.com/Demystifying_FDA.pdf. Accessed 17 March 2019.

4. Kesselheim AS, Misono AS, Lee J, et al. Clinical Equivalence of Generic and Brand-Name Drugs Used in Cardiovascular Disease A Systematic Review and Meta-analysis. *JAMA*. 2008;300(21):2514-2526. doi:10.1001/jama.2008.758.
5. Henney JE. Review of Generic Bioequivalence Studies. *JAMA*. 1999;282(21):1995. doi:10.1001/jama.282.21.1995-JFD90010-2-1.
6. Gaffney A, Mezher M, Brennan Z. Regulatory Explainer: Everything You Need to Know About FDA's Priority Review Vouchers. Regulatory Focus. RAPS website. https://www.raps.org/regulatory-focus/news-articles/2017/12/regulatory-explainer-everything-you-need-to-know-about-fdas-priority-review-vouchers. Accessed 22 March 2019.

Chapter 3

Clinical Trials: GCPs, Regulations and Compliance for Drugs, Biologics and Medical Devices

Updated by Monique Carter, MS, RAC and Samantha Zappia, MS, RAC

OBJECTIVES

- Define Good Clinical Practices (GCPs)
- Discuss the purpose of GCPs
- Provide a historical overview of GCPs
- Provide an overview of clinical trials
- Define Institutional Review Board (IRB), sponsor, CRO and Principal Investigator requirements and responsibilities
- Discuss clinical trial monitoring and auditing
- Define and discuss Good Documentation Practice (GDP)
- Provide an overview of important distinctions between medical device ISO GCPs (ISO 114155) and ICH GCPs for drugs (ICH E6) in the US

US LAWS, REGULATIONS AND GUIDANCE DOCUMENTS COVERED IN THIS CHAPTER

- *Pure Food and Drug Act* of 1906
- *Federal Food, Drug, and Cosmetic Act* of 1938 (*FD&C Act*)
- *National Research Act* of 1974
- *Medical Device Amendments* of 1976
- *Safe Medical Devices Act* of 1990
- *Mammography Quality Standards Act* of 1992
- *Medical Device User Fee and Modernization Act* of 2002
- *Medical Device User Fee Stabilization Act* (*MDUFSA*) of 2005
- 21 CFR Part 11 Electronic Records
- 21 CFR 50 Protection of Human Subjects
- 21 CFR 54 Financial Disclosure by Clinical Investigators
- 21 CFR 56 Institutional Review Board
- 21 CFR 312 Investigational New Drug Application
- 21 CFR Part 812 Investigational Device Exemptions
- 45 CFR 45 Public Welfare
- 45 CFR 46 Protection of Human Subjects
- *E6(R1) Good Clinical Practice: Consolidated Guidance* (10 June 1996)

Chapter 3

- E6(R2): Guideline for Good Clinical Practice (9 November 2016)
- ISO 14155: 2011 Clinical investigation of medical devices for human subjects—Good clinical practice (Second Edition)
- ISO 14971:2007 Medical devices—Application of Risk Management to Medical Devices
- Guidance for Industry: Submitting and Reviewing Complete Responses to Clinical Holds (October 2000)
- Guidance for Industry and Clinical Investigators: The Use of Clinical Holds Following Clinical Investigator Misconduct (September 2004)
- Guidance for Industry, Investigators, and Reviewers: Exploratory IND Studies (January 2006)
- Guidance for Industry: Using a Centralized IRB Review Process in Multicenter Clinical Trials (March 2006)
- Guidance for Industry: Computerized Systems Used in Clinical Investigations (May 2007)
- Guidance for Clinical Investigators, Sponsors, and IRBs: Adverse Event Reporting to IRBs—Improving Human Subject Projection (January 2009)
- Guidance for Institutional Review Boards (IRBs): Frequently Asked Questions—IRB Registration (July 2009)
- Guidance for Industry: Investigator Responsibilities—Protecting the Rights, Safety, and Welfare of Study Subjects (October 2009)
- Guidance for Sponsors, Investigators, and Institutional Review Boards. Questions and Answers on Informed Consent Elements, 21 CFR 50.35(c) (February 2012)
- Guidance for Clinical Investigators, Industry, and FDA Staff: Financial Disclosure by Clinical Investigators (February 2013)
- Guidance for IRBs, Clinical Investigators, and Sponsors: IRB Responsibility for Reviewing Qualifications of Investigators, Adequacy of Research Sites, and the Determination of Whether an IND/IDE is Needed (August 2013)
- Guidance for Industry: Oversight of Clinical Investigations—A Risk-Based Approach to Monitoring (August 2013)
- Guidance for Industry: Electronic Source Data in Clinical Investigations (September 2013)
- Guidance for IRBs, Clinical Investigators, and Sponsors: Informed Consent Information Sheet (July 2014)
- A Guide to Informed Consent—Information Sheet (January 1998)
- Institutional Review Boards Frequently Asked Questions—Information Sheet (January 1998)
- Sponsor—Investigator—IRB Interrelationship—Information Sheet (January 1998)
- Information Sheet Guidance for Sponsors, Clinical Investigators, and IRBs: Waiver of IRB Requirements for Drug and Biological Product Studies (January 2006)
- Information Sheet Guidance for IRBs, Clinical Investigators, and Sponsors: FDA Institutional Review Board Inspections (January 2006)
- Information Sheet Guidance for Sponsor, Clinical Investigators, and IRBs, Frequently Asked Questions—Statement of Investigator (Form FDA 1572) (May 2010)
- Information Sheet Guidance for IRBs, Clinical Investigators, and Sponsors: FDA Inspections of Clinical Investigators (June 2010)
- Information Sheet Guidance for Institutional Review Boards, Clinical Investigators, and Sponsors: Clinical Investigator Administrative Actions—Disqualification (March 2014)
- Use of Electronic Informed Consent. Questions and Answers—Guidance for Institutional Review Boards, Investigators, and Sponsors (December 2016)
- Institutional Review Board (IRB) Written Procedures: Draft Guidance for Institutions and IRBs (August 2016)

❑ *Use of Electronic Health Record Data in Clinical Investigations—Draft Guidance for Industry* (May 2016)

❑ *Minutes of Institutional Review Board (IRB) Meetings—Guidance for Institutions and IRBs* (November 2015)

❑ *Guidance for Industry and Food and Drug Administration Staff: Investigational Device Exemptions (IDEs) for Early Feasibility Medical Device Clinical Studies, Including Certain First in Human (FIH) Studies* (October 2013)

❑ *Draft Guidance for Industry and Food and Drug Administration Staff: Technical Considerations for Additive Manufactured Devices* (May 2016)

❑ *Guidance for Industry and Food and Drug Administration Staff: Applying Human Factors and Usability Engineering to Medical Devices* (February 2016)

❑ *Guidance for Industry and FDA Staff: Guidance for the Content of Premarket Submissions for Software Contained in Medical Devices* (May 2005)

❑ *The Least Burdensome Provisions of the FDA Modernization Act of 1997: Concept and Principles: Final Guidance for FDA and Industry* (October 2002)

Note on the Scope of this Chapter
This chapter includes salient topics related to both ICH and ISO GCPs associated with drug or biologic and medical device development, respectively. This chapter focuses particularly on unique drug or biologic and medical device trial elements and applicable US regulations governing human clinical trials.

Introduction

Clinical trials in humans are conducted to assess whether a new drug, biologic or medical device provides a safe and effective way to treat, prevent or diagnose a disease in a particular patient population. Good Clinical Practice (GCP) is an internationally accepted, scientific and ethical quality standard for the design, conduct, performance, auditing, recordkeeping, analysis and reporting of clinical trials involving human subjects.[1] Global regulatory authorities (e.g., US Food and Drug Administration (FDA), European Medicines Agency (EMA), UK Medicines and Healthcare products Regulatory Agency (MHRA), Japan's Pharmaceuticals and Medical Devices Agency (PMDA), China Food and Drug Administration (CFDA)) have published numerous regulations, reflection papers, guidance documents and information sheets defining GCP requirements. However, it generally is accepted that many industry standards for conducting clinical trials are "best practices," based on regulations and guidance documents, but not found in the black letter text of the regulations. When a GCP compliance issue or event is not addressed specifically by local GCP regulations and guidelines, regulatory professionals should consult internal and external resources, including their companies' quality assurance, regulatory compliance and regulatory intelligence departments and/or local Ethics Committees (ECs), Institutional Review Boards (IRBs) and regulatory authorities.

Significant distinctions exist between drug, biologic and medical device clinical trials, ranging from process requirements to different international standards. While drug and biologic studies are subject to the International Council on Harmonisation (ICH) *E6(R2) Good Clinical Practice Guideline*, the analogous ISO 14155:2011 *Clinical investigation of medical devices for human subjects—Good clinical practice* (Second edition) standard published by the International Standards Organization (ISO) is recognized by FDA and other international agencies as Good Clinical Practice (GCP) for medical device clinical trials.[2,3]

Note, ISO/DIS 14155 *Clinical investigation of medical devices for human subjects—Good clinical practice* is currently under development and will replace ISO14155:2011 when available.

Purpose of GCPs

GCPs establish the minimum standards and guidelines for conducting human clinical research. Complying with GCP regulations and guidance documents ensures human subjects' rights, safety, confidentiality and well-being participating in clinical research are protected.[4] Subjects' rights include the right to be informed, to not participate, to withdraw at any time and to have their privacy respected. GCPs also ensure the data collected and reported during the trial are high quality, credible, accurate and reliable. Regulatory agencies rely on data integrity to make scientifically sound decisions on sponsors' marketing applications. GCPs also serve to define the roles and responsibilities of the groups involved in clinical research, including study sponsors, clinical research investigators, IRBs and monitors. All parties involved in conducting clinical research are required to comply with applicable laws and regulations to ensure subjects' risks are minimized.

Drug, biologic and medical device GCPs have many commonalities of scope, including ensuring data integrity and setting forth monitoring and core study document

Table 3-1. Significant Legislation Relevant to Clinical Trials in the US

Legislation	Significance
Pure, Food and Drug Act (1906)	• Prohibited the manufacturing and interstate shipment of adulterated drugs or foods in the US • All products must have proper labeling and list all ingredients (products cannot be misbranded)
Food, Drug and Cosmetic Act (1938)	• Revised the misbranding standard for therapeutic claims • Changed the definition of misleading from "false and fraudulent" to "false or misleading in any particular" • Required drug labels with adequate directions for safe use • Introduced the NDA premarket review process • The drug must be safe before it can be marketed • Provided an initial definition of medical devices, with some problematic overlap with drugs
National Research Act (1974)	• Authorized federal agencies to develop human research regulations for government-funded research involving human subjects • Required the development of IRBs for the protection of human research subjects
Medical Device Amendments (1976)	• Established premarket requirements for Class III devices • Established the 510(k) process
Belmont Report (1979)	• Report released by the National Commission establishing ethical principles for research in human subjects
Common Rule (1981–91)	• Department of Health and Human Services (HHS) issued regulations based on the Belmont Report and Code of Federal Regulations (CFR), 45 CFR (public welfare) Part 46 (protection of human subjects) to protect human subjects • In 1991, core DHHS regulations (45 CFR 46 Subpart A) were adopted formally by more than 17 departments and agencies
Safe Medical Devices Act (1990)	• Established quality system and postmarket surveillance requirements • Provided discretion on PMA panel review • Clarified Humanitarian Use Devices (HUD) for humanitarian device exemption (HDE) applications are not required to contain the results of clinical effectiveness investigations
Food and Drug Administration Modernization Act (1997)	• Established the Biologics License Application and harmonized it with the New Drug Application • Exempted most Class I and some Class II devices from 510(k) process, reducing clinical trial requirements • Established the "least burdensome" approach provision • Improved dispute resolution and mandated interested parties' free and open participation • Enabled evaluation of automatic Class III designation, allowing sponsors to request lower classification in cases of minimal risk (*de novo* review)
Medical Device User Fee and Modernization Act (2002)	• Established a fee schedule for most device submission types to achieve shorter review times • Requires FDA to include pediatric experts on the panel for a product intended for pediatric use
Medical Device User Fee and Stabilization Act (2005)	• Amended *MDUFMA* to limit the provision to reprocess single-use devices (SUDs) and the manufacturers who reprocess them
Food and Drug Administration Amendments Act (2007)	• Required all clinical trials (except Phase 1) to be registered in the clinical trial registry databank (ClinicalTrials.gov) • Required results from clinical trials that serve as the basis for efficacy claims and postmarketing studies to be posted on ClinicalTrials.gov • Reauthorized *PDUFA* • Reauthorized and expanded *MDUFMA*

requirements, as well as describing study sponsor, clinical research investigators, ethics and monitors' responsibilities. Medical device GCPs uniquely address device and component issuance, device malfunction and use error documentation.

Overview of GCP History

GCPs and associated regulations were developed, primarily, in response to tragic events where individuals' rights and safety were ignored or put at risk. Examples are described below, including but not limited to the 1937 Sulfanilamide disaster, experiments performed during World War II and the Tuskegee Syphilis Study. **Table 3-1** illustrates significant drug, biologic and medical device legislation relevant to US clinical trials.

Sulfanilamide Disaster and the Food, Drug and Cosmetic Act (1937–38)

Prior to the *Pure Food and Drug Act*, passed in 1906, the US had no regulations on the ethical involvement of human subjects in clinical research.[5] The most widely recognized standard was the *Hippocratic Oath*, traditionally taken by physicians, the primary tenet of which is to cause no harm to the patient.

In 1937, the S.E. Massengill Company produced a treatment for streptococcal infections, composed of the antimicrobial, sulfanilamide, dissolved in diethylene glycol (i.e., a chemical analog of antifreeze) and raspberry flavoring. The elixir was tested for appearance, flavor and fragrance. However, under the *Pure Food and Drug Act*, toxicity testing was not required and was not performed.[6] Some 240 gallons of the elixir were distributed in 15 states, and 105 people, including 34 children, died. FDA was able to retrieve 228 gallons of the elixir. It was estimated that if all 240 gallons had been consumed, the number of deaths would have exceeded 4,000. In response to the sulfanilamide disaster, Congress passed the *Federal Food, Drug, and Cosmetic Act* in 1938 (*FD&C Act*), which required manufacturers to show a drug was safe before it could be marketed.[7]

Device Regulation Under the Federal Food, Drug, and Cosmetic Act of 1938

When Congress revisited the 1906 law in the 1930s, the initial legislation did not include premarket review of medical devices or pharmaceutical agents. Instead, it focused on such broad prohibitions on "adulterated" and "misbranded" products intended for medicinal applications, enabling enforcement primarily through noncompliant product seizures, injunctions for future violations or making recommendations to the Department of Justice (DoJ) regarding criminal prosecutions of persons responsible for these infractions.[8,9] In response to increasing attention on public safety issues involving drugs, the new legislation included premarket drug review through the New Drug Application (NDA) process, and the *Federal Food, Drug, and Cosmetic Act* (*FD&C Act*) became law in 1938.[10] However, the *FD&C Act*'s scope did not differentiate completely the terms "device" and "drug." Medical devices were defined broadly as any "instrument, apparatus, ... [or] contrivance" from an official compendium (like the *US Pharmacopeia*), while drugs were any "article." In the *FD&C Act*, drugs and devices shared the common purpose of being "intended for use in the diagnosis, cure, mitigation, treatment, or prevention of disease."[11] This overlap provided the basis for early medical device regulatory actions and legal cases and, ultimately, further medical device regulation definition and distinction in the 1960s and 1970s.

WW II Holocaust (1938–45)

During WW II, the German Nazi party systematically persecuted and killed six million Jewish and five million non-Jewish victims.[12] Many were subjects of medical experiments designed to advance German medicine and the war effort. Victims were exposed to high altitude and extreme cold, in an effort to aid the German Luftwaffe's investigation into the effects of high-altitude flying. Subjects were exposed to mustard gas and burned with materials used in incendiary bombs to investigate treatments for injuries resulting from air raids and battlefield conditions. They also were infected with malaria, epidemic jaundice, tuberculosis and typhus, in an effort to find treatments for diseases to which German soldiers were exposed in occupied territories. Rapid, large-scale sterilization experiments were conducted to ensure the eventual elimination of enemy populations, while maintaining a captive labor force during the war. Individuals who survived the experiments almost always were killed and dissected shortly thereafter to determine why they survived.[13] While some of these experiments may have had a legitimate scientific purpose, they were conducted without the subjects' consent and with total disregard for their suffering or survival.

Nuremberg Doctors' Trials (1946) and the Nuremberg Code (1947)

On 9 December 1946, an American military tribunal began criminal proceedings against 23 German physicians and administrators for their willing participation in WW II war crimes and crimes against humanity.[14] Of the 16 doctors found guilty, seven were sentenced to death. In their defense, several doctors argued that no international law or standard existed to differentiate between legal and illegal human experimentation.[15]

Dr. Andrew Ivy, an American doctor working with the US Counsel for War Crimes during the trial, was disturbed by the legitimacy of this defense and, on 17 April 1947, submitted a memorandum to the counsel defining legitimate research. Information from Dr. Ivy's memorandum was included in the trial's verdict in a section entitled "Permissible Medical Experiments," which subsequently became known as the *Nuremberg Code*.[16]

The *Nuremberg Code* lists 10 basic moral, ethical and legal principles for human medical research:

1. Voluntary consent is essential. The individual must have "sufficient knowledge and comprehension of the research to make an understanding and enlightened decision."
2. Research must benefit the good of society, unprocurable by other means.
3. Research must be based on a preclinical animal study.
4. Research should avoid all unnecessary physical and mental suffering and injury.
5. Research should not be conducted when there is reason to believe death or a disabling injury will occur.
6. Research risk must be minimized and relative to the anticipated research benefit.
7. Proper preparations and adequate facilities are required to ensure subjects are protected against even the remote possibilities of injury, disability or death.
8. Research should be conducted only by scientifically qualified persons.
9. Subjects have the right to end their participation in research.
10. Research should be terminated if, at any time, continuation is likely to result in subject injury, disability or death.[17]

Declaration of Helsinki (1964)

In 1964, the World Medical Association (WMA), an international organization representing physicians, established ethical principles for medical doctors involved in human biomedical research. Between 1964 and 2013, the *Declaration of Helsinki* was revised seven times. The original declaration was divided into three sections: Basic Principles, Medical Research Combined with Professional Care (Clinical Research) and Non-Therapeutic Biomedical Research Involving Human Subjects (Nonclinical Biomedical Research), and included 22 points, including the 10 from the *Nuremberg Code*.[18] The 2013 declaration was expanded into nine sections, containing 37 points. Sections in the 2013 declaration include Preamble, General Principles, Risks, Burdens and Benefits, Vulnerable Groups and Individuals, Scientific Requirements and Research Protocols, Research Ethics Committees, Privacy and Confidentiality, Informed Consent, Use of Placebo, Post-Trial Provisions, Research Registration and Publication and Dissemination of Results and Unproven Interventions in Clinical Practices.[19]

The declaration includes a number of important human research ethical codes of practice, such as the necessity of informed consent, research protocol review by an independent committee prior to initiation, ensuring research risk does not exceed its benefits, precedence of subjects' well-being over the interests of science and society, confidentiality of subjects' personal information, post-trial access provisions for subjects still needing the intervention identified as beneficial during the trial, and the ethical obligation to publish and disseminate research results.

While the declaration has been codified in or influenced national and regional legislation and regulations, it is not, itself, a legally binding instrument in international law. Regulatory professionals should regard the declaration as an important human research guidance document that does not supersede local regulations and laws.

Mid-Century "Drug-Device" Regulation (1969)

Marketed medical devices with safety or labeling issues were subject primarily to enforcement through the *FD&C Act*'s adulteration and misbranding provisions. In the 1960s, however, the agency extended drug premarket requirements to some medical device products by classifying them as drugs, an extension of the agency's authority supported by federal court rulings. These controversial "drug-device" products included applicators and nylon loop surgical components (where some device material potentially could remain in the patient's body after the procedure)[20] and antibiotic-sensitivity disks.[21] The latter, a product called Bacto-Unidisk, was the Supreme Court's first ruling on the issue of "drug-device" regulation, which set the stage for FDA regulation of such devices in 1969.[22] The decision to classify some medical devices as drugs for regulatory purposes prompted renewed interest in medical device regulation, with Congress and Presidents Nixon, Kennedy and Johnson all weighing in on the pressing need to develop more comprehensive medical device regulation authority, including premarket safety assessments and clinical evidence.[23] In 1969, President Nixon called for "certain minimum standards… for medical devices… [including] pre-marketing clearance in certain cases."[24]

Tuskegee Syphilis Study (1932–72)

In 1932, the US Department of Health sponsored a study entitled 'The Tuskegee Study of Untreated Syphilis in the Negro Male" conducted at Tuskegee University Alabama. The objective was to study the effects of untreated syphilis in 400 impoverished and poorly educated African

American men diagnosed with a latent form of the disease. For 40 years researchers did not tell the subjects they were participating in an experiment. Instead, most of the subjects thought they were receiving treatments for "bad blood." Researchers withheld treatment even after penicillin became the standard treatment for syphilis in the 1947. Many subjects died of syphilis during the study, more than 40 of their wives contracted syphilis and 19 babies were born with congenital syphilis.[25]

The study was stopped in 1972 after its existence was publicized by the media. By that time, only 74 of the subjects were still alive.[26] Survivors eventually received financial compensation and in May 1997 US President Bill Clinton apologized to the subjects and their families, acknowledging the government's actions were morally wrong and an outrage to the US commitment to integrity and equality for all citizens.[27,28]

National Research Act (1974)

Due to Tuskegee Syphilis Study publicity, the *National Research Act* of 1974 was passed, authorizing federal agencies to develop human research regulations for government-funded research involving human subjects. It also required the development of Institutional Review Boards (IRBs) to protect human research subjects.

The act also established the US Office for Human Research Protection and created the National Commission for the Protection of Human Subjects of Biomedical and Behavioral Research, which developed the *Belmont Report*, a foundational document for human research participants' ethical treatment in the US.[29]

Cooper Committee and the Dalkon Shield Incident (1970–76)

In September 1970, a joint report was developed by the Cooper Committee, reflecting its chair's name (Theodore Cooper, director of the National Heart and Lung Institute, now the National Heart, Lung, and Blood Institute) and the secretary of the Department of Health, Education, and Welfare (now the Department of Health and Human Services). The Cooper Committee report followed closely on the 1969 drug-device rulings and made recommendations to improve medical device definition and premarket requirements. In particular, the committee called for risk-based medical device assessment based on potential hazards and specific mechanisms, as well as requirements for reporting and recordkeeping, Good Manufacturing Practices (GMPs) and agency inspections.[30] As Congressional controversy continued regarding the contentious draft medical device legislation, FDA began to classify devices by risk as part of an early and voluntary initiative Peter Barton Hutt, FDA's chief counsel 1971–74, described as the motivating factor that "finally got the attention of the House as well as the Senate… [who] both began to show renewed interest in late 1974."[31] At the same time, the public became increasingly aware of unsafe and ineffective medical devices' health impact through widely publicized controversies. Of these, the most widely recognized was the Dalkon Shield Intrauterine Device (IUD) incident, in which 209 US cases of septic spontaneous abortion and 11 maternal deaths were reported from the time the device entered the market in 1970 until its removal in 1976.[32] The committee responsible for the subsequent 1976 legislation included this and other examples, such as occurrences of device-related pacemaker and intraocular lens failures and infection.[33] Premarket controls—and, in some cases, clinical trials—were needed to establish evidence that would protect the public.

Medical Device Amendments (1976)

In response to this need, the landmark *Medical Device Amendments* of 1976 (*MDA*) were passed. This legislation clearly defined medical devices and provided the basis for extensive new requirements beyond those on general adulteration and misbranding in the *FD&C Act*. *MDA* officially established medical device inventory and risk-based classification requirements, including premarket requirements for Class III devices and the medical device 510(k) mechanism (subsequently modified in 1990 and 1997).[34] This law has been amended several times, most significantly in 1990, 1992, 1997, 2002, 2004, 2005 and 2007, although the fundamental regulatory regime established in 1976 remains primarily intact.[35] Since the 1997 amendments, most Class I devices remain exempt from 510(k) review, while most Class III devices are subject to the premarket approval (PMA) process rather than the 510(k) pathway. However, more than 20 Class III device types are still eligible for commercialization via the 510(k) clearance process.

Belmont Report (1979)

In 1979, the National Commission for the Protection of Human Subjects of Biomedical and Behavioral Research released the *Belmont Report*, establishing ethical principles for human subjects' research. The report is a key document in US human research ethics regulations, emphasizing three basic ethical principles: respect for persons, beneficence (i.e., the moral obligation to act for the benefit of others) and justice.[36]

Under respect for persons, there is a duty to respect subjects' autonomy and their choices, as well as provide extra protections to those with diminished autonomy (e.g., vulnerable populations—prisoners, children, cognitively impaired individuals, etc.). Key to beneficence is to do no harm, protect subjects' welfare and maximize

Chapter 3

Table 3-2. Comparison of 21 CFR and ISO-GCP Requirements for Protocol Deviations in Medical Device Clinical Trials

21 CFR Requirements	ISO 14155:2011 (ISO-GCP) Requirements	Conclusion
21 CFR 812.140 (a) (4): A participating investigator shall maintain the following accurate, complete, and current records relating to the investigator's participation in an investigation: The protocol, with documents showing the dates of and reasons for each deviation from the protocol.	ISO 14155 9.6 (g): The principal investigator shall document and explain any deviation from the approved clinical investigation plan that occurred during the course of the clinical investigation.	Following CFR requirements will satisfy ISO-GCP.
21 CFR 812.150 (a) (4): An investigator shall notify the sponsor and the reviewing IRB of any deviation from the investigational plan to protect the life or physical well-being of a subject in an emergency. Such notice shall be given as soon as possible, but in no event later than 5 working days after the emergency occurred. Except in such an emergency, prior approval by the sponsor is required for changes in or deviations from a plan, and if these changes or deviations may affect the scientific soundness of the plan or the rights, safety, or welfare of human subjects, FDA and IRB in accordance with 21 CFR 812.35 (a) also is required.	ISO 14155 9.4 (e): Under emergency circumstances, deviations from the CIP to protect the rights, safety and well-being of human subjects may proceed without prior approval of the sponsor and the ethics committee. Such deviations shall be documented and reported to the sponsor and ethics committee as soon as possible.	US regulations set an additional maximum of five days for reporting emergency events, which is beyond the "as soon as possible" requirement of ISO-GCP.

possible benefits while minimizing possible harms. Duties under justice include treating people fairly, distributing benefits and burdens fairly and allowing individuals who do not want to participate in the study, but would like treatment, to receive the usual standard of care and not be turned away. The application of these principles is seen in the informed consent process and respect for privacy (respect for persons), good research design, competent investigators and favorable benefit-risk analysis (beneficence) and equitable selection of study subjects (justice).[37]

Common Rule (1981-91)

In 1981, the Department of Health and Human Services (HHS) issued regulations based on the *Belmont Report* and Code of Federal Regulations (CFR), 45 CFR (public welfare) Part 46 (protection of human subjects). In 1991, core HHS regulations (45 CFR 46 Subpart A) were adopted formally by more than 17 departments and agencies. Most universities and agencies have adopted this rule (Common Rule). HHS also has promulgated regulations providing additional protections for vulnerable populations involved in research, codified as Subpart B (pregnant women, human fetuses and neonates), Subpart C (prisoners) and Subpart D (children).[38]

In 2011, the Office of Human Research Protections (OHRP) announced significant proposed Common Rule changes, for the first time since 1981, to enhance human subject protections and reduce investigator burden. In its Advance Notice of Proposed Rulemaking, HHS invited comments on proposed changes, including:

- All studies conducted at institutions receiving federal funding from a Common Rule agency must comply with the rule for research. Previously, compliance was required for only federally funded studies.
- A single IRB review would be required for multi-site studies; previously, this was optional.
- Data security and information protection standards, consistent with those of the *Health Insurance Portability and Accountability Act (HIPAA)*, would be mandatory for all studies involving identifiable or potentially identifiable data.
- Study participants would have an opportunity to decide whether their biological specimens could be used for future research and, if so, to specify the research types in which those might be used.
- Informed consent forms and processes would be updated.
- A systematic approach would be implemented for data collection and analysis on unanticipated problems and adverse effects occurring during clinical trials.[39]

This was followed by a Notice of Proposed Rulemaking published 8 September 2015. Comments were received through 6 January 2016, and the text of revised rules currently is in development.[40]

The Safe Medical Devices Act (1990)

The *Safe Medical Devices Act* of 1990 (*SMDA*) amended *MDA* to provide greater protections against dangerous medical devices. A number of important statutory changes were made to the premarket notification (510(k)) process that resulted in the addition of Section 513(i), which codifies FDA review practice in applying the "substantial equivalence" review standard central to the 510(k) process.

International Ethical Guidelines for Biomedical Research (1993)

In 1993, the Council for International Organizations of Medical Science (CIOMS), in collaboration with the World Health Organization (WHO), developed an international ethics guideline for biomedical research, with special attention on protecting subjects' rights in developing counties. An updated version was released in 2002. Important elements include:

1. Any intervention, product or knowledge generated will be made available for the benefit of the population or community (Guideline 10).
2. Placebo control is justified when (Guideline 11):
   o there is no established intervention
   o withholding an established intervention would expose the subject to temporary discomfort
   o using an established intervention would not yield scientifically reliable results
   o using a placebo does not present a risk of serious irreversible harm to the subject
3. Compensation for research injury (Guideline 19)[41]

International Council on Harmonisation Good Clinical Practice (1996)

In 1996, ICH published the GCP (E6) guideline to eliminate unnecessary delay in the global development and availability of new medicines, while maintaining appropriate safeguards on quality, safety and efficacy and regulatory obligations to protect public health. By establishing a minimum acceptable standard, the guideline allows the mutual acceptance of clinical trial data by regulatory agencies, avoiding redundancies and duplicative requirements in different regions. However, regulatory professionals should remember compliance with ICH GCP alone is insufficient. Clinical trials also must comply with regulations at the clinical trial site.

ICH GCP is the official GCP guideline adopted by the regulatory agencies of the EU, Japan, US and, most recently, China. Through the ICH Global Cooperation Group, many other countries, including Australia, Canada, Russia, South Korea and others, also recognize ICH GCP as a standard for clinical trial conduct.[42]

ICH GCP also forms the basis of:

- World Health Organization (WHO) Technical Report Series No. 850 Annex 3, 1995—Guidelines for good clinical practice (GCP) on pharmaceutical products http://apps.who.int/medicinedocs/en/d/Jh3009e/22.9.html
- WHO Handbook for Clinical Research Practice (GCP) Guidance for Implementation, 2005 http://whqlibdoc.who.int/publications/2005/924159392X_eng.pdf

The ICH GCP guideline comprises 13 principles and details the responsibilities of ECs, IRBs, investigators and sponsors or Contract Research Organizations (CROs). ICH GCP principles include:

1. Clinical trials should be conducted in accordance with the ethical principles originating in the *Declaration of Helsinki*, consistent with GCP and applicable regulatory requirement(s).
2. Before a trial is initiated, foreseeable individual trial subject and society risks and inconveniences should be weighed against the anticipated benefit. A trial should be initiated and continued only if anticipated benefits justify the risks.
3. Trial subjects' rights, safety and well-being are the most important considerations and should prevail over interests of science and society.
4. Available investigational product nonclinical and clinical information should be adequate to support the proposed clinical trial.
5. Clinical trials should be scientifically sound and described in a clear, detailed protocol.
6. A trial should be conducted in compliance with a protocol that has received prior IRB/EC approval or a favorable opinion.
7. The medical care provided to, and medical decisions made on behalf of subjects always should be the responsibility of a qualified physician or, when appropriate, a qualified dentist.
8. Each individual involved in conducting a trial should be qualified by education, training and experience to perform his or her respective task(s).
9. Freely given informed consent should be obtained from every subject prior to clinical trial participation.
10. All clinical trial information should be recorded, handled and stored in a way that allows its accurate reporting, interpretation and verification.
11. Confidentiality of records that could identify subjects should be protected, respecting the privacy and confidentiality rules in accordance with the applicable regulatory requirement(s).
12. Investigational products should be manufactured, handled and stored in accordance with applicable Good Manufacturing Practice (GMP). They

Chapter 3

Figure 3-1. Types of Pharmaceutical and Biologic Clinical Trials and Typical Pathway

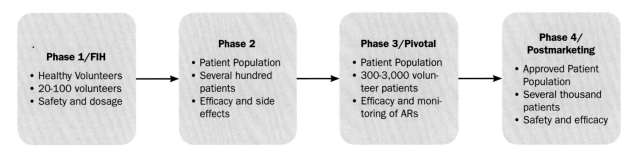

FIH = First-In-Human; ARs = adverse reactions; *The clinical trial pathway for pharmaceuticals and biologics is a linear progression. In some cases with rare diseases and oncology products, Phase 1 studies may be conducted in the patient population, and with adaptive trial designs, some clinical trials may include more than one phase.*

should be used in accordance with the approved protocol.
13. Systems with procedures to ensure the quality of every trial aspect should be implemented.[43]

First published in 1996, ICH GCP was last revised in 2016.

Modern Medical Device Legislative Milestones (1992–2005)

Other laws and regulations also play important roles in medical device clinical trials and regulatory submissions and are influential in developing and applying GCPs for medical devices. Some of these are discussed briefly in this chapter.[44] Specific legislation also impacts certain device types and their clinical use and reimbursement pathways, which also influence the medical device trial development and the facilities and investigators qualified to perform these activities (**Table 3-2**). For instance, the *Mammography Quality Standards Act* (*MQSA*) of 1992 provides requirements for certified mammography facilities. Review fees and regulatory reforms were addressed further in the *Medical Device User Fee and Modernization Act* of 2002 (*MDUFMA*) and the *Medical Device User Fee Stabilization Act* of 2005 (*MDUFSA*), which aimed to bring safe and effective devices to the public more quickly. These acts were developed alongside modern GCP requirements; it is important to note the overlap in thinking and philosophy underscored in these acts, which broadly attempt to balance making innovative new technologies available to the public with minimal burden while ensuring medical device safety and effectiveness.

Clinical Trial Overview

Clinical Trials—Drugs and Biologics

Drug and biologic clinical trials are conducted in phases. Each phase describes the general information the trial is collecting about a new treatment, such as its dose, safety and efficacy, and is designed to answer a separate research question (**Figure 3-1**).

Preclinical

During the Preclinical Phase, the drug or biologic is tested in animals to collect efficacy, toxicology and pharmacokinetic information.[45]

Phase 1

Phase 1, or first-in-human trials, represent the initial human exposure to an investigational drug or biologic. Researchers usually test a new drug or biologic, which has been proven safe for use in animals, in a small group of healthy human volunteers (i.e., 10–80 subjects). A Phase 1 trial's objective is to evaluate the product's metabolism and pharmacologic action, determine a safe dosage range, identify side effects and, if possible, gain early effectiveness evidence. In some circumstances, real patients are used when the treatment is likely to make healthy individuals ill. Phase 1 study subjects usually receive 24-hour medical attention and monitoring. Phase 1 doses often are subtherapeutic, but with ascending or escalating doses, to establish the best and safest dose.[46]

In 2006, FDA recognized "exploratory IND study," a new early Phase 1 study category, to collect baseline information, such as biodistribution of an extremely low dose of the new agent. Investigators use this information to determine whether to pursue additional human trials. Exploratory IND studies are smaller and shorter than the usual Phase 1 study, often involving fewer than 10 subjects and lasting a week or less.[47]

Phase 2

Once a dose or range of doses has been established, the drug or biologic is given to a larger group of subjects (i.e., 100–300) to study its effectiveness and further evaluate its safety. Genetic testing is not uncommon at this stage. Doses in Phase 2 are at a therapeutic level, although the product is not presumed to have any therapeutic effect at this stage. Phase 2 studies sometimes are separated into Phase 2a or 2b studies, with dosing requirements assessed in Phase 2a and study efficacy evaluated in Phase 2b.[48]

Phase 3

During Phase 3 studies, the drug or biologic is given to larger groups of subjects (hundreds to thousands, depending on the condition being studied) to confirm its effectiveness, monitor side effects, compare it to commonly used treatments and collect information to allow the drug or biologic to be used safely. Phase 3 studies are randomized, multicenter trials and usually have a longer duration, sometimes lasting several years. Phase 3 studies of chronic conditions or diseases often have a short follow-up period, three to six months, for ongoing evaluation.[49]

Drug and biologic manufacturers frequently continue enrollment in Phase 3 trials while the marketing application is undergoing regulatory review. These studies are usually categorized as Phase 3b studies and allow patients to continue to receive beneficial investigational drugs until the drug is available commercially.

Phase 4

Postmarketing studies are conducted in Phase 4 to gather information on the drug's effect in various populations and any side effects associated with its long-term use. Regulatory authorities may require manufacturers to conduct Phase 4 studies to collect additional safety information among the general population or in specific populations (e.g., pregnant or nursing women) normally excluded from clinical trials.[50]

Protocols and Protocol Amendments

FDA regulations require both drug and biologic studies to be conducted in compliance with the investigational plan, signed agreement, federal regulations and conditions of approval imposed by the IRB. Prior to starting a clinical trial, drug and biologic sponsors must submit a protocol for the planned study to FDA.

Protocol information for drug and biologic studies must contain:
- a statement of the study's objectives and purpose
- the name and address and a statement of qualification for each investigator, the name of each sub-investigator, the name and address of the research facilities to be used and the name and address of each IRB reviewing the study
- subject selection criteria (i.e., inclusion and exclusion criteria) and the estimated number of subjects to be enrolled in the study
- the study design, including the control group type to be used, if any, and a description of the methods (e.g., blinding) to be used to minimize bias on the part of subjects, investigators and analysts
- the method for determining the dose(s) to be administered, the planned maximum dosage and the duration of each individual subject's exposure to the drug or biologic
- a description of the observations and measurements to be made during the study
- a description of clinical procedures, laboratory tests or other measures taken to monitor the drug's effects on the subjects and to minimize risk[51]

Drug and biologic study sponsors must submit protocol amendments to describe any changes that affect subject safety significantly (Phase 1) or any Phase 2 or 3 protocol change that significantly affects subject safety, scope of the investigation or the study's scientific quality. Examples include:
- increase in dosage or duration of exposure of individual subjects to the drug or biologic, or a significant increase in the number of subjects to be enrolled in the study
- significant study design change (e.g., adding or dropping a control group)
- adding a new test or procedure to improve monitoring for, or reduce the risk of, a side effect or adverse event, or dropping a test intended to monitor subject safety
- a new investigator added to a previously submitted protocol[52]

Protocol amendments can be implemented once the sponsor has submitted the amendment to FDA for review and the responsible IRB has approved the change. However, sponsors may implement the change to the protocol immediately if it is intended to eliminate an apparent immediate hazard to subjects, provided FDA and the reviewing IRB subsequently are notified in a timely manner.[53]

Informed Consent

Informed consent from prospective subjects is required for participation in FDA-regulated clinical investigations, except in limited circumstances, such as life-threatening situations, military operations or public health emergencies and emergency research. FDA has stated informed consent involves more than just obtaining the subject or legally authorized representative's signature on the informed consent form (ICF); it is an information exchange between the individual obtaining the subject's consent and the subject.

The consent process involves providing a potential subject with sufficient information to allow an informed decision about participating in the clinical investigation, facilitating the potential subject's understanding of the information, providing adequate opportunity for a potential subject to ask questions and consider whether to participate, obtaining the potential subject's voluntary agreement to participate and continuing to provide information as the clinical investigation progresses or as the subject or situation requires.[54] To be effective, the process must provide the subject sufficient opportunity to consider whether to participate and must occur under circumstances that minimize the possibility of coercion or undue influence.[55]

The ICF serves multiple purposes. It ensures the subject is presented with the required information about the drug or biologic and the trial, allowing the subject to make an informed decision about participating in a clinical investigation. The ICF also provides the subject with a take-home reminder of the clinical investigation's elements, as well as contact information in case additional questions or concerns arise. Additionally, it documents the subject's voluntary agreement to participate. The consent process often continues after the ICF is signed. Through the course of the trial, additional information may need to be given to the subject, and the subject may need additional opportunities to ask questions and receive answers.

FDA regulations do not specifically require study sponsors to submit a copy of the ICF with the IND application. However, if FDA determines an ICF review is necessary to determine whether the clinical investigation may safely proceed, the agency will request the sponsor to submit the ICF. This is likely to occur for treatment INDs, treatment protocols and INDs conducted under the exception from informed consent requirements for emergency research. FDA reviews the ICF to ensure it conforms to 21 CFR 50 requirements. After review, FDA may send the sponsor a letter citing deficiencies regarding the ICF, in which case the clinical investigation may not begin until the sponsor has corrected them. In the event an IRB makes substantive changes to the ICF (i.e., changes that affect subjects' rights, safety or welfare), the sponsor must submit the revised ICF to FDA for review and approval prior to implementing the document changes.[56]

All parties involved in clinical research (i.e., sponsors or CROs, IRBs and clinical investigators) share responsibility for ensuring the informed consent process is adequate. For example, FDA's review of the consent form does not negate or replace the IRB's responsibility to review and approve the consent form, all materials used in the consent process and the consent process itself, as a condition for the clinical investigation to begin. FDA regulations mandate IRB review and approval of modifications (to secure approval) or disapproval of all research activities covered by the IRB regulations. IRB oversight is critical to ensuring an adequate informed consent process is in place to protect clinical investigation subjects' rights and welfare.[57]

IRB review ensures the ICF received by subjects contains the eight required elements (e.g., description of the clinical investigation, risks and discomforts, benefits, alternate procedures or treatments, confidentiality, compensation and medical treatment in the event of injury, contacts and voluntary participation) identified in 21 CFR 50.25, as well as any additional elements (e.g., unforeseeable risks, involuntary termination of subject's participation, additional costs to subjects, consequences of subject's decision to withdraw, provision of significant new findings to subjects and approximate number of subjects involved in the trial) required under 21 CFR 50.25(b), as appropriate.

The IRB also has the authority to require information, in addition to that specifically mentioned in 21 CFR 50.25, be given to subjects when, in the IRB's judgment, the information would be relevant to the protection of subjects' rights and welfare. Additionally, the IRB should be aware of who will conduct the consent interview on site, the timing for obtaining informed consent and any waiting period (between informing the subject and obtaining the consent) that will be observed.

The clinical investigator is responsible for protecting subjects' rights, safety and welfare during a clinical investigation and for ensuring a legally effective ICF is obtained from each subject prior to study participation. Although the investigator may delegate the task of obtaining consent to another study staff member who has the appropriate training, credentials, medical expertise and protocol knowledge, the investigator retains ultimate responsibility for the consent process.[58]

Sponsors often provide clinical investigators with a model consent form they may adapt to meet local needs. Because the clinical investigator must receive IRB approval before starting the clinical investigation, the sponsor should work closely with the clinical investigator to ensure the IRB reviews and approves the modified consent form. FDA recommends the clinical investigator provide the sponsor with a copy of the IRB-approved consent form.[59]

Responsibilities

IRBs

Organization and Purpose

Under FDA regulations, an IRB is an appropriately constituted group formally designated to review and monitor biomedical research involving human subjects to ensure subjects' rights and welfare are protected.[60]

An IRB is designated or formed to review research conducted at an institution or with its support. For multicenter studies, an institution's IRB can serve as a central IRB, can rely on a centralized IRB's review (in whole or in part) in place of its own study review or can conduct its own study review. Because the goal of the centralized process is to increase efficiency and decrease duplicative efforts, it may be more effective for a central IRB to take responsibility for all reviews at each site. Other approaches may be appropriate as well. For example, an institution may permit a central IRB to take responsibility for initial and ongoing study review or apportion IRB review responsibilities between the central IRB and its own.[61]

Whether the study utilizes a central or institutional IRB or a combination of both, FDA regulations require each IRB to have at least five members, with varying backgrounds (i.e., no IRB can consist entirely of members of one discipline) to promote complete and adequate research activity review. The IRB must be sufficiently qualified through its members' experience and expertise and their diversity, including race, gender, cultural backgrounds and sensitivity to such issues as community attitudes.[62] When a centralized IRB is used, the review process should include mechanisms to ensure meaningful consideration of relevant local factors. Possible mechanisms include:
- providing important local information to the central IRB in writing from individuals or organizations familiar with the local community, institution and/or clinical research
- utilizing consultants with relevant expertise or members from the institution's IRB in the central IRB's deliberations
- limited review of a central IRB-reviewed study by the institution's IRB, focused on issues of concern to the local community[63]

IRBs must include at least one member whose primary concern is in the scientific area, and at least one whose primary concern is in a nonscientific area. The IRB also must include at least one member who is not otherwise affiliated with the institution and whose immediate family does not include a person affiliated with the institution. FDA regulations allow convened IRBs to review and approve studies if at least a majority of its members, including the non-scientific member, is present.[64]

IRB members with conflicting interests associated with the study may not participate in the IRB's initial or continuing study review, except to provide information the IRB requests. For example, a clinical investigator involved with a study may be a member of the IRB but would have to absent him- or herself from deliberation and abstain from voting due to potential conflicts of interest.[65]

IRB Review

The three IRB review situations are: exempt from IRB review, expedited review and full board (convened) IRB review. The review type is driven by the study type and associated risk. An exemption from the prospective IRB review requirement is permitted for one emergency use of a test article in an institution, provided the product's emergency use is reported to the IRB within five working days. An emergency use is defined as a single use (or single course of treatment, e.g., multiple doses of an antibiotic) with one subject. Subsequent use would be a second use with that subject or the use with another subject.

If, in reviewing the emergency use, it is anticipated the test article may be used again, the IRB would ask the sponsor to develop a protocol and consent document(s), so an approved protocol would be in place if needed. However, FDA notes, despite the clinical investigator and IRB's best efforts, a situation may arise requiring a second emergency use. FDA has stated it is inappropriate to deny emergency treatment to an individual when the only obstacle is lack of time for the IRB to convene to review and approve the use.[66]

Expedited review is a procedure through which certain types of research may be reviewed and approved without convening an IRB meeting. FDA regulations permit, but do not require, an IRB to review certain research categories through an expedited procedure if the research involves no more than minimal risk. Examples of activities eligible for expedited review include:
- research on drugs or biologics for which an IND is not required
- collecting blood samples by finger, heel or ear stick or by venipuncture from subjects meeting defined age, weight and heath criteria, and the blood draws do not exceed volume/frequency limits
- prospectively collecting biological specimens (i.e., hair or nail clippings, saliva, sweat, etc.) for research purposes by noninvasive means

The IRB also may use the expedited review procedure to review minor changes to previously approved research during the period covered by the original approval. Under an expedited review procedure, the IRB chairperson or one or more experienced IRB members designated by the chairperson may review research changes. The reviewer(s) may exercise all the IRB's authorities except disapproval. Research may be disapproved only following review by the full committee, and the IRB is required to adopt a method to keep all members advised of research studies approved by expedited review.[67]

Although IRB review and approval generally are required before a study can be initiated under an IND, FDA may waive any of the IRB requirements for specific research activities or classes of research activities otherwise covered by the IRB regulations. The waiver provision is used only when alternative mechanisms are available to ensure human subjects' rights and welfare protection. The most common circumstance for a waiver request is when a sponsor wishes to conduct a foreign clinical study under an IND. In this case, sponsors typically utilize an Independent EC (IEC) that operates in accordance with GCP. Although its membership and functions for ensuring human subject protection are comparable to those of an IRB, an IEC may not meet all the Part 56 IRB requirements.[68]

Regulatory Oversight
In January 2009, FDA issued a final rule requiring all US IRBs that review FDA-regulated clinical studies to register through a system maintained by HHS. Registration information includes:
- contact information (i.e., addresses and telephone numbers)
- number of active protocols involving FDA-regulated products reviewed during the preceding 12 months
- description of the types of FDA-regulated products in the protocols reviewed

IRB registration provides FDA and other interested parties (e.g., sponsors, clinical investigators) with a comprehensive listing of all US IRBs that review FDA-regulated research and non-US IRBs, Independent or Research Ethics Committees (IECs/RECs) that review FDA-regulated research and voluntarily choose to register. This makes it easier for FDA to inspect IRBs and convey educational information to them.[69]

FDA conducts IRB inspections to determine whether they are operating in compliance with current agency regulations and statutory requirements and are following their own written procedures.

FDA inspections of IRBs generally fall into two categories:
- surveillance inspections—periodic, scheduled inspections to review the IRB's overall operations and procedures
- directed inspections—unscheduled inspections focused on the IRB's review of a specific clinical trial(s) (Directed inspections generally result from a complaint, clinical investigator misconduct or safety issue pertaining to a trial or site.)

During an inspection, FDA interviews IRB personnel to obtain information about the IRB's policies and procedures. The IRB's performance is evaluated by tracking one or more studies subject to IRB review under FDA regulations. During the inspection, FDA typically reviews:
- IRB membership records
- IRB procedures and guidelines
- IRB meeting minutes for the past year
- clinical investigator study documents sent to the IRB
- IRB study documents sent to the clinical investigator
- other study materials[70]

At the end of the inspection, FDA will discuss inspection findings and, if deficiencies are found, issue a written Form FDA 483 (inspectional observations) to the responsible IRB representative. The IRB can respond to the observations verbally during the exit interview and/or in writing. After the inspection, FDA personnel will forward the Establishment Inspection Report (EIR), the 483 (if issued), copies of materials collected during the inspection and any IRB responses to the appropriate FDA center for further evaluation. Following this review, the center will send one of three types of letters to the IRB chairperson:
- a letter stating FDA observed no significant deviations from the regulations
- an Informational or Untitled Letter identifying deviations, for which voluntary corrective action is sufficient; these letters may request an IRB response
- a Warning Letter, which identifies serious deviations; a Warning Letter generally requests prompt corrective action and a formal written response by the IRB

In addition to issuing letters, FDA can take other administrative actions against IRBs, including:
- withholding approval of new studies conducted at the institution or reviewed by the IRB
- directing that no new subjects be added to ongoing studies
- terminating ongoing studies, when doing so would not endanger the subjects
- notifying relevant state and federal regulatory agencies and other parties with direct interest in the agency's action on the IRB's operational deficiencies, in instances when the apparent noncompliance creates a significant threat to human subjects' rights and welfare

The FDA commissioner also can begin disqualification proceedings against an IRB or the institution if the IRB has refused or repeatedly failed to comply with FDA's IRB regulations and the noncompliance adversely affects human subjects' rights or welfare.

IRB violations cited most commonly in FDA inspections include:
1. failure to have adequate written procedures governing the IRB's functions and operations
2. failure to ensure the IRB reviews proposed research at convened meetings at which a majority of the members are present
3. failure to prepare and maintain IRB meeting minutes in adequate detail
4. failure to prepare and maintain adequate documentation of IRB activities, including a list of IRB members identified by: name, earned degrees, representative capacity, indications of experience and any other employment or other relationship between each member and the institution
5. failure to conduct continuing research reviews at intervals appropriate to the degree of risk but not less than once per year[71]

One of the most publicized IRB Warning Letters was the Coast IRB letter, issued 14 April 2009. In 2009, after concerns were raised in Congress that many for-profit IRBs routinely approved clinical trials' design and conduct without adequately monitoring subjects' safety, the Government Accountability Office (GAO) created a fictitious clinical trial for a fake surgical adhesive gel, conducted by a non-existent medical device company. The GAO wrote a fake protocol, based on an actual high-risk study for a product FDA ultimately withdrew from the market because of deaths and infections among patients, and submitted the package to three central IRBs. Two of the IRBs declined approval, citing serious subject safety concerns. However, Coast IRB of Colorado Springs, CO approved the study.

The FDA Warning Letter cited Coast for failing to determine risks to subjects were minimized and that those risks were reasonable in relation to anticipated benefits, for failing to make a risk determination, for failing to ensure basic informed consent elements were present in the ICF and for failing to demonstrate its ability to ascertain the acceptability of the proposed research. Coast was instructed to halt all new IRB operations, including enrolling additional subjects to ongoing studies.[72] As a result of the GAO actions and FDA's Warning Letter, several companies withdrew their business from Coast IRB, resulting in the IRB's closure on 29 April 2009.[73]

Sponsors and Contract Research Organizations (CROs)
Responsibilities
Under FDA regulations, the sponsor is responsible for all the trial's operational aspects. Specifically, sponsors are responsible for ensuring: 1) clinical studies are conducted properly for submission to FDA and 2) clinical study subjects' right and welfare are protected. These regulations are designed to protect human subjects and promote quality data collection.[74]

Drug and Biologic Studies
FDA regulations define a sponsor as "a person who takes responsibility for and initiates a clinical investigation. The sponsor may be an individual or a pharmaceutical company…" Sponsors' regulatory responsibilities are identified in 21 CFR 312 and include:
- obtaining agency approval, where necessary, before studies begin
- manufacturing and labeling investigational products appropriately
- initiating, withholding or discontinuing clinical trials as required
- refraining from investigational product commercialization
- selecting investigators qualified by training and experience as appropriate experts to investigate the drug or biologic
- providing investigators with the information needed to conduct an investigation
- ensuring proper investigation monitoring by trained and experienced monitors
- ensuring the investigation(s) is conducted in accordance with the IND's general investigational plan and protocols
- maintaining an effective IND with respect to the investigations
- ensuring FDA and all participating investigators are informed promptly of significant new adverse effects or risks with respect to the drug
- shipping the investigational drug only to investigators participating in the trial
- reviewing and evaluating the evidence relating to the drug's safety and effectiveness as it is obtained from the investigator (If determining its investigational drug presents an unreasonable and significant risk to subjects, the sponsor will discontinue those investigations presenting the risk and notify FDA, all IRBs and all investigators who have at any time participated in the investigation of the discontinuance.)
- maintaining and retaining adequate records and reports and permitting FDA to inspect records and reports relating to the clinical investigations
- maintaining written records of the investigational drug's disposition

Under 21 CFR 312.52, the sponsor may transfer responsibility for any or all of its obligations, with the exception of overall study oversight, to a CRO. All obligations the sponsor transfers to a CRO must be documented in writing. If the sponsor is transferring only some obligations, the documentation must describe each obligation being transferred. If all obligations are transferred, a general statement that all obligations have been transferred is acceptable. Any obligation not documented in the written description will remain with the sponsor. A CRO assuming any sponsor obligations must comply with the regulations applicable to those obligations and shall be subject to the same regulatory action as a sponsor for failure to comply with any regulations related to the obligation.

Recordkeeping and Record Retention
Drug and biologic sponsors must retain all records associated with a clinical study, including:
- all correspondence with another sponsor, monitor, clinical investigator, IRB and FDA
- investigational drug or biologic receipt, shipment and disposition
- signed investigator agreements and financial disclosure information

Drug and biologic study sponsors also must retain reserve samples of any test article or reference standards associated with the trial.

Drug and biologic study sponsors must retain all records and reports for two years after a marketing application is approved or, if the application is not approved, until two years after discontinuing drug shipment and delivery and FDA has been notified.[75]

Regulatory Oversight
FDA conducts various types of sponsor inspections. The most common are routine surveillance inspection; preapproval inspection used to determine whether a product approval is granted, delayed or denied; or a for-cause inspection arising from a product complaint, a recall or information provided to FDA by a "whistleblower." FDA sponsor inspections are used to confirm subjects' rights, safety and welfare were protected appropriately, to determine the accuracy and reliability of the clinical data submitted in support of marketing applications and to assess compliance with FDA regulations. In addition to determining whether FDA violations occurred during the trial, FDA inspections are used to obtain voluntary corrections by the inspected entity and the evidence necessary to support FDA enforcement action if voluntary correction is ineffective or does not occur.[76]

Findings cited most frequently during sponsor regulatory inspections include: 1) failure to ensure proper monitoring and 2) failure to ensure the trial was conducted in accordance with the investigational plan or protocol. Examples of both compliance issue types were cited in the October 2007 Sanofi-Aventis Warning Letter,[77] the August 2009 Johnson & Johnson Pharmaceuticals Warning Letter,[78] the November 2009 Icon Clinical Research Inc. Warning Letter[79] and the April 2010 Pfizer Inc. Warning Letter.[80]

FDA enforcement actions (e.g., 483s, Untitled Letters, Warning Letters, Notice of Initiation of Disqualification Proceedings and Opportunity to Explain (NIDPOE) letters, debarment, etc.) against clinical trial sponsors and CROs are similar to those used for IRBs. Additionally, FDA can utilize the Application Integrity Policy (AIP), formally entitled "Fraud, Untrue Statement of Material Facts, Bribery, and Illegal Gratuities Policy," implemented in 1991. Under the AIP, FDA can stop all scientific review of a pending submission when an applicant commits a "wrongful act" that raises significant questions about the integrity of data and information submitted to the agency in support of marketing approval. FDA will not resume substantive scientific review until all the data in question have been validated. If the data are not validated, the applicant must withdraw the submission, conduct additional clinical trials or abandon the product altogether. If FDA detects a pattern or practice of wrongful conduct, it can freeze review of all pending submissions until the integrity of the company's entire quality assurance system is verified. FDA also may require previously approved products to be recalled from the market.

Currently, six firms have been included on the AIP list from the Center for Drug Evaluation and Research (CDER) and the Center for Biologics Evaluation and Research (CBER). This list represents firms notified by FDA that it is deferring substantive scientific review of one or more of the firm's applications and/or is proceeding to withdraw the approved applications.[81]

Clinical Investigators
Responsibilities
Drug and biologic study investigators are responsible for:
- ensuring the trial is conducted according to the signed investigator statement for clinical investigations, the investigational plan and applicable regulations
- protecting study subjects' rights, safety and welfare
- controlling the drug and biological products under investigation
- ensuring informed consent is obtained from each subject in accordance with 21 CFR 50[82]

Clinical investigators for drug and biologic studies must ensure an IRB complies with FDA regulations and conducts initial and continuing ethical review of the study. They also must notify the IRB of changes in the research activity or unanticipated problems involving risks to human subjects or others and must not make any changes in the protocol without IRB and sponsor approval, unless necessary to eliminate apparent immediate hazards to human subjects. Investigators also are responsible for following the signed investigator statement (Form FDA 1572) and the investigational plan. In addition, they must report their financial interests to the sponsor to permit conflict of interest assessments.[83]

Recordkeeping and Retention
Investigators for drug studies are required to maintain the following records:
- disposition of the drug or biologic, including dates, quantity and subject use
- adequate and accurate case histories, recording all observations and other data pertinent to the investigation on each subject involved in the clinical trial
- annual clinical trial progress reports
- safety reports
- final report when the investigator's involvement in the trial is completed
- financial disclosure reports, including any updates for relevant changes occurring during the investigation and for one year following the trial's completion

The investigator is responsible for retaining all relevant records for two years following the date the drug or biologic marketing application is approved for the indication under investigation or, if no application is filed, or the application is not approved for the indication, until two years after the investigation is discontinued and FDA is notified.[84]

Regulatory Oversight
The various types of FDA investigator inspections include: data audits, in which the focus is on verifying study data submitted as part of a marketing application; information gathering; and for-cause inspections, where the focus is on the study's conduct by the investigator and usually is triggered by FDA's notification of a problem or complaint about the investigator. Generally, FDA conducts inspections of investigator sites to determine whether clinical investigators are conducting studies in accordance with applicable regulations.

FDA conducts both announced and unannounced clinical investigator site inspections for various reasons, including:
- verifying the accuracy and reliability of data submitted to the agency
- in response to a complaint about the study conduct at the site
- in response to sponsor concerns about the site
- upon termination of the clinical site
- during ongoing clinical trials to provide real-time assessment of the investigator's conduct of the trial and protection of human subjects
- at the request of an FDA review division
- related to certain classes of investigational products FDA has identified as products of special interest in its current work plan (i.e., targeted inspections based on current public health concerns)[85]

At the end of an inspection, the FDA investigator conducts an exit interview with the clinical investigator to review the findings and, if deficiencies are found, issues a written Form FDA 483. Common deficiencies observed by FDA investigators during clinical investigator inspections include:
- failure to follow the investigational plan and signed investigator statement/agreement (e.g., failure to conduct or supervise the study in accordance with the relevant, current protocol)
- failure to appropriately document and report medically necessary protocol deviations
- inadequate recordkeeping
- inadequate accountability for the investigational product
- inadequate subject protection, including informed consent issues

FDA enforcement actions (e.g., 483s, Untitled Letters, Warning Letters, NIDPOE letters, debarment, etc.) against investigators are similar to those used against clinical trial sponsors and CROs. If FDA determines there have been serious violations, and corrective action by the investigator cannot resolve the matter, FDA may elect to initiate an enforcement action against the investigator. If the findings indicate the investigator has violated FDA regulations or submitted false information repeatedly or deliberately, the agency may disqualify the investigator from conducting future studies it regulates. Additionally, FDA may initiate a civil or criminal enforcement action in federal court. However, both of these actions can take several months, or years, to complete.[86]

In the interim, FDA can issue a clinical hold, which will immediately suspend or impose restriction on an ongoing or proposed drug or biologic clinical study. The clinical hold order may apply to one or more investigations covered by an IND. When a proposed study is placed on clinical hold, subjects may not be given the investigational drug. When an ongoing study is placed on clinical hold, no new subjects may be recruited to the study and placed on the investigational drug; patients already in the study should be taken off therapy involving the investigational drug unless specifically permitted by FDA in the interest of patient safety. A clinical hold may be complete or partial; delay or suspension of all clinical work under an

IND is considered a complete clinical hold, while delay or suspension of only part of the clinical work under an IND is considered a partial clinical hold. A partial clinical hold could be imposed to delay or suspend one of several protocols in an IND, a part of a protocol or a specific study site (i.e., investigator) in a multi-site investigation.

FDA will impose a clinical hold if it finds subjects are, or would be, exposed to an unreasonable and significant risk of illness or injury. Examples of investigator actions that may result in a clinical hold include:
- failure to report serious or life-threatening adverse events
- serious protocol violations (e.g., enrolling subjects who do not meet the entrance criteria, failing to carry out critical safety evaluations)
- repeated or deliberate failure to obtain adequate informed consent
- failure to obtain IRB review and approval for significant protocol changes
- failure to supervise the clinical trial adequately such that human subjects are, or would be, exposed to an unreasonable and significant risk of illness or injury

FDA will lift a clinical hold when the grounds for the hold no longer apply. While the hold is in place, the sponsor of the affected study may present evidence to FDA to show it has taken steps to protect study subjects, e.g., by replacing the investigator who is charged with misconduct. If FDA concludes the study subjects no longer are exposed to an unreasonable and significant risk of illness or injury, the hold will be lifted.[87]

Monitors and Monitoring

Purpose of Monitoring

Effective clinical investigation monitoring is critical to protecting human subjects; collecting complete, accurate and verifiable study data; and conducting high-quality studies, compliant with the protocol, applicable regulations and GCPs. Sponsors of drug and biologic clinical investigations are required to provide adequate oversight of trials to ensure human subjects' rights, welfare and safety are protected and to ensure the quality of the clinical trial data submitted to FDA. FDA regulations require sponsors to monitor their clinical investigations' conduct and progress. While the monitoring task can be delegated, it ultimately remains the sponsor's responsibility.[88]

Monitor Qualifications

Monitors appointed by the sponsor should be trained appropriately and have the scientific and/or clinical knowledge to monitor the trial adequately. They should be thoroughly familiar with the investigational product(s), the protocol, written informed consent form and any other written information to be provided to subjects, the sponsor's Standard Operating Procedures (SOPs), GCP and the applicable regulatory requirement(s).[89]

Monitor Responsibilities

While the sponsor determines the appropriate extent and nature of monitoring, the monitor, by following the sponsor's monitoring plans, ensures the trial is conducted and documented properly. The monitor's responsibilities include:
- acting as the main line of communication between the sponsor and the investigator
- verifying the investigator has adequate qualifications and resources throughout the trial period
- verifying investigational product storage time and conditions are acceptable, and an adequate supply is available throughout the trial
- verifying the investigational product is supplied only to eligible subjects, and the subjects are provided with necessary instruction on the investigational product's proper use, handling, storage and return
- verifying the investigational product's receipt, use, return and disposition at the trial sites are controlled and documented adequately
- verifying the investigator and the trial staff follow the approved protocol and all approved amendments
- verifying written informed consent was obtained before each subject's participation in the trial
- ensuring the investigator receives the current Investigator's Brochure, all documents and all trial supplies needed to conduct the trial properly and comply with applicable regulatory requirements
- verifying source data, documents and other trial records are accurate, complete, kept up-to-date and maintained
- checking the accuracy and completeness of case report form (CRF) entries, source data and documents and other trial-related records against each other
- determining whether all adverse events (AEs) are reported appropriately within the required time periods[90]

Monitoring Activities

On-Site Monitoring

On-site monitoring is an in-person visit to the clinical investigation site. On-site monitoring is important early in a study, especially if the protocol is complex and includes novel procedures with which the investigator and site staff may be unfamiliar. On-site monitoring is used to:

- verify appropriate study subject enrollment
- assess the site's consenting process
- identify data entry errors (e.g., discrepancies between source records and CRFs, and missing data in source records or CRFs)
- verify the presence of study documentation
- assess the site's familiarity with the protocol and required procedures
- assess the site's compliance with the protocol, investigational product control and GCPs

Experienced on-site monitors also can provide the sponsor with an overall sense of the quality of a site's trial conduct (e.g., investigator oversight, attention to detail, thoroughness of study documentation and appropriate delegation of study tasks).[91]

Remote or Centralized Monitoring
Centralized or remote monitoring is an off-site evaluation performed by clinical monitors, data management personnel, medical monitors and/or statisticians. Centralized monitoring depends on various factors, including the sponsor's use of electronic systems, the sponsor's access to the site's data (i.e., either through electronic records or timely data entry from paper CRFs) and communication tools available to the sponsor and study site.

Centralized monitoring is used to supplement or reduce the frequency and extent of on-site monitoring by replacing the on-site activities with those that can be done as well or better remotely. Examples of activities well suited for remote monitoring include:
- monitoring data quality through routine review of submitted data to identify and follow-up on missing data, inconsistent data, data outliers and potential protocol deviations that may indicate systemic or significant errors in site data collection and reporting
- conducting statistical analyses to identify data trends not easily detected by on-site monitoring, such as checks of data range, consistency and completeness, and checks for unusual data distribution within and between study sites
- analyzing site characteristics, performance metrics (e.g., high screen failure or withdrawal rates, high eligibility violation frequency, data reporting delays) and clinical data to identify trial sites with characteristics correlated with poor performance or noncompliance
- verifying critical source data remotely[92]

Risk-Based Monitoring
Risk assessment generally involves identifying risks, analyzing them and determining whether they need to be modified by implementing controls (e.g., processes, policies or practices). In a recent guidance document, FDA stated risk-based monitoring could improve sponsors' clinical investigation oversight. FDA recommended sponsors prospectively identify critical data and processes, perform a risk assessment to identify and understand risks that could affect the collection of critical data or the performance of critical processes and develop a monitoring plan focusing on the important and likely risks to critical data and processes. Risk-based monitoring activities focus on preventing or mitigating important and likely sources of error in the conduct, collection and reporting of critical data and processes necessary for human subject protection and trial integrity.

Under risk-based monitoring, sponsors prospectively identify critical data and processes that, if inaccurate, not performed or performed incorrectly, would threaten human subjects' protection or study result integrity. Examples of critical data and processes include:
- verifying informed consent was obtained appropriately
- adhering to protocol eligibility criteria designed to exclude individuals for whom the investigational product may be less safe than intended and to include only subjects from the targeted study population for whom the test article is most appropriate
- procedures for documenting appropriate investigational product accountability and administration (e.g., ensuring the integrity of randomization at the site level, where appropriate)
- conducting and documenting procedures and assessments related to study endpoints—protocol-required safety assessments—evaluating, documenting and reporting serious adverse events and unanticipated adverse effects, subject deaths and withdrawals, especially when a withdrawal may be related to an adverse event
- conducting and documenting procedures essential to trial integrity, such as ensuring the study blind is maintained, at both the site level and sponsor level, as appropriate, referring specified events for adjudication and allocation concealment[93]

Monitor Reports
To ensure the sponsor remains informed of clinical trial progress, monitors submit a written report after each trial-site visit or trial-related communication. These reports include the date, site, monitor name and name of the investigator or other individual(s) contacted. They also summarize what the monitor reviewed and the monitor's statements concerning significant findings or facts, deviations and deficiencies, conclusions, actions taken

or to be taken and/or actions recommended to secure compliance.[94]

Consequences of Inadequate Monitoring

FDA clearly signaled the consequences of inadequate monitoring practices in the August 2009 Johnson & Johnson Pharmaceuticals Warning Letter, the November 2009 Icon Clinical Research Inc. Warning Letter and the April 2010 Pfizer Inc. Warning Letter. In all three cases, the first deficiency cited was "Failure to ensure proper monitoring of the clinical investigation (21 CFR 312.50; 312.56(a))."[95-97] Additionally, in the J&J and Icon letters, many observations start with the words, "Study monitors failed to identify that …."

The monitor's role is to ensure human subjects' protection; complete, accurate and verifiable study data collection; and the conduct of high-quality studies, compliant with the protocol, applicable regulations and GCPs. Considering the approval of any drug or biologic marketing application will depend on the quality of the scientific evidence that supports product use, the criticality of the monitor's role and activities cannot be over-emphasized.[98]

Quality Assurance (Auditing)

No general guidance or industry standard clarifies the requirements for a quality assurance program for clinical trials. FDA's Compliance Program Guidance Manual 7348.810 (Sponsors, CROs, and Monitors) notes clinical trial quality assurance units (QAUs) are not required by regulation. However, where the sponsor utilizes audits to determine protocol compliance, GCPs, clinical trial regulations and SOPs, auditing personnel should be independent of, and separate from, routine monitoring or quality control functions.

ICH E6, Section 5.19, Audit, notes sponsors should select qualified auditors who are trained and experienced and have written procedures describing what to audit, how to audit, audit frequency and audit report form and content. The audit plan should be guided by the trial's importance to regulatory submissions, the number of trial subjects, the trial's type and complexity, the level of risks to trial subjects and any identified problem(s). Additionally, all audit observations and findings must be documented.

Good Documentation Practices (GDPs)

All individuals associated with a clinical trial are responsible for creating and maintaining complete and accurate records. The IRB is required to create and maintain complete and accurate records of all its activities, including its members and procedures, research proposals reviewed, meeting minutes, correspondence with investigators and ongoing review activities. The investigator is required to create and maintain complete and accurate records of the investigational drug or biologic's disposition and case histories that record all observations and data pertinent to the investigation. The sponsor is required to create and maintain complete and accurate records of the investigational drug or biologic's receipt, shipment and disposition, agreement of obligations transferred to a CRO, and all records associated with clinical study oversight, including but not limited to investigator selection, monitoring activities, quality assurance, safety reporting and data handling. The monitor is required to create and maintain complete and accurate records of all trial-site visits and trial-related communications.

Good documentation practices are important because the regulatory agency's ultimate decision to approve a marketing application is based on the submitted data's accuracy and integrity, which should allow an independent observer to reconstruct the trial as it occurred by examining the study records.

FDA uses the acronym ALCOA (attributable, legible, contemporaneous, original and accurate) to describe the key attributes of good documentation practices.[99]

- Attributable—Does the document clearly indicate who observed and recorded the information, and the time?
- Legible—Can the information be understood easily? Is it recorded permanently on a durable medium? Are the original entries clearly readable (e.g., not obscured)?
- Contemporaneous—Was the information recorded at the time of the occurrence or observation?
- Original—Is the source information accessible and preserved in its original form?
- Accurate—Does the recorded information clearly, and without error, describe the documented study events?

Clinical Trial Overview

Clinical Trials—Medical Devices

Development of Harmonized Medical Device GCPs (ISO-GCP)

By the 1970s and 1980s, drug and device clinical trial practices had advanced dramatically worldwide, underscored by technological advancement and growing public health concerns. The US, Japan, UK and other European countries each had developed varying clinical trial requirements and, as a result, divergent clinical trial practices were burdensome and often repetitious for regulatory submissions in various regions, frequently extending the cost and time for new products to enter the market even after their safety and effectiveness had been established in other global regions.[100] In response, GCP standards were developed with the intent to establish and harmonize global clinical trial requirements.

Predecessors of ISO-GCP: ISO 10993 and BS EN 540
The International Organization for Standardization (ISO) is a worldwide federation of national standard organizations (ISO member bodies) that collaborates closely with the International Electrotechnical Committee (IEC). In 1996, the same year that the International Conference on Harmonisation of Technical Requirements for Pharmaceuticals for Human Use (now International Council on Harmonisation, ICH) convened to produce the harmonized GCP guideline for drugs, an international initiative was undertaken to specify harmonized guidelines for medical device clinical trials. This initiative led to the development of ISO 10993 *Biological testing of medical and dental materials and devices—Part 8: Clinical investigation*.[101,102] ISO 10993 attempted to harmonize international medical device GCPs and was based primarily on earlier European initiatives, such as the British standard EN 540:1993 *Clinical Investigation of Medical Devices for Human Subjects*.[103-105] In 2001, the Vienna Agreement formalized the relationship between the Center for European Normalization (CEN) and ISO. This collaboration was recently extended from European states to both the US and Asia. As working group member Nancy Stark recounts, momentum on medical device GCP development was strongly influenced by the entrance of the US and Japan into these discussions, a fundamental shift away from a primarily pan-European collaboration to a true international standard, which was reflected in the shift to using the term "global" rather than "international" (conventionally understood as pan-European in prior standards) in this standard.[106]

Development of ISO 14155 GCP
ISO's GCP for medical devices was introduced in 2003 as ISO 14155-1:2003 *Clinical investigation of medical devices for human subjects—Part 1: General requirements*, a product of ISO technical committee (ISO/TC) 194 Biological evaluation of medical devices. However, critics found the newly minted medical device GCP standard lacking the rigor of ICH's GCP recognized by FDA in 2000.[107] The battle for a harmonized standard for medical devices was far from over, as the new medical device GCP was further challenged when Japan elected to abstain from the vote on ISO 14155-1:2003. Despite this controversy, committee members from the US and other regions voted to recognize the standard, a decision based on the increasing technological differences between drugs and innovative new devices, requiring different testing methods and controls.[108]

In response, a New Work Item Proposal was introduced by the US in 2003, paving the way for harmonization of the 2003 standard with ICH's GCP. By April that same year, political sensitivities existed between the ISO organization, responsible for leading Part 1 under a Swiss convener, and CEN, the organization that led Part 2 with a British convener, which led the US to take a step back; additional politically sensitive issues between Europe and the US arose during US involvement in Iraq.[109] However, international work continued on this standard, with an emphasis on harmonizing it with ICH's GCP.

Current ISO GCP (ISO 14155:2011)
The current ISO GCP standard was published in 2011 as ISO 14155:2011 *Clinical investigation of medical devices for human subjects—Good clinical practice*. This standard, further addressed later in this chapter, included sweeping changes in content and format. Centrally, both Part 1 and Part 2 of the original 2003 standard were combined into a single comprehensive document, and to reflect alignment with ICH's GCPs, the standard's title clearly includes "Good Clinical Practices," signaling the working group's intent that this be the seminal standard for international medical device clinical trials. This version of the standard was developed through collaboration among international regulatory agencies, with FDA's Center for Devices and Radiological Health (CDRH) highly involved in its development.[110] Notably, while the standard was accepted by most member bodies, Japan subsequently voted against the latest form (ISO 14155-2:2011 GCP), and the standard has earned varying recognition across global regions.[111] The ISO 14155:2011 standard commonly is referenced as medical device GCP, and its scope broadly parallels ICH's GCP, but it is intended for medical devices, excluding in vitro diagnostics.

FDA Recognition of ISO-GCP for Medical Device Trials
ISO-GCP Recognition in the US
FDA has formally recognized ISO 14155:2011, publishing it as a recognized consensus standard in the *Federal Register* in 2012 as part of the *FDAMA* Modifications to the List of Recognized Standards, Recognition List Number: 028, which enables manufacturers to declare conformity to satisfy regulatory requirements.[112] In February 2013, FDA published a *Federal Register* notice indicating its proposed rule to amend current device regulations to require device clinical trials conducted outside the US to support FDA regulatory applications to comply with ISO GCP.[113] Thus, ISO 14155 compliance is an issue for both US domestic medical device trials and a consideration for regulatory personnel in determining whether evidence from trials in other global regions may be used for regulatory purposes in the US. Since January 2014, ISO 14155:2011 also has been listed online in FDA's Recognized Consensus Standards database.[114]

Chapter 3

ISO-GCP for Non-US Trials Supporting US Submissions

ISO GCP compliance extends to trials conducted in global regions that may be used to support US regulatory submissions. On 28 April 2008, FDA issued a final rule that modified 21 CFR 312.120, which states that the agency will accept foreign clinical study involving a medical device not conducted under an IDE only if the study adheres to the Declaration of Helsinki's (1983 version) ethical principles or the laws and regulations of the country in which the clinical trial was conducted, whichever provides greater protection to the study subjects.[115]

Global Recognition of ISO-GCP

While ISO 14155 is formally recognized in the US and EU, not all global member bodies exercise the same recognition and enforcement practices for medical devices (see recommended reading at the end of this chapter). When applying ISO 14155 in global regions, including multicenter trials, it is important to consult regulatory professionals in the regions to understand regional differences in GCP recognition.

US CFR and ISO GCP

While the US formally recognizes ISO 14155:2011 (ISO GCP) as a consensus standard, it is important to note the standard itself is not mandated by US law. Thus, US medical device clinical trials declaring conformity with ISO GCP face the unique challenge of complying with both the ISO 14155:2011 standard and applicable sections of 21 CFR, including:

- Part 11 Electronic Records
- Part 50 Protection of Human Subjects, which includes informed consent requirements (Subpart B) and additional safeguards for children in clinical investigations (Subpart D)
- Part 54 Financial Disclosure
- 486 Part 56 Institutional Review Boards
- Part 812 Investigational Device Exemptions, addressing IDEs required for some US Class II and all Class III investigational devices

FDA regulations and ISO 14155 standards include numerous unique requirements, some overlapping in content. To comply with both requirements, it is important to note these differences, which impact adherence to requirements specific to the investigational plan, deviations, recordkeeping, device accountability and subject protections (particularly, AE and consent issues), have been the subject of extensive prior review[116] and are, in part, addressed in this chapter. In general, CFR compliance results in ISO compliance, although additional requirements may be found in each that are applicable to medical device trials.

When are clinical trials required for medical devices?

Not all medical device submissions require clinical trials and, for many, the device development stage and various trial types overlap instead of following a linear process, as scientists invent, refine and test medical devices iteratively prior to entering the market.[117] Unlike drug and biologic clinical trials conducted in clear phases (i.e., Phases 1–4), medical device clinical trials are classified broadly into feasibility and pivotal trials.

Clinical trial research questions are governed by the device's potential hazard, which is reflected in both its classification (Class I, II or III) and whether it will enter the market through a 510(k) or PMA mechanism. Although PMA applications require clinical trials, only some 510(k) submissions require preclinical or clinical trials, and the trial research questions supporting a 510(k) vary widely. Minimal risk devices subject to Class I general controls (e.g., elastic bandages, dental floss and enemas) and some 510(k)-exempt Class II devices typically do not require clinical trials. Conversely, all Class III devices (e.g., replacement heart valves, pacemakers, breast implants) require clinical trials when submitted through the PMA process, as do most Class III devices that enter the market through the 510(k) process. Class III devices (e.g., implantable pacemakers and breast implants) subject to PMAs require clinical trials; however, special exemptions to the clinical trial effectiveness requirement exist for humanitarian use devices (HUD) that come to market via a humanitarian device exemption (HDE) application, which is similar in both form and content to the PMA application but without the clinical trial effectiveness requirement.

Perhaps the most subjectivity in whether a clinical trial is required lies in the 510(k) mechanism. Virtually all Class I devices are considered exempt from 510(k). Class II devices subject to 510(k) (e.g., ultrasound scanners, condoms and wheelchairs) are considered intermediate risk and may or may not require clinical trials. FDA maintains a specific listing of Class I and II devices exempt under *FDAMA*, which includes general chemistry, hematology/pathology, dental and many other device types not considered to have a significant potential public health impact.[118]

To understand why medical device clinical trials are conducted and how to design their aims, it is important to note the 510(k) and PMA processes' underpinnings. Premarket notification (510(k)) medical device submissions are reviewed by CDRH, specifically the Office of Device Evaluation (ODE) and Office of In Vitro Diagnostics and Radiological Health (OIR).[119] Submission of a 510(k) leads to a determination of "substantially equivalent" (SE) or "not substantially equivalent" (NSE) to an existing marketed (predicate) device. In effect, a substantive submission portion is dedicated to allowing the manufacturer to make the case

Figure 3-2. Types of Medical Device Clinical Trials and Typical Pathway

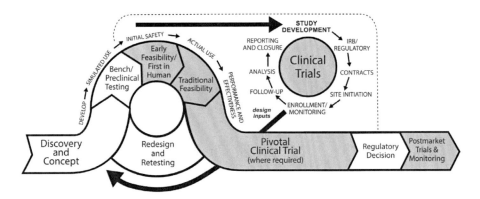

Grey regions show clinical trials, including early feasibility studies ("pilot trials")/first in human (FIH) studies, traditional feasibility studies, pivotal device trials and subsequent postmarket trials. It is important to note that various medical device trials are not always required for all device types, and these may be conducted concurrently or with overlap (unlike the phased trials in pharmaceuticals). An important reason for this is that information about the device performance and use from clinical trials provides input into the design or redesign of the device prior to commercial release. While early and traditional feasibility studies may often include more than one device configuration or version with iterative optimizations, a final or near final configuration is required for pivotal clinical trials.

the new device is, in fact, substantially equivalent to the predicate. For simple existing product improvements (next-generation devices), this often is straightforward and requires little or no clinical evidence. As the difference from the predicate increases, e.g., for new technology, more robust clinical testing may be required to build sufficient evidence. Based on relevant guidance, standards, existing literature and a variety of other factors, clinical trials may or may not be required. The subjectivity of balancing regulation and innovation in the substantial equivalence paradigm of 510(k) has been debated widely in modern scientific and legal literature.[120–122]

While the 510(k) process enables some potentially high-risk devices to come to market without clinical trials, regulatory professionals should approach these cases with caution and seek scientific and agency input on the evidence required for a specific product. A recent, but not entirely rare example, highlighted in the *New England Journal of Medicine*, provides a cautionary tale about challenges associated with determining complex medical devices' safety without clinical testing.[123] In the case of artificial hip implants (historically consisting of a ball and polymer cup), a new metal-on-metal design known as the DePuy (Johnson & Johnson) ASR XL Acetabular System came to market via the 510(k) process without clinical trials; this device was marketed in the US in 2005–10. Because the device borrowed a metal alloy cup from another device already on the market, the manufacturer successfully built a body of evidence that the re-engineered device was "substantially equivalent," primarily using bench testing to simulate the biomechanical stresses inside the patient's body. The failure rate, however, was found to be as high as one in eight, and the device was recalled, but only after it had already been implanted in nearly 100,000 patients.[124]

On the other side of the argument, Congressman Cliff Stearns (R-FL), the chairman of the 2011 US House Energy and Commerce Subcommittee on Oversight and Investigations hearing on "Medical Device Regulation: Impact on American Patients, Innovation, and Jobs," argued the burden of regulation and additional clinical trial requirements is burdensome, stifles innovation and leads manufacturers and innovators to market their devices overseas. Thus, manufacturers and regulatory professionals face numerous considerations in determining the most appropriate type of evidence for a given device and when preclinical or bench testing may be used to support 510(k) filings without the need for clinical trials.

Types of Medical Device Clinical Trials
Medical devices follow a widely recognized path to US commercialization that, unlike the phased approach in pharmaceuticals, may involve a good deal of overlap between types of trials and device development activities. This section outlines the major types of medical device clinical trials.

Discovery and Concept
The medical device development process begins when an unmet medical need is identified and scientists conceptualize a new device. During this part of medical device development, scientists and engineers build a "proof of concept" document and prototypes. Early studies may be conducted in engineering environments as part of medical

device design and development to ensure the device functions properly, user needs are met, and FDA requirements for certain design controls are met (verification and validation) prior to further testing.[125] This testing is completed before clinical trials, where required.

Preclinical Trials and Bench Testing
Although medical device preclinical testing often is not required, based on the new device's risk level, preclinical testing may be warranted prior to testing in humans. In some cases, particularly for devices that are iterative improvements to technology already commercialized as another medical device, preclinical and laboratory trials may be used as evidence to support a substantial equivalence determination in the 510(k) process without the need for clinical trials.

For many established device technologies, recognized standards exist that provide additional details for preclinical and bench test methods. For many innovative new devices, however, such recognized standards may not yet be in place.

Early Feasibility Studies (Pilot Trials)
Unlike drug trials, which emphasize dosage in early stage trials, early medical device feasibility trials focus primarily on prototype development and may include First-in-Human (FIH) studies. FDA guidance defines early feasibility studies as synonymous with pilot trials and defines such a study as "a limited clinical investigation of a device early in development, typically before the device design has been finalized, for a specific indication."[126] When the trial also represents the first use in human subjects, FDA considers it to be FIH.

Early feasibility studies may be conducted for various reasons, including:[127]
- determining the procedure's device-specific clinical safety aspects
- determining whether the device can be delivered, implanted or used successfully
- identifying device operator technique use challenges
- learning more about human factors (e.g., procedural step comprehension difficulties)
- initially evaluating device clinical safety (e.g., evaluating device-related serious adverse events)
- determining whether the device performs according to its intended purpose (e.g., mechanical function, making intended measurements)
- identifying device failures
- identifying patient characteristics that may impact device performance (e.g., anatomical limitations)
- determining device use therapeutic parameters (e.g., energy applied, sizing, dose released)

Particularly for nonsignificant risk devices (as defined in 21 CFR 812.3(m)) eligible for an investigational device exemption (IDE), early feasibility trials may be iterative in nature and involve testing, optimization, and re-testing of multiple prototypes in the course of a single trial. Such testing often involves a cross-disciplinary team of engineers, scientists, materials and mechanical specialists and, in some cases, other experts in electrical, software/firmware and interoperability.

Unlike traditional feasibility studies, these early studies are iterative in nature and may be used to provide input into appropriate future clinical or bench-testing procedures to optimize user experience and to refine the intended use population prior to subsequent clinical study protocols. Early feasibility studies also are not strictly required prior to the start of traditional studies, but rather are conducted as needed for device development, optimization and user testing.

Further, early feasibility studies may be conducted concurrently with traditional feasibility or pivotal trials, enabling exploration of specific design elements prior to the final commercial configuration. Such concurrent studies are common practice for those medical devices where human factors play an important role, as "actual-use" testing can be used to understand user interactions with a medical device rapidly and can be conducted as part of a clinical study. According to FDA's *Applying Human Factors and Usability Engineering to Medical Devices: Guidance for Industry and Food and Drug Administration Staff,* while clinical trials may be used to collect actual-use testing data, it is important to consider that these users are supervised more closely than real-world users, and thus findings should be considered in the appropriate context; the guidance recommends that such data be supplemented to the extent practicable with real-world observational data (see more in recommended reading at the end of this chapter).[128]

Traditional Feasibility Studies
FDA defines a traditional feasibility study as "a clinical investigation that is commonly used to capture preliminary safety and effectiveness information on a near-final or final device design to adequately plan an appropriate pivotal study."[129] While these studies are similar in design to early feasibility studies, the central difference is use of a final or near-final device configuration. These studies occur later in development than early feasibility studies, and IDE applications for traditional feasibility studies are typically expected to contain some prior clinical or preclinical or bench-test results. However, conducting an early feasibility study prior to a traditional feasibility study is not always necessary.

Pivotal Study
A pivotal study is a clinical investigation designed to collect definitive safety and effectiveness evidence for a device within its specified intended use.[130] These studies are required for some 510(k) and all PMA submissions. Pivotal trials often are similar in design and somewhat analogous to Phase 3 pharmaceutical studies and typically are required to have a statistically justified number of subjects. Early or traditional feasibility studies may or may not be required prior to pivotal studies.

Postmarket Surveillance Studies
In the US, postmarket surveillance studies may be required under Section 522 at the time of approving a PMA, HDE or product development protocol (PDP) application.[131] For high-risk devices that come to market through the PMA process, clinical evidence generation is shifting from a premarket activity to continual study throughout the total product lifecycle. The clinical evidence required to support a PMA varies in size and quality, and about 13% of initiated postmarket studies are completed within three to five years after FDA approval.[132] In some cases, postmarket studies may continue under the same protocols as those approved by FDA.

Medical Device Trial Pathway—Putting it all Together
Medical device clinical trials play an important role not only in establishing safety and effectiveness, but also in providing use, performance and functionality information to help optimize the device prior to entering the market. Early feasibility and/or traditional feasibility testing play an important role in identifying how users interact with devices and in optimizing device performance in actual-use cases, and much literature has been dedicated to this subject.[133] Not all study types are necessary for all devices, and use and performance information from all study types should provide inputs into the device's final commercial configuration (**Figure 3-2**).

Registering Medical Device Trials to ClinicalTrials.gov
Clinical trial transparency is an increasing concern, and information about many medical device studies is available through ClinicalTrials.gov and other publicly available FDA documents.[134] The registration portal formats for ClinicalTrials.gov and others, however, are designed primarily with pharmaceutical trials in mind, and can pose some challenges to medical device industry users. Once registered, certain information about registered trials is available to the public.

Applicable Device Clinical Trials
Under the final rule implementing *Food and Drug Administration Amendments Act* (*FDAAA*) Section 801, Applicable Clinical Trials (ACTs) per 42 CFR 11.22(b) are defined as either Applicable Device Clinical Trials or Applicable Drug Clinical Trials. All ACTs must be registered on ClinicalTrials.gov.

To be considered an ACT, a medical device trial must meet all the following requirements (these appear in abbreviated form here; the ClinicalTrials.gov checklist and associated regulation provide additional details):[135]
- be a prospective interventional clinical study of health outcomes
- employ an FDA-regulated device
- be conducted in the US or with devices planned for export from the US
- be other than a small clinical trial to determine the device's feasibility (typically a trial testing a device prototype, not health outcomes)

Certain other trial types also must register, such as pediatric postmarket surveillance trials of devices conducted under *FD&C Act* Section 522 (21 U.S.C. 3601) and certain combination products meeting these criteria.

Notably, the requirements of *FDAAA* Section 801 were expanded and clarified in The Final Rule for Clinical Trials Registration and Results Information Submission (42 CFR Part 11) released in September 2016 and in effect for all new trials initiated after 18 January 2017.

Registering Feasibility Trials
It is important to note, like Phase 1 pharmaceutical and biologics studies, medical device studies consisting primarily of feasibility studies do not meet the ACT requirements and, thus, are not required to register on ClincialTrials.gov (see recommended reading at the end of this chapter).[136] However, medical device manufacturers increasingly are opting to register some feasibility studies voluntarily, particularly if these early studies collect some exploratory data that could be considered related to health outcomes or if the material may be published in scientific journals, which are requiring more clinical data reports to be linked to registered trials.

Protocols and Protocol Amendments
US regulations and ISO GCP requirements require medical device clinical trials to be conducted in accordance with an investigational plan, signed agreements, federal regulations and IRB-imposed conditions of approval.

When an FDA Protocol Review is Required
In the US, device studies must be conducted under an IDE. For Class II and III devices considered significant-risk devices, the sponsor submits the protocol in the investigational plan when the IDE application is submitted to FDA (Part 812.20) and the IRB for approval. For nonsignificant risk devices, only IRB approval is required, and FDA considers the trial to have an approved

IDE when the IRB concurs with the nonsignificant risk determination. In the event an IRB disagrees with the nonsignificant risk determination, this must be reported to FDA within five working days per §812.150(b)(9).[137,138]

Clinical Investigation Plan (Protocol) Structure and Content

According to ISO GCP, the terms "protocol" and "clinical investigation plan (CIP)" are synonymous; this document also explains the medical device clinical investigation rationale, objectives, design and proposed analysis, methodology, monitoring, conduct and recordkeeping (ISO 14155:2011 3.7). Its required contents are detailed in ISO GCP standard 14155:2011, Annex A:

- introduction, including required contents or appropriate references to other documents (i.e., the Investigator's Brochure)
- identification (study title, reference number, CIP version or date, summary of revisions or amendments, version or issue number)
- sponsor name and address
- Principal Investigator name, address and professional position; identity of investigation coordinator (where applicable); names and addresses of all participating institutions and clinical investigation sites (Note: Per ISO GCP, a final list of investigators, sites and institutions may be maintained outside the CIP and is not grounds for amendment, so long as this information is treated as a controlled document stored alongside the CIP by both sponsor and sites, as per ISO 14155:2011 Annex A A.1.4(c).)
- overall synopsis, with inclusion and exclusion criteria, number of subjects, clinical investigation duration, follow-up (or lack thereof), objective(s) and endpoint(s)
- device identification and description, including summary, intended purpose, manufacturer details, name, number and version (for the device and any accessories), traceability information (i.e., serial or batch numbers), populations and indications studied, description of device and materials contacting patients' bodies, operator training and experience summary, and description of any applicable medical or surgical procedures used in testing
- clinical investigation design justification, including evaluation of relevant preclinical and clinical data
- device and investigation risks and benefits, including anticipated clinical benefits and adverse device effects, residual risks, possible medication interactions and risk mitigations (per ISO 14971)
- objectives and hypotheses, including primary and secondary objectives, statistical hypotheses (or lack thereof where no analysis is performed, as in some small feasibility studies)
- study design, including blinding, masking and other rationale(s)
- investigational device and comparator description, where applicable (Note: For many medical device studies, the comparator will be the "predicate" device for which substantial equivalence is required per the 510(k) process. It also is important to note ancillary devices, device accessories (which may or may not be regulated separately as medical devices in their own right) and device components should be documented.)
- subject information, including inclusion and exclusion, withdrawal and discontinuation criteria, point of enrollment, total expected investigation duration and subject participation, number of subjects and estimated time to enroll (enrollment period) (Note: Unlike ICH GCPs for pharmaceuticals and biologics, a trial's enrollment point may be defined in the protocol based on when the subject completes recruitment and signs and dates the informed consent form (ISO 14155:2011 3.32). Due to some studies' nature, it is possible complex recruiting activities are required that can alter the trial's point of enrollment. In these cases, recruitment activity details and the actual point of enrollment should be defined prospectively in the protocol.)
- procedures, including those subjects will undergo, and, where applicable, which will be performed by the sponsor or staff (Note: For some medical device studies, particularly early feasibility, scientists or engineering personnel may need to be onsite to examine human factors issues or make iterative adjustments to the device. This is permissible if specified in the protocol and reviewed by the responsible IRB. Such sponsor activities during medical device development, however, should be prospectively documented in the protocol along with such personnel's required experience, training or qualifications.)
- general monitoring plan outline (Note: Monitoring arrangements may be detailed more specifically outside the CIP (ISO 14155:2011 Annex A A.6.5). Best practice, however, is to include a general summary and reference to the monitoring plan document.)
- statistical considerations, including the design, method and analytical procedures, sample size, level of significance and power calculations, expected drop-out rate, pass/fail criteria,

- provisions for interim analysis (where applicable), criteria for statistical termination, procedures for statistical plan deviations, treatment of missing data, data exclusions and minimum/maximum enrollment for multi-center investigations (Note: Many medical device feasibility studies may not have statistical powering, statistical hypotheses or pass/fail criteria. The sampling rationale in these cases may be related to device development needs or prior research experience, which ISO GCP defines as "special reasoning" that should be noted in the protocol rather than omitting these sections (ISO 14155:2011 Annex A A.7). If statistical section changes to the protocol are foreseen, this section may reference a separate statistical plan document or other supplementary documents outside the protocol that will document these changes and ultimately be considered part of the governing CIP.)
- data management, including data review and cleaning, electronic system verification and validation, data retention (with retention period) procedures and other applicable aspects of quality assurance (Note: The sponsor typically establishes a Data Management Plan (DMP) that supplements this information in detail, and typically is presented more generally in the site-facing protocol.)
- protocol amendment procedure description
- device accountability procedure description
- statements of compliance with requirements, including the Declaration of Helsinki, ISO 14155:2011 GCP, and regional or national requirements as appropriate
- statements that insurance will be provided for subjects, and additional IRB or governing regulatory agency(ies) (e.g., FDA) requirements will be followed
- informed consent process description, including how subjects unable to consent will be handled
- adverse events, serious adverse events, adverse device effects and device deficiency definitions and details of foreseeable events and their reporting process
- vulnerable population definitions and, if included, their informed consent process and any medical care provided after the investigation is complete
- premature investigation suspension or termination criteria, breaking blinding or masking and any subject follow-up (Note: Procedures for subject contact and follow-up after the trial are critical, particularly for significant risk devices, such as implants and life-supporting devices, where trial participation may have lasting health effects.)
- publication policy, including a statement of whether the results may be submitted or offered for publication (Note: In practice, although not specified in the ISO GCP standard, best practice dictates publication is not limited to academic or scientific journals, and also may include other public uses, as manufacturer presentations, training or commercial public uses. These may be detailed in the contract/agreement(s) for the trial as well, and it is important to ensure agreement between publication policy language in the contract/agreement(s) and the protocol.)
- bibliography/references

While not explicitly required by the ISO GCP standard, most institutions' protocols also include several additional best practice sections:
- core abbreviation and terminology definitions
- reference to specific documents required for the study, such as device operator manuals or training modules
- participation details for any sponsor or manufacturer representatives (other than the monitor) who may interact with sites or participate materially in the study in other ways, which is common in feasibility studies (e.g., engineers or scientists involved with optimizing the device used)
- calibration, cleaning, electrical safety, interoperability or software or hardware requirement instructions

Protocol Amendments and Changes

ISO GCP requires protocol and core study document amendments to be controlled by version number and date (ISO 14155:2011 6.5.1) and to provide a rationale for any protocol amendments (ISO 14155:2011 D.6.2). The governing IRB must review and approve amendments prior to their implementation at the clinical site. Generally, sponsors should submit notices of changes impacting an IDE application to FDA within five business days after making the change, while some will require prior notice; however, FDA recently has published guidance that interprets this requirement more liberally for certain changes in early feasibility studies where iteration and changes are expected.[139]

Because changes are expected during early feasibility studies, FDA has allowed more iterative approaches throughout the Pre-Sub and IDE processes, specifically designed to reduce the burden on early feasibility trials, including:[140]
- permitting a broader array of feasibility study device and protocol modifications with five-day notice (and without advance FDA approval)

- enabling sponsors to seek advance "contingent approval" for changes that would require FDA approval for early feasibility studies
- utilizing a 30-day "interactive review process" for early feasibility studies

While all medical device studies should document amendments in accordance with regulations and ISO GCP, special considerations apply for feasibility studies that may enable broader scope changes to procedures and device use during the study, as detailed in *Guidance for Industry and Food and Drug Administration Staff: Investigational Device Exemptions (IDEs) for Early Feasibility Medical Device Clinical Studies, Including Certain First in Human (FIH) Studies* (October 2013).

Protocol Deviations

ISO GCP defines a deviation as any instance(s) of failure to follow, whether intentionally or unintentionally, CIP (synonymous with protocol) requirements. While 21 CFR requirements are similar to ISO GCPs, important additional requirements exist. Primarily, US GCP places additional emphasis on specific deviation element documentation, with a mandatory five-day reporting window for emergency deviations. Except in such emergency cases, sponsor prior approval is required for protocol changes or deviations. Both 21 CFR and ISO GCP contain provisions for addressing protocol compliance issues (**Table 3-2**).

Informed Consent

Informed consent is required for participation in FDA-regulated clinical investigations, except in special circumstances (detailed below), and all clinical investigations must adhere to 21 CFR Part 50, Subpart B Informed Consent of Human Subjects.

ISO GCP specifically defines informed consent as the process by which an individual is provided with information and is asked to participate voluntarily in a clinical trial (ISO 14155:2011 3.21). Both 21 CFR 812.140 (a) and ISO 14155:2011 (3.2.1 and 4.7.1) require informed consent to be obtained prior to a subject's participation in a clinical study, and informed consent requirements are quite similar to those of pharmaceutical and biologic trials. Further, ISO GCP specifies that informed consent be:
- written, i.e., the informed consent form (ICF)
- signed
- dated

The information should be presented in lay language understandable to patients, which can be challenging for technologically complex medical devices. A study staff member at the investigational site should deliver the consent and ensure any potential subject's questions or concerns are answered prior to participation.

Special Informed Consent Circumstances

ISO GCP makes allowances for legally authorized representatives (LARs, ISO 14155:2011 3.26) to consent on the behalf of a prospective subject, where authorized by individual or judicial authority to do so. Informed consent also may be attained by supervised processes where the subject is unable to read or write and in emergency treatment cases. The challenge of conveying ethical and accurate informed consent in simple language often is addressed in the scientific literature.[141,142]

These standards' portions correspond to applicable 21 CFR requirements, specifically those stating that, except under the limited circumstances described in 21 CFR 50.23 (i.e., certain life-threatening situations, military operations, or public health emergencies) and 21 CFR 50.24 (i.e., emergency research), informed consent is required.

Feasibility Trial Informed Consent

If an early or traditional feasibility study is being conducted to collect data to support either a future subsequent clinical investigation or a marketing application, the study must comply with 21 CFR Part 50 informed consent requirements and 21 CFR Part 56. 21, CFR 50.1(a), 21 CFR 50.20, 21 CFR 56.101(a) and 21 CFR 56.103. In certain cases, early feasibility research may not be subject to these provisions if the device does not meet requirements; however, all trials still will be subject to the regulatory provisions imposed by the governing IRB and local requirements, which typically include informed consent.[143]

Early feasibility studies, as for all clinical investigations, must adhere to 21 CFR Part 50, Subpart B informed consent requirements. However, FDA has provided specific instruction to supplement these requirements, including specific recommendations for executing informed consent for early feasibility studies, in *Guidance for Industry and Food and Drug Administration Staff—Investigational Device Exemptions (IDEs) for Early Feasibility Medical Device Clinical Studies, Including Certain First in Human (FIH) Studies* (October 2013). The specific recommendations relevant to early feasibility studies are found under each applicable general consent requirement. Some of these recommendations may be appropriate for other types of clinical studies, but are particularly relevant for early feasibility studies.[144]

Informed Consent in HUD Research

HDE regulations do not require informed consent but, because HDE provides for marketing approval, FDA has stated an HUD does not constitute research or an investigation that typically would require study subjects' consent.[145] Despite not being required by regulation, most institutions and IRBs still may insist on informed consent for these studies, at their discretion.

Table 3-3. Comparison of 21 CFR and ISO GCP Requirements for Investigator Responsibilities in Medical Device Clinical Trials

21 CFR Requirements	ISO 14155:2011 (ISO-GCP) Requirements	Conclusion
21 CFR 812.110 (b): An investigator shall conduct an investigation in accordance with the signed agreement with the sponsor, the investigational plan, this part and other applicable FDA regulations, and any conditions of approval imposed by an IRB or FDA.	ISO 14155 9.6 (b): The principal investigator shall conduct the clinical investigation in compliance with the clinical investigation plan.	Compliance with CFR requirements is inclusive of the ISO GCP requirement and contains additional elements specific to US regulation.
21 CFR 812.110 (a): An investigator may determine whether potential subjects would be interested in participating in an investigation, but shall not request the written informed consent of any subject to participate, and shall not allow any subject to participate before obtaining IRB and FDA approval.	ISO 14155 6.1: The clinical investigation shall not commence until written approval/favourable opinion from the ethics committee and, if required, the relevant regulatory authorities of the countries where the clinical investigation is taking place has been received.	The IRB is given additional governance of methods for determining subject interest prior to IRB approval. In both, subjects may not consent or participate until IRB approval is received and FDA requirements are met.

Studies of New Uses of Cleared/Approved Devices

FDA also has stated that trials of cleared or approved devices being researched for new uses must comply with human subject protection (informed consent and additional safeguards for children in research) and IRB and IDE regulations.[146]

Responsibilities

This section does not attempt to provide an exhaustive list of IRB, sponsor and investigator responsibilities in clinical research, but highlights some of their core unique and differentiated roles in medical device trials. Further, ISO GCP states explicitly that all parties involved in clinical investigations share ethical responsibility for the study conduct according to their roles (ISO 14155:2011 4.4).

IRBs and ECs

ISO GCP defines an EC as synonymous with an IRB, the term most commonly used in the US. The EC or IRB is defined as the independent body whose responsibility it is to review clinical investigations to protect clinical trial subjects' rights, safety and well-being. In addition to the IRB's general responsibilities in reviewing core study documents and providing ethical oversight, which are similar for device and pharmaceutical or biologics trials and detailed elsewhere, IRBs overseeing medical device trials also are responsible for reviewing the sponsor's nonsignificant risk determinations and requesting additional information, where appropriate, to make a risk determination. Because an IDE is considered issued upon the IRB's approval of the determination (unlike significant risk devices, for which the IDE must be filed with FDA), this is a significant additional responsibility.

For early feasibility studies, IRBs face notable additional challenges that merit consideration, in part due to these trials' iterative and inherently dynamic nature. This results in much greater uncertainty about risks that can be mitigated, in part, by:[147]

- agreement on goals among the IRB, sponsor and investigator
- parallel contract and legal review processes
- establishing FDA liaison relationships with the IRB
- accepting central IRB and uniform consent forms, where possible (rather than introducing a wide degree of variation from the governing IRB at each participating site for multi-center trials)

Sponsor Responsibilities

General sponsor responsibilities for medical device trials are identified in 21 CFR 812.40, including:

- ensuring proper monitoring
- ensuring IRB review and approval
- submitting the IDE application to FDA, where applicable
- ensuring the IRB and FDA are informed of significant new information about an investigation

As detailed in both ISO 14155:2011 8.2.4 and 21 CFR 812.3(j), the sponsor is responsible for designating monitors to oversee the investigation and ensuring they are qualified by training and experience (21 CFR 812.43(d)). This task may be delegated, but it ultimately is the sponsor's responsibility (21 CFR 812.3(j)).

While some of these general responsibilities are similar between devices and pharmaceutical or biologic products (as detailed elsewhere), medical device trial sponsors are

Table 3-4. Comparison of 21 CFR and ISO-GCP Requirements for Recordkeeping in Medical Device Clinical Trials

21 CFR Requirements	ISO 14155:2011 (ISO-GCP) Requirements	Conclusion

• 21 CFR 812.140 (a): A participating investigator shall maintain the following accurate, complete and current records relating to the investigator's participation in an investigation:
  - Correspondence
  - Device disposition
  - Subject case history, including informed consent, relevant observations such as adverse device effects, and exposure to the investigational device
  - Protocol, including dates and reasons for deviations
  - Any other records FDA requires
	• ISO 14155 4.7.1: Informed consent
	• ISO 14155 6.4: Adverse events and device deficiencies
	• ISO 14155 6.9: Investigational device accountability
	• ISO 14155 6.10: Accounting for subjects
	• ISO 14155 4.5: Communication with the ethics committee
		• Following requirements in 21 CFR will ensure ISO-GCP compliance. Additional reporting details are provided in ISO-GCP.

responsible for some very specific responsibilities unique to medical devices:[148–150]

- selecting qualified investigators and providing them with information needed to conduct a study (21 CFR 812.40) and initiate the study (21 CFR 812.3(n)), which may involve complying with additional device use regulations (e.g., in the case of mammography facilities, which require certain qualifications to use these devices)
- for NSR studies, providing information to support determinations and informing the IRB of its determination(s) (21 CFR 812.2(b)(1)(ii)), which includes providing supporting information that may help the IRB evaluate the study's risk
- ensuring medical device-specific reporting requirements are met, including filing IDE and changes thereto that impact the clinical investigation.
- device feasibility and pivotal trials may overlap or be conducted concurrently, so the sponsor assumes responsibility for ensuring new information about safety and effectiveness, learned across a portfolio of studies, is communicated and updated regularly across all ongoing studies (This includes connecting information learned in one or more clinical trials with design inputs for device design or redesign.)
- providing the device's technical description, reports of its prior investigations, the proposed investigational plan, subject selection criteria and other information the IRB may need
- shipping the investigational device(s) only to qualified investigator(s), selecting qualified monitors, obtaining signed investigator agreements and financial disclosures (21 CFR 812.33) and maintaining accountability for all devices and their components and accessories used in the trial

Investigator Responsibilities
Similar responsibilities apply to medical device and pharmaceutical or biologic clinical trial investigators (an investigator as defined in 21 CFR 312.3(b) and 21 CFR 812.3(i)), although they are not identical. Medical device clinical investigations are conducted under 21 CFR part 812, which details the investigators' general responsibilities:[151]

- ensuring a clinical investigation is conducted according to the agreement, the investigational plan and applicable regulations
- protecting the rights, safety and welfare of subjects under the investigator's care
- controlling the medical devices used in the investigation (21 CFR 812.100), which includes device supervision, disposal and, in some cases, return to the sponsor (In practice, for electronic devices with storage, this may also include removing patient data from the device.)

There also are subtle legal and contractual issues that vary among sites and investigators, and important differences between 21 CFR and ISO GCP regarding medical device investigations can cause issues and delays (**Table 3-3**).[152,153] Notably, ISO GCP requires medical device investigations to be conducted in accordance with the CIP, whereas FDA regulations additionally require such investigations to be conducted in accordance with the signed agreement, FDA regulations and IRB conditions. Following 21 CFR requirements means the investigation is compliant with ISO GCP.

Further, investigators and sponsors are confronted with requirements to submit reports of unanticipated adverse device effects (UADE) and device deficiencies throughout medical device clinical trials.

The medical device regulations are distinct from those for drugs in that they do not require a specific

Table 3-5. Comparison of 21 CFR and ISO-GCP Requirements for Device Accountability in Medical Device Clinical Trials

21 CFR Requirements	ISO 14155:2011 (ISO-GCP) Requirements	Conclusion
21 CFR 812.140 (a): A participating investigator shall maintain the following accurate, complete and current records relating to the investigator's participation in an investigation: ...Device disposition ...Any other records FDA requires	ISO 14155 6.9: Investigational device accountability	Following 21 CFR requirements will ensure ISO-GCP compliance. Additional reporting details are provided in ISO-GCP.

form to be used for an investigator's statement. There also are additional medical device regulation and ISO GCP requirements and distinctions not listed above. Investigators and sponsors should refer to 21 CFR Parts 11, 50, 54, 56 and 812 and ISO GCP for a comprehensive list of medical device clinical trial requirements.

Reporting and Monitoring Medical Device Trials
While monitoring practices are similar for medical device and drug or biologic trials, important distinctions exist. The most visible of these are reporting device deficiencies and adverse device effects, and maintaining device accountability and recordkeeping.

Monitoring and Data Monitoring Committee (DMC)
In medical device clinical trial conduct, monitoring is a different process than oversight by a Data Monitoring Committee (DMC). Monitoring is conducted primarily by qualified individuals the sponsor delegates under 21 CFR 812.46 to:
- secure investigator compliance
- evaluate unanticipated adverse device effects
- obtain FDA and IRB approval before resuming a terminated study

As in drug research, risk-based monitoring, centralized or de-centralized monitoring and remote monitoring may be used, when appropriate, to ensure compliance. While these are beyond the scope of this chapter, other texts and guidance documents provide comprehensive detail on monitoring practices.[154]

Comparatively, a DMC may be utilized when it is necessary to have a group with additional oversight of the clinical trial data. It often advises the sponsor on study enrollment and evaluates the data's continuing validity and scientific merit.[155]

Reporting Adverse Events/Adverse Device Effects
The ISO GCP standard defines the following terms:
- adverse device effect—adverse event related to the use of an investigational medical device (ISO 14155:2011 3.1), including adverse events related to instructions, labeling or use error.
- adverse event—any untoward medical occurrence, unintended disease or injury, or untoward clinical signs (including abnormal laboratory findings) in subjects, users or other persons, whether or not related to the investigational medical device (ISO 14155:2011 3.2), including those related to the device or comparator, subject procedures or user/operator device events
- serious adverse device effect—adverse device effect that has resulted in any of the consequences characteristic of a serious adverse event (ISO 14155:2011 3.36)
- serious adverse event—adverse event that (a) led to death, (b) led to serious deterioration in the health of the subject that resulted in either (1) a life-threatening illness or injury, (2) a permanent impairment of a body structure or a body function, (3) in-patient or prolonged hospitalization or (4) medical or surgical intervention to prevent life-threatening illness or injury or permanent impairment to a body structure or a body function, (c) led to fetal distress, fetal death or a congenital abnormality or birth defect, (ISO 14155:2011 3.37) except planned hospitalization
- unanticipated serious adverse device effect—serious adverse device effect that by its nature, incidence, severity or outcome has not been identified in the current version of the risk analysis report (ISO 14155:2011 3.42) (Anticipated serious adverse device effects (ASADEs) are those listed in the risk analysis report (presumably serious and non-serious, although this is not defined).

In the US, an unanticipated adverse device effect (UADE) in a medical device clinical trial is defined as "any serious adverse effect on health or safety or any life-threatening problem or death caused by, or associated with, a device, if that effect, problem, or death was not previously identified in nature, severity, or degree of incidence in the investigational plan or application (including a supplementary plan or application), or any other unanticipated serious problem associated with a device that relates to the rights, safety, or welfare of subjects" (21 CFR 812.3(s)). Investigators must submit UADE reports to the reviewing IRB and sponsor as soon as possible, but in no event later than 10 working days after the investigator first learns of the effect (21 CFR 812.150(a)(l)). The sponsor is responsible for timely UADE evaluation, reporting results to FDA and reviewing IRBs and participating investigators within 10 working days after notice is received (21 CFR 812.46(b), 812.150(b)(l)).

Reporting Device Deficiencies

An important distinction unique to medical device trials is the ISO GCP requirement to document device deficiencies, which are defined as any "inadequacy of a medical device with respect to its identity, quality, durability, reliability, safety or performance" (ISO 14155:2011 3.15, 6.4.2). Device deficiencies should be documented and reported to the sponsor even when the deficiency did not lead to an adverse event if it is possible it could have led to an adverse event under the following conditions:
- if suitable action had not been taken
- if intervention had not been made
- if circumstances had been less fortunate

Further, device deficiencies should be classified as related to one or more of three primary areas, which include use error, malfunction or inadequate labeling (ISO 14155:2011 3.15) and managed by the sponsor accordingly.

Because many sponsors and investigational sites engage in both medical device and pharmaceutical research, there often is a misunderstanding about device deficiency reporting among clinical trial investigators engaged primarily in pharmaceutical research. Thus, it is essential for on-site investigators and key personnel and the sponsor o be trained in the ISO GCP device deficiency reporting requirements, which are not identical to those found for drugs in ICH GCP.

Recordkeeping

It is important to note some specific ISO GCP requirements apply in addition to the minimum requirements in 21 CFR and are distinct, in some cases, from ICH GCP. ISO GCP requires the principal investigator or designee to sign and date both printed and electronic CRFs. ISO GCP also requires printed versions of electronic source documents to contain signature and date alongside a statement indicating the contents represent a true reproduction of the original source data and the use of a Delegation Log (**Table 3-4**).

Device Accountability

Device accountability refers to control of the investigational devices used in the clinical investigation, which should be only those in the protocol or CIP. Certain differences exist between 21 CFR requirements and ISO GCP, with ISO GCP providing additional rigor on device accountability, requiring device trial investigator records to include the following specific details on medical device receipt, use, return and disposal (ISO 14155:2011 6.9):
- receipt date
- identification of each device (batch, serial number or other unique code)
- expiry date, when applicable
- use date(s)
- subject identification corresponding to device use
- date on which a device was returned or explanted from subject
- return date for unused, expired or malfunctioning investigational devices

In addition, ISO GCP requires sponsors to keep records of all investigational devices' physical locations, from shipment to return or disposal. These requirements overlap those contained in 21 CFR (**Table 3-5**).

Essential Clinical Investigation Documents and Archival

ISO 14155 7.2(a) requires that "arrangements are made for archiving and record retention," and 7.4 requires the sponsor and Principal Investigator to take measures to prevent the accidental or premature destruction of these documents and transfer changes of custody for records at both the site and sponsor facilities. ISO 14155:2011 Annex E specifies "Essential Clinical Investigation Document" subject to archiving, which include:
- Investigator's Brochure
- CIP (inclusive of the protocol)
- device labeling sample
- Principal Investigator's signed and dated CV, key investigational staff and other individuals who "materially contribute to the clinical investigation" (CV or other qualifications apply to individuals in this category, including any new members added during the study.)
- investigational site list
- per-site log of Principal Investigator and key individuals
- Ethics Committee (IRB in US) notification, correspondence and opinion or approval and IRB list for the clinical investigation
- regulatory authority notification(s), correspondence and approval (where required)
- signed agreements among the Principal Investigator, investigational sites and applicable

- third parties (contract research organizations, laboratory or core lab services, electronic data or image storage, etc.) and financial agreements (if separate)
- insurance certificates
- shipping records for investigational devices and clinical investigational documents and materials (although not specified in the standard, these commonly include documents such as the operator manual, calibration, PACS/HER interoperability requirements for software-driven devices and cleaning/sterilization instructions for the device, among many others)
- sample of approved informed consent form, subject information and advertisements and translations (where applicable)
- decoding procedures for blinded/masked trials (where applicable)
- investigational site selection report
- clinical investigation initiation monitoring report (although not specified in the standard, this often is termed the "Site Initiation Visit" or SIV report, and close-out monitoring report "Close Out Visit" or COV), and monitoring follow-up letter, and monitor(s) name and contact information
- case report forms, AE forms, device deficiency forms
- training records
- confirmation of equipment adequacy (where applicable)
- normal value and range of laboratory tests (where applicable) and evidence of laboratory director certification, accreditation, quality assessment, validation and identity, where relevant to the clinical investigation
- conflict of interest disclosures
- Investigator's Brochure, protocol, and Informed Consent amendments, if any, with IRB opinion/approval of each
- correspondence related to the investigation, including emails, letters, meeting notes and phone reports
- signed, dated and fully executed informed consent forms
- source documents
- fully executed CRFs and any corrections made
- AE and device deficiency reports, including reports to the IRB and sponsor (where required)
- subject screening and identification logs
- audit certificate (if required or conducted)
- sponsor's statistical analysis and clinical investigation report

An important ISO GCP requirement that often confuses regulatory professionals coming from a pharmaceutical background hinges on the additional requirements surrounding device labeling, accountability (including shipping and storage of devices) and device deficiencies, which all are considered essential documents for the clinical investigation of medical devices.

Additionally, US law specifies these records be retained for two years, and the manufacturer has 10 working days to notify FDA of applicable records transfers.

Quality Assurance and BIMO

CDRH's Division of Bioresearch Monitoring (DBM or BIMO) is responsible for the development and execution of inspections as well as the review and classification of resultant establishment inspection reports (EIRs) for:[156]
- IDEs
- PMAs
- PDPs
- HDEs
- 510(k)s
- routine surveillance of IRBs and nonclinical laboratories conducting animal research with medical devices (Good Laboratory Practice)

Because the scope of these mechanisms may involve preclinical and clinical medical device trials, BIMO's inspection process is important. In evaluating inspections, BIMO reviewers may consider such parameters as:[157]
- time elapsed since the clinical study's initiation
- device's nature (e.g., breakthrough product, first of a kind)
- study's risk to human subjects, concerns regarding nonclinical study results
- study sponsor's compliance history

Conclusion

GCPs establish the minimum standards and guidelines for conducting clinical research. GCP is an internationally accepted, scientific and ethical quality standard for the design, conduct, performance, auditing, recordkeeping, analysis and reporting of clinical trials involving human subjects. Compliance with GCP regulations and guidance documents provides assurance human subjects' rights, safety, confidentiality and well-being are protected. GCPs also ensure data collected and reported during the trial are of high quality, credible, accurate and reliable.

This chapter provides a basic overview of the key considerations and challenges associated with drug, biologic and medical device clinical trials. Due to the complex regulatory environment in which these products are developed, regulatory professionals are advised to consult internal and external resources, including their companies' quality assurance, regulatory compliance and regulatory intelligence departments and/or local EC/IRB and regulatory authorities, when resolving GCP compliance issues.

Chapter 3

References

1. ICH E6(R1) Good Clinical Practice guideline. ICH website. https://www.ich.org/fileadmin/Public_Web_Site/ICH_Products/Guidelines/Efficacy/E6/E6_R1_Guideline.pdf. Accessed 5 April 2019.
2. Ibid.
3. ISO 10993 Biological testing of medical and dental materials and devices—Part 8: Clinical investigation.
4. Op cit 1.
5. Ballentine C. "Sulfanilamide Disaster". *FDA Consumer Magazine*. June 1981. https://www.fda.gov/downloads/AboutFDA/WhatWeDo/History/ProductRegulation/UCM593517.pdf. Accessed 5 April 2019.
6. Ibid.
7. Jarrell K. "Regulatory History: Elixir Sulfanilamide." *Journal of GXP Compliance*, Summer 2012 Vol. 16 No 3: 12-14. Institute of Validation Technology website. http://www.ivtnetwork.com/sites/default/files/IVTGXPxxxx_CoverStory-2%20pr1.pdf. Accessed 5 April 2019.
8. "Appendix A: History of Medical-Device Legislation and Regulation in the United States." Institute of Medicine." Medical Devices and the Public's Health: The FDA 510(k) Clearance Process at 35 Years. Washington, DC: The National Academies Press. 2011.
9. *FD&C Act* §§301-04, 52 Stat. at 1042-45. FDA website. https://www.fda.gov/RegulatoryInformation/LawsEnforcedbyFDA/FederalFoodDrugandCosmeticActFDCAct/FDCActChapterIIIProhibitedActsandPenalties/default.htm. Accessed 5 April 2019.
10. FD&C Act §505, 52 Stat. at 1052-53. FDA website. https://www.fda.gov/regulatoryinformation/lawsenforcedbyfda/federalfooddrugandcosmeticactfdcact/fdcactchaptervdrugsanddevices/default.htm. Accessed 5 April 2019.
11. FD&C Act §201(g)-(h), 52 Stat. at 1041 (1938). House Legal Counsel website. https://legcounsel.house.gov/Comps/Federal%20Food,%20Drug,%20And%20Cosmetic%20Act.pdf. Accessed 5 April 2019.
12. World War II in Europe. US Holocaust Memorial Museum website. http://www.ushmm.org/wlc/en/article.php?ModuleId=10005137. Accessed 5 April 2019.
13. Research Starters: The Holocaust. National WWII Museum website. http://www.nationalww2museum.org/learn/education/for-students/research-starters/holocaust.html. Accessed 5 April 2019.
14. Military Legal Resources. Nuremberg Trials. Library of Congress website. http://www.loc.gov/rr/frd/Military_Law/Nuremberg_trials.html. Accessed 5 April 2019.
15. *Nürnberg Trials: World War II Trials* (14 February 2019). Encyclopedia Britannica website. https://www.britannica.com/event/Nurnberg-trials. Accessed 5 April 2019.
16. Ibid.
17. The *Nuremberg Code*. HHS website. https://history.nih.gov/research/downloads/nuremberg.pdf. Accessed 5 April 2019.
18. *Declaration of Helsinki*. British Medical Journal (7 December) 1996;313(7070):1448-1449.
19. *Declaration of Helsinki*—Ethical Principles for Medical Research Involving Human Subjects. 2013. World Medical Association website. https://www.wma.net/policies-post/wma-declaration-of-helsinki-ethical-principles-for-medical-research-involving-human-subjects/. Accessed 5 April 2019.
20. AMP, Inc. v. Gardner, 389 F.2d 825 (2d Cir. 1968), cert. denied, 393 U.S. 825 (1968). Casetext.com website. https://casetext.com/case/amp-incorporated-v-gardner. Accessed 5 April 2019.
21. U.S. v. Bacto-Unidisk, 394 U.S. 784 (1969). Justia website. https://supreme.justia.com/cases/federal/us/394/784/case.html. Accessed 5 April 2019.
22. Munsey R. "Trends and Events in FDA Regulation of Medical Devices over the Last Fifty Years." Food & Drug LJ. Vol. 163. (1995).
23. H.R. REP. No. 94-853, at 9.
24. H.R. Rep. No. 94-853, at 9-10; U.S. Department of Health, Education & Welfare, MEDICAL DEVICES: A LEGISLATIVE PLAN passim (1970) (Cooper Committee Report).
25. The Tuskegee Syphilis Study and Its Implications for the 21st Century. The New Social Worker website. http://www.socialworker.com/feature-articles/ethics-articles/The_Tuskegee_Syphilis_Study_and_Its_Implications_for_the_21st_Century/. Accessed 5 April 2019.
26. Tuskegee Syphilis Study. Explorable website. https://explorable.com/tuskegee-syphilis-study. Accessed 5 April 2019.
27. Ibid.
28. US Public Health Service Syphilis Study at Tuskegee, Presidential Apology. CDC website. http://www.cdc.gov/tuskegee/clintonp.htm. Accessed 5 April 2019.
29. *The Belmont Report* (18 April 1979). HHS website. http://www.hhs.gov/ohrp/humansubjects/guidance/belmont.html. Accessed 5 April 2019.
30. Link D. "Cooper Committee Report and its Effect of Current Medical Device Activities." *Food Drug Cosm*. Vol. 624 (1972).
31. Rados C. "Medical Device and Radiological Health Regulations Come of Age." *FDA Consumer*. The Centennial Edition (January-February 2006).
32. Tatum HJ et al. "The Dalkon Shield Controversy Structural and Bacteriological Studies of IUD Tails." *JAMA*. Vol. 231; Iss. 7, pp. 711-717. (1975)
33. H.R. Rep. No. 94-853, at 8 (1976).
34. Op cit 8.
35. Ibid.
36. Op cit 29.
37. Ibid.
38. Federal Policy for the Protection of Human Subjects ('Common Rule'). HHS website. http://www.hhs.gov/ohrp/humansubjects/commonrule/. Accessed 5 April 2019.
39. ANPRM for Revision to Common Rule. HHS website. http://www.hhs.gov/ohrp/humansubjects/anprm2011page.html. Accessed 5 April 2019.
40. NPRM 2015—Summary. Office for Human Research Protections website. https://www.hhs.gov/ohrp/regulations-and-policy/regulations/nprm-2015-summary/index.html. Accessed 5 April 2019.
41. *International Ethical Guidelines for Biomedical Research Involving Human Subjects*. CIOMS website. https://cioms.ch/shop/product/international-ethical-guidelines-for-biomedical-research-involving-human-subjects-2/. Accessed 5 April 2019.
42. Op cit 40.
43. Op cit 1.
44. Op cit 31.
45. Step 2: Preclinical Research (4 January 2018). FDA website. http://www.fda.gov/ForPatients/Approvals/Drugs/ucm405658.htm. Accessed 5 April 2019.
46. The FDA's Drug Review Process: Ensuring Drugs Are Safe and Effective (24 November 2017). FDA website. http://www.fda.gov/drugs/resourcesforyou/consumers/ucm143534.htm. Accessed 5 April 2019.
47. *Guidance for Industry: Investigators, and Reviewers—Exploratory IND Studies* (January 2006). FDA website. www.fda.gov/downloads/drugs/guidancecomplianceregulatoryinformation/guidances/ucm078933.pdf. Accessed 5 April 2019.
48. Op cit 46.
49. Ibid.
50. "Phase" definition (February 2019). Clinical trials.gov website. https://www.clinicaltrials.gov/ct2/about-studies/glossary#P. Accessed 5 April 2019.
51. 21 CFR Part 312 Investigational New Drug Applications. Electronic CFR website. https://www.ecfr.gov/cgi-bin/text-idx?SID=b3a7f3448e8f494e02dc86098591804a&mc=true&node=pt21.5.312&rgn=div5. Accessed 5 April 2019.
52. Ibid.

53. Ibid.
54. *Informed Consent Information Sheet—Draft Guidance for IRBs, Clinical Investigators and Sponsors* (July 2014). FDA website. http://www.fda.gov/downloads/RegulatoryInformation/Guidances/UCM405006.pdf. Accessed 5 April 2019.
55. 21 CFR Part 50 Protection of Human Subjects. Electronic CFR website. https://www.ecfr.gov/cgi-bin/text-idx?SID=b3a7f3448e8f494e02dc86098591804a&mc=true&node=pt21.1.50&rgn=div5. Accessed 5 April 2019.
56. Op cit 54.
57. 21 CFR Part 56 Institutional Review Boards. Electronic CFR website. https://www.ecfr.gov/cgi-bin/text-idx?SID=b3a7f3448e8f494e02dc86098591804a&mc=true&node=pt21.1.56&rgn=div5. Accessed 5 April 2019.
58. Op cit 54.
59. Ibid.
60. Op cit 57.
61. *Guidance for Industry: Using a Centralized IRB Review Process in Multicenter Clinical Trials* (May 2006). FDA website. http://www.fda.gov/downloads/RegulatoryInformation/Guidances/ucm127013.pdf. Accessed 5 April 2019.
62. *Institutional Review Boards Frequently Asked Questions—Information Sheet: Guidance for Institutional Review Boards and Clinical Investigators* (12 July 2018). FDA website. http://www.fda.gov/RegulatoryInformation/Guidances/ucm126420.htm. Accessed 5 April 2019.
63. Op cit 61.
64. Op cit 57.
65. Ibid.
66. *Information Sheet Guidance for Sponsors, Clinical Investigators and IRBs—Waiver of IRB Requirements for Drug and Biological Product Studies* (October 2017). FDA website. http://www.fda.gov/downloads/RegulatoryInformation/Guidances/UCM126500.pdf. Accessed 5 April 2019.
67. Conditions for IRB Use of Expedited Review (3 April 2018). FDA website. http://www.fda.gov/ScienceResearch/SpecialTopics/RunningClinicalTrials/GuidancesInformationSheetsandNotices/ucm118099.htm. Accessed 5 April 2019.
68. *Information Sheet Guidance for Sponsors, Clinical Investigators, and IRBs, Frequently Asked Questions—Statement of Investigator (Form FDA 1572)* (May 2010). FDA website. http://www.fda.gov/downloads/RegulatoryInformation/Guidances/UCM214282.pdf. Accessed 5 April 2019.
69. Institutional Review Boards; Registration Requirements. Federal Register, Volume 74, No. 10:2358–2369. GPO website. http://www.gpo.gov/fdsys/pkg/FR-2009-01-15/html/E9-682.htm. Accessed 5 April 2019.
70. *Information Sheet guidance for IRBs, Clinical Investigators, and Sponsors, FDA Institutional Review Board Inspections* (January 2006). FDA website. http://www.fda.gov/downloads/RegulatoryInformation/Guidances/UCM126555.pdf. Accessed 5 April 2019.
71. Ibid.
72. Coast Institutional Review Board Warning Letter (14 April 2009). Citizens for Responsible Care and Research (CIRCARE) website. http://www.circare.org/fdawls/coastirb_20090414.pdf. Accessed 5 April 2019.
73. Coast Institutional Review Board. Citizens for Responsible Care and Research (CIRCARE) website. http://www.circare.org/info/coastirb.htm. Accessed 5 April 2019.
74. Op cit 51.
75. Ibid.
76. Compliance Program 7348.810 Bioresearch Monitoring, Sponsors, Contract Research Organizations and Monitors (19 April 2017). FDA website. http://www.fda.gov/ICECI/EnforcementActions/BioresearchMonitoring/ucm133777.htm. Accessed 5 April 2019.
77. Sanofi-Aventis U.S. LLC Warning Letter (23 October 2007). Citizens for Responsible Care and Research (CIRCARE) website. http://www.circare.org/fdawls2/sanofiaventis_20071017.pdf. Accessed 5 April 2019.
78. Johnson & Johnson Pharmaceutical Research & Development LLC Warning Letter (10 August 2009). Citizens for Responsible Care and Research (CIRCARE) website. http://www.circare.org/fdawls2/jnjprandd_20090810.pdf. Accessed 5 April 2019.
79. ICON Clinical Research Inc. Warning Letter (27 November 2009). Citizens for Responsible Care and Research (CIRCARE) website. http://www.circare.org/fdawls2/icon_wl_20091127.pdf. Accessed 5 April 2019.
80. Pfizer Inc. Warning Letter (9 April 2010). Citizens for Responsible Care and Research (CIRCARE) website. http://www.circare.org/fdawls2/pfizer_fdawl_20100409.pdf. Accessed 5 April 2019.
81. Application Integrity Policy List (18 May 2015). FDA website. http://www.fda.gov/icecl/enforcementactions/applicationintegrity-policy/ucm134453.htm. Accessed 5 April 2019.
82. Op cit 51.
83. Ibid.
84. Ibid.
85. *Information Sheet Guidance for IRBs, Clinical Investigators, and Sponsors: FDA Inspection of Clinical Investigators* (June 2010). FDA website. https://www.fda.gov/downloads/regulatoryinformation/guidances/ucm126553.pdf. Accessed 5 April 2019.
86. Ibid.
87. *Guidance for Industry and Clinical Investigators: The Use of Clinical Holds Following Clinical Investigator Misconduct* (September 2004). FDA website. http://www.fda.gov/downloads/RegulatoryInformation/Guidances/UCM126997.pdf. Accessed 5 April 2019.
88. Op cit 1.
89. Ibid.
90. Ibid.
91. *Guidance for Industry: Oversight of Clinical Investigations—A Risk-Based Approach to Monitoring* (August 2013). FDA website. http://www.fda.gov/downloads/Drugs/Guidances/UCM269919.pdf. Accessed 5 April 2019.
92. Ibid.
93. Ibid.
94. Op cit 1.
95. Op cit 78.
96. Op cit 79.
97. Op cit 80.
98. Op cit 1.
99. *Guidance for Industry: Electronic Source Data in Clinical Investigations* (September 2013). FDA website. http://www.fda.gov/downloads/drugs/guidancecomplianceregulatoryinformation/guidances/ucm328691.pdf. Accessed 5 April 2019.
100. Abraham S, Grace D, Parambi T, Pahuja S. "Milestones in Development of Good Clinical Practice." *Internet Journal of Health.* Vol. 9; No. 1. pp. 75–81 (2008).
101. Op cit 1.
102. Op cit 3.
103. Stark N. A Standard Development Tale: ISO/FDIS 14155 (2010): ISO/FDIS 14155 *Clinical investigation of medical devices in human subjects—good clinical practices* (2010). CDG Whitepapers website. http://clinicaldevice.typepad.com/cdg_whitepapers/2010/09/a-standard-development-tale-isofdis-14155-2010.html. Accessed 5 April 2019.
104. BS EN 540:1993 Clinical Investigation of Medical Devices for Human Subjects. Freestd website. http://www.freestd.us/soft2/658973.htm. Accessed 5 April 2019.
105. Op cit 31.
106. Op cit 103.
107. Ibid.
108. Ibid.

109. Ibid.
110. ISO 14155:2011 *Clinical Investigation of Medical Devices for Human Subjects—Good Clinical Practice.* Second Edition.
111. Final Document: International Medical Device Regulators Forum. Statement regarding Use of ISO 14155:2011. *Clinical investigation of medical devices for human subjects—Good clinical practice.* IMDRF website. http://www.imdrf.org/docs/imdrf/final/procedural/imdrf-proc-150326-statement-iso141552011.docx. Accessed 5 April 2019.
112. *Food and Drug Administration Modernization Act* of 1997: Modifications to the List of Recognized Standards, Recognition List. Federal Register, Volume 77(52), p. 15775 (2012). GPO website. https://www.gpo.gov/fdsys/pkg/FR-2012-03-16/html/2012-6389.htm. Accessed 5 April 2019.
113. Op cit 111.
114. Recognized Consensus Standards [Search Agent]. FDA website. https://www.accessdata.fda.gov/scripts/cdrh/cfdocs/cfStandards/search.cfm. Accessed 5 April 2019.
115. *Acceptance of Foreign Clinical Studies - Information Sheet* (12 July 2018). FDA website. https://www.fda.gov/RegulatoryInformation/Guidances/ucm126426.htm. Accessed 5 April 2019.
116. Kennedy S. FDA Medical Device Regulations vs. ISO 14155. *Journal of Clinical Research Best Practices.* Vol. 11, No. 9 (2015).
117. Step 1: Device Discovery and Concept (4 January 2018). FDA website. https://www.fda.gov/ForPatients/Approvals/Devices/ucm405378.htm. Accessed 5 April 2019.
118. Medical Device Exemptions 510(k) and GMP Requirements. FDA website. https://www.accessdata.fda.gov/scripts/cdrh/cfdocs/cfpcd/315.cfm. Accessed 5 April 2019.
119. 510(k) Submission Process (27 September 2018). FDA website. https://www.fda.gov/MedicalDevices/DeviceRegulationandGuidance/HowtoMarketYourDevice/PremarketSubmissions/PremarketNotification510k/ucm070201.htm. Accessed 5 April 2019.
120. Goldberger BA. The Evolution of Substantial Equivalence in the FDA's Premarket Review of Medical Devices. *Food Drug Law J.* Vol. 53, No. 3, pp. 317-37 (2001).
121. Miller HI. Substantial equivalence: Its uses and abuses. *Nature Biotechnology.* Vol. 17, pp. 1042-43 (1999).
122. Curfman GD, Redberg RF. Medical Devices—Balancing Regulation and Innovation. *NEJM.* Vol. 365, pp. 975-977.
123. Ibid.
124. Ibid.
125. *Design Control Guidance for Medical Device Manufacturers* (11 March 1997). FDA website. https://www.fda.gov/downloads/MedicalDevices/DeviceRegulationandGuidance/GuidanceDocuments/ucm070642.pdf . Accessed 5 April 2019.
126. Op cit 122.
127. *Guidance for Industry and Food and Drug Administration Staff: Investigational Device Exemptions (IDEs) for Early Feasibility Medical Device Clinical Studies, Including Certain First in Human (FIH) Studies: Guidance for Industry and Food and Drug Administration* (October 2013). FDA website. https://www.fda.gov/downloads/medicaldevices/deviceregulationandguidance/guidancedocuments/ucm279103. Accessed 5 April 2019.
128. *Guidance for Industry and Food and Drug Administration Staff: Applying Human Factors and Usability Engineering to Medical Devices* (3 February 2016). https://www.fda.gov/downloads/MedicalDevices/.../UCM259760.pdf. Accessed 5 April 2019.
129. Op cit 127.
130. Ibid.
131. Postmarket Requirements (Devices) (2014) FDA website. https://www.fda.gov/MedicalDevices/DeviceRegulationandGuidance/PostmarketRequirements/. Accessed 5 April 2019.
132. Holmes et al. (2015) Overcoming the Challenges of Conducting Early Feasibility Studies of Medical Devices in the United States. *J Am Coll Cardiol.* 68(17):1908-15.
133. Ibid.
134. Checklist for Evaluating Whether a Clinical Trial or Study is an Applicable Clinical Trial (ACT) Under 42 CFR 11.22(b) for Clinical Trials Initiated on or After January 18, 2017. ClinicalTrials.gov, a service of the National Institutes of Health. Clinicaltrials.gov website. http://prsinfo.clinicaltrials.gov/ACT_Checklist.pdf. Accessed 5 April 2019.
135. Ibid.
136. IDE Approval Process (2016). FDA website. https://www.fda.gov/MedicalDevices/DeviceRegulationandGuidance/HowtoMarketYourDevice/InvestigationalDeviceExemptionIDE/ucm046164.htm. Accessed 5 April 2019.
137. Rath VK, Krumholz HM, Masoudi FA, et al. Characteristics of Clinical Studies Conducted Over the Total Product Life Cycle of High-Risk Therapeutic Medical Devices Receiving FDA Premarket Approval in 2010 and 2011. *JAMA.* 2015;314(6):604-612.
138. Op cit 127.
139. Ibid.
140. Rosen C. "New Devices and Truly Informed Consent." *Virtual Mentor.* Vol. 12, No. 2: 73-76. (2010).
141. Spatz ES, Krumholz, HM, Moulton BW. "The New Era of Informed Consent: Getting to a Reasonable-Patient Standard Through Shared Decision Making." *JAMA*, Vol. 315, No. 19:2063-2064 (2016).
142. Op cit 127.
143. *Information Sheet Guidance for IRBs, Clinical Investigators, and Sponsors: Frequently Asked Questions About Medical Devices* (January 2006). FDA website. https://www.fda.gov/downloads/RegulatoryInformation/Guidances/UCM127067.pdf. Accessed 5 April 2019.
144. Op cit 141.
145. Ibid.
146. Op cit 132.
147. Op cit 143.
148. *Information Sheet Guidance for IRBs, Clinical Investigators, and Sponsors: Significant Risk and Nonsignificant Risk Medical Device Studies* (January 2006). FDA website. https://www.fda.gov/downloads/RegulatoryInformation/Guidances/UCM126418.pdf. Accessed 5 April 2019.
149. *Guidance for Industry: Investigator Responsibilities - Protecting the Rights, Safety, and Welfare of Study Subjects* (October 2009). FDA website. https://www.fda.gov/downloads/Drugs/.../Guidances/UCM187772.pdf. Accessed 5 April 2019.
150. Parker C. The Sponsor: Responsibilities in Medical Device Clinical Trials (2016). FDA website. https://www.fda.gov/downloads/training/cdrhlearn/ucm176457.pdf. Accessed 5 April 2019.
151. Op cit 116.
152. Op cit 132.
153. *Guidance for Industry: Oversight of Clinical Investigations—A Risk-Based Approach to Monitoring* (August 2013). FDA website. https://www.fda.gov/downloads/Drugs/Guidances/UCM269919.pdf. Accessed 5 April 2019.
154. Op cit 150.
155. *Guidance for Clinical Trial Sponsors: Establishment and Operation of Clinical Trial Data Monitoring Committees* (March 2006). FDA website. https://www.fda.gov/downloads/RegulatoryInformation/Guidances/ucm127073.pdf. Accessed 5 April 2019.
156. Bioresearch Monitoring Initiatives (2014). FDA website. https://www.fda.gov/MedicalDevices/DeviceRegulationandGuidance/Overview/BioresearchMonitoring/ucm052083.htm. Accessed 5 April 2019.
157. Ibid.

Recommended Reading
- History of medical device clinical trial and ISO GCP legislation and regulation: Committee on the Public Health Effectiveness of the FDA 510(k) Clearance Process; Institute of Medicine. *Medical*

- *Devices and the Public's Health: The FDA 510(k) Clearance Process at 35 Years.* Washington, DC. The National Academies Press (2011). NAP website. https://www.nap.edu/read/13150/chapter/1. Accessed 5 April 2019.
- Countries recognizing ISO-GCP: IMDRF. Statement regarding Use of ISO 14155:2011 "Clinical investigation of medical devices for human subjects – Good clinical practice" (2015). IMDRF website. http://www.imdrf.org/docs/imdrf/final/procedural/imdrf-proc-150326-statement-iso141552011.docx. Accessed 5 April 2019.
- Early feasibility study designs: Holmes et al. (2016) Overcoming the Challenges of Conducting Early Feasibility Studies of Medical Devices in the United States. *J Am Coll Cardiol.* 68(17):1908-15.
- Human factors: *Guidance for Industry and Food and Drug Administration Staff: Applying Human Factors and Usability Engineering to Medical Devices* (3 February 2016). FDA website. https://www.fda.gov/downloads/MedicalDevices/.../UCM259760. pdf (accessed 5 April 2019) and Wiklund ME et al. *Usability Testing of Medical Devices.* Second edition. CRC Press: Boca Raton, FL (2015).
- Applicable Device Clinical Trials and ClinicalTrials.gov registration requirements: Checklist for Evaluating Whether a Clinical Trial or Study is an Applicable Clinical Trial (ACT) Under 42 CFR 11.22(b) for Clinical Trials Initiated on or After (18 January 2017). ClinicalTrials.gov, a service of the National Institutes of Health. ClinicalTrials.gov website. http://prsinfo.clinicaltrials.gov/ACT_Checklist.pdf. Accessed 5 April 2019.
- Comparison of ISO-GCP (ISO 14155:2011) and ICH-GCP (E6): "S603—Comparing ICH E6 with ISO 14155 Medical Device GCPs. ACRP (2016). ACRP Online website. http://www.prolibraries.com/acrp/?select=session&sessionID=1388. Accessed 5 April 2019.

Chapter 4

Current Good Manufacturing Practices and Quality System Design

Updated by Joscelyn Bowersock, MS-RA, and Richard Vincins, CQP, MCQL, CBA, CQA, RAC

OBJECTIVES

❑ Understand medical device, drug and biologics current Good Manufacturing Practice (CGMP) requirements

❑ Understand the "quality-by-design" concept and how it is embodied in CGMP regulations

❑ Understand the "quality system" concept and how it ensures product safety and efficacy

❑ Recognize the need for CGMP compliance at all levels of an organization

❑ Describe how CGMP regulations go beyond product "manufacture" and impact all levels of an organization

❑ Understand the difference between medical device verification and validation

❑ Recognize the different device documentation requirements, including Design History File, Device Master Record and Device History Record

❑ Develop awareness of the management responsibilities defined by CGMP regulations

❑ Differentiate between medical device and pharmaceutical/biologics CGMP regulations

❑ Understand pharmaceutical CGMPs

❑ Understand biologics CGMPs

❑ Understand the differences and similarities among pharmaceutical, biologics, medical device and combination product CGMPs

❑ Understand the most significant CGMP regulations and guidance documents affecting device, drug and biologics manufacturing

LAWS, REGULATIONS AND GUIDELINES COVERED IN THIS CHAPTER

❑ 21 CFR 820 Quality System Regulations

❑ Design Control Guidance for Medical Device Manufacturers (March 1997)

❑ Compliance Program Guidance Manual, Program 7382.845: Inspection of Medical Device Manufacturers (February 2011)

❑ Quality System Inspection Technique—QSIT (August 1999)

❑ 21 CFR Part 4, Regulation of Combination Products

❑ 21 CFR Parts 808, 812, and 820, Medical Devices; Current Good Manufacturing Practice (CGMP) Final Rule; Quality System Regulation, *Federal Register*: October 7, 1996 (Volume 61, Number 195)

Chapter 4

- *Quality System Information for Certain Premarket Application Reviews: Guidance for Industry and FDA Staff* (February 2003)

- *Current Good Manufacturing Practice Requirements for Combination Products*: Guidance for Industry and FDA Staff (January 2015)

- *Guidance for Industry: Quality Systems Approach to Pharmaceutical CGMP Regulations* (September 2006)

- 21 CFR 210, current Good Manufacturing Practice in manufacturing, processing, packing, or holding of drugs: General

- 21 CFR 211, current Good Manufacturing Practice for Finished Pharmaceuticals

- 21 CFR 600, Biological Products: General

- 21 CFR 606, Current Good Manufacturing Practice for Blood and Blood Components

- *Guidance for Industry: Q7A Good Manufacturing Practice Guidance for Active Pharmaceutical Ingredients* (August 2001)

- *Guidance for Industry: Q10 Pharmaceutical Quality System* (April 2009)

- *Guidance for Industry: CGMP for Phase 1 Investigational Drugs* (July 2008)

- *Questions and Answers on Current Good Manufacturing Practice (CGMP) for Drugs* (updated December 2015)

- *FDA Staff Manual Guides, Volume IV – Agency Program Directives – Combination Products – Inter-Center Consult Request Process, SMG 4101, Effective: June 11, 2018*

- *Guidance for Industry and FDA Staff: Current Good Manufacturing Practice Requirements for Combination Products*

Introduction

Title 21 of the Code of Federal Regulations (CFR) provides specific regulations that define the minimum current Good Manufacturing Practice (CGMP) requirements for drugs, biologics and medical devices. For example, 21 CFR 210, 211 and 600 provide the CGMP framework within which drug and biologics manufacturers must operate to manufacture compliant products. Similarly, 21 CFR 820 provides detailed requirements for medical device manufacturing under CGMP, also known as the Quality System Regulation (QSR), with which device manufacturers must comply to market their devices in the US. These regulations exist to ensure healthcare products in the US are manufactured according to a quality standard that ensures their safety and effectiveness.

The CGMP regulations are based on the "quality-by-design" (QbD) principle. This principle is derived from the idea that "quality should be built into the product, and testing alone cannot be relied on to ensure product quality."[1] Using a QbD approach means the product is designed and manufactured to conform to its specifications consistently following the manufacturing process. This also ensures a finished medical device's safety and efficacy are maintained throughout the product's lifecycle. Therefore, CGMPs do not apply only to a drug, biologic or medical device's manufacturing process; rather, CGMPs apply to the entire product design, development, testing, manufacturing and commercialization process. FDA intended the CGMP regulations to be flexible enough to allow manufacturers to determine which quality system controls are most appropriate for their specific products and operations while maintaining compliance.[2,3] In addition, because these regulations must apply to so many different product types, FDA describes what must be done, but does not prescribe how this should be accomplished. CGMPs are intended to prevent manufacturing defects, performance or efficacy failures, contamination, mix-ups, deviations and nonconformities. Manufacturers are responsible for establishing policies, procedures and processes to meet CGMP requirements. Although different regulations apply to medical devices, pharmaceuticals and biologics, their intent is the same: to ensure healthcare product safety and effectiveness on the US market.

Quality Management System

CGMP regulations require establishment of a Quality Management System (QMS). The QMS determines how healthcare product manufacturers implement CGMP regulations through a formal, documented system. It is a framework or organizational structure that maximizes conformity with policies and procedures, promotes process efficiency and accuracy and ensures product safety and efficacy. The QMS impacts an organization's daily activities at every level, from the manufacturing floor to executive leadership. Manufacturers with robust QMS processes can ensure a QbD approach to product development, manage risk and initiate continuous improvement activities, when necessary. If the QMS is implemented thoughtfully and maintained well, a manufacturer may experience fewer product failures and recalls and be subject to shorter and less frequent FDA inspections.

Management Responsibility

QMS establishment, implementation and maintenance are critical organizational management CGMP responsibilities. The regulations clearly hold executive leadership accountable for CGMP compliance. The implication is management must be actively involved with the organization's QMS; although it can delegate authority, it cannot abdicate responsibility for the organization's compliance with these regulations. Management must participate by establishing quality policies, modeling compliance in its organizational role, leading management reviews and making compliant quality management a company priority.

Documentation: SOPs, Work Instructions, Policies

All aspects of a manufacturer's QMS must be governed by policies, standard operating procedures (SOPs), work instructions or other process document types (**Figure 4-1**). The figure displays a typical QMS documentation structure describing the lower levels, which have more detail and documentation. Under the regulations, each of these documents must be controlled. When controlled, each policy, procedure or process document must undergo a review and approval process before being implemented and must have a revision history. Controlled documents ensure everyone is using the most recent and approved version of a particular procedure, policy instruction or process.

Change Control

FDA also requires manufacturers to implement change control for all QMS-related documents. When executed properly, change control ensures any revisions made are critically reviewed and approved prior to implementation. Change control procedures must be established and should include the method by which changes are communicated within the organization. In some cases, a change may need further verification and/or validation prior to implementation. For example, if a change is made to a manufacturing process step, that process may need to be revalidated before the change can be implemented. Similarly, changes to suppliers, raw materials or inspection criteria also may require verification before implementation. Change control is critical to ensuring changes are implemented only after appropriate review, validation and approval.

Medical Device CGMP

QSR

The QSR, codified in 21 CFR 820, covers medical device CGMP regulations. The QSR details how FDA expects medical device manufacturers to implement QbD and CGMPs throughout the product lifecycle. Depending on

Figure 4-1. Quality System Documentation Elements

the device type and class, a manufacturer must implement only the parts of the regulation appropriate for its device. Detailed FDA guidance provides insight into the agency's thinking about implementing these important regulations.

Design Control

The QSR includes regulations on design control, which detail FDA's required activities for medical device design and development. Design control regulations provide specific details on how FDA expects manufacturers to implement QbD during the product's lifecycle design phase. Design control is an iterative process following a structured methodology to ensure the device under development will be safe, effective and meet end-user needs (**Figure 4-2**). These regulations typically apply to all Class II and III devices. Most Class I devices are exempt from this QSR requirement, although there are exceptions, including devices automated with software, tracheobronchial suction catheters, surgeons' gloves, protective restraints, manual radionuclide applicator systems and radionuclide teletherapy sources. Design control activities must be documented and recorded in a Design History File (DHF).

Design and Development Plan

FDA regulations require manufacturers to establish a detailed design and development plan for each product. The plan must specify the development process, compliance with design control and assign responsibility for each activity. It also must detail how different groups in the company will interact and provide a review and approval schedule. The development plan is a dynamic,

Figure 4-2. Design Control "V" Model Process Flow

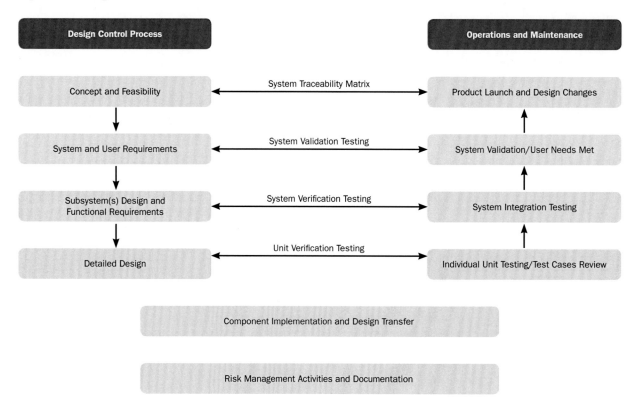

living document and should be maintained and updated throughout the design control process.

Design Inputs and Outputs

Design inputs are device requirements and should encompass end-user and patient wants and needs. Design inputs also may include regulatory requirements, patient preference data or postmarket surveillance feedback on similar products. Inputs may include specific performance characteristics, device specifications, reliability requirements, clinical constraints (e.g., must be sterile) and handling and storage requirements, among others. Design inputs can be gathered from many different information sources, including physician and surgeon requests, regulations, published literature or an emerging medical need.

Design outputs are device characteristics that manifest the design inputs confirming device requirements and specifications are met. These include things like materials, dimensional specifications, power source and electronic components, sterility, packaging and usability, etc. Design outputs must be measurable through verification or validation to determine whether they manifest the design inputs correctly. Design outputs often are captured in descriptive materials such as design/assembly drawings, material specifications, production specifications and software code, among others.

Verification and Validation

Verification and validation are critical iterative design control testing processes and, typically, are achieved via bench, animal and/or clinical testing. Although they may appear similar, verification and validation are distinctly different activities in the design control process. Verification is the process of determining whether the design outputs match the design inputs for detailed requirements related to the finished device. Verification is when the manufacturer ensures the product is made correctly and specified requirements have been fulfilled. In contrast, validation is the process of determining whether the device meets its intended use and function. Validation is when a manufacturer determines whether the right product was manufactured and whether it meets end-user requirements. Verification and validation are key design control activities during which feedback and iterative changes occur. If testing at this stage fails (e.g., the device does not achieve performance specifications or meet the user need), design controls revert to where changes can be made and further testing conducted.

Design Transfer

Design transfer is a process by which final device specifications are transferred to manufacturing and documented in the Device Master Record (DMR). This transfer should be detailed specifically in SOPs that ensure information is transitioned accurately from the development team to manufacturing. Design transfer is an iterative process that can start at any point in the development process, allowing components or sub-assemblies to be manufactured in a normal production environment. This allows transition of responsibility for finished product assembly into manufacturing, which is anticipated for representative performance testing.

Design Changes
Design changes can occur prior to or after product launch, which may be handled differently through the design and development process. Design changes prior to product launch may be less-restrictive to facilitate timely change processing through development activities. These changes still must be managed, controlled and recorded in a manner to allow reviewing impact of changes on finished product development activities to be understood. Design changes after product launch must be managed and controlled to understand how those changes impact the finished device. A change assessment and review of the document control process should support any required verification or validation testing. Post-product launch design changes, depending on their significance, may require a return to the design and development process to update finished medical device requirements, specifications or function.

Design Review
Pre-planned and documented design reviews must occur at regular intervals during device design and development. These reviews should be included in the design plan, and those responsible for the design stage being reviewed should participate, with at least one individual not responsible for the design stage being reviewed. It is recommended individuals with specialized knowledge be included in design review activities. Design reviews allow the manufacturer to examine the design process up to the review point. These reviews typically are done at specified design and development stages to accept design activities and proceed to the next step. If the review necessitates design changes, design control ensures the device process cycles back to a point where changes can occur. Once changes are completed, design review must be repeated before the next design step is initiated. Design review meetings should be documented thoroughly in the DHF.

Production and Process Controls
Device CGMPs require manufacturers to control all manufacturing and production processes to ensure the final device meets specifications. Manufacturers are expected to establish, implement and maintain procedures, work instructions, inspection methods and acceptance criteria under strict controls to ensure each lot is manufactured uniformly. Such monitoring and measuring practices as in-process inspections or automatic recording are required to ensure each product meets production specifications at critical points in the manufacturing process. Where appropriate, processes must conform to reference standards or established internal requirements. Production, testing, labeling, packaging and other product realization activities are documented in the Device Master Record (DMR); this file typically describes how a finished device is made. Whenever a process change is made, change control procedures, including process validation, must be followed.

Production and process control regulations also apply to facility and equipment controls. These include requirements for establishing and maintaining procedures to prevent equipment or product contamination that would affect device quality. Similarly, the QSR requires manufacturing sites to be located in buildings adequate to manufacture devices meeting specifications and complying with internal and regulatory requirements. Equipment must be installed, inspected, calibrated and validated. This is known as "Installation Qualification, Operational Qualification, Process Qualification" or "IQ-OQ-PQ." Each piece of equipment must be qualified and calibrated when it is installed (IQ). Its ability to perform the function for which it was designed then must be verified (OQ). Finally, the manufacturing process related to equipment performance must be validated (PQ). Periodic inspections are required to ensure all equipment performs as intended to assure devices are manufactured to specification. Equipment software also must be validated to ensure automated processes are functioning as intended. All of these activities must be planned and documented under a manufacturer's QMS.

Other regulations include posting acceptable equipment and process tolerances for operator reference through automated equipment or in documented instructions related to processes. Documenting activities related to finished device production ensures personnel follow cleanliness and behavior procedures in the manufacturing space and implement methods to remove manufacturing material that could affect device quality. Personnel also are required to be fully trained for their jobs or supervised when working in specialized environments or conditions.

Acceptance Activities and Nonconforming Product
The QSR requires manufacturers to establish acceptance activity procedures and criteria for receiving in-process and final product inspections. Acceptance criteria must be objective and may include testing, inspection activities or other means of establishing the product meets specifications. Receiving acceptance may apply when raw materials

or components are initially received or upon device return after being treated or sterilized. In-process inspection occurs during the manufacturing process to ensure the device is being made to specification. Final acceptance occurs at the completion of the manufacturing process, when it is decided whether the product should be released to market. All activities related to production, testing and inspection should be documented in the Device History Record (DHR) with what product was made, typically a single unit assigned a serial number or a number of units assigned a lot number.

Any product not meeting specifications is considered nonconforming product. FDA requires manufacturers to establish handling procedures for nonconforming products, which include means to identify nonconforming product, designating space to quarantine nonconforming products and developing review processes for nonconforming product disposition. In addition, manufacturers must determine whether an investigation is necessary to identify the nonconformity's root cause and whether to initiate corrective action. All nonconforming product handling and disposition must be documented in the DHR.

Labeling and Packaging Control

All device labeling and packaging must be controlled to ensure proper labels meeting specifications and FDA requirements are affixed to each product. In addition, labeling must be inspected for accuracy, contain all required information and be approved prior to product release. Package labeling must include information related to manufacturer, product description, Unique Device Identification (UDI), lot or serial number, applicable expiration date, etc. Labels are controlled documents subject to change control. Further, manufacturers must ensure packaging and shipping containers will protect the device, allow for proper sterilization (when required) and maintain device integrity during processing, storage, handling and distribution.

Resource Management

This encompasses a broad area defining the resources, needs and requirements throughout an organization to support how activities are performed and controlled.

Corrective and Preventive Action

Corrective action (CA) and preventive action (PA) is a critical CGMP component impacting the entire device manufacturing operation. CA and PA are the means by which device manufacturers implement continuous improvement in operations, QMS compliance, device performance, manufacturing process function, personnel training, etc. An effective CA and PA program can impact a medical device manufacturer's compliance significantly with documenting these activities. CA initiates a process to address a nonconformity that has occurred in order to prevent the failure from occurring again. PA initiates a process to address a trend or potential issue in order to prevent the failure from occurring. A distinction should be made between CA and PA for how these are handled based on issues, potential issues, nonconformities or trends observed in the QMS.

Under the QSR, a device manufacturer must establish, implement and maintain CA and PA procedures and policies, including ongoing quality data analysis from operations, complaints, quality records, published literature, management and design reviews or any other quality data source. Quality data analyses should be conducted regularly using appropriate statistical techniques to identify quality system deficiencies, recurring quality problems, trends in adverse event occurrences or other quality issues and nonconformities. Once a nonconformity or trend is identified, the CA or PA process should be initiated. CA and PA activities may include establishing a team to investigate an issue or potential issue, conducting a root cause analysis, implementing product testing or gathering additional quality data. Under the corrective or preventive action processes, a root cause analysis' extent is expected to be commensurate with the nonconformity's associated risk. The greater the nonconformity's risk or severity, the more thorough the investigation must be. If corrective or preventive action is deemed necessary, the regulations require all actions to be verified or validated to ensure the corrective or preventive action effectively addresses the issue. Management review must be an integral part of a CA and PA program; FDA expects these activities to undergo management review and approval. All corrective and preventive action-related actions, including trending reports, analyses, testing and meeting minutes, must be documented fully.

Complaint Handling

All device manufacturers, regardless of their device's class, must comply with regulations pertaining to product complaint handling. The QSR requires device manufacturers to establish, implement and maintain policies and procedures to handle product complaints. Further, each complaint must be reviewed to determine whether it must be reported to FDA under 21 CFR 803, Medical Device Reporting. In addition, each complaint must be evaluated to determine whether an investigation is necessary; if no investigation is needed, the rationale for this decision and the person making it must be recorded in the complaint file. It is important to note the manufacturer's device must have been involved in the occurrence of an adverse event to determine a complaint's reportability to FDA.

Manufacturers must treat every complaint as though their devices may have contributed to failure and report adverse events to FDA if the complaint meets reporting requirements. FDA regulations are very specific about the details required for each complaint, including the context in which the device problem occurred and whether the device failed to meet specifications. Complaint records must detail the complainant, device identity, failure conditions, investigation, corrective action, etc., in a formal method. The manufacturer also must include in the complaint file whether the device was in clinical use at the time of the incident, whether an investigation or Medical Device Report (MDR) was required and whether any corrective action was needed.

Documentation

Each CGMP regulation section provides detailed expectations for required documentation. Every aspect of design and development, improvement-related activities, review functions, complaint handling, training and device manufacturing activities must be documented. All quality system documents must be maintained per QSR requirements and must be retained for a period of time equivalent to the device's expected life, but no less than two years. Records should be accurate, complete, traceable and have dates and signatures. Controlled documents must be easily accessible from all locations at which they are needed. Similarly, controlled documents must be readily available upon FDA request during an inspection. Documents should be kept in a manner to prevent damage or loss, whether maintained in hard copy or electronically.

All QMS documents not specific to a device (e.g., quality policy, quality system procedures, etc.) make up the manufacturer's Quality System Record. FDA also requires three device-specific document assemblies (DHF, DMR and DHR) to be compiled and maintained.

DHF

The DHF includes documents detailing a specific device's entire design and development process. It should document every design control step and demonstrate accordance with an approved design plan and product requirements. A device DHF, at minimum, should include the design plan and subsequent iterations; design inputs, design outputs and product specification documents; verification and validation testing protocols and reports; design transfer records; design change information; and design review minutes. A DHF also may include drawings, equipment qualifications (IQ/OQ/PQ), labeling and packaging specifications and manufacturing process validations. A specific device's inspection and acceptance criteria also may appear in a DHF. It is common for multiple iterations and revisions of each design and development step to appear in a DHF, documenting the cyclical design process expected under the design control regulations. For manufacturers marketing multiple devices, a DHF is expected for each device to which these regulations apply. Similarly, for devices marketed before QSR implementation in 1997, a retrospective DHF should be in place to document, to the best of the manufacturer's ability, each device's design and development history.

DMR

The DMR contains all the information necessary to manufacture a particular device. The DMR is the device "recipe," containing all specifications and steps needed to produce a finished device that conforms to all specifications and performance criteria. The DMR is created during the design transfer process (see Design Control). A final DMR usually is a complete document record or index referencing applicable product realization activities such as manufacturing instructions, testing, inspection and labeling. This document should contain only the most recent and approved revisions of all procedures, work instructions, drawings, inspection and acceptance criteria, tolerances, equipment controls and settings and any other methods or procedures needed to manufacture the device. As such, the DMR must be updated and approved whenever changes are made.

DHR

The DHR, also known as a lot or batch record, is a record of a specific device or device lot's production history. This record should include the manufacturing date, documents showing the device's progression through manufacturing steps, forms detailing in-process inspection and acceptance activities, detailed manufacturing information, a copy of any labeling affixed to or packaged with the device, device packaging, evidence of sterilization, if applicable, and final acceptance and approval for release to market. The DHR also must contain Unique Device Identification (UDI) information, and, in the case of surgical implants or devices that support or sustain life, full traceability of data. In addition, the DHR must include the number of devices in the lot, the number of devices passing in-process and final inspection and the final number of devices accepted and released to market.

Other Device CGMP Requirements

A number of additional QSR requirements may apply, including device handling, storage, distribution, installation and servicing requirements. In addition, the QSR requires valid statistical techniques to be implemented whenever applicable, including the use of appropriate sampling plans and methods. These statistical techniques are used in monitoring and measuring processes to define what information is recorded and how it is managed. Device manufacturers must determine which QSR parts apply to their products and establish appropriate compliance programs.

International standard ISO 13485 was revised in 2016, with a significant number of changes, including placing a much stronger emphasis on regulatory requirements, process-approach and using a risk-based approach in quality systems. This revision strengthens alignment with the FDA QSR, including new sections such as design transfer and complaint handling. It is important to note that ISO 13485 has not been a traditional CGMP requirement; however, this is the *de facto* standard for regulatory compliance that would be interpreted as meeting CGMP requirements. In addition, many medical device manufacturers today are certified to ISO 13485 to meet quality system and CGMP requirements stipulated by other regulatory agencies around the world.

Pharmaceutical CGMP

Definitions

Per 21 CFR 210.3, drug product means a finished dosage form, e.g., tablet, capsule, solution, etc., that generally contains an active drug ingredient but, not necessarily, in association with inactive ingredients. The term also includes a finished dosage form that does not contain an active ingredient but is intended to be used as a placebo.

Component is any ingredient intended for use in drug product manufacture.

Active ingredient (AI) means any component intended to furnish pharmacological activity or other direct effect in the diagnosis, cure, mitigation, treatment or prevention of a disease, or to affect the structure or any function of the body of man or other animals. AIs also include those components that may undergo chemical change in the drug product's production and be present in the drug product in a modified form intended to furnish the specified activity or effect.

Inactive ingredient is any drug product component that is not the active ingredient.

A batch is a specific quantity of a drug or other material intended to have uniform character and quality, within specified limits, and produced according to a single manufacturing order during the same manufacturing cycle.

A lot refers to a batch, or a specific identified portion thereof, having uniform character and quality within specified limits; or, in the case of a drug product produced by continuous process, a specific identified amount produced in a unit of time or quantity in a manner that ensures its uniform character and quality within specified limits.

Lot, control or batch number is any distinctive combination of letters, numbers or symbols, from which a drug product batch or lot or other material's complete manufacture, processing, packing, holding and distribution history can be determined.

Strength is the drug substance's concentration (e.g., weight/weight, weight/volume or unit dose/volume basis) and/or the drug product's potency (therapeutic activity) as indicated by appropriate laboratory tests or by adequately developed and controlled clinical data (expressed, for example, in terms of units by reference to a standard).

Acceptance criteria are the product specifications and acceptance or rejection criteria, such as acceptable quality level and unacceptable quality level, with an associated sampling plan, necessary for making a decision to accept or reject a lot or batch.

Organization and Personnel

A quality assurance (QA) unit is the group responsible for overseeing a pharmaceutical or biological facility's administration and adherence to CGMPs. All quality-related drug product matters must be maintained by QA, including documents, internal audits, self-inspections, process validations, maintenance of critical equipment, batch record reviews, vendor and supplier audits and proper stability and storage requirements. Complaint investigations also are under QA's purview.

Under CGMP, a quality control (QC) unit must be established (with written procedures) and has the responsibility and authority to approve or reject all components including drug products, containers, closures, in-process materials, packaging materials and labeling. Adequate laboratory facilities must be available for testing the items listed above. If procedures or specifications impact the drug product's identity, purity, strength or quality, the QC unit can approve or reject those procedures or specifications.

QA and QC form a pharmaceutical organization's quality unit. The two entities can be one group, separate groups or a single individual or group, depending on the organization's size and structure.

There should be an adequate number of trained, educated and experienced persons involved in drug product manufacture, processing, packing or holding. Additionally, they must wear the correct personal protective equipment to ensure the drug product is free from contamination. Personnel with illnesses, open lesions or not practicing good hygiene habits will not be allowed access to or contact with drug products. It is imperative personnel follow all necessary steps and procedures to prevent drug product contamination.

Consultants must be trained, experienced and educated in the area in which they are retained. Records for each consultant must be maintained and include name, address, qualifications and services provided.

Facilities and Equipment
Buildings and facilities should be located and designed to eliminate or reduce the risk of cross-contamination or microbial infection, and constructed to facilitate cleaning, maintenance and operations, as appropriate for the manufacturing, packing, processing and holding type and stage. Adequate space and lighting must be available for necessary equipment and materials to prevent mix-ups or contamination. Adequate cleaning and personnel toilet facilities must be provided. Facilities should include defined areas for control of materials, production operations, labeling operations and release.

Equipment should be of adequate size and design and be placed in the proper environment to ensure it works correctly. Any part of the equipment that touches the drug product or active pharmaceutical ingredient (API) cannot be reactive, additive or absorptive; this ensures strength, purity, identity, safety and quality are not compromised. Equipment must be cleaned and maintained regularly to ensure proper function and prevent contamination issues.

Water
According to USP 1231, water can be categorized as drinking water, bulk water or sterile water. Drinking water is the minimum quality of water that should be used for the preparation of official substances and other bulk pharmaceutical ingredients. Bulk water is produced and distributed on site, typically through a piping system. Sterile water is produced, packaged and sterilized to preserve microbiological properties and contains no added substances or anti-microbial agents. USP states that water quality must be assessed through continuous monitoring of conductivity and total organic carbon (TOC), which allows a more quantitative purity and variability assessment, while current CGMP guidelines specify that levels of endotoxin and microbial counts be established, monitored and maintained.

Air
Adequate ventilation, air filtration and exhaust systems should be provided in the manufacturing facility and any testing laboratories. These systems should be designed and constructed to minimize contamination and cross-contamination risks. Equipment to ensure adequate control over air pressure, microorganisms, dust, humidity and temperature must be provided as appropriate for the drug product's manufacture, processing, packing or holding.

Air filtration systems, including prefilters and particulate matter air filters, must be used on air supplied to all production areas. If recirculated air is used in production areas, measures must be taken to control recirculation of dust and other contaminants from production.

Sanitation and Cleaning
Any building used for drug product manufacture, packing, processing or holding must be maintained in a sanitary and clean condition. The facility should be free of infestation from rodents, birds, insects and other vermin. Trash and organic waste matter should be held and disposed of in a timely and sanitary manner.

Written sanitation procedures should be available, including responsibilities and descriptions of cleaning schedules, methods, equipment and materials to be used in cleaning buildings and facilities. Procedures should cover the use of appropriate rodenticides, insecticides, fungicides, fumigating agents and cleaning and sanitizing agents. Procedures should describe how to prevent equipment, component, drug product container, closure, packaging, labeling material and drug product contamination adequately. These procedures apply not only to employees, but also to contractors and temporary staff.

Controls
Components and Drug Product Containers
Written procedures should exist describing receipt, identification, storage, handling, sampling, testing and approval or rejection for components, containers and closures. All components should be visually inspected for damage, broken seals and evidence of tampering or contamination prior to use and release. Representative lots should be tested for conformity to specifications while maintaining sterility, before they are mixed with existing stock. The vendor or supplier's certificate of analysis can be used in lieu of testing as long as the manufacturing facility has processes and procedures in place to ensure the certificate is sufficient. Drug containers and closures should be additionally tested to ensure each component is not reactive, additive or absorptive so as to alter any established drug product requirements. Inventory should be stored in a manner that facilitates use of the oldest stock first.

A unique code on containers and closures should identify each lot in each shipment and be used to record each lot's disposition. Each lot should be identified appropriately as quarantined, approved or rejected. Each container and closure lot should be withheld from use until the lot has been sampled, tested or examined and released for use by the QC unit.

Container closure systems should provide adequate protection against foreseeable external factors in storage and use that can cause drug product deterioration or contamination. If applicable, containers and closures should be sterilized and processed to remove pyrogenic properties to ensure they are suitable for their intended use. The sterilization and pyrogenic removal processes must be validated.

Production and Process
Written procedures should exist for the production and process control to ensure drug products, including those from re-processed batches, have the identity, strength, quality and purity as reported. Testing is conducted on appropriate samples of in-process materials. Weights, measures, components, additions and yield calculations should all be independently verified by a second person unless that action is performed by automated equipment, in which case only one person is required to verify.

Packaging and Labeling
Written procedures should describe in sufficient detail the receipt, identification, storage, handling, sampling, examination and/or testing of labeling and packaging materials. Labeling and packaging materials shall be representatively sampled and examined or tested upon receipt and before use in packaging or labeling of a drug product. Labeling materials issued for a batch shall be carefully examined for identity and conformity to the labeling specified in the master or batch production records. A representative lot of final released packaging must be visually inspected and results recorded on the batch or production record. Labels are required to contain expiration dates. Products requiring reconstitution must include the product's expiration prior to and post-reconstitution. Exceptions to this include new drug products for investigational use, provided there are appropriate stability studies included in the clinical trial use.

All OTC drug products that are not dermatologicals, dentifrices, insulins or lozenges must be in tamper-resistant packages. Tamper-evident packaging is required for products accessible to the public while being held for sale. To reduce the likelihood of successful tampering and to increase the likelihood that consumers will discover whether someone has tampered with a product, the package is required to be distinctive by design. Packages with such designs are required to have labeling that is prominently displayed and unaffected by the tamper-evident feature, which identifies such features. FDA requires notification of any change in packaging and labeling under §314.70.

Laboratory
Written procedures should exist for the sampling and testing of all components, including packaging, for each drug product lot or batch. There also shall be established, scientifically sound specifications to ensure all components conform to standards of identity, strength, quality and purity.

Instruments, apparatus, gauges and recording devices must be calibrated at appropriate intervals in accordance with established written procedures containing specific directions, schedules, accuracy and precision limits and provisions for remedial action in the event accuracy and/or precision limits are not met. If the instruments, apparatus, gauges and recording devices do not meet established specifications, they cannot be used.

Method Validation
Any test (including in-process control tests) or analytical method used must be validated. Written procedures describing how to conduct specific test method validation also should contain acceptance criteria for the results. Typically, a method validation protocol or procedure will contain all the information necessary to perform the validation. If test results do not meet the predefined acceptance criteria in the specified protocol or procedure, the test fails. Retesting can be conducted only if the validation protocol or procedure provides guidance on retesting steps.

If the analytical method being used is included in a relevant pharmacopoeia or recognized standard reference, method validation is not needed. However, the test method's suitability should be verified under actual use conditions and documented.

Stability Testing
A written testing program must be established to assess the drug product's stability characteristics. Stability testing results should be used to determine appropriate storage conditions and expiration dates. The written testing program should include:
- sample size and test intervals based on statistical criteria for each attribute examined to ensure valid stability estimates
- sample retention storage conditions for testing
- reliable, meaningful and specific methods
- drug product testing in the same container-closure system as that in which the drug product is marketed
- drug product testing for reconstitution at the time of dispensing (as directed in the labeling) as well as after they are reconstituted

An adequate number of drug product batches should be tested to determine an appropriate expiration date, and a record of such data should be maintained. Accelerated studies, combined with basic component, drug product and container-closure system stability information may be used to support tentative expiration dates if full shelf-life studies are unavailable and being conducted.

Records

Production, control and distribution records specifically associated with a drug product batch shall be retained for at least one year after the batch expiration date or, in the case of OTC drug products lacking expiration dating because they meet the criteria for exemption, three years after batch distribution.

Master Production

Master production and control records are created to ensure batch-to-batch uniformity. Records for each intermediate and API should be prepared, dated and signed by one person and independently checked, dated and signed by a second person. Master production records should contain:
- intermediate or API being manufactured and an identifying document reference code
- complete raw material and intermediate list designated by names or codes sufficiently specific to identify any special quality characteristics
- an accurate quantity or ration statement of each raw material or intermediate to be used, including the unit of measure
- production location and major production equipment to be used
- detailed production instructions, including:
  o sequences to be followed
  o ranges of process parameters to be used
  o sampling instructions and in-process controls with their acceptance criteria, where appropriate
  o expected yield ranges at appropriate processing or time phases
  o where appropriate, special notations and precautions to be followed or cross-references to them
  o instructions for intermediate or API storage to ensure its suitability for use, including labeling and packaging materials and special storage conditions with time limits, if applicable

Batch Records

Batch production records should be prepared for each intermediate and API and include complete information relating to the batch's production and control. These records should use a unique batch or identification number and be dated and signed when issued. Batch records may contain:
- major equipment identity
- date and, if appropriate, times
- any sampling performed
- weights, measures and batch numbers of raw materials, intermediates or any reprocessed materials used during manufacturing
- signatures of personnel performing, directly supervising or checking each critical step in the operation
- actual yield
- release testing results

Distribution

These records should contain the product's name and strength and description of dosage form, consignee name and address, date and quantity shipped and the drug product's lot or control number.

Complaint Files

Written procedures describing how all written and oral drug product complaints are handled must be established and followed. The procedures should contain QC unit review provisions for any complaint involving a drug product's possible failure to meet any of its specifications and, for such drug products, a determination as to the need for an investigation. Complaint records should contain:
- complainant's name and address
- complainant's name, title (if applicable) and phone number
- complaint nature (including the API name and batch number)
- date the manufacturer, agent or manufacturer employee receives the complaint
- action initially taken (including dates and identity of the person taking the action)
- any follow-up action taken
- responses provided to the complainant (including the date the response was sent)
- final decision on the intermediate or API batch or lot

Complaint records should be retained to evaluate trends, product-related frequencies and severity, with a view to taking additional and, if appropriate, immediate corrective action.

Additionally, written procedures should define the circumstances under which an intermediate or drug product recall should be considered. The procedure should designate who should evaluate the information, how a recall should be initiated, who should be informed and how the recalled material should be disposed.

Investigational Use Only

Investigational use only (IUO) drug products and biologics are not required to be manufactured according to 21 CFR 211 if used in a Phase 1 clinical trial. Because a Phase 1 clinical trial initially introduces an investigational new drug into human subjects, appropriate CGMPs must be applied to ensure subject safety. Therefore, IUO products are required to comply with CGMP requirements in Section 501(a)(2)(B) of the *Federal Food, Drug, and Cosmetic Act (FD&C Act)*. However, drug product to be used in Phase 2 and 3 trials are subject to 21 CFR 210 and 211. In addition, any already approved drug or biologic used in a Phase 1 clinical trial must comply with 21 CFR 210 and 211.

Adherence to CGMPs during Phase 1 IUO drug manufacture occurs primarily through:
- well-defined written procedures
- adequately controlled equipment and manufacturing environment
- accurately and consistently recorded manufacturing (including testing) data

Methods, facilities and manufacturing controls must be in place to meet the appropriate standards for IUO product identity, safety, purity, strength and quality. The important CGMP aspects that should be adapted for IUO products are:
- personnel
- QC function
- facility and equipment
- component, containers and closure control
- manufacturing and records
- laboratory controls (including testing and stability)
- packaging, labeling and distribution
- recordkeeping

Chemistry, manufacturing and controls (CMC) information must be submitted to FDA as part of an Investigational New Drug (IND) application. FDA will determine whether the IUO drug or biologic to be used in a Phase 1 clinical trial is sufficiently safe to permit the trial to proceed. The agency can conduct an inspection if insufficient information is submitted in the IND to allow it to determine the risks to clinical trial subjects or if clinical trial subjects could be subjected to unreasonable and significant risk. A manufacturer or sponsor's clinical trial could be put on hold, or the IND could be terminated if sufficient information concerning the IUO drug or biologic's CMC is not provided in the IND.

Biologics CGMP

Definitions

The term "biological product" is defined in *Public Health Service Act (PHS Act)* Section 351(i)(1) to mean:

"a virus, therapeutic serum, toxin, antitoxin, vaccine, blood, blood component or derivative, allergenic product, protein (except any chemically synthesized polypeptide), or analogous product, or arsphenamine or derivative of arsphenamine (or any other trivalent organic arsenic compound), applicable to the prevention, treatment, or cure of a disease or condition of human beings."

General Information

The CGMP requirements discussed above also are applicable to biologics and biotechnology products. However, because biological products are made from living organisms, additional CGMP requirements specific to biologics apply. This is true especially when using live viruses, spore-forming microorganisms and animals to manufacture a biological product. Ensuring facilities are well maintained and do not promote contamination is vital, as are animal care and handling. Adequate space to quarantine animals and perform necropsies is equally essential. It is critical these areas are separate from the actual manufacturing or processing areas and equipment. CGMP requirements specific to biologics are discussed below.

Personnel

Personnel working with pathogenic viruses or spore-forming microorganisms who are engaged in the care of animals or animal quarters should be excluded from areas where other products are manufactured or should change outer clothing, including shoes or wear protective covering prior to entering such areas.

Personnel cannot enter live vaccine processing areas if they have been working with other infectious agents during the same workday. Only personnel actually performing culture propagation, vaccine production and unit maintenance should be allowed in the live vaccine processing area. Personnel caring for animals used in the live vaccine manufacture are excluded from other animal quarters and from contact with other animals during the same working day.

Plant and Facilities

All equipment, manufacturing facilities and structures must be of a suitable size and construction for the product being manufactured. Additionally, manufacturing facilities must have proper air handling (i.e., ventilation, exhaust system) and water. For biologics manufacturing, the ventilation system must be designed to prevent dissemination of microorganisms from one manufacturing area to another and to avoid other conditions affecting product safety. Cleaning procedures must ensure airborne contaminants are minimized.

Work areas where products are manufactured or stored must be kept orderly, clean and free of dirt, dust, vermin and objects not required for manufacturing. Precautions should be taken to avoid clogging and back-siphonage of drainage systems. Workrooms must be well lighted and ventilated. Filling rooms and other rooms where open, sterile operations are conducted must be adequate to meet manufacturing needs and cleaning must be permitted. Refrigerators, incubators and warm rooms must be maintained at temperatures within applicable ranges and should be free of extraneous material that might affect product safety.

Laboratory and Bleeding Rooms
Any room used for product processing, including bleeding rooms, must be fly-proofed and kept free of flies and vermin. The rooms should be constructed to ensure no dust, smoke or other deleterious substances are present and to permit thorough cleaning and disinfection. Rooms used for animal testing, such as animal injection and bleeding and smallpox vaccine testing, will be disinfected and be provided with the necessary water, electrical and other services.

Animal Quarters and Stables
Animal quarters, stables and food storage must be of appropriate construction, fly-proofed, adequately lighted and ventilated and maintained in a clean, vermin-free and sanitary condition. No manure or refuse should be stored in or near these areas to ensure fly breeding is not engendered.

Sufficient personnel are required to ensure adequate animal care. The animals must be inspected daily if they are used in production to check for any ill effects from production. If an animal falls ill, it must be quarantined and cannot be used for production until its recovery is complete. Competent veterinary care should be provided as needed.

Any cases of actual or suspected infection with foot and mouth disease, glanders, tetanus, anthrax, gas gangrene, equine infectious anemia, equine encephalomyelitis or any of the pock diseases among animals intended for manufacture or used to manufacture products require the manufacturer to notify the directors of both CBER and CDER.

Spore-Forming Microorganisms
Some spore-forming microorganisms are used as sterilization process controls. They can be introduced only into manufacturing facility areas where they will be used and only immediately prior to use. They cannot be pathogenic to man or animals and cannot produce pyrogens or toxins. Steps must be taken to avoid spore contamination of other manufacturing facility areas.

Live Vaccine Processing
Live vaccine processing must be performed under appropriate controls to prevent cross-contamination of other products and manufacturing areas within the building. At minimum, live vaccine processing should be in a dedicated manufacturing area in another building, a separate wing of a building or quarters at the blind end of a corridor. The building or area should include adequate space and room for equipment for all processing steps, excluding final container filling.

CGMP for Blood and Blood Components
Definitions
21 CFR 606.3 describes blood as a fluid containing dissolved and suspended elements collected from a human's vascular system.

A blood component is a product containing a part of human blood separated by physical or mechanical means.

Personnel
CGMPs require personnel responsible for blood or blood component collection, processing, compatibility testing, storage or distribution to be adequate in number, educational background, training and experience, including professional training as necessary, to ensure competent performance of their assigned functions and that the final product has the safety, purity, potency, identity and effectiveness it is represented to possess.

Facilities
Facilities must be maintained in a clean and orderly manner, and should be of suitable size, construction and location to facilitate adequate cleaning, maintenance and proper operations.

Per 21 CFR 606.40, facilities should:
a. Provide adequate space for the following, when applicable:
   1. private and accurate examinations of individuals to determine their eligibility as blood donors
   2. blood withdrawal from donors with minimal risk of contamination or exposure to activities and equipment unrelated to blood collection
   3. blood or blood component storage pending completion of tests
   4. blood or blood component quarantine storage in a designated location pending repetition of those tests that initially gave questionable serological results
   5. finished product storage prior to distribution
   6. quarantine storage, handling and disposition of products and reagents not suitable for use
   7. orderly collection, processing, compatibility testing, storage and distribution of blood and blood components to prevent contamination
   8. adequate and proper performance of all steps in plasmapheresis, plateletpheresis and leukapheresis procedures

Chapter 4

      9. orderly conduct of all packaging, labeling and other finishing operations
- b. Provide adequate lighting, ventilation and screening of open windows and doors.
- c. Provide adequate, clean and convenient handwashing facilities for personnel and adequate, clean and convenient toilet facilities for donors and personnel. Drains should be of adequate size and, where connected directly to a sewer, shall be equipped with traps to prevent back-siphonage.
- d. Provide for safe and sanitary disposal of:
  1. trash and items used during blood and blood component collection, processing and compatibility testing for management of biohazardous materials
  2. blood and blood components not suitable for use or distribution

Equipment
Equipment used in blood and blood component collection, processing, compatibility testing, storage and distribution should be maintained in a clean and orderly manner and located in a place that facilitates cleaning and maintenance. Cleaning and disinfecting processes shall be defined and validated ensuring cross-contamination is prevented. A table in 21 CFR 606.60(b) details the frequency for observing, standardizing and calibrating different equipment types. In addition, all equipment used in the manufacturing process must meet specified requirements and be appropriately designed, constructed, placed and installed to facilitate maintenance, adjustment, cleaning and use.

Supplies and Reagents
As discussed previously, CGMPs require supplies to be stored in a safe, sanitary and orderly manner. Additionally, any surface that comes into contact with blood and blood components intended for transfusion must be sterile, pyrogen-free and cannot interact with the product in a manner that would adversely affect its safety, purity, potency or effectiveness. Blood collection containers should be examined for seal breakage, abnormal discoloration or any other defects. If defects are noted, the containers cannot be used. Material storage, conditions of storage and expiration dating need to be controlled to prevent the use of expired supplies or supplies that may be compromised through storage and handling.

Certain reagents and solutions used in manufacturing blood and blood components must be tested on a regular schedule per the manufacturer's SOPs to determine their capacity to perform as required. The list of reagents and solutions with testing frequency is contained in 21 CFR 606.65(c).

Production and Process Controls
Standard Operating Procedures
Medical device, pharmaceutical and biologic CGMPs all require the manufacturing facility to have written procedures in place for processing products, QC testing and inspection, methods, finished product testing and labeling. These procedures are required for blood and blood component manufacturers as well. For these specific products, which will be used in transfusion and further manufacturing purposes, written procedures must cover collection, processing, compatibility testing, storage and distribution. Proper quarantine and notification procedures are required for those donors testing positive for HIV or HCV after donation. These procedures should include determining suitability for release, notifying the transfusion recipient's physician of record or legal representative and donor deferral. For more information on what the SOPs should describe, see 21 CFR 606.100(b).

Labeling
In *Guidance for Industry: Recognition and Use of a Standard Uniform Blood and Blood Component Container Labels*, FDA adopted the use of the "United States Industry Consensus Standard for the Uniform Labeling of Blood and Blood Components Using ISBT 128." This standard outlines the format, structure and readability of all blood and blood component labeling. These requirements are outlined in 21 CFR 606.121.

Circular of Information
This document must be available for distribution if the product is intended for transfusion. It must contain adequate instructions for use. Additional information required in a circular of information can be found in 21 CFR 606.122.

Laboratory Control System
Laboratory Controls
Laboratory controls described above for pharmaceutical products also apply to blood and blood components. Scientifically sound and appropriate specifications, standards and test procedures must be established to ensure blood and blood components are safe, pure, potent and effective.

Compatibility Testing
Compatibility testing must be performed according to written and approved SOPs. A method must be in place for collecting and identifying recipients' blood samples to ensure positive identification. Procedures should be in place to demonstrate incompatibility between the donor's cell type and the recipient's serum or plasma type. There also should be a procedure to expedite transfusion in life-threatening emergencies.

Records

Donor Records

While not all-inclusive, the following information is required to be collected:
- donor selection, including medical interview, examination and, if necessary, informed consent
- donor adverse reaction complaints and reports, including results of all investigations and follow-ups
- immunization, including informed consent, identification of the antigen, dosage and route of administration
- records to relate the donor with the unit number of each of his or her previous donations from that donor

Other Records

Other records the manufacturer must maintain for blood or blood components per CGMP are: processing, storage and distribution, compatibility test, transfusion reaction reports and complaints, quality control and general records, including biological product deviations. These records are described in 21 CFR 606 and shall be maintained according to an established time period and shall comply with any specific state regulatory requirements for blood donor and recipient information.

Adverse Event Files

Per 21 CFR 606.170, records shall be maintained of any adverse reaction complaint reports regarding each unit of blood or blood product resulting from blood collection or transfusion. A thorough investigation of each reported adverse reaction is required. A written report of the adverse reaction investigation, including conclusions and follow-ups, must be prepared and maintained as part of the record for the lot or unit of final product.

If a blood collection complication or transfusion results in a fatality, CBER must be notified by telephone, facsimile, express mail or email as soon as possible. A written report of the investigation must be submitted to CBER within seven days after the fatality.

Combination Product CGMPs

Background

FDA's final rule on CGMP requirements for combination products is at 21 CFR Part 4. Combination product definitions are presented in *Guidance for Industry and FDA Staff: Current Good Manufacturing Practice Requirements for Combination Products*.[4] CGMP requirements must be applied to the constituent parts, e.g., the drug or device, regardless of the final combination product. However, the final rule provides two options for how CGMP requirements are applied to combination products. In the first option, a manufacturer demonstrates compliance separately for each product constituent part by implementing the drug CGMP or device QSR in its entirety. The second option is where manufacturers demonstrate compliance to the applicable parts of 21 CFR 211 or 21 CFR 820 rather than demonstrating compliance to both full regulatory requirements. This second option, considered a streamlined approach, has identified specific parts of 21 CFR 211 and 21 CFR 820 that would be applicable to either a drug or device. As an example, a drug/device combination product manufactured in a facility primarily for drug manufacturing would comply with 21 CFR 211, and the device constituent part would comply with applicable 21 CFR 820 parts.

Implementing CGMP Compliance

Demonstrating CGMP implementation compliance for combination products would be the same as for any individual product type, i.e., drug, biologic, blood product or device. The final rule allows combination product manufacturers to comply with regulations applicable to constituent parts, whether the final product is co-packaged or a single-entity combination product. The final rule contains combination product definitions that must be clearly understood to prevent confusion with other definitions contained in CGMP (drug, biologic) or QSR (device) requirements. This final rule clarifies terms used throughout those individual regulations, such as defining 'constituent part,' not to be confused with 'component.' FDA's guidance on combination product CGMP requirements discusses this further for various terms used in the regulations.

Implementing 21 CFR Part 4 allows combination product or constituent part manufacturers to apply respective CGMP or QSR requirements appropriate to the facility. The regulation focuses on the facility where product is manufactured, not finished product composition. It is important that manufacturers implement requirements "where appropriate" and that applicable processes for establishing, implementing and monitoring of processes are completed for compliance. Consideration also should be given to documented justification for those CGMP or QSR requirements that are not implemented for a facility. While this final rule is intended for compliance by an individual facility, there are many circumstances where multiple facilities are involved for different aspects of processing those constituent parts. Coordination and/or quality agreements should exist between those facilities.

Changes to combination products shall be controlled appropriately to ensure the safety and efficacy of each constituent part and the final combination product. Manufacturers should have procedures in place notifying each other of any changes or intended changes to be made. These changes should be coordinated between the drug and device component manufacturers and should consider whether a change to one of the constituent parts necessitates additional activities, such as CMC changes for drugs or design verification for devices.

Individual CGMP Requirements
Certain provisions need to be considered for implementing QSR requirements for device constituent parts, CGMP requirements for drug constituent parts and those requirements applicable to biological products and HCT/Ps.

QSR Provisions
Compliance with a number of primary processes identified in 21 CFR 820 is important, such as management responsibility, design controls, purchasing controls and CA and PA. While 21 CFR Part 4 does not address these individually, several other guidance documents address medical device QSR compliance. FDA guidance documents are not intended to be all-encompassing, as many different types of medical devices exist. Manufacturers shall implement the appropriate and applicable parts of the regulation.

Provisions of CGMP Requirements
Special requirements for drug manufacturing, including testing and approval or rejection, calculation of yield, tamper-evident packaging, expiration dating, testing and release for distribution, stability testing and reserve samples, are identified in 21 CFR 211. This list does not fully encompass CGMP requirements for drug products, but helps medical device manufacturers understand specific compliance areas. The combination product CGMP regulation also defines constituent part batches or lots and how to link specific batches or lots together. Master production and control records in drug manufacturing should be clearly defined to allow traceability among all constituent parts.

Provisions for Biological Products and HCT/Ps
Biological product requirements are defined in 21 CFR Parts 600–680, although a biological product must comply with either CGMP or QSR requirements. The requirements in 21 CFR Parts 600–680 augment CGMP requirements for drug and device counterparts. HCT/Ps not regulated under *PHS Act* Section 361 are regulated under the drug, device and/or biological requirements. Specific manufacturing requirements for HCT/Ps are intended to prevent transmission or spread of communicable diseases and protect public health. Biological and HCT/P products intended to be used in combination products also are subject to the requirements under 21 CFR Part 4.

Summary
FDA CGMP regulations exist to ensure the safety and effectiveness of all pharmaceutical, biologic and medical device products manufactured and commercialized in the US. The importance of compliance with these regulations cannot be minimized. Quite simply, failure to adhere to CGMP requirements results in adulterated product and puts public health at risk. Compliance with all CGMP regulations is the responsibility of every manufacturer that commercializes pharmaceutical, biologic, medical device and combination products in the US. QMS process and procedure establishment, implementation and maintenance must be management's priority to ensure a culture of compliance at all levels within their organizations.

As regulations change, it is imperative manufacturers stay informed and have regulatory intelligence operations to provide timely updates to leadership and compliance teams. Training personnel on CGMPs' importance and requirements will ensure everyone understands their roles in the compliance program. Attention to process and procedure validation is critical, as are timely identification of and response to deviations and failures. Continuous improvement activities following internal audits, corrective and preventive action activities and FDA inspections will help ensure all products are manufactured under the QbD objectives of these regulations.

References
1. *Guidance for Industry: Quality Systems Approach to Pharmaceutical CGMP Regulations* (September 2006). FDA website. http://www.fda.gov/downloads/Drugs/.../Guidances/UCM070337.pdf. Accessed 28 March 2019.
2. Ibid.
3. *Design Control Guidance for Medical Device Manufacturers* (11 March 1997). FDA website. https://www.fda.gov/downloads/MedicalDevices/DeviceRegulationandGuidance/GuidanceDocuments/ucm070642.pdf. Accessed 28 March 2019.
4. *Guidance for Industry and FDA Staff: Current Good Manufacturing Practice Requirements for Combination Products* (January 2015). FDA website. https://www.fda.gov/downloads/RegulatoryInformation/Guidances/UCM429304.pdf. Accessed 28 March 2019.
5. *Revisions to Labeling Requirements for Blood and Blood Components, Including Source Plasma.* (January 2012). FDA website. https://www.federalregister.gov/documents/2012/01/03/2011-33554/revisions-to-labeling-requirements-for-blood-and-blood-components-including-source-plasma. Accessed 28 March 2019

Chapter 5

Prescription Product Drug Submissions

By Shyamala Jayaraman, PhD, Lean Six Sigma Black Belt and Glen D. Park, PharmD, MSJ

OBJECTIVES

❑ Define regulatory submission requirements associated with new therapeutic entity development and approval

❑ Define and describe Investigational New Drug Application (IND) components, review process and different IND types

❑ Explain clinical hold reasons

❑ Define IND maintenance submissions

❑ Define and describe New Drug Application (NDA) components and review process

❑ Define NDA maintenance submissions

❑ Describe programs for expediting drug development and review

LAWS, REGULATIONS, GUIDANCE DOCUMENTS COVERED IN THIS CHAPTER

❑ *Federal Food, Drug, and Cosmetic Act of 1938*

❑ *Public Health Service Act of 1944*

❑ *Drug Price Competition and Patent Term Restoration Act of 1984 (Hatch-Waxman Act)*

❑ *Prescription Drug Marketing Act of 1987*

❑ *Prescription Drug User Fee Act of 1992*

❑ *Federal Advisory Committee Act of 1972*

❑ *Food and Drug Administration Modernization Act of 1997*

❑ *Food and Drug Administration Amendments Act of 2007*

❑ *Food and Drug Administration Safety and Innovation Act of 2012*

❑ *Food and Drug Administration Reauthorization Act of 2017*

❑ 21 CFR 310 New Drugs

❑ 21 CFR 312 Investigational New Drug Application

❑ 21 CFR 314 Applications for FDA Approval to Market a New Drug

❑ 21 CFR 601 Licensing (biologics)

❑ *Guidance for Industry: Providing Clinical Evidence for Effectiveness for Human Drugs and Biological Products* (May 1998)

❑ *Guidance for Industry on Advisory Committee Meetings — Preparation and Public Availability of Information Given to Advisory Committee Members* (August 2008)

- *Guidance for Industry: Reports on the Status of Postmarketing Study Commitments—Implementation of Section 130 of the Food and Drug Administration Modernization Act of 1997* (February 2006)

- *Guidance for Industry: Postmarketing Studies and Clinical Trials—Implementation of Section 505(o)(3) of the Federal Food, Drug, and Cosmetic Act* (April 2011)

- *Draft Guidance for Industry and Review Staff: Good Review Management Principles and Practices for New Drug Applications and Biologics License Applications* (September 2018)

- *Guidance for Industry: Fixed Dose Combinations, Co-Packaged Drug Products, and Single-Entity Versions of Previously Approved Antiretrovirals for the Treatment of HIV* (October 2006)

- *Guidance for Industry: Expedited Programs for Serious Conditions – Drugs and Biologics* (May 2014)

- *Draft Guidance for Industry: Providing Regulatory Submissions in Electronic and Non-Electronic Format—Promotional Labeling and Advertising Materials for Human Prescription Drugs* (May 2015) *Guidance for Industry: Formal Meetings with Sponsors and Applicants for PDUFA Products* (December 2017)

- *Draft Guidance for Industry: Applications Covered by Section 505(b)(2)* (October 1999)

- Manual of Policies and Procedures 6020.3 Rev. 2: Review Classification Policy: Priority (P) and Standard (S) (June 2013)

- *Guidance for Industry: Providing Regulatory Submissions in Electronic Format—Certain Human Pharmaceutical Product Applications and Related Submissions Using the eCTD Specifications* (April 2018)

- *Guidance for Industry: Providing Regulatory Submissions in Electronic Format—Content of Labeling* (April 2005)

- *Guidance for Industry: Contents of a Complete Submission for the Evaluation of Proprietary Names* (April 2016)

- *Guidance for Industry: M4 Organization of the Common Technical Document for the Registration of Pharmaceuticals for Human Use* (October 2017)

- *Draft Guidance for Industry: How to Comply with the Pediatric Research Equity Act* (September 2005)

- *Draft Guidance for Industry: Qualification Process for Drug Development Tools* (January 2014)

- *Draft Guidance for Industry Format and Content of a REMS Document* (October 2017)

- *Draft Guidance for Industry and Review Staff: Target Product Profile—A Strategic Development Process Tool* (March 2007)

- *Draft Guidance for Industry: Labeling for Human Prescription Drug and Biological Products—Implementing the PLR Content and Format Requirements* (February 2013)

- *Guidance for Industry: Dosage and Administration Section of Labeling for Human Prescription Drug and Biological Products Content and Format* (March 2010)

- *Guidance for Industry: Information Program on Clinical Trials for Serious or Life-Threatening Diseases and Conditions* (March 2002)

- *Guidance for Industry: Changes to an Approved NDA or ANDA* (April 2004)

- *Guidance for Industry: Content and Format of Investigational New Drug Applications (INDs) for Phase 1 Studies of Drugs, Including Well-Characterized, Therapeutic, Biotechnology-Derived Products* (November 1995)

- *Draft Guidance for Industry: Formal Meetings Between the FDA and Sponsors or Applicants of PDUFA Products* (December 2017)

- *Guidance for Industry: Indexing Structured Product Labeling* (June 2008)

- *Guidance for Industry: Part 11, Electronic Records; Electronic Signatures—Scope and Application* (August 2003)

- *Guidance for Industry: Providing Regulatory Submissions in Electronic Format—General Considerations* (January 1999)

- *Guidance for Industry: Expedited Programs for Serious Conditions—Drugs and Biologics* (May 2014)

- *Draft Guidance for Industry: Providing Regulatory Submissions in Electronic Format—Postmarketing Expedited Safety Reports* (June 2014)

- *Guidance for Industry: Providing Regulatory Submissions in Electronic Format—Submissions Under Section 745A(a) of the Federal Food, Drug, and Cosmetic Act* (December 2014)

- *The Comprehensive Table of Contents Headings and Hierarchy* (Version 2.3.2 2018-11-01)

- *Guidance for Industry: Providing Regulatory Submissions in Electronic Format—Standardized Study Data* (December 2014)

- *Guidance for Industry: E2F Development Safety Update Report* (August 2011)

- *Guidance for Industry: Submitting and Reviewing Complete Responses to Clinical Holds* (October 2000)

Introduction

This chapter provides an overview of the regulations, regulatory process and submission requirements associated with developing new therapeutic entities (i.e., new prescription products or new drugs). Specifically, it covers the Investigational New Drug (IND) application, which establishes an exemption from regulations prohibiting the use and distribution of unapproved drugs. It focuses on the requirements sponsors must meet when developing a new drug before seeking drug product approval through a New Drug Application (NDA), although high-level information associated with biological products also is presented. Full information regarding biological products is found in Chapter 25. For full information on generic drug submissions, see Chapter 16.

Overall, as described in Chapters 2 and 3, drug products are regulated under the *Federal Food, Drug, and Cosmetic Act* of 1938 (*FD&C Act*) and subsequent amendments. The *FD&C Act* also applies to biological products subject to regulation under *Public Health Service Act* (*PHS Act*) Section 351. Generally, a new drug is any drug containing an ingredient or combination of ingredients whose safety and effectiveness under the labeled conditions for use are unknown. However, a new drug also may be one with a known safety and effectiveness profile under the labeled conditions for use but that has not been used to a material extent or for a material time under different conditions.

Unless a drug is covered under an Over-the-Counter (OTC) product monograph, the *FD&C Act* prohibits its introduction into interstate commerce if the drug manufacturer has not submitted an NDA to the US Food and Drug Administration (FDA) and obtained agency approval. Likewise, the *PHS Act* prohibits the introduction of any biological product into interstate commerce unless an approved Biologics License Application (BLA) is in effect, and each package is marked plainly and properly with specific requirements (e.g., proper name). The NDA or BLA must contain substantial evidence of effectiveness from adequate and well-controlled investigations, including nonclinical and clinical tests conducted by qualified experts. In addition to providing evidence of the drug's effectiveness, the application must demonstrate it is reasonably safe when used under the labeled conditions. Further, the application must demonstrate that the product can be manufactured under a quality system that preserves its identity, strength, quality and purity throughout its shelf life.

The IND's purpose is to provide the structure for communicating product development activities that will provide the information on the product's effectiveness, safety and quality to FDA that will allow the agency to conduct a substantial review and approve the product for marketing. The IND regulations define the fundamental roles of the IND sponsor and the investigators conducting clinical studies with the new drug, with the overriding objective of protecting the human subjects participating in the studies.

The NDA's purpose is to present a comprehensive picture of the information that supports the efficacy, safety and quality of the product the sponsor intends to market and to provide the information in a standardized format to facilitate FDA review.

INDs

An IND is a potential therapy a sponsor wants to test in human clinical trials. In the US, such testing must be covered by an IND Application (synonymous with a Notice of Claimed Investigational Exemption for a New Drug, Form FDA 1571). Essentially, an IND is a claim of exemption from certain *FD&C Act* labeling requirements, allowing drug shipment in interstate commerce for the purpose of conducting clinical trials in the US. An IND sponsor is the entity named in Item 1 of Form FDA 1571 and may be a company, institution, organization or individual physician, and is defined as the entity who takes responsibility for and initiates clinical investigations. An IND may be sponsored by a sponsor-investigator, which is when a single investigator files the IND as the sponsor.

Original IND Content

The minimum information required to file an original IND is nonclinical pharmacology and toxicity, information regarding the manufactured product's quality and a clinical protocol with investigator information. However, the totality of information depends on such factors as the drug's novelty, the extent to which it has been studied previously, its known or suspected risks and the drug's developmental phase. For example, any additional information on previous human experience with the drug not conducted under an IND should be included in an original IND. Also, an original IND may be filed for a new formulation or new indication and cross-referenced to an existing IND or NDA for information relevant to the new IND.

Nonclinical Testing

Prior to submitting an IND, FDA requires a sponsor to conduct nonclinical (preclinical) testing to develop the initial toxicological and pharmacological information needed to evaluate the new drug's safety before initiating human clinical trials. Nonclinical studies consist of *in vitro* and *in vivo* animal toxicology and pharmacology tests, including assessing the drug's mechanism of action and efficacy in specific indications using animal models. A full nonclinical testing program can take one to four or more years, including one to two years before filing an IND, with further testing conducted in parallel with the clinical testing.

Nonclinical studies are used to:
- assess pharmacodynamic activity and mechanism of action
- assess drug absorption, distribution to organ systems and tissues, and metabolism and excretion (ADME) pathways
- assess pharmacokinetics
- detect overt toxicity and identify toxic effects and principal target organs
- assess genotoxic or mutagenic potential
- assess carcinogenicity
- assess reproductive toxicity and teratogenic potential
- assess drug impurity safety
- estimate pharmacological dose-response relationships and toxic effects
- estimate a safe human starting dose
- suggest clinical safety assessments

Pharmacology

Pharmacology information usually includes studies to identify the mechanism of action, dose- and concentration-response relationship for pharmacodynamic endpoints, ADME, safety pharmacology (cardiovascular, respiratory and neurologic effects) and toxicokinetics. The studies to be included in an original IND are dependent on the drug and its intended use but should provide sufficient information to justify study in humans and to identify any special concerns that should be considered in the design and conduct of the initial clinical trials.

Toxicity

The International Council on Harmonisation (ICH) M3 and S series guidance documents discuss animal toxicity study types and durations required to support safe human clinical trials. Toxicology studies must be conducted in accordance with current Good Laboratory Practice (CGLP) if they are intended to support safety assessments. Alternate standards can be proposed with an accepted scientific rationale.

Toxicity testing generally must be conducted in two mammalian species (one non-rodent), usually involving rats and dogs. The duration of the toxicity studies depends on the desired human dosing duration. For example, first-in-human single and multiple dosing can be supported by one- to four-week studies, whereas 30- to 90-day subchronic toxicity studies are required for the full drug development program. Chronic dosing may require six-month studies in rats and nine-month studies in dogs. In principle, the duration of animal toxicity studies should equal or exceed that of proposed human clinical trials (up to the maximum recommended duration of the repeated-dose toxicity studies). Exceptions to these general guidelines exist for such cases as intermittent exposure or life-threatening disease. For example, multiple intermittent chemotherapy cycles of one-month duration can be supported with one-month toxicity studies.

Genotoxicity

A standard test battery of *in vitro* genotoxicity studies generally is required prior to initial clinical testing and includes mutagenicity assessment in bacteria and chromosomal damage in mammalian cells. *In vivo* assessments of genotoxicity are typically required prior to conducting Phase 2 clinical trials.

Carcinogenicity

Carcinogenicity studies usually are conducted in parallel to Phase 3 testing, once proof of concept studies for a clinical indication are completed, and normally are required for all chronic dosing indications. Usually, carcinogenicity studies also are required for products that may not be chronically administered, but total exposure over a lifetime from repeated administrations result in total exposure of more than six months. Carcinogenicity studies may not be required at all for some products (e.g., known carcinogens or life-threatening diseases with short life-expectancy). Carcinogenicity studies are conducted for two years in rats and 18 months in mice. A shorter mouse study (six months) using knockout mice may be negotiated. The carcinogenicity study plan should be agreed upon by End-of-Phase 2 meetings with FDA and consideration given to submitting the protocols for Special Protocol Assessment.

Reproductive Toxicity
Fertility and reproduction studies are divided into three segments and generally must be completed before starting Phase 3 studies:
1. Segment I: fertility and early embryonic development to implantation
2. Segment II: embryo-fetal development
3. Segment III: prenatal and postnatal development, including maternal function, in addition to a requirement for mutagenicity studies

Other Nonclinical Considerations
Depending on the intended population, drug use and characteristics, additional nonclinical evaluations might be necessary. These include ensuring nonclinical data are appropriate for pediatric populations, understanding the product's abuse potential, the product's potential to produce immunotoxicity, the product's potential to be phototoxic and understanding the toxicity of combining two separate products (either in a single dosage form or co-packaged products).

Chemistry, Manufacturing and Controls (CMC)
Products manufactured for human administration are required to be manufactured under current Good Manufacturing Practices (CGMP) (see Chapter 8). FDA allows some flexibility for CGMP application in manufacturing products for early Phase 1 clinical trials, in which a limited number of healthy subjects or patients are exposed to the product. However, quality control principles still apply. The original IND will provide information that supports an agency determination that the investigational product has the identity, strength, quality and purity, and purported effect described in the IND application. In some cases, where the drug substance is manufactured by a contract manufacturing organization (CMO), the CMO may file a Drug Master File (DMF), and the IND will merely reference the DMF and include a letter of authorization from the CMO for FDA to access the file.

Clinical Protocol
An original IND for a new molecular entity (NME) usually will include a first-in-human protocol, commonly a single ascending dose design. However, it is possible to file an IND with any protocol for any development phase depending on the information already known about the drug. The protocol's detail and complexity are dependent on the investigational phase: the protocol for Phase 1 studies is less detailed than Phase 2 and 3 protocols. Regardless, the protocol must be accompanied by information on at least one investigator who will conduct the study, showing the investigator is qualified by training and experience. In addition, information on facilities involved in the study's conduct and the Institutional Review Board (IRB) that will review the protocol for human subject protection should be provided.

IND Application Preparation and Submission
Regulations pertaining to INDs can be found in 21 CFR 312. The IND utilizes Form FDA 1571, which lists the aspects and applicable CFR section outlined below:
- Form FDA 1571 (21 CFR 312.23(a)(l))
- Table of contents (21 CFR 312.23(a)(2))
- Introductory statement and general investigation plan (21 CFR 312.23(a)(3))
- Investigator's Brochure (IB) (21 CFR 312.23(a)(5))
- Protocol(s) (21 CFR 312.23(a)(6), including investigator, facilities and IRB data (Form FDA 1572))
- CMC data (21 CFR 312.23(a)(7), including labeling and environmental analysis)
- Pharmacology and toxicology data (21 CFR 312.23(a)(8))
- Previous human experience (21 CFR 312.23(a)(9))
- Additional information (21 CFR 312.23(a)(10))
- Biosimilar User Fee Cover Sheet (Form FDA 3792)
- Clinical Trials Certification of Compliance (Form FDA 3674)

Original INDs from commercial sponsors must be submitted electronically. Non-commercial INDs may be submitted in paper format in triplicate (an original for archives and two review copies).

The IND in electronic format is assembled according to the Common Technical Document (CTD) defined by ICH in 5 Modular sections. The structure and headings of the CTD are strictly defined:
- Module 1—administrative information such as cover letters and forms

- Module 2—summaries of information presented in detail in Modules 3, 4 and 5
- Module 3—quality information on drug substance and drug product CMC, investigational product labeling and environmental analysis
- Module 4—reports of nonclinical studies and nonclinical publications
- Module 5—clinical protocols and reports of clinical studies and publications

Documents are "published" in PDF format according to prescribed standards and assembled on an extensible markup language (XML) backbone using specialized software. These standards are fully explained in guidance documents related to electronic data standards and submissions. All electronic IND files are submitted through FDA's electronic submissions gateway (ESG).

The first step in assembling IND documents is to obtain an IND number from FDA. Form FDA 1571 is required for any submission, including a pre-IND meeting request and briefing document as well as any other correspondence prior to submitting the original IND. Each submission is assigned a serial number starting with 0000, with each subsequent submission numbered sequentially.

IND Application Review

After receiving the IND, FDA assigns it to a reviewing division, based on the indication identified on Form FDA 1571, which then assigns a review team consisting of the various disciplines responsible for evaluating the information, and may include a medical officer, a clinical pharmacologist, a pharmacologist, a statistician and a chemist. A regulatory project manager (RPM) will work with the team to handle administrative matters, including sponsor contact. An acknowledgment letter, stating the date on which the IND was received and identifying the RPM, is sent to the sponsor.

The IND is reviewed to determine whether there is sufficient information to allow the investigational drug's safe administration to humans and to ensure the rights of the subjects are protected. The pharmacologist reviews the nonclinical information to identify whether the toxicity and pharmacology studies provide ample information to identify a reasonably safe starting dose and what, if any, specific safety monitoring tests may be required in the clinical studies. The medical officer reviews the proposed clinical study to determine whether it is designed in a way that protects human subjects' safety. The chemist reviews the CMC information to determine whether the manufacturing process produces a product that provides identity, purity and stability information for the intended initial clinical study.

INDs are not approved; instead, the IND becomes effective within 30 days of FDA receipt unless the agency places the proposed trial on clinical hold (**Figure 5-1**). If IND deficiencies are found, FDA generally will contact the sponsor and provide an opportunity to correct the deficiencies within the 30-day review time, although this is not required. If issues cannot be resolved within 30 days, FDA may place a clinical hold on the IND or study. Generally, FDA will contact the sponsor by telephone within the 30-day period and inform it the IND is being placed on full or partial clinical hold. The initial clinical hold contact may or may not provide a full explanation for the basis of FDA's action, but is followed within 30 days by a written explanation of the reasons for the hold. FDA lifts the clinical hold when it determines the sponsor has satisfactorily corrected the deficiencies and that the investigation may proceed safely (see below for additional information on clinical holds after the IND is active).

Reasons for clinical hold imposition during original IND review include:
- unreasonable risk of human subject harm or insufficient information to allow risk assessment
- unqualified investigators
- misleading, incomplete or erroneous IB
- insufficient information to assess risk to humans
- exclusion of subjects with a life-threatening disease from participation in an early phase clinical trial because of a perceived risk or potential risk of reproductive or developmental toxicity due to the drug

Once the IND is open, the sponsor may conduct human clinical trials. It also is the sponsor's responsibility to keep the IND updated through the amendment and annual report processes, as described below. No public communication should promote an investigational drug as safe and effective for use, and no advertising or promotion is allowed during the drug's clinical testing. Study recruitment advertising is reviewed and approved by site IRBs prior to use.

IND Amendments

During development, the IND must be updated continually. Each submission is an IND amendment and is assigned a sequentially numbered and signed Form FDA 1571. Types of submissions available after the IND is open include:
1. Protocol amendments: used to change a previously submitted protocol, submit a new study protocol, and/or add investigator information. Protocols for new investigations must be submitted prior to the study's start; however, there is no 30-day review period after the initial IND is active. If adding

Figure 5-1. FDA IND Review Process

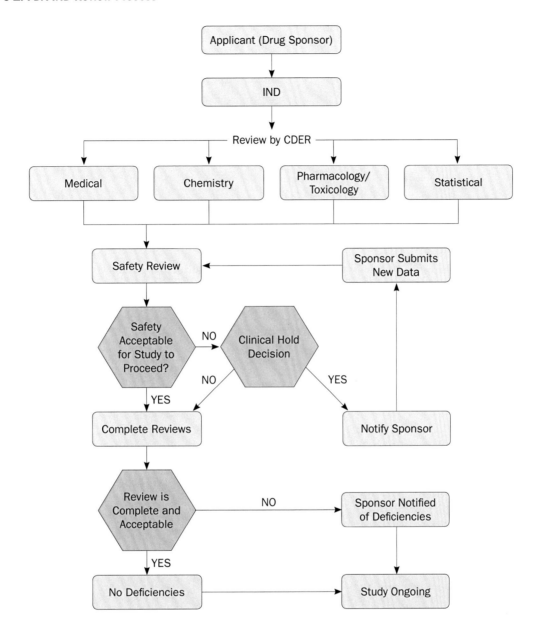

new investigators or updating investigator information (e.g., Form FDA 1572) to a previously submitted protocol, the investigator's information may be batched and submitted monthly.
2. Information amendments: new animal toxicology and pharmacology, CMC, technical information or discontinued clinical trials. Notification of a clinical trial discontinued for safety reasons must be submitted promptly.
3. IND safety reports must be communicated in writing to FDA within seven calendar days for deaths and life-threatening events, or within 15 calendar days for other serious adverse events from when the sponsor initially becomes aware, including the following kinds of information:
   a. any Suspected Unexpected Serious Adverse Reaction (SUSAR) associated with the drug's use (including information from non-IND studies)
   b. any finding in laboratory animals or literature reports that suggests a significant risk for human subjects
4. Annual reports to the IND must be submitted to FDA within 60 days of the anniversary date of the IND becoming effective. In place of an annual report, the same information may be submitted

as a Development Safety Update Report (DSUR) upon approval of the review division. The DSUR is an internationally accepted format for annual reporting of development safety information. If the DSUR is submitted, the submission date can be changed to reflect the Development International Birthdate (date of the first international clinical trial application approval) if it is different from the IND effective date. Regardless of the format, the report must include:
   a. individual study information, including identifying each study, its purpose, patient population, enrollment status and demographics, number completed and number dropped out
   b. a brief description of any available study results, including:
      i. a summary showing the most frequent and most serious adverse experiences by body system
      ii. a summary of IND safety reports submitted during the year
      iii. a list of all subjects who died during participation, including cause of death
      iv. a list of all subjects who dropped out due to any adverse experience
      v. a brief description of what, if anything, has been learned that is pertinent to understanding the drug's action
      vi. a list of nonclinical studies completed or in progress during the past year and a summary of their major findings
      vii. a summary of any significant manufacturing or microbiological changes
   c. a general investigational plan for the coming year
      i. a description of any IB revisions and a copy of the new brochure
      ii. a description of any significant Phase 1 modifications not previously reported through a protocol amendment(s)
      iii. a summary of such significant foreign marketing developments as marketing approvals or withdrawals in any country
      iv. a log of any outstanding IND business for which the sponsor expects or requests a response from FDA also may be included
5. General correspondence can be submitted to the IND. These submissions generally include all other types of miscellaneous correspondence. These can be requested by FDA or be unsolicited.

Administrative Actions on an IND

INDs can be placed on clinical hold, withdrawn by the sponsor, terminated by FDA or inactivated by the sponsor or FDA.

As noted above, during an initial IND review, FDA can place the IND on clinical hold for various reasons to protect a human subject's safety and rights. Accordingly, any time during development, the IND can be placed on full or partial clinical hold for the same reasons or if the investigational plan's design is clearly insufficient to meet its stated objectives. Once the sponsor receives information on why the clinical hold was imposed and recommendations on the information FDA would require to lift it, the sponsor may request a Type A meeting with the review division to discuss the hold's details and plan a response. A formal complete response to the clinical hold that addresses all issues raised is required for the hold to be lifted. FDA has a 30-day clock to respond. FDA will notify the sponsor that the clinical hold is lifted so clinical investigations may resume, or that the clinical hold will continue due to an insufficient response.

If no subjects are entered into clinical studies for a period of two years, or all investigations are on clinical hold for one year or more, the IND may be placed on inactive status, at either the sponsor's request or FDA's initiative. If the IND remains on inactive status for five years, or if FDA is unable to resolve deficiencies through a clinical hold or other alternative, it may be terminated following notification by FDA.

Clinical Trials Data Bank (clinicaltrials.gov)

ClinicalTrials.gov was mandated by the *Food and Drug Administration Modernization Act* of 1997 (*FDAMA*). *FDAMA* required the US Department of Health and Human Services (HHS), through the National Institutes of Health (NIH), to establish a registry of clinical trial information for both federally and privately funded trials conducted under INDs to test the effectiveness of experimental drugs for serious or life-threatening diseases or conditions. NIH and FDA worked together to develop the site, which was made available to the public in February 2000. Information on non-effectiveness trials, or trials for drugs to treat conditions not considered serious or life-threatening, also may be submitted. Data requested include brief descriptions of clinical study protocols that include:
- summary of the study's purpose
- recruiting status
- patient participation criteria
- research study design
- trial phase
- disease or condition and drug or therapy under study

- trial investigational site locations and specific contact information
- trial location
- contact information
- study sponsor

If the sponsor does not want to disclose the information, it must submit a detailed certification to FDA, stating the disclosure will interfere substantially with timely subject enrollment. However, FDA makes the final determination of whether to disclose the information. NIH maintains the database, which is available online (http://clinicaltrials.gov/). The ClinicalTrials.gov registration requirements were expanded after Congress passed the *Food and Drug Administration Amendments Act* of 2007 (*FDAAA*). Section 801 requires more types of trials to be registered and additional trial registration information to be submitted. The law also requires the submission of results for certain trials and imposes penalties for noncompliance. Requirements and procedures for submitting trial information is available on CDER's guidance page and the Protocol Registration System (http://prsinfo.clinicaltrials.gov/).

A Clinical Trials Certification of Compliance (Form FDA 3674) is required to be submitted to the IND for a covered clinical trial.

Special INDs

Various special INDs are described in the regulations that may differ in scope from the typical IND sponsored by a pharmaceutical company or organization such as NIH. The typical IND described above is a commercial IND and is sponsored by an entity intending to commercialize following NDA approval.

Sponsor-Investigator IND

A Sponsor-Investigator IND is submitted by an individual investigator to study a new drug that does not currently have commercial interest or intent. An Investigator IND may cross-reference a commercial IND, NDA or published literature for the technical information required to support the proposed clinical investigation. Generally, a commercial IND or NDA holder provides a letter to the sponsor-investigator, authorizing FDA to access its application.

Expanded Access

"Expanded access" refers to various procedures employed to facilitate investigational drugs' availability to patients with serious diseases or conditions when there is no comparable or satisfactory alternative therapy to diagnose, monitor or treat the patient's disease or condition, and the patient is not eligible for participation in a clinical trial being conducted under a commercial IND because they do not meet inclusion or exclusion criteria or cannot travel to an investigational location. Various terms have been used to mean what is now consolidated under expanded access, including treatment use, compassionate use and preapproval access. Expanded access policies are evolving, as increased public and political pressure has been applied, particularly those resulting in passage of the *Right to Try Act* of 2017 (see below).

The *21st Century Cures Act* amended *FD&C Act* Section 561A to require an investigational drug manufacturer or distributor to make its expanded access policy publicly available, but did not require the entity to provide guaranteed access under an expanded access program.

The general criteria for participation in the Expanded Access program are:
- The drug is intended for a serious or immediately life-threatening disease, and there is no comparable or satisfactory alternative drug or other therapy available to treat the disease stage in the intended patient population.
- The potential patient benefit justifies the treatment's potential risks, and those potential risks are not unreasonable in the context of the disease or condition to be treated.

and
- Providing the investigational drug for the requested use will not interfere with the initiation, conduct or completion of clinical investigations that could support marketing approval of the expanded access use or otherwise compromise the potential development of the expanded access use.

Expanded Access for Individual Patients, Including Emergency Use

Also referred to as a "single patient IND," this allows a single patient to be treated in an emergency situation before the usual paperwork can be processed. FDA has acted to facilitate the process and reduce the burden on the patient, treating physician and sponsor by providing Form FDA 3926 (Individual Patient Expanded Access Investigational New Drug Application (IND)) that can be completed, theoretically, in 45 minutes. FDA will respond on the same day to submission of this form and sponsor agreement to supply the drug.

Expanded Access Protocol

An expanded access protocol may be submitted under an existing IND, usually a commercial IND sponsored by a company developing the drug for marketing approval. Consolidation under an IND, rather than opening a separate expanded access IND, facilitates identification of safety issues and reduces the administrative burden on the sponsor and FDA.

Chapter 5

Expanded Access IND
An Expanded Access IND can be submitted when there is no IND for the drug or when the IND sponsor declines to participate in expanded access use.

Right to Try
Right to Try legislation has been enacted in a number of states and federally in the *Right to Try Act* of 2017 (S-204). The act allows patients to request access to an investigational drug that has completed Phase 1 safety trials and who:
- have been diagnosed with life-threatening diseases or conditions
- have exhausted approved treatment options
- are unable to participate in a clinical trial involving the eligible investigational drug, as certified by a doctor, who is in good standing with his or her licensing organization and will not be compensated directly by the manufacturer for so certifying and
- give written informed consent regarding the risks associated with the investigational treatment

The requested product must be under active development in a clinical trial intended to form the basis of an application for approval, providing the treatment is voluntary on the part of the physician treating the patient, and the treatment is provided by the drug manufacturer. The patient may request treatment from his or her physician and obtain the drug without FDA involvement. The act indemnifies the physician and manufacturer against liability for supplying the drug or deciding not to supply the drug unless the relevant conduct constitutes reckless or willful misconduct, gross negligence or an intentional tort under any applicable state law. However, the act requires the manufacturer to report annually on the drug's supply.

New Drug Applications

Pre-Submission Activities

The applicant needs to complete many activities prior to submitting an application, including proprietary name submission and review, establishment registration, labeler code assignment and a Pre-Submission Meeting request to the review division.

Nonproprietary (INN) Names
In early development, most products are assigned a company-specific code or a name from common use of a chemical to identify the molecule or product. As development progresses, a manufacturer is expected to obtain an International Nonproprietary Name (INN) for the active moiety designated by the World Health Organization. Typically, the manufacturer then will submit the INN to the United States Adopted Names Council for adoption as the USAN and publication in the US Pharmacopeia Dictionary of USAN. This name, which is not trademarked, is used as the generic name for the product under development and any future generic product of the same active moiety.

Pediatric Study Plan
An initial Pediatric Study Plan is required to be submitted no later than 60 days after an End-of-Phase 2 meeting. Details on pediatric development are presented in Chapter 37.

Proprietary Name Submission and Review
One important development phase activity is crafting the product's proprietary name (i.e., brand name). The proprietary name is one of the product's critical identifiers for healthcare professionals and consumers. Companies can expend a lot of time and money creating the perfect proprietary name. Equally, FDA allocates substantial resources to review proposed proprietary names to help prevent medication errors, with a focus on being able to distinguish among many possible drug products to avoid names that are similar phonetically (sound-alike), in spelling or orthographic appearance (look-alike names) or are otherwise confusing or misleading.

The proprietary name approval request must be submitted when the application is submitted, although applicants should submit the request prior to application submission (perhaps as early as completion of Phase 2 trials). It is recommended the proposed proprietary name be submitted as early as possible, since it could take multiple submissions to gain FDA agreement on a name. If product indications are not sufficiently clear to evaluate a name to prevent potential medication errors, FDA does not evaluate proposed names until products have completed Phase 2 trials.

A proprietary name submission should include primary and alternate proposed proprietary names, the proprietary name's intended pronunciation, name derivation, intended proprietary name modifier meanings, the name's pharmacologic/therapeutic category and dosage form and administration instructions. Some of this information can be included in draft labeling, if available. In addition, applicants commonly conduct trademark searches, their own phonetic and orthographic analysis, and even physician and consumer research, to evaluate and select the best proprietary name. While this information is not required for the proprietary name request, it can be helpful.

FDA's proprietary name review includes evaluating both the proposed name's safety and promotional aspects. The safety review focuses primarily on preventing medication errors and evaluating other products that may have similar dosage regimens, overlapping strengths, similar names when spoken or a similar appearance when written by hand. The promotional review is to determine whether the name implies superiority, attempts to minimize risk or implies efficacy.

For a proposed proprietary name submitted during the IND phase, FDA will review and communicate a decision about the name within 180 days of the submission's receipt. Once a proprietary name is provisionally accepted, the proposed proprietary name must be submitted again with the original NDA or BLA. FDA will review and communicate a decision within 90 days of the submission's receipt to ensure it is still acceptable. Lack of acceptability at this stage could be because information about the intended use may be different in the NDA, or another product has been approved in the meantime with a conflicting name.

Establishment Registration and National Drug Code
A company manufacturing human drugs, certain biological products and animal drugs must register the manufacturing facility before FDA will approve a marketing application. Specifically, owners or operators of all drug establishments not exempt under *FD&C Act* Section 510(g) or Part 207 Subpart B engaging in drug manufacture, preparation, propagation, compounding or processing shall register and submit a list of every drug in commercial distribution (21 CFR 207.20(a)).

The National Drug Code (NDC) system is designed to provide drugs in the US with a specific number that describes the product. Per 21 CFR 207.33, the NDC is limited to 10 or 11 digits. The *Health Insurance Portability and Accountability Act* of 1996 (*HIPAA*) propagated more-consistent 11-digit codes to allow for proper reimbursement billing. FDA assigns the first NDC segment that identifies the vendor (or labeler) involved in the drug's manufacture, packaging or distribution. The second segment conveys product codes and comprises entity, strength, dosage form and formulation. The third segment, or package code, indicates package forms and sizes. The manufacturer assigns the second and third product code segments.

Prior to June 2009, FDA input the full NDC number and information into a database known as the Drug Registration and Listing System (DRLS). However, the use of electronic submissions and electronic DRLS (eDRLS) makes this process automatic. More recently, the *Food and Drug Administration Safety and Innovation Act* (*FDASIA*) of 2012 amended the *FD&C Act*, requiring additional information to be submitted to register domestic or foreign drug facilities. This additional information includes each drug establishment's unique facility identifier and a point-of-contact email address. Further, as of 1 October 2012, the domestic and foreign drug manufacturers' registration period was changed to 1 October to 31 December of each year, instead of the previously more open-ended period of on or before 31 December. A link providing more direction on listing and registering products properly is included under Electronic Drug Registration and Listing Instructions below.

FDA utilizes eDRLS database information to update the NDC directory on a daily basis (see the NDC Directory, www.accessdata.fda.gov/scripts/cder/ndc/default.cfm). Additionally, FDA relies on establishment registration and drug listing information to administer many of its programs, such as postmarketing surveillance (including risk-based scheduling and inspection planning), protection against bioterrorism, drug shortage prevention, drug recall management and user fee assessment.

Presubmission Meeting
Meeting with FDA for a pre-NDA or pre-BLA meeting is highly recommended once data are available from the Phase 3 trials intended to provide substantial evidence of effectiveness. The meeting's goal is to gain general agreement that the information to be submitted will be sufficient to allow FDA to conduct a substantive review and will be presented according to the data and other information standards expected.

The New Drug Application or Biologics License Application
Goals
An NDA or BLA's goals are to provide enough information to permit FDA reviewers to reach key decisions within a scheduled timeframe. These decisions include assessing:
- the drug's safety and efficacy profile when used for the indications described in the labeling
- drug manufacturing methods and controls used to maintain drug quality, and ensuring they are adequate to preserve the drug's identity, strength, quality and purity through product expiry

Content and Format
An application must provide all pertinent drug development information, the quantity of which can vary from one application to another; however, the application structure is consistent. Per 21 CFR 314.50 and 601.2 (NDA and BLA, respectively), a submission must include an application form, index, summary, three technical sections, case report forms and tabulations, patent information, financial disclosure or certification and labeling. Technical sections may include product quality, nonclinical pharmacology and toxicology, human pharmacokinetics and bioavailability, microbiology and statistical and clinical data. The product quality section

should describe both the drug substance and drug product's composition, manufacture and specifications, as well as fairly detailed manufacturing control and stability data descriptions. Historically, information on developing the file's technical portion has not always been provided or required, but it now is expected to help FDA reviewers understand the product and process better. The nonclinical pharmacology and toxicology section should describe any animal and *in vitro* drug studies that help define the drug's pharmacologic properties and address toxicity related to its administration. The clinical section should include a description of all clinical investigations completed to support the drug's efficacy and safety, as well as study protocols and copies of case report forms for each patient who died during a clinical study or did not complete a study because of an adverse event, regardless of the incident's relationship to the study drug.

Copies of the proposed drug product labeling should be included in the application. This includes the package insert, carton and container labels and, if necessary, a Medication Guide. FDA requires labeling to be submitted electronically in a format the agency can review and process. The labeling content must be in structured product labeling (SPL) format with an XML backbone. SPL has several advantages: information exchange between computer systems, text comparison automation by section and exchange of information needed for other submissions (i.e., cross-referencing). SPL allows labeling content to be searched, moved between systems and combined with other data sources, and lends itself to supporting electronic healthcare initiatives.

Required labeling content and format for prescription drugs and biological products is in 21 CFR 201.56. On 24 January 2006, FDA published a final rule amending human prescription drug and biological product labeling content and format requirements. The rule commonly is referred to as the Physician Labeling Rule (PLR) because it addresses prescription drug labeling used by prescribers and other healthcare practitioners. It was designed to make prescription drug labeling information easier for healthcare practitioners to access, read and use to facilitate prescribing decisions. The PLR format is described further in FDA's February 2013 *Guidance for Industry: Labeling for Human Prescription Drug and Biological Products—Implementing the PLR Content and Format Requirements.*

CTD Format
As outlined above, a marketing application submission requires a huge amount of information. Generally, comparable scientific and clinical information is required in countries where a manufacturer (or applicant or sponsor) plans to market the drug. Because the information is similar, and to allow manufacturers to proceed more quickly and consistently with the submission and application process, ICH developed the CTD format (**Figure 5-2**). The CTD provides a harmonized new marketing application structure and format for the US, EU, Japan and other countries adhering to ICH guidance. Regional content requirements continue to vary in some areas, but harmonized formatting has allowed regulatory professionals to work more efficiently on global projects.

The CTD is divided into five modules. Module 1 contains region-specific information, and Modules 2 through 5 provide information common across all regions. Module 1 contains administrative and prescribing information (e.g., application forms, proposed labeling and applicable patent information). Module 2 contains CTD summaries (e.g., quality overall summary and nonclinical and clinical overview and summaries). Module 3 contains quality data or product quality information (e.g., drug substance and drug product data). Module 4 includes nonclinical study reports (e.g., pharmacodynamic, pharmacokinetic and toxicology data, as well as relevant literature references cited in the Module 2 nonclinical summaries). Module 5 contains clinical study reports (e.g., study protocols, case report forms, integrated safety and efficacy summaries and relevant clinical literature references and references cited in the Module 2 clinical summaries).

Electronic CTD (eCTD) Format
Historically, submissions to FDA have been in paper format. Paper submissions require many sponsor and agency resources and a lot of storage space. FDA attempted to address this issue by creating electronic submission standards (eSubs). FDA started accepting electronic CTDs (eCTDs) in 2003; they became the recommended standard in 2008 and have been required since May 2017.

The value of electronic submissions is well recognized. Under *FDASIA*, FDA, working with stakeholders, will issue draft and final guidance on e-submission standards and format. E-submission requirements have been phased in over the last few years, starting with original NDA and ANDA submissions, DMFs and certain INDs and BLAs.

The paper CTD has a different format than the eCTD. With an eCTD submission, each document is separate (granular) and named according to ICH specifications. Each submission has its own eCTD XML backbone file, which allows FDA to receive, archive and review the submission. Once an application is submitted in electronic format, all subsequent submissions to the application also are submitted electronically and should include eCTD backbone files. Without these backbone files, FDA will be unable to process subsequent submissions. Unless submitted through the ESG, as described below, FDA recommends electronic file cover letters include a description of the submission's approximate size (e.g., 4 gigabytes), the type and number of electronic

Figure 5-2. Diagram of the ICH Common Technical Document (CTD)

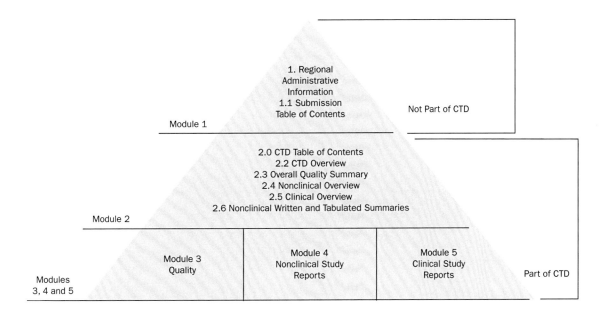

media used (e.g., two DVDs), a regulatory and technical point of contact and a statement that the submission is virus-free, with a description of the software used to virus-check the file.

At any time, a sponsor can decide to convert its paper application to an electronic filing. If a sponsor decides to convert to an electonic filing, there is no requirement for all previous submissions to be in electronic format with eCTD backbone files; instead, the electronic filing may begin with the planned submission. For ease of conversion, the Comprehensive Table of Contents Headings and Hierarchy maps the application to the eCTD format. When converting and cross-referencing past submissions, the applicant should be sure to include specific information, such as the date of the previous submission, document name, page number(s), volume number and approval dates, or may consider including any items critical for review of the current submission within the electronic format submission, so the reviewer can find it more easily.

Types of Applications

There are several types of drug applications:
- Traditional 505(b)(1) NDA—*FD&C Act*, Section 505(b)(1)
- 505(b)(2) NDA—*FD&C Act*, Section 505(b)(2)
- Abbreviated NDA (ANDA)—*FD&C Act*, Section 505(j)
- Original BLA—*PHS Act*, Section 351(a)
- Biosimilar BLA—*PHS Act*, Section 351(k)

505(b)(1) NDA (Traditional NDA)

A 505(b)(1) application is a complete NDA containing all the applicant's studies necessary to demonstrate a drug's safe and effective use. A 505(b)(1) application contains all information outlined in 21 CFR 314.50.

505(b)(2) NDA

A 505(b)(2) application also contains information required in a 505(b)(1) application necessary to demonstrate a drug's safe and effective use; however, the applicant can provide some of the required information from studies it did not conduct and for which it has not obtained a right of reference.

Section 505(b)(2) was added to the *FD&C Act* by the *Drug Price Competition and Patent Term Restoration Act* of 1984 (*Hatch-Waxman Act*) to allow companies to develop alternative therapies more quickly by relying on existing data. Applicants may rely on published literature supporting an application's approval and/or on previous FDA findings of safety and effectiveness of an approved drug. For example, a 505(b)(2) application can be submitted if the applicant desires to introduce a new route of administration, such as an intramuscular injection, versus an approved product available as an oral tablet. In this instance, the applicant can rely on the efficacy data and some of the safety data established for the drug's oral formulation already approved by FDA, but the applicant is required to conduct studies showing safety and efficacy relating to the change to the intramuscular dosage form. In addition, the applicant may need to establish a bridge (e.g., via comparative bioavailability data) between the proposed drug and the approved listed drug to demonstrate reliance on FDA's previous findings of safety and effectiveness is justified scientifically. These applications need to include product quality information, unless the applicant has the right to reference a currently approved application for quality information when the same product will be used. *FD&C Act* Sections 505(b)(2) and 505(j) replaced FDA's paper NDA policy, which had permitted an applicant to rely on studies published in the scientific literature to demonstrate the safety and effectiveness of duplicates of certain post-1962 pioneer drug products.

505(j) Abbreviated NDA (ANDA)
A 505(j) application is considered abbreviated because, generally, the applicant is not required to include nonclinical and clinical data necessary to demonstrate safety and effectiveness. Instead, it contains CMC and bioequivalence data to show the proposed product is identical in active ingredient, dosage form, strength, route of administration, labeling, quality, performance characteristics and intended use to the previously-approved reference listed drug (RLD). For some well-characterized products, a bioequivalence waiver may be requested based on FDA's current guidance. Additional detailed information on generic drug submissions can be found in Chapter 16.

351(a) BLA (Original BLA)
A 351(a) application is a complete BLA containing all the applicant's studies conducted to demonstrate a drug's safe and effective use. A 351(a) BLA contains all information outlined in 21 CFR 601.2. Biologic products are derived from living material, making them much more complex and more difficult to fully characterize than drugs covered under NDAs and ANDAs. Additional detailed information on biologics submissions can be found in Chapter 25.

351(k) BLA (Biosimilar BLA)
A 351(k) application is an abbreviated BLA for a biological product demonstrated to be biosimilar to or interchangeable with an FDA-licensed biological product. Due to biologics' complex nature, these abbreviated applications carry more requirements than ANDAs, including nonclinical and clinical studies. For additional information, see Chapter 27.

Submission of the Marketing Application and Next Steps
eCTD submissions are submitted through FDA's ESG.

Upon application receipt, FDA has 60 days to determine whether the application is sufficiently complete to allow for a substantive review. If FDA determines the application is complete, it will be filed on Day 60. If FDA determines the application is not complete (see 21 CFR 314.101[d]), it may Refuse to File (RTF) it and, if so, will issue a formal RTF letter by Day 60, providing the reasons for its decision. By eliminating incomplete applications from the review queue, FDA can focus its resources on complete applications. The agency tends to be more flexible in accommodating drugs intended for critical diseases, particularly when there is no alternative therapy. In such cases, FDA and the applicant often work together to find a balanced resolution to allow application review to begin as quickly as possible.

Additionally, FDA may accept some parts of an application and RTF others (e.g., file one of two proposed indications for use and RTF another). The applicant may resubmit the application after addressing FDA's RTF issues. The agency then determines whether the resubmitted application can be filed.

If an applicant strongly disagrees with FDA's decision to RTF an application, it has 30 days after receiving the RTF letter to request an informal meeting with the agency. Following the meeting, the applicant can request the agency to file the application over protest. In this event, the date of filing will be 60 days after the date the applicant requested the meeting.

FDA performs an initial application filing review by Day 60 to identify any issues, such as substantive deficiencies or concerns that may impact FDA's ability to complete the review and approve the application. Filing review issues are distinct from application deficiencies that serve as the basis for an RTF action. Note, FDA's initial filing review is a preliminary application review and is not indicative of deficiencies (minor or major) that may be identified later in the review cycle.

FDA then will inform the applicant in writing whether there are filing review issues by issuing a *PDUFA-mandated letter* within 14 days of the determination (also called a Day 74 Letter). The Day 74 Letter states the date the application was received, which is the date the review clock begins. It also provides the planned review timeline and includes an action date when FDA will provide a decision on the application, as well as dates the applicant can expect to receive feedback from the review division on proposed labeling and postmarketing requirements or commitments. In addition, the Day 74 Letter identifies FDA's review classification (i.e., Standard Review or Priority Review).

For applications reviewed under the *PDUFA VI* Program, the Day 74 Letter also states whether the division is considering convening an Advisory Committee Meeting. For additional information on filing review issues and the Day 74 Letter, refer to MaPP 6010.5 NDAs and BLAs: Filing Review Issues.

During the review period, FDA may ask the applicant for additional information (solicited information), or the applicant may submit additional information on its own initiative (unsolicited information). If the new information constitutes a major amendment, FDA may determine an extension to the *PDUFA* action date is needed to review it. This type of extension is more likely further into the review due to internal FDA action dates that are not always transparent to the applicant. Only one three-month extension can be given per review cycle. For a solicited major amendment that extends the *PDUFA* action date, FDA also provides a new timeline for feedback on proposed labeling and postmarketing requirements or commitments. Thus, an applicant's strategy for providing information in the application should be planned very carefully.

Food and Drug Administration Review Process

Once an application is received and validated, it is routed to the RPM in the appropriate review division. The RPM will ask supervisory team leaders from appropriate disciplines to assign reviewers. The first review task is to determine, from each specific discipline, whether the application is fileable (see Submission of the Marketing Application and Next Steps above).

The review team consists of various disciplines, such as clinical, pharmacology and toxicology, CMC, clinical pharmacology, etc.

It is recommended that NDA amendments after submission be minimized, with the exception of the 120-Day Safety Update. Specifically, for all filed NDAs, a Safety Update is required 120 days after the NDA is submitted.

Each disciplinary group completes its review and determines whether the data can support the drug's approval. During this process, a reviewer may identify a minor deficiency, may need a topic clarified or may need additional information to facilitate his or her review. These requests for additional information usually are communicated through an information request, or advice letter, and these requests generally are handled via email, telephone or regular mail. As the regulatory contact for the application, the RPM facilitates these communications. Applicants submit amendments to the application in an attempt to address all additional information requests. If serious deficiencies exist, the review division has the option of notifying applicants via a discipline review (DR) letter after each reviewer has completed its section of the pending application. DR letters have been used sparingly since the release of FDA's 2001 *Guidance for Industry: Information Request and Discipline Review Letters Under the Prescription Drug User Fee Act*.

If additional scientific expertise is needed outside the core review team, the review division may consult with other parts of the center or beyond (e.g., the Center for Devices and Radiological Health). For certain applications, opinions from outside experts also may be sought through the Advisory Committee process or by special government employees (SGEs).

As the review proceeds, FDA determines whether any bioresearch monitoring (BIMO) or CGMP inspections are required prior to approval. Those inspections' results allow the agency to determine the credibility and accuracy of the application's data (see Preapproval Inspections (PAI) below).

FDA will determine whether Postmarketing Requirements (PMRs) and/or Postmarketing Commitments (PMCs) are necessary. If so, this is communicated to the applicant, and FDA and the applicant discuss and agree on specific studies and milestone dates, including final protocol submission, study or trial completion and final report submission.

In parallel with PMR and PMC determinations, FDA reviews product labeling and determines whether it accurately reflects the product's safety and efficacy and allows physicians, healthcare professionals and consumers to determine whether the drug's benefits outweigh its risks. The agency then will decide if it is ready to act on the application.

Application review consists of several stages and involves a multidisciplinary team (see **Figure 5-3** for standard review process and timelines). The priority review process shortens the timeframe for the main review from 10 months to six months. The primary review staff summarizes preliminary review findings at a mid-cycle meeting. Discussions at the mid-cycle meeting can include the need for additional information from the applicant and/or additional scientific expertise within the center and, potentially, initial discussions regarding the need for a Risk Evaluation and Mitigations Strategy (REMS) or postmarketing commitments or requirements if the product is approved. During the review, the applicant's proposed labeling is reviewed, and comprehensive comments are conveyed to the applicant. At the wrap-up meeting, discussions can include issues that preclude the application's approvability and details of any needed REMS or postmarketing commitments or requirements.

If the product is an NME or an original BLA, the application signatory authority is the office director; the signatory authority for all other applications, including efficacy supplements, is usually the division director.

REMS

FDAAA Title IX, Subtitle A, Section 901 amended the *FD&C Act* by creating Section 505-1, which authorizes FDA to require applicants of certain prescription drug products to submit a proposed Risk Evaluation and Mitigation Strategy (REMS) if the agency determines one

Figure 5-3. Timeline and Product Review Clock

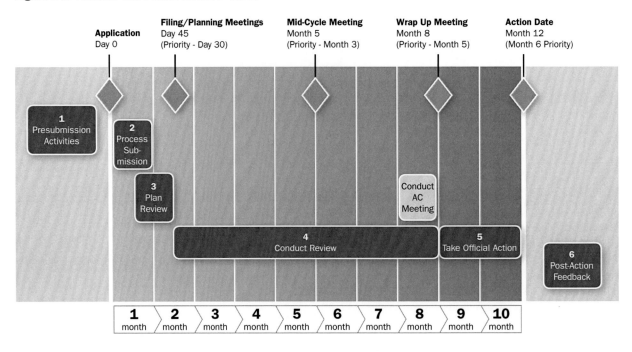

is necessary to ensure a drug's benefits outweigh its risks. An applicant also may voluntarily submit a proposed REMS without having been required to do so by FDA. FDA can request the REMS at the time of the original application's initial submission or at any time after its approval (if the agency becomes aware of new safety information and determines a REMS is necessary). Once FDA notifies the applicant a REMS is necessary, the applicant must submit a proposed REMS within 120 days.

A proposed REMS' content should describe its intended goals and specific elements adequately. The proposed REMS must include, at a minimum, a timetable for submitting assessments at 18 months, three years and seven years after FDA approval. The proposed REMS also may include one or more of the following elements: Medication Guide (21 CFR 208); Patient Package Insert; communication plan to healthcare providers; and Elements to Assure Safe Use (ETASU). The proposed REMS should contain a thorough explanation of the rationale for, and supporting information about, its content and a timetable specifying when each element will be implemented.

ETASU may be required if a drug has been shown to be effective but is associated with a serious adverse event. In such a case, the drug can be approved only if, or would be withdrawn unless, the REMS includes elements to mitigate the specific serious risks listed in the product's labeling. ETASU may be required for approved products when an assessment and Medication Guide, Patient Package Insert or communication plan are not sufficient to mitigate these risks. An example of an ETASU would be a system or process to ensure certain laboratory test result outcomes are obtained before a drug may be dispensed.

The applicant must reach agreement with FDA on REMS submission elements and implementation timelines. FDA will determine which REMS elements are necessary to ensure the drug's benefits outweigh its risks and decide on its approvability. FDA also must approve REMS that are voluntarily submitted. An approved REMS submitted voluntarily is subject to the same requirements and enforcement as a required REMS. FDA will notify applicants that submit proposed REMS voluntarily whether the strategy will be required. If FDA determines a REMS is not required, an applicant may undertake voluntary risk management measures to be performed without a REMS.

Once FDA approves the REMS, the strategy will serve as the basis for inspection and enforcement. A drug will be considered misbranded if the applicant fails to comply with a requirement of the approved REMS. An applicant that violates a REMS requirement is subject to civil monetary penalties of up to $250,000 per violation, not to exceed $1 million in a single proceeding. These penalties increase if the violation continues more than 30 days after FDA notifies the applicant. Penalties double for the second 30-day period and continue to double for subsequent 30-day periods, up to $1 million per period and $10 million per proceeding. In addition, the sponsor may not introduce an approved drug noncompliant with REMS' conditions into interstate commerce.

Advisory Committee Meetings

Advisory Committee Meetings are an integral part of the approval process and are discussed in Chapter 5. Situations that frequently lead FDA to convene an Advisory Committee meeting are described in the relevant draft guidance. According to *FDAAA*, a drug characterized by "…no active ingredient (including any ester or salt of the active ingredient) of which has been approved in any other application under this section or section 351 of the Public Health Service Act" needs to be evaluated by an independent FDA Advisory Committee, unless FDA delineates why such a review will be unnecessary.

FDAAA also amended the *FD&C Act* to limit conflicts of interest and restrict eligibility criteria for FDA Advisory Committee members. It was felt these provisions made the recruitment of suitable individuals for Advisory Committees more difficult. More recently, *FDASIA* reduced those restrictions to help individuals whose scientific expertise is much needed on Advisory Committees dealing with extremely complex issues. Detailed discussions and analysis of the changes can be found in a number of recent third-party newsletters.

PAIs

Another product aspect FDA assesses during its review is whether the methods used in, and the facilities and controls used for, the drug's manufacture, processing, packing and testing are adequate to ensure and preserve the drug's identity, strength, quality and purity.

Prior to approving an application, FDA may conduct manufacturing and analytical facility (CGMP) inspections, as well as nonclinical or clinical testing facility or site (BIMO) inspections. A PAI is performed to contribute to FDA's assurance that a manufacturing establishment listed in a drug product application is capable of manufacturing a drug and that data are accurate and complete.

Although the risk-based decision is left to the agency's discretion, BIMO and CGMP inspections generally are conducted for most new NDA and original BLA applications. FDA is likely to conduct PAI inspections in the following instances:
- NMEs or original BLAs
- Priority Reviews
- sponsor filing its first application
- for-cause inspections (e.g., if one clinical site has a significantly better trial outcome than other sites)
- original or supplemental applications if the CGMP status is unknown (e.g., it has been more than two years since the domestic facility was last inspected, or the establishment is new and has yet to be inspected by FDA or another global regulatory authority)

CDER evaluates the adequacy of the applicant's data and relies on facility inspections to verify the data are authentic and accurate. This ensures applications are not approved if it is determined the applicant cannot demonstrate the ability to operate with integrity and comply with all applicable requirements.

All applicants are expected to include a comprehensive and readily located list of facilities and establishments. FDA will use this list to determine the need for potential inspections of foreign and domestic sites that will manufacture a drug for the US market or have completed a study to support the approval of a drug that will be marketed in the US. The FDA-EU Mutual Recognition Agreement (MRA) allows drug inspectors to rely upon information from drug inspections conducted within each other's borders. Under *FDASIA*, FDA has the authority to enter into agreements to recognize drug inspections conducted by foreign regulatory authorities if it has determined those authorities are capable of conducting inspections that meet US requirements. As of December 2018, FDA has recognized 20 European drug regulatory authorities as capable of conducting inspections of manufacturing facilities that meet FDA requirements, with remaining EU Member States to be added by June 2019.

FDA Decision on the Application

One of two actions may be taken on an application: approval or a complete response. The actions are communicated by either an Approval Letter or a Complete Response letter. The latter lists all review deficiencies FDA identified and describes steps the applicant should take to address these deficiencies by amending the application before it can be approved. Approval Letters are issued when FDA has determined a drug is safe and effective, can be manufactured acceptably and is labeled appropriately. An approval is effective on the issue date of the Approval Letter granting authorization to market the drug in the US.

Postmarketing Requirements and Commitments

The approval letter also stipulates any postmarketing requirements and commitments. A postmarketing requirement is a study (e.g., an observational epidemiologic study, an animal study or a laboratory experiment) or clinical trial the applicant must conduct after the application is approved. It includes studies that may be required under the *Pediatric Research Equity Act* (*PREA*, 21 CFR 314.55[b]), the Animal Efficacy Rule (21 CFR 314.610[b][1]), Accelerated Approval regulations (21 CFR 314.510 and 601.41) or *FDAAA* (Title IX, Section 901). Postmarketing commitments also can include studies and additional reporting for the application's quality aspects. The applicant must report the status of each postmarketing requirement annually. A postmarketing commitment is a written commitment by the applicant to FDA to provide additional information after application approval. *FD&C Act* Section 506B mandates annual status reports and obligates FDA to make certain information about postmarketing commitments available publicly. FDA maintains a database listing postapproval commitments relating to clinical or nonclinical studies. It is important for applicants to monitor this database for their own products, and it also can be a useful regulatory intelligence resource.

Maintaining the Application

After the application is approved, the applicant is expected to continue a variety of activities, including submitting expedited reports of serious, unexpected adverse events that occur in the postmarketing setting. An analysis of these reports is submitted in a Periodic Safety Update Report. These reports review the drug's safety profile since approval. Additionally, applicants are required to submit annual reports. These reports include updated stability data and annual updates to establishment registrations, including supporting documentation. Annual drug listings also are necessary. Please refer to Chapter 15 for more information on postmarketing activities.

Programs for Expediting Drug Development and Review

FDA currently uses four programs to expedite the development and review of new drugs for serious and life-threatening diseases with an unmet medical need:
- Fast Track
- Accelerated Approval
- Priority Review
- Breakthrough Therapy

An investigational product may be eligible for any combination of these programs if it meets the requirements. For example, approximately 80% of applications approved under a Fast Track designation also were Priority Review drugs (six-month application review). Sponsors need to apply for these different programs separately. A novel product with breakthrough designation is subject to the same drug development and review programs as those with Fast Track designation, although breakthrough products receive more development advice and are assigned top division reviewers. Accelerated Approval will apply, if appropriate, and if all the criteria under 21 CFR 314 Subpart H or Subpart E are met.

A comprehensive guidance has been issued on this subject, *Guidance for Industry: Expedited Programs for Serious Conditions—Drugs and Biologics* (May 2014). A summary of the programs and their impact follows. This guidance helps companies focusing on these types of products to develop a strategy to get them to the market as quickly as possible.

Fast Track Designation

FDAMA added Fast Track designation to *FD&C Act* Section 506(b), which then was amended by *FDASIA*. This designation was designed to facilitate the development and expedite the review of drugs: 1) to treat serious or life-threatening diseases and 2) having the potential to address unmet medical needs. Addressing an unmet medical need is defined as providing a therapy where none exists or replacing an available therapy that does not address the need adequately. Fast Track designation may apply to drugs or biologics intended to treat a broad range of serious diseases, including AIDS, Alzheimer's disease, cancer, epilepsy and diabetes. Once a drug receives Fast Track designation, FDA offers the sponsor early and frequent communication to facilitate an efficient development program. The communication frequency ensures questions and issues are resolved in a timely manner, often leading to earlier drug approval. Fast Track drug sponsors also are eligible for rolling reviews of applications, allowing earlier submission and review initiation. A Fast Track designation request can be submitted simultaneously with the IND, or at any time thereafter, prior to receiving marketing approval. To maximize the use of Fast Track incentives, it is best to include the designation request in the original IND submission or as soon as possible thereafter. Note, the Fast Track designation request can be granted by FDA only upon IND submission. The agency will respond to a Fast Track designation request within 60 days of receipt. If FDA determines Fast Track criteria have been met, the review division will issue a letter stating Fast Track designation is granted for the product's development for treating the specific serious or life-threatening condition. The letter also will request sponsors to design and perform studies that can show whether the product fulfills unmet medical needs. FDA can issue a non-designation letter either because the Fast Track request package was incomplete or the drug development program failed to meet the required criteria. The non-designation letter will explain the reasons for FDA's decision.

FDA will respond to a subsequent Fast Track designation request after a non-designation determination within 60 days of receiving the new request. Sponsors must continue to meet the Fast Track criteria throughout product development to retain the designation. The sponsor should expect the appropriateness of continuing the drug development program's Fast Track designation to be discussed and evaluated at different times during the process, including at the End-of-Phase 2 and Presubmission meetings. If FDA determines a product is no longer eligible, it will notify the sponsor of that decision. Sponsors can appeal FDA's decision through the dispute resolution process (21 CFR 10.75, 312.48 and 314.103).

Accelerated Approval
The Accelerated Approval process under Subpart H (Drugs, 21 CFR 314) and Subpart E (Biologics, 21 CFR 601) was created by FDA in 1992 at the height of the HIV/AIDS crisis and amended by *FDASIA*. It allows drug approvals based on surrogate endpoints that are reasonably likely to predict clinical benefit under the following conditions: the disease to be treated must be serious or life-threatening, and the treatment must provide meaningful therapeutic benefit over existing treatments. In cancer drug development, a surrogate endpoint could be tumor shrinkage, and the clinical benefit could be increased overall survival.

Under these provisions, approval requires the applicant to study the drug further to verify and describe its clinical benefit where there is uncertainty about the relation of the surrogate endpoint to clinical benefit or the observed clinical benefit to ultimate outcome.

Priority Review
In 1992, under *PDUFA*, FDA agreed to specific goals for improving drug review times using a two-tiered review time system: priority review and standard review. Priority Review designation is given to drugs that offer major advances in treatment or provide a treatment where no adequate therapy exists. FDA reviews priority applications more quickly than standard applications, in six months versus 10 months (in eight months versus 12 months for applications in the program). Prior to *PDUFA*, CDER application review was subject to the 180-day review period described in 21 CFR 314.100 (the regulatory clock), with review extensions allowed for receipt of major amendments. In addition, prior to 1992, CDER used a three-tiered therapeutic-potential classification system (type A—important therapeutic gain; type B—modest therapeutic gain; and type C—little or no therapeutic gain) to determine application review priorities. Drugs possibly eligible for Priority Review have the potential to provide significant advances in treatment in at least one of the following instances:
- provide evidence of increased effectiveness in disease treatment, prevention or diagnosis
- eliminate or substantially reduce a treatment-limiting drug reaction
- provide documented evidence of enhanced patient compliance to treatment schedule and dose
- provide evidence of safety and effectiveness in a new subpopulation, such as children

An applicant may submit a Priority Review request to FDA if it has adequate evidence its drug product meets one of the above criteria. Although Fast Track- and Breakthrough Therapy-designated products generally are eligible for Priority Review because they are intended to treat serious or life-threatening conditions and address unmet medical needs, those designations do not automatically convey Priority Review. The applicant should request Priority Review, with appropriate justification in the cover letter, when filing the initial NDA, BLA or efficacy supplement. CDER currently grants Priority Review for drugs that provide a significant improvement, compared to marketed products, in the disease's treatment, diagnosis or prevention, i.e., eligibility is not limited to drugs for a serious or life-threatening disease. A Fast Track- or Breakthrough Therapy-designated product ordinarily would meet Priority Review criteria.

FDA determines within 60 days whether a Priority Review or Standard Review designation will be assigned. If Priority Review is granted, the applicant still must provide the same amount of scientific and medical evidence as required under Standard Review classification for FDA to approve the drug.

Breakthrough Therapy Designation
In 2012, *FDASIA* gave FDA a new pathway to expedite the development of therapies that show substantial promise in early clinical trials. This new authority arose from discussions between FDA, NIH, industry, academia and patient groups on how to create a novel pathway for developing breakthrough therapies. A drug company may seek Breakthrough Therapy designation of a drug for a serious and life-threatening disease, and preliminary clinical evidence must show the drug may offer substantial improvement over existing therapies on one or more clinically significant endpoints. Once FDA designates a drug as a Breakthrough Therapy, the drug qualifies for the same benefits as Fast Track-designated products, in addition to an organizational commitment from FDA and intensive agency guidance and interaction throughout the development process to streamline the drug's clinical trials and review process.

Rolling Review
In addition to the standard expedited programs, FDA may consider reviewing portions of a marketing application before the complete NDA or BLA is submitted (Rolling Review). To qualify for a Rolling Review, Fast Track or Breakthrough Therapy designation must have been granted. In addition, the pivotal study must be complete or near completion. A sponsor seeking a Rolling Review may submit such a request simultaneously with a Fast Track-designation request. The sponsor should provide a schedule for submitting portions of the application. If the Rolling Review request is granted, FDA may review portions of the application as they become

available. However, FDA is not obligated to start the review upon receipt of a portion of the application. The *PDUFA* goal date is determined upon receipt of the application's final portion, whereas the user fee is due upon receipt of the first portion. Applicants are advised to initiate discussion about their plans for submitting a Rolling Review NDA or BLA at the Presubmission Meeting.

Special Drug Development Incentive Programs

Orphan Drug Act and *PREA* programs are the most well-known special incentive programs and are discussed in detail in other chapters of this book. This section briefly introduces programs designed to stimulate the development of new antimicrobial drugs, drugs for certain tropical diseases and the Presidential Emergency Plan for AIDS Relief (PEPFAR).

Antibiotics

FDASIA contains specific provisions to incentivize antibiotic development, known as Generating Antibiotic Incentives Now (GAIN). GAIN is designed to stimulate development of drugs for the treatment of serious or life-threatening infections caused by bacteria or fungi. Eligible drugs must be designated as qualified infectious disease products (QIDPs). QIDP designation benefits include Fast Track designation, FDA Priority Review and a five-year marketing exclusivity extension granted at the time of NDA approval (e.g., five-year NCE exclusivity, three-year new product exclusivity, seven-year orphan drug exclusivity). CDER has created an Antibacterial Drug Development Task Force (www.fda.gov/Drugs/DevelopmentApprovalProcess/DevelopmentResources/ucm317207.htm). As part of its work, the task force assists in developing and revising GAIN-required guidance related to antibacterial drug development.

Priority Review Vouchers: Tropical Diseases and Pediatric Rare Diseases

A guidance describing tropical disease priority review voucher policies and procedures described in *FD&C Act* Section 524(a)(3) (21 79 U.S.C. 360n(a)(3)) is available and should be used in conjunction with FDA's *Guidance for Industry: Neglected Tropical Diseases of the Developing World: Developing Drugs for Treatment or Prevention* (July 2014). *FDASIA* Section 908, the Rare Pediatric Disease Priority Review Voucher Incentive Program, extends the voucher program on a trial basis to rare pediatric diseases.

Briefly, under the law, sponsors of certain marketing applications approved for preventing or treating designated tropical diseases (e.g., malaria, tuberculosis and cholera) or rare pediatric diseases receive Priority Review Vouchers (PRVs) from FDA to be used with products of their choice. These vouchers can be transferred to other developers. A PRV entitles the bearer to Priority Review for a future new drug application that otherwise would not qualify for the program. When sponsors use the PRV, they are required to pay FDA an additional user fee (independent of other user fees). The previous one-year notice before redeeming the voucher has been eliminated, and tropical vouchers now may be redeemed in just 90 days and resold an unlimited number of times. As of November 2018, seven PRVs had been granted in the following tropical disease categories: malaria, tuberculosis, leishmaniasis, cholera, river blindness and Chagas disease. To date, FDA has granted 17 rare pediatric disease vouchers.

AIDS Relief

Working with implementing organizations and governments in more than 32 countries, the President's Emergency Plan for AIDS Relief (PEPFAR) has contributed to the rapid acceleration of HIV treatment access, availability of care and support services and HIV prevention interventions. To support PEPFAR's goals, FDA introduced an initiative in 2004 to ensure antiretroviral drugs produced by manufacturers worldwide could be reviewed rapidly, their quality assessed and their acceptability for purchase with PEPFAR funds supported.

More than 150 antiretroviral drugs have been approved or tentatively approved by FDA in association with PEPFAR. Tentative approval means, although existing patents and/or marketing exclusivity prevent the product from being approved for marketing in the US, FDA has found the product meets all manufacturing quality, safety and effectiveness requirements for marketing in the US.

New Drug Product Exclusivity (Hatch-Waxman Exclusivity)

New Drug Product Exclusivity, under *FD&C Act* Sections 505(c)(3) (E) and (j)(5)(F) (*Hatch-Waxman Act*), provides the approved NDA holder limited protection from new marketplace competition for the innovation its approved drug product represented. A five-year exclusivity period is granted for drugs containing an NCE. An NCE is a drug containing an active moiety not previously approved by FDA in any other application submitted under *FD&C Act* Section 505(b). An active moiety is the molecule or ion responsible for the drug substance's physiological or pharmacological action. Excluded from the active moiety concept are those appended portions of the molecule that cause the drug to be an ester, salt (including a salt with hydrogen or coordination bonds) or other noncovalent derivative (such as a complex, chelate or clathrate) of the molecule (see 21 CFR 314.108). A three-year period of exclusivity may be granted for drug products containing an active moiety that has been approved previously if the application contains reports of new clinical investigations (other than bioavailability studies) conducted or sponsored by the applicant that were essential to the application's approval. For example, changes in an approved drug product that affect its active ingredient, strength, dosage form, route of administration or conditions of use may be granted exclusivity if the application meets the criteria.

Summary

- A prescription drug is any drug approved or licensed for distribution by FDA that requires a healthcare practitioner's authorization before it can be obtained.
- The *FD&C Act* prohibits introduction of a prescription drug product into interstate commerce unless the drug manufacturer has submitted an application and obtained FDA approval.
- An *FD&C Act* exemption can be obtained through the IND to allow sponsors to conduct clinical trials to demonstrate a proposed product's safety and efficacy.
- A well-thought-out regulatory strategy is essential to the ultimate success of an applicant's drug development program and could shave months, or even years, off the product launch timeline.
- A marketing application is required to contain all information pertaining to the drug's development, including CMC; nonclinical; and clinical data. The application's ultimate goal is to provide adequate information to allow FDA to complete its review and provide a decision on the drug's safety, effectiveness and quality.
- There are three types of NDAs and two types of BLAs. All these applications should provide adequate information to allow FDA reviewers to conclude the drug is safe and effective when used for the proposed indication and can be manufactured consistently under controlled conditions.
- FDA will act on a submitted application by issuing either a complete response letter or an approval letter, based on its application assessment. Complete response letters are issued when deficiencies are identified. Approval letters are issued once FDA has determined the drug is safe, effective, can be acceptably manufactured and is labeled appropriately. FDA can require a REMS, postmarketing studies or clinical trials following approval.
- Ongoing application maintenance is required for the application's lifetime. Maintenance includes, but is not limited to, adverse event reporting, annual report submission and submission of advertising and promotional labeling.
- Many incentives and programs are available to expedite drug development, review and approval. Many of these incentives focus on the development, review and approval of drugs intended to treat serious or life-threatening conditions and/or address unmet medical needs.

Chapter 6

Postapproval Submissions and Compliance: Prescription Drugs and Biologics

Updated by Emily Rapp, RAC and Dar Rosario, MBA, RAC

OBJECTIVES

❑ Define and review postmarketing requirements and commitments

❑ Define and review postapproval reporting requirements for prescription marketing applications, including chemistry, manufacturing and controls (CMC) and labeling changes, postmarketing surveillance and annual reports

❑ Understand the impact of changes to an approved product and the information that must be communicated to the agency when such changes are made

LAWS, REGULATIONS AND GUIDELINES COVERED IN THIS CHAPTER

❑ 21 CFR 7.40–7.59 Recalls (Including Product Corrections)—Guidance on Policy, Procedures, and Industry Responsibilities

❑ 21 CFR 207 Requirements for Foreign and Domestic Establishment Registration and Listing for Human Drugs, Including Drugs That Are Regulated Under a Biologics License Application, and Animal Drugs, and the National Drug Code

❑ 21 CFR 210 Current Good Manufacturing Practice in Manufacturing, Processing, Packing, or Holding of Drugs; General

❑ 21 CFR 211 Current Good Manufacturing Practice for Finished Pharmaceuticals

❑ 21 CFR 211.198 Complaint files

❑ 21 CFR 314.70 Supplements and other changes to an approved NDA

❑ 21 CFR 314.71 Procedures for submission of a supplement to an approved application

❑ 21 CFR 314.72 Change in ownership of an application

❑ 21 CFR 314.80 Postmarketing reporting of adverse drug experiences

❑ 21 CFR 314.81 Other postmarketing reports

❑ 21 CFR 314.97 Supplements and other changes to an approved ANDA

❑ 21 CFR 314.98 Postmarketing reports

❑ 21 CFR 314.99 Other responsibilities of an applicant of an ANDA

❑ 21 CFR 314.150 Withdrawal of approval of an application or abbreviated application

❑ 21 CFR 314.151 Withdrawal of approval of an abbreviated new drug application under 505(j)(5) of the act

- 21 CFR 314.152 Notice of withdrawal of an application or abbreviated application for a new drug

- 21 CFR 314.153 Suspension of approval of an abbreviated new drug application

- 21 CFR 314.170 Adulteration and misbranding of an approved drug

- 21 CFR 314.420 Drug Master Files

- 21 CFR 600.80 Postmarketing reporting of adverse experiences

- 21 CFR 600.81 Distribution reports

- 21 CFR 600.82 Notification of a permanent discontinuance or an interruption in manufacturing

- ICH, Medical Dictionary for Regulatory Activities (MedDRA) M1

- *Guideline for Drug Master Files* (September 1989)

- *Guideline for Postmarketing Reporting of Adverse Drug Experiences* (March 1992)

- *Guidance for Industry: Guideline for Adverse Experience Reporting for Licensed Biological Products* (October 1993)

- *Guidance for Industry: Format and Content for the CMC Section of an Annual Report* (September 1994)

- *Guidance for Industry: SUPAC-IR: Immediate-Release Solid Oral Dosage Forms: Scale-Up and Postapproval Changes: Chemistry, Manufacturing and Controls, In Vitro Dissolution Testing and In Vivo Bioequivalence Documentation* (November 1995)

- *SUPAC-IR: Questions and Answers about SUPAC-IR Guidance* (February 1997)

- *Guidance for Industry: SUPAC-SS: Nonsterile Semisolid Dosage Forms; Scale-Up and Post-Approval Changes: Chemistry, Manufacturing and Controls; In Vitro Release Testing and In Vivo Bioequivalence Documentation* (May 1997)

- *Guidance for Industry: Changes to an Approved Application for Specified Biotechnology and Specified Synthetic Biological Products* (July 1997)

- *Guidance for Industry: Postmarketing Adverse Experience Reporting for Human Drug and Licensed Biological Products: Clarification of What to Report* (August 1997)

- *Guidance for Industry: SUPAC-MR: Modified Release Solid Oral Dosage Forms Scale-Up and Postapproval Changes: Chemistry, Manufacturing, and Controls; In Vitro Dissolution Testing and In Vivo Bioequivalence Documentation* (October 1997)

- *Guidance for Industry: PAC-ATLS: Postapproval Changes—Analytical Testing Laboratory Sites* (April 1998)

- ICH, *Good Manufacturing Practice Guide for Active Pharmaceutical Ingredients Q7* (November 2000)

- *Guidance for Industry: Changes to an Approved NDA or ANDA: Questions and Answers* (January 2001)

- *Draft Guidance for Industry: Postmarketing Safety Reporting for Human Drug and Biological Products Including Vaccines* (March 2001)

- *Guidance for Industry: Changes to an Approved NDA or ANDA* (April 2004)

- *Guidance for Industry: Changes to an Approved NDA or ANDA; Specifications—Use of Enforcement Discretion for Compendial Changes* (November 2004)

- *Guidance for Industry: Providing Regulatory Submissions in Electronic Format—Drug Establishment Registration and Drug Listing* (May 2009)

- ICH, *Pharmaceutical Development Q8 (R2)* (August 2009)

- *Guidance for Industry: CMC Postapproval Manufacturing Changes To Be Documented in Annual Reports* (March 2014)

- ❏ *Draft Guidance for Industry: Providing Submissions in Electronic Format – Postmarketing Safety Reports* (June 2014)

- ❏ *Draft Guidance for Industry: SUPAC: Manufacturing Equipment Addendum* (December 2014)

- ❏ ICH, *Guideline on Clinical Safety Data Management—Data Elements for Transmission of Individual Case Safety Reports E2B(R3)* (April 2015)

- ❏ *Draft Guidance for Industry: Established Conditions: Reportable CMC Changes for Approved Drug and Biologic Products* (May 2015)

- ❏ *Draft Guidance for Industry: Comparability Protocols for Human Drugs and Biologics: Chemistry, Manufacturing, and Controls Information* (April 2016)

- ❏ *Guidance for Industry: Providing Postmarket Periodic Safety Reports in the ICH E2C(R2) Format* (November 2016)

- ❏ *Draft Guidance for Industry: CMC Postapproval Manufacturing Changes for Specified Biological Products to be Documented in Annual Reports* (August 2017)

- ❏ *Draft Guidance for Industry: Format and Content of a REMS Document* (October 2017)

- ❏ ICH, *Draft Guideline for Technical and Regulatory Considerations for Pharmaceutical Product Lifecycle Management Q12* (November 2017)

- ❏ *Draft Guidance for Industry: Chemistry, Manufacturing, and Controls Changes to an Approved Application: Certain Biological Products* (December 2017)

- ❏ *Guidance for Industry: Field Alert Report Submission Questions and Answers* (July 2018)

- ❏ *Draft Guidance for Industry: Postapproval Changes to Drug Substances* (September 2018)

- ❏ *The Comprehensive Table of Contents Headings and Hierarchy* (November 2018)

- ❏ *Guidance for Industry: Providing Regulatory Submissions in Electronic Format—Certain Human Pharmaceutical Product Applications and Related Submissions Using the eCTD Specifications* (January 2019)

Introduction

Prescription product manufacturers, distributors and marketers are required to comply with regulations throughout the product lifecycle, from early development through product commercial marketing, discontinuation or withdrawal. Preapproval requirements differ from those in the postapproval stage; however, both stages focus on product safety and quality. In the clinical development phases, product manufacturers are required to adhere to current Good Manufacturing Practice (CGMP) regulations, and sponsors are required to report changes that potentially may affect the product's safety and quality to the US Food and Drug Administration (FDA) during clinical evaluation. These same requirements apply to approved marketing applications and commercial production. After approval, commercial experience is gained, and changes, such as those that can reduce the possibility of supply disruption due to quality problems, lower production costs and improve quality, may be identified. Postapproval maintenance and lifecycle management must be reported as required through codified regulation and guidance. These requirements are similar for products approved under a New Drug Application (NDA), Biologics License Application (BLA) or an Abbreviated New Drug Application (ANDA).

This chapter discusses important postapproval activities, including postmarketing requirements, postmarketing commitments and establishment registrations and product listings. It also examines the application holder's postapproval responsibilities. An approved marketing application holder is required to comply with CGMPs; communicate any change with a potential to impact product identity, strength, quality, purity or potency and safety to FDA; establish product complaint monitoring and complaint handling procedures; and promptly investigate adverse experience reports and initiate action if needed.

Postmarketing Requirements and Commitments

Postmarketing requirement and commitment studies and clinical trials occur after a drug or biological product has been approved by FDA. A sponsor may commit to conducting postapproval studies or clinical trials for a product, known as postmarketing commitments (PMC). Alternately, in some instances, FDA may require certain studies or clinical trials, referred to as Postmarketing Requirements (PMR). The 2007 *Food and Drug Administration Amendments Act* (*FDAAA*) specifically provides FDA with authority to require manufacturers to conduct postmarket safety studies and clinical trials to further evaluate a potential safety issue, better characterize risk factors for a known safety issue and to further characterize a product's use in the therapeutic arsenal. Postmarketing studies the agency may require include:[1]

- postmarketing studies or clinical trials to demonstrate clinical benefit for products approved under the accelerated approval requirements in 21 CFR 314.510 and 21 CFR 601.41
- deferred pediatric studies (21 CFR 314.55(b) and 601.27(b)), where studies are required under the *Pediatric Research Equity Act* (*PREA*)
- studies or clinical trials to demonstrate safety and efficacy in humans that must be conducted at the time products approved under the Animal Efficacy Rule (21 CFR 314.610(b)(1) and 601.91(b)(1)) are used
- studies to assess a known serious risk related to product use
- studies to assess signals of serious risk related to product use
- studies to identify a potential unexpected serious risk indicated by available data

To keep the public informed, the agency maintains a database of postmarketing requirements and commitments, including study status, at http://www.accessdata.fda.gov/scripts/cder/pmc/index.cfm. The *Food and Drug Administration Modernization Act* of 1997 (*FDAMA*) requires the agency to publish an annual notice in the *Federal Register*, with information on postmarket study and clinical trial performance FDA had required or requested manufacturers to perform. The annual report is intended to summarize the data in FDA's internal PMR and PMC databases, which are used to track the PMR and PMC status. PMR and PMC status is tracked as submitted, fulfilled or released. Once the agreed-upon studies and trials are completed, the manufacturer submits a final report to FDA. The agency reviews the final reports and issues fulfillment or release letters as appropriate.

There also are postmarketing requirements and commitments agreed with the applicant related to the application's chemistry, manufacturing and controls (quality) aspects, which are not typically included in formal requirement and commitment discussions or included in the FDA database. Nonetheless, it is still critical for applicants to track and meet quality requirements and commitments in addition to the PMRs and PMCs.

Changes to an Approved Application

After approval, the product transitions to lifecycle management and postapproval maintenance. Applicants, for a variety of reasons, often implement changes in established product, production process, quality controls, equipment, facilities, or labeling in an approved application. For example, changes may be proposed due to raw material availability, compendial updates, technological advances or manufacturing process improvements. Recognizing the need for continual process performance and product quality improvements, the regulations provide a mechanism for product application holders to report postapproval changes. Under the *Food, Drug, and Cosmetic Act* of 1938 (*FD&C Act*), nearly all changes to an approved marketing application must be reported to FDA. *FD&C Act* Section 506A identifies the requirements for making and reporting manufacturing changes to an approved application or license and distributing a product made with such changes. An applicant must assess the change's potential to adversely impact the product; the associated postapproval submission provides data to demonstrate the change's lack of an adverse effect on product identity, strength, quality, purity or potency related to its safety or effectiveness.[2] FDA has issued guidance to assist applicants in determining which reporting mechanism is appropriate for reporting a change, based on assessing the effect, to reduce the applicant's burden when reporting changes, and to facilitate the approval process for the proposed change. Submissions of editorial changes, such as typographical and spelling error corrections or formatting changes to standard operating procedures or batch records, are not required.[3]

It is critical that an application holder maintain a robust change management process to ensure the impact of proposed product changes are assessed appropriately and are well-documented. A successful change management process will ensure the change's impact is categorized correctly to reduce any risk of FDA re-categorization, which can lead to review, approval and product distribution delays. Additionally, good postapproval change documentation will ensure all necessary information is available when preparing application supplements and/or annual reports.

Specific regulations for supplements and other changes to an approved application are codified in 21 CFR 314.70 and 21 CFR 601.12 for drugs and biologics, respectively. General rules for approved marketing application supplements include:

- an applicant must assess a proposed change's effects
- only the applicant may submit a supplement to the application
- only information supporting the proposed change(s) is required to be submitted

- all FDA procedures and actions applicable to original applications also apply to supplements

Under *FD&C Act* Section 745A and in accordance with *Guidance for Industry: Providing Regulatory Submissions in Electronic Format—Certain Human Pharmaceutical Product Applications and Related Submissions Using the eCTD Specifications* (January 2019), supplements to approved NDAs, ANDAs and certain BLAs are required to be submitted in electronic Common Technical Document (eCTD) format as of May 2017.

As briefly discussed above, the change category (i.e., the change's potential to adversely impact the product) determines the submission reporting category.

Three postapproval CMC change categories are described in 21 CFR 314.70 and 21 CFR 601.12:
- major (314.70(b))/601.12(b)—prior approval before distribution or Prior Approval Supplement (PAS)
- moderate (314.70(c))/601.12(c)—changes being effected in 30 days (CBE-30) or CBE-0
- minor (314.70(d))/601.12(d)—annual report

An applicant may ask FDA to expedite its review of a supplement for public health reasons or if a delay in making the change would impose an extraordinary hardship on the applicant (21 CFR 314.70(b)(4) and 21 CFR 601.12 (b)(4)). As indicated previously, these changes are categorized based on their potential to adversely affect the product's identity, strength, quality, purity or potency. **Figure 6-1** summarizes the reporting categories for approved application changes.

Proposed product labeling changes also must be evaluated to determine the reporting category. Labeling changes are classified as major, moderate or minor and reported to FDA as described above. For example, a change to the product labeling's clinical pharmacology or clinical study sections would be classified as a major change and would require submission and approval of a PAS to FDA before distribution. Alternatively, an editorial change, such as adding a distributor's name, is considered an annual reportable change; annual reportable changes can be implemented and the product distributed without formal FDA approval.

A supplement or annual report must include a list of all changes being proposed or implemented. FDA recommends the applicant describe each change in enough detail to allow the agency to determine quickly whether the appropriate reporting category was used. If the agency determines an incorrect reporting category was assigned to a change, the change will be re-categorized, and the sponsor must adhere to the new categorization distribution requirements. For example, if FDA re-categorizes a change from a CBE-30 to a PAS, the product incorporating the change cannot be marketed until the agency reviews and approves the change. For supplements, the cover letter must list the changes.[4] In annual reports, the CMC summary section should include the list of changes.[5] The applicant must describe each change fully in the supplement or annual report body.[6] An applicant making a change to an approved application under *FD&C Act* Section 506A also must conform to other applicable laws and regulations, including CGMP requirements under the act (21 U.S.C. 351(a)(2)(B)) and applicable regulations in 21 CFR 210, 211 and 314.

FDA will review each supplement and annual report for completeness and adequate justification and/or data to support the change, if needed. If FDA determines a supplement or annual report is deficient, the sponsor cannot distribute the product until it addresses the deficiency required by the agency. If the product with the proposed change is in commercial distribution already (e.g., the product was distributed after a Changes Being Effected (CBE) supplement was submitted), and FDA believes the supplement is deficient, the agency may order the manufacturer to cease product distribution until the supplement is amended and subsequently approved.

To aid sponsors in interpreting the regulations set forth in 21 CFR 314.70 and 21 CFR 601.12, FDA has issued several guidance documents:
- *Guidance for Industry: Changes to an Approved Application: Biological Products* (July 1997)
- *Guidance for Industry: PAC-ATLS: Postapproval Changes—Analytical Testing Laboratory Sites* (April 1998)
- *Guidance for Industry: Changes to an Approved NDA or ANDA: Questions and Answers* (January 2001)
- *Guidance for Industry: Changes to an Approved NDA or ANDA* (April 2004)
- *Guidance for Industry: Changes to an Approved NDA or ANDA: Specifications—Use of Enforcement Discretion for Compendial Changes* (November 2004)
- *Draft Guidance for Industry: Chemistry, Manufacturing and Controls Changes to an Approved Application: Certain Biological Products* (December 2017)

Additionally, the agency issued *Guidance for Industry: CMC Postapproval Manufacturing Changes To Be Documented in Annual Reports* (March 2014) and *Draft Guidance for Industry: CMC Postapproval Manufacturing Changes for Specified Biological Products To Be Documented in Annual Reports* (August 2017) to further clarify its thinking on annual reportable CMC changes considered to have minimal potential to have an adverse effect on product quality.

Chapter 6

Figure 6-1. Summery of Reporting Categories for Postapproval Changes

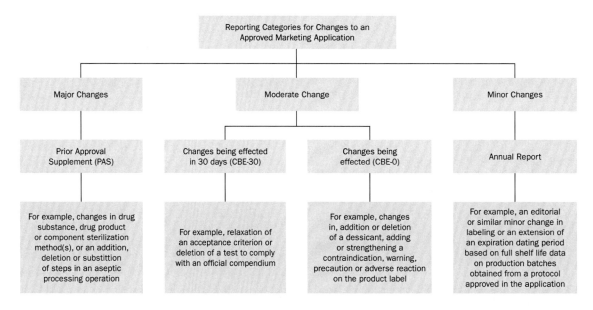

Source: Guidance for Industry: Changes to an Approved NDA or ANDA (April 2004)

These guidance documents provide direction on postapproval changes to:[7]
- components and composition
- manufacturing sites
- analytical testing laboratory sites
- manufacturing process, batch size and equipment
- specifications
- container closure system
- labeling
- miscellaneous changes
- multiple related changes

It is important to note FDA guidance documents do not establish legally enforceable responsibilities. Guidances describe the agency's current thinking on a topic and should be viewed as recommendations, unless specific regulatory or statutory requirements are cited. Alternative approaches may be acceptable if the approach satisfies the requirements of the applicable statutes and regulations. Not all changes are addressed directly by guidance or regulation; in such cases, the application holder is encouraged to consider consulting FDA. If this approach is pursued, it is important to understand the change's scope and its potential impact on product identity, strength, quality, purity or potency, safety and effectiveness. Having a proposed plan regarding the product's filing category, documentation and data package is key in obtaining FDA feedback and agreement on the regulatory strategy.

Further to the pursuit of postapproval changes, FDA issued guidance documents to aid applicants or manufacturers in determining the documentation required to support certain postapproval changes. The most notable of these for drug products, particularly, are the Scale-Up and Postapproval Changes (SUPAC) guidance documents, which detail the chemistry information and potential bioequivalence study requirements associated with scale-up postapproval changes. Additionally, these guidance documents assess the changes' associated risk levels (e.g., manufacturing process, manufacturing site, product formula, equipment, batch size, etc.). The SUPAC documents classify changes into three levels that correspond to minor, moderate and major changes, respectively. Level 1 changes are annual reportable changes, e.g., site changes within a single facility or process changes within validated ranges. Level 2 changes, such as certain changes in composition or manufacturing equipment, are filed in CBE-0 or CBE-30 supplements (Changes Being Effected immediately or in 30 days, respectively). Level 3 changes require a PAS and can range from site changes to the use of a new manufacturer with no experience with the product type. Due to the complexity of manufacturing biological products, SUPAC guidance documents are available only for small molecule products. However, the SUPAC principles may assist biological product applicants in establishing strategies that might support postapproval BLA changes.

The following SUPAC guidance documents provide information on the expected documentation and data when certain changes are filed:

- *Guidance for Industry: SUPAC-IR: Immediate-Release Solid Oral Dosage Forms: Scale-Up and Post-Approval Changes: Chemistry, Manufacturing and Controls, In Vitro Dissolution Testing, and In Vivo Bioequivalence Documentation* (November 1995)
- *SUPAC-IR: Questions and Answers about SUPAC-IR* (February 1997)
- *Guidance for Industry: SUPAC-SS: Nonsterile Semisolid Dosage Forms; Scale-Up and Post-Approval Changes: Chemistry, Manufacturing and Controls; In Vitro Release Testing and In Vivo Bioequivalence Documentation* (May 1997)
- *Guidance for Industry: SUPAC-MR: Modified Release Solid Oral Dosage Forms Scale-Up and Postapproval Changes: Chemistry, Manufacturing, and Controls; In Vitro Dissolution Testing and In Vivo Bioequivalence Documentation* (October 1997)
- *Guidance for Industry: SUPAC: Manufacturing Equipment Addendum* (December 2014)

Postapproval changes also can be implemented by using a comparability protocol (CP) to NDAs, ANDAs and BLAs. A CP is a comprehensive, prospectively written plan to assess a proposed CMC change's effect on a drug or biological product's identity, strength, quality, purity and potency related to the product's safety or effectiveness (i.e., quality). A CP submitted in an original application, or as a PAS after approval, allows the agency to review the description of one or more proposed CMC postapproval change(s), supporting information (including an analysis and risk assessment), a specific plan to implement the change(s) and, if appropriate, a proposed reduced change reporting category. A CP should clearly describe the change(s) the protocol covers, including specifying tests and studies to be performed, analytical methods to be used and acceptance criteria to demonstrate specified CMC changes do not adversely affect product quality. Submitting a comparability protocol is optional. In many cases, it facilitates potential and planned changes so distribution and product availability are not delayed. Although this option can help reduce future changes' review timeline(s), a very detailed CP sometimes can be a challenge to follow and implement, as circumstances often change over time. If the CP's terms cannot be met, an applicant will have to file either a PAS to amend the approved protocol or a new protocol via a PAS.[8]

Postapproval changes in a Quality-by-Design (QbD) development and validation program, as detailed in the International Council for Harmonisation (ICH) guidelines on Pharmaceutical Development Q8(R2), Quality Risk Management Q9, and Pharmaceutical Quality System Q10, also may reduce reporting requirements.

FDA issued *Draft Guidance for Industry: Established Conditions: Reportable CMC Changes for Approved Drug and Biologic Products* (May 2015) to provide additional clarification on which CMC changes the agency considers reportable and which may be managed by the sponsor's Pharmaceutical Quality System (PQS). A description of established conditions is intended to support development of the forthcoming *ICH Q12 Guideline for Technical and Regulatory Considerations for Pharmaceutical Product Lifecycle Management.*[9] The ICH Q12 guideline will provide a framework to efficiently manage postapproval CMC changes throughout the product lifecycle.[10]

CGMP Compliance for Manufacturing, Processing, Packing or Holding of Drugs and Finished Pharmaceuticals

Manufacturers of approved products and those undergoing human clinical trials are required to adhere to CGMP regulations, 21 CFR 210 and 21 CFR 211. CGMP regulations establish minimum requirements for manufacturing and process controls, personnel, equipment, product container and closure controls, facilities, packaging, holding and distribution procedures, laboratory controls and records. The regulations are intended to ensure products are safe and meet all quality, identity, strength and purity requirements through the entire product lifecycle. Additionally, CGMP regulations require all manufacturing and testing equipment to be qualified as suitable for use, and all operational methodologies and procedures (such as manufacturing, cleaning and analytical testing) utilized in the manufacturing process to be validated (according to predetermined specifications) to demonstrate they can perform their purported function(s) in a reliable and consistent manner.

Active Pharmaceutical Ingredients (APIs) are subject to the adulteration provisions of *FD&C* Act Section 501(a)(2)(B), which requires all drugs to be manufactured in conformance with CGMPs. The act makes no distinction between an API and a finished pharmaceutical, and failure of either to comply with CGMPs violates the act. FDA has not promulgated CGMP regulations specifically for APIs or drug and biologic components because it is recognized the CGMP regulations for finished pharmaceuticals (21 CFR 210 and 211) are valid and applicable to API manufacturing in the context of both drugs and biologics. These concepts include designing quality into the product by using suitable equipment and employing appropriately qualified and trained personnel, establishing adequate written procedures and controls to ensure manufacturing processes are valid, establishing a system of in-process material testing and final product tests, and ensuring the product's stability for its intended period of use. In 2001, FDA adopted an internationally harmonized guidance for industry on API CGMPs in conjunction with ICH regulatory partners. This guidance, *Good Manufacturing Practice Guidance for Active Pharmaceutical Ingredients Q7,* represents FDA's current thinking on API CGMPs and covers APIs manufactured by chemical synthesis, extraction, cell culture or fermentation, recovery from natural sources or any combination of these processes. Thus, API and related manufacturing and testing facilities following this guidance generally will be considered to be in compliance with the statutory CGMP requirements.

Postmarketing Reporting of Adverse Experiences

Each applicant of an approved application under 21 CFR 314.98, 21 CFR 314.80 and 21 CFR 600.80, for an ANDA, NDA and BLA, respectively, are required to review adverse experiences. An applicant must promptly review all adverse drug experiences or adverse product experiences, herein referred to as adverse experiences (AEs), regardless of the source (foreign or domestic).

Potential AE information also may be derived from:
- information from commercial marketing experience
- postmarketing clinical investigations
- postmarketing epidemiological or surveillance studies
- reports in scientific literature
- unpublished scientific papers

It is important to recognize the existence of additional adverse experience data sources not specified in the regulations. For example, the internet and social media play significant roles in how patients interact with each other and their care providers. Approved application holders should review AE reports received on websites they sponsor; however, the agency currently does not hold sponsors responsible for AEs posted to sites they do not sponsor.[11] Approved application holders should, at minimum, assess the information to determine whether it should be reported to FDA. FDA also will submit AE reports to applicants. Although the applicant is not required to resubmit information FDA has forwarded to it, regulations do require the applicant to provide all follow-up information on such reports to the agency.

In addition to AE review requirements, the application holder is required to develop written procedures for surveillance, receipt, evaluation and postmarketing reporting of AEs to FDA.[12]

Postmarketing AE reporting requirements apply to any company whose name appears on an approved product label as a manufacturer, packer or distributor. However, the regulations permit non-applicants to satisfy these reporting requirements by submitting all serious AE reports to the applicant. If a non-applicant chooses to submit AE reports to the applicant rather than FDA, the non-applicant must submit each report to the sponsor within five calendar days of receiving it; then, the applicant is responsible for submitting these AE reports to FDA.[13]

The applicant is required to submit the following AE reports to FDA within the specified timeframes in electronic format:
- Postmarketing 15-Day Alert Reports—A sponsor must report all AEs (foreign or domestic) that are both serious and unexpected to FDA as soon as possible but no later than 15 calendar days from the initial receipt of information. The applicant must investigate all AE reports promptly and submit follow-up reports within 15 calendar days of receipt of new information, or as requested by FDA. If additional information is not obtainable, records should be maintained of the unsuccessful attempts to seek the additional information.
- Periodic Adverse Drug Experience Reports (PADER) and Periodic Adverse Experience Reports (PAER)—For the first three years following product approval, a sponsor shall submit the PADER or PAER on a quarterly basis. It is due within 30 days after the end of each quarter. Unless otherwise requested by FDA, after three years, the sponsor shall submit a PADER or PAER at annual intervals, due 60 days from the anniversary of the application's approval. Each periodic report should contain:
  o a narrative summary and analysis of the report's information, including all AE information obtained during the reporting period
  o analysis of 15-Day Alert Reports submitted during the reporting interval
  o a history of actions taken during the reporting period due to AEs (e.g., labeling changes or additional studies initiated)
  o an index including the applicant's patient identification code and adverse reaction term(s) for all individual case safety reports
  o Individual Case Safety Reports (ICRSs) for serious, expected and non-serious adverse experiences

FDA has provided guidance regarding submitting AE reports in electronic format in *Draft Guidance for Industry: Providing Submissions in Electronic Format—Postmarketing Safety Reports* (June 2014).

In November 1996, ICH endorsed the E2C Periodic Safety Update Guideline (ICH E2C(R1) guideline), which established the Periodic Safety Update Report (PSUR) as a harmonized format for postmarketing periodic safety reports for drug and biologic products and described the format, content and timing of PSUR submissions. FDA adopted the guideline, which was published in 1997 as *Guidance for Industry: E2C Clinical Safety Data Management: Periodic Safety Update Reports for Marketed Drugs,* and published an addendum to clarify some aspects of the guideline.

Since introducing the PSUR reporting format, FDA has granted waivers under 314.90(b) and 600.90(b) to allow applicants to substitute the PSUR for the PADER or PAER (PSUR waiver).

As described in *Guidance for Industry: Providing Postmarket Periodic Safety Reports in the ICH E2C(R2) Format Periodic Benefit-Risk Evaluation Report (PBRER)* (November 2016), applicants can use an alternative reporting format, the PBRER, in place of the US PADER, PAER or PSUR to satisfy the periodic postmarketing safety report requirements in 21 CFR 314.80 (c)(2) and 21 CFR 600.60 (c)(2). Like the PSUR, the harmonized PBRER is intended to promote a consistent approach to periodic postmarketing safety reporting among the ICH regions and enhance efficiency by reducing the number of reports submitted to regulatory authorities. If applicants already have a PSUR waiver for an approved application, FDA will consider the existing PSUR waiver to allow applicants to submit a PBRER instead of a PSUR under certain conditions because the PBRER replaces the PSUR for postmarketing safety reporting. If applicants do not already have a PSUR waiver and wish to submit a PBRER format, a waiver must be requested under 21 CFR 314.90(a) or 21 CFR 600.90(a).

To encourage healthcare professionals to collect, evaluate and report serious AEs, FDA developed the MedWatch educational and publicity program in 1993 (www.fda.gov/Safety/MedWatch/default.htm). Sponsors, manufacturers, distributors and user facilities use MedWatch Form 3500A for mandatory reporting of both adverse events and problems with human drugs and other FDA-regulated products. Healthcare professionals, consumers and patients may use MedWatch Form 3500 (or Form 3500B for a consumer-friendly form) for spontaneous AE reporting to the sponsor or directly to FDA. Foreign reportable AEs also may be submitted on forms developed by the Council for International Organizations of Medical Sciences (CIOMS).

FDA tracks adverse product reaction reports by entering all safety reports for approved drugs and therapeutic biological products into the FDA Adverse Event Reporting System (FAERS) database, which uses standardized international terminology from the Medical Dictionary for Regulatory Activities (MedDRA). FDA uses FAERS to facilitate postmarketing surveillance and compliance activities, with the goal of improving public health by providing the best available tools for storing and analyzing safety data and reports. Data and trends from FAERS may lead to FDA action on products, such as safety alerts communicated via FDA's website, "Dear Health Care Professional" letters or requests to sponsors for additional safety studies. This is part of an FDA initiative to collect, analyze and disseminate product safety information rapidly and is highlighted in *Guidance: Drug Safety Information—FDA's Communication to the Public* (March 2007 and March 2012). FDA also uses this information to update product labeling and, on rare occasions, to re-evaluate the approval and marketing decision.

Risk Evaluation and Mitigation Strategies

In 2007, the Food and Drug Administration Amendments Act *(FDAAA),* renewing the *Prescription Drug User Fee Act (PDUFA IV),* gave FDA authority to require manufacturers to create risk management plans, called Risk Evaluation and Mitigation Strategies (REMS), in addition to a product's current labeling, to ensure a drug or biological product's benefits outweigh its risks. A sponsor may propose a REMS as part of an application if it is deemed necessary. FDA may require a REMS during initial application review or any time after a product is approved for marketing if the agency becomes aware of new safety information and determines a REMS is necessary to ensure the drug or biological product's benefits continue to outweigh its risks. If FDA determines a REMS is necessary, it may require one or more REMS elements, which could include a Medication Guide, a patient package insert and/or a communication plan and implementation system. FDA also may require elements to assure safe use (ETASU) as part of a REMS *(FD&C Act* Section 505-1(f)). All REMS should include one or more overall goals, and if it has ETASU, the REMS must include one or more goals to mitigate any specific serious risk listed in the product's labeling and for which the ETASU is required. The REMS generally must include a timetable for assessing the REMS' effectiveness in achieving its stated goals and submit the assessment to FDA by 18 months, three years and seven years after its initial approval. Assessment of results may support eliminating the REMS after three years. Additional assessment dates can be added if more frequent assessments are required to ensure the product's benefits continue to outweigh its risks.[14] As noted in *Draft Guidance for Industry: Format and Content of a REMS Document* (October 2017*),* ANDA sponsors are not mandated to submit assessments of REMS' effectiveness per a timetable; however, FDA can require the submissions from any application holder, including ANDA sponsors.

Elements of a REMS may include:
- Medication Guide and/or a Patient Package Insert—materials written for the patient to help ensure the product's safe use

- Communication Plan—explains to healthcare providers the strategy being employed to ensure the product's benefits outweigh its risks
- Elements to Assure Safe Use (ETASU)—e.g., requiring healthcare providers who prescribe the product to have particular training or experience or be specially certified; dispensing the product to patients only in certain healthcare settings, such as hospitals; monitoring patients using the product
- Implementation System

FDA maintains a list of approved REMS (http://www.accessdata.fda.gov/scripts/cder/rems/index.cfm).

A sponsor may propose modifying an approved REMS, and such a proposal must include a REMS assessment. Additionally, FDA may determine new safety information requires an element of the REMS to be modified; this also will require the sponsor to assess the REMS. A proposal to modify an approved REMS should be submitted in a new PAS if it is not already associated with an existing application.[15]

If an approved brand-name drug utilizes a REMS, any generic versions also requires a REMS. In these cases, the brand-name and generic manufacturers may work together to create a joint REMS known as a shared system REMS. In November 2017, FDA published *Draft Guidance for Industry: Use of a Drug Master File for Shared System REMS Submissions* to recommend use of a Type V Drug Master File for shared system REMS submissions. It is important to note that brand-name and generic manufacturers also may have different REMS, but both documents would have the "same goal(s), the same requirements, and comparable processes in place to meet those goals and requirements."[16]

Reporting Field Alert Events

The purpose of Field Alert Reports (FARs), required under 21 CFR 314.81(b), is to quickly identify quality defects in distributed product that may pose a potential safety threat. Approved NDA, BLA or ANDA holders are required to submit FARs within three working days (Monday through Friday) of becoming aware of any significant problem with a distributed product.[17]

FDA recommends that applicants use Form FDA 3331a to submit FARs electronically, as this will expedite FDA's review process. FARs submitted initially by telephone or other rapid means in 21 CFR 314.81(b)(1) must submit Form 3331a. Once a Form FDA 3331a is submitted, the information will be available to CDER or CBER and the FDA district responsible for the facility.

21 CFR 314.81(b)(1) requires the following information be reported in an FAR:[18]
- incidents causing the product or its labeling to be mistaken for or applied to another article
- bacterial contamination
- any significant chemical, physical or other change or deterioration in the distributed product
- any failure of one or more distributed product batches to meet the specifications established in the approved application

Annual Reports

As outlined in 21 CFR 314.81(b)(2), approved NDA and ANDA application holders are required to submit annual reports to FDA. Routine annual reports, such as those required under NDA and ANDA regulations, are not mandatory for BLAs. The regulations require annual reports for products marketed under a BLA for certain changes made to the application per 21 CFR 601.12 (d), summaries on submissions related to pediatric studies per 21 CFR 601.28, and status reports on postmarketing requirements and commitments related to clinical safety, clinical efficacy, clinical pharmacology or nonclinical toxicology per 21 CFR 601.70.[19] The annual report is sent to the division responsible for the application's review. The reporting period is defined as one full year from the anniversary date of the application's approval; the annual report must be submitted within 60 days of this anniversary date. Annual report content is outlined below.

FDA Forms and Cover Letter

The annual report should include a cover letter, which indicates product name, application number, reporting period and any additional information the sponsor may wish to bring to the agency's immediate attention. Additionally, a completed Form FDA 2252 (Transmittal of Annual Reports for Drugs and Biologics for Human Use) is to be submitted with the annual report.[20] Per the *Comprehensive Table of Contents Headings and Hierarchy*, much of the information described below is compiled in Section 1.13 Annual Report. Labeling information is compiled in Section 1.14. Nonclinical and clinical literature are compiled in Modules 4 and 5, respectively.

Summary of Significant New Information[21]
- a brief summary of significant new information from the previous year that might affect the product's safety, effectiveness or labeling, and a description of actions the sponsor has taken or intends to take as a result of this new information
- indication of whether labeling supplements for pediatric use have been submitted, and whether new studies in the pediatric population have been initiated to support appropriate labeling for the pediatric population
- where possible, an estimate of patient exposure to the product, with special reference to the pediatric

population (neonates, infants, children and adolescents), including dosage form

Distribution Data[22]
- quantity of product distributed under the approved application, including amounts provided to distributors (The distribution data must include the National Drug Code (NDC) number and total number of dosage units of each strength or potency.)
- quantities distributed for domestic and foreign use
- disclosure of financial or pricing data is not required

Authorized Generic Drugs[23]
- for any authorized generics for a product, the dates the product(s) entered the market and ceased being distributed

Labeling[24]
- current professional labeling, patient brochures or package inserts and representative samples of package labels
- content of labeling required under 21 CFR 201.100(d)(3) (i.e., the package insert or professional labeling), including all text, tables and figures provided in electronic format in a form FDA can process, review and archive
- a summary of any labeling changes made since the last report, listed by date in the order in which they were implemented or, if no changes, a statement of that fact

Chemistry, Manufacturing and Controls[25]
- reports of experiences, investigations, studies or tests involving the physical or chemical properties, or any other properties of the product (The reports are only required for new information that may affect FDA's previous conclusions about the safety or effectiveness of the product.)
- CMC index: a current list of approved CMC information intended to aid the agency's review of the annual report (i.e., list of approved analytical methods, specifications, manufacturing sites, etc.); this should include the type and date of each change to each component, the submission type used to report the change (original, supplement or annual report) and the date the change was reported and approved, if an application was submitted (See **Figure 6-2** for an example of a CMC index.)
- a complete description of CMC changes not requiring a supplemental application under 21 CFR 314.70(b) and (c) (i.e., "annual reportable" changes) listed in order of implementation
- stability data obtained during the reporting period

Nonclinical Laboratory Studies[26]
- copies of unpublished reports and summaries of published reports of new toxicological findings in animal or *in vitro* studies (e.g., mutagenicity)
- nonclinical laboratory study reports, including all studies conducted by, or otherwise obtained by, the application holder

Clinical Data[27]
- published clinical trials (or abstracts) of the product, including clinical trials on safety and effectiveness; clinical trials on new uses; biopharmaceutic, pharmacokinetic and clinical pharmacology studies; and reports of clinical experience related to safety, conducted by the sponsor or found in the public domain
- summaries of completed unpublished clinical trials or available prepublication manuscripts conducted by the sponsor or otherwise obtained by the applicant; supporting information should not be reported (A study is consider completed one year after its conclusion.)
- analysis of available safety and efficacy data in the pediatric population and changes in labeling based on this information, including an assessment of data needed to ensure appropriate labeling for the pediatric population

Status Reports of Postmarketing Study Commitments[28]
- status report on each PMR or PMC concerning clinical safety, clinical efficacy, clinical pharmacology and nonclinical toxicology (status report content is prescribed in 314.81 (b)(2)(vii)(a))
- pediatric studies: the status report shall include a statement indicating whether postmarketing clinical studies in pediatric populations were required by FDA under §201.23 (The status of these postmarketing studies shall be reported annually until FDA notifies the applicant, in writing, that the agency concurs with the applicant's determination that the study commitment has been fulfilled or that the study is either no longer feasible or would no longer provide useful information.)

Status of Other Postmarketing Studies[29]
- status report of any postmarketing study not included in the PMR/PMC section above;

Figure 6-2. Example of a CMC Index

ATTACHMENT 1

NDA/ANDA/AADA ######
INDEX OF APPROVED CHEMISTRY, MANUFACTURING AND CONTROLS
INFORMATION

			SUBMISSION TYPE	SUBMISSION DATE	APPROVAL DATE
I.	DRUG SUBSTANCE				
	A.	Manufacturer(s)	_____	_____	_____
	B.	Method(s) of Manufacture	_____	_____	_____
	C.	Container and Closure	_____	_____	_____
	D.	Stability Protocol	_____	_____	_____
	E.	Specifications and Analytical Methods*	_____	_____	_____
II.	DRUG PRODUCT				
	A.	Composition	_____	_____	_____
	B.	Manufacturer(s)	_____	_____	_____
	C.	Method(s) of Manufacture and Packaging	_____	_____	_____
	D.	Specifications and Analytical Methods*	_____	_____	_____
	E.	Container(s) and Closure(s)	_____	_____	_____
	F.	Expiration Dating Period ___ Months	_____	_____	_____
	G.	Stability Protocol	_____	_____	_____

*Please attach a complete listing of the Specifications and Analytical Methods for the drug substance and drug product in the format provided.

Source: Guidance for Industry: Format and Content for the CMC Section of an Annual Report (September 1994)

primarily relates to CMC postmarketing studies and for all product stability studies

Log of Outstanding Regulatory Business[30]
- at the sponsor's discretion, a listing of any open regulatory business with FDA concerning the application (e.g., a list of unanswered correspondences between the sponsor and FDA, or vice-versa).

Advertising and Labeling
Under 21 CFR 314.81(b)(3)(i), the sponsor must submit specimens of mailing pieces and any other labeling or advertising devised for product promotion at the time of the promotional material's initial use and the time of initial publication of a prescription product

advertisement. A copy of the current labeling and a completed Form FDA 2253 (Transmittal of Advertisements and Promotional Labeling for Drugs and Biologics for Human Use) are required for each submission. These submissions are made to the Office of Prescription Drug Promotion (OPDP) for products regulated by CDER, and to the Advertising and Promotional Labeling Branch (APLB) for products regulated by CBER.[31] These submissions are not approved as are other submissions to FDA. Often, the agency does not respond to these submissions unless there are questions or concerns about them.

Orange Book and Purple Book

Upon marketing application approval, the drug product is listed in FDA's *Approved Drug Products with Therapeutic Equivalence Evaluations*. Commonly referred to as the *Orange Book* because the original print version had an orange cover, this reference lists patent and marketing exclusivity information associated with each approved drug product. FDA maintains an electronic version of the *Orange Book* (www.accessdata.fda.gov/scripts/cder/ob/default.cfm).

Drug products are considered to be therapeutic equivalents (generics) only if they are pharmaceutical equivalents for which bioequivalence has been demonstrated, and they can be expected to have the same clinical effect and safety profile when administered to patients under the conditions specified in the labeling.[32]

Patent information is listed in the *Orange Book* via Form FDA 3542a, which is submitted with an application, amendment or supplement, and Form FDA 3452, which is submitted upon application, amendment or supplement approval.

Under the *Drug Price Competition and Patent Term Restoration Act* of 1984, also known as the *Hatch-Waxman Act*, a company can seek FDA approval to market a generic drug before the expiration of patents related to the associated brand-name drug. To seek this approval, a generic applicant must certify that a patent submitted to FDA by the brand-name drug's sponsor and listed in the *Orange Book* is invalid, unenforceable or will not be infringed by the generic drug. This is called a paragraph IV certification.[33]

The *Purple Book* lists biological products, including any biosimilar and interchangeable biological products, licensed by FDA under the *Public Health Service Act* (the *PHS Act*). The *Purple Book* includes the date a biological product was licensed under *PHS Act* Section 351(a) and whether FDA evaluated the biological product for reference product exclusivity under Section 351(k)(7).

The *Purple Book* also indicates whether FDA has determined a biological product licensed under *PHS Act* Section 351(k) to be biosimilar to—or interchangeable with—a reference biological product (an already-licensed FDA biological product). The *Patient Protection and Affordable Care Act* (*Affordable Care Act*), signed into law by President Obama on 23 March 2010, amends the *PHS Act* to create an abbreviated licensure pathway for biological products that are demonstrated to be "biosimilar" to or "interchangeable" with an FDA-licensed biological product. This pathway is provided in the part of the *Affordable Care Act* known as the *Biologics Price Competition and Innovation Act* of 2009 (*BPCI Act*). Biosimilar and interchangeable biological products licensed under Section 351(k) will be listed under the reference product to which biosimilarity or interchangeability was demonstrated.[34] Separate lists for those biological products regulated by the Center for Drug Evaluation and Research (CDER) and the Center for Biologics Evaluation and Research (CBER) are updated periodically.

Product Complaints

The regulations outlining CGMPs for finished pharmaceuticals require the sponsor and manufacturing control sites to establish and follow written procedures describing the handling of all written and oral product complaints, per 21 CFR 211.198 Complaint files. Established procedures should include a mechanism for the organization's quality control unit to review any complaint involving an approved product's possible failure to meet any of its specifications.[35] Additionally, the procedures must include criteria to determine whether an investigation is needed in accordance with 21 CFR 211.192.

The established procedures also should include provisions to determine whether the complaint represents a serious and unexpected ADE or AE. A serious and unexpected ADE or AE is required to be reported to FDA in accordance with 21 CFR 314.80 and 21 CFR 600.80.

In addition, the sponsor is required to maintain a written record of each complaint in a designated product complaint file. The file should be maintained in a location where it can be accessed easily for review during a regulatory inspection. Written records on a product complaint should be maintained until at least one year after the product's expiration date or one year after the date the complaint was received, whichever is longer.[36]

Product Recalls

A recall is a voluntary action taken by manufacturers and distributors to remove products from the market that are in violation of laws or may present a risk of injury to the public. Recall actions may be taken on the manufacturer or distributor's initiative, or FDA may request a firm to recall a product. While FDA can take other formal administrative or civil actions to remove products from the market, recalls are more effective in removing products from the market quickly, particularly when a product has been distributed widely.[37] Industry responsibilities in conducting recalls are delineated in 21 CFR 7.40–7.59.

Additionally, recall guidance is provided in *Guidance for Industry: Product Recalls, Including Removals and Corrections* (November 2003).

Recalls are classified as Class I, II or III:
- Class I—when there is a reasonable probability the use of or exposure to a suspected product will cause serious adverse health consequences or death
- Class II—when the use of or exposure to a suspected product may cause temporary or medically reversible adverse health consequences, or where the probability of serious adverse health consequences is remote
- Class III—when use of or exposure to a suspected product is not likely to cause adverse health consequences, but the product violates FDA labeling or manufacturing laws

The agency will review a firm's proposed recall strategy and recommend changes if necessary. The firm will conduct the recall in accordance with the approved recall strategy, but should not delay initiating a recall pending review of its recall strategy.[38]

Under 21 CFR 7.42(b), the product recall strategy should address:[39]
- recall depth—depending on the product's degree of hazard and extent of distribution, the recall strategy should specify the level in the distribution chain to which the recall is to be extended, (i.e., consumer/user level, retail level or the wholesale level)
- public warnings—to alert the public a product poses a serious hazard (Public warnings are reserved for urgent situations. Whether or not a public warning is warranted will be specified in the recall strategy.)
- effectiveness checks—to ensure all affected parties have received the recall notification and have taken appropriate action

Changes to Drug Master Files Affecting Approved Applications

Drug master files (DMFs) are a way for a contract manufacturer, or an active pharmaceutical ingredient (API), excipient or packaging supplier to submit confidential information to FDA to protect intellectual property. DMFs are not required; however, they provide detailed information about facilities, processes or materials used in human drugs and biological products' manufacturing, processing, packaging, storing and shelf-life to support an application while maintaining confidentiality. The five types of US DMFs and their content are detailed in 21 CFR 314.420 and associated guidance. Unlike EU and Canadian master files, all parts of a US DMF are 'open' to FDA for review and remain 'closed' to the applicant that references the DMF in an application. DMFs also can be submitted for biological products. Specifically, biologics contract manufacturing facilities can file Type V Master Files involving proprietary information that should include all products manufactured at the facility and any non-compendial test procedures. A DMF is not a substitute for an NDA, ANDA or BLA; it is not approved or disapproved. DMF technical contents are reviewed only in connection with the review of an NDA, ANDA or BLA.

DMF holders must issue a Letter of Authorization to allow FDA to review this confidential information in support of an NDA, ANDA, BLA supplement or amendment to an NDA, ANDA, BLA or another DMF.[40]

The holder also should send a copy of the Letter of Authorization to the affected applicant, sponsor or other holder who is authorized to incorporate by reference the specific information the DMF contains. The applicant, sponsor or other holder referencing a DMF is required to include a copy of the DMF holder's Letter of Authorization in the application.

DMF holders have regulatory requirements to keep the DMF current and accessible. Once filed, DMF holders are required to submit an annual report, due on the anniversary date of the original submission, that includes a list of all parties authorized to access the DMF, and a summary of amendments reporting changes since the last annual report (or a statement that no amendments have been submitted since the last annual report).

DMF changes are submitted in the form of DMF amendments, and the firms authorized to reference the DMF are notified of any change. Similar to changes made to an approved application, the impact of changes to a DMF referenced in the application also must be evaluated to determine the appropriate reporting category (PAS, CBE-30, CBE-0 or annual report) and, thus, the timing for distributing product manufactured using the change. The marketing application sponsor must report changes to FDA as appropriate and reference the associated DMF amendment.

Since 5 May 2018, new DMFs other than Type III (packaging material) DMFs, as well as all documents submitted to existing DMFs other than Type III DMFs, are required to be submitted using the eCTD. DMF submissions after this date not in eCTD format are rejected. For Type III DMFs, the requirement goes into effect 5 May 2020.

Establishment Registration and Product Listing

All owners or operators of domestic establishments that manufacture, repack, relabel or salvage a drug or biological product must register the establishment within five calendar days after beginning the activity. All owners or operators of foreign establishments must register before a drug or biological product that is manufactured, repacked, relabeled or salvaged at the site is imported into the US. In addition, registrants must list each product in commercial distribution with FDA within three calendar days after the initial establishment registration. The product listing also must include bulk drugs for commercial distribution, whether they are involved in interstate commerce or not. Among other things, establishment registration and product listing allow FDA to track commercially distributed products, monitor product shortages, conduct postmarket surveillance and prepare user fee assessments. The regulations permit submission registration and listing by the parent, subsidiary or affiliate company for operations conducted at more than one establishment, and by those with joint ownership and control among all the establishments. FDA requires all drug or biologic establishment registration and product listing information to be submitted electronically in Structured Product Labeling (SPL) format. The FDA website advises on SPL authoring software, and registrants transmit the information through FDA's Electronic Submission Gateway (ESG) after creating a WebTrader account.[41]

After the initial registration, establishments are required to renew their registrations annually. Per 21 CFR 207.29, registrants must renew registrations between 1 October and 31 December each year. These renewals allow establishments to report the required updates to their drug or biologic listings, including information on drugs or biologics not previously submitted, drugs or biologics for which commercial distribution has been discontinued, and products previously discontinued for which distribution has resumed. Additionally, owners and operators of all registered establishments must update their drug or biologic listing information every June and December or at the registrant's discretion when a change occurs. Foreign establishments whose drugs or biologics are imported or offered for import into the US also must comply with establishment registration and drug or biologic listing requirements. However, if the drug or biological products enter a foreign trade zone and are re-exported from that foreign trade zone without having entered US commerce, compliance is not required.[42] Each foreign drug or biologic establishment must submit its US agent's name, address and phone number as part of its initial and updated registration information. US agents representing foreign firms must reside or maintain a place of business in the US. Only one US agent is allowed per foreign drug or biologic establishment. The foreign drug or biologic establishment or the US agent should report changes in the agent's name, address or telephone number to FDA within 10 business days of the change. The information required for each establishment, foreign or domestic, includes:[43]

- name and D-U-N-S number of the establishment
- contact information of someone responsible for receiving FDA communication related to the establishment
- applicable business operations performed at the establishment
- for foreign establishments, the name and D-U-N-S of a US agent and all importers

For each drug or biologic in commercial distribution, the product listing information must include:
- full 10-digit NDC
- proprietary and non-proprietary name
- dosage form and route of administration
- the name (with unique ingredient identifier or UNI code) and amount/strength of each active ingredient
- each inactive ingredient (name and UNI) only
- a copy of the most up-to-date labeling, including a JPG file of the outer packaging and principal display panel
- name and D-U-N-S number for each establishment involved in manufacturing the product

The 2017 *PDUFA* reauthorization (*PDUFA VI*) eliminated user fees associated with drug or biologic product and establishment fees; however, there are no changes in the requirements for establishment registration and product listing described above.[44]

Approved Application Inactivation or Withdrawal

Under 21 CFR 314.150, FDA may withdraw approval of an application or abbreviated application; under 21 CFR 601.5, FDA may revoke a biologics license. When the agency intends to withdraw approval or revoke an application, it may notify the sponsor and, if appropriate, all other persons who manufacture or distribute identical, related or similar products, and the application holders will be afforded the opportunity for a hearing.[45] FDA will propose withdrawing an approved application if:

- The agency finds clinical data, tests or other scientific evidence showing the product is unsafe for use under the conditions of use on the basis of which the application or abbreviated application was approved (21 CFR 314.150(a)(2)(i)).
- New clinical data, not contained in the application or not available to FDA until after the application or abbreviated application was approved, indicate the product is not safe under the conditions of use (21 CFR 314.150(a)(2)(ii)).

- New information indicates there is insufficient evidence from adequate and well-controlled studies, as defined in 21 CFR 314.126, to support the efficacy claims under the conditions of use prescribed, recommended or suggested in its labeling (21 CFR 314.150(a)(2)(iii)).
- The agency determines the application or abbreviated application contains any untrue statement of a material fact (21 CFR 314.150(a)(2)(iv)).
- Required patent information is not submitted (21 CFR 314.150(a)(2)(v)).

Additionally, approval may be suspended summarily if FDA determines the product poses an imminent hazard to public health (21 CFR 314.150(a)(1)). In this case, FDA will provide the application holder an opportunity for an expedited hearing on this finding. Under 21 CFR 314.150(b), FDA may propose withdrawing an approved application for a number of other reasons including noncompliance issues, inaccurate labeling, and lack of bioavailability/bioequivalence data.

The regulations also allow the sponsor to voluntarily request withdrawal of an approved application. A sponsor may choose to withdraw an application if the product is no longer being marketed (21 CFR 314.150(c)). Voluntary application holder withdrawal of an approval is permissible if the product does not fall into any of the categories previously discussed relating to involuntary withdrawal. The sponsor must continue to maintain postapproval activities such as submitting annual reports and other postapproval reporting until the agency publishes notification of the withdrawal in the *Federal Register*, including the withdrawal reason.

If the agency believes a product or product class poses a significant risk to public health, it may contact approved application holders and ask them to waive the opportunity for a hearing and allow FDA to withdraw application approval. If the application holder agrees, the agency will not make an official finding as to the reason for withdrawal but will withdraw approval of the application and publish a notice containing a brief summary of the agency's and the application holder's reasons for withdrawal in the *Federal Register*. For example, in 2011, FDA announced it was requesting holders of approved applications for combination prescription products containing more than 325 mg of acetaminophen to withdraw these products voluntarily.[46] In this case, FDA concerns about the incidence of liver damage associated with high-dose acetaminophen prompted the voluntary withdrawal of these products.

For biological products, under 21 CFR 601.6, whenever FDA has reasonable grounds to believe any of the grounds for revocation of a license exist and, by reason thereof, there is a danger to health, the commissioner may notify the licensed manufacturer that the biologics license is suspended and require the licensed manufacturer to:
- Notify the selling agents and distributors to whom such product or products have been delivered of such suspension.
- Furnish complete records of such deliveries and notice of suspension to CBER or CDER.

Upon suspension of a license, the commissioner shall either:
- Proceed to revoke the license under 21 CFR 601.5(b).

or
- Defer revocation pending resolution by the licensed manufacturer of the matters involved.

Change in Sponsor (Transfer of Ownership) of an Approved Application

21 CFR 314.72 covers the transfer of ownership of an approved application. The application holder must submit a letter or other documentation to FDA, indicating all rights to the application have been transferred to the new owner as of the transfer date.

When ownership of an approved application is transferred, the new owner assumes all the former owner's commitments to application agreements, promises and conditions. The new owner must submit a signed application form and a letter stating acceptance of such commitments. The new application holder also must provide FDA with the effective date for the change in ownership and a statement that either the new owner has a complete copy of the approved application, including supplements and records, or has requested a copy of the application from FDA's files.

Once transferred, the new application holder assumes all regulatory responsibility for the application. As such, the new application holder must inform FDA of any change to the approved application under 21 CFR 314.70. Associated changes to the product's labeling to change the product's brand or the name of its manufacturer, packer or distributor can be submitted in the next annual report.[47]

Summary
- Postmarketing requirements and commitments are studies and clinical trials conducted after a product is approved. The purpose of these studies is to collect additional safety, efficacy or optimal use data on the approved product.
- Approved marketing application sponsors are required to report all changes to FDA under the *FD&C Act*. The agency has provided numerous guidance documents to aid application holders in determining the appropriate reporting category

- for postapproval changes to components and composition, manufacturing sites, analytical testing sites, manufacturing process, specifications, container closure systems and labeling. These guidance documents also provide advice on the documentation and data to justify changes, as well as handling multiple related changes. The reporting categories are classified based on their potential to adversely impact the product (major—PAS, moderate—CBE-30 or CBE-0 or minor—annual report).
- Manufacturers of approved products are required to adhere to CGMP regulations per 21 CFR 210 and 211.
- Approved marketing application sponsors are required to review ADE/AE information obtained from all potential sources. They must report postmarketing safety information to FDA in 15-Day Alert Reports and periodic ADE or AE reports either quarterly or annually.
- A REMS may be proposed by application holders or required by FDA when deemed necessary to ensure a drug or biological product's benefits outweigh its risks. Modification of an approved REMS must be submitted in a PAS and requires the sponsor to perform a REMS assessment.
- Field Alert Reports (FARs) are intended to quickly identify quality defects in distributed product that may pose a potential safety threat. Approved NDA, BLA or ANDA holders are required to submit FARs within three working days (Monday through Friday) of becoming aware of any significant problem with a distributed product.
- Sponsors of approved NDA and ANDA applications are required to submit an annual report. Each copy of the report must be accompanied by a completed Form FDA 2252 (Transmittal of Annual Reports for Drugs and Biologics for Human Use). For a BLA, certain information is required to be reported in an annual report. The period covered in the report is defined as one full year from the approval anniversary date. The report should include a summary; distribution data; labeling status; chemistry, manufacturing and controls information; nonclinical laboratory studies; clinical data; postmarketing study requirement and commitment status; other postmarketing study status; and a log of outstanding regulatory business.
- A sponsor must submit specimens of mailing pieces and any other labeling or advertising devised for product promotion at the time of the promotional material's initial use and initial publication of a prescription product advertisement. A copy of the current labeling and a completed Form FDA 2253 (Transmittal of Advertisements and Promotional Labeling for Drugs and Biologics for Human Use) are required for each submission.
- FDA maintains an electronic version of the *Orange Book* (*Approved Drug Products with Therapeutic Equivalence Evaluations*) to list patent and marketing exclusivity information associated with each approved drug product. The *Purple Book* lists biological products, including any biosimilar and interchangeable biological products, licensed by FDA under the *PHS Act*.
- Product sponsors are required to establish and follow written procedures to handle, review and investigate product complaints.
- A recall is a voluntary action taken by manufacturers and distributors to remove products from the market that are in violation of laws or may present a risk of injury to the public. Recalls are classified as Class I (reasonable probability for serious adverse health effects), Class II (remote probability for serious adverse health effects) or Class III (unlikely to cause adverse health effects).
- DMFs are voluntary submissions to FDA containing detailed, confidential CMC information about APIs, intermediates, drug or biological products, excipients or packaging materials that may be used for human drugs. DMFs are not 'approved' by the agency; these files are retained by the agency and accessed when referenced in support of an application, supplement to an application or another DMF. Changes to DMFs are submitted in DMF amendments. The DMF holder will notify companies authorized to reference the file of any change, so they can assess the impact of the change on associated finished products.
- Manufacturers are required to register establishments on an annual basis and provide a current product list to FDA on a semi-annual basis. Establishment registration must be submitted in electronic format.
- A detailed process exists for the withdrawal or revocation of an approved application.
- A detailed process exists for application ownership transfer to ensure clear communication between the sponsor and FDA, as well as the sponsors involved in the transfer.

References
1. *Guidance for Industry: Postmarketing Studies and Clinical Trials—Implementation of Section 505(o)(3) of the Federal Food, Drug, and Cosmetic Act*. FDA website. https://www.fda.gov/downloads/Drugs/GuidanceComplianceRegulatoryInformation/Guidances/UCM172001.pdf. Accessed 18 March 2019.

Chapter 6

2. 21 CFR 314.71 Procedures for submission of a supplement to an approved application. Electronic Code of Federal Regulations website. https://www.ecfr.gov/cgi-bin/text-idx?SID=3f154a53a57b123f2fd65e559cf8e7cd&mc=true&node=se21.5.314_171&rgn=div8. Accessed 18 March 2019.
3. *Guidance for Industry: Changes to an Approved NDA or ANDA* (April 2004). FDA website. https://www.fda.gov/downloads/drugs/guidancecomplianceregulatoryinformation/guidances/ucm077097.pdf. Accessed 18 March 2019.
4. 21 CFR 314.70(a)(1) Supplements and other changes to an approved NDA. Electronic Code of Federal Regulations website. https://www.ecfr.gov/cgi-bin/text-idx?SID=628f734596d98835ac41396097507011&mc=true&node=se21.5.314_170&rgn=div8. Accessed 18 March 2019.
5. 21 CFR 314.70(a)(6) Supplements and other changes to an approved NDA. Electronic Code of Federal Regulations website. https://www.ecfr.gov/cgi-bin/text-idx?SID=628f734596d98835ac41396097507011&mc=true&node=se21.5.314_170&rgn=div8. Accessed 18 March 2019.
6. 21 CFR 314.81(b)(2)(iv)(b) Other postmarketing reports. Electronic Code of Federal Regulations website. https://www.ecfr.gov/cgi-bin/text-idx?SID=628f734596d98835ac41396097507011&mc=true&node=se21.5.314_181&rgn=div8. Accessed 18 March 2019.
7. *Guidance for Industry: CMC Postapproval Manufacturing Changes To Be Documented in Annual Reports* (March 2014). FDA website. https://www.fda.gov/downloads/Drugs/.../Guidances/UCM217043.pdf. Accessed 18 March 2019.
8. *Draft Guidance for Industry: Comparability Protocols—Chemistry, Manufacturing, and Controls Information* (February 2003). FDA website. https://www.fda.gov/downloads/drugs/guidancecomplianceregulatoryinformation/guidances/ucm070545.pdf. Accessed 18 March 2019. *Draft Guidance for Industry: Comparability Protocols for Human Drugs and Biologics—Chemistry, Manufacturing, and Controls Information* (April 2016). FDA website. https://www.fda.gov/downloads/Drugs/GuidanceComplianceRegulatoryInformation/Guidances/UCM496611.pdf. Accessed 18 March 2019.
9. Boam AB. FDA Perspectives on Established Conditions and ICH Q12. CMC Strategy Forum website. https://cdn.ymaws.com/www.casss.org/resource/resmgr/2016_CMCS_BoamAshley.pdf. Accessed 18 March 2019.
10. ICH Q12 Technical and Regulatory Considerations for Pharmaceutical Product Lifecycle Management. ICH website. https://www.ich.org/products/guidelines/quality/quality-single/article/technical-and-regulatory-considerations-for-pharmaceutical-product-lifecycle-management.html. Accessed 18 March 2019.
11. *Draft Guidance for Industry: Postmarketing Safety Reporting for Human Drug and Biological Products Including Vaccines* (March 2001). FDA website. https://www.fda.gov/ucm/groups/fdagov-public/@fdagov-bio-gen/documents/document/ucm092257.pdf. Accessed 18 March 2019.
12. 21 CFR 314.80(b) Postmarketing reporting of adverse drug experiences. Electronic Code of Federal Regulations website. https://www.ecfr.gov/cgi-bin/text-idx?SID=628f734596d98835ac41396097507011&mc=true&node=se21.5.314_180&rgn=div8. Accessed 18 March 2019.
13. 21 CFR 314.80(c)(1)(iii) Postmarketing reporting of adverse drug experiences. Electronic Code of Federal Regulations website. https://www.ecfr.gov/cgi-bin/text-idx?SID=628f734596d98835ac41396097507011&mc=true&node=se21.5.314_180&rgn=div8. Accessed 18 March 2019.
14. A Brief Overview of Risk Evaluation and Mitigation Strategies (REMS). FDA website. http://www.fda.gov/downloads/aboutfda/transparency/basics/ucm328784.pdf. Accessed 18 March 2019.
15. *Draft Guidance for Industry: Format and Content of a REMS Document* (October 2017). FDA website. https://www.fda.gov/downloads/Drugs/.../Guidances/UCM184128.pdf. Accessed 18 March 2019.
16. Frequently Asked Questions about REMS. FDA website. https://www.fda.gov/Drugs/DrugSafety/REMS/ucm592627.htm. Accessed 18 March 2019.
17. Field Alert Reports. FDA website. https://www.fda.gov/drugs/guidancecomplianceregulatoryinformation/surveillance/ucm529729.htm. Accessed 18 March 2019.
18. 21 CFR 314.81(b)(1) Other postmarketing reports. Electronic Code of Federal Regulations website. https://www.ecfr.gov/cgi-bin/text-idx?SID=628f734596d98835ac41396097507011&mc=true&node=se21.5.314_181&rgn=div8. Accessed 18 March 2019.
19. Postmarketing Requirements and Commitments: Frequently Asked Questions (FAQ). FDA website. https://www.fda.gov/Drugs/GuidanceComplianceRegulatoryInformation/ucm070766.htm#q6. Accessed 18 March 2019.
20. 21 CFR 314.81(b)(2) Other postmarketing reports. Electronic Code of Federal Regulations website. https://www.ecfr.gov/cgi-bin/text-idx?SID=628f734596d98835ac41396097507011&mc=true&node=se21.5.314_181&rgn=div8. Accessed 18 March 2019.
21. 21 CFR 314.81(b)(2)(i) Other postmarketing reports. Electronic Code of Federal Regulations website. https://www.ecfr.gov/cgi-bin/text-idx?SID=628f734596d98835ac41396097507011&mc=true&node=se21.5.314_181&rgn=div8. Accessed 18 March 2019.
22. 21 CFR 314.81(b)(2)(ii)(a) Other postmarketing reports. Electronic Code of Federal Regulations website. https://www.ecfr.gov/cgi-bin/text-idx?SID=628f734596d98835ac41396097507011&mc=true&node=se21.5.314_181&rgn=div8. Accessed 18 March 2019.
23. 21 CFR 314.81(b)(2)(ii)(b) Other postmarketing reports. Electronic Code of Federal Regulations website. https://www.ecfr.gov/cgi-bin/text-idx?SID=628f734596d98835ac41396097507011&mc=true&node=se21.5.314_181&rgn=div8. Accessed 18 March 2019.
24. 21 CFR 314.81(b)(2)(iii) Other postmarketing reports. Electronic Code of Federal Regulations website. https://www.ecfr.gov/cgi-bin/text-idx?SID=628f734596d98835ac41396097507011&mc=true&node=se21.5.314_181&rgn=div8. Accessed 18 March 2019.
25. 21 CFR 314.81(b)(2)(iv) Other postmarketing reports. Electronic Code of Federal Regulations website. https://www.ecfr.gov/cgi-bin/text-idx?SID=628f734596d98835ac41396097507011&mc=true&node=se21.5.314_181&rgn=div8. Accessed 18 March 2019.
26. 21 CFR 314.81(b)(2)(v) Other postmarketing reports. Electronic Code of Federal Regulations website. https://www.ecfr.gov/cgi-bin/text-idx?SID=628f734596d98835ac41396097507011&mc=true&node=se21.5.314_181&rgn=div8. Accessed 18 March 2019.
27. 21 CFR 314.81(b)(2)(vi) Other postmarketing reports. Electronic Code of Federal Regulations website. https://www.ecfr.gov/cgi-bin/text-idx?SID=628f734596d98835ac41396097507011&mc=true&node=se21.5.314_181&rgn=div8. Accessed 18 March 2019.
28. 21 CFR 314.81(b)(2)(vii) Other postmarketing reports. Electronic Code of Federal Regulations website. https://www.ecfr.gov/cgi-bin/text-idx?SID=628f734596d98835ac41396097507011&mc=true&node=se21.5.314_181&rgn=div8. Accessed 18 March 2019.
29. 21 CFR 314.81(b)(2)(viii) Other postmarketing reports. Electronic Code of Federal Regulations website. https://www.ecfr.gov/cgi-bin/text-idx?SID=628f734596d98835ac41396097507011&mc=true&node=se21.5.314_181&rgn=div8. Accessed 18 March 2019.
30. 21 CFR 314.81(b)(2)(ix) Other postmarketing reports. Electronic Code of Federal Regulations website. https://www.ecfr.gov/cgi-bin/text-idx?SID=628f734596d98835ac41396097507011&mc=true&node=se21.5.314_181&rgn=div8. Accessed 18 March 2019.
31. 21 CFR 314.81(b)(3) Other postmarketing reports. Electronic Code of Federal Regulations website. https://www.ecfr.gov/cgi-bin/text-idx?SID=628f734596d98835ac41396097507011&mc=true&node=se21.5.314_181&rgn=div8. Accessed 18 March 2019.

32. Orange Book Preface. FDA website. https://www.fda.gov/Drugs/DevelopmentApprovalProcess/ucm079068.htm. Accessed 18 March 2019.
33. Patent Certifications and Suitability Petitions. FDA website. https://www.fda.gov/drugs/developmentapprovalprocess/howdrugsaredevelopedandapproved/approvalapplications/abbreviatednewdrugapplicationandagenerics/ucm047676.htm. Accessed 18 March 2019.
34. Purple Book Preface. FDA website. https://www.fda.gov/Drugs/DevelopmentApprovalProcess/HowDrugsareDevelopedandApproved/ApprovalApplications/TherapeuticBiologicApplications/Biosimilars/ucm411418.htm. Accessed 18 March 2019.
35. 21 CFR 211.198(a) Complaint files. Electronic Code of Federal Regulations website. https://www.ecfr.gov/cgi-bin/text-idx?SID=87476cec0b520f673ba2b79044975983&mc=true&node=se21.4.211_1198&rgn=div8. Accessed 18 March 2019.
36. 21 CFR 211.198(b) Complaint files. Electronic Code of Federal Regulations website. https://www.ecfr.gov/cgi-bin/text-idx?SID=87476cec0b520f673ba2b79044975983&mc=true&node=se21.4.211_1198&rgn=div8. Accessed 18 March 2019.
37. 21 CFR 7.40(a) Recall policy. Electronic Code of Federal Regulations website. https://www.ecfr.gov/cgi-bin/text-idx?SID=87476cec0b520f673ba2b79044975983&mc=true&node=se21.1.7_140&rgn=div8. Accessed 18 March 2019.
38. 21 CFR 7.42(a)(2) Recall strategy. Electronic Code of Federal Regulations website. https://www.ecfr.gov/cgi-bin/text-idx?SID=87476cec0b520f673ba2b79044975983&mc=true&node=se21.1.7_142&rgn=div8. Accessed 18 March 2019.
39. 21 CFR 7.42(b) Recall strategy. Electronic Code of Federal Regulations website. https://www.ecfr.gov/cgi-bin/text-idx?SID=87476cec0b520f673ba2b79044975983&mc=true&node=se21.1.7_142&rgn=div8. Accessed 18 March 2019.
40. Drug Master Files: Guidelines. FDA website. http://www.fda.gov/Drugs/GuidanceComplianceRegulatoryInformation/Guidances/ucm122886.htm. Accessed 18 March 2019.
41. Electronic Drug Registration and Listing Instructions. FDA website. https://www.fda.gov/Drugs/GuidanceComplianceRegulatoryInformation/DrugRegistrationandListing/ucm078801.htm. Accessed 18 March 2019.
42. 21 CFR 207.13(j)(1) Who is exempt from the registration and listing requirements? Electronic Code of Federal Regulations website. https://www.ecfr.gov/cgi-bin/text-idx?SID=87476cec0b520f673ba2b79044975983&mc=true&node=se21.4.207_113&rgn=div8. Accessed 18 March 2019.
43. Op cit 41.
44. PDUFA IV: A Time for Change. FDA CDER SBIA Chronicles. FDA website. https://www.fda.gov/downloads/Drugs/DevelopmentApprovalProcess/SmallBusinessAssistance/UCM586625.pdf. Accessed 18 March 2019.
45. 21 CFR 314.150(a) Withdrawal of approval of an application or abbreviated application. Code of Federal Regulations website. https://www.ecfr.gov/cgi-bin/text-idx?SID=9d6799e95569f58355ad428e0388e31c&mc=true&node=se21.5.314_1150&rgn=div8. Accessed 18 March 2019.
46. FDA Drug Safety Communication: Prescription Acetaminophen Products to be Limited to 325 mg Per Dosage Unit; Boxed Warning Will Highlight Potential for Severe Liver Failure. FDA website. https://www.fda.gov/Drugs/DrugSafety/ucm239821.htm. Accessed 18 March 2019.
47. 21 CFR 314.72. Change in ownership of an application. Electronic Code of Federal Regulations website. https://www.ecfr.gov/cgi-bin/retrieveECFR?gp=&SID=9ceee5d3603bbd857a697bc77a849b65&mc=true&n=pt21.5.314&r=PART&ty=HTML#se21.5.314_172. Accessed 18 March 2019.

Chapter 7

Generic Drug Submissions

Updated by Amrita Ghosh, RAC and Sharry Arora, MPharm

OBJECTIVES

❑ Understand the history of US generic drug development

❑ Understand FDA's generic drug approval process and requirements, including various approval pathways

❑ Understand bioequivalence and therapeutic equivalence concepts

❑ Understand the *Generic Drug User Fee Act* and amendments

LAWS, REGULATIONS AND GUIDELINES COVERED IN THIS CHAPTER

❑ *Federal Food, Drug, and Cosmetic Act* of 1938

❑ *Drug Efficacy Amendments* of 1962

❑ *Drug Regulation Reform Act* of 1978

❑ *Drug Price Competition and Patent Term Restoration Act* of 1984 (Hatch-Waxman Act)

❑ *Medicare Prescription Drug, Improvement, and Modernization Act* of 2003

❑ *Prescription Drug User Fee Act* of 1992

❑ *Pediatric Research Equity Act* of 2003

❑ *Generic Drug User Fee Amendments* of 2012

❑ 21 CFR 314 Applications for FDA Approval to Market a New Drug

❑ 21 CFR 320 Bioavailability and Bioequivalence Requirements

❑ 43 FR 39,126 (1 September 1978) Abbreviated New Drug Applications; Proposed Related Drug Amendments

❑ 44 FR 2932 (12 January 1979) Therapeutically Equivalent Drugs; Availability of List

❑ 45 FR 72,582 (31 October 1980) Therapeutically Equivalent Drugs; Availability of List

❑ 45 FR 82,052 (12 December 1980) Response to Petition Seeking Withdrawal of the Policy Described in the Agency's "Paper" NDA Memorandum of 31 July 1978

❑ 46 FR 27,396 (19 May 1981), Publication of "Paper NDA" Memorandum

❑ 54 FR 28,872 (10 July 1989), Proposed ANDA Regulations

❑ 74 FR 2849 (16 January 2009) Requirements for submission of bioequivalence data

Chapter 7

- 81 FR 69,580 (6 October 2016) Abbreviated New Drug Applications and 505(b)(2) Applications

- Manual of Policies and Procedures 5240.3: Review Order of Original ANDAs, Amendments, and Supplements (October 2006)

- *Guidance for Industry: Bioavailability and Bioequivalence Studies for Orally Administered Drug Products—General Considerations* (March 2003)

- Generic Drug User Fee Act Program Performance Goals and Procedures

- *ANDA Submissions—Content and Format: Guidance for Industry* (September 2018)

- *Waiver of In Vivo Bioavailability and Bioequivalence Studies for Immediate-Release Solid Oral Dosage Forms Based on a Biopharmaceutics Classification System: Guidance for Industry* (December 2017)

Introduction

The term "generic drug" is not defined in the *Federal Food, Drug, and Cosmetic Act* of 1938 (*FD&C Act*) or in US Food and Drug Administration (FDA) regulations. It refers to a medication created to be equivalent to an existing approved brand-name drug in dosage form, safety, strength, route of administration, quality and performance characteristics. Since generic medicines use the same active ingredients as brand-name medicines and work the same way, they have the same risks and benefits as the brand-name medicines. Approved generic medicines generally are sold only after patents and exclusivities protecting the brand-name version end. Generic medicines tend to cost about 85% less than their brand-name counterparts because animal and clinical (human) studies to demonstrate safety and effectiveness are not repeated. In addition, multiple applications for generic drugs often are approved to market a single product, resulting in market competition and, hence, lower prices.

The first generic drugs were marketed between enactment of the *FD&C Act* (Pub. L. No. 75-717, 52 Stat 1040 (1938)) and the *Drug Efficacy Amendments* of 1962 (Pub. L. No. 87-781, 76 Stat. 780 (1962)). These products were marketed without FDA approval, on the theory the agency's approval of the brand-name drug under a New Drug Application (NDA) (based only on safety) applied to the next version of an "old" drug.[1] With passage of the 1962 *Drug Efficacy Amendments*, FDA required submission of an Abbreviated New Drug Application (ANDA) for each generic version of a "pre-62" brand-name drug FDA had found to be effective under the Drug Efficacy Study Implementation (DESI) program. However, the agency did not permit ANDAs to be submitted for brand-name drugs approved after 1962.[2] This meant a full NDA had to be filed for a post-1962 brand-name drug which, in some cases, was economically prohibitive.

Competitive pressure drove some generic drug companies to market both pre- and post-1962 drugs without FDA approval, arguing an active ingredient became available as an "old" drug after initial FDA approval. FDA's attempts to suppress this practice culminated in the 1983 Supreme Court decision in *United States v. Generix Drug Corp.*, 460 US 453 (1983). The court accepted FDA's position that "old drug" status applied not to the active ingredient, but to the individual finished product. Hence, each alternative version of a drug was a "new drug"[3] requiring FDA approval, no matter how many times FDA had approved its active ingredient.

Aware its own policies and interpretations were preventing post-1962 generic drug competition, FDA took two steps during the 1970s to address the need for a post-1962 drug ANDA program:
1. developing the so-called "paper NDA" policy
2. developing ANDA regulations for post-1962 drug products

In 1978, FDA adopted the paper NDA policy, under which the agency accepted a combination of product-specific data and published literature about an active ingredient to satisfy full NDA approval requirements.[4] FDA's paper NDA policy essentially permitted the sponsor of a post-1962 product "duplicate" (i.e., a drug product containing the same active ingredients as an already marketed product, in a similar or identical dosage form and for the same indications) to submit published studies and bridging data to support its application.[5] However, because the paper NDA approach required published literature rather than information not publicly available, it had limited utility for most drugs.[6]

In 1978, FDA issued proposed regulations announcing its intent to extend its pre-1962 ANDA regulations to post-1962 drugs.[7] FDA began to develop these regulations in the early 1980s. The agency's initiative was controversial because it reportedly would have required a substantial waiting period after initial approval of the brand-name drug before any ANDA could be approved for a generic version. Congressional interest in FDA's initiative, however, coincided with a broader effort to develop legislation promoting both drug industry competition and innovation.[8]

The *Drug Price Competition and Patent Term Restoration Act* of 1984 (*Hatch-Waxman Act*) was a compromise allowing manufacturers of new drugs extra patent protection while permitting generic manufacturers an opportunity to introduce affordable alternatives. Thus, an innovator pharmaceutical manufacturer may obtain longer market exclusivity in exchange for allowing generic manufacturers to submit, and FDA to approve, ANDAs.

The *Hatch-Waxman Act* amended the *FD&C Act*'s new drug approval provisions to add Section 505(j). Section 505(j) formalized the generic drug legal structure, under which an ANDA containing bioequivalence data to a brand-name drug—the Reference Listed Drug (RLD)—among other data and information, was sufficient for FDA to consider approval. As explained below, the *Hatch-Waxman Act* also amended patent laws to authorize a patent term extension that could be as long as five years for time lost during the regulatory review period.[9] The new law also required brand-name drug firms to "list" patents with FDA that claimed the branded drug (ingredient or product) or a method for using the branded product. FDA lists these patents—and all drug approvals—in a publication known as the *Orange Book* (named after its cover's original color), the formal name of which is *Approved Drug Products with Therapeutic Equivalence Evaluations*.

Under the *FD&C Act* (as amended by the *Hatch-Waxman Act*), ANDA approval is subject to several restrictions. First, the *Hatch-Waxman Act* added non-patent market exclusivity provisions of three or five years to compensate brand-name manufacturers for allowing reliance on their proprietary research. Second, an ANDA applicant must "certify" to all *Orange Book*-listed patents and, if seeking approval prior to patent expiration, notify the NDA holder and patent owner (if different). If the NDA owner files a patent infringement suit, ANDA approval is deferred. Third, an ANDA drug product must contain the "same" active ingredient as the brand-name drug and have essentially the same labeling, including indications, warnings, contraindications, etc.

ANDA Contents

FD&C Act Section 505(j) describes an ANDA's contents, including bioequivalence information, patent certification requirements and criteria for a petitioned ANDA. An ANDA contains information to show that the proposed product is the same as the RLD with respect to active ingredient, conditions of use, dosage form, route of administration, strength and (with certain permissible differences) labeling, among other characteristics.[10] The RLD is defined as "the listed drug identified by FDA as the drug product upon which an applicant relies in seeking approval of its abbreviated application" (21 CFR 314.3(b)).[11] Differences may be allowed in route of administration, dosage form and strength, as well as in a single active ingredient in case of a combination drug product, if FDA first approves them under a suitability petition not requiring clinical investigations.[12]

An ANDA must include sufficient information to: 1) demonstrate the proposed product is bioequivalent to the RLD[13] and 2) ensure the product's identity, strength, quality and purity.[14] An ANDA must contain, among other things, a certification describing the applicant's belief regarding each patent's status claiming the RLD.[15] Additional required ANDA information is identified in the *FD&C Act* and FDA's ANDA format and content regulations in 21 CFR 314.94, including, but not limited to, information showing the generic's proposed labeling is the same that of the RLD.

Demonstrating Bioequivalence

A drug product is considered bioequivalent to the RLD if: the drug's rate and extent of absorption does not show a significant difference from the RLD's when administered at the same therapeutic ingredient's molar dose under similar experimental conditions in either a single dose or multiple doses.

When the listed drug's absorption rate difference is intentional (e.g., in certain extended-release dosage forms), bioequivalence is considered if there is no significant difference in the extent to which the active ingredient or moiety from each product becomes available at the site of drug action. This applies only when the difference in drug absorption rate at the site of action is intentional, is reflected in its proposed labeling, is not essential to attaining effective body drug concentrations on chronic use and is considered medically insignificant for the drug (*FD&C Act* Section 505(j)(8)(B); 21 CFR 320.1(e)).

Bioequivalence studies involve both clinical and analytical components.[16] A typical bioequivalence study's objective is to demonstrate the test (generic) and reference (brand-name) products achieve a similar pharmacokinetic profile in plasma, serum and/or urine.[16] Under FDA regulations, an applicant must use "the most accurate, sensitive, and reproducible approach available among those set forth" in 21 CFR 320.24(b) to demonstrate bioequivalence. In general, the descending order of preference includes pharmacokinetic, pharmacodynamic, clinical and *in vitro* studies.[17] As noted in 21 CFR 320.24, *in vivo* and/or *in vitro* methods can be used to establish bioequivalence. However, the "gold standard" for establishing two drug products' bioequivalence is the *in vivo* comparative bioavailability (BA) study measuring the active ingredient's concentration in a biological fluid as a function of time.[18] Bioequivalence (BE) testing determines whether differences in formulation or manufacturing between the proposed generic drug product and the brand-name product affect the rate or extent to which the active ingredient reaches the primary site of action.

The choice of which *in vivo* BE study design to use is based on the design's ability to compare the drug delivered by the test and reference drug products at the drug's particular site of action. In a standard *in vivo* BE study, single doses of the test and reference drug products are administered to volunteers (usually 24–36 healthy adults), and the drug's absorption rate and extent are determined from measured plasma concentrations over time for each study subject. The absorption extent (i.e., how much of a given drug's dose was absorbed) is reflected through various measurements. The preferred oral dosage form study design is a single-dose, fasting, two-treatment, two-sequence crossover design with a washout period between treatments, although a study in the "fed" condition usually is required as well.[19] To demonstrate *in vitro* BE, FDA recommends an *in vitro* test (e.g., a dissolution rate test) correlating with *in vivo* data.[20]

Bioequivalence Waivers

Although data and information demonstrating *in vivo* BE often are required, FDA may waive this requirement if *in vivo* BE is considered self-evident (e.g., in the case of many injectable drugs) or for other reasons (21 CFR 320.22)(b).[21] Specifically, 21 CFR 320.22(a) provides, "any person submitting a full or abbreviated new drug application . . . may request FDA to waive the requirement for the submission of evidence measuring the in vivo bioavailability or demonstrating the in vivo bioequivalence of the drug product that is the subject of the application." Thus, an ANDA applicant seeking a BE waiver must submit an official request for such waiver with the application. Additionally, BE waivers commonly are used for oral solutions and injectable drugs, provided the proposed generic formulation is qualitatively and quantitatively the same (Q1–Q2 the same) as the RLD formulation (21 CFR 320.22(b)). For immediate release (IR) solid oral dosage forms based on the Biopharmaceutics Classification System (BCS) approach, demonstration of *in vivo* BA or BE may not be necessary for drug products containing class 1 and class 3 drug substances, as long as the inactive ingredients used in the dosage form do not significantly affect absorption of the active ingredients.[22]

Patent Certification

The *Hatch-Waxman Act* provided advantages for both the brand and generic drug industries. First, it established a five-year exclusivity period for a new chemical entity (NCE exclusivity), protecting a brand manufacturer from a generic ANDA submission. Second, if a drug was not eligible for the NCE exclusivity, the *Hatch-Waxman Act* allowed a shorter three-year period of exclusivity for certain changes to previously approved drugs. Thus, if a brand manufacturer submitted one or more new clinical studies to support a change in the conditions of an approved drug's use, the *FD&C Act* conferred a three-year period of marketing exclusivity, so long as FDA considered those studies to have been essential to the agency's approval of the change.[23] In exchange, the *Hatch-Waxman Act* provided the generic drug industry the ability to challenge brand-drug patents prior to marketing and bestowed a 180-day market exclusivity under certain conditions.

A brand manufacturer that files an NDA is required to submit those patents that reasonably cover the drug product, drug substance or drug use method to FDA.[24] When a brand manufacturer obtains FDA approval for a new drug product or method of treatment, it submits a list of relevant patents and their expiration dates to FDA. FDA regulations also require a description of any method-of-use patent, known as a "use code."[25] FDA does not attempt to verify the accuracy of the use codes the brand manufacturers supply. Instead, it simply publishes the codes, patent numbers and expiration dates in the *Orange Book*.

"Paragraph" Certification

After consulting the *Orange Book*, an ANDA applicant must enter one of four possible certifications with respect to each patent listed in the applicable RLD (*FD&C Act* Section 505(j)(2)(A)(vii)).[26] Accordingly, an ANDA applicant must submit one or more of the following patent certifications:

1. "Paragraph I" certification—patent certification has not been filed, and FDA may approve an ANDA when ready
2. "Paragraph II" certification—patent listed in the *Orange Book* has expired, and FDA may approve an ANDA when ready
3. "Paragraph III" certification—the date when the patent will expire, meaning FDA can approve an ANDA only when the patent expires and the ANDA is ready
4. "Paragraph IV" certification—patent listed in the *Orange Book* is invalid, unenforceable or will not be infringed by the drug product proposed in the ANDA, which involves a complex approval landscape

"Paragraph IV" Litigation Landscape and 180-Day Exclusivity

An ANDA applicant that submits a paragraph IV certification is required to provide notice of such certification to the RLD NDA holder and the patent owner (if different) subject to the certification. Filing an ANDA with a paragraph IV certification constitutes patent infringement.[27] Thus, a notice of a paragraph IV certification subjects the ANDA applicant to the risk of being sued for patent infringement. If the NDA holder or patent owner sues the ANDA applicant within 45 days of receiving the notice of a paragraph IV certification, there generally will be a statutory 30-month stay of ANDA approval while the patent infringement litigation is pending. In summary, the timing for approval of an ANDA is subject to certain patent and marketing exclusivity protections

Nevertheless, ANDA applicants have an incentive to submit a paragraph IV certification and challenge listed patents that may be invalid, unenforceable or not infringed by the ANDA drug product. The first applicant to submit a "substantially complete" ANDA (as defined below under Timelines Surrounding ANDA Filing) containing a paragraph IV certification may be eligible for a 180-day exclusivity period, during which FDA may not approve a subsequent ANDA containing a paragraph IV certification. If multiple applicants submit paragraph IV certifications on the first day they are accepted, all will be considered first applicants. In addition, different ANDA applicants each can qualify as a first applicant by certifying to different listed patents on the same first day.[28]

In October 2016, FDA issued a final rule implementing Title XI of the *Medicare Prescription Drug, Improvement, and Modernization Act* of 2003 (*MMA*) (hereafter, the final rule), which amended *FD&C Act* provisions governing the *Hatch-Waxman* litigation landscape.[29] The final rule, which became effective 5 December 2016, set forth, among other revisions, significant updates on patent information filing. For example, under the new regulations, an ANDA applicant must send a paragraph IV certification no later than 20 days after the "Paragraph IV Acknowledgment Letter" postmark date.[30] Additionally, the statutory 30-month stay begins on the date of paragraph IV certification notification receipt by any listed patent owner or the NDA holder (or its representative(s)). This revision codified FDA's then-existing practice, providing an efficient means of ensuring each patent owner or NDA holder received the full 30-month stay. Finally, the final rule clarified the type of federal district and appellate court patent litigation decisions that would terminate a 30-month stay leading to ANDA approval.

"Section VIII" Carve-Out
As mentioned above, an ANDA applicant must consult the *Orange Book* and submit a certification for each RLD patent listed. However, there is an exception for certain patents that claim a method of using the RLD. The *Hatch-Waxman Act* permits ANDA applicants to submit a "Section VIII" statement, asserting it will not market the drug for those methods of use covered by the brand-drug's patents and proposing a label that "carves out" the patented method(s) of use (*FD&C Act* Section 505(j)(2) (A)(viii) and 21 CFR 314.94(a)(8)(iv)). FDA will not approve an ANDA with a "Section VIII" statement if the proposed labeling fails to completely carve out the conditions set forth in the applicable patent use code.

In effect, a "Section VIII" carve-out enables an ANDA to be approved immediately by limiting its application to unpatented uses. *FD&C Act* Section 505(j)(5)(C)(ii) (I), as interpreted by the US Supreme Court in *Caraco Pharmaceutical Laboratories v. Novo Nordisk*, also permits a generic manufacturer to challenge the scope of a patent's *Orange Book*-listed use code.[31]

Inactive Ingredients
As mentioned previously, an ANDA may be submitted when the generic drug is the same as the RLD. However, while different inactive ingredients may be acceptable, novel inactive ingredients are not acceptable (21 CFR 314.94(a)(9)). The goal is to ensure any inactive ingredient differences do not change the generic's risk profile compared to the RLD.

FD&C Act Section 505(j)(4)(H) states FDA must approve an ANDA unless, among other things:

> (I)nformation submitted in the application or any other information available to [FDA] shows that (i) the inactive ingredients of the drug are unsafe for use under the conditions prescribed, recommended, or suggested in the labeling proposed for the drug or (ii) the composition of the drug is unsafe under such conditions because of the type or quantity of inactive ingredients included or the manner in which the inactive ingredients are included.

FDA's regulations implementing *FD&C Act* Section 505(j)(4)(H) generally are found in the agency's ANDA content and format regulations at 21 CFR 314.94. Pertinent regulations on inactive ingredient changes for certain generic drug product types are set forth in 21 CFR 314.94(a)(9). For example, FDA's regulations for parenteral drug products at 21 CFR 314.94(a)(9)(iii) state:

> Generally, a drug product intended for parenteral use shall contain the same inactive ingredients and in the same concentration as the [RLD] identified by the applicant under paragraph (a)(3) of this section. However, an applicant may seek approval of a drug product that differs from the reference listed drug in preservative, buffer, or antioxidant provided that the applicant identifies and characterizes the differences and provides information demonstrating the differences do not affect the safety or efficacy of the proposed drug product.

Preservative, buffer and antioxidant changes in generic parenteral drug products are referred to as "exception excipients," which may differ qualitatively or quantitatively from the RLD formulation. Other regulations under 21 CFR 314.94(a)(9)(iv) identify exception excipients for generic ophthalmic and otic drug products (i.e., preservative, buffer, substance to adjust tonicity and thickening agent). Excipients not identified in these regulations are referred to as "non-exception excipients."

FDA's exception excipient regulations under 21 CFR 314.94(a)(9) find their parallel in 21 CFR 314.127(a)(8)(ii), which addresses the grounds for an FDA refusal to approve an ANDA for a parenteral, ophthalmic or otic drug product. For example, one regulation states: "FDA will consider an inactive ingredient in, or the composition of, a drug product intended for parenteral use to be unsafe and will refuse to approve the [ANDA] unless it contains the same inactive ingredients, other than preservatives, buffers, and antioxidants, in the same concentration as the listed drug."[32] Thus, it is important for a company to understand the possible implications of changing certain drug product formulations. If such a change is for a non-exception excipient, FDA would, unless under a narrow exception, refuse to receive or approve an ANDA. Instead, a company would need to submit a 505(b)(2) application for the proposed drug product, which, like other NDAs, is subject to much higher user fees.

Inactive Ingredients Database (IID)

During ANDA development, sponsors consult FDA's Inactive Ingredient Database (IID) to gather information on "acceptable levels" of excipients utilized in previously approved products. Maximum potency is the amount of the excipient used in the approved product that is the basis for the IID listing. The IID lists the highest amount of the excipient per unit dose in each dosage form in which it is used. The amounts shown for maximum potency do not reflect the excipient's maximum daily intake (MDI), unless the maximum daily dose of the product that is the basis for the listing is only a single unit. FDA also weighs whether the excipient's conditions of use in the previously approved product are equivalent to (or greater than) those of the proposed new product. Additional factors FDA considers in this analysis are the route of administration, exposure duration, patient population and exposure level.

Many inactive ingredients have CAS Registry Numbers, which are useful in searching other databases for chemical information.

New Substance Registration System (SRS) nomenclature has been used for specific grades and resulted in several IID references disappearing, which has caused many commonly used excipients to be treated like new excipients that require significant safety assessment. However, recent IID and SRS updates have enabled consistencies when searching for specific excipients. For example, certain excipients that were listed in error were removed from the IID.

Timelines Surrounding ANDA Filing

Once a generic manufacturer submits an ANDA application, FDA strives to review and send the applicant either an approval letter or a complete response letter (21 CFR 314.100). However, before it makes this determination, FDA makes a threshold determination that the application is "substantially complete."[33] Substantially complete means the ANDA contains all the information required under *FD&C Act* Section 505(j)(2)(A) and does not contain any ANDA or regulatory deficiencies described in 21 CFR 314.101(d) and (e).[34] If the ANDA is substantially complete, FDA will receive the ANDA and notify the applicant in writing. The agency will consider the ANDA to have been received as of the submission date.

However, if the ANDA is not substantially complete (i.e., due to an ANDA or regulatory deficiency), FDA may "refuse to receive" the application, at which time the applicant may withdraw the ANDA, correct the deficiencies and resubmit it or take no action.[35] If the ANDA applicant does not take any action, FDA may consider the ANDA withdrawn after one year. A "refuse to receive" (RTR) decision will cause a company to lose some or all of its ANDA filing fee and the potential 180-day exclusivity if the applicant was eligible for "first to file" status.

GDUFA Commitments Letter

The *Generic Drug User Fee Act* (*GDUFA*) was enacted 9 July 2012 as part of the *Food and Drug Administration Safety and Innovation Act* (*FDASIA*), based on an agreement between FDA and the generic drug industry to accelerate generic drugs' movement onto the market. Prior to *GDUFA*, the median ANDA approval times averaged 42–44 months. Consequently, in an effort to provide FDA with industry funds through a user fee structure, generic drug manufacturers agreed to pay approximately $300 million in fees each year throughout the five-year program. In exchange, FDA committed to providing a more-rapid "first action" on an application. Under the *GDUFA* program, FDA was tasked with either granting an approval or tentative approval or, if there were deficiencies that prevented approval, identifying those deficiencies to the applicant in a complete response letter or in a refusal to receive notification. A major *GDUFA* commitment was to take "first action" on 90% of the pre-*GDUFA* "backlog" applications pending before FDA by the end of Fiscal 2017. Consequently, the median ANDA approval time decreased from approximately 24 months in 2013 to less than 15 months in Fiscal 2015.[36]

GDUFA II

Under *GDUFA*, FDA collects user fees that help fund ANDA reviews. The agency generally collects four types of user fees for an ANDA review: 1) an ANDA filing fee, 2) a prior approval supplement (PAS) fee, 3) a drug master file (DMF) fee and 4) an active pharmaceutical ingredient (API) or finished dosage form (FDF) facility fee. *GDUFA II* helps FDA increase the generic drug application review program's overall capacity and capabilities through a user fee structure that provides stable, predictable funding.

Modifications to the user fees are:

1. Annual fees—To improve the predictability of the fees base and to align the fee responsibility with program cost and fee-paying ability, FDA and industry have agreed to shift the burden toward annual program fees.
2. Eliminating supplemental fees—Previously, if the sponsor made any changes to the approved ANDA, it submitted the change via a PAS with a fee. Over the years, the unpredictability of the number of annual PAS submissions became apparent, so industry and FDA agreed to eliminate the PAS fee.
3. Small Business Considerations (facility fee)—Under *GDUFA I*, a facility would pay an annual facility listing fee, whether or not its ANDA was approved or pending. Under *GDUFA II*, no facility or ANDA sponsor would be charged an annual fee until an ANDA in which the facility is listed is approved. Under this fee structure, the firm and its affiliates will pay one fee for the number of approved ANDAs the firm and its affiliates collectively own. A firm will not pay a per-ANDA fee, but will be split into three tiers that represent different positions held by the firm and its affiliates. The other *GDUFA II* fee structures are explained below:
   A. A CMO will pay one-third of the annual fee paid by firms manufacturing under ANDAs they or their affiliates own. A foreign fee differential will still apply.
   B. Fee relief is available for noncommercial drug distribution in which the sponsor or drug manufacturer does not pay user fees if it is not involved in its products' commercial distribution.
   C. Partial refund for withdrawal is available when an ANDA sponsor knows it will not be received by FDA and withdraws the ANDA voluntarily before FDA makes a decision whether to receive it.
   D. Facilities that qualify for both API and FDF would pay just the FDF fee under *GDUFA II*, whereas *GDUFA I* required them to pay both fees.
   E. Under *GDUFA I*, FDA could charge foreign facilities anywhere from $15,000 to $30,000 more per facility than domestic facilities, depending on its calculations each year for foreign and domestic inspections. Each year under *GDUFA I*, FDA determined the differential would be $15,000. *GDUFA II* sets the foreign fee differential at $15,000.[37]

Marketing a Generic Drug

FDA works with pharmaceutical companies to ensure all drugs marketed in the US meet identity, strength, quality, purity and potency specifications. In approving a generic drug product, FDA requires many rigorous tests and procedures to ensure the generic drug is interchangeable with the brand-name drug under all approved indications and conditions of use. Brand-name drug products and therapeutically equivalent generic drug products are listed in the *Orange Book*.[38]

The *Orange Book* identifies drug products approved under *FD&C Act* Section 505 and reflects FDA's evaluations of approved drug products' therapeutic equivalence.[39] One of the *Orange Book*'s primary purposes is to provide state agencies and officials with information relating to drug products that may be selected for dispensing under applicable state law. Drug product substitutions must be made in accordance with each individual state's pharmacy practice act. While some state pharmacy laws require the *Orange Book*'s use when making generic drug substitutions, others make no such reference.

In addition, state pharmacy laws may extend the prescribing authority granted to pharmacists beyond substituting a generic drug. For example, pharmacists may be permitted to substitute a product from the same drug class, even though the drug is not identified in the *Orange Book* as therapeutically equivalent to the prescribed drug product. This procedure is known as "therapeutic interchange." The laws covering therapeutic interchange vary widely from state to state.[40] Thus, the "clinical appropriateness" of substituting drug products FDA does not consider to be therapeutically equivalent is handled on a state-by-state basis. The consequences for violating a particular state substitution law also are governed by that state's laws.[41]

Therapeutic Equivalence

The term "therapeutic equivalence" simply refers to drug products that are otherwise safe and effective and can be expected to have equivalent therapeutic effect and equivalent potential for adverse effects when used under the conditions set forth in their labeling.[42] "FDA believes that products classified as therapeutically equivalent can be substituted with the full expectation that the substituted product will produce the same clinical effect and safety profile as the prescribed product."[43] Thus, if one therapeutically equivalent drug product is substituted for another under state law, with due professional regard for the individual patient, there is no substantial reason to believe the patient will receive a drug product that is different in terms of the intended therapeutic effect.

Drug products are considered therapeutic equivalents if they are pharmaceutical equivalents and can be expected to have the same clinical effect and safety profile when administered to patients under the conditions specified in the labeling (i.e., are bioequivalent). The term "bioequivalence" is defined in the *FD&C Act* and FDA regulations as explained above.[44]

FDA's regulations define the term "pharmaceutical equivalents" to mean:

> (D)rug products in identical dosage forms that contain identical amounts of the identical active drug ingredient, i.e., the same salt or ester of the same therapeutic moiety, or, in the case of modified release dosage forms that require a reservoir or overage or such forms as prefilled syringes where residual volume may vary, that deliver identical amounts of the active drug ingredient over the identical dosing period; do not necessarily contain the same inactive ingredients; and meet the identical compendial or other applicable standard of identity, strength, quality, and purity, including potency and, where applicable, content uniformity, disintegration times, and/or dissolution rates.[45]

Pharmaceutically equivalent prescription drug products usually are identified in the *Orange Book* with either an "A" or "B" code designation. "A-rated" drug products are considered therapeutically equivalent to other pharmaceutically equivalent products because there are no known or suspected bioequivalence problems, or such problems have been resolved with adequate evidence supporting bioequivalence. "B-rated" drug products are not considered therapeutically equivalent to other pharmaceutically equivalent drug products because actual or potential bioequivalence problems identified by FDA have not been resolved by adequate bioequivalence evidence.[46]

Drug products assigned an "A" rating fall under one of two categories:

- those active ingredients or dosage forms for which no *in vivo* bioequivalence issue is known or suspected, and for which RLD bioequivalence is presumed and considered self-evident based on other data in an application, or by showing an acceptable *in vitro* dissolution standard is met (e.g., approved based on a waiver of bioequivalence)

- those active ingredients or dosage forms presenting a potential bioequivalence problem, but the applicant's approved application contains adequate scientific evidence establishing (through *in vivo* and/or *in vitro* studies) the product's therapeutic equivalence to a selected RLD[47]

Drug products falling under the first category are assigned a therapeutic equivalence code, depending on the dosage form. These codes include AA, AN, AO, AP or AT. Drug products falling under the second category are coded AB, the most common code assignment.

Drug products assigned a "B" rating fall under one of three categories:

- FDA has documented bioequivalence problems or a significant potential for such problems (and no adequate studies demonstrating bioequivalence have been submitted to the agency).
- FDA has an insufficient basis to determine therapeutic equivalence (e.g., quality standards are inadequate).
- The drug products are under regulatory review.[48]

Drug products falling under these categories are assigned a therapeutic equivalence code largely based on dosage form. These codes are B*, BC, BD, BE, BN, BP, BR, BS, BT or BX.[51] FDA's assignment of a "B" rating does not mean a particular drug product is not safe and effective. (Indeed, the applicant has provided sufficient data to meet the statutory and regulatory approval criteria.) Rather, a "B" rating means FDA has identified unresolved actual or potential bioequivalence problems and, as a result, a particular drug product cannot be considered therapeutically equivalent to other pharmaceutically equivalent drug products.

"Pharmaceutical alternatives" are not pharmaceutically equivalent to the RLD and, therefore, are not substitutable for the RLD. FDA's regulations define "pharmaceutical alternatives" as:

> (D)rug products that contain the identical therapeutic moiety, or its precursor, but not necessarily in the same amount or dosage form or as the same salt or ester. Each such drug product individually meets either the identical or its own respective compendial or other applicable standard of identity, strength, quality, and purity, including potency and, where applicable, content uniformity, disintegration times and/or dissolution rates.[549]

A generic drug that is a pharmaceutical alternative to an RLD (e.g., tablet versus capsule) is not assigned a therapeutic equivalence code (such drug products, by definition, are not therapeutic equivalents). Instead, they are listed separately in the *Orange Book* as single-source drug products. However, because each *Orange Book*-listed drug product may be designated as an RLD (pursuant to a request to FDA to assign RLD status), a generic applicant could cite the approved drug as the RLD and obtain ANDA approval for a pharmaceutically equivalent drug product. In such a case, if the drug also is shown to be bioequivalent to the RLD, FDA could assign both drug products an "A" therapeutic equivalence code appropriate for such a multi-source drug product.[50]

Summary

The term "generic drug" is not defined in the *FD&C Act* or in FDA regulations. It generally is used, however, to refer to a drug product that is the same as a brand-name drug in these key aspects: active ingredient, dosage form, route of administration and strength; and for which FDA has determined the generic version is therapeutically equivalent to the branded drug. As a result of these "sameness" aspects, state law typically allows a pharmacist to substitute the generic for a branded drug when filling a prescription. When combined with the lower costs of a generic drug—because the brand-name drug company already has done the work necessary to develop the active ingredient and show it is safe and effective for its indications—the generic can be sold for a fraction of the brand-name price. Generic drug approval in the US is governed by a tapestry of laws, regulations and FDA policies developed over the past few decades. While a complex regime, the generic drug approval process has allowed these products to grow to more than 80% of all prescriptions filled in the US and is estimated to have saved Americans billions of dollars.

References

1. Karst KR. "Marketed Unapproved Drugs–Past, Present and Future?" *Regulatory Affairs Focus*, Vol. 12, No. 2, pp 37–42 (February 2007).
2. ANDAs were permitted under FDA regulations for duplicates (i.e., generic versions). The term "duplicate" applied to a drug product that was the same as an already approved drug product in dosage form, route of administration, kind and amount of active ingredient, indication(s) and any other conditions of use. FDA regulations permitted ANDAs for "similar" and "related" products only if the agency had made a separate finding (following a firm's petition) that an ANDA was appropriate for that drug product.
3. A product that is a "new drug" within *FD&C Act* Section 201(p) may not be introduced into interstate commerce unless there is an approved marketing application (e.g., an NDA), or an exemption has been granted permitting the drug's introduction into interstate commerce (e.g., an effective Investigational New Drug Application (IND)).
4. The "paper NDA" policy is described in a 31 July 1978 FDA staff memorandum. The policy originally was not published in the *Federal Register* because FDA determined rulemaking procedures were not required because "the policy is a lawful exercise of FDA's statutory authority..." 45 *Fed. Reg.* 82,052 (12 December 1980). FDA was challenged on this issue in court and won. See *Burroughs Wellcome Co. v. Schweiker*, 649 F.2d 221, 225 (4th Cir. 1981). Subsequently, in separate litigation, the US District Court for the Northern District of Illinois ruled that upon the FDA policy's publication in the *Federal Register*, the agency could implement it without rulemaking procedures. See *American Critical Care v. Schweiker*, Food, Drug, Cosm. L. Rep. (CCH) 1980-81 Transfer Binder 38, 110 (N.D. Ill. 1981).
5. The published studies requirement could be met by referencing data available in published literature, laboratory reports, physician evaluation forms and even unpublished reports when available and necessary. However, the underlying data did not have to be included or referenced, as was required under FDA's old interpretation of "full reports" in *FD&C Act* Section 505(b)(1). Reference to information not publicly available was not permitted, including information in the brand-name product's NDA. The "bridging" data requirement could be met by submitting data from a bioavailability/bioequivalence study comparing the drug that was the subject of the "paper NDA" to the approved drug "to show that the drug is comparable in blood levels (or dissolution rate, as required) to the innovator's product." 46 *Fed. Reg.* 27396, 27,397 (19 May 1981).
6. FDA revoked the "paper NDA" policy in 1989 when it proposed regulations implementing the *Drug Price Competition and Patent Term Restoration Act*, Pub. L. No. 98-417, 98 Stat. 1585 (1984) (*Hatch-Waxman Act*). See FDA, Proposed Rule, ANDA Regulations, 54 *Fed. Reg.* 28,872, 28, 890 (10 July 1989).
7. 43 *Fed. Reg.* 39126, 39128 (1 September 1978).
8. *Drug Regulation Reform Act*, 95th Cong., 2d Sess. (1978); *Drug Regulation Reform Act*, 96th Cong., 1st Sess. (1979).
9. The *Hatch-Waxman Act* also replaced the "paper NDA" with the 505(b)(2) application. The *FD&C Act* describes a 505(b)(2) application as an application "for a drug for which the investigations... relied upon by the applicant for approval of the application were not conducted by or for the applicant and for which the applicant has not obtained a right of reference or use from the person by or for whom the investigations were conducted." *FD&C Act* Section 505(b)(2). A 505(b)(2) application differs from a "paper NDA" in that it permits the sponsor of a drug that may differ substantially from a drug listed in FDA's *Orange Book* to rely on FDA's determination of the reference drug's safety and effectiveness and/or on published studies or studies in an NDA (or NDAs) sponsored by another person, together with studies generated on its own drug product, as a way to satisfy the requirement of "full reports" of safety and effectiveness. As with the old "paper NDA" policy, "bridging" studies to the referenced drug are necessary. An application for a duplicate of a drug listed in the *Orange Book* and eligible for approval as a generic drug under the ANDA *FD&C Act* Section 505(j) provisions may not be submitted as a 505(b)(2) application.
10. Abbreviated New Drug Applications and 505(b)(2) Applications. Federal Register website. https://www.federalregister.gov/documents/2016/10/06/2016-22690/abbreviated-new-drug-applications-and-505b2-applications. Accessed 24 March 2019.
11. While an ANDA applicant must identify an RLD in its application, a 505(b)(2) applicant must identify a "listed drug" (or drugs) in its application if it seeks to rely on FDA's previous safety or efficacy findings for that listed drug(s). While there are no FDA regulations governing how a 505(b)(2) applicant should choose a listed drug when various options are present, the agency has spoken to the issue in guidance and Citizen Petition responses. FDA has stated, "[i]f there is a listed drug that is the pharmaceutical equivalent of the drug proposed in the 505(b)(2) application, the 505(b)(2) applicant should provide patent certifications for the patents listed for the pharmaceutically equivalent drug" (FDA, *Draft Guidance for Industry: Applications Covered by Section 505(b)(2)*, at 8 (October 1999)). This serves to "ensure that the 505(b)(2) applicant does not use the 505(b) (2) process to end-run patent protections that would have applied had an ANDA been permitted" (FDA, Citizen Petition Response, Docket No. FDA-2004-P-0089 (formerly 2004P-0386), at 9 (30 November 2004) (hereinafter "RLD Choice Petition Response")). Additionally, these provisions "further ensure that the

505(b)(2) applicant (and FDA) can rely, to the maximum extent possible, on what is already known about a drug without having to re-prove (or re-review) what has already been demonstrated."

"When there is no listed drug that is a pharmaceutical equivalent to the drug product proposed in the 505(b)(2) NDA, neither the statute, the regulations, nor the Draft Guidance directly addresses how to identify the listed drug or drugs on which a 505(b)(2) applicant is to rely." In FDA's RLD Choice Petition Response, however, the agency stated:

it follows that the more similar a proposed drug is to the listed drug cited, the smaller the quantity of data that will be needed to support the proposed change. Accordingly, to avoid unnecessary duplication of research and review, when a section 505(b)(2) application has been submitted and no pharmaceutically equivalent drug product has previously been approved, the 505(b)(2) applicant should choose the listed drug or drugs that are most similar to the drug for which approval is sought. Similarly, if all the information relied on by FDA for approval...is contained in a single previously approved application and that application is a pharmaceutical equivalent or the most similar alternative to the product for which approval is sought, the 505(b)(2) applicant should certify only to the patents for that application. This is the case even when another application also contains some or all of the same information. FDA has not defined the factors that should be taken into account when determining "similarity" of drug products; however, FDA likely considers factors, such as active ingredient, dosage form, route of administration and strength. See 21 CFR 320.1(c).

12. See *FD&C Act* Section 505(j)(2)(C); 21 CFR 314.93.
13. See *FD&C Act* Section 505(j)(2)(A)(iv).
14. *Guidance for Industry: ANDA Submissions—Content and Format* (September 2018). FDA website. https://www.fda.gov/downloads/drugs/guidances/ucm400630.pdf. Accessed 24 March 2019.
15. *FD&C Act*, Section 505(j)(2)(A)(vii).
16. *Draft Guidance for Industry, on Bioavailability Studies Submitted in NDAs or INDs—General Considerations* (February 2019). FDA website. https://www.fda.gov/ucm/groups/fdagov-public/@fdagov-drugs-gen/documents/document/ucm631943.pdf. Accessed 31 March 2019.
17. *Draft Guidance for Industry, on Bioequivalence Studies with Pharmacokinetic Endpoints for Drugs Submitted under an ANDA* (December 2013). The guidance generally is applicable to dosage forms intended for oral administration and to non-orally administered drug products relying on systemic exposure measures that are suitable for documenting bioequivalence (e.g., transdermal delivery systems and certain rectal and nasal drug products). FDA website. https://www.fda.gov/downloads/drugs/guidances/ucm377465.pdf. Accessed 24 March 2019.
18. 21 CFR 320.24(b) Types of evidence to measure bioavailability or establish bioequivalence, on listing in vivo and in vitro approaches in descending order of accuracy, sensitivity, and reproducibility, with the primary test being an in vivo test in humans in which concentrations of the active ingredient in whole blood, plasma, serum, or other biological fluid is measured as a function of time. FDA website. https://www.accessdata.fda.gov/scripts/cdrh/cfdocs/cfcfr/CFRSearch.cfm?fr=320.24. Accessed 24 March 2019.
19. *Draft Guidance for Industry: Bioavailability and Bioequivalence Studies for Orally Administered Drug Products—General Considerations* (July 2002). Although *in vivo* testing is FDA's preferred method for an ANDA applicant to demonstrate bioequivalence, agency regulations state "bioequivalence may be demonstrated by several in vivo and in vitro methods," which are described at 21 CFR 320.24 in descending order of accuracy, sensitivity and reproducibility. FDA website. https://www.fda.gov/downloads/Drugs/Guidances/ucm154838.pdf. Accessed 24 March 2019.
20. 21 CFR 320.24(b)(5) Types of evidence to measure bioavailability or establish bioequivalence. FDA recently amended its ANDA bioequivalence regulations to require applicants to submit data from all bioequivalence studies the applicant conducts on the "same drug product formulation" submitted for approval. FDA website. https://www.accessdata.fda.gov/scripts/cdrh/cfdocs/cfcfr/CFRSearch.cfm?fr=320.24. Accessed 24 March 2019. See also 21 CFR 314.94(a) (7), 320.21(b)(1) and *Final Rule, Requirements for Submission of Bioequivalence Data*, 74 Fed. Reg. 2849 (16 January 2009).
21. The *FD&C Act* states an ANDA must include, among other things, "information to show the new drug is bioequivalent to the [RLD]...," *FD&C Act* Section 505(j)(2)(A)(iv), and that FDA must approve an ANDA unless, among other things, "information submitted in the application is insufficient to show that the drug is bioequivalent to the [RLD] . . ." at Section 505(j)(4)(F). However, FDA has discretion to determine how the bioequivalence requirement is met (*FD&C Act* Section 505(j)(7)(A)(i)(III)). FDA's discretion need only be based on a "reasonable and scientifically supported criterion, whether [the agency] chooses to do so on a case-by-case basis or through more general inferences about a category of drugs..." *Bristol-Myers Squibb Co. v. Shalala*, 923 F. Supp. 212, 218 (D.D.C. 1996) (quoting *Schering Corp. v. Sullivan*, 782 F. Supp. 645, 651 (D.D.C. 1992), vacated as moot sub nom, *Schering Corp. v. Shalala*, 995 F.2d 1103 (D.C. Cir. 1993)); see also *Fisons Corp. v. Shalala*, 860 F. Supp. 859, 865 (D.D.C. 1994) (upholding FDA's authority to waive the requirement for submission of *in vivo* evidence of bioequivalence where bioequivalence can be determined by other available science).
22. *Waiver of In Vivo Bioavailability and Bioequivalence Studies for Immediate-Release Solid Oral Dosage Forms Based on a Biopharmaceutics Classification System: Guidance for Industry*. FDA website. https://www.fda.gov/downloads/Drugs/GuidanceComplianceRegulatoryInformation/Guidances/UCM070246.pdf. Accessed 24 March 2019.
23. Unlike the five-year exclusivity provision, which prohibits FDA from even accepting an application during the exclusivity period, the three-year exclusivity provision only precludes FDA from making a new ANDA effective before the end of the three-year period (see Sections 505(j)(5)(F)(ii)-(iii) of the *FD&C Act*).
24. *FD&C Act* Section 505(b)(1) allows an NDA applicant to "file with the application the patent number and expiration date of any patent which claims the drug for which the applicant submitted the application or which claims a method of using such drug and with respect to which a claim of patent infringement could reasonably be asserted if a person not licensed by the owner engaged in the manufacture use, or sale of the drug."
25. CFR 314.53(c)(2)(ii)(P)(3) and 21 CFR 314.53(e) Submission of patent information. FDA website. https://www.accessdata.fda.gov/scripts/cdrh/cfdocs/cfcfr/CFRSearch.cfm?fr=314.53. Accessed 24 March 2019.
26. 21 CFR 314.94(a)(12)(i) Content and format of an abbreviated application. FDA website. https://www.accessdata.fda.gov/scripts/cdrh/cfdocs/cfcfr/CFRSearch.cfm?fr=314.94. Accessed 24 March 2019.
27. See 21 USC 271(e)(2) (noting it is an act of infringement to file an ANDA "for a drug claimed in a patent or the use of which is claimed in a patent).
28. *Draft Guidance for Industry: 180-Day Exclusivity: Questions and Answers* (January 2017). FDA website. https://www.fda.gov/downloads/Drugs/GuidanceComplianceRegulatoryInformation/Guidances/UCM536725.pdf. Accessed 24 March 2019.
29. FDA Final Rule, *Abbreviated New Drug Applications and 505(b)(2) Applications*, 81 Fed. Reg. 69,580 (6 February 2015). Federal Register website. https://www.federalregister.gov/documents/2016/10/06/2016-22690/abbreviated-new-drug-applications-and-505b2-applications. Accessed 24 March 2019.

30. Ibid; see also Karst KR. "*FDA Issues Final Hatch-Waxman Regulations to Implement Some of the Provisions of the 2003 Medicare Modernization Act*." HPM FDA Law Blog website. http://www.fdalawblog.net/fda_law_blog_hyman_phelps/2016/10/fda-issues-final-hatch-waxman-regulations-to-implement-some-of-the-provisions-of-the-2003-medicare-m.html. Accessed 24 March 2019.
31. *Caraco Pharm. Laboratories, Ltd. v. Novo Nordisk A/S*, 566 US 399 (2012) (holding that a generic manufacturer could bring a counterclaim seeking to correct patentee's use code on the ground that it was overbroad).

    At the time Caraco submitted its ANDA, there was only one method-of-use patent listed in the *Orange Book* covering the use of repaglinide in combination with metformin to lower blood glucose. Caraco initially filed a Paragraph IV certification for this patent stating it was "invalid or [would] not be infringed;" however, FDA advised Caraco that if it did not seek to market repaglinide for use with metformin, it could submit a "Section VIII" statement. Caraco submitted a "Section VIII" statement with proposed labeling carving out Novo Nordisk's patented metformin therapy. However, Novo Nordisk later changed its use code to describe "[a] method for improving glycemic control in adults with type 2 diabetes." Since Caraco's label now overlapped with Novo Nordisk's use code, the proposed carve-out was insufficient. The Supreme Court held that the counterclaim provision enables a generic manufacturer to obtain a judgment directing a brand company to "correct or delete" certain patent information that is blocking FDA's approval of a generic product. McAndrews, Held & Malloy Ltd. website. https://www.orangebookblog.com/orange_book_patent_listingdelisting/. Accessed 31 March 2019.
32. 21 CFR 314.127(a)(8)(ii)(B) Refusal to approve an abbreviated new drug application. FDA website. https://www.accessdata.fda.gov/scripts/cdrh/cfdocs/cfcfr/CFRSearch.cfm?fr=314.127. Accessed 24 March 2019.
33. 21 CFR 314.101(b)(1) Filing an application and receiving an abbreviated new drug application. FDA website. https://www.accessdata.fda.gov/scripts/cdrh/cfdocs/cfcfr/CFRSearch.cfm?fr=314.101. Accessed 24 March 2019.
34. Preamble to the Final Rule on ANDAs, *Abbreviated New Drug Applications and 505(b)(2) Applications*, 81 Fed. Reg. 69580, 69622 (6 October 2016); see also *ANDA Submissions—Refuse-to-Receive Standards: Guidance for Industry* (December 2016). FDA website. https://www.fda.gov/downloads/drugs/guidancecomplianceregulatoryinformation/guidances/ucm370352.pdf. Accessed 24 March 2019.
35. 21 CFR 314.101(b)(3). Filing an application and receiving an abbreviated new drug application. FDA website. https://www.accessdata.fda.gov/scripts/cdrh/cfdocs/cfcfr/CFRSearch.cfm?fr=314.101. Accessed 24 March 2019.
36. *GDUFA II Fee Structure Summary*. FDA website. http://www.fda.gov/downloads/ForIndustry/UserFees/GenericDrugUserFees/UCM525236.pdf. Accessed 24 March 2019.
37. Ibid.
38. 2019 Orange Book. FDA website. https://www.fda.gov/ucm/groups/fdagov-public/@fdagov-drugs-gen/documents/document/ucm071436.pdf. Accessed 31 March 2019.
39. Ibid
40. State laws also vary regarding how the final product selection is determined. In the majority of states, prescribers must indicate expressly substitution is not permitted by writing "Brand Necessary," "Do Not Substitute," "Dispense as Written," "Medically Necessary" or other approved wording on the prescription form. Some states include lines on the prescription form with the phrases "Product Selection Permitted" (or similar wording) and "Do Not Substitute." The prescriber can prevent product substitution by signing on the line. See generally National Association of Boards of Pharmacy, Survey of Pharmacy Law, 2003–2004.
41. Vivian JC. "Legal Aspects of Therapeutic Interchange Programs." *US Pharmacist* (2003).
42. *Orange Book* Preface, 39th ed. The *Orange Book* Preface further states:
    FDA classifies as therapeutically equivalent those products meeting the following general criteria: (1) they are approved as safe and effective; (2) they are pharmaceutical equivalents in that they (a) contain identical amounts of the same active drug ingredient in the same dosage form and route of administration and (b) meet compendial or other applicable standards of strength, quality, purity, and identity; (3) they are bioequivalent in that (a) they do not present a known or potential bioequivalence problem, and they meet an acceptable *in vitro* standard or (b) if they do present such a known or potential problem, they are shown to meet an appropriate bioequivalence standard; (4) they are adequately labeled; [and] (5) they are manufactured in compliance with current Good Manufacturing Practice regulations. (https://www.fda.gov/drugs/developmentapprovalprocess/ucm079068.htm)
43. Ibid.
44. 21 CFR 320.1(c) Definitions. FDA website. https://www.accessdata.fda.gov/scripts/cdrh/cfdocs/cfcfr/CFRSearch.cfm?fr=320.1. Accessed 24 March 2019.
45. Ibid.
46. Op Cit 42
47. Op Cit 38
48. Ibid.
49. Op Cit 42
50. Ibid.

Chapter 8

Patents and Exclusivity

Updated by Kurt R. Karst, JD

OBJECTIVES

❑ Understand the laws and regulations governing patent and non-patent market exclusivity available to sponsors of brand-name drugs and their effects on generic drug approval

❑ Understand how FDA interprets many of these laws and regulations

❑ Understand the patent certification process for generic drugs and the 180-day marketing exclusivity available to certain generic drug sponsors

LAWS, REGULATIONS AND GUIDELINES COVERED IN THIS CHAPTER

❑ *Federal Food, Drug, and Cosmetic Act* of 1938

❑ *Drug Price Competition and Patent Term Restoration Act* of 1984 (*Hatch-Waxman Act*)

❑ *Food and Drug Administration Modernization Act* of 1997

❑ *Orphan Drug Act* of 1983

❑ *Uruguay Rounds Agreements Act* of 1994

❑ *Leahy-Smith America Invents Act* of 2011

❑ *Generating Antibiotics Incentives Now Act* (*GAIN Act*), *Food and Drug Administration Safety and Innovation Act* (*FDASIA*) Section VIII

❑ Humane Use Device provisions, *FDASIA* Title VI, Part L

❑ *PDUFA V*, *FDASIA* Title I

❑ 21 CFR 314 Applications for FDA Approval to Market a New Drug

❑ 21 CFR 320 Bioavailability and Bioequivalence Requirements

❑ 21 CFR 316 Orphan Drugs

❑ 54 *Federal Register* 28,872 (10 July 1989), Proposed ANDA Regulations

❑ 59 *Federal Register* 50,338 (3 October 1994), ANDA regulations; patent and exclusivity provisions

❑ 68 *Federal Register* 36,676 (18 June 2003), Applications for FDA approval to market a new drug: patent submission and listing requirements and application of 30-month stays on approval of Abbreviated New Drug Applications certifying that a patent claiming a drug is invalid or will not be infringed

Regulatory Affairs Professionals Society

Chapter 8

- 81 Federal Register 69,580 (6 October 2016), Abbreviated New Drug Applications and 505(b)(2) Applications

- *Guidance for Industry: Qualifying for Pediatric Exclusivity Under Section 505A of the Federal Food, Drug, and Cosmetic Act* (September 1999)

- *Manual of Policies and Procedures 5240.3, "Review Order of Original ANDAs, Amendments and Supplements"* (October 2006)

- *Draft Guidance for Industry: Applications Covered by Section 505(b)(2)* (October 1978)

Introduction

As discussed in Chapter 16, the *Drug Price Competition and Patent Term Restoration Act* of 1984 (*Hatch-Waxman Act*) amended the *Federal Food, Drug, and Cosmetic Act* of 1938 (*FD&C Act*) to create the Abbreviated New Drug Application (ANDA) generic drug approval pathway under Section 505(j), as well as a hybrid approval pathway under Section 505(b)(2). The ANDA applicant relies entirely on FDA's findings of the third party's clinical data (the Reference Listed Drug or RLD), and its product is approved solely on the basis of its sameness to the RLD, while the 505(b)(2) applicant may conduct some clinical trials of its own and relies on FDA's findings of a third party's clinical data (or on published literature) to fill in any gaps needed to prove its drug is safe and effective under the *FD&C Act*. The *Hatch Waxman Act* also put mechanisms into place to protect the RLD's patent rights from companies that rely on the RLD's clinical data, while allowing drug developers (of innovators and generics alike) to conduct the work necessary to secure approval without infringing the RLD owner's patents, and ensuring these drugs come to market as early as possible after an RLD's patents have expired.

The *Hatch-Waxman Act* also gave drug companies that perform clinical studies several things in return for these allowances, including the opportunity to obtain a patent term extension for time lost during a patent's early life while its product was undergoing regulatory development. In addition, 505(b)(1) and (b)(2) applicants can submit certain types of patents to FDA to list in the *Orange Book* and also may be eligible for several periods of non-patent exclusivity. Certain ANDA sponsors may be eligible for a 180-day marketing exclusivity period for challenging patents for the RLD listed in FDA's *Orange Book*. Under the current law, an ANDA sponsor's eligibility for a period of 180-day market exclusivity can be forfeited under various scenarios.

Various other laws have been enacted in addition to the *Hatch Waxman Act* to incentivize the development of certain drug types. These laws include the *Orphan Drug Act*, which rewards sponsors for developing products to treat rare diseases and conditions; the *Best Pharmaceuticals for Children Act* (*BPCA*), which rewards sponsors for developing products for children; and the *Generating Antibiotic Incentives Now Act* (*GAIN Act*), which rewards companies for developing antibiotics against difficult-to-treat microorganisms. Each of these non-patent exclusivities is discussed in this chapter.

Patent-Related Market Exclusivity

Patent Term Extensions

Under Title II of the *Hatch-Waxman Act*, a patent related to an FDA-regulated product is eligible for extension if patent life was lost during a period when the product was being reviewed by FDA for approval.[1] This extension is known as a "patent term extension" (PTE). Only one patent can be extended for each regulatory review period, and that patent can be extended only once, even if it covers more than one drug product.[2] The extended patent protects all subsequently approved drug product uses and formulations, as long as the uses and formulations are covered by the underlying patent.[3] However, the PTE does not apply to any drug product uses or formulations that do not share the same active ingredient, or salt or ester thereof.[4]

The period of regulatory review for which the PTE is intended to compensate is composed of a "testing phase" and a "review phase." For a drug product, the testing phase begins on the effective date of an Investigational New Drug (IND) Application and ends on the date a New Drug Application (NDA) is submitted to FDA.[5] The review phase is the period between NDA submission and approval.[6] A patent term may be extended for a period of time that is the sum of one-half of the time in the testing phase, plus all the time in the review phase.[7] The regulatory review period must be reduced by any amount of time the applicant "did not act with due diligence."[8] The total (calculated) extension of the patent term may not exceed five years, and the extended patent term may not exceed 14 years from the date of NDA approval.[9]

Over the years, questions have cropped up as to when the review phase begins—i.e., when an application is considered initially submitted to FDA—in the context of "rolling" or modular submissions. Insofar as NDA and Biologics License Application (BLA) "fast track" submissions are concerned, FDA has determined receipt of the last module (or application component) makes the application complete and, thus, "initially submitted" for PTE purposes.[10] Similarly, the review phase for a New Animal Drug Application (NADA) reviewed under FDA's Phased

Data Review Policy and Administrative Applications for NADA begins when the company submits the final technical section to its application.[11]

As applied to drugs, the PTE law provides the term of a patent claiming the drug (or a use of the drug or a method of manufacturing a drug) to be extended from the original patent expiration date if:
1. the patent term has not expired
2. the patent has not previously been extended
3. the extension application is submitted by the patent owner of record within 60 days of NDA approval
4. the product, use or method of manufacturing claimed has been subject to a "regulatory review period" before it is marketed commercially
5. the NDA is the drug product's first permitted commercial use[12]

Criterion 5, a drug product's first permitted commercial use, has been the most controversial. The law defines *drug product* as a new drug's active ingredient, including any salt or ester of the active ingredient.[13] The question becomes whether the term refers to the ingredient's "active moiety," or the active ingredient itself. The definition chosen can have interesting implications when, for example, one is determining whether a new ester of an old active moiety is entitled to a PTE when the active moiety was approved previously as a different ester.

Until 2010, the US Patent and Trademark Office (PTO) relied on decisions by the US Court of Appeals for the Federal Circuit in *Fisons v. Quigg*, 8 U.S.P.Q.2d 1491 (D.D.C.1988), affirmed 876 F.2d 99 U.S.P.Q.2d 1869 (Fed.Cir.1989), and *Pfizer Inc. v. Dr. Reddy's Labs.*, 359 F.3d 1361 (Fed. Cir. 2004) to support the office's interpretation of the term *product* in 35 U.S.C. §156(a)(5)(A) to mean active moiety (i.e., the molecule in a drug product responsible for pharmacological action, regardless of whether the active moiety is formulated as a salt, ester or other non-covalent derivative) rather than "active ingredient" (i.e., the active ingredient physically found in the drug product, which would include any salt, ester or other non-covalent derivative of the active ingredient). In contrast, the Federal Circuit's 1990 decision in *Glaxo Operations UK Ltd. v. Quigg*, 894 F.2d 392, 13 USPQ2d 1628 (Fed. Cir. 1990), construed the term *product* in 35 U.S.C. §156(a) (5)(A) to mean active ingredient. In 2010, the US Court of Appeals for the Federal Circuit ruled in *Photocure ASA v. Kappos*, 603 F.3d 1372, 1375 (Fed. Cir. 2010) that the term *product* in 35 U.S.C. §156(a)(5)(A) means active ingredient rather than active moiety. Post-*Photocure,* PTO has framed patent term extension eligibility as a three-part inquiry: 1) Has the active ingredient been previously approved?; 2) Has a salt of the active ingredient been approved?; and 3) Has an ester of the active ingredient been approved? A "yes" to any of these questions means that the first permitted commercial marketing prong of the statute (i.e., criterion 5 above) has not been met.

In some cases, a patent scheduled to expire before an application for extension can be submitted to PTO may be granted an interim patent extension.[14] This can occur, for example, if the patent will expire before the NDA is approved. Two types of interim patent extensions are available:
1. interim patent extensions available during the review phase of the statutory regulatory review period[15]
2. interim patent extensions available during PTO's review of an application for patent term extension[16]

The cumulative patent time granted under either interim patent type extension cannot exceed the patent term extension a company could obtain under regular patent extension provisions. PTO reviews each application for an interim patent extension to ensure a patent will not be extended longer than its eligibility under the law.

Orange Book Patent Listing

The *FD&C Act* and FDA regulations require each NDA sponsor to submit with its application "the patent number and the expiration date of any patent which claims the drug for which the applicant submitted the [NDA] or which claims a method of using[17] such drug and with respect to which a claim of patent infringement could reasonably be asserted if a person not licensed by the owner engaged in the manufacture, use, or sale of the drug."[18] FDA regulations clarify "such patents consist of drug substance (active ingredient) patents, drug product (formulation and composition) patents, and method-of-use patents."[19] Patents that cover the drug's manufacturing method cannot be listed.

Thus, to be listed in the *Orange Book*, the patent must claim the drug or a method of using the drug that is the subject of the NDA; and a claim of patent infringement must be reasonably capable of assertion by the NDA holder or patent owner for the unauthorized manufacture, use or sale of the drug that is the subject of the NDA.[20] Once an NDA is approved, FDA is required to publish information in the *Orange Book* on the patents claiming the drug or its method of use.[21] If a new patent meeting the requirements of *FD&C Act* Section 505(b)(1) and FDA patent listing regulations is issued while an NDA is pending FDA review, or has received NDA approval, the NDA sponsor must submit information on the patent to FDA within 30 days of issuance.[22]

An ANDA or 505(b)(2) application that cites an RLD (which, in the context of a 505(b)(2) NDA is technically referred to as a "listed drug" rather than an RLD) for approval must contain one of four possible certifications "with respect to each patent which claims the [listed] drug...or which claims a use for such listed drug...and for which information is required to be filed" by the RLD/NDA holder and listed in the *Orange Book*.[23] If there are patents on the drug, and the ANDA or 505(b)(2) applicant decides not to challenge them, the applicant submits a Paragraph III certification, and FDA cannot approve the application until the patents have expired.[24] If the patents have expired already, or the required patent information has not been filed, the ANDA or 505(b)(2) applicant submits a Paragraph II or Paragraph I certification, respectively, and FDA can approve the application.[25] If the ANDA or 505(b)(2) applicant decides to challenge a patent listed in the *Orange Book*, the applicant submits a Paragraph IV certification claiming the patent is "invalid or will not be infringed by the manufacture, use, or sale of the new drug for which the [ANDA or 505(b)(2) application] is submitted."[26]

ANDA applicants also have an alternative to these four certifications if the patent is a "method of use patent which does not claim a use for which the applicant is seeking approval." In this case, the application instead may contain "a statement that the method of use patent does not claim such a use."[27] This often is referred to as a "section viii statement" and permits a generic applicant to "carve out" a patent-protected use from its proposed labeling, provided the omission of such protected information does not "render the proposed drug product less safe or effective than the listed drug for all remaining, non-protected conditions of use."[28] An ANDA applicant that submits a section viii statement is not entitled to the 180-day exclusivity period discussed below based on that statement, although it still might be entitled to the exclusivity based on a paragraph IV certification to another patent.[29] Similarly, an ANDA is not barred from approval by the 180-day exclusivity period of another ANDA applicant, based on the ANDA's containing a section viii statement, although the ANDA still might be barred if it contains a paragraph IV certification to a different patent.[30]

An NDA or patent owner may choose to sue a generic applicant that submits a Paragraph IV certification. If suit is brought, FDA is prohibited statutorily from approving the ANDA for 30 months, with certain limited exceptions (i.e., the so-called "30-month stay").[31] If a patent infringement suit is not brought by the NDA or patent owner, FDA can approve the ANDA once it has determined all conditions required for approval have been met.

FDA has developed various procedural tools to carry out its obligations under the *Hatch Waxman Act*, including its use code system for evaluating a section viii statement's propriety. Under this system, the RLD owner submits to FDA a use code for any method of use patents listed in the *Orange Book* that describe what the patent covers.[32] When evaluating a section viii statement's propriety, FDA will compare the ANDA labeling to the use code and determine whether the label describes a use claimed in the patent. If the patent covers a use described in the label, FDA will deny the section viii statement and require the ANDA holder to include an appropriate patent certification.[33] In 2011, in *Caraco Pharm. Labs., Ltd. v. Novo Nordisk A/S*, 132 S. Ct. 1670 (U.S. 2012), the US Supreme Court held that an ANDA applicant that objects to the use code could bring a lawsuit against the patent owner for a declaration the use code is written too broadly.

Until recently, questions also have arisen regarding FDA's RLD policies, with some believing FDA would require an application submitted under Section 505(b)(2) to cite the closest RLD as its supporting drug, and to furnish patent certifications for any RLD patents listed in the *Orange Book*. In January 2015, a district court affirmed FDA's determination that a 505(b)(2) application for colchicine capsules that did not rely on any clinical data from an earlier approval for colchicine tablets did not need to provide patent certifications for patents listed in the *Orange Book* for the colchicine tablets.[34] That decision was affirmed in July 2016 by the US Court of Appeals for the District of Columbia Circuit.

Non-Patent Statutory Market Exclusivity

Five-Year Exclusivity

Under the *FD&C Act* (as amended by *Hatch-Waxman Act* Title I), five-year exclusivity is available to the sponsor of an application (either a full 505(b)(1) NDA or a 505(b)(2) application) for a drug product that does not contain an active moiety previously approved under Section 505(b) of the *FD&C Act* (i.e., an NDA for a New Chemical Entity (NCE)). Five-year exclusivity prevents the submission of an ANDA (and a 505(b)(2) application) that "refers to the drug for which the [approved Section 505(b) NCE NDA] was submitted before the expiration of five years from the date of the approval" of the NCE NDA.[35] Thus, five-year exclusivity sometimes is called "NCE exclusivity." NCE exclusivity prevents the submission of a generic application for the approved active ingredient or any salt or ester of the approved active ingredient for five years. However, five-year exclusivity does not prevent FDA from approving, or a company from submitting, a full Section 505(b)(1) NDA for the same drug.

As with the PTE provisions for new molecules approved under the *FD&C Act*, the statutory provisions governing the term "drug," and whether a drug is new for purposes of NCE exclusivity under Sections 505(c)(3)(E)

(ii) and 505(j)(5)(F)(ii), are ambiguous. Neither provision addresses whether drug means the particular drug product that is the subject of a previously approved NDA with five-year exclusivity or, more generally, the approved active moiety. FDA identified this ambiguity in the preamble to its proposed rule implementing the exclusivity provisions of the *Hatch-Waxman Act*:

> The language of sections 505(c)(3)(E) and 505(j)(5)(F)[36] of the act is ambiguous as to which ANDAs or 505(b)(2) applications are affected by an innovator's exclusivity. The statutory language allows at least two interpretations. The narrower interpretation of the protection offered by exclusivity is that exclusivity covers only specific drug products and therefore protects from generic competition only the first approved version of a drug...The broader interpretation of the coverage of exclusivity is that it covers the active moieties in new chemical entities...FDA has concluded that the broader interpretation of the scope of exclusivity should be applied to all types of exclusivity conferred by sections 505(c)(3)[(E)] and 505(j)[(5)(F)] of the act. Therefore, when exclusivity attaches to an active moiety or to an innovative change in an already approved drug, the submission or effective date of approval of ANDAs and 505(b)(2) applications for a drug with that active moiety or innovative change will be delayed until the innovator's exclusivity has expired, whether or not FDA has approved subsequent versions of the drugs entitled to exclusivity, and regardless of the specific listed drug product to which the ANDA or 505(b)(2) application refers.[37]

This policy, known as FDA's Umbrella Policy, effectively replaces the term "drug" in the statutory text with the term "active moiety."[38] However, this should not be taken to mean a drug cannot qualify for NCE exclusivity simply because it yields the same active moiety as a previously approved drug. If the molecule has structural differences from those of a previously approved molecule, other than a difference in salt or ester form, it still might qualify for NCE exclusivity, even though it yields the same active moiety *in vivo*.

Combination products also have presented interesting issues of statutory interpretation for FDA. Until 2014, FDA required all the active ingredients in a new drug product not to have been approved previously to qualify for NCE exclusivity. FDA changed its policy in 2014 in response to several industry-sponsored Citizen Petitions and now will grant NCE exclusivity for a combination product as long as one of the active ingredients satisfies its requirements for a new chemical entity.[39]

Three-Year Exclusivity

Under the *FD&C Act* (as amended by Title I of the *Hatch-Waxman Act*), a sponsor may qualify for a three-year period of exclusivity for an application (a full 505(b)(1) NDA, a 505(b)(2) application or a supplement to either) if the application contains "reports of new clinical investigations (other than bioavailability studies)" that were "essential to approval" of the application and were "conducted or sponsored by" the applicant.[40] All three of these criteria must be satisfied to qualify for three-year exclusivity.[41] Three-year exclusivity often is referred to as "new clinical investigation" or "new use" exclusivity.

Each criterion is defined in FDA's implementing regulations. A "new clinical investigation" is:

> an investigation in humans the results of which have not been relied on by FDA to demonstrate substantial evidence of effectiveness of a previously approved drug product for any indication or of safety for a new patient population and do not duplicate the results of another investigation that was relied on by the agency to demonstrate the effectiveness or safety in a new patient population of a previously approved drug product.[42]

An investigation is "essential to approval" of an application if "there are no other data available that could support approval of the application."[43] FDA explained that if the agency were aware of "published reports of studies other than those conducted or sponsored by the applicant, or other information...sufficient for FDA to conclude that a proposed drug product or change to an already approved drug product is safe and effective," exclusivity would not be appropriate.[44] The applicant must submit a list of all publicly available reports of clinical investigations "that are relevant to the conditions for which the applicant is seeking approval" and explain why these studies or reports do not provide a sufficient basis for approval.[45]

Finally, an investigation is "conducted or sponsored by the applicant" if:

> (B)efore or during the investigation, the applicant was named...as the sponsor of the [IND]...under which the investigation was conducted, or the applicant or the applicant's predecessor in interest, provided substantial support for the investigation. To demonstrate "substantial support," an applicant must either provide a certified statement from a certified public accountant that the applicant provided 50 percent or more of the cost of conducting the study or provide an explanation why FDA should consider the applicant to have conducted or sponsored the study if the applicant's financial contribution to the study is less than 50 percent or the applicant did not sponsor the investigational new drug. A predecessor in interest is an

entity, e.g., a corporation, that the applicant has taken over, merged with, or purchased, or from which the applicant has purchased all rights to the drug. Purchase of nonexclusive rights to a clinical investigation after it is completed is not sufficient to satisfy this definition.[46]

Three-year exclusivity prevents FDA from approving[47] an ANDA or a 505(b)(2) application for the protected "conditions of approval" until three years after the date of the original NDA's or NDA supplement's FDA approval.[48] Specifically, the statute states:

> If an application submitted under subsection (b) for a drug, which includes an active ingredient (including any ester or salt of the active ingredient) that has been approved in another application approved under subsection (b), is approved after the date of the enactment of this clause and if such application contains reports of new clinical investigations (other than bioavailability studies) essential to the approval of the application and conducted or sponsored by the applicant, the Secretary may not make the approval of an application submitted under subsection (b) for the conditions of approval of such drug in the approved subsection (b) application effective before the expiration of three years from the date of the approval of the application under subsection (b) if the investigations described in clause (A) of subsection (b)(1) and relied upon by the applicant for approval of the application were not conducted by or for the applicant and if the applicant has not obtained a right of reference or use from the person by or for whom the investigations were conducted.[49]

The emphasized clause above, often referred to as the "bar clause," describes which 505(b)(2) NDAs will be barred or blocked from approval by the three-year exclusivity and thus describes the scope of three-year exclusivity. FDA's interpretation of the bar clause, and thus a determination of the scope of three-year exclusivity under *FD&C Act* Section 505(c)(3)(E)(iii), generally involves two aspects.

The first aspect of the scope inquiry focuses on the drug at issue. The phrase "such drug in the approved subsection (b) application" in the bar clause refers to the earlier use of the term "drug" in the eligibility clause. The "drug" in the eligibility clause refers to "a drug, which includes an active ingredient (including any ester or salt of the active ingredient) that has been approved in another application;" that is, the drug that includes a previously approved active moiety. FDA interprets this cross-reference to mean, for a single-entity drug to be potentially barred by three-year exclusivity for another single-entity drug, the drug must contain the same active moiety as the drug with three-year exclusivity.[50]

The second aspect of the scope inquiry focuses on the "new clinical investigations" "essential to approval" "conducted or sponsored by the applicant." Under this aspect of the inquiry, the scope of the "new clinical investigations" "essential to approval" "conducted or sponsored by the applicant" informs the "conditions of approval" relevant to three-year exclusivity.[51]

Although neither the statute nor FDA's regulations define the phrase "conditions of approval," for purposes of determining the scope of three-year exclusivity, the preamble to FDA's 1989 proposed rule governing exclusivity provides the agency's interpretation. It makes clear FDA's view that three-year exclusivity covers the innovative change supported by the "new clinical investigations:"

> Exclusivity provides the holder of an approved new drug application limited protection from new competition in the marketplace for the innovation represented by its approved drug product. Thus, if the innovation relates to a new active moiety or ingredient, then exclusivity protects the pioneer drug product from other competition from products containing that moiety or ingredient. If the innovation is a new dosage form or route of administration, then exclusivity protects only that aspect of the drug product, but not the active ingredients. If the innovation is a new use, then exclusivity protects only that labeling claim and not the active ingredients, dosage form, or route of administration.[52]

FDA thus interprets the scope of exclusivity to be related to the scope of the underlying "new clinical investigations" that were essential to the approval. Exclusivity does not extend beyond the scope of the approval and does not cover aspects of the drug product for which "new clinical investigations" were not essential. Courts have upheld FDA's view of the relationship between "new clinical investigations" that were essential to the approval and the scope of three-year exclusivity.[53]

The general rule is that a generic drug product's labeling approved under an ANDA must have the "same" labeling as the RLD.[54] This is to prevent NDA holders from continually supplementing their labels with new data that could repeatedly extend the three-year exclusivity period, and thereby indefinitely bar FDA from approving the ANDA. FDA regulations permit the ANDA labeling to omit "an indication or other aspect of labeling protected by patent or accorded exclusivity under [505(j)(5)(F)] of the [*FD&C Act*]."[55] FDA can approve an ANDA with labeling "carve outs" if a particular use of the innovator drug is protected by a patent or period of exclusivity, and other uses are not protected. Before approving such a drug, FDA first must determine the "carve out" of the protected information does not "render the proposed drug product less safe or effective than the listed drug for all remaining, non-protected conditions of use."[56]

Pediatric Exclusivity

BPCA amended the *FD&C Act* to create Section 505A, which provides an additional six months of exclusivity to pharmaceutical manufacturers that conduct acceptable pediatric studies[57] of new and currently marketed drug products identified by FDA in a Pediatric Written Request (PWR) for which pediatric information would be beneficial. A grant of pediatric exclusivity extends to all *Orange Book*-listed patents[58] and non-patent market exclusivity periods granted to an application holder under the *FD&C Act*. The exclusivity does not extend the term of a patent, but it does extend by six months the date on which FDA is permitted to approve an ANDA that contains a Paragraph III certification.[59] The *Food and Drug Administration Safety and Innovation Act* of 2012 (*FDASIA*) made the *BPCA* amendments permanent, and they are not required to be reauthorized by future user fee negotiations.

An important aspect of an initial grant of pediatric exclusivity is additional market exclusivity for not just the pediatric indications or formulations, but for all protected indications and formulations of that sponsor's drug. Thus, an initial grant of pediatric exclusivity attaches to the patent and non-patent market exclusivities for any of the sponsor's approved drug products (including certain combination products) that contain the active moiety for which pediatric exclusivity was granted, and not to a specific drug product.[60]

While an initial period of pediatric exclusivity is broad, a second exclusivity period is narrow. Specifically, a second period of pediatric exclusivity attaches only to any three-year period of new clinical investigation exclusivity granted by FDA with respect to a pediatric use supplement containing studies submitted in response to a second PWR issued by FDA.[61] A second period of pediatric exclusivity does not apply to any existing *Orange Book*-listed patent exclusivity or any existing five-year periods of NCE exclusivity or orphan drug exclusivity. FDA's September 1999 guidance document further explains the scope of a second period of pediatric exclusivity:

> Pediatric studies submitted in a supplemental application for a drug that has already received one period of pediatric exclusivity may qualify the drug to receive a different 6-month period of pediatric exclusivity if submitted in response to a [PWR]. The different 6-month period of pediatric exclusivity will attach only to any exclusivity period under sections 505(c)(3)(D)(iv) and 505(j)(5)(D)(iv) [(i.e., three-year exclusivity)] granted to the supplemental application for which the studies were completed.[62]

An important exception to the applicability of pediatric exclusivity relative to new PWRs was added to the law in 2007. Under the exception, FDA will not apply a period of pediatric exclusivity to an unexpired period of patent or non-patent exclusivity if the agency's decision to grant pediatric exclusivity "is made later than 9 months prior to the expiration of such period."[63]

Orphan Drug Exclusivity

Under the *Orphan Drug Act* of 1983 (Pub. L. No. 97-414, 96 Stat. 2049 (1983)), as amended, a manufacturer or sponsor may submit a written request for FDA to designate a drug for a rare disease or condition (i.e., an "orphan drug"). A rare disease or condition affects fewer than 200,000 people in the US, or affects more than 200,000 people but the sponsor can show it will be unable to recover its development and marketing costs from sales of the product in the US.[64]

Once FDA approves a marketing application for a drug designated as an orphan drug, the agency may not approve another company's version of the "same drug" for the same disease or condition for seven years, unless the subsequent drug is "different" from the approved orphan drug.[65]

A drug is different from an approved orphan drug if it is chemically or structurally distinct. The degree of chemical or structural similarity that allows FDA to determine whether two drugs are the same depends on whether the drugs are small molecules or macromolecules.[67] However, even a drug that is structurally the same as an approved orphan drug may be approved for the same condition if it is "clinically superior" to the approved orphan drug. For decades, FDA's orphan drug regulations have defined a *clinically superior* drug as "a drug...shown to provide a significant therapeutic advantage over and above that provided by an approved orphan drug (that is otherwise the same drug)" in one of three ways:

1. greater effectiveness as assessed by effect on a clinically meaningful endpoint in adequate and well-controlled trials
2. greater safety in a substantial portion of the target populations
3. a demonstration the drug makes a major contribution to patient care[68]

In 2017, the statute was amended to codify FDA's clinical superiority regulations.[69]

In addition, the *FD&C Act* and FDA's orphan drug regulations identify circumstances under which the agency can approve another version of the same drug for the same orphan disease or condition during the term of another sponsor's orphan drug exclusivity (e.g., failure to assure a sufficient quantity of the drug).[66]

Paragraph IV Litigation and 180-Day Exclusivity

An ANDA or 505(b)(2) applicant making a Paragraph IV certification must notify the NDA holder and patent owner of its application once FDA determines the application is substantially complete. The applicant must give notice to the NDA holder and patent owner "not later than 20 days after the date of the postmark on the notice with which [FDA] informs the applicant that the application has been filed."[70] If the patent certification is in an amendment or supplement to the ANDA, the applicant must give notice to the NDA holder and patent owner "at the time at which the applicant submits the amendment or supplement, regardless of whether the applicant has already given notice with respect to another such certification contained in the application or in an amendment or supplement to the application."[71] The notice to the NDA owner and patent owner must include a "detailed statement of the factual and legal basis of the applicant's opinion that the patent is not valid or will not be infringed" and must "state that an application that contains data from bioavailability or bioequivalence studies has been submitted for the drug with respect to which the certification is made to obtain approval to engage in the commercial manufacture, use, or sale of the drug before the expiration of the patent referred to in the certification."[72]

The NDA holder or patent owner has 45 days from the date of receipt of such notice to file a suit for patent infringement to benefit from the 30-month stay provided by the *Hatch Waxman Act*.[73] If a patent infringement suit is brought within this 45-day period, FDA cannot approve the ANDA or 505(b)(2) application until the earlier of:

- the expiration of a single 30-month stay of approval, which may be shortened or lengthened by the court if "either party to the action fail[s] to reasonably cooperate in expediting the action"[74]
- the date on which a district court enters judgment in favor of the defendant (i.e., the ANDA or 505(b)(2) applicant) that the patent is invalid or not infringed (or on the date of a settlement order or consent decree signed and entered by the court stating that the patent that is the subject of the certification is invalid or not infringed)
- if the district court enters judgment in favor of the plaintiff (i.e., the NDA holder or patent owner) and that decision is appealed by the ANDA or 505(b)(2) applicant, the date on which the court of appeals enters judgment in favor of the ANDA or 505(b)(2) applicant that the patent is invalid or not infringed (or on the date of a settlement order or consent decree signed and entered by the court of appeals stating that the patent that is the subject of the certification is invalid or not infringed)

If the district court's judgment is not appealed or is affirmed by the court of appeals, an ANDA or 505(b)(2) approval can be made effective immediately. An ANDA or 505(b)(2) applicant also may assert a counterclaim "seeking an order requiring the [NDA] holder to correct or delete the patent information submitted by the [NDA] holder on the grounds that the patent does not claim either the drug for which the application was approved or an approved method of using the drug."[75] A counterclaimant is not entitled to damages resulting from inappropriate patent information listing.[76]

If a patent infringement suit is not brought by the NDA holder or the patent owner within the 45-day period, FDA can approve the ANDA or 505(b)(2) application as soon as it is satisfied the application meets its requirements. In addition, an applicant whose application contains a Paragraph IV certification may bring an action for declaratory judgment on patent infringement or invalidity if it is not sued within the 45-day period.[77] To file a declaratory judgment on non-infringement grounds, an applicant must provide an offer of confidential access to its application to allow the NDA holder or patent owner the opportunity "of evaluating possible infringement of the patent that is the subject of the [Paragraph IV] certification."[78] An applicant is not entitled to damages in such an action even if it obtains a declaratory judgment in its favor.[79]

FD&C Act Section 505(j)(5)(B)(iv) establishes an incentive for generic manufacturers to submit Paragraph IV certifications and to challenge *Orange Book*-listed patents as invalid or not infringed by providing a 180-day period of market exclusivity.[80] This means, in certain circumstances, the applicant that submits an ANDA containing the first Paragraph IV certification to an *Orange Book*-listed patent is protected from competition from other generic versions of the same drug product for 180 days.

Prior to enactment of the *Medicare Prescription Drug, Improvement, and Modernization Act* of 2003 (*MMA*), 180-day exclusivity was patent based, such that a period of 180-day exclusivity could arise from each *Orange Book*-listed patent. Pre-*MMA*, 180-day exclusivity (which applies to a dwindling number of pending ANDAs) began on the date FDA "receives notice from the applicant of the first commercial marketing of the drug" under the first ANDA or "the date of a decision of a court in [a patent infringement action] holding the patent which is the subject of the certification to be invalid or not infringed," whichever is earlier. Post-*MMA*, 180-day exclusivity generally is drug based, providing a single 180-day exclusivity period (that can be shared by multiple first applicants) with respect to each listed drug. Also, post-*MMA*, there is a single trigger to 180-day exclusivity—first commercial marketing.

Under *MMA* changes to the *FD&C Act*, the first applicant that qualifies for 180-day exclusivity can forfeit

Table 8-1. 180-Day Exclusivity Forfeiture Snapshot

"Failure to Market:" A first applicant forfeits exclusivity if it fails to market the drug by the *later of* –
(1) The *earlier of* 75 days after ANDA *approval*, or 30 months after ANDA *submission*; and
(2) Either:
- 75 days after favorable court decision on all qualifying patents (appeals court, or unappealed district court, decision): or
- 75 days after favorable court settlement or consent decree on all qualifying patents; or
- 75 days after all qualifying patents are delisted from the *Orange Book*.

Immediate Forfeiture:
- If the ANDA applicant withdraws the ANDA or the application is withdrawn because the applicant failed to meet approval requirements;
- If the ANDA applicant amends or withdraws its Paragraph IV certification;
- If the ANDA applicant fails to obtain tentative approval within 30 months after filing the application (unless the failure is caused be a review of or change in approval requirements imposed after the ANDA is filed or because of a related Citizen Petition);
- If the ANDA applicant enters into an agreement with another generic applicant, the NDA holder, or patent owner, and the Federal Trade Commission (FTC) files a complaint, and either the FTC or an appeals court rules that the agreement violates antitrust laws; or
- If all of the patents certified to in the generic applicant's Paragraph IV certification have expired.

eligibility for exclusivity under various circumstances. While some of the statutory forfeiture provisions are straightforward—e.g., 180-day exclusivity is forfeited if the ANDA sponsor withdraws its exclusivity-qualifying Paragraph IV certification—others are more complex. In particular, the so-called "failure to market" forfeiture provisions under *FD&C Act* Section 505(j)(5)(D)(i)(I) require FDA to calculate a forfeiture date based on the later of two events (see **Table 8-1**). Although FDA has not issued formal regulations implementing the 180-day exclusivity forfeiture provisions, *MMA* added to the *FD&C Act* by the agency has applied them on a case-by-case basis, and has issued several letter decisions describing its interpretation of these provisions. Congress enacted the forfeiture provisions to "ensure that the 180-day exclusivity period enjoyed by the first generic to challenge a patent cannot be used as a bottleneck to prevent additional generic competition."[81]

Of the six 180-day exclusivity forfeiture provisions created by the *MMA*, the one invoked by FDA most often is *FD&C Act* Section 505(j)(5)(D)(i)(IV), which states that 180-day exclusivity eligibility is forfeited if:

The first applicant fails to obtain tentative approval of the application within 30 months after the date on which the application is filed, unless the failure is caused by a change in or a review of the requirements for approval of the application imposed after the date on which the application is filed.

The *Food and Drug Administration Amendments Act* of 2007 (*FDAAA*) clarified *FD&C Act* Section 505(j)(5)(D)(i)(IV) such that if "approval of the [ANDA] was delayed because of a [citizen] petition, the 30-month period under such subsection is deemed to be extended by a period of time equal to the period beginning on the date on which the Secretary received the petition and ending on the date of final agency action on the petition (inclusive of such beginning and ending dates) . . ."[82] The large number of 180-day exclusivity forfeitures under *FD&C Act* Section 505(j)(5)(D)(i)(IV) likely is due, in part, to the significant amount of time FDA's Office of Generic Drugs has historically taken to review and act on ANDAs. *FDASIA* further clarified and modified the timeframe within which an ANDA must receive tentative approval to avoid forfeiting the 180-day marketing exclusivity. *FDASIA* shortened the time for FDA to respond to certain Citizen Petitions related to generic drugs and biologics from 180 to 150 days (see **Table 8-1**).

Exclusivity for Antibiotic Drugs

Until 1997, antibiotic drugs were approved under *FD&C Act* Section 507 and were not entitled to any *Hatch-Waxman Act* benefits.[83] In 1997, the *Food and Drug Administration Modernization Act* (*FDAMA*) (Pub. L. No. 105-115, 111 Stat. 2295 (1997)), among other things, repealed *FD&C Act* Section 507 and required all NDAs for antibiotic drugs to be submitted under *FD&C Act* Section 505.

FDAMA included a transition provision declaring an antibiotic application approved under Section 507 before the enactment of *FDAMA* would be considered an application submitted, filed and approved under *FD&C Act* Section 505.[84] Congress created an exception to this transition provision. *FDAMA* Section 125(d)(2) exempted certain applications for antibiotic drugs from those provisions of *FD&C Act* Section 505 that provide patent listing, patent certification and market exclusivity. Specifically, *FDAMA* Section 125(d)(2) exempted an

Table 8-2. Differences Among Applications Submitted and Approved Under FD&C Act Section 505

	505(b)(1) NDA	505(b)(2) Application	ANDA
Patent and Exclusivity Information	Submit information on patents claiming the drug or a method of use; exclusivity request claiming exclusivity	Submit information on patents claiming the drug or a method of use (if any); generally, a patent certification (Paragraph I, II, III or IV) or "section viii" statement is required; exclusivity request claiming exclusivity and exclusivity statement that the listed drug is subject to exclusivity (if any exists)	Patent certification (Paragraph I, II, III or IV) or a "section viii" statement is required; exclusivity statement that the RLD is subject to exclusivity (if any exists)
Five-Year Exclusivity	Prevents the submission of an ANDA or 505(b)(2) application for five years after NDA approval, except that an ANDA or 505(b)(2) application with a Paragraph IV certification to an *Orange Book*-listed patent may be submitted after four years	Only for applications for NCEs; prevents the submission of an ANDA or another 505(b)(2) application for five years after application approval, except that an ANDA or other 505(b)(2) application with a Paragraph IV certification to an *Orange Book*-listed patent may be submitted after four years; also subject to NDA holder's exclusivity	No exclusivity; subject to five-year exclusivity of NDA or 505(b)(2) applicant
Three-Year Exclusivity	Only if one or more of the clinical studies, other than BA/BE studies, was essential to the product's approval; prevents FDA from making effective an ANDA or 505(b)(2) application for the NDA conditions of approval	Only if one or more of the clinical studies, other than BA/BE studies, was essential to the product's approval; prevents FDA from making an ANDA or other 505(b)(2) application effective for the conditions of approval of the 505(b)(2) application; also subject to NDA holder's exclusivity	Subject to three-year exclusivity of NDA or 505(b)(2) applicant
Orphan Drug Exclusivity	Prevents FDA from approving an application for the same drug (moiety) for the same orphan indication for seven years	Prevents FDA from approving an application for the same drug for the same condition for seven years; also subject to NDA holder's exclusivity	Subject to seven-year exclusivity of NDA or 505(b)(2) applicant
Antibiotic Exclusivity	Provides an additional five-year exclusivity for qualified infectious disease products	Not applicable	Not applicable
Pediatric Exclusivity	Extends by six months all other types of patent and non-patent market exclusivity an NDA holder may have under the *FD&C Act* for a particular active moiety, provided there is no less than nine months of term remaining when FDA grants pediatric exclusivity	Extends by six months all other types of patent and non-patent market exclusivity an NDA holder may have under the *FD&C Act* for a particular active moiety; also subject to NDA holder's exclusivity	Subject to exclusivity of NDA or 505(b)(2) applicant
180-Day Exclusivity	Not applicable	Not applicable	Available to any "first applicant" that submits an ANDA with a Paragraph IV certification; prevents FDA from approving subsequent Paragraph IV ANDAs submitted by applicants that are not first applicants
Orange Book Listing	Included in the *Orange Book* as a listed drug; may be identified as an RLD	Included in the *Orange Book* as a listed drug; can be identified as a therapeutic equivalent (e.g., "AB-rated") to the listed drug if BE is demonstrated and also is a pharmaceutical equivalent	Included in the *Orange Book* as a listed drug; can be identified as a therapeutic equivalent (e.g., "AB-rated") to RLD if BE is demonstrated and also is a pharmaceutical equivalent; listed in the *Orange Book* as a "pharmaceutical alternative" without a therapeutic equivalence evaluation code if approved under a suitability petition

antibiotic application from *Hatch-Waxman* benefits when "the drug that is the subject of the application contains an antibiotic drug and the antibiotic drug was the subject of an application" received by FDA under *FD&C Act* Section 507 before the enactment of *FDAMA* (i.e., 21 November 1997). Thus, antibiotic drug applications received by FDA prior to 21 November 1997, and applications submitted to FDA subsequent to that date for drugs containing an antibiotic drug that was the subject of an application received by FDA prior to 21 November 1997, are within the *FDAMA* Section 125(d)(2) exemption, and not eligible for *Hatch-Waxman* benefits. These drugs are referred to as "old antibiotics." Applications for antibiotic drugs not subject to the *FDAMA* Section 125(d)(2) exemption (i.e., so-called "new antibiotics") are eligible for *Hatch-Waxman* benefits.

In October 2008, Congress effectively repealed *FDAMA* Section 125(d)(2), so old antibiotic drugs now are eligible for some *Hatch-Waxman* benefits. Specifically, Section 4 of the *QI Program Supplemental Funding Act* of 2008 (*QI Act*)—"QI" stands for Qualifying Individual—amended the *FD&C Act* to add a new Section 505(v) "Antibiotic Drugs Submitted Before November 21, 1997," to create certain *Hatch-Waxman* benefits for old antibiotics.

The *Generating Antibiotic Incentives Now Act* (*GAIN Act*), which was a part of *FDASIA* Title VIII, adds a new Section 505E (21 U.S.C. 355E). It grants an additional five years of market protection at the end of the existing exclusivity for Qualified Infectious Disease Products (QIDPs). This protection is added to any applicable *Hatch-Waxman* five-year NCE exclusivity, *Hatch-Waxman* three-year new clinical studies exclusivity or seven-year orphan drug exclusivity. The five-year extension also is in addition to any six-month pediatric exclusivity. However, as *FD&C Act* Section 505E(c) states, not all QIDP applications are eligible for the additional market exclusivity.[85] In addition, an application for a drug designated as a QIDP is eligible for Priority Review and Fast Track designation (*FD&C Act* Sections 524A and 506(a)(1) (21 U.S.C. 356(a)(1))), respectively.

Exclusivity for Enantiomers of Previously Approved Racemates

For decades, FDA has treated single enantiomers of approved racemates as previously approved active moieties not eligible for five-year NCE exclusivity (but eligible for three-year exclusivity).[86] (In chemistry, enantiomers are stereoisomers that are non-superimposable complete mirror images of one another. Enantiomers may be either "right-handed" or "left-handed." A racemic mixture has equal amounts of left- and right-handed enantiomers of a particular chiral molecule.) *FDAAA*, however, amended the *FD&C Act* to add Section 505(u), which permits an NDA applicant for an enantiomer (that is contained in a previously approved racemic mixture) containing full reports of clinical investigations conducted or sponsored by the applicant to "elect to have the single enantiomer not be considered the same active ingredient as that contained in the approved racemic drug," and, thus, be eligible for five-year NCE exclusivity.[87] The enantiomer NDA applicant cannot "rely on any investigations that are part of an application submitted under [*FD&C Act* Section 505(b)] for approval of the approved racemic drug."[88]

There are certain limitations under *FD&C Act* §505(u). The enantiomer NDA must not be for a condition of use "(i) in a therapeutic category in which the approved racemic drug has been approved; or (ii) for which any other enantiomer of the racemic drug has been approved."[89] In addition, if the enantiomer NDA applicant elects to receive exclusivity, FDA may not approve the enantiomer drug for any condition of use in the "therapeutic category" in which the racemic drug is approved until 10 years after approving the enantiomer.[90] The term *therapeutic category* is defined in *FD&C Act* Section 505(u) to mean "a therapeutic category identified in the list developed by the United States Pharmacopeia pursuant to section 1860D-4(b)(3)(C)(ii) of the *Social Security Act* and as in effect on [27 September 2007]," which FDA must publish and that may be amended by regulation.[91]

Summary

Brand-name drug sponsors may qualify for patent and non-patent exclusivities of various durations, which could delay the submission or final approval of a marketing application for a generic version of the brand-name drug. In addition, certain generic drug sponsors may qualify for their own 180-day period of market exclusivity. Each type of exclusivity is different in scope and subject to different rules and interpretations (**Table 8-2**).

References
1. Before 8 June 1995, patents typically had 17 years of life from the date of issue by the US Patent and Trademark Office (PTO). The *Uruguay Rounds Agreements Act* (*URAA*), Pub. L. No. 103-465, 108 Stat. 4809 (1994), changed the patent term in the US so that patents granted after 8 June 1995 (the effective date of *URAA*) have a 20-year life from the date of the first filing of the patent application with PTO. Under a transition provision in *URAA*, a patent in effect on 8 June 1995 was awarded a term of the greater of 20 years from the filing of the patent or 17 years from the date of patent issuance. See 35 U.S.C. §154(c)(1).
2. 35 U.S.C. §156(a).
3. 35 U.S.C. §156(b).
4. 35 U.S.C. §156(b)(1).
5. 35 U.S.C. §156(g)(1)(B)(i).
6. 35 U.S.C. §156(g)(1)(B)(ii).
7. 35 U.S.C. §§156(c)(2) and 156(g)(1)(B).
8. 35 U.S.C. §156(c)(1).
9. 35 U.S.C. §§156(g)(6)(A) and 156(c)(3).
10. This has been the topic of several letter decisions, including in Docket No. FDA-2005-E-0310 concerning KEPIVANCE, in

Docket No. FDA-2009-E-0237 concerning DEXILANT and in Docket No. FDA-2007-E-0278 concerning ZOLINZA.
11. *Wyeth Holdings Corp. v. Sebelius*, 603 F.3d 1291 (Fed. Cir. 2010).
12. 35 U.S.C. §156(a)(1)-(5). The patent term extension law defines the term "drug product" to mean "the active ingredient of a new drug [as defined in §201(p) of the FD&C Act]...including any salt or ester of the active ingredient, as a single entity or in combination with another active ingredient." Id. §156(f)(2). With respect to the applicability of patent term extensions to combination drugs, the US Court of Appeals for the Federal Circuit ruled in 2004 that "the statute places a drug product with two active ingredients, A and B, in the same category as a drug product with a single ingredient.... To extend the term of a patent claiming a composition comprising A and B, either A or B must not have been previously marketed." *Arnold Partnership v. Dudas*, 362 F.3d 1338, 1341 (Fed. Cir. 2004).
13. 35 U.S.C. §156(f).
14. 35 U.S.C. §§156(a)(1), 156 (d)(5) and 156 (e)(2).
15. 35 U.S.C. §156(d)(5).
16. 35 U.S.C. §156(e)(2).
17. Method-of-use patents listed in the *Orange Book* are typically assigned a "patent use code." The *Orange Book* contains hundreds of such use codes.
18. *FD&C Act* §505(b)(1).
19. FDA regulations at 21 CFR 314.53(b)(1) further state:
For patents that claim the drug substance, the applicant must submit information only on those patents that claim the drug substance that is the subject of the pending or approved NDA or that claim a drug substance that is the same as the active ingredient that is the subject of the approved or pending NDA. For patents that claim only a polymorph that is the same as the active ingredient described in the approved or pending NDA, the applicant must certify in the required FDA declaration form that the applicant has test data, as set forth in paragraph (b)(2) of this section, demonstrating that a drug product containing the polymorph will perform the same as the drug product described in the NDA. For patents that claim a drug product, the applicant must submit information only on those patents that claim the drug product, as is defined in §314.3, that is described in the pending or approved NDA. For patents that claim a method of use, the applicant must submit information only on those patents that claim those indications or other conditions of use for which approval is sought or has been granted in the NDA.
20. FDA, Final Rule; Applications for FDA Approval to Market a New Drug: Patent Submission and Listing Requirements and Application of 30-Month Stays on Approval of Abbreviated New Drug Applications Certifying That a Patent Claiming a Drug Is Invalid or Will Not Be Infringed, 68 Fed. Reg. 36,676 (18 June 2003).
21. *FD&C Act* Sections 505(b)(1) & 505(c)(2).
22. Ibid. Section 505(c)(2); see also 21 CFR 314.53(c)(2)(ii).
23. *FD&C Act* Section 505(j)(2)(A)(vii).
24. Ibid. Section 505(j)(2)(A)(vii)(III) and Section 505(j)(5)(B)(ii).
25. Ibid. Sections 505(j)(2)(A)(vii)(I)-(II) & (j)(5)(B)(i).
26. Ibid. Sections 505(j)(2)(A)(vii)(IV) & 505(j)(5)(B)(iii).
27. Ibid. Section 505(j)(2)(A)(viii). For a listed drug covered by a period of five-year NCE exclusivity, generally an ANDA and 505(b)(2) applicant may not reference the listed drug until such exclusivity (described in the next sections) applicable to that listed drug has expired. For this reason, the information in the NDA for the listed drug is sometimes said to be under "data exclusivity."
28. 21 CFR 314.127(a)(7). An ANDA applicant must make an additional certification (or submit an additional section viii statement) as to any new patent listed in the *Orange Book* while its application is pending if the NDA holder submits the new patent to FDA for *Orange Book* listing within 30 days of patent issuance. See 21 CFR 314.94(a)(12)(vi). A Paragraph IV certification to a later-listed patent will not result in an additional 30-month stay of ANDA approval.
29. *FD&C Act* Section 505(j)(5)(A)(iv)(I) states that "Subject to subparagraph (D), if the application contains a certification described in paragraph (2)(A)(vii)(IV) and is for a drug for which a first applicant has submitted an application containing such a certification, the application shall be made effective on the date that is 180 days after the date of the first commercial marketing of the drug (including the commercial marketing of the listed drug) by any first applicant." Section 8 does not yield exclusivity.
30. Ibid.
31. *FD&C Act* Section 505(j)(5)(B).
32. 21 CFR 314.53(c)(2)(ii)(P)(3) requires the NDA owner to submit "[t]he description of the patented method of use as required for publication." This description is the use code.
33. *Caraco Pharm. Labs., Ltd. v. Novo Nordisk A/S*, 132 S. Ct. 1670 (U.S. 2012). In 2016, FDA finalized regulations that, among other things, are intended to clarify the agency's policies concerning method-of-use patents and patent use codes. See generally 81 Federal Register 69,580 (6 October 2016), Abbreviated New Drug Applications and 505(b)(2) Applications.
34. *Takeda Pharms., U.S.A., Inc. v. Burwell*, 2015 U.S. Dist. LEXIS 5908 (D.D.C. Jan. 13, 2015).
35. Specifically, five-year exclusivity prevents the submission of an ANDA or 505(b)(2) application for five years unless the applicant submits a Paragraph IV patent certification. See *FD&C Act* Sections 505(b) (2)(A) and 505(j)(2)(A)(vii). In this case, the ANDA or 505(b)(2) application can be submitted after four years; however, "if an action for patent infringement is commenced during the one-year period beginning [four years] after the date of the approval of the [NCE NDA], the thirty-month [stay] period...shall be extended by such amount of time which is required for seven and one-half years to have elapsed from the date of approval of the [NCE NDA]." *FD&C Act* Sections 505(c)(3)(E)(ii) & 505(j)(5)(F)(ii).
36. The original citations are to Sections 505(c)(3)(D) and 505(j)(4)(D) of the *FD&C Act*. These sections were recodified in the *MMA*.
37. 54 Fed. Reg. at 28,897.
38. FDA's regulations define the term *active moiety* to mean "the molecule or ion, excluding those appended portions of the molecule that cause the drug to be an ester, salt (including a salt with hydrogen or coordination bonds), or other noncovalent derivative (such as a complex, chelate or clathrate) of the molecule, responsible for the physiological or pharmacological action of the drug substance." 21 CFR 314.108(a).
39. Combination PTE CP response.
40. 21 CFR 314.108(b)(4), (5); see also *FD&C Act* Sections 505(j)(5) (F) (iii) and (iv).
41. 21 CFR 314.50(j)(4).
42. 21 CFR 314.108(a).
43. Ibid.
44. FDA, Final Rule, ANDA Regulations; Patent and Exclusivity Provisions, 59 Fed. Reg. at 50,338, 50,357 (3 October 1994).
45. 21 CFR 314.50(j)(4)(ii).
46. 59 Fed. Reg. at 50,368-69; see also 21 CFR 314.50(j)(4)(iii).
47. This is an important difference compared to five-year exclusivity, which prevents the submission of a generic application.
48. 21 CFR 314.108(b)(4), (5).
49. *FD&C Act* §505(c)(3)(E)(iii) (emphasis added).
50. *See* FDA, Citizen Petition Response, Docket No. FDA-2015-P-2482 (Oct. 5, 2015).
51. FDA considered the meaning of the phrase "conditions of approval" in a decisional letter regarding whether Astellas Pharma US, Inc.'s ("Astellas'") three-year exclusivity for its tacrolimus drug, ASTAGRAF XL, blocks approval of Veloxis Pharmaceuticals, Inc.'s ("Veloxis") tacrolimus drug, ENVARSUS XR. See Letter from FDA to Veloxis (12 January 2015) (Veloxis Letter), *aff'd Veloxis Pharms., Inc. v. FDA*, 109 F. Supp. 3d 104 (D.D.C. 2015), available at https://ecf.dcd.uscourts.gov/cgi-bin/show_public_doc?2014cv2126-57. ENVARSUS XR, the subject of

a second-in-time 505(b)(2) NDA, did not reference or otherwise rely on the approval of ASTAGRAF XL. In the Veloxis Letter, FDA considered whether approval of ENVARSUS XR was blocked. In interpreting the statutory phrase "conditions of approval of such drug in the subsection (b) application," FDA considered the conditions of approval for tacrolimus. FDA ruled that the three-year exclusivity for ENVARSUS XR covered "a once-daily, extended-release dosage form of tacrolimus for prophylaxis of organ rejection for use in de novo kidney transplant patients." Because the active moiety was the same for the two products at issue, FDA then considered the scope of the new clinical investigations essential to the approval conducted or sponsored by the applicant to determine the "conditions of approval of such drug," and thus the scope of exclusivity. FDA's decision that the approval of ENVARSUS XR was blocked from approval because of the exclusivity applicable to ASTAGRAF XL was challenged in court, which upheld FDA's determination. In particular, the court ruled that regardless of other allegedly clinically meaningful differences, "[t]he effect of marketing exclusivity in [FDC Act § 505(c)(3)(E)(iii)] turns on whether a second-in-time 505(b)(2) NDA shares any conditions of approval with the first-in-time 505(b) drug granted exclusivity." Veloxis at *25 (emphasis added).
52. FDA, Proposed Rule, Abbreviated New Drug Application Regulations, 54 *Fed. Reg.* 28,872, 28,896-97 (July 10, 1989).
53. See *Veloxis Pharms, Inc. v. U.S. Food & Drug Admin.*, 109 F. Supp. 3d 104, at 115-24 (D.D.C. 2015); *Zeneca Inc. v. Shalala*, Case No. 99-307, 1999 WL 728104, at *12 (D. Md. Aug. 11, 1999) aff'd, 213 F.3d 161 (4th Cir. 2000) ("The exclusivity extends only to the 'change approved in the supplement'"); *AstraZeneca Pharm. LP v. Food & Drug Admin.*, 872 F. Supp. 2d 60, 79 (D.D.C. 2012) aff'd, 713 F.3d 1134 (D.C. Cir. 2013) ("[T]he Court concludes that [FDC Act § 505(j)(5)(F)(iv)] is ambiguous. The FDA has reasonably interpreted and applied the applicable statute . . ."). Although the latter two cases involved the parallel statutory provision for ANDAs, rather than the provision at issue here (i.e., FDC Act § 505(c)(3)(E)(iii)), the provision pertaining to ANDAs interpreted by the courts includes the same language regarding the scope of three-year exclusivity. The courts upheld as reasonable FDA's interpretation of the relationship between the scope of clinical studies that earned exclusivity, the change in the product that resulted, and the scope of the exclusivity earned.
54. *FD&C Act* Section 505(j)(2)(A)(v).
55. 21 CFR 314.94(a)(8)(iv).
56. 21 CFR 314.127(a)(7).
57. The term "pediatric studies" is defined as "at least one clinical investigation (that, at [FDA's] discretion, may include pharmacokinetic studies) in pediatric age groups (including neonates in appropriate cases) in which a drug is anticipated to be used." *FD&C Act* Section 505A(a).
58. *FD&C Act* Section 505A does not extend the term of the patent itself, but only the period during which FDA cannot approve (or accept for review) an ANDA or 505(b)(2) application that includes a Paragraph II or Paragraph III certification, or a Paragraph IV certification that concerns a patent that a court has determined is valid and would be infringed. See *FD&C Act* Section 505A(c)(2).
59. Exclusivity does not extend term of patent.
60. See *National Pharmaceutical Alliance v. Henney*, 47 F. Supp. 2d 37 (D.D.C. 1999); and *Guidance for Industry: Qualifying for Pediatric Exclusivity Under Section 505A of the Food, Drug, and Cosmetic Act* (September 1999).
60. *FD&C Act* Section 505A(g).
62. *Guidance for Industry: Qualifying for Pediatric Exclusivity Under Section 505A of the Food, Drug, and Cosmetic Act*, at 14.
63. *FD&C Act* Sections 505A(b)(2), 505A(c)(2).
64. *FD&C Act* Section 526(a)(2).
65. Orphan drug exclusivity operates independently of patent protection and independently of five- and three-year exclusivity (and therefore, pediatric exclusivity as well).
66. *FD&C Act* Sections 527(b)(1) and (2); see also 21 CFR 316.31(a).
67. 21 CFR 316.3(13).
68. 21 CFR 316.3(b)(3)(i)-(iii).
69. See *FD&C Act* §527(c). The statutory change was made after FDA's regulation was repeatedly invalidated by the courts. See *Depomed, Inc. v. HHS*, 66 F. Supp. 3d 217 (D.D.C. 2014); Order, *Eagle Pharms., Inc. v. Azar*, No. 16-790 (D.D.C. June 8, 2018), ECF No. 64. Indeed, the D.C. District Court held in both *Depomed* and *Eagle* that *FD&C Act* Section 527's plain language compels FDA to award exclusivity to any orphan-designated drug upon approval, regardless of whether the sponsor actually demonstrates clinical superiority.
70. *FD&C Act* Section 505(j)(2)(B)(ii)(I).
71. *FD&C Act* Section 505(j)(2)(B)(ii)(II).
72. *FD&C Act* Sections 505(j)(2)(B)(iv)(I)–(II).
73. *FD&C Act* Section 505(j)(5)(B)(iii).
74. *FD&C Act* Section 505(j)(5)(B)(iii).
75. *FD&C Act* Section 505(j)(5)(C)(ii).
76. *FD&C Act* Section 505(j)(5)(C)(iii).
77. *FD&C Act* Section 505(j)(5)(C)(i).
78. Ibid.
79. *FD&C Act* Section 505(j)(5)(C)(iii).
80. A 505(b)(2) application is not eligible for 180-day exclusivity.
81. 149 Cong. Rec. S15746 (daily ed. Nov. 24, 2003) (statement of Sen. Schumer).
82. *FD&C Act* Section 505(q)(1)(G)
83. *Glaxo, Inc. v. Heckler*, 623 F. Supp. 69 (E.D.N.C. 1985).
84. FDAMA Section 125(d)(1).
85. In 2018, FDA issued draft guidance interpreting the statutory limitations. *Qualified Infectious Disease Product Designation; Questions and Answers: Draft Guidance for Industry* (January 2018). FDA website. https://www.fda.gov/downloads/Drugs/GuidanceComplianceRegulatoryInformation/Guidances/UCM594213.pdf. Accessed 26 April 2019.
86. See 54 *Fed. Reg.* at 28,898. "FDA will consider whether a drug contains a previously approved active moiety on a case-by-case basis. FDA notes that a single enantiomer of a previously approved racemate contains a previously approved active moiety and is therefore not considered a new chemical entity."
87. *FD&C Act* Section 505(u)(1).
88. *FD&C Act* Section 505(u)(1)(A)(ii)(II).
89. *FD&C Act* Section 505(u)(1)(B).
90. *FD&C Act* Section 505(u)(2)(A).
91. *FD&C Act* Section 505(u)(3).

Helpful References and Resources
- FDA's Office of Generic Drugs webpage, including exclusivity decisions. FDA website. www.fda.gov/Drugs/DevelopmentApprovalProcess/HowDrugsareDevelopedandApproved/ApprovalApplications/AbbreviatedNewDrugApplicationANDAGenerics/ucm142112.htm. Accessed 26 April 2019.
- *Federal Food, Drug, and Cosmetic Act*. Legal Information Institute website. https://www.law.cornell.edu/uscode/text/21/chapter-9. Accessed 26 April 2019.
- The Electronic *Orange Book*. FDA website. www.accessdata.fda.gov/scripts/cder/ob/default.cfm. Accessed 26 April 2019.
- FDA's Paragraph IV Patent Certification List. FDA website. www.fda.gov/Drugs/DevelopmentApprovalProcess/HowDrugsareDevelopedandApproved/ApprovalApplications/AbbreviatedNewDrugApplicationANDAGenerics/ucm047676.htm. Accessed 26 April 2019.

Chapter 9

Over-the-Counter (Nonprescription) Drug Products

Updated by Valerie Ramsey, DRSc, MS, RAC

OBJECTIVES

- Learn OTC drug product definition and characteristics
- Understand OTC drug development and regulation
- Understand OTC drug development through the NDA and OTC drug monograph processes
- Understand regulatory pathways available for industry to request an OTC drug monograph be reopened and/or amended
- Understand Rx-to-OTC switch
- Understand OTC "Drug Facts" label
- Learn packaging requirement for OTC drugs, tamper evident packaging

LAWS, REGULATIONS AND GUIDELINES COVERED IN THIS CHAPTER

- *Federal Food, Drug, and Cosmetic Act* of 1938
- 1951 *Durham-Humphrey Amendment*
- *Kefauver-Harris Amendments* of 1962
- *Controlled Substances Act* of 1970
- *Poison Prevention Packaging Act* of 1970
- *Food and Drug Administration Modernization Act* of 1997
- *Combat Methamphetamine Epidemic Act* of 2005
- *Dietary Supplement and Nonprescription Drug Consumer Protection Act* of 2006
- *Methamphetamine Production Prevention Act* of 2008
- 76 FR 74696 Implementation of the Methamphetamine Production Prevention Act of 2008
- 63 FR 59463, 21 CFR 211 Tamper-evident packaging requirements for over-the-counter human drug products
- 21 CFR 10.30 Citizen petition
- 21 CFR 201.66 Format and content requirements for over-the-counter (OTC) drug product labeling
- 21 CFR 210 Current good manufacturing practice in manufacturing, processing, packing or holding of drugs: General
- 21 CFR 211 Tamper-Evident Packaging Requirements for Over-the-Counter Human Drug Products

- ❑ 21 CFR 211.132 Packaging and label control

- ❑ 21 CFR 314.108 Application for FDA Approval to Market a New Drug

- ❑ 21 CFR Part 330.10 Procedures for classifying OTC drugs as generally recognized as safe and effective and not misbranded, and for establishing monographs

- ❑ 21 CFR Part 330.14 Additional criteria and procedures for classifying OTC drugs as generally recognized as safe and effective and not misbranded

- ❑ 21 CFR 331.80 Labeling of nasal decongestant drug products

- ❑ 21 CFR 341.90 Professional labeling

- ❑ 21 CFR 343 Internal analgesic, antipyretic, and antirheumatic drug products for over-the-counter human use

- ❑ 21 CFR 1314 Retail sale of scheduled listed chemical products

- ❑ 21 CFR 1700 Poison prevention packaging

Introduction

Over-the-counter (OTC) drugs are defined as drugs that are safe and effective for use by the general public without a prescription. More than 300,000 OTC drug products are marketed in the US, encompassing about 800 significant active ingredients.[1] These include more than 80 OTC drug classes (therapeutic categories), ranging from acne drug products to weight control drug products. As with prescription drugs, the Center for Drug Evaluation and Research (CDER) oversees OTC drugs to ensure they are labeled properly and their benefits outweigh their risks.[2] These drugs often are located on pharmacy shelves easily accessible by patients, but also may be located in non-pharmacy outlets, such as grocery and convenience stores and large discount retailers.[3]

Prior to 1951, there was no legal basis for designating what was acceptable as an OTC drug product. The 1951 *Durham-Humphrey Amendment* to the *Federal Food, Drug, and Cosmetic Act (FD&C Act)* established three criteria that would limit a drug to prescription status (21 USC 353):
- habit-forming drugs
- not safe for use unless supervised by a healthcare professional
- limited to prescription use under a New Drug Application (NDA)

The *Food and Drug Administration Modernization Act* of 1997 (*FDAMA*) repealed the requirement for a prescription for habit-forming drugs from the *FD&C Act*; however, a drug could still be limited to prescription under the *Controlled Substances Act* (*CSA*) of 1970 if sufficient potential abuse evidence exists (21 USC 829(d)).

In contrast, OTC drugs generally have the following characteristics:[4]
- their benefits outweigh their risks
- the potential for misuse and abuse is low
- consumers can use them for self-diagnosed conditions
- they can be labeled adequately
- healthcare practitioners are not needed for the product's safe and effective use

An OTC drug subset in the US, such as drugs containing ephedrine, pseudoephedrine or phenylpropanolamine, have restrictions on retail sale. For example, the *Combat Methamphetamine Epidemic Act* of 2005 banned over-the-counter sales of cold medicines containing pseudoephedrine, which commonly is used to make methamphetamine. This ban effectively limited the sale of cold medicine with pseudoephedrine to behind-the-counter. The *Methamphetamine Production Prevention Act* of 2008 clarified requirements for information entry and purchaser signature in a logbook, further strengthening the behind-the-counter requirements (76 FR 74696). These products, while considered OTC, are kept behind the counter to prevent customers from having direct access and are dispensed by a pharmacist when a purchaser presents a state- or federal government-issued identification (21 CFR 1314). Although this OTC subset exists, the drug classification system in the US still is officially considered a two-class system consisting of OTCs and prescription drugs.

In March 2012, FDA considered expanding the nonprescription drug definition to include cholesterol, blood pressure, migraine headache and asthma medications.[5] Under this *Nonprescription Safe Use Regulatory Expansion (NSURE)* initiative, FDA held a public hearing to obtain information and public comments on the feasibility of allowing nonprescription (OTC) use of prescription drugs.[6] However, FDA still is working on a practical regulatory framework and has not issued a ruling for this potential Rx-to-OTC switch.

OTC medications can carry risks, including the possibility of side effects, drug or food interactions or harm due to excessive doses. These risks are disclosed on the "Drug Facts" label on all OTC products.

OTC Drug Development and Regulation

OTC drugs are developed under either the OTC Monograph or OTC New Drug Application (NDA) process. FDA's OTC drug review is handled primarily by two divisions within CDER's Office of Drug Evaluation IV (ODE-IV). The Division of Nonprescription Regulation Development (DNRD) is responsible for the OTC drug monograph process and products marketed under those monographs. Conversely, the Division of Nonprescription Clinical Evaluation (DNCE) is responsible for managing Investigational New Drug (IND) applications and the associated NDAs for those products approved under the NDA route.

Regulations relating to all drug manufacture and testing aspects (current Good Manufacturing Practices (CGMPs)), facility listing and inspection, drug registration, clinical trials and safety oversight apply equally to prescription and OTC drug products. All OTC drug manufacturing activities must comply with 21 CFR 210 and 211, current Good Manufacturing Practices for Pharmaceuticals. Drug substance and drug product manufacturing sites are required to register with FDA and are subject to Prior Approval Inspections (PAIs) for NDA products and routine FDA inspections. OTC drug products also are required to be drug listed; the National Drug Code (NDC) is suggested, but not required, to be displayed on the product label. Both establishment registration and drug listing are submitted electronically to FDA using Structured Product Labeling (SPL) format. Medical oversight activities for OTC drug products also mimic those required for prescription products. The *Dietary Supplement and Nonprescription Drug Consumer Protection Act* of 2006 mandated safety reporting requirements for OTC drug products marketed without an NDA.[8] Prior to this, only NDA products were subject to adverse event reporting requirements. NDA OTC drug lifecycle management and maintenance activities are identical to those of their prescription counterparts.

OTC Drugs Developed Under the OTC Drug Monograph Process

DNRD is responsible for OTC drug monograph development. Supporting data for different active ingredients' safety and efficacy for a particular drug monograph are reviewed by appropriate scientific personnel. Efficacy data may require a prescription review division medical officer and/or statistician's input. Carcinogenicity or other animal toxicology data may require input from a CDER pharmacologist. While DNRD is considered the lead division in developing an OTC drug monograph, reviewers from multiple divisions within the Office of New Drugs (OND) also are involved in this process.

How is an OTC Monograph Established?

An OTC drug monograph provides specific guidance on the conditions under which that category's drugs generally are recognized as safe and effective (GRASE). These conditions may relate to active ingredients (strength and dosage form) and labeling requirements (indications, warnings and directions for use) necessary and appropriate for the safety or effectiveness of drugs the monograph covered (21 CFR 330.10). Currently, more than 300,000 OTC drug products are on the market, and many of these were approved via the OTC monograph route.[9]

In 1972, FDA initiated an OTC drug review process as part of implementing the *Kefauver-Harris Amendments* of 1962. The OTC drug review process encompassed the review of marketed products' safety and efficacy. FDA reviewed the active ingredients and labeling of more than 80 therapeutic categories of drugs, rather than reviewing individual drug products. By grouping products into categories and evaluating active ingredients rather than each product, FDA was able to make the process more efficient. Following the review of each category, an OTC drug monograph is developed and published in the *Federal Register*. **Table 9-1** details more than 80 therapeutic categories reviewed by an expert Advisory Panel and the three-step public rulemaking process (call for information, proposed rules and a codified final rule) resulting in publication in the *Federal Register*.[10]

The review process begins with appointing subject matter experts to a therapeutic category-specific Advisory Panel. Review panel formation is followed by a *Federal Register* notice from the commissioner (i.e., FDA) for the public to submit data within a defined time period. Under 21 CFR 330.10, data regarding OTC monographs can be submitted by anyone, including a drug company, health professional, consumer or citizen's group. Open Advisory Panel meetings are held to review the data and provide recommendations, including assigning active ingredients to one of three categories:

- Category I: generally recognized as safe and effective for the claimed therapeutic indication
- Category II: not generally recognized as safe and effective or unacceptable indications
- Category III: insufficient data available to permit final classification

Advisory Panel recommendations are published as an Advance Notice of Proposed Rulemaking (ANPR) for public review and comment within a defined time period. An opinion regarding the ANPR must be submitted as correspondence to an established monograph docket. After collecting public comments, FDA publishes its conclusions in a Tentative Final Monograph (TFM) (Proposed Rule). The TFM also is published for public review and comment. FDA reviews any additional

Table 9-1. OTC Monograph Therapeutic Category Subtopics Evaluated as Part of the OTC Review Process

Acne	Callus Remover	Nighttime Sleep Aid
Allergy	Corn Remover	Ophthalmic
Analgesic	Dandruff	Oral Health Care
Analgesic, Internal	Daytime Sedative	Oral Wound Healing
Anorectal	Decongestant, Nasal	Otic
Antacid	Dental Care	Overindulgence, Food & Drink
Anthelmintic	Deodorant	Internal Pancreatic Insufficiency
Antibiotic, First Aid	Diaper Rash	Pediculicide
Anticaries	Digestive Aid	Poison Oak/Ivy
Anticholinergic	Drink Overindulgence	Poison Treatment
Antidiarrheal	Exocrine Pancreatic Insufficiency	Prostatic Hypertrophy
Antiemetic	Expectorant	Psoriasis
Antiflatulent	External Analgesic	Seborrheic Dermatitis
Antifungal	Fever Blister	Sedative, Daytime
Antihistamine	First Aid Antibiotic	Skin Bleaching
Antimalarial	Food Overindulgence	Skin Protectant
Antimicrobial	Hair Growth & Loss	Sleep Aid, Nighttime
Antiperspirant	Hormone	
Antipyretic	Hypophosphatemia/Hyperphosphatemia	Smoking Deterrent
Antirheumatic	Ingrown Toenail	Stimulant
Antitussive	Insect Bite & Sting	Stomach Acidifier
Aphrodisiac	Insect Repellent	Sunscreen
Astringent	Internal Analgesic	Thumbsucking
Benign Prostatic Hypertrophy	Internal Deodorant	Topical Analgesic
Boil Treatment	Laxative	Vaginal Contraceptive
Bronchodilator	Leg Muscle Cramps	Vaginal Drug Products
Camphorated Oil	Male Genital Desensitizers	Vitamins & Minerals
Cholecystokinetic	Menstrual	Wart Remover
Cold & Cough	Nailbiting	Weight Control
Colloidal Silver	Nasal Decongestant	

information submitted prior to publishing a Final Monograph (FM) (Final Rule). An example is provided in **Table 9-2**, with citations for ANPR, TFM and FM for acne drug products containing benzoyl peroxide, a specific active ingredient.[11] Once the FM is published, manufacturers of products not complying with FM requirements are given a defined timeframe to withdraw their products from the market, bring the products into monograph compliance or submit an NDA. FMs are codified in the CFR. According to 21 CFR 330.1, products complying with monographs can be marketed without FDA preapproval, provided they are listed appropriately, comply with CGMPs and are manufactured in a registered facility.

The monograph process can be very lengthy, as FDA timelines for moving a TFM to an FM have not been defined. Hence, a number of monographs still have not been finalized. For example, the oral healthcare drug products monograph is not final, even though the original Advisory Panel provided its expert opinion in 1979. Products meeting the conditions of in-process TFMs can be marketed. FDA can amend or repeal FMs as new information becomes available. For example, the *OTC Internal Analgesic Drug Products* monograph (21 CFR 343) was amended in 2009 to include an organ-specific warning statement for acetaminophen and NSAIDs. In addition to monograph changes initiated by FDA, two regulatory pathways are available for someone to request an OTC drug monograph be reopened and/or amended:

1. citizen petition
2. Time and Extent Application (TEA)

The citizen petition process, codified in 21 CFR 10.30, can be used to amend or repeal conditions in a proposed or final OTC drug monograph. According to agency guidance, the citizen petition process should not be used to make an initial request to amend or repeal conditions in the OTC drug monograph system marketed under *FD&C Act* Section 505 after the beginning of the OTC drug review in 1972 or those without any US marketing experience. These conditions must undergo a review through submission of a TEA.[12] Under the TEA process, codified in 21 CFR 330.14, a condition could include an ingredient, botanical drug substance, dosage form, dosage strength or route of administration marketed for a specific OTC use. This process can be utilized only when the condition has been marketed for a significant time (five or more continuous years in the same country) with a significant marketing distribution (tens of millions of dosage units sold).

The TEA is only the first step in the process. If the condition the TEA proposes is considered eligible for a monograph, a notice requesting safety and effectiveness data is published in the *Federal Register*. The agency may use an Advisory Panel to review safety and effectiveness data. Once an ingredient is determined to be GRASE for a condition, the agency may propose amending an existing monograph or establishing a new one.

OTC Drugs Developed Through the NDA Process

Products not covered by or not marketed under the OTC drug monograph system (i.e., not GRASE) are subject to FDA preapproval through the NDA process under *FD&C Act* Section 505 prior to marketing. Four NDA routes are available for OTC products:
- direct-to-OTC NDA
- Rx-to-OTC switches
  - full switch (NDA supplement)
  - partial switch (new NDA)
- NDA monograph deviation (§330.11)
- generic (ANDA)

A sponsor seeking to market an OTC product, as either a new NDA or a switch from a prescription product, can submit an application to DNCE. DNCE will oversee drug development, including IND review and regulatory action, and may obtain specific subject matter review division (SSMRD) input during the development process. After a sponsor submits an NDA, DNCE reviews the consumer studies, postmarketing safety data, OTC labeling and any regulatory issues. SSMRD collaborates with DNCE and typically reviews the controlled clinical trial efficacy and safety data. Additional input is obtained as needed from other disciplines outside DNCE, including clinical pharmacology, statistics and chemistry.[13,14] **Table 9-3** summarizes the differences between the NDA/ANDA and OTC drug monograph marketing pathways.

Direct-to-OTC NDA

A product can be approved as OTC by the NDA route even if it was never available as a prescription drug. The same requirements apply for direct-to-OTC NDA products as for new prescription drug products, except the applicant also must prove the product can be used safely by the wider consumer population without healthcare professional oversight. Colgate Total® toothpaste (active ingredients: Sodium Fluoride and Triclosan) and Abreva® (active ingredient: docosanol) are examples of direct-to-OTC NDAs.

Rx-to-OTC Switch

An Rx-to-OTC route is used when it can be demonstrated a prescription product can be used by the wider consumer population without healthcare professional oversight.

Table 9-2. Acne Drug Products: Benzoyl Peroxide

Advance Notice of Proposed Rulemaking	Date	FR Citation
Advance Notice of Proposed Rulemaking	3/23/1982	47 FR 12430
Correction	4/23/1982	47 FR 17575
Proposed Rule	**Date**	**FR Citation**
Tentative Final Monograph	1/15/1985	50 FR 2172
Proposed Rule: Reclassifies benzoyl peroxide from GRASE to Category III	8/7/1991	56 FR 37622
Correction	10/8/1991	56 FR 50754
Proposed Rule: Additional Labeling	2/17/1995	60 FR 9554
Extension of Comment Period	5/19/1995	60 FR 26853
Final Rule	**Date**	**FR Citation**
Final Monograph	3/4/2010	75 FR 9767

Table 9-3. NDA vs. OTC Drug Monograph

NDA Route	OTC Monograph Route
Premarket approval	No premarket approval (conditions of marketing are codified) • The onus is on the manufacturer/distributor to assure compliance
Confidential filing	Public process
Drug product-specific	Active ingredient-specific • OTC drug therapeutic category
May require a user fee	No user fees
Potential for marketing exclusivity	No marketing exclusivity
Mandated FDA review timelines	No mandated FDA review timelines
May require clinical studies for application • Safety and efficacy • Label comprehension • Actual use • Demonstration of appropriate consumer	May require clinical studies • Label comprehension and actual use studies not required

FDA evaluates the product's toxicity and safe consumer use as well as whether the condition can be self-diagnosed and recognized without a healthcare professional's intervention. This route has gained popularity because a supplementary NDA for the switch can be timed to coincide with patent expiry. Under the *Hatch-Waxman Act*, a sponsor may qualify for three-year market exclusivity for a change involving new clinical investigation reports (21 CFR 314.108), allowing an innovator company to market a product for a longer time period without generic competition and to a wider consumer base.

One of the challenges in the switch process is transcribing information from the prescription drug product label to the "Drug Facts" OTC label, which has a limited amount of space, and ensuring the information is presented in a format consumers can comprehend and apply. Some examples of product switches are Prilosec OTC® (proton pump inhibitor for frequent heartburn), Nicorette® (smoking cessation aid), Zyrtec® (antihistamine) and Plan B® (emergency contraceptive). Several attempts to switch cholesterol-lowering medication to date have failed to meet FDA's criteria for appropriate self-selection.

An Rx-to-OTC switch that creates a new OTC product category is referred to as a first-in-class switch and often is subject to FDA Advisory Panel (composed of applicable prescription drug Advisory Committee members and members of the Nonprescription Drug Advisory Committee) review. Examples of first-in-class switches are Prilosec OTC, Alli® (weight loss aid) and Claritin® (a non-sedating antihistamine). Rx-to-OTC switches also can be partial or complete. For a complete switch (e.g., Claritin, Nicorette), the full product range and indications are switched. For a partial switch, either the product strength or indication remains prescription (e.g., Prilosec OTC). To address partial switch rules, an ANPR was published in the *Federal Register* in 2005 to elicit comments on whether clarification was necessary in circumstances when an active substance can be marketed simultaneously as OTC and prescription. While rulemaking for this issue has not been finalized, FDA indicated it will not allow the same active substance to be marketed with a prescription in a certain population and as an OTC for a subset of that population.

NDA Monograph Deviation

This route can be used when the drug product deviates in any aspect from the OTC drug monograph. The applicant submits an NDA referencing the monograph, with data to support the drug product's safety and efficacy with the deviation. This route was utilized for approval of a head lice aerosol foam product, Rid Mousse®. This drug product met all the conditions of the Pediculicide Final Monograph, with the exception of dosage form.

Generic (ANDA)

The ANDA (505)(j) route can be used when a company intends to market an OTC drug product equivalent to one already on the market. The same regulations apply here as for prescription products; however, a company must submit bioequivalence data in lieu of safety and efficacy studies. In addition, the product's labeling must be the same as the original product.

OTC NDA Products and Specific Studies

As with prescription products, OTC product manufacturers conduct preclinical studies (and clinical studies, as appropriate) to assess safety and efficacy. However, three additional studies are required for OTC products:

- label comprehension
- self-selection
- actual use or OTC simulation trials

Label comprehension studies are used to evaluate the extent to which a consumer can understand the proposed OTC drug label's information and apply that information when making drug-product use decisions in a hypothetical situation.[15] Label comprehension studies are open label and uncontrolled. No drug product is used in these studies, and they do not have to be conducted under an IND; however, it is recommended manufacturers submit these studies under an IND to obtain CDER advice on the protocol. FDA issued a guidance document on label comprehension testing design aspects in August 2010, which describes test standards, hurdle rates and test population literacy demographics.

Identifying a suitable label may take several iterations and should achieve a satisfactory comprehension level prior to running self-selection and actual use trials (AUT). Self-selection studies are used to evaluate whether a consumer can make a correct decision about using a drug product based on the drug product label information and knowledge of the customer's personal medical history. No drug product is used in these studies, although a self-selection measure can be incorporated into AUT design. AUTs are used to evaluate consumer behavior—whether a consumer actually will use the product safely without healthcare practitioner supervision and as per label instructions. These trials typically are designed as "all comers" studies, to measure consumer behavior against product usage intent the labeling describes, and conducted under an IND. The product label tested in AUTs should have been evaluated previously in the label comprehension study. The sponsor must follow the same process as for a prescription drug when selecting an OTC product's proprietary name when submitting an NDA. Ideally, primary and alternate proposed proprietary names should be submitted for review and approval.[16]

OTC "Drug Facts" Label

An OTC product's label must include specific information that will help the consumer understand the product's usage and safety information without a healthcare professional's oversight. A final rule on the use of "Drug Facts" became effective in 1999. The rule standardized the format, content, headings, graphics and minimum type size required for all OTC drug products.

All OTC drug labels have detailed usage and warning information to help consumers determine whether the product is appropriate to treat their conditions and how to take the product correctly. Specific information on the OTC label must include:[17]

- active ingredient(s)
- purpose
- uses
- warnings
- directions
- other information
- inactive ingredients
- questions

Figure 9-1 provides an example of a "Drug Facts" label. In accordance with 21 CFR 201.66, all OTC drug products must bear the "Drug Facts" label, which must be visible to consumers at the time of purchase.

FDA regulations require OTC labeling to be written and tested for ordinary people's use, including those with low comprehension skills, to ensure product information is easy to find and understand, including:

- product's intended uses and results
- active and inactive ingredients
- adequate directions for proper use
- warnings against unsafe use, side effects and adverse reactions

Some OTC drug monographs also provide professional labeling information, including specific information for healthcare professionals on uses outside the scope permitted by OTC consumer drug labeling. These uses may contain additional dosage information or indications not provided to the general public. Some examples include professional labeling for use of OTC antacid (21 CFR 331.80) or antitussive (cough) (21 CFR 341.90) drug products.

Packaging Requirements

In 1982, seven people in the Chicago area died after ingesting cyanide-laced Extra-Strength Tylenol® capsules resulting from a tampering incident. As a result of this incident, FDA issued tamper-resistant packaging regulations. The regulations required, among other things, any OTC drug product (except a dermatologic, dentifrice, insulin or lozenge product) for retail sale to be packaged in a tamper-resistant package, so a package breach would provide visible evidence to consumers tampering had occurred. In response to another incident in 1986, FDA amended the regulations to require OTC drug products marketed in two-piece, hard gelatin capsules to be packaged using at least two tamper-resistant packaging features, or with at least one tamper-resistant packaging feature if a tamper-resistant capsule seal was employed. FDA later changed "tamper-resistant" to "tamper-evident" (63 FR 59463). Tamper-evident packaging, as required by 21 CFR 211.132, is becoming the standard for most OTC drug products. Statements must be included on both outer and inner cartons clearly describing the tamper-evident features utilized.

Figure 9-1. Example of an OTC Drug Facts Label

```
Drug Facts
Active ingredient (in each tablet)                    Purpose
Chlorpheniramine maleate 2 mg..........................Antihistamine

Uses temporarily relieves these symptoms due to hay fever or other upper respiratory
allergies:  ■ sneezing    ■ runny nose    ■ itchy, watery eyes    ■ itchy throat

Warnings
Ask a doctor before use if you have
■ glaucoma      ■ a breathing problem such as emphysema or chronic bronchitis
■ trouble urinating due to an enlarged prostate gland
Ask a doctor or pharmacist before use if you are taking tranquilizers or sedatives
When using this product
■ you may get drowsy        ■ avoid alcoholic drinks
■ alcohol, sedatives, and tranquilizers may increase drowsiness
■ be careful when driving a motor vehicle or operating machinery
■ excitability may occur, especially in children
If pregnant or breast-feeding, ask a health professional before use.
Keep out of reach of children. In case of overdose, get medical help or contact a Poison
Control Center right away.

Directions
adults and children 12 years and over    take 2 tablets every 4 to 6 hours;
                                         not more than 12 tablets in 24 hours
children 6 years to under 12 years       take 1 tablet every 4 to 6 hours;
                                         not more than 6 tablets in 24 hours
children under 6 years                   ask a doctor
```

```
Drug Facts (continued)
Other information  ■ store at 20-25°C (68-77°F)   ■ protect from excessive moisture
Inactive ingredients  D&C yellow no. 10, lactose, magnesium stearate, microcrystalline
cellulose, pregelatinized starch
```

Source: 21 CFR 201.66

In addition, OTC drugs must comply with child-resistant packaging requirements as defined in the *Poison Prevention Packaging Act* of 1970 *(PPPA)*. Congress passed this act, authored by Senator Frank E. Moss (D-UT), in response to incidents of children opening household packaging and ingesting the contents. The US Consumer Product Safety Commission (CPSC) enforces child-resistant packaging requirements (16 CFR 1700). A provision is in place for one container size to be marketed in non-child-resistant packaging for elderly or handicapped persons unable to use the child-resistant packaging, as long as it is adequately labeled and child-resistant packages also are supplied.

Challenges in Assigning a Product Class

Products are classified as drugs based on their intended use as defined by the *FD&C Act*. Intended use can be determined through product indications or claims, consumer perception or drug ingredients. Because product positioning can define product classification, some cosmetics can be considered unapproved drugs. This is why some cosmetics' manufacturers making drug claims, either on product labeling or through advertising and promotion, have been subject to FDA regulatory actions. Some OTC drug products containing cosmetic-like claims (cleaning)—such as toothpastes—are considered drugs based on the presence of the anti-caries drug ingredient, fluoride.

Many OTC products meet the *FD&C Act*'s definition of both a cosmetic and a drug because they have two intended uses.[18] Examples of such products include anti-dandruff shampoo, deodorants containing antiperspirant active ingredients, moisturizers and makeup with sunscreens. These products must comply with both cosmetic and drug requirements, e.g., drugs that also are cosmetics are required to list inactive ingredients in descending order of predominance as required by the cosmetic regulations, rather than in alphabetical order as required by drug regulations.

Advertising

OTC drug product advertising is regulated by the Federal Trade Commission (FTC).[19] In 1971, a Memorandum of Understanding between FDA and FTC gave FTC primary responsibility for OTC drug advertising and gave FDA primary responsibility for OTC drug labeling. Unlike prescription products, OTC drugs have no fair balance requirement and promotional material is not required to be submitted to FTC prior to distribution. FTC has a number of advertising policy guides.[20] The National Advertising Division (NAD) of the Council of Better Business Bureaus also oversees advertising, either by challenging the advertisement directly or resolving the advertisement challenge submitted by a competitor. Since this council is a nongovernmental organization, advertising oversight by the council is a private process. In addition, the Consumer Healthcare Products Association (CHPA), a not-for-profit trade association representing the OTC drug industry, established an advertising code of practice. The regulatory professional should ensure advertising standards are followed, including quality claim support data, prior to initiation of advertising.

OTC Monograph Modernization

The OTC drug review program was initiated more than 45 years ago and has been successful in facilitating the efficient review of countless OTC medicines. However, OTC products have become more challenging to regulate, and the existing monograph framework and rulemaking process has inherent limitations in speed and flexibility. At this point, the monograph program does not receive user fee funding, thereby limiting the resources that can be dedicated to it. In 2015, FDA began discussions with industry to develop ways to reform the OTC monograph review program and, in 2017, proposed an agreement that was transmitted to Congress. The agreement includes an OTC monograph user fee program, FDA performance and procedural goals, infrastructure development, development and implementation of an information technology platform, enabling industry-initiated innovation, FDA in-review meetings and guidance development for innovation.[21] In July 2018, the US House of Representatives passed legislation to reform the monograph system but, to date, the Senate has not passed it, and it has not been enacted into law.

Summary

OTC drug manufacturers must comply with the same quality standards and regulatory requirements as prescription product manufacturers. However, unlike prescription products, OTC products must be proven to be safe and effective for use without healthcare professional supervision. Hence, the information on an OTC drug product label is critical. A number of regulatory pathways are available to market OTC drug products in the US. The regulatory professional's role in creating a strategy for product innovation and product differentiation through claims and/or promotion and advertising, while ensuring compliance with the applicable rules and regulations, is essential in the dynamic and challenging arena of OTC drugs.

References

1. OTC Ingredient List. FDA website. http://www.fda.gov/downloads/AboutFDA/CentersOffices/OfficeofMedicalProductsandTobacco/CDER/UCM207938.xls. Accessed 6 April 2019.
2. Over-the-Counter (OTC) Drug Product Review Process. FDA website. https://www.fda.gov/Drugs/DevelopmentApprovalProcess/SmallBusinessAssistance/ucm052786.htm. Accessed 6 April 2019.
3. Over-the-Counter Medications. Drugs.com website. http://www.drugs.com/otc. Accessed 6 April 2019.
4. Regulation of Nonprescription Products. FDA website. http://www.fda.gov/aboutfda/centersoffices/officeofmedicalproductsandtobacco/cder/ucm093452.htm. Accessed 6 April 2019.
5. Nonprescription Drug Safe Use Regulatory Expansion (NSURE). FDA website. https://www.fda.gov/downloads/ForHealthProfessionals/UCM330650.pdf. Accessed 6 April 2019.
6. Behind the counter availability of certain drugs; Public Meeting. Regulations.gov website. https://www.regulations.gov/docket?D=FDA-2007-N-0083. Accessed 6 April 2019.
7. Regulation of Over-the-Counter (OTC) Drug Products: ODE IV. FDA website. https://www.fda.gov/downloads/AboutFDA/CentersOffices/CDER/UCM148055.pdf. Accessed 6 April 2019.
8. *Guidance for Industry: Postmarketing Adverse Event Reporting for Nonprescription Human Drug Products Marketed Without an Approved Application* (July 2009). FDA website. https://www.fda.gov/Drugs/GuidanceComplianceRegulatoryInformation/Guidances/UCM171672. Accessed 6 April 2019.
9. Drug Applications for Over-the-Counter (OTC) Drugs. FDA website. http://www.fda.gov/drugs/developmentapprovalprocess/howdrugsaredevelopedandapproved/approvalapplications/over-the-counterdrugs/default.htm. Accessed 6 April 2019.
10. Status of OTC Rulemakings. FDA website. http://www.fda.gov/Drugs/DevelopmentApprovalProcess/DevelopmentResources/Over-the-CounterOTCDrugs/StatusofOTCRulemakings. Accessed 6 April 2019.
11. Rulemaking History for OTC Acne Drug Products. FDA website. http://www.fda.gov/Drugs/DevelopmentApprovalProcess/DevelopmentResources/Over-the-CounterOTCDrugs/StatusofOTCRulemakings/ucm069967.htm. Accessed 6 April 2019.
12. *Guidance for Industry: Time and Extent Applications for Nonprescription Drug Products* (September 2011). FDA website. http://www.fda.gov/downloads/Drugs/Guidances/ucm078902.pdf. Accessed 6 April 2019.
13. OTC (Nonprescription) Drugs. FDA website. http://www.fda.gov/Drugs/DevelopmentApprovalProcess/HowDrugsareDevelopedandApproved/ucm209647.htm. Accessed 6 April 2019.
14. FDA MAPP 6020.5R Good Review Practice: OND Review Management of INDs and NDAs for Nonprescription Drug Products. FDA website. http://www.fda.gov/downloads/aboutfda/centersoffices/cder/manualofpoliciesprocedures/ucm082003.pdf. Accessed 6 April 2019.
15. *Guidance for Industry: Label Comprehension Studies for Nonprescription Drug Products* (August 2010). FDA website. http://www.fda.gov/downloads/drugs/guidancecomplianceregulatoryinformation/guidances/ucm143834.pdf. Accessed 6 April 2019.
16. *Contents of a Complete Submission for the Evaluation of Proprietary Names: Guidance for Industry* (February 2010). FDA website. http://www.fda.gov/downloads/drugs/guidancecomplianceregulatoryinformation/guidances/ucm075068.pdf. Accessed 6 April 2019.
17. *Guidance for Industry: Labeling OTC Human Drug Products—Questions and Answers* (December 2008). FDA website. http://www.fda.gov/downloads/drugs/guidancecomplianceregulatoryinformation/guidances/ucm078792.pdf. Accessed 6 April 2019.
18. Is It a Cosmetic, a Drug, or Both? (Or Is It Soap?). FDA website. http://www.fda.gov/cosmetics/guidanceregulation/lawsregulations/ucm074201.htm. Accessed 6 April 2019.
19. FTC, Bureau of Consumer Protection, Business Center. Health Claims. FTC website. https://www.ftc.gov/tips-advice/business-center/advertising-and-marketing/health-claims. Accessed 2 March 2019.
20. FTC, Bureau of Consumer Protection, Business Center. Advertising FAQ's: A Guide for Small Business. FTC website. https://www.ftc.gov/tips-advice/business-center/guidance/advertising-faqs-guide-small-business. Accessed 6 April 2019.
21. Modernizing FDA's Regulation of Over-the Counter Drugs. FDA website. https://www.fda.gov/NewsEvents/Testimony/ucm575941.htm. Accessed 6 April 2019.

Chapter 10

Prescription Drug Labeling, Advertising and Promotion

Updated by Anu Gaur, PhD, MBA, MSRA, RAC

OBJECTIVES

❑ Understand the scope of FDA's regulatory authority over prescription drug labeling and advertising.

❑ Learn general FDA requirements for prescription drug labeling, advertising and promotion.

❑ Recognize the importance of agency enforcement actions pertaining to prescription drug labeling, advertising and promotion.

LAWS, REGULATIONS AND GUIDELINES COVERED IN THIS CHAPTER

❑ *Federal Food, Drug, and Cosmetic Act* of 1938

❑ *Federal Trade Commission Act* of 1914

❑ *Kefauver-Harris Drug Amendments* of 1962

❑ 21 CFR 99 Dissemination of information on unapproved/new uses for marketed drugs, biologics and devices

❑ 21 CFR 200.5 General; mailing of important information about drugs

❑ 21 CFR 201 Labeling

❑ 21 CFR 201.56 Labeling; requirements on content and format of labeling for human prescription drug and biological products

❑ 21 CFR 201.57 Labeling; specific requirements on content and format of labeling for human prescription drug and biological products described in 201.56(b)(1)

❑ 21 CFR 202 Prescription drug advertising

❑ 21 CFR 203 Prescription drug marketing

❑ 21 CFR 208 Medication Guides for prescription drug products

❑ 21 CFR 312.7 Investigational new drug application; promotion of investigational drugs

❑ 21 CFR 314.50(l)(i) Applications for FDA approval to market a new drug; content and format; labeling

❑ 21 CFR 314.70 Applications for FDA approval to market a new drug; supplements and other changes to an approved application

❑ 21 CFR 314.81(b)(2)(iii) Applications for FDA approval to market a new drug; reporting requirements; annual report; labeling

❑ 21 CFR 314.81(b)(3)(i) Applications for FDA approval to market a new drug; reporting

Chapter 10

requirements; other reporting; advertisements and promotional labeling

- 21 CFR 314.126 Applications for FDA approval to market a new drug; adequate and well-controlled studies

- 21 CFR 314.550 Applications for FDA approval to market a new drug; promotional materials

- 21 CFR 601.12(f)(4) Licensing; changes to an approved application; labeling changes; advertisements and promotional labeling

- 21 CFR 601.45 Licensing; promotional materials

- *Guidance for Industry: Consumer-Directed Broadcast Advertisements* (August 1999)

- *Guidance for Industry: Content and Format for Geriatric Labeling* (October 2001)

- *Guidance for Industry: Providing Regulatory Submissions in Electronic Format-Content of Labeling* (April 2005)

- *Guidance for Industry: Adverse Reactions Section of Labeling for Human Prescription Drug and Biological Products-Content and Format* (January 2006)

- *Guidance for Industry: Clinical Studies Section of Labeling for Human Prescription Drug and Biological Products-Content and Format* (January 2006)

- *Draft Guidance for Industry: Public Availability of Labeling Changes in "Changes Being Effected" Supplements* (September 2006)

- *Guidance for Industry: Indexing Structured Product Labeling* (June 2008)

- *Draft Guidance for Industry: SPL Standard for Content of Labeling Technical Qs & As* (October 2009)

- *Draft Guidance for Industry: Presenting Risk Information in Prescription Drug and Medical Device Promotion* (May 2009)

- *Guidance for Industry and Review Staff: Labeling for Human Prescription Drug and Biological Products-Determining Established Pharmacologic Class for Use in the Highlights of Prescribing Information-Good Review Practice* (October 2009)

- *Guidance for Industry: Good Reprint Practices for the Distribution of Medical Journal Articles and Medical or Scientific Reference Publications on Unapproved New Uses of Approved Drugs and Approved or Cleared Medical Devices* (January 2009)

- *Guidance for Industry: Dosage and Administration Section of Labeling for Human Prescription Drug and Biological Products-Content and Format* (March 2010)

- *Draft Guidance for Industry: Responding to Unsolicited Requests for Off-Label Information About Prescription Drugs and Medical Devices* (December 2011)

- *Guidance for Industry: Warnings and Precautions, Contraindications, and Boxed Warnings Sections of Labeling for Human Prescription Drug and Biological Products-Content and Format* (October 2011)

- *Guidance: Medication Guides-Distribution Requirements and Inclusion in Risk Evaluation and Mitigation Strategies (REMS)* (November 2011)

- *Draft Guidance for Industry: Direct-to-Consumer Television Advertisements-FDAAA DTC Television Ad Pre-Dissemination Review Program* (March 2012)

- *Draft Guidance for Industry: Drug Interaction Studies-Study Design, Data Analysis, Implications for Dosing, and Labeling Recommendations* (February 2012)

- *Guidance for Industry: Labeling for Human Prescription Drug and Biological Products-Implementing the PLR Content and Format Requirements* (February 2013)

- *Draft Guidance for Industry and Review Staff: Pediatric Information Incorporated Into Human Prescription Drug and Biological Products Labeling-Good Review Practice* (February 2013)

- ❏ *Draft Guidance for Industry: Safety Considerations for Container Labels and Carton Labeling Design to Minimize Medication Errors* (April 2013)

- ❏ *Draft Guidance for Industry: Product Name Placement, Size, and Prominence in Advertising and Promotional Labeling-Revision 1* (November 2013)

- ❏ *Guidance for Industry and FDA Staff: Dear Health Care Provider Letters: Improving Communication of Important Safety Information* (January 2014)

- ❏ *Draft Guidance for Industry: Labeling for Human Prescription Drug and Biological Products Approved Under the Accelerated Approval Regulatory Pathway* (March 2014)

- ❏ *Draft Guidance for Industry: Fulfilling Regulatory Requirements for Postmarketing Submissions of Interactive Promotional Media for Prescription Human and Animal Drugs and Biologics* (January 2014)

- ❏ *Draft Guidance for Industry: Internet/Social Media Platforms with Character Space Limitations-Presenting Risk and Benefit Information for Prescription Drugs and Medical Devices* (June 2014)

- ❏ *Draft Guidance for Industry: Internet/Social Media Platforms: Correcting Independent Third-Party Misinformation About Prescription Drugs and Medical Devices* (June 2014)

- ❏ *Draft Guidance for Industry: Distributing Scientific and Medical Publications on Risk Information for Approved Prescription Drugs and Biological Products-Recommended Practices* (June 2014)

- ❏ *Revised Draft Guidance for Industry: Distributing Scientific and Medical Publications on*

- ❏ *Unapproved New Uses - Recommended Practices* (February 2014)

- ❏ *Guidance for Industry: Patient Counseling Information Section of Labeling for Human Prescription Drug and Biological Products-Content and Format* (December 2014)

- ❏ *Draft Guidance for Industry: Pregnancy, Lactation, and Reproductive Potential: Labeling for Human Prescription Drug and Biologics Products* (December 2014)

- ❏ *Revised Draft Guidance for Industry: Brief Summary and Adequate Directions for Use: Disclosing Risk Information in Consumer-Directed Print Advertisements and Promotional Labeling for Prescription Drugs* (August 2015)

Introduction

The *Federal Food, Drug, and Cosmetic Act* of 1938 (*FD&C Act*) grants the US Food and Drug Administration (FDA) broad authority over prescription drug labeling and advertising.

The term "labeling" includes the actual product label affixed to the container; the broader definition of *labeling* encompasses any words or graphics on the drug product and its containers or wrappers, and any material issued in association with the drug (i.e., package insert). Title 21 of the Code of Federal Regulations (CFR) Part 201 provides the full scope of drug labeling.[1]

The term "advertising" includes advertisements intended to overtly sell a drug product to consumers, as well as material called "promotional labeling." Such labeling is any material intended to promote a drug's use and, typically, is directed at physicians through such various media such as product detail aids, professional convention displays, booklets, videotapes and even sales representatives' oral statements.

FDA is responsible for protecting and advancing public health and upholds its responsibility on both fronts by ensuring prescription drug information is truthful, balanced and communicated accurately. Misinformed consumers and physicians create the potential for serious injury, while well-informed consumers and physicians are empowered to make better-informed health decisions.

Summary of Labeling Requirements

The terms label and labeling represent specific compliance. Explicit container label requirements are discussed below, as are requirements for professional and patient labeling. No matter the requirements, FDA requires labeling content submission in a predetermined electronic format.

Electronic Labeling, Including Structured Product Labeling (SPL)

FDA requires "content of labeling" submission in electronic format for initial New Drug Application (NDA) submissions (21 CFR 314.50(l)), labeling supplements and annual reports for approved NDAs (21 CFR

314.81(b)). *Content of labeling* is defined as the complete professional labeling, including all text, tables and figures.

SPL is the electronic document markup standard FDA adopted for electronic content of labeling submissions. The SPL standard uses the extensible markup language (XML) file format with specifications (schema and controlled terminology) defined by FDA's Data Standards Council. Additional information on SPL, including both technical and nontechnical guidance, can be found on FDA's Structured Product Labeling Resources website (www.fda.gov/ForIndustry/DataStandards/StructuredProductLabeling/default.htm).

General Label Requirements (21 CFR 201 Subparts A and B)

Some of the most broadly applicable label requirements are:
- manufacturer, packager or distributor name and address (21 CFR 201.1)
- National Drug Code (NDC) number location (requested but not required) (21 CFR 201.2) (note: NDC number determination is included in 21 CFR 207.35)
- statement of ingredients (21 CFR 201.10), including required warning statements for specific ingredients (e.g., FD&C Yellow No. 5 (21 CFR 201.20))
- expiration date location (21 CFR 201.17) and control numbers' significance (21 CFR 201.18)
- bar code label requirements (21 CFR 201.25)
- statement of identity (21 CFR 201.50)
- declaration of net quantity of contents (21 CFR 201.51)
- statement of dosage (21 CFR 201.55)

The appropriate label content placement and prominence also are key concerns in FDA's regulation of drug labeling (21 CFR 201.10). Apart from FDA, the US Pharmacopeia sets voluntary standards for prescription container labels and the Institute for Safe Medicine Practices recommends the following:
- words in easy-to-read 12-point type
- patient name, drug name and drug instructions in the largest letters, displayed prominently at the top of the label
- warnings typed directly onto labels
- images or physical descriptions of the container's pills
- no extra zeroes (5.0 mg could be misread as 50 mg)
- dispensing pharmacy's information

Package Insert and the Physician Labeling Rule (PLR)

The drug product's professional labeling, or package insert, is a compilation of product information based on FDA's comprehensive review of the sponsor's approved NDA or Biologics License Application (BLA). The package insert is considered "adequate directions for use," written to direct healthcare professionals in the drug product's use.

The PLR format also requires contact information to help make reporting adverse events easier. FDA has issued several guidance documents articulating standards for professional labeling content.

On 24 January 2006, FDA issued final regulations governing the content and format of prescribing information (PI) for human drug and biological products. This rule is referred to as the "Physician Labeling Rule" (PLR). The rule's goal in terms of PLR contents and format requirements have been documented and described in 21 CFR 201.56, and 21 CFR 201.57, with an objective to enhance the safe and effective use of prescription drug products by providing healthcare providers with clear and concise PI that is easier to access, read and use. Therefore, the PI information required with New Drug Applications (NDAs), Biologics License Applications (BLAs), and efficacy supplements must conform to the PLR content and format regulations. On 3 December 2014, FDA published the Pregnancy and Lactation Labeling Rule (PLLR). The PLLR's goal is to enhance the safe and effective use of prescription drug products in pregnant women, lactating women, and females and males of reproductive potential.[2]

The PLR and labeling requirements incorporate the following:[3]
- PLR—content and format of labeling for human prescription drug and biological products (24 January 2006; Federal Register Notice)
- 21 CFR 201.56—labeling content and format for human prescription drug and biological products
- 21 CFR 201.57—content and format of PLR labeling for human prescription drug and biological products described in §201.56(b)(1)
- 21 CFR 201.80—"Old" Format Labeling: content and format of labeling for human prescription drug and biological products; older drugs not described in §201.56(b)(1)

Overall, the PLR requirements are intended to improve healthcare professionals' ability to access, read and use the package insert.

PLR format includes three main sections:
- Highlights of Prescribing Information—intended to provide prescribers with the location of information they overtly reference and consider most important

- Full Prescribing Information (FPI): FPI contents commonly referred to as the FPT Table of Contents (TOC)
- FPI—in fixed numbered sections (1–17), starting with the boxed warning

In February 2013, FDA published *Guidance for Industry: Labeling for Human Prescription Drug and Biological Products—Implementing the PLR Content and Format Requirements*. **Table 10-1** provides an overview of the PLR format, associated regulations and available guidance documents.

Note, the PLR regulations establish minimum requirements for font size and certain other graphic elements (21 CFR 201.57(d)). These requirements vary depending on the product's intended use (e.g., whether labeling is to accompany the drug product or be used in accompanying promotional materials). Refer to *Guidance for Industry: Labeling for Human Prescription Drug and Biological Products—Implementing the PLR Content and Format Requirements* (February 2013) for additional information. This guidance sets forth the labeling format requirements, including the package insert highlights section, to address labeling changes or updates. For example, major changes within the previous 12 months to boxed warnings, indications and usage, dosage and administration, contraindications and warnings must be listed in both the highlights section and the FPI's body.

Professional labeling for all drugs approved after June 2001 (or for which an efficacy supplement was approved after June 2001), must be converted to the PLR format (21 CFR 201.56(c)). In addition, for drug products approved in or after June 2006, efficacy supplements may necessitate labeling revisions to the PLR format; however, as a general rule, bioequivalence or CMC supplements would not trigger a revision.

Since converting a product's professional labeling from the old format to PLR is a difficult and time-consuming process, FDA suggests manufacturers develop new sections; assess whether new information warrants a data reanalysis or new studies to avoid being misleading; and evaluate labeling information systematically to identify and revise and/or remove unsubstantiated claims and outdated information.

FDA has instituted a staggered implementation schedule that prioritizes label revision from the most recently approved products to older products. The deadline for submitting revised labeling to meet the new requirement is based on the most recent NDA efficacy supplement's date (or original approval, if no approved efficacy supplements have been submitted). However, manufacturers are encouraged to convert product labeling to the PLR format voluntarily. In any case, all label conversions must be submitted as Prior Approval Supplements. Refer to the table outlining FDA's implementation schedule in Appendix A of the above-mentioned February 2013 guidance.

Patient Labeling, Including Medication Guides

Patient labeling is product information derived from professional labeling and written in consumer- or user-friendly language. Patient labeling usually focuses on directions for use and product-associated risks. For certain products, FDA determines the serious and significant risks and, in these cases, the agency may require a patient Medication Guide (21 CFR 208).

All Medication Guides must comply with specific content and format requirements (21 CFR 208.20), including being written in English in easily understandable, nontechnical language, which should not be promotional in tone, content or messaging, and is expected to meet the not less than 10-point text font size requirement. In addition, Medication Guides must be distributed to patients each time the prescription drug product is dispensed (21 CFR 208.24). Since a manufacturer cannot be present when each prescription is distributed or dispensed, the manufacturer is required to ensure adequate means exist for dispensers to comply with this requirement. (This usually is achieved by providing sufficient numbers of printed Medication Guides with each unit of drug product.) FDA clarifies its expectations for Medication Guide distribution in its *Guidance for Industry: Medication Guides—Distribution Requirements and Inclusion in Risk Evaluation and Minimization Strategies (REMS)* (November 2011).

Labeling Changes

Any approved drug product labeling change is considered an NDA or BLA change and is required to be reported to FDA according to the approved application supplement regulations (21 CFR 314.70). FDA has the authority to require approved NDA holders to make safety-related labeling changes and updates based on any new safety information that becomes available after a drug's marketing approval. NDA holders have a limited time to respond and implement these FDA-requested labeling changes (see *FD&C Act* Section 505(o)(4) for details).

Summary of Prescription Drug Promotion and Advertising

No Preapproval Promotion

According to 21 CFR 312.7, sponsors or investigators "shall not represent in a promotional context that an investigational new drug is safe or effective for the purposes for which it is under investigation or otherwise promote the drug."

Table 10-1. PLR Format, Associated Regulations and Guidance Documents

PLR Format	Associated Regulations/Guidance (if any)
Overall	21 CFR 201.56 and 21 CFR 201.57 Guidance for Industry: Labeling for Human Prescription Drug and Biological Products—Implementing the PLR Content and Format Requirements (February 2013)
Highlights of Prescribing Information Product Names, Other Required Information Boxed Warning Recent Major Changes Indications and Usage Dosage and Administration Dosage Forms and Strengths Contraindications Warnings and Precautions Adverse Reactions Drug Interactions Use in Specific Populations	21 CFR 201.57(a) Guidance for Industry: Labeling for Human Prescription Drug and Biological Products—Implementing the PLR Content and Format Requirements (February 2013) Guidance for Industry and Review Staff: Labeling for Human Prescription Drug and Biological Products—Determining Established Pharmacologic Class for Use in the Highlights of Prescribing Information (October 2009)
Full Prescribing Information: Contents	21 CFR 201.57(b)
Full Prescribing Information	21 CFR 201.57(c)
Boxed Warning (if applicable)	21 CFR 201.57(c)(1) Guidance for Industry: Warnings and Precautions, Contraindications, and Boxed Warning Sections of Labeling for Human Prescription Drug and Biological Products—Content and Format (October 2011) Guidance for Industry: Labeling for Human Prescription Drug and Biological Products—Implementing the PLR Content and Format Requirements (February 2013)
Indications and Usage	21 CFR 201.57(c)(2) Guidance for Industry: Labeling for Human Prescription Drug and Biological Products—Implementing the PLR Content and Format Requirements (February 2013)
Dosage and Administration	21 CFR 201.57(c)(3) Guidance for Industry: Dosage and Administration Section of Labeling for Human Prescription Drug and Biological Products—Content and Format (March 2010) Guidance for Industry: Labeling for Human Prescription Drug and Biological Products—Implementing the PLR Content and Format Requirements (February 2013)
Dosage Forms and Strengths	21 CFR 201.57(c)(4) Guidance for Industry: Labeling for Human Prescription Drug and Biological Products—Implementing the PLR Content and Format Requirements (February 2013)
Contraindications	21 CFR 201.57(c)(5) Guidance for Industry: Warnings and Precautions, Contraindications, and Boxed Warning Sections of Labeling for Human Prescription Drug and Biological Products—Content and Format (October 2011) Guidance for Industry: Labeling for Human Prescription Drug and Biological Products—Implementing the PLR Content and Format Requirements (February 2013)
Warnings and Precautions	21 CFR 201.57(c)(6) Guidance for Industry: Warnings and Precautions, Contraindications, and Boxed Warning Sections of Labeling for Human Prescription Drug and Biological Products—Content and Format (October 2011) Guidance for Industry: Labeling for Human Prescription Drug and Biological Products—Implementing the PLR Content and Format Requirements (February 2013)
Adverse Reactions	21 CFR 201.57(c)(7) Guidance for Industry: Adverse Reactions Section of Labeling for Human Prescription Drug and Biological Products—Content and Format (January 2006) Guidance for Industry: Labeling for Human Prescription Drug and Biological Products—Implementing the PLR Content and Format Requirements (February 2013)
Drug Interactions	21 CFR 201.57(c)(8) Guidance for Industry: Labeling for Human Prescription Drug and Biological Products—Implementing the PLR Content and Format Requirements (February 2013)
Use in Specific Populations	21 CFR 201.57(c)(9) Guidance for Industry: Content and Format for Geriatric Labeling (October 2001) Guidance for Industry: Labeling for Human Prescription Drug and Biological Products—Implementing the PLR Content and Format Requirements (February 2013) Draft Guidance for Industry and Review Staff: Pediatric Information Incorporated Into Human Prescription Drug and Biological Products Labeling (February 2013)

Table 10-1. PLR Format, Associated Regulations and Guidance Documents (cont'd.)

PLR Format	Associated Regulations/Guidance (if any)
Drug Abuse and Dependence	21 CFR 201.57(c)(10)
Overdosage	21 CFR 201.57(c)(11)
Description	21 CFR 201.57(c)(12)
Clinical Pharmacology	21 CFR 201.57(c)(13) Draft Guidance for Industry: Clinical Pharmacology Labeling for Human Prescription Drug and Biological Products—Considerations, Content, and Format (August 2014)
Nonclinical Toxicology	21 CFR 201.57(c)(14)
Clinical Studies	21 CFR 201.57(c)(15) Guidance for Industry: Clinical Studies Section of Labeling for Human Prescription Drug and Biological Products—Content and Format (January 2009)
References	21 CFR 201.57(c)(16)
How Supplied/Storage and Handling	21 CFR 201.57(c)(17)
Patient Counseling Information	21 CFR 201.57(c)(18) Guidance for Industry: Labeling for Human Prescription Drug and Biological Products—Implementing the PLR Content and Format Requirements (February 2013)
Medication Guide (if applicable)	21 CFR 208 Guidance: Medication Guides—Distribution Requirements and Inclusion in Risk Evaluation and Mitigation Strategies (REMS) (November 2011)

The only exceptions to the preapproval promotion prohibition are disease-state-only promotions, institutional promotions (linking the drug manufacturer's name with a research field) and "Coming Soon" promotions. "Coming Soon" advertisements reveal only the name of a product that will be available soon, without any written, verbal or graphic suggestions of potential indications or any safety or effectiveness claims. During the preapproval period, a company may choose one promotional campaign type, but may switch back and forth between those available. This is because, if a disease awareness campaign is underway (e.g., "Company X is involved in research in the field of diabetes" followed by a "Coming Soon from Company X: Product Y" campaign), the audience could link the drug's name with the disease state, which is considered tantamount to preapproval promotion.

Promotional Material Submission and Preclearance

The Office of Prescription Drug Promotion (OPDP) has an active research program designed to investigate applied and theoretical issues of relevance to direct-to-consumer (DTC) and professional promotional prescription drug materials. This research program utilizes a number of different research methodologies, including survey and experimental research as well as qualitative research for development purposes. OPDP's research supports FDA's goal of science-based policy while maintaining its commitment to protect the public health.

The OPDP research team also provides technical assistance to outside organizations on designing and implementing studies concerning prescription drug promotion. Some of these organizations include groups of academic researchers, pharmaceutical companies and nonprofit groups.[4]

With only one exception, all promotional materials must be submitted to OPDP at the time of their initial publication or dissemination using Form FDA 2253 (21 CFR 314.81).

Manufacturers of drug products approved under Subpart H (Accelerated Approval of New Drugs for Serious or Life-Threatening Illnesses) are required to submit drafts of all promotional labeling for review at least 30 days prior to dissemination (21 CFR 314.550 and 601.45). Additionally, for products anticipating accelerated approval during the NDA preapproval review period, all promotional materials intended to be used in the first 120 days following marketing approval must be submitted to OPDP for advisory review prior to approval.

For drugs approved under standard conditions, a common industry practice (although not required) is to submit the drug's launch materials to OPDP for advisory comment. OPDP pays careful attention to launch materials during the first year after a drug's approval. For example, OPDP issued a letter to a company for violations found in a promotional launch journal advertisement, taking issue with claims such as "novel," "next generation" and "unique." The company was asked to pull the advertisement and run a corrective advertising campaign. Another company received an Untitled Letter from OPDP for a branded story that was part of the launch campaign. The branded story included a patient testimonial that overstated efficacy, omitted key information and minimized important risk information. Although a company spokeswoman told the press the patient testimonial was never circulated to the public, this did not stop issuance of the FDA letter.

Additionally, while not required, it is common industry practice to send DTC television advertisements to OPDP for preclearance prior to dissemination. OPDP's website explains the submission process for preclearance of television advertisements and other materials.

Substantial Evidence Standard

Promotional materials may not suggest a product use that is not approved or otherwise permitted for use in the FPI. This is referred to as "off-label" product use.

In addition to the "on-label" requirement, promotional materials may not suggest a drug is better, safer or more effective than demonstrated by "substantial evidence." Generally, FDA's standard for "substantial evidence" in support of a drug product claim is two adequate and well-controlled clinical trials (21 CFR 314.126). Although certain claims may be allowable based on a single study, on numerous occasions OPDP has articulated the requirement for two studies for claims of a product's superiority.

Even if product claims are on-label, if they are either overt or implied and not supported by substantial evidence, FDA will consider the materials to be misleading and, therefore, violative.

Prescription drug advertising is covered under 21 CFR Part 202, and CFR Part 202.1 includes the full scope of those advertisements.[5] 21 CFR 202.1(e)(6) and (7) detail the general principles by which FDA evaluates whether promotional materials are misleading (e.g., are inaccurate, fail to reveal material facts or improperly use graphics or statistics). Importantly, OPDP enforcement letters reflect the agency's expectations in this regard.

21 CFR Part 203 covers the scope of required information for prescription drug marketing. This includes such information as the list of ingredients; order for listing ingredients in the advertisement; proprietary name for the drug; list of inert or inactive ingredients; established name; text font and format; and requirements for two or more active ingredients. Additionally, there must be a true statement of information in brief summary relating to drug's side effects, contraindications and effectiveness, when required. The overall scope also covers exempt advertisements, reminder advertisements, bulk-sale drug advertisements, prescription-compounding drug advertisements, scope of information to be included; applicability to the entire advertisement, effectiveness of the drug, side effects and contraindications, and related areas.[6]

Fair Balance

All prescription drug advertising and promotion effectiveness claims must be accompanied by information about the product's risks, and the risk information must have prominence comparable to that of the promotional claims (21 CFR 202.1(e)(5)). This commonly is known as "fair balance." Risk information omission or minimization are the most commonly cited concerns in OPDP's enforcement letters.

OPDP considers many factors when determining fair balance, including whether the safety and efficacy messages have equal prominence, typography and layout, contrast and white space, or other methods used to achieve emphasis (21 CFR 202.1(e)(7)(viii)). In addition, if promotional material is directed to a consumer audience, the fair balance information should be written in consumer-friendly language.

FDA's 2009 *Draft Guidance for Industry: Presenting Risk Information in Prescription Drug and Medical Device Promotion* sheds more light on factors the agency considers when evaluating risk information presentation in advertisements and promotional labeling. This draft guidance includes many helpful, concrete examples to illustrate FDA's thinking on this important topic.

Drug Safety Oversight Board

The Drug Safety Board (DSB) was created in 2005 and mandated by law in the *Food and Drug Administration Amendments Act* of 2007 (*FDAAA*). It advises the Center for Drug Evaluation and Research (CDER) director on handling and communicating important and emerging drug safety issues. DSB meets monthly and provides a forum for discussion and input on how to address potential drug safety issues.

DSB is composed of representatives from two FDA centers and eight other federal government agencies:

1. Agency for Healthcare Research and Quality (AHRQ)
2. Centers for Disease Control and Prevention (CDC)
3. Centers for Medicare and Medicaid Services (CMS)
4. Department of Defense (DOD)
5. Health Resources and Services Administration (HRSA)
6. Indian Health Service (IHS)
7. National Institutes of Health (NIH)
8. Department of Veterans Affairs (VA)

An important DSB role is helping FDA assess the impact of its safety decisions on its federal partners' healthcare systems.[7]

Product Name Placement, Size and Prominence

Promotional labeling must reference the drug's established (generic) name, per 21 CFR 202.1(b)(1). The regulations require the brand name's most prominent mention to be accompanied by the generic name "in letters at least half as large as the letters comprising the proprietary name or designation with which it is joined." In January 2012, with a subsequent revision in November 2013, FDA issued *Guidance for Industry: Product Name Placement, Size, and Prominence in Advertising and Promotional Labeling* to clarify issues in this area.

Advertising

Brief Summary Requirement

Under 21 CFR Part 202(l) regulations, materials constituting advertising from other forms of promotional labeling are differentiated. The regulations require prescription drug advertising to contain a "[t]rue statement of information in brief summary relating to side effects, contraindications, and effectiveness" (21 CFR 202.1(e)). Promotional labeling that is not an advertisement must be disseminated with a copy of the FPI.

In August 2015, FDA issued *Revised Draft Guidance for Industry: Brief Summary and Adequate Directions for Use: Disclosing Risk Information in Consumer-Directed Print Advertisements and Promotional Labeling for Human Prescription Drugs* to explain the agency's expectations regarding the brief summary in print advertisements directed to consumers. As with fair balance, FDA encourages sponsors to write a brief summary for consumer pieces in easily understandable language. FDA also recommends sponsors include a statement in the advertisement to remind consumers the risk information is not comprehensive. Sponsors should provide a toll-free telephone number or website where more information can be found.

Direct-To-Consumer (DTC) Advertising

Both promotional labeling and advertising are used to market and sell prescription drugs. Promotional labeling differs from advertising in how it is distributed. Under the scope of 21 CFR 203.1, advertisements subject to FD&C Act Section 502(n) include appearing in:
- published journals
- magazines, other periodicals
- newspapers
- advertisements broadcast through such media as radio, television and telephone communication systems[8]

Promotional labeling about a drug is said to "accompany" that drug, or accompanying materials, even if the promotional labeling is not physically attached to a drug container. Promotional labeling must be accompanied by the drug's prescribing information.[9]

Consumer-directed broadcast advertisements (i.e., television and radio) must include a "major statement" of the product's primary risk in the audio portion for both media and, for television, in the video portion. In addition, the advertisement should make "adequate provision…for dissemination of the approved or permitted package labeling in connection with the broadcast presentation" (21 CFR 202.1(e)(1)). This sometimes is referred to as the "adequate provision" requirement. In August 1999, FDA issued *Draft Guidance for Industry: Consumer-Directed Broadcast Advertisements* to clarify the approach manufacturers may take to fulfill it. As noted previously, most companies submit their television advertisements to FDA for advisory comment prior to broadcast.

Draft Guidance for Industry: Direct-to-Consumer Television Advertisements—FDAAA DTC Television Ad Pre-Dissemination Review Program has more information about submitting DTC television advertisement for pre-dissemination review.

In addition to other requirements, *FDAAA* requires published DTC advertisements to include the following statement printed in conspicuous text: "You are encouraged to report negative side effects of prescription drugs to FDA. Visit https://www.fda.gov/safety/medwatch/."

For safety alert information, see https://www.fda.gov/Safety/MedWatch/SafetyInformation/default.htm.

While FDA oversees prescription drug advertisements, the Federal Trade Commission (FTC) oversees advertising for over-the-counter (non-prescription) drugs including:
- product claim advertisements
- reminder advertisements
- help-seeking advertisements
- other promotional materials containing product claims
- risk disclosure requirements for different advertising types[10]

Reminder Advertisements and Items

Reminder advertisements provide only the drug's name, not its uses. These advertisements assume the audience already knows the drug's uses. Therefore, a reminder advertisement does not have to contain the drug's risk information because it does not demonstrate how the drug works or its uses.

Unlike product claim advertisements, reminder advertisements cannot suggest, in words or illustrations, anything about the drug's benefits or risks. Additionally, reminder advertisements are not allowed for certain prescription drugs with serious risks. In general, drugs with serious risks have special warnings, referred to as "boxed warnings," in their FDA-approved prescribing information. If a drug has a boxed warning, this fact should be referenced in all advertisements.[11]

Print product claim and reminder advertisements must include the following statement:

> "You are encouraged to report negative side effects of prescription drugs to the FDA. Visit MedWatch or call 1-800-FDA-1088."[12]

In the past, pharmaceutical companies commonly distributed reminder items. In July 2008, the Pharmaceutical Research and Manufacturers of America (PhRMA) issued an update to the PhRMA Code on Interactions with Healthcare Professionals addressing the topic of reminder items. The Advanced Medical Technology Association (AdvaMed) issued similar guidelines to medical device manufacturers.

The PhRMA Code, which is a voluntary standard, prohibits distribution of non-educational and practice-related promotional materials, including such reminder items as pens, notepads and mugs with product logos on them, even if the item is of minimal value and is related to the healthcare professional's work or for the patient's benefit. Most manufacturers have adopted the PhRMA Code and no longer distribute reminder items.

Help-Seeking, Bulk Sale and Compounding Drug Advertising

Other exceptions to the brief summary and certain advertisement requirements include "help-seeking advertisements," bulk-sale and compounding drug advertisements. A help-seeking advertisement is intended to inform consumers about a specific medical condition and encourage them to discuss it with their healthcare professional. These advertisements must not mention any product name or imply a certain prescription drug is intended to treat the medical condition.

Help-seeking advertisements describe diseases or conditions, but do not recommend or suggest any specific drug treatment. Because these are not considered drug advertisements, FDA does not regulate true help-seeking advertisements; rather, FTC does. However, if an advertisement recommends or suggests a specific drug's use, it is considered a product claim advertisement that must comply with FDA's rules.[13]

Bulk-sale drugs intended to be used for further processing or manufacturing also are exempt from the brief summary requirement, as are drugs sold to pharmacies for compounding. As with help-seeking advertisements, neither bulk-sale drugs nor compounding drugs are permitted to make safety or efficacy claims (21 CFR 202.1(e)(2)(ii) and (iii)).

Promotion

Pharmacoeconomic Claims and Promotion to Formulary Decision Makers

Pharmaceutical companies may promote their drug products to formularies or other related entities primarily responsible for managed care coverage and reimbursement decisions. This kind of promotion often focuses on healthcare economic information (pharmacoeconomic claims).

FDAAA Section 114 provides a legal mechanism to allow the promotion of pharmacoeconomic claims using a less-stringent standard than the "substantial evidence" standard described above. The law states pharmacoeconomic claims may be made based on "competent and reliable" evidence, as long as the information relates directly to an approved indication and is provided only to formularies or other similar managed care decision makers.

Press Releases

Press releases often cause confusion regarding where the appropriate regulatory jurisdiction lies. Typically, the Securities and Exchange Commission (SEC) regulates how information is communicated to the investment community. Nevertheless, FDA believes product-specific press releases fall under its promotional regulations, thus requiring fair balance and avoidance of false or misleading content or preapproval promotion. Many companies have received Warning Letters and Untitled Letters from OPDP for violative statements in their press releases. In February 2013, a company received an Untitled Letter for a video press release that was cited for omission of risk information, unsubstantiated superiority claims and inadequate communication of indication.

Product Detailing

Product detailing, including oral statements by company representatives about their firms' prescription drug products, is considered promotional labeling. While it is difficult for FDA to monitor conversations, OPDP has issued Warning Letters and Untitled Letters to companies for presentations made to healthcare professionals by sales representatives. FDA also has issued letters to companies for professional telephone scripts. In July 2014, a company received an Untitled Letter citing its script, which omitted risk information and material facts and inadequately disclosed the product's name in direct conjunction with the proprietary name.

Historically, many conversations resulting in enforcement letters have occurred and been overheard at exhibit halls at major medical meetings. This is an enforcement area for OPDP; FDA representatives may attend major medical meetings and pay close attention to exhibit hall activities, including collecting materials distributed at those meetings.

Reprints

FDA-cleared or -approved prescription drugs, biologics and medical devices frequently are the subject of medical research, with study results typically published in medical journals, textbooks and other scientific reference publications. Often, these studies describe or suggest product uses that go beyond the prescription information to include off-label use. Since manufacturers must limit product promotion to approved, labeled uses, the promotional use of reprints can be challenging.

FDA helped address the appropriate use of reprints by publishing *Guidance for Industry on Good Reprint Practices for the Distribution of Medical Journal Articles and Medical or Scientific Reference Publications on Unapproved New Uses of Approved Drugs and Approved or Cleared Medical Devices* (Good Reprint Practices Guidance) (January 2009). This guidance describes the kind of material FDA considers a true reprint (e.g., a peer-reviewed publication versus one that is funded by the manufacturer), what information should accompany a reprint and appropriate reprint dissemination.

Internet and Social Media

The internet—from drug-specific websites to sponsored links to social media sites—commonly is used for prescription drug promotion. OPDP's predecessor, the Division of Drug Marketing, Advertising and Communication (DDMAC), issued its first letter regarding a promotional website in 1996. FDA has never issued formal regulations, citing rapidly changing technology as the reason. However, FDA took its first step in addressing social media in June 2014 with the release of two draft guidances.

The first, *Draft Guidance for Industry: Internet/Social Media Platforms with Character Space Limitations—Presenting Risk and Benefit Information for Prescription Drugs and Medical Devices*, provides recommendations for presenting benefit-risk information for prescription drugs or medical devices using media sources with character space limitations, such as Twitter and paid search results links on Google, Yahoo and Bing. The takeaway, even if there are character space limitations, is that the promotion must satisfy FDA's fair balance requirement. Moreover, these character space-limited promotions should link consumers to a website containing a complete discussion of product risks.

The second, *Draft Guidance for Industry: Internet/Social Media Platforms: Correcting Independent Third-Party Misinformation About Prescription Drugs and Medical Devices*, provides recommendations to companies that choose to correct third-party misinformation related to their own prescription drugs and medical devices (e.g., a manufacturer that chooses to correct inaccurate information about its product on a highly trafficked blog or Facebook page). The takeaway is that manufacturers are not required to correct misinformation controlled by independent third parties. However, if manufacturers choose to correct such misinformation, they should follow FDA's recommendations to be relevant and responsive to the misinformation; limited and tailored to the misinformation; nonpromotional in nature, tone and presentation; and consistent with FDA-required product labeling.

While the above-mentioned FDA guidances were groundbreaking as the first two to address the internet and social media, their recommendations are limited in scope—a scope that does not communicate FDA's standards for online promotion. To determine such standards, regulatory professionals must continue to review examples of improper internet promotion cited in OPDP enforcement letters to develop their own best judgment and practices for online promotion. Some notable examples include a letter for a video posted on YouTube (25 September 2008), a letter for a Facebook widget placed on a product site (29 July 2010), a letter for a video posted on WebMD (20 June 2012) and a letter for an online banner advertisement (31 July 2013). Even an FDA district office issued a Warning Letter in December 2012 to a company regarding Facebook "likes" of off-label content.

Product Promotion Versus Scientific Exchange

FDA does distinguish between drug promotion and scientific information exchange. Historically, manufacturers were involved in setting up continuing medical education (CME) programs to facilitate an exchange of scientific information. These events and the manufacturers organizing them fell under harsh scrutiny, however, when it was alleged the CME events were merely "dressed up product promotion." Truly independent and nonpromotional industry-supported activities serving as a scientific information exchange, if done properly, may not be deemed promotional labeling, even if the information being exchanged is considered off-label.

Enforcement of Prescription Drug Promotion and Advertising

The *FD&C Act* grants FDA regulatory authority over prescription drug advertising and promotion and allows monitoring of company promotional activity through OPDP. It also addresses prescription drug advertising. The law requires that prescription drug advertisements be accurate and not misleading.[14]

While *FD&C Act* Section 502 information is relatively brief and does not define *advertising* or *promotion* specifically, FDA has interpreted the act broadly in its regulations and guidance covering drug advertising and promotion. With the passage of the 1962 *Kefauver-Harris Amendments*, the agency gained greater authority over prescription drug marketing. Regulations covering prescription drug promotion are found in 21 CFR 202 and cross-referenced to 21 CFR 201.

If OPDP finds advertising or promotion to be violative, the agency has both administrative and judicial tools at its disposal. FDA's administrative tools include issuing Notice of Violation (NOV) letters, often referred to as Untitled Letters; Warning Letters; ordering a recall; and calling for product approval delay, suspension or withdrawal. Of these, FDA's most common administrative actions are NOVs and Warning Letters.

NOVs are different from Warning Letters in that they typically require the company to stop using the materials that make the claim(s) FDA finds violative. Warning Letters typically are addressed to the company CEO, with a warning that FDA will take further action if the company does not address and correct the matter immediately. If the matter is a product advertisement, this correction typically is a remedial advertisement in each venue where the violative advertisement was run. Warning Letters also may require the company to issue a "Dear Health Care Provider" letter to physicians as described in both 21 CFR 200.5(c)(3) and *Draft Guidance for Industry and FDA Staff: Dear Health Care Provider Letters: Improving Communication of Important Safety Information* (November 2010). All letters OPDP issues are posted publicly on FDA's Enforcement Activities webpage and often include a copy of the violative promotion; these postings also serve as one of the most important tools in understanding OPDP's position on certain topics.

As in other FDA enforcement areas, the agency's judicial tools include injunction, seizure or criminal prosecution. However, OPDP rarely seeks judicial action on its own for promotional violations. FDA is more likely to work with the Office of the Inspector General (OIG), Department of Justice (DOJ) or individual states' attorneys general in pursuing companies for significant promotional violations.

To supplement its enforcement activities, OPDP administers a program, started in 2010, called Truthful Prescription Drug Advertising and Promotion (or, more commonly, the "Bad Ad" program). The Bad Ad program's stated goal is to educate prescribers about their role in reporting false or misleading detailing by sales representatives and other forms of drug promotion to FDA. Since the Bad Ad program's inception, OPDP has attended a number of major medical meetings each year to continue educating attendees about the program. FDA distributes materials helping prescribers to recognize and encouraging them to report any activities and promotional messages they believe are false or misleading.

Prescription drug advertising resources can be found at https://www.fda.gov/Drugs/ResourcesForYou/Consumers/PrescriptionDrugAdvertising/.

Enforcement by Agencies Beyond FDA

FDA is not the only agency closely tracking prescription drug advertising and related activities. Many other federal agencies, including DOJ, the Department of Health and Human Services' (DHHS) OIG, states' attorneys general, FTC and Congress, closely monitor drug companies' activities.

US government enforcement efforts against the pharmaceutical industry were enhanced greatly beginning in 2001. The original focus was suspected kickbacks and violations of the pricing statutes (the *Anti-Kickback Statute*).

This law makes it illegal for any person—e.g., healthcare provider, office manager or sales agent—to knowingly and willfully solicit, offer, pay or receive "remuneration" (including kickbacks, bribes, rebates or anything of value) directly or indirectly in cash or in kind to any person to induce or cause that person to prescribe a product for which payment may be made in whole or in part under a federal healthcare program (42 USC 1320a-7b).

More recently, government agencies have focused on pharmaceutical and medical device manufacturers' off-label promotion in connection with the *False Claims Act* (*FCA*). The *FCA* was enacted during the Civil War when fraud was pervasive, particularly by defense contractors who unscrupulously sold bad goods (defective guns, putrid rations, etc.) to the US government and sought payment for them. Under the *FCA*, an individual not affiliated with the government can bring a suit claiming fraud. In such cases, the person filing the claim is known as a "whistleblower."

While this legislation has undergone some changes over the years, the tenets remain the same: it is unlawful to knowingly present or cause to be presented to the US government a false claim for payment. Among other things, modern-day changes to the laws impose treble damages and civil fines of $5,000–$10,000 per false claim. In practical application, today's whistleblowers, working with DOJ and states' attorneys general, have investigated and brought many high-profile claims against companies for off-label drug promotion, resulting in false claims for payment submitted to federal insurance programs, such as Medicare and Medicaid, which do not provide coverage for off-label uses. In these cases, each off-label prescription is considered one false claim. Many healthcare product manufacturers that settle *FCA* claims also agree to enter into Corporate Integrity Agreements

(CIAs) with HHS, placing strict requirements on corporate compliance for a number of years.

In recent years, some settlements have reached $1 billion plus. In July 2012, the largest settlement in history was reached with a manufacturer over allegations it engaged in unlawful promotion of some of its drugs, failed to report certain safety data and engaged in false price reporting practices. The company agreed to pay $3 billion and plead guilty to charges, which included introducing misbranded drugs into interstate commerce. The company also agreed to enter into a strict five-year CIA with HHS. The CIA requires individual accountability of the company's executives and board of directors.

More recently, in February 2014, the DOJ reached a settlement with a manufacturer over a prescription drug's labeling and promotion. The allegations included lack of adequate directions for use and certain sales representatives' being instructed how to expand sales conversations with healthcare providers beyond the product's approved indication. While not in the billions, this approximately $192.7 million settlement was the largest in 2014.

Finally, manufacturers must consider their competition as they develop advertising and promotional materials. Competitors have brought suit against manufacturers for violations of the *Lanham Act*. While this legislation often is thought of in terms of trademark protection, it also allows manufacturers to sue competitors for false advertising. Manufacturers have used courts' interpretations of the act to bring suits charging comparative claims in advertising are false and misleading, deceive a substantial part of the audience viewing the advertisements and could influence purchasing decisions. If a plaintiff prevails on a *Lanham Act* false advertising claim, the court can not only bar the advertising, but also order corrective advertising or a product recall.

Summary

- Drug product labeling includes the affixed container label as well as any material issued in association with the drug, including package inserts, patient labeling and Medication Guides.
- FDA requires the submission of labeling content in electronic format using Structured Product Labeling (SPL). SPL uses extensible markup language (XML) that permits a standardized mechanism for exchanging drug information.
- Container labels must contain the specific content outlined in 21 CFR 201 and must display such content with appropriate placement and prominence.
- Prescribing information (PI) is for healthcare professionals and is intended to direct their use of a drug product. The Physician Labeling Rule (PLR) guides new drug products' required prescribing information format and content.
- Patient labeling is product information, usually taken from the package insert, but written in consumer-friendly language. A Medication Guide is a type of patient labeling for drugs with serious risks and is required to be distributed to the consumer each time a prescription is filled or refilled.
- Advertising includes advertisements and promotional material called "promotional labeling."
- FDA monitors prescription drug advertising and promotion through OPDP. No drug can be promoted until FDA has approved the NDA.
- All advertising and promotional labeling must be submitted at the time of first use with Form FDA 2253, except materials for products receiving accelerated approval, which must be submitted for advisory opinion 30 days prior to initial dissemination. Although not generally required, it is strongly recommended that launch materials and new television advertisements be submitted to OPDP for advisory comment prior to dissemination.
- Promotional materials may not suggest a drug's use that is not approved or otherwise permitted in FDA-approved labeling; this is considered "off-label" use. Additionally, materials cannot claim a product is safer or more effective than has been established by "substantial evidence." Such evidence typically is obtained through two adequate and well-controlled clinical trials. *FDAMA* Section 114 allows pharmacoeconomic data distribution using a less-stringent standard as long as certain requirements are met.
- All promotional materials must include a "fair balance" of efficacy and risk information, with the exception of reminder labeling (not allowed for products with a boxed warning).
- Prescription drug advertisements must contain a "brief summary" of the Full Prescribing Information (FPI), and broadcast advertisements must include a "major statement" of risk and make "adequate provision" for disseminating the drug's permitted labeling.
- Promotional labeling that is not an advertisement must be disseminated with a copy of the FPI.
- Beyond traditional advertising, ways to promote a prescription drug product include press releases, oral statements by drug company representatives, medical journal reprints and, more commonly, the internet and social media. In June 2014, FDA entered the social media space by issuing two draft guidances: one covering social media

- with character space limitations and the other addressing the correction of online drug product misinformation.
- FDA takes strict action to enforce its labeling and advertising regulations. Typical FDA enforcement actions include Notices of Violation (NOVs) and Warning Letters. Although they are rarely used, the agency has other tools at its disposal to deal with violative advertising and promotional materials.
- FDA works with other agencies, such as the US Attorney's Office and OIG, in prosecuting companies alleged to be in violation of the *FCA* or *Anti-Kickback Statute* through off-label promotion. Companies found in violation of the *FD&C Act, Anti-Kickback Statute* and /or *FCA* risk disbarment from participation in federal programs (e.g., Medicare), imposition of Corporate Integrity Agreements and payment of large fines.

References
1. 21 CFR 201 Labeling. FDA website. https://www.accessdata.fda.gov/scripts/cdrh/cfdocs/cfcfr/CFRSearch.cfm?CFRPart=201. Accessed 17 April 2019.
2. PLR Requirements for Prescribing Information. https://www.fda.gov/Drugs/GuidanceComplianceRegulatoryInformation/LawsActsandRules/ucm084159.htm. Accessed 17 April 2019.
3. Ibid.
4. Office of Prescription Drug Promotion (OPDP) Research. FDA website. https://www.fda.gov/AboutFDA/CentersOffices/OfficeofMedicalProductsandTobacco/CDER/ucm090276.htm. Accessed 17 April 2019.
5. 21 CFR 202 Prescription Drug Advertising. FDA website. https://www.accessdata.fda.gov/scripts/cdrh/cfdocs/cfcfr/CFRSearch.cfm?CFRPart=202. Accessed 17 April 2019.
6. 21 CFR 203 Prescription Drug Marketing. FDA website. https://www.accessdata.fda.gov/scripts/cdrh/cfdocs/cfcfr/CFRSearch.cfm?CFRPart=203. Accessed 17 April 2019.
7. Drug Safety Oversight Board. FDA website. https://www.fda.gov/AboutFDA/CentersOffices/OfficeofMedicalProductsandTobacco/CDER/ucm082129.htm. Accessed 17 April 2019.
8. Promotional Labeling. FDA website. https://www.fda.gov/Drugs/ResourcesForYou/Consumers/PrescriptionDrugAdvertising/ucm072025.htm#promotional_labeling. Accessed 17 April 2019.
9. Ibid.
10. Basics of Drug Ads. FDA website. https://www.fda.gov/Drugs/ResourcesForYou/Consumers/PrescriptionDrugAdvertising/ucm072077.htm. Accessed 17 April 2019.
11. Reminder Advertisements. FDA website. https://www.fda.gov/Drugs/ResourcesForYou/Consumers/PrescriptionDrugAdvertising/ucm072077.htm#reminder. Accessed 17 April 2019.
12. Ibid.
13. Ibid.
14. Background on Advertising. FDA website. https://www.fda.gov/Drugs/ResourcesForYou/Consumers/PrescriptionDrugAdvertising/ucm071964.htm. Accessed 17 April 2019.

Chapter 11

Pharmacovigilance and Risk Management

Updated by Stacy Woeppel, MBA and Robert Falcone, PhD

OBJECTIVES

❑ Understand Investigational New Drug (IND) safety data reporting requirements

❑ Understand safety data drug and biologic requirements

❑ Understand safety data medical device postmarketing requirements

❑ Understand Risk Evaluation and Mitigation Strategy (REMS) requirements

❑ Understand drug and biologic proprietary name review requirements

LAWS, REGULATIONS, AND GUIDELINES COVERED IN THIS CHAPTER

❑ CDER Manual of Policies and Procedures (MAPP) 4151.3R3: Drug Safety Oversight Board (DSB)

❑ CDER MAPP 5240.8: Handling of Adverse Experience Reports and Other Generic Drug Post Marketing Reports

❑ CDER MAPP 6004.2R: Procedures for Completing and Processing the Form "Annual Status Report Review Form: PMR and PMC Summary"

❑ CDER MAPP 6010.R: Responsibilities for Tracking and Communicating the Status of Postmarketing Requirements and Commitments

❑ CDER MAPP 6010.9: Procedures and Responsibilities for Developing Postmarketing Requirements and Commitments

❑ CDER MAPP 6700.1: Risk Management Plan Activities in OND and ODS

❑ CDER MAPP 6700.9: FDA Posting of Potential Signals of Serious Risks Identified by the Adverse Event Reporting System

❑ CDER MAPP 6720.2 Rev.1: Procedures for Handling Requests for Proprietary Name Review

❑ CBER Manual of Regulatory Standard Operating Policies and Procedures (SOPP) 8401.6: The Responsibilities of the Division of Epidemiology (DE/OBE) in the BLA Review Process

❑ CBER SOPP 8413: Postmarketing Commitment Annual Reports, Final Reports, and Related Submissions—Administrative Handling, Review and CBER Reporting CBER SOPP 8415: Procedures for Developing Postmarketing Requirements and Commitments

Chapter 11

- CBER SOPP 8420: FDAAA Section 921: Posting of Potential Signals of Serious Risk

- CBER SOPP 8508: Procedures for Handling Adverse Reaction Reports Related to "361" Human Cells, Tissues, and Cellular and Tissue-Based Products (HCT/Ps)

- Compliance Program Guidance Manual 7353.001: Enforcement of the Postmarketing Adverse Drug Experience Reporting Regulations

- *Guidance for Industry: Good Pharmacovigilance Practices and Pharmacoepidemiologic Assessment* (March 2005)

- *Guidance for Industry: Postmarketing Adverse Event Reporting for Nonprescription Human Drug Products Marketed Without an Approved Application* (July 2009)

- *Guidance for Industry: Postmarketing Adverse Event Reporting for Medical Products and Dietary Supplements During an Influenza Pandemic* (February 2012)

- *Guidance for Industry: Reports on the Status of Postmarketing Study Commitments—Implementation of Section 130 of the Food and Drug Administration Modernization Act of 1997* (February 2006)

- *Guidance for Industry: Format and Content of Proposed Risk Evaluation and Mitigation Strategies (REMS), REMS Assessments and Proposed REMS Modifications* (September 2009)

- *Draft Guidance for Industry: Risk Evaluation and Mitigation Strategies: Modifications and Revisions* (April 2015)

- *Draft Guidance for Industry: FDA's Application of Statutory Factors in Determining When a REMS Is Necessary* (September 2016)

- *Final Guidance for Industry and Investigators: Safety Reporting Requirements for INDs and BA/BE Studies* (December 2012)

- *Final Guidance for Industry and Investigators: Safety Reporting Requirements for INDs and BA/BE Studies—Small Entity Compliance Guide* (December 2012)

- *Draft Guidance for Industry: Safety Assessment for IND Safety Reporting* (December 2015)

- *Guidance for Industry and Investigators: Enforcement of Safety Reporting Requirements for Investigational New Drug Applications and Bioavailability/Bioequivalence Studies* (June 2011)

- *Guidance for Industry: Development and Use of Risk Minimization Action Plans* (March 2005)

- *Guidance: Medication Guides—Distribution Requirements and Inclusion in Risk Evaluation and Mitigation Strategies (REMS)* (November 2011)

- *Draft Guidance: Drug Safety Information—FDA's Communication to the Public* (March 2012)

- Final Rule: Postmarketing Safety Reports for Human Drug and Biological Products; Electronic Submission Requirement (effective June 2015)

- *Draft Guidance: Classifying Significant Postmarketing Drug Safety Issues* (March 2012)

- *Guidance for Industry and Food and Drug Administration Staff: Postmarket Surveillance Under Section 522 of the Federal Food, Drug, and Cosmetic Act* (May 2016)

- *Final Guidance: Best Practices for Conducting and Reporting Pharmacoepidemiologic Safety Studies Using Electronic Healthcare Data Sets* (May 2013)

- *Final Guidance: Drug-Induced Liver Injury: Premarketing Clinical Evaluation* (July 2009)

- *Final Guidance: Postmarketing Studies and Clinical Trials—Implementation of Section 505(O)(3) of the Federal Food, Drug, and Cosmetic Act* (March 2011)

- *Final Guidance: Providing Postmarket Periodic Safety Reports in the ICH E2C(R2) Format (Periodic Benefit-Risk Evaluation Report)* (November 2016)

- *Draft Guidance: Safety Considerations for Container Labels and Carton Labeling Design to Minimize Medication Errors* (April 2013)

- *Final Guidance for Industry: Safety Considerations for Product Design to Minimize Medication Errors* (April 2016)

- *Final Guidance: Safety Labeling Changes—Implementation of Section 505(o)(4) of the Federal Food, Drug, and Cosmetic Act* (July 2013)

- *Draft Guidance for Industry: Best Practices in Developing Proprietary Names for Drugs* (May 2014)

- *Final Guidance for Industry: Over-the-Counter Pediatric Oral Liquid Drug Products Containing Acetaminophen* (August 2015)

- *Final Guidance for Industry: Adverse Event Reporting for Outsourcing Facilities Under Section 503B of the Federal Food, Drug, and Cosmetic Act* (October 2015)

- *Guidance for Industry: Questions and Answers Regarding Adverse Event Reporting and Recordkeeping for Dietary Supplements as Required by the Dietary Supplement and Nonprescription Drug Consumer Protection Act* (September 2013)

- ICH Clinical Safety Data Management: Definitions and Standards for Expedited Reporting E2A (Final) (1 March 1995)

- ICH Pharmacovigilance Planning E2E (Final) (April 2005)

- ICH Electronic Transmission of Individual Case Safety Reports E2B (R2)

Introduction

Safety is a critical component of investigating and marketing drugs, biologics and medical devices in the US. Reporting requirements are rigorous and compliance with these requirements is significant. Currently, the US Food and Drug Administration (FDA) has no legal authority to require postmarketing surveillance of dietary supplements by their manufacturers or distributors, unlike drugs, biologics and medical devices. When an FDA-regulated product is approved, not everything is known about it due to the limitations of clinical trial data. Additional information is learned continuously throughout the product lifecycle as more and more individuals use it in a real-world setting. Postmarketing safety data monitoring is required by both industry and FDA to protect and promote patient safety. Other regulatory agencies also require postmarketing follow-up and safety databases are maintained globally. The International Council on Harmonization (ICH) defines safety reporting standards and requirements globally and US legislation is consistent with these requirements. As new safety information is generated through postmarketing surveillance, this may result in regulatory actions, including labeling changes and issuance of safety alerts, Dear Health Care Professional (DHCP) letters, Drug Safety Communications, Field Alert Reports (FAR) and rare product withdrawals or recalls. Regulatory and pharmacovigilance professionals serve critical functions in monitoring product safety together with patients and consumers, who remain the most significant spontaneous report contributors to FDA's Adverse Event Reporting System (FAERS) database.[1]

Clinical Trials

Definitions of adverse events or suspected adverse reactions are slightly different when used in a clinical trial setting. Definitions below are consistent with ICH definitions used worldwide.

Definitions of Adverse Events in Clinical Studies

- Adverse event—any untoward medical occurrence associated with the use of a drug in humans, whether or not considered drug-related.
- Life-threatening adverse event or life-threatening suspected adverse reaction—an adverse event or suspected adverse reaction that, in the view of either the investigator or sponsor, places the patient or subject at immediate risk of death. It does not include an adverse event or suspected adverse reaction that, had it occurred in a more severe form, might have caused death.
- Serious adverse event or serious suspected adverse reaction—an adverse event or suspected adverse reaction that, in the view of either the investigator or sponsor, results in any of the following outcomes: death, a life-threatening adverse event, inpatient hospitalization or prolongation of existing hospitalization, a persistent or significant incapacity or substantial disruption of the ability to conduct normal life functions, or a congenital anomaly or birth defect. Important medical events that may not result in death, but are life-threatening or require hospitalization may

be considered serious when, based on appropriate medical judgment, they may jeopardize the patient or subject and may require medical or surgical intervention to prevent one of the outcomes listed in this definition. Examples of such medical events include allergic bronchospasm requiring intensive treatment in an emergency room or at home, blood dyscrasias or convulsions that do not result in inpatient hospitalization or the development of drug dependency or drug abuse.
- Suspected adverse reaction—any adverse event for which there is a reasonable possibility the drug was the cause. For Investigational New Drug (IND) application safety reporting, "reasonable possibility" means there is evidence to suggest a causal relationship between the drug and the adverse event. Suspected adverse reaction implies a lesser degree of certainty about causality than adverse reaction, which means any adverse event caused by a drug.[2]
- Unexpected adverse event or unexpected suspected adverse reaction—an adverse event or suspected adverse reaction is considered "unexpected" if it is not listed either in the Investigator's Brochure (IB) or at the specificity or severity observed; or, if an IB is not required or available, the adverse event or suspected adverse reaction is not consistent with the risk information described in the general investigational plan or elsewhere in the current application, as amended. For example, under this definition, hepatic necrosis would be unexpected (under greater severity) if the IB referred only to elevated hepatic enzymes or hepatitis. "Unexpected," as used in this definition, also refers to adverse events or suspected adverse reactions mentioned in the IB as occurring with a class of drugs or as anticipated from the drug's pharmacological properties, but not explicitly mentioned as occurring with the particular drug under investigation.

Clinical Trial Reporting Requirements

The clinical trial investigator is required to report all adverse events encountered with the drug to the sponsor promptly.

1. The sponsor is responsible for reviewing all information relevant to the drug's safety, obtained or otherwise received by the sponsor from any source, foreign or domestic, including information derived from any clinical or epidemiological investigations, animal investigations, commercial marketing experience, reports in the scientific literature and unpublished scientific papers, as well as reports from foreign regulatory authorities not reported to the agency already.
2. The sponsor must notify FDA and all participating investigators promptly in a written IND safety report of:
   o any adverse experience associated with the drug's use that is both serious and unexpected

   or

   o any laboratory animal test finding that suggests a significant risk for human subjects, including reports of mutagenicity, teratogenicity or carcinogenicity

As a result of the final rule on Drug Safety Reporting Requirements for Human Drug and Biological Products and Safety Reporting Requirements for Bioavailability and Bioequivalence studies in Humans, the following information must be reported to the agency within 15 days of the sponsor becoming aware of any of the following:[3]

- findings from clinical or epidemiological studies that suggest a significant risk to study participants
- severe suspected adverse reactions occurring at a rate higher than expected
- serious adverse events from bioavailability studies and bioequivalence studies conducted without an IND

For clinical studies, an adverse experience or fatal outcome need not be submitted to FDA unless the applicant concludes there is a reasonable possibility the product caused the adverse experience or fatal outcome (See 21 CFR 310.305(c)(1)(ii), 314.80(e)(1) and 600.80(e)(1)). Each written notification may be submitted on a Form FDA 3500A or in a narrative format (foreign occurring events may be submitted on either a Form FDA 3500A or, if preferred, a Council for International Organizations of Medical Sciences (CIOMS) I form). Reports from animal or epidemiological studies should be submitted in a narrative format. All reports should be labeled prominently as "IND Safety Report." Each written notification to FDA should be transmitted to the Center for Drug Evaluation and Research's (CDER) New Drug Review Division or the Center for Biologics Evaluation and Research's (CBER) product review division responsible for the IND.

The sponsor is required to notify FDA by telephone or facsimile of any unexpected fatal or life-threatening experience associated with the drug's use as soon as possible, but no later than seven calendar days after the sponsor's initial receipt of the information. Each telephone call or facsimile to FDA shall be transmitted to the CDER new drug review division or CBER product review division responsible for the product's review.

The sponsor must provide follow-up information for each IND safety report submitted. The follow-up information should be submitted as soon as all available information has been gathered. If, upon further investigation into an adverse event, a sponsor establishes that an event not initially determined to be reportable now is reportable, it shall report this event as soon as possible but no later than 15 calendar days after the event has been made clear. FDA may require a sponsor to submit IND safety reports in a different format or frequency than those established in the regulations. The sponsor shall provide all additional safety information it has obtained regarding the drug in an information amendment or an annual report.[4]

For bioavailability (BA) and bioequivalence (BE) studies conducted without an IND, the person conducting the study, including any contract research organization (CRO), is required to notify FDA of any serious adverse event within 15 days of its occurrence, and of any fatal or life-threatening adverse event from the study within seven days of its occurrence. Each notification under this paragraph must be submitted to the director, Office of Generic Drugs in CDER. Relevant follow-up information to a BA/BE safety report must be submitted as soon as the information is available and must be identified as such, i.e., "Follow-up BA/BE safety report." Upon FDA's request, the person conducting the study, including any CRO, must submit any additional data or information the agency deems necessary to FDA within 15 days of receiving the request.

The sponsor's submission of an IND safety report for a drug product under a clinical study does not constitute the sponsor or FDA's admission that the drug caused or contributed to the adverse event.

Postmarketing Surveillance of Drugs and Biologics

Postmarketing surveillance is the systematic collection, analysis, interpretation and dissemination of health-related data to improve public health and reduce morbidity and mortality. FDA requires marketed prescription and nonprescription drug manufacturers, packagers and distributors to establish and maintain records and report all serious, unexpected adverse drug experiences associated with the use of their medical products to the agency. Healthcare professional reporting outside the industry is voluntary.

Definitions
The following definitions apply to postmarketing adverse drug experience reporting:[5]
- Adverse drug experience—any adverse event associated with the use of a drug, whether or not considered drug-related, including:
  - an adverse event occurring in the course of the drug product's use in professional practice
  - an adverse event occurring from a drug overdose, whether accidental or intentional
  - an adverse event occurring from drug abuse
  - an adverse event occurring from drug withdrawal
  - any failure of expected pharmacological action
- Associated with the use of the drug—there is a reasonable possibility the drug may have caused the experience.
- Disability—An adverse event that results in a substantial disruption of a person's ability to conduct normal life functions.
- FAERS—a computerized information database designed to support FDA's postmarketing safety surveillance program for drug and non-vaccine biological products.
- VAERS—a national vaccine safety surveillance program co-sponsored by FDA and the Centers for Disease Control and Prevention (CDC).
- Individual Case Safety Report (ICSR)—a description of an adverse experience related to an individual patient or subject.
- Life-threatening adverse drug experience—any adverse drug experience that places the patient, in the initial reporter's view, at immediate risk of death from the adverse drug experience as it occurred, i.e., does not include an adverse drug experience that, had it occurred in a more severe form, might have caused death.
- Serious adverse drug experience (See Definitions of Adverse Events in Clinical Studies)
- Unexpected adverse drug experience—any adverse drug experience not listed in the drug product's current labeling. This experience could include events that may be related symptomatically and patho-physiologically to an event listed in the labeling, but differ from the event because of greater severity or specificity. "Unexpected," as used in this definition, refers to an adverse drug experience that has not been observed previously (i.e., included in the labeling) rather than from the perspective of such experience not being anticipated from the pharmaceutical product's pharmacological properties.

Authorities
CDER's Office of Surveillance and Epidemiology (SE) consists of two offices, with a total of six divisions under these offices:
- Office of Pharmacovigilance and Epidemiology
  - Division of Pharmacovigilance I and II

- o Division of Epidemiology I and II
- Office of Medication Error Prevention and Risk Management
  - o Division of Medication Error Prevention and Analysis
  - o Division of Risk Management

Office of Pharmacovigilance and Epidemiology
Division of Pharmacovigilance (DPV)
The Division of Pharmacovigilance (DPV) includes staff who provide critical analysis of postmarketing data sources to identify and evaluate safety signals for all marketed drug products. Team coverage is aligned with the Office of New Drugs (OND) review divisions' therapeutic areas. Each SE covers assigned product group(s) aligned with a therapeutic area. The DPV staff also includes medical officers (MOs) who provide clinical expertise in various therapeutic areas, such as dermatology, oncology and rheumatology. Both SEs and MOs collaborate and work closely with relevant OND staff, so potential safety signals are placed in the context of existing preclinical, clinical or pharmacologic knowledge of the products in question.

Division of Epidemiology
The role of epidemiologists in the Division of Epidemiology (DEPI) is assessing and evaluating preapproval data and postmarketing safety data, including spontaneous reports of adverse events and epidemiological studies. Responsibilities include critiquing industry safety submissions, including pharmacoepidemiology studies and risk management plans; advising review divisions in designing and developing epidemiological protocols for studies to explore and/or confirm signals to assess risk in areas of significant CDER concern; conducting active drug safety surveillance using the Sentinel Initiative and reviewing drug safety-related epidemiological study protocols and study reports required from manufacturers as postmarketing requirements (PMRs) and commitments. They serve as agency leads in ensuring sponsors' PMR activities meet best practices in epidemiology and can provide robust and actionable evidence to inform regulatory decision making following initial approval. They evaluate safety signals by putting them into the context of drug use, including calculating reporting rates, the existing body of evidence in the scientific literature and by mounting FDA-sponsored epidemiological studies, as needed, to quantify and characterize drug safety risks detected through spontaneous reports or systematic scientific literature review. Also, the drug utilization team provides denominator data, or context, for understanding adverse event reports; modeling drug risk based on usage patterns; and calculating patient-based reporting rates. Epidemiologists also provide data to aid in increasing FDA's ability to request regulatory impact studies, such as those authorized under the *Best Pharmaceuticals for Children Act* (*BPCA*), to understand how clinicians can better use drug labeling.

Office of Medication Error Prevention and Risk Management (OMEPRM)
Division of Medication Error Prevention and Analysis (DMEPA)
DMEPA is responsible primarily for the premarket review of proposed proprietary medication names, labels/labeling, packaging and human factors studies to reduce the potential for CDER-regulated product medication errors. DMEPA also conducts review and analysis of postmarketing medication errors to determine whether regulatory actions are needed, such as label or labeling revisions, product redesign or postmarketing communications to stakeholders. DMEPA works with external stakeholders, regulators and researchers to understand the causes of medication errors and the effectiveness of preventative interventions, and to provide guidance to industry on drug development considerations from a medication errors perspective.

Division of Risk Management
The Division of Risk Management (DRISK) serves as the focal point for CDER risk management activities. DRISK provides risk management expertise on developing and implementing programs and initiatives to support CDER's policies related to Risk Evaluation and Mitigation Strategies (REMS) authorities under the *Food and Drug Administration Amendments Act* (*FDAAA*) of 2007. It reviews all proposed REMS, REMS modifications and REMS assessments for all products with approved REMS for conformance with current FDA standards.

Other CDER Authorities
CDER's Drug Safety and Risk Management Advisory Committee advises the commissioner on risk management, risk communication and quantitative evaluation of spontaneous reports for drugs for human use and any other product for which FDA has regulatory responsibility. The committee also advises the commissioner regarding the scientific and medical evaluation of all information gathered by the Department of Health and Human Services (HHS) and the Department of Justice regarding drugs and other substances' safety, efficacy and abuse potential and recommends actions to HHS regarding the marketing, investigation and control of such drugs or other substances.

CDER's Drug Safety Oversight Board (DSB), created in 2005 and mandated by law by *FDAAA*, advises CDER's director on the handling and communicating of essential and often emerging drug safety issues. It meets monthly and provides a forum for discussion and input on how to address potential drug safety issues. DSB is composed of representatives from two FDA centers and eight other federal government agencies. An important DSB role is helping FDA assess the impact of its safety decisions on its federal partners' healthcare systems. DSB, with its broad representation from federal healthcare organizations, can provide valuable input and allows FDA to hear other perspectives on drug safety issues.

Postmarketing Drug/Biologic Surveillance: Individual Case Safety Reports (ICSRs)

Sponsors of approved New Drug Applications (NDAs), Abbreviated New Drug Applications (ANDAs) and antibiotic applications, manufacturers of marketed prescription drugs for human use without approved NDAs or ANDAs, and licensed manufacturers of approved Biologic License Applications are required to report adverse experiences to FDA under 21 CFR 310.305, 314.80, 314.98 and 600.80. Before considering any clinical incident for submission to FDA in an individual case safety report (ICSR), applicants should, at minimum, know the five categories applicable to all products, including vaccines. Examples of some of the types of information in each category are:
- patient information (e.g., age or age category, gender)
- adverse experience information (e.g., date and description of the experience)
- suspect medical product information (e.g., drug name, dose, indication and National Drug Code (NDC) number)
- initial reporter information (e.g., name and contact information)
- applicant, manufacturer or responsible person information (e.g., name and contact information)

The following two categories apply to vaccine products only:
- information about other vaccines administered in the previous four weeks
- information on the facility and personnel where the vaccine was administered (e.g., the name of the person who administered the vaccine, name of responsible physician and facility where the vaccine was administered)

If any one of these essential elements remains unknown after being pursued actively by the applicant, the applicant should maintain records of efforts to obtain the necessary elements for an individual case in its corporate drug or biological safety files.

It is notable that FDA has moved to an electronic requirement for ICSR submissions. Electronic ICSR submission enhances global pharmacovigilance by facilitating electronic transmission and exchange of appropriate information from ICSRs among regulatory bodies and regulated entities, using common data elements and transmission standards.

An applicant actively seeking information on an adverse experience should use direct verbal contact with the initial adverse experience reporter (e.g., in person, by telephone or other interactive means, such as a videoconference). The applicant should not send the initial reporter a letter requesting information concerning the adverse experience. Applicants should use a healthcare professional (e.g., physician, physician assistant, dentist, pharmacist, nurse) for initial contact with reporters to be able to understand the case's medical consequences and ask appropriate questions to acquire relevant information rapidly to determine the case's significance.

In reports concerning an "identifiable" patient, statements, such as "some patients got anaphylaxis," should be excluded until further patient information is obtained. However, a report stating that "an elderly woman had anaphylaxis" should be included because there is enough information to suspect specific patients were involved. Patients should not be identified by name or address. Instead, the applicant should assign a unique code as the patient identifier for reporting purposes. The exception to using the unique code is if the patient is the reporter. FDA has determined it is relevant for the reporter's name to be included, even when the reporter is the patient, to allow agency follow-up, as needed. Names of patients, healthcare professionals, hospitals and geographic identifiers in adverse drug experience reports are not releasable to the public under FDA's public information regulations.

For spontaneous reports, the applicant should assume an adverse experience or fatal outcome was thought to be due to the suspect drug or biological product (implied causality). An adverse experience should, at minimum, consist of signs (including abnormal laboratory findings, if appropriate), symptoms or disease diagnosis (including any colloquial descriptions) obtained for reporting purposes. Thus, a report stating that a patient "experienced unspecified injury" or "suffered irreparable damages" should not be included until more specific information about the adverse experience can be determined.

Current regulations dealing with postmarketing adverse drug experience (ADE) reporting include 21 CFR 314.80 and 310.305. US regulations are consistent with ICH and CIOMS standards.[6]

Under 21 CFR 314.80, the sponsor is required to review ADE information obtained from all potential sources (foreign and domestic), including:
- marketing experience
- scientific literature (peer-reviewed and non-peer-reviewed)
- unpublished reports

- postmarketing clinical investigations
- postmarketing epidemiological or surveillance studies

Further, the sponsor is required to develop written procedures for surveillance, receipt, evaluation and reporting of postapproval ADEs to FDA and maintain records of all ADEs known to the applicant for 10 years, including raw data and any correspondence relating to ADEs. Any company (sponsor, manufacturer, distributor or packer) listed on the approved product labeling must meet these ADE reporting requirements. A non-sponsor's obligations may be met by submitting all serious ADE reports to the sponsor. If a non-sponsor elects to submit ADE reports to the sponsor rather than to FDA, the non-sponsor shall submit and report to the sponsor within five calendar days of receiving the report, and the sponsor would be responsible for submitting ADEs to FDA. The non-sponsor should document the submission to the sponsor.

Serious and unexpected adverse experiences from all sources, whether domestic or foreign, must be submitted to FDA. Possible sources include, for example, scientific literature, postmarketing studies or commercial marketing experience. Scientific literature reports may comprise published and unpublished scientific papers known to the applicant. All adverse events (domestic and foreign) that are both serious and unexpected must be submitted within 15 calendar days of initial receipt by anyone in the applicant's employ.

For marketed products with an approved application, manufacturers, packers or distributors that do not hold the application continue to have the option of submitting 15-Day Alert reports directly to FDA or the application holder under Sections 314.80(c)(1)(iii) and 600.80(c)(1)(iii). If they opt to submit reports directly to FDA, they are required to do so electronically. If they choose to report to the applicant, they may submit the report in any format acceptable to the reporter and applicant. The applicant, however, is required to use electronic reporting when subsequently reporting the information to FDA.[7]

Unlike IND Safety Reports, causality does not enter into the decision for postmarketing reports, except postmarketing clinical investigations or studies (whether or not conducted under an IND). In these instances, if the reporter concludes there is a reasonable possibility the drug caused a serious, unexpected adverse experience, the report is subject to a 15-Day Alert. This instance is considered the one exception to reporting postmarketing ADEs where a causality assessment is required. Postmarketing study reports should be separate and identified as coming from those studies to differentiate them from spontaneous reports.

Reports from scientific literature, i.e., medical journals, are required to be submitted as either case reports or the result of a formal clinical trial. Reports based on scientific literature also should be reported and accompanied by a copy of the published article.

The sponsor is required to investigate all ADEs that are the subject of postmarketing 15-Day Alert reports and submit follow-up reports. If additional information is not obtainable, records should be maintained of unsuccessful steps taken to seek additional information. Postmarketing 15-Day Alert reports and their follow-ups shall be submitted under separate cover. The mailing label should prominently say "15-Day Alert Report" or "15-Day Alert Report Follow-up."

A sponsor should protect the patient's privacy by assigning a unique code instead of using the patient's name and address in the reports. A sponsor can include a disclaimer statement in the report, indicating it is not admitting or denying the ADE report submitted constitutes an admission the drug caused or contributed to an adverse effect.

The *Dietary Supplement and Nonprescription Drug Consumer Protection Act* (*DSNDCA*) (PL 109-462) was signed into law in 2006. The *DSNDCA* amended the *Food, Drug, and Cosmetic Act* (*FD&C Act*) to add safety reporting requirements for nonprescription drug products marketed without an approved application. Section 760(b) states the manufacturer, packager or distributor whose name appears on the label of a nonprescription drug marketed in the US without an approved application (referred to as the responsible person) must submit to FDA any report of a serious adverse event associated with such drug when used in the US, accompanied by a copy of the label on or within the drug's retail package. Also, the responsible person must submit follow-up reports of new medical information related to a submitted serious adverse event report received within one year of the initial report.

Postmarketing Drug/Biologic Surveillance: Periodic Reporting

The sponsor is required to submit the following periodic reports to FDA quarterly for the first three years following approval. Unless otherwise requested by FDA, after three years, the sponsor shall submit the periodic ADE report at annual intervals. Quarterly reports are required to be filed within 30 days of the close of the quarter, with the first quarter beginning on the date of the application's approval. Annual reports are required to be submitted within 60 days of the close of the year. FDA may extend or reestablish the requirement for an applicant to submit quarterly reports after a significant supplement's approval. Applicants have the option of submitting ICSRs at any time up until the periodic report due date to allow flexibility with electronic reporting.

The regulations require a postmarketing periodic report to contain:
- a narrative summary and analysis of the information in the report and an analysis of any 15-Day Alert reports submitted during the reporting interval
- ICSRs for serious, expected and non-serious adverse experiences
- a history of actions taken since the last report due to adverse experiences

An applicant may request a waiver from submitting postmarketing periodic safety reports in the format described in the regulations. Instead, applicants can prepare these reports using the Periodic Safety Update Report (PSUR) or Periodic Benefit Risk Evaluation Report (PBRER) formats described in ICH E2C. Even if a waiver has been obtained to submit in PSUR format, a separate waiver must be requested to submit in PBRER format.

Postmarketing Drug and Biologic Surveillance: Safety Monitoring by FDA

FDA tracks adverse drug reactions by entering all approved drugs and therapeutic biological products' safety reports into the FAERS database, which uses standardized international terminology from the Medical Dictionary for Regulatory Activities (MedDRA). FDA uses FAERS to facilitate postmarketing drug surveillance and compliance activities. FAERS' goal is to improve public health by providing the best available tools for storing and analyzing safety data and reports.[8] FAERS data and trends may lead to FDA action on products, such as DHCP letters or requests to a sponsor for additional safety studies. DHCP letters are part of an FDA initiative to collect, analyze and disseminate drug safety information rapidly. FDA's *Draft Guidance: Drug Safety Information—FDA's Communication to the Public* (March 2012) highlights the elements required in all safety communications.

FDA also posts potential signals of serious risks or new safety information identified from FAERS on its website quarterly. A drug's appearance on this list does not mean FDA has concluded the drug has the risk. It means FDA has identified a potential safety concern, not that it has identified a causal relationship between the drug and the listed risk. If, after further evaluation, FDA determines the drug is associated with the risk, it may take a variety of actions, including requiring drug labeling changes or development of a REMS, or gathering additional data to characterize the risk better. FDA posts these quarterly reports per *FDAAA* Title IX, Section 921. CDER and CBER staff examine the FAERS database regularly as part of routine safety monitoring. When a severe potential risk signal is identified from FAERS data, it is entered as a safety issue into CDER's Document Archiving, Reporting and Regulatory Tracking System (DARRTS) or CBER's Therapeutics and Blood Safety Branch Safety Signal Tracking (SST) system. The table in each quarterly report lists the product names and potential safety issues entered into the above tracking systems. Additional information on each issue, such as an FDA Drug Safety Communication is also provided. **Table 11-1** provides a summary on the categories and entities responsible for submitting safety reports for drugs and biologics to FDA.

Proprietary Name Review

FDA has made the role of medical product names and the naming processes in medication errors part of its focus on safe medical product use. The agency has developed internal procedures and processes as part of its marketing application review to evaluate a proposed product name's (submitted as part of an NDA, Biologics License Application (BLA) or ANDA) potential to cause or contribute to medication errors. *Guidance for Industry: Contents of a Complete Submission for the Evaluation of Proprietary Names* is intended to assist industry in submitting a complete package of information for FDA's use in assessing a proposed proprietary name's safety aspects (to reduce medication errors) and a proposed name's promotional implications (to ensure compliance with other labeling and promotion requirements).

Risk Management and REMS

FDAAA created *FD&C Act* Section 505-1, which authorizes FDA to require sponsors of specific product applications to submit and implement a REMS. Risk management is defined in FDA's *Guidance for Industry: Good Pharmacovigilance Practices and Pharmacoepidemiologic Assessment* as an iterative process of:
- assessing a product's benefit-risk balance
- developing and implementing tools to minimize a product's risks while preserving its benefits
- evaluating tool effectiveness and reassessing the benefit-risk balance
- making adjustments, as appropriate, to the risk minimization tools to further improve the benefit-risk balance

FDA's *Draft Guidance for Industry: Format and Content of Proposed Risk Evaluation and Mitigation Strategies (REMS), REMS Assessment: Planning and Reporting: Draft Guidance for Industry*, and *Risk Evaluation and Mitigation Strategies: Modifications and Revisions: Guidance for Industry* provide information on:
- the proposed REMS format and content, including supporting documentation

Table 11-1. Safety Reporting Requirements for Drugs/Biologics

Responsible	Category	Initial Reporting Timeframe
Clinical Trials ICSR[a,b]		
Sponsor[c]	Unexpected, serious adverse event (SAE), associated with product[d,e]	7 calendar days
Sponsor[f]	SAE associated with product[g,h]	15 calendar days
Postmarketing ICSR		
Company[i]	Unexpected, serious adverse event (SAE)[j]	15 calendar days
Periodic Reports		
Sponsor	IND Safety Reports (DSUR)[k]	Annually from DIBD[l]
Company[m]	Postmarketing Safety Reports (PSUR/PBRER)[n]	Quarterly for first 3 years after approval and thereafter annually
Field Alert Reports (FAR)		
Sponsor	• Incident that caused a product or its labeling to be mistaken for or applied to another article • Information concerning any quality change or deterioration in distributed product or failure of distributed product batches to meet established product specifications	3 working days[o]

a. Includes postmarketing clinical trials.
b. FDA and all participating investigators must be notified.
c. For BE/BA studies not conducted under an IND, the individual conducting study or CRO is responsible for submitting report.
d. Causal association is determined by the sponsor whose, judgement may supersede that of the investigator.
e. BE/BA studies not conducted under an IND are reported whether or not associated with drug.
f. Op cit d.
g. Op cit d.
h. Op cit e.
i. Sponsor, manufacturer, distributor or packer listed on the approved product labeling. Compounding facilities also are expected to adhere to this reporting requirement.
j. From all sources, whether domestic or foreign (e.g., scientific literature, postmarketing studies or commercial marketing experience).
k. Op cit d.
l. Development International Birth Date (DIBD)—the sponsor's first authorization to conduct a clinical trial or date of commencement of first clinical trial.
m. Op cit i.
n. Op cit e.
o. To be submitted even if product approved under an NDA/ANDA is only distributed outside US.

- approved REMS assessment content and proposed modifications
- identifiers to use on REMS documents
- communicating with FDA about REMS

Guidance for Industry: Medication Guides—Distribution Requirements and Inclusion in Risk Evaluation and Mitigation Strategies (REMS) outlines the use of a Medication Guide as required as part of a REMS. The guidance also provides information on enforcement discretion regarding Medication Guide dispensing requirements.

The *Food and Drug Administration Safety Innovation Act* of 2012 (*FDASIA*) requires an assessment strategy to determine whether a REMS is effective. Under the law, the assessment could determine whether a modification is necessary to maintain an acceptable benefit-risk balance and keep the burden on the healthcare system at an acceptable level. Applicants may propose a REMS modification at any time, FDA may propose a REMS modification at any time or FDA may request an applicant to submit a modification. If the agency makes such a request, the applicant must respond within 120 days (or another timeframe agreed upon by FDA and applicant), and the agency must review and act on the submitted strategy within 180 days of the request or 60 days for minor modifications or modifications based on safety label changes.

In some cases, FDA may initiate discussions about the formation of a shared system REMS.[9] A shared system REMS uses a single REMS document, supporting document and REMS materials for drugs and biologics in a class with similar severe risks. Details on the requirements, benefits and recommendations for a shared system REMS can be found in *Guidance for Industry: Development of a Shared System REMS* and *Guidance for Industry: Waivers of the Single, Shared System REMS Requirement*.[10]

Table 11-2. Safety Reporting Requirements for Medical Devices

Medical Device Reports (MDR)		
Responsible	**Category**	**Initial Reporting Timeframe**
Manufacturer[a,b]	• May have caused or contributed to a death or serious injury • Malfunctioned and the malfunction of the device or a similar device manufactured by the manufacturer would likely cause or contribute to a death or serious injury	30 calendar days
Manufacturer[c,d]	• May have caused or contributed to a death or serious injury • Malfunctioned and the malfunction of the device or a similar device manufactured by the manufacturer would likely cause or contribute to a death or serious injury AND • Requires remedial action to prevent an unreasonable risk of substantial harm to the public	5 working days
IDE Reporting		
Company[g]	Unanticipated Adverse Device Effects	10 working days

a. Manufactures, prepares, propagates, compounds, assembles or processes a device by chemical, physical, biological or other procedure.
b. Includes US manufacturers whose devices are not cleared in US but are exported to foreign locations.
c. Op cit a.
d. Op cit b.
e. Any action other than routine device maintenance or servicing necessary to prevent recurrence of an MDR. FDA does not consider an action to correct only a single device involved in an MDR to be a remedial action.
f. Remedial actions associated with MDRs not taken to prevent an unreasonable risk of substantial harm to the public can be reported within 30 calendar days.
g. Ibid.

Postmarketing Device Surveillance

Medical device postmarketing surveillance presents unique challenges compared to drugs and biologics due to medical devices' great diversity and complexity, the iterative medical device product development process, the technology adoption learning curve and the relatively short product lifecycle. Proper medical device operation depends on optimal device design, the use environment, user training and adherence to directions for use and maintenance. In some cases, these features limit the utility of systems designed for identifying device-related adverse events.[11]

The primary regulations governing device postmarketing reporting requirements are included in:
- 21 CFR 803 Medical device reporting:
    - Device user facilities must report deaths and serious injuries a device has or may have caused or contributed to, establish and maintain adverse event files and submit annual summary reports.
    - Manufacturers or importers must report deaths and serious injuries their device has or may have caused or contributed to the incident. They also must report certain device malfunctions and establish and maintain adverse event files. Also, manufacturers must submit specified follow-up information.
    - Medical device distributors must maintain records of incidents but are not required to file these incidents.
- 21 CFR 806 Medical devices; reports of corrections and removals
- 21 CFR 822 Postmarket surveillance

In 2012, *FDASIA* expanded FDA's Sentinel network to apply to devices. The agency is required to establish procedures for tracking device risk and analyzing public health trends. FDA also was given the authority to require postmarketing studies at any time in the product's marketed lifetime.

The current US medical device postmarket surveillance system depends primarily on:
- Medical Device Reporting (MDR)—See above.
- Medical Product Safety Network (MedSun)— MedSun is an enhanced surveillance network comprised of approximately 280 hospitals nationwide that work interactively with FDA to understand and report on device use and adverse outcomes in the real-world clinical environment better. The overall quality of reports received annually via MedSun is significantly higher than those received via MDR. Specialty networks within MedSun focus on device-specific areas such

as cardiovascular devices (HeartNet) and pediatric intensive care unit devices (KidNet). Also, the network can be used for targeted surveys and focused on clinical research.
- Postapproval studies—FDA may order a postapproval study as a condition of device approval under a Premarket Approval (PMA) application. Typically, postapproval studies are used to assess device safety, effectiveness and/or reliability, including longer-term, real-world device performance. Status updates for postapproval studies may be found on FDA's website (www.accessdata.fda.gov/scripts/cdrh/cfdocs/cfpma/pma_pas.cfm).
- Postmarket surveillance studies—FDA may order certain Class II or III device manufacturers to conduct postmarket surveillance studies (often referred to as "522 studies"). Study approaches vary widely and may include nonclinical device testing, existing clinical database analysis, observational studies and, rarely, randomized controlled trials. Status updates for ongoing postmarket surveillance studies covering approximately a dozen device types may be found on FDA's website (www.accessdata.fda.gov/scripts/cdrh/cfdocs/cfPMA/pss.cfm).
- FDA discretionary studies—In addition to medical device adverse event reports, postapproval and postmarket surveillance studies, FDA also conducts research to monitor device performance, investigate adverse event signals and characterize device-associated benefits and risks to patient subpopulations. A variety of privacy-protected data sources are used, including national registries, Medicare and Medicaid administrative and claims data, data from integrated health systems, electronic health records and published scientific literature.
- Other tools—FDA has other tools it may use postmarket to track devices, restrict or ban device use and remove unsafe, adulterated or misbranded products from the market. **Table 11-2** summarizes the categories and entities responsible for submitting safety reports for medical devices to FDA.

Postmarketing Surveillance of Dietary Supplements

Currently, FDA has no legal authority to require postmarketing dietary supplement surveillance as it does for other regulated products. The *Dietary Supplement Health and Education Act* of 1994 (*DSHEA*) made supplement manufacturers responsible for ensuring their products are safe.

The Sentinel Initiative in Drug, Biologic and Device Postmarket Surveillance

The Sentinel Initiative (SI) began in 2008 as a multi-year effort to create a national electronic system for monitoring FDA-regulated medical product performance. The SI is FDA's response to *FDAAA*'s requirement to work with public, academic and private entities to develop a system to obtain information from existing electronic healthcare data from multiple sources to assess approved medical product safety. The SI's work focuses on drugs, vaccines and other biologics (e.g., blood products). Since its inception, the SI has continued to refine and expand its data infrastructure and capabilities. In recent years, new analytical tools and data method enhancements have unlocked access to more diverse data sources to improve evidence quality for safety surveillance operations. As of January 2017, the SI distributed database had 223 million unique member IDs; 425 million person-years of observation time; 43 million people currently accruing new data; 5.9 billion dispensations; 7.2 billion unique encounters; and 42 million people with more than one laboratory test result. Sentinel now is an integral part of FDA's routine safety surveillance system and is used to generate real-world evidence to support regulatory actions aimed at protecting the public health.

Conclusion

This chapter has reviewed both clinical trial and postmarketing reporting requirements for manufacturers and distributors of drugs, biologics and medical devices, including IND reporting requirements.

Periodic update reports also have been discussed. In addition, FDA's activities in monitoring healthcare products' postmarketing safety through the Sentinel Initiative and other safety monitoring efforts have been reviewed along with proprietary nomenclature for pharmaceutical products and the need for a REMS. Safety is one of both FDA's and the pharmaceutical industry's highest priorities when developing products for patients and consumers. For regulatory and pharmacovigilance professionals, careful attention to product safety also is of paramount importance.

References
1. 21 CFR Part 312.64(b) Investigator reports. FDA website. http://www.accessdata.fda.gov/SCRIPTs/cdrh/cfdocs/cfcfr/CFRSearch.cfm?fr=312.64. Accessed 29 March 2019.
2. 21 CFR Part 312.32(b) IND safety reporting. FDA website. http://www.accessdata.fda.gov/scripts/cdrh/cfdocs/cfcfr/cfrsearch.cfm?fr=312.32. Accessed 29 March 2019.
3. Investigational New Drug Safety Reporting Requirements for Human Drug and Biological Products and Safety Reporting Requirements for Bioavailability and Bioequivalence Studies in Humans, 21 CFR Parts 312 and 320 (Final Rule). *Federal Register*, 29 September 2010. Federal Register website. https://www.federalregister.gov/articles/2010/09/29/2010-24296/

investigational-new-drug-safety-reporting-requirements-for-human-drug-and-biological-products-and. Accessed 29 March 2019.
4. Postmarketing Safety Reports for Human Drugs and Biological Products; Electronic Submission Requirements (Final Rule). *Federal Register*. Federal Register website. https://www.federalregister.gov/articles/2014/06/10/2014-13480/postmarketing-safety-reports-for-human-drug-and-biological-products-electronic-submission. Accessed 29 March 2019.
5. 21 CFR Part 312.32(d) IND safety reporting. FDA website. https://www.accessdata.fda.gov/scripts/cdrh/cfdocs/cfcfr/CFRSearch.cfm?fr=312.32. Accessed 29 March 2019.
6. 21 CFR Part 314.80 Postmarketing reporting of adverse drug experiences. FDA website. https://www.accessdata.fda.gov/scripts/cdrh/cfdocs/cfcfr/CFRSearch.cfm?fr=314.80. Accessed 29 March 2019.
7. *Adverse Event Reporting for Outsourcing Facilities Under Section 503B of the Federal Food, Drug, and Cosmetic Act: Guidance for Industry* (October 2015). FDA website. https://www.fda.gov/downloads/Drugs/GuidanceComplianceRegulatoryInformation/Guidances/UCM434188.pdf. Accessed 29 March 2019.
8. *Field Alert Report Submission—Questions and Answers: Draft Guidance for Industry* (July 2018). FDA website. https://www.fda.gov/downloads/Drugs/GuidanceComplianceRegulatoryInformation/Guidances/UCM613753.pdf. Accessed 29 March 2019.
9. *Development of a Shared System REMS: Draft Guidance for Industry* (June 2018). FDA website. https://www.fda.gov/downloads/Drugs/GuidanceComplianceRegulatoryInformation/Guidances/UCM609045.pdf. Accessed 29 March 2019.
10. *Waivers of the Single Shared System REMS Requirement: Draft Guidance for Industry* (June 2018). FDA website. https://www.fda.gov/downloads/Drugs/GuidanceComplianceRegulatoryInformation/Guidances/UCM609048.pdf. Accessed 29 March 2019.
11. *Medical Device Reporting for Manufacturers: Guidance for Industry and Food and Drug Administration Staff* (8 November 2016). FDA website. https://www.fda.gov/downloads/medicaldevices/deviceregulationandguidance/guidancedocuments/ucm359566.pdf. Accessed 29 March 2019.

Chapter 12

Biologics Submissions

Updated by Jocelyn Jennings, MS, RAC

OBJECTIVES

- Explain basic biologics submission concepts
- Understand the organizational structure and responsibilities of the Center for Biologics Evaluation and Research (CBER) and the Center for Drug Evaluation and Research (CDER) in reviewing premarket biologics submissions
- Understand the Investigational New Drug (IND) process
- Review US Food and Drug Administration (FDA) recommendations for developing biologics, including requirements for preclinical, clinical and chemistry, manufacturing and control development to support regulatory submissions
- Understand Biologic License Application (BLA) contents and the BLA review process
- Become familiar with biosimilars
- Become familiar with FDA and sponsor meeting procedures and requirements
- Review postmarketing compliance and biologic commercial manufacturing and supply

LAWS, REGULATIONS AND GUIDELINES COVERED IN THIS CHAPTER

- *Public Health Service Act*, Section 351, including new Subsection (k) Licensure of Biological Products as Biosimilar or Interchangeable
- *Federal Food, Drug, and Cosmetic Act* of 1938
- 21 CFR 210 Current Good Manufacturing Practice in Manufacturing, Processing, Packing, or Holding of Drugs, General
- 21 CFR 211 Good Manufacturing Practice for Finished Pharmaceuticals
- 21 CFR 600 Biological Products: General
- 21 CFR 601 Biologics Licensing
- 21 CFR 610 General Biological Products Standards
- 21 CFR 312 Investigational New Drug Application
- 21 CFR 314 Applications for FDA Approval to Market a New Drug
- 21 CFR 25 Environmental Impact Considerations
- *ICH M4: The Common Technical Document*
- Administrative Processing of Biologics License Applications (BLA), SOPP 8401

Chapter 12

- Guidance for Sponsors, Industry, Researchers, Investigators, and Food and Drug Administration Staff: Certifications To Accompany Drug, Biological Product, and Device Applications/Submissions: Compliance with Section 402(j) of The Public Health Service Act, Added By Title VIII of The Food and Drug Administration Amendments Act of 2007

- Draft Guidance for the Public and the Food and Drug Administration Staff on Convening Advisory Committee Meetings (August 2008)

- Guidance for Industry: Formal Dispute Resolution: Appeals Above the Division Level (February 2000)

- Intercenter Consultative/Collaborative Review Process (August 2002), SOPP 8001.5

- Guidance for Industry: Cooperative Manufacturing Arrangements for Licensed Biologics (November 2008)

- Guidance for Industry: Submitting Type V Drug Master Files to the Center for Biologics Evaluation and Research (August 2001)

- Investigational and Marketable Applications: Submission of Regulatory Documents to CBER (October 2014), SOPP 8110

- Draft Guidance for Industry: Investigational New Drugs (INDs)—Determining Whether Human Research Studies Can Be Conducted Without an IND (October 2010)

- Guidance for Industry Preclinical Assessment of Investigational Cellular and Gene Therapy Products (November 2013)

- Draft Guidance for Industry: Investigating and Reporting Adverse Reactions Related to Human Cells, Tissues, and Cellular and Tissue-Based Products (HCT/Ps) Regulated Solely under Section 361 of the Public Health Service Act and 21 CFR Part 1271 (February 2015)

- Draft Guidance for Industry: Current Good Manufacturing Practice Requirements for Combination Products (January 2015)

- Guidance for Industry: Providing Regulatory Submissions in Electronic Format—Submissions Under Section 745A(a) of the Federal Food, Drug, and Cosmetic Act (December 2014)

- Draft Guidance for Industry: The Effect of Section 585 of the FD&C Act on Drug Product Tracing and Wholesale Drug Distributor and Third-Party Logistics Provider Licensing Standards and Requirements: Questions and Answers (October 2014)

- Draft Guidance for Industry, Food and Drug Administration Staff, and Clinical Laboratories: Framework for Regulatory Oversight of Laboratory Developed Tests (LDTs) (September 2014)

- Guidance for Industry: Immunogenicity Assessment for Therapeutic Protein Products (August 2014)

- Draft Guidance for Industry and Food and Drug Administration Staff: De Novo Classification Process (Evaluation of Automatic Class III Designation) (August 2014)

- Draft Guidance for Industry: Reference Product Exclusivity for Biological Products Filed Under Section 351(a) of the PHS Act (August 2014)

- Guidance for Industry: Expedited Programs for Serious Conditions—Drugs and Biologics (May 2014)

- Draft Guidance for Industry: Product Development Under the Animal Rule (May 2014)

- Draft Guidance for Industry: Clinical Pharmacology Data to Support a Demonstration of Biosimilarity to a Reference Product (May 2014)

- Draft Guidance for Industry: Best Practices in Developing Proprietary Names for Drugs (May 2014)

- Draft Guidance for Industry and Food and Drug Administration Staff: Balancing Premarket and Postmarket Data Collection for Devices Subject to Premarket Approval (April 2014)

- Draft Guidance for Industry and Food and Drug Administration Staff: Expedited Access for Premarket Approval Medical Devices Intended *for Unmet Medical Need for Life Threatening or Irreversibly Debilitating Diseases or Conditions* (April 2014)

☐ *Draft Guidance for Industry: Fulfilling Regulatory Requirements for Postmarketing Submissions of Interactive Promotional Media for Prescription Human and Animal Drugs and Biologics* (January 2014)

☐ *Guidance for Industry: Providing Regulatory Submissions to the Center for Biologics Evaluation and Research (CBER) in Electronic Format—Biologics Marketing Applications [Biologics License Application (BLA), Product License Application (PLA)/Establishment License Application (ELA) and New Drug Applications (NDA)]* (November 1999)

Basic Biologics Submission Concepts

FDA's Definition of Biologic and Implications of Product Application Review and Postmarket Surveillance Process

Biotechnology has led to the development of many of today's most important medicines, including: monoclonal antibodies for treating cancer; human insulin for treating diabetes; cloning of the naturally occurring protein, erythropoietin, to stimulate the production of red blood cells in the treatment of chronic anemia; and products used for tissue regeneration (e.g., cartilage and skin). Biological products can be made of sugars, proteins or nucleic acids, or complex combinations of these substances, or may be living entities, such as cells and tissues.

A product's classification as a drug, biologic, medical device or combination product depends primarily on its intended use and principal mode of action. Biological products, or biologics, are medical products. Biologics are made from a variety of natural sources (human, animal or microorganism). Like drugs, biologics are intended to treat diseases and medical conditions. Some biologics are used to prevent or diagnose diseases. Examples of biologics regulated by FDA include:
- vaccines (bacterial and viral)
- blood and blood products for transfusion and /or manufacturing into other products
- allergenic extracts used for both diagnosis and treatment (e.g., allergy shots)
- human cells and tissues used for transplantation (e.g., tendons, ligaments and bone)
- gene therapies
- cellular therapies, including somatic cells
- tests to screen potential blood donors for infectious agents, such as HIV
- toxins, antitoxins, growth factors and monoclonal antibodies

Public Health Service Act (*PHS Act*) Section 351(i) defines a "biological product" as "any virus, therapeutic serum, toxin, antitoxin, vaccine, blood, blood component or derivative, allergenic product, protein (except any chemically modified synthetic polypeptide), or analogous product…that is intended for use in the diagnosis, cure, mitigation, treatment, or prevention of disease." Biological products are approved for marketing under the *PHS Act* but, because most also meet the definition of "drug" under the *Federal Food, Drug, and Cosmetic Act* of 1938 (*FD&C Act*), they also are regulated under this law.

Pursuant to *PHS Act* Section 351(a), a biologics license must be in place for any biological product introduced or delivered into interstate commerce. Biological products subject to the *PHS Act* must comply with Title 21 of the Code of Federal Regulations (CFR) Parts 210 and 211, current Good Manufacturing Practices (CGMPs). A biological product submission might be accomplished through a Biologics License Application (BLA); however, those meeting the definition of a drug are submitted through a New Drug Application (NDA).

Biological medicines are proteins derived from living organisms, often by genetically modifying cell constructs or cell lines. Biologic medical products also might be made using processed allogenic or autologous cells (e.g., stem cells, mononucleous cells) or tissues to stimulate patient tissue or bone regeneration.

Biologic products are known for complex manufacturing processes and require product testing and safety and efficacy evaluation. A DNA technology platform is used to insert desirable genes or remove undesirable ones within a living cell or via a vector such as a virus, prompting a specific function, e.g., producing a protein to treat disease. The DNA sequence of a chosen protein, such as human insulin or an immune system antibody, is identified and introduced into a vector suitable for introduction into a bacterial, yeast or mammalian cell line's genetic material, which will produce it. Genetically modified cell lines are selected carefully and cultured in bioreactors before the biologic is extracted through complex and lengthy purification processes. During selection, the cell line that produces the biologic most effectively is identified and expanded to manufacture the medicine. This cell line is unique to each manufacturer and is the source of all future product. Each of the thousands of steps in the manufacturing process is intricate, sensitive and often specific to a particular medicine, requiring robust quality systems and significant experience, expertise and financial investment. Even minor alterations to the cell line or process may lead to changes in cell behavior and differences in the end product's structure, stability or other quality aspects. Any of these differences has the potential to affect the treatment's safety, efficacy or shelf life, and can increase the risk of an unwanted immune response.

Like drugs, biologics are eligible for postmarket safety evaluations. In that respect, FDA assesses several data sources including:
- the product's preapproval safety profile
- the product's current FDA-approved label
- reports made to the FDA Adverse Event Reporting System (FAERS)
- reports made to the Vaccine Adverse Event Reporting System (VAERS)
- manufacturer-submitted periodic safety reports
- medical literature
- drug utilization databases
- data from postapproval clinical trials and other studies, where applicable

Beginning no later than 18 months after approval, scientists from the Center of Biologics Evaluation and Research (CBER) Office of Biostatistics and Epidemiology and the relevant product office (Office of Blood Research and Review (OBRR), Office of Vaccine Research and Review (OVRR) or Office of Tissues and Advanced Therapies (OTAT)) conduct a safety review and evaluation. FDA compiles the postmarket safety evaluations and posts summary reports on its website periodically.

History of Biologics Regulation

In 1902, Congress passed the *Biologics Control Act*, which applied to "any virus, therapeutic serum, toxin, antitoxin, or analogous product applicable to the prevention and cure of diseases of man" and required licensure of facilities making these products. Over the next 100+ years, Congress expanded this list of covered products to include the following products and those "analogous" to them: vaccines, blood, blood products, allergenic products and proteins (except chemically synthesized polypeptides), among others.

The overlapping definition of drug added to this complexity. The *Food and Drug Act* of 1906 and the *FD&C Act* defined drug broadly to include substances intended for use in the cure, mitigation or prevention of disease, and the latter statute mandated NDA submission before marketing a drug. Although these drug definitions encompassed many biologics, the statutes did not provide concrete parameters for distinguishing nonbiological drugs from biological products. In 1944, when Congress revised and recodified the 1902 act in the *PHS Act*, it clarified that the NDA requirement did not apply to biologics or define the biological product's scope. Regulators attempted to fill this gap by promulgating regulatory definitions of *virus*, *therapeutic serum*, *toxin*, *antitoxin* and *analogous product*. For example, the 1947 regulations, which were essentially similar to current regulations, defined products analogous to a toxin or antitoxin as those intended for preventing, treating or curing diseases or injuries "through specific immunization." The 1947 definition of products analogous to therapeutic serums excluded hormones. Hormones, such as insulin and human growth hormone, were approved under the *FD&C Act*, not the *PHS Act*. Despite the 1947 regulations, differentiating biologics from drugs remained challenging at the margins.

The advent of biotechnology and agency organizational disputes brought this issue to the forefront of FDA's focus. In 1986, FDA issued a policy stating it would determine whether biotechnology products constituted biologics "based on the intended use of each product on a case-by-case basis." Thus, FDA continued to make product-specific determinations informed by history and precedent, and different agency offices had to agree on a given product's approval pathway. This proved to be difficult, with press reports of "turf battles" between Center for Drug Evaluation and Research (CDER) and CBER for jurisdiction over blockbuster biotechnology products and claims the decisions were inconsistent. For example, epidermal growth factors were regulated as drugs because their first approved indications traditionally were drug indications. Most monoclonal antibodies (mAbs) were licensed as biologics because of their biological source material and immunologic function. Recombinant insulin and human growth hormone, similar to their naturally derived counterparts, were approved pursuant to NDAs.

CDER and CBER executed an Intercenter Agreement (ICA) to attempt to clarify the governing authorities for products derived from living material. The agreement determined the specific following products were subject to licensure under the *PHS Act*: vaccines, proteins, peptides and carbohydrates produced by cell culture (other than hormones and products previously derived from human or animal tissue and approved as drugs), proteins made in transgenic animals, blood and blood products, and allergenic products. NDAs were required specifically for hormones (regardless of method of manufacture), synthetic mononucleotide and polynucleotide products, and naturally derived products other than vaccines or allergenics.

FDA consolidated review of most therapeutic proteins in CDER 12 years later, but this transfer did not include any modification to the governing statutory scheme for any ICA product. The agency continued to decide whether new products were biological or nonbiologic drugs on a case-by-case basis using ICA principles and historical precedents.

In February 2012, FDA issued draft guidance intended to implement recent legislation adding "protein

Table 12-1. Key Milestones in the Regulatory Oversight of Biologics

Year	Regulatory Action
1902	*Biologics Control Act (Virus-Toxin Law)*, later called the *Public Health Service Act (PHS Act)*—required regulation of vaccine and antitoxin producers, including licensing and inspections of manufacturers and the interstate sale of serum, vaccines and related products
1903	First biologics regulations by Public Health Service Hygienic Laboratory's "Poison Squad," on the effect of food preservatives and artificial colors on public health
1906	*Pure Food and Drug Act*—prohibited "misbranding and adulteration"
1930	PHS Hygienic Laboratory became National Institutes of Health (NIH)
1937	NIH reorganized; Hygienic Laboratory became Division of Biologics Standardization
1938	*Federal Food, Drug and Cosmetics Act (FD&C Act)*—products must be shown to be "safe;" authorized factory inspections
1944	*PHS Act*—required Product License Application/Establishment License Application (PLA/ELA, precursor to the BLA); gave seizure power
1955	The Division of Biologics Control became an independent entity within NIH after polio vaccine thought to have been inactivated was associated with about 260 cases of polio
1972	The Division of Biologics Standardization, which was responsible for regulation of biologics, including serums, vaccines and blood products, transferred from NIH to FDA; became what is now called CBER
1982	Bureau of Drugs and Bureau of Biologics combined to form the Center for Drugs and Biologics (CDB)
1988	FDA became part of Department of Health and Human Services (HHS); Center for Drug Evaluation and Research (CDER) and Center for Biologics Evaluation and Research (CBER) established
1995	Regulatory Initiative Reinventing government (REGO IIb)—eliminated ELA requirement and lot release requirement for specified biotechnology products
1997	*Food and Drug Administration Modernization Act (FDAMA)*—Revised *PHS Act* and eliminated the ELA for all biologics
1998	FDA promulgated the Pediatric Rule—requires manufacturers of selected new and extant drug and biological products to conduct studies to assess their safety and efficacy in children
2003	Review of "well-characterized" proteins transferred to CDER FDA given authority under the *Pediatric Research Equity Act* to require sponsors to conduct clinical research into pediatric applications of new drugs and biological products
2009	*Biologics Price Competition and Innovation Act* of 2009 *(BPCI Act)* created an abbreviated licensure pathway for biosimilars
2010	*BPCI Act* contained in *Affordable Care Act* signed into law
2012	*Food and Drug Administration Safety and Innovation Act (FDASIA)* expanded FDA's authority to collect user fees from industry, including for biosimilar biological products
2014	US Government Policy for Institutional Oversight of Life Sciences Dual Use Research of Concern was released FDA released new draft guidance document explaining how biological products approved under *PHS Act* Section 351(a) are given periods of market exclusivity
2016	FDA released draft guidance for human drugs and biologics on implementing a chemistry, manufacturing and controls (CMC) postapproval change through the use of a comparability protocol (CP)

(except any chemically synthesized polypeptide)" to the biological product definition. This draft guidance proposed a bright-line rule distinguishing proteins from "peptides" and "chemically synthesized polypeptide[s]" approved by FDA under the *FD&C Act*. The agency proposed defining *protein* as "any alpha amino acid polymer with a specific defined sequence that is greater than 40 amino acids in size." According to the draft guidance, peptides have 40 or fewer amino acids and are not proteins. The agency also proposed defining a *chemically synthesized polypeptide* as an alpha amino acid polymer made entirely by chemical synthesis and with fewer than 100 amino acids.

CBER and CDER Organizational Structures

As discussed previously, the responsibility for reviewing biologics submissions is divided primarily between CBER and CDER.

Table 12-2. Applications Regulated by *PHS Act*

351(a) Application	351(k) Application
Application used for approval of a new biological entities. Requires extensive data on: • preclinical studies • clinical safety and efficacy • quality	Application used for approval of a biosimilar product *BPCI Act* (2009): • biosimilarity to a reference/innovator product • highly similar to an FDA-approved biological product with respect to quality, safety and efficacy • no "clinically meaningful" differences in terms of safety and efficacy between innovator and biosimilar product • interchangeability assessment • extensive CMC comparability with the innovator product

The following sections describe FDA's biologic product review responsibilities.

CBER

CBER is FDA's primary biological product review center.

Effective 30 June 2003, "well-characterized" or "therapeutic" biological product oversight responsibility was transferred from CBER to CDER. These reviews are conducted by the appropriate therapeutic review division in CDER's Office of New Drugs (OND). These products continue to be regulated as licensed biologics (i.e., requiring a BLA) per 21 CFR 601.2(a). CDER also has responsibility for hormone protein products, e.g., insulin, growth hormone and pituitary hormones, as part of an October 1991 ICA between CBER and CDER; these products were regulated as NDAs. However, under the *Biologics Price Competition and Innovation Act (BPCI)* of 2009, proteins (with the exception of synthetic polypeptides) approved under NDAs will be considered licensed biologics and will be required to comply with *PHS Act* Section 351 by 23 March 2020, 10 years after *BPCI* was enacted. *BPCI*'s goal is similar, in concept, to that of the *Drug Price Competition and Patent Term Restoration Act* of 1984 (the *Hatch-Waxman Act*), which created abbreviated pathways for drug products under the *FD&C Act*. *BPCI* aligns with FDA's longstanding policy of permitting appropriate reliance on what already is known about a drug, thereby saving time and resources and avoiding unnecessary duplication of human or animal testing. FDA interprets this provision to mean that on 23 March 2020, applications for biological products approved under *FD&C Act* Section 505 no longer will exist as NDAs (or, as applicable, Abbreviated New Drug Applications (ANDAs)) and will be replaced by approved BLAs under *FD&C Act* Section 351(a) or (k).

CBER's regulatory authority is derived from *PHS Act* Section 351. Following approval of the *Biologics Control Act* in 1902, the Division of Biologics Standards (DBS) within the National Institutes of Health (NIH) was responsible for biologics' control and release until 1972. DBS was transferred from NIH to FDA and renamed the Bureau of Biologics, which ultimately became CBER. **Table 12-1** lists key milestones in biologics' regulatory oversight.

Biologic product submission review responsibility is divided among three main review offices within CBER: the Office of Blood Research and Review (OBRR), the Office of Tissues and Advanced Therapies (OTAT) and the Office of Vaccine Research and Review (OVRR).

Through the ICA, CBER also regulates all medical devices associated with the collection and testing of licensed blood and cellular products. The devices also must comply with all appropriate medical device laws and regulations. **Table 12-2** presents the applications the *PHS Act* regulates.

CDER's Function in Review of Biologic Products

In 2003, FDA transferred some therapeutic biological products previously reviewed and regulated by CBER to CDER, giving it regulatory responsibility, including premarket review and continuing oversight for those products. CBER and CDER consult regularly and, whenever necessary, discuss regulating the products assigned to them.

On 1 October 2003, CBER's Office of Therapeutics Research and Review also was transferred to CDER, which created two new offices to accommodate the former CBER staff:
- Office of Drug Evaluation VI, within CDER's OND
- Office of Biotechnology Products, within CDER's Office of Pharmaceutical Science

Table 12-3 shows how most new chemical entities and a few biologics' molecules are covered by the *FD&C Act*.

Table 12-4 lists biologics handled by CDER and CBER.

Investigational New Drug (IND) Process

IND Process for Biologics

FDA regulates US clinical investigations of drugs, biological products and medical devices regardless of their funding sources. Clinical investigations of an unapproved biologic must be conducted under an Investigational New Drug Application (IND).

An IND is a formal submission to FDA, with a defined structure and content, submitted by a sponsor seeking an exemption from restrictions on interstate commerce of an unapproved new biologic's shipment (21 USC 355).

IND requirements are outlined in 21 CFR 312:
- §312.23 IND Content and Format
- §312.42 Clinical Holds
- §312.50–312.69 Responsibilities of Sponsors/Investigators

An IND is a living document, updated by the sponsor over time to include protocol amendments, study data, safety reports, manufacturing changes, preclinical reports and annual reports.

IND Submission Process
- Step 1: Pre-IND meeting
  - highly recommended for new products, new dosage forms, new routes of administration and new indications
- Step 2: Submission of complete IND package
- Step 3: IND Review
  - FDA will notify the sponsor within 30 calendar days of IND receipt of whether the study may proceed or is placed on clinical hold.
  - Studies may not begin until the 30-day review is complete or FDA notifies the sponsor that the studies may proceed. (This scenario is applicable for only some applications. For most INDs, the sponsor needs to wait 30 days for FDA's reponse; if FDA does not respond within 30 days, the sponsor can initiate the trials. The sponsor does so at its own risk. FDA has been known to provide comments after 30 days with most leading to substantial protocol amendments.)

According to 21 CFR 312, three clinical investigation categories are exempt from IND requirements: 1) clinical research involving marketed drug products; 2) bioavailability or bioequivalence studies in humans; and 3) radioactive drugs for certain research uses. Clinical investigations not meeting these three criteria, by regulation, must be conducted under an IND. Most IND regulations for small molecule drugs also apply to biologics, including requirements related to the IND's format and content, financial disclosure, informed consent, special INDs, orphan products, clinical holds and pediatric studies.

A biological product IND may be submitted electronically using the electronic Common Technical Document (eCTD) format. The IND application must contain:
- administrative information—a cover letter and forms, such as Forms FDA 1571, 1572 (Statement of Investigator) and 3674 (Certificate of Compliance), should be included in the IND (Form FDA 3674 is an FDA requirement for sponsors to include clinical trial registration and results on ClinicalTrials.gov)
- preclinical (animal pharmacology and toxicology) studies—preclinical data to permit an assessment as to whether the product is reasonably safe for initial testing in humans
- previous human experience—any previous experience with the drug in humans, such as results from clinical trials conducted outside the US
- chemistry, manufacturing and controls—information pertaining to the drug substance and drug product composition, manufacturer, testing, stability and controls

Table 12-3. Applications Regulated by the *FD&C Act*

505(b)(1)	505(b)(2)[a]	505(j)
New drug or new biological application (as applicable)	Application for new drug approval relying, at least in part, on data not developed by the applicant, e.g., new dosage form, strength, route of administration, substitution of an active ingredient in a combination product, formulation, dosage regimen, combination product	Generic drug approval application
Requires extensive data on: • preclinical studies • clinical safety and efficacy • quality	*Hatch-Waxman Act* (1984) • Safety and efficacy: the applicant may rely on published literature, safety and effectiveness findings for already approved products or studies conducted by others/innovator	Requires establishing bioequivalence and bioavailability with the innovator/reference drug approved by 505 b(1)

[a] *505(b)(2) pathway is applicable for a relatively narrow category of biologics (e.g., insulin, hormones, etc.), specifically those approved under an NDA before BPCIA was signed into law 23 March 2010, and is available only for that narrow category of biologics until 23 March 2020. After 23 March 2020, all biological drugs approved under FD&C Act Section 505 will be transferred to PHS Act Section 351.*

Table 12-4. Biologics Controlled by CDER and CBER

CDER	CBER
Monoclonal antibodies for *in vivo* use	Allergenic extracts (e.g., for allergy shots and tests)
Cytokines (types of proteins involved in immune response)	Blood and blood components Human tissue and cellular products used in transplantation
Growth factors (proteins that affect cell growth)	Gene therapy products
Enzymes (types of proteins that speed up biochemical reactions), such as thrombolytics (used to dissolve blood clots)	Certain medical devices and test kits
Immunomodulators (agents that affect immune response)	Vaccines

- clinical protocols and investigator information—protocols for proposed clinical studies to assess whether initial clinical trials will expose subjects to unnecessary risks; information on clinical investigators' qualifications to assess their ability to fulfill their clinical trial duties; clinical development plan for the next 12 months, Investigator's Brochure (IB) and commitments to obtain informed consent from research subjects, to obtain study approval from an institutional review board (IRB), and to adhere to IND regulations and study protocols

Regulatory Basis of IND Application Elements
- Form FDA 1571—21 CFR 312.23(a)(1)
- Table of Contents—21 CFR 312.23(a)(2)
- Introductory statement and general investigational plan—21 CFR 312.23(a)(3)
- Investigator's Brochure—21 CFR 312.23(a)(5)
- Protocols—21 CFR 312.23(a)(6)
- Product/CMC information—21 CFR 312.23(a)(7)
- Pharmacology/Toxicology information—21 CFR 312.23(a)(8)
- Previous human experience—21 CFR 312.23(a)(9)
- Additional Information—21 CFR 312.23(a)(10)

Recommended Preclinical Information:
- scientific basis for conducting the clinical study
- data from animal or *in vitro* studies to establish an initial safe dose in humans
- proof-of-concept animal models, if appropriate
- toxicology studies in relevant animal model
- submission of complete study reports

As noted, once the IND is submitted, the sponsor must wait 30 calendar days before initiating the clinical trial. During this time, FDA has an opportunity to review the IND for efficacy and safety to ensure research subjects will not be subjected to unreasonable risk.

To accommodate biologic-related issues, both CDER and CBER have developed a number of guidance documents, including those entitled "Points to Consider," representing FDA's current thinking on a variety of topics. In addition, guidance from the International Council on Harmonisation (ICH) is applicable to biologics.

After an IND is opened and active, the sponsor submits various supporting documents to the original IND as a part of an amendment, specific requests or annual reports during its life cycle. **Tables 12-5–12-8** summarize FDA's timelines, evaluation types and communication (if needed) for the sponsor's submitted supporting documents. The IND submission and amendment types are separated into four categories:

1. submissions with a specific, regulatory-mandated timeline (e.g., Special Protocol Assistance (SPAs)) or an FDA-established timeline (e.g., proposed pediatric study request reviews) (**Table 12-5**)
2. safety-related submissions (e.g., initial telephone safety reports or seven- or 15-day reports, where communication with sponsors may or may not be needed) (**Table 12-6**)
3. drug development submissions without regulatory-mandated timelines, where communication to the sponsor often is critical and recommended (e.g., new nonclinical, clinical, or protocol amendments) (**Table 12-7**)
4. other submissions that may overlap any of the three preceding three categories and where communication with the sponsor may be needed (e.g., general correspondence, final reports, annual reports, drug quality amendments) (**Table 12-8**)

FDA Processes to Review Biological Product IND Submissions

FDA's primary objectives in reviewing an IND in all investigation phases are to ensure subjects' safety and rights, and in Phases 2 and 3, to ensure the scientific evaluation's quality is adequate to permit an evaluation of the product's effectiveness and safety (21 CFR 312.22).

FDA takes a team approach to IND review. The review team typically consists of:
- regulatory project manager
- product/CMC reviewer
- pharmacology/toxicology reviewer
- clinical reviewer
- statistical reviewer
- consults as needed (e.g., from CDRH for review of a device component if it is a combination product)

Within 30 days, FDA determines whether the file is active or on hold, and issues outstanding hold and non-hold orders by phone, email or detailed letter. All hold issues must be satisfactorily resolved to proceed.

IND Review Status Stages
- pending—within the initial 30-day review period
- active—study may proceed
- hold—an order issued by FDA to delay a proposed clinical investigation or suspend an ongoing investigation (21 CFR 312.42)
- partial hold—a delay or suspension of part of the clinical work under an IND (e.g., IND with two protocols where one can proceed and one is on clinical hold)

FDA Biologic Development Review Recommendations (Preclinical, Clinical and Manufacturing) to Support Regulatory Submissions

When developing a biologic product, the sponsor must determine how to begin to prove its safety and efficacy.

Preclinical Development for Biologics

Successful and efficient new biological product development requires planning an integrated development program to coordinate the product manufacture trilogy—chemistry, manufacturing, and controls (CMC); preclinical studies (absorption, distribution, metabolism, elimination (ADME), pharmacology and toxicology) and clinical trials—within the regulatory development strategy framework. Preclinical safety studies must support each successive clinical development phase, as well as any significant changes to product manufacturing, formulations or methods of administration. The preclinical safety package for biologics (large molecules) can be different from the toxicology package for small molecule drugs. Special considerations for biologics' toxicological assessments are described in ICH *S6: Preclinical Safety Evaluation of Biotechnology-Derived Pharmaceuticals*. S6's important points:

- Pharmacology/biological activity/proof of concept—pharmacology and biological activity may be evaluated using *in vitro* and/or *in in vivo* studies to determine which product effects may be related to clinical activity. The use of cell lines and/or primary cell cultures can be useful to examine direct effects on cellular phenotype and proliferation.
- Animal model selection—due to the species specificity of many biotechnology-derived pharmaceuticals, it is important to select relevant animal species for toxicity testing. The biological activity, together with many biotechnology-derived products species and/or tissue specificity, often preclude standard toxicity testing designs in commonly used species (e.g., rats and dogs).
- Safety evaluation/toxicity/toxicokinetics studies—safety evaluation normally requires data from two relevant species. However, in certain justified cases, one relevant species may suffice (e.g., when only one relevant species can be identified, or where the biopharmaceutical's biological activity is well understood). In addition, even where two species may be necessary to characterize toxicity in short-term studies, it may be possible to justify the use of only one species for subsequent long-term toxicity studies when the two species' toxicity profiles are comparable in the short term. Molecule toxicity profiles also are assessed based on single- and repeat-dose toxicity studies.
- Analogous products—where there is no animal in which the biologic can function, due to either lack of specificity or anti-drug antibodies, preparing an analogous product, such as an animal homologue of the product intended for humans (e.g., a mouse monoclonal antibody that binds to the same intended target in mice), can be used to assess potential safety issues.
- Maximum Tolerated Dose (MTD)—because biologics typically are not inherently toxic, it is difficult to provide drug concentrations at high enough levels to induce overt toxicity. Consequently, clinical dosing may be based on the biologically effective dose rather than the MTD. However, an attempt to cover the planned maximum human dose (preferably with up to a 10-fold safety margin) should be assessed in the safety studies.
- Safety pharmacology and acute chronic toxicity studies—safety pharmacology endpoints normally are incorporated into multiple-dose toxicity testing rather than conducted as separate studies. Safety evaluation needs to be conducted on the cardiovascular, central nervous and respiratory systems.

Table 12-5. Submissions With Specific Regulatory Mandated Timelines (e.g., SPAs) or FDA Established Timelines (e.g., Reviews of Proposed Pediatric Study Requests)

Description	Timeline	Type of Evaluation	Communication With Sponsor
Treatment IND/ treatment protocol	Less than 30 days for complete review. CDER/CBER-established interim dates: • Day 19 after receipt for discipline review • Day 21 for team leader reviews • Day 26 for division director review • Day 30 for office director review 30 days to send acknowledgement letter Issue hold letter within 30 calendar days of hold action	Written review by appropriate discipline(s) Treatment IND/protocol executive summary review	Required: Acknowledgement letter from CDER/CBER to sponsor for IND and protocol(s) Hold letter required if the IND/protocol is put on clinical hold
Single-patient IND	Up to 30 days	Brief written review	Required: Acknowledgement letter from CDER/CBER to sponsor Hold letter required if the IND is put on clinical hold
Single-patient protocol	Up to 30 days	Brief written review	Hold letter required if the protocol is put on clinical hold
Emergency IND or protocol	Immediately	Brief written review	Acknowledgement letter from CDER/CBER to sponsor
Intermediate-size access IND	Up to 30 days	Brief written review	Required: Acknowledgement letter from CDER/CBER to sponsor Hold letter required if the IND is put on clinical hold
Intermediate-size access protocol	Up to 30 days	Brief written review	Hold letter required if the protocol is put on clinical hold
Request to charge	30 days for complete review and response	Clinical evaluation	Required: Letter from CDER/CBER to sponsor
Request for SPA	45 days for review and response	Written review by appropriate discipline(s) (including consult with appropriate OPQ reviewer for updated drug information) or Exec CAC meeting minutes	Required: See Type of evaluation column
Pediatric exclusivity, PPSR	120 days for response Must be reviewed internally by PeRC before issuance	Written review by appropriate discipline(s), issued as an FDA Written Request or notification of an inadequate or incomplete PPSR	Required: See Type of evaluation column
Pediatric exclusivity, amendment to request for studies	120 days for response Must be reviewed by PeRC if there are substantive changes	Written review by appropriate discipline(s), issued as pediatric revised or reissued Written Request	Required: Acknowledgement letter from CDER/CBER to sponsor
Initial PSP	90 days for initial response Must be reviewed internally by PeRC before issuance Additional 90 days to reach agreement with sponsor on agreed initial PSP	Meeting with appropriate disciplines and sponsor, or written review by appropriate discipline(s) if meeting is not necessary, for initial response	Required Review letter from CDER/CBER

Table 12-5. Submissions With Specific Regulatory Mandated Timelines (e.g., SPAs) or FDA Established Timelines (e.g., Reviews of Proposed Pediatric Study Requests) (cont'd.)

Description	Timeline	Type of Evaluation	Communication With Sponsor
Agreed initial PSP	30 days for response Must be reviewed by PeRC before issuance	Written response	Required: Agreement letter from CDER/CBER
Amendment to agreed initial PSP	90 days for initial response Must be reviewed internally by PeRC before issuance Additional 90 days to reach agreement with sponsor on agreed initial PSP	Meeting with appropriate disciplines and sponsor, or written review/response by appropriate discipline(s) if meeting is not necessary for initial response Further negotiations and revisions needed	Required: Review letter from CDER/CBER
Agreed amendment to initial PSP	30 days for response Must be reviewed by PeRC before issuance	Written response	Required: Agreementl letter from CDER/CBER
Fast track designation request	60 days for response	Letter to the sponsor denying or granting fast track status Fast track form—medical reviewer to complete	Required: See Type of evaluation column
Breakthrough designation request	60 days for response	Letter to the sponsor denying or granting breakthrough status	Required: See Type of evaluation column
Proprietary name review (submitted to the IND)	180 days for response	Written review	Required: Acceptance or non-acceptance letter from CDER/CBER
Request for formal dispute resolution	30 days for response	Letter to the sponsor from the office or center director/deputy	Required: See Type of evaluation column

Exec CAC—Executive Carcinogenicity Assessment Committee; PPSR—proposed pediatric study request; PeRC—Pediatric Review Committee; PSP—pediatric study plan, OPQ—Office of Pharmaceutical Quality

- Immunogenicity—many biotechnology-derived pharmaceuticals intended for humans are immunogenic in animals. Therefore, measurement of antibodies associated with administering these products should be performed when conducting repeat-dose toxicity studies to aid in study interpretation. Antibody responses should be characterized, and their appearance should be correlated with any pharmacological and/or toxicological changes.
- Metabolism (e.g., CYP450 Inhibition/Induction)—the expected consequence of biotechnology-derived pharmaceutical metabolism is degradation to small peptides and individual amino acids. Therefore, metabolic pathways generally are understood. Classic biotransformation studies for pharmaceuticals are not needed. Instead, understanding the biopharmaceutical's behavior in the biologic matrix and the possible influence of binding proteins is important.
- Pharmacokinetics—this involves assessing the molecule's absorption, distribution, metabolism and excretion (ADME).
- Immunotoxicity—many biotechnology-derived pharmaceuticals are intended to stimulate or suppress the immune system and, therefore, may affect not only humoral but also cell-mediated immunity. Inflammatory reactions at the injection site may be indicative of a stimulatory response. Immunotoxicological testing strategies may require screening studies followed by mechanistic studies to clarify such issues. Routine tiered-testing approaches or standard testing batteries are not recommended for biotechnology-derived pharmaceuticals.
- Genotoxicity studies—the range and type of these studies, conducted routinely for pharmaceuticals, are not applicable to biotechnology-derived pharmaceuticals and, therefore, are not needed. Moreover, administering large quantities of peptides or proteins may yield uninterpretable

Table 12-6. Safety-Related Submissions

Description	Timeline	Type of Evaluation	Communication With Sponsor
Unexpected fatal or life-threatening suspected adverse reaction report	1 day	Written documentation of the call (OND RPM) or electronic archiving of emails and faxes and any advice or recommendations (in consultation with medical reviewer)	Inherent
IND safety report	Up to 15 days	Written review if needed, or electronic sign-off that "Safety report was reviewed and did not identify new safety concerns or items that required additional action" (medical reviewer)	As needed
Follow-up to an IND safety report	Up to 30 days	Written review if needed, or electronic sign-off that "Safety report was reviewed and did not identify new safety concerns or items that required additional action" (medical reviewer)	As needed

IRT—Interdisciplinary Review Team, OND—Office of New Drugs, RPM—Regulatory Program Manager

results. Studies should be conducted in available and relevant systems. The Ames test, chromosome aberration test and *in vivo* micronucleus test are some tests used to study the molecule's genotoxicity.

- Carcinogenicity studies—standard carcinogenicity bioassays generally are inappropriate for biotechnology-derived pharmaceuticals. However, product-specific carcinogenic potential assessments still may be needed, depending on clinical dosing duration, patient population and/or the product's biological activity. When there is concern about carcinogenic potential, a variety of risk-evaluation approaches may be taken.
- Local tolerance studies—these should be conducted using the formulation intended for marketing. The product's potential adverse effects can be evaluated in single- or repeat-dose toxicity studies, obviating the need for a separate local tolerance study.
- Reproductive toxicity studies—developmental and reproductive toxicology (DART) studies should be considered during biotechnology-derived pharmaceutical product development. DART studies are categorized into three segments (Segment 1: male/female fertility, Segment 2: teratogenicity and Segment 3: pre- and postnatal).

Clinical Development Considerations for Biologics

Clinical study designs and requirements are similar for biological products and small molecule drugs; however, there may be additional immunogenicity safety concerns with biological products. Thus, additional testing may be required during clinical trials to assess immunogenicity and the potential development of autoimmunity. Biologics' initial safety is evaluated in Phase 1 trials. Phase 2 trials assess how well the biologic works in patients and evaluate safety and dosing in a larger group of subjects. Phase 2 studies sometimes are divided into Phase 2A and Phase 2B. Phase 2A is designed to assess dosing requirements and also can include combination dosing studies if the biologic is to be administered in combination with another therapy. Phase 2B is designed to study efficacy and can include exploratory endpoints to assess other pharmacodynamic markers, safety and efficacy endpoints, and patient populations to enable better Phase 3 trial design. Phase 3 studies typically are randomized controlled studies in larger patient groups and are intended to be the definitive assessment of the drug's effectiveness, which sometimes is compared to the current standard of care. Certain Phase 3 trial parts or stages continue while the regulatory submission is being reviewed. This allows patients to continue to receive potentially life-saving drugs until the drug is approved, and allows additional safety and efficacy data to be collected. While not required in all cases, two successful Phase 3 trials demonstrating a drug's safety and efficacy normally are recommended to obtain approval from the appropriate regulatory agencies.

ICH efficacy and multidisciplinary guidelines cover topics relevant to biologics' clinical development. In addition, FDA has issued a number of guidance documents that provide general guidelines on clinical trial designs. Selected guidances are listed below:

- *Guidance for Industry: Clinical Pharmacogenomics: Premarket Evaluation in Early-Phase Clinical Studies and Recommendations for Labeling*—This guidance focuses on evaluating how human genome variations or specific DNA sequence variants could affect a drug's pharmacokinetics (PK), pharmacodynamics (PD), efficacy and safety. The guidance provides recommendations on when and how genomic information should be considered to address questions arising during drug development and regulatory review.
- *Draft Guidance for Industry: Enrichment Strategies for Clinical Trials to Support Approval of Human Drugs and Biological Products*—This document

focuses on enrichment strategies that can be used in clinical trials to support effectiveness and safety claims, including strategies to decrease heterogeneity and improve prognostic enrichment and predictive enrichment.
- *Draft Guidance for Industry Premarketing Evaluation in Early Phase Clinical Studies*—This draft guidance focuses specifically on using and evaluating genomic strategies in early drug development and identifying enrichment options for later trials.
- *Draft Guidance for Industry and Food and Drug Administration Staff: In Vitro Companion Diagnostic Devices*—This draft guidance describes FDA's policies for approving companion diagnostics concurrently with the therapeutic product's approval and labeling.
- *Draft Guidance for Industry: Adaptive Design Clinical Trials for Drugs and Biologics*—This document considers enrichment approaches introduced only after randomization and based on interim evaluations. It discusses designing clinical trials with adaptive features (i.e., design or analytical changes guided by examining the accumulated data at an interim trial point). These adaptive trial designs may improve study efficiency (e.g., shorter duration, fewer patients) and are more likely to demonstrate drug efficacy if one exists, or generate more information (e.g., by providing broader dose-response information). Such retrospective findings must be implemented carefully.
- *Guidance for Industry: Providing Clinical Evidence of Effectiveness for Human Drug and Biological Products*—This guidance describes the amount and type of evidence needed to demonstrate effectiveness.
- *Draft Guidance for Industry: Determining the Extent of Safety Data Collection Needed in Late-Stage Premarket and Postapproval Clinical Investigations*—This draft guidance provides advice on how and when to simplify data collection to maintain a balance between eliminating collecting unuseful data and sufficient data to allow a drug's safety profile to be characterized adequately, given its potential benefits. Safety data amounts and types collected during clinical trials and safety evaluations vary based on a range of factors, including the disease, patient population, subgroup of interest, preclinical results, prior experience with the drug, experience with the drug class, development phase and study design.
- *Draft Guidance for Industry: Non-Inferiority Clinical Trials*—This draft guidance describes the underlying principles involved in the use of noninferiority (NI) study designs to provide evidence of a drug's or biologic's effectiveness. It provides advice on when NI studies can be interpretable, how to choose the NI margin and how to analyze the results.
- *Guidance for Industry: Postmarketing Studies and Clinical Trials—Implementation of Section 505(o)(3) of the Federal Food, Drug, and Cosmetic Act*—The *FD&C Act* was amended in September 2007, adding a new Section 505(o). Section 505(o)(3) authorizes FDA to require certain postmarketing studies and clinical trials for prescription drugs and biological products approved under *PHS Act* Section 351. This guidance discusses postmarketing study requirements and describes the postmarketing study types generally required under the amended legislation.
- *Guidance for Industry: Population Pharmacokinetics*—This document makes recommendations on using population pharmacokinetics during the drug development process to help identify differences in drug safety and efficacy among population subgroups. It summarizes scientific and regulatory issues that should be addressed using population pharmacokinetics.
- *Draft Guidance for Industry: General Considerations for Pediatric Pharmacokinetic Studies for Drugs and Biological Products*—This draft guidance addresses general considerations for conducting studies to enable drug and biological products to be labeled for pediatric use.
- *Guidance for Industry: Providing Clinical Evidence of Effectiveness for Human Drug and Biological Products*—This guidance provides FDA's current thinking about the quantitative and qualitative standards for demonstrating drugs' and biologics' effectiveness.
- *Guidance for Industry: Pharmacokinetics in Patients with Impaired Renal Function—Study Design, Data Analysis, and Impact on Dosing and Labeling*—This document focuses on how to conduct studies to assess the influence of renal impairment on an investigational drug's pharmacokinetics, when PK studies should be conducted with patients with impaired renal function, and study design. It also covers PK study conduct in patients with end-stage renal disease.
- *Guidance for Industry: Multiple Endpoints in Clinical Trials*—This draft guidance focuses on the problems multiple endpoints pose in study result analysis and interpretation, and how these problems can be managed in drug and biologic clinical trials.

Table 12-7. IND Drug Development Submissions

Description	Timeline	Type of Evaluation	Communication With Sponsor
Nonclinical			
Nonclinical information: • Priority amendments supporting new clinical protocols (general, genetic, toxicology) • Standard (toxicology studies by routes of administration other than planned clinical route, pharmacology, abuse/dependence)	Reviewer/team leader should screen within seven business days of receipt to determine priority status and review level. • Priority amendments: preliminary evaluation within 14–30 days; review up to 180 days • Standard: within 6–12 months	Written review for priority Written review as needed for nonpriority	As needed
New animal protocol (excluding SPA)	Up to 60 days	Written review if CDER feedback is requested	As needed
Carcinogenicity information	Reviewer/team leader should screen within seven business days of receipt to determine priority status. Within 6–12 months	Written review	As needed
Nonclinical: Response to information request	Reviewer/team leader should screen within seven business days of receipt to determine priority status and review level. Up to 90 days	Written review as needed, or electronic sign-off that "Response reviewed and satisfactorily addresses CBER's information request."	As needed
Clinical Pharmacology			
Clinical pharmacology information: High priority (1) Submissions where input on use of quantitative drug development methods can be influenced (2) Decision-making by CBER or the sponsor will be based on clinical pharmacology review Standard	Reviewer/team leader should screen within seven business days of receipt to determine priority status and review level. Up to 60 days Up to 60 days Up to 180 days	 Written review Written review Written review, as needed	 Required Required As needed
Clinical pharmacology: Response to information request	Up to 90 days	Written review, as needed	As needed
Clinical			
Clinical information	Reviewer/team leader should screen within seven business days of receipt to prioritize and determine review level. Safety-related: within 15 days Other: up to 180 days	Written review as needed	As needed
Clinical: Response to information request	Reviewer/team leader should screen within seven business days of receipt to prioritize and determine review level. Up to 90 days	Written review for safety (including abuse/dependence) concern as needed, or electronic sign-off that "Response reviewed and satisfactorily addresses CDER's information request."	As needed
Biometrics			
Biometrics information	Up to 60 days	Written efficacy or safety review if submission addresses statistical aspects of Phase 3 clinical protocol	As needed
Biometrics: Response to information request	Up to 90 days	Written efficacy or safety review as needed, or electronic sign-off that "Response reviewed and satisfactorily addresses CBER's information request."	As needed
Statistical analysis plan	Up to 60 days	Written review	As needed

Table 12-7. IND Drug Development Submissions (cont'd.)

Protocols			
New Phase 1 protocol	Up to 30 days	Written safety review, as needed, by appropriate discipline(s)	As needed

New Phase 2 protocol	Reviewer/team leader should screen within seven business days of receipt to determine priority status; potential clinical hold issues; and need for consult with quality, clinical pharmacology (including pharmacogenomics and pharmacometrics) or other disciplines.
	
	Up to 60 days
		Written safety and/or efficacy review by appropriate discipline(s):
		• As needed for dose-response Phase 2 or proof-of-concept studies/trials (clinical pharmacology)
		• Required for:
		  o Trial intended to support accelerated or full approval, as stated by sponsor
		  o Novel trial design, endpoint or other new element
		• Recommended if requested by sponsor and workload permits
			As needed

New Phase 2/3 adaptive trial design	Up to 60 days	Written review as needed by appropriate discipline(s)	As needed
New Phase 3 protocol (excluding SPA)	Reviewer/team leader should screen within seven business days of receipt to determine priority status and need for consult with quality, clinical pharmacology (including pharmacogenomics or pharmacometrics) or other disciplines. Up to 60 days.	Written safety and efficacy review by appropriate discipline(s) if trial is intended to support approval or novel endpoints Recommended if requested by sponsor and workload permits	As needed (required if intended to support approval; as workload permits if requested by sponsor)
Clinical trial intended to support a demonstration of biosimilarity (excluding SPA)	Reviewer/team leader should screen within seven business days of receipt to determine priority status and need for consult to quality, clinical pharmacology (including pharmacogenomics or pharmacometrics) or other disciplines. Up to 60 days.	Written review by appropriate discipline(s)	As needed
Pediatric protocol (part of Written Request or PREA)	60 days	Written safety or efficacy review by appropriate discipline(s)	Required
Postmarketing study/clinical trial protocol	Up to 60 days	Written safety and efficacy review by appropriate discipline(s), including assessment of whether it will fulfill stated objectives, as needed	As needed
Protocol change	30 days for safety up to 60 days for development concerns	Written review by appropriate discipline(s) for: • safety concerns • change in analysis plan for Phase 3 trial • major change in design element	As needed

IRT—Interdisciplinary Review Team

Table 12-8. Other Submission Types

Description	Recommended Timeline	Type of Evaluation	Communication With Sponsor
General correspondence	Up to six months	As needed by relevant discipline(s)	As needed

DSUR	• screen contents within two months
	• review within 12 months
	• other disciplines:
	  o screen contents within 14–30 days
	  o review within six months
		Written review as needed, or electronic sign-off that "Annual report was reviewed and did not identify new concerns that required CDER action."	As needed

Study/trial final report	Screen within 14 days Review within 60–120 days	Written review as needed, (and see below), or electronic sign-off for Phase 1 or early Phase 2 trials that "Trial was reviewed and did not identify new concerns that required CDER action." Targeted brief written review of critical elements generally needed for Phase 3 trials or important Phase 2 trials (e.g., dose selection; possible use for accelerated approval).	As needed
Rolling review designation	60 days	Letter denying or granting request	Required
Change of sponsor/change of address/transfer obligation	Up to 60 days	Letter (RPM)	Required
IND inactivation	Up to 30 days	Letter (RPM)	Required
IND withdrawal	Up to 30 days	Up to 30 days	Required

DSUR—Development Safety Update Report;

- *Guidance for Industry : Evaluating Drug Effects on the Ability to Operate a Motor Vehicle*—This guidance focuses on evaluating psychoactive drugs' effects on the ability to operate a motor vehicle. Specifically, this guidance addresses FDA's current thinking regarding the agency-regulated drugs for which such evaluation may be needed and the types of studies required.
- *Draft Guidance for Industry: Physiologically Based Pharmacokinetic Analyses-Format and Content'*—This guidance outlines the recommended format and content for a sponsor-submitted, physiologically based pharmacokinetic (PBPK) analysis to FDA to support IND, NDA, BLA and ANDA applications.
- *Guidance for Industry: General Clinical Pharmacology Considerations for Pediatric Studies for Drugs and Biological Products*—This draft guidance focuses on clinical pharmacology information (e.g., exposure response, pharmacokinetics and pharmacodynamics) to support effectiveness and safety findings and help identify appropriate doses in pediatric populations. This guidance also describes the use of quantitative approaches (i.e., pharmacometrics) to employ disease- and exposure-response knowledge from relevant prior clinical studies to design and evaluate future pediatric studies.
- *Draft Guidance: E17 General Principles for Planning and Design of Multi-Regional Clinical Trials (MRCTs)*—This guideline's purpose is to describe general principles for MRCT planning and design, with the aim of increasing MRCT acceptability in global regulatory submissions. The guideline addresses some strategic program issues and issues specific to planning and design of confirmatory MRCTs.

FDA has issued several guidances on the use of pharmacogenomics (PGx) in drug development. PGx studies can contribute to a greater understanding of inter-individual differences in an investigational biologic's efficacy and safety. Across the drug development continuum, genomic data may be used to understand PK variations and clinical response variability; elucidate the molecular basis for lack of efficacy or adverse events; and to design clinical trials that test for effects in identified subgroups, possibly for use in study enrichment strategies.

Draft Guidance for Industry: Immunogenicity, Assay Development for Immunogenicity Testing of Therapeutic Proteins (December 2009) and *Draft Guidance for Industry: Immunogenicity Assessment for Therapeutic Protein*

Products (February 2013) are particularly relevant for biologics because therapeutic protein treatments frequently stimulate immune responses. The clinical efficacy of these immune responses to therapeutic proteins, however, have ranged from none to extremely harmful. Such varied immune responses can affect product safety, efficacy and immunogenicity rates observed during clinical trials, which are included in the product labeling. Thus, development of a valid, sensitive immune assay is a key product enabler. Because immunogenicity poses a high risk, real-time data concerning patient responses are needed. Generally, a preliminary validated assay should be used during clinical studies. Even though animal model immunogenicity is not predictive of human immunogenicity, it may reveal potential antibody-related toxicities that should be monitored in clinical trials. Multiple immunogenicity testing approaches may be appropriate during clinical trials; however, testing strategies should address sensitivity, interference, functional or physiological consequences and risk-based application. The IND should provide the immunogenicity testing paradigm's rationale.

Chemistry, Manufacturing and Controls(CMC) for Biologics

Investigational biological products are subject to *FD&C Act* Section 501(a)(2)(B) (21 U.S.C. 351(a)(2)(B)) and the IND regulations in 21 CFR Part 312. During Phase 1 studies, emphasis generally should be placed on elements to ensure subjects' safety. This should include identification, control and stability of raw materials, drug substances and drug products. In each investigational phase, sufficient information is required to ensure proper investigational drug identification, potency, quality, purity and strength. The amount of information necessary for that assurance will vary with the investigational phase, proposed duration, dosage form and amount of information known.

In 2008, FDA issued *Guidance for Industry: CGMP for Phase 1 Investigational Drugs*. This guidance recognizes that manufacturing controls, and the extent of those controls needed to achieve appropriate product quality, can differ between investigational and commercial manufacture, and also among the various clinical trial phases.

CMC information requirements for biologics IND submission include:
- biological name and strain—original cell source from which the drug substance was derived, product strains with special attention to biological activity, and modifications
- characterization—description of acceptable limits and analytical methods used to ensure drug substance and drug product identity, strength, quality and purity
- master cell bank (MCB)—complete MCB history and characterization, including the original cell source used in establishing cell banks, cell culture/passage history, method used to derive the cell bank, phenotypic and genotypic characterization, culture purity and a description of all media components
- working cell banks (WCBs)—cell banking procedure description, including banking system; cell banks' size; methods, reagents and media used for cell bank preparation; conditions employed for cryopreservation and storage; in-process controls; storage conditions; and procedures used to avoid extraneous microbial contamination
- cell growth and harvesting—step-by-step description from cell bank retrieval to culture harvest; media used at each step, with preparation and sterilization details; initial and sub-culture inoculation and growth; incubationtime and temperature; transfer performance details; in-process testing conducted to control contamination; and the main culture system's nature, including operating conditions and control parameters
- purification and downstream processing—step-by-step description of the concentrate intermediate and final bulk forms' methods and materials. (The description of each downstream processing step also should include the accompanying analytical tests the manufacturer developed or adopted to show identity, purity and concentration and the levels of impurities.)

Adventitious agents are a particular concern with biological products, especially vaccines containing animal materials and/or cellular substrates. An adventitious agent is an infectious agent extraneous to the product; potential agents include transmissible spongiform encephalopathy (TSE), viruses and oncogenic agents. Known agents' testing and clearance must be demonstrated to be sufficiently sensitive; testing also should be capable of detecting unsuspected agents. Suitable tests may include such techniques as cell culture, polymerase chain reaction (PCR), electron microscopy, and egg or animal inoculation. In addition, material sourcing to avoid animal-derived materials can help reduce material and substrate exposure to specified TSE-risk materials. Viral clearance capacity testing should be performed (viral validation studies) on plasma-derived therapeutic products. The testing provides evidence to FDA that the biologic's manufacturing process demonstrates the capacity to remove or inactivate a specific panel (i.e., HIV, Hepatitis C, Hepatitis A etc.) of enveloped and non-enveloped virus challenges, which assures safety from the risk of infection viruses' transmission.

Table 12-9. Key CMC Guidance for Biological Product Development

ICH Guidelines Specifically Targeted at Biotechnological Products
Q5C: Quality of Biotechnological Products: Stability Testing of Biotechnological/Biological Products (November 1995)
Q5B Quality of Biotechnological Products: Analysis of the Expression Construct in Cells Used for Production of r-DNA Derived Protein Products (February 1996)
Q5D: Derivation and Characterization of Cell Substrates Used for Production of Biotechnological/Biological Products (July 1997)
Q5A Viral Safety Evaluation of Biotechnology Products Derived From Cell Lines of Human or Animal Origin (September 1998)
Q6B: Specifications: Test Procedures and Acceptance Criteria for Biotechnological/Biological Products (August 1999)
Q5E: Comparability of Biotechnological/Biological Products Subject to Changes in Their Manufacturing Process (June 2005)
Q4B Annex 14: Bacterial Endotoxins Test General Chapter (July 2010)
S6(R1) Preclinical Safety Evaluation of Biotechnology-Derived Pharmaceuticals (May 2012)
FDA Points to Consider and Other Applicable CMC Guidance Documents
Points to Consider in the Production and Testing of New Drugs and Biologicals Produced by Recombinant DNA Technology (April 1985)
Guideline on Validation of the Limulus Amebocyte Lysate Test as an End-Product Endotoxin Test For Human and Animal Parenteral Drugs, Biological Products, and Medical Devices (December 1987)
Points to Consider in the Collection, Processing, and Testing of Ex-Vivo Activated Mononuclear Leukocytes for Administering to Humans (August 1989)
Guidance for Industry: Content and Format of Investigational New Drug Applications (INDs) for Phase 1 Studies of Drugs, Including Well-Characterized, Therapeutic, Biotechnology-Derived Products (November 1995).
Guidance for Industry: Content and Format of INDs for Phase 1 Studies of Drugs, Including Well-Characterized, Therapeutic, Biotechnology-Derived Products. Questions and Answers (November 1995)
Demonstration of Comparability of Human Biological Products, Including Therapeutic Biotechnology-derived Products (April 1996)
Guidance on Applications for Products Comprised of Living Autologous Cells Manipulated ex vivo and Intended for Structural Repair or Reconstruction (May 1996)
Guidance for Industry for the Submission of Chemistry, Manufacturing, and Controls Information for a Therapeutic Recombinant DNA-Derived Product or a Monoclonal Antibody Product for In Vivo Use (August 1996)
Proposed Approach to Regulation of Cellular and Tissue-Based Products (February 1997)
Points to Consider in the Manufacture and Testing of Monoclonal Antibody Products for Human Use (February 1997)
Guidance for Industry: Changes to an Approved Application for Specified Biotechnology and Specified Synthetic Biological Products (July 1997)
Guidance for Industry: Guidance for Human Somatic Cell Therapy and Gene Therapy (March 1998)
Guidance for Industry: Environmental Assessment of Human Drug and Biologics Applications (July 1998)
Guidance for Industry: Monoclonal Antibodies Used as Reagents in Drug Manufacturing (March 2001)
Guidance for Industry: IND Meetings for Human Drugs and Biologics Chemistry, Manufacturing, and Controls Information (May 2001)
Guidance for Industry: Container Closure Systems for Packaging Human Drugs and Biologics—Questions and Answers (May 2002)
Draft Guidance for Industry: Drugs, Biologics, and Medical Devices Derived from Bioengineered Plants for Use in Humans and Animals (September 2002)
Draft Guidance for Industry: Comparability Protocols—Protein Drug Products and Biological Products—Chemistry, Manufacturing, and Controls Information (September 2003)
Draft Guidance for Industry: Labeling for Human Prescription Drug and Biological Products—Implementing the New Content and Format Requirements (January 2006)
Draft Guidance for Industry: Characterization and Qualification of Cell Substrates and Other Biological Starting Materials Used in the Production of Viral Vaccines for the Prevention and Treatment of Infectious Diseases (September 2006)
Draft Guidance for Industry: Validation of Growth-Based Rapid Microbiological Methods for Sterility Testing of Cellular and Gene Therapy Products (February 2008)

Table 12-9. Key CMC Guidance for Biological Product Development (cont'd.)

Guidance for Food and Drug Administration Reviewers and Sponsors: Content and Review of Chemistry, Manufacturing, and Control (CMC) Information for Human Somatic Cell Therapy Investigational New Drug Applications (INDs) (April 2008)
Guidance for Food and Drug Administration Reviewers and Sponsors: Content and Review of Chemistry, Manufacturing, and Control (CMC) Information for Human Gene Therapy Investigational New Drug Applications (INDs) (April 2008)
Guidance for Industry: CGMP for Phase 1 Investigational Drugs (July 2008)
Draft Guidance for Industry: Potency Tests for Cellular and Gene Therapy Products (October 2008)
Guidance for Industry: Labeling for Human Prescription Drug and Biological Products—Determining Established Pharmacologic Class for Use in the Highlights of Prescribing Information (October 2009)
Draft Guidance for Industry: Assay Development for Immunogenicity Testing of Therapeutic Proteins (December 2009)
Draft Guidance for Industry: CMC Postapproval Manufacturing Changes Reportable in Annual Reports (June 2010)
Draft Guidance for Industry: Early Clinical Trials with Live Biotherapeutic Products: Chemistry, Manufacturing, and Control Information (December 2010)
Guidance for Industry: Process Validation: General Principles and Practices (January 2011)
Draft Guidance for Industry: Guidance for Industry on Biosimilars: Q & As Regarding Implementation of the BPCI Act of 2009 (February 2012)
Draft Guidance for Industry: Scientific Considerations in Demonstrating Biosimilarity to a Reference Product (February 2012)
Draft Guidance for Industry: Quality Considerations in Demonstrating Biosimilarity to a Reference Protein Product (February 2012)
Guidance for Industry: Limiting the Use of Certain Phthalates as Excipients in CDER-Regulated Products (December 2012)
Draft Guidance for Industry: Immunogenicity Assessment for Therapeutic Protein Products (February 2013)
Draft Guidance for Industry: Allowable Excess Volume and Labelled Vial Fill Size in Injectable Drug and Biological Products (March 2014)
Draft Guidance for Industry: Current Good Manufacturing Practice Requirements for Combination Products (January 2015)
Draft Guidance for Industry: Established Conditions: Reportable CMC Changes for Approved Drug and Biologic Products (May 2015)
Guidance for Industry: Analytical Procedures and Methods Validation for Drugs and Biologics (July 2015)
Draft Guidance for Industry: Selection of the Appropriate Package Type Terms and Recommendations for Labeling Injectable Medical Products Packaged in Multiple-Dose, Single-Dose, and Single-Patient-Use Containers for Human Use Guidance for Industry (October 2015)
Draft Guidance for industry: Comparability Protocols for Human Drugs and Biologics: Chemistry, Manufacturing, and Controls Information (April 2016)
Draft Guidance for Industry: Assay Development and Validation for Immunogenicity Testing of Therapeutic Protein Products (April 2016)
Draft Guidance for Industry: Elemental Impurities in Drug Products (June 2016)
Guidance for Industry: Q7 Good Manufacturing Practice Guidance for Active Pharmaceutical Ingredients (September 2016)

Information amendments are required during the IND stage for significant changes and any changes likely to affect safety and efficacy prior to the revised process material's use in clinical studies. During development through Phase 3, testing specifications will evolve and become more defined; critical assays will need to be validated and determined to be reproducible, quantitative, sensitive, specific and biologically relevant; and the manufacturing process will be optimized.

Requirements unique to biologics are found in 21 CFR 610 General Biological Product Standards. Under these standards, the data submitted to FDA for BLA or NDA review must demonstrate the product is "safe, pure, and potent." In addition, an inspection must confirm the production facility can manufacture the product to meet these standards. Biological standards provide specific tests to be performed on each lot prior to release:

- potency—ideally, via a product-specific bioassay correlating with the *in vivo* mechanism of action or predictive of function
- sterility—similar to tests described in *United States Pharmacopeia* (*USP*) Chapter 71
- purity—essentially free of extraneous materials, such as residual solvents, antibiotics, animal products, contaminating cell populations and co-purifying proteins; also includes residual moisture and pyrogenic substances (e.g., endotoxin)

- identity—if a product comprises multiple components (e.g., cell lines and proteins), the test method should identify all components
- constituent materials—all ingredients should meet general purity and quality standards
- mycoplasma—if applicable

Alternative methods are permitted if they provide assurance equal to or greater than that of the specified tests. They are required to be be validated by the end of Phase 3 to show equivalency to the established tests. The standards also include testing requirements for communicable disease agents, product dating periods and product labeling requirements (i.e., the product package to be labeled with the biologic's proper name; the manufacturer's name, address and applicable license number; and the expiration date).

The amount of analytical procedure and methods validation information necessary for submissions will vary according to the investigational phase (21 CFR 312.23(a)(7)). For general guidance on analytical procedures and validation methods to be submitted for Phase 1 studies, sponsors can refer to FDA's *Guidance for Industry: Content and Format of Investigational New Drug Applications (INDs) for Phase 1 Studies of Drugs, Including Well-Characterized, Therapeutic, Biotechnology-Derived Products* (November 1995). All analytical procedures should be fully developed and validated when the BLA is submitted. The requested BLA analytical procedure format and content are the same as for an NDA.

A number of appropriate CMC development guidances are available, including ICH guidelines, CBER Points to Consider and other FDA guidances. Key CMC-related guidances are listed in **Table 12-9**. In addition, several general and specific USP chapters are relevant to biologics, including testing methods and viral safety evaluation.

Drug Master Files

A Drug Master File (DMF) is a submission to FDA containing confidential CMC information about a drug substance, intermediates, container closures and excipients that allows FDA to review the confidential information to support a third party's submission. DMFs are optional and are categorized in 21 CFR 314.420 as follows:
- Type I: reserved, no longer applicable
- Type II: drug substance, drug substance intermediate and material used in their preparation
- Type III: packaging material
- Type IV: excipient, colorant, flavor, essence
- Type V: FDA-accepted reference material

Submitted DMFs are reviewed only in conjunction with a sponsor's IND, NDA or BLA when that DMF is referenced and there is a letter of authorization granting FDA permission to access the DMF to support the submission. If there are deficiencies in the DMF, the DMF holder will be asked to provide additional information. The sponsor also will be notified in either an Information Request (IR) or Complete Response (CR) letter; however, no confidential details about the deficiency will be included in this communication. If there are no deficiencies, the DMF holder will not receive any communication. DMFs should be updated annually, although FDA does not send reminders. After three years' inactivity (i.e., no annual updates), FDA will notify the holder that the DMF is considered inactive; the holder has 90 days to either close the DMF or provide an annual update to keep it open.

A DMF's content should be based on applicable guidance, and the submission should follow the M4Q CTD-Quality format. The submission also must contain a statement of commitment to CGMP compliance. One commonly used DMF submission for CBER is the Type V DMF, under which CBER accepts:
- facility information in support of gene- and cell-based therapies (may be used to support clinical trials and facilitate IND review)
- production information for a contract manufacturer to provide a list of other products manufactured in the facility (formerly filed as a Type I DMF)
- submissions from contract testing facilities, such as cell bank testing and viral clearance studies

Before submitting any Type V DMF, a letter of intent should be submitted to FDA to determine the DMF submission's suitability.

Animal Rule

FDA's regulations concerning whether human efficacy studies are ethical or feasible for biological products are codified in 21 CFR 601.90, the Animal Rule. The Animal Rule states FDA may grant marketing approval based on adequate and well-controlled animal studies that establish a drug is reasonably likely to produce clinical benefit for products developed to ameliorate or prevent serious or life-threatening conditions caused by exposure to lethal or permanently disabling toxic substances, for which performing human challenge studies would be unethical, and field trials to study effectiveness after accidental or intentional human exposure are not feasible. Products evaluated for efficacy under the Animal Rule also should be evaluated for safety under the existing requirements for establishing new drugs' safety. The Animal Rule states FDA will rely on evidence from animal studies to provide

substantial evidence of effectiveness only when all four of these criteria are met:
1. There is a reasonably well-understood pathophysiological mechanism of the substance's toxicity and its prevention or substantial reduction by the product.
2. The effect is demonstrated in more than one animal species expected to react with a response predictive for humans, unless the effect is demonstrated in a single animal species that represents a sufficiently well-characterized animal model for predicting the response in humans.
3. The animal study endpoint clearly is related to the desired benefit in humans, generally the enhancement of survival or prevention of major morbidity.
4. Data or information on the product's kinetics and pharmacodynamics or other relevant data, or information in animals and humans, allows selection of an effective dose in humans.

BLA Submission and Review Process

BLA Format and Content

A BLA is an application for a biologics license under *PHS Act* Section 351 (21 CFR 601.2). BLAs are required for all biological products submitted to CBER or, for well-characterized proteins, to CDER. The BLA must be submitted according to ICH eCTD requirements. Major NDA and BLA sections are the same, with a few exceptions. For instance, biologics typically are excluded categorically from requiring an environmental assessment under 21 CFR 25.5(c); however, the reason must be stated in the BLA. The manufacturing process needs to be validated for biologics prior to BLA submission; validation is reviewed as part of the Preapproval Inspection (PAI) requirements.

A BLA must provide the multidisciplinary FDA review team (medical officers, microbiologists, chemists, biostatisticians, etc.) with the efficacy and safety information necessary to make a benefit-risk assessment and recommend or oppose the biologic product's approval.

BLAs are regulated under 21 CFR Parts 600–680. A BLA can be submitted by any legal person or entity taking responsibility for compliance with product and establishment standards. Form FDA 356h specifies BLA requirements, including:
- administrative information, including applicant information
- product and manufacturing (CMC) information, including facilities information
- preclinical studies
- clinical studies
- labeling

Timetable for BLA Review

The BLA review process is divided into five phases:
1. filing determination and review planning
2. review
3. Advisory Committee meeting preparation and conduct
4. action
5. post-action

Table 12-10 is a representative timetable of the NDA/BLA review process.

Per 21 CFR 601.2, an application for licensure is not considered filed until CBER has received all pertinent information and data from the applicant. A refuse-to-file (RTF) decision may be made on applications containing incomplete or inadequate information required under *PHS Act* Section 351, the *FD&C Act* or in FDA regulations (e.g., 21 CFR 601.2). RTF decisions can be based on:

- an application's administrative incompleteness
- an application's scientific incompleteness (i.e., omission of critical data, information or analyses needed to evaluate safety, purity and potency or provide adequate directions for use (21 CFR 601.2))
- an application's inadequate information content or organization, precluding a substantive and meaningful review
- a technically deficient electronic submission

In summary, CBER's initial decision on whether to file a BLA will be based on a threshold determination of whether the information submitted to support the license application is sufficient to permit a substantive and meaningful review. An RTF may apply if the application contains uncorrected deficiencies (e.g., manufacturing or product specifications) clearly communicated to the applicant before the application was submitted or, for electronic submissions, technical deficiencies sufficient to require resolution before a meaningful review can occur. An RTF is not a final determination concerning potential approvability; it can be an early opportunity for the applicant to develop a complete application, but will delay a full review of the application.

Applicants may receive additional information requests as a result of ongoing reviews and are encouraged to respond promptly and completely. During the first cycle, the FDA division ordinarily reviews all amendments solicited by the agency during the review and any amendments to the application previously agreed upon during the pre-BLA meeting. Substantial amendments submitted late in the review cycle may be reviewed in a subsequent cycle, depending on other identified application deficiencies. Following FDA's review of a license application,

Table 12-10. NDA/BLA Standard and Priority Review Process (*PDUFA VI*)

Day/Month	Activity
Day 0	Application received
Day 0–14	RPM is assigned, regulatory filing review begins
By Day 14	RPM sends a letter acknowledging application receipt to the applicant
By Day 38 (Day 23 for Priority Review)	BIMO site selection meeting
By Day 45 (Day 23 for Priority Review)	Filing review is conducted Inspection actions are identified Potential RTF issues are communicated to applicant
By Day 60	Applicant is informed in writing of a priority designation Filing determination to applicant is communicated (for BLAs and priority NDAs) Applicant is notified of RTF determination
By Day 74	Filing review issues communicated to applicant
Month 5 (Month 3 for Priority Review)	Mid-cycle meeting: • REMS requirement discussed • Decision is confirmed, any issues that could preclude an approval action are identified; for expedited reviews, possible early target date(s) for completion of reviews and action are discussed
Month 8 (Month 5 for Priority Review)	Late-cycle meeting: • Labeling/postmarketing requirements and commitments are sent to applicant with FDA's rationale for major changes requiring explanation
Month 10 (Month 6 for Priority Review)	Action Date: Issue action letter to applicant

BIMO—Bioresearch monitoring; RTF—Refuse to file; REMS—Risk Evaluation and Mitigation Strategy, RPM—Regulatory Program Manager

the applicant and FDA may present their findings to FDA's related Biological Products Advisory Committee. This non-FDA expert committee (scientists, physicians, biostatisticians and a consumer representative) provides advice to the agency regarding the product's safety and efficacy for the proposed indication. Based on Advisory Committee discussions and committee recommendations, FDA may ask an applicant to submit additional data or analyses for review.

A *Complete Response* (CR) Letter after a complete review can be issued based on either critical data or analyses omissions or an adverse judgment about the data, conclusions, rationale, etc., the application presented. For example, a CR Letter could be issued if CBER concludes effectiveness has not been demonstrated, an analysis was carried out incorrectly, clinical trials were poorly designed or conducted, safety has not been adequately demonstrated or outstanding compliance issues remain. These judgments would not serve as the basis for an RTF unless the deficiencies were so severe as to render the application incomplete.

Other action letters include the I*nformation Request* (IR) Letter and the Discipline Review (DR) Letter. An IR Letter requests further information or clarification necessary to complete the discipline review. A DR Letter is sent to convey early thoughts on possible deficiencies found by a discipline review team at the conclusion of its review. A single DR Letter may contain comments from multiple discipline reviews.

A PAI will be conducted for the proposed manufacturing facilities during the application review process.

A biologic is approved for marketing by issuing a biologics license (including US license number) as part of the approval letter. A license represents a determination that the product, the manufacturing process and the manufacturing facilities meet applicable requirements to ensure the product's continued safety, purity and potency. Among other things, safety and purity assessments must consider the storage and testing of cell substrates often used to manufacture biologics. A potency assay is required due to biologics' complexity and heterogeneity.

Product approval also requires product labeling adequate to allow healthcare providers to understand the product's proper use, including its potential benefits and risks; effectively communicate with patients and parents (for minors); and safely deliver the product to the public.

On 18 August 2017, the *Food and Drug Administration Reauthorization Act* of 2017 *(FDARA)* was signed into law. This new law included the reauthorization of the *Prescription Drug User Fee Act (PDUFA),* which provided FDA with the necessary resources to maintain a predictable and efficient human drug and biologic product review process. Under *PDUFA VI*, FDA will promote innovation through enhanced communication with sponsors during drug development. As part of its commitments in *PDUFA VI*, FDA continued the review program to promote greater transparency and increased communication between the FDA review team and the applicant on the most innovative products reviewed by the agency. The program applies to all New Medical Entity (NME) NDAs and original BLAs received 1 October 2018–30 September 2022.

PDUFA VI maintains the review timelines for priority reviews (six months) and for standard reviews (10 months) after an initial 60-day filing review. The increase in review duration is intended to increase the likelihood of an on-time (first-cycle) approval.

Under *PDUFA* provisions, submitting a major amendment during the last three months of a review may trigger a three-month extension of the review clock. Under *PDUFA VI* a major amendment can extend the review clock by three months at any time during the review.

Nonproprietary Biological Product Naming

Originator biological products, related biological products and biosimilar products previously licensed and newly licensed under *PHS Act* Section 351(a) or 351(k), and biological products approved under the *FD&C Act* on or before 23 March 2020, when such products are deemed to be licensed under *PHS Act* Section 351 (*BPCI Act* Sections 7002(e)(2)–(e)(4)), are covered under the guidance for "non-proprietary naming of biological products."

Per FDA, the nonproprietary naming convention facilitates pharmacovigilance for originator biological products, related biological products and biosimilar products containing related drug substances when other means to track a specific dispensed product are not readily accessible or available. Nonproprietary names that include distinguishing suffixes can serve as key elements to identify specific products in spontaneous adverse event reporting and to reinforce accurate product identification in billing and claims records used for active pharmacovigilance. Other product-specific identifiers, such as proprietary names or National Drug Codes (NDCs), may not be available or could change over time. A distinguishing suffix also supports tracking product-specific events over time, thereby enhancing the accurate attribution of product-specific adverse event reports.

FDA suggests the proposed suffix be:
- unique
- devoid of meaning
- four lowercase letters, of which at least three are distinct
- nonproprietary
- attached to the core name with a hyphen
- free of legal barriers that would restrict its usage

Example:
- replicamab-cznm
- replicamab-hjxf

The proposed suffix should not:
- be false or misleading, such as making misrepresentations with respect to safety or efficacy
- include numerals and other symbols aside from the hyphen attaching the suffix to the core name
- include abbreviations commonly used in clinical practice in a manner that may lead the suffix to be misinterpreted as another element on the prescription or order
- contain or suggest any drug substance name or core name
- look similar to or be capable of being mistaken for the name of a currently marketed product (e.g., should not increase the risk of confusion or medical errors with the product and/or other products in the clinical setting)
- look similar to or otherwise connote the name of the license holder
- be too similar to any other FDA-designated nonproprietary name suffix

But, these suffix rules do not necessarily apply to all related biologics. FDA notes, in some instances, it has designated a proper name, including an identifier attached as a prefix to distinguish products from previously licensed biologics. For example, with ado-trastuzumab emtansine, FDA includes a unique prefix, which it says was necessary to minimize certain medication errors and facilitate pharmacovigilance.

However, in March 2019, FDA released *Draft Guidance for Industry: Nonproprietary Naming of Biological Products: Update*, in which it reassessed the implementation of FDA-designated suffixes. The draft guidance states that nonproprietary names of biological products licensed under *PHS Act* Section 351 do not need to be revised to meet the naming convention's objectives. Additionally, FDA does not intend to apply the naming convention to biological products that are the subject of an approved application under *FD&C Act* Section 505 as of 23 March 2020 when that application is deemed to be a biologics license application under *PHS Act* Section 351 on the same date (transition biological products). FDA also is rethinking whether vaccines should be included in the scope of the naming convention guidance.

Biologics Advertising and Promotional Labeling

CBER reviews draft and final professional and direct-to-consumer (DTC) advertising and promotional labeling materials submitted for licensed biological

products. CBER reviews promotional materials to ensure information about the product's risks and benefits is communicated in a truthful, nonmisleading and balanced manner, and the materials comply with pertinent federal laws and regulations. Final advertising and promotional labeling materials submissions must contain:
- Form FDA-2253: Transmittal of Advertisements and Promotional Labeling for Drugs and Biologics for Human Use
- two copies of final advertisements and promotional labeling materials
- two copies of the product's current professional labeling (e.g., approved Package Labeling (PI), Patient Package Insert (PPI), Medication Guide and Instructions for Use)

CBER's Advertising and Promotional Labeling Branch (APLB) reviews and evaluates proposed biological product proprietary names in accordance with SOPP 8001.4: Review of Proprietary Names for CBER Regulated Products. Proposed proprietary names are evaluated to avoid potential medication errors related to look-alike and sound-alike proprietary names and to avoid fanciful or misleading names.

APLB also evaluates other factors that could contribute to medication errors, such as unclear label abbreviations, acronyms, dose designations and error-prone label and packaging design. Additional information on advertising and promotional labeling can be found in Chapter 28: Biologics Labeling, Advertising and Promotion.

Biosimilars

The *BPCI Act* created an abbreviated licensure pathway in *PHS Act* Section 351(k) for biological products shown to be biosimilar to, or interchangeable with, an FDA-licensed reference product. Objectives are similar to those of the *Hatch-Waxman Act*. The *BPCI Act* aligns with FDA's policy of permitting appropriate reliance on what already is known about a biologic, thereby saving time and resources and avoiding unnecessary duplication of human or animal testing.

A biological product may be deemed "biosimilar" if data show it is "highly similar" to the reference product, notwithstanding minor differences in clinically inactive components, and there are no clinically meaningful differences between the biological product and the reference product in terms of safety, purity and potency. To meet the higher interchangeability standard, a sponsor must demonstrate the biosimilar product can be expected to produce the same clinical result as the reference product in any given patient and, for a biological product administered more than once, the risk of alternating or switching from the reference product to the biosimilar product is no greater than the risk of maintaining the patient on the reference product. Interchangeable products may be substituted for the reference product by a pharmacist without the prescribing healthcare provider's intervention. To be approved as a biosimilar, the product must meet the following criteria:
- The biological product and reference product utilize the same mechanism or mechanisms of action for the condition(s) of use prescribed, recommended or suggested in the proposed labeling.
- The condition(s) of use prescribed, recommended or suggested in the labeling proposed for the biological product previously has been approved for the reference product.
- The biological product's route of administration, dosage form and strength are the same as those of the reference product.
- The facility in which the biological product is manufactured, processed, packed or held meets standards designed to ensure the product continues to be safe, pure and potent.

A biosimilar application under *PHS Act* Subsection 351(k) may not be approved until 12 years from the reference product's initial licensing date. In addition, an application under Subsection 351(k) may not be accepted for review until four years after the reference product's first licensing date.

Additional information on biosimilars can be found in Chapter 27 Biosimilars.

Preapproval Inspections

The pre-license inspection is performed as part of the BLA review process. There are circumstances under which a pre-license inspection can be waived, but an inspection generally is necessary. An applicant can be either a non-FDA-licensed firm applying for its first license, in which case it will definitely get an inspection, or an FDA-licensed firm with a new product. A licensed firm would submit a new BLA, but its facility could be licensed for other products already. The pre-license inspection may become more complicated if it involves multiple sites. A pre-license inspection is necessary for licensure under 21 CFR 601.20, which requires that a BLA be approved only after establishments listed in the application are inspected and determined to comply with the application's standards and requirements prescribed in the applicable regulations.

A preapproval inspection is slightly different from a pre-license inspection.

The preapproval inspection may be completed for a new manufacturing facility or a new contract manufacturing facility, or due to significant manufacturing process changes. With pre-license and preapproval inspections, the sponsor is supposed to be ready for an inspection at the time of its submission. CBER wants the investigator to see all of the facility's pertinent operations. With respect to pre-license and preapproval inspections, per 21CFR 601.20, CBER will make a determination of compliance with the application and applicable standards, including GMP standards, to approve the application or supplement. The product to be introduced into interstate commerce must be available for inspection during all phases of manufacturing.

Inspections occur about halfway through the review cycle. For a new BLA, that would be about five months after the application was received, since the review timeframe is 10 months. For a prior approval supplement, the inspection would occur at about two months because that submission type has a four-month review timeframe. CBER sometimes determines an inspection in support of an application or supplement is unnecessary (e.g., if CBER has inspected the production or processing area recently, and the sponsor has a good compliance history, the inspection might be waived). FDA Standard Operating Procedure 8410 (SOP 8410), is used as a guide in determining when pre-license or preapproval inspections are necessary. CBER's Office of Compliance and Biologics Quality's (OCBQ) Division of Manufacturing and Product Quality serves as the lead on pre-license or preapproval inspections of biologic drugs and devices. For inspection of blood and blood products, CBER OBRR's Division of Blood Applications takes the lead.

Preapproval inspections also are performed for prior approval supplements. In this case, the inspection is for changes to an approved application, defined in 21 CFR 601.12, and covers the general regulation for changes to an approved application.

Market Exclusivity

Biologics receive 12-year market exclusivity instead of the five years allowed for NDA drugs (seven years for orphan products). The *BPCI Act* allows biologics to receive an additional six months of market exclusivity for pediatric indications.

Communications and Meetings With FDA

Three types of meetings occur between sponsors or applicants and FDA staff: Type A, B and C. Each meeting type is subject to different procedures:
- Type A—to resolve a clinical hold or RTF or to resolve a dispute or discuss a special protocol assessment (SPA)
- Type B—key milestone meetings to include Pre-IND, End-of-Phase 1 (for products developed under 21 CFR 601 Subpart E), End-of-Phase 2/Pre-Phase 3 and Pre- BLA
- Type C—for any other purpose

If applicants are considering requesting a Type A meeting, they should contact the review division in either CBER or CDER to discuss the request's appropriateness before submitting it. Type A meetings should be scheduled to occur within 30 days of FDA's receipt of a written meeting request.

FDA should schedule Type B meetings to occur within 60 days of receiving the written meeting request. In general, the agency will not grant more than one of each Type B meeting for each potential application.

A Type C meeting is any meeting other than a Type A or Type B meeting between CBER or CDER and a sponsor regarding a product's development and review. Type C meetings should be scheduled to occur within 75 days of FDA's receipt of the written meeting request.

A meeting background package should be submitted to the appropriate review division in accordance with the following timeframes:
- Type A meeting—at least two weeks before the formal meeting
- Type B meeting—at least four weeks before the formal meeting
- Type C meeting—at least four weeks before the formal meeting

Additional information on FDA meetings can be found in Chapter 4: FDA Communications and Preparing for FDA Meetings.

Advisory Committee Meetings

The *Federal Advisory Committee Act* is the legal foundation defining how these committees operate. The law places special emphasis on open meetings, chartering, public involvement and reporting. Advisory Committees are groups of experts from outside the agency that FDA turns to for advice on complex scientific, technical and policy issues. Advisory Committees provide independent, professional expertise related to the development and evaluation of FDA-regulated products, such as allergenic products; blood products; cellular, tissue and gene therapies; transmissible spongiform encephalopathies; and vaccines and related biological products. In general, Advisory Committees include a chairman and several members, plus representatives of consumer groups, industry representatives and, sometimes, patients. Additional experts with special knowledge may be added for individual meetings, as needed. Although the committees provide advice to the agency, FDA makes the final decisions. In some cases, FDA is legally required to refer an issue to an

Advisory Committee. In others, the agency has discretion whether to refer a matter to an Advisory Committee. For all first-of-a-kind or first-in-class products for human use, FDA either refers the product to an Advisory Committee or summarizes the reasons it does not do so before approval in the action letter.

Once the review has progressed within the reviewing division, CBER will notify the sponsor 55 days in advance if it has determined an Advisory Committee meeting is required. The sponsor prepares materials for Advisory Committee review and designates which materials are publicly releasable under the *Freedom of Information Act* (*FOIA*) and which are to be treated as proprietary, nonpublic materials. FDA may disagree with the sponsor's designations and request additional information be made public. In general, product information not in the labeling, such as manufacturing processes, formulation information and quality control testing, as well as the raw data from preclinical and clinical studies, can be considered exempt from *FOIA*. Advisory Committee members receive both public and proprietary materials. During the meeting, sponsors may be permitted to make presentations, but they are not allowed to approach committee members without a federal officer's consent. Additional information on advisory committee meetings can be found in Chapter 5: Preparing for FDA Advisory Committee Meetings.

FDA Biologics Postapproval and Compliance Regulations

Under 21 CFR 601.12, a change in the approved product, labeling, production process, quality control, equipment or facility must be reported to FDA. The change can be reported in a supplement requiring approval prior to distribution (Prior Approval Supplement—PAS), a supplement submitted at least 30 days prior to distributing the product made using the change (Changes Being Effected in 30 Days—CBE-30), a supplement submitted prior to distribution of the product made using the change (Changes Being Effected—CBE) or an annual report, depending on its potential to affect the biological product's "identity, strength, quality, purity, or potency" adversely. Before distributing a licensed product manufactured using a change, the manufacturer is required to demonstrate, through appropriate validation and/or clinical or nonclinical laboratory studies, the change's lack of adverse effect on the product's safety or effectiveness.

Due to the sometimes limited ability to identify clinically active component(s) of complex biological products, such products often are defined by their manufacturing processes. In 1996, FDA provided recommendations in its *Guidance Concerning Demonstration of Comparability of Human Biological Products, Including Therapeutic Biotechnology Products*, which explains how an applicant may demonstrate—through a combination of analytical testing, functional assay, assessment of PK, PD and toxicity in animals and clinical studies—a manufacturing change does not adversely affect its FDA-approved product's identity, purity or potency. Since 1996, FDA has approved many manufacturing process changes for licensed biological products based on demonstrating product comparability before and after the process change, as supported by quality criteria and analytical testing, but without the need for additional nonclinical data and clinical safety and/or efficacy studies. In cases where the change's effects are uncertain, additional data may be required, including nonclinical and/or clinical studies, to demonstrate product comparability. In July 1997, CBER issued *Guidance for Industry: Changes to an Approved Application for Specified Biotechnology and Specified Synthetic Biological Products* to assist applicants in determining which reporting mechanism is appropriate for a change to an approved license application. These concepts were developed further by ICH and resulted in *Q5E Comparability of Biotechnological/Biological Products Subject to Changes in their Manufacturing Process* (November 2004).

Applicable Types of Submissions

The three reporting categories for changes to an approved application are defined in 21 CFR 601.12:
- PAS—changes with a substantial potential to affect the product's safety or effectiveness adversely, requiring submission of a supplement and FDA approval prior to distributing the product made using the change (major changes)
- Changes Being Effected (CBE) 30 or CBE—changes with a moderate potential to affect the product's safety or effectiveness adversely, requiring submission of a supplement to FDA at least 30 days prior to distributing the product made using the change; for some changes, the 30 days may be waived (moderate changes)
- annual report—changes with minimal potential to affect the product's safety or effectiveness adversely (minor changes)

Monitor the Approved Biological Product's Safety and Stability

Manufacturers must report certain problems to FDA's Biological Product Deviation Reporting System. They also must report and correct product problems within established timeframes. If a significant problem is detected, a manufacturer may need to recall a product or even stop manufacturing it.

GMP Inspections

CBER regularly inspects manufacturing facilities to assess whether biological products are made in compliance with appropriate laws and regulations and to assist in identifying any changes needed to help ensure product quality.

GMP inspections are mandated by 21 CFR Part 600, requiring each licensed establishment and any of its additional locations to be inspected at least every two years. These facility inspections determine whether the establishment is meeting the regulation's minimal requirements for licensed biologics. They also determine whether the facility is in compliance with the *PHS Act*, the *FD&C Act* and any particular BLA requirements. If the biologics license is for a device regulated by CBER, 21 CFR Part 600 and/or Part 1271 (as applicable) regulations establish the minimal requirements, and the facility also must comply with the *PHS Act*, *FD&C Act* and the BLA. If the device is approved under a PMA, it would be subject to the *FD&C Act* and specific PMA provisions.

For CBER products, per 21 CFR Part 600.21, each licensed establishment shall be inspected biannually. For human cell and tissue establishments, there is a risk-based approach to prioritizing inspections. There is no statutory or regulatory requirement regarding inspectional frequency for human cells, tissues and cellular-based products, known as HCT/Ps. For flu vaccine manufacturers, inspections occur annually and early in the manufacturing cycle so problems or issues can be detected and resolved in a timely fashion to ensure an adequate vaccine supply for the upcoming flu season.

Routine GMP inspections cover CGMPs for all products or high-risk products manufactured at the location. Again, for flu vaccine manufacturers, this occurs every year. Production processes are inspected for all high-risk products manufactured at that location. Additionally, any complaints or adverse event reports the firm has received, any trends it has seen (e.g., in its environmental monitoring), all Biological Product Deviation Reports it has submitted to CBER, any medical device reports (similar to the Adverse Event Reporting System or AERS, but specific to devices), any recalls and any changes made since the last inspection are reviewed. If the manufacturer has had to change its process, it is important to make sure it has submitted appropriate supporting documentation, as outlined in 21 CFR 314.81.

Biologics Establishment Registration and Listing

Biological drug product manufacturers are required to update their registration and listing information with CDER or CBER in the proper electronic format. FDA has adopted Structured Product Labeling (SPL) as the electronic means for submitting registration and listing information to the agency. As of 1 June 2009, FDA no longer accepts paper registration and listing submissions unless a waiver is granted. Under *FD&C Act* Section 510 and the regulations in 21 CFR Part 207, biological drug product manufacturers must:
- register their establishments annually on or before 31 December of each year
- list all of their products in commercial distribution at the time of initial registration, with semi-annual updates to their listings in June and December, as necessary

Special Circumstances—Commercial Biologics Manufacturing and Supply

Lot Release

After a BLA is approved, some products may be subject to official lot release. As part of the manufacturing process, the manufacturer is required to perform certain tests on each product lot before it is released for distribution. If the product is subject to official release by CBER, the manufacturer submits samples of each product lot to CBER together with a release protocol showing a summary of the lot's manufacturing history and the lot testing results performed by the manufacturer. CBER also may perform certain confirmatory tests on lots of some products, such as viral vaccines, before releasing the lots for distribution.

Short Supply

When a licensed biologic is in short supply, the manufacturer may obtain an initial or partially manufactured version of the product from an unlicensed, but registered, facility when the product is shipped solely to the licensee, and the licensee can ensure the product made at the unlicensed facility will be manufactured in full compliance with applicable regulations. The license holder must update its license with FDA to explain this arrangement. This provision is used most commonly to obtain source materials, such as those used in producing allergenic extracts; specific types of human plasma containing rare antibodies; venoms used in producing antitoxins and antivenins; and recovered plasma.

Divided Manufacturing

Divided manufacturing is an arrangement in which two or more manufacturers, each registered with FDA and licensed to manufacture a specific biological product in its entirety, participate jointly in manufacturing that product by performing only part of the approved process. BLAs should be updated to describe each manufacturer's role and may need to demonstrate the intermediate products' equivalency and stability during shipment. The intermediate also should be labeled "for further manufacturing use" as part of the proper name. Each licensed manufacturer must notify the other licensee(s) and appropriate FDA center regarding proposed changes in its product's manufacture, testing or specifications, in accordance with 21 CFR 601.12.

Shared Manufacturing

Shared manufacturing is an arrangement in which two or more manufacturers are registered and licensed for specific aspects of a product's manufacture, but neither is licensed for the product's total manufacturing process. A common shared manufacturing arrangement makes one manufacturer responsible for an intermediate product and another for the final product. All license applications or supplements under a shared manufacturing arrangement should be submitted concurrently to FDA for BLA review. Lack of one or more related applications may result in an RTF.

Contract Manufacturing

A sponsor holdng a BLA license must establish, maintain and follow procedures for receiving information from the contract manufacturer on all deviations, complaints and adverse events that may affect product quality. Specific contractor identification in product labeling is not required, since the contractor does not hold the license.

Summary

- Biologics are products or live cells derived from living sources, e.g., humans, animals and microorganisms, approved for licensure under the *PHS Act*, unlike small molecule drugs, which are approved under the *FD&C Act*. CBER is the primary reviewing center for biologics and is organized into three offices for the review of blood products; vaccines; and cell, tissue and gene therapy products.
- Per current regulations, biologics are handled both by CDER and CBER.
- The review of "well-characterized" biological products was moved from CBER to CDER in 2003. This category comprises biotechnology products and naturally and synthetically derived proteins and includes such products as monoclonal antibodies, cytokines, growth factors, enzymes, immunomodulators and thrombolytics.
- The IND process for biologics is much the same as for drugs. A number of preclinical, clinical and manufacturing guidance documents have been published to assist sponsors with issues unique to the development of biological products.
- The BLA format and general review process also are similar to that for NDAs, including utilizing the eCTD format for submissions.
- It now is possible for a sponsor to seek approval of a "biosimilar" product under new *PHS Act* Section 351(k). The sponsor must demonstrate the product is highly similar to the reference product and there are no clinically meaningful differences between the biological product and the reference product in terms of safety, purity and potency. However, to meet the higher standard of interchangeability, a sponsor must demonstrate the risk of alternating or switching between the biosimilar product and the reference product is no greater than the risk of maintaining the patient on the reference product.

Chapter 13

Biologics Compliance

Updated by Anne Marie Woodland, MS, RAC

OBJECTIVES

- Understand and learn general regulatory compliance principles for biologics preapproval, including chemistry, manufacturing and controls (CMC); change control; Investigational New Drug (IND) safety reports; role of bioresearch monitoring; product naming; and pre-license inspections

- Understand and learn general regulatory postapproval compliance principles for biologics, including inspections, postapproval commitments, change control, biologic deviations reporting and import/export

- Understand the organization, roles and responsibilities of the Office of Compliance and Biologics Quality at the US Food and Drug Administration's (FDA) Center for Biologics Evaluation and Research

- Understand risk management plans for biologics, including setting up Risk Evaluation and Mitigation Strategies (REMS)

- Understand FDA enforcement activities for biologics

LAWS, REGULATIONS AND GUIDANCE DOCUMENTS COVERED IN THIS CHAPTER

- *Public Health Service Act* of 1946, Sections 351 and 361

- *Federal Food, Drug, and Cosmetic Act* of 1938

- *Food and Drug Administration Amendments Act* of 2007

- 21 CFR 600 Biologics General

- 21 CFR 601 Biologics Licensing

- 21 CFR 610 General Biological Products Standards

- Compliance Program Guidance Manual—Inspection of Biological Drug Products—7345.848

- Regulatory Procedures Manual, Chapter 9, Subchapter 9.3, "Importation of Biological Products," Office of Regulatory Affairs, US Food and Drug Administration

- *Comparability Protocols for Human Drugs and Biologics: Chemistry, Manufacturing, and Controls Information: Draft Guidance for Industry* (April 2016)

- *Guidance for Industry: Comparability Protocols—Protein Drug Products and Biological Products—Chemistry, Manufacturing, and Controls Information* (September 2003)

- *Comparability of Biotechnological/ Biological Products Subject to Changes in Their Manufacturing Process Q5E* (June 2005)

Chapter 13

- *Guidance for Industry: Changes to an Approved Application for Specified Biotechnology and Specified Synthetic Biological Products* (July 1997)
- *SOPP 8410: Determining When Pre-license/Preapproval Inspections are Necessary* (December 2001)
- *SOPP 8001.4: Review of Proprietary Names for CBER Regulated Products Version* (September 2016)
- *Contents of a Complete Submission for the Evaluation of Proprietary Names: Guidance for Industry* (April 2016)
- *Guidance for Industry: Regulation of Human Cells, Tissues, and Cellular and Tissue-Based Products (HCT/Ps)—Small Entity Compliance Guide* (August 2007)
- Exports Under the FDA Export Reform and Enhancement Act of 1996 (July 2007)
- *Draft Guidance for Industry: Postmarketing Safety Reporting for Human Drug and Biological Products Including Vaccines* (March 2001)
- *Guidance for Industry: Biological Product Deviation Reporting for Licensed Manufacturers of Biological Products Other than Blood and Blood Components* (October 2006)
- *SOPP 8404: Refusal to File Procedures for Biologics License Applications, New Drug Applications and Efficacy Supplements* (January 2017)
- *Guidance for Industry: Good Pharmacovigilance Practices and Pharmacoepidemiologic Assessment* (March 2005)
- *Guidance for Industry: Premarketing Risk Assessment* (March 2005)
- *Guidance for Industry: Changes to an Approved Application: Biological Products* (July 1997)
- *Guidance for Industry: Format and Content of Proposed Risk Evaluation and Mitigation Strategies (REMS), REMS Assessments, and Proposed REMS Modifications* (September 2009)

- *Guidance for Industry: Risk Evaluation and Mitigation Strategies: Modifications and Revisions* (April 2015)
- *Safety Assessment for IND Safety Reporting: Draft Guidance for Industry* (December 2015)
- *Guidance for Industry: Postmarketing Studies and Clinical Trials—Implementation of Section 505(o)(3) of the Federal Food, Drug, and Cosmetic Act* (April 2011)
- *Guidance: Medication Guides—Distribution Requirements and Inclusion in Risk Evaluation and Mitigation Strategies (REMS)* (December 2011)
- *Guidance for Industry and Investigators: Safety Reporting Requirements for INDs and BA/BE Studies* (December 2012)
- *Guidance for Industry: Electronic Submission of Lot Distribution Reports* (March 2015)
- *Nonproprietary Naming of Biological Products: Guidance for Industry* (January 2017)
- *Deviation Reporting for Human Cells, Tissues, and Cellular and Tissue-Based Products Regulated Solely Under Section 361 of the Public Health Service Act and 21 CFR Part 1271: Guidance for Industry* (September 2017)

Introduction

Compliance is a key part of ensuring a robust product lifecycle, starting with successful product development and approval to commercialization and postapproval monitoring. Biologics compliance follows a risk-based approach and focuses specifically on US Food and Drug Administration (FDA) requirements (Code of Federal Regulations (CFR), FDA guidances and International Council for Harmonisation (ICH) guidelines). Biologics encompass many products, such as fractionated blood and their recombinant analogues; antitoxins; toxins; allergenic products; vaccines; oncolytic viruses; products of manipulated, cultured or expanded human cells; and tissue therapy, gene therapy and therapeutic serum or analogous products that aid in the prevention, treatment or cure of disease or injuries.[1]

Regulations

FDA's Center for Biologics Evaluation and Research (CBER) is responsible for ensuring biological products are safe and effective and comply with applicable laws and regulations. Biological products are licensed under Section 351 of the *Public Health Service Act* (*PHS Act*) (42 U.S.C.) and fall within the definition of a drug, found in *Food, Drug, and Cosmetic Act* (*FD&C Act*) Section 201(g)(1). Biological products are subject to inspection under the provisions of both the *PHS Act* and the *FD&C Act*.

Biological products are subject to applicable regulations promulgated under both acts, including the current Good Manufacturing Practice (CGMP) regulations, found in 21 CFR Parts 210 and 211, and the biologics regulations, found in 21 CFR Parts 600–680. In addition, human cells, tissues and cellular and tissue-based products regulated as biological products are subject to the registration and listing, donor eligibility and Current Good Tissue Practice (CGTP) regulations in 21 CFR Part 1271. CGMP regulations apply to the manufacture of biological products under *FD&C Act* Section 501(a)(2)(b), and CGMP principles apply to the manufacture of biological intermediates and drug substances under the biologics regulations in 21 CFR Part 600.

Establishments also must comply with FDA-approved Biologics License Application (BLA) commitments and applicable standards. Biological products include a wide variety of indications, dosage forms and manufacturing processes, all of critical importance in promoting and protecting the public health. To help ensure manufacturers consistently produce safe, pure, potent and effective biological products, FDA conducts CGMP inspections of each establishment at least biennially. Pre-license inspections (PLIs) for new biological products and preapproval inspections (PAIs) for significant changes to a BLA are performed to ensure compliance with the regulations prior to approval of a new license or significant license change.[2]

To provide more effective and efficient biological product regulation, the Office of Regulatory Affairs (ORA) and CBER established Team Biologics in 1997 to conduct routine and compliance follow-up CGMP inspections of biological drug product manufacturers, including blood establishments.[3] Team Biologics uses ORA's investigative skills and the Bioresearch Monitoring Program's (BIMO) medical, scientific and product expertise to promote and protect the public health through coordinated, integrated assessments of biologics manufacturers' compliance status. CBER conducts PLIs and PAIs utilizing CGMP requirements and CBER reviewer's scientific expertise.[4]

This compliance program builds on knowledge gained during previous FDA inspections of biological drug and tissue industries. It reflects the objectives identified in FDA's Strategic Action Plan for developing and implementing new inspection approaches using a resource-efficient, risk-based approach to provide high-quality, cost-effective oversight of biological drug product manufacturing, processing and distribution to reduce risk.[5]

This approach identifies key systems and critical elements common to biological product establishments. Most biological products covered under this compliance program were identified as critical to public health and processed aseptically. These factors help form the basis for establishing appropriate inspection coverage levels under this program.

The program also establishes two inspection levels to evaluate an establishment's compliance with applicable CGMP regulations: Level I (Full)—a comprehensive evaluation of at least four systems; and Level II (Abbreviated)—an evaluation of one mandatory system plus one additional system on a rotating basis.[6] This approach is similar in concept to that set forth in CBER's CPG 7342.001—Inspection of Licensed and Unlicensed Blood Banks, Brokers, Reference Laboratories, and Contractors, which incorporates a systems-based approach covering critical elements within each system and a Level I/II inspection option.[7]

This quality management approach focuses on facilities' key operating systems, and the two-tiered inspection option provides a method to focus the inspectional coverage and resources appropriate for each inspection with applicable advisory, administrative or regulatory action taken when necessary.

Continued biennial inspections under this compliance program will:[8]
- safeguard the public health by reducing the risk of adulterated or misbranded biological products reaching the marketplace
- increase communication between industry and the agency
- provide timely feedback during inspections to improve industry compliance with CGMPs

Subsequent to implementation, CBER will evaluate this inspection program annually to determine its effectiveness and assess and improve its quality.

FDA requirements for biologics licensing standards and 21 CFR 600.3 provide biologics must be "safe, pure, and potent." Under 21 CFR 601.20, upon inspection, the production facility must demonstrate assurance the product meets these standards and complies with applicable regulations. Therefore, during the Investigational New Drug (IND) application stage, the manufacturer must develop processes and methods to ensure these attributes are in place before the product is licensed. These attributes are defined as follows:
- safety—relative freedom from harmful effect to persons affected, directly or indirectly, by a product when it is administered prudently, taking

into consideration the product's character in relation to the recipient's condition at the time
- purity—relative freedom from extraneous matter in the finished product, whether or not harmful to the recipient or deleterious to the product; purity includes, but is not limited to, relative freedom from residual moisture or other volatile and pyrogenic substances
- potency—specific product ability or capacity, as indicated by appropriate laboratory tests or adequately controlled clinical data obtained through the product's administration in the manner intended, to effect a given result

Upon BLA approval, a manufacturer receives a license to market its product in interstate commerce. The compliance and surveillance activities related to biologics licenses during the product's lifecycle are overseen by the Office of Compliance and Biologics Quality (OCBQ). OCBQ comprises four divisions, plus additional staff within OCBQ's Immediate Office of the Director (IOD):
- Division of Case Management (DCM)
- Division of Inspections and Surveillance (DIS)
- Division of Manufacturing and Product Quality (DMPQ)
- Division of Biological Standards and Quality Control (DBSQC)

OCBQ performs the following tasks and activities to ensure pre- and postapproval compliance.[9]
- ensure the quality of products regulated by CBER over their entire lifecycle, from premarket review and inspection to postmarket review, surveillance, inspection, outreach and compliance
- monitor the quality of marketed biological products through surveillance, inspections and compliance programs; review, evaluate and take appropriate compliance action, in coordination with other agency components
- review and evaluate all administrative action recommendations, including suspension, revocation, denial of license, disqualification of investigators and recommended civil and criminal actions, including seizures, injunctions and prosecution based on findings of inspections and investigations
- direct the biologic product shortages program for CBER-regulated products
- direct the recall program for CBER-regulated products
- direct CBER's bioresearch monitoring program and take appropriate compliance actions in coordination with other agency components
- direct CBER's program for Biological Product Deviation Reports (BPDRs) and reports of complications of blood collection and transfusion confirmed to be fatal
- review, evaluate and take appropriate action on manufacturing supplements submitted by manufacturers (except blood and plasma establishments), and lead preapproval and pre-license inspections supporting BLA submissions and supplements as part of the CBER managed review process
- assess the compliance status of regulated establishments within CBER's purview (compliance status checks)
- evaluate proposed proprietary names to avoid potential medication errors related to look-alike and sound-alike proprietary names and other mitigating factors that contribute to medication errors, such as unclear label abbreviations, acronyms, dose designations and error-prone label and packaging design
- provide consultative reviews of proposed product labeling
- plan and conduct tests on biological products and conduct research to develop and improve procedures to evaluate biological products' safety, efficacy and purity
- in cooperation with other center components, test biological products submitted for release by manufacturers, as appropriate
- advise the center director and other agency officials on emerging and significant compliance issues for biological products and serve as CBER's focal point for surveillance and enforcement policy
- develop, with other CBER and agency components, biological products' policies and compliance standards, including CGMP regulations; ensure the uniform interpretation of standards and evaluate industry's conformance with CGMPs in manufacturing biological products

Preapproval Compliance

CMC Change Control

During the IND stage, any changes to the manufacturing or testing process are submitted by filing information amendments to the IND, with sufficient data to justify the comparability or improvements related to manufacturing changes, prior to making the change. During product development, multiple changes are likely to arise in the manufacturing process that could impact drug product quality, safety and efficacy. Comparability studies generally are performed to demonstrate nonclinical and clinical data generated with pre-change product are equivalent to post-change product, to facilitate further development and, ultimately, support marketing approval.

An important focus while conducting comparability studies is that product quality, safety and efficacy are not impacted and/or decreased with the intended change. Comparability studies conducted during product development are influenced by such factors as the availability of validated analytical procedures and the extent of product and process knowledge, which can vary based on manufacturer experience. Due to analytical tools' limitations in early clinical development, physicochemical and biological tests alone might not be adequate to determine comparability, and it may be necessary to bridge nonclinical and/or clinical studies.

When process changes are introduced in later development stages, and no additional clinical studies are planned to support the marketing authorization, the comparability study should be as comprehensive as that for an approved product. However, some comparability study outcomes on quality attributes still may require additional nonclinical or clinical studies.

IND Safety Reporting

During premarketing, expedited safety reports are required for serious and unexpected adverse experiences associated with the biological product's use, as is the case for drugs (21 CFR 312.32). These requirements were amended in 2012 to update the definitions for safety reporting and to clarify when to submit expedited safety reports. In summary, expedited safety reporting applies to suspected adverse reactions that are both serious and unexpected and where there is a reasonable possibility of a causal relationship between the biologic and the adverse event. For other adverse events, the sponsor should collect the information and develop a process for ongoing evaluation of accumulating safety data and submitting it periodically to regulatory agencies.[10]

FDA issued final regulations addressing IND safety reporting requirements in 21 CFR Part 312. *Draft Guidance for Industry: Safety Assessment for IND Safety Reporting Guidance for Industry* (December 2015) is aimed at improving the quality of safety reports submitted to FDA by developing a systematic approach for IND safety reporting where there is a prospective identification of anticipated serious adverse events. The guidance is most applicable to sponsors managing a drug development program with multiple studies. The guidance lays out clear definitions and standards to ensure critical safety information on investigational new drugs is reported to FDA quickly and accurately, minimizing uninformative reports and enhancing reporting of meaningful, interpretable information.

Additional safety reporting guidance is available for specific biological products, such as those used in gene therapy clinical trials. In gene therapy trials, where there is heightened concern about the potential for delayed adverse events as a consequence of the transferred genetic material's persistent biological activity, long-term follow-up safety studies are recommended. Adverse events associated with gene therapy trials also may need to be reported to the National Institutes of Health (NIH), via the Recombinant DNA Advisory Committee, if the trial includes NIH-funded sites.[11] In August 2018, NIH released a proposal to amend the NIH guidelines to streamline the oversight for gene transfer research protocols. To that end, while NIH is reviewing the comments and proposals, no new submissions are being accepted, but these clinical studies are still under the oversight of FDA, Institutional Review Boards (IRBs) and other relevant approvals.[12]

BIMO

BIMO is FDA's compliance program for Good Clinical Practice (GCP) and Good Laboratory Practice (GLP) inspections during development. BIMO covers clinical investigators, IRBs, sponsors, contract research organization (CRO) monitors, *in vivo* bioequivalence laboratories and facilities and GLP facilities. Clinical inspections focus on how sponsors ensure the validity of clinical data submitted to FDA and the adherence of sponsors, CROs and monitors to applicable regulations, such as adverse event reporting and article integrity from the time of manufacture until investigator receipt. To carry out these responsibilities, BIMO staff conduct preapproval data audit inspections, investigate complaints, answer questions about GCP and help evaluate data integrity concerns.

Biological Product Naming

The nonproprietary or proper name for a new biological product,[13] as for a drug, is determined by submitting an application and fee to the United States Adopted Names Council (USANC), which is part of the American Medical Association (see www.ama-assn.org/). Sponsors should provide several selections and the naming rationale to USANC. When submitting suggested names, consideration should be given to the naming conventions used by USANC to assess submissions (i.e., use of common stems and/or syllables for existing products or product classes).[14] For biologics, CBER has developed naming conventions for certain product categories, e.g., cellular therapies, which must be followed to the extent possible. Under this naming convention, the nonproprietary name designated for each originator biological product, related biological product and biosimilar product will be a proper name that is a combination of the core name and a distinguishing suffix that is devoid of meaning and composed of four lowercase letters.[15] Thus, sponsors needing assistance may want to discuss nonproprietary name selection with

CBER prior to submission to USANC. For well-characterized proteins, certain suffixes are standard and must be included in the nonproprietary name, e.g., monoclonal antibodies use "-mab" as the final syllable.

The proprietary name for a new biological is approved by CBER and reviewed by OCBQ's Advertising and Promotional Labeling Branch (APLB). Two names may be submitted with a clear indication of the sponsor's preference. The rationale for the choice, with summaries from marketing research studies, should be included. These studies should assess similar-sounding names and how names may be interpreted, including foreign language translations. The application also should include full descriptions of the product, therapeutic category and/or indication and the setting for use (e.g., doctor's office, hospital or home). Proprietary name submissions can be made any time after Phase 2, but a recommendation made prior to product approval will be reevaluated within 90 days of approval to ensure no new products have entered the marketplace that could give rise to confusion because of similarity in spelling or pronunciation.

Pre-License Inspection

A pre-license inspection entails inspecting all facilities involved in the drug substance and drug product manufacture and testing for each biologic CBER has not yet licensed or approved. These inspections apply to the company itself and any contract sites. The inspection also can include establishments that already have one or more biologics license(s) or other product approvals. *PHS Act* Section 351 and *FD&C Act* Section 704 allow the regulatory authority to conduct inspections at any biological product manufacturing establishment.

CBER's general policy is that a pre-license or preapproval inspection will be necessary for a BLA or supplement if any of the following criteria are met:

- The manufacturer does not hold an active US license or, in the case of a contract manufacturer, the facility is not approved for use in manufacturing a licensed product.
- FDA has not inspected the establishment in the last two years.
- The previous inspection revealed significant GMP deficiencies in areas related to the processes in the submission (similar processes) or systemic problems, such as quality control or quality assurance oversight.
- The establishment is performing a significant manufacturing step(s) in new (unlicensed) areas using different equipment (representing a process change). This would include currently dedicated areas that have not been approved as multiproduct facilities, buildings or areas.
- The manufacturing process is sufficiently different (new production methods, specialized equipment or facilities) from that of other approved products produced by the establishment.
- Other points to be considered: differences in the process (e.g., different types of columns) or particulars (e.g., different production cell lines) that require an on-site GMP compliance determination; analytical methods that are accurate or sensitive enough to detect problems and if different equipment or processes are being used.

Even if the above criteria otherwise would call for an inspection, the inspection may be waived if the establishment only performs ancillary testing (testing not impacting drug substance or drug product release) for the submission under consideration. An inspection should not be waived if the applicant receives a request to submit additional information that normally would not be submitted to a BLA or supplement.

In some cases, CBER relies on inspections to obtain validation and facility information that previously may have been submitted in the BLA; thus, greater coordination and efficiency are required in planning and conducting inspections. However, some BLAs and supplements include manufacturing establishments that use production areas common to other licensed products, so conducting a pre-license or preapproval inspection may not be necessary. In such cases, both the director of the division with product responsibility and the director of OCBQ's DMPQ must agree to waive an inspection, or the inspection should be scheduled according to established procedures.

Inspections for biologics are much the same as those for drugs. Systems-based inspections include review of:
- quality systems (e.g., change controls, deviations/investigations, training, etc.)
- buildings and facilities
- equipment cleaning and maintenance
- laboratory controls

In addition, the BLA's CMC section will be compared to manufacturing site documents to establish the submission's accuracy and integrity. Because of biological products' manufacturing process complexity, the investigator is likely to spend considerably more time observing the process than is typical for small-molecule inspections. The investigator usually works with the manufacturer to schedule an appropriate time to conduct the inspection, so the entire manufacturing process can be observed; any delay by the sponsor in this activity may delay BLA review. Another difference is the product specialist responsible for the BLA's CMC section review generally will participate in a biologics inspection.

The regulations require Annual Reports, provided within 60 days after the application approval anniversary date, for products marketed under a BLA for certain situations, such as: making changes to the application (21 CFR 601.12(d)); providing information on pediatric studies (21 CFR 601.28); and providing status reports on postmarket study requirements related to clinical safety, clinical efficacy, clinical pharmacology or nonclinical toxicology (21 CFR 601.70).

The *Food and Drug Administration Amendments Act of 2007* (*FDAAA*) authorized FDA to require additional postmarketing studies to assess known safety risks, including both serious risk signals and potential serious risks associated with the drug's use. *FDAAA* also gave FDA authority to require labeling changes based on such studies' results. *FD&C Act* Section 505(o)(3)(E)(ii), enacted under *FDAAA*, stipulates the following information be provided in the Annual Report for required postmarketing studies: a timetable for the completion of each study; periodic reports on required studies' status, including whether enrollment has begun, the number of participants enrolled and whether any difficulties in completing the study have been encountered; and registration information with respect to clinical trial certification.[16] In addition, *FDAAA* requires applicants to report on each study "otherwise undertaken by the applicant to investigate a safety issue." The status of other postmarketing commitments (e.g., those concerning chemistry, manufacturing, production controls and studies conducted on an applicant's own initiative) are not required to be reported under Sections 314.81(b)(2)(vii) and 601.70.

Once a required postmarketing study commitment has been made, an Annual Report is due each year within 60 days after the anniversary date and must be accompanied by a completed transmittal Form FDA 2252. Sponsors must continue to report on the commitment's progress until the postmarketing study is completed or terminated, unless the postmarketing study commitment is either no longer feasible or no longer would provide useful information (as agreed with FDA). Failure to comply with the timetable, the periodic reporting submissions or other requirements of Section 505(o)(3)(E)(ii) will be considered a violation unless the applicant demonstrates good cause for the noncompliance (only as agreed with FDA). Violations could result in civil penalties of up to $250,000 per violation, and the penalties can be increased (i.e., doubled) if the violation continues for more than 30 days, and can continue to double for subsequent 30-day periods.

Inspections[17]

After approval, two other types of inspections may take place: routine, periodic inspections that should occur every two years (biennial) and directed (for cause) inspections. CBER and ORA have built a partnership to focus resources on inspectional and compliance issues in the biologics area. To accomplish this, Team Biologics, as mentioned earlier, inspects licensed biological drug and device product facilities regulated by CBER. The goal of Team Biologics is to ensure biological products' quality and safety and resolve inconsistencies quickly.

Import/Export

CBER oversees biologic products' import and export to determine whether imported products, drugs and devices regulated by the center comply with the requirements of the *FD&C Act*, the *PHS Act* and the regulations promulgated under these statutes. Imported products regulated by FDA are subject to inspection at the time of entry by the US Customs and Border Protection (CBP) (https://www.cbp.gov/). Shipments found not to comply with the law are subject to detention. For imports, FDA works with CBP to verify licensure; FDA may perform random sampling and will issue import alerts for noncompliant products. A foreign manufacturer must have a US license to import a biological product into the US. Per FDA's Regulatory Procedures Manual, Chapter 9, Subchapter 9.5, "Importation of Biological Products," licensed biologics that have been lot-released (or are exempt) by CBER may be imported into the US and may proceed through CBP without FDA examination. Entry documents for IND biologics must declare a valid, active IND number. Products in short supply also may be imported under 21 CFR 601.22; however, these products must be registered with CBER, which CBP will verify. Under 7 CFR Chapter III, overseen by the US Department of Agriculture (USDA), biological products also may require an Animal and Plant Health Inspection Service (APHIS) permit to enter the country if the product contains certain microbial, plant- or animal-derived materials or is otherwise a regulated product, such as a genetically engineered organism.

A licensed biologic may be exported without FDA authorization (*Guidance for Industry: FDA Export Certificates* (August 2002)) and in accordance with *FD&C Act* Section 801(e) Exports or 802 Export of Certain Unapproved Products or *PHS Act* Section 351(h), which states a biologic is not adulterated or misbranded if it:
- accords to the foreign purchaser's specifications
- is not in conflict with the laws of the country to which it is intended for export
- is labeled on the outside of the shipping package that it is intended for export
- is not sold or offered for sale in domestic commerce

FDA supplies a Certificate to Foreign Government, if requested, for the export of products that can be marketed legally in the US. It also supplies a Certificate of Exportability for the export of products that cannot be marketed legally in the US but meet *FD&C Act* requirements.

Import for export, per the *FDA Export Reform and Enhancement Act* of 1996, allows the importation of drug and device components for incorporation into a finished product that then can be exported in accordance with 801, 802 and *PHS Act* 351(h).

Postapproval Changes

In accordance with *FD&C Act* Section 506A(b), the effect of any postapproval CMC changes on a product's identity, strength, quality, purity or potency, as they may relate to the product's safety or efficacy, must be assessed.

Before distributing a product made following a change, sponsors are required to demonstrate, through appropriate validation and/or other clinical or nonclinical laboratory studies, the lack of the change's adverse effect on identity, strength, quality, purity or potency as they may relate to the product's safety or effectiveness.

Sponsors should assess the change to determine the correct product reporting category:

- Prior Approval Supplement (PAS)—major changes that require supplement submission and approval prior to distribution of the product made using the change (21 CFR 601.12(b)). A PAS is used to report changes with substantial potential to affect a product's identity, strength, quality, purity or potency adversely as they may relate to the product's safety or effectiveness. Examples include: a change in manufacturing processes or analytical methods resulting in a change of specification limits; a change to larger-scale production; major construction; a change in the stability protocol or acceptance criteria; and extension of the expiration dating period.
- Changes Being Effected in 30 Days (CBE-30)—moderate changes (CBE-30) require a supplement to FDA 30 days prior to distribution (21 CFR 601.12(c)(3)). A CBE-30 is used to report changes with moderate potential to affect a product's identity, strength, quality, purity or potency adversely as they may relate to the product's safety or effectiveness. Examples include: addition of a duplicated process chain or unit process; change in the testing site from one facility to another (e.g., from a contract laboratory to the sponsor; from an existing contract laboratory to a new contract laboratory; from the sponsor to a new contract laboratory).
- Changes Being Effected in 0 Day (CBE-0)—these changes have minimal potential to affect a product's identity, strength, quality, purity or potency adversely as they may relate to the product's safety or effectiveness. A CBE-0 supplement would be received by FDA before, or concurrently with, distribution of the product made using the change. A CBE-0 typically is filed when a manufacturer wants to inform FDA immediately, even though the change does not require FDA approval.
- Annual Report—minor changes can be included in the Annual Report, which is submitted within 60 days of the product's anniversary date. These are changes with minimal potential to affect a product's identity, strength, quality, purity or potency adversely as they may relate to the product's safety or effectiveness. Examples include: an increase in the scale of aseptic manufacturing for finished product without a change in equipment, e.g., increased number of vials filled; modifications in analytical procedures with no change in the basic test methodology or existing release specifications, provided the change is supported by validation data; and establishment of a new working cell bank derived from a previously approved master cell bank according to an SOP on file in the approved license application.

A comparability protocol is a well-defined, detailed, written plan for assessing the effect of specific CMC changes on a particular drug product's identity, strength, quality, purity and potency as they may relate to the product's safety and effectiveness. A comparability protocol describes the changes it covers and specifies the tests and studies to be performed, including establishing analytical procedures and acceptance criteria to demonstrate specified CMC changes do not affect the product adversely. However, it is important to note comparability protocols are not recommended for CMC changes that cannot be evaluated definitively, require a new IND, or require efficacy, safety (clinical or nonclinical) or pharmacokinetic/pharmacodynamic data to evaluate the change's effect (e.g., certain formulation changes or clinical or nonclinical studies to qualify new impurities).

By using a comparability protocol previously reviewed by FDA, the sponsor may be able to file certain CMC changes under a less-restrictive reporting category, e.g., a change that normally would be a PAS may be allowed as a CBE-30 if it has been approved already as a comparability protocol. While submitting a comparability protocol is not required for changes, in many cases, it will facilitate the subsequent CMC change implementation and reporting requirements, which could result in moving a product into distribution more quickly. For marketing applications or postapproval implementations, "Submission of a comparability protocol in an original application or prior approval supplement (PAS) allows the agency to review a description of one or more proposed CMC postapproval changes, supporting information including any analysis and risk assessment activities, a plan to implement the change(s) and, if appropriate, a proposed reduced reporting category for the change(s)."[18] The comparability protocol should include a summary of the changes, description and rationale for the proposed change, supporting information and analysis, comparability protocol for the proposed change and proposed reduced reporting category.[19]

An FDA review committee will determine whether the changes reported in the supplement require on-site review. If the review committee determines an inspection is necessary for one or more establishments included in the supplement, the inspection(s) will be performed prior to sending the action letter for the supplement. Failure to comply with the reporting requirements outlined in 21 CFR 601.12 could result in an FDA request that all changes be submitted as a PAS. Two examples of failure to comply are the constant downgrading of changes (e.g., from a PAS to a CBE) and failing to supply sufficient information to support the changes.

Similarly, under 21 CFR 601.12(f), changes to a product package label, container label and package insert require one of the following:
- submission of a supplement with FDA approval needed prior to product distribution, e.g., the addition of superiority claims or changes based on additional preclinical and/or postmarketing clinical studies
- submission of a supplement with product distribution allowed at the time of supplement submission (does not require a 30-day waiting period), e.g., strengthening cautionary statements or instructions
- submission of the final printed label in an Annual Report, e.g., editorial changes and changes in how the product is supplied, provided there is no change in dosage form or strength

Additionally, under 21 CFR 601.12(f)(4), changes to advertising and promotional labeling must comply with the provisions of 21 CFR 314.81(b)(3)(i), which require sponsors to submit specimens of mailing pieces and any other labeling or advertising devised for a drug product's promotion to FDA at the time of initial dissemination of the labeling, and at the time of initial publication of the advertisement for a prescription drug product. Mailing pieces and labeling designed to contain samples of a drug product are required for the submission to be considered complete, except the drug product sample (see Chapter 28 Biologics Labeling, Advertising and Promotion for more on labeling).

Postmarketing Reporting Requirements

Expedited postmarketing reporting requirements for serious and unexpected adverse experiences from all sources (domestic and foreign) related to biologics are similar to those for drugs and are stated in 21 CFR 600.80 and 600.81. Reporting requirements include: Postmarketing 15-day "Alert Reports," which include reports based on scientific literature; Postmarketing 15-day Alert Report follow-ups, which also are required to be reported within 15 days of receiving new information; and periodic adverse experience reports. The reporting format for individual case study reports is the MedWatch mandatory Form FDA 3500A. However, adverse events related to vaccines must be reported on a separate form under the Vaccine Adverse Event Reporting System (VAERS). Foreign adverse experience may be reported using either Form FDA 3500A or, if preferred, a CIOMS I form. Sponsors may request waivers of the requirement to file Form FDA 3500A for nonserious, expected adverse experiences; however, FDA does not intend to grant waivers within one year of licensure for new biological molecular entities, blood products, plasma derivatives or vaccines. For biological combination products, reports must be filed with both relevant centers. Adverse events related to vaccines also are monitored by the Centers for Disease Control (CDC). The VAERS reporting system is not linked to the vaccine injury compensation program.

Periodic adverse experience reports (PADERs) include serious and unexpected adverse experience summaries as well as reports of nonserious expected adverse experiences. Periodic reports are made at quarterly intervals for three years from the date of BLA issuance, and annually thereafter. The licensed manufacturer is required to submit each quarterly report within 30 days of the close of the quarter (the first quarter beginning on the date of BLA issuance) and each Annual Report within 60 days of the anniversary date.

Distribution reports for biological products, including vaccines, also are required under 21 CFR 600.81; this requirement is unique for biologics with approved BLAs. The distribution report includes the bulk, fill and label lot numbers for the total number of dosage units of each strength or potency distributed, expiration date, distribution date and quantity returned. The licensed manufacturer submits this report every six months to either CBER or CDER, as applicable. *Guidance for Industry: Electronic Submission of Lot Distribution Reports*, issued March 2015, outlines the electronic submission requirements for lot distribution reports. The information required for the distribution reports remains the same, but electronic submission requirements now are formalized.[20]

Risk Assessment[21]

Risk assessment should occur throughout a product's lifecycle, from early potential product identification and preclinical testing, through the premarketing development process and postapproval during marketing. Premarketing risk assessment is a key step in this process, and product approval requires adequate assessment of the product's underlying risks and benefits. The adequacy of this risk assessment is a matter of both quantity (ensuring enough patients are studied) and quality (the appropriateness of the assessments performed, appropriateness and breadth of the patient populations studied and how results are analyzed). In reaching a final approvability decision, both existing risk information and any outstanding safety questions are considered in a product's risk assessment and weighed against its demonstrated benefits. The fewer a product's demonstrated benefits, the less acceptable are its higher levels of demonstrated risks.

For postapproval risk assessment, labeling and routine reporting requirements are sufficient to mitigate risks and preserve benefits for the majority of approved products. However, in other cases, FDA has requested additional risk minimization strategies, originally called Risk Minimization Action Plans, or RiskMAPs. *FDAAA* created Risk Evaluation and Mitigation Strategies (REMS). A REMS is a strategy to manage a drug or biological product's serious safety risk(s) while preserving the product's benefits. Proposed changes to approved REMS should be submitted as follows:
- revisions, to be submitted as "REMS Revisions" and documented in the next Annual Report, or
- REMS modifications, which are categorized as either:
  o minor, to be submitted as a CBE-30 supplement, defined as changes that may affect the risk message nominally
  o major, to be submitted as a PAS, defined as changes that may substantially affect the risk message and/or substantially change REMS requirements

FDA also has the authority to apply a REMS retroactively and require sponsors to submit a REMS for an already approved product.

A REMS can include a Medication Guide, a Patient Package Insert, a communication plan for healthcare professionals, various Elements to Assure Safe Use (ETASU) and an implementation system. The Medication Guide is the most common REMS component, now required for more than 80 approved drugs.[22] Medication Guides are utilized when specific information is necessary to prevent serious adverse effects, when patient decision making should include knowledge about a serious side effect, or if patient adherence to directions for use is essential for the product's effectiveness. The responsibility for ensuring Medication Guides are available to patients lies with the sponsor, not the pharmacist.

ETASU may include one or more of the following requirements:
- Healthcare providers who prescribe the drug must have particular training or experience or be specially certified.
- Pharmacies, practitioners or healthcare settings dispensing the drug must be specially certified.
- The drug is dispensed to patients only in certain healthcare settings, such as hospitals.
- The drug is dispensed to patients with evidence or other documentation of safe use conditions, such as laboratory test results.
- Each patient using the drug is subject to certain monitoring requirements.
- Each patient using the drug is enrolled in a registry.

Biological Product Deviation Reporting (BPDR)
Licensed biological product manufacturers are required to report events representing unexpected or unforeseeable events or deviations from CGMPs, applicable regulations or applicable standards or established specifications that may affect a product's safety, purity or potency per 21 CFR 600.14. Prior to 2001, this was termed "error and accident" reporting. The BPDR is reported on Form FDA 3486—Biological Product Deviation Report Form—and must include the appropriate event type deviation code. The report must not be dated more than 45 calendar days from the date of discovery of information reasonably suggesting a reportable event has occurred. Reportable events are those that occur at the sponsor's facility or a facility under the sponsor's control, e.g., a contract manufacturer, and include events for distributed products no longer under the sponsor's control. Therefore, investigation procedures for an unexplained discrepancy or failure of a lot to meet any of its specifications should include provisions for timely investigation; an appropriate corrective action plan to prevent recurrence; procedures to gain control of unsuitable products in a timely manner; and appropriate disposition of all affected products (in-date and expired). All BPDRs should be submitted to OCBQ, except those for biological products transferred to CDER starting in 2003.

FDA Enforcement Actions

Regulatory Action Letters
CBER may issue several types of regulatory action letters. These letters ordinarily are issued to biological product manufacturers in an attempt to stop practices that violate the regulations and promote corrective action. Examples of regulatory action letters issued by CBER include:
- Warning Letters

- Notice of Initiation of Disqualification Proceedings and Opportunity to Explain (NIDPOE) Letters
- Untitled Letters
- Administrative License Action Letters
- Orders of Retention, Recall, Destruction and Cessation of Manufacturing Related to Human Cell, Tissue, and Cellular and Tissue-Based Products (HCT/Ps)

Warning Letters are issued for violations of regulatory significance to achieve voluntary compliance. Significant violations are those that may lead to enforcement action if not corrected promptly and adequately. A Warning Letter is issued to a responsible individual or firm to establish prior notice that the agency considers one or more products, practices, processes or other activities to be in violation of the *FD&C Act*, its implementing regulations and/or other federal statutes. A Warning Letter is one of FDA's principal means of achieving prompt voluntary *FD&C Act* compliance.

A NIDPOE Letter informs the recipient clinical investigator the agency is initiating an administrative proceeding to determine whether the investigator should be disqualified from receiving investigational products pursuant to FDA regulations. Generally, the agency issues a NIDPOE letter when it believes it has evidence the clinical investigator repeatedly or deliberately violated FDA's regulations governing proper clinical study conduct involving investigational products or submitted false information to the sponsor.

An Untitled Letter is an initial correspondence with a sponsor citing violations that do not meet the regulatory significance threshold for a Warning Letter. CBER has issued Untitled Letters, for example, after reviewing a manufacturer's advertising and promotional labeling, after an inspection under CBER's BIMO program or by Team Biologics and as a result of internet website surveillance.

Administrative License Action Letters include license revocation and suspension. License revocation is the cancellation of a license and withdrawal of the authorization to introduce biological products into interstate commerce. Examples of revocation grounds include: FDA inability to gain access for inspection; manufacturer failure to report a change as required; product or establishment failure to conform to standards in the license or comply with CGMPs; or the product not being safe or effective, or being misbranded. Except in the case of license suspension or willful violations, CBER will issue a Notice of Intent to Revoke License Letter and provide the sponsor an opportunity to demonstrate or achieve compliance before initiating revocation proceedings and issuing a license revocation letter. The licensee has 10 days to notify FDA of its commitment to, and plans for, achieving compliance, and then has 30 days to submit a comprehensive report with rigid timetables.

License suspension is a summary action that provides for immediate withdrawal, without prior notice or a hearing, of the authorization to introduce biological products into interstate commerce when there are reasonable grounds to believe the product is a danger to public health (*PHS Act* Section 351). The Department of Justice does not need to concur. All product shipping and manufacturing activities must cease until the license is reactivated.

Recalls

Recalls generally are voluntary sponsor acts because FDA has limited statutory authority to prescribe a recall. However, the *National Childhood Vaccine Injury Act* of 1986 amended the *PHS Act* to provide recall authority for biological products (42 U.S. 262). Therefore, FDA can order a recall if the biological product constitutes an imminent or substantial hazard to public health per *PHS Act* Section 351(a), or if it is considered a "dangerous" medical device per the *FD&C Act*. Recalls can be ordered for any reason, but if a recall is due to misbranding or adulteration, FDA should be notified to prevent further action. Companies should work closely with the agency during a recall. There are four key stages in the recall process: discovery, planning, implementation and termination of the recall event. Final disposition of the recalled product should be discussed with FDA and typically involves destruction.

Judicial Enforcement

FDA's civil and criminal enforcement actions include:
- Seizure—an action taken to remove a product from commerce because it is in violation of the law. FDA initiates a seizure by filing a complaint with the US District Court where the product is located. A US Marshal then is directed by the court to take possession, i.e., seize the goods where they are found, until the matter is resolved.
- Injunction—a civil action taken against an individual or firm seeking to stop continued production or distribution of a violative product until the firm complies with FDA requirements.
- Prosecution—a criminal action taken as the result of acts prohibited in the *FD&C Act* that can be directed at the responsible persons in management.

Conclusion

Compliance and surveillance activities related to biologics licenses during the product lifecycle are overseen by CBER's Office of Compliance and Biologics Quality. Manufacturers are required to comply with FDA's preapproval and postapproval requirements, and noncompliance may include REMS, Medication Guides or postmarketing studies. If CBER identifies areas of noncompliance, it may issue one of several types of regulatory action letters, up to and including license revocation to stop practices found to be in violation of the regulations and to promote corrective action. CBER also has options for judicial enforcement, including seizure, injunction and prosecution, if warranted.

References
1. 21 CFR 600.3 Biological Products: General Provisions—Definitions. FDA website. https://www.accessdata.fda.gov/scripts/cdrh/cfdocs/cfcfr/CFRSearch.cfm?fr=600.3. Accessed 2 March 2019.
2. FDA. Office of Compliance and Biologics Quality (OCBQ). FDA website. http://www.fda.gov/BiologicsBloodVaccines/GuidanceComplianceRegulatoryInformation/ucm331317.htm Accessed 2 March 2019.
3. Biological Products FY2015 Program Alignment Action Plan. https://www.fda.gov/AboutFDA/CentersOffices/ucm416820.htm. Accessed 2 March 2019.
4. Compliance Program Guidance Manual—Inspection of Biological Drug Products (CBER) 7345.848. FDA website. https://www.fda.gov/downloads/BiologicsBloodVaccines/GuidanceComplianceRegulatoryInformation/ComplianceActivities/Enforcement/CompliancePrograms/UCM095419.pdf. Accessed 2 March 2019.
5. Op cit 2.
6. Op cit 4.
7. SOPP 8410: Determining When Pre-License/Pre-Approval Inspections are Necessary (September 2018). FDA website. https://www.fda.gov/BiologicsBloodVaccines/GuidanceComplianceRegulatoryInformation/ProceduresSOPPs/ucm073506.htm. Accessed 2 March 2019.
8. Ibid.
9. Op cit 2.
10. *Guidance for Industry: E2F Development Safety Update Report* (August 2011). FDA website. https://www.fda.gov/downloads/Drugs/GuidanceComplianceRegulatoryInformation/Guidances/UCM073109.pdf. Accessed 2 March 2019.
11. *Oversight and Review of Clinical Gene Transfer Protocols. Assessing the Role of the Recombinant DNA Advisory Committee.* Editors: Lenzi RN, Altevogt BM and Gostin LO. Washington (DC): National Academies Press (US); 2014. ISBN-13:978-0-309-29662-5.
12. Proposal to Streamline Review of Gene Therapy Trials and Restore the Original Vision of the RAC—August 2018. https://osp.od.nih.gov/biotechnology/nih-guidelines/. Accessed 2 March 2019.
13. *Guidance for Industry: Nonproprietary Naming of Biological Products* (January 2017). FDA website. https://www.fda.gov/downloads/drugs/guidances/ucm459987.pdf. Accessed 2 March 2019.
14. *Guidance for Industry: Contents of a Complete Submission for the Evaluation of Proprietary Names* (April 2016). FDA website. https://www.fda.gov/downloads/Drugs/Guidances/ucm075068.pdf. Accessed 2 March 2019.
15. Op cit 13.
16. *Guidance for Industry: Postmarketing Studies and Clinical Trials—Implementation of Section 505(o)(3) of the Federal Food, Drug, and Cosmetic Act* (April 2011). FDA website. https://www.fda.gov/downloads/Drugs/GuidanceComplianceRegulatoryInformation/Guidances/UCM172001.pdf. Accessed 2 March 2019.
17. Op cit 3.
18. *Comparability Protocols for Human Drugs and Biologics: Chemistry, Manufacturing, and Controls Information Guidance for Industry: Draft Guidance for Industry* (April 2016). FDA website. https://www.fda.gov/downloads/Drugs/GuidanceComplianceRegulatoryInformation/Guidances/UCM496611.pdf. Accessed 2 March 2019.
19. Ibid.
20. *Electronic Submission of Lot Distribution Reports: Guidance for Industry* (March 2015). FDA website. https://www.fda.gov/downloads/biologicsbloodvaccines/guidancecomplianceregulatoryinformation/guidances/general/ucm412006.pdf. Accessed 2 March 2019.
21. *Risk Evaluation and Mitigation Strategies: Modifications and Revision: Guidance for Industry* (April 2015). FDA website. https://www.fda.gov/downloads/drugs/guidances/ucm441226.pdf. Accessed 2 March 2019.
22. Approved Risk Evaluation and Mitigation Strategies (REMS). FDA website. https://www.accessdata.fda.gov/scripts/cder/rems/. Accessed 2 March 2019.

Chapter 14

Biosimilars

Updated by Nathalie Innocent, MS, RAC and Jennifer Wilhelm, MSc, MBA, RAC

OBJECTIVES

❑ Learn basic concepts of biosimilar regulatory submissions

❑ Understand the provisions of the *Biologics Price Competition and Innovation Act* and its impact on biosimilar approvals

❑ Understand biosimilar application similarities and differences compared to biologics submissions

❑ Review US Food and Drug Administration recommendations for developing biosimilars, including requirements to support regulatory submissions

❑ Understand the abbreviated Biologics License Application pathway used for biosimilar approvals under *Public Health Service Act (PHS Act)* Section 351(k)

LAWS, REGULATIONS AND GUIDELINES COVERED IN THIS CHAPTER

❑ *Federal Food, Drug, and Cosmetic Act* of 1938 (*FD&C Act*)

❑ *Patient Protection and Affordable Care Act* of 2010 (*Affordable Care Act*) (including *Biologics Price Competition and Innovation Act (BPCI Act)*)

❑ *Public Health Service Act (PHS Act)* Section 351, including new Section (k) Licensure of Biological Products as Biosimilar or Interchangeable

❑ *Biosimilar User Fee Act* of 2012 (*BsUFA*)

❑ 21 CFR 210 Current Good Manufacturing Practice in Manufacturing, Processing, Packing, or Holding of Drugs, General

❑ 21 CFR 211 Good Manufacturing Practice for Finished Pharmaceuticals

❑ 21 CFR 600 Biological Products: General

❑ 21 CFR 601 Biologics Licensing

❑ 21 CFR 610 General Biological Products Standards

❑ 21 CFR 312 Investigational New Drug Application

❑ 21 CFR 314 Applications for FDA Approval to Market a New Drug

❑ 21 CFR 25 Environmental Impact Considerations

❑ *ICH Final Concept Paper Q5E: Comparability of Biotechnological/Biological Products Subject to Changes in Their Manufacturing Process* (February 2002)

Chapter 14

- ICH Q5E Comparability of Biotechnological/Biological Products Subject to Changes in Their Manufacturing Process (November 2004)

- Draft Guidance for Industry: Reference Product Exclusivity for Biological Products Filed Under Section 351(a) of the PHS Act (August 2014)

- Guidance for Industry: Scientific Considerations in Demonstrating Biosimilarity to a Reference Product (April 2015)

- Guidance for Industry: Quality Considerations in Demonstrating Biosimilarity of a Therapeutic Protein Product to a Reference Product (April 2015)

- Guidance for Industry: Questions and Answers on Biosimilar Development and the BPCI Act (December 2018)

- Draft Guidance for Industry: New and Revised Draft Q&As on Biosimilar Development and the BPCI Act (December 2018)

- Guidance for Industry: Formal Meetings Between the FDA and Biosimilar Biological Product Sponsors or Applicant (November 2015)

- Guidance for Industry: Labeling for Biosimilar Products (July 2018)

- Guidance for Industry: Clinical Pharmacology Data to Support a Demonstration of Biosimilarity to a Reference Product (December 2016)

- Draft Guidance for Industry Implementation of the 'Deemed to be a License' Provision of the Biologics Price Competition and Innovation Act of 2009

- The United States Pharmacopeial Convention, 2016, Guiding Principles for Coining United States Adopted Names for Drugs

Introduction

The *Biologics Price Competition and Innovation Act* (*BPCI Act*)[1] was signed into law 23 March 2010 as part of the *Patient Protection and Affordable Care Act*.[2] The *BPCI Act* amended the *Public Health Service Act* (*PHS Act*)[3] by inserting Section 351(k), which created an abbreviated pathway for biological products that are highly similar to, or interchangeable with, products approved by the US Food and Drug Administration (FDA). Under Section 351(k), a proposed biosimilar product can rely on certain already existing knowledge regarding the reference product's safety, purity and potency to support a Biologics License Application (BLA).

Due to the significant cost of biological product development and product cost to patients, the *BPCI Act* was implemented to reduce the research and development requirements to make less-expensive alternative products available. Until the *BPCI Act*, an abbreviated pathway existed only for products approved under the *Food, Drug, and Cosmetic Act* (*FD&C Act*), not those approved under the *PHS Act*.

The *BPCI Act*'s aim parallels that of the *Drug Price Competition and Patent Term Restoration Act* of 1984 (*Hatch-Waxman Act*),[4] which established the abbreviated approval pathway for drug products at *FD&C Act* Sections 505(b)(2) and 505(j).[5] Both of these acts were implemented to ensure this balance between innovation and competition. However, while the abbreviated drug approval pathway under the *FD&C Act* requires the product's active pharmaceutical ingredient and formulation to be identical to the reference product in order to claim 'sameness,' 'similarity' or 'comparability,' for biosimilar biological products, the abbreviated drug approval does not mean the products are identical. The *BPCI Act* was intended to strike a balance between access and innovation, providing a period of exclusivity for originator biologics and enabling a pathway for competitive biosimilars once exclusivity periods have lapsed. The new Section 351(k) allows FDA to rely on certain available data established by a reference biological product it has approved through a BLA under Section 351(a)[6] during the biosimilar product approval process. To qualify for the abbreviated pathway, the sponsor must provide data demonstrating the biosimilar product's quality attributes are, among other things, highly similar to an already approved biological product. A detailed history of the regulation of biological product development may be found in Chapter 25.

Biological products' complexity differs significantly from chemical products, and related scientific and regulatory issues need to be taken into account when developing a program (see Chapter 25). Individual versions of biological products can differ in: a) their primary amino acid sequence, b) modifications of amino acids such as glycosylation status or other changes and c) higher order structure. Small deviations in manufacturing conditions, such as temperature, pH, nutrient mix sustaining the production cultures, etc., may change molecular key sites necessary for the molecule's intended mechanism of action (e.g., receptor binding, effector cell activation, immunogenicity). Each small modification could have a major impact on the product's safety and effectiveness, which needs to be determined during the development program. During product development, a stepwise approach is taken to eliminate residual uncertainty, starting with the extensive characterization of quality attributes followed by nonclinical testing and a product-specific clinical study program aimed at eliminating any remaining uncertainty. Formulation and environmental factors, such as light, temperature, moisture and packaging can influence protein modifications and higher structure. Additionally, impurities—process- and/or product-related—can influence an adverse event's occurrence and severity, including an immune reaction to the proposed biosimilar product. A proposed biosimilar product will not be considered acceptable as a biosimilar product if the modifications lead to clinically meaningful differences (see *Guidance for Industry: Scientific Considerations in Demonstrating Biosimilarity to a Reference Product*).[9]

Since the US biosimilars regulation is fairly new, much of the guidance aligning the regulations' interpretation and providing specific considerations to be taken into account still is under development. FDA continually issues new guidance addressing various biosimilar development aspects and has identified priorities as part of their Biosimilars Action Plan: Balancing Innovation and Competition, with key deliverables to be implemented over the coming years. Therefore, by the time this book is published, new guidance not covered in this chapter likely will have been published. However, regulatory professionals strive to stay current with guidance updates by the various means available.[7,8]

Key Terms and Concepts

The biosimilars regulation and assessment process introduces specific terminology. Key terms and concepts include:

- biosimilar or biosimilarity—For the purpose of a biological product subject to a Section 351(k) application, a biosimilar product is a) a "biological product that is highly similar to the reference product notwithstanding minor differences in clinically inactive components" and b) there are "no clinically meaningful differences between the biological product and the reference product in terms of safety, purity, and potency of the product."[10]
- bridging studies—Studies conducted to provide nonclinical, clinical or analytical data to allow data to be extrapolated based on existing data for the reference product. In *Guidance for Industry: Questions and Answers Regarding Implementation of the Biologics Price Competition and Innovation Act of 2009*,[11] FDA addresses the issue of using comparative nonclinical or clinical data from a non-US licensed product. Although certain information available from non-US comparators can be used, sponsors need to provide adequate comparative data linking the non-US licensed comparator to a US-licensed reference product and a scientific justification regarding the relevance of the non-US comparator's data. More specifically, FDA states: "As a scientific matter, the type of bridging data needed will always include data from analytical studies (e.g., structural and functional data) that directly compare all three products (i.e., the proposed biosimilar product, the US-licensed reference product, and the non-US-licensed comparator product), and is likely to also include bridging clinical pharmacokinetics (PK) and/or pharmacodynamics (PD) study data for all three products. All three pairwise comparisons should meet the prespecified acceptance criteria for analytical and PK and/or PD similarity."[12]
- comparable/comparability—As defined under the International Council on Harmonisation's (ICH) Q5E, "A conclusion that products have highly similar quality attributes before and after manufacturing process changes and that no adverse impact on the safety or efficacy, including immunogenicity, of the drug occurred." Although ICH Q5E addresses comparability of changes the same manufacturer made during product development, the principle applies to biosimilar products.[13]
- interchangeability: The interchangeability demonstration follows a higher standard than required to demonstrate biosimilarity. The proposed biosimilar sponsor has to demonstrate biosimilarity to a reference product and show no meaningful clinical differences are observed between the products. Additionally, if the biological product is administered more than once, the sponsor needs to demonstrate the risk of alternating or switching between the reference product and the biosimilar is the same as taking the reference product without alternation or switching (*PHS Act* Section 351(k)(4)).[14]
- reference product: The reference product is "the single biological product licensed" under *PHS Act* Section 351(a) "against which a biological product is evaluated in an application submitted under subsection" 351(k).[15]
- totality-of-the-evidence: FDA first introduced its approach to scientific evidence in *Guidance for Industry: Providing Clinical Evidence of Effectiveness for Human Drug and Biological Products* (May 1998).[16] This approach includes "considerations of both the quantity and quality of the evidence to support effectiveness." Specifically, in determining biosimilarity, "FDA will consider the totality of the

Table 14-1. BsUFA Fees Financial Year 2019a

BPD	Initial	$ 185,409
	Annual	$ 185,409
		$ 370,818
Application	With clinical data	$1,746745
	Without clinical data	$ 873,373
Product		$ 304,162

Abbreviations: BsUFA—Biosimilars User Fee Act; BPD—Biosimilar Biological Product Development
a. Biosimilar User Fee Act, Latest News. FDA website. http://www.fda.gov/ForIndustry/UserFees/BiosimilarUserFeeActBsUFA/. Accessed 1 April 2019.

data and information submitted in the application, including structural and functional characterization, nonclinical evaluation, human PK and PD data, clinical immunogenicity data, and comparative clinical study(ies) data. The FDA intends to use a risk-based approach to evaluate all available data and information submitted in support of the biosimilarity of the proposed product."[17]

Biosimilar User Fee Act

Following *BPCI Act* enactment, the *FD&C Act* was amended to include the *Biosimilar User Fee Act* of 2012 (*BsUFA*),[20] which was introduced as part of the *Food and Drug Administration Safety and Innovation Act* (*FDASIA*) (Public Law 112-144).[21] *BsUFA* permitted FDA to collect fees for the Biosimilar Biological Product Development (BPD), October 2012–September 2017, and was amended by the *Biosimilar User Fee Amendments* of 2017 (*BsUFA II*) to collect fees through September 2022. Unlike user fees for other medicinal products, the biosimilar fee assessment begins at the Investigational New Drug (IND) phase. The program includes an initial fee required when requesting a BPD Type 1, 2, 3 or 4 meeting with FDA or when submitting an initial clinical protocol to initiate the IND, whichever comes first[22] (the fee is not applicable for the initial advisory meeting—see **Table 14-1** for the current fee schedule[23]). Biosimilar sponsors then are required to pay an annual fee throughout the IND period and until a marketing application or 351(k) BLA is filed or the development program discontinued. Should the sponsor discontinue the program and later decide to restart product development, a reactivation fee will be required[24] (for more information, see FDA's BsUFA website[25]).

As part of FDA's agency-wide program performance management system, FDA-TRACK, the Center for Drug Evaluation and Research (CDER) established the "Number of biosimilar INDs received in the month" as a *BsUFA* performance measure.[26] **Figure 14-1** presents the number of biosimilar INDs submitted to CDER by fiscal year.[27] FDA's fiscal year is 1 October–30 September.

IND and BLA submission requirements for a proposed biosimilar biological product generally are very similar to those for biological products. While the process does not differ for INDs, the FDA center responsible for the product is dependent upon the product type. Biological therapeutics (monoclonal antibodies, peptides or well-characterized proteins) are regulated by CDER, while the Center for Biologics Evaluation and Research (CBER) regulates more-complex products such as gene therapies, vaccines and blood products.[28] Chapter 1 summarizes the specific product types the two centers regulate.

Despite IND process similarities, the proposed biosimilar product needs to be compared extensively to the reference product by physicochemical and biological tests, and its development may require fewer clinical studies if the two products' similarity can be established early. The biosimilar development program takes a stepwise approach to eliminating residual uncertainty for demonstrating quality comparability and no clinically meaningful difference.[29]

FDA Meetings

As the BLA approval data requirement will vary by specific product, product type and particular product candidate, FDA stresses the importance of conducting an initial advisory meeting to discuss the product candidate and product development plan. FDA has established five types of meetings to foster timely and efficient product development plan discussion.[30]

Draft Guidance for Industry: Formal Meetings Between the FDA and Sponsors or Applicants of BsUFA Products (June 2018)[31]

A biosimilar product applicant or sponsor may request a formal meeting with FDA review staff via a set procedure at various times throughout the development program. Depending on the product type and development program status, FDA will determine whether a meeting is granted and whether it will be face-to-face, a teleconference or videoconference. The meeting types for proposed biosimilar products are specific to the product type and do not apply to other medical products. Specifically, five different types of meetings may be requested to discuss the development program:
1. Biosimilar Initial Advisory meeting:
    o initial discussion to determine whether the 351(k) biosimilar pathway is viable for the proposed product
    o product development plan discussion

- general development program overview also should be included
- supportive data including initial comparative analytical similarity data between the potential biosimilar product and the reference product
- should be scheduled within 75 days of meeting request submission
2. BPD Type 1 meeting:
- aims to facilitate a stalled BPD program, similar to a Type A meeting for other medical products
- meetings should be requested to discuss such issues as clinical holds, special protocol assessments, safety issues and dispute resolution
- Type 1 meetings should be scheduled within 30 days of meeting request submission
3. BPD Type 2 meeting:
- discussion of specific issues or questions for which FDA can provide direction
- substantive review of summary data may be required to address the issues
- should be scheduled within 75 days of meeting request submission
4. BPD Type 3 meeting:
- in-depth development program data review and advice
- questions may address product similarity, study proposals and design, and additional study requirements and indication extrapolation
- should include comprehensive analytical similarity data and full study reports for any clinical studies conducted
- should be scheduled within 120 days of meeting request submission
5. BPD Type 4 meeting:
- discussion of proposed 351(k) biosimilar product application content and format, similar to a Type B Pre-BLA meeting for other biological products
- should be scheduled within 60 days of meeting request submission

Table 14-2 summarizes the types of BPD meetings and compares them to equivalent *Prescription Drug User Fee Act* (*PDUFA*) meetings.

As discussed in the *BsUFA* section, all granted BPD Type 1, 2, 3 or 4 meeting requests trigger the fee requirement if an IND is not in place. The fee is charged per product, not per meeting. Once granted, the meeting request triggers the fee requirement; the sponsor or applicant needs to pay the initial fee within five calendar days and annual fees for that product thereafter, independent of how many further meetings are requested. Failure to pay the applicable fees results in meeting cancellation and denial of any further meeting requests.[32]

BPD meeting package content and format are comparable to those for *PDUFA* drug and biological development program meeting packages submitted to FDA. However, for all biosimilar product meetings, the request must be accompanied by the meeting package. Meeting requests without the meeting package will be regarded as incomplete, and the request likely will be denied. FDA will contact the sponsor and/or applicant

Figure 14-1. Number of Biosimilar INDs Received by CDER by Fiscal Year[a]

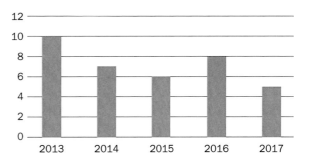

Abbreviations: CDER—Center for Drug Evaluation and Research, IND—Investigational New Drug (application)
*Data collection began in January 2013.
a. Food and Drug Administration. Number of biosimilar investigational new drug applications (INDs) received in the month. FDA website. http://www.accessdata.fda.gov/scripts/fdatrack/view/track.cfm?program=cder&id=CDER-RRDS-Number-of-biosimilar-INDs. Accessed 1 April 2019.

Figure 14-2. Number of Biosimilar Type 1–4 Meetings Held by CDER by Fiscal Year[a]

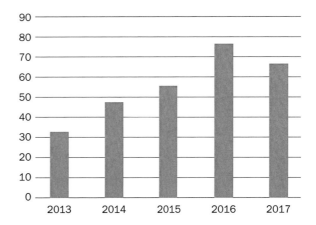

Abbreviations: BPD—Biosimilar Biological Product Development, CDER—Center for Drug Evaluation and Research
* Data collection began in January 2013.
a. Biosimilar User Fee Act, Latest News. FDA website. http://www.fda.gov/ForIndustry/UserFees/BiosimilarUserFeeActBsUFA/. Accessed 1 April 2019.

Table 14-2. Meetings Between FDA and Biosimilar Biological Product Sponsors

Meeting Type	Purpose	Meeting Timeline	Equivalent *PDUFA* Meeting
Biosimilar Initial Advisory	351(k) biosimilar pathway viability assessment	75 days from receipt of meeting request submission	Type B: Pre-IND
BPD Type 1	• Stalled program • Clinical holds • Special protocol assessment • Safety issues • Dispute resolution	30 days from receipt of meeting request submission	Type A
BPD Type 2	Development issues	90 days from receipt of meeting request submission	Type C
BPD Type 3	Assessment of need for additional studies/data, study design and analysis	120 days from receipt of meeting request submission	Type C
BPD Type 4	BLA format and content	60 days from receipt of meeting request submission	Type B: Pre-BLA

Abbreviations: BLA—Biologics License Application, BPD—Biosimilar Biological Product Development, FDA—US Food and Drug Administration, PDUFA—Prescription Drug User Fee Act

with a decision on the meeting request within 14 days of BPD Type 1 meeting request receipt and within 21 days for the Initial Advisory Meeting and all BPD Type 2, 3 and 4 meeting requests. Meeting requests following denial based on a substantive reason for an earlier meeting request will be considered a new meeting request. Following a meeting, FDA will provide finalized meeting minutes within 30 days. FDA guidance also advises on pre-meeting communication, meeting conduct, rescheduling and cancellation procedures.[33]

Another *BsUFA* performance measure established under CDER for FDA-TRACK is "Number of biosimilar BPD Type 1–4 meetings held in the month."[34] **Figure 14-2** shows the number of biosimilar BPD meetings CDER has held per fiscal year.

Biosimilar products generally are biological products and need to fulfill all biological products' regulatory requirements. However, because they claim to be similar to an already approved reference product, applicants also have to provide evidence the biosimilar, in fact, has highly similar properties to, and no clinically meaningful difference from, the reference biological product. Therefore, a biosimilar product developer needs to take into account regulations, FDA and the International Council for Harmonisation (ICH) guidances and US Pharmacopeial Convention (USP) monographs for biological product development, outlined in applicable sections of Chapters 26–28.

However, rather than establishing biological product patient safety and effectiveness, biosimilar products require direct comparison of the proposed biosimilar product's quality attributes to the reference biological product. The reference biological product's safety and effectiveness were established during its development program and approval under *PHS Act* Section 351(a). Therefore, it is assumed the biosimilar product is equally safe and effective as long as biosimilarity is demonstrated. The aim of biosimilar development programs is not to establish the product's safety and effectiveness independently.[38]

The biosimilar development program follows a stepwise approach, with the aim of eliminating residual uncertainty regarding quality attribute similarity to the reference product at each step, i.e., chemistry, manufacturing and controls (CMC), nonclinical and clinical. The amount of nonclinical and clinical data required depends largely on residual uncertainty remaining after conducting a CMC-level comparability exercise and evaluating nonclinical data. The less the residual uncertainty, the less investigation required. Totality-of-the-evidence is evaluated in determining biosimilarity—there is no pivotal clinical study to demonstrate biosimilarity. These concepts are explained in more detail in *Guidance for Industry: Scientific Considerations in Demonstrating Biosimilarity to a Reference Product*[39] and *Guidance for Industry: Quality Considerations in Demonstrating Biosimilarity of a Therapeutic Protein Product to a Reference Product*,[40] released by FDA in 2015.

Generally, a biosimilar development program consists of three components:
- analytical studies demonstrating the proposed biosimilar product's high similarity to the reference product
- animal studies including toxicity studies
- clinical study or studies assessing immunogenicity, pharmacodynamics and pharmacokinetics, which demonstrate the proposed biosimilar product's safety, purity and potency are highly similar to those of the reference product

Although comparability assessment requirements may vary from one biosimilar development program to another based on the involved biological product's special characteristics, in general, an extensive comparative structure and function characterization with the reference biological product and in-depth understanding of critical quality attributes are required for the assessment and elimination of residual uncertainty. FDA has the sole discretion to decide biosimilar product development study requirements and also can determine the development program elements outlined above are unnecessary. Early development program and guidance discussions with FDA are pertinent.[41,42]

Topics related to general biological product development are addressed by ICH.[43] ICH aims to achieve greater harmonization to ensure safe, effective, high-quality medicines are developed globally. It issues international guidelines that recommend standards to be used in product development; those addressing biologics also would be applicable to proposed biosimilar products. They include efficacy guidelines (E1–E18)[44] and safety guidelines (S1A–S11).[45] Some multidisciplinary guidelines also apply, such as those on nonclinical safety studies (M3(R2))[46] and bioanalytical method validation (M10).[47] Several ICH quality guidelines are referenced in FDA guidance documents as applicable to the biosimilar development program (ICH Q1A(R2), Q2(R1), Q2B, Q3A, Q5A, Q5B, Q5C, Q5D, Q5E, Q6B, Q7(A), Q8(R2), ICH Q9–11).[48] Of particular interest is ICH Q5E *Comparability of Biotechnological/Biological Products Subject to Changes in Their Manufacturing Process*.[49] Although this guidance addresses manufacturing process changes by a biological product manufacturer during the development process and not the manufacturing differences inevitable for a biosimilar product, many of the principles discussed also apply to biosimilar products. As a biosimilar sponsor does not have insight into the reference product license holder's manufacturing process, it is paramount to address the impact of any manufacturing differences on safety, purity and potency using the appropriate analytical tests, functional assays, animal and clinical studies. ICH Q5E's principles also apply to biosimilars, but FDA expects more data and information than would be necessary for a manufacturing change made by the license holder.

Biosimilar Product Development Guidances

FDA has issued three guidance documents that provide scientific and quality considerations and address clinical pharmacology requirements for biosimilar product development:

Guidance for Industry: Scientific Considerations in Demonstrating Biosimilarity to a Reference Product (April 2015)[50]

This guidance provides an overview of FDA's approach for determining biosimilarity and a discussion of key scientific considerations for demonstrating a proposed therapeutic protein product's biosimilarity to a reference product.

FDA's biosimilar product review is a stepwise process using a risk-based totality-of-evidence evaluation. A biosimilar development program's aim is to assess the effects of any quality differences between the proposed biosimilar product and the reference product, rather than establishing safety and effectiveness independently. At each step of quality, nonclinical and clinical investigation, study planning should focus on eliminating residual uncertainty and maximizing information that demonstrates biosimilarity. This approach applies to all development stages, including analytical, animal and clinical studies.

Extensive comparison studies to collect as much information demonstrating product similarity are important because FDA will evaluate the totality-of-evidence to determine whether a proposed biosimilar product is highly similar to a reference product. Data evaluated include structural and functional evaluation, nonclinical evaluation and human PK, PD and immunogenicity data. Minor differences, e.g., in post-translational modifications or certain inactive excipients, may not prevent a determination of highly similar as long as the submitted data support biosimilarity and no clinically meaningful difference is associated with the product. Clinically meaningful differences include those in the expected safety, purity or potency range between the proposed biosimilar product and the reference product.

Biologics licensing through *PHS Act* Section 351(k) requires the proposed biosimilar biological product's comparison to a US-licensed biological product.[51] However, in certain situations, a sponsor may want to rely on data from a comparator not licensed in the US. In this situation, an acceptable bridge comparing the non-US comparator with the US-licensed reference product must be established and an adequate scientific justification with supporting data provided.[52,53] FDA retains the final decision on data adequacy and the justification provided.

Developing supportive evidence to demonstrate biosimilarity is a stepwise process that starts in the analytical stage.[54] Comparing the proposed product to the reference product means evaluating structure, function, animal toxicity, human PK and PD, clinical immunogenicity and clinical safety and effectiveness.

The guidance provides detailed scientific considerations for demonstrating biosimilarity:
- Structural analysis should provide an extensive structural characterization of both the proposed biosimilar product and the reference product.

- Functional assays analyzing the product's pharmacologic activity should be conducted *in vitro* and/or *in vivo*.
- Animal studies including toxicity assessment are required unless determined unnecessary by FDA. Considerations for PK and PD studies and interpreting animal immunogenicity are included.
- Clinical studies include pharmacology data, immunogenicity assessment and comparative clinical studies.

Immunogenicity studies are particularly important to demonstrate any product characteristic differences between the proposed biosimilar and the reference product do not affect its safety profile and product effectiveness. Even small differences could affect adverse event incidence and severity. Additionally, neutralizing immunogenicity is a concern since it would lead to loss of the therapeutic product's activity. Since animal models are not always ideal for predicting human subjects' immunogenicity due to the physiological differences between animals and humans, clinical studies generally are required to evaluate this aspect. Demonstrating no clinically meaningful differences in immune response between the proposed biosimilar and the reference product is particularly pertinent for establishing biosimilarity.

Generally, a comparative clinical study will be required to remove any residual uncertainty to support the biosimilarity claim unless the sponsor can provide a scientifically substantiated justification for why it is not required. The comparative studies' type and extent depend on the reference product's nature and complexity, the extent to which analytical and nonclinical studies predict any differences' effects, the extent to which PK and PD data can predict clinical outcomes, previous clinical experience with the reference product and information available on the proposed product, e.g., through studies conducted outside the US.

A proposed biosimilar product applicant may extrapolate one or more additional conditions licensed for the reference product if the biosimilarity demonstration through clinical, animal and analytical studies shows the safety, purity and potency for a condition of use licensed for the reference product. A scientific justification for extrapolation is required and should include the mechanism of action for each condition of use, PK, biodistribution and immunogenicity in different populations, differences in expected toxicities and any other factor affecting safety and efficacy. Again, FDA uses totality-of-evidence to assess the data provided, and differences between conditions may not preclude the automatic demonstration of biosimilarity.

A solid postmarketing program is required and should address any remaining safety and effectiveness concerns. Sponsors should have mechanisms in place to detect any new and unique adverse biosimilar product-related events not previously observed in the reference product. Particularly, some immunogenicity issues may not have been detected before product approval, due to the limited clinical trial population.

The guidance also stresses sponsors should consult FDA on their product development and postmarketing programs to receive feedback on a case-by-case basis.

Guidance for Industry: Quality Considerations in Demonstrating Biosimilarity of a Therapeutic Protein Product to a Reference Product (April 2015)[55]
A second FDA guidance addresses quality issues to be considered during the proposed biosimilar product's characterization.

FDA began receiving New Drug Applications (NDAs) and BLAs for products derived by recombinant DNA-technology (rDNA) in the 1980s. Associated policies were developed, recognizing the challenges in characterizing protein products by physicochemical and functional testing alone.[56,57] Further, biological systems' involvement in the manufacturing process can significantly affect product safety and efficacy. Originally, FDA required an NDA under *FD&C Act* Section 505(b)(1) or a BLA. However, rDNA-derived protein products can be characterized extensively and compared before and after manufacturing changes using advanced analytical technologies. Manufacturing process, process control, material and product testing changes may not have any significant product safety and effectiveness impact. Therefore, new clinical studies and/or a new NDA or BLA may not be necessary. In 1996, FDA released *Guidance for Industry: Demonstration of Comparability of Human Biological Products, Including Therapeutic Biotechnology-Derived Products*,[58] explaining how manufacturers can demonstrate a manufacturing change does not adversely influence the approved product's identity, purity or potency without performing new clinical studies or submitting a new BLA. ICH Q5E[59] develops these concepts further. This ICH guideline and FDA's 1996 guidance only address manufacturing changes made by the same manufacturer to the approved product; however, many of the principles discussed also apply to biosimilars.

The guidance addresses analytical studies relevant to demonstrating biosimilarity.[60]

A biosimilar BLA under *PHS Act* Section 351(k) requires a complete and thorough CMC section providing necessary information concerning, e.g., characterization, adventitious agents, process controls and specifications. In addition to the regular CMC data submission required for a Section 351(a) application, a Section 351(k) biosimilar application must include CMC data supporting the proposed biosimilar product's quality similarity to the reference product. The reference product's known quality attributes and performance-related characteristics need to be considered when developing the similarity assessment rationale. Comparative analytical data should be available as early as possible in the development program, as they are the foundation for further biosimilar development. Ideally, these data should be available for the initial advisory meeting, as they can influence decisions on animal and clinical data requirements (amount and type). The more data available, the more specific data requirement feedback FDA will be able to provide. Physicochemical and functional studies may include biological assays, binding studies and enzyme kinetics to determine whether the proposed biosimilar and reference product are highly similar. The capabilities and limitations of methods used to establish quality attributes should be explained clearly. In addition, product-related impurities, product-related substances and process-related impurities need to be characterized clearly and compared to those of the reference product (see *ICH Q6B Specifications: Test Procedures and Acceptance Criteria for Biotechnological/Biological Products*[61]). Biosimilar products will have minor differences from reference products, so FDA's principal goal is to understand the impact those differences could have on the biosimilar product's safety, efficacy, potency and quality as supported by comparative data.

The guidance provides a detailed discussion of the analytical assessment expectations and notes manufacturers should perform "comparisons with side-by-side analysis of an appropriate number of lots of the proposed product and the reference product."[62] The type and extent of animal studies can be influenced by the analytical data's ability to discern differences between the proposed biosimilar and the reference product.

A robust characterization is key as FDA's quality guidance addresses specific consideration with respect to the expression system, manufacturing process, assessment of physicochemical properties, functional assays, receptor binding, immunochemical properties, impurities, reference product and reference standards, and finished drug product and stability.

The guidance cautions that if state-of-the-art technology cannot characterize the reference product or proposed biosimilar adequately, a submission under *PHS Act* Section 351(k) is not appropriate.

Guidance for Industry: Clinical Pharmacology Data to Support a Demonstration of Biosimilarity to a Reference Product (December 2016)[63]

PHS Act Section 351(k) applications must contain information demonstrating biosimilarity to a reference product, including, among other things, analytical studies, animal studies and clinical studies assessing immunogenicity, PK and PD unless FDA determines, on a case-by-case basis, that certain studies are unnecessary. This guidance states, "the types of clinical pharmacology studies to be conducted will depend on the residual uncertainties about biosimilarity that these studies can address to add to the Totality-of-the-Evidence for biosimilar product development."[64]

Three concepts are particularly relevant to stepwise biosimilar development:

1. PK and PD response assessment—these studies aim to characterize and compare the proposed biosimilar and reference product's PK and PD profiles. Ideally, they should include, where possible, exposure and exposure-response information and provide an indication of any potential clinically meaningful differences.
2. Residual uncertainty evaluation—FDA sequentially considers the totality of data, sponsor-provided information and the need for additional studies. A risk-based approach is used to evaluate data from structural and functional characterizations, nonclinical evaluations, clinical PK and PD studies, immunogenicity testing and clinical safety investigations, including clinical effectiveness, if appropriate.
3. Analytical quality and similarity—meaningful biosimilar assessment, in part, depends on state-of-the-art analytical assay and method capabilities and limitations. An extensive analytical analysis should aid in determining any differences between the reference product and the proposed biosimilar and their potential effects. The assessment will result in one of four classifications: insufficient analytical similarity, analytical similarity with residual uncertainty, tentative analytical similarity and fingerprint-like analytical similarity.

This guidance lists appropriate PK and PD bioanalytical methods and various considerations; more detail is available in *Guidance for Industry: Bioanalytical Method Validation*[65] and ICH guidance.[66]

Biosimilar immunogenicity assessment is crucial for assessing product safety, PD effect, efficacy loss or immune-mediated toxicity, and the response's incidence and severity. Even small proposed biosimilar characteristic differences might change the product's immunogenicity fundamentally compared to the reference product.

FDA encourages sponsors to discuss study program and design early in the development program at a meeting specifically available for biosimilar sponsors (see FDA meeting guidance, earlier in this chapter). The guidance discusses study design, reference product, study population, dose selection, route of administration, PK and PD measure considerations, definition of the appropriate PD time profile and PK and PD statistical comparison results.

Table 14-3. Comparison of Development Programs Between Chemical Drugs and Biological Products

	Testing	New Chemical Entity	Generic	New Biologic	Biosimilar
Legal Basis		505(b)(1) *FD&C Act*	505(j) *FD&C Act*	351(a) *PHS Act*	351(k) *PHS Act*
Objective		Demonstrate safety and effectiveness with patient benefit superior to placebo	Demonstrate generic is identical to approved chemical drug in active ingredient, dosage form, strength, etc.	Demonstrate safety and effectiveness with patient benefit superior to placebo	Demonstrate similarity to approved reference product with no clinically meaningful differences
Quality	Characterization	Noncomparative	Noncomparative	Noncomparative	Comparative
	Release Testing	Yes	Yes	Yes	Yes
Nonclinical	In vitro	Extensive analytical and functional characterization for prediction of in vivo effect	No	Extensive analytical and functional characterization for prediction of in vivo effect	Extensive structure/function comparison
	Animal studies	Yes (PK/PD)	No	Yes (PK/PD, immunogenicity)	Yes (PK/PD, immunogenicity) comparative
Clinical	Phase 1	Yes	PK	Noncomparative PK, PD, safety	Comparative PK, PD, safety
	Phase 2	Yes	No	Yes	No
	Phase 3	Yes	Small comparative	Large-scale placebo controlled	Large-scale comparative
	Phase 4/Pharmacovigilance	Yes	No	Yes	Yes

Abbreviations: PD—Pharmacodynamics; PHS Act—Public Health Service Act; PK—Pharmacokinetics

Although the biosimilar product approval pathway is abbreviated, the study requirements for approval required in *PHS Act* Section 351(k) differ fundamentally from those of the abbreviated pathway applicable for drugs and certain biologics under Section 505(b)(2) for drugs (See **Table 14-3**).

NDA Application and Approval

The *BPCI Act*[67] also changed the biological product approval pathway; with its enactment, all biological products including proteins (except chemically synthesized polypeptides) are subject to a BLA under *PHS Act* Section 351. However, FDA's practice has been to approve some biological products with active ingredients derived from natural sources or rDNA technology under *FD&C Act* Section 505 instead of *PHS Act* Section 351.[68,69] During a 10-year transition period (expiring 23 March 2020), biological products similar to a reference product approved under *FD&C Act* Section 505 may be approved under Section 505(b)(2) if:

1. a product in that class with the same gene code was subject to an application under *FD&C Act* Section 505 submitted before *BPCI Act* enactment

2. the application is submitted within 10 years of *BPCI Act* enactment

After the transition period, all biological products approved under *FD&C Act* Section 505 will be deemed to have a biologics license approved under *PHS Act* Section 351(a).[70]

Biologics license requirements apply to biotechnology-derived products, including proteins, but specifically excluding "chemically synthesized polypeptides." Chemically synthesized polypeptides are alpha amino acid polymers that are: a) entirely produced by chemical synthesis and b) less than 100 amino acids in size. The total number of amino acids determines molecule size. If a chemically synthesized molecule is more than 99 amino acids, and a naturally occurring peptide of shorter length exists, FDA will determine whether the additional amino acids raise concerns about the benefit-risk profile.

On the other hand, a peptide with more than 40 amino acids becomes a protein requiring a biologics license, with the exception of chemically synthesized polypeptides previously described. A peptide with 40 or fewer amino acids will be regulated under the *FD&C Act* unless it meets other statutory biological product definitions, such as a peptide vaccine.

The *BPCI Act* specifies sponsors applying for a BLA under *PHS Act* Section 351(k) must submit information demonstrating:
1. The biological product's similarity to a reference product is supported by analytical studies, animal studies and clinical studies.
2. The reference biological product and biosimilar product have the same mechanism(s) of action.
3. Condition(s) of use for labeling purposes have been used previously.
4. Biosimilar product and reference product route of administration, dosage form and strength are the same.
5. The manufacturing facility meets current Good Manufacturing Practices (CGMP) standards.

BLAs are subject to regulation under 21 CFR 600,[71] 601[72] and 610.[73] Chapter 25 provides additional details on the BLA process.

FDA has released question and answer (Q&A) documents to address sponsors' common concerns.[74]

Guidance for Industry: Questions and Answers on Biosimilar Development and The BPCI Act (December 2018)[75]
The first Q&A document primarily addresses acceptable differences and conditions of acceptability between the proposed biosimilar and the reference product, as well as questions regarding the use of a non-US-licensed comparator, extrapolation to other indications and pediatric study program requirements.

A number of high-level product expectations include:
- Biosimilars can be formulated differently than the reference product, but must have supporting data demonstrating such differences are minor and do not result in "clinically meaningful differences" in terms of safety, purity and potency.
- Delivery device or container closure system differences also can be acceptable if they do not result in "clinically meaningful differences," have the same route of administration and do not introduce a condition of use (e.g., indication or dosing regimen) for which the reference product has not previously been approved.
- A biosimilar product does not need to be approved for all reference product strengths. However, to be biosimilar to a reference product, the product must have the same strength, which generally means the same amount of drug substance and same concentration.
- Generally, a non-US licensed comparator product is considered an investigational new drug and would require an IND submission and have to fulfill 21 CFR 312 requirements to be imported into the US.[76] However, a sponsor may include the non-US licensed comparator in the proposed biosimilar's IND and, therefore, will need to file only one IND for the proposed biosimilar product and the non-US licensed comparator.
- Comparative animal or clinical assessment data using a non-US-licensed comparator can be used to support a biosimilarity indication if it is supported by appropriate analytical studies and at least one PK and, where appropriate, PD study. The application also likely will need to include bridging data comparing all three products (proposed biosimilar, non-US reference product and US reference product).
- Extrapolating indications is possible, but requires a scientific justification addressing mechanism(s) of action, PK, biodistribution and immunogenicity in different patient populations, expected toxicities for each condition of use, patient population and any other factor(s) that might affect safety and/or efficacy.
- The guidance further provides information on sample retention length (five years) and the number of dosage units to be retained as well as what constitutes publicly-available information.
- Under the *Pediatric Research Equity Act* (*PREA*), pediatric assessments[77] are required for all biosimilars except where the biosimilar product has been determined to be interchangeable with the reference product, or the requirement is waived, deferred or is inapplicable. Biosimilars not deemed interchangeable with the reference product are considered to have a "new active ingredient" with respect to *PREA* according to *Affordable Care Act* Section 7002(d)(2).[77,78] By contrast, interchangeable products are not considered to have new active ingredients.
- The guidance also discusses initial Pediatric Study Plan (PSP) submission timing and content. Since the initial PSP agreement process between FDA and sponsor described under Sections 505B(E)(2)(C) and 505B(e)(3) can take up to 210 days, the guidance suggests a biosimilar product sponsor should submit the PSP as soon as feasible but no later than 210 days before the proposed study start.

Draft Guidance for Industry: New and Revised Draft Q&As on Biosimilar Development and the BPCI Act (December 2018)[79]
This draft guidance provides new and revised Q&As from FDA's 2015 *Guidance for Industry: Biosimilars: Questions and Answers: Regarding Implementation of the Biologics Price Competition and Innovation Act of 2009*. The additional Q&As contain more-detailed explanations

for certain issues and address new questions not raised in prior versions of the Q&A document:

- The proposed biosimilar and reference product must have the same dosage form, i.e., the same physical manifestation containing the active and inactive ingredients, to be considered biosimilar or interchangeable under *PHS Act* Section 351(k)(2)(A)(i)(IV). In this respect, various injectable products, including "injection" (solution), "for injection" (lyophilized powder), suspensions and emulsions, all are different dosage forms. However, this distinction may not apply to products approved under *FD&C Act* Section 505(c) or *PHS Act* Section 351(a).

- The guidance highlights the differences in the interpretation of "extrapolation" for biosimilar application purposes and for *PREA* purposes. A proposed biosimilar may extrapolate biosimilarity to a reference product demonstrated in one condition to other conditions for which the reference product is approved. However, under *PREA*, a single sponsor may extrapolate efficacy findings from one population (e.g., adults or older pediatric populations) to additional populations (e.g., younger pediatrics) for the same single product or product line. Sponsors must ensure applicable extrapolation requirements are verified.

The guidance also considers information required to support postapproval manufacturing changes for licensed biosimilars. The sponsor should follow the principles in the International Council for Harmonisation (ICH) guidance for industry *Q5E Comparability of 334 Biotechnological/Biological Products Subject to Changes in their Manufacturing Process* (June 2005). The sponsor should provide data to demonstrate the biosimilar product's comparability before and after the manufacturing change.

Biosimilar Naming

All original biological products, related biological products and biosimilars approved under the *PHS Act* are required to bear a nonproprietary name made up by the combination of a core name and a hyphenated distinguishable suffix. This requirement applies to all newly and previously approved biologics licensed under *PHS Act* Section 351(a) or 351(k).[81]

FDA generally uses nonproprietary names determined by USP,[82] where the United States Adopted Names Council (USAN) plays a large role.[83,84] This nonproprietary name formerly was known as the "proper name." However, according to *Guidance for Industry: Nonproprietary Naming of Biological Products*[85] the "proper name" is a combination of the "core name" and a hyphenated suffix. The core name is the compendial/USP name, e.g., filgrastim and epoetin alfa, unless none existed, and FDA assigned it during the BLA. The core name generally reflects certain scientific product characteristics (e.g., chemical structure, pharmacological characteristics) and helps healthcare providers identify the drug substance. This also is true for the international nonproprietary name (INN), which is determined independently by the World Health Organization (WHO) and intended to be used globally.[86] Many jurisdictions have accepted WHO's INN in their national naming systems, including USAN. The original product and biosimilar's core names generally will be the same.

Guidance for Industry: Nonproprietary Naming of Biological Products (January 2017)[87]

The requirement for the proper name to include a hyphenated suffix in addition to the core name was implemented to enhance biological product pharmacovigilance, ensure safe use of biologics and advance appropriate practices and perceptions.

A pharmacovigilance system should allow biological product tracking back to its manufacturer, so adverse events can be associated appropriately and safety signals can be detected throughout the product lifecycle. Pharmacovigilance systems differ in their use of identifiers, which may include one or more of the proprietary name, proper name, manufacturer, national drug code number, lot number and billing code. If two biological products share the same core name, as would be the case for a reference biologic and a biosimilar product if no suffix was provided, it will be impossible to determine the manufacturer unless another identifier, such as the national drug code or proprietary name, is used. Including the suffix as part of the proper name through hyphenation will allow the different biological products to be distinguished based on the same biologic compound by just the proper name. The naming requirement aims to provide a critical tool for accurate product identification and pharmacovigilance activity facilitation.

Moreover, adding a unique hyphenated suffix guards against inadvertent substitutions based on the nonproprietary name alone. As interchangeability is an additional standard to meet, the accidental switching or alternating between originator and biosimilar product should be avoided unless a product clearly has been determined to be interchangeable with the reference product. A biosimilar product may be approved for all or fewer indications than the reference product; therefore, inadvertent switching might lead to off-label use for an unapproved indication. Healthcare providers or pharmacists might assume products are interchangeable if only the core name is used, as with small molecule drugs. However, due to biologics' added complexity, the distinction between the products must be ensured to preserve patient safety and enable safe use.

Products are identified individually by adding a hyphenated distinguished suffix composed of four lower-case letters devoid of any meaning. In combination, the core name and suffix form the proper name.

Sponsors can propose up to 10 options for the hyphenated suffix, which should be:
- unique and devoid of any meaning
- four lower-case letters, with at least three distinct letters
- nonproprietary and free of legal barriers limiting usage

Sponsors must ensure the proposed suffix:
- is not false or misleading and does not make misrepresentations with respect to safety and efficacy
- does not include numerals or symbols, except for the hyphen attaching it to the core name
- does not contain abbreviations commonly used in clinical practice, leading to misinterpretation
- does not contain any other drug substance name or core name
- cannot easily be mistaken for the name of an already marketed product
- does not look similar to or otherwise connote the license holder's name
- is not too similar to any other FDA-designated nonproprietary name suffix

In addition, FDA recommends "including supporting analyses demonstrating that the proposed suffixes meet the factors described in the guidance for FDA's consideration" in the sponsor's submission.

One important point to note is FDA's naming convention differs from WHO's proposed biological qualifier for naming biosimilars, which recommends acceptance "at will" without changing the INN itself.[90]

The requirement for three distinct letters in the four-letter suffix means the two approved Sandoz biosimilar proper names do not conform to the FDA guidance: filgrastim-sndz—the suffix is a connotation of the company name and etanercept-szzs is a connotation of the company name in addition to only two distinct letters.

Although applicants should conduct their own due diligence on a suffix's acceptability, FDA will make the final determination and inform applicants whether a proposed suffix is acceptable, or if none are acceptable. If all suffixes are unacceptable, applicants can resubmit further suffixes for FDA evaluation within a reasonable time. If the applicant does not submit further suggestions, and no suggested suffix is acceptable, FDA may elect to assign an appropriate suffix to be used in the proper name at the time of BLA approval.

These naming requirements also will apply to all other biological products approved under the *PHS Act* or the *FD&C Act* on or before 23 March 2020. After the transition period, all *FD&C Act*-approved biological products will be deemed to have a biologics license and the *BPCI Act* naming requirements apply.[91] Guidance on the transition and retroactive application to already approved products is expected to be forthcoming from FDA.

As part of a BLA, sponsors and/or applicants also need to submit draft labeling to FDA along with the proposed nonproprietary name. In July 2018, FDA finalized *Guidance for Industry: Labeling for Biosimilar Products*[92] to guide sponsors in developing labeling for proposed biosimilar products submitted under *PHS Act* Section 351(k). Product labeling provides summary scientific information needed by healthcare personnel and patients to enable safe and effective product use.

Guidance for Industry: Labeling for Biosimilar Products (July 2018)

This guidance indicates biosimilar product labeling should include "relevant data and information from the reference product labeling, including clinical data that supported FDA's finding of safety and effectiveness of the reference product." Generally, clinical studies conducted with proposed biosimilar products should not be included in labeling, as the studies aim to compare safety and effectiveness to the approved comparator rather than demonstrate the proposed biosimilar product's safety and effectiveness *per se*.[93] Therefore, they are not relevant to health practitioners' assessments of safety and effectiveness. Biosimilar product labeling must meet all the content and format requirements under 21 CFR 201.56(C)(1), 21 CFR 201.56(d)[94] and 21 CFR 201.57(c)(9)(i)–(iii)[95] (also see Final Rule on Content and Format for Labeling[96] and Final Rule for Requirements for Pregnancy and Lactation Labeling[97]).

FDA's guidance[98] recommends including relevant information from the reference product in the biosimilar product label. To ensure appropriate biosimilar product identification, sponsors should use the proprietary name, if available and wherever possible, when referring to the biosimilar product. For example, the reference product's proper name (core name with suffix, see Biosimilar Naming) should be used when describing clinical studies conducted with the reference product. Since "the overall risk-benefit profile of the reference product is relevant to the biosimilar product, even if a particular serious adverse reaction or other risk included in the reference product labeling may not have been reported with the biosimilar product at the time of licensure," the core name (INN) followed by 'products' should be used in the benefit-risk profile.

A biosimilar product label also generally should contain a statement of the fact the product is a biosimilar and name the appropriate reference product as well as explain the meaning of biosimilar.

Although the biosimilar product sponsor may not be seeking approval for all the same indications, or is not approved for the same indications as the reference product, "it may be necessary to include information in the biosimilar product labeling relating to an indication(s) for which the biosimilar product applicant is not seeking licensure, in order to help ensure safe use (e.g., when safety information in the reference product labeling is related to use of the product and is not specific to a particular approved indication(s) or when information specific to only the biosimilar product's indication(s) cannot be easily extracted)."[99] The label should be very clear about the reference product indication(s) or intended use(s) for which the biosimilar product has been approved.

The labeling may contain information specific to the biosimilar product as it is necessary to provide product safety and efficacy information. This specific biosimilar product information may include differences in administration, preparation, storage or safety information that do not impact the biosimilarity demonstration. The guidance states: "In cases where the biosimilar product applicant is not seeking approval for all the indications for which the reference product is licensed, the pooled data described in the reference product labeling should be included in the biosimilar product labeling in a manner that is not indication-specific. However, any text that refers to an indication for which licensure has not been sought by the biosimilar product applicant and is included to ensure safe use of the biosimilar product should be revised to avoid an implication that the biosimilar has been approved for that indication(s)."

The immunogenicity information usually is placed in a subsection in the "Adverse Reactions" section of the label entitled "Immunogenicity." To aid healthcare practitioners in understanding the immunogenicity information's significance, the first label subsection paragraph should include explanatory text, such as: "As with all therapeutic proteins, there is potential for immunogenicity. The detection of antibody formation is highly dependent on the sensitivity and specificity of the assay. Additionally, the observed incidence of antibody (including neutralizing antibody) positivity in an assay may be influenced by several factors, including assay methodology, sample handling, timing of sample collection, concomitant medications, and underlying disease. For these reasons, comparison of the incidence of antibodies to [reference product's proper name] in the studies described below with the incidence of antibodies in other studies or to other products may be misleading."

In summary, the proposed biosimilar product's labeling text should be based on, and similar to, the reference product's label, but does not have to be identical. In contrast, generic product and reference product labels are not only similar, but identical.

Commercialization

During the new drug approval process and before marketing, the biosimilar product sponsor must provide the reference product's sponsor with confidential information regarding the BLA under *PHS Act* Section 351(k).[100] Generally, a multi-step procedure detailed in *PHS Act* §351(l)(2)–(6) (*PHS Act* as codified in 42 U.S.C. §262(l)(2)–(6)) is initiated and often referred to as the "patent dance." The multi-step procedure is as follows:

1. provide biosimilar application to reference product sponsor (no later than 20 days after application under *PHS Act* Section 351(k) has been accepted)
2. reference product sponsor provides list of patents to biosimilar applicant (*PHS Act* §351(l)(2)) (no later than notification by biosimilar sponsor)
3. biosimilar applicant provides patent list and response to each patent listed by the reference product sponsor (*PHS Act* §351(l)(3)(A)) (no later than 60 days after receipt of patent list from reference product sponsor)
4. reference product sponsors provide a detailed statement to biosimilar sponsors for each patent on a claim-by-claim basis and factual and legal basis of opinion (*PHS Act* §351(l)(3)(B))
5. patent resolution negotiations (*PHS Act* §351(l)(4))
6. patent resolution (*PHS Act* §351(l)(5)) and/or filing for infringement action (*PHS Act* §351(l)(6))

Under *PHS Act* Section 351(k), the applicant also must provide notice of the first commercial marketing to the reference product sponsor at least 180 days prior to intended commercialization. This 180-day notice can be provided only after the proposed biosimilar product has been approved as a biosimilar, according to a recent Federal Appeals Court ruling (Amgen vs Sandoz 2015-1499[101]). The reference product sponsor may seek a preliminary injunction when it receives the notice of intended marketing, up to the marketing date stated to prevent biosimilar launch before all patent issues are resolved.

As of 31 January 2019, FDA had approved 17 biosimilar products, and six had been commercialized, as listed in **Table 14-4**.

Market Exclusivity

BsUFA provides market exclusivity for the first approved interchangeable product. However, none of the currently approved products has been deemed interchangeable with the reference biological product. FDA is working on providing guidance on the requirements to meet this

Table 14-4. FDA-Approved Biosimilars

Biosimilar Product Name	Nonproprietary Name	Sponsor	Reference Product	Approval Date
Zarxio*	filgrastim-sndz	Sandoz	Neupogen	6 March 2015
Inflectra*	infliximab-dyyb	Celltrion/Pfizer	Remicade	5 April 2016
Erelzi	etanercept-szzs	Sandoz	Enbrel	31 August 2016
Amjevita	adalimumab-atto	Amgen	Humira	23 September 2016
Renflexis*	infliximab-abda	Samsung Bioepis/Merck	Remicade	21 April 2017
Cyltezo	adalimumab-adbm	Boehringer Ingelheim	Humira	29 August 2017
Mvasi	bevacizumab-awwb	Amgen/Allergan	Avastin	14 September 2017
Ogivri	trastuzumab-dkst	Mylan/Biocon	Herceptin	3 December 2017
Ixifi	infliximab-qbtx	Pfizer	Remicade	14 December 2017
Retacrit*	epoetin-epbx	Pfizer (Hospira)	Epogen	15 May 2018
Fulphila*	pegfilgrastim-jmdb	Mylan/Biocon	Neulasta	4 June 2018
Nivestym*	filgrastim-aafi	Pfizer	Neupogen	20 July 2018
Hyrimoz	adalimumab-adaz	Sandoz	Humira	31 October 2018
Udenyca	pegfilgrastim-cbqv	Coherus Biosciences	Neulasta	2 November 2018
Truxima	rituximab-abbs	Teva/Celltrion	Rituxan	28 November 2018
Herzuma	trastuzumab-pkrb	Teva/Celltrion	Herceptin	14 December 2018
Ontruzant	trastuzumab-dttb	Samsung Bioepis	Herceptin	18 January 2019

*Commercialized product
Source: https://www.fda.gov/drugs/developmentapprovalprocess/howdrugsaredevelopedandapproved/approvalapplications/therapeuticbiologicapplications/biosimilars/ucm580432.htm. Accessed 1 April 2019.

higher standard of interchangeability in addition to biosimilarity. During the exclusivity period, second or further interchangeable products for any condition of use covered by the first interchangeable product cannot be determined to be interchangeable until the earlier of:[102]

- one year after the first interchangeable product's commercialization
- 18 months after a) the final court decision (court decision with no appeal filed but excluding *writ certiorari* US Supreme Court petitions) or b) the dismissal with or without prejudice of any action
- a) 42 months after the first interchangeable product was approved if the candidate was sued or b) 18 months after approval if the candidate was not sued

The 12-year reference biological product market exclusivity granted at first licensing as a biological product under *PHS Act* Section 351(a) must be respected. Therefore, a biosimilar approval cannot be made effective until the reference product's 12-year market exclusivity period has expired (*BsUFA*[103]), as further explained in the reference product exclusivity draft guidance.

Draft Guidance for Industry: Reference Product Exclusivity for Biological Products Filed Under Section 351(a) of the PHS Act (August 2014)

This guidance[104] outlines how FDA establishes the reference product's date of first licensure and outlines the types of information reference BLA product sponsors should provide to facilitate agency determination of the date of their products' first licensure. "In most instances, the date of first licensure will be the initial date the particular product at issue was licensed in the US." Under the *BPCI Act*, there is no reference product exclusivity for a BLA or licensed product supplement that results in a new "indication, route of administration, dosing schedule, dosage form, delivery system, delivery device, or strength." The guidance stays consistent with the statute, stating the date such a product is licensed will not constitute a "date of first licensure" that begins an exclusivity period, unless there is "a modification to the structure of the biological product" that "result[s] in a change in safety, purity or potency." The onus is on sponsors to demonstrate when a new licensure meets the exclusivity standards.

The guidance clarifies the following three conditions in *PHS Act* Section 351(k)(7)(C): (a) "licensor, predecessor in interest, or other related entity," (b) "modification to the structure of the biological product" and (c) "does not result in a change in safety, purity, or potency."

a. "Licensor, Predecessor in Interest, or Other Related Entity"
The following definitions are important in clarifying the wide legal categories of entities whose prior licensures of certain structurally related products could potentially weaken a BLA sponsor's first licensure exclusivity claim:
o A "licensor" is "any entity that has granted the sponsor a license to market the biological product, regardless of whether such license is exclusive."
o A "predecessor in interest" is "any entity that the sponsor has taken over, merged with, or purchased, or that has granted the sponsor exclusive rights to market the biological product under the [BLA], or had exclusive rights to the data underlying that application."
o An entity is an "other related entity" if "(1) either entity owns, controls or has the power to own or control the other entity (either directly or through one or more other entities) or (2) the entities are under common ownership or control," or if "the entities are or were engaged in certain commercial collaborations relating to the development of the biological product(s) at issue."

b. "Modification to the Structure of the Biological Product"
The reference product exclusivity guidance seems to put the burden on the reference drug product sponsor to demonstrate the new licensure is a "modification to the structure of the biological product." This guidance outlines additional contexts for the specific structural modification categories in a reference product that may be a basis for applying first licensure exclusivity, even where the sponsor or its predecessor-in-interest, licensor or related entity previously may have licensed a related product.
For example, the sponsor should "demonstrate that the product has been structurally modified" and "describe the structural similarities and differences between its proposed product and any previously licensed biological product that was the subject of a [BLA] application filed by the same sponsor or manufacturer (or its licensor, predecessor in interest, or other related entity)." For a therapeutic protein product, this includes outlining the "differences in amino acid sequence, glycosylation patterns, tertiary structures, post-translational events (including any chemical modifications of the molecular structure such as pegylation), and infidelity of translation or transcription."

c. "Does Not Result in a Change in Safety, Purity, or Potency"
The guidance also seems to put the burden on the reference drug product sponsor to demonstrate a structural modification to the biological product will "result in a change in safety, purity, or potency," before exclusivity will be granted. The guidance indicates exhibiting a change in safety, purity or potency "may include evidence that the change will result in a meaningful benefit to public health, such as a therapeutic advantage or other substantial benefit when compared to the previously licensed biological product." The reference drug product sponsor should submit data demonstrating "measurable effects (typically demonstrated in preclinical or clinical studies and shown by relevant methods such as bioassays) clearly describing how the modification resulted in a change in safety, purity, or potency compared to the previously licensed product." However, FDA will consider this obligation is satisfied "if the sponsor of the proposed product demonstrates that it affects a different molecular target than the original product."

These conditions seem to offer additional guidance on what clinical effects FDA might consider relevant to showing a "change in safety, purity, or potency," as well as the evidence FDA might require. The proposed evidence to demonstrate the requirements to qualify for the exclusivity set forth in Section 351(k)(7) includes:
- a list of all structurally similar BLA products related to the proposed BLA product
- a list of those BLA products currently or previously owned by the sponsor or one of its affiliates, including any licensors, predecessors in interest or related entities, and also:
  o a description of structural differences between those products and the proposed BLA product
  o supportive data on the change(s) in safety, purity and/or potency between those products and the proposed BLA product

The Case of Zarxio®

Zarxio® (filgrastim, Sandoz) was the first biosimilar approved in the US in March 2015.[105] Zarxio is biosimilar to Amgen's Neupogen,® originally approved in 1991.

Soon after Zarxio's approval, Amgen filed a lawsuit in the US District Court of Northern California to obtain a preliminary injunction preventing Sandoz from launching Zarxio[106] and a Citizen Petition[107] requesting FDA to require a certification making the "patent dance" mandatory.

In Amgen's case, both the preliminary injunction[108] and the Citizen Petition[109] were denied. Both decisions were based on the interpretation of certain *BPCI Act* sections and wording. Amgen's motion for preliminary injunction and the Citizen Petition requesting FDA to implement the outlined patent dance hinge on the interpretation of the *BPCI Act*'s creation of *PHS Act* §351(l)(2),[110] which reads:

> "No later than 20 days after the Secretary notifies the subsection (k) applicant [biosimilar pathway applicant—*ed. Note*] that the application has been accepted for review, the subsection (k) applicant:
> (A) Shall provide to the reference product sponsor [Amgen in this case—*ed. Note*] a copy of the application submitted…
> (B) May provide to the reference product sponsor additional information requested…"

Amgen interpreted the "shall provide" in point (A) as meaning the biosimilar applicant must provide the application and manufacturing information to the reference product sponsor (as opposed to the "may provide" in point (B) being voluntary). Amgen took this section to be a mandatory disclosure to the reference product sponsor similar to the patent certification requirement in the *Hatch-Waxman Act*[111] for generic applications (21 CFR Section 314.94 (a)(12)).

FDA denied the request for requiring a certification procedure in Amgen's Citizen Petition, which would make the patent dance, according to *PHS Act* §351(l)(2)–(6), mandatory in future, based on the competing interpretations, and referred a legal resolution to the ongoing litigation.[112]

District Court Judge Richard Seeborg[113] also interpreted the relevant *BPCI Act* section as an option for the 351(k) applicant to provide the information and allow the applicant's decision not to do so. Further, the decision not to provide the information does not permit the reference product sponsor to obtain injunctive relief based on that decision alone.

Amgen also claimed in the lawsuit that Sandoz committed an act of conversion (definition: unlawful taking or use of someone else's property) by basing its biosimilar application for Zarxio on Amgen's prior demonstration of Neupogen's safety, purity and potency without Amgen's authorization and without providing the application information. This claim was dismissed with prejudice (i.e., it cannot be litigated again).

Amgen also argued Subparagraph 42 of U.S.C. §262(l)(8)(A) requires the biosimilar manufacturer to give 180-day notice before first commercialization, but after FDA approval. Judge Seeborg dismissed that claim stating: if "Congress intended to make the exclusivity period twelve and one-half years (by adding the 180-day notice 'wait period' – author's note), it could not have chosen a more convoluted method of doing so." The judge concluded it was not wrong for Sandoz to give notice to Amgen while the application was pending.

Amgen appealed the decision[114] and filed an emergency motion resulting in a *per curiam* order in May 2015.[115] In June, the Federal Circuit Court heard arguments presented by Amgen and Sandoz.

Amgen's attorney held the position Sandoz did not follow the *BPCI Act*'s steps laying out the "patent dance." However, Sandoz's lawyer affirmed the company had followed the disclosure rules. In July 2015, the Federal Circuit Court of Appeals ruled the biosimilar sponsor does not need to engage in the information exchange but must wait to receive FDA approval before it can notify the originator developer of the intent to market.[116] That *de facto* adds 180 days of exclusivity for the originator product. This delayed the launch of Zarxio until 2 September 2015.

In February 2016, Sandoz filed a petition in the US Supreme Court to review the Federal Circuit Court's decision to require giving the 180-day notice of commercialization after product approval,[117] while Amgen asked the Supreme Court to reject the challenge.[118]

In December 2016, the Solicitor General of the US filed an *amicus* brief with the Supreme Court requesting the granting of *certiorari* (grant of the review of the lower courts' decision) and to reverse the Federal Circuit Court decision on the 180-day notice following product approval.[119,120]

The Supreme Court ultimately decided Amgen v. Sandoz in June 2017. It ruled that federal injunction is not available to force biosimilar applicants to participate in the patent exchange process (patent dance); however, it remanded to the Federal Circuit to address whether an injunction is available under state law.[121] Additionally, the Court held that a biosimilar sponsor may provide 180-day notice of commercial marketing before the biosimilar product is licensed.[122]

Zarxio was the first biosimilar approved and paved the way for the 351(k) pathway; however, several legal and regulatory challenges remained.

Biosimilars Action Plan

As described in this chapter, FDA already has made substantial progress in implementing the biosimilars pathway, including organizational changes, providing access to meetings and releasing guidelines. However, challenges still remain. As described in the Biosimilars Action Plan, FDA expects to take key actions to improve the 351(k) pathway including:

1. improving the efficiency of the development and approval process—This will include development of application review templates and transitioning

responsibility to an Office of Therapeutic Biologics and Biosimilars.
2. maximizing scientific and regulatory clarity for biosimilars product development—FDA plans to hold public meetings and hearings to seek additional input on possible alternative approaches, as well as develop additional guidance on biosimilars product development and postapproval changes.
3. taking a proactive role in educating clinicians, patients and payors about biosimilar and interchangeable products—Educational resources will include webinars, forums and video format communications that can be used on social media.
4. supporting market competition by reducing gaming of FDA requirements or other attempts to unfairly delay competition—FDA is expected to clarify its position on issues affecting reference product exclusivity and coordinate with the Federal Trade Commission to address anticompetitive practices that may delay biosimilar competition beyond exclusivity periods.

Conclusion

The *BPCI Act*, signed into law in 2010, amended the *PHS Act* by inserting new Section 351(k) to create an abbreviated pathway for biological products that are highly similar to or interchangeable with already approved biological products. Under Section 351(k), a proposed biosimilar product can rely on certain already existing knowledge regarding the reference product's safety, purity and potency to support the BLA. Implementation considerations for the new pathway are addressed in two FDA question and answer documents: *Guidance for Industry: Questions and Answers on Biosimilar Development and the BPCI Act* (December 2018) and *Draft Guidance for Industry: New and Revised Draft Q&As on Biosimilar Development and the BPCI Act* (December 2018).

As a result of the new pathway and the stepwise case-by-case decision approach, FDA established a specific process for granting meetings with sponsors to discuss development plans, outlined in *Guidance for Industry: Formal Meetings Between the FDA and Biosimilar Biological Product Sponsors or Applicant*.

FDA has released several guidance documents providing its current thinking on biosimilars' regulatory requirements. The requirements for quality, nonclinical and clinical studies are provided in *Guidance for Industry: Scientific Considerations in Demonstrating Biosimilarity to a Reference Product*; *Guidance for Industry: Quality Considerations in Demonstrating Biosimilarity of a Therapeutic Protein Product to a Reference Product*; and *Guidance for Industry: Clinical Pharmacology Data to Support a Demonstration of Biosimilarity to a Reference Product*. FDA uses a risk-based approach to evaluate the totality-of-evidence to determine what data are required to support a biosimilar product's marketing approval.

Other guidances address reference product exclusivity, biosimilar labeling and biologic naming.

FDA is working with WHO and other international partners toward harmonization. In 2011, EMA and FDA biosimilar clusters were established, which now also include Health Canada and the Japanese Pharmaceuticals and Medical Devices Agency, to align biosimilar product evaluation scientific approaches. The overall aim is to harmonize regulatory requirements to allow a global biosimilar product development approach.[123]

References
1. *Biologics Price Competition and Innovation Act* of 2009 (*BPCI Act*). FDA website. http://www.fda.gov/downloads/Drugs/GuidanceComplianceRegulatoryInformation/UCM216146.pdf. Accessed 1 April 2019.
2. *Patient Protection and Affordable Care Act* of 2010 (*PPACA*). HHS website. https://www.hhs.gov/healthcare/about-the-law/read-the-law/#. Accessed 1 April 2019.
3. *Public Health Service Act* (*PHS Act*). 42 US Code §262, page 356. GPO website. https://www.gpo.gov/fdsys/pkg/USCODE-2010-title42/pdf/USCODE-2010-title42-chap6A.pdf. Accessed 1 April 2019.
4. *Drug Price Competition and Patent Term Restoration Act* of 1984 (*Hatch-Waxman Act*). Public Law 98-417. GPO website. https://www.gpo.gov/fdsys/pkg/STATUTE-98/pdf/STATUTE-98-Pg1585.pdf. Accessed 1 April 2019.
5. *Food, Drug, and Cosmetics Act* of 1938 (*FD&C Act*). 21 US Code 9. GPO website. https://www.gpo.gov/fdsys/pkg/USCODE-2011-title21/pdf/USCODE-2011-title21-chap9.pdf. Accessed 1 April 2019.
6. Op cit 1.
7. Information on Biosimilars. FDA website. http://www.fda.gov/drugs/developmentapprovalprocess/howdrugsaredevelopedandapproved/approvalapplications/therapeuticbiologicapplications/biosimilars/default.htm. Accessed 1 April 2019.
8. Biosimilars Guidances. FDA website. http://www.fda.gov/Drugs/GuidanceComplianceRegulatoryInformation/Guidances/ucm290967.htm. Accessed 1 April 2019.
9. *Scientific Considerations in Demonstrating Biosimilarity to a Reference Product: Guidance for Industry* (April 2015). FDA website. http://www.fda.gov/ucm/groups/fdagov-public/documents/document/ucm291128.pdf. Accessed 1 April 2019.
10. Op cit 1.
11. *Questions and Answers on Biosimilar Development and the BPCI Act: Guidance for Industry* (December 2018). FDA website. http://www.fda.gov/ucm/groups/fdagov-public/@fdagov-drugs-gen/documents/document/ucm444661.pdf. Accessed 1 April 2019.
12. Ibid.
13. *Comparability of Biotechnological/Biological Products Subject to Changes in Their Manufacturing Process Q5E* (November 2004). ICH website. http://www.ich.org/fileadmin/Public_Web_Site/ICH_Products/Guidelines/Quality/Q5E/Step4/Q5E_Guideline.pdf. Accessed 1 April 2019.
14. Op cit 3, page 357.
15. Op cit 3, page 356.
16. *Guidance for Industry—Providing Clinical Evidence of Effectiveness for Human Drug and Biologic Products* (May 1998).
17. Op cit 9, page 8.
18. Search for FDA Guidance Documents. FDA website. http://www.fda.gov/RegulatoryInformation/Guidances/default.htm. Accessed 1 April 2019.

19. Op cit 9.
20. *Biosimilar User Fee Act* of 2012 (*BsUFA*). FDA website. https://www.fda.gov/forindustry/userfees/biosimilaruserfeeactbsufa/default.htm. Accessed 1 April 2019.
21. *Food and Drug Administration Safety and Innovation Act* of 2012 (*FDASIA*). Public Law 112-144. GPO website. https://www.gpo.gov/fdsys/pkg/BILLS-112s3187enr/pdf/BILLS-112s3187enr.pdf. Accessed 1 April 2019.
22. Op cit 20, pp. 4–5.
23. *Biosimilar User Fee Act*, Latest News. FDA website. http://www.fda.gov/ForIndustry/UserFees/BiosimilarUserFeeActBsUFA/. Accessed 17 January 2019.
24. Op cit 20, pp. 5–6.
25. Op cit 23.
26. Ibid.
27. Number of biosimilar investigational new drug applications (INDs) received in the month. FDA website. http://www.accessdata.fda.gov/scripts/fdatrack/view/track.cfm?program=cder&id=CDER-RRDS-Number-of-biosimilar-INDs. Accessed 1 April 2019.
28. Transfer of Therapeutic Products to the Center for Drug Evaluation and Research (CDER). FDA website. http://www.fda.gov/AboutFDA/CentersOffices/OfficeofMedicalProductsandTobacco/CBER/ucm133463.htm. Accessed 1 April 2019.
29. Op cit 9, pp. 7–8.
30. *Formal Meetings Between the FDA and Sponsors or Applicants of BsUFA Products* (June 2018). FDA website. https://www.fda.gov/downloads/Drugs/GuidanceComplianceRegulatoryInformation/Guidances/UCM609662.pdf. Accessed 1 April 2019.
31. Ibid.
32. Op cit 20.
33. Op cit 30, pp. 12–14.
34. Number of biosimilar biological product development (BPD) Type 1–4 meeting requests received in the month. FDA website. http://www.accessdata.fda.gov/scripts/fdatrack/view/track.cfm?program=cder&id=CDER-RRDS-Number-of-BPD-meetings. Accessed 1 April 2019.
35. Op cit 23.
36. Biosimilar User Fee Act; Public Meeting. 19 September 2016. Federal Register Docket No. FDA-2015-N-3326. GPO website. https://www.gpo.gov/fdsys/pkg/FR-2016-09-19/pdf/2016-22442.pdf. Accessed 17 January 2019.
37. Biosimilar biologic product reauthorization performance goals and procedure fiscal years 2018–2022. FDA website. http://www.fda.gov/downloads/ForIndustry/UserFees/BiosimilarUserFeeActBsUFA/UCM521121.pdf. Accessed 1 April 2019.
38. Op cit 9, page 3.
39. Op cit 9.
40. *Quality Considerations in Demonstrating Biosimilarity of a Therapeutic Protein, Product to a Reference Product: Guidance for Industry* (April 2015). FDA website. http://www.fda.gov/downloads/drugs/guidances/ucm291134.pdf. Accessed 1 April 2019.
41. Op cit 9.
42. Op cit 40.
43. ICH Guidelines. ICH website. http://www.ich.org/products/guidelines.html. Accessed 1 April 2019.
44. ICH Efficacy Guidelines. ICH website. http://www.ich.org/products/guidelines/efficacy/article/efficacy-guidelines.html. Accessed 1 April 2019.
45. ICH Safety Guidelines. ICH website. http://www.ich.org/products/guidelines/safety/article/safety-guidelines.html. Accessed 1 April 2019.
46. *Guidance on Nonclinical Safety Studies for the Conduct of Human Clinical Trials and Marketing Authorization for Pharmaceuticals M3(R2)* (11 June 2009). ICH website. http://www.ich.org/fileadmin/Public_Web_Site/ICH_Products/Guidelines/Multidisciplinary/M3_R2/Step4/M3_R2__Guideline.pdf. Accessed 1 April 2019.
47. Final Endorsed Concept Paper M10: Bioanalytical Method Validation (7 October 2016). ICH website. http://www.ich.org/fileadmin/Public_Web_Site/ICH_Products/Guidelines/Multidisciplinary/M10/ICH_M10_Concept_paper_final_7Oct2016.pdf. Accessed 1 April 2019.
48. ICH Quality Guidelines. ICH website. http://www.ich.org/products/guidelines/quality/article/quality-guidelines.html. Accessed 1 April 2019.
49. *Comparability of Biotechnological/Biological Products Subject to Changes in Their Manufacturing Process Q5E* (18 November 2004). ICH website. http://www.ich.org/fileadmin/Public_Web_Site/ICH_Products/Guidelines/Quality/Q5E/Step4/Q5E_Guideline.pdf. Accessed 1 April 2019.
50. Op cit 9.
51. Op cit 3.
52. Op cit 9, page 6.
53. Op cit 11, page 8.
54. Op cit 9.
55. Op cit 40.
56. Coordinated Framework for Regulation of Biotechnology. 51 *Federal Register* 23303 (26 June 1986). Executive Office of the President, Office of Science and Technology Policy. https://www.aphis.usda.gov/brs/fedregister/coordinated_framework.pdf. Accessed 1 April 2019.
57. Points to Consider in the Production and Testing of New Drugs and Biologicals Produced by Recombinant DNA Technology (10 April 1985). FDA website. http://www.fda.gov/downloads/BiologicsBloodVaccines/GuidanceComplianceRegulatoryInformation/OtherRecommendationsforManufacturers/UCM062750.pdf. Accessed 1 April 2019.
58. Demonstration of Comparability of Human Biological Products, Including Therapeutic Biotechnology-Derived Products (April 2016). FDA website. http://www.fda.gov/Drugs/GuidanceComplianceRegulatoryInformation/Guidances/ucm122879.htm. Accessed 1 April 2019.
59. Op cit 49.
60. Op cit 40.
61. *Guidance for Industry: Q6B Specifications: Test Procedures and Acceptance Criteria for Biotechnological/Biological Products*. (August 1999). FDA website. http://www.fda.gov/downloads/drugs/guidancecomplianceregulatoryinformation/guidances/ucm073488.pdf. Accessed 1 April 2019.
62. Op cit 40.
63. *Clinical Pharmacology Data to Support a Demonstration of Biosimilarity to a Reference Product: Guidance for Industry* (December 2016). FDA website. http://www.fda.gov/downloads/drugs/guidancecomplianceregulatoryinformation/guidances/ucm397017.pdf. Accessed 1 April 2019.
64. Ibid.
65. *Bioanalytical Method Validation: Guidance for Industry* (May 2018). FDA website. http://www.fda.gov/downloads/Drugs/Guidance/ucm070107.pdf. Accessed 1 April 2019.
66. Op cit 47.
67. Op cit 1.
68. Woodcock J, et al. The FDA's assessment of follow-on protein products (June 2007). Nat Rev Drug Discov. PubMed website. https://www.ncbi.nlm.nih.gov/pubmed/17633790. Accessed 1 April 2019.
69. *Draft Guidance for Industry: Applications Covered by Section 505(b)(2)* (October 1999). FDA website. http://www.fda.gov/downloads/Drugs/Guidances/ucm079345.pdf. Accessed 1 April 2019.
70. Op cit 1.
71. 21 CFR Part 600 Biological Products: General. FDA website. https://www.accessdata.fda.gov/scripts/cdrh/cfdocs/cfCFR/CFRSearch.cfm?CFRPart=600. Accessed 1 April 2019.

72. 21 CFR Part 601 Licensing. FDA website. http://www.accessdata.fda.gov/scripts/cdrh/cfdocs/cfcfr/CFRsearch.cfm?CFRPart=601. Accessed 1 April 2019.
73. 21 CFR Part 610 General Biological Product Standards. FDA website. https://www.accessdata.fda.gov/scripts/cdrh/cfdocs/cfcfr/CFRSearch.cfm?CFRPart=610. Accessed 1 April 2019.
74. Op cit 11.
75. Ibid.
76. *New and Revised Draft Q&As on Biosimilar Development and the BPCI Act* (December 2018). FDA website. http://www.fda.gov/downloads/Drugs/Guidances/UCM273001.pdf. Accessed 1 April 2019.
77. *Pediatric Research Equity Act* of 2003 (*PREA*). FDA website. http://www.fda.gov/downloads/Drugs/DevelopmentApprovalProcess/DevelopmentResources/UCM077853.pdf. Accessed 1 April 2019.
78. Op cit 2, page 699.
79. Op cit 11.
80. 21 CFR Part 312 Investigational New Drug Application. e-CFR website. https://www.ecfr.gov/cgi-bin/ECFR?page=browse. Accessed 1 April 2019.
81. *Nonproprietary Naming of Biological Products: Guidance for Industry* (January 2017). FDA website. http://www.fda.gov/downloads/drugs/guidances/ucm459987.pdf. Accessed 1 April 2019.
82. *USP Dictionary of U.S. Adopted Names and International Drug Names Released; 51st Edition of a Comprehensive Guide on Drug Substances* (7 January 2015). USP website (subscription required). http://www.usp.org/news/usp-dictionary-us-adopted-names-and-international-drug-names-released-51st-edition-comprehensive-guide-drug-substances. Accessed 1 April 2019.
83. United States Adopted Names Naming Guidelines. AMA website. https://www.ama-assn.org/about/united-states-adopted-names/united-states-adopted-names-naming-guidelines. Accessed 1 April 2019.
84. 21 CFR Part 299, Subpart A §299.4 Established Names for Drugs. GPO website. http://www.ecfr.gov/cgi-bin/text-idx?SID=3a3b62f973e6140ccbe4a138d95ea969&mc=true&node=pt21.4.299&rgn=div5#se21.4.299_14. Accessed 1 April 2019.
85. Op cit 81.
86. International Nonproprietary Names (INN) for biological and biotechnological substances (a review). WHO website. http://www.who.int/medicines/services/inn/BioRev2013.pdf. Accessed 1 April 2019.
87. Op cit 81.
88. *Nonproprietary Naming of Biological Products; Draft Guidance for Industry* (Availability). *Federal Register* Docket No. FDA-2013-D-1543. GPO website. https://www.gpo.gov/fdsys/pkg/FR-2017-01-13/html/2017-00694.htm. Accessed 1 April 2019.
89. Agency Information Collection Activities; Submission for Office of Management and Budget Review; Comment Request; Guidance for Industry on Nonproprietary Naming of Biological Products (2 June 2016). *Federal Register* Docket No. FDA-2013-D-01543. *Federal Register* website. https://www.federalregister.gov/documents/2016/06/02/2016-12885/agency-information-collection-activities-submission-for-office-of-management-and-budget-review. Accessed 1 April 2019.
90. Op cit 85.
91. *Implementation of the "Deemed to be a License" Provision of the Biologics Price Competition and Innovation Act of 2009: Guidance for Industry* (March 2016). FDA website. http://www.fda.gov/downloads/drugs/guidancecomplianceregulatoryinformation/guidances/ucm490264.pdf. Accessed 1 April 2019.
92. *Labeling for Biosimilar Products: Guidance for Industry* (July 2018). FDA website. http://www.fda.gov/downloads/drugs/guidancecomplianceregulatoryinformation/guidances/ucm493439.pdf. Accessed 1 April 2019.
93. Ibid.
94. 21 CFR 201.56(c)(1) and 201.56(d) (the latter known as part of the *Physician Labeling Rule*). FDA website. https://www.accessdata.fda.gov/scripts/cdrh/cfdocs/cfcfr/CFRSearch.cfm?fr=201.56. Accessed 11 April 2019.
95. 21 CFR Part 201 Labeling Sections 201.57 and 201.57(c)(9)(i)–iii). FDA website. https://www.accessdata.fda.gov/scripts/cdrh/cfdocs/cfCFR/CFRSearch.cfm?fr=201.57. Accessed 11 April 2019.
96. 21 CFR 201, 314, and 601: Requirements on Content and Format of Labeling for Human Prescription Drug and Biological Products and Draft Guidances and Two Guidances for Industry on the Content and Format of Labeling for Human Prescription Drug and Biological Products; Final Rule and Notices. (24 January 2006) *Federal Register* Vol. 17 No. 15. FDA website. http://www.fda.gov/OHRMS/DOCKETS/98fr/06-545.pdf. Accessed 11 April 2019.
97. Content and Format of Labeling for Human Prescription Drug and Biological Products; Requirements for Pregnancy and Lactation Labeling (4 December 2014) *Federal Register Docket* No. FDA-2006-N-0515. FDA website. https://www.fda.gov/downloads/aboutfda/reportsmanualsforms/reports/economicanalyses/ucm427798.pdf. Accessed 1 April 2019.
98. Op cit 92.
99. Ibid.
100. Op cit 1.
101. United States Court of Appeals for the Federal Circuit. Amgen Inc., Amgen Manufacturing Limited v. Sandoz Inc. 2015-1499 (21 July 2015), Court Ruling. uscourts.com website. http://www.cafc.uscourts.gov/sites/default/files/s15-1499.pdf. Accessed 1 April 2019.
102. *Guidance for Industry: Reference Product Exclusivity for Biological Products filed Under Section 351(a) of the PHS Act* (August 2014). FDA website. http://www.fda.gov/downloads/drugs/guidancecomplianceregulatoryinformation/guidances/ucm407844.pdf. Accessed 1 April 2019.
103. Op cit 20.
104. Op cit 102.
105. Drugs@FDA: FDA Approved Drug Products. FDA website. https://www.accessdata.fda.gov/scripts/cder/daf/index.cfm?event=overview.process&ApplNo=103353. Accessed 1 April 2019.
106. Mueller L. Unwrapping the BPCIA Patent Dance Riddle for Biosimilar Companies (June 2016). Biosimilar Development website. https://www.biosimilardevelopment.com/doc/unwrapping-the-bpcia-patent-dance-riddle-for-biosimilar-companies-0001. Accessed 1 April 2019.
107. Citizen Petition From Sidney Austin LLP (29 October 2014). Regulations.gov website. https://www.regulations.gov/document?D=FDA-2014-P-1771-0001. Accessed 1 April 2019.
108. Sullivan T. District Court Denies Amgen's Motion for Preliminary Injunction to Prevent Marketing of Sandoz's Biosimilar Zarxio (May 2018). Policy & Medicine website. https://www.policymed.com/2015/03/district-court-denies-amgens-motion-for-preliminary-injunction-to-prevent-marketing-of-sandozs-biosi.html. Accessed 1 April 2019.
109. Citizen Petition Denial Response (25 March 2015) Docket No. 2014-P-1771. Regulations.gov website. https://www.regulations.gov/document?D=FDA-2014-P-1771-0004. Accessed 1 April 2019.
110. Op cit 3.
111. Op cit 4.
112. Op cit 109.
113. Op cit 108.
114. United States District Court Northern District of California. Amgen's motion and Motion for an Injunction Pending Appeal. Amgen Inc. and Amgen Manufacturing, Limited vs. Sandoz Inc., Sandoz International GMBH, and Sandoz GMBH (24 March 2015) Case No. 3:14-cv-04741-RS. FDA Law Blog. http://www.fdalawblog.net/NEUPOGEN%20-%20Amgen%20Injunction%20Pending%20Appeal.pdf. Accessed 1 April 2019.

115. United States Court of Appeals for the Federal Circuit. On Motion Per Curiam Order. Amgen Inc, Amgen Manufacturing Limited vs Sandoz Inc. (5 May 2015) Case No. 2015-1499. Orange Book Blog website. http://orangebookblog.typepad.com/files/order-3.pdf. Accessed 1 April 2019.
116. Op cit 107.
117. Noonan KE. Sandoz Petitions High Court to Review the Federal Circuit's Decision on the BPCI Act's 180-Day Notice of Commercial Marketing Provision (17 February 2016). Patent Law Weblog. http://www.fdalawblog.net/fda_law_blog_hyman_phelps/2016/02/sandoz-petitions-high-court-to-review-the-federal-circuits-decision-on-the-bpcias-180-day-notice-of-.html. Accessed 1 April 2019.
118. Shehan JC. Amgen Asks the Supreme Court to Reject Challenge on Ruling that Notice of Commercial Marketing is Mandatory, But Asks for Review of Patent Dance Ruling Just in Case (28 March 2016). FDA Law Blog website. http://www.fdalawblog.net/fda_law_blog_hyman_phelps/2016/03/amgen-asks-the-supreme-court-to-reject-challenge-to-ruling-that-notice-of-commercial-marketing-is-mandatory-but-asks-for-rev.html. Accessed 1 April 2019.
119. Karst KR. Solicitor General Urges SCOTUS to Take Up Sandoz and Amgen Petitions on the BPCIA's Notice and Patent Dance Provisions (8 December 2016). FDA Law Blog website. http://www.fdalawblog.net/fda_law_blog_hyman_phelps/2016/12/solicitor-general-urges-scotus-to-take-up-sandoz-and-amgen-petitions-on-the-bpcias-notice-and-patent.html. Accessed 1 April 2019.
120. Supreme Court of the United States Blog. Amgen Inc. v Sandoz Inc. SCOTUSblog website. http://www.scotusblog.com/case-files/cases/amgen-inc-v-sandoz-inc/. Accessed 1 April 2019.
121. Ibid.
122. Fischer A. Supreme Court Decides Amgen v. Sandoz: Patent Dance Cannot Be Enforced by Federal Injunction, Notice of Commercial Marketing Can Be Given at Any Time. Biologics Blog website. https://www.biologicsblog.com/supreme-court-decides-amgen-v-sandoz-patent-dance-cannot-be-enforced-by-federal-injunction-notice-of-commercial-marketing-can-be-given-at-any-time. Accessed 1 April 2019.
123. Cluster Activities. EMA website. http://www.ema.europa.eu/ema/index.jsp?curl=pages/partners_and_networks/general/general_content_000655.jsp&mid=WC0b01ac0580953d98. Accessed 1 April 2019.

Chapter 15

Biologics Labeling, Advertising and Promotion

By Kathrin Schalper, PhD, RAC

OBJECTIVES

- Understand FDA requirements for labeling of biological drugs under CBER or CDER's jurisdiction

- Review FDA requirements for advertising and promotion of biological drugs under CBER or CDER's jurisdiction

- Understand these regulations' application through FDA compliance and enforcement

- Learn how to differentiate promotional activities from educational, scientific exchange and disease awareness activities

LAWS, REGULATIONS AND GUIDELINES COVERED IN THIS CHAPTER

- *Federal Food, Drug, and Cosmetic Act (FD&C Act) of 1938*

- *Public Health Service Act (PHS Act)*

- *Kefauver-Harris Drug Amendments (1962)*

- *Drug Supply Chain Security Act (DSCSA) of 2013*

- 21 CFR 99 Dissemination of information on unapproved/new uses for marketed drugs, biologics and devices

- 21 CFR 201 Labeling

- 21 CFR 202.1 Prescription drug advertisements

- 21 CFR 203 Prescription drug marketing

- 21 CFR 208 Medication guides for prescription drug products

- 21 CFR 312.6–7 Labeling and promotion for investigational new drugs

- 21 CFR 314.70 Supplements and other changes to an approved application

- 21 CFR 314.81 Other postmarketing reports

- 21 CFR 601.2 Applications for biologics licenses; procedures for filing

- 21 CFR 601.12 Changes to an approved application

- 21 CFR 601.25 Review procedures to determine that licensed biological products are safe, effective, and not misbranded under prescribed, recommended, or suggested conditions of use

- 21 CFR 601.45 Promotional materials

- 21 CFR 610 Subpart G Labeling standards

Chapter 15

- ❑ 21 CFR 606.120–122 Labeling, general requirements

- ❑ 21 CFR 660 Additional standards for diagnostic substances for laboratory tests

- ❑ 21 CFR 660.2(c) General requirements, labeling

- ❑ 21 CFR 660.28 Blood grouping reagent labeling

- ❑ 21 CFR 660.35 Reagent red blood cells labeling

- ❑ 21 CFR 660.45 Hepatitis B surface antigen labeling

- ❑ 21 CFR 660.55 Anti-human globulin labeling

- ❑ *Draft Guidance for Industry: Brief Summary and Adequate Directions for Use: Disclosing Risk Information in Consumer-Directed Print Advertisements and Promotional Labeling for Human Prescription Drugs (February 2015)*

- ❑ Patient Counseling Information Section of Labeling for Human Prescription Drug and Biological Products—Contents and Format (December 2014)

- ❑ Pregnancy, Lactation, and Reproductive Potential: Labeling for Human Prescription Drug and Biological Products—Contents and Format (December 2014)

- ❑ Structured Product Labeling (SPL) Implementation Guide with Validation Procedures (May 2018)

- ❑ *Guidance for Industry: Labeling for Human Prescription Drug and Biological Products Approved Under the Accelerated Approval Regulatory Pathway (January 2019)*

- ❑ *Guidance for Industry: Clinical Pharmacology Labeling for Human Prescription Drug and Biological Products—Considerations, Content and Format (December 2016)*

- ❑ *Guidance for Industry: Product Name Placement, Size, and Prominence in Advertising and Promotional Labeling (December 2017)*

- ❑ *Guidance for Industry: Labeling for Human Prescription Drug and Biological Products— Implementing the PLR Content and Format Requirements (February 2013)*

- ❑ *Draft Guidance for Industry: Pediatric Information Incorporated Into Human Prescription Drug and Biological Products Labeling Good Review Practice (February 2013)*

- ❑ *Guidance for Industry: Providing Regulatory Submissions in Electronic Format—Certain Human Pharmaceutical Product Applications and Related Submissions Using the eCTD Specifications (January 2019)*

- ❑ *Draft Guidance for Industry: Direct-to-Consumer Television Advertisements—FDAAA DTC Television Ad Pre-Dissemination Review Program (March 2012)*

- ❑ *Draft Guidance for Industry: Fulfilling Regulatory Requirements for Postmarketing Submissions of Interactive Promotional Media for Prescription Human and Animal Drugs and Biologics (January 2014)*

- ❑ *Draft Guidance for Industry: Internet/Social Media Platforms with Character Space Limitations—Presenting Risk and Benefit Information for Prescription Drugs and Medical Devices (June 2014)*

- ❑ *Draft Guidance for Industry: Presenting Quantitative Efficacy and Risk Information in Direct-to-Consumer Promotional Labeling and Advertisements Guidance for Industry (October 2018)*

- ❑ *Guidance: Medication Guides—Distribution Requirements and Inclusion in Risk Evaluation and Mitigation Strategies (REMS) (November 2011)*

- ❑ *Guidance for Industry: Warnings and Precautions, Contraindications, and Boxed Warning Sections of Labeling for Human Prescription Drug and Biological Products— Content and Format (October 2011)*

- ❑ *Guidance for Industry: Bar Code Label Requirements (August 2011)*

- Guidance for Industry: Content and Format of the Dosage and Administration Section of Labeling for Human Prescription Drug and Biological Products (March 2010)

- Guidance for Industry: Contents of a Complete Submission for the Evaluation of Proprietary Names (April 2016)

- Draft Guidance for Industry: SPL Standard for Content of Labeling Technical Qs & As (October 2009)

- Guidance for Industry: Labeling for Human Prescription Drug and Biological Products—Determining Established Pharmacologic Class for Use in the Highlights of Prescribing Information, Good Review Practice (October 2009)

- Draft Guidance for Industry: Presenting Risk Information in Prescription Drug and Medical Device Promotion (May 2009)

- Guidance for Industry: Indexing Structured Product Labeling (June 2008)

- Guidance for Industry: Adverse Reactions Section of Labeling for Human Prescription Drug and Biological Products—Content and Format (January 2006)

- Guidance for Industry: Clinical Studies Section of Labeling for Human Prescription Drug and Biological Products—Content and Format (January 2006)

- Draft Guidance for Industry: Public Availability of Labeling Changes in "Changes Being Effected" Supplements (September 2006)

- Guidance for Industry: Providing Regulatory Submissions in Electronic Format—Content of Labeling (April 2005)

- Guidance for Industry: Consumer-Directed Broadcast Advertisements (August 1999)

- Final Guidance on Industry-Supported Scientific and Educational Activities (November 1997)

- Guidance for Industry: Changes to an Approved Application: Biological Products (July 1997)

- Guidance for Industry: Labeling of Biosimilar Products (July 2018)

- Guidance for Industry: Content and Format for Geriatric Labeling (October 2001)

- Draft Guidance for Industry: Internet/Social Media Platforms: Correcting Independent Third-Party Misinformation About Prescription Drugs and Medical Devices. Food and Drug Administration (June 2014)

Introduction

The *Federal Food, Drug, and Cosmetic Act* of 1938 (*FD&C Act*) grants the US Food and Drug Administration (FDA) authority over "labeling" for prescription drug and biological products. The *FD&C Act* defines a "label" as a display of written, printed or graphic material on the immediate container of a drug, and Section 201(m) of the *FD&C Act* defines "labeling" to mean "all labels and other written, printed, or graphic matter (1) upon any article or any of its containers or wrappers, or (2) accompanying such article." Therefore, it includes container labels, professional labeling (generally referred to as the package insert or United States Prescribing Information (USPI)), patient labeling (Patient Package Insert (PPI)), Medication Guides, Instructions for Use and risk management materials.

The umbrella term "labeling" also is used to describe promotional materials. The US Supreme Court has explained the language "accompanying such article" in the "labeling" definition is interpreted broadly, and no physical attachment between the materials and the article is necessary. As such, FDA generally recognizes two types of labeling for drugs, including biologics:
1. FDA-approved labeling
2. promotional labeling

Promotional labeling is any product material (other than FDA-required labeling as defined above) intended to promote a product's use, e.g., a sales aid.

Labeling Regulations and Requirements

The *FD&C Act* provides the legal basis for labeling drugs, devices and biological products. 21 CFR Part 201 provides general label provisions, labeling requirements for prescription and over-the-counter drugs, exemptions and specific labeling claims; 21 CFR Part 601 also provides general label provisions for biological products.

Labeling Filed With Original Biologics License Application (BLA) Submissions

FDA's initial review of biological products' labeling begins when the first Biologics License Application (BLA) is filed. The BLA is a request for permission to introduce or deliver for introduction a biological product into interstate commerce, and labeling information is required in BLA submissions to FDA (21 CFR 601.2), with review and approval by FDA's Center for Biologics Evaluation and Review (CBER) or Center for Drug Evaluation and Review (CDER). There is no designated labeling division within either CBER or CDER; the content of the proposed labeling is reviewed by the assigned product review division's labeling team.

The content and format of the labeling submitted in the BLA is regulated by 21 CFR 201.56–57 and 21 CFR 610.60–68 and further explained in various guidance documents. Typically, four types of prescription drug labeling are submitted in the original BLA:

1. professional labeling with annotated draft labeling text, i.e., the USPI
2. patient labeling, e.g., a Medication Guide
3. draft container and carton labels
4. Structured Product Labeling (SPL)

Professional Labeling: USPI

"Prescribing information," commonly referred to as USPI, professional labeling, content of labeling, package insert, physician labeling, direction circular, circular of information or package circular, is a component of prescription drug labeling and contains the information necessary for safe and effective product use by healthcare professionals.

In 2006, FDA issued final regulations governing prescribing information content and format for human drug and biological products, commonly referred to as the "Physician Labeling Rule" (PLR), since it applies to labeling used by prescribers and healthcare providers.[1] The requirements' goal in 21 CFR 201.56–57 is to enhance prescription drugs' safe and effective use with a clear and concise USPI that is easier to access, read and use, thus facilitating practitioners' use of labeling to make informed prescribing decisions.

Professional labeling submitted with original BLAs and postapproval submissions must conform to the PLR as described in 21 CFR 201.56–57.

USPI includes three sections:
1. Full Prescribing Information (FPI) containing the detailed information necessary for the drug's safe and effective use
2. Highlights of Prescribing Information (Highlights) containing selected FPI information healthcare practitioners most commonly reference and consider most important
3. Table of Contents (Contents) listing FPI sections and subsections

A USPI template according to PLR format is available on FDA's website. Further changes to the PLR format were introduced in 2014 when the final Pregnancy and Lactation Labeling Rule (PLLR) was issued. In addition, several guidances describing prescription drug and biological product labeling content and format requirements are available.

An annotated version of the draft labeling text needs to be included in the BLA submission to substantiate each labeling claim by linking each USPI section to the respective BLA data submitted. This annotated version is a separate file from the draft labeling text required in the initial submission and is called "annotated labeling."

Patient Labeling: Medication Guides, Instructions for Use (IFU) and Patient Package Inserts (PPIs)

"Patient labeling" is another component of FDA-approved labeling for some prescription drugs and biological products intended for patient use, and includes PPIs, Instructions for Use (IFUs) and Medication Guides. FDA requires a Medication Guide for prescription drugs and biological products (21 CFR Part 208.1(a)) when:

- patient labeling could help prevent serious adverse effects
- the patient should be informed about a known serious side effect for decision making
- patient adherence to directions for use is crucial to the drug's effectiveness

Medication Guides are approved by FDA and distributed to patients when the agency determines such a guide is necessary for a drug product's safe and effective patient use (21 CFR 208.1 (b)). Medication Guides also may be required as an element to ensure safe use as part of a drug's Risk Evaluation and Mitigation Strategies (REMS). Of CDER-regulated biological products approved between 2008 and 2016, about 34% had a REMS required at product approval, and the requirement for a Medication Guide has been the most common REMS element.[2]

IFUs are dispensed with biological products regulated as combination products (e.g., a monoclonal antibody supplied in an auto-injector). Such products tend to have complicated dosing instructions, and IFUs help the patient use the product properly.

PPIs also are approved by FDA and are required to be dispensed with specific classes of drug products (i.e., oral contraceptives). For biologics, manufacturers submit PPIs to FDA voluntarily for approval by the agency, but their distribution is not mandated.

Container and Carton Labels

Based on the *FD&C Act* definitions of label and labeling, any outer container, carton or package is "labeling." Biological product labeling regulations further differentiate a "container label," i.e., label on the immediate packaging, from a "package label," i.e., labeling on the outer package (21 CFR 610.60 and 610.61). Per 21 CFR 610.60, biological products' container labels should bear:
1. proper product name
2. manufacturer name, address and license number
3. lot number or other lot identification
4. expiration date
5. recommended individual dose, for multiple dose containers
6. statement, "Rx only," for prescription biologicals

If a Medication Guide is required under 21 CFR Part 208, a statement is required under 21 CFR 208.24(d), instructing the authorized dispenser to provide a Medication Guide to each patient to whom the drug is dispensed and stating how the Medication Guide is provided; in case the container label is too small, the required statement may be placed on the package label.

In special cases, certain information may be expanded or omitted. For example, expansion may be needed if the container is not inserted in any package, or text can be omitted if the container is too small to affix a label containing all the information listed above (see 21 CFR 610.60(b), (c) and (d)). To allow visual content inspection, the label should not cover the container completely.

Per 21 CFR 610.61, biological products' package labels should contain:
1. proper product name
2. manufacturer name, address and license number
3. lot number or other lot identification
4. expiration date
5. preservatives used, if any, and concentration
6. number of containers, if more than one
7. amount of product in the container, expressed as:
    o number of doses
    o volume
    o units of potency
    o weight
    o equivalent volume (for dried product to be reconstituted)
    or
    o such combination of the foregoing as needed for an accurate description of the contents
8. recommended storage temperature
9. the words, "Shake Well" or "Do not Freeze," as required
10. recommended individual dose, for multi-dose container
11. recommended route of administration or reference to such directions in an enclosed circular
12. known sensitizing substances or reference to an enclosed circular containing appropriate information
13. type and calculated amount of antibiotics added during manufacture
14. inactive ingredients, when a safety factor, or reference to an enclosed circular containing appropriate information
15. adjuvant, if present
16. product source, when it is a factor in safe administration
17. identity of each microorganism used in manufacture, where applicable, production medium and inactivation method or reference to an enclosed circular containing appropriate information
18. minimum product potency or the statement, "No US standard of potency"
19. statement, "Rx only," for prescription biologicals

The container and package label font size, type, color, position and legibility should meet the requirements in 21 CFR 610.62. Divided manufacturing responsibility also should be shown on either the package or the container label. Bar code label requirements under 21 CFR 201.25 apply to all biologics except biological devices or blood and blood components intended for transfusion, which follow the requirements in 21 CFR 606.121(c)(13). *Guidance for Industry: Bar Code Label Requirements Questions and Answers* (August 2011) covers requirements for machine-readable blood and blood component label requirements.

As part of the FDA *Drug Supply Chain Security Act*'s (*DSCSA*) product tracing scheme, manufacturers also have been required since November 2018 to place a unique product identifier on each prescription drug package (i.e., serialization) intended to be introduced into interstate commerce. The *DSCSA* also applies to biological products, with a few exceptions, e.g., radioactive biological products. The purpose of the serialization requirement is to enable product tracing throughout the supply chain and facilitate the detection of illegitimate products.

SPL

Labeling changes submitted electronically as part of a regulatory submission must be filed in a specific format FDA can process, review and archive. SPL is a key component for making regulated product information publicly available on FDA's Online Label Repository (http://labels.fda.gov/) and on the National Library of Medicine's DailyMed website (https://dailymed.nlm.nih.gov/dailymed/).

The SPL standard is based on extensible markup language (XML). Instructions for preparing SPL are detailed in *Guidance for Industry: Providing Regulatory Submissions in Electronic Format—Content of Labeling* (April 2005) and *Guidance for Industry: Indexing Structured Product Labeling* (June 2008). The SPL standard should be used when submitting labeling content for biological products to CBER or CDER in XML with original submissions, supplements and annual reports.

Labeling is expected to move toward fully electronic distribution rather than paper format, based on a proposed rule published in 2014. The proposed rule would require sponsors to submit labeling in SPL format for each content change, and labeling would be distributed via FDA's publicly accessible labeling repository. The aim is to ensure the most current prescribing information is available at a single, comprehensive website, so healthcare professionals can access the information readily and be better informed at the time of clinical decision making and dispensing.[3]

Postapproval Labeling Changes and Lifecycle Management

The labeling lifecycle begins when draft labeling is submitted to FDA. During the BLA review phase, labeling content may be revised by the sponsor or at the agency's request. Once labeling is modified and approved by FDA, the sponsor can begin to commercialize the product by promoting and advertising the approved labeling information to both healthcare providers and consumers through various marketing channels such as television, newspapers, magazines, radio or promotional labeling items, such as mailers. However, changes to the initially approved labeling may be required to add new information, or delete or clarify specific information to prevent misunderstanding in the marketplace.

Postapproval labeling changes are managed per *Guidance for Industry: Changes to an Approved Application—Biological Products* (July 1997). Any postapproval labeling changes to a BLA must comply with 21 CFR 314.70 (recombinant DNA-derived protein/polypeptide products and drug antibody conjugates) or 601.12 (all other licensed biologics), to notify FDA about changes to approved applications (21 CFR 314.70(a) and 601.12(a)). Depending on their type, changes may be submitted through a supplement for prior approval (prior approval supplement or PAS) before distribution as a Changes Being Effected (CBE) supplement or by including the information in the Annual Report (21 CFR 314.70(b), (c) and (d); and 601.12(b), (c) and (d)). Depending on the change category, the sponsor needs to develop a strategy, collect necessary information and submit the relevant regulatory documents to FDA.

Advertising and Promotion

Overview of Nonpromotional and Promotional Materials

FDA traditionally has recognized important reasons not to regulate all industry-supported scientific and educational activities as advertising, since this can restrict participants' freedom to discuss data or express views. To permit industry support for scientific and educational discussions, including unapproved uses, FDA has distinguished between nonpromotional and promotional activities and materials. Activities the agency has deemed to be independent from influence by the supporting company and nonpromotional have been neither treated as advertising or labeling, nor subjected to the agency's regulatory scrutiny.

Nonpromotional Scientific and Educational Activities

Scientific media include journal publications and scientific abstracts and presentations at purely scientific forums. To determine whether a communication truly is a scientific exchange, FDA looks at the communicator, disclosures and the program's focus, as described in *Final Guidance on Industry: Supported Scientific and Educational Activities* (November 1997). If a promotional individual (e.g., pharmaceutical sales representative) provides the communication in a promotional venue (e.g., promotional presentation), it is unlikely to be considered nonpromotional. However, if a clinical researcher from the company, in response to a request from a medical society, provides a presentation on current findings in a purely scientific forum, this may qualify as a scientific exchange.

The nuances are slight and sometimes difficult to discern; therefore, this is an area of much discussion. Consequently, in one-on-one communications, sponsors generally do not allow any proactive communication of information that may be deemed inconsistent with the label and restrict any additional information sharing to reactive responses to unsolicited requests from medical customers.

FDA also has made clear on various occasions that it holds the medical affairs department to the same standards as it does sales reps to prevent blurring the lines between promotion and responses to unsolicited requests.[4] As Tom Abrams, Office of Prescription Drug Promotion (OPDP) Director, stated: "Just because you have a person with a different hat in a different booth, if they are promoting a drug [providing off-label information is still] against the law." In line with these requirements, various major biopharmaceutical companies have been fined since 2010 due to, for example, failure to adequately separate medical affairs and sales activities or using scientific advisory boards to promote off-label promotion.

Nonpromotional Disease Awareness and "Help-Seeking" Communications

"Help-seeking" communications or advertisements are disease-awareness communications directed at consumers or healthcare practitioners, discussing a particular disease or health condition, to encourage consumers to seek appropriate treatment from healthcare practitioners. FDA believes this is particularly important for underdiagnosed and undertreated conditions (such as osteoporosis and diabetes).[5] Unlike promotional labeling and prescription drug advertising, disease awareness communications (also called "disease state" communications) are not subject to the requirements of the *FD&C Act* or FDA regulations due to their unbranded nature without the mention of specific products.

However, in the past, there have been instances where FDA felt that companies "masqueraded" promotional material as "disease-state" communication using unbranded website addresses while providing references to their branded websites.[6] Any unbranded communication needs to be clearly distinguishable and separated from branded material the company publishes. If a disease awareness or help-seeking piece and a reminder advertisement are presented in a manner that causes their messages to be linked together by the audience, the failure of the combined communication to include the risk information required under the *FD&C Act* and FDA regulations would cause the advertised product to be misbranded.

In determining whether two communications together qualify as promotional labeling or advertising, FDA considers elements like graphic, visual and thematic presentation, and the physical or temporal proximity of the presentation of the two pieces.

Preapproval Product Communications

FDA generally prohibits any promotional activity and safety and efficacy claims for investigational products, including biologics, prior to approval. Specifically, 21 CFR 312.7(a) states: "A sponsor or investigator, or any person acting on behalf of a sponsor or investigator, shall not represent in a promotional context that an investigational new drug is safe or effective for the purposes for which it is under investigation or otherwise promote the drug." However, companies often need to provide product information to the public prior to approval (e.g., clinical trial recruitment, press releases, etc.). In these instances, the following recommendations can help ensure product information is not linked to promotional safety and efficacy claims:

- when presenting efficacy information, data should be presented objectively, and endpoints and data provided without bias
- when presenting safety information, all adverse event grades with material percentages and/or incidences should be included
- data should not be presented as well-tolerated, revolutionary or robust
- the product's lack of approval should be clarified by using descriptions such as "investigational" or "study medication"
- the presentation should not imply that agency approval to market the product is guaranteed or highly probable.

Promotional Materials: Advertising vs. Promotional Labeling

The *FD&C Act* does not define what constitutes an "advertisement," but per 21 CFR 202.1(l), regulated promotional materials include advertisements in published journals, magazines, other periodicals and newspapers, and advertisements broadcast through such media as radio, television and telephone. Promotional labeling, in contrast, generally is any labeling, other than FDA-required labeling, devised to promote the product, e.g., sales aids or professional mailers. Promotional labeling, in contrast to advertisements, is required to be accompanied by the full USPI instead of just a brief summary. These distinctions are further discussed in the following sections.

Regulatory Oversight of Biologics Advertising and Promotion Labeling

FDA has primary jurisdiction over prescription advertising under the 1962 *Kefauver-Harris Drug Amendments* to the *FD&C Act*, and over biologics advertising under the *Public Health Service Act* (*PHS Act*). Both CDER and CBER have regulatory responsibility for therapeutic biological products, including premarket review and oversight. In some cases, guidance differs between CDER and CBER due to differences in the centers' procedures and infrastructure.

At CBER, the Advertising and Promotional Labeling Branch (APLB) within the Office of Compliance and Biologics Quality is responsible for reviewing and monitoring biological product promotion. Specific oversight activities include reviews of final and draft advertising and promotional labeling of licensed biological products to ensure product communications are fairly balanced (with risks and benefits), truthful, non-misleading and in compliance with federal laws and regulations.

At CDER, OPDP is responsible for promotional materials for biological products, including monoclonal antibodies and recombinant proteins. OPDP consists of two divisions, Division I and Division II, which both handle professional and consumer-directed promotion. Each division oversees different therapeutic classes of drugs. OPDP's primary roles include establishing policy for regulating prescription drug promotion, including advertisements and promotional labeling, and planning and supervising research studies.

FDA does not preapprove or "clear" drug advertising prior to its dissemination except in certain instances, such as accelerated approval applications. Regulatory oversight of promotion serves to ensure the following advertising and promotional labeling overarching principles:
- Drug promotion must be consistent with approved product labeling.
- Promotion (with the exception of reminder labeling) must clearly state at least one FDA-approved use for the drug.
- Claims must be supported by substantial evidence.
- Promotion must not be false or misleading.
- Promotion must be fairly balanced.
- Promotion must reveal all material information.

General Content and Format Requirements

Requirements for information to be included in prescription drug product advertisements, including biologics, are described in detail in 21 CFR 202.1(e)(1)–(5) and in various guidance documents.

The applicable requirements and concepts are briefly reviewed in the following.

Product Name Presentation

As outlined in 21 CFR 202.1 and *Guidance for Industry: Product Name Placement, Size, and Prominence in Advertising and Promotional Labeling*, product names in advertising and promotional labeling for biologics should be presented as follows:
- The entire proprietary (brand or trade) name should be presented together, without any intervening written or graphic matter.
- The established (generic) name must be printed in letters at least half as large as the letters comprising the proprietary name, and the established name's prominence must be comparable with the proprietary name's prominence.
- Ingredients and respective quantities should be listed in the same order as on the product label, and each ingredient's quantity also should correspond to the product label.

Substantiation of Product Claims

As per 21 CFR 202.1, all biological products' advertising and promotional labeling may recommend or suggest only the product's approved use as indicated in the USPI. Any suggestions or recommendations inconsistent with the label's specific product use or indication could constitute off-label promotion or broadening of the indication, causing the advertised product to be misbranded.

To determine whether a product claim is consistent with its approved use, FDA looks at not just the product indication, but also the USPI's clinical trial section. The USPI's clinical trial section provides study background, included patient populations and study results. Generally, if a product is promoted for use in a patient population broader than was tested in the clinical trials used for product approval, it may be construed as broadening the indication and considered a violation of the regulations.

Product claims held to this standard include not just verbal and textual communications, but also graphics. Advertising and promotional labeling graphics must be consistent with the FDA-approved product label and be supported by substantial evidence. For instance, a patient depicted in an advertisement should represent the average patient in the product's clinical trials. An example of an inconsistent advertising claim would contain a graphic of a patient climbing a mountain when the product is indicated for a seriously physically disabling disease; if the majority of patients in the clinical trial had seriously debilitating physical disabilities, this depiction could constitute overstating the product's efficacy.

Consistent with these requirements, CBER issued an Untitled Letter in 2018 covering various promotional pieces for a biological product for treatment of hemophilia, stating "… claims and presentations misleadingly overpromise the effect that the drug will have on a hemophilic patient's activities and overall quality-of-life. Specifically, your promotional materials contain an image of a man playing soccer, which is considered a moderate to dangerous high-risk activity for hemophilic patients because of the bleeding risk associated with the cuts, scrapes, contusions, and similar injuries that occur when people engage in such activity."[7]

In general, all promotional pieces with the exception of reminder advertising (further defined below) must clearly state at least one FDA-approved use for the drug.

Fair Balance and Presentation of Risk Information

The presentation of a product's risks in advertising and promotional labeling in comparison to the efficacy information is of utmost importance. Essentially, safety and effectiveness claims in advertising and promotional labeling must be fairly balanced with risk information. In addition, the risk information must be presented with equal prominence to the promotional claims (21 CFR 202.1(e)(5)). Material facts about the product being promoted also must be communicated, including facts about possible consequences from using the product as suggested in the promotional piece (21 CFR 202.1

(e)(5)(iii)). *Revised Draft Guidance for Industry: Brief Summary and Adequate Directions for Use, Disclosing Risk Information in Consumer-Directed Print Advertisements and Promotional Labeling for Human Prescription Drugs* (February 2015) provides insight into FDA's thinking on appropriate risk presentation and the various factors used to evaluate adequate risk disclosure.

In addition, *FD&C Act* Section 502(n) specifies that prescription drug advertisements need to describe the advertised product's side effects, warnings, precautions, contraindications and effectiveness in the form of a brief summary.

To fulfill the regulatory requirements for fair balance and the brief summary, sponsors typically have included risk information about the product in direct-to-consumer (DTC) print advertisements in both the main part of the advertisement, where the product claims appear, and in a separate brief summary page. The section of the main advertisement where the risks appear often is referred to as the "Important Safety Information" (ISI). Through the revised draft guidance, it has become clear FDA believes the brief summary should focus on the most important risk information rather than an exhaustive list of risks and information, presented in a way consumers are most likely to understand.[8]

When FDA evaluates promotional pieces' risk communication, it looks not only at specific risk statements, but also the net impression. The net impression is the message the promotional piece communicates in its entirety; the piece as a whole should convey an accurate and non-misleading impression of the product's benefits and risks.

Further, even if individual claims are not misleading, if the piece as a whole provides a misleading impression (e.g., the drug is safer than has been proven by substantial evidence), the piece may be deemed violative.

The fair balance requirement applies to any type of promotion for prescription products, regardless of the medium by which it is communicated. Thus, the aforementioned concept of "Important Safety Information" also is frequently used in other marketing channels such as the internet.

Lack of fair balance and omission of risk information is one of the most frequently cited violations. CBER issued an Untitled Letter in 2015 for a video promoting an influenza vaccine, stating "specifically, the video presents multiple efficacy claims ..., such as 'helps you fight the flu,' but fails to present any important safety information ..."

Advertising Requirements for Specific Media

Content and format requirements apply to any biological product promotional piece, regardless of the medium by which it is communicated—including broadcast advertising (on television or radio), print media and the internet or social media. Generally, advertising and promotional labeling are treated in the same manner, with a few distinctions.

One of the key differences is that promotional labeling is required to be accompanied by the full prescribing information, while advertisements include a brief summary of the prescribing information instead.

Broadcast Advertising (Television/Radio)

Prescription drug, including biologics, television and radio broadcast advertisements have specific requirements. First, the advertisement must include a statement of risk-related information relating to the major side effects and contraindications in the audio or audio/video advertisement sections, referred to as the "Major Statement" (21 CFR 202.1(e)(1)). Second, FDA recognizes the medium's inherent limitations by allowing broadcast advertising to include only the most important risk information if the advertisement makes "adequate provision" and directs viewers and/or listeners to a source for full FDA-approved prescribing information. Broadcast advertisements can meet the "adequate provision" requirement, described in *Guidance for Industry Consumer-Directed Broadcast Advertisements* (August 1999), by communicating a drug's prescribing information location, e.g., website address or toll-free telephone number or a healthcare provider (e.g., a doctor or pharmacist).

Print Advertising

A biological product's print advertisements must contain the product's established, quantitative composition; a 'brief summary" relating to side effects, contraindications and effectiveness; direct-to-consumer advertisements must contain a statement encouraging adverse event reporting to FDA (21 CFR 202.1(e)). As consumers are unlikely to understand the traditional approach of including the USPI's risk-related sections verbatim and in small font, FDA believes the brief summary in consumer-directed biologic advertisements, referred to as the consumer brief summary, should focus on the most important risk information, excluding certain information from the USPI or FDA-approved patient labeling. Since the consumer brief summary's risk information is not complete, statements must be included to advise consumers the information is not comprehensive and to speak with their healthcare provider or pharmacist, and the advertisement should contain a toll-free number or website address where FDA-approved labeling can be obtained.

Internet/Social Media Platforms

FDA has issued draft guidances on its thinking on promotion of FDA-regulated medical products, including biologics, on electronic or digital platforms such as the internet and through social media or other technological venues. Internet and social media platforms, such as online microblogs, messaging services (e.g., Twitter) and online paid search (e.g., "sponsored links" on search engines such as Google and Bing) can limit character spaces, as discussed in the *Draft Guidance for Industry Internet/Social Media Platforms with Character Space Limitations—Presenting Risk and Benefit Information for Prescription Drugs and Medical Devices* (June 2014). FDA's policy, regardless of character space constraints, is that a product benefit claim also should incorporate risk information within the same character-space-limited communication.

Sponsors also have devised various mechanisms to meet fair balance requirements for branded websites, such as general product landing pages. One option to ensure fair balance, for example, is designing the website in a way that a box including the ISI stays on top of the page, even if the user is scrolling through the webpage.

A mechanism to allow direct access to a more-complete discussion of risks also must be provided. With respect to user-generated content and misinformation, FDA has determined that firms correcting misinformation about medicinal products may benefit public health and, in addition, has provided recommendations for firms choosing to correct third-party, user-generated misinformation.[9]

In contrast to print or broadcast advertisements, any promotional activity on the internet is considered promotional labeling and, thus, is required to include access to the full prescribing information.

Reminder Labeling
"Reminder labeling," per 21 CFR 201.100(f), calls attention to the drug product's name, but does not include indications for use or dosage recommendations. Reminder labeling must contain the drug product's proprietary name and, optionally, each active ingredient's established name and descriptive information about quantitative ingredient statements, dosage form, package content quantity or price. The assumption behind reminder advertisements is the audience knows what the drug is for and does not need to be told. Reminder advertisements must not include indication(s), dosage recommendation(s) or claims, and are not considered appropriate for drugs whose labeling contains a "black box" warning.

Note, merely indicating a patient population in the material, either through text or a graphic, would violate this exemption and require the sponsor to provide risk disclosure. For instance, if, along with the name (Product X), there was a graphic of a child in the background, it would provide a representation that the product is appropriate for use in a pediatric population and would make

the piece a product claim ad; therefore, the sponsor would have to include the appropriate risk disclosure.

Generally, the distribution of promotional items qualifying as "reminder advertisements," e.g., pens or mugs with product logos, has decreased significantly over the last decade, as they do not advance disease or treatment-related education. The Pharmaceutical Research and Manufacturers of America (PhRMA), one of the leading biopharmaceutical industry associations in the US, instituted a voluntary code in 2009 prohibiting the distribution of "reminder" items.[10]

Promotional Submissions to FDA

Submission at the Time of First Use ("2253 Submissions")
Sponsors are required to submit all biological product advertisements and promotional labeling at the time of dissemination, also referred to as "time of first use," on Form FDA 2253, "Transmittal of Advertisements and Promotional Labeling for Drugs and Biologics for Human Use" (21 CFR 314.81(b)(3)(i). The form requires sponsors to indicate the advertising or promotional labeling type being submitted (using the form's specific coding), as well as the target audience and the initial dissemination date. CBER's APLB requires the same form as CDER's OPDP; however, each center provides slightly different directions on completing the form, so the sponsor should be careful to note these differences. Failure to submit advertising and promotional labeling on Form FDA 2253 constitutes a violation of 21 CFR 314.81(b)(3)(i).

A common industry misconception is if FDA does not comment on an item when submitted at first use on Form FDA 2253, it is deemed to be "approved." This misconception can encourage the continued use of inappropriate or violative materials. In general, submission of Form FDA 2253 is for documentation purposes and does not constitute any type of "approval."

Request for Advisory Comments
While not a requirement, sponsors have the option to request advisory comments on draft advertising and promotional materials. Advisory comments can be requested only for draft materials not yet published or disseminated and currently not in use or in the public domain. When sponsors are uncertain about promotional campaigns or language, this can be a very valuable option. APLB strongly encourages this option's use when launching a new product or indication. Specific directions on how to submit draft materials for advisory comments can be found on the CBER and CDER websites. Note, even after submitting material for advisory comments or withdrawing a submission for advisory comments, the sponsor

still is required to submit the items on Form FDA 2253 at time of dissemination or first use.

Presubmission for Accelerated Approval Products
While most products' promotional materials initially can be submitted to FDA at the time of dissemination, there is an exception that requires prior submission for products approved under the Accelerated Approval program (21 CFR 601.45) and for those that may cause fatalities or serious damage, but for which the information has not been widely publicized (as described in 21 CFR 202.1(j)(1). In these cases, FDA approval prior to dissemination is required.

During the preapproval review period, an Accelerated Approval product sponsor must submit all advertisements and promotional materials intended to be published within 120 days after approval. After 120 days following marketing approval, the applicant must submit all promotional materials at least 30 days prior to the advertisement's intended initial dissemination or publication. Once submitted, the sponsor must wait a minimum of 30 days to receive FDA's advisory comments (often referred to as "pre-clearance"). If no comments are received within 30 days, the sponsor can choose to withdraw the submission and move ahead to use the piece.

FDA Advertising and Promotion Enforcement Activities

FDA can enforce *FD&C Act* or regulation violations through a variety of mechanisms, including: Notices of Violations (NOVs), also known as Untitled Letters; Warning Letters; and, if the violation warrants, referral for judicial action. All three mechanisms are intended to induce compliance with regulations. CBER's APLB reviews complaints about promotional activities or materials related to CBER-regulated products, and OPDP reviews complaints for prescription drug advertising and promotional labeling, including many therapeutic biological products. OPDP's mission is to protect public health by ensuring prescription drug information is truthful, balanced and accurately communicated. The majority of advertising and promotion NOVs are issued by OPDP and can be found on FDA's website. Likewise, APLB publishes Untitled Letters on its website.[11]

NOVs generally are reserved for less-serious violations that do not jeopardize public health greatly but are significant concerns. An NOV usually requires the sponsor to discontinue use of the violative materials along with any other pieces that may contain a similar violation.

Warning Letters usually are reserved for more serious violations that may pose a risk to public safety. They typically contain stronger language and commonly are addressed to the company's CEO. In addition to ceasing use of the violative materials, Warning Letters also may require the company to conduct corrective actions. For example, a company may be required to run a remedial advertisement to reach the same audience as the original violative advertisement or disseminate corrective information through a "Dear Healthcare Professional" letter as described in 21 CFR 200.5(c)(3). Generally, the corrective action is meant to be communicated in the same medium as the original violative piece. Warning Letters frequently direct the sponsor to provide information to FDA on any other promotional items containing similar messages. All FDA Warning Letters, regardless of issuing center or office, are available on FDA's website.[12]

In determining whether a sponsor should be issued an enforcement letter and, if so, which level, FDA often looks at the following elements:
- Do the product materials have recurrent violations?
- Is there a pattern and/or consistency of these violations through different forms of media?
- Is there a risk to public health?

If FDA is not satisfied by the sponsor's Warning Letter response, it may recommend such enforcement actions as injunctions, seizures and/or criminal prosecution. The Department of Justice carries out these activities. One possible outcome is the company agreeing to an arrangement with the government, called a consent decree, which places severe restrictions on the company's operations to ensure it comes into compliance.

Corrective actions FDA can take on inadequate dissemination of medical and scientific information relating to an unapproved use of an approved biologic are outlined in 21 CFR 99.401–405.

Summary
- The umbrella term "labeling" generally is used to describe two types of labeling for biologics: 1) FDA-approved labeling and 2) promotional labeling.
- Typically, four prescription labeling information types are submitted in the original BLA: 1) professional labeling with annotated draft labeling text; 2) patient labeling; 3) draft container and carton labels; and 4) Structured Product Labeling (SPL). Upon approval, the labeling content can be applied appropriately to promotional and advertising activities.
- Biologics' labeling information content and format are subject to FDA regulations, commonly referred to as the "Physician Labeling Rule" (PLR).
- Postapproval changes to original labeling, promotional labeling and advertising content need to be reported to FDA. Depending on the change's nature, it is reported via one of three mechanisms:

Prior Approval Supplement, Changes Being Effected or Annual Report.
- FDA has distinguished differences between promotional and nonpromotional activities, such as scientific and educational activities and disease awareness communications. However, product communications intended to be "nonpromotional" in nature can be subject to FDA regulations if they make product claims.
- Regulated promotional materials include advertisements in published journals, magazines, other periodicals and newspapers and advertisements broadcast via radio, television and telephone.
- FDA has jurisdiction over prescription advertising; both CBER and CDER have regulatory responsibility for biological products' promotional labeling. In CBER, APLB is responsible for promotional materials, while in CDER, OPDP oversees all labeling activities.
- Advertising and promotional labeling must be consistent with FDA-approved product labeling, supported by substantial evidence, not be false or misleading and reveal all material information.
- Generally, advertising and promotional labeling are treated in the same manner; however, some specific requirements exist for broadcast, print and internet or social media platforms.
- Sponsors are required to submit all biological product advertisements and promotional labeling at the time of dissemination, also referred to as "time of first use," and advisory comments can be requested. An exception requires prior submission for products approved under the Accelerated Approval program and those that may cause fatalities or serious damage but for which information has not been widely publicized.
- FDA uses a variety of enforcement tools, such as Notices of Violations, Warning Letters and other corrective actions to ensure industry compliance with the *FD&C Act* and safe and effective use of biologics in patients. Most NOVs related to prescription drug advertising, including many therapeutic biological products, are issued by OPDP.

References

1. PLR Requirements for Prescribing Information. FDA website. https://www.fda.gov/Drugs/GuidanceComplianceRegulatoryInformation/LawsActsandRules/ucm084159.htm. Accessed 14 February 2019.
2. Johnson NA. Assessment of the United States REMS Program Requirements for NDAs and BLAs. Poster Presentation. Drug Information Association Annual Conference (2018).
3. Electronic Distribution of Prescribing Information for Human Prescription Drugs, Including Biological Products. A Proposed Rule by the Food and Drug Administration (December 2014). https://www.federalregister.gov/documents/2014/12/18/2014-29522/electronic-distribution-of-prescribing-information-for-human-prescription-drugs-including-biological. Accessed 14 February 2019.
4. Faget K. The Fine Line between Medical Affairs and Commercial. CBI Events. http://www.cbinet.com/sites/default/files/compendiums/pc17170/Faget_Kyle_pres.pdf. Accessed 14 February 2019.
5. Sullivan T. FDA to Study Disease Awareness Programs. *Policy and Medicine*. https://www.policymed.com/2012/10/fda-to-study-disease-awareness-programs.html. Accessed 14 February 2019.
6. Martin CS. DDMAC Digs Deep to Link Unbranded Websites to Violative Promotional Practices. FDA Law Blog. http://www.fdalawblog.net/2010/05/ddmac-digs-deep-to-link-unbranded-websites-to-violative-promotional-practices-/. Accessed 14 February 2019.
7. IDELVION Untitled Letter (February 2018). FDA website. https://www.fda.gov/downloads/BiologicsBloodVaccines/GuidanceComplianceRegulatoryInformation/ComplianceActivities/Enforcement/UntitledLetters/UCM599432.pdf. Accessed 14 February 2019.
8. Sullivan T. FDA Brief Summary and Adequate Directions for Use: Disclosing Risk Information in Consumer-Directed Print Advertisements and Promotional Labeling for Human Prescription Drugs. Policy and Medicine. https://www.policymed.com/2015/02/brief-summary-and-adequate-directions-for-use-disclosing-risk-information-in-consumer-directed-print.html. Accessed 14 February 2019.
9. *Draft Guidance for Industry: Internet/Social Media Platforms: Correcting Independent Third-Party Misinformation About Prescription Drugs and Medical Devices* (June 2014). FDA website. https://www.fda.gov/downloads/drugs/guidances/ucm401079.pdf. Accessed 14 February 2019.
10. *Code on Interactions with Healthcare Professionals*. PhRMA website. http://phrma-docs.phrma.org/sites/default/files/pdf/phrma_marketing_code_2008-1.pdf. Accessed 14 February 2019.
11. Enforcement Actions (CBER). FDA website. https://www.fda.gov/BiologicsBloodVaccines/GuidanceComplianceRegulatoryInformation/ComplianceActivities/Enforcement/default.htm. Accessed 14 February 2019.
12. Warning Letters and Notice of Violation Letters to Pharmaceutical Companies. FDA website https://www.fda.gov/Drugs/GuidanceComplianceRegulatoryInformation/EnforcementActivitiesbyFDA/WarningLettersandNoticeofViolationLetterstoPharmaceuticalCompanies/default.htm. Accessed 14 February 2019.

Recommended Reading List
- An Introduction to the Improved Prescription Drug Labeling. FDA website. https://www.fda.gov/downloads/training/forhealthprofessionals/ucm090796.pdf. Accessed 14 February 2019.
- OPDP Frequently Asked Questions. (FAQs). FDA website. https://www.fda.gov/AboutFDA/CentersOffices/OfficeofMedicalProductsandTobacco/CDER/ucm090308.htm. Accessed 14 February 2019.
- Basics of Drug Ads. FDA website. https://www.fda.gov/Drugs/ResourcesForYou/Consumers/PrescriptionDrugAdvertising/ucm072077.htm. Accessed 14 February 2019.
- Drug Advertising: A Glossary of Terms. FDA website. https://www.fda.gov/Drugs/ResourcesForYou/Consumers/PrescriptionDrugAdvertising/ucm072025.htm. Accessed 14 February 2019.

Glossary of Terms

21st Century Cures Act (CCA)
Amends various *FD&C Act* and PHS Act sections to include provisions for:
- patient-focused drug development
- advancing new drug therapies
- modern trial design and evidence development
- patient access to therapies and information
- antimicrobial innovation and stewardship
- medical device innovations
- improving FDA scientific expertise and outreach
- medical countermeasures innovation
- vaccine access, certainty and innovation

30-day hold
Time period between filing a protocol under an IND and FDA approval to proceed with enrollment. Also, the time period between when a company submits an IND and when it can initiate a protocol. This timeline may be extended if FDA does not agree with the proposed protocol. (See "Clinical Hold.")

120-day Safety Report
Amendment to an NDA containing a safety update due 120 days after the NDA is filed.

180-day Exclusivity
Protects an ANDA applicant from competition from subsequent generic versions of the same drug product for 180 days.

351(k) Application
An abbreviated BLA for a biological product demonstrated to be biosimilar to or interchangeable with an FDA-licensed biological product.

505(b)(2) Application
An application submitted under FD&C Act Section 505(b)(2) for a drug for which one or more of the investigations relied on by the applicant for approval "were not conducted by or for the applicant and for which the applicant has not obtained a right of reference or use from the person by or for whom the investigations were conducted" (21 U.S.C. 355(b)(2)).

510(k)
- Traditional 510(k): A premarket notification submitted to FDA to demonstrate the medical device to be marketed is as safe and effective or "substantially equivalent" to a legally marketed device. 510(k) refers to the FD&C Act section authorizing the submission of the premarket notification.
- Special 510(k): A type of 510(k) submission for device modifications neither affecting the intended use nor altering its fundamental scientific technology. FDA processing time is 30 days.
- Abbreviated 510(k): A type of 510(k) submission supported by conformance with guidance document(s), special controls or standards.

513(g) Request for Information
When it is unclear into which classification a device falls, a provision in FD&C Act Section 513(g) allows the device sponsor to request a classification determination and regulatory information from FDA. This requires a letter with a description of the device and a fee payment

515 Program Initiative
Created to facilitate reclassification action on the remaining pre-amendments Class III 510(k)s.

Glossary of Terms

522 Postmarket Surveillance Studies Program
Encompasses design, tracking, oversight and review responsibilities for medical device studies mandated under section 522 of the Federal Food, Drug, and Cosmetic Act.

A

AABB
American Association of Blood Banks

ACBTSA
Advisory Committee on Blood and Tissue Safety and Availability

Accelerated Approval
Allows earlier approval of drugs to treat serious diseases and those filling an unmet medical need based on a surrogate endpoint.

Accredited Persons Program
FDA program accrediting third parties to conduct the primary 510(k) review for eligible devices.

ACE
Adverse Clinical Event

ACRP
Association for Clinical Research Professionals

ACT
Applicable Clinical Trial

Action Letter
Official communication from FDA informing an NDA or BLA sponsor of an agency decision; includes approvable, not approvable and clinical hold.

Active Ingredient
Any drug component intended to furnish pharmacological activity or other direct effect in the diagnosis, cure, mitigation, treatment or prevention of disease, or to affect the structure or any function of the body of man or other animals.

ADE
Adverse Drug Event or Adverse Drug Experience

ADME
Absorption, Distribution, Metabolism and Excretion

ADR
Adverse Drug Reaction

Adulterated
Product containing any filthy, putrid or decomposed substance; or prepared under unsanitary conditions; or not made according to GMPs; or containing an unsafe color additive; or not meeting the requirements of an official compendium (FD&C Act, Section 501 [351]).

AdvaMed
Advanced Medical Technology Association

Advisory Committee
Committees and panels used by FDA to obtain independent expert advice on scientific, technical and policy matters.

AE
Adverse Event

AERS
See FAERS

AFDO
Association of Food and Drug Officials

AHRQ
Agency for Healthcare Research and Quality

AIA
America Invents Act of 2011

AIDC
Automatic Identification and Data Capture

AIP
Application Integrity Policy—FDA's approach to reviewing applications that may be affected by wrongful acts raising significant questions regarding data reliability.

ALCOA
Attributable, legible, contemporaneous, original and accurate—Acronym used by FDA to describe data quality.

Amendment
Additions or changes to an ANDA, NDA, BLA, PMA or PMA supplement still under review. Includes safety updates. Any updates to an IND or an IDE prior to approval also are called amendments.

AMS
Agricultural Marketing Service (USDA)

Analyte
In a clinical trial, the part of the sample the test is designed to find or measure.

Glossary of Terms

ANDA
Abbreviated New Drug Application—Used for generic drugs.

Animal Rule
Provides for approval of certain new drug and biological products based on animal data when adequate and well-controlled efficacy studies in humans cannot be conducted ethically because the studies would involve administering a potentially lethal or permanently disabling toxic substance or organism to healthy human volunteers and field trials are not feasible prior to approval.

Anti-Kickback Statute
Prohibits offering, paying, soliciting or receiving anything of value to induce or reward referrals or generate federal healthcare program business.

Annual Report
An annual periodic report or progress report required to be submitted to FDA. Depending on the type of application for which the report is submitted, it may include new safety, efficacy and labeling information; preclinical and clinical investigation summaries; CMC updates; nonclinical laboratory studies; and completed unpublished clinical trials.

ANPR
Advance Notice of Proposed Rulemaking

APhA
American Pharmacists Association

APHIS
Animal and Plant Health Inspection Service

API
Active Pharmaceutical Ingredient

APLB
Advertising and Promotional Labeling Branch (CBER)

Approved
FDA designation given to drugs, biologics and medical devices granted marketing approval.

AQL
Acceptable Quality Level

ASTM
American Society of Testing and Materials

ASQ
American Society for Quality (formerly ASQC)

ASR
Analyte Specific Reagent

ATF
Bureau of Alcohol, Tobacco, Firearms and Explosives

AUT
Actual Use Trials

B

BA/BE Studies
Bioavailability and bioequivalence studies.

Bad Ad Program
Truthful Prescription Drug Advertising and Promotion—Education program for healthcare providers to ensure prescription drug advertising and promotion are truthful and not misleading. Administered by CDER's Office of Prescription Drug Promotion (OPDP).

Banned Device
Device presenting a substantial deception, unreasonable risk of injury or illness, or unreasonable direct and substantial danger to public health.

BCES
Blood establishment computer software

BIMO
Bioresearch Monitoring Program

BIO
Biotechnology Industry Organization

Bioequivalence
The absence of a significant difference in the rate and extent to which the active ingredient or active moiety in pharmaceutical equivalents or pharmaceutical alternatives becomes available at the site of drug action when administered at the same molar dose under similar conditions in an appropriately designed study.

Biologic
A virus, therapeutic serum, toxin, antitoxin, vaccine, blood, blood component or derivative, allergenic product, protein (except any chemically synthesized polypeptide), or analogous product, or arsphenamine or derivative of arsphenamine (or any other trivalent organic arsenic compound) applicable to the prevention, treatment or cure of a disease or condition of human beings.

Regulatory Affairs Professionals Society

Glossary of Terms

Biosimilar
Under the BPCI Act, a biological product may be demonstrated to be "biosimilar" if data show, among other things, the product is "highly similar" to an already-approved biological product.

Bioterrorism Act
Public Health Security and Bioterrorism Preparedness and Response Act of 2002

BLA
Biologics License Application

Blinded Study
Clinical trial in which the patient (single-blind) or patient and investigator (double-blind) are unaware of which treatment the patient receives. Involves use of multiple treatment groups such as other active, placebo or alternate dose groups. Sometimes referred to as "masked."

Boxed Warning
Drugs with special problems, particularly ones that may lead to death or serious injury, may have this warning information displayed within a box in the prescribing information. This often is referred to as a "boxed" or "black box" warning. Drugs with such boxed warnings are not permitted to have reminder advertisements.

BPCA
Best Pharmaceuticals for Children Act of 2002

BPCI Act
Biologics Price Competition and Innovation Act of 2009

BPDR
Biological Product Deviation Report

Breakthrough Therapy Designation
A new pathway to expedite the development of therapies showing substantial promise in early clinical trials. A drug company may seek Breakthrough Therapy designation if the drug is developed for a serious and life-threatening disease and preliminary clinical evidence shows the drug may offer substantial improvement over existing therapies on one or more clinically significant endpoints.

BsUFA
Biosimilar User Fee Act

BsUFA II
Biosimilar User Fee Act of 2017

C

CAP
Color additive petition

CAPA
Corrective and Preventive Actions

CBE-30
Changes Being Effected in 30 days—A submission to an approved application reporting changes FDA has identified as having moderate potential to affect drug product identity, strength, quality, purity and potency adversely. The supplement must be received by FDA at least 30 days before product distribution.

CBER
Center for Biologics Evaluation and Research

CBP
US Customs and Border Protection

CDC
Centers for Disease Control and Prevention

CDER
Center for Drug Evaluation and Research

CDRH
Center for Devices and Radiological Health

CDx
Companion Diagnostic

CF
Consent Form—Document used to inform a potential subject of a clinical trial's risks and benefits per the Declaration of Helsinki. Sometimes referred to as ICF (Informed Consent Form) or ICD (Informed Consent Document).

CFG
Certificate to Foreign Government—Required by certain countries to prove an exported product can be legally marketed in the US.

CFR
Code of Federal Regulations

CFSAN
Center for Food Safety and Applied Nutrition

CGMP
Current Good Manufacturing Practice

CGT Products
Cellular and gene therapy products

CGTP
Current Good Tissue Practice

CH
Clinical Hold

CHIP
Children's Healthcare Insurance Program

CHPA
Consumer Healthcare Products Association

CIOMS
Council for International Organizations of Medical Sciences

CIP
Clinical Investigation Plan

Class I Device
Low-risk device requiring general controls to ensure safety and effectiveness.

Class II Device
Requires general and special controls to ensure safety and effectiveness. Special controls may include guidance documents, mandatory performance standards, patient registries for implantable devices and postmarket surveillance. Requires a 510(k), unless exempted; may require clinical trials.

Class III Device
Requires general controls and premarket approval (PMA); includes devices that are life-sustaining, life-supporting, pose significant potential for risk to patient, or are not substantially equivalent to Class I or Class II devices. PMAs almost always require clinical trials.

Clearance
Devices that receive marketing permission through the 510(k) process based on demonstrating substantial equivalence to a pre-amendment device or another device reviewed under FD&C Act Section 510(k).

CLIA
Clinical Laboratory Improvement Amendments of 1988

Clinical Hold
FDA order to delay proposed clinical investigation or suspend an ongoing investigation.

Clinical Investigator
A medical researcher in charge of carrying out a clinical trial protocol.

ClinicalTrials.gov
A registry and results database of federally and privately supported clinical trials conducted in the US and around the world. Operated by NIH.

CLSI
Clinical and Laboratory Standards Institute (formerly National Committee for Clinical Laboratory Standards)

CMC
Chemistry, Manufacturing, and Controls

CME
Continuing Medical Education

CMS
Centers for Medicare & Medicaid Services

COA
Clinical outcomes assessment—Directly or indirectly measures how patients feel or function and can be used to determine whether a drug has been demonstrated to provide a treatment benefit.

Codex Alimentarius Commission
Develops harmonized international food standards, guidelines and codes of practice to protect the health of consumers and ensure fair practices in the food trade.

COE
Certificate of Exportability—Required by certain countries for the export of unapproved devices not sold or offered for sale in the US; issued by FDA to the exporter.

Combination Product
Defined in 21 CFR 3.2(e) as a combination of two or more different types of regulated products, i.e.:
- a drug and a device
- a device and a biological product
- a drug and a biological product
- a drug, a device and a biological product

Commercial Distribution
Any distribution of a device intended for human use, which is offered for sale but does not include internal or interplant transfer within the same parent, subsidiary or affiliate company or any device with an approved exemption for investigational use.

Glossary of Terms

Common Rule
Requires the research institution's IRB to ensure each research protocol contains adequate provisions to protect a subject during the course of the study.

Companion Diagnostic
An in vitro diagnostic device or an imaging tool providing information essential for the safe and effective use of a corresponding therapeutic product.

Complaint
Any written, electronic or oral communication alleging deficiencies related to a product's identity, quality, durability, reliability, safety, effectiveness or performance after release for distribution.

Component
Any ingredient or part intended for use in the manufacture of a drug, device, cosmetic, biologic or IVD product, including those not appearing in the finished product.

Consent Decree
Enforcement action carried out by the Department of Justice. An agreement between FDA and a company outlining steps to correct CGMP violations by placing severe restrictions on company operations to ensure the firm comes into compliance.

COOL
Country of Origin Labeling—Requirements for source labeling for food products (USDA).

CPG
Compliance Policy Guide

CPGM
Compliance Program Guidance Manual

CPSC
Consumer Product Safety Commission

CRA
Clinical Research Associate

CRC
Clinical Research Coordinator

CRF
Case Report Form—Paper or electronic document used to record data collected in a clinical trial.

CR Letter
Complete response letter—Communicates FDA's decision to a drug company its new drug application (NDA) or abbreviated new drug application (ANDA) to market a new or generic drug will not be approved in its present form.

CRO
Contract Research Organization

CSO
Consumer Safety Officer—Often the FDA contact person for sponsors. Also known as the regulatory project manager.

CTD
Common Technical Document

CTP
Center for Tobacco Products

D

DARRTS
Document Archiving, Reporting and Regulatory Tracking System (CDER)

DBSQC
Division of Biological Standards and Quality Control (CBER)

DDT
Drug Development Tools

DEA
Drug Enforcement Administration

Dear Health Care Professional (DHCP) letter
Correspondence mailed by a manufacturer and/or distributor to physicians and/or other healthcare professionals to convey important information about drugs or devices. DHCP letters are considered promotional labeling and may be associated with recalls or device corrections or removals. These letters can be requested by FDA or initiated by the applicant.

Debarment
An official action in accordance with 21 CFR 1404 to exclude a person from directly or indirectly providing services in any capacity to a firm with an approved or pending drug or device product application. A debarred corporation is prohibited from submitting or assisting in the submission of any NDA or ANDA. Equivalent to disqualification for devices requiring a PMA submission.

Glossary of Terms

Declaration of Helsinki
Ethical principles for medical research involving human subjects. Trials conducted under Good Clinical Practice (GCP) generally follow the Declaration of Helsinki.

Default Decree
A court order entered when a seized article is not claimed or defended. The order condemns the article as being in violation of the law and provides for its destruction, donation to charity, sale or disposal as the court may elect to decree.

De Novo Process
Provides a route to market for low- to moderate-risk medical devices that have been classified in Class III because FDA has found them to be "not substantially equivalent" (NSE) to legally marketed predicate devices.

DESI
Drug Efficacy Study Implementation

DFUF
Device Facility User Fee

DHF
Design History File—Describes a finished device's design.

DHR
Device History Record—Contains a device's production history.

DIA
Drug Information Association

Discipline Review Letter
Used by FDA to convey early thoughts on possible deficiencies found by a discipline review team for its portion of the pending application at the conclusion of the discipline review.

DMC
Data Monitoring Committee

DMEPA
Division of Medication Error Prevention and Analysis (CDER)

DMF
Drug Master File—Submission to FDA that may be used to provide confidential detailed information about facilities, processes or articles used in the manufacturing, processing, packaging and storing of one or more human drugs.

DMPQ
Division of Manufacturing and Product Quality (CBER)

DMR
Device Master Record—Compilation of records containing a finished device's procedures and specifications.

DNCE
Division of Nonprescription Clinical Evaluation (CDER)

DNRD
Division of Nonprescription Regulation Development (CDER)

DRC
Direct Recall Classification Program (CBER)

DRISK
Division of Risk Management (CDER)

DRLS
Drug Registration and Listing System

Drug
Any article intended for use in the diagnosis, cure, mitigation, treatment or prevention of disease in man.

Drugs@FDA
A searchable database of brand-name and generic prescription and OTC human drugs and biological therapeutic products approved since 1939.

Drug Competition Action Plan
FDA action to reduce gaming by branded companies that can delay generic drug entry; resolve scientific and regulatory obstacles that can make it difficult to win approval of generic versions of certain complex drugs; and improve the efficiency and predictability of FDA's generic review process to reduce the time it takes to get a new generic drug approved and lessen the number of review cycles undergone by generic applications before they can be approved.

"Drug Facts" Label
Labeling requirement for all nonprescription, over-the-counter (OTC) medicine labels with detailed usage and warning information so consumers can choose and use the products properly.

Glossary of Terms

Drug Product
A finished dosage form (e.g., tablet, capsule, solution, etc.) containing an active drug ingredient. It generally, but not necessarily, also is associated with inactive ingredients. This includes a finished dosage form not containing an active ingredient but intended to be used as a placebo.

DQSA
Drug Quality and Security Act. Also called the Compounding Quality Act.

DSB
Drug Safety Oversight Board (CDER)

DSCSA
Drug Supply Chain Security Act

DSHEA
Dietary Supplement Health and Education Act of 1994

DSNDCA
Dietary Supplement and Nonprescription Drug Consumer Protection Act

DTC
Direct-to-Consumer (advertising)

D-U-N-S
Data Universal Numbering System—A unique nine-digit sequence provided by Dun & Bradstreet that is specific to each physical location of an entity (e.g., branch, division and headquarters).

E

EA
Environmental Assessment

EA
Expanded access program—also called "compassionate use," provides a potential pathway for patients with an immediately life-threatening condition or serious disease or condition to gain access to an investigational medical product (drug, biologic or medical device) for treatment outside clinical trials when no comparable or satisfactory alternative therapy options are available.

EAP
Expedited Access Pathway Program—A voluntary program for certain medical devices demonstrating the potential to address unmet medical needs for life-threatening or irreversibly debilitating diseases or conditions and subject to PMAs or de novo requests.

eBPDR
Electronic Biological Product Deviation Reports

EC
European Commission, European Community or Ethics Committee

ECO
Emergency Change Order

eCopy (CDRH)
Required format for medical device submissions to FDA. eCopy is an exact duplicate of the paper submission, created and submitted on a CD, DVD or flash drive. The eCopy application must pass certain technical standards before it will be accepted by FDA for review.

eCTD
Electronic Common Technical Document

eDRLS
Electronic Drug Registration and Listing System

EFTA
European Free Trade Association

EIR
Establishment Inspection Report

EMA
European Medicines Agency

eMDR
Electronic Medical Device Reporting requirement for manufacturers and importers to submit MDRs to FDA in an electronic format FDA can process, review and archive. The two options for submitting eMDRs are eSubmitter or Health Level 7 Individual Case Safety Reports (HL7 ICSR).

Emergency Use IND
FDA authorization for shipping a drug for a specific emergency use for a life-threatening or serious disease for which there is no alternative treatment.

EPA
Environmental Protection Agency

Establishment Listing and Registration
In accordance with 21 CFR 807, manufacturers (both domestic and foreign) and initial distributors (importers) of medical devices must register their establishments electronically with FDA. Manufacturers must also list their devices with FDA.

eSubmitter
Under the eMDR program, a free downloadable application allowing submission of MDRs one at a time. This option is suitable for low volume reporters.

ETASU
Elements to Ensure Safe Use

EU
European Union has 28 Member States: Austria, Belgium, Bulgaria, Croatia, Cyprus, Czech Republic, Denmark, Estonia, Finland, France, Germany, Greece, Hungary, Ireland, Italy, Latvia, Lithuania, Luxembourg, Malta, Netherlands, Poland, Portugal, Romania, Slovakia, Slovenia, Spain, Sweden and the UK. EU policies also apply to members of the European Free Trade Association: Iceland, Norway, Switzerland and Liechtenstein.

Excipient
An ingredient contained in a drug formulation that is not a medicinally active constituent.

Expected Life
Time a device is expected to remain functional after being placed into service.

Expiration Date
Date printed on product label indicating the end of the product's useful life. Expiration period length is determined by stability studies and negotiated with FDA.

F

FAERS
FDA Adverse Event Reporting System—A database containing information on adverse event and medication error reports submitted to FDA (CDER).

FALCPA
Food Allergen Labeling and Consumer Protection Act of 2004

FAP
Food additive petition

FAR
Field Alert Report

Fast Track
FDA program to facilitate the development and expedite the review of new drugs intended to treat serious or life-threatening conditions demonstrating the potential to address unmet medical needs. Accelerated NDA review.

FCA
False Claims Act

FCC
Federal Communications Commission

FCS
Food-contact substance

FD&C Act
Federal Food, Drug, and Cosmetic Act of 1938

FDA
Food and Drug Administration

FDAAA
Food and Drug Administration Amendments Act of 2007

FDA ESG
FDA Electronic Submissions Gateway—Enables the secure submission of regulatory information for review.

FDAMA
FDA Modernization Act of 1997

FDARA
FDA Reauthorization Act of 2017

FDASIA
Food and Drug Administration Safety and Innovation Act of 2012

FDLI
Food and Drug Law Institute

FIFRA
Federal Insecticide, Fungicide, and Rodenticide Act

FIH
First in human study

FOIA
Freedom of Information Act

FPI
Full prescribing information

FPLA
Fair Packaging and Labeling Act

FR
Federal Register

Glossary of Terms

FSIS
Food Safety and Inspection Service

FSMA
Food Safety Modernization Act of 2011

FSMP
Food for special medical purposes

FTC
Federal Trade Commission

FURLS
FDA Unified Registration and Listing System for establishment registration of medical device operators and distributors.

G

GAIN Act
Generating Antibiotic Incentives Now Act of 2011

GAO
Government Accountability Office

GARD
National Institute of Health Genetic and Rare Diseases

GCP
Good Clinical Practice—Regulations and requirements with which clinical studies must comply. These regulations apply to manufacturers, sponsors, clinical investigators and Institutional Review Boards.

GDUFA I
Generic Drug User Fee Amendments

GDUFA II
Generic Drug User Fee Amendments of 2017

GE
Genetically engineered

Generic Drug
Drugs manufactured and approved after the original brand-name drug has lost patent protection. Sponsor files an Abbreviated New Drug Application (ANDA) for marketing approval.

GLP
Good Laboratory Practice—Regulations governing the conduct of nonclinical laboratory studies supporting or intended to support research or marketing applications.

GMP
Good Manufacturing Practices (for devices, see Quality System Regulation)

GO
Office of Global Regulatory Operations and Policy (CDER)

GPO
Government Printing Office and Group Purchasing Organization

GPR
General Purpose Reagents

Grandfathered
Tacit approval of drugs marketed before 1938 and devices marketed before May 1976.

GRAS(E)
Generally Recognized as Safe (and Effective)

Group Purchasing Organization (GPO)
An entity consisting of two or more hospitals or other healthcare entities formed to offer its members access to purchasing contracts for health supplies (i.e., pharmaceuticals, biologics, medical/surgical equipment, laboratory supplies and other capital equipment).

GRP
Good Review Practice or Global Regulatory Plan

GTP
Good Tissue Practice

GUDID
Global Unique Device Identification Database

Guidance
Documents published by FDA to provide current interpretation of regulations.

H

HAACP
Hazard Analysis and Critical Control Point (inspection technique)

Hatch-Waxman Act
Drug Price Competition and Patent Restoration Act of 1984

HCEI
Healthcare economic information

HCFAC
Health Care Fraud and Abuse Control Program

HCT/P
Human Cells, Tissues and Cellular and Tissue-Based Products

HDE
Humanitarian Device Exemption

HeartNet
A subnetwork of MedSun (CDRH's adverse event reporting program) focusing on identifying, understanding and solving problems with medical devices used in electrophysiology laboratories.

HEAT
Health Care Fraud Prevention and Enforcement Action Team

HHS
Department of Health and Human Services

HIPAA
Health Insurance Portability and Accountability Act of 1996, also known as the Privacy Rule, established the minimum federal requirements for protecting the privacy of individually identifiable health information.

Homeopathic Drug
Any drug labeled as being homeopathic listed in the Homeopathic Pharmacopeia of the United States (HPUS), an addendum to it or its supplements. Homeopathy is based on the belief disease symptoms can be cured by small doses of substances producing similar symptoms in healthy people.

HPC-C
Hematopoietic progenitor cells derived from cord blood.

HPCUS
Homeopathic Pharmacopoeia Convention of the United States

HPUS
Homoeopathic Pharmacopoeia of the United States

HUD
Humanitarian Use Device

Human Factors
The study or evaluation of how people use technology, specifically the interaction of human abilities, expectations and limitations with work environments and system design.

I

IB
Investigator's Brochure

IC (ICF) (ICD)
Informed Consent (Form) (Document)

ICA
Intercenter Agreement

ICCBBA
International Council for Commonality in Blood Banking Automation

ICH
Founded in 1990, the International Council on Harmonisation of Technical Requirements for Registration of Pharmaceuticals for Human Use develops guidelines intended to simplify the multi-region marketing approval application process for pharmaceutical and biologic manufacturers. Member regulatory bodies include the European Commission, Japan's Ministry of Health, Labour and Welfare and Pharmaceuticals and Medical Devices Agency, the US FDA, Health Canada and Swissmedic. Additional agencies hold membership or observer status.

ICSR
Individual case safety report

IDE
Investigational Device Exemption

IDMC
Independent Data Monitoring Committee

IID
Inactive Ingredient Database

IMDRF
International Medical Device Regulators Forum—A voluntary group of medical device regulators from around the world who have come together to build on the foundational work of the Global Harmonization Task Force on Medical Devices (GHTF) and aims to accelerate international medical device regulatory harmonization and convergence.

Glossary of Terms

Immunogenicity
The ability of a substance to provoke an immune response or the degree to which it provokes a response.

Inactive Ingredient
Any drug product component other than the active ingredient, such as excipients, vehicles and binders.

IND
Investigational New Drug (application)

Information Amendment
Includes most submissions under an active IND, such as new protocols, final study reports, safety reports, CMC information, etc. The initial IND ends with 000; each serial amendment receives the next consecutive number.

INN
International Nonproprietary Names

Intended Use
Objective labeled use of a device.

Investigator IND
Protocol and IND submitted by an individual investigator instead of a manufacturer. A letter of authorization allows FDA to review the sponsor's DMF or cross-reference CMC information. The investigator, not the manufacturer, is responsible for maintaining the IND.

IOM
Investigations Operations Manual or Institute of Medicine

iPSP
Initial Pediatric Study Plan

IRB
Institutional Review Board or Independent Review Board

IR Letter
A communication FDA sends to an applicant during an application or supplement review to request further information or clarification needed or helpful in completing the discipline review.

ISAO
Information Sharing Analysis Organization—cybersecurity information sharing focal points among different private sector and government stakeholders, with an obligation to protect any shared confidential information.

ISI
Important Safety Information

ISO
International Organization for Standardization

IUO
Investigational Use Only

IVD
In Vitro Diagnostic

K

KidNet
A subnetwork of MedSun (CDRH's adverse event reporting program) focusing on identifying, understanding and solving problems with medical devices used in neonatal and pediatric intensive care units.

L

Label
Any display of written, printed or graphic matter on the immediate container or package of, or affixed to, any article.

Labeling
All written, printed or graphic matter accompanying an article at any time while such article is in interstate commerce or held for sale after shipment in interstate commerce; includes user manuals, brochures, advertising, etc.

LDT
Laboratory developed test—A subset of in vitro diagnostic devices designed, manufactured and offered for clinical use by a single laboratory.

LOA
Letter of Authorization—A letter from a Drug Master File holder to FDA authorizing another party to reference the DMF (also Letter of Agreement).

Lookback Procedure
Donor screening procedure used by blood establishments to retrieve and quarantine units previously collected from a donor who originally tested negative for HIV or another infectious disease but subsequently tested positive at a later donation.

M

Major Statement
Refers to the presentation in a television or radio advertisement of a prescription drug's most important risks. This presentation must be spoken. It also can be included in the video part of television advertisements.

Market Withdrawal
Firm-initiated removal or correction of a device, drug or biologic product involving a minor violation of the FD&C Act, not subject to legal action by FDA, or involving no violation, e.g., normal stock rotation practices, routine equipment adjustments and repairs, etc.

MAF
Device Master File—Analogous to a Drug Master File, this submission to FDA may be used to provide confidential detailed information about a medical device or a component used in the manufacture of a medical device to FDA in support of another party's obligation.

MAPP
Manual of Policies and Procedures—Approved instructions for internal practices and procedures followed by CDER staff to help standardize the new drug review process and other activities.

MAUDE
Manufacturer and User Facility Device Experience database (CDRH)—Contains reports of adverse events involving medical devices.

Master Protocol
A protocol with multiple substudies, which may have different objectives and involve coordinated efforts to evaluate one or more investigational drugs, in one or more disease subtypes, within the overall trial structure.

MCB
Master Cell Bank—A collection of cells of uniform composition derived from a single source prepared under defined culture conditions.

MDR
Medical Device Reporting

MDSAP
Medical Device Single Audit Program—Pilot program allowing FDA and other international partners to conduct a single audit of a medical device manufacturer that will satisfy the relevant requirements of the medical device regulatory authorities participating in the pilot program. FDA will accept the MDSAP audit reports as a substitute for routine agency inspections.

MDUFA IV
Medical Device User Fee Amendments of 2018

MDUFMA
Medical Device User Fee and Modernization Act of 2002

MedDRA
Medical Dictionary for Regulatory Activities—Global standard international medical terminology designed to supersede or replace all other terminologies used within the medical product development process including COSTART and WHO-ART.

Medical Device
An instrument, apparatus, implement, machine, contrivance, implant, in vitro reagent or other similar or related article, including any component, part or accessory:
- recognized in the official National Formulary or US Pharmacopeia, or any supplement to them
- intended for use in diagnosis of disease or other conditions, or in cure, mitigation, treatment or prevention of disease in man or other animals intended to affect the structure or any function of the body of man or other animals, and which does not achieve its primary intended purposes through chemical action within or on the body of man or other animals, and which is not dependent upon being metabolized for the achievement of its primary intended purposes (FD&C Act Section 201(h))

Medical Food
A food formulated to be consumed or administered enterally under the supervision of a physician and intended for the specific dietary management of a disease or condition for which distinctive nutritional requirements, based on recognized scientific principles, are established by medical evaluation.

Medication Guide
Paper handouts accompanying many prescription medicines, addressing issues specific to particular drugs and drug classes, containing FDA-approved information to help patients avoid serious adverse events.

MedSun
Medical Product Safety Network—An adverse event reporting program for healthcare professionals launched in 2002 by CDRH.

MedWatch
FDA program for voluntary and mandatory reporting of AEs and product problems (Form FDA 3500 or 3500A).

Glossary of Terms

Misbranded
Designation given to an incorrectly labeled product (i.e., false or misleading or fails to include information required by law). Other violations also may render a product misbranded (e.g., failure to obtain a 510(k) for a device).

MMA
Medicare Prescription Drug, Improvement and Modernization Act of 2003

Modular PMA
Allows a company to file completed PMA portions or modules for an ongoing FDA review.

MOU
Memorandum of Understanding—An agreement between FDA and another country's regulatory authority allowing mutual recognition of inspections.

MQSA
Mammography Quality Standards Act of 1992

MRCT
Multi-regional clinical trial

MTD
Maximum Tolerated Dose

N

NAFTA
North American Free Trade Agreement

NAI
No Action Indicated—Most favorable FDA post-inspection classification.

NCE
New Chemical Entity

NCTR
National Center for Toxicological Research

NDA
New Drug Application

NDA Number
A six-digit number assigned by FDA to each application for new drug marketing approval in the US. A drug can have more than one application number if it has different dosage forms or routes of administration.

NDA Field Alert
Report filed with FDA within three working days of obtaining information on any distributed drug product with contamination, significant chemical or physical change, deterioration, batch failure or labeling causing mistaken identity.

NDC
National Drug Code—The first five digits identify establishment and last five digits identify drug name, package size and drug type.

NDIN
New dietary ingredient notification

Next-Generation Sequencing
Technologies that parallelize the genetic sequencing process, allowing the production of thousands or millions of sequences concurrently (also referred to as "high-throughput sequencing").

NF
National Formulary (incorporated into the USP-NF)

NIDPOE
Notice of Initiation of Disqualification Proceedings and Opportunity to Explain Letter

NIH
National Institutes of Health

NLEA
Nutrition Labeling and Education Act of 1990

NLM
National Library of Medicine

NME
New Molecular Entity

NORD
National Organization for Rare Disorders

NOV
Notice of Violation letter

NRC
National Research Council or Nuclear Regulatory Commission

NSE
Not Substantially Equivalent—Designation for a device not qualifying for 510(k) clearance; generally requires a PMA.

NSR
Nonsignificant Risk

Nuremberg Code of 1947
A set of research ethics principles for human experimentation created as a result of atrocities involving medical experimentation on humans during World War II.

O
OAI
Official Action Indicated—Serious FDA post-inspection classification.

OBRR
Office of Blood Research and Review (CBER)

OC
Office of the Commissioner (FDA)

OCBQ
Office of Compliance and Biologics Quality (CBER)

OCC
Office of the Chief Counsel (FDA)

OCE
Oncology Center of Excellence

OCET
Office of Counterterrorism and Emerging Threats (FDA)

OCI
Office of Criminal Investigation (FDA)

OCP
Office of Combination Products (FDA)

OCTGT
Office of Cellular, Tissue and Gene Therapies (CBER)

ODA
Orphan Drug Act of 1983

ODE
Office of Device Evaluation (FDA)

OECD
Organization for Economic Cooperation and Development

Off-Label Drug Use
When a drug is used in a way different from that described in the FDA-approved drug label.

Office of the Chief Scientist
Includes the following offices:
- Office of Counterterrorism and Emerging Threats
- Office of Health Informatics
- Office of Regulatory Science and Innovation
- Office of Scientific Integrity
- Office of Scientific Professional Development
- Office of Minority Health
- FDA's National Center for Toxicological Research

OFM
Office of Financial Management (FDA)

OGD
Office of Generic Drug Products (CDER)

OIG
Office of the Inspector General (FDA)

OIP
Office of International Programs (FDA)

OIR
Office of In Vitro Diagnostics and Radiological Health (formerly the Office of In Vitro Diagnostic Device Evaluation and Safety)

OIRA
Office of Information and Regulatory Affairs (OMB)

OMEPRM
Office of Medication Error Prevention and Risk Management (CDER)

OND
Office of New Drugs (CDER)

ONDQA
Office of New Drug Quality Assessment (CDER)

ONPLDS
Office of Nutritional Products, Labeling and Dietary Supplements (CFSAN)

OOPD
Office of Orphan Products Development (FDA)

OPA
Office of Public Affairs (FDA)

Glossary of Terms

OPDP
Office of Prescription Drug Promotion (CDER)

Open Label Study
A clinical trial in which subjects and investigators are aware of the treatment received.

OPQ
Office of Pharmaceutical Quality (CDER)

ORA
Office of Regulatory Affairs (FDA); oversees FDA's field organization.

Orange Book
FDA-published listing of Approved Drug Products with Therapeutic Equivalence Evaluations generally known as generics (original print version had an orange cover).

Orphan Drug
Drugs for a disease or condition affecting fewer than 200,000 persons in the US or occurring in more than 200,000 but for which there is no reasonable expectation the drug development and manufacturing costs will be recovered from US sales.

OSB
Office of Surveillance and Biometrics (CDRH)

OSHA
Occupational Safety Health Administration

OSI
Office of Scientific Integrity (FDA)

OTAT
Office of Tissues and Advanced Therapies (CBER)

OTC
Over-the-Counter—Nonprescription drugs receive this designation.

OTC Monograph
Rules for a number of OTC drug categories.

OVRR
Office of Vaccine Research and Review (CBER)

P
PADER
Periodic Adverse Drug Experiences Report

PAI
Preapproval Inspection

PAS
Prior Approval Supplement or Postapproval Study

PAT
Process Analytical Technology

PBRER
Periodic benefit-risk evaluation reports

PCM
Payment confirmation number

PD
Pharmacodynamics—Study of the reactions between drugs and living structures.

PDA
Parenteral Drug Association

PDMA
Prescription Drug Marketing Act of 1987

PDP
Product Development Protocol (for medical devices) or Principal Display Panel (for product labels)

PDUFA
Prescription Drug User Fee Act of 1992

PDUFA II
Prescription Drug User Fee Act of 1997

PDUFA III
Prescription Drug User Fee Act of 2002

PDUFA IV
Prescription Drug User Fee Act of 2007

PDUFA V
Prescription Drug User Fee Act of 2012

PDUFA VI
Prescription Drug User Fee Act of 2018

Pediatric Rule
Requires manufacturers to assess the safety and effectiveness of certain drug and biological products in pediatric patients.

PEPFAR
President's Emergency Plan for AIDS Relief

Personalized Medicine
Tailoring medical treatment to a patient's individual characteristics, needs and preferences during all stages of care, including prevention, diagnosis, treatment and follow-up.

PGx
Pharmacogenomics—The study of DNA and RNA characteristics' variations to drug response.

Pharmaceutical Equivalents
Drug products containing the same active ingredient(s), same dosage form and route of administration and identical in strength or concentration.

Pharmacovigilance
Adverse event monitoring and reporting

PhRMA
Pharmaceutical Research and Manufacturers of America

Phase I
Initial clinical safety studies in humans. May be as few as 10 subjects, often healthy volunteers, includes PK, ADME and dose escalation studies. Usually open label.

Phase II
Well-controlled clinical trials of approximately 100–300 subjects who have the condition of interest, includes PK, dose ranging, safety and efficacy.

Phase III
Larger, well-controlled clinical trials of hundreds to thousands of subjects, including both safety and efficacy data. Generally, two well-controlled studies are needed to establish a drug product's efficacy.

Phase IV
Postmarket clinical trials performed to support labeling and advertising or fulfill FDA safety requirements noted at the time of NDA approval.

PHI
Protected Health Information

PHS
Public Health Service

PHS Act
Public Health Service Act

PI
Package Insert (approved product labeling) or Principal Investigator

PK
Pharmacokinetics—The study of the chemicals and medicines' ADME processes.

Placebo
A drug product fashioned to look like an active drug but containing no active ingredient. Used in clinical trials to blind or mask the patient, investigator or both as to the treatment received.

PLR
Physician Labeling Rule

PMA
Premarket Approval—Marketing application required for Class III devices.
- Traditional PMA—The complete PMA application is submitted to FDA at one time.
- Modular—The complete contents of a PMA are broken down into well-delineated components (or modules) and submitted to FDA as soon as the applicant has completed the module, compiling a complete PMA over time.
- Product Development Process (PDP)—The clinical evaluation of a device and the development of necessary information for marketing approval are merged into one regulatory mechanism. Ideal candidates for the PDP process are those devices in which the technology is well established in industry.

PMC
Postmarketing commitment—Studies or clinical trials a sponsor has agreed to conduct but not required by a statute or regulation.

PMDSIA
Pediatric Medical Device Safety and Improvement Act of 2007

PMN
Premarket Notification—A premarket notification is also called a 510(k).

PMOA
Primary Mode of Action—A combination product's single mode of action providing its most important therapeutic action; used to assign a combination product to a lead FDA center.

PMR
Postmarketing Requirements—Studies and clinical trials sponsors are required to conduct under one or more statutes or regulations.

Glossary of Terms

PMS
Postmarketing Surveillance—Ongoing monitoring of approved medical products' safety; may include Phase IV studies and AE reporting.

PPA
Poison Prevention Act

PPACA
Patient Protection and Affordable Care Act of 2010

PPI
Patient Package Insert—Contains information explaining how patients should use a drug product safely.

PPI
Patient preference information—Qualitative or quantitative assessments of the relative desirability or acceptability to patients of specified alternatives or choices among outcomes or other attributes that differ among alternative health interventions.

PPSR
Proposed Pediatric Study Request

PREA
Pediatric Research Equity Act of 2003

Preclinical Studies
Animal PK and toxicity studies generally performed prior to clinical studies. These studies must comply with GLP.

Pre-Sub Meeting
Provides the opportunity for an applicant to obtain FDA feedback prior to intended submission of an IDE or device marketing application.

Priority Review
FDA review category for drugs appearing to represent an advance over available therapy. Designated NDAs or BLAs receive faster review than standard applications.

PRO
Patient-reported outcome

Protocol
Document describing a clinical trial's objectives, design and methods. All GLP and GCP studies must follow a protocol.

PSUR
Periodic Safety Update Report

PTC
Points to Consider—Type of guidance published by FDA, usually CBER.

PTCC
Pharmacology/Toxicology Coordinating Committee (CDER)

PTE
Patent term extension

PTO
Patent and Trademark Office

Public Health Security and Bioterrorism Preparedness and Response Act **of 2002**
Also known as the Bioterrorism Act

Purple Book
Lists biological products, including any biosimilar and interchangeable biological products, licensed by FDA under the PHS Act.

Q

QA
Quality Assurance

QAU
Quality Assurance Unit

QC
Quality Control

QbR
Question-based review (CDER)—Chemistry, Manufacturing, and Controls (CMC) evaluation of ANDAs incorporating the most important scientific and regulatory review questions focused on critical pharmaceutical attributes essential for ensuring generic drug product quality.

QbD
Quality by Design—This concept emphasizes building quality into a product with a thorough understanding of the product and process by which it is developed and manufactured along with a knowledge of the risks involved in manufacturing the product and how best to mitigate those risks.

QIDP
Qualified Infectious Disease Product

QoL
Quality of Life

QSIT
Quality System Inspection Technique

Q-Submission Program
Provides submitters an opportunity to have early collaboration and discussions about medical device submissions.

QSR
Quality System Regulation (21 CFR 820)—Identifies GMPs for medical devices.

Qualified Health Claim
Food labeling health claim supported by scientific evidence, but not meeting the more rigorous "significant scientific agreement" standard required for an authorized health claim.

R

R&D
Research and Development

RAC
Regulatory Affairs Certification

RAPS
Regulatory Affairs Professionals Society

Rare Pediatric Disease Priority Review Voucher
A voucher FDA issues to a rare pediatric disease product application sponsor at the time of marketing application approval. This voucher entitles the holder to designate a single human drug application submitted under FD&C Act Section 505(b)(1) or PHS Act Section 351 as qualifying for a priority review.

RCDAD
Relevant communicable disease agents and diseases

RCT
Randomized Clinical Trial or Randomized Controlled Trial

Real-Time PMA Supplement
A supplement to an approved premarket application or premarket report under Section 515 requesting a minor change to the device, such as a minor change to the device design, software, sterilization or labeling, and for which the applicant has requested and the agency has granted a meeting or similar forum to jointly review and determine the supplement's status.

Reminder Labeling
Calls attention to the drug product's name but does not include indications for use or dosage recommendations.

Recall
A firm's removal or correction of a marketed product FDA considers to be in violation of the laws it administers and against which the agency would initiate legal action, e.g., seizure. Recall does not include a market withdrawal or a stock recovery.

Recall Classification
Assigned by FDA and applicable to firm-initiated device recalls based on reasonable probability and relative degree of health hazard.
- Class I—violative device would cause serious adverse health consequences
- Class II—violative device may cause temporary or medically reversible adverse health consequences or such consequences are remote
- Class III—violative device is not likely to cause adverse health consequences

Reference Product
The single biological product licensed under PHS Act Section 351(a) against which a biological product is evaluated in an application submitted under subsection 351(k).

Regenerative Medicine
A group of medicinal products comprising cell therapy, gene therapy and tissue engineering.

Regulation
Refers to Code of Federal Regulations

REMS
Risk Evaluation and Mitigation Strategies

Restricted Device
A device restricted by regulation to sale, distribution and/or use only upon the written or oral authorization of a licensed practitioner or other conditions prescribed by the commissioner.

Glossary of Terms

RFA
Request for Application

RFD
Request for Designation—A written submission to the Office of Combination Products (OCP) requesting designation of the center with primary jurisdiction for a combination or non-combination product.

RFR
Request for Reconsideration—A request for OCP to reconsider an RFD determination.

RFR
Reportable Food Registry—An electronic portal used to report foods suspected of causing serious adverse health consequences.

***Right to Try Act* of 2018**
Provides a way for patients who have been diagnosed with life-threatening diseases or conditions who have tried all approved treatment options and who are unable to participate in a clinical trial to access certain unapproved treatments.

RiskMAP
Risk Minimization Action Plan—A strategic safety program designed to meet specific goals and objectives in minimizing a product's known risks while preserving its benefits.

RLD
Reference Listed Drug—Drug product listed in the Approved Drug Products with Therapeutic Equivalence Evaluations book (also known as the Orange Book).

RMAT
Regenerative Medicine Advanced Therapy Designation—grants eligible products the same benefits as fast track and breakthrough therapy designation, including early interactions with FDA.

Rolling NDA Submission
Allows a company to file the completed portions of an NDA for ongoing FDA review. Permitted only for drugs and biologics FDA has granted Fast Track designation.

RPM
Regulatory Procedures Manual—A reference manual for FDA personnel containing information on internal procedures to be used in processing domestic and import regulatory and enforcement matters.

RTA Policy
Refuse to accept—FDA will conduct an acceptance review of all traditional, special or abbreviated 510(k)s and PMAs based on objective criteria using the applicable Acceptance Checklist to ensure the 510(k) or PMA is administratively complete.

RTF
Refusal to File—Letter sent by FDA when an incomplete NDA or ANDA is filed. FDA will not review the application until complete. Letter is sent within 60 days of submission.

RUO
Research Use Only

Rx
Prescription Use Only

Rx to OTC Switch
The process of transferring FDA-approved prescription medications to nonprescription, over-the-counter (OTC) products for the same dosage form, population and route of administration.

S

SAE
Serious Adverse Event

SAHCODHA
Severe adverse health consequence or death in humans or animals

SBA
Summary Basis of Approval

SC
Study Coordinator

SDWA
Safe Drinking Water Act

SE
Substantially Equivalent

SECG
Small entity compliance guide

Sentinel Initiative
Program FDA has in place aimed at developing and implementing a proactive system to complement existing systems to track reports of adverse events linked to the use of its regulated products.

SGE
Special government employee

Shelf Life
Maximum time a device will remain functional from the date of manufacture until it is used in patient care (See Expiration Date).

Significant Risk Device
An investigational device:
- intended as an implant
- represented to be for use in supporting or sustaining human life
- for a use of substantial importance in diagnosing, curing, mitigating or treating disease or otherwise preventing impairment of human health and presents a potential for serious risk to the subject's health, safety or welfare

SMDA
Safe Medical Devices Act of 1990

SoCRA
Society of Clinical Research Associates

SOP
Standard Operating Procedure

Source Documents
Original documents and records containing information captured in a clinical study. Case Report Forms are monitored against source documents. Includes office charts, laboratory results, x-rays, etc.

SPA
Special Protocol Assessment

SPL
Structured Product Label. Content of package insert in XML format.

SR
Significant Risk (device)

Sponsor
Company, person, organization or institution taking responsibility for initiating, managing or financing a clinical trial or a product marketing application.

SSED
Summary of Safety and Effectiveness Data—An FDA document intended to present a reasoned, objective and balanced summary of the scientific evidence, both positive and negative, that served as the basis of the decision to approve or deny the PMA.

SST
Safety Signal Tracking

Standard Review (S)
FDA review category for drugs with therapeutic qualities similar to those already approved for marketing.

Subject
Clinical trial participant; may be a healthy volunteer or a patient.

Subpart E
21 CFR 312—Accelerated review for life-threatening and severely debilitating illness.

Subpart H
21 CFR 314.500—Approval based upon a surrogate endpoint or a product approved with restrictions and/or requirements for Phase IV trials.

Substantial Equivalence
Comparison of a new device to a legally marketed predicate device; substantial equivalence establishes a device is as safe and as effective as another 510(k)-cleared device.

Suitability Petition
A request to FDA to submit an ANDA for a product varying from a Reference Listed Drug in indication, strength, dosage form, route of administration, etc.

SUPAC
Scale Up and Post-Approval Changes

Supplement (sNDA)
NDA submission for changes to an approved NDA, including SUPAC.

Supplement (sPMA)
PMA submission for changes to an approved PMA that affect the device's safety or effectiveness.

SUPPORT Act **of 2018**
Substance Use-Disorder Prevention that Promotes Opioid Recovery and Treatment (SUPPORT) for Patients and Communities Act

Glossary of Terms

Surrogate Endpoint
A laboratory or physical sign used in trials as a substitute for a clinically meaningful endpoint that is a direct measure of how a patient feels, functions or survives and is expected to predict the therapy's effect.

T

Target Product Profile (TPP)
A format for a drug development program summary described in terms of labeling concepts. A TPP can be prepared by a sponsor and shared with the appropriate FDA review staff to facilitate communication regarding a particular drug development program.

TEA
Time and extent application—Demonstrates a drug product can meet the statutory standard of marketing to a material extent and for a material time.

Team Biologics
A group of specialized investigators who conduct routine and CGMP follow-up inspections of biological product manufacturers regulated by CBER. Partnership program between ORA and CBER.

TFM
Tentative Final Monograph

Therapeutic Equivalence
Drug products that are otherwise safe and effective and can be expected to have equivalent therapeutic effect and equivalent potential for adverse effects when used under the conditions set forth in their labeling.

Third-party Review
Under FDAMA, FDA has accredited third parties authorized to conduct the primary review of 510(k)s for eligible devices.

THOMAS
Public federal legislation database (Library of Congress)

TK
Toxicokinetics

Tobacco Control Act
The Family Smoking Prevention and Tobacco Control Act of 2009

TOPRA
The Organisation for Professionals in Regulatory Affairs

TPLC
Total product lifecycle

TPP
Target Product Profile

Transitional Device
Devices regulated as drugs prior to 28 May 1976, when the Medical Device Amendments were signed into law. Any device approved by the New Drug Application process now is governed by the PMA regulations.

Treatment IND (tIND)
Allows limited use of an unapproved drug for patients with a serious or life-threatening disease.

TRG
Tissue Reference Group

TRO
Temporary restraining order—Temporarily stops distribution of an allegedly violative product; FDA uses this in cases where it believes a violation is serious enough to require immediate control to protect the public health.

TSCA
Toxic Substances Control Act

TTB
Alcohol and Tobacco Tax and Trade Bureau

U

UADE
Unexpected Adverse Device Effect—Any serious adverse effect on health or safety or any life-threatening problem or death caused by, or associated with, a device, if that effect, problem or death was not identified previously in nature, severity or degree of incidence in the investigational plan or application, or any other unanticipated serious problem associated with a device relating to the rights, safety or welfare of subjects.

UDI
Unique Device Identification—Requires a device's label to bear a unique identifier, unless an alternative location is specified by FDA or an exception is made for a particular device or group of devices.

Umbrella Policy
After a drug product becomes eligible for five-year NCE exclusivity, certain drug products subsequently developed that contain the same active moiety would also benefit from the original product's five-year NCE exclusivity until the exclusivity period for the original product has expired.

Unexpected AE
An AE, the nature or severity of which is not described in the Investigator's Brochure (for an unapproved product) or in the package insert (for an approved product).

Unmet medical need
A condition whose treatment or diagnosis is not addressed adequately by available therapy.

USAN
US Adopted Name

USANC
US Adopted Names Council

USC
US Code

USDA
US Department of Agriculture

User Fees
Fees authorized by Congress to fund various FDA activities. The fee schedule for different application types is published annually in the Federal Register. Initially established by the Prescription Drug User Fee Act and later extended to medical devices, generic drugs and animal drugs.

USP
United States Pharmacopeia

V
VA
Department of Veterans Affairs

VAERS
Vaccine Adverse Event Reporting System

VAI
Voluntary Action Indicated—Moderately serious FDA post-inspection classification.

VSTA
Virus-Serum-Toxin Act

W
Warning Letter
Serious enforcement letter issued by FDA notifying a regulated entity of violative activity; requires action within 15 days.

Warning Letter Database
Contains Warning Letters issued from November 1996 to present, searchable by company, subject, issuing office or date.

WCB
Working Cell Bank—Cells derived from one or more vials of cells from the master cell bank, which are expanded by serial subculture.

Well-Characterized Biologic
A biological product whose identity, purity, impurities, potency and quantity can be determined and controlled.

WHO
World Health Organization

WR
Written Request—issued by FDA to allow companies to conduct pediatric studies under Section 505A of the Federal Food, Drug, and Cosmetic Act.

Y
Yates Memo
A memo issued by deputy attorney general Sally Quillian Yates that amended the False Claims Act, limiting any discretionary credit the government would provide violators to only those who would reveal the responsible parties at all levels of an organization.

Index of Laws and Guidances

The entries in this index represent only substantive discussion of the law or guidance document. Draft guidance is included under the Guidance for Industry heading without notation. Reauthorizations of user fee laws have not been indexed separately.

A

Administrative Procedure Act (APA), 3
Affordable Care Act (Patient Protection and Affordable Care Act)
    biological products, 5
    biosimilar product approval pathway, 24
Animal Generic Drug User Fee Act (AGDUFA I), 13
Anti-Kickback Statute, 188

B

Biologics Control Act (Virus Serum and Toxin Act), 24
Biologics Price Competition and Innovation Act (BPCI)
    biosimilar approval pathway, 24, 210
    biosimilar product approval, 7
Biosimilar User Fee Act (BsUFA), 24, 248–250, 258

C

Combat Methamphetamine Epidemic Act, 168
Compounding Quality Act, 9
Controlled Substances Act (CSA)
    control schedules, 9, 21
    habit-forming drug status, 168

D

Dietary Supplement and Nonprescription Drug Consumer Protection Act (DSNDCA)
    nonprescription drug safety reporting, 198
    OTC drug development and regulation, 169

Dietary Supplement Health Education Act (DSHEA)
    CGMP application to supplements, 34
    dietary supplement packaging, 34
    dietary supplements regulation under, 34–35, 42
    dietary supplements/ingredients safety, 202
    regulatory structure for, 34
    safety responsibility under, 202
Drug Amendments of 1962. *See Kefauver-Harris Amendments*
Drug Efficacy Amendments, 142
Drug Price Competition and Patent Term Restoration Act
Drug Quality and Security Act (DQSA)
    supply chain security/compounding, 8–9
    supply security and compounding, 9
Drug Supply Chain Security Act (DSCSA), 9
Durham-Humphrey Amendment
    criteria for OTC exclusion, 168
    OTC drug clarification, 35
    prescription vs. nonprescription drugs, 6

F

False Claims Act (FCA), 188, 190
Family Smoking Prevention and Tobacco Control Act
    product regulation by FDA, 6
    response to Supreme Court decision, 4
    user fee programs, 13
FDA Reauthorization Act (FDARA), 8
Food, Drug, and Cosmetic Act (FD&C Act)
    adulteration provisions, 50, 127
    amendments by *FDAAA*, 115
    ANDA contents, 143
    approved application changes, 124
    changes made by, 5
    device regulation under, 49

Index of Laws and Guidances

Durham-Humphrey Amendment, 168
expanded access publication, 107
labeling prescription drugs and biologicals, 269
medical device regulation, 36–37
repeal of *Pure Food and Drug Act* by, 5
sulfanilamide disaster, 49
Food Additives Amendment
    adulteration criteria, 6
Food and Drug Administration Amendments Act (FDAAA)
    Advisory Committee requirements, 115
    Applicable Clinical Trials (ACT), 69
    clinical trial registration requirements, 69
    ClinicalTrials.gov website, 18
    delayed ANDA approval, 161
    Drug Safety Board creation, 184
    DTC advertising/promotion, 185
    enantiomer/racemic mixture approvals, 163
    PDUFA IV renewal, 129
    pharmacoeconomic claims, 186
    postmarket drug safety, 4
    postmarket requirement/commitments, 115
    postmarket safety studies, 124
    postmarketing surveillance, 239
    rare pediatric/tropical disease priority, 26
    Reagan-Udall Foundation, 25
    REMS requirements by, 30, 196, 199, 242
    safety information report requirements, 199
    serious/life-threatening disease products, 29
    submission of trial results, 107
    user fee programs reauthorization, 8
Food and Drug Administration Modernization Act (FDAMA)
    amendments to *Orphan Drug Act*, 25
    clinical trial registration requirements, 106–107
    habit-forming drug caution, 6
    habit-forming drug status, 168
    postmarket surveillance, 8
    postmarketing study data, 124
    postmarketing study requirements, 8
Food and Drug Administration Safety and Innovation Act (FDASIA)
    ANDA approval time, 161
    assessment of REMS efficacy, 200
    breakthrough therapy designation, 26
    committments letter, 146–147
    development incentives under, 8–9
    generic drug user fees, 8
    MDUFA III, 39
    NDC requirements for, 109
    priority product review, 27
    provisions and reauthorizations, 8–9
    user fee extension, 8
Food Safety Modernization Act (FSMA)
    FDA enforcement authority under, 8

traceability and supply chain, 8
Foreign Corrupt Practices Act (FCPA), 22
Freedom of Information Act (FOIA)
    CDRH responses to, 9–10
    citizen petitions to, 26
    civil litigation in response to, 21
    CTP offices and, 11
    exempt materials, 230
    oversight of, 8

G

Generating Antibiotic Incentives Now (GAIN) Act
    difficult-to-treat organisms, 154
    exclusivity and patents, 8–9, 163
    incentives for, 118
    QIDPs designation, 26
    QIDPs incentives, 4
Generic Drug User Fee Act (GDUFA)
    commitments letter, 146
    marketing approval process, 34
    modifications with *II*, 147
Government in the Sunshine Act, 3
Guidance for Industry
    180-Day Exclusivity When Multiple ANDAs are Submitted on the Same Day, 34
    Applying Human Factors and Usability Engineering to Medical Devices, 68
    approved application changes, 125
    Best Practices in Developing Proprietary Names for Drugs, 30
    Brief Summary and Adequate Directions for Use: Disclosing Risk Information in Consumer-Directed Print Advertisements and Promotional Labeling for Human Prescription Drugs, 185
    Changes to an Approved Application—Biological Products, 272
    CMC Postapproval Manufacturing Changes for Specified Biological Products To Be Documented in Annual Reports, 125
    Consumer-Directed Broadcast Advertisements, 185, 275
    Contents of a Complete Submission for the Evaluation of Proprietary Names, 30
    Dear Health Care Provider Letters: Improving Communication of Important Safety Information, 188
    Direct-to-Consumer Television Advertisements—FDAAA DTC Television Ad Pre-Dissemination Review Program, 185
    E2C Clinical Safety Data Management: Periodic Safety Update Reports for Marketed Drugs, 129
    Expedited Programs for Serious Conditions—Drugs and Biologics, 25–26

Final Rule on CGMP in Manufacturing, Packaging, Labeling, or Holding Operations for Dietary Supplements, 34
Format and Content of Proposed Risk Evaluation and Mitigation Strategies (REMS), REMS Assessment: Planning and Reporting: Draft Guidance for Industry, 199
Good Pharmacovigilance Practices and Pharmacoepidemiologic Assessment, 199
Good Reprint Practices Guidance, 187
Indexing Structured Product Labeling, 272
Internet/ Social Media Platforms: Correcting Independent Third-Party Misinformation About Prescription Drugs and Medical Devices, 187
Internet/Social Media Platforms with Character Space Limitations—Presenting Risk and Benefit Information for Prescription Drugs and Medical Devices, 187, 276
Investigational Device Exemptions (IDEs) for Early Feasibility Medical Device Clinical Studies, Including Certain First in Human (FIH) Studies, 72
Labeling for Human Prescription Drug and Biological Products—Implementing the PLR Content and Format Requirements, 110, 180
Medication Guides—Distribution Requirements and Inclusion in Risk Evaluation and Mitigation Strategies (REMS), 181, 200
The New 510(k) Paradigm—Alternate Approaches to Demonstrating Substantial Equivalence in Premarket Notification, 39
Product Name Placement, Size, and Prominence in Advertising and Promotional Labeling, 185, 274
Product Recalls, Including Removals and Corrections, 134
Providing Postmarket Periodic Safety Reports in the ICH E2C(R2) Format Periodic Benefit-Risk Evaluation Report (PBRER), 129
Providing Regulatory Submissions in Electronic Format—Certain Human Pharmaceutical Product Applications and Related Submissions Using the eCTD Specifications, 125
Providing Regulatory Submissions in Electronic Format—Content of Labeling, 272
Providing Submissions in Electronic Format—Postmarketing Safety Reports, 128
Recognition and Use of a Standard Uniform Blood and Blood Component Container Labels, 199
Risk Evaluation and Mitigation Strategies: Modifications and Revisions, 199
Special Protocol Assessment (SPA), 22
SUPAC documents, 126–127
Supported Scientific and Educational Activities, 272

H

Hatch-Waxman Act
   antibiotic drug exclusivity, 161–162
   drug approval process, 7
   generic drug legal framework, 142–143
   generic drug marketing, 133
   patent extension and generic licensing, 7
   regulatory changes, 5
   RLD patent protection, 154
   safety/efficacy information on NDA, 111–112
   Section 505(j), 142–143
   "Section VIII" statement, 145
Health Insurance Portability and Accountability Act (HIPAA)
   National Drug Code (NDC) system, 109
   proposed Common Rule changes, 52

I

Improving Regulatory Transparency for New Medical Therapies Act
   control schedule final rule, 9
   drug scheduling by DEA, 9

K

Kefauver-Harris Amendments
   abbreviated NDA for 505(j) generics, 32
   advertising/promotion enforcement, 188
   drug safety reform, 6
   OTC review process, 169
   prescription advertising jurisdiction, 273

L

Lanham Act, 189

M

Mammography Quality Standards Act of 1992 (MQSA), 54
Meat Inspection Act, 5
Medical Device Amendments (MDA)
   device classification and manufacture, 6
   device regulation, 6–7
   regulation changes with, 36–37
   risk-based classification, 51
   safety reporting standards, 7
Medical Device User Fee and Modernization Act (MDUFMA)
   review fees and regulatory reform, 54
   user fee programs, 8
Medical Device User Fee Stabilization Act (MDUFSA), 54
Medicare Prescription Drug, Improvement, and Modernization Act (MMA), 144, 160–161
Methamphetamine Production Prevention Act, 168

Index of Laws and Guidances

N

National Childhood Vaccine Injury Act, 243
National Environmental Policy Act (NEPA), 14–15
National Research Act, 51
Nonprescription Safe Use Regulatory Expansion (NSURE), 168

O

Orphan Drug Act (ODA)
    amendments to, 25
    documentation for orphan status, 25
    orphan drug defined, 7

P

Poison Prevention Packaging Act (PPPA), 174
Prescription Drug User Fee Act (PDUFA)
    REMS requirements by, 129
    Special Protocol Assessment procedures, 22
    user fee authorization, 7–8
    user fee changes with *VI*, 135
Privacy Act, 9
Public Health Service Act (PHS Act)
    biologics development, 24
    CBER regulatory authority, 210
    FDA authority over biologics, 5
    NIH authority, 24
    regulatory structure, 19
    vaccine and serums regulation, 5
Pure Food and Drug Act
    history of, 4–5
    toxicity testing requirements under, 49

R

Ransdell Act, 24
Right to Try Act
    patient requests, 108
    unapproved treatment access, 10–11

S

Safe Medical Devices Act (SMDA)
    adverse event reporting, 37
    combination products introduced, 40
    device definition and reporting standards, 7
    premarket notification process, 53
Sherley Amendment, 5

T

Tobacco Control Act
    product regulation by FDA, 6
    response to Supreme Court decision, 4
    user fee programs, 13
21st Century Cures Act (CCA)
    combination product premarket expectations, 40–41
    expanded access program, 107
    patient-focused product development, 9–10

V

Virus Serum and Toxin Act (Biologics Control Act), 24

Index by Subject

Some agencies, e.g. Center for Devices and Radiological Health, that are referred to most often in the text by the acronym (CDRH) have been indexed under that acronym. Numbers such as 510(k) have been indexed as if spelled out. The contents of tables and figures have not been indexed. Subjects, laws, and guidance documents have been indexed only where there has been substantive discussion of that topic.

NUMBERS
351(a). *See* Biologics License Application
351(k). *See* Biologics License Application
505(b)(1) NDA. *See* New Drug Application
505(b)(2). *See* "paper" NDA
505(b)(2) NDA. *See* New Drug Application
505(j) Abbreviated NDA. *See* Abbreviated New Drug Application
510(k). *See* Premarket Notification

A
Abbreviated New Drug Application (ANDA), 505(j)
   adverse experience reporting, 128
   comparability protocol for changes, 127
   DMF review with, 134
   generic drug submissions, 142
   generic drugs, 32–34
   "Section VIII" carve-out, 145
Accelerated Approval
   expedited development programs, 117
   promotional material for, 183
   promotional material submissions, 277
acceptance criteria, 90
active ingredient (AI), 90
Active Pharmaceutical Ingredients (APIs)
   adulteration provisions for, 127
actual use trials (AUT), 173
ADME pathways, 102, 213, 215
Advance Notice of Proposed Rulemaking (ANPR)
   OTC Advisory Panel recommendation, 169
   proposed Common Rule changes, 52
Advanced Medical Technology Association (AdvaMed)
   advertising/promotion guidelines, 186
adverse event reporting
   adverse drug experience (ADE)
      defined, 195
      postmarketing surveillance reporting, 197–198
   adverse event defined, 193–194, 198
   adverse event definitions, 195
   blood/blood components, 97
   clinical trials/studies, 193–195
   for gene therapy, 237
   MedDRA use for, 129, 199
   for medical devices, 75–76
   safety reporting forms, 129, 194, 197, 241
Adverse Event Reporting System (FAERS) database, 193
advertising/promotion
   for Accelerated Approval products, 277
   biologics, 272–277
   bulk-sale drugs, 186
   direct-to-consumer (DTC) advertising, 185–186
   Drug Safety Board (DSB), 184–185
   general content and format for, 274–276
      fair balance and risk presentation, 274–275
      product name presentation, 274
      substantiation of product claims, 274
   help-seeking advertisements, 186
   media requirements

broadcast advertising, 275
internet/social media, 275–276
print, 275
over-the-counter (OTC) drug products, 174
preapproval product communications, 273
prescription drug advertising, 185–186
prescription drug promotion, 181, 183–185
principles for, 274
promotional submission to FDA
first use, 276
reminder labeling, 276
request for advisory comments, 276–277
Warning Letters for violations, 277
Advisory Committee Meetings
FDA review process (NDA/BLA), 115
Agency for Healthcare Research and Quality (AHRQ)
Drug Safety Board (DSB), 184
ALCOA, 64
Animal Rule, 224
antibiotic drug exclusivity, 161–163
Applicable Device Clinical Trials, 69
Applicable Drug Clinical Trials, 69
Application Integrity Policy (AIP), 60
Approved Drug Products with Therapeutic Equivalence Evaluations, 133

B
Bacto-Unidisk court ruling, 50
batch (pharmaceutical), 90
bioavailability (BA)
for generic drugs, 7
safety reporting for, 195
bioequivalence (BE)
definition, 143
safety reporting for, 195
biological products/HCT/Ps
labeling, 110
biologics
advertising/promotion labeling, 272–277
compliance, 233–244
distinguished from drugs, 24
enforcement, 242–243
enforcement for advertising/promotion activities, 277
Full Prescribing Information (FPI), 189, 270
Highlights of Prescribing Information (Highlights), 270
import/export, 239–240
labeling
with BLA submissions, 270
container/carton label requirements, 271
SPL use, 271–272
USPI, 270
labeling lifecycle, 272
labeling regulations and requirements, 269–272

postapproval changes, 240–242
postapproval submissions/compliance, 121–139
postmarketing surveillance, 195–199
regulatory milestones, 209t
submissions, 205–232
Biologics License Application (BLA)
adverse experience reporting, 128
biosimilar application, 112
biosimilar BLA (351(k)), 111, 112, 252
comparability protocol for changes, 127
content and format of, 109
CTD format for, 24
development and approval, 24
DMF review with, 134
original BLA (351(a)), 111, 112, 113, 115, 270, 277
prescribing information (PI) for, 180–181
professional/USPI labeling, 270
purpose of, 109
submission and review of, 112–113
biologics submissions, 205–232
biosimilars, 245–265
Biosimilars Action Plan, 261–262
commercialization, 258–259
Purple Book listing, 133
Biosimilars Action Plan, 261–262
Breakthrough Therapy designation
accelerated approval pathway, 22, 26
drug development and review, 116–117
expedited development programs, 117
British standard EN 540:1993, 65
bulk-sale drugs, advertising/promotion, 186

C
CAS Registry Numbers, 146
CBER (Center for Biologics Evaluation and Research)
Advertising and Promotional Labeling Branch (APLB), 273
AIP list from, 60
history of, 24
product regulation, 234–236
safety reporting to, 194
CDER (Center for Drug Evaluation and Research)
AIP list from, 60
biologics regulation by, 24
Drug Safety and Risk Management Advisory Committee, 196
Drug Safety Board (DSB), 184
Drug Safety Oversight Board (DSB), 196–197
New Drug Review Division, 194
OPDP regulation of labeling, 273–274
oversight of OTC drug products, 168
surveillance offices, 195–196
Centers for Disease Control and Prevention (CDC)
Drug Safety Board (DSB), 184

regulatory structure, 19
vaccine safety surveillance, 195
Centers for Medicare and Medicaid Services (CMS)
Drug Safety Board (DSB), 184
CGMPs for biologic products, 94–97
See also Current Good Manufacturing Practices
definitions for, 94
general information, 94
personnel for, 94
plant and facilities, 94–95
plant and facilities, animal quarters/stables, 95
plant and facilities, laboratory/bleeding rooms, 95
plant and facilities, live vaccine processing, 95
plant and facilities, spore-forming microorganisms, 95
CGMPs for blood/blood components
See also Current Good Manufacturing Practices
adverse event files, 97
circular information, 96
compatibility testing, 96–97
definitions for, 95
donor records, 97
equipment, 96
facilities, 95–96
personnel for, 95
production/process controls, labeling, 96
SOPs for, 96
supplies and reagents, 96
CGMPs for combination products
See also Current Good Manufacturing Practices
application to constituent parts, 97
biological products/HCT/Ps, 98
compliance implementation, 97
drug manufacturing requirements, 98
individual requirements, 98
QSR provisions, 98
CGMPs for medical devices
See also Current Good Manufacturing Practices
acceptance activities, 87–88
appropriate statistical techniques, 89–90
complaint handling, 88–89
corrective/preventive actions, 88
design and development plan, 85–86, 86f
design changes, 87
Design History File (DHF)., 89
design inputs/outputs, 86
design review, 87
design transfer, 86–87
documentation, 85f, 88–89
labeling/packaging control, 88
medical devices, 85–90
nonconforming product, 88
production/process controls, 87
QSR for, 85
resource management, 88

verification/validation, 86
CGMPs for pharmaceutical products, 90–93
See also Current Good Manufacturing Practices
CMC information for, 103
controls
component handling, 91
containers, 91–92
laboratory operation, 92
method validation, 92
packaging/labeling, 92
production and process, 92
stability testing, 92
definitions for, 90
facilities and equipment, 91
air/ventilation, 91
sanitation and cleaning, 91
water, 91
finished pharmaceuticals, 127
investigational use only (IUO), 93–94
organization
personnel, 90–91
QA/QC units, 90
recordkeeping/retention
batch records, 93
complaint files, 93
distribution, 93
master production record, 93
change control in Quality Management System (QMS), 85
Changes Being Effected (CBE) supplement
biologics labeling lifecycle, 272
proposed labeling changes, 125
chemistry, manufacturing and controls (CMC)
changes to approved product, 125–126
IUO products, 94
post approval annual reports, 131
postapproval submissions/compliance, 127
prescription drug submissions, 103
citizen petitions
OTC drug approval, 35
reopening/amending OTC monograph, 170–171
clinical hold, 61–62
clinical superiority to approved orphan drug, 159
clinical trials for drugs/biologics, 54–81
adverse events, 193–195
clinical investigator
clinical hold, 61–62
FDA oversight of, 61
recordkeeping/retention, 61
responsibilities of, 60–61
clinical investigators, 60
FDA sponsor regulatory inspections, 60
good documentation practices (GDPs), 64
informed consent, 55–56

Index by Subject

IRB responsibilities
    organization/purpose, 56–57
    registration requirements for oversight, 58
    reviews by, 57–58
laws and regulations, 45–81
legislation relevant to, 48t
monitors/monitoring
    consequences of inadequate, 63–64
    purpose of, 62
    qualifications for, 62
    remote/centralized, 63
    reporting by, 63–64
    responsibilities of, 62
    risk-based, 63
    on-site, 62–63
pharmaceutical/biologic pathway, 54f
phases of, 54–55
protocols/amendments, 55
quality assurance (auditing), 64
recordkeeping/retention, 60
sponsor/CRO responsibilities, 59–60

clinical trials for medical devices, 64–77
14155:2011, 65–66
Applicable Clinical Trials (ACTs), 69
BIMO, 77
CFR and ISO GCP, 66
ClinicalTrials.gov registration, 69
device accountability, 76
discovery and concept, 67–68
early feasibility (pilot), 68
harmonized GCPs for, 64–65
informed consent
    feasibility trials, 72
    HUD research, 72
    new use of approved device, 73
    special circumstances, 72
pathway for, 67f
pivotal study, 69
postmarketing surveillance studies, 69
preclinical and bench testing, 68
protocols/amendments, 69
protocols for
    clinical investigation plan (CIP), 70–71
    FDA protocol review, 69–70
    protocol deviations, 71–72
    protocols/amendments/changes, 71–72
quality assurance, 77
recordkeeping/retention, 74t, 76
    essential documents, 76–77
reporting/monitoring
    adverse device effects, 75
    Data Monitoring Committee, 75
    device deficiencies, 76
    monitoring, 75

responsibilities
    investigator, 73t
    IRB and ECs, 73–75
traditional feasibility studies, 68
trial pathway, 67f

ClinicalTrials.gov registration, IND application, 106–107
CMC index, 131, 132f
Coast IRB letter, Warning Letters, 59
Code of Federal Regulations (CFR)
compilation of regulations, 19
minimum current CGMPs, 84–85
monograph codification, 170
organization of, 3, 19, 20t
Quality System Regulation (QSR), 7, 84
color additive petition (CAP), 35
combination product request for designation (RFD), 40–41
Common Technical Document (CTD) format
BLA/NDA, 24
contents and format, 111f
drug application types
    ANDA, 112
    NDA (505(b)(2)), 111
    original BLA, 112
    traditional NDA, 111
eCTD format, 110–111
eCTD submissions, 112
fast track designation, 26
ICH harmonization of, 41
NDA or BLA, 109
NDC requirements for, 109
submission contents, 27f
comparability protocol (CP), 127
compliance, biologics, 233–244
Compliance Program Guidance Manuals (CPGMs), 20, 64
Congress, user fee reauthorization, 8
Consumer Product Safety Commission (CPSC), child-resistant packing enforcement, 174
container/carton labels for biologics, 271
contract research organization (CRO) responsibilities, 59–60
Cooper Committee/Report, 6, 51
Corporate Integrity Agreements (CIAs), 188–189
corrective action (CA), 88
Council for International Organizations of Medical Science (CIOMS)
biomedical research guidelines, 53
safety reporting forms, 129, 194, 197, 241
Current Good Manufacturing Practices (CGMPs), 83–98
See also specific products
biologics, 94

combination products, 96–97
dietary supplements/ingredients, 34
medical devices, 85–90
pharmaceutical products, 89–93
Quality Management System (QMS), 84

D

Dalkon Shield Intrauterine Device (IUD) incident, 51
Data Monitoring Committee (DMC), 75
Dear Health Care Professional (DHCP) letters
    for advertising/promotional violations, 277
    safety alerts, 193
decision trees for premarket review, 21f
Declaration of Helsinki, 50
Department of Justice (DOJ), advertising/promotion enforcement, 188
Department of Veterans Affairs (VA), Drug Safety Board (DSB), 184
Design History File (DHF), 85, 87, 89
Device History Record (DHR), 88
Device Master Record (DMR), 86, 87, 89
Device Registration and Listing Module (DRLM), 40
dietary supplements/ingredients, defined, 34
direct-to-consumer (DTC) advertising/promotion
    broadcast advertisements, 185
    fair balance and risk presentation, 275
    promotional material preclearance, 183–184
Division of Biologics Standards (DBS), 210
Division of Epidemiology (DEPI), 196
Division of Medication Error Prevention and Analysis (DMEPA), 196
Division of Nonprescription Clinical Evaluation (DNCE), 169
Division of Nonprescription Regulation Development (DNRD), 169
Division of Pharmacovigilance (DPV), 196
Division of Risk Management (DRISK), 196
Document Archiving, Reporting and Regulatory Tracking System (DARRTS), 199
Drug Enforcement Administration (DEA, new drug development, 9–10, 19
Drug Facts label, risk disclosure on, 168
drug master files (DMFs)
    in biologics submissions, 224
    postapproval changes to, 134
drug products
    definition of, 22, 90
    distinguished from biologics, 24
    postmarketing surveillance, 195–199
Drug Safety Board (DSB), creation, 184
Drug Safety Communications, safety alerts, 193

E

856 Advance Ship Notice (ASN), 201
Electronic Submission Gateway (ESG)
    eCTD format, 110–111
    establishment registration/listing submission, 135
    IND submissions, 104
    SPL submissions, 135
Elements to Assure Safe Use (ETASU)
    in development process, 30
    in REMS process, 114, 129–130, 242
enantiomers of approved racemates, 163
enforcement actions
    advertising/promotion
        biologics, 277
        prescription drugs, 187–190
    Application Integrity Policy (AIP), 60
    biologics, 242–243
    CBER regulatory action letters, 242
    clinical hold, 61–62
    clinical investigators, 61
    Coast IRB letter, 60
    FDA advertising and promotion, 277
    NIDPOE, 60
establishment registration/product listing
    medical devices, 40
    New Drug Application (NDA), 109
    postapproval renewal, 134–135
Ethics Committees (ECs), 47, 53, 73
excipients, 137, 145–146, 224, 251
exclusivity and patents, Orange Book listing for, 133
expanded access (EA) program
    individual patient/emergency use, 107
    protocols for, 107

F

FAERS, drug/biologics postmarket surveillance, 195
fair balance
    in advertising/promotion, 274–275
    promotional material for, 184
Fast Track designation
    facilitated development and review, 25–26
    QIDPs designation, 8–9, 163
FDA communications and meetings, presubmission NDA/BLA meetings, 109
FDA Offices
    Human Research Protections (OHRP)
        proposed Common Rule changes, 52
    Medication Error Prevention and Risk Management (OMEPRM), 174
    Orphan Products Development (OOPD)
        request for designation, 25
    Prescription Drug Promotion (OPDP), 183–184

Index by Subject

FDA review process (NDA/BLA)
   Advisory Committee Meetings, 115
   AIDS relief, 118
   expedited review programs
      accelerated approval pathway, 117
      breakthrough therapy designation, 117
      fast track designation, 116–117
      priority review, 117
      rolling review, 117–118
   incentive programs
      antibiotics, 118
      exclusivity, 118
      ODA/PREA, 118
      priority review vouchers, 118
   postapproval activities, 116
   postmarket requirement/commitments, 115
   preapproval inspection, 115
   REMS requirements by, 113–114
   timeline for, 113, 114f
FDA v. Brown & Williamson Tobacco Corp., 4
Field Alert Reports (FARs), 130, 193
15-Day Alert report, causality in, 198, 199
Final Monograph (FM) (Final Rule), 170
first-in-human (FIH) trials, device studies, 68, 72
513(g) Request for Information, 333
five-year exclusivity, 156–157
food additive petition (FAP), 35
Food and Drug Administration (FDA)
   authority expansion, 5–11
   dietary supplements/ingredients safety, 34
   drug development and approval, 22–24, 23t
   electronic submission gateway (ESG), 104, 110, 135
   expedited development programs, 116–118
   guidelines for interpretation, 19
   IRB oversight by, 58–59
   NDA/BLA review process, 113–119
   Orange Book listing, 133
   premarket review, 21f
   prescription-to-OTC switch approvals, 35
   regulatory oversight of sponsor/CRO, 60
   Special Protocol Assessment (SPA), 22
food, drug and cosmetic laws, 1–11
   21st century, 8–11
   early food and drug legislation, 4–5
   early legislation
      FD&C Act, 5
      Pure Food and Drug Act, 4–5
      Sherley Amendment, 5
   electronic resources, 3t
   FDA authority expansion, 5–11
      Biologics Price Competition and Innovation Act, 7–8
      CCA (21st Century Cures Act), 9–10
      Compounding Quality Act, 9
      Controlled Substances Act, 9
      Drug Quality and Security Act (DQSA), 9
      Durham-Humphrey Amendment, 5
      FDAMA (Food and Drug Administration Modernization Act), 8
      Food Additives Amendment, 6
      Food and Drug Administration Amendments Act, 8–9
      Food and Drug Administration Safety and Innovation Act (FDASIA), 8
      Food Safety Modernization Act (FSMA), 8
      Hatch-Waxman Act, 7
      Improving Regulatory Transparency for New Medical Therapies Act, 9
      Kefauver-Harris Amendment, 6
      Medical Device Amendments, 6, 7
      Medical Device User Fee and Modernization Act (MDUFA), 8
      Orphan Drug Act, 7
      other laws and regulations, 10–11, 10t
      PHS Act, 5
      Right to Try Act, 10–11
      Safe Medical Devices Act, 7
   history of, 1–11
   legislative process
      Code of Federal Regulations (CFR), 3
      executive branch, 2–3
      judicial branch, 3–4
      legislative branch, 2
   other laws and regulations, 10t
   traceability and supply chain, 8
Form FDA 1571 (Notice of Claimed Investigational Exemption for a New Drug), 101
Full Prescribing Information (FPI), biologics, 270

G

generally are recognized as safe and effective (GRASE), 169
generic drug submissions, 141–151
   ANDA contents, 142–143
      bioequivalence demonstration, 143–144
      bioequivalence waivers, 144
   DMF fee, 147
   GDUFA commitments letter, 146–147
   inactive ingredients in, 145
   legal framework for, 142–143
   marketing
      therapeutic equivalence, 147–149
      therapeutic interchange, 147
   patent certification, "paragraph IV", 144–145
   regulatory pathways, 32–34
   "Section VIII" statement, 145
Good Clinical Practices (GCPs)
   Belmont Report, 51–52
   CIOMS/WHO ethical guidelines, 53
   Common Rule, 52

Cooper Committee/Dalkon Shield, 51
Declaration of Helsinki, 50
device regulation under, 49
"Drug-Device" Regulation, 260–261
Holocaust/WW II, 49
ICH principles for, 53
Medical Device Amendments (MDA), 51
medical device legislation, 54
medical devices
    FDA recognition of ISO-GCPs, 64–66
    ISO-GCP, 64–65
National Research Act, 50–51
Nuremberg Doctors' Trials, 49
purpose of, 47–54
SMDA (Safe Medical Devices Act), 53
sulfanilamide disaster, 49
Tuskegee syphilis study, 50–51

good documentation practices (GDPs)
    ALCOA criteria for, 64
    clinical trials for drugs/biologics, 64
    DHR for, 89
    in GCP monitoring, 49
    IRB activities, 59
    key attributes in GCP, **64**
    manufacturer's change in process, 231
    for manufacturer's QMS, 85, 88
    postapproval change, 124, 126–127
    production/control records, 92
    for protocol deviation, 72
    REMS supporting documentation, 199
    in on-site monitoring, 63
    sponsor/CRO transfer, 60, 136–137

Good Laboratory Practice (GLP) regulations, toxicology studies, 102

GRAS (generally recognized as safe), 6

H

Health and Human Services Department (HHS)
    advertising/promotion enforcement, 188
    Common Rule, 52
    Corporate Integrity Agreements (CIAs) with, 188–189
    Drug Safety Board (DSB), 184
    postmarketing surveillance, 196
    regulatory structure, 19

Health Resources and Services Administration (HRSA)
    Drug Safety Board (DSB), 184

help-seeking advertisements/communications, 186, 273

Highlights of Prescribing Information (Highlights), 270

Hygienic Laboratory of the Public Health and Marine Hospital Service, 24

I

Icon Clinical Research Inc., Warning Letters, 60, 64
import/export, biologics, 239–240
"Important Safety Information" (ISI), 275
inactive ingredient, 90
Inactive Ingredients Database (IID), 146
IND Safety Report, 194, 198
Indian Health Service (IHS), 184
individual case safety reports (ICSRs)
    content of, 197
    definition of, 195
    drug/biologic postmarket surveillance, 197
    periodic reporting, 199

informed consent form (ICF), 55–56
inspections
    biologics pre-license, 238
    FDA clinical investigator inspections, 61
    FDA sponsor regulatory inspections, 60
    pre-license, 235
    preapproval, 42, 115, 169, 235
    preapproval inspections (PAIs), 42, 115, 169, 235

installation qualification (IQ), 87
installation qualification, operational qualification, process qualification (IQ-OQ-PQ), 87

Institutional Review Board (IRB)
    FDA oversight of, 58–59
    HUD/IDE supervision, 38–39
    in informed consent process, 56
    organization/purpose, 56–57
    responsibilities
        medical device trials, 73–75
    reviews by, 57–58

Instructions for Use (IFUs)
    for biologics, 270
    biologics, 270–271

International Council on Harmonisation (ICH)
    Active Pharmaceutical Ingredients (APIs), 128
    GCP principles, 53–54
    guidelines for interpretation, 19
    guidelines issued by, 27–28
    harmonization recommendations, 41
    Periodic Safety Update Guideline, 128
    pharmaceutical development guidelines, 127
    safety reporting standards, 193
    toxicology studies, 102

International Electrotechnical Commission (IEC), 65
international nonproprietary name (INN)
    biosimilar naming, 256, 257
    for NDA, 108

International Organization for Standardization (ISO), 64–66

Investigational Device Exemptions (IDEs)
    CBER review of submissions, 37
    clinical study use of, 39
    conformity declaration for, 66
    quality assurance and BIMO, 77

Investigational New Device Exemptions (IDEs)
    MDA changes in route to market, 37
    for premarket safety/effectiveness data, 42

Investigational New Drug (IND) application
    administrative actions on, 106
    amendments to, 104–106
    annual reports, 29
    biosimilar product approval pathway, 24
    clinical protocol, 103
    CMC information for, 94
    Expanded Access IND, 108
    ICF form submission, 56
    nonclinical testing
        carcinogenicity, 102–103
        CMC information for, 103
        genotoxicity, 102
        other evaluations, 103
        pharmacology, 102
        reproductive toxicity, 103
        toxicity, 102
    original content of, 102
    preparation/submission, 103–104
    purposes of, 101–102
    review of, 104, 105f
    review process, 105f
    safety reporting, 29, 29t
    special instances
        expanded access program, 107–108
        Right to Try Act, 108
        sponsor-investigated, 107

investigational use only (IUO) drug products, 93–94

IQ (installation qualification), 87

IQ-OQ-PQ (installation qualification, operational qualification, process qualification), 87

ISO 10993 in GCP harmonization, 65

ISO 13485, *de facto* device compliance standard, 90

ISO 14155:2011
    recognition in the US, 65
    as US consensus standard, 66

ISO-GCP (harmonized GCPs)
    current GCP, 65
    development of, 64–65
    device trial requirements, 69–71
    global recognition of, 66
    ISO 14155 development, 65
    non-US trials/US submissions, 66
    predecessors of, 65
    recognition in the US, 65
    US CFR compliance with, 66

J

Johnson & Johnson Pharmaceuticals, Warning Letters, 60, 64

L

label requirements
    Drug Facts label, 168, 173, 174f
    National Drug Code number location, 180
    prescription drugs, 180
    specific studies for OTC NDA, 172–173

labeling
    biologics, 269–272
        package label contents, 270–271
        regulatory oversight, 273–274
    biologics regulations and requirements, 269
    blood/blood product global standardization, 95
    blood/blood products, 96
    changes based on postmarket studies, 239
    changes to approved product, 125
    DSHEA, 34
    medical devices, 88
    patient labeling/medication guides, 181
    pharmaceutical product CGMPs, 92
    postapproval annual reports, 131
    postapproval current, 132–133

laws and regulations
    codified laws by subject, 19
    compilation of regulations, 19, 20t

legal actions
    Bacto-Unidisk court ruling, 50
    FDA v. Brown & Williamson Tobacco Corp., 4
    Supreme Court "labeling" interpretation, 269
    United States v. Generix Drug Corp., 142
    United States v. Johnson, 5
    Zarxio, 260–261

Letter of Authorization, 134

life-threatening adverse drug experience, 195

lifecycle management
    labeling, 272

lot/batch records
    batch-to-batch uniformity, 92
    device traceability, 70, 81, 89
    pharmaceutical products, 89, 92
    postapproval changes to, 126
    product labeling/packaging, 91
    Scale-Up and Postapproval Changes, 126

lot-release testing, commercial biologics manufacturing, 231

M

market exclusivity
   biosimilars, 258–259
   under *Orphan Drug Act*, 25
   patent-related, 154–156
   QIDPs extension of, 8–9

MedDRA (Medical Dictionary for Regulatory Activities)
   for adverse product reaction tracking, 129, 199
   ICH harmonization of, 27, 28, 41

medical devices
   documentation of device definition, 38
   postmarketing surveillance, 202

Medical Product Safety Network (MedSun), 201–202

Medication Guides
   for biologics, 270–271
   prescription drugs, 181
   in REMS process, 242

MedWatch program
   Form 3500A for, 129, 241
   safety alerts, 185–186

N

National Drug Code (NDC) system
   in commercial distribution, 135
   in distribution data, 131
   individual case safety reports, 197
   label requirements, 180
   New Drug Application (NDA), 109
   for OTC products, 169
   peri-approval activities, 31

National Institutes of Health (NIH)
   biologic product development, 24
   biological product development, 24, 209t
   biologics control and release, 210
   clinical trials registry, 106–107
   Drug Safety Board (DSB), 184
   gene therapy adverse event reporting, 237
   regulatory structure, 19

New Chemical Entities (NCEs) development and approval, 22–24

new dietary ingredient (NDI) notifications (NDINs), 35

New Drug Application (NDA)
   adverse experience reporting, 128
   after FM noncompliance, 170
   comparability protocol for changes, 127
   content of labeling in, 179–180
   CTD format for, 24
   development and approval, 22–24
   DMF review with, 134
   establishment registration/requirements, 109
   general information, 29
   National Drug Code (NDC) system, 109
   pediatric study plan, 108
   pre-submission activities
      naming, 108
   prescribing information (PI) for, 29, 180–181
   prescription-to-OTC switch approvals, 35–36
   presubmission meetings, 109
   presubmission NDA/BLA meetings, 109
   proprietary name submission, 108–109
   purpose of, 101, 109
   submission and review of, 112–113
   submission contents, 29–31

New Drug Product Exclusivity, 118–119

new molecular entities (NMEs), clinical protocol for, 103

New Substance Registration System (SRS), 146

nonprescription drug safety reporting, 198

nonpromotional materials
   disease awareness/help-seeking communications, 273
   scientific and educational, 272

not-substantially-equivalent (NSE) determination
   device clinical trials for determination, 66
   device submission alternatives for, 39

Notice of Claimed Investigational Exemption for a New Drug (Form FDA 1571), 101

Notice of Initiation of Disqualification Proceedings and Opportunity to Explain (NIDPOE), 60, 61

Notice of Proposed Rulemaking, proposed Common Rule changes, 52

Nuremberg Code/Doctors' Trials, 49–50

Nutrient Content Claims
   dietary supplements/ingredients, 35

O

off-label promotion/marketing
   in biosimilar use, 256
   False Claims Act (FCA), 188
   labeling and, 274
   "off-label" product use, 184, 187, 272

Office of Medication Error Prevention and Risk Management, 196

Office of Pharmacovigilance and Epidemiology, 195, 196

Office of Surveillance and Epidemiology (SE), 195–196

180-day exclusivity
   eligibility for, 156
   forfeiture of, 154, 161t
   MMA consequences on, 160–161
   with multiple ANDAs, 34
   paragraph IV certification, 144–145
   refuse to receive decision, 146

Online Label Repository, 271

operational qualification (OQ), 87

Orange Book listing, 133

orphan drug exclusivity, 159

over-the-counter (OTC) drug products, 167–175
- advertising/promotion, 174
- characteristics of, 168
- Drug Facts label, 173, 174f
- drug monograph development
  - active ingredient categories, 169
  - Advisory Panel review process, 169
  - reopening/amending, 170–171
  - therapeutic category evaluation, 169, 170t
- monograph modernization, 174–175
- NDA routes for development, 171–173
  - direct-to-OTC NDA, 171
  - generic (ANDA), 172
  - NDA monograph deviation, 172
  - Rx-to-OTC switch, 171–172
- packaging requirements, 91, 173
- product class assignment for, 174
- product monograph approval, 101
- regulations applicable to development, 169
- safety reporting, 198
- specific studies for OTC NDA
  - actual/simulation use trials, 173
  - label comprehension, 173
  - self-selection, 173

P

packaging requirements
- APLB evaluation of, 228
- biologics, 247, 271
- CGMPs for, 91
- for devices, 87
- dietary supplement packaging, 34
- dietary supplements/ingredients, 34
- DMEPA review of, 196
- DMF for packing materials, 224
- for elderly/handicapped persons, 174
- for OTC products, 91, 173–174

"paper" NDA, safety and efficacy requirements, 31
paragraph IV litigation exclusivity, 160–161, 161t
patent term extension (PTE), 154–155
patents and exclusivity, 153–165
- non-patent statutory exclusivity, 156–163
  - antibiotic drug exclusivity, 161–163
  - application types and, 162t
  - enantiomers of approved racemates, 163
  - five-year exclusivity, 156–157
  - orphan drug exclusivity, 159
  - paragraph IV litigation, 160–161, 161t
  - pediatric exclusivity, 159
  - three-year exclusivity, 157–159
- patent-related exclusivity, 154–156
  - *Orange Book* listing, 155–156
  - patent term extension (PTE), 154–155

patient labeling
- *See also* labeling; Medication Guides
- components for drugs and biologics, 270–271
- components of, 270
- Patient Package Insert (PPI), 269

pediatric exclusivity, 159
performance qualification (PQ), 87
Periodic Adverse Drug Experience Reports (PADER), 128
Periodic Adverse Experience Reports (PAER), 128
Periodic Benefit Risk Evaluation Report (PBRER), 199
Periodic Safety Update Report (PSUR), 128, 199
Pfizer Inc., Warning Letters, 64
pharmaceutical products, clinical trials/studies, 54–64
Pharmaceutical Quality System (PQS), 127
Pharmaceutical Research and Manufacturers of America (PhRMA) guidelines, 186
pharmacoeconomic claim evidence requirements, 186
pharmacovigilance, 191–203
- bioavailability/bioequivalence studies, 195
- clinical trials/studies
  - adverse events, 193
  - reporting requirements, 194
- Division of Risk Management (DRISK), 196
- drug/biologics
  - postmarket periodic reporting, 198–199
- drugs/biologics
  - authorities for, 195–196
  - FDA safety monitoring, 199
  - ICSRs, 197
  - propriety name review, 199
  - reporting requirements, 200t
  - Sentinel Initiative (SI), 202
- postmarketing surveillance, 195

physician labeling rule (PLR)
- for biologics, 270
- biologics, 270–272
- Full Prescribing Information (FPI), 270
- prescription drugs, 180–181, 182–183t

postapproval submissions/compliance (drugs/biologics), 121–139
- adverse experience reporting, 128
  - Periodic Adverse Drug Experience Reports (PADER), 128
  - Periodic Adverse Experience Reports (PAER), 128
  - Postmarketing 15-Day Alert Reports, 128
- advertising and labeling, 132
- annual reports
  - authorized generic drugs, 131
  - clinical data, 131
  - CMC information, 131
  - distribution data, 131
  - FDA forms and cover letter, 130
  - labeling and changes, 131

new information summary, 130–131
nonclinical studies, 131
outstanding regulatory business log, 132
PMR, PMC and study status, 131–132
application supplements, 124–125
approved application inactivation/withdrawal, 135–136
change management process, 124
comparability protocol for implementation, 127
complaints, 133
DMF changes, 134, 137
establishment registration/product listing, 134–135
expedited supplement review, 125
Field Alert Reports, 129–130
Orange and Purple Book listings, 133
postmarketing requirements (PMR), 123
postmarketing surveillance, 196
prescription drugs/biologics, 121–139
in product lifecycle, 123
product recalls, 133–134
proposed labeling changes, 125
Quality by Design changes, 127
quality requirements, 124
REMS requirements, 129–130
reporting categories for changes, 126f
sponsor change/ownership transfer inactivation/withdrawal, 136
summary, 136–137
SUPAC documents for, 126
Postmarketing 15-Day Alert Reports, 128
Postmarketing Commitments (PMCs), 113
Postmarketing Requirements (PMR), 113, 124
postmarketing surveillance
dietary supplements/ingredients, 202
FAERS in, 199
medical devices, 201
product lifecycle and, 193
Sentinel Initiative (SI), 202
pre-license inspection (PLIs), 235
preapproval inspections (PAIs), 115, 169, 235
preapproval inspections (PAIs) for NDA/BLA, 42
preapproval product communications, advertising/promotion, 273
predicate (marketed) device, 38, 66
Pregnancy and Lactation Labeling Rule (PLLR), 180, 270
premarket approval
dietary supplements/ingredients, 34
MDA changes in route to market, 37
Premarket Approval Application (PMA)
clinical study data for, 39–40
for device classes, 36t
medical devices, 37
postapproval study requirements, 202

premarket notification (510(k))
device classifications and, 37
device submission review, 66–67
IDE for safety/effectiveness data, 42
MDA changes in route to market, 37
submission and exemptions, 38–39
submission review, 66–67
substantial equivalence review standard in, 53
prescribing information
with advertisements, 275
for Biologics License Application (BLA), 180–181
in CTD modules, 110
FDA final regulations on, 270
FPI in prescription drug advertising, 189
for internet promotion, 276
for New Drug Application (NDA), 29, 180–181
in PLR format, 180–181, 189
prescription drugs, 180
with promotional labeling, 185, 275
prescription drug submissions, 99–119
expediting development and review, 116–119
FDA review process, 113–116
IND application preparation/submission, 101–109
NDA or BLA, 109–113
new therapeutic product requirements, 101
prescription drugs
advertising/promotion
brief summary exceptions in, 186
brief summary requirement, 185
defined, 179
direct-to-consumer (DTC), 185
reminder advertisements, 185
advertising/promotion enforcement
by FDA, 187–188
other agencies, 188–189
labeling, 177–185
changes to approved product, 181
definitions of, 179, 180
electronic/SPL, 179–180
general requirements, 180
PLR format, 110
product name/placement, 185
summary, 179
package insert and PLR, 180–181, 182–183t
patient labeling/medication guides, 181
postapproval submissions/compliance, 121–139
promotion
for formulary, 186
internet and social media, 187
pharmacoeconomic claims, 186
press releases, 186
product detailing, 186–187
reprints, 187
promotional material for

fair balance, 184
substantial evidence standard, 184
regulation summary, 189–190
scientific exchange, 187
prescription-to-OTC switch, 35
President's Emergency Plan for AIDS Relief (PEPFAR), 118
preventive action (PA), 88
prior approval supplement (PAS), biologics labeling lifecycle, 272
Priority Review
expedited development programs, 117
QIDPs designation, 163
vouchers for serious/life-threatening disease products, 27
product naming, biologics, 237–238
promotional materials
advertisement vs. promotional labeling, 273
FDA evaluation of risk communication, 275
proprietary name, 30, 108–109
PSUR waiver, 129

Q

qualified health claims, dietary supplements/ingredients, 35
Qualified Infectious Disease Product (QIDP)
definition, 26
exclusivity extensions for, 163
expedited marketing approval, 22
incentives for, 8–9, 118
quality assurance unit (QAU)
personnel for, 64
pharmaceutical products, 90
quality-by design (QbD) principle, 84, 85, 127
quality control (QC) unit, pharmaceutical products, 90
Quality Management System (QMS), 83–98
for CGMPs, 84–85
change control in, 85
corrective/preventive actions in, 88
documentation elements, 85f
management responsibility in, 85
Quality System Regulation (QSR), 85–90
acceptance activities, 87–88
additional CGMP requirements, 89–90
complaint handling procedures, 88–89
corrective/preventive action procedures, 88
corrective/preventive actions in, 88
design and development plan, 85–86
design changes, 87
design control, 86t
design inputs/outputs, 86
design review, 87
design transfer, 86–87
documentation, 89

for IDEs, 39
labeling and packaging control, 88
production/process controls, 87
resource management, 88
verification and validation, 86

R

rare pediatric disease, priority product review, 26–27
recalls, 133–134
Refuse to File (RTF), 112
refuse to receive (RTR) decision, 146
regulatory information resources
CAS Registry Numbers, 146
Orange Book listing, 137
regulatory pathways
ANDA, 32–34
antibacterial development, 26
biologics regulation by, 24
biosimilar product approval pathway, 24
CTD format for, 27–28
development and approval
Biologics License Application (BLA), 24
New Chemical Entities, 22–24
dietary supplements/ingredients
CGMPs for, 34
claims allowed, 35
Fast Track designation, 25
FDA
overview, 19–20
premarket review, 21f
relationships and meetings, 20–22
Special Protocol Assessment (SPA), 22
federal executive departments/agencies, 19
generic drugs, 32–34
ICH guidelines, 27–28
IND annual reports, 29
IND application and amendments to, 28–29
IND safety reporting, 29
medical devices, 40
de novo classification, 39
establishment registration/device listing, 40
HUD classification, 38
IDE and PMA process, 39
IDE submissions, 37–38
PMA for, 37
premarket notification and exemptions, 38–39
regulatory milestones, 36–37
substantial equivalence, 39
user fees for, 40
NDA 505(b)(1), 29–31
new dietary ingredient (NDI), 35
orphan drug designation, 25
over-the-counter (OTC) drug products
monographs for, 35

vs. prescription, 35
overview, 13–44
paper NDA, 31–32
rare disease products, 26–27
regulatory project manager (RPM)
application review, 28, 104, 113
sponsor contact, 31
reminder advertisements, 185, 276
Request for Designation (RFD), combination products, 40–41
Risk Evaluation and Mitigation Strategy (REMS)
in drug development, 30
drugs/biologics postapproval, 129–130
efficacy assessment of, 200
Medication Guides, 270
pharmacovigilance, 199–200
prescription drug products, 113
RiskMAP in development process, 30
shared system for, 200
risk management, 199–203
Risk MAP in development process, 30
rolling review
BLA/NDA, 26
request for, 117–118

S

safety alerts
Dear Health Care Professional (DHCP) letters, 193
Drug Safety Communications, 193
Field Alert Reports (FARs), 193
safety reporting
biologics IND, 237
FAERS, 193
forms for, 129, 194, 197, 241
harmonized format for, 128–129
for OTC drug products, 169
product lifecycle and, 193
vaccine safety surveillance, 195
Sanofi-Aventis, Warning Letters, 60
Scale-Up and Postapproval Changes (SUPAC) guidance documents, 126
S.E. Massengill Company (sulfanilamide disaster), 49
"Section VIII" carve-out, 145
Securities and Exchange Commission (SEC), 186
Sentinel Initiative (SI), 202
serious adverse event
defined, 193–194
reporting of, 198
serious disease definition, 26
serious suspected adverse reaction, defined, 193–194
single patient IND, 107
Special Protocol Assessment (SPA), eligibility for, 22, 41
sponsor responsibilities

promotional submission to FDA, 276
safety reporting, 194–195
Standard Operating Procedures (SOPs)
blood/blood products, 96
CGMP compatibility testing, 96
CGMP documentation for, 85
CGMPs facility requirements, 95
for design transfer, 86
documentation of CGMPs, 85, 85f
for *FD&C Act* compliance, 20
in GCP monitoring, 62, 64
strength (pharmaceutical), 90
Structure Function Claims, dietary supplements/ingredients, 35
Structured Product Label (SPL) format
for advertising/promotional labeling, 179–180
biologics establishment registration/listing information, 231
BLA/NDA requirements, 29–30
with BLA submissions, 270, 271–272
defined, 180
electronic submission of, 30
OTC development, 169
for prescription products, 110, 135
substantial equivalence
defined by *SMDA*, 37, 53
determining factors for, 38–39
investigational devices, 70
medical devices, 8, 39
premarketing submissions for, 42, 66–68
substantial evidence standard, 184
substantially equivalent (SE) determination, 66–67, 70
sulfanilamide disaster, 49
supply chain management, globalization of, 8
Supreme Court "labeling" interpretation, 269
suspected adverse reaction defined, 194

T

Table of Contents (Contents) for PLR, biologics, 270
tamper-evident packaging, 91, 97, 173
tamper-resistant packaging, 173
Tentative Final Monograph (TFM) (Proposed Rule), 169–170
therapeutic equivalence, 147–149
therapeutic interchange, 147
Therapeutics and Blood Safety Branch Safety Signal Tracking (SST) system, 199
three-year exclusivity, 157–159
Time and Extent Application (TEA) for OTC monograph, 170–171
traceability and supply chain (pharmaceutical), 8
tropical diseases, priority product review, 26–27
Tuskegee syphilis study, 50–51

U

unanticipated adverse device effect (UADE), 75–76
unexpected adverse drug experience
    defined, 195
    reporting of, 198
unexpected adverse event, defined, 194
unexpected suspected adverse reaction, defined, 194
Unified Registration and Listing System (FURLS), 40
Unique Device Identification (UDI) in device labeling/packaging control, 88
United States Prescribing Information (USPI), 269
    print advertising, 275
    product claim substantiation, 274
    promotional labeling, 273
    template for PLR format, 270
United States v. Generix Drug Corp., 142
United States v. Johnson, 5
unmet medical need definition, 26
Untitled Letters
    press release statements, 186
    for risk information omissions, 275
US Code (USC), codified laws by subject, 19
user fee programs
    biosimilars, 24
    expansion of, 7

V

vaccine safety surveillance, ICSRs for, 197–198
vaccines, live vaccine processing, 95
VAERS, drug/biologics postmarket surveillance, 195

W

Warning Letters
    for advertising/promotional violations, 277
    Coast IRB letter, 59
    Icon Clinical Research Inc., 60, 64
    Johnson & Johnson Pharmaceuticals, 60, 64
    Pfizer Inc., 64
    press release statements, 186
    Sanofi-Aventis, 60
warning statements, habit-forming drug caution, 6
World Health Organization (WHO)
    biomedical research guidelines, 53
    nonproprietary name assignment, 108

Z

Zarxio®, 260–261

SECTION II
Fundamentals of Canadian Pharmaceutical and Biologics Regulations

Copyright © 2018 by the Regulatory Affairs Professionals Society.
All rights reserved.

ISBN: 978-1-947493-15-5

Every precaution is taken to ensure accuracy of content; however, the publisher cannot accept responsibility for the correctness of the information supplied. At the time of publication, all Internet references (URLs) in this book were valid. These references are subject to change without notice.

RAPS Global Headquarters
5635 Fishers Lane
Suite 550
Rockville, MD 20852
USA

RAPS.org

Acknowledgements

RAPS and CAPRA would like to thank the following individuals for their contributions to this book and willingness to share their knowledge and experiences on Canadian pharmaceutical and biologics' regulations.

Christopher Antonio
Regulatory Affair Supervisor
Office of Regulatory Affairs
Biologics and Genetic Therapies Directorate
Health Products and Food Branch
Health Canada

Roshni Celeste
Unit Head, Regulatory Affairs and Quality Assurance Unit
Data Management and Integrity Section
Marketed Health Safety and Effectiveness Information Bureau
Marketed Health Products Directorate
Health Products and Food Branch
Health Canada

Junyi Chen, JD, PhD
Partner
Blane McMurtry

Mahdis Dorkalam, MSc, RHN
President
CRM Pharma Consulting Inc.

Danny Germain, MSc, MBA, RAC, CCPE
Director, Regulatory Affairs
Avir Pharma Inc./Laboratoire Riva Inc.

Jenna Griffiths, MSc, PhD
Manager, Office of Science
Bureau of Policy, Science and International Programs
Therapeutic Products Directorate
Health Products and Food Branch
Health Canada

Bocar Guisse, MSc
Manageer, Regulatory Affairs—CMC
Pharmascience Inc.

Gordon Jepson, MA, LLB
Partner
Deeth Williams Wall LLP

Carole Légaré, MD, CCFP, Cert PE& PV
Director, Office of Clinical Trials
Therapeutic Products Directorate
Health Products and Food Branch
Health Canada

Hetal Mokashi
Director, Canadian Regulatory Affairs
Mapi Group

Bhavesh Patel, CChem
Associate, Regulatory Affairs
Natco Pharma (Canada) Inc.

Regulatory Affairs Professionals Society

Ajay Babu Pazhayattil, MPharm, CPGP, CKM
Director, Quality and Compliance
Eurofins Alphora Research Inc

Susanne Picard, MSc
President
SPharm Inc.

Marc F. Poitras, PhD, MBA
Scientific Manager
Marketed Pharmaceuticals and Medical Device Bureau
Health Products and Food Branch
Health Canada

Tanya Ramsamy, PhD
Associate Director, Office of Clinical Trials
Therapeutic Products Directorate
Health Products and Food Branch
Health Canada

Marcia Sam
Manager, Regulatory Affairs
Shire Pharma Canada ULC

Naheed Sayeed-Desta, MBA Candidate
Manager, Technical Operations Process Validation
Apotex Inc.

Navneet Sekhon
President
AxSource Consulting Inc.

Fraidianie Sévigné
Director, Regulatory Affairs—CMC
Pharmascience Inc.

Thanh Vu, PharmD, RPh
Regional Coordinator
Marketed Health Products Safety and Effectiveness
   Information Bureau
Marketed Health Product Directorate (MHPD)
Health Products and Food Branch
Health Canada

Janice Weiler
President
J. Weiler Regulatory Affairs Inc.

Penny Wilks, ND, RAC
Senior Manager, Regulatory Services
Mapi Group

Kristin Willemsen
Director of Scientific and Regulatory Affairs
Consumer Health Products Canada

Bruce Wozny, MA
Senior Policy Officer
Marketed Health Products Directorate
Healt4h Products and Food Branch
Health Canada

Raymond Yang, PhD
Assessment Officer
Natural and Non-prescription Health Products
   Directorate
Health Product and Food Branch
Health Canada

Khaled Yahiaoui, MSc, RAC
President
eCTD Now Inc.

Section II
Table of Contents

Chapter 1	Health Canada Organization and Its History of Regulating Health Products in Canada ....1 *Updated by Hetal Mokashi, MBA and Penny Wilks, ND, RAC*	
Chapter 2	Good Laboratory Practice for Nonclinical Laboratory Studies ....11 *Updated by Navneet Sekhon*	
Chapter 3	Clinical Trial Applications, Good Clinical Practices ....19 *By Mahdis Dorkalam, MSc, RHN, and Navneet Sekhon*	
Chapter 4	Good Manufacturing Practices and Establishment Licensing in Canada ....29 *By Bocar Guisse, MSc and Fraidianie Sévigné*	
Chapter 5	New Drug Submission Process..45 *Updated by Susanne Picard and Janice Weiler*	
Chapter 6	Postmarketing and Other Activities ....59 *Updated by Janice Weiler and Danny Germain, RAC*	
Chapter 7	Health Product Vigilance and Risk Management ....69 *Updated by Christopher Antonio, Roshni Celeste, Jenna Griffiths, Carole Légaré, Marc Poitras, Tanya Ramsamy, Thanh Vu, Bruce Wozny and Raymond Yang*	
Chapter 8	An Overview of Pharmaceutical Intellectual Property Protection in Canada ....79 *By Junyi Chen, JD, PhD, Danny Germain, RAC, Gordon Jepson, MA, LLB, and Bhavesh Patel, CChem*	
Chapter 9	Abbreviated New Drug Submissions...95 *Updated by Bhavesh Patel, CChem, Bocar Guisse, MSc and Fraidianie Sevigne*	
Chapter 10	Nonprescription Drugs ....105 *Updated by Kristin Willemsen*	
Chapter 11	Biologics Submission, Approval and Postmarketing ....115 *Updated by Marcia Sam and Mahdis Dorkalam, MSc, RHN*	
Chapter 12	Labelling, Advertising and Promotion: Prescription Pharmaceutical Drugs, Biologics and Radiopharmaceuticals...127 *Updated by Marcia Sam, Veronica Yip and Sandra Alderdice*	
Chapter 13	electronic Common Technical Document (eCTD)..133 *By Khaled Yahiaoui, MSc, RAC*	

Chapter 14   Product Lifecycle Management Guidance 143
             by Ajay Babu Pazhayattil, Naheed Sayeed-Desta and Queenia Lee

Index..............149

Figures
Figure 1-1.   Health Canada..............2
Figure 1-2.   Branches with Responsibility for the Regulation of Healthcare Products..............3
Figure 5-1.   Diagram of the NDS Submission and Approval Procedure..............51
Figure 5-2.   Example Boxed Text for Product Approved Under the NOC/c Policy..............52
Figure 6-1.   Form IV Patent List..............64
Figure 13-1. Structure of a Regulatory Transaction in eCTD Format..............135
Figure 13-2. End-to-End Process for Preparing and Filing Regulatory Transactions in eCTD Format..............141

Tables
Table 1-1.   Timeline—Regulating Health Products in Canada..............6
Table 2-1.   Examples of Studies and the Requirement for GLP Compliance..............14
Table 3-1.   Contents of a CTA Submission Package..............22
Table 3-2.   Quality Changes—Biologics and Radiopharmaceuticals..............24
Table 3-3.   Quality Changes—Pharmaceuticals..............25
Table 3-4.   Postapproval Requirements..............27
Table 4-1.   Definitions for Terms in This Chapter..............30
Table 4-2.   GMP Regulations Applicable to Licensable Activities..............33
Table 5-1.   Presentation of Information in the Common Technical Document (CTD) Format..............49
Table 5-2.   Target Review Times..............53
Table 7-1.   Clinical Trial Definitions..............71
Table 7-2.   Postapproval Stage Definitions..............74
Table 9-1.   Target Review Times..............102
Table 10-1. NAPRA Scheduling Factors..............110
Table 11-1. Drug Substance (Biologics and Radiopharmaceuticals)..............118
Table 11-2. Drug Product (Biologics and Radiopharmaceuticals)..............119
Table 11-3. Sample Table of Contents for a Schedule D (Biological) Product Monograph (PM)..............120
Table 11-4. Summary of Requirements for Evaluation Groups..............123
Table 13-1. Localization of Main XML Files Within an eCTD Sequence..............136
Table 13-2. Canadian eCTD Envelope Elements..............136
Table 13-3. m2-m5 eCTD Attributes..............137
Table 13-4. Validation Rule Samples and Their Descriptions and Severities..............137
Table 13-5. Document Formats Health Canada Expects for Specific Documents..............138
Table 13-6. Lifecycle Management Table Template..............138
Table 13-7. Lifecycle Management Table Example with Three Regulatory Activities and Related Regulatory Transactions..............139
Table 13-8. Lifecycle Management of Specific Documents..............140

Chapter 1

Health Canada Organization and Its History of Regulating Health Products in Canada

Updated by Hetal Mokashi, MBA and Penny Wilks, ND, RAC

OBJECTIVES

❑ Understand the mission of Health Canada.

❑ Understand the organization of Health Canada.

❑ Provide a concise timeline of events that influenced the *Food and Drugs Act*.

❑ Discuss current status of health product legislation and regulations.

LAWS AND REGULATIONS COVERED IN THIS CHAPTER

❑ *Constitution Act (1867)*

❑ *Department of Health Act*

❑ *Patent Act*

❑ *Patented Medicines (Notice of Compliance) Regulations*

❑ *Food and Drugs Act*

❑ *Food and Drug Regulations*

❑ *Medical Devices Regulations*

❑ *Natural Health Products Regulations*

Introduction

A century ago, most Canadians believed it was a family's duty to look after members who were poor, unemployed, sick or old. Industrialization and the Great Depression caused this philosophy to change. The *British North America Act* gave provinces control over social welfare, including health. After World War II, both federal and provincial government levels saw a need for change, and the federal government agreed to pay half the cost of provincial healthcare programs. To obtain access to the federal money, each province had to ensure its system met national standards. Both governments, therefore, are responsible for assisting with Canadians' health and well-being.

The federal government enacts legislation regulating what products can be sold as drugs, how different drug categories (prescription, nonprescription, narcotics or natural health products) are controlled and how drug abuse is avoided. Provincial governments legislate how drugs are distributed and, for certain citizens, pay for listed drugs, limited-use drug products, some nutritional products and some diabetic testing products. Provinces and territories plan, finance and evaluate the provision of hospital care, physician and allied healthcare services, some aspects of prescription care and public health.

This chapter focuses on the federal government's involvement in Canadians' healthcare. A discussion of the relevant federal department's organization and structure is followed by an overview of the legislative framework.

Health Canada

Health Canada is the federal government department responsible for enforcing food and drug regulations and administering national health-related functions such as health promotion programs. The minister of health's

Chapter 1

Figure 1-1. Health Canada

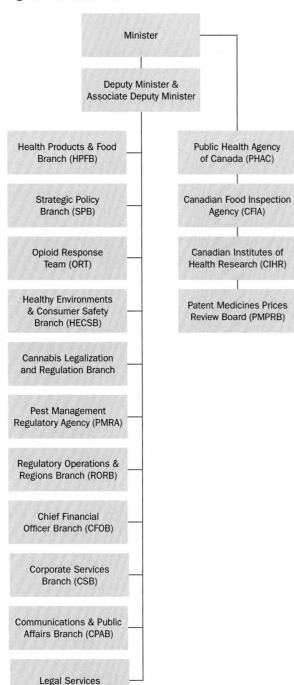

powers, duties and functions are assigned via Section 4(2) of the *Department of Health Act*; Section 79 of the *Patent Act* assigns patented medicine regulation (i.e., Sections 80-103) to the minister of health. These functions flow from the federal government's constitutional criminal law, patent and spending powers.

The *Food and Drugs Act* (*F&DA*) and its regulations form the key legislative framework administered by Health Canada. They enable Health Canada to regulate the sale of food, drugs, cosmetics and medical devices in Canada, whether manufactured in Canada or imported. They also enable regulation for these products' safety, efficacy and quality and prohibit misleading advertising.

Health Canada is the federal organization responsible for helping Canadians maintain and improve their health. In partnership with provincial and territorial governments, Health Canada provides national leadership to develop health policy, communicate health risks and promote healthy lifestyles, promote disease prevention and monitor risks related to the sale and use of drugs, food, chemicals, pesticides, medical devices and other consumer products across Canada.

Health Canada Organization and Structure of Departments

Health Canada is organized into branches, each of which is responsible for a different aspect of health governance. The deputy minister and associate deputy minister of health, working with the secretariat, support the minister of health in managing these operations. See **Figure 1-1** for more information.

The Health Canada branches are broadly divided into:
- Health Products and Food Branch (HPFB)
- Strategic Policy Branch
- Opioid Response Team (ORT)
- Healthy Environment and Consumer Safety Branch
- Cannabis Legalization and Regulation Branch
- Pest Management Regulatory Agency
- Regulatory Operations and Regions Branch
- Chief Financial Officer Branch
- Communications and Public Affairs Branch
- Corporate Services Branch
- Communications and Public Affairs Branch
- Legal Services

Additionally, the following independent agencies are included in the portfolio of, and report directly to, the minister of health:
- Public Health Agency of Canada—the agency, headed by the chief public health officer, reports directly to the minister of health and focuses on efforts to prevent chronic diseases such as cancer and heart disease, prevent injuries and respond to public health emergencies and infectious disease outbreaks
- Canadia Food Inspection Agency (CFIA)—a science-based regulatory body dedicated to protecting Canadians from preventable health risks related to food and zoonotic diseases.

- Canadian Institutes of Health Research—Canada's premier federal funding agency for health research
- Patented Medicine Prices Review Board—a quasi-judicial body regulating the prices of patented medicines

Some Health Canada branches are managed by assistant deputy ministers located in Ottawa, while other offices or services are independent and report directly to the deputy minister and assistant deputy minister of health. Additionally, the Regions and Programs Branch has regional directors representing departmental interests and providing a presence through regional offices. Health Canada maintains eight regional operations throughout the provinces from coast to coast: British Columbia Region, Alberta Region, Manitoba Region, Saskatchewan Region, Ontario Region, Quebec Region, Atlantic Region and Northern Region. The regional offices are found under the Regions and Programs Branch.

Health Products and Food Branch (HPFB)

The most important Health Canada branch for the regulatory field is HPFB, which seeks to minimize Canadians' health risk factors while maximizing health product and food safety, promoting conditions enabling Canadians to make healthy choices and providing information to allow them to make informed decisions about their health.

HPFB helps Canadians maintain and improve their health by:
- evaluating and monitoring the safety, quality and efficacy of:
  o health products (including drugs, medical devices, biologic and genetic therapies and natural health products)
  o foods
  o veterinary drugs (to protect the safety of Canada's food supply)
- developing, promoting and implementing nutrition and food policies and standards
- providing timely, evidence-based and authoritative information to allow healthy and informed decisions
- anticipating and responding to public health and safety issues associated with health products, food and nutrition

HPFB's activities are carried out through offices in the National Capital Region and five regional offices: Atlantic, Quebec, Ontario and Nunavut, Manitoba-Saskatchewan and Western (British Columbia, Alberta, Northwest Territories and Yukon).

HPFB's organization is shown in **Figure 1-2**.

HPFB is divided into several directorates, including:

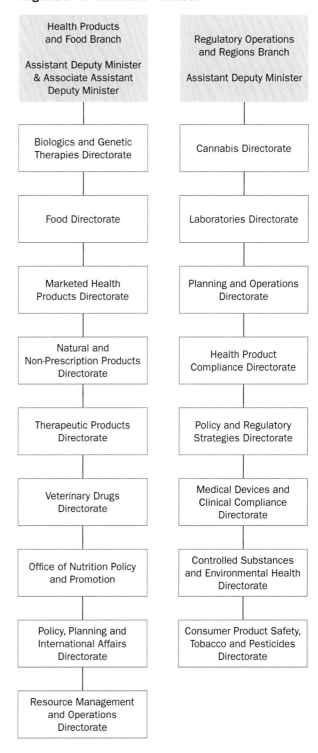

Figure 1-2. Branches with Responsibility for the Regulation of Healthcare Products

- The Biologics and Genetic Therapies Directorate (BGTD) regulates biological drugs (products derived from living sources) and radiopharmaceuticals for human use. BGTD reviews the safety and effectiveness evidence provided by manufacturers to determine whether the product's benefits outweigh its risks and whether those risks can be mitigated. BGTD then monitors the product's safety and effectiveness in concert with the Regulatory and Regions Operations Branch (RORB),[1] the Marketed Health Products Directorate (MHPD) and the Public Health Agency of Canada (PHAC).
- The Food Directorate establishes policies, sets standards and provides advice and information on the safety and nutritional value of food. Additionally, under the *Canadian Food Inspection Agency Act*, this directorate assesses the effectiveness of the Canadian Food Inspection Agency's (CFIA) activities related to food safety.
- The Marketed Health Products Directorate (MHPD) ensures HPFB programs take a consistent approach to postapproval safety surveillance, assessment of issues and safety trends and risk communications concerning all regulated marketed health products. Its activities include collecting and analyzing adverse reaction data and communicating risk assessments.
- The Natural and Non-prescription Health Products Directorate (NNHPD) is the regulating authority for natural health products and over-the-counter (OTC) drugs for sale in Canada. It processes applications and submissions and grants licences for natural health products and Drug Identification Numbers (DINs) for OTC drugs.
- The Therapeutic Products Directorate (TPD) regulates pharmaceutical drugs and medical devices for human use. TPD reviews scientific evidence of a product's safety, efficacy and quality submitted by a manufacturer, as required by the *F&DA* and *Food and Drug Regulations* (*FDR*). The directorate's activities concern medical devices, clinical trials, drug submissions, patented medicines and a variety of other matters.
- The Veterinary Drugs Directorate evaluates and monitors product safety, quality and effectiveness, sets standards and promotes the prudent use of veterinary drugs administered to food-producing and companion animals.
- The Research Management and Operations Directorate fulfils management and stewardship obligations with respect to resources. These obligations are set out in legislation and accountability requirements and the federal public service values and ethics code.

HPFB's policy development arms include:
- Office of Nutrition Policy and Promotion
- Office of the Assistant Deputy Minister
- Policy, Planning and International Affairs Directorate

Regulatory Operations and Regions Branch (RORB)

It is worth noting HPFB's licensing and regulatory requirements' arm is separate from its enforcement arm. RORB is responsible for operating a national compliance and enforcement program for all products under HPFB's mandate, with the exception of food products, which are CFIA's responsibility, as it performs analagous functions regarding food products. RORB is divided into eight different directorates (see **Figure 1-2**). RORB core functions include compliance monitoring such as industry inspection and product investigation, supported by drug and medical device establishment listing and laboratory analysis. RORB develops and implements enforcement strategies in these areas. RORB's activities apply to all drugs and devices, as defined by the *F&DA*. These include medical devices and human drugs, natural health products, blood and blood components for transfusion, semen for assisted conception, cells, tissues, organs for transplantation and veterinary drugs.

Modernization and the Future of Health Product Legislation

Canadian food and drug legislation has a rich history (**Table 1-1**). First introduced in 1875 to fight fraud, frequent, incremental legislative changes were made to address gaps identified, as regulators gained experience administering the statutes and as regulated parties continued to innovate. When legislation was no longer sufficient to protect Canadians, it was renewed and modernized, e.g., the *Adulteration Act of 1884*, the *Proprietary or Patent Medicine Act* in 1909 and the first *Food and Drugs Act* in 1920. The current *F&DA* structure dates back to 1953, and the regulations date back to 1963, with the addition of Division 8—New Drugs.

The pursuit of a new *Health Protection Act* was part of a legislative renewal exercise (1998) aimed at replacing four acts with one. Regulatory renewal was to follow. The legislation proposed incorporating such principles as science-based evidence, benefit-risk and the precautionary principle. Extensive consultations were undertaken in 2003, but legislation was never moved forward in Parliament.

In 2003, Health Canada embarked on the Therapeutic Access Strategy, focused on improving regulatory processes and eliminating the submission backlog. Under the strategy, work was initiated to update user fees and transparency projects aimed at increasing the amount and quality of information available to the public (e.g., product monograph, summary basis of decision, performance reporting, etc.).

International harmonization initiatives were undertaken to reduce unnecessary duplication, thereby contributing to the efficiency of new drug development, registration and surveillance. The strategy also sought to make greater use of expert science advice in the regulatory review of submissions and to benefit from other regulatory authorities' experiences through increased regulatory collaboration and foreign review reports.

The 2006 Blueprint for Renewal once again embarked on modernizing the *F&DA*. Like Legislative Renewal, Blueprint was launched with extensive consultations, followed by the 2008 Blueprint II document outlining the plan forward. The legislation was aimed at progressive health product licensing or a lifecycle approach that would allow product safety, efficacy and quality to be evaluated continuously before and after introduction to the Canadian market. Bill C-51, the *Canada Health Protection Act*, was introduced in Parliament to replace the *F&DA*. The 39th Parliament ended on 7 September 2008, and Bill C-51 did not become law.

Despite Bill C-51's end in Parliament, significant progress was made on various "Blueprint" regulatory and policy projects. For example:
- *Cells, Tissues and Organs for Transplant Regulations* came fully into force June 2008.
- New user fee regulations were completed and came into force in April 2011.
- *Blood Regulations* were published in *Canada Gazette, Part II* in 2013.
- A statutory review of the clinical trials regulations was undertaken and, although the regulations themselves did not require adjustments, various guidance documents were either developed or updated.
- The *Natural Health Products (Unprocessed Product Licence Applications) Regulations (NHP-UPLAR)* came into force in August 2010 as a backlog reduction measure. These temporary regulations allowed lower-risk products that met safety and efficacy requirements to be sold legally (and labelled with exemption numbers (ENs)) while awaiting full review. The regulations were rescinded in February 2013 when they were no longer needed.
- Guidance for the consideration of special populations was published, e.g., *Inclusion of Women in Clinical Trials* (May 2013).

Modernization efforts continued to build on previous initiatives and are summarized in the *2012 Regulatory Roadmap for Health Products and Food*, which was implemented in phases over a five-year period from 2012 to 2017. The roadmap focused on the *F&DA*'s various product-specific regulations, with the intent to develop an efficient, sustainable and science-based regulatory system that:

- maintains protections against unsafe health products' sale and advertising
- responds to the evolution in science, patient and consumer behaviour as well as healthcare practices
- moves from a "benefit-risk" to "benefits, harms and uncertainties" paradigm
- allows for greater international regulatory collaboration
- provides meaningful transparency about health products

Since October 2013, Health Canada has moved forward on several transparency initiatives, such as posting Regulatory Decision Summaries (RDSs), Summary Basis of Decisions (SBDs), Summary Safety Reviews (SSRs), inspection summary reports and drug safety reviews.

Schedule F, a regulatory list previously updated through Order in Council, was replaced with the administrative Prescription Drug List, under the minister of health's authority. Although the 2005 Schedule F Memorandum of Understanding had shortened the regulatory process by permitting *Canada Gazette, Part I* pre-publication to be bypassed, the new process to update the list is intended to reduce the timelines further. The Prescription Drug List came into effect in December 2013.

On 22 June 2013, Health Canada pre-published proposed regulatory amendments requiring "plain language" labelling (PLL) and packaging of drugs for human use, and the submission of data to support a Look-Alike/Sound-Alike assessment of the brand name in *Canada Gazette, Part I*. The proposed regulations link "plain language" with label readability, standardise nonprescription drug labels and require label and package mock-ups to be submitted for review. Contact information for reporting suspected harms would be required for all drugs, prescription and nonprescription. On 12 June 2014, these PLL regulations were published in *Canada Gazette, Part II*. The regulations took effect for prescription products and those administered or obtained through a healthcare professional on 13 June 2015. The PLL regulations took effect for nonprescription drugs on 13 June 2017.

Vanessa's Law, also known as the *Protecting Canadians from Unsafe Drugs Act*, was launched, with the purpose of strengthening therapeutic product safety and its regulation. Following the death of 15-year-old Vanessa Young from a prescription drug in 2000, this law was initiated to propose amending the *F&DA*. With its introduction, 6 December 2013, Bill C-17 received Royal Assent on 6 November 2014. This act applies to therapeutic products, including prescription drugs, OTC drugs, vaccines, medical devices (including combination drug-devices), gene therapies, cells, tissues and organs; however, it does not apply to natural health products.

Chapter 1

Table 1-1. Timeline—Regulating Health Products in Canada

1875	The first food and drugs legislation in Canada was triggered by the rampant adulteration of spirits. The *Act to Impose License Duties on Compounders of Spirits; to Amend the Act Respecting the Inland Revenue; and to Prevent the Adulteration of Food, Drink and Drugs*, which became known as the *Inland Revenue Act of 1875*, dealt with fraud and set out penalties. It provided for the appointment of inspectors responsible for collecting and analysing samples. The legislation was not implemented until March 1876, with the Order-in-Council (Privy Council) appointment of four analysts as the first administration body of food and drugs within the Department of Inland Revenue.
1884	The 1875 legislation was found deficient. Little attention had been given to the analysis of drugs, and few samples of liquor had been examined, despite liquor's influence in motivating the original legislation. Also, there were few successful prosecutions for adulterated foods. The legislation was amended and consolidated into the *Adulteration Act of 1884*. It defined drugs as all medicine for internal or external use and required them to meet the standards set out in the *British Pharmacopoeia*, the *US Pharmacopeia* or other recognized standards. The legislation also provided for the appointment of a chief analyst. An 1890 amendment expanded the definition of adulterated food and allowed standards to be set by Orders-in-Council.
1909	The *Proprietary or Patent Medicine Act* addressed gaps in adulteration laws, notably the sale of potentially dangerous "secret-formula, non-pharmacopoeial packaged medicines," particularly preparations containing cocaine. It was the first legislation to require the registration of medicines. The formulae would be inspected by a government official and if its claims, such as the claimed therapeutic value, were accurate, a licence could be granted for its distribution. This act is the first statute to protect the public against drugs administered without medical supervision.
1919	Federal government departments were reorganized after World War I. The first federal Department of Health was assigned the administration of the *Adulteration Act* and the *Proprietary or Patent Medicine Act*. The *Proprietary or Patent Medicine Act* was amended in 1919 to give the government authority and control over advertising and to prohibit claims of a cure for specific diseases.
1920	*An Act Respecting Food and Drugs* received royal assent. This act replaced the *Adulteration Act* and incorporated the concept of "delegated legislation," giving the governor-in-council the authority to make regulations for the purpose of carrying out the provisions of the act.
1927	The development of vaccines for smallpox, diphtheria and tetanus led to amendments giving the minister of health the authority to license manufacturers of drugs listed in schedules to the act, including endocrine preparations, serums, toxins, vaccines and analogous biological products. The amendment also required manufacturers to submit test samples of each lot to the department. Authority was given to the minister to cancel or suspend a licence for violation of the regulations.
1941	The *Food and Drugs Act* was amended so potent and dangerous drugs were only available by prescription. The prescription requirement at the federal level ensured pan-Canadian uniformity in the conditions of sale.
1951	Drug manufacturers were required to file New Drug Submissions and to establish their new drugs were safe prior to advertising. If the Department of Health was satisfied with the submission, it would issue a Notice of Compliance.
1953	The 1920 *Food and Drugs Act* was, by now, a patchwork of incremental changes, no longer effective in regulating the rapid development of new drugs during and after World War II. Extensive amendments were made to the act. Significant features were added to the basic principles of the 1920 act, including the prohibition of the manufacture, preparation, preservation, storage or sale of foods, drugs or cosmetics in unsanitary conditions. This act came into force in August 1954 and continues to provide the legal authority for drug and device regulation today.
1954	New *Food and Drug Regulations* came into force in December 1954. Although defined in the new act, these regulations did not contain provisions specific to medical devices. Devices were nevertheless subject to the administrative provisions of the regulations.
1958	The *Food and Drugs Act* was amended to make it an offence to possess drugs listed on Schedule G (e.g., methamphetamine and barbituric acid) for the purpose of trafficking. These amendments introduced mandatory licences for listed drug manufacturers and importers.
1963	In 1961, it was discovered that thalidomide—a drug previously approved for use by pregnant women to alleviate the symptoms of morning sickness—was responsible for serious birth defects and fetal deaths. The case led to major changes to the *Food and Drugs Act* and the regulations aimed at preventing similar tragedies. The act was amended in 1962 to include an outright prohibition to sell certain scheduled substances, including thalidomide, and to significantly increase the scope of regulation-making authorities. In 1963, substantive revisions to the regulations pertaining to "New Drugs" came into effect. These included requirements to file submissions for clinical trials, to present substantial evidence of safety and efficacy for new drugs and to submit manufacturing and control information. The minister was also given the authority to suspend a clinical trial or a Notice of Compliance.

1966	Gaps in information about marketed not-new drugs became apparent. Notification regulations came into effect, requiring manufacturers to notify Health Canada within 30 days following a drug first being sold and provide information about its ingredients, use and dosage. Notification also was required regarding changes to already marketed drugs or when a drug is removed from the market. Finally, the regulations required annual notification of drugs sold in Canada. These changes allowed for the 1995 introduction of "right to sell" fees and for the eventual development of the Drug Product Database. Regulations came into effect allowing the sale of a new drug to a physician for the emergency treatment of a patient. The sale was exempt from the requirements of the *Food and Drugs Act* and the regulations. Emergency release is now called the Special Access Programme.
1969	The first medical device-specific regulations come into force with the addition of "Part K—Devices" in the *Food and Drug Regulations*. Part K required that no person sell a medical device that was not labelled as required by the regulations.
1974	Part K of the *Food and Drug Regulations* was amended to require the provision of safety and effectiveness evidence when requested by Health Canada. The amendment also provided for the suspension of the sale of a device.
1975	Standalone *Medical Devices Regulations* came into force; Part K was repealed. The regulations required manufacturers to notify Health Canada of the first sale or proposed first sale of a medical device in Canada. The regulations reiterated the responsibility of manufacturers and importers to conduct safety and effectiveness testing prior to marketing a medical device in Canada.
1993	The *Patented Medicines (Notice of Compliance) Regulations* became part of the *Patent Act*. These regulations were intended to prevent generic drugs from infringing on drug patents. The regulations tie patent protection to the drug approval system of the *Food and Drugs Act*.
1995	The *Food and Drug Regulations* were amended to include data protection provisions (C.08.004.1) for innovative drugs (i.e., new chemical entities and biologics). Health Canada implemented user fee regulations for the review of drug and medical device submissions, and for annual "Right to Sell" fees for licensed drugs and medical devices.
1998	New *Medical Devices Regulations* (*MDR*) came into force and employed a risk-based regulatory approach. The *Notice of Compliance with Conditions Policy* was published for new drugs for serious, life-threatening or severely debilitating diseases or conditions with promising evidence of efficacy. The policy responded to rapid developments in HIV and some cancers and was similar, in scope, to the 1996 *Priority Review Policy*, which provided for an expedited review process. Health Canada started the Legislative Renewal exercise to address "shortcomings in Health Canada's legislative basis for health protection." Consultations on the legislative proposal were carried out in 2003. The new act was to replace the *Hazardous Products Act* (1969), the *Radiation Emitting Devices Act* (1970), the *Food and Drugs Act* (1953) and the *Quarantine Act* (1872). However, the 2003 SARS crisis made the *Quarantine Act* a priority. It was tabled separately as Bill C-12 and received Royal Assent in May 2005.
2001	New *Clinical Trial Regulations (Division 5)* came into effect. New requirements include: Research Ethics Board approval; adherence to Good Clinical Practices (GCPs); demonstration of the quality of drugs used in clinical trials; filing amendments and notifications; timelines for adverse drug reaction reporting; record retention; and requirements pertaining to discontinuation, suspension or cancellation of a trial.
2003	Health Canada launched the Therapeutic Access Strategy, aimed at process efficiency and elimination of backlogs, increasing the information available to Canadians about regulatory decisions and marketed drugs. International harmonization of standards and collaboration with other regulatory authorities received increased emphasis to address the globalization of the regulated industry.
2004	The *Natural Health Products Regulations* came into force under the drug authorities of the *Food and Drugs Act*. These regulations flowed from the March 2000 recommendations from the Standing Committee on Health. The *Assisted Human Reproduction Act* received Royal Assent in March 2004. The act responded to the 1993 recommendations of the Royal Commission on New Reproductive Technologies, entitled "*Proceed with Care*." The legislation created Assisted Human Reproduction Canada—a national agency to administer the act. The government of Quebec challenged the constitutionality of the act. In December 2010, the Supreme Court ruled that certain sections of the act exceeded the federal government's legislative power and significantly reduced the scope of the act. Significant portions of the act were repealed in 2012 via Division 56 of the *Budget Implementation Act*. The agency was wound down and the remaining responsibilities assigned to the minister of health.
2007	*Cells, Tissues and Organs for Transplant Regulations* came into force in December 2007, addressing safety in the processing and handling of these products. Subsection 26(1), which deals with in vitro diagnostic devices, was delayed until June 2008. The new regulations referenced standards developed by the Canadian Standards Association, an approach known as "incorporation by reference."

Year	
2008	Amendments to the *Natural Health Products Regulations*, the *Food and Drug Regulations* and the *Medical Devices Regulations* came into force to allow for labelling and advertising of preventive health claims to the general public for Schedule A diseases. Regulations to update the diseases listed on Schedule A to the *Food and Drugs Act* also came into force. Supporting guidances were published in 2010. Bill C-51, the *Canada Health Protection Act* was introduced in Parliament to replace the *Food and Drugs Act*. Bill C-51 did not become law before the 39th Parliament ended on 7 September 2008.
2011	The 1995 cost recovery framework was updated, and the new *Fees in Respect of Drugs and Medical Devices Regulations* came into force. The regulations, which are made under the *Financial Administration Act*, provide for annual fee increases and tie fees to meeting published performance targets.
2012	Health Canada published the *Regulatory Road Map for Health Products and Food*. Building on Legislative Renewal (1998), the Blueprint for Renewal and the Progressive Licensing Project (2004–06), the new roadmap focuses on updating old regulatory frameworks and increased international cooperation. The *Food and Drugs Act* was amended via Division 19 of the *Budget Implementation Act*, giving the minister of health the power to establish an administrative list that sets out prescription drugs or classes of prescription drugs and to enable "incorporation by reference" of such lists in the regulations. The amendments set the stage for replacing Schedule F, a list updated through an Order-in-Council, with the administrative Prescription Drug List under the authority of the minister of health. The new Prescription Drug List came into effect in December 2013, following *Food and Drug Regulations* amendments (SOR/2013-122) and the publication of process and guidances. The *Food and Drugs Act* was amended, so non-corrective contact lenses are regulated as a "device" pursuant to the *Medical Devices Regulations*. An amendment to the *Food and Drug Regulations* effective 13 May 2012 requires nonmedicinal ingredients to be declared on the label of nonprescription drug products. Proposed *Blood Regulations* were published in *Canada Gazette, Part I* for consultation. Final regulations were expected in 2013.
2013	In spring 2013, Division 2 of the *Food and Drug Regulations* was amended to extend GMP requirements to active pharmaceutical ingredients. The *Sale of New Drugs for Emergency Treatment Regulations*, unchanged since 1966, were amended to "remove doctors' ability to prescribe dangerous drugs" through the Special Access Programme. Under the new regulations, products containing heroin, unauthorized forms of cocaine or other Part J restricted drugs will not be eligible for authorization under the programme. The amendments came into immediate effect on 2 October 2013. Blood Regulations were published in *Canada Gazette, Part II* on 23 October 2013 and came into force over the course of one year after publication.
2014	On 6 November 2014, the *Protecting Canadians from Unsafe Drugs Act* (aka, *Vanessa's Law*) received Royal Assent. The act introduced amendments to the *Food and Drugs Act* and includes new rules strengthening the regulation of therapeutic products. The changes' intent is to improve Health Canada's ability to collect postmarket safety information and take appropriate action when a serious health risk is identified. Upon Royal Assent, key provisions of *Vanessa's Law* immediately came into force enabling the government to recall unsafe therapeutic products, impose tougher fines and penalties, require label updates to clearly reflect health risk information and seek an injunction. To fully implement *Vanessa's Law*, both additional changes to current regulations and new regulations are needed. These changes will allow Health Canada to require tests and studies, to order a reassessment, to attach terms and conditions to market authorizations and to require mandatory reporting of serious adverse drug reactions and medical device incidents by healthcare institutions. *Regulations Amending the Food and Drug Regulations (Labelling, Packaging and Brand Names of Drugs for Human Use)* (aka, *Plain Language Labelling Regulations*) were written into regulation on 13 June 2014. The regulations aim to improve the safe use of drugs by making drug labels and packaging easier to read and understand. The regulations impose new obligations on health products sponsors to: • provide information in plain language • assess the name of their health products to avoid confusion • submit label and package mock-ups for review • indicate how to report harms on product labels • provide information in an easy-to-read format While these obligations form a coherent set of regulatory obligations, not all these obligations apply to all health products.

2015	*Plain Language Labelling Regulations* came into effect for prescription products and those administered or obtained through a health professional as of 13 June 2015.
2016	The *Access to Cannabis for Medical Purposes Regulations* were registered on 5 August 2016. Health Canada published a consultation document on 7 September 2016, seeking input on modernizing the approach to regulating self-care products. The proposals outlined in the document represented building blocks for a modernized approach. A What We Heard summary report was posted on 30 March 2017. On 22 February 2018, Health Canada announced their plans for a phased approach over the course of 2018–20. Changes are expected to be made to the *Natural Health Product Regulations* (e.g., improved labelling) and *Food and Drug Regulations*. Information on the self-care framework as it develops can be found at: https://www.canada.ca/en/health-canada/services/self-care-framework.html.
2017	*Plain Language Labelling Regulations* came into effect for nonprescription drugs 13 June 2017. *Regulations Amending the Food and Drug Regulations (Shortages of Drugs and Discontinuation of Sale of Drugs)* were published in the *Canada Gazette*, Part II on 29 June 2016 and came into force on 14 March 2017. On 17 June 2017, *Regulations Amending the Food and Drug Regulations—Labelling and Risk Management Plans for Opioid Drugs* were published in *Canada Gazette I*. *Certificate of Supplementary Protection Regulations* (*CSP Regulations*) under the *Patent Act* is a new regulation registered 1 September 2017. A Certificate of Supplementary Protection (CSP) allows up to two additional years of 'patent-like' protection for an eligible authorization of a new medicinal ingredient (or combinations of medicinal ingredients) protected by an eligible patent. The *Patented Medicines (Notice of Compliance) Regulations* (*PM (NOC) Regulations*) were amended effective 21 September 2017. The proposed amendments seek to facilitate the just and expeditious resolution of patent infringement and validity disputes under the regulations. In October 2017, a fee proposal for drugs and medical devices was issued. With the new *Service Fees Act*, the minister of health can adjust fees under the *Food and Drugs Act* with greater flexibility and apply changes in a timely manner.
2018	Regulations supporting the proposed *Cannabis Act* are expected in July 2018 for the legalization of recreational cannabis use. The following regulatory initiatives (regulations amending the *Food and Drug Regulations* to support *Vanessa's Law*) are expected to be implemented 2017–19: • Regulations Amending the Food and Drug Regulations—Foreign Risk Communications; Tests and Studies; Reassessment • Regulations Amending the Food and Drug Regulations and Medical Devices Regulations—Recall of Therapeutic Products • Regulations Amending the Food and Drug Regulations and Medical Devices Regulations—Public Release of Clinical Information in Drug Submissions and Medical Device Applications • Regulations Amending the Food and Drug Regulations and Medical Device Regulations—Mandatory Reporting of Serious Adverse Drug Reactions and Medical Device Incidents by Health Care Institutions

The new legislation is intended to increase patient safety and will enable the government to require strong drug safety surveillance (including mandatory adverse drug reaction reporting by healthcare institutions) and unsafe therapeutic product recalls. In addition, it will impose tough penalties for unsafe products, impose even stronger fines if violations were caused intentionally, require drug companies to revise labels to reflect health risk information and compel drug companies to do further testing on a product, including when issues are identified with certain at-risk populations, e.g., children.

The *Access to Cannabis for Medical Purposes Regulations* (*ACMPR*) replaced the *Marihuana for Medical Purposes Regulations* (*MMPR*) effective 24 August 2016. *ACMPR* was implemented as a result of the Federal Court ruling in the case of *Allard v. Canada*. The *ACMPR* allows Canadians reasonable access to cannabis for medical purposes if authorized by their healthcare practitioners. Under the *ACMPR*, Canadians whose healthcare practitioners have authorized them to access cannabis for medical purposes will continue to have the option of purchasing safe and quality-controlled cannabis from Health Canada-licenced producers. Canadians are able to produce a limited amount of cannabis for their own medical purposes or designate someone to produce it for them. Regulations supporting the legalization of recreational cannabis use are expected to be implemented in July 2018.

A modernized self-care framework is under development, with the goal of streamlining and updating the current legislation and regulations for self-care products, which include cosmetics, natural health products, and nonprescription drugs. The proposed approach is to tailor the oversight level for these products to a level commensurate with their risk to the consumer, require similar evidence for similar claims and provide Health Canada the appropriate powers to address safety concerns and noncompliance.

Health Canada also has undertaken a regulatory review of drugs and devices. Some examples of initiatives include the use of foreign reviews and decisions to gain submission review efficiency, Special Access Programme renewal, strengthening use of real-world evidence for drugs and medical devices, developing an appropriate cost recovery framework and public release of sponsor clinical information.

Health Canada's ongoing modernization efforts continue. The strategic priorities outlined in HBFB Strategic Plan 2016-2021 include openness and transparency, collaboration (international and domestic) and innovation. Some HBFB objectives for 2016–21 are to be a credible source of scientific health information, lead health dialogues on the latest research and trends, maximize safety and minimise regulatory burden, use a flexible, risk-based regulatory framework and harmonize efforts with other domestic and international regulators.

Summary
- Health Canada is the federal organization responsible for helping Canadians maintain and improve their health.
- Health Canada is organized into branches and agencies, each of which is responsible for a different aspect of health governance.
- Health product regulation has evolved, and continues to evolve, as highlighted in this chapter.

References
1. Formerly the Health Products and Food Branch Inspectorate (HPFBI); the Inspectorate. RORB was created 4 April 2016.

Recommended Reading
- *Blueprint for renewal: Transforming Canada's Approach to Regulating Health products and Food* (2006). Health Canada website. http://publications.gc.ca/collections/collection_2014/sc-hc/H164-173-2006-eng.pdf. Accessed 7 April 2018.
- *Blueprint for renewal II: Modernizing Canada's Regulatory System for Health Products and Food* (2007). Health Canada website. http://publications.gc.ca/site/eng/308178/publication.html. Accessed 7 April 2018.
- Canada Gazette website: http://www.gazette.gc.ca/accueil-home-eng.html. Accessed 7 April 2018.
- *Canada's Health Care System (Medicare),* Health Canada website. https://www.canada.ca/en/health-canada/services/canada-health-care-system.html. Accessed 7 April 2018.
- Chapman RA. The Evolving Role of the Canadian Government in Assessing Drug Safety, Canad. Med. Ass. J. 1968:98:294.
- Consolidated Regulations. Justice Laws website. http://laws.justice.gc.ca/eng/regulations/. Accessed 7 April 2018.
- Linton DA. The Genesis and Growth of Food and Drug Administration in Canada, 1950. Department of Health and Welfare.
- External Advisory Committee on Smart Regulation, Smart Regulation: A Regulatory Strategy for Canada, September 2004. Health Canada website. http://publications.gc.ca/collections/Collection/CP22-78-2004E.pdf Accessed 7 April 2018.
- Forward Regulatory Plan: 2017-2019. Health Canada website. https://www.canada.ca/en/health-canada/corporate/about-health-canada/legislation-guidelines/acts-regulations/forward-regulatory-plan/2016-2018.html. Accessed 7 April 2018.
- Health Canada website on Assisted Human Reproduction. http://www.hc-sc.gc.ca/dhp-mps/brgtherap/legislation/reprod/index-eng.php. Accessed 7 April 2018.
- Health Canada and Health Products and Food Branch Organization. Health Canada website. https://www.canada.ca/en/health-canada/corporate/about-health-canada/branches-agencies.html. Accessed 7 April 2018.
- *Health Protection Legislative Renewal,* Health Canada 2003. Library and Archives Canada website. http://publications.gc.ca/site/eng/245150/publication.html. Accessed 7 April 2018.
- HPFB Strategic Plan 2016-2021. Health Canada website. https://www.canada.ca/content/dam/hc-sc/migration/hc-sc/ahc-asc/alt_formats/pdf/pubs/hpfb-dgpsa/2016-2021-strat-plan-eng.pdf. Accessed 7 April 2018.
- Improving the regulatory review of drugs and devices. Health Canada website. https://www.canada.ca/en/health-canada/corporate/transparency/regulatory-transparency-and-openness/improving-review-drugs-devices.html.
- Accessed 7 April 2018.
- Jackman M. *Constitutional Jurisdiction Over Health in Canada,* Health Law Journal. 2000;8;95–117.
- Leeson H. "*Constitutional Jurisdiction Over Health and Health Care Services in Canada,*" Discussion Paper 12, Commission on the Future of Health Care in Canada, August 2002.
- All Bills for the Current Session. LEGISinfo website. http://www.parl.ca/LEGISinfo/Home.aspx?Language=E&Parliament Session=42-1. Accessed 7 April 2018.
- *Proceed with Care, Final Report of the Royal Commission on New Reproductive Technologies* (1993). Government of Canada Publications website. http://publications.gc.ca/site/eng/38077/publication.html. Accessed 7 April 2018.
- *Regulatory Roadmap for Health Products and Food* (2012). Government of Canada website. http://www.hc-sc.gc.ca/ahc-asc/activit/strateg/mod/roadmap-feuillederoute/index-eng.php. Accessed 7 April 2018.
- Stieb EW. "*Drug Adulteration: Detection and Control in Canada II. A step Forward: The Adulteration Act of 1884"* Pharmacy in History Vol. 18, No 1(1976), pp 17–24. JStor website. http://www.jstor.org/stable/41108947. Accessed 7 April 2018.
- Teevens LP. *The Proprietary or Patent Medicines Act and Improper Medicines. CMAJ* 1929 January; 20(1): 69–70.
- Wright J. *Progressive Licensing: An opportunity to achieve transparency and accountability? CMAJ. 2007;* 173(13); 1849.

Chapter 2

Good Laboratory Practice for Nonclinical Laboratory Studies

Updated by Navneet Sekhon

OBJECTIVES

❑ Review Health Canada's expectations for nonclinical data submitted in applications or submissions for market authorization.

❑ Assist sponsors in demonstrating compliance with Good Clinical Practice (GLP) principles.

❑ Understand the Standards Council of Canada's (SCC) role in the recognition of GLP compliance.

GUIDANCE DOCUMENTS COVERED IN THIS CHAPTER

❑ *Guidance Document—Submission and Information Requirements for Extraordinary Use New Drugs (EUNDs)* (16 May 2014)

❑ *Guidance Document: Non-Clinical Laboratory Study Data Supporting Drug Product Applications and Submissions: Adherence to Good Laboratory Practice* (30 April 2010)

❑ *Questions and Answers—Guidance Document Non-Clinical Laboratory Study Data Supporting Drug Product Applications and Submissions: Adherence to Good Laboratory Practice* (30 April 2010)

❑ *OECD Principles of Good Laboratory Practice* (as revised in 1997)

Introduction

Canada is a founding member of the Organisation for Economic Co-operation (OECD), established in 1961. By signing the OECD Convention, Canada committed to assist governments in achieving economic growth and development. OECD is an intergovernmental organisation comprised of representatives from industrialised market economy countries and developing countries in North America, Europe, the Pacific and the European Commission. OECD follows a two-pronged approach: harmonization of national economic and social policies, and information sharing and common problem solving among member countries.

Since its establishment, member countries have tackled various issues of mutual interest and concern in other areas: economy, society, development, finance, governance, innovation and sustainability. Among the sustainability indicators, environmental health policies and safety activities, chemical safety guidelines were introduced to prevent future occurrences of pharmaceutical research malpractice, as reported by the US Food and Drug Administration (FDA) in the 1970s. Following these US findings, FDA and the US Environmental Protection Agency (EPA) instituted Good Laboratory Practice (GLP) regulations, and many regulatory authorities worldwide followed suit.

In the 1980s, the OECD Council published its GLP principles and called for the global standardization of safety testing, test facility management and GLP compliance verification procedures to promote the compatibility, quality and mutual acceptance of data (MAD). OECD member states have signed agreements that make the GLP principles binding, thereby formalizing GLP as an international standard.

Implementing Canadian GLP standards for nonclinical data development supporting pharmaceuticals, biologics

Chapter 2

and radiopharmaceuticals, and establishing GLP compliance monitoring procedures, are an integral part of Canada's OECD member country obligations.

Health Canada is the federal department responsible for helping Canadians maintain and improve their health. In collaboration with provincial and territorial governments, Health Canada provides national leadership to develop health policy, enforce health regulations, promote disease prevention and enhance healthy living for all Canadian citizens. Health Canada's Health Products and Food Branch (HPFB) administers the *Food and Drugs Act* (*F&DA*), which governs the sale, importation and advertisement of drugs, cosmetics, food additives and feed additives and veterinary drugs in Canada.

HPFB and the Standards Council of Canada (SCC) have entered into a Memorandum of Understanding (MOU) that designates SCC as the monitoring authority for GLP compliance of Canadian test facilities. SCC is a federal Crown corporation that promotes efficient and effective standardization in Canada by accrediting laboratories and recognizing GLP compliance, which sponsors can use in turn to support a Canadian drug application for market authorization. SCC takes its mandate from the *Standards Council of Canada Act* (*SCCA*), its governing legislation. Under the MOU, SCC conducts conformity assessments and grants GLP recognition in accordance with the *OECD Revised Guidelines for Compliance Monitoring Procedures for Good Laboratory Practice, Environment Monograph No. 110* (Paris 1995) or subsequent versions. Given SCC is an OECD-recognized body, the GLP recognition for Canadian test facilities also can be used internationally.

This chapter focuses on the underlying principles of GLP and Health Canada's national GLP framework for nonclinical laboratory studies, as outlined in *Guidance Document Non-Clinical Laboratory Study Data Supporting Drug Product Applications and Submissions: Adherence to Good Laboratory Practice*. The application of these requirements to new drug submissions types will be identified.

GLP

A drug's lifecycle is characterized by a benefit-risk profile assessment based on nonclinical studies, clinical trials, chemistry and manufacturing data, literature reviews and postmarket experiences. To meet the *Food and Drug Regulations'* (*F&DR*) standards of evidence for safety, efficacy and quality, a manufacturer must be able to demonstrate the scientific and clinical data were obtained following quality assurance systems overseeing test data integrity. Compliance with GLP, Good Clinical Practice (GCP) and Good Manufacturing Practice (GMP) enhances data reliability; provides safeguards for subjects' rights, safety and well-being; and offers assurance the drug was consistently produced and handled. It should be emphasized that, unlike GMP and GCP, for which the Health Products and Food Branch Inspectorate (HPFBI) performs the compliance functions, it is SCC's role to carry out the national GLP compliance monitoring program by conducting conformity assessments and granting GLP recognition.

GLP's purpose is to standardize practices; enhance data quality, integrity and reproducibility; and provide assurance to other regulatory authorities in both OECD member and non-member adherent countries that study data can confidently be relied on without further verification. GLP governs the conduct of nonclinical studies and defines the organizational process and conditions under which nonclinical studies are planned, performed, monitored, recorded, archived and reported. The fundamental GLP principles pertain to test facility organization and personnel, facility design and equipment, protocols and written procedures, characterization of test items and test systems, documentation and the quality assurance program. Additional information and clarification regarding these principles may be obtained by referring to OECD's GLP documents on its website.

Nonclinical data include all *in vitro* and *in vivo* testing, not involving human subjects, performed to determine the safety of human drugs. Data gathered from nonclinical studies support Clinical Trial Applications (CTAs), which are submitted by sponsors prior to initiating clinical testing in human subjects. Data gathered from nonclinical studies and clinical trials support a drug application or submission for market authorization.

Status of GLP Implementation in Canada

Similar to an international treaty, the 1989 *OECD Decision Concerning the GLP Principles and Compliance Monitoring* is legally binding on all member countries. It requires procedures for monitoring GLP compliance with GLP principles be established based on laboratory inspections and study audits; an authority or authorities be designated to discharge the functions required by the monitoring compliance procedures; and that test facility management issue a declaration, where applicable, that a study was carried out in accordance with GLP principles, pursuant to any other provisions established by national GLP legislation or administrative procedures.

All OECD members are mandated to implement OECD's GLP principles for nonclinical testing of items contained in industrial chemicals, pharmaceutical products, veterinary drugs, pesticide products, food additives, feed additives and cosmetic products, as required for the purposes of assessment related to protecting health and the environment. "These test items are frequently synthetic chemicals, but may be of natural or biological origin and, in some circumstances, may be living organisms."[1]

In Canada, GLP principles originally were introduced in the pesticide, agrochemical and industrial chemical sectors. Health Canada's Pest Management Regulatory

Agency (PMRA) issued mandatory GLP requirements in 1998, with the publication of regulatory directive Dir98-01 for studies supporting the premarket authorization of pesticides and agrochemicals. In 2005, Environment Canada targeted the industrial chemicals industry, with the adoption of the *New Substances Notification Regulations (Chemicals and Polymers)*, which include GLP requirements under Section 89 of the *Canadian Environmental Protection Act, 1999 (CEPA 1999)*.

At the time of writing, Health Canada continues to explore the applicability of GLP requirements to veterinary drugs, natural health products, medical devices, food additives and cosmetics, and fully intends to pursue implementation, as capacities and priorities permit. For cosmetics, there are no regulatory requirements to supply premarket data for HPFB preapproval. Natural Health Products also are exempt. With FDA issuing *The Applicability of Good Laboratory Practice in Premarket Device Submissions: Questions and Answers - Draft Guidance for Industry and Food and Drug Administration Staff* (August 2013), Health Canada may be expected to follow suit and expand the SCC mandate to the medical device field.

Through the release of the finalized Health Canada *Guidance Document Non-Clinical Laboratory Study Data Supporting Drug Product Applications and Submissions: Adherence to Good Laboratory Practice* (April 2010), the pharmaceutical industry became the third major Canadian sector to have formal GLP data requirements consistent with OECD's GLP principles and subject to verification by SCC, an OECD-approved compliance monitoring authority.

In the pre-GLP implementation era, adherence to the GLP framework was achieved informally through the wide international acceptance of the OECD standard by both industry and regulatory authorities, as well as the adoption of various international guidance documents referencing the application of GLP. These include the technical guidelines regarding nonclinical data for human pharmaceuticals issued by the International Council on Harmonisation (ICH).

Therefore, Health Canada received a large number of nonclinical studies conducted in accordance with GLP requirements and observed that the majority of test facilities were using quality processes and systems to ensure data reliability. However, in the absence of a designated Canadian monitoring authority, Canadian test facilities' GLP compliance status could be verified only by foreign monitoring authorities.

Canadian GLP Framework Applicability

The OECD principles of GLP (ENV/MC/CHEM(98)17 and subsequent revisions) are recognized as the GLP standard by HPFB and form the basis of Canada's GLP framework. The nonclinical study guidance is an interpretation of OECD's GLP principles, with the addition of a records retention period, which regulatory authorities are required to define.

On 30 April 2010, the GLP requirements became formalized and applicable to all nonclinical studies (domestic and foreign) submitted to Health Canada in support of pharmaceutical, radiopharmaceutical or biologic drugs. A one-year transition period, ending 30 April 2011, was granted to Canadian test facilities to provide flexibility for sponsors and SCC to complete the GLP recognition process.

The GLP guidance document states the general expectations for nonclinical data relating to pharmaceutical (including disinfectants), radiopharmaceutical or biologic drugs for human use included in the following submission types:
- CTA
- CTA Amendment (CTA-A)
- Drug Identification Number (DIN) application
- DIN application to support a post-DIN change
- Extraordinary Use New Drug Submission (EUNDS)
- Abbreviated Extraordinary Use New Drug Submission (AEUNDS)
- New Drug Submission (NDS)
- Abbreviated New Drug Submission (ANDS)
- Submissions to support a Post-Notice of Compliance (Post-NOC) change
  - Supplement to an NDS (SNDS)
  - Supplement to an ANDS (SANDS)
  - Notifiable Change (NC)

More specifically, nonclinical studies considered pivotal to supporting a drug's safety profile are expected to be obtained from well-designed studies conducted under the GLP framework. Any study not conducted in accordance with GLP should be appropriately justified. Study data generated in a facility that is not shown to have employed GLP principles will be considered neither sufficiently credible nor reliable for regulatory decision making and will be considered only as supplementary information rather than primary evidence.

Examples of studies requiring GLP compliance are provided in the guidance document that assists investigators and their staffs in assessing GLP applicability (**Table 2-1**). This list is not exhaustive.

Filing Requirements
For Studies
- All nonclinical studies (domestic or foreign), as defined in the guidance document and initiated since 30 April 2010 are expected to comply with the GLP guidance document requirements that complement OECD's GLP principles.
- As of 16 May 2014, EUNDS/AEUNDS application also are expected to comply with GLP principles.

Chapter 2

Table 2-1. Examples of Studies and the Requirement for GLP Compliance

Examples of Studies	Requirement for GLP Compliance
Bioanalysis in support of human bioequivalence	No. Should be conducted under GCP.
Safety pharmacology and pharmacodynamic studies	Yes/No*
Primary pharmacodynamic studies during the discovery phase of pharmaceutical development	No
Pivotal or core battery toxicity studies, including repeated-dose, pharmaco- or toxicokinetics, reproductive, developmental, local tolerance, photosafety, immunotoxicity, etc., as applicable	Yes
Carcinogenicity studies	Yes
Genotoxicity studies	Yes
Physical-chemical testing including dissolution studies, stability studies and studies on impurities and degradation products	Yes, if conducted solely under a nonclinical study. Other standards may apply (i.e., GCP, GMP) if testing is done to support the marketing authorization of a drug.
Data that cannot be obtained in clinical studies for ethical reasons	Yes

Studies that are considered to be core battery or pivotal as per the ICH guidelines, Health Canada guidelines, or other international guidelines should be conducted under GLP conditions. Certain nonclinical studies may not need to adhere to GLP depending on the importance of the studies and whether any claims are made based on such studies.
Source: Health Canada, Guidance Document Non-Clinical Laboratory Study Data Supporting Drug Product Applications and Submissions: Adherence to Good Laboratory Practice, 30 April 2010

- Health Canada expects a GLP compliance statement consistent with the OECD GLP principles to be provided in the aforementioned drug submission packages. Each study report, when applicable, should include a declaration issued by test facilities' management that the study was carried out in accordance with OECD's GLP principles.
- OECD's Mutual Acceptance of Data (MAD) directive states data generated in a facility recognized by the national GLP compliance monitoring authority must be accepted for purposes of assessment by both OECD member countries and non-member countries adherent to the MAD Decision (1981). All signatories to the OECD Council Act Decisions on MAD are to mutually accept nonclinical GLP studies.

For Facilities
- Additionally, Health Canada requires GLP recognition for both domestic and foreign sites. Evidence, in the form of a letter or certificate declaring the facility was assessed and found to be compliant with GLP by an OECD-approved GLP monitoring authority, should be provided to the regulator. Alternatives may be considered acceptable when the standard used to assess the facility's compliance is deemed to be equivalent and, therefore, comparable to OECD's, e.g., FDA's.
- Documentation should include details of the GLP area of expertise for which the facility is GLP-compliant and inspection dates. In instances where documentation cannot be provided, Health Canada evaluators may ask SCC to provide the facility's compliance history. Study-specific evidence may be requested upon evaluation.
- Any evidence declaring the facility was assessed and found to be GLP-compliant should be included in the current Good Manufacturing Practices/Establishment License (GMP/EL) information section—Common Technical Document (CTD) Module 1.2.5 Compliance and Site Information.
- Health Canada does not require retrospective GLP recognition for facilities conducting nonclinical studies. Nonetheless, although the facility conducting the studies may not have been inspected for GLP compliance, it is expected the studies be conducted under GLP principles (same quality processes). Proof of study quality will need to be provided and assessed on a case-by-case basis.

Records Retention
OECD's GLP principles defer to the regulatory authorities to specify an archiving period for records and materials' storage and retention. However, OECD recommends the manner in which all documentation, electronic records, samples of tests, reference items and specimens should be kept. Health Canada provides further guidance by recommending sponsors store all documentation, the study plan, raw data and the final report of each study supporting an approved drug product for a minimum of 10 years (from the market notification date) and for a longer period when

required by the *F&DR*. Archive conditions should protect the contents from untimely deterioration.

International records retention requirements vary from two to 15 years. It is felt the clinical experience gathered with a product that has been on the market for a period of approximately 10 years is sufficient to cover uncertainties regarding the nonclinical safety database. This record retention period is appropriate to support facility inspections and study audits as well.

Computerized Systems and Validation

With the increasing use of computer systems in GLP environments, OECD issued a revision to the advisory document, *Application of GLP Principles to Computerised Systems. No. 17* (Paris, 2016).

The guideline requires test facility management to ensure raw data capture, processing, reporting and storage during the planning, conduct and postmarket stages of nonclinical studies are conducted in accordance with recognized standards for validation. A risk management plan is devised to support the qualification or validation level necessary for any given computer system, from simple laboratory instrument to a major Laboratory Information Management System (LIMS). These requirements are applicable to controlling computer systems used in test facilities, laboratories, equipment, communications and data management.

SCC Recognition Process Application

SCC recognition of GLP compliance is based on inspections and study audits conducted in accordance with the *Revised Guidance for the Conduct of Test Facility Inspections and Study Audits* and the *SCC Monitoring Authority Requirements for the Recognition of GLP Compliant Test Facilities* (CAN-P-1583). Compliance with the conditions found in the OECD *Principles of Good Laboratory Practice* (No. 1) is the prerequisite for obtaining GLP recognition. SCC inspects test facilities and issues proof of compliance in the form of a certificate specifying the GLP expertise areas for which the facility is recognized. This certificate of compliance is recognized by HPFB as evidence the test data have been generated in accordance with GLP principles and are acceptable to support a drug's eventual marketing authorization in Canada.

To obtain GLP recognition, a facility applies to the SCC GLP Monitoring Authority by submitting the following:
   a. a completed application form
   b. facility information as described in the application form
   c. appropriate non-refundable application fee according to the current published SCC fee structure (Inspection costs are borne by the recipient facility.)

Inspection

A team of inspectors is assembled and may be vetoed by the facility management with a written rationale. The team makeup reflects the facility's areas of study expertise and the complexity of its study expertise. A mutually acceptable date is arranged for an inspection. A facility is always given appropriate advance notice of any impending inspection or specific study audit. The lead inspector and site personnel set the inspection schedule.

GLP compliance recognition is based on the acceptability of submitted documentation and evaluation of the facility inspection and associated study audits.

The inspection team will audit a representative number of studies to ensure proper evaluation of the organisation's competence. Study selection is based on the number of studies the organization performs, the number and type of test systems and/or test items and the fields of the studies. At least one study is selected from each field of expertise in which studies were done. SCC usually selects studies that are completed, ongoing and started, to determine whether the facility complies with the GLP principles at each stage of a study and at every step of the processes.

SCC inspectors verify all documentation, i.e., standard operating procedures and instructions related to data transfer, data handling, changes to data, data storage, archiving and validation records.

Inspection findings are discussed with facility management during a closing conference in accordance with the *Revised Guidance for the Conduct of Test Facility Inspections and Study Audits*. During this meeting, a written List of Findings signed and dated by the inspector(s) and facility management is presented to facility staff as evidence of any GLP noncompliance. The report is based on individual observations and interviews and lists the noncompliant findings, each referenced to the applicable item from OECD's GLP principles. The List of Findings report contains all required actions, minor actions and suggestions identified by the inspection team. A facility may appeal findings within 10 days following the inspection.

Upon completion of all required actions (if applicable), the inspectors review the facility's response and determine whether a reinspection is needed to verify actions have been implemented. The inspectors review and approve the facility responses and put forward a recommendation to SCC. The facility may appeal the decision.

The timeline between the inspection and receipt of the GLP recognition varies. A decision usually is rendered within two weeks of the final report's issuance. However, the timeline is dependent on both the facility and SCC. The faster the facility responds to the findings, the faster the process can be completed.

Chapter 2

Peer Review

In its capacity as the GLP monitoring authority, SCC is evaluated periodically by an OECD mutual joint visit (MJV) peer review team. The MJV includes a site visit to the GLP monitoring authority by a team of observers from GLP monitoring authorities in other OECD member countries, with the objective of providing assurance about the manner in which inspections and study audits are conducted and for the mutual acceptance of test data. Monitoring authorities have key requirements, including maintaining a team of trained inspectors, publishing program documents and maintaining records of inspected facilities. They also report annually to one another, the OECD and the European Commission on all activities. Any change in the compliance status of a facility is reported immediately to other member countries and regulatory authorities.

Part of the MOU between SCC and HPFB is to maintain open communication. The details of specific SCC inspections are readily available to Health Canada. It is anticipated the program will be reviewed at five-year intervals by Health Canada and the results shared with SCC.

Summary

- Canadian GLP requirements are found in *Guidance Document Non-Clinical Laboratory Study Data Supporting Drug Product Applications and Submissions: Adherence to Good Laboratory Practice*.
- OECD's *Principles of Good Laboratory Practice* (ENV/MC/CHEM(98)17 and subsequent revisions) are recognized as the GLP standard by Health Canada's Health Products and Food Branch.
- GLP compliance and monitoring in Canada are undertaken by the Standards Council of Canada.
- GLP requirements became formalized on 30 April 2010 and applicable to all nonclinical studies (domestic and foreign) submitted to Health Canada effective 30 April 2011.
- All signatories to the OECD Council Act Decisions on MAD are to mutually accept nonclinical GLP studies.
- Through the OECD, member countries are required to establish monitoring authorities that inspect and monitor the test facilities within their countries. Generally, OECD member countries recognize the inspections conducted by one another's monitoring authorities.

Useful Links

In addition to the Health Canada and SCC websites, periodically checking publications on OECD, WHO and ICH websites is highly recommended.

Besides the OECD *Principles of GLP*, the OECD website provides GLP documents that address responsibilities of quality assurance, study directors, test facility management and suppliers, and expectations regarding multisite studies, computerized systems and archives.
- http://www.oecd.org/chemicalsafety/testing/good-laboratory-practiceglp.htm

The World Health Organization (WHO) published a *GLP Handbook and Training Manual* that can be found at:
- http://www.who.int/tdr/publications/training-guideline-publications/good-laboratory-practice-handbook-ver1/en/

Since 1990, the International Council on Harmonisation (ICH) has brought together the regulatory authorities and pharmaceutical industries of the EU, Japan and the US to discuss scientific and technical aspects of drug registration. The ICH website provides quality, safety, efficacy and multidisciplinary guidelines.
- http://www.ich.org/products/guidelines.html

The revised ICH guidance, *Non-clinical Safety Studies for the Conduct of Human Clinical Trials and Marketing Authorization for Pharmaceuticals M3 (R2)* (11 June 2009), provides consensus regarding the type and duration of nonclinical safety studies and their timing to support the conduct of human clinical trials and marketing authorization for pharmaceuticals, while ICH's *Questions & Answers: Guidance on Non-clinical Safety Studies for the Conduct of Human Clinical Trials and Marketing Authorization for Pharmaceuticals M3 (R2)* (5 March 2012) provides further clarification regarding limit dose for toxicity studies and addresses four additional sections: safety pharmacology, exploratory clinical trials, reproductive toxicity and juvenile animal studies.

ICH's *Preclinical Safety Evaluation of Biotechnology-Derived Pharmaceuticals S6(R1)* (12 June 2011) covers the preclinical safety testing requirements for biotechnological products. It addresses the species selection, study design, immunogenicity, reproductive and developmental toxicity, assessment of carcinogenic potential, etc.

References
1. OECD, *OECD Series on Principles of Good Laboratory Practice and Compliance Monitoring*, Number 1, Paris 1998.

Recommended Reading
- Standards Council of Canada, *Fee Schedule for the Good Laboratory Practice Program Specialty Area (Laboratories)*, June 2002.
- Standards Council of Canada, *Guidelines for the Recognition of GLP Compliant Test Facilities*, CAN-P-1583, April 1998.
- Standards Council of Canada, *SCC Monitoring Authority Requirements for the Recognition of GLP Compliant Facilities*, CAN-P-1583 February 2008.

- OECD, *OECD Series on Principles of Good Laboratory Practice and Compliance Monitoring*, Number 1 to Number 18, Paris 1998.
- Health Canada, *Guidance Document Non-Clinical Laboratory Study Data Supporting Drug Product Applications and Submissions: Adherence to Good Laboratory Practice*, 30 April 2010.
- Health Canada, *Questions and Answers—Guidance Document Non-Clinical Laboratory Study Data Supporting Drug Product Applications and Submissions: Adherence to Good Laboratory Practice,* 30 April 2010.
- ICH *Harmonized Tripartite Guidance on Non-clinical Safety Studies for the Conduct of Human Clinical Trials and Marketing Authorization for Pharmaceuticals M3 (R2),* (11 June 2009).
- ICH *Harmonized Tripartite Questions & Answers: Guidance on Non-clinical Safety Studies for the Conduct of Human Clinical Trials and Marketing Authorization for Pharmaceuticals M3 (R2),* (5 March 2012).
- ICH *Harmonized Tripartite Guideline Preclinical Safety Evaluation of Biotechnology-Derived Pharmaceuticals S6(R1),* (12 June 2011).
- ICH *Note for Guidance on Toxicokinetics: The Assessment of Systemic Exposure in Toxicity Studies S3A* (October 1994).
- ICH *Detection of Toxicity to Reproduction for Medicinal Products S5A* (July 1997).
- ICH *Safety Pharmacology Studies for Human Pharmaceuticals S7A* (November 2000).
- ICH *The Nonclinical Evaluation of the Potential for Delayed Ventricular Repolarization (QT Interval Prolongation) by Human Pharmaceuticals QT/QTc Interval Prolongation S7B* (May 2005).

Chapter 3

Clinical Trial Applications, Good Clinical Practices

By Mahdis Dorkalam, MSc, RHN, and Navneet Sekhon

OBJECTIVES

- Provide an overview of clinical trials in Canada for drugs, biologics and natural health products (NHPs).

- Understand the clinical trial application (CTA) regulatory framework in Canada and when a CTA is required.

- Classify and understand postapproval requirements for the conduct of clinical trials in Canada.

- Become familiar with Good Clinical Practices (GCPs).

REGULATIONS AND GUIDELINES COVERED IN THIS CHAPTER

Drugs, Biologics and Natural Health Products

- *Food and Drug Regulations*, Part C, Division 5

- *Natural Health Products Regulations*, Part 4

- Health Canada, *Guidance for Industry: General Considerations for Clinical Trials ICH Topic E8* (1997)

- Health Canada, *Guidance Document for Clinical Trial Sponsors: Clinical Trial Applications* (29 May 2013)

- Health Canada, *Clinical Trials for Natural Health Products* (October 2005)

- Health Canada, *Notice to: Stakeholders of Clinical Trials for Natural Health Products* (1 August 2012)

- Health Canada, *Notice to: Stakeholders of Clinical Trials for Biologic-Type Natural Health Products* (5 October 2012)

- Health Canada, *Guidance for Industry: Good Clinical Practice: Consolidated Guideline ICH Topic E6* (1997)

- Health Canada, *Guidance Document, Good Clinical Practice: Integrated Addendum to E6(R1) ICH Topic E6(R2)* (25 May 2017)

- Health Canada, *Guidance Document—Quality (Chemistry and Manufacturing) Guidance: Clinical Trial Applications (CTAs) for Pharmaceuticals* (1 June 2009)

- Health Canada, *Guidance Document: Annex 13 to the Current Edition of the Good Manufacturing Practices Guidelines Drugs Used in Clinical Trials, GUI-0036* (7 August 2009)

- Health Canada, *Guidance Document: Conduct and Analysis of Comparative Bioavailability Studies and Comparative Bioavailability Standards: Formulations used for Systemic Effects* (22 May 2012)

- Health Canada Notice: *Preparation of Clinical Trial Regulatory Activities in the "Non-eCTD Electronic-Only" Format* (2 March 2016)

Clinical Trial Applications—Drugs, Biologics and Natural Health Products

Introduction

A clinical trial, as defined in the *Food and Drug Regulations (FDR)* Section C.05.001 and the *Natural Health Product Regulations (NHPR)* Part 4, is "an investigation in respect of a drug (natural health product) for use in humans that involves human subjects and that is intended to discover or verify the clinical, pharmacological or pharmacodynamic effects of the drug, identify any adverse events in respect of the drug (natural health product), study the absorption, distribution, metabolism and excretion of the drug, or ascertain the safety or efficacy of the drug (natural health product)." For information on the conduct of clinical trials, consult Health Canada's *Guidance for Industry: General Considerations for Clinical Trials ICH Topic E8* (1997).

Clinical trials typically are categorized in four phases (Phase I, II, III and IV). Each phase number represents a successive phase in drug development as follows:

- Phase I—Clinical trials designed to determine the drug's pharmacokinetic/pharmacological actions and any side effects associated with increasing doses. Drug interaction studies usually are considered Phase I trials, regardless of when they are conducted during drug development. Phase I trials generally are conducted in healthy volunteers but may be conducted in patients where administration of the drug to healthy volunteers is not ethical.
- Phase II—Clinical trials to evaluate the drug's efficacy in patients with medical conditions to be treated, diagnosed or prevented and to determine the side effects and risks associated with it. If a new indication for a marketed drug is to be investigated, those clinical trials generally may be considered Phase II trials.
- Phase III—Controlled or uncontrolled trials conducted after preliminary evidence suggesting drug efficacy has been demonstrated. These are intended to gather additional information about clinical efficacy and safety under the proposed conditions of use.
- Phase IV—All studies performed within the approved indication after the regulator has approved the drug for the market, as per the Notice of Compliance (NOC) or DIN (Drug Identification Number). These studies often are important for optimizing the drug's use to provide real-world and observational data. Common Phase IV studies include long-term safety studies or studies designed to support use under the approved indication, e.g., mortality and morbidity studies or epidemiological studies.

Sponsors must conduct clinical trials according to generally accepted Good Clinical Practice (GCP) principles that ensure the protection of clinical trial subjects and other persons' rights, safety and well-being. Also, Research Ethics Boards (REBs) play an important role in the oversight of clinical trial conduct. The regulations require sponsors to obtain REB approval for each trial site prior to commencing the trial [C.05.006(1) (c)]. These regulations are generally consistent with International Council on Harmonisation (ICH) guidance documents.

All clinical trial sponsors (industry, academic institutions, contract research organizations, etc.) must submit a clinical trial application (CTA) to Health Canada to receive authorization to sell or import a drug for the purpose of a clinical trial in the following scenarios:

- clinical trials of a product not authorized for sale in Canada, including clinical trials for drug development Phases I–III and comparative bioavailability studies
- clinical trials for marketed drugs where the drug's proposed use is outside the parameters of the NOC or DIN application for drugs and biologics or its Product Licence for NHPs
- Clinical Trial Application Amendments (CTA-A) [C.05.008] and Notifications (CTA-N) [C.05.007]

A CTA is not required for Phase IV studies.

Regulatory Framework Governing Clinical Trials in Canada

The drug clinical trial regulatory requirements originally were developed in the early 1960s. On 1 September 2001, the regulatory amendments to Part C, Division 5 of the *FDR* (Drugs for Clinical Trials Involving Human Subjects) came into force to strengthen clinical trial subjects' protections in Canada. In 2004, the *NHPR* came into force, and Part 4 addresses the regulatory requirements for conducting NHP clinical trials. This section's requirements are similar to those for a clinical trial for a conventional pharmaceutical but take unique NHP clinical trial aspects into consideration.

Pre-CTA Consultation Meetings

Clinical trial sponsors are welcome to request a pre-CTA consultation meeting to solicit agency feedback on their proposed trials but are not required to do so. Such consultations may be particularly useful for new active substances or applications that include complex issues that may be new to Health Canada.

The pre-CTA consultation meeting provides the sponsor an opportunity to present relevant data and discuss concerns and issues regarding drug development. This meeting also gives Health Canada an opportunity to provide guidance on a proposed trial's acceptability.

A pre-CTA consultation request should be submitted in writing to the appropriate directorate at Health Canada at least 30 days prior to the meeting date. Requests should include a cover letter proposing four meeting dates and times (three for NHPs). The request also should include:
- a brief synopsis of the proposed study
- a list of preliminary questions for the directorate to address during the meeting
- sufficient information for Health Canada to assess the meeting's utility and identify the appropriate staff necessary to discuss the proposed issues

The directorate will acknowledge the consultation request in a timely manner. If the directorate agrees to the request, an acknowledgement letter will be sent to confirm the meeting date and indicate the number of copies of the pre-CTA information package to be provided 30 days before the confirmed meeting (two weeks for NHPs).

The pre-CTA consultation package should contain:
- proposed agenda, any prepared slides, a finalized list of questions and a complete list of attendees
- brief data summary including:
  o tabular listing of completed nonclinical and clinical studies
  o outline of observed toxicological manifestations and discussion of their impact on the drug's use in humans
  o outline of observed adverse events and discussion of potential safety problems
- proposed global clinical plan for the current state of drug development, including regulatory status in other countries
- details of proposed clinical trials be conducted in Canada, within the intended CTA's scope including:
  o trial design statement
  o parameters, values, ranges or limits for indication(s) and clinical use(s), patient study population(s) and route(s) of administration
  o parameters, values and ranges or limits for dosage form(s), dosage regimen(s) and formulation(s)
  o proposed procedures and/or criteria for patient monitoring, clinical efficacy and safety assessments, alternative treatments, premature patient discontinuation and other considerations, as appropriate
- summary of significant drug quality (chemistry and manufacturing) aspects, if applicable:
  o drug substance and dosage form manufacturing method summary
  o relevant flow charts
  o quality control procedures and specifications list
  o summary of product characteristics
  o list of all production site(s) (biologics and radiopharmaceuticals only)

Copies of the most recent study protocol and informed consent documents should be provided if available.

The sponsor is required to prepare and send a written record of the consultation meeting's discussions and conclusions to the appropriate directorate within 14 days of the consultation date. The agency will review the minutes for approval. The subsequent CTA should include a copy of the record of discussions and conclusions approved by all parties attending the meeting.

CTA

FDR Section C.05.005 and *NHPR* Section 61 outline what is required in a CTA. CTA submissions should utilize the Common Technical Document (CTD) format, including Modules 1, 2 and 3, and be filed directly to the appropriate directorate. The shipping carton's outer label should clearly identify the contents as a "Clinical Trial Application." **Table 3-1** outlines the CTA submission structure. Refer to Health Canada's *Guidance Document for Clinical Trial Sponsors: Clinical Trial Applications* (29 May 2013) and *Clinical Trials for Natural Health Products* (October 2005) for detailed information on submission requirements.

For CTAs for biologics, drugs and radiopharmaceuticals (or a combination of the above), a hard copy of the cover letter is acceptable, provided the application is submitted in accordance with current electronic specifications (see below). For NHPs, two hard copies and two electronic copies of the submission should be provided. CTAs containing a medical device and drug (or biologic or radiopharmaceutical) combination classified as a drug should be submitted in duplicate. Similarly, if the trial includes an NHP and a drug (or biologic or radiopharmaceutical), the submission should be provided in duplicate. Separate Investigational Testing Applications (ITAs) and CTAs must be filed and authorized before the trial can commence for protocols involving a drug and the use of an unlicensed Class II, III or IV medical device that is not a combination product.

The lead directorate is responsible for communicating the regulatory decision to the sponsor.

The CTA is composed of three parts (modules) in accordance with the CTD format:

Table 3-1. Contents of a CTA Submission Package

Drugs and Biologics		NHPs	
Module	Contents	Module	Contents
1	Administrative and Product Information	1	Administrative/Clinical Information
1.0	Correspondence	1.1	Table of Contents (Module 1-3)
1.0.1	Cover Letter	1.2.	Application Information
1.0.5	Meeting Information	1.2.1	NHPD Clinical Trial Application Form
		1.2.2	Information on Prior-related applications
1.1	Table of Contents	1.2.3	Investigator's Brochure (IB)
1.2	Administrative Information	1.2.4	Protocol Synopsis and Evaluation Review Template (PCERT)
1.2.1	Application Forms	1.2.5	Study Protocol
1.2.3	Certification and Attestation Forms	1.2.6	Informed Consent Documents
1.2.5	Compliance and Site Information	1.2.7	Clinical Trial Site Information Form
1.2.5.1	Clinical Trial Site Information Form	1.2.8	Canadian Research Ethics Board Refusals
1.2.6	Authorization for Sharing Information	1.2.9	Foreign Refusals
1.2.7	International Information	1.2.10	Letters of Access
1.2.9	Other Administrative Information	1.2.11	Other Application Information
1.3	Product Information	1.3	Electronic Review Documents
1.3.4	Investigator's Brochure (IB)	2	Common Technical Document Summaries
1.4	Health Canada Summaries	2.1	CTD Table of Contents
1.4.1	Protocol Safety and Efficacy Template – Clinical Trial Application (PSEAT-CTA)	2.3	Quality Overall Summary
1.7	Clinical Trial Information	3	Quality Data (supporting data)
1.7.1	Protocol	3.1	Table of Contents of Module 3
1.7.2	Informed Consent Forms (ICF)	3.2	Body of Data
1.7.3	Canadian Research Ethics Board (REB) Refusals	3.3	Quality Literature References
1.7.4	Information on Prior-related Applications		
1.A	Appendices		
1.A.1	Electronic Review Package		
2	Common Technical Document Summaries		
2.1	Table of Contents		
2.3	Quality Overall Summary (QOS)		
3	Quality (if submitted)		
3.1	Table of Contents		
3.2	Body of Data		
3.3	Literature References		

Note: When no information is required in section or subsection, that section or subsection can be omitted from the submission.

- Module 1—administrative and clinical information about the proposed trial
- Module 2—quality (chemistry and manufacturing) summaries about the drug product(s) to be used in the proposed trial
- Module 3—additional supporting quality information

CTA Amendments—Clinical

CTA Amendments (CTA-As) are applications in which a sponsor proposes information to support changes to a previously authorized application (*FDR* Section C.05.008 and *NHPR* Section 71). CTA-As are required for changes to clinical trial drug supplies that affect the drug's quality or safety, changes to an authorized protocol that alter clinical trial subjects' risk, or both. CTA-As must be authorized by Health Canada prior to implementing changes.

A CTA-A must be filed when the proposed amendment to the protocol:
- affects clinical trial subject selection, assessment or dismissal
- affects the drug's clinical efficacy evaluation
- alters the clinical trial subjects' health risk
- affects the drug's safety evaluation
- extends the treatment's duration

Protocol changes should be reflected in the appropriate corresponding documents (e.g., informed consent form (ICF) and Investigator's Brochure (IB)) and provided, with changes clearly indicated (annotated), in the CTA-A. For a CTA-A submission, the sponsor is required to include only the sections outlined in **Table 3-1** relevant to the amendment. Refer to Health Canada's *Guidance Document for Clinical Trial Sponsors: Clinical Trial Applications* (29 May 2013) and *Clinical Trials for Natural Health Products* (October 2005) for detailed submission filing requirements. It is important to note CTA-As must be authorized by Health Canada prior to implementing the changes [C.05.008]. If any of the changes must be implemented immediately, the sponsor must provide Health Canada a rationale per C.05.008 Subsection (2) no later than 15 days after implementing the amendment [C.05.008(4)].

CTA Amendments and Notifications—Quality (Chemistry and Manufacturing)

Sponsors must file a CTA-A or CTA-Notification (CTA-N) to a previously authorized application when changes that may affect clinical trial drug supply quality or safety are proposed. It should be noted, for biologics and radiopharmaceuticals, manufacturing strategy differences can lead to the production of a novel drug product requiring both nonclinical and clinical data to support its use and are considered beyond the scope of an authorized CTA. In such cases, a new CTA is required. Changes requiring a CTA-A or CTA-N filing include, but are not limited to, those outlined in **Tables 3-2 and 3-3**. Refer to Health Canada's *Guidance Document for Clinical Trial Sponsors: Clinical Trial Applications* (29 May 2013) and *Clinical Trials for Natural Health Products* (October 2005) for detailed information on submission filing requirements.

Notifications

Notifications must be provided for CTA changes that do not meet the CTA-A criteria. The changes may be implemented immediately, but Health Canada must be informed in writing within 15 calendar days of the change (*FDR* C.05.007 and *NHPR* Section 70). Information regarding the change should be submitted in a cover letter accompanied by any supporting documentation. This information will be reviewed and added to the file.

Notifications include:
- protocol changes that do not affect (or increase) trial participants' safety and would not be considered an amendment
- changes to quality (chemistry and manufacturing) information that does not affect the drug's quality or safety
- information on foreign regulatory authorities or REB refusals
- information on the importation of additional drugs (comparator, concomitant and rescue medication)
- information on a trial's premature discontinuation

Review Process

Health Canada reviews the documents submitted in CTAs and CTA-As to assess a product's quality and to determine whether the drug's use for the clinical trial purposes does not endanger clinical trial subjects or other persons' health, the clinical trial is not contrary to the clinical trial subjects' best interests and the new clinical trials' objectives may be achieved (C.005.006(1)(b)(ii)). All CTAs for drugs, biologics and radiopharmaceuticals are subject to the 30-day default period from the completed application receipt's date per *FDR* C.05.005 or C.05.008. Comparative bioavailability studies meeting the requirements (see below) are targeted to be reviewed within seven days. This is an administrative target only. There is no regulatory review period for NHP CTAs and CTA-As outlined in the *NHPR*.

CTAs and CTA-As will be screened for completeness; if the application is considered complete, an acknowledgement letter will be issued. For *FDR* products, this letter will indicate the beginning of the 30-day review. If deficiencies are identified at screening, the sponsor will receive a Request for Clarification (called a Processing Deficiency Notice for NHPs) or a Screening Rejection Letter. Once accepted for review, any issues identified during review will result in the issuance of an Information Request Notice. All requests for information require a response within two calendar days, unless otherwise indicated as per C.05.009. Should the sponsor be unable to provide the requested information within the specified timeframe, the submission may be withdrawn and resubmitted without prejudice. If significant deficiencies are identified during the review, a Not Satisfactory Notice (NSN) may be issued. If the CTA or CTA-A is deemed acceptable, a No Objection Letter (NOL) for drugs/biologics, or Notice of Authorization (NOA) for NHPs, will be issued.

For NHPs, Health Canada has begun a transition for reviewing CTAs and CTA-As for which the proposed primary indication is not appropriate for self-care to be

Table 3-2. Quality Changes—Biologics and Radiopharmaceuticals

DRUG SUBSTANCE			
Type of Change			**Submission Type**
1.	Replacement or addition of a manufacturing site involving:		
	a.	the production of the starting material, intermediate or drug substance	Amendment
	b.	testing (e.g., release, stability)	Notification
2.	Change in the manufacturing process for the drug substance intermediate, involving:		
	a.	the fermentation process (e.g., scale-up, new bioreactor technology, use of new raw materials of biological origin); or change in the route of synthesis of the radiopharmaceutical drug substance or critical component	Amendment
	b.	the purification process (e.g., addition/removal/replacement of a purification step)	Amendment
3.	Change in the specifications for the drug substance involving:		
	a.	deletion or replacement of a test, relaxation of an acceptance criterion or addition of a test for a new impurity	Amendment
	b.	Addition of a test (other than a test for new impurity or tightening of an acceptance criterion)	Notification
4.	Change in the primary container closure system(s) for the storage and shipment of the drug substance provided the proposed container closure system is at least equivalent to the approved container closure system with respect to its relevant properties, and the change does not concern a sterile drug substance		Notification
5.	Change in the shelf life for the drug substance, involving:		
	a.	extension	
		i. if the approved shelf life is less than or equal to 18 months	Amendment
		ii. if the approved shelf life is more than 18 months	Notification
	b.	reduction (due to stability concerns)	Amendment
DRUG PRODUCT			
1.	Replacement or addition of a drug product manufacturing site involving:		
	a.	production of a drug product (including primary packaging)	Amendment
	b.	secondary packaging	Notification
	c.	testing (e.g., release, stability)	Notification
2.	Change in the drug product manufacturing process (e.g., scale-up, changes to the formulation process); change from manual synthesis of positron-emitting radiopharmaceutical to use of Automatic Synthesis Unit (ASU) or change in type of ASU		Amendment
3.	Deletion of a drug product manufacturer/manufacturing site, primary or secondary packaging site or testing site		Notification
4.	Change in the specifications for the drug product, involving:		
	a.	deletion or replacement of a test, relaxation of an acceptance criterion or addition of a test for a new impurity	Amendment
	b.	addition of a test (other than a test for new impurity) or tightening of an acceptance criterion	Notification
5.	Change in the shelf life for the drug product, involving:		
	a.	Extension	
		i. if the approved shelf life is less than or equal to 18 months	Amendment
		ii. if the approved shelf life is more than 18 months	Notification
	b.	Reduction (due to stability concerns)	Amendment
6.	Change in the storage conditions for the drug product		Amendment
7.	Changes in final product dosage form (e.g., liquid to lyophilized formulation)		Amendment
8.	Changes in final product strength		Amendment
9.	Change in diluent, involving replacement or addition of a diluent for a lyophilized powder or concentrated solution by a diluent which is commercially available in Canada, is water for injection (WFI) or a salt solution, and after reconstitution, there is no change in the drug product specifications outside of the approved ranges.		Notification
10.	Change in radiolytic protective agent or antioxidant		Amendment

Table 3-3. Quality Changes—Pharmaceuticals

DRUG SUBSTANCE	
Type of Change	**Submission Type**
1. Replacement or addition of a manufacturing site involving:	
a. production of drug substance	Amendment
b. testing (e.g., release, stability)	Notification
2. Change in the manufacturing process for the drug substance intermediate or starting material (e.g., reaction conditions, solvents, catalysts, synthetic routes, reagents, etc.)	Amendment
3. Change in the batch size for the drug substance (no impact on quality)	Notification
4. Change in the specification for the drug substance involving test and acceptance criteria:	
a. deletion or replacement of a test, relaxation of an acceptance criterion, or addition of a test for a new impurity	Amendment
b. addition of a test (other than a test for new impurity) or tightening of an acceptance criterion	Notification
5. Change in the re-test period (or shelf life) for the drug substance, involving:	
a. extension	Notification
b. reduction (due to stability concerns)	Amendment
DRUG PRODUCT	
1. Addition of a dosage form or strength	Amendment
2. Change in the composition of a dosage form	Amendment
3. Qualitative or quantitative addition, deletion or replacement of a colour or flavour with no negative impact on stability	Notification
4. Change in diluent, involving replacement or addition of a diluent for a lyophilized powder or concentrated solution	Amendment
5. Replacement or addition of a drug product manufacturer/manufacturing site involving:	
a. production of an immediate-release drug product (tablet, capsule, liquids, semi-solids) within the same manufacturer	Notification
b. production of an immediate-release drug product (tablet, capsule, liquids, semi-solids) to a new manufacturer	Amendment
c. production of a modified-release product	Amendment
d. production of a sterile drug product	Amendment
e. primary packaging (non-sterile products)	Notification
f. testing (e.g., release, stability)	Notification
6. Change in the drug product manufacturing process	Amendment
7. Change in the specification for the drug product tests and acceptance criteria, involving:	
a. deletion or replacement of a test, relaxation of an acceptance criterion, or addition of a test for a new impurity	Amendment
b. addition of a test (other than a test for a new impurity) or tightening of an acceptance criterion	Notification
8. Change in the shelf life for the drug product, involving:	
a. extension	Notification
b. reduction (due to stability concerns)	Amendment
9. Change in the storage conditions for the drug product	Amendment

reviewed by either the Therapeutic Products Directorate (TPD) or the Biologics and Genetic Therapies Directorate (BGTD), as applicable. Refer to Health Canada's *Notice to: Stakeholders of clinical trials for natural health products* (1 August 2012) and *Notice to: Stakeholders of clinical trials for biologic-type natural health products* (5 October 2012) for additional information.

Health Canada also has begun an initiative to publish the following information regarding authorized clinical trials for *FDR* products in the clinical trial database (https://health-products.canada.ca/ctdb-bdec/index-eng.jsp) shortly after NOL issuance:
- protocol number and title
- drug name

- medical condition and study population
- authorization date and sponsor name
- Health Canada control number
- start and end date of the clinical trial, if known

Comparative Bioavailability Trials

Bioavailability is an important attribute of drug formulations used to determine systemic effects. It is defined as the rate and extent of drug entry into the systemic circulation. These studies are conducted with normal, healthy volunteers (male and/or female).

Pharmaceutical comparative bioavailability studies to which the seven-day administrative review applies include:
- single-dose studies to be performed on healthy volunteers
- studies where the reference drug product is marketed in Canada, the US, the EU, Australia, Switzerland or Japan
- studies where the study drug's maximum dose does not exceed that specified in the reference drug product's labelling

This administrative review target does not apply to biologics, radiopharmaceuticals or comparative bioavailability studies, such as those conducted during new active substance development to assess the impact of dosage form or manufacturing changes or studies comparing different routes of administration.

Comparative bioavailability study filing requirements are the same as those outlined for other studies, with the following exceptions:
- cover letter outlines the study rationale
- current reference product labelling or product monograph/prescribing information is provided in lieu of the IB
- bioavailability study quality overall summary is provided

CTA-A and CTA-N bioavailability filing requirements are the same as outlined for other studies.

Electronic Requirements

As Health Canada completes its move to the electronic filing process, sponsors must provide electronic documents for CTAs and related submissions.

As of 1 June 2016, Health Canada accepts only clinical trial applications in the non-eCTD electronic format. Paper copies are not accepted.

As of this writing, eCTD CTA and CTA-A submissions will be accepted as part of Health Canada's pilot program from 1 April 2018 to 31 March 2019. All applicable Module 1, 2 and 3 sections (see **Table 3-1**) must be provided in eCTD format. With the exception of the Protocol Safety and Efficiency Table (PSEAT), the Protocol Synopsis and Evaluation Review Template (PCERT) for NHPs and the Quality Overall Summary (QOS) must be provided in Microsoft Word 2010 or earlier, and all sections should be provided in PDF format. Electronic media contents should be organized in folders and named according to the format outlined in **Table 3-1**. A letter of attestation should be provided in submission Section 1.2.3 (Section 1.2.11 for NHPs), attesting the electronic documents are identical to the paper-based documents. Refer to Health Canada's *Notice: Release of Electronic Specifications for Clinical Trial Applications and Amendments Filed in accordance with Guidance Document for Clinical Trial Sponsors: Clinical Trial Applications* (29 May 2013) for acceptable media formats and additional details on the electronic requirements.

Postapproval Requirements

Sponsors are required to comply with **Table 3-4**'s numerous postapproval requirements. Refer to Health Canada's *Guidance Document for Clinical Trial Sponsors: Clinical Trial Applications* (29 May 2013), *FDR*'s Sections C.05.012, C.05.014 and C.05.015 for drugs/biologics and *Clinical Trials for Natural Health Product* (October 2005) and *NHPR*'s Sections 69, 70 and 71 for NHPs and notice to stakeholders (2012).

GCP

In addition to the postapproval requirements with which the sponsor must comply, each sponsor should ensure the clinical trial is conducted in accordance with GCPs (*NHPR* Section 74). Consult Health Canada's *Guidance for Industry: Good Clinical Practice: Consolidated Guideline ICH Topic E6* (1997). Health Canada extends the GCP general guidelines to include the following, to which sponsors should adhere as closely as possible:
- The clinical trial is scientifically sound and clearly described in a protocol.
- The clinical trial is conducted, and the drug is used, in accordance with the protocol and *FDR* Section C.05 or *NHPR* Part 4.
- Systems and procedures ensuring every clinical trial quality aspect is implemented.
- For each clinical trial site, REB approval is obtained before starting the clinical trial.
- Only one qualified investigator is at each clinical trial site.
- Trial-related medical care and medical decisions are under the qualified investigator's supervision at each clinical trial site.
- Each person involved in clinical trial conduct is qualified by education, training and experience to perform his or her tasks.

Table 3-4. Postapproval Requirements

Research Ethics Board (REB) Refusals • The sponsor must submit a notification to Health Canada to advise of any REB refusals available after the approval of the CTA/CTA-A. • The proposed protocol and informed consent must be reviewed and approved by an REB before the trial can begin; a copy of the research ethics board attestation should be retained by the sponsor and made available upon request by Health Canada. For NHPs, the REB approval must be provided with the CTSI form.
Qualified Investigators • There must be only one qualified investigator at each clinical trial site who is responsible for the trial. • Only a licensed physician or dentist can be a qualified investigator. • A copy of the qualified investigator undertaking (QIU) form should be completed and made available upon request from Health Canada. For NHPs, the QIU must be submitted with the CTSI form.
Filing of Trial Commencement Information • Sponsors must complete and submit a Clinical Trial Site Information (CTSI) form for each site prior to the commencement of the trial or the implementation of a CTA-A.
Lot Release (for Biologics) • Prior to use in the trial, sponsors must provide lot numbers of material being used during the trial as well as lot numbers and manufacturing source of any associated human-derived excipient for the final product and the bulk product. • The sponsor will certify that all testing on the drug substance or human-derived excipient is within specification. This certification will be provided to the agency as a faxback.
Importation • Sponsors importing a drug for the purposes of a trial need to provide the NOL with the shipment. • If clinical trial materials are to be imported, the Canadian importer must be authorized by the sponsor by completing Appendix 1 of the HS/SC 3011 form and providing it with the application. Appendix 1 should be included with shipments. For NHPs, the Authorization for a Third Party to Import should be submitted with the CTA and provided with the clinical trial material shipment. • For *FDR* products, additional drugs (comparator, concomitant and rescue medications) that are being imported for the trial must be provided in Section 1.2.3 of the CTA using the Summary of Additional Drugs (SOAD) form found in Appendix 4 of Health Canada's guidance document, *For Clinical Trial Sponsors: Clinical Trial Applications* (29 May 2013). The SOAD should also be included with the shipment.
Premature Discontinuation • The sponsor must notify Health Canada within 15 days in the event that the trial has to be discontinued prematurely at one or all of its clinical sites. • This notification should include the rationale, impact on the proposed trials in Canada, confirmation that the drug distribution has stopped and unused drugs have been returned and that the investigators have been notified. • The trial may be resumed upon the approval of a CTA-A containing the name of the investigator and REB, information related to REB refusals and the proposed date of re-initiation. • Notification of a premature discontinuation of a clinical trial outside Canada, for which there are ongoing trials in Canada, should also be submitted to the appropriate directorate. • Sponsors may resume a trial following the submission of a notification indicating the name of the investigator, the name of the REB that approved the re-initiation, the proposed date of re-initiation and the name of any REB that refused the re-initiation. Changes to the protocol or the quality of the information requires the submission of a CTA-A.
Study Completion • Sponsors should submit a notification to advise Health Canada when a clinical trial is completed or a clinical trial site is closed. • A study is considered to be completed after the last subject globally completes the end of study visit as defined in the protocol.
Adverse Drug Reaction (ADR) Reporting • Serious, unexpected and related events in Canada and at international sites related to the study products must be reported (non-fatal or life-threatening events: within 15 days; fatal or life-threatening events: within seven days). • Within eight days after Health Canada is informed of fatal or life-threatening events, a complete report that includes the assessment of importance and implication of findings must be submitted. • Each event should be submitted individually by fax only, with an ADR expedited reporting summary form. • NHP ADRs are to be submitted to BGTD or TPD, not NHPD, as appropriate.
Updated Investigator's Brochure • Updated IBs should be submitted annually and contain all safety information and global status, including previous expedited ADR reports.
Records (to be retained for 25 years) • Retain all versions of the IB, including the change history. • Retain records of all ADRs, enrollment, dropouts and information regarding the drug lifecycle (shipment, receipt, disposition, return and destruction). • Retain copies of qualified investigator undertaking forms, REB approvals, protocols, informed consent and amendments. • Records must be available to Health Canada, upon request, within two calendar days if they are safety related; otherwise, they must be made available within seven calendar days.

- Written informed consent is obtained from each person before he or she participates in the trial.
- Every person who considers participating in the trial is informed of the risks and anticipated benefits to his or her health arising from clinical trial participation and all other trial aspects necessary to decide whether to participate in the clinical trial.
- Requirements related to *FDR* Section C.05.012 information and records and *NHPR* Section 76 are met.
- The drug is manufactured, handled and stored in accordance with applicable Good Manufacturing Practice (GMP) referred to in Divisions 2–4, except *FDR* Sections C.02.019, C.02.025 and C.02.026 and Part 3, except *NHPR* Section 61.

It also should be noted that Canadian GMP drug regulations also apply to clinical trial supplies. *FDR* Section C.05.010(j) and *NHPR* Section 63 require the sponsor to ensure drugs for use in clinical trials are manufactured, handled and stored in accordance with the applicable GMP requirements referenced in *FDR* Divisions 2–4 (*NHPR* Part 3), except *FDR* Sections C.02.019, C.02.025 and C.02.026 and *NHPR* Section 61 (these regulations address sample retention and lot testing requirements in Canada). For additional information, refer to Health Canada's *Guidance Document: Annex 13 to the Current Edition of the Good Manufacturing Practices Guidelines Drugs Used in Clinical Trials GUI-0036* (7 August 2009).

Conclusion

- Clinical trials are categorized into four phases (Phase I, II, III and IV). Each successive phase typically involves a larger number of subjects as the drug is tested to establish its dosage, safety and efficacy. Various study designs can be used in clinical trials in any of the four phases.
- Health Canada regulates drug sale and importation in Canada through the *Food and Drug Regulations* and *Natural Health Products Regulations*. Various *FDR* Part C Sections and *NHPR* Part 4 stipulate certain requirements on drugs by restricting their sale and importation in Canada.
- Sponsors that wish to conduct Phase I, II or III drug development and comparative clinical trials, or Phase I, II or III marketed product clinical trials for which the proposed use is outside the product's approved indications and conditions must submit a CTA to Health Canada.
- Electronic CTA requirements in CTD format apply; NHP submissions are made in non-eCTD format, and drug, biologic and radiopharmaceutical submissions are in eCTD format.
- *FDR* Sections C.05.005 and 64 define what a CTA submission requires, and Sections C.05.008(3) and 71 specify what a CTA Amendment (CTA-A) requires for an *FDR* and *NHPR* product, respectively.
- A sponsor submitting a CTA is applying for authorization to sell or import a drug for the purpose of conducting a clinical trial as regulated under *FDR* Division C.05 or *NHPR* Part 4.
- CTAs and CTA-As for *FDR* submissions are subject to the 30-day review default period. There is no defined review for *NHPR* products.
- Following CTA approval, postapproval requirements include amendments, notifications, lot release, adverse event reporting and annual Investigator's Brochure updates.
- The clinical trial application process and regulatory requirements for medical devices and in vitro diagnostic devices (IVDDs) vary significantly from the CTA process.

Chapter 4

Good Manufacturing Practices and Establishment Licensing in Canada

By Bocar Guisse, MSc and Fraidianie Sévigné

OBJECTIVES

❑ Describe the framework of legislation, regulations and guidelines governing the manufacture and import of drugs in Canada.

❑ Provide an overview of the key activities related to the manufacture of drugs and the requirements for Drug Establishment Licences (DELs).

❑ Describe the key elements of the quality management system as laid out in the Canadian Good Manufacturing Practices (GMP) regulations and guidelines.

❑ Provide an overview of the applicability of GMPs to the manufacture of clinical trial materials, veterinary drugs and active pharmaceutical ingredients.

❑ Provide an overview of enforcement of GMPs through inspections.

LEGISLATION, REGULATIONS AND GUIDELINES COVERED IN THIS CHAPTER

❑ *Food and Drugs Act*, R.S.C., 1985, c. F-27, Current to March 18, 2018. Last amended on 22 June 2017

❑ *Food and Drug Regulations*, C.R.C., c.870, Current to 18 March 2018, Last amended on 27 December 2017

❑ *Good Manufacturing Practices (GMP) Guidelines–2009 edition*, Version 2

❑ *Guidance on Drug Establishment Licences and Drug Establishment Licencing Fees* (GUI-0002)

❑ *Risk Classification of GMP Observations* (GUI-0023) Published: 28 February 2018

❑ *Guidance Document—Annex 13 to the Current Edition of the Good Manufacturing Practices Guidelines Drugs Used in Clinical Trials* (GUI-0036)

❑ *Annex 4 to the Current Edition of the Good Manufacturing Practices Guidelines—Veterinary Drugs* (GUI-0012)

❑ *Good Manufacturing Practice Guidance for Active Pharmaceutical Ingredients ICH Q7A*

❑ *Good Manufacturing Practices (GMP) Guidelines for Active Pharmaceutical Ingredients (APIs)* (GUI-0104)

❑ *Annex 1 to the Good manufacturing practices guide—Manufacture of sterile drugs* (GUI-0119) Published: 28 February 2018

Introduction

This chapter covers the specific Canadian legislation, regulations and guidelines for the manufacture of drugs. The primary focus is on requirements related to Good

Chapter 4

Definitions for Terms in This Chapter

Term	Definition
Active Pharmaceutical Ingredient (API)	Any substance or mixture of substances intended to be used in the manufacture of a drug (medicinal) product and that, when used in the production of a drug, becomes an active ingredient of the drug product. Such substances are intended to furnish pharmacological activity or other direct effect in the diagnosis, cure, mitigation, treatment or prevention of disease or to affect the structure and function of the body.
Distributor or Manufacturer	"A person, including an association or partnership, who under their own name, or under a trade, design or word mark, trade name or other name, word, or mark controlled by them, sells a food or drug." (A.01.010)
Dosage Form	A drug product that has been processed to the point at which it is in a form that may be administered in individual doses.
Drug	Any substance or mixture of substances manufactured, sold, or represented for use in *(a)* the diagnosis, treatment, mitigation, or prevention of a disease, a disorder, an abnormal physical state, or the symptoms thereof, in humans or animals, *(b)* restoring, correcting, or modifying organic functions in humans or animals, or *(c)* "disinfection" in premises in which food is manufactured, prepared, or kept. (Section 2 of the *Food and Drugs Act*). In Division 1A and Division 2 of the *Food and Drug Regulations*, "drug" means a drug in a dosage form, or a drug that is a bulk process intermediate that can be used in the preparation of a drug.
Drug Establishment Licence (DEL)	A licence issued to a person in Canada to conduct licensable activities in a building that has been inspected and assessed as being in compliance with the requirements of Divisions 2–4 of the *Food and Drug Regulations*.
Fabricate	"To prepare and preserve a drug for the purpose of sale." (C.01A.001)
Import	"To import into Canada a drug for the purpose of sale" (C.01A.001)
Marketing Authorization	A legal document issued by Health Canada, authorizing the sale of a drug (or a device) based on the health and safety requirements of the *Food and Drugs Act* and the *Food and Drug Regulations*.
Mutual Recognition Agreement (MRA)	An international agreement that provides for the mutual recognition of compliance certification for Good Manufacturing Practices for drugs.
MRA Country	A country that is a participant in a mutual recognition agreement with Canada.
Package/Label	"To put a drug in its immediate container or to affix the inner or outer label to the drug." (C.01A.001)
Specifications	A detailed description of a drug, the raw material used in a drug or the packaging material for a drug including: *(a)* a statement of all properties and qualities of the drug, raw material or packaging material that are relevant to the manufacture, packaging and use of the drug, including the identity, potency and purity of the drug, raw material or packaging material; *(b)* a detailed description of the methods used for testing and examining the drug, raw material or packaging material; and *(c)* a statement of tolerances for the properties and qualities of the drug, raw material or packaging material.
Test	To perform the tests, including any examinations, evaluations and assessments, as specified in Division 2 of the *Food and Drug Regulations*.
Wholesale	"To sell any of the following drugs, other than at retail sale, where the seller's name does not appear on the label of the drugs: *(a)* a drug listed in Schedule C or D to the *Act* or in Schedule F to these *Regulations* or a controlled drug as defined in subsection G.01.001 (1); or *(b)* a narcotic as defined in the *Narcotic Control Regulations*." (C.01A.001)

Source: Good Manufacturing Practices (GMP) Guidelines - 2009 Edition, Version 2 (GUI-0001).

Manufacturing Practices (GMPs) and Drug Establishment Licences (DELs).

The *Food and Drugs Act*, R.S.C., 1985 (*F&DA*) is the legislation enacted by Parliament covering food, drugs, cosmetics and devices. Broadly, the *F&DA* is divided into two parts. The law specific to drugs is defined in Part I of the act under the "Drugs" section. The other sections in Part I refer to food, cosmetics and devices. Part II outlines the law relating to "Administration and Enforcement." It includes the mandate for powers granted to government agencies for developing regulations to put this law into effect and ensure compliance. Health Canada is the federal department responsible for all activities concerning *F&DA* compliance and enforcement (except products regulated as foods, which are the responsibility of the Canadian Food Inspection Agency (CFIA)) and the *Controlled Drugs and Substances Act* (*CDSA*) and their associated regulations.

Based on the *F&DA*, the regulations through which this legislation is enforced are laid out under the *Food and Drug Regulations*, C.R.C., c. 870 (*FDR*). Health Canada, under the authority of the act, develops and enforces regulations. The *FDR* includes seven parts. These parts contain requirements covering enforcement of all matters the *F&DA* defines, e.g., foods, drugs and their administration. The drug regulations are contained in Part C. Each part is subdivided into divisions. Regulations governing drugs in Part C contain nine divisions. The requirements related to a DEL are provided in Division 1A, and the requirements related to GMPs are provided in Division 2. The other divisions in Part C cover other topics, such as clinical trials, new drugs, nonprescription drugs, etc. Each division has sections that define specific requirements related to it. For example, Section C.01A.05 relates to the requirements for a DEL "application," and Section C.02.005 defines requirements for "equipment" used in drug manufacture. Hence, a regulation's requirement hierarchy runs from part->division->section. As is apparent, the "C" in C.01A.005 represents the "part" of the "drug" regulation; "01A" represents the "division" number containing DEL information; and "005" is the specific division section describing "application" submission requirements for a DEL.

Health Canada also prepares guidelines and policies to help interpret and clarify the legislation surrounding drugs and other health products. Drug manufacture guidelines are documented in the *Good Manufacturing Practices (GMP) Guideline*. Some of this guideline's elements are described later in this chapter. Overall, the regulatory framework has a hierarchy, with the "act" at the highest level, describing the "what," followed by the "regulations" that describe "how" the mandate laid down in the "act" can be met, followed by implementation "guidelines" that provide a more detailed interpretation of the regulations and the act.

Health Canada has several branches under its organizational structure. Health Canada's Therapeutic Products Directorate (TPD) is the Canadian federal authority that regulates pharmaceutical drugs (small molecule) and medical devices for human use. Prior to being given authorization to market a drug, a manufacturer must present substantive scientific evidence of a product's safety, efficacy and quality, as required by the *F&DA and FDR*. As part of its regulatory responsibilities, Health Canada is responsible for compliance monitoring and enforcement activities related to health products to verify regulatory requirements are being applied appropriately. Its Health Products and Food Branch Inspectorate (HPFBI) is the directorate primarily responsible for health product compliance monitoring activities, such as industry inspection and product investigation. HPFBI develops and implements enforcement strategies in these areas. Establishment licensing (explained in more detail later in this chapter) and related investigation and laboratory functions support the inspectorate's compliance and enforcement activities.

Drug Establishment Licence (DEL)

This section contains some excerpts from *FDR* Division 1A on DELs. References to applicable guidelines on DELs also are provided. For details on these requirements, refer to the *FDR* and the guidance documents.

Since 1 January 1998, all Canadian drug establishments have been required to hold a DEL to fabricate, package, label, distribute, import, wholesale or test a drug. This licensing requirement applies to all drug establishments (with few exceptions detailed in the regulations, e.g., some natural health products, traditional medicines, such as Chinese and ayurvedic, homeopathic preparations and vitamin and mineral supplements). It is not permitted, except in accordance with a DEL, to fabricate, package, label, distribute, import or wholesale a drug, or to perform tests required under *FDR* Division 2 noted above.

An applicant wishing to perform any of the six drug licensing activities mentioned above must submit an application in the prescribed form, FRM-0033. *Guidance on Drug Establishment Licences and Drug Establishment Fees* (GUI-002) describes the responsibilities of persons involved in all licensable activities, what a DEL is, when it is required, who is required to hold a licence and the activities it covers.

Drug establishments are inspected by the Inspectorate Program to assess whether they are performing licensable activities in compliance with the requirements of *FDR* Part C, Divisions 2–4 pertaining to GMPs. A DEL will be issued only when the inspectorate has assessed the applicant as being in compliance with these requirements.

Foreign sites whose drugs are to be imported also fall under the scope of drug establishment licensing. These sites are inspected or evaluated according to the FDR pertaining to GMP compliance. A foreign site will be listed on a DEL site annex only after it has been assessed as being compliant with these requirements.

Guidance on Evidence to Demonstrate Drug Compliance of Foreign Sites (GUI-0080) provides details on how foreign sites can satisfy this requirement. For sites in a Mutual Recognition Agreement (MRA) country, the Canadian Inspectorate would obtain a Certificate of Compliance (CoC) from the MRA country's regulatory authority. For sites not located in an MRA country, the type of evidence required for the establishment may include:

- Certification for compliance from a Canadian inspector—this may require an on-site evaluation by a Canadian inspector.
- Providing other evidence that establishes that the site meets the applicable GMP requirements—this may include documentation of GMP compliance from other recognized regulatory authorities, e.g., UK Medical and Healthcare products Regulatory Agency (MHRA) inspection report for a site in India, or US Food and Drug Administration (FDA) inspection report for a site located in the

US, along with other associated documentation. If these reports are not available, the inspectorate recommends submitting a corporate or consultant audit report with other supporting documentation specified in the guideline. FRM-0211 is recommended for conducting corporate/consultant audits.

Updated GUI-0080, *How to demonstrate foreign building compliance with drug good manufacturing practices*, was released 18 January 2018 in line with canada.ca posting requirements. This version includes: new template for guidance documents and visual call-out boxes within the document to highlight important information, tips or general knowledge items. The renewal process provides more flexibility, since the expiry date is replaced by the NERBY (new evidence required by) date. Renewal applications must be submitted by the NERBY date. As long as an application with GMP evidence is filed by the NERBY date, an importer can continue importation from the foreign building. A NERBY date is generally three to four years. NERBY date assignment is determined by whether the foreign building is located in an MRA country and conducts activities covered by the MRA and the DEL Annex on which the foreign building is listed. Standard operating procedures (SOPs) and written quality agreements no longer are required to be submitted as part of the application. GMP evidence also may be submitted by a foreign building directly to Health Canada.

It is important to note finished product importers must include active pharmaceutical ingredient (API) sites on the foreign building license. The application must be submitted with a comprehensive Table A and without GMP evidence package for APIs.

Good Manufacturing Practices (GMPs)—Regulations

As noted above, a DEL holder must conform to GMP requirements in *FDR* Division 2. Section C.02.003 (Sale) requires "no distributor referred to in paragraph C. 01A.003(b) and no importer shall sell a drug unless it has been fabricated, packaged/labelled, tested and stored in accordance with the requirements of this Division." Excerpts from some GMP sections in the *FDR* are listed below. For details of the listed and other GMP requirements, refer to *FDR*:

"1. C.02.004—Premises: The premises in which a lot or batch of a drug is fabricated, packaged/labelled or stored shall be designed, constructed and maintained in a manner that (*a*) permits the operations therein to be performed under clean, sanitary and orderly conditions; (*b*) permits the effective cleaning of all surfaces therein; and (*c*) prevents the contamination of the drug and the addition of extraneous material to the drug.

2. C.02.005—Equipment: The equipment with which a lot or batch of a drug is fabricated, packaged/labelled or tested shall be designed, constructed, maintained, operated and arranged in a manner that (*a*) permits the effective cleaning of its surfaces; (*b*) prevents the contamination of the drug and the addition of extraneous material to the drug; and (*c*) permits it to function in accordance with its intended use.

3. C.02.006—Personnel: Every lot or batch of a drug shall be fabricated, packaged/labelled, tested and stored under the supervision of personnel who, having regard to the duties and responsibilities involved, have had such technical, academic and other training as the director considers satisfactory in the interests of the health of the consumer or purchaser.

4. C.02.007 and C.02.008—Sanitation: Every person who fabricates or packages/labels a drug (*a*) shall have a written sanitation program that shall be implemented under the supervision of qualified personnel (*b*) shall have, in writing, minimum requirements for the health and the hygienic behaviour and clothing of personnel to ensure the clean and sanitary fabrication and packaging/labelling of the drug.

5. C.02.009 and C.02.010—Raw Material Testing: Each lot or batch of raw material shall be tested against the specifications for that raw material prior to its use in the fabrication of a drug.

6. C.02.011 and C.02.012—Manufacturing Control: The fabricator, packager/labeller, distributor and importer of a drug shall have written procedures prepared by qualified personnel in respect of the drug to ensure that the drug meets the specifications for that drug and all activities are performed in compliance with the procedures.

7. C.02.013, C.02.014 and C.02.015—Quality Control Department: No lot or batch of raw material or of packaging/labelling material shall be used in the fabrication or packaging/labelling of a drug unless the material is approved for that use by the person in charge of the quality control department. Except in the case of a wholesaler, no lot or batch of a drug shall be made available for sale unless the sale of that lot or batch is approved by the person in charge of the quality control department.

8. C.02.016—Packaging Material Testing: Each lot or batch of packaging material shall, prior to its use in the packaging of a drug, be examined or

Table 4-1. GMP Regulations Applicable to Licensable Activities

Section	Regulation	F	P/L	I	D	W	T
1. Premises	C.02.004	√	√	√	√	√	
2. Equipment	C.02.005	√	√				√
3. Personnel	C.02.006	√	√	√	√	√	√
4. Sanitation	C.02.007	√	√				
	C.02.008	√	√				
5. Raw Material Testing	C.02.009	√					*
	C.02.010	√					*
6. Manufacturing Control	C.02.011	√	√	√	√		
	C.02.012	√	√	√	√	√	
7. Quality Control	C.02.013	√	√	√	√	√	
	C.02.014	√	√	√	√	√	
	C.02.015	√	√	√	√	√	√
8. Packaging Material Testing	C.02.016	√	√				*
	C.02.017	√	√				*
9. Finished Product Testing	C.02.018	√	√	√	√		*
	C.02.019		√	√	√		*
10. Records	C.02.020	√	√	√	√		√
	C.02.021	√	√	√	√	√	√
	C.02.022			√	√	√	
	C.02.023	√	√	√	√	√	
	C.02.024	√	√	√	√	√	
11. Samples	C.02.025	√		√	√		
	C.02.026	√		√	√		
12. Stability	C.02.027			√	√		*
	C.02.028			√	√		*
13. Sterile Products	C.02.029	√	√				*

F = Fabricator P/L = Packager/Labeller I = Importer (MRA and non-MRA) D = Distributor
W = Wholesaler T = Tester
* Where applicable depending on the nature of the activities

tested against the specifications for that packaging material.

9. C.02.018 and C.02.019—Finished Product Testing: (1) Each lot or batch of a drug shall, prior to its availability for sale, be tested against the specifications for that drug. (2) No lot or batch of a drug shall be available for sale unless it complies with the specifications for that drug. (3) The specifications shall (*a*) be in writing; (*b*) be approved by the person in charge of the quality control department; and (*c*) comply with the *Act* and these *Regulations*.

10. C.02.020 through C.02.024—Records: The DEL holder shall maintain records, for example (*a*) master production documents for the drug; (*b*) evidence that each lot or batch of the drug has been fabricated, packaged/labelled, tested and stored in accordance with the procedures described in the master production documents; (*c*) evidence that the conditions under which the drug was fabricated, packaged/labelled, tested and stored are in compliance with the requirements of this Division; (*d*) evidence of the testing referred to in section C.02.018 (e) sanitation program.

Chapter 4

11. C.02.025 and C.02.026—Samples: The fabricator shall retain a sample of each lot or batch of raw materials used in the fabrication of a drug for a period of at least two years after the materials were last used in the fabrication of the drug.
12. C.02.027 and C.02.028—Stability: The DEL holder shall ensure establishment of the period of time during which each drug in the package in which it is sold will comply with the specifications.
13. C.02.029—Sterile Products: In addition to the other requirements of this Division, a drug that is intended to be sterile shall be fabricated and packaged/labeled (*a*) in separate and enclosed areas; (*b*) under the supervision of personnel trained in microbiology; and (*c*) by a method scientifically proven to ensure sterility."

On 28 February 2018, the Health Products Compliance Directorate posted four drug GMP documents to the Health Canada website. These documents included:
- Good manufacturing practices guide for drug products (GUI-0001)[1]
- Risk classification guide for drug good manufacturing practices observations (GUI-0023)[2]
- Annex 1 to the Good manufacturing practices guide – Manufacture of sterile drugs (GUI-0119)[3]

GUI-0001 and GUI-0023 are revised versions of currently posted documents, and GUI-0119 is a new document to replace the sterile products section of GUI-0001. These documents, except GUI-0023, have an implementation date of 1 October 2018.

These documents have been updated to:
- address emerging issues such as increased reliance on foreign fabricators, packagers, labellers and testers, and emerging trends such as data integrity
- incorporate additional sample observations
- help industry comply with the regulations related to sterile drugs
- use plain language principle reformatting in accordance with new Canada.ca requirements, soon to be in effect

GMP Guidelines (GUI-0001)

The GMP guidelines provide a quality management system (QMS) framework designed to facilitate compliance by industry and enhance consistency in applying regulatory requirements. This section contains excerpts from the GMP guidelines (GUI-0001). For details on these requirements, refer to the GMP guidelines. Although this document does not constitute part of the *F&DA* or *FDR*, it is an administrative document whose purpose is to provide interpretive guidance for *FDR* Part C, Division 2, which applies to pharmaceutical, radiopharmaceutical, biological and veterinary drugs. These guidelines were developed by Health Canada in consultation with stakeholders.

This document's content should not be regarded as the only GMP regulations' interpretation and is not intended to cover every conceivable case. Alternative means of complying with the regulations can be considered with the appropriate scientific justification.

This guidance is meant to harmonize with GMP standards from other countries and from the World Health Organization (WHO), the Pharmaceutical Inspection Cooperation/Scheme (PIC/S) and the International Council on Harmonisation (ICH). It takes into consideration the implementation of Canada's current MRAs with other countries regarding drug manufacture. The MRAs establish mutual recognition of GMP compliance certification between regulatory authorities designated as equivalent in the MRA countries.

As mentioned earlier, *FDR* Division 1A, Part C defines the six GMP activities with which compliance must be demonstrated prior to DEL issuance. **Table 4-1** (Chart 1.0 excerpted from GUI-0001 Section 1) provides the list of GMP regulations applicable to each corresponding licensable activity.

1. Quality Management (Reference–GMP Guidelines Section 4.0)

"1.1 Guiding Principle: The holder of an Establishment Licence under the requirements of Division 2, Part C of the *Food and Drug Regulations,* must ensure that the fabrication, packaging, labelling, distribution, testing and wholesaling of drugs comply with these requirements and the marketing authorization, and do not place consumers at risk due to inadequate safety and quality.

The attainment of this quality objective is the responsibility of senior management and requires the participation and commitment of personnel in many different departments and at all levels within the establishment and its suppliers. To ensure compliance, there must be a comprehensively designed and correctly implemented quality management system (QMS) that incorporates GMP and quality control. The system should be fully documented and its effectiveness monitored. All parts of the QMS should be adequately resourced with qualified personnel, suitable premises, equipment, and facilities.

1.2 Relationship among Quality Elements: The basic concepts of quality assurance, GMP, and quality control are inter-related. They are described here in order to emphasize their relationships and their fundamental importance to the production and control of drugs.

    1.2.1 Quality Assurance: Quality assurance is a wide-ranging concept that covers all matters that individually or collectively influence the quality of a drug. It is the total of the organized arrangements made with the objective of ensuring that drugs are of the quality required for their intended use. Quality assurance therefore incorporates GMPs, along with other factors.

A system of quality assurance appropriate for the fabrication, packaging, labelling, testing, distribution, importation, and wholesale of drugs should ensure that:

(i) Drugs are designed and developed in a way that takes into account the GMP requirements;
(ii) Managerial responsibilities are clearly specified;
(iii) Systems, facilities and procedures are adequate and qualified;
(iv) Production and control operations are clearly specified;
(v) Analytical methods and critical processes are validated;
(vi) Arrangements are made for the supply and use of the correct raw and packaging materials;
(viii) All necessary control on intermediates, and any other in-process monitoring is carried out;
(ix) Outsourced activities are subject to appropriate controls and meet GMP requirements;
(x) Fabrication, packaging/labelling, testing, distribution, importation, and wholesaling are performed in accordance with established procedures;
(xi) Drugs are not sold or supplied before the quality control department has certified that each lot has been produced and controlled in accordance with the marketing authorization and of any other regulations relevant to the production, control and release of drugs;
(xii) Satisfactory arrangements exist for ensuring that the drugs are stored, distributed, and subsequently handled in such a way that quality is maintained throughout their shelf life;
(xiii) The quality risk management system should ensure that:
   a. the evaluation of the risk to quality is based on scientific knowledge, experience with the process and ultimately links to the protection of the patient
   b. the level of effort, formality and documentation of the quality risk management process is commensurate with the level of risk.
(xiv) The effectiveness, applicability, and continuous improvement of the quality management system is ensured through regular management review and self-inspection;
(xv) An annual product quality review of all drugs should be conducted with the objective of verifying the consistency of the existing process, the appropriateness of current specifications for both raw materials and finished product to highlight any trends and to identify product and process improvements.

1.2.2. Good Manufacturing Practices (GMP) for Drugs
GMP are the part of quality assurance that ensures that drugs are consistently produced and controlled in such a way to meet the quality standards appropriate to their intended use, as required by the marketing authorization.

GMP basic requirements are as follows:

(i) Manufacturing processes are clearly defined and controlled to ensure consistency and compliance with approved specifications;
(ii) Critical steps of manufacturing processes and significant changes to the process are validated;
(iii) All necessary key elements for GMP are provided, including the following:
   a. qualified and trained personnel,
   b. adequate premises and space,
   c. suitable equipment and services,
   d. correct materials, containers and labels,
   e. approved procedures and instructions,
   f. suitable storage and transport.
(iv) Instructions and procedures are written in clear and unambiguous language;
(v) Operators are trained to carry out and document procedures;
(vi) Records are made during manufacture that demonstrate that all the steps required by the defined procedures and instructions were in fact taken and that the quantity and quality of the drug was as expected. Deviations are investigated and documented;
(vii) Records of fabrication, packaging, labelling, testing, distribution, importation, and wholesaling that enable the complete history of a lot to be traced are retained in a comprehensible and accessible form;
(viii) Control of storage, handling, and transportation of the drugs minimizes any risk to their quality;
(ix) A system is available for recalling of drugs from sale;
(x) Complaints about drugs are examined, the causes of quality defects are investigated,

Chapter 4

and appropriate measures are taken with respect to the defective drugs and to prevent recurrence.

1.2.3. Quality Control

Quality control is the part of GMP that is concerned with sampling, specifications, testing, documentation, and release procedures. Quality control ensures that the necessary and relevant tests are carried out and that raw materials, packaging materials, and products are released for use or sale, only if their quality is satisfactory. Quality control is not confined to laboratory operations but must be incorporated into all activities and decisions concerning the quality of the product.

The basic requirements of quality control are that adequate facilities, trained personnel, and approved procedures are available for sampling, inspecting and testing of raw materials, packaging materials, intermediate bulk and finished products, and, where appropriate monitoring environmental conditions for GMP purposes."

2. Rationale and Interpretation of the Specific Regulations in the Guideline

"The following section provides excerpts of the rationale and examples of interpretation from the GMP guideline to its corresponding section in the *GMP Regulations* (shown in parentheses). For a detailed interpretation, the reader is advised to refer to the GMP guideline document.

(i) Premises (Regulation C.02.004)

Rationale: The pharmaceutical establishment should be designed and constructed in a manner that permits cleanliness and orderliness while preventing contamination. Regular maintenance is required to prevent deterioration of the premises. The ultimate objective of all endeavours is product quality.

Example of Interpretation:

The premises are designed, constructed, and maintained such that they prevent the entry of pests into the building and also prevent the migration of extraneous material from the outside into the building and from one area to another.

- Doors, windows, walls, ceilings, and floors are such that no holes or cracks are evident (other than those intended by design).
- Doors giving direct access to the exterior from manufacturing and packaging areas are used for emergency purposes only. These doors are adequately sealed. Receiving and shipping area(s) do not allow direct access to production areas.
- Production areas are segregated from all non-production areas. Individual manufacturing, packaging, and testing areas are clearly defined and if necessary segregated. Areas where biological, microbiological or radioisotope testing is carried out require special design and containment considerations.
- Laboratory animals' quarters are segregated.
- Engineering, boiler rooms, generators, etc. are isolated from production areas.

(ii) Equipment (Regulation C.02.005)

Rationale: The purpose of these requirements is to prevent the contamination of drugs by other drugs, by dust, and by foreign materials such as rust, lubricant and particles coming from the equipment. Contamination problems may arise from poor maintenance, the misuse of equipment, exceeding the capacity of the equipment and the use of worn-out equipment. Equipment arranged in an orderly manner permits cleaning of adjacent areas and does not interfere with other processing operations. It also minimizes the circulation of personnel and optimizes the flow of materials. The fabrication of drugs of consistent quality requires that equipment perform in accordance with its intended use.

Example of Interpretation:

The design, construction and location of equipment permit cleaning, sanitizing, and inspection of the equipment.

- Equipment parts that come in contact with raw materials, in-process intermediates or drugs are accessible to cleaning or are removable.
- Tanks used in processing liquids and ointments are equipped with fittings that can be dismantled and cleaned. Validated Clean-In-Place (CIP) equipment can be dismantled for periodic verification.
- Filter assemblies are designed for easy dismantling.
- Equipment is located at a sufficient distance from other equipment and walls to permit cleaning of the equipment and adjacent area.
- The base of immovable equipment is adequately sealed along points of contact with the floor.
- Equipment is kept clean, dry and protected from contamination when stored.

(iii) Personnel (Regulation C.02.006)

Rationale: People are the most important element in any pharmaceutical operation, without the proper personnel with the appropriate attitude and sufficient training, it is almost impossible to fabricate, package/label, test, or store good quality drugs.

It is essential that qualified personnel be employed to supervise the fabrication of drugs. The operations involved in the fabrication of drugs are highly technical in nature and require constant vigilance, attention to details and a high degree of competence on the part of employees. Inadequate training of personnel or the absence of an appreciation of the importance of production control, often accounts for the failure of a product to meet the required standards.

Example of Interpretation:

The individual in charge of the quality control department of a fabricator, packager/labeller, tester, importer, and distributor; and the individual in charge of the manufacturing department of a fabricator or packager/labeller:

- holds a Canadian university degree or a degree recognized as equivalent by a Canadian university or Canadian accreditation body in a science related to the work being carried out;
- has practical experience in their responsibility area;
- directly controls and personally supervises on site, each working shift during which activities under their control are being conducted; and
- may delegate duties and responsibility (e.g., to cover all shifts) to a person in possession of a diploma, certificate or other evidence of formal qualifications awarded on completion of a course of study at a university, college or technical institute in a science related to the work being carried out combined with at least two years of relevant practical experience, while remaining accountable for those duties and responsibility.

(iv) Sanitation (Regulation C.02.007, C.02.008)

Rationale: Sanitation in a pharmaceutical plant, as well as employee attitude, influences the quality of drug products. The quality requirement for drug products demand that such products be fabricated and packaged in areas that are free from environmental contamination and free from contamination by another drug.

Employee's health, behaviour, and clothing may contribute to the contamination of the product. Poor personal hygiene will nullify the best sanitation program and greatly increase the risk of product contamination. Hence, health requirements and hygiene programs must be clearly defined.

Example of Interpretation:

The sanitation program contains procedures that describe the following:
1. cleaning requirements applicable to all production areas of the plant with emphasis on manufacturing areas that require special attention;
2. requirements applicable to processing equipment;
3. cleaning intervals;
4. products for cleaning and disinfection, along with their dilution and the equipment to be used;
5. the responsibilities of any outside contractor;
6. disposal procedures for waste material and debris;
7. pest control measures;
8. precautions required to prevent contamination of a drug when rodenticides, insecticides, and fumigation agents are used;
9. microbial and environmental monitoring procedures with alert and action limits in areas where susceptible products are fabricated or packaged; and
10. the personnel responsible for carrying out cleaning procedures.

(v) Raw Material Testing (Regulation C.02.009, C.02.010)

Rationale: The testing of raw materials before their use has three objectives: to confirm the identity of the raw materials, to provide assurance that the quality of the drug in dosage form will not be altered by raw material defects, and to obtain assurance that the raw materials have the characteristics that will provide the desired quantity or yield in a given manufacturing process.

Section C.02.010 outlines options as to when the testing prescribed by Section C.02.009 is carried out. The purchase of raw materials is an important operation that requires a particular and thorough knowledge of the raw materials and their fabricator. To maintain consistency in the fabrication of drug products, raw materials should originate from reliable fabricators.

Examples of Interpretation:
a) Each raw material used in the production of a drug is covered by specifications (see regulation C.02.002) that are approved and dated by the person in charge of the quality control department or by a designated alternate who meets the requirements described under Regulation C.02.006, interpretation 1.4.
b) Specifications are of pharmacopoeial or equivalent status and are in compliance with the current marketing authorization. Where appropriate, additional properties or qualities not addressed by the pharmacopoeia (e.g., particle size, etc.) are included in the specifications.
c) Identity testing: Specific identity testing is conducted on all lots of any raw material received on the premises of the person who formulates the raw material into dosage forms.

(vi) Manufacturing Control (Regulation C.02.011)

Rationale: This regulation requires that measures be taken to maintain the integrity of a drug product from the moment the various raw materials enter the plant to the time the finished dosage form is released for sale and distributed. These measures ensure that all manufacturing processes are clearly defined, systematically reviewed in light of experience, and demonstrated to be capable of consistently manufacturing pharmaceutical products of the required quality that comply with their established specifications.

(Regulation C.02.012) The purpose of a recall is to remove from the market, a drug that represents an undue health risk. Drugs that have left the premises of a fabricator, packager/labeller, distributor, wholesaler and importer can be found in a variety of locations. Depending on the severity of the health risk, it may be necessary to recall a product to one level or another. Fabricators, packagers/labellers, distributors, wholesalers, and importers are expected to be able to recall to the consumer level if necessary. Additional guidance on recalls can be found in Health Canada's document entitled *Recall Policy* (POL-0016).

Examples of Interpretation:
a) All handling of raw materials, products, and packaging materials such as receipt, quarantine, sampling, storage, tracking, labelling, dispensing, processing, packaging and distribution is done in accordance with pre-approved written procedures or instructions and recorded.
b) All critical production processes are validated. Detailed information is provided in various Health Canada validation guidelines.
c) Validation studies are conducted in accordance with predefined protocols. A written report summarizing recorded results and conclusions is prepared, evaluated, approved, and maintained.
d) Changes to production processes, systems, equipment, or materials that may affect product quality and/or process reproducibility are validated prior to implementation.

(vii) Quality Control Department (Regulation C.02.013)
Rationale: Quality control is the part of GMP concerned with sampling, specifications, and testing and with the organization, documentation, and release procedures. This regulation ensures that the necessary and relevant tests are actually carried out and that raw materials and packaging materials are not released for use, nor products released for sale, until their quality has been judged to be satisfactory. Quality control is not confined to laboratory operations but must be incorporated into all activities and decisions concerning the quality of the product.

Although manufacturing and quality control personnel share the common goal of assuring that high-quality drugs are fabricated, their interests may sometimes conflict in the short run as decisions are made that will affect a company's output. For this reason, an objective and accountable quality control process can be achieved most effectively by establishing an independent quality control department. The independence of quality control from manufacturing is considered fundamental. The rationale for the requirement that the quality control department be supervised by qualified personnel is outlined under Regulation C.02.006.

(Regulation C.02.014) The responsibility for the approval of all raw materials, packaging materials and finished products is vested in the quality control department. It is very important that adequate controls be exercised by this department in order to guarantee the quality of the end product.

To maintain this level of quality, it is also important to examine all returned drugs and to give special attention to reprocessed drugs.

(Regulation C.02.015) Pharmaceutical processes and products must be designed and developed taking GMP requirements into account. Production procedures and other control operations are independently examined by the quality control department. Proper storage, transportation, and distribution of materials and products minimize any risk to their quality. Complaints may indicate problems related to quality. By tracing their causes, one can determine which corrective measures should be taken to prevent recurrence. Having tests carried out by a competent laboratory provides assurance that test results are genuine and accurate.

Written agreements for consultants and contract laboratories describe the education, training, and experience of their personnel and the type of services provided and are available for examination and inspection. Records of the activities contracted are maintained.

Examples of Interpretation:
a) A person responsible for making decisions concerning quality control requirements of the fabricator, packager/labeller, distributor, importer, and wholesaler is on site or fully accessible to the quality control department and has adequate knowledge of on-site operations to fulfill the responsibilities of the position.
b) The quality control department has access to adequate facilities, trained personnel, and equipment in order to fulfill its duties and responsibilities.
c) Approved written procedures are available for sampling, inspecting, and testing raw materials,

packaging materials, in-process drugs, bulk drugs, and finished products.

d) The quality control department ensures that raw materials and packaging materials are quarantined, sampled, tested, and released prior to their use in the fabrication or packaging/labelling of a drug.

e) Establishing a change control system to provide the mechanisms for ongoing process optimization and for assuring a continuing state of control. All changes are properly documented, evaluated, and approved by the quality control department and are identified with the appropriate effective date. Any significant change may necessitate re-validation.

f) Computerized systems are validated, and spreadsheets are qualified.

g) Out of Specification (OOS) test results are investigated to determine the cause of the OOS.

(viii) Packaging Material Testing (Regulation C.02.016)
Rationale: Where a drug product is presented in an inadequate package, the entire effort put into the initial research, product development and manufacturing control is wasted. Drug quality is directly dependent on packaging quality. In many cases (e.g., metered-dose aerosols), packaging quality is critical to the overall performance and effectiveness of the drug product. Faults in the packaging and labelling of a drug product continue to be a cause of drug recalls. Packaging materials are required to be tested or examined prior to their use in a packaging operation to ensure that materials of acceptable quality are used in the packaging of drugs.

(Regulation C.02.017) Regulation C.02.017 outlines options as to when the testing or examination prescribed by Regulation C.02.016 is carried out. As with raw materials, the purchase of packaging materials is an important operation that involves personnel who have thorough knowledge of the packaging materials and vendor. Packaging materials originate only from vendors named in the relevant specifications. It is of benefit that all aspects of the production and control of packaging materials be discussed between the manufacturer and the vendor. Particular attention is paid to printed packaging materials; labels are examined or tested after receipt on the premises of the person who packages a drug.

Examples of Interpretation:
a) Each packaging material used in the packaging/labelling of a drug is covered by specifications.

b) Where applicable, specifications are of pharmacopoeial or equivalent status and are in compliance with the marketing authorization.

c) The adequacy of test or examination methods that are not of pharmacopoeial or equivalent status is established and documented.

d) Only packaging materials released by the quality control department are used in packaging/labelling.

e) Outdated or obsolete packaging material is adequately segregated until its disposition.

f) The testing or examination of the packaging material is performed on a sample taken after their receipt on the premises of the person that packages the drug unless the vendor is certified. A packaging material vendor certification program, if employed, is documented in a standard operating procedure.

(ix) Finished Product Testing (Regulation C.02.018)
Rationale: Finished product tests complement the controls employed during the manufacturing process. It is the responsibility of each fabricator, packager/labeller, distributor, and importer to have adequate specifications and test methods that will help ensure that each drug sold is safe and meets the standard under which it is represented.

Example of Interpretation:
a) Written specifications are approved by the person in charge of the quality control department.

b) Test methods are validated, and the results of such validation studies are documented. Method transfer studies are conducted when applicable.

c) All tests are performed according to the approved specifications.

d) Any lot or batch of a drug that does not comply with specifications is quarantined pending final disposition and is not made available for sale.

(x) Records (Regulation C.02.020)
Rationale: Good documentation is an essential part of the quality assurance system and should therefore be related to all aspects of GMP. Its aims are to define the specifications for all materials and methods of fabrication, packaging/labelling, and control; to ensure that the quality control department has all the information necessary to decide whether or not to release a batch of a drug for sale; and to provide an audit trail that will permit investigation of the history of any batch that is suspected to be defective.

Evidence that drugs have been fabricated and packaged/labelled under prescribed conditions can be maintained only after developing adequate record systems. The information and evidence should provide assurance that imported drugs are fabricated and packaged/labelled in a like manner to those produced in Canada.

Examples of Interpretation:

For all sections of Good Manufacturing Practices guidelines, standard operating procedures (SOPs) are retained for reference and inspection. These SOPs are regularly reviewed and kept up to date by qualified personnel. The reasons for any revisions are documented. A system is in place to ensure that only current SOPs are in use. Records of SOPs for all computer and automated systems are retained where appropriate.

All relevant GMP documents (such as associated records of actions taken or conclusions reached) and SOPs are approved, signed, and dated by the quality control department. Documents are not altered without the approval of the quality control department. Any alteration made to a document is signed and dated; the alteration permits the reading of the original information. Where appropriate, the reason for the change is recorded.

(xi) Samples (Regulation C.02.025, C.02.026)

Rationale: These requirements help ensure that responsible officials at the establishment and Health Canada have ready access to those samples that are essential for re-examination should a product quality concern arise.

Examples of Interpretation:
a) A sample of each lot or batch of a raw material (including both active and inactive ingredients), is retained by the fabricator of the drug.
b) In determining the size of sample to be maintained, it is to be kept in mind that Health Canada needs at least enough of the material to carry out tests to determine whether the drug or the raw material complies with its specifications.

(xii) Stability (Regulation C.02.027, C.02.28)

Rationale: The purpose of the written stability program is to ascertain the normal shelf life of the products that is to determine how long the products can be expected to remain within specifications under recommended storage conditions. The requirements for the stability studies (primary and commitment batches) are outlined in the various Health Canada, ICH, and Veterinary International Conference on Harmonisation (VICH) Guidelines. Each packaged dosage form must be covered by a sufficient amount of data to support its shelf life in its trade package.

Examples of Interpretation:
a) The stability of the drug is determined prior to marketing and prior to adoption of significant changes in formulation, fabrication procedures, or packaging materials that may affect the shelf life of the drug.
   i. Accelerated stability data are considered to be preliminary information only. The accelerated data are supported by long term testing. When the shelf-life is assigned based on accelerated data and extrapolated long-term data, it should be verified by additional long term stability data as these data become available.
   ii. Stability studies are carried out on the drug in each package type in which it is to be sold in Canada.
b) A continuing stability program is implemented to ensure compliance with the approved shelf life specifications. A protocol is available and is implemented for each drug marketed in Canada. A summary of all the data generated, including the evaluation and the conclusions of the study, is prepared.

(xiii) Sterile Products (Regulation C.02.029)

Rationale: Sterile drugs are susceptible to particulate, pyrogenic and microbiological contamination. Due to the health hazard associated with the use of contaminated sterile products, special precautions are required in the production of these products. The skill, training, and competency of all personnel involved are critical.

Quality assurance is important and the production must follow carefully established and validated methods of preparation and sterilization.

Examples of Interpretation:
a) All aqueous-based sterile products must be subjected to terminal steam sterilization, with the following exceptions:
   • Instances where terminal steam sterilization is not practicable (e.g., where the sterilization process would cause product or packaging degradation). The rationale for the departure from the standard is fully evaluated and documented; and
   • Aseptic processes that exclude human intervention (e.g., robotics, form-fill-seal, and barrier systems) may be employed in lieu of terminal sterilization, provided that the data developed demonstrate an acceptable level of sterility assurance. Any such methods introduced are fully validated, taking into account all critical factors of the technology used as well as the routine monitoring to be carried out.
b) Parenterals sterilized by filtration, are formulated in an environment with a minimum classification

of a Grade C. Sterile filtration requires a minimum filter rating of 0.2 µm. The integrity of the filter is verified before and after use by an appropriate method such as a bubble point, diffusion or pressure hold tests.
c) Access to clean and aseptic areas is provided only through air-locks.
d) The filtered air supply for clean and aseptic areas is designed to provide a fabrication environment that meets the required grade classifications. Under all operational conditions, a positive pressure of filtered airflow is maintained in relation to surrounding areas of a lower grade."

Internationally Harmonized Requirements for Batch Certification

GMP guidelines' Appendix A provides an explanatory note for internationally harmonized requirements of batch certification falling within the MRAs' framework.

The internationally harmonized requirements for a drug or medicinal product's batch certificate content also are provided in this appendix. The batch importer is to receive and maintain the batch certificate the fabricator or manufacturer issued. This manufacturer certification of each batch's conformity is essential to exempt the importer from re-control (re-analysis). Upon request, the batch certificate must be readily available to the importing country's regulatory authority.

Each batch shipped between countries with an MRA in force must be accompanied by the exporting country's fabricator or manufacturer batch certificate. This certificate will be issued after a full qualitative and quantitative analysis of all active and other relevant constituents to ensure the product's quality complies with the importing country's marketing authorization requirements.

Clinical Trial Material GMPs

Drug products in development and used for clinical trial purposes also are required to be manufactured under GMP conditions. Because drugs in development do not have fully defined and validated manufacturing processes, there are certain modifications to GMP guidelines' applicability for clinical trial material manufacture. *FDR* Section C.05.010*(j)* requires the sponsor to ensure drugs for use in clinical trials are manufactured, handled and stored in accordance with the applicable GMP requirements referenced in Divisions 2–4, except Sections C.02.019, C.02.025 and C.02.026 (which are mentioned above). Clinical trial sponsors shall ensure imported drugs are fabricated, packaged and labelled in accordance with these requirements.

Annex 13 to the Current Edition of the Good Manufacturing Practices Guidelines Drugs Used in Clinical Trials (GUI-0036) provides more detailed guidance relevant to the fabrication, packaging and labelling of drugs intended for use in human clinical trials, including the placebo and comparator product.

Veterinary Drug Product GMPs

Although *FDR's* rationale and the quality management principles outlined in the GMP guidelines (GUI-0001) apply to all veterinary drugs, it is recognized that some of the interpretations provided in the GMP guidelines may not always be applicable or appropriate in certain situations. For example, the requirements for fabrication premises for veterinary drugs containing penicillin, or those for manufacturing drug premixes, have certain requirements that differ from drugs manufactured for human use. For such types of veterinary drugs, feed ingredients are used in large quantities and invariably contain some light, powdery, flour-like material, which may lead to extremely dusty conditions. This problem can be controlled with sophisticated dust extraction equipment. However, the main concern in drug premix production is the potential for cross-contamination. Also, drug premix production methods and handling characteristics do not necessarily call for the same complex techniques requiring highly skilled production and control staff as other veterinary drugs. For this reason, Health Canada has issued *Guidance Document Annex 4 to the Current Edition of the Good Manufacturing Practices Guidelines—Veterinary Drugs* (GUI-0012). Only those interpretations that differ from the ones included in the GMP guidelines (GUI-0001) are contained in this annex. Below are two examples of modified interpretation from the Annex 4 guidance for veterinary drugs for the corresponding section in the GMP guidelines for premises (C.02.004):

1. For all veterinary drug products except drugs and drug premixes:
    In the case of facilities producing other veterinary drugs, campaign production of veterinary drugs containing penicillin is considered acceptable, provided the following conditions are met:
    - non-penicillin drug products for human use are not fabricated, packaged, labelled or stored in the same facility
    - validated decontamination and cleaning procedures are in place to minimize any risk of cross-contamination
2. For drug premixes:
    Work areas used for the production or storage of drug premixes or components thereof shall not be used for, and shall be physically separated from, work areas used for the manufacture and storage of fertilizers, herbicides, insecticides, fungicides, rodenticides and other pesticides.

GMPs for Active Pharmaceutical Ingredients

The extension of GMPs to Active Pharmaceutical Ingredients (APIs) has increasingly been recognized as a necessary element in ensuring the overall quality and consistency of marketed drug products. Health Canada, like its international regulatory counterparts, adopted the ICH Q7 guidance initially on a voluntary basis and has now implemented internationally aligned regulatory GMP requirements for APIs destined for human use.

The ICH Q7 guidance provides a framework for a quality management system that covers APIs (or AIs) manufactured by chemical synthesis, extraction, cell culture/fermentation, recovery from natural sources or any combination of these processes. Conceptually, the GMPs for APIs are similar to the GMPs for drug products described previously. ICH Q7 is intended to help ensure APIs meet the requirements for quality and purity that they purport to possess.

While the scope of the ICH Q7 guidance is limited to APIs that will be used in the manufacture of human use pharmaceuticals by virtue of ICH's mandate, the principles and practices described also have relevance to APIs for veterinary use.

Health Canada issued *Good Manufacturing Practices (GMP) Guidelines for Active Pharmaceutical Ingredients (APIs)—(GUI-0104)* on 6 December 2013. Supplier qualification and management through on-site audits, quality assurance agreements and compliance with Table A are mandatory for importation of API from foreign suppliers.

Requirements C.02.027 and C.02.028 (described below) are unique to Canada only and are required in addition to ICH Q7 requirements.

Stability

Section C.02.027 (2): Every fabricator and importer of an active ingredient shall establish the period during which each drug in the package in which it is sold will comply with the specifications for that drug.

Section C.02.028 (2): Every fabricator and importer of an active ingredient shall monitor, by means of a continuing program, the stability of the drug in the package in which it is sold.

GMP Inspections

Canadian establishments involved in the fabrication, packaging, labelling, testing, distribution, importation or wholesaling of listed drugs (*FDR* Section C.01A.008) must comply with the requirements of *FDR* Division 2 (GMP). Compliance is assessed by conducting inspections of these establishments based on a priority ranking scale and a risk-based approach. HPFBI has established the following targets for inspection cycles:
- fabricator, packager, labeller and testing laboratory: 24 months
- importer, distributor and wholesaler: 36 months

These inspections are the basis for the issuance of Establishment Licences (ELs) to domestic sites according to the requirements described in *FDR* Division 1A. New establishments applying for an EL must be ready for an inspection when submitting their applications.

All GMP observations are based on the current GMP guidelines, and a risk is assigned to each observation according to *Risk Classification of GMP Observations* (GUI-0023). New (GUI-0023) is effective immediately and will provide a better understanding of how Health Canada currently assigns the risk rating to GMP inspection findings and the compliance rating for a GMP inspection. There are important changes in this guide related to lower-risk products and activities.

Inspection results are used for issuing ELs and Certificates of Compliance (exchanged in the MRA framework). Either a C rating (recommended for the continuation or issuance of the Establishment Licence) or NC rating (not recommended for the continuation or issuance of the Establishment Licence) is assigned following the inspection.

The inspector assigns a risk classification to each observation: 1 is "critical," 2 is "major" and 3 is "other."
- Critical observation (Risk 1)—describes a situation likely to result in a product with an immediate or latent health risk, or that involves fraud, misrepresentation or process, product or data falsification
- Major observation (Risk 2)—describes a situation that may produce a drug not consistently meeting its marketing authorization (Some Risk 2 observations may be upgraded to Risk 1, e.g., in cases where the issue identified is not isolated to one area or system.)
- Other observation (Risk 3)—describes a situation that is neither critical nor major, but is a departure from the GMPs (Any Risk 3 observation could be upgraded to Risk 2.)

Key GMP Concepts Presented
- GMPs derive their structure from the applicable *Food and Drugs Act* and *Food and Drug Regulations'* sections and specific guidelines associated with drug manufacturing activities.
- GMPs provide a quality management system (QMS) framework for drug manufacture. The QMS is comprised of different elements, with specific requirements that work together to ensure quality and purity. These elements include

premises, equipment, personnel, sanitation, raw material testing, manufacturing control, quality control, packaging material testing, finished product testing, records, samples, stability and requirements for sterile products.
- An Establishment Licence is required to fabricate, package, label, distribute, import or wholesale a drug or to perform tests; all these activities must comply with the applicable GMPs.
- Finished product importers must include API manufacturing sites in the Table A Annex.
- Batch certification requirements are harmonized between Canada and several countries through Mutual Recognition Agreements. These ensure product quality complies with the importing country's marketing authorization requirements.
- GMPs for manufacture of both clinical trial materials for human use and veterinary products include certain modifications of the GMPs for the manufacture of drugs for human use.
- GMPs for APIs used in the manufacture of drug products are required to conform to the ICH Q7 guidance on APIs. Health Canada issued *Good Manufacturing Practices (GMP) Guidelines for Active Pharmaceutical Ingredients (APIs)* (GUI-0104) on 6 December 2013. The Health Canada website contains current information.
- To ensure GMP compliance, Health Canada has a GMP inspection program that rates establishments as able to continue or not continue a facility's Establishment Licence.

Reference
1. *Good Manufacturing Practices Guide for Drug Products* (GUI-0001). Health Canada website. https://www.canada.ca/en/health-canada/services/drugs-health-products/compliance-enforcement/good-manufacturing-practices/guidance-documents/gmp-guidelines-0001.html. Accessed 9 April 2018.
2. *Risk classification guide for drug good manufacturing practices observations* (GUI-0023)—Summary. Health Canada website. https://www.canada.ca/en/health-canada/services/drugs-health-products/compliance-enforcement/good-manufacturing-practices/guidance-documents/risk-classification-drug-gmp-observations-0023.html. Accessed 9 April 2018.
3. *Annex 1 to the Good Manufacturing Practices Guide—Manufacture of Sterile Drugs*—(GUI-0119). Health Canada website. https://www.canada.ca/en/health-canada/services/drugs-health-products/compliance-enforcement/good-manufacturing-practices/guidance-documents/gmp-guidelines-annex-1-manufacture-sterile-drugs-0119.html. Accessed 9 April 2018.

Recommended Reading
Drug Establishment Good Manufacturing Practices—Pre-Application Package (Importers, Distributors and Wholesalers)
Drug Establishment Licence Application: Forms and Instructions (FRM-0033)
Drug Good Manufacturing Practices (GMP) and Establishment Licencing (EL) Enforcement Directive (POL-0004)
GMP Inspection Policy for Canadian Drug Establishments (POL-0011)
Compliance and Enforcement Policy (POL-0001)
Guidance on Evidence to Demonstrate Drug GMP Compliance of Foreign Sites (GUI-0080)
Good Manufacturing Practices—Audit Report Form (FRM-0211)
Good Manufacturing Practices—Request for an Inspection of a Foreign Site Form (FRM-0213)
Good Manufacturing Practices—Foreign Site Inspection Services Agreement Form (FRM-0214)
Annex 1 to the Current Edition of the Good Manufacturing Practices Guidelines—Selected Category IV Monograph Drugs (GUI-0066)
PIC/S Annex 11: Computerised Systems
ICH Q2(R1): Validation of Analytical Procedures: Text and Methodology
Guidelines for Temperature Control of Drug Products during Storage and Transportation (GUI-0069)
Medical Devices Regulations (SOR/98-282)
Recall Policy (POL-0016)

Chapter 5

New Drug Submission Process

Updated by Susanne Picard, MSc and Janice Weiler

OBJECTIVES

❑ Gain an overview of the New Drug Submission (NDS) process.

❑ Understand the submission process in the electronic Common Technical Document (eCTD) format.

❑ Understand the criteria for Priority Review status.

❑ Understand the criteria for a Notice of Compliance with Conditions.

REGULATIONS AND GUIDELINES COVERED IN THIS CHAPTER

❑ *Food and Drugs Act (F&DA)*

❑ *Food and Drug Regulations (FDR)*, Division 8, Part C

❑ International Council on Harmonisation (ICH) Guidelines

❑ *Guidance Document: Preparation of Drug Regulatory Activities in the Common Technical Document (CTD) Format* (22 June 2012)

❑ *Guidance for Industry: Management of Drug Submissions* (19 December 2013)

❑ *Guidance for Industry: Reconsideration of Decisions Issued for Human Drug Submissions* (1 April 2015)

❑ *Guidance Document: Preparation of Drug Regulatory Activities in the Electronic Common Technical Document Format* (14 May 2015)

❑ *Guidance Document Creation of the Canadian Module 1 Backbone* (30 September 2012)

❑ *Guidance on Evidence to Demonstrate Drug GMP Compliance of Foreign Sites (GUI-0080)* (1 August 2009)

❑ *Guidance Document: Fees for the Review of Drug Submissions and Applications* (20 November 2015)

❑ *Notice: Submission Filing Requirements: Good Manufacturing Practices (GMP)/Establishment Licences (EL)* (10 February 2017)

❑ *Guidance for Industry: Priority Review of Drug Submissions* (18 December 2008)

❑ *Policy: Priority Review of Drug Submissions* (18 December 2008)

❑ *Guidance for Industry: Notice of Compliance with Conditions* (16 September 2016)

❑ *Guidance Document: Review of Drug Brand Names* (13 June 2015)

Regulatory Affairs Professionals Society

- *Guidance Document: Data Protection under C.08.004.1 of the Food and Drug Regulations* (16 May 2017)
- *Guidance Document: Patented Medicines (Notice of Compliance) Regulations* (16 April 2012)
- *Guidance Document: Submission of Risk Management Plans and Follow-up Commitments* (26 June 2015)
- *Guidance Document: Drug Submissions Relying on Third-Party Data (Literature and Market Experience)* (1 May 2015)
- *Guidance Document: Product Monograph* (9 June 2017)
- *Guidance Document: Labelling of Pharmaceutical Drugs for Human Use* (13 June 2015)
- *Good Label and Package Practices Guide for Prescription Drugs* (30 June 2016)
- *Guidance Document: Questions and Answers: Plain Language Labelling Regulations* (8 September 2016)
- *Guidance Document: Certified Product Information Document—Chemical Entities (CPID-CE)* (30 January 2018)
- *Guidance Document: Quality (Chemistry and Manufacturing) Guidance: New Drug Submissions (NDSs) and Abbreviated New Drug Submissions (ANDSs)* (1 January 2018)
- *Guidance Document: ADDENDUM—Quality (Chemistry and Manufacturing) Guidance: Questions and Answers* (1 January 2018)
- *Guidance for Industry: Preparation of the Quality Information for Drug Submissions in the CTD Format: Conventional Biotherapeutics* (25 May 2004)
- *Guidance for Industry: Preparation of the Quality Information for Drug Submissions in the CTD Format: Biotechnological/Biological (Biotech) Products* (25 May 2004)
- *Guidance for Industry: Harmonized Requirements for the Licensing of Vaccines and Guidelines for the Preparation of an Application* (6 June 2016)
- *Guidance for Industry: Preparation of the Quality Information for Drug Submissions in the CTD Format: Blood Products* (25 May 2004)

Introduction

The *Food and Drugs Act* (*F&DA*), Section 2, defines a drug as:
"Drug" includes any substance or mixture of substances manufactured, sold or represented for use in
   a. the diagnosis, treatment, mitigation or prevention of a disease, disorder or abnormal physical state, or its symptoms, in human beings or animals
   b. restoring, correcting or modifying organic functions in human beings or animals, or
   c. disinfection in premises in which food is manufactured, prepared or kept

A Drug Identification Number (DIN) is an eight-digit numeric code assigned to each drug product approved under the *F&DA* and its regulations, except Schedule C drugs (radiopharmaceuticals). A DIN uniquely identifies the following
- product information:
- manufacturer
- product name
- active ingredient(s)
- active ingredient(s) strength(s)
- pharmaceutical form
- route of administration

In accordance with the *Food and Drug Regulations* (*FDR*) C.01.014, no manufacturer can sell a drug in dosage form unless a DIN has been assigned, or the DIN has not been previously cancelled pursuant to Section C.01.014.6.

In Canada, drug products are divided into "new drugs" and "old drugs" and regulated under either Division 8 or Division 1 of the regulations, respectively.

A new drug is defined in *FDR* Section C.08.001 as:
"New Drug" means a drug, other than a veterinary health product,
   a. that contains or consists of a substance, whether as an active or inactive ingredient, carrier, coating, excipient, menstruum or other component, that has not been sold as a drug in Canada for sufficient time and in sufficient quantity to establish in Canada the safety and effectiveness of that substance for use as a drug;
   b. that is a combination of two or more drugs, with or without other ingredients, and that has not been sold in that combination or in the proportion in which those drugs are combined in that drug, for sufficient time and in sufficient quantity

to establish in Canada the safety and effectiveness of that combination and proportion for use as a drug; or

c. with respect to which the manufacturer prescribes, recommends, proposes or claims a use as a drug, or a condition of use as a drug, including dosage, route of administration or duration of action, and that has not been sold for that use or condition of use in Canada for sufficient time and in sufficient quantity to establish in Canada the safety and effectiveness of that use or condition of use of that drug.

Old drugs (i.e., drugs that are not on the Listing of Drugs Regulated as New Drugs or have not been moved from old drug status by Health Canada) are registered for sale through a DIN. Old drugs are approved through the DIN application process.

A New Drug Submission (NDS) is an application to the Therapeutic Products Directorate (TPD) or to the Biologics and Genetic Therapies Directorate (BGTD) of Health Canada, the Canadian federal authority that regulates pharmaceutical drugs and medical devices for human use and grants marketing approval for a new drug. To be granted market authorization, a manufacturer must present substantive scientific evidence of a product's safety, efficacy and quality (chemistry and manufacturing) as required by the act and its regulations.

International Council on Harmonisation (ICH) Guidances

ICH's founding and standing regulatory members are the EU, US, Japan, Canada and Switzerland. Through the ICH process, considerable harmonization has been achieved in efficacy, safety and quality (chemistry and manufacturing) technical requirements for the registration of pharmaceuticals for human use. The ICH guideline, *The Common Technical Document (CTD) for the Registration of Pharmaceuticals for Human Use (M4)*, primarily addresses information organization for new pharmaceutical registration applications (including biotechnology-derived products). The CTD is divided into five modules: Module 1 contains region-specific information, and Modules 2–5 contain common clinical, nonclinical and chemistry and manufacturing information with limited regional variation. The organization of these modules is described in the M4Q, M4S and M4E guidelines, which can be found on the ICH website, www.ich.org, as well as in the relevant Canadian guidances.

Pre-NDS Meetings With Health Canada

Providing strategic drug development advice is a key responsibility of regulatory personnel. Canada-specific requirements can be overlooked in the global environment. Proactively meeting with Health Canada to discuss the drug development program at both the preclinical trial application (CTA) and pre-NDS stages is critical for informing Health Canada of the global development strategy and addressing specific national requirements.

It cannot be presumed a drug submission approved in the EU and/or US will be approvable in Canada or vice versa. Sponsors, therefore, are encouraged to request a meeting with Health Canada before filing NDS applications. Holding a pre-NDS meeting is advantageous for several reasons. In particular, this meeting provides an opportunity for Health Canada to become familiar with the sponsor and the forthcoming submission and provides a forum to discuss the data in the submission to facilitate its review. This allows the sponsor to ascertain whether the reviewers have any concerns (e.g., with the drug class, data adequacy or specific requirements in special populations) that the NDS must address. The sponsor then may address these concerns before filing the submission to facilitate the drug's review and approval process. During this meeting, the sponsor also may discuss the submission's potential eligibility for a Priority Review or consideration for a Notice of Compliance with conditions (NOC/c).

For more information on presubmission meetings, consult Section 5.1 Presubmission Meetings and Package Requirements of the *Guidance for Industry: Management of Drug Submissions*.

NDS Preparation and Submission in the CTD Format

The guidance, *Preparation of Drug Regulatory Activities in the Common Technical Document (CTD) Format*, applies to the preparation of all drug regulatory activities for human use, filed pursuant to the *FDR*, including Clinical Trial Applications (CTAs), their amendments (CTA-As) and Master Files (MFs). With this guidance, Health Canada applies a more inclusive approach for the CTD format, with documents that may be submitted only for specific regulatory activity types or upon request; therefore, many sections and subsections may not be applicable for a given regulatory activity. When no information is required in a specific section or subsection, that section or subsection should be omitted. The numbering of an omitted section should not be reused for another section.

The guidance, *Preparation of Drug Regulatory Activities in the Common Technical Document (CTD) Format*, is to be used to prepare drug submissions for human use filed pursuant to *FDR* Division 8, Part C. The CTD's purpose is to provide a common format for preparing a well-structured submission according to the ICH modular framework (ICH Topic M4). This guidance helps integrate the CTD format into the Canadian drug registration framework by defining the regional administrative (Module 1) and general filing requirements.

Currently, CTD use is mandatory for original filings and subsequent filings (NDS, abbreviated NDS (ANDS), supplemental NDS (SNDS), supplemental abbreviated NDS (SANDS) and notifiable change (NC)), regardless of the original submission's format.

CTD Format Structure and Content Submitted Electronically (eCTD)

The guidance documents: *Preparation of Drug Regulatory Activities in the Common Technical Document (CTD) Format* and *Preparation of Drug Regulatory Activities in the Electronic Common Technical Document Format* are to be used for submitting information in relation to drugs for human use, filed over that product's lifecycle in Canada. **Table 5-1** outlines the eCTD modular structure and main headings.

For the Canadian Module 1 format, refer to *Preparation of Drug Regulatory Activities in the Common Technical Document (CTD) Format* and *Creation of the Canadian Module 1 Backbone*.

As of 1 June 2016, Health Canada no longer accepts paper copies of transactions related to Division 8 regulatory activities. Further, on 1 January 2018, the eCTD format became mandatory for filing all NDS, SNDS, SANDS and ANDS regulatory activities for human drugs. The guidance, *Preparation of Drug Submissions in Electronic Common Technical Document Format,* defines the electronic format requirements and process and provides additional guidance on the information structure and content of the eCTD.

When possible, it is strongly recommended electronic data in eCTD format be provided via the Common Electronic Submissions Gateway (CESG). For more information, see Health Canada's *Frequently Asked Questions—Common Electronic Submissions Gateway*.

When an eCTD regulatory activity or transaction is not submitted via the CESG, the following media formats are acceptable:
- Compact Disc-Recordable (CD-R) conforming to the Joliet specification
- Digital Versatile Disc-Random Access Memory (DVD-RAM) Universal Disc Format (UDF) standard
- Single- and dual-layer Recordable Digital Versatile Discs
- Single- and dual-layer Blu-ray discs
- Universal Serial Bus (USB) 2.0 or 3.0 drive
- Portable External Hard Drive with USB 2.0 or 3.0 interface

The package should include the paper cover letter and all documents on a single disc or drive. Duplicate copies are not required.

For detailed information on the content of Modules 2–5, refer to the appropriate ICH guidance cited below.
- Module 3 is discussed in greater detail in *The Common Technical Document for the Registration of Pharmaceuticals for Human Use: Quality—M4Q, Quality Overall Summary of Module 2. Module 3: Quality.*
- Safety is addressed in *The Common Technical Document for the Registration of Pharmaceuticals for Human Use: Safety, M4S Nonclinical Overview and Nonclinical Summary of Module 2, Organisation of Module 4.*
- Efficacy is addressed in *The Common Technical Document for the Registration of Pharmaceuticals for Human Use: Efficacy—M4E. Clinical Overview and Clinical Summary of Module 2. Module 5: Clinical Study Reports.*

Every effort should be made to complete all CTD sections as outlined. Depending on the nature of the drug product's development, this may not always be possible. In some instances, it may be possible to supplement the submission with literature data. If the data are not available, another option is to provide a sound rationale for why it is not pertinent or, if possible, to cross-reference other parts of the submission.

Module 1 Requirements

Intellectual Property Information

Drug products containing a new chemical entity are entitled to an eight-year market exclusivity period. A further six-month extension may be possible if acceptable pediatric data are submitted within the first five years of the eight-year period. Data protection eligibility also requires the generation of data supporting the medicinal ingredient's approval. Supporting information should be submitted as part of the NDS. Health Canada will conduct a preliminary assessment while the drug is under review and notify the sponsor of the outcome.

A subsequent-entry manufacturer is not allowed to file a submission for a copy of the innovative drug for the first six years of the eight-year period. For more details, refer to *Data Protection under C.08.004.1 of the FDR*.

For products with eligible patents, patent form submission with every eligible NDS and SNDS is critical. Failure to list the patents may result in the loss of rights and generic entries to the market. Eligibility requires a patent claim for a medicinal ingredient, formulation, dosage form or use of the medicinal ingredient. For more details, refer to Chapter 8 and *Patented Medicines (Notice of Compliance) Regulations*.

Table 5-1. Presentation of Information in the Common Technical Document (CTD) Format

Module 1: Administrative and Product Information	Binder/Label Colour	Number of Copies
1.0 Correspondence	Red	1*
1.1 Table of Contents (Modules 1 to 5)		
1.2 Administrative Information		
1.3 Product Information		
1.4 Health Canada Summaries		
1.5 Environmental Assessment Statement		
1.6 Regional Clinical Information		
1.7 Clinical Trial Application and Clinical Trial Application- Amendment Specific Requirements		
1.A Appendix		
Module 2: Common Technical Document (CTD) Summaries	Yellow	1*
2.1 CTD Table of Contents (Modules 2 to 5)		
2.2 CTD Introduction		
2.3 Quality Overall Summary		
2.4 Nonclinical Overview		
2.5 Clinical Overview		
2.6 Nonclinical Written and Tabulated Summaries		
2.7 Clinical Summary		
Module 3: Quality	Blue	1*
3.1 Table of Contents of Module 3		
3.2 Body of Data		
3.3 Literature References		
Module 4: Nonclinical Study Reports	Green	1
4.1 Table of Contents of Module 4		
4.2 Study Reports		
4.3 Literature References		
Module 5: Clinical Study Reports	Black	1
5.1 Table of Contents of Module 5		
5.2 Tabular Listing of All Clinical Studies		
5.3 Clinical Study Reports		
5.4 Literature References		

*For combination products that require a joint review, an additional copy of Modules 1, 2, and 3 is required.
Source: Table 1 of the Guidance Document: Preparation of Drug Regulatory Activities in the Common Technical Document (CTD) Format

GMP Compliance

On 10 February 2017, TPD clarified its requirements for evidence of Good Manufacturing Practices (GMPs) for drug submissions. Evidence of GMP compliance must be included in Module 1 for the submission to be accepted for review.

For drug submission purposes, "evidence of GMP compliance" for facilities in which a specific activity occurs would include:

- a valid Health Canada Drug Establishment Licence (DEL)
- a current GMP compliance rating issued by the HPFB Inspectorate (HPFBI)
- evidence of a signed Quality Agreement with the third party selected for GMP activities

Eligible submissions are those where:
1. All required buildings and activities are listed on the current DEL.

2. A site has a GMP compliance rating in Canada for the required activities and dosage form(s).
3. A complete DEL application has been filed with the minister for any new buildings and activities.

Where a DEL application is needed, the sponsor may file the drug submission 90 days after the minister issues the DEL Acknowledgment of Application Acceptance. Drug submissions that do not meet the requirements listed above will be issued a screening rejection letter.

In addition, where any site listed in a drug submission is considered by Health Canada to be noncompliant for GMP, a screening rejection letter will be issued.

Likewise, it is recommended Master File(s) (MFs) be submitted to Health Canada no more than one year but no less than two months prior to the NDS filling. For Type I and IV MFs (drug substance and drug product), the dossier must include "Open" and "Restricted" parts. The sponsor must include a copy of the Open part in the NDS, along with the appropriate letter of access (LoA). The MF owner also must send a copy of the LoA directly to Health Canada.

Refer to Chapter 4, GUI-0080, *Guidance on Evidence to Demonstrate Drug GMP Compliance of Foreign Sites* and *Guidance Document—Master Files (MFs)—Procedure and Administrative Requirements.*

International Information

The provision of foreign review reports in an NDS is not mandatory. However, they usually are requested at screening if not included within the submission. Review reports from the US Food and Drug Administration (FDA) and the European Medicines Agency (EMA) generally are preferred. However, review reports from other regulatory authorities also may be considered, e.g., Australia's Therapeutic Goods Administration (TGA) and Switzerland's Swissmedic.

Also, in the Screening Acceptance letter, Health Canada usually requests the sponsor to share foreign regulatory agency review questions and the answers provided during the NDS review. Consequently, if Health Canada has questions that already have been addressed in a response to questions from a foreign agency, it will likely reduce the number of questions it raises with the sponsor accordingly.

Product Monograph

The product monograph (PM) is a critical part of the NDS. Its purpose is to provide information for the new drug's safe and effective use and also to serve as a standard for all promotion and advertising materials. Templates are available for standard pharmaceuticals, biologicals and NOC/c products. For more details, refer to Chapter 12 and the guidance, *Product Monograph*.

Labelling

Full colour, full-size mock-ups of the inner and outer labels and packages and package insert(s) must be provided with the NDS. Bilingual requirements (French and English) must also be taken into consideration. For more details, refer to Chapter 12 and *Labelling of Pharmaceutical Drugs for Human Use, Good Label and Package Practices Guide for Prescription Drugs,* and *Guidance Document Questions and Answers: Plain Language Labelling Regulations.*

The provision of approved foreign labelling is encouraged by Health Canada.

Certified Product Information Document

The certified product information document (CPID) is a template-based, concise summary of the drug substance and drug product's key quality information. Separate templates are available for pharmaceuticals and biologicals. The information contained in the CPID must be cross-referenced to the appropriate modules (e.g., 2.3 Quality Overall Summary and/or Module 3). For more details, refer to Chapter 9 and *Draft Guidance Document: Certified Product Information Document- Chemical Entities (CPID-CE), Preparation of the Quality Information for Drug Submissions in the CTD Format: Conventional Biotherapeutic Products, Preparation of the Quality Information for Drug Submissions in the CTD Format: Biotechnological/Biological (Biotech) Products,* and *Harmonized Requirements for the Licensing of Vaccines and Guidelines for the Preparation of an Application and Preparation of the Quality Information for Drug Submissions in the CTD Format: Blood Products.*

Look-Alike/Sound-Alike Assessment

Brand names are reviewed by Health Canada to determine whether they could be misleading or confused with another approved product available in Canada. For submissions with a target review period of at least 180 days, two brand names may be submitted, and the brand name with priority must be identified. For submissions with a target review period of less than 180 days, only one brand name may be submitted.

The initial review is to be completed within 90 days of the submission being accepted (i.e., screening acceptance). A second review is to be conducted 30 days prior to approval to ensure no other products with potentially confusing brand names have been approved since the first review. If the first brand name is not acceptable, Health Canada will provide a timeframe for a second brand name to be submitted and at least 90 days prior to the review target. If an acceptable brand name is not submitted, the NOC/DIN will be issued with the proper or common name.

Although a brand name assessment may have been completed for another jurisdiction, an additional assessment will be required for Canada to confirm the foreign information's relevance in the Canadian context. For more details, refer to *Review of Drug Brand Names*.

Risk Management Plan
The NDS should include a risk management plan (RMP). The EU format is acceptable, as are others that include all essential EU RMP elements. A Canada-specific RMP may be provided, or relevant Canadian information may be incorporated into an RMP prepared for another jurisdiction. Canada-specific information should include, but is not limited to: epidemiology, patient exposure, regional, rare genetic disorders. For more details, refer to Chapter 7 and *Submission of Risk Management Plans and Follow-up Commitments*.

Environmental Assessment
Since September 2001, all drug products including active ingredients and excipients have been subject to the *Canadian Environmental Protection Act* (*CEPA*) and the *New Substances Notification Regulations* (*NSNR*). An environmental assessment statement is required for new substances in *F&DA*-regulated products. A New Substances Notification package is submitted to Environment Canada in respect of new ingredients that are not on the Domestic Substances List (DSL).

Company Core Data Sheets
Core data sheets contain the minimum information to be included in the product labelling and should be included in the NDS.

NDS Submission Types and Review Process

Submission Types
NDSs may be filed as one of three types: standard, priority review or advance consideration Notice of Compliance with conditions (NOC/c).

Review Process
Prior to filing the first regulatory transaction for an eCTD dossier (e.g., Pre-NDS meeting request), the sponsor should request a Dossier Identifier (see section 4.5 of *Preparation of Drug Regulatory Activities in Electronic Common Technical Document Format*).

The eReview Unit will validate an eCTD dossier and advise the sponsor if the dossier is found unacceptable in this regard. When the submission is filed, a control number is assigned to the original information and material. The Office of Submissions and Intellectual Property (OSIP) will acknowledge receipt of the submission by fax or email. OSIP's target for forwarding the submission to the reviewing bureau or center is 10 calendar days.

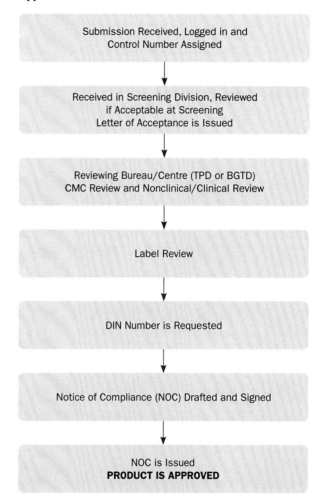

Figure 5-1. Diagram of the NDS Submission and Approval Procedure

The submission then enters screening where, if the original information and material are found acceptable, it will be accepted for review and considered a submission. All submission types are considered workload from the date of acceptance. The sponsor is notified by fax or email of the submission's acceptability. The target screening timeline is 25 days for a priority or NOC/c review and 45 days for a standard review.

If the submission is not acceptable, a Screening Deficiency Notice will be issued. The sponsor will be required to file a response within 15 (priority or NOC/c review) or 45 calendar days (standard review).

The submission then enters the review and approval process. **Figure 5-1** diagrams the NDS evaluation process for a priority or standard review. **Figure 5-2** diagrams the process for an advance consideration NOC/c NDS. Review times are all targeted. There are no regulated timeframes. Target review timelines are 300 days for a standard NDS, 200 days for an advance consideration NOC/c and 180 days

Figure 5-2. Example Boxed Text for Product Approved Under the NOC/c Policy

> "Product, indicated for < > has been issued marketing authorization with conditions, pending the results of studies to verify its clinical benefit. Patients should be advised of the nature of the authorization."

for a priority review. Information requests, referred to as "clarifaxes" or "clarimails," may be issued at any time during the review, and the sponsor must file a response within 15 calendar days.

Table 5-2 presents the target standard NDS review performance standards. For a detailed explanation of the TPD and BGTD submission management processes, consult *Guidance for Industry: Management of Drug Submissions* and *Guidance for Industry: Reconsideration of Final Decisions Issued for Human Drug Submissions*.

Notice of Deficiency

If deficiencies and/or significant omissions precluding the review are identified in a submission, a Notice of Deficiency (NOD) will be issued. For NDSs, SNDSs, SNDS–confirmatory (SNDS-C), ANDSs and SANDSs, the sponsor will be given 90 calendar days, or such time as the bureau or centre director and sponsor may agree, to submit all solicited information. The response is screened, and another review period begins (same timelines as original submission). If the response if found to contain unsolicited information, is incomplete or deficient, an NON-Withdrawal Letter will be issued.

Adding Information to an NDS Under Review

Certain unsolicited information may be submitted to Health Canada after the original application has been filed. Specifically:

- Final data (where interim data were permissible at the time of filing) may be submitted within 180 days of the original filing's receipt.
- Safety information that would enhance the product's safe use and result in contraindications, warnings and precautions and/or adverse reactions section changes to the product monograph may be submitted at any time.
- Final ongoing safety study reports previously identified in the original filing may be submitted within 180 days along with a revised product monograph.
- Foreign regulatory information may be submitted within 120 days of filing.
- Correspondence between the sponsor and other regulatory agencies is recommended to be submitted at any time.
- Expert advisory reports may be submitted after a Notice of Noncompliance (NON) is issued.
- Changes in sponsor name may be submitted at any time without prejudice.

If the submission review does not begin before the Health Canada performance target date, the sponsor has the opportunity to update the submission following receipt of an Update Notice. There are no restrictions on the type of information that may be added or removed from the original submission, such as new dosage forms, new routes of administration, new strengths and new indications.

For more information on these processes, consult Section 5.5 of *Guidance for Industry: Management of Drug Submissions* and *Guidance for Industry: Reconsideration of Final Decisions Issued for Human Drug Submissions*.

Finalization of Review

The label-negotiating period is the final review stage. Shortly after the labelling review has been completed, and the final version of the product monograph has been submitted, the drug identification number(s) (DIN) is issued, followed by the NOC.

Potential Health Canada Decisions Following an NDS Review

Notice of Compliance

This decision means the submission has been reviewed and found to be acceptable. The product will be able to proceed to marketing.

Notice of Compliance with Conditions Qualifying Notice (NOC/c-QN)

An NOC/c-QN will be issued by the responsible reviewing bureau or centre director upon completion of a review if a submission is determined to qualify for further consideration under the NOC/c policy. The NOC/c-QN will indicate the submission qualifies for an NOC under the NOC/c policy, as well as outline the additional clinical evidence to be provided in confirmatory studies, postmarket surveillance responsibilities and any requirements related to advertising, labelling or distribution. Submission review will cease upon issuance of the QN. The sponsor must submit the required information to Health Canada within 30 calendar days of NOC/c-QN receipt. The information will be subject to a 30-day review target by Health Canada. If the information is acceptable, Health Canada and the sponsor will finalize the conditions associated with issuance of the

Table 5-2. Target Review Times

Type of Submission	Content	Performance Standards (calendar days)			
		First Review		Second Review	
		Screening 1	Review 1	Screening 2 Response to NON	Review 2 Response to NON
NDS or Response to NOD	New Active Substance	45	300	45	150
	Clinical or Nonclinical Data/Chemistry and Manufacturing/Quality	45	300	45	150
	Clinical or Nonclinical Only	45	300	45	150
	Comparative Clinical, Biological or Pharmacodynamic/ Chemistry and Manufacturing/Quality	45	180	45	150
	Chemistry and Manufacturing/Quality/ Labelling	45	180	45	150
	Published Data	45	300	45	150
	Labelling Only	7	60	0	0
	Administrative	45	0	0	0

Source: Appendix 3 of the Guidance for Industry: Management of Drug Submissions

NOC/c, and the Letter of Undertaking and the NOC/c will be issued.

Notice of Noncompliance

After the comprehensive submission review is complete, a Notice of Noncompliance (NON) will be issued if the submission is deficient or incomplete in complying with *F&DA* and *FDR* requirements. The difference between an NON and an NOD is that the review of the submission is not considered complete when an NOD is issued. The deficiencies identified in all parts of the review will be specified. Only one NON per submission will be issued. Review of the submission will stop on the date of the NON.

New drug submission sponsors will be given 90 calendar days, or such time as the directorate and sponsor may agree, to submit all the solicited information. The response is screened, and a second review period begins (90 or 150 days for priority or standard review, respectively). Following the response review, if the submission is still found to be deficient, an NON-Withdrawal Letter will be issued.

Appeal (Reconsideration) Procedures

Sponsors may appeal some of these decisions by submitting a letter of intent to appeal to the bureau or centre director within 30 calendar days of receiving Health Canada's decision. If deemed eligible for reconsideration, the sponsor submits a full Request for Reconsideration package that includes relevant background information and the rationale within 45 days of the Eligibility Letter. Depending on whether the review is conducted internally or sent to a Reconsideration Panel, the process takes approximately 70 or 140 days, respectively. For more detailed information, refer to *Reconsideration of Decisions Issued for Human Drug Submissions*.

Publication of Decisions

NOC decisions are published on the Health Canada website. They also are published in the NOC database (https://health-products.canada.ca/noc-ac/index-eng.jsp) with the drug's full name, the date it was authorized, the active/medicinal ingredient, the manufacturer, the drug's therapeutic class and its DIN number.

Health Canada publishes Summary Basis of Decisions (SBD) for NDSs for New Active Substances when they are approved. An SBD is a document outlining the scientific and benefit-risk-based considerations factored into Health Canada's decision to grant a drug market authorization. The document includes regulatory, safety, efficacy and quality considerations. SBDs are published within four months of authorization.

Health Canada publishes the NOC/c Qualifying Notices with any proprietary information redacted.

Health Canada also publishes Regulatory Decision Summaries (RDS) for positive and negative decisions and for cancellations of:
- NDSs
- SNDSs for new uses

- new class IV licence applications for medical devices

Submission Fees

Submissions with fees of less than $10,000 (Can) require the payment to be provided at the time of filing. Where the fee exceeds this amount, 10% of the fee is payable upon notification that the drug submission, supplement or application has been found to be incomplete following screening. Where the submission is accepted through screening and through review, 75% of the fee is payable. Upon the review's completion (issuance of an NOC or NON), the remaining 25% of the fee must be paid. An invoice is issued via regular mail, and payment is due within 30 days of the transaction date.

The examination is considered complete with the issuance of an NOC or NON at the end of Review 1. The final invoice is billed as follows:
- NOC—payment is due within 30 days of receipt of the NOC.
- No response to NON—payment is due within 30 days of receipt of a NON withdrawal letter (NON-WD). Note, if the sponsor does not respond to an NON within a 90-day timeframe, the directorate will issue a letter withdrawing the submission (NON-WD).
- NON-WD—payment is due within 30 days of receipt of NON-WD letter.

If a sponsor has not completed its first full fiscal year on the drug submission filing date, a two-year deferral of payment is granted from that filing date.

A fee remission may be filed when the drug submission fee is greater than 10% of that drug's actual gross revenue in Canada during the fee verification period (three years from the date of first sale in Canada).

For information on submission evaluation fees, refer to *Fees for the Review of Drug Submissions and Applications*.

Priority Review

Priority Review status permits expedited approval, with a shortened review target of 180 days. Refer to *Guidance for Industry: Priority Review of Drug Submissions* and the Priority Review of Drug Submissions policy.

Scope

Priority Review may apply to an NDS or supplemental NDS (SNDS) for a serious, life-threatening or severely debilitating illness or condition when no drug is presently marketed in Canada, or when the new drug has an improved benefit-risk profile over existing therapies.

"Serious" conditions generally are associated with morbidity that has a substantial impact on day-to-day functioning. The likelihood that the disease, if left untreated, will progress from a less-severe condition to a more-serious one is taken into consideration. Examples include AIDS, Alzheimer's dementia and cancer. "Severely debilitating" conditions include many chronic illnesses, such as inflammatory bowel disease, asthma and diabetes mellitus.

Applying for Priority Review Status

Before filing a Priority Review status request, sponsors are encouraged to deliver a pre-NDS presentation to discuss the submission's potential eligibility for that status. When applying for Priority Review status, the sponsor is required to submit, in advance of the drug submission, a written request and a complete clinical assessment package. After Priority Review status has been granted, the sponsor is required to file the submission within 60 calendar days of, but not prior to, the acceptance letter's date of issuance.

If a Priority Review request is rejected, the sponsor may appeal the decision. A written letter of intent to appeal should be sent to the bureau director within 30 calendar days of the letter of rejection. The appeal will proceed as outlined in *Guidance for Industry: Management of Drug Submissions* and *Guidance for Industry: Reconsideration of Final Decisions Issued for Human Drug Submissions*. If an initial request for Priority Review status is rejected, sponsors may file a second request for the same indication, following a period of 60 days from the date of the original request, provided new supporting information is evident. Note, sponsors may only file a Request for Reconsideration of the first rejection or file a second request for Priority Review; they cannot file both.

Discontinuation of Priority Review Status

Priority Review status will be re-evaluated upon issuance of an NON or NOD. Sponsors will receive formal notification of Health Canada's decision to continue or reject Priority Review status based on whether the conditions for Priority Review status still apply.

NOC With Conditions

For more information, refer to *Guidance Document: Notice of Compliance with Conditions (NOC/c)*. The drug development, submission and review processes are arduous, expensive and time-consuming. Because Canada is under increasing pressure to provide timely access to drugs for serious, life-threatening or severely debilitating diseases or conditions (e.g., AIDS, cancer and amyotrophic lateral sclerosis), an accelerated approval mechanism has been developed to facilitate patient access to these potential therapeutic breakthroughs. To expedite the application, review and approval of these drugs, a sponsor may consider or request an NOC/c.

Initially, the available data on these types of drugs may be limited due to the small number of patients who could be eligible for clinical trials. Even with a larger patient population, data on final outcomes, such as morbidity and mortality, may be insufficient. The only data available may be on the drug's effect on surrogate markers. Surrogate markers are parameters that, when measured directly, are reasonably likely, based on available evidence, to predict a drug's effect on recognized clinical outcomes.

The benefits of the NOC/c policy are two-fold:
1. It facilitates earlier physician and patient access to the drug.
2. It provides the means to effectively monitor and report on promising new therapies' safety and efficacy through enhanced postmarket surveillance initiatives.

Scope

The NOC/c guidance applies to:
1. An NDS or SNDS for a serious, life-threatening or severely debilitating disease or condition for which data show promising evidence that a drug has the potential to provide:
   - effective treatment, prevention or diagnosis of a disease or condition for which no drug presently is marketed in Canada, or
   - a significant increase in efficacy and/or significant decrease in risk such that the overall benefit-risk profile is improved over that of existing therapies, or preventive or diagnostic agents for a disease or condition not adequately managed by a drug marketed in Canada
2. An ANDS or SANDS where the Canadian Reference Product (CRP) still holds the NOC/c status. In instances where the CRP does not hold the NOC/c status, the ANDS can be considered only under the NOC/c policy via an NDS/SNDS for a new indication that fits the NOC/c policy objective.

For NDS or SNDS sponsors, a prerequisite for issuance of an NOC/c is the sponsor's written commitment to pursue confirmatory studies acceptable to Health Canada. ANDS sponsors will not automatically be requested to complete the confirmatory trials. The need to conduct confirmatory trials by ANDS sponsors will be decided on a case-by-case basis through an appropriate clinical bureau evaluation.

Review and Authorization

If a drug product meets NOC/c guidance Section 1.3 criteria outlined above, consideration of NOC/c status then may be granted under one of the two following circumstances:
- Post-review—Health Canada, upon review, has determined the sponsor must undertake additional confirmatory postmarketing studies, to be outlined in the letter of undertaking, to substantiate the promising clinical evidence submitted in the application.
- Pre-review—Sponsor requests advance consideration under the NOC/c policy prior to submission review.

For the second option, the sponsor is required to deliver a pre-NDS presentation outlining the evidence of clinical effectiveness to the appropriate Health Canada directorate. Within 10 working days after the pre-NDS meeting minutes are final, the sponsor will be notified of the drug submission's eligibility for filing and consideration under the NOC/c policy. Advance consideration under the NOC/c policy permits a shortened review target of 200 days.

Note, submissions filed for advance consideration under the NOC/c policy on the basis of promising clinical evidence are not eligible for Priority Review status.

Appeal Procedures

Sponsors may appeal the eligibility decision. A letter of intent to appeal should be sent to the bureau or centre director within 30 calendar days of receiving Health Canada's decision. The appeal will proceed as outlined in *Guidance for Industry: Management of Drug Submissions*. See also *Guidance for Industry: Reconsideration of Final Decisions Issued for Human Drug Submissions*. Health Canada will issue the outcome of the appeal within 30 days.

Issuance of the NOC/c Qualifying Notice

After Health Canada has reviewed the submission, determined it qualifies under the NOC/c policy and contacted the sponsor to discuss the submission and postapproval commitments, an NOC/c Qualifying Notice (NOC/c-QN) is issued. The NOC/c-QN outlines the additional clinical evidence to be provided in the confirmatory studies, postmarket surveillance responsibilities and any requirements related to advertising, labelling or distribution. Submission review ceases when the NOC/c-QN is issued. Within 30 calendar days of receiving the NOC/c-QN, the sponsor must submit the following to Health Canada:
- any additional information requested by Health Canada (e.g., Dear Healthcare Professional Letters and product monographs consistent with the recommendations outlined in the NOC/c guidance document)
- an initial outline of the proposed confirmatory trials and a rationale bridging the "Promising Clinical Evidence" with the proposed confirmatory studies; similarly, an initial outline of any agreed-upon safety monitoring studies

- a letter signed by the sponsor's chief executive officer, indicating the sponsor agrees to have the submission considered under the NOC/c policy
- a draft letter of undertaking signed by the sponsor's chief executive officer, in a form and content satisfactory to Health Canada

Letter of Undertaking

As outlined in the guidance, a sponsor must submit a draft letter of undertaking in response to the NOC/c-QN. The letter should include the following:
- list of confirmatory studies
- postmarket surveillance commitments
- paragraph outlining agreed-upon advertising, labelling or distribution requirements imposed on the product
- notification of specific issues of concern
- details about other ongoing clinical studies
- copies of marketing approvals from any other regulatory agency for the drug under review

For the product to qualify for a full NOC, Health Canada must deem all components of the letter of undertaking acceptable.

Specific Advertising, Labelling and Educational Material Requirements

Products approved under the NOC/c policy are subject to enhanced labelling requirements. Any advertising, labelling or educational material must clearly disclose the nature of the granted market authorization and the need to conduct studies to confirm the product's clinical benefit. For example, on the product monograph's cover page and in Parts I and II, boxed text is used to denote a product that has been granted approval with conditions (see **Figure 5-2**).

Postmarket Commitments

The sponsor is required to submit annual confirmatory trial progress reports. Final results are submitted in the form of an SNDS-C, within the agreed-upon timeframe, so the sponsor can apply for an NOC.

In addition, products granted an NOC/c can be subject to enhanced postmarket surveillance activities. All serious adverse drug reactions (ADRs) that occur in Canada, and all serious unexpected ADRs that occur outside Canada, must be reported within 15 days to the Marketed Health Products Directorate. Sponsors may obtain information regarding the adverse reactions (ARs) received by Health Canada, including those received directly from healthcare professionals and/or consumers, by accessing the searchable subset of the Canada Vigilance Database, which is available on the Health Canada website. Additional safety information may be required periodically, as established by Health Canada. The requirements may be determined at the time of the pre- or postmarket assessment.

Additional active postmarket surveillance may be required on a case-by-case basis.

Removal of Conditions from the NOC/c

Sponsors submit the results from confirmatory studies (efficacy and safety) in the form of an SNDS-C. When all undertakings have been satisfied, and the drug's clinical benefits have been confirmed, conditions associated with the NOC will be removed.

The sponsor is required to submit a new letter of undertaking if, based on the outcome of the SNDS-C review, not all undertakings have been satisfied, or the sponsor foresees an inability to adhere to the agreed-upon studies or timelines for confirmatory trial commencement or completion, as outlined in the letter of undertaking.

If subsequent reviews determine undertakings have not been satisfied, the sponsor may receive a stop-sale letter, and the product may be recalled from the market, or the product may remain in limited availability through the Special Access Programme. In addition, at Health Canada's discretion and consistent with the regulations of all marketed products, the following may be discussed on a case-by-case basis:
- restriction of the patient population for which the drug was approved
- further education material dissemination for informed use
- enhanced postmarket surveillance analysis

Summary

- A New Drug Submission (NDS) is an application to Health Canada for approval to market a new drug as defined by the *F&DA* and *FDR*. The standard target review time is approximately 355 days (300 days for scientific review, 45 days screening and 7–10 days for submission login.
- An NDS for a new drug product is reviewed by the appropriate bureau of the Therapeutics Products Directorate. A biologic product NDS is reviewed by the Biologics and Genetic Therapies Directorate.
- Health Canada requires NDSs to be submitted in the electronic Common Technical Document (eCTD) format. The eCTD consists of five modules: Modules 2, 3, 4 and 5 are intended to be common for all regions (technical information such as efficacy, safety and quality); Module 1 is region-specific.
- When a sponsor wishes to submit a drug for a serious, life-threatening or severely debilitating illness or condition for expedited review

consideration, it may do so in one of two ways. The sponsor may request either Priority Review status before submitting the NDS (Priority Review status provides a substantially shorter review and approval timeframe, with a target of 25 days for screening and 180 days for scientific review) or an NOC-c when the only data available may be the drug's effect on surrogate markers (this status also shortens the review period to a target of 200 days of scientific review after the 25 days screening, when eligible for advance consideration).

Chapter 6

Postmarketing and Other Activities

Updated by Janice Weiler and Danny Germain, RAC

OBJECTIVES

❑ Categorize levels of postapproval changes for Division 8 drugs (new drugs).

❑ Define postapproval changes for Division 1 drugs (old drugs).

❑ Identify other postmarketing activities.

REGULATIONS AND GUIDELINES COVERED IN THIS CHAPTER

❑ *Food and Drugs Act*

❑ *Food and Drug Regulations*

❑ *Guidance Document: Labelling of Pharmaceutical Drugs for Human Use* (13 June 2015)

❑ *Patent Act*

❑ *Patented Medicines Regulations*

❑ *Patented Medicines (Notice of Compliance) Regulations*

❑ Patented Medicines Prices Review Board Compendium of Policies, Guidelines and Procedures (February 2017)

❑ Patented Medicines Prices Review Board, *Patentees Guide to Reporting* (July 2015)

❑ *Post-Notice of Compliance (NOC) Changes: Framework Document* (15 September 2011)

❑ *Post-Notice of Compliance (NOC) Changes: Quality Document* (14 October 2016)

❑ *Post-Notice of Compliance (NOC) Changes: Safety and Efficacy Document* (2 February 2016)

❑ *Post-Drug Identification Number (DIN) Changes Guidance Document* (17 March 2017)

❑ *Protecting Canadians from Unsafe Drugs Act (Vanessa's Law) Amendments to the Food and Drugs Act* (Bill C-17) (6 December 2013)

Introduction

During a drug's regulatory lifecycle, various postapproval changes occur. Some of these require Health Canada preapproval, some require notification or reporting and others are maintained on file. This chapter addresses postapproval changes and other routine maintenance activities, including Patented Medicines Prices Review Board (PMPRB) reporting and annual drug notification, drug shortages and discontinuation reporting.

Other maintenance activities such as adverse reaction reporting requirements, preparation of annual reports and risk management plans are addressed in Chapter 7 Health Product Vigilance and Risk Management. Requirements for Establishment Licensing and Good Manufacturing Practices are discussed in Chapter 4. For biologics, there also is a requirement to prepare and submit a Yearly Biologic Product Report, and there is a lot release program that applies postapproval. See Chapter 11 Biologics Submission,

Approval and Postmarketing. Advertising is addressed in Chapter 12.

Postapproval Changes

Post-NOC Changes

Postapproval changes to drugs that have received an NOC pursuant to *Food and Drug Regulations'* (*FDR*) Section C.08.004 (New Drugs) are assigned to one of four categories, with different submission requirements for each level.[1] Post-NOC changes guidance documents are applicable to drugs for both human use (pharmaceuticals, biologics and radiopharmaceuticals) and veterinary use (pharmaceuticals, radiopharmaceuticals and certain biotechnological products).

Level I changes require a supplemental submission (Supplemental New Drug Submission (SNDS) or Supplemental Abbreviated New Drug Submission (SANDS)), with variable fees and agency timelines, depending on specific changes. These changes have the highest potential to impact a drug product's safety, efficacy, quality and/or effective use. They cannot be implemented without the issuance of a Notice of Compliance (NOC). Level I changes are those that are "significantly different" as it relates to the matters specified in *FDR* C.08.003(2).[2]

Examples of a Level I change include:
- labeling modifications involving a new route of administration or indication
- for human pharmaceuticals for sterile drug substances, replacing the sterility test with process parametric release

Level II changes are processed as Notifiable Change (NC) submissions, with approval indicated by the issuance of a No Objection Letter (NOL). Timelines for an NC are seven days for screening, and a target review of 90 or 120 days. There are no associated fees. Multiple Level II changes for the same drug product may be filed in a single submission, provided those changes are related and/or supported by the same information and fall within the same category (90-day or 120-day). Level II quality changes do not apply to human pharmaceuticals.

Level II (120-day) NCs include any changes to the label that do not affect the conditions of use (i.e., do not involve risk management or have the potential to increase the drug's exposure level) but require prior approval. Level II (90-day) NCs include label changes with the potential to improve risk management within the population indicated for use of, or in any other way exposed to, the drug. These changes improve adverse event identification or characterization; add or strengthen risk management measures for the adverse event; improve subgroup or conditions of use identification for which the new drug's benefit-risk profile may be less favourable; and add or strengthen risk management measures, including dosing instructions or any other conditions of use. From a chemistry perspective, Level II changes include quality modifications that have a moderate potential to have an adverse effect on the drug product's identity, strength, quality, purity or potency. In comparison with Level I changes, Level II NCs have a lower relative potential to impact a product's safety, efficacy, quality and/or effective use. Level II changes should not be implemented until an NOL has been issued. An NC requires a level of detail in information and amount of supporting data similar to those required for a SNDS/SANDS.

Examples of 90-day NCs are:
- for a biologic, a major change to the following process validation protocols used during drug substance manufacture: protocol for the manufacture of cell bank/seed bank, protocol for introducing the product into an approved multi-product facility, protocol for cleaning equipment (e.g., change in the worst-case scenario during cleaning validation process)
- addition of a drug interaction or better characterization of an existing drug interaction
- alteration to an existing indication, including a reduction in scope, for risk management purposes

Examples of 120-day NCs are:
- any change to the Product Monograph's pharmacology, microbiology or toxicology section that does not alter the conditions of use
- any change to the Product Monograph's clinical trial section that does not alter the conditions of use

Level III changes may be implemented immediately without agency preapproval and have minimal potential to adversely affect the drug product's identity, strength, quality, purity or potency, as these factors may relate to the drug product's safety or effectiveness.

These changes should be annotated in the affected documents when filing the next Health Canada submission, to indicate those Level III changes have been implemented. Supporting data are not filed unless requested by Health Canada. The Level III Changes Form should be provided to Health Canada at the time changes are implemented. The forms should not be provided with the Annual Notification.[3,4]

Examples of Level III labeling changes include:
- changing a publication in the REFERENCE section of the Product Monograph/Package Insert listed as "in press" to a published listing
- the existing text of the labels (for human drugs) have been revised to add clarity as it relates to maintaining consistency with common label phrase standards (e.g., change from "Product Monograph available on request" to "Product

Monograph available to healthcare professional on request," change from "Not recommended for children" to "Not for use in children," etc.)
- revisions to Product Monograph Part III, Patient Medication Information/Consumer Information section (for human drugs) to standardize text in each of the following sections: Overdose, Missed Dose, How to Store It or Reporting Suspected Side Effects
- any change in spelling of the text of the label (e.g., "adition" is replaced by "addition")
- sponsor contact information (e.g., customer service number, website addresses, etc.)

For prescription products and those administered or obtained through a health professional for human use, as of 13 June 2015, examples of Level III labeling-related changes include but are not limited to:
- nonsignificant label changes
- updating bar codes and technical codes
- removing graphics
- removing non-regulatory label information
- changing colour of graphics where there is no text overlay or changing colour of company logo
- correcting spelling errors
- updating contact information

Examples of Level III labeling quality changes include:
- for a pharmaceutical, a change to the product markings involving a change in embossing, debossing or engraving (except scorelines/break lines) (e.g., plain tablet to engraved, engraved to plain, change in engraving) or a change in imprinting (e.g., plain tablet/capsule to imprinted tablet/capsule) where the change does not affect the drug product's stability or performance characteristics (e.g., release rate) and changes to the drug product specifications are necessitated only by the change to the markings

Level IV changes to a new drug are not expected to impact the product's safety, efficacy, quality and/or effective use. The changes in this category are quality only. They are documented and filed internally, subject to internal change controls, with no notification to Health Canada needed.

Examples of Level IV changes are:
- non-critical changes to the licensed application that have no impact on the product's safety, efficacy and quality, including editorial changes to add clarity or correct spelling mistakes in documents such as Validation Summaries and/or Reports, Analytical Procedures, SOPs, Production Documentation Summaries, QOS.

- change in stopper cap colour for an injectable product
- modification to a WFI system's pretreatment stages, including purified water systems used solely for pretreatment in WFI production
- change in the floor plan that does not affect production process or contamination precautions
- addition of vial reject chute
- change to in-process controls performed at non-critical manufacturing steps or change to a non-critical manufacturing area
- rooms upgrades, such as installation of improved finishes on floors or walls
- addition of a new GMP storage warehouse for raw materials, master and working cell banks and drug substance
- installation of non-process-related equipment or rooms to improve the facility, such as warehousing refrigerators or freezers
- replacement of equipment with identical equipment
- introduction of additional laboratory facility in a manufacturing facility to perform drug substance or drug product testing
- for biologics and radiopharmaceuticals, with the exception of a potency assay or a bioassay, transfer of the QC testing responsibilities for a pharmacopoeial assay to a different facility within the same company
- for biologics and radiopharmaceuticals, with the exception of a potency assay or a bioassay, transfer of the QC testing responsibilities for a pharmacopoeial assay to a different company listed on the sponsor's establishment licence
- change in supplier for non-critical excipients
- change in drug substance or drug product tertiary packaging components that do not affect stability

Further information on postapproval changes of new drugs is provided in the Post-Notice of Compliance (NOC) guidance documents at: www.hc-sc.gc.ca/dhp-mps/prodpharma/applic-demande/guide-ld/postnoc_change_apresac/index-eng.php.[5-7]

When considering labeling updates, *Guidance Document: Labelling of Pharmaceutical Drugs for Human Use* should be consulted to facilitate compliance with the labeling requirements pursuant to sections 3, 9, and 10 of the *Food and Drugs Act* (*F&DA*) as well as related provisions of the *Food and Drug Regulations* (*FDR*) and the *Controlled Drugs and Substances Act* and its related regulations, including the *Narcotic Control Regulations*, *FDR* Parts G and J and the *Benzodiazepines and Other Targeted Substances Regulations*.[8]

Guidance Document Questions and Answers: Plain Language Labelling Regulations also provides information for industry on how Health Canada's Health Products and Food Branch interprets and applies the 2014 *Regulations Amending the Food and Drug Regulations (Labelling, Packaging and Brand Names of Drugs for Human Use)* for prescription products and those administered or obtained through a health professional.[9]

Advisement Letters—Health Canada-Mandated Safety Changes

In 2014, the *Protecting Canadians from Unsafe Drugs Act* (*Vanessa's Law*) amended the *F&DA* to include new rules that strengthen the regulation of a therapeutic product by providing Health Canada with the necessary authorities to take quick and appropriate action when a serious health risk is identified.

Under the new *F&DA* Section 21.2, enacted through *Vanessa's Law*, the minister may order a therapeutic product authorization holder to modify the product's label and/or modify or replace its package if such changes are deemed to be "necessary to prevent injury to health." The safety changes to a product's label and/or packaging, as ordered by the minister, must be filed as a supplement. Since *Vanessa's Law* came into force, when Health Canada identifies a label change necessary to prevent injury to health, the sponsor will receive an Advisement Letter to request the filing of an S(A)NDS-labeling-only submission. Examples of label changes that may be requested include, but are not limited to: addition of a new contraindication, change in an existing contraindication, addition of a serious Warning or Precaution or tightening clinical monitoring requiring a change to the Product Monograph's Warnings and Precautions section. Health Canada's request for a label change will be supported by data reviewed by the department, and a copy of Health Canada's review will be included with each request.[10]

Post-DIN Changes (Division 1 Drugs)

For product changes after the Drug Identification Number (DIN) has been issued, the provisions of *FDR* C.01.014.4 apply.

Content of the initial DIN application is referenced in C.01.014.1. Depending on the types of changes to the initial content, either a new DIN application is required, or the new information needs to be submitted as a notification within 30 days of the change.

C.01.014.1

"(1) A manufacturer of a drug, a person authorized by a manufacturer or, in the case of a drug to be imported into Canada, the importer of the drug may make an application for a drug identification number for that drug.

(2) An application under subsection (1) shall be made to the Director in writing and shall set out the following information:
  (a) the name of the manufacturer of the drug as it will appear on the label
  (b) the pharmaceutical form in which the drug is to be sold
  (c) in the case of any drug other than a drug described in paragraph (d), the recommended route of administration
  (d) in the case of a drug for disinfection in premises, the types of premises for which its use is recommended
  (e) a quantitative list of the medicinal ingredients contained in the drug by their proper names or, if they have no proper names, by their common names
  (f) the brand name under which the drug is to be sold
  (g) whether the drug is for human use, veterinary use or disinfection in premises
  (h) the name and quantity of each colouring ingredient that is not a medicinal ingredient
  (i) the use or purpose for which the drug is recommended
  (j) the recommended dosage of the drug
  (k) the address of the manufacturer referred to in paragraph (a) and, where the address is outside the country, the name and address of the importer of the drug
  (l) the name and address of any individual, firm, partnership or corporation, other than the names and addresses referred to in paragraphs (a) and (k), that will appear on the label of the drug
  (m) the written text of all labels and package inserts to be used in connection with the drug and of any further prescribing information stated to be available on request
  (n) the name and position of the person who signed the application and the date of signature"

DIN Application

Section C.01.014.4 of the *FDR* states:

"If the information referred to in subsection C.01.014.1(2) in respect of a drug is no longer correct owing to a change in the subject matter of the information,
  (a) in the case of a change in the subject matter of any of the information referred to in paragraphs C.01.014.1(2)(a) to (f)
    (i) that occurs prior to the sale of the drug, a new application shall be made, or

(ii) that occurs after the sale of the drug, no further sale of the drug shall be made until a new application for a drug identification number in respect of that drug is made and a number is assigned."[11]

Changes in this category must be filed along with the required supporting data and may not be implemented prior to Health Canada's review. If the change is acceptable, a new DIN may be issued, or an active DIN may be retained for the changed drug and an NOL issued.[12]

Notification (30 Days)
Section C.01.014.4 of the *FDR* states:
"If the information referred to in subsection C.01.014.1(2) in respect of a drug is no longer correct owing to a change in the subject matter of the information,
"(b) in the case of a change in the subject matter of any of the information referred to in paragraphs C.01.014.1(2)(g) to (k)
  (i) that occurs prior to the sale of the drug, the particulars of the change shall be submitted with the return of the document referred to in section C.01.014.3, or
  (ii) that occurs after the sale of the drug, the person to whom the drug identification number in respect of that drug was issued shall, within 30 days of the change, inform the Director of the change."[13]

Changes in this category need to be filed with the supporting data within 30 days of the change. Upon notification, Health Canada will update its record, uphold the change, request that the change be undone or request that a DIN application be filed in support of the change. Although a notification can be submitted within 30 days of a change, Health Canada advises the notification be provided prior to implementing the change. If the change is considered acceptable, Health Canada will issue an NOL.

Further information on postapproval changes of Part C, Division 1 drugs that have received a DIN pursuant to Section C.01.014.2 is provided in *Guidance Document on Post-Drug Identification (DIN) Changes* at: www.hc-sc.gc.ca/dhp-mps/prodpharma/applic-demande/guide-ld/change_din-eng.php. Note, this guidance applies to pharmaceuticals for human and veterinary use, as well as disinfectant drugs, but excludes biologics and radiopharmaceuticals.[14]

In the absence of a guidance specific to quality changes to drugs approved through a Drug Identification Application—Biologics (DIN-B drugs), the post-NOC-Quality guidance document applies to those products.[15]

Other Activities

Drug Notification following receipt of a NOC/DIN
Following issuance of a DIN or NOC (as per C.01.014.3), the manufacturer, importer or authorized person, within 30 days after commencing sale of a drug, must date and sign the Drug Notification Form (DNF) issued by Health Canada. The DNF comprises three parts (product information, company information and notified information). This form is returned with a confirmation the information recorded is correct (or corrections are made on the form). The date on which the drug was first sold in Canada also is indicated.[16]

Annual Drug Notification
The Annual Drug Notification Form (ADNF) is intended to assist sponsors in complying with *FDR* Section C.01.014.5, which states "every manufacturer of a drug shall, annually before the first day of October, and in a form authorized by the Director, furnish the Director with a notification signed by the manufacturer or by a person authorized to sign on his behalf, confirming that all the information previously supplied by the manufacturer with respect to that drug is correct."

A fee schedule is provided for ADNFs, based on the amount of product sales (in Canadian dollars) for the company's fiscal year. Fees are paid only after the invoice is issued by Health Canada; payment instructions are included with the invoice.[17,18]

DIN Inactivation
As per C.01.014.7, when a DIN owner discontinues sale of a drug in Canada, it should notify the director within 30 days of such discontinuation that it is no longer selling the drug.[19]

Drug Shortages and Discontinuations Reporting
On 14 March 2017, amendments to *FDR* (C.01.014.7 to C.01.014.13) came into force, requiring drug authorization holders to publicly report drug shortages and discontinuations to a new, independent website: https://www.drugshortagescanada.ca/ and https://www.penuries-demedicamentscanada.ca/. Drug authorization holders now are required to report drug shortages and discontinuations of sale as follows:
- no less than six months in advance if it is likely to begin in more than six months
- within five days of becoming aware of the drug shortage or discontinuation of sale if it will begin within six months; and
- update any posted information on the website within two days of becoming aware of the change

The following product types are impacted:

Figure 6-1.

Health Canada Santé Canada

FORM IV PATENT LIST
PATENTED MEDICINES (NOTICE OF COMPLIANCE) REGULATIONS
COMPLETE ONE FORM PER PATENT PER SUBMISSION

(•) English ( ) Français

* denotes a mandatory field
\+ denotes a field with validation error or missing data

[Show Instructions] [Hide Instructions] Guidance Document

PART 1: PATENT FILING INFORMATION

Please select from the Patent List Filing Option below, and then enter the required information.

Patent List Filing Option *

Related Submission *

PART 2: MEDICINAL INGREDIENT(S)

[Add an Ingredient]

x

Brand Name

Human/Veterinary *

Strength per Unit *

Dosage Form *

Route(s) of Administration * DIN

Uses(s) of Medicinal Ingredient(s) *

PART 3: PATENT INFORMATION

Patent Number*	Code*	Canadian Filing Date of Patent Application (YYYY-MM-DD)*	Date Granted (YYYY-MM-DD)*	Expiration Date (YYYY-MM-DD)*
	☐ A ☐ B ☐ C			

PART 4: SERVICE IN CANADA

NAME & ADDRESS (FOR SERVICE IN CANADA)

Company Name *

Canada

FORM IV: PATENT LIST

VERSION 2.11 FINAL DRAFT Access date: 2018-05-21

Health Canada   Santé Canada

Street/Suite *

City - Town * | Country* Canada | Province * | Postal Code *

PART 5: MANUFACTURER INFORMATION AND CERTIFICATION ☐ Same Name and Address as Service in Canada

Company Name *

Street/Suite/PO Box *

City/Town * | Country * | Province/State | Postal/ZIP Code

MANUFACTURER CONTACT

Salutation * | Given Name * | Initial | Surname * | Title *

Telephone No. * | Ext. | Fax No. * | Email

CERTIFICATION

In accordance with paragraph 4(4)(f), I certify that the information included in this Patent List is accurate and that the patent on the list meets the eligibility requirements of subsection 4(2) or 4(3) of the Patented Medicines (Notice of Compliance) Regulations.

Salutation * | Given Name * | Surname * | Position Title *

[Finalize]   [Modify]

FORM IV: PATENT LIST
VERSION 2.11 FINAL DRAFT   Access date: 2018-05-21

Regulatory Affairs Professionals Society

- drugs included in *Controlled Drugs and Substances Act* Schedule I, II, III, IV or V
- prescription drugs
- drugs that are listed in *F&DA* Schedule C or D
- drugs permitted to be sold without a prescription but administered only under a pracitioner's supervision[20]

For further details, refer to the *Guide to reporting drug shortages and discontinuations*: https://www.canada.ca/en/public-health/services/publications/drugs-health-products/reporting-drug-shortages-discontinuations.html.

Patent Forms

If any patents relating to the drug are still pending at the time of submission, Patent Form IV (**Figure 6-1**) must be submitted within 30 days of the patent's being granted in order to be added to the Patent List and receive the protection of the *Patented Medicines (NOC) Regulations*. Form IV is found at: https://www.canada.ca/en/health-canada/services/drugs-health-products/drug-products/applications-submissions/forms.html.[21]

Patent Medicines Prices Review Board (PMPRB)

PMPRB (www.pmprb-cepmb.gc.ca) is an independent quasi-judicial body established by Parliament in 1987 under the *Patent Act*.

The *Patent Act* sets out dual roles for PMPRB. The regulatory role is to ensure the prices patentees charge for patented medicines sold in Canada are not excessive; the reporting role is to report on trends in pharmaceutical sales and pricing for all medicines and to report on patentees' research and development (R&D) spending.

With the exception of medicines sold under compulsory licenses granted by the commissioner of patents before 20 December 1991, which were not terminated before the day amendments to the act came into force on 15 February 1993, all patented medicines, including those sold in any market in Canada for human or veterinary use, are covered by PMPRB's price review jurisdiction, including patented medicines sold pursuant to NOCs, under the Special Access Programme and through Clinical Trial Applications.

PMPRB is responsible for reviewing the prices of all patented medicines sold in Canada. It regulates the "factory gate" prices and does not have jurisdiction over prices charged by wholesalers or pharmacies, or over pharmacists' professional fees. PMPRB does not set the prices at which patented medicines can be sold but determines the Maximum Average Potential Price and the Non-Excessive Average Prices at which these medicines can be sold in Canada.

The *Patent Act* and the *Patented Medicines Regulations* set out the filing requirements pertaining to patentee or former patentee price regulation for an invention pertaining to a patented medicine that falls under the PMPRB's jurisdiction.

A patentee is expected to notify PMPRB of the intent to sell a drug product and the expected sales start date as soon as it is practical to do so. Information relating to price need not be provided more than 60 days before the intended date of sale.

Revenues and R&D expenditures are reported on Form 3 within 60 days of the end of each calendar year. All patentees that filed a Form 2 during the calendar year must report gross revenues (net of taxes) and Scientific Research and Experimental Development expenditures on Form 3.

Form 1, Form 2 and Form 3 information should be filed using the electronic documents in the format and file type available on the PMPRB website.[22-25]

Summary

Changes to a drug following issuance of a DIN or an NOC should be carefully assessed to ascertain whether filing and preapproval requirements are applicable. There also are routine maintenance activities for drugs, such as the annual drug notification.

References

1. *Food and Drug Regulations*. Government of Canada Justice Laws website. http://laws.justice.gc.ca/eng/regulations/c.r.c.,_c._870/index.html. Accessed 13 April 2018.
2. Ibid.
3. Post Notice of Compliance (NOC) Changes: Level III Form (2016). Health Canada website. https://www.canada.ca/en/health-canada/services/drugs-health-products/drug-products/applications-submissions/guidance-documents/post-notice-compliance-changes.html. Accessed 15 April 2018.
4. Notice - Post-Notice of Compliance (NOC) Changes: Notices of Change (Level III) Form (2016). Health Canada website: https://www.canada.ca/en/health-canada/services/drugs-health-products/drug-products/applications-submissions/guidance-documents/post-notice-compliance-changes/change-level-form.html. Accessed 15 April 2018.
5. Health Canada. *Guidance Document Post-Notice of Compliance (NOC) Changes: Framework Document* (September 2011). Health Canada website. http://www.hc-sc.gc.ca/dhp-mps/prodpharma/applic-demande/guide-ld/postnoc_change_apresac/noc_pn_framework_ac_sa_cadre-eng.php. Accessed 15 April 2018.
6. Health Canada. *Guidance Document Post-Notice of Compliance (NOC) Changes: Quality Document* (October 2016). Health Canada website. http://www.hc-sc.gc.ca/dhp-mps/prodpharma/applic-demande/guide-ld/postnoc_change_apresac/noc_pn_quality_ac_sa_qualite-eng.php. Accessed 15 April 2018.
7. Health Canada. *Guidance Document Post-Notice of Compliance (NOC) Changes: Safety and Efficacy Document* (February 2016). Health Canada website. http://www.hc-sc.gc.ca/dhp-mps/prodpharma/applic-demande/guide-ld/postnoc_change_apresac/noc_pn_saf_ac_sa_inn-eng.php. Accessed 15 April 2018.
8. Health Canada. *Guidance Document: Labelling of Pharmaceutical Drugs for Human Use* (2015). Health Canada website. https://www.canada.ca/en/health-canada/services/drugs-health-products/drug-products/applications-submissions/guidance-documents/labelling-pharmaceutical-drugs-human-use-2014-guidance-document.html. Accessed 15 April 2018.

9. Health Canada. *Guidance Document Questions and Answers: Plain Language Labelling Regulations* (2016). Health Canada website. https://www.canada.ca/en/health-canada/services/drugs-health-products/drug-products/applications-submissions/guidance-documents/questions-answers-plain-language-labelling-regulations.html. Accessed 15 April 2018.
10. *Food and Drugs Act.* Government of Canada Justice Laws website. http://laws-lois.justice.gc.ca/eng/acts/F-27/. Accessed 15 April 2018.
11. Op cit 1.
12. Health Canada. *Guidance Document on Post-Drug Identification (DIN) Changes* (March 2017). Health Canada website. http://www.hc-sc.gc.ca/dhp-mps/prodpharma/applic-demande/guide-ld/change_din-eng.php. Accessed 15 April 2018.
13. Op cit 1.
14. Op cit 11.
15. Op cit 6.
16. Op cit 1.
17. Ibid.
18. Op cit 3.
19. Op cit 1.
20. Ibid.
21. Patent Form IV. Health Canada website. https://www.canada.ca/en/health-canada/services/drugs-health-products/drug-products/applications-submissions/forms.html. Accessed 20 May 2018.
22. *Patent Act.* Government of Canada Justice Laws website. http://laws-lois.justice.gc.ca/eng/acts/p-4/. Accessed 15 April 2018.
23. *Patented Medicines Regulations.* Government of Canada Justice Laws website. http://laws-lois.justice.gc.ca/eng/regulations/SOR-94-688/index.html. Accessed 15 April 2018.
24. *Compendium of Policies, Guidelines and Procedures—Updated February 2017.* Patented Medicines Prices Review Board website. http://www.pmprb-cepmb.gc.ca/view.asp?ccid=492. Accessed 15 April 2018.
25. *Patentees' Guide to Reporting—Updated July 2015.* Patented Medicines Prices Review Board website. http://pmprb-cepmb.gc.ca/view.asp?ccid=523&lang=en. Accessed 15 April 2018.

Chapter 7

Health Product Vigilance and Risk Management

Updated by Christopher Antonio, Roshni Celeste, Jenna Griffiths, Carole Légaré, Marc Poitras, Tanya Ramsamy, Thanh Vu, Bruce Wozny and Raymond Yang

OBJECTIVES

❑ Understand the reporting requirements for safety information arising during clinical trials for pharmaceuticals, biologics, radiopharmaceuticals and natural health products

❑ Understand the reporting requirements for post-approval safety information for pharmaceuticals, biologics, radiopharmaceuticals and natural health products

❑ Understand the requirements for Risk Management Plans

LAWS, REGULATIONS AND GUIDELINES COVERED IN THIS CHAPTER

Drugs, Biologics and Natural Health Products

❑ *Reporting Adverse Reactions to Marketed Health Products - Guidance Document for Industry* (May 2018)

❑ *Guidance for Industry: Clinical Safety Data Management Definitions and Standards for Expedited Reporting ICH Topic E2A* (1995)

❑ *Notice: Adoption of the International Conference on Harmonisation (ICH) Guidance on Periodic Benefit Risk Evaluation Report - ICH Topic E2C (R2)* (March 2013)

❑ *Development Safety Update Report (DSUR) E2F* (July 2012)

❑ *Guideline for Good Clinical Practice E6(R2)* (November 2016)

Drugs and Biologics

❑ *Food and Drug Regulations* (C.R.C., c. 870)

❑ *Good Pharmacovigilance Practices (GVP) Guidelines GUI-0102* (August 2013)

❑ *Guidance Document for Clinical Trial Sponsors: Clinical Trial Applications* (May 2013)

❑ *Notice Regarding Implementation of Risk Management Planning including the adoption of ICH Guidance Pharmacovigilance Planning—ICH Topic E2E* (February 2009)

❑ *Post-approval safety data management: Definitions and standard for expedited reporting E2D*

Natural Health Products

❑ *Guidance Document: Clinical Trials for Natural Health Products* (October 2005)

❑ *Natural Health Products Regulations* (SOR/2003-196)

Introduction

Health product vigilance is an evolving science. This chapter discusses pharmacovigilance and natural health product vigilance. In Canada, the health product vigilance system is governed by regulations describing the responsibilities of the clinical trial sponsor, the Market Authorization Holder (MAH), the importer and Health Canada for collecting, analyzing and notifying safety data. Health Canada is developing a Health Product Vigilance Framework with the aim of moving to a "product lifecycle" approach, where what is known about a product's benefit-risk profile is assessed and applied on an ongoing basis, starting at the preclinical stage and continuing after market authorization. Within this framework, the industry's vigilance responsibilities will be emphasized, consistent with international harmonization objectives, wherever possible. Health Canada has committed to the full integration of ICH vigilance tools.[1]

Clinical Trial Surveillance

Part C, Division 5 of the *Food and Drug Regulations* (*FDR*) and Part 4 of the *Natural Health Products Regulations* (*NHPR*) form the framework for monitoring and reporting safety data originating from clinical trials. In addition, Health Canada has adopted ICH E2A and will implement the ICH E6(R2) guideline by April 2019. The agency endorses the principles and practices described in these guidelines. Health Canada also has implemented ICH's *Guidelines on Development Safety Update Reports (DSURs) E2F*.

This section covers the safety reporting requirements for pharmaceuticals (prescription and non-prescription), biologics, radiopharmaceuticals and natural health products during:

- clinical trials of products not authorized for sale in Canada, including Phases I to III of development and comparative bioavailability studies
- clinical trials for marketed products where the drug's proposed use is outside the parameters of the Notice of Compliance (NOC), Drug Identification Number (DIN) application, Natural Product Number (NPN) or Drug Identification Number-Homeopathic Medicine (DIN-HM)
- Clinical Trial Application amendments and notifications

Note, Phase IV clinical trials involving marketed products, where the investigation is to be conducted within the parameters of the approved NOC, DIN, NPN or DIN-HM, will be discussed in the post-approval section of this chapter.

The definitions in **Table 7-1** are applicable to clinical trials involving human subjects conducted in Canada.

Health Canada Directorates

Office of Clinical Trials, Therapeutic Products Directorate (TPD)
- pharmaceuticals (prescription and non-prescription); natural health products not appropriate for self-care and not considered biologic substances

Biologics and Genetic Therapies Directorate (BGTD)
- biologics; biologic substances meeting the NHP definition that are not appropriate for self-care (e.g., some probiotics); radiopharmaceuticals

Natural and Non-Prescription Health Products Directorate (NNHPD)
- natural health products appropriate for self-care

Reporting of Individual Case Safety Reports

The clinical trial sponsor is responsible for managing risk during drug and natural health product development, taking nonclinical and clinical data into account.[2] The sponsor also is responsible for expedited safety information reporting to Health Canada, investigator(s) and Research Ethics Boards.

The sponsor must collect all adverse events, both non-serious and serious, regardless of a presumed relationship with the study agent by the investigator or sponsor. This allows subsequent assessment of causality using standardized methods for individual cases and aggregate data.[3]

The investigator responsible for conducting the clinical trial must report all serious adverse events (SAEs) immediately to the sponsor. Adverse events of special interest and laboratory abnormalities identified in the protocol as critical to safety evaluations also must be reported promptly to the sponsor, even if the event is considered non-serious according to the usual regulatory criteria.[4,5] For reports of deaths, the investigator also should provide any additional available information (e.g., autopsy reports and terminal medical reports).

Under Part C, Division 5 of the *FDR* and Section 78 of the *NHPR*, the sponsor is required to inform Health Canada, in an expedited manner, of any serious unexpected adverse drug reaction (ADR) or adverse reaction (AR) that has occurred in Canada or outside Canada, regarding the drug or natural health product. In addition, serious expected ARs that occur in Canada regarding a natural health product also require expedited reporting.

The expedited reporting requirement applies to reports from spontaneous sources and any type of clinical or epidemiological investigation, independent of design or purpose. It also applies to cases not reported directly to a sponsor or manufacturer (e.g., those found in regulatory authority-generated ADR registries or in publications). The timeframe for expedited reporting is:

- Serious unexpected ADRs/ARs that are neither fatal nor life-threatening should be reported to Health Canada within 15 calendar days after the sponsor becomes aware of the information.
- Fatal or life-threatening unexpected ADRs/ARs should be reported (e.g., by telephone, facsimile transmission, or in writing) as soon as possible but no later than seven calendar days after the sponsor's

Table 7-1. Clinical Trial Definitions

Adverse Event*	An adverse event is any adverse occurrence in the health of a clinical trial subject administered a drug, that may or may not be caused by the drug's administration, and includes an adverse drug reaction.
Adverse Event**	Adverse event is any adverse occurrence in the health of a clinical trial subject administered a natural health product, that may or may not be caused by the natural health product's administration, and includes an adverse reaction, a serious adverse reaction and a serious unexpected adverse reaction.
Adverse Drug Reaction (ADR)*	Adverse drug reaction (ADR) is any noxious and unintended response to a drug caused by the administration of any dose of the drug.
Drug**	A drug (pharmaceutical, biologic, gene therapy, blood product, vaccine or radiopharmaceutical) for human use that is to be tested in a clinical trial.
Investigator's Brochure*	Investigator's Brochure (IB) is a document containing the drug's preclinical and clinical data that are described in the *Food and Drug Regulations*' Paragraph C.05.005(e).
Investigator's Brochure**	Investigator's Brochure (IB) is a document containing the preclinical and clinical information regarding the natural health product that is described in Paragraph 66(e),
Serious Adverse Drug Reaction*	Serious adverse drug reaction is an adverse drug reaction that: requires inpatient hospitalization or prolongation of existing hospitalization; causes congenital malformation; results in persistent or significant disability or incapacity; is life threatening; or results in death. Important medical events that may not be immediately life-threatening or result in death or hospitalization but may jeopardize the patient or require intervention to prevent one of the other outcomes listed in the definition also should usually be considered serious. **Note:** The term "life-threatening" in the definition of "serious" refers to an event in which the patient was at risk of death at the time of the event; it does not refer to an event that hypothetically might have caused death if it were more severe.*****
Serious Unexpected Adverse Drug Reaction*	Serious unexpected adverse drug reaction is a serious adverse drug reaction that is not identified in nature, severity or frequency in the risk information set out in the Investigator's Brochure or on the drug's label.
Sponsor*	A sponsor is an individual, corporate body, institution or organization that conducts a clinical trial.
Sponsor**	A sponsor is an individual, corporate body, institution or organization that conducts a clinical trial.

**Food and Drug Regulations* (C.R.C., c. 870)
***Natural Health Products Regulations* (SOR/2003-196)
****Guidance Document for Clinical Trial Sponsors: Clinical Trial Applications*
*****Guidance for Industry: Clinical Safety Data Management: Definitions and Standards for Expedited Reporting, E2A* (1995)

first knowledge that a case qualifies. Within eight calendar days after having initially informed Health Canada of the fatal or life-threatening ADR/AR, the sponsor should submit as complete a report as possible. This report must include an assessment of the importance and implication of the findings, including relevant previous experience with the same or similar health products.

The sponsor must submit initial reports within the prescribed timeframe as long as the following minimum criteria are met: an identifiable patient (e.g., age and gender); a suspect health product; an identifiable reporting source; and a reaction or outcome that can be identified as serious and unexpected, and for which there is a reasonable, suspected causal relationship. The sponsor must actively seek follow-up information and submit it as it becomes available.

When the clinical trial involves a drug or natural health product not yet approved for marketing in Canada, the sponsor should use the Investigator's Brochure as the source document for the assessment of expectedness. During clinical trials for a marketed drug or natural health product, the approved Product Monograph or product label is used instead of an Investigator's Brochure to assess expectedness.

The sponsor and the investigator are required to assess the clinical trial adverse reaction's causality. All reactions judged by either the reporting healthcare professional or the sponsor as having a reasonable, suspected causal relationship to the drug or to the natural health product qualify as ADRs.

When a serious adverse reaction is judged reportable on an expedited basis, the blind may have to be broken, but a number of issues need to be taken into consideration when doing so. When possible and appropriate, the sponsor should maintain the blind for those persons responsible for analyzing and interpreting results at the study's conclusion (e.g., biometrics personnel).

When a fatal or other serious outcome occurs in a clinical trial, the investigation's integrity may be compromised if the blind is broken. If serious adverse events become predominant, the trial should be immediately discontinued. Under these and similar circumstances, the sponsor should reach agreement with Health Canada in advance concerning serious events that would be treated as disease-related and not subject to routine expedited reporting.

Serious adverse reactions are reported to the sponsor after the patient has completed a clinical study (including any protocol-required, post-treatment follow-up) and should be assessed for expedited reporting purposes in the same manner as study reports. Therefore, a sponsor should conduct a causality assessment and determination of expectedness to decide whether expedited reporting is required.

The sponsor should submit electronically via a secure gateway, fax or mail (if necessary) individual cases requiring expedited reporting to Health Canada's Biologics and Genetic Therapies Directorate (BGTD) for (biologics, including biologic substances that meet the NHP definition and radiopharmaceuticals,) or to the Therapeutic Products Directorate (TPD) for pharmaceuticals and non-biologic natural health products, as applicable. The report should be in a completed Council for International Organizations of Medical Sciences (CIOMS) I Form or FDA Form 3500A format. In addition, the sponsor must submit either a completed Health Canada Form 01-03 (Adverse Drug Reactions (ADRs) for Clinical Trials Expedited Reporting Summary Form) or the equivalent Natural and Non-Prescription Health Products Directorate Form "Adverse Reaction Report Form for Clinical Trials."

The Health Products and Food Branch (HPFB) has implemented a gateway-to-gateway e-Reporting solution for AR reports that is capable of handling the electronic receipt of AR reports. To register for e-Reporting, an entity or organization must meet several technical requirements. For more information on e-Reporting, the Trading Partner Management Office can be contacted at TPMO_BGPC@hc-sc.gc.ca.

Reporting Other Information

Rapid communication to Health Canada also may be necessary for information that might influence a drug or natural health product's benefit-risk assessment or would warrant changes in administration or in the clinical trial's overall conduct. The sponsor is required to apply appropriate medical judgment in such situations. Examples may include:

- an increase in the occurrence rate of an "expected" serious ADR/AR, which is judged to be clinically important
- a significant hazard to the patient population, such as lack of a drug or natural health product's efficacy in treating life-threatening disease
- a major safety finding from a newly completed animal study (such as carcinogenicity)

The sponsor must submit this information to the BGTD for (biologics, biologic substances that meet the NHP definition and radiopharmaceuticals,) or to the Office of Clinical Trials, TPD for (pharmaceuticals and natural health products that are not considered biologic substances), as applicable.

At any time during a clinical trial's conduct, Health Canada may ask a sponsor to submit information or records to assess the drug's safety. The safety report could include a line listing of all serious reactions and/or other expected and unexpected ADRs.[6]

In accordance with ICH E6(R2), the sponsor should review the Investigator's Brochure, including all safety information and global status, at least annually and revise it as necessary. More frequent revision may be appropriate, depending on the stage of development and emerging relevant new information.

Under *FDR* Paragraph C.05.012(4) and *NHPR* Section 76(3)(c), the sponsor must maintain, for a period of 25 years, complete and accurate records of all adverse reactions related to the drug or the natural health product that have occurred within or outside Canada, including information that specifies the drug or natural health product's indication for use and dosage form at the time of the adverse reaction. Under *FDR* Paragraph C.05.013 and *NHPR* Section 77, records must be made available to the relevant directorate within two calendar days of a request if there is a concern regarding the drug or natural health product's use for the purposes of a clinical trial and if there is a concern of risk to health of the subjects involved in that trial. In any other case, records must be provided within seven days of a request.

Periodic Reporting

Health Canada conducted a pilot project to integrate the review of ICH's *Development Safety Update Reports (DSURs) E2F* into the safety surveillance of drugs in development. The agency implemented. E2F 4 December 2015. Unless specifically requested, a clinical trial sponsor should submit a DSUR to Health Canada only when significant new safety information or any important changes to the drug's safety profile need to be conveyed. In these cases, the DSUR should be accompanied by a rationale or justification in the cover letter.

Post-Approval Surveillance

Post-market safety information monitoring and reporting are governed by *FDR* Part C, Division 1 (C.01016-020) and Part C, Division 8 (C.08.007 and C.08.008) and *NHPR* Part 1, Section 24. In addition, Health Canada has adopted ICH's E2C, E2D and E2E guidelines and the CIOMS Working Group V report. During the post-approval stage, MAHs are responsible for the safety of any products they sell, manufacture, import or distribute to the Canadian public.[7] MAHs should consult Health Canada's guidance documents for industry for detailed interpretations of the regulations.

The term "marketed health products" in this section includes:
- pharmaceuticals (prescription and non-prescription products)
- biologics, as set out in Schedule D to the *Food and Drugs Act* (*F&DA*), (which includes biotechnology products, vaccines and fractionated blood products), excluding blood and blood components, and cells, tissues and organs
- radiopharmaceutical drugs as set out in *F&DA* Schedule C
- natural health products as defined in *NHPR* Section 1

All importers should have evidence that the foreign MAH is meeting reporting requirements. In addition, importers who have been delegated activities related to pharmacovigilance by the foreign MAH are required to meet all requirements outlined in this section.[8]

The definitions in **Table 7-2** apply in Canada during the post-approval stage.

Adverse Reaction Reporting

ARs for marketed health products are to be reported to the MHPD's Canada Vigilance Program. This section covers collecting individual AR reports by MHPD for the above-mentioned marketed health products.

Under *FDR* Section C.01.017 and *NHPR* Section 24, MAHs must report to MHPD, within 15 calendar days of receipt or awareness (whichever occurs first), all Canadian serious ARs and all foreign serious unexpected ARs. A foreign AR is one that occurs outside Canada, involving a product with the same combination of active ingredients marketed in Canada, regardless of variations in the formulation, dosage form, strength, route of administration or indication.

For products with a "new drug status," under *FDR* Part C, Division 8, the MAH is required to submit Canadian reports of unusual failure in efficacy to MHPD within 15 calendar days of receipt or awareness. In cases where the MAH is uncertain whether a report of lack of efficacy is "unusual," it should submit the report to MHPD.

MAHs' reporting obligations commence when it sells a drug, which can include instances when an MAH offers a drug for sale, exposes a drug for sale or has a drug in its possession for sale and distribution whether or not the distribution is made for consideration. The regulatory reporting time clock is considered to start on the day the MAH first has all the information that satisfies the minimum criteria for an AR report. This date should be considered Day 0.

For both domestic and foreign reports, expectedness is determined from relevant Canadian labelling, such as the product monograph, labelling standards, information approved for market authorization or the product label. Whenever expectedness is uncertain, the MAH should assess the reaction as "unexpected." Adverse reactions with a fatal outcome should be considered "unexpected" unless the Canadian product labelling specifically states that the adverse reaction may be associated with a fatal outcome. Similarly, "Class Adverse Reactions" should be considered "expected" only if described in the Canadian labelling as specifically occurring with the suspect product.

For post-market regulatory reporting purposes, the minimum data elements for an individual case are the same as those for clinical trials, i.e., an identifiable reporter (source), an identifiable patient, an adverse reaction and a suspect product. The term "identifiable" refers to the verification of the existence of both a patient and a reporter. Reports containing a reference to "a patient" or the patient's age, age category, gender or identification number should be considered as having an identifiable patient. Reports referring to a group of patients, e.g., "a few patients," should be followed up to for identifiable patient information before reporting to MHPD.

When additional information is needed to fully evaluate an individual report, the MAH is expected to follow-up with the reporter, giving highest priority to serious unexpected reports and to reports involving ARs under enhanced or active surveillance. Furthermore, the MAH is expected to follow-up with a healthcare professional on all reports where an embryo or foetus could have been exposed to a health product. Care should be taken when reporting ARs related to the embryo or foetus to ensure the patient and the parent/child relationship are accurately identified in the report and that the AR information is attributed to the correct patient. Routine follow-up also is required in cases of overdose, medication error or occupational exposure associated with serious ARs that are subject to expedited reporting in accordance with the *FDR*.

An unsolicited report is a spontaneous report, defined by ICH as an unsolicited communication from a health professional or consumer to an MAH, regulatory authority (i.e., Health Canada) or other organization that describes one or more ARs in a patient who was given one or more health

Table 7-2. Postapproval Stage Definitions

Adverse Reaction (AR)*	An adverse reaction (AR) is a noxious and unintended response to a natural health product that occurs at any dose used or tested for the diagnosis, treatment or prevention of a disease or the modification of an organic function.
Adverse Drug Reaction (ADR)**	An adverse drug reaction (ADR) is a noxious and unintended response to a drug, which occurs at doses normally used or tested for the diagnosis, treatment or prevention of a disease or the modification of an organic function.
Serious Adverse Reaction*	A serious adverse reaction is a noxious and unintended response to a natural health product that occurs at any dose and requires inpatient hospitalization or prolongation of existing hospitalization, causes congenital malformation, results in persistent or significant disability or incapacity, is life-threatening or results in death.
Serious Adverse Drug Reaction**	A serious adverse drug reaction is a noxious and unintended response to a drug that occurs at any dose and requires inpatient hospitalization or prolongation of existing hospitalization, causes congenital malformation, results in persistent or significant disability or incapacity, is life-threatening or results in death. Medical and scientific judgment should be exercised in deciding whether other situations should be considered serious, such as important medical events that might not be immediately life-threatening or result in death or hospitalization but might jeopardize the patient or require intervention to prevent one of the other outcomes listed in the definition above. Examples of such events are intensive treatment in an emergency room or at home for allergic bronchospasm, blood dyscrasias or convulsions that do not result in hospitalization, or development of drug dependency or drug abuse. **Note:** The term "life-threatening" in the definition of "serious" refers to an event or reaction in which the patient was at risk of death at the time of the event or reaction; it does not refer to an event or reaction that hypothetically might have caused death if it were more severe.***
Serious Unexpected Adverse Reaction*	A serious unexpected adverse reaction is a serious adverse reaction that is not identified in nature, severity or frequency in the risk information set out on the natural health product's label.
Serious Unexpected Adverse Drug Reaction**	A serious unexpected adverse drug reaction is a serious adverse drug reaction that is not identified in nature, severity or frequency in the risk information set out on the drug's label.
Solicited Report**	A solicited report is one that is derived from organized data collection systems, which include clinical trials, registries, postapproval named-patient use programs, other patient support and disease management programs, surveys of patients or healthcare providers or information gathering on efficacy or patient compliance. Adverse event reports obtained from any of these should not be considered spontaneous.
Unsolicited Reports**	An unsolicited report is an unsolicited communication from a healthcare professional or consumer to a company, regulatory authority or other organization (e.g., WHO, Regional Center, Poison Control Center) that describes one or more adverse drug reactions in a patient who was given one or more medicinal products and does not derive from a study or any organized data collection scheme.
New Drug***	Generally, if a Notice of Compliance (NOC) was issued for a drug in Canada, that drug is considered a "new drug," regardless of how long it has been on the market. *Food and Drug Regulations:* A new drug is: (a) a drug that contains or consists of a substance, whether as an active or inactive ingredient, carrier, coating, excipient, menstruum or other component, that has not been sold as a drug in Canada for sufficient time and in sufficient quantity to establish in Canada that substance's safety and effectiveness for use as a drug; (b) a drug that is a combination of two or more drugs, with or without other ingredients, and has not been sold in that combination or in the proportion in which those drugs are combined in that drug, for sufficient time and in sufficient quantity to establish in Canada the safety and effectiveness of that combination and proportion's use as a drug; or (c) a drug, with respect to which the manufacturer prescribes, recommends, proposes or claims a use as a drug or a condition of use as a drug, including dosage, route of administration or duration of action and that has not been sold for that use or condition of use in Canada for sufficient time and in sufficient quantity to establish in Canada that drug's use or condition of use's safety and effectiveness.

Natural Health Products Regulations (SOR/2003-196)
**Food and Drug Regulations* (C.R.C., c. 870)
****ICH *Post-approval Safety Data Management: Definitions and Standards for Expedited Reporting: E2D*
*****Health Products and Food Branch Inspectorate Good Pharmacovigilance Practices (GVP) Guidelines* (GUI-0102)

products, and the report is not derived from a study or any organized data collection scheme. These can include spontaneous reports from medical sources, all nonmedical sources (e.g., consumers, lay press and media), stimulated reports (e.g., reports prompted by Health Canada Public Advisory) and reports identified in the published literature and on the Internet. To determine reportability, the same minimum criteria (i.e., identifiable reporter, identifiable patient, suspect product and AR) should apply as for other reports.

ICH defines solicited reports as those derived from organized data collection systems, which include clinical trials (e.g., Phase IV studies), registries, post-approval named patient use programs, other patient support and disease management programs, surveys of patients or health professionals, or information gathering on efficacy or patient compliance. The MAH's qualified healthcare professional must determine whether there is a reasonable possibility the health product caused the AR. The MAH should submit the report to MHPD only if the relationship between the product and the AR cannot be ruled out. In its *Guidance Document for Industry: Reporting Adverse Reactions to Marketed Health Products,* Health Canada advises any case report that falls within the World Health Organization (WHO) causality criteria of certain, probable, possible or unlikely must be reported to MHPD. Solicited reports should be submitted only if there is a reasonable possibility that the health product caused the AR as determined by a qualified MAH health professional. A "reasonable possibility" means the relationship cannot be eliminated. For example, using the WHO criteria for causality applicable to AR reporting, any case reports that fall within the certain, probable, possible or unlikely criteria must be reported to MHPD. In any case where an underlying illness or another health product may have contributed to the adverse event, the report still should be considered an AR, as the causality cannot be eliminated. In Phase IV studies, the drug sponsor is responsible for deciding whether to report adverse reactions to the MAH or directly to MHPD in cases where the active comparator or a concomitant product is the suspect product.

It is recommended the MAH regularly screen the worldwide medical and scientific literature to identify ARs in published articles, as well as published abstracts from meetings and draft manuscripts. For serious unexpected ARs identified in foreign literature reports, products with the same combination of active ingredients as those marketed in Canada must be reported to Health Canada regardless of variations in the formulation, dosage form, strength, route of administration or indication. The publication reference should be considered the reporting source. ARs that meet expedited reporting requirements must be submitted to MHPD with the relevant article or abstract in English or French. The MAH must consider its own product to be the "suspect drug" for reports associated with active ingredient(s) it markets, where the source, brand or trade name of the "suspect drug" is not specified. Whenever multiple products are mentioned in one article, the MAH should submit the report to MHPD only if the author identifies its product as a "suspect product."

The MAH also is responsible for screening websites under its management for potential AR reports. MAHs should consider using their websites to facilitate AR data collection.

The preferred AR reporting method is electronic. HPFB has implemented a gateway-to-gateway e-Reporting solution for AR reports that is capable of handling the electronic receipt of AR reports. To register for e-Reporting, an entity or organization must meet several technical requirements. For more information on e-Reporting, the Trading Partner Management Office can be contacted at TPMO_BGPC@hc-sc.gc.ca.

For MAHs that do not meet the technical-reporting requirements, MHPD accepts drug ARs by fax and mail to the Canada Vigilance Program using the CIOMS Form I, and natural health product ARs via the Mandatory Adverse Reaction Reporting Form for Industry.

As part of their surveillance activities, MAHs should consult the Canada Vigilance Adverse Reaction Online Database to identify reports for their products that were sent directly to the Canada Vigilance Program. If an MAH becomes aware of a report that has been submitted by a health professional or consumer to the Canada Vigilance Program, the MAH also must submit the report to the Canada Vigilance Program. To assist the program in identifying duplicates, Canada Vigilance should be indicated as the source, with the Canada Vigilance Adverse Event Report (AER) number listed. If additional information is required (e.g., complete case narratives), the MAH may request copies of AR reports through the Access to Information and Privacy Division of Health Canada, which will require applicable fee payment.

Summary Reports for Drugs and Natural Health Products

Under *FDR* Section C.01.018, the MAH must, on an annual basis and whenever requested by the minister of health, conduct a concise, critical analysis of all ADRs and serious ADRs received during the previous 12 months for a drug and prepare a summary report. When preparing the report, the MAH must determine whether there has been a significant change in the drug's benefit-risk profile. If the MAH concludes there has been a significant benefit-risk profile change, it must notify the minister in writing, without delay, unless this already has been done. The primary focus should be on the change's clinical significance.

In accordance with *NHPR* Section 24, the MAH must prepare an annual summary report (ASR) that contains a concise and critical analysis of all domestic ARs to a natural health product, and all foreign serious unexpected ARs to a natural health product taken at the recommended dose and reported during the previous 12 months. If the minister has reasonable grounds to believe the natural health product no longer may be safe when used under the recommended conditions of use, the minister may request any summary reports, interim summary reports and all adverse reactions for which a case report is required to be submitted to Health Canada within 30 days after the day on which the request is received by the MAH/licensee.

The MAH must maintain the annual summary report on site or in an easily accessible location. Depending on the product's nature and the MAH's preference, a number of formats are considered to be acceptable for preparing ASRs. Health Canada prefers that MAHs prepare ASRs in the Periodic Benefit-Risk Evaluation Report (PBRER) format in accordance with the standards defined in ICH E2C(R2)10. The Periodic Safety Update Report (PSUR) format, in accordance with the standards defined in ICH E2C(R1), also is acceptable to Health Canada. An ASR using a non-ICH format, taking into account not only adverse reaction reports but also other sources of information that might be necessary for the analysis, also is acceptable. The *NHPR* ASR requirements differ from those in *FDR* Division 1 (Appendix 1: Legislation and Regulations Pertaining to Annual Summary Reports and Issue-Related Summary Reports). Although the ICH format is preferred for ASR preparation, a simpler format also is acceptable for NHP ASRs.

Although standardized periodic summary reports (i.e., PBRERs and PSURs) are used globally, regional differences may exist. Manufacturers should consider the need for a Canada-specific section when preparing an ASR for Health Canada.

For more detailed information, interpretation and instructions regarding ASRs, including content, periodicity, document retention, notifying Health Canada, etc., please refer to *Preparing and Submitting Summary Reports for Marketed Drugs and Natural Health Products—Guidance Document for Industry*.

Issue-Related Summary Reporting for Drugs

At any time, Health Canada may require the MAH to analyze a specific drug safety or effectiveness issue by requesting an issue-related summary report (IRSR) to be submitted for the specific safety issue. Pursuant to *FDR* Section C.01.019(1), Health Canada, for the purposes of assessing a drug's safety and effectiveness, may request in writing that the manufacturer submit an IRSR. An IRSR contains a concise, critical analysis of the adverse drug reactions and serious adverse drug reactions to a drug known to the manufacturer with respect to a specific issue the minister directs the manufacturer to analyse. The minister, after giving the manufacturer an opportunity to be heard, shall specify a reasonable period under the circumstances for submitting the report. Typically, a 30-day period is requested for report submission; however, the period may be shorter if the information is required on an expedited basis to determine whether the drug poses a serious and imminent risk to human health.

There are no *NHPR* provisions for IRSRs. However, to assess natural health products' safety and effectiveness, Health Canada may ask the MAH, in writing, to submit an IRSR.

For more detailed IRSR information, interpretation and instructions, including content, document retention, submissions to Health Canada, etc., please refer to *Preparing and Submitting Summary Reports for Marketed Drugs and Natural Health Products—Guidance Document for Industry*.

Risk Management

Risk management planning's objectives are to identify safety issues early in a product's lifecycle, develop methods to assess and quantify those risks, implement risk management measures that will be assessed to determine their effectiveness in minimizing the risk and allow for identification of risks that only may be observed in the post-market setting.[9]

In 2009, Health Canada issued a notice regarding the interim implementation of risk management planning, including adoption of ICH's *Guidance on Pharmacovigilance Planning E2E*. In Canada, natural health products currently are outside the scope of risk management planning.

MAHs are encouraged to start a dialogue with Health Canada regarding risk management plans (RMPs) early in the submission process (i.e., pre-submission meetings). Health Canada may request RMPs when they are considered relevant to decisions regarding a drug's benefit-risk profile, including but not limited to:

- any product containing a new active substance
- potentially, products with a significant change in indication
- products new to a class for which a serious or potentially serious safety risk previously has been identified
- where a safety risk has been identified, such that the product's associated risk is perceived to potentially outweigh its benefit

The sponsor or MAH can prepare a Canadian RMP by providing a Canadian context to an existing European RMP, according to the guidelines provided in the 2009 Notice Appendix. Alternatively, other recognized formats can be used, e.g., the US Risk Evaluation and Mitigation Strategy system (REMS), if the elements described in the EU guidance are covered. The following key sections must be included in all RMPs:

1. Safety Specification—a summary of the known important safety information about the health product and a means to identify gaps in knowledge
2. Pharmacovigilance Plan—based on the Safety Specification and identifying and characterizing known or potential safety concerns
3. Risk Minimization Plan—providing proposals on minimizing any identified or potential safety risks

Conclusion

Timely health product safety information monitoring and reporting by industry are important means of identifying previously unrecognized rare or serious safety issues. The regulations and guidances governing the industry's reporting obligations are updated periodically and harmonized with emerging international standards. Continuous surveillance, therefore, is required of the sponsor and MAH for new safety information (drawn from domestic and foreign reporting sources) and developments in the vigilance framework itself.

References

1. Health Product Vigilance Framework. Health Canada. (9 December 2012). Health Canada website. http://www.hc-sc.gc.ca/dhp-mps/alt_formats/pdf/pubs/medeff/fs-if/2012-hpvf-cvps/dhpvf-ecvps-eng.pdf. Accessed 12 June 2018.
2. Council for International Organizations of Medical Sciences (CIOMS) Working Group VI, *Management of Safety Information from Clinical Trials,* Geneva, 2005.
3. Ibid.
4. Ibid.
5. *ICH Guideline for Good Clinical Practice: E6(R1)* (1996). EMA website. http://www.ema.europa.eu/docs/en_GB/document_library/Scientific_guideline/2009/09/WC500002874.pdf. Accessed 12 June 2018.
6. Health Canada, *Guidance Document for Clinical Trial Sponsors: Clinical Trial Applications.* Health Canada website. http://www.hc-sc.gc.ca/dhp-mps/prodpharma/applic-demande/guide-ld/clini/ctdcta_ctddec-eng.php. Accessed 12 June 2018.
7. Op cit 1.
8. *Inspection Strategy for Good Pharmacovigilance Practices (GVP) for Drugs (POL-0041)* Health Canada website. http://www.hc-sc.gc.ca/dhp-mps/compli-conform/gmp-bpf/docs/pol-0041_gvp-eng.php. Accessed 12 June 2018.
9. Op cit 1.

Chapter 8

An Overview of Pharmaceutical Intellectual Property Protection in Canada

By Junyi Chen, JD, PhD, Danny Germain, RAC, Gordon Jepson, MA, LLB, and Bhavesh Patel, CChem

OBJECTIVES

- To provide an overview of intellectual property protection for pharmaceuticals in Canada, including:

    - *Patented Medicines (Notice of Compliance) Regulations* (Patent Linkage Regulations)

    - *Certificate of Supplementary Protection Regulations* (Patent Term Extension)

    - Data protection

    - Patented medicine price control

LEGISLATION, REGULATIONS AND GUIDELINES COVERED IN THIS CHAPTER

- Patent Linkage Regulations

    - *Patent Act*, Section 55.2 (last amended 21 September 2017)

    - *Patented Medicines (Notice of Compliance) Regulations* (last amended 21 September 2017)

    - *Guidance Document: Patented Medicines (Notice of Compliance) Regulations* (27 October 2016)

    - *Notice: Patented Medicines (Notice of Compliance) Regulations* (19 September 2017)

- Patent Term Extension

    - *Patent Act*, Sections 104–134 (came into force 21 September 2017)

    - *Certificate of Supplementary Protection Regulations* (21 September 2017)

    - *Guidance Document: Certificate of Supplementary Protection Regulations* (21 September 2017)

- Data Protection

    - *Food and Drug Regulations*, Section C.08.004.1 (last amended 4 June 2014)

    - *Guidance Document: Data Protection under C.08.004.1 of the Food and Drug Regulations* (16 May 2017)

- Patented Medicine Price Control

    - *Patent Act*, Sections 79–103 (last amended 21 September 2017)

    - *Patented Medicines Regulations* (last amended 10 December 2013)

Regulatory Affairs Professionals Society

o   *Compendium of Policies, Guidelines and Procedures* (February 2017)

Introduction

Canada's intellectual property (IP) protection regime for pharmaceuticals consists of the following elements: 1) the *Patent Act*, 2) the *Patented Medicines (Notice of Compliance) Regulations* (*PM(NOC) Regulations*), 3) Certificate of Supplementary Protection (CSP) under the *Patent Act* and *Certificate of Supplementary Protection Regulations* (*CSP Regulations*), 4) data protection provisions under the *Food and Drug Regulations* and 5) price control of patented medicine under the *Patent Act* and *Patented Medicines Regulations* and administered by the Patented Medicine Prices Review Board (PMPRB).

Generally, under the *Patent Act*, owners of new and useful inventions obtain 20 years of exclusivity for making, constructing and using their inventions and selling them to others, commencing from the Canadian patent filing date. In return, the owners must disclose their inventions to the public.[1] Pharmaceutical drug patents usually cover active medicinal ingredients, including compounds, salts, enantiomers, polymorphs, prodrugs and antibodies, formulations, dosage forms, kits, therapeutic indications, dosing regimens and manufacturing methods.

With the elimination of compulsory licences for pharmaceutical products, a statutory "early working exception" was added to the *Patent Act* in 1993. The exception allows a party, usually a generic drug manufacturer, to make, construct, sell or use a patented invention "solely for uses reasonably related to" obtaining a regulatory approval to sell its product, while the relevant patent is still in force.[2] Pursuant to *Patent Act* Subsection 55.2(4), the *PM(NOC) Regulations* were enacted in 1993 to govern how granting of a Notice of Compliance (NOC) for a subsequent entry drug product is linked to the corresponding brand name Canadian reference product's patent status.[3] This is similar but not identical to the US Hatch-Waxman system. Under the *PM(NOC) Regulations*, the subsequent entry company (called the second person), usually a generic drug manufacturer, must successfully address the patents of the brand name company (called the first person) listed on the Register to obtain an NOC. The *PM(NOC) Regulations* provide requirements and procedures regarding: 1) the listing of patents on the Patent Register, 2) the second person's obligations to address the patents listed on the Patent Register, 3) litigation commenced by the first person against the second person, 4) the timing of issuing an NOC to the second person and 5) compensation to the second person for wrongly delayed market entry by the first person.

The CSP regime was introduced in September 2017 to meet Canada's obligations under the *Canada-European Union Comprehensive Economic and Trade Agreement* (*CETA*). The CSP regime is intended to partially compensate a patentee for time spent in obtaining marketing authorization in Canada for a drug containing a new medicinal ingredient or combination of medicinal ingredients. It provides a maximum two-year period of patent-like rights for the drug from the date of the eligible pharmaceutical patent's expiry based on the first authorization for sale of the drug in Canada. Specifically, Sections 104-134 were added to the *Patent Act* to introduce a framework for the issuance and administration of CSPs, for which patentees with patents relating to human and veterinary drugs may apply.[4] *CSP Regulations* also were enacted in 2017 to specify the various timelines and requirements for the CSP regime's administration.[5]

In 2006, data protection provisions were introduced to the *Food and Drug Regulations* (*FDR*) as Section C.08.004.1.[6] They grant an innovator drug manufacturer (including pharmaceutical, biological and radiopharmaceutical drugs) a market exclusivity period of eight years (extended by an additional six months if information regarding paediatric use is provided). In addition, a second entry manufacturer is prevented from filing a regulatory submission with Health Canada for a copy of that innovative drug for the first six years of the eight-year period.

In Canada, prices of patented medicines are regulated federally by the PMPRB. The PMPRB was established under the *Patent Act* to ensure that the prices charged for patented medicines are not excessive. Patentees also are responsible for ongoing reporting requirements pursuant to the *Patent Act*[7] and *Patented Medicines Regulations*.[8]

This chapter describes key elements of the *PM(NOC) Regulations*, CSP, data protection provisions and price control of patented medicines by the PMPRB. For ease of reference, the terms "generic" and "subsequent entry" are used interchangeably throughout this chapter, and both include biosimilars.

PM(NOC) Regulations

Introduction

The *PM(NOC) Regulations* were introduced in 1993 with Bill C-91, which eliminated compulsory licenses for pharmaceutical products and created a statutory "early working exception." This early working exception allows a manufacturer to make and use a patented invention, while the relevant patents are in force, to obtain regulatory approval to sell an equivalent product after the patents have expired. Under *Patent Act* Subsection 55.2(1), before the patents relating to a drug expire, a manufacturer can develop a generic version of the drug, taking the necessary steps to meet the regulatory requirements pertaining to its authorization (generally known as NOC) for sale.

The purpose of the *PM(NOC) Regulations* is to permit the early working of patented inventions,[9] balancing an effective patent enforcement for new and innovative drugs with a timely entry of their lower-priced generic competitors.[10]

The *PM(NOC) Regulations* detail how granting an NOC for a generic drug is linked to the brand-name Canadian reference product's patent expiry. For this reason, the *PM(NOC) Regulations* often are sometimes called the "linkage regulations." Essentially, the *PM(NOC) Regulations* provide that, unless 1) a patented drug manufacturer provides consent to a generic manufacturer to make a generic copy of its patented drug or 2) the patents relevant to the patented drug are invalid or not infringed, the minister of health (minister) cannot issue an NOC to a generic manufacturer until the relevant patents expire.

The *PM(NOC) Regulations* were based in part on the US *Drug Price Competition and Patent Term Restoration Act* of 1984 (the *Hatch-Waxman Act*);[11] however, there are significant differences, and complications and problems arose. The *PM(NOC) Regulations* have been amended several times since 1993. The most recent 2017 amendments implement Canada's CETA obligation to "afford all litigants equivalent and effective rights of appeal" under the *PM(NOC) Regulations*, by replacing summary prohibition applications (shortened and simplified processes) with full actions, resulting in final determinations of patent infringement and validity.[12] To increase efficiency, a limited number of procedural rules have been introduced to the *PM(NOC) Regulations* to facilitate early exchange of key information and allow timely resolution of interlocutory issues (described in detail below).

Administration of the PM(NOC) Regulations

The Office of Patented Medicines and Liaison (OPML) within Health Canada's Therapeutic Products Directorate (TPD) administers the *PM(NOC) Regulations*. All drug submissions seeking an NOC, including those submitted to the Biologics and Genetic Therapies Directorate (BGTD) and the Veterinary Drugs Directorate (VDD), are assessed to determine whether they fall within the scope of the *PM(NOC) Regulations*. All these directorates are part of Health Canada's Health Products and Food Branch (HPFB).

Health Canada has published *Guidance Document: Patented Medicines (Notice of Compliance) Regulations*,[13] most recently updated 26 October 2017. A notice for updated information related to OPML's administration of the 2017 amendments to the *PM(NOC) Regulations* also has been published.[14]

Listing Patents
The Patent Register and Patent List

As part of its *PM(NOC) Regulations* administration duties, OPML maintains a patent register containing patents (including their expiry dates and other information) a first person has listed successfully for each drug it has regulatory authorization to market (i.e., drugs for which NOCs have been issued). The register is similar to the US Food and Drug Administration's (FDA) *Orange Book* and covers eligible patents associated with pharmaceutical, biological or radiopharmaceutical drugs.

A first person wishing to add patents to the register and patent list must provide Health Canada with a list of patents (patent lists or Patent Form IVs) for each product. Based on the information provided by the first person, OPML will determine each patent's eligibility for listing on the register, using the requirements provided by *PM(NOC) Regulations* Section 4 (described in detail below). Eligible patents are added to the register and patent list after the drug's NOC is issued. Generally, a second person seeking to copy a patented Canadian reference product is required to address the patents listed on the register for that reference product before it can receive an NOC for a generic or biosimilar version. However, as described in detail below, the second person is not required to address any patents added to the register on or after the second person's regulatory submission filing date.

The register is available at http://pr-rdb.hc-sc.gc.ca/pr-rdb/index-eng.jsp (accessed 15 May 2018).

Patent Eligibility

PM(NOC) Regulations' Section 4 outlines the requirements for including a patent on the patent register. The section outlines the timing requirements for patent list filing, the information required, the type of drug submissions for which a patent list may be filed and substantive eligibility requirements related to the patent claims.

Patent List in Relation to a New Drug Submission (NDS)

A first person that files an NDS may submit patent lists related to its drug submission it wishes to be listed on the register to the minister. One patent listing requirement is that it contains a claim:

    a)   for the medicinal ingredient
    b)   for the formulation containing the medicinal ingredient
    c)   for the dosage form (delivery system for the medicinal ingredient or a formulation containing it)

or

    d)   for the medicinal ingredient's use

OPML will not list patents purely for process, for a medical device, for an intermediate used in the medicinal ingredient manufacture, for a metabolite, for an impurity present in the final drug product or for a different chemical form of the medicinal ingredient or its uses, including salts, esters and other medicinal ingredient derivatives.

Claim of types a–d must be relevant to the drug, meaning there must be a high degree of specificity between the claim's wording and the NOC (product specificity requirement).[15]

Chapter 8

Patents Claiming the Medicinal Ingredient
A "claim for the medicinal ingredient" is defined in *PM(NOC) Regulations* Section 2. According to the definition, in addition to compound patents, product-by-process patents and patents claiming biological drugs are eligible, as are patents claiming different medicinal ingredient polymorphs. According to the Regulatory Impact Analysis Statement (RIAS) accompanying the 2006 *PM(NOC) Regulations*' amendments,[16] the term "polymorph" includes different crystalline, amorphous, hydrated and solvated forms of the approved medicinal ingredient. The definition specifically excludes different chemical forms of the medicinal ingredient, such as salts and esters.

Since the creation of the *PM(NOC) Regulations*, Health Canada's practice has been to list patents containing a claim for the medicinal ingredient on the register for any approved drug that includes that medicinal ingredient. This practice was confirmed in Subsection 4(2.1)(a), added to the *PM(NOC) Regulations* in 2015.[17] According to this subsection, a patent claiming a single medicinal ingredient as a compound will be eligible for listing for a drug that contains that medicinal ingredient in combination with other medicinal ingredients, notwithstanding that the medicinal ingredient on the NOC is the combination of medicinal ingredients. However, patents claiming a combination of medicinal ingredients are not eligible for listing for a drug containing only one of the claimed medicinal ingredients.

Similarly, a patent claiming a specific enantiomer is not eligible for listing against a racemic drug, and neither is a patent that claims a racemate for listing against an enantiomeric drug.

Patents Claiming the Formulation
For formulation patents, the *PM(NOC) Regulations* specify a relevant claim must include both the approved drug formulation's medicinal and nonmedicinal ingredients as essential elements. Like a medicinal ingredient patent claim, the formulation's claimed medicinal ingredient(s) must be those specifically approved in the NOC. Therefore, a single medicinal ingredient formulation claim cannot be listed against an approved multi-medicinal ingredient formulation. The specificity standard applicable to the nonmedicinal component is lower. Where a nonmedicinal component is specifically claimed in the formulation patent, it is listable only if that nonmedicinal component is specifically present in the drug. However, the patent is not made ineligible for listing if there are additional nonmedicinal components approved for the drug.[18]

Patents Claiming the Dosage Form
According to the definition of "claim for the dosage form" in *PM(NOC) Regulations*' Section 2, a listable dosage form patent must contain a claim for a delivery system for a medicinal ingredient or formulation, with both the delivery system and medicinal ingredient or formulation being specifically approved in the NOC. Eligible dosage form patents may claim extended-release dosage forms, implants and patches. Patents are not listable if they are directed solely to the delivery system (for example, IV bags or stents) or if they fail to claim the approved medicinal ingredient or formulation.

Patents Claiming Use of the Medicinal Ingredient
Patents with a "claim for the use of the medicinal ingredient" must contain a claim for the medicinal ingredient's exact use approved through the issuance of an NOC.[19] To determine whether the patent claims an approved use, OPML will refer to the "indication" section of the drug's Product Monograph (PM). Patents claiming the use of a combination of medicinal ingredients generally will not be eligible for listing against a drug containing only one component of the combination, unless the combination use is found in the drug's approved PM indication section. In addition, a patent that contains a claim for the medicinal ingredient's use is eligible for listing if the submission includes the use claimed in the patent, even if: 1) the submission includes additional medicinal ingredients, 2) the submission includes other additional uses of the medicinal ingredient or 3) the use included in the submission requires the medicinal ingredient's use in combination with another drug.[20]

Patent in Relation to a Supplement to a New Drug Submission (SNDS)
A first person also may submit a patent list in relation to an SNDS. A patent may be submitted for listing against an SNDS only for a change in formulation, dosage form or the medicinal ingredient's use; that is, a mere corporate or product name change or similar administrative amendment does not provide a listing opportunity.[21] The patent will be eligible only if it contains a claim for the change for which approval is being sought in the SNDS.[22]

Listing of Certificate of Supplementary Protection (CSP)
The CSP regime (described in detail below) was implemented in September 2017. A CSP is eligible for listing on the register for an NDS or SNDS if: 1) the patent set out in the CSP is listed and 2) the NDS or SNDS relates to a drug for which the CSP is granted.[23]

Once issued, all CSPs will be assessed by TPD for eligibility for the patent register, without requiring a separate form or request from the first person.

Timing Requirements for Listing
A first person wishing to submit a patent list must do so at the time its NDS or SNDS is filed. The information must be provided on a Form IV: Patent List.[24]

The *PM(NOC) Regulations* provide one exception to this rule: a first person also may submit a patent list for a previously filed drug submission, provided: 1) the Canadian patent filing date precedes the drug submission filing date (in other words, the patent is pending at the time of the submission filing); and 2) the patent list is submitted to OPML within 30 days of the patent being granted.[25]

The timing requirements are strictly enforced, and only patent lists submitted in accordance with these timelines will be accepted. There is no mechanism for listing a patent on the register if a patent list is submitted outside these timelines. For this reason, first persons should closely monitor their pending patent applications' status.

For a patent granted after an NOC has been granted, the first person must identify the submission number assigned by TPD to add the newly granted patent.[26]

Carry-Forward Provisions

PM(NOC) Regulations' Subsection 4.1(2) is a "carry-forward" provision. Under this subsection, a first person that submits a patent list for an NDS may, if the list is added to the patent register, resubmit the same list for an SNDS but may not submit a new patent list for a supplement except in accordance with Subsection 4(3).[27] In other words, a patent on a patent list that has been added to the register for an NDS under Subsection 4(2) will be carried forward for a supplement for the same drug product, but only for a supplement for the same drug product, provided it also meets drug product specificity requirements.

Obligations of First Person

Pursuant to *PM(NOC) Regulations*' Subsection 4(7), the first person is responsible for keeping patent list information updated.[28] The register includes the name and address of the first person on whom the second person must serve a Notice of Allegation (NOA) (described in detail below). A first person's failure to maintain this information can lead to delays and missed communications, so it is critical the information in the register be current.

Patent List Audit by OPML

Upon receipt of the first person's patent list, OPML will audit it to verify the information required under *PM(NOC) Regulations*' Subsection 4(4) is accurate and in compliance with the regulations. OPML also will review the patent and the associated drug submission(s) when conducting its patent eligibility assessment. If the patent is determined to be ineligible, the first person will be notified in writing and will have 30 days to make written representations as to the patent's eligibility.

If a first person disagrees with an OPML patent listing decision, it can bring an application to the Federal Court of Canada for judicial review of the decision.

Obligations of Second Person

Under the early working provision in *Patent Act* Section 55.2, a second person can make or use a copy of a patented Canadian reference product to obtain regulatory approval without being liable for infringing any patents, including those listed on the patent register. Therefore, where a second person files an Abbreviated New Drug Submission (ANDS) or a supplement to an ANDS (SANDS) seeking an NOC for a drug, and the submission or supplement directly or indirectly compares the drug with, or makes reference to a Canadian reference product marketed by a first person and for which patents have been listed on the patent register, the second person must, in the submission or supplement, comply with *PM(NOC) Regulations*' Section 5 regarding each listed patent.[29] Specifically, the second person is required to address all patents on the register listed against the Canadian reference product as of its ANDS or SANDS filing date.[30] The second person is not required to address any patents added to the register after its regulatory submission has been filed. The register, thus, will be "frozen" after filing in terms of that second person's regulatory submission.

The first step in addressing each patent listed against the drug on the patent list is to submit a Form V: Declaration re Patent List (Form V). In Form V, the second person may accept that an NOC for its generic product will not be issued until the declared expiration of the listed patent or the CSP, or the second person may challenge the patent or CSP by making one or more of the following allegations:

- the statement made by the first person about patent or CSP ownership or licensing is false
- the patent or CSP has expired
- the patent or CSP is not valid or void
- the patent or CSP is ineligible for inclusion on the patent register
- the patent or CSP would not be infringed by the second person making, constructing, using or selling the generic drug
- in the case of a CSP, that CSP cannot take effect, for example, where a CSP has been issued and listed on the patent register, but the patent set out in the CSP has lapsed or otherwise terminated by operation of law prior to expiry of the 20-year patent term[31]

Note, if any allegation above has been checked, it is required to comply with *PM(NOC) Regulations* Subsection 5(3) requiring the provision of an NOA.

NOA

If a second person files a Form V containing one of the above allegations, it must serve an NOA on the first person on or after its regulatory filing date. The NOA must include a description of the medicinal ingredient, dosage form, strength, route of administration and the drug's use for which the ANDS or SANDS has been filed. It also must include a statement of the allegation's legal and factual basis. In the case of an allegation of a listed patent or CSP's invalidity, the statement must be detailed.[32] In addition, the second person must address all claims in a listed patent that is the NOA's subject. The second person must provide proof to the minister that the NOA has been served on the first person, along with a copy of the NOA.

In addition, the second person must serve the following documents with the NOA:
1. a certification by the minister of the submission or supplement's filing date
2. a document setting out the second person's address for service for the purpose of any action that may be brought against it under *PM(NOC) Regulations*' Section 6 along with the names of and contact information for their anticipated solicitors of record, if that action is brought
3. a searchable electronic copy of the submission or supplement's portions under the second person's control that are relevant to determine whether any patent or CSP referred to in the NOA would be infringed
4. if the second person is alleging patent or CSP invalidity, an electronic copy of any document—along with an electronic copy of it in English or French if available—on which the person is relying in support of the allegation[33]

If the second person makes an invalidity allegation, when serving the NOA, the second person may request the following information:
1. the name of and contact information for any inventor who might have information relevant to the allegation, along with an indication as to whether that inventor is an employee of the first person or of the patent owner

and/or

2. any laboratory notebook, research report or other document (collectively, internal invention documents) that may be relevant to determine whether a particular property, advantage or use asserted by the second person to be part of the invention was established as of the filing date of the patent application, if the second person identifies the specific allegation in the NOA that is relevant to the request and the portion of the patent in which that property, advantage or use is set out[34]

Patent Infringement Actions Commenced by First Person

The *PM(NOC) Regulations*' Subsection 6(1) allows a first person served with an NOA to commence an action in the Federal Court of Canada for a declaration that making, constructing, using or selling a second person's drug would infringe the patent or CSP that is the NOA's subject. The first person must bring the action within 45 days after being served with an NOA. If the first person is not the patent or CSP owner, the owner is a required party to the action. If a first person or patent owner chooses not to commence an action, subsequent actions are prohibited unless the first person or patent owner did not have a reasonable basis for bringing an action within the prescribed 45-day period.[35]

The commencement of a patent infringement action automatically triggers a 24-month stay, which prevents the minister from issuing an NOC to the second person while the action proceeds, unless the first person renounces the stay when commencing the action.[36] In addition, during the 24-month stay, the *PM(NOC) Regulations* prohibit joinder of any action, other than an action in relation to an allegation of the second person included in a submission or supplement in the main action or an action in respect of a CSP that sets out a patent at issue in the main action.[37]

When commencing an action under the *PM(NOC) Regulations*, the first person must serve the following documents on the second person:
a. the statement of claim
b. a document setting out the information regarding inventors and the internal invention documents, if requested by the second person
c. a document setting out an explanation of the steps that have been and are being taken to locate item b above, along with a statement they will be provided as soon as feasible

or

d. a document setting out the reasons for not providing item b above[38]

Since the mandatory documents produced by the first or second person pursuant to the *PM(NOC) Regulations* often contain commercially sensitive confidential information, the producing party is allowed to impose reasonable rules for maintaining the information's confidentiality, as between the parties.[39]

In addition to defending a patent infringement action, the second person may commence a counterclaim seeking to invalidate the patent or CSP.[40]

Exceptions to the 24-Month Stay Against NOC Issuance

The *PM(NOC) Regulations* contain several exceptions to the 24-month stay against NOC issuance to the second person, including:

- if the patent owner has consented to the second person making, constructing, using or selling the drug in Canada
- if the patent or CSP is deleted from the patent register
- if the Federal Court declares the patent or CSP is ineligible for register listing
- if the infringement action under the *PM(NOC) Regulations* is discontinued or dismissed

or

- each party that brings an action in response to the NOA renounces application of the 24-month stay against NOC issuance[41]

Noninfringement and Invalidity

The most commonly litigated issues in actions under the *PM(NOC) Regulations* surround allegations of noninfringement and invalidity of the patents on the register.

An analysis of either infringement or validity first requires a construction of the claims, which is a legal exercise undertaken by the court in arriving at the patent claims' monopoly boundaries. Once determined, this claim scope is then either: 1) compared to the second person's drug, to determine the issue of infringement; or 2) compared to the prior art references to determine validity.

Allegations of invalidity can take numerous forms, including a listed patent:
- is anticipated by a previously disclosed reference
- is obvious to a person of skill in the art as of the claim date
- has not been demonstrated or soundly predicted to deliver the utility of the patent
- is ambiguously claimed
- is claimed too broadly

and/or
- is insufficiently described to support the claims

PM(NOC) Regulations' Section 6.08 allows a second person to bring a motion for summary dismissal of the action in whole or in part, on the grounds it is redundant, scandalous, frivolous or vexatious or is otherwise an abuse of process.[42] One abuse of process that may serve as the basis for summary dismissal occurs when a first person's infringement claim is bereft of any possibility of success.[43]

Remedies for the First Person

In addition to a declaration of infringement, the court may order any other remedy available under the *Patent Act*, or at law or in equity, in respect of patent infringement. For example, if an NOC issues prior to a declaration of infringement being made, the availability of injunctive relief against the second person may be obtained.[44]

Remedies for the Second Person

The *PM(NOC) Regulations*' Section 8 allows second persons to seek compensation for losses suffered during the period its product was kept off the market as a result of an unsuccessful or discontinued proceeding having been brought against them under the *PM(NOC) Regulations*. If an action brought under the *PM(NOC) Regulations* is discontinued, dismissed or if a declaration of infringement is reversed on appeal, all plaintiffs in the action are jointly and severally, or solitarily, liable to the second person for any loss suffered after the later of: 1) the date of service of the NOA that allowed the action to be brought and 2) the date the NOC would have issued in the absence of the *PM(NOC) Regulations*. The court has discretion to specify another start date, provided the date is determined to be more appropriate than the date specified in the *PM(NOC) Regulations*. No end date is specified in the *PM(NOC) Regulations*, thus allowing a second person to seek compensation for any loss suffered due to delayed market entry after the NOC date. The court may make any order for relief by way of damages the circumstances require.[45]

The remedy available under Section 8 is not available to the second person if the first person renounces the 24-month stay.[46]

Related Rights of Action

Because not all patents are eligible for listing on the patent register, and not all eligible patents are listed on the register, the *PM(NOC) Regulations* allow the parties to address unlisted patents to reach legal certainty regarding patent infringement. In particular, on receipt of an NOA, the first person or patent owner may bring an action for infringement of an unlisted patent, effectively permitting the first person or patent owner to bring an action prior to the occurrence of actual infringement.[47] If the second person has reasonable grounds to believe making, constructing, using or selling the drug might be alleged to infringe an unlisted patent or CSP, that person is deemed to be an "interested person" and can seek a declaration of noninfringement or invalidity.[48]

Summary

- The *PM(NOC) Regulations*' intent is to balance innovative drug patent protection with the timely entry of generic drugs to the market.
- The *PM(NOC) Regulations* link drug approval regulations with patent protection law and are administered by OPML for Health Canada.
- Patented drug manufacturers may list eligible patents for approved medicines on the patent register. Timing requirements are stringent. Generic companies must address the patents and CSPs listed on the patent register as part of their drug approval process.

- OPML decisions about listing patents on the register may be challenged in the Federal Court of Canada through an application for judicial review.
- If a generic drug manufacturer does not wait for a listed patent or CSP to expire before it seeks an NOC, it must serve an NOA on the patented drug manufacturer.
- In response to an NOA, the patented drug manufacturer may initiate an action in the Federal Court of Canada seeking a patent infringement declaration. Commencing the action will result in an automatic 24-month stay, preventing the minister from issuing an NOC to the generic drug manufacturer during that time, unless the patented drug manufacturer renounces the stay.
- To balance an innovator company's right to initiate an action, the *PM(NOC) Regulations* permit a generic drug manufacturer to apply to the Federal Court for a summary dismissal of the action as an abuse of process.
- The *PM(NOC) Regulations* contain procedural rules intended to facilitate early exchange of key information, allow for timely resolution of interlocutory issues and efficient resolution of the action within the 24-month stay.
- The *PM(NOC) Regulations* allow a second person to seek compensation for losses suffered during the period its product was kept off the market as a result of an unsuccessful or discontinued proceeding having been brought against them under the *PM(NOC) Regulations*.

Certificate of Supplementary Protection

Introduction

In September 2017, to meet its CETA obligations,[49] Canada implemented a new CSP (or patent term restoration) regime for patents related to human or veterinary drugs containing a new medicinal ingredient or a combination thereof. This regime, administered by the minister, is similar to patent term extensions granted in some countries and is intended to give additional patent-like protection to compensate in part for on-the-market time lost due to research and regulatory review.

Details of CSP are fleshed out in the *CSP Regulations*,[50] issued under the *Patent Act*. Regulatory and legal professionals also should review Health Canada's *Guidance Document on the Certificate of Supplementary Protection Regulations*, published 21 September 2017.[51]

The CSP regime's effective date was 21 September 2017; the implications of this and transitional issues are discussed below.

As noted above, the *PM(NOC) Regulations* also have been updated to include "Certificate of Supplementary Protection" in Section 3(2).

Term and Scope of CSP

As noted above, the normal patent protection term in Canada is 20 years from the Canadian filing date. The CSP regime permits a new protection acting as an extension of up to two years if the patent and product meet the prescribed conditions. Lesser extensions also can be given if circumstances demand it.[52]

A CSP's term is the difference between the date of the filing of the patent application and the date of authorization for sale, reduced by five years, and capped at two years.

CSP term = [Notice of Compliance date − Patent filing date] − five years, with a cap of two years

For example, if a patent was filed on 1 January 2000, and the marketing approval was issued for the drug product on 1 January 2010, the patent would expire on 31 December 2020; however, due to the long approval time, a full two-year CSP would be available. (Eligibility rules requiring prompt filing and prosecution of drug submissions by the sponsor must be met, and the company cannot be dilatory in seeking approval; this is discussed more below.)

The scope of CSP protection can be no broader than that afforded by the patent in the CSP and is subject to the same limitations and exceptions as the patent. However, it is not a CSP infringement for any person to make, construct, use or sell the medicinal ingredient or combination of medicinal ingredients for export from Canada. In addition, the CSP can be exercised only in connection with the drug product for which it was issued. For example, an infringement action using a CSP against an alleged infringer would be possible if that infringer were using the patented invention in manufacturing a similar product; however, were it incorporated in another drug product, or the invention used in some way not related to the drug product for which the CSP was issued, no infringement proceeding could be brought only due to the CSP.

A CSP may issue for human use, and a separate CSP may issue for veterinary use for a medicinal ingredient or combination of medicinal ingredients that otherwise would be considered the same.

Eligibility

For a patent and a drug to qualify for a CSP, a number of eligibility requirements must be met. In essence, a CSP can be issued only for a new eligible medicinal ingredient or a new combination of all medicinal ingredients, where the patent in fact claims that ingredient or combination either on its own or as obtained by a process, or a use of that ingredient or combination. Eligible medicinal ingredients and eligible patents are described in detail below.

Eligible Medicinal Ingredients
Eligible medicinal ingredients or combinations of medicinal ingredients must meet the requirements of *Patent Act* Subsections 106(1)(c)(d) and (e), applying *Patent Act* Subsections 105(3) and (4) and *CSP Regulations*' Section 2. According to the CSP guidance, Health Canada determines which medicinal ingredients or combinations of medicinal ingredients are eligible by considering:
- whether the authorization for sale of the underlying submission was "an authorization for sale of the prescribed kind"
- if yes, whether the authorization for sale is the first authorization for sale issued with respect to the medicinal ingredient or combination of medicinal ingredients

and
- if yes, whether any other CSP has been issued with respect to that medicinal ingredient or combination[53]

According to *CSP Regulations*' Section 2, a medicinal ingredient is to be treated as the same as any other medicinal ingredient if they differ from each other only with respect to one or more of the following variations:
- a) a variation in any appendage within a medicinal ingredient's molecular structure that causes it to be an ester, salt, complex, chelate, clathrate or any noncovalent derivative
- b) a variation that is a medicinal ingredient's enantiomer or a mixture of enantiomers
- c) a variation that is a medicinal ingredient's solvate or polymorph
- d) an *in vivo* or *in vitro* post-translational modification of a medicinal ingredient
- e) any combination of the variations set out in paragraphs a) to d) above[54]

According to *Patent Act* Subsections 105(5) and (6), if combinations of medicinal ingredients differ from each other only with respect to a variation in the ratio between those ingredients, they are deemed to be the same combination.[55]

First Authorization for Sale in Canada
Eligible authorizations for sale are NOCs for drugs, biologics or veterinary drugs issued on or after 21 September 2017. The authorization for sale in connection with which a CSP is sought also must be the first such authorization for that drug or combination of drugs issued in Canada. There are specific rules on how to decide whether such an authorization is indeed "first," as further described in the CSP guidance.[56]

Further, there must be no earlier CSP issued for that medicinal ingredient (or combination) under any circumstances. For example, a CSP is considered to have been issued even if it subsequently is held to be invalid or void, never takes effect or ceases to have effect.[57]

Eligible Patents
An eligible patent must pertain to a medicinal ingredient or medicinal ingredient combination that actually is contained in a drug product for which the marketing approval is issued. This means the patent must meet the requirements of *Patent Act* Subsection 106(1)(c) and *CSP Regulations*' Subsection 3(2):
- the patent must pertain to a medicinal ingredient or combination of medicinal ingredients, contained in a drug for which an authorization for sale of the prescribed kind was issued on or after 21 September 2017
- the patent must contain
  a) a claim for the medicinal ingredient or combination of all the medicinal ingredients contained in a drug or their use or process for manufacture, for which the authorization for sale set out in the application for a CSP was issued
  b) a claim for the medicinal ingredient or combination of all the medicinal ingredients as obtained by a specified process (i.e., product by process claim) contained in a drug for which the authorization for sale set out in the CSP application was issued

or
  c) a claim for a use of the medicinal ingredient or combination of all medicinal ingredients contained in a drug for which the authorization for sale set out in the CSP application was issued

According to the CSP guidance, the claimed use does not need to match the use approved in an NOC for the NDS set out in the CSP application, as long as the claimed use includes use in humans or animals.[58]

Timing Requirements
There are timing requirements based on the patent issue date, the Canadian regulatory submission filing date and, in most cases, the date of the first foreign regulatory submission filing in countries as prescribed in *CSP Regulations*' Subsection 6(1).

For patents, there are two very specific windows of time during which a patent holder may apply for a CSP. The first is, if the patent is granted before the drug product NOC is issued, the CSP application must be made within 120 days of NOC issuance. If the NOC has been issued and the patent is granted later, the CSP application must be made within 120 days of the patent being granted.[59]

To prevent patent holders from extending their monopolies beyond the time needed for regulatory review, the application (in most cases, an NDS) also must have been submitted in a timely fashion *vis-à-vis* corresponding foreign approvals. This is referred to as the "Timely Submission Requirement." Under *CSP Regulations*, if an application for "authorization for sale" has been filed in the EU, any constituent EU country, the US, Australia, Switzerland or Japan, the Canadian application must be filed within 12 months of the first foreign application. There is an extra year available (i.e., 24 months total) if the CSP application is filed no later than 21 September 2018.[60] Filing for a CSP also is permitted if Canada is the first country in which an application is filed, i.e., the company has not previously sought approval in any of the listed countries.

CSP Regulations and guidance explicitly provide the following regarding an "application for a marketing approval equivalent to an authorization for sale:"

> ". . . In order to determine the date of submission (filing date) of an "application for a marketing approval equivalent to an authorization for sale", the applicable regulatory provisions or practices in the foreign country of that application apply. In making a determination of what type of approval is equivalent (i.e., one that permits the regular sale and what does not), applicants should have regard to the exceptions in the definition of 'authorization for sale' in subsection 1(2) of the *Certificate of Supplementary Protection Regulations*."

The exceptions to an authorization for sale—i.e., permitted sales that are not "regular" authorizations for CSP purposes—are set out in *CSP Regulations*' Subsection 1(2) and also apply to equivalent foreign exceptions. These include interim orders to deal with significant risks, experimental study certificates, urgent public health needs, clinical trials or sales of new drugs for emergency treatment.

CSP Application Details

The application procedure is set out in detail in the CSP guidance. The CSP form, a payment details form (credit card and wire transfer information) and the required fee are needed. The form requires certain critical attestations as to the patent's eligibility for a CSP. The application is intended to be entirely electronic; however, this requirement is not in the *Patent Act* or *CSP Regulations* and does not have the force of law. The fee for an application is currently $9,192 (CAD); this increases every year on 1 April by an amount equal to 2% of the fee payable in the previous year, rounded up to the nearest dollar.

Priority and Conflicts

The amendments to the *Patent Act* and the new *CSP Regulations* have attempted to anticipate all possible conflicts caused by co-pending CSP applications, as only one CSP will be granted for any given medicinal ingredient or combination of medicinal ingredients (*Patent Act* Sections 108–112). If more than one CSP application has been filed for the same authorization for sale, a CSP application for a patent granted on or before the day the NOC was issued will have the same priority as any other such application, and these CSP applications will have priority over CSP applications for a patent granted after the NOC issue date. For CSP applications based on patents issued after the NOC issue date, the application with the earlier patent grant date has priority.

It is possible for CSP applications citing the same NOC to have the same priority, referred to as a "conflict." The *Patent Act* and *CSP Regulations* contemplate a notice will be sent to the parties in such a case. Each then has 90 days to commence a "noncompliance proceeding."

Noncompliance Proceedings

A third party (i.e., a competitor) may bring a legal proceeding in the Federal Court to have a pending CSP application declared invalid within 90 days of the administrative notice of the conflict.[61]

Processing CSP Applications

The TPD is entitled to request additional information once it has completed its preliminary review. The CSP guidance establishes a "service standard" for processing as follows:
- Sixty calendar days (average) for the first eligibility decision beginning the day there are no conflicting CSP applications of the highest priority, and the time for filing a CSP application having the same or higher priority has ended.
- If there are no CSP applications filed before the end of the 120-day period that begins on the day on which the NOC is issued, the highest priority CSP application will be the one that sets out the earliest patent grant date. Measurement of the 60 calendar days will start from the day following the end of the 120-day period that begins on the day on which the patent is granted, since a CSP application will not be assessed until after it is determined there are no other conflicting or higher priority CSP applications.

Register of CSPs and Applications

Information on both CSP applications and issued CSPs is publicly available (https://www.canada.ca/en/health-canada/services/drugs-health-products/drug-products/

applications-submissions/guidance-documents/register-certificates.html); as of the date of writing (1 April 2018), one CSP has been issued, and nine more are pending.

CSPs and the PM(NOC) Regulations

CSPs can be listed on the register and, like patents, can be asserted as part of proceedings under the *PM(NOC) Regulations*. Generic companies will have to address CSPs in the same way as patents under the *PM(NOC) Regulations*, and CSP owners will have the same rights as patent owners.

Summary

- CSPs now are available for eligible patents in Canada that claim eligible medicinal ingredients or combinations of medicinal ingredients or the use thereof in a first-to-market drug.
- The maximum CSP term is two years.
- There are strict timing requirements for CSP applications, based on both the underlying patent grant date and the timing of the drug submission embodying the claimed medicinal ingredient or combination of medicinal ingredients.
- The Canadian regulatory drug submission must be the first submission for that drug worldwide or be filed within 12 months of filing the first corresponding application in any constituent country of the EU, the US, Australia, Switzerland or Japan. This period will extend to 24 months if the CSP application is filed no later than 21 September 2018.
- Only one CSP can be issued per drug obtaining a first NOC on or after 21 September 2017.
- CSPs give the patent holders all the same rights as those provided by in-force patents; however, export from Canada during the CSP term is not regarded as infringement.
- CSPs can be listed on the register and must be addressed by subsequent entry manufacturers in the same way as a patent before an NOC can issue.
- Health Canada has issued detailed guidance setting out many of the ins and outs of dealing with the CSP process, including disputes and conflicts.

Data Protection

Introduction

In 2006, in the wake of North American Free Trade Agreement requirements, Canada amended data protection provisions of the Food and Drug Regulations, CRC c. 870 as new Section C.08.004.1 (data protection provisions). These provisions provide, where an NOC is issued for a "new chemical entity" (NCE), the sponsor is entitled to eight years of exclusivity before a third party (in practice, a generic) can rely on the NCE's approval to leverage its own approval. Further, such a generic cannot even file a regulatory submission (normally an ANDS) until six years after the exclusivity date.

Data protection is available for pharmaceutical, biological and radiopharmaceutical drugs that receive NOCs, including veterinary drugs. The protection can be extended for a further six months if pediatric trial information is provided (described below).

Administration of Data Protection Provisions

Health Canada has issued a *Guidance Document [for] Data Protection under C.08.004.1 of the Food and Drug Regulations* (data protection guidance).[62] This was updated most recently in May 2017 in response to court decisions interpreting the meaning of "innovative drug."[63]

An application for data protection is made in accordance with Health Canada's *Guidance Document: Preparation of Drug Regulatory Activities in the Electronic Common Technical Document Format* Section 1.2.4.2 and related guidances. Once an application is received, TPD conducts a preliminary assessment while the submission is under review to determine whether the drug qualifies for data protection. The sponsor is kept informed throughout the process.

If two manufacturers have products containing the same medicinal ingredient, only the first drug issued an NOC can qualify for the protection. Whether other similar data protection applications are pending can be determined from the public database, the Register of Innovative Drugs (https://www.canada.ca/en/health-canada/services/drugs-health-products/drug-products/applications-submissions/register-innovative-drugs/register.html).

What constitutes an "innovative drug"?

The data protection provisions define an "innovative drug" as a drug that contains a medicinal ingredient not previously approved in a drug by Health Canada and is not a variation of a previously approved medicinal ingredient such as a salt, ester, enantiomer, solvate or polymorph. Under the old system, this was known as a "new chemical entity." Data protection is not available for drugs issued an NOC for a new indication, dosage form or other changes made through a supplement to an SNDS, with the exception of SNDSs containing pediatric clinical trial data.

Some variations, e.g., molecules, with a molecular structure similar to a previously approved medicinal ingredient but not a variation enumerated in the definition of "innovative drug" are considered to be "arguable variations" and may constitute innovative drugs. Health Canada assesses these instances on case-by-case bases, and the data protection guidance discusses this in detail, although it does not appear in the data protection provisions.[64]

A further requirement to qualify for protection is the drug submission must have involved "considerable effort." This is a somewhat subjective test but is discussed in the data protection guidance.

Pediatric Extension
To encourage research on the use of innovative drugs for children, a further six months of data exclusivity can be obtained if the company benefitting from the data protection can show significant research has been done on pediatric use. Clinical trial data must be submitted to Health Canada to gain this benefit, and its sufficiency is open to review. Such research need not necessarily lead to a change in the drug's PM to permit on-label pediatric use, although this may be necessary in most cases. The pediatric clinical trial data must be provided within five years of the beginning of the data protection period.

Product-Line Extensions
In some cases, a drug from the same company may contain a medicinal ingredient plus a customization, optimization or other change but have the same medicinal ingredient as found in an innovative drug for which a data protection period is still in effect. Such drugs would have the same data protection period as the first innovative drug. The brand name of all drugs subject to the same data protection will be shown on the publicly available Register of Innovative Drugs.[65]

Summary
- Data protection is available for an initial innovative drug in Canada.
- The data protection term is eight years from the time the innovative drug's NOC is granted to the time a second product relying on the first product's approval can receive its NOC; this is subject to six months' extension if the sponsor submits the results of pediatric clinical trials for the product.
- A subsequent entry ANDS cannot be filed with Health Canada until six years have passed from the innovative drug's NOC date.
- A public register of such protections and pending applications for same is available online.

Patented Medicine Price Control

Introduction
The *Patent Act* was amended in 1987 to introduce provisions for controlling patented medicines' prices. Under the 1987 amendments, PMPRB[66] was established as the consumer protection agency to ensure patented medicines' prices in Canada are not excessive. PMPRB also was tasked with reporting on pharmaceutical trends and contributes to informed decisions and healthcare policy making in Canada. Further amendments to the patented medicine price provisions of the *Patent Act* were made in 1993, 1994, 1996 and 1999.[67] The *Patented Medicines Regulations* were enacted to provide details on implementing the *Patent Act*'s patented medicine price provisions.

PMPRB has published *Compendium of Policies, Guidelines and Procedures* (last updated, February 2017)[68] to inform patentees of PMPRB's price review policies, guidelines and procedures for the prices of patented medicines sold in Canada, and the procedures normally undertaken in the scientific and price review processes, including identifying when a price appears to be excessive.

PMPRB
The *Patent Act* sets out dual PMPRB roles:
1. regulatory—to ensure the prices patentees charge for patented medicines sold in Canada are not excessive[69]
2. reporting—to report on pharmaceutical trends and patentee research and development (R&D) spending[70]

PMPRB is an independent, autonomous quasi-judicial body composed of board members and board staff. Board members perform the PMPRB's adjudicative function, while board staff carry out the board's day-to-day work, including administering the *Patented Medicines Regulations* to ensure compliance with the prescribed filing requirements and patented medicines' price reviews to identify instances of possible excessive pricing.

PMPRB Jurisdiction Pertaining to Price Regulation
The *Patent Act* grants PMPRB jurisdiction whether a patentee or former patentee of an invention pertaining to a medicine is selling or has sold the medicine at an excessive price in any market in Canada. In determining PMPRB's jurisdiction, the following terms provided in the *Patent Act* apply and have been considered by the courts: 1) "patentee," 2) "invention pertaining to a medicine" and "sale in any market in Canada." The courts tend to interpret these terms liberally to confer jurisdiction on PMPRB.

Patentee
Subsection 79(1) of the *Patent Act* provides the following definition for "patentee":
> "patentee, in respect of an invention pertaining to a medicine, means the person for the time being entitled to the benefit of the patent for that invention and includes, where any other person is entitled to exercise any rights in relation to that patent other than under a licence continued by subsection 11(1) of the *Patent*

Act Amendment Act, 1992, that other person in respect of those rights"[71]

According to the compendium, PMPRB also has jurisdiction over a former patentee of an invention while it was a patentee.[72]

Patent Pertains to the Medicine
The *Patent Act* Subsection 79(1) provides the following definition for "invention pertaining to a medicine:"
> "an invention pertains to a medicine if the invention is intended or capable of being used for medicine or for the preparation or production of medicine"[73]

In the compendium, PMPRB provides a non-exhaustive list of patents it considers as pertaining to a medicine:
- active ingredients
- processes of manufacture
- a particular delivery system or dosage form integral to the medicine's delivery
- indications/use
- formulations[74]

Essentially, according to PMPRB, a patent pertains to a medicine if it is capable of being used, whether or not it is being worked. For example, if a patent pertains to an unapproved indication in Canada, PMPRB still can assert jurisdiction because it is capable of being used as a medicine.

Therefore, on the face of a patent, if there is a rational connection or nexus, which can be one of the merest slender thread, between the invention described in the patent and the medicine, PMPRB can assert jurisdiction.[75] In determining a rational connection, PMPRB is not required to construe a patent's claims; however, it must review the whole patent to determine the invention the patent describes on its face.[76]

In addition to medicines commonly understood to be any substance or mixture of substances administered to humans or in animals to aid in the diagnosis, treatment, mitigation or prevention of disease, symptoms, disorders, abnormal physical states, or in modifying organic functions in humans or animals, PMPRM regards vaccines, topical preparations, anaesthetics and diagnostic products used *in vivo*, regardless of delivery mechanism, as medicines. However, this definition of medicine excludes medical devices, in vitro diagnostic products and disinfectants not used *in vivo*.[77]

If a pending patent application pertains to a medicine being sold in any market in Canada, when the patent is granted, PMPRB will review the price as of the date of first sale or the date on which the patent application was published, whichever comes later. In other words, once the patent is granted, PMPRB's jurisdiction over the price at which the medicine was sold extends to the pre-grant period, as the party selling the medicine derives the benefit of the patent during this period and so is a "patentee."[78] Accordingly, patents should consider the implications of PMPRB jurisdiction before paying grant fees.

PMPRB has asserted jurisdiction over the price of a "patented generic drug," which is a drug falling within a patent for an "invention pertaining to a medicine" as defined in *Patent Act* Subsection 79(2) and has been approved by Health Canada on the basis of a licensed version of an existing brand reference product sold in Canada (e.g., a drug product approved by Health Canada pursuant to a cross-reference to an original drug submission or a generic subsidiary of the brand). In this instance, board staff will review only information relating to the medicine's identity and/or pricing upon the commencement of a board staff investigation. Board staff will commence an investigation into a patented generic drug's price if the following three conditions are met:
- a complaint has been received regarding the patented generic drug
- the patented generic drug's patentee is the only company in Canada selling a generic version of the drug in Canada
- the patented generic drug is not the subject of a pricing agreement with the pan-Canadian Pharmaceutical Alliance (pCPA) to which it is compliant[79]

Sale in Any Market in Canada
For PMPRB to assert jurisdiction, the patentee or former patentee must be selling or have sold the patented medicine in any market in Canada. The sale "in any market in Canada" covers patented medicines sold pursuant to NOCs and may, in some circumstances, include sales under the Special Access Programme, through Clinical Trial Applications and as Investigational New Drugs.[80]

PMPRB reviews the prices of a patented medicine's first sale by the patentee, directly to a class of customer (e.g., a wholesaler, hospital, pharmacy or other) at arm's-length. It has no authority over prices charged by wholesalers or retailers or over pharmacists' professional fees. Further, PMPRB does not need to approve prices before patented medicines are sold in Canada, although at a patentee's request, board staff may provide pre-sale and/or pre-patent advisory assistance on whether a price would appear to be excessive.

PMPRB does not set the prices at which patented medicines can be sold, but determines the Maximum Average Potential Price.[81]

Price Regulation Factors
Patent Act Subsection 85(1) lists factors PMPRB must consider when determining whether a patented medicine is being sold or has been sold at an excessive price in any

market in Canada by a patentee or former patentee. These factors include:
- the prices at which the medicine has been sold in the relevant market
- the prices at which other medicines in the same therapeutic class have been sold in the relevant market
- the prices at which the medicine and other medicines in the same therapeutic class have been sold in countries other than Canada
- changes in the Consumer Price Index
- such other factors as may be specified in any regulations made for the purposes of this subsection[82]

At present, comparator countries for excessive pricing include: France, Germany, Italy, Sweden, Switzerland, the UK and the US.

Remedies

In the event PMPRB finds a patentee or former patentee is selling a patented medicine in any market in Canada at an excessive price, it may order the patentee or former patentee to reduce the maximum price at which its medicine is being sold in that market and to offset revenues received as a result of excessive prices. In many instances, the manufacturer usually will sign a Voluntary Compliance Undertaking (VCU) with PMPRB that includes adjusting its price to a non-excessive level and offsetting any excess revenues collected, instead of going through a formal hearing before a panel of board members. PMPRB decisions are subject to judicial review in the Federal Court of Canada.

PMPRB has published *The Rules of Practice and Procedure* hearings for PMPRB hearings.

Summary

- PMPRB reviews and regulates the patented medicines' prices sold in any market in Canada to ensure they are not excessive.
- When fulfilling its regulatory mandate, PMPRB asserts a very broad jurisdiction over the prices of patented medicines being sold by a patentee or former patentee in any market in Canada.

References

1. *Patent Act*, R.S.C., 1985, c. P-4. Government of Canada Justice Laws website. http://laws-lois.justice.gc.ca/eng/acts/P-4/FullText.html. Accessed 24 April 2018.
2. Ibid, Subsection 55.2(1).
3. *Patented Medicines (Notice of Compliance) Regulations*, S.O.R./93-133 (*PM(NOC) Regulations*). Government of Canada Justice Laws website. http://laws-lois.justice.gc.ca/eng/regulations/sor-93-133/FullText.html. Accessed 24 April 2018.
4. Op cit 1, Sections 104–134.
5. *Certificate of Supplementary Protection Regulations (CSP Regulations)*, SOR/2017-165. Government of Canada Justice Laws website. http://laws-lois.justice.gc.ca/eng/regulations/SOR-2017-165/FullText.html. Accessed 24 April 2018.
6. *Food and Drug Regulations*, C.R.C., c. 870, section C.08.004.1. Government of Canada Justice Laws website. http://laws.justice.gc.ca/eng/regulations/C.R.C.%2C_c._870/page-136.html#docCont. Accessed 24 April 2018.
7. Op cit 1, Sections 79–103.
8. *Patented Medicines Regulations*, SOR/94-688. Government of Canada Justice Laws website. http://laws-lois.justice.gc.ca/eng/regulations/SOR-94-688/FullText.html. Accessed 24 April 2018.
9. *AstraZeneca Canada Inc v Canada (Minister of Health)*, 2006 SCC 49, at paragraph 39.
10. Regulatory Impact Analysis Statement, *Canada Gazette* 2006.II.1510 (*RIAS*).
11. *Drug Price Competition and Patent Term Restoration Act of 1984*, Pub. L. No. 98-417, 98 Stat. 1585 (1984) (*Hatch-Waxman Act*).
12. Regulatory Impact Analysis Statement (RIAS) to the *Regulations Amending the Patented Medicines (Notice of Compliance) Regulations*, 2017, P.C. 2017-1115, 31 August 2017.
13. Office of Patented Medicines and Liaison, *Guidance Document: Patented Medicines (Notice of Compliance) Regulations* (26 October 2017). Health Canada website. https://www.canada.ca/content/dam/hc-sc/migration/hc-sc/dhp-mps/alt_formats/pdf/prodpharma/applic-demande/guide-ld/patmedbrev/pmreg3_mbreg3-eng.pdf. Accessed 24 April 2018.
14. Notice—Patented Medicines (Notice of Compliance) Regulations, 19 September 2017. Health Canada website. http://www.hc-sc.gc.ca/dhp-mps/prodpharma/activit/announce-annonce/pmnoc-notice-rmbac-avis-eng.php. Accessed 24 April 2018.
15. Op cit 3, Subsection 4(2).
16. Op cit 10.
17. *Regulations Amending the Patented Medicines (Notice of Compliance) Regulations*, SOR/2015-0169.
18. Op cit 3, Subsection 4(2.1)(b).
19. *G.D. Searle & Co. v. Canada (Health)*, 2009 FCA 35.
20. Op cit 3, Subsection 4(2.1)(c).
21. Op cit 3, Subsection 4(3).
22. Ibid.
23. Op cit 3, Subsection 4(3.1).
24. Op cit 3, Subsection 4(5).
25. Op cit 3, Subsection 4(6).
26. Op cit 3, Subsection 4(4)(a).
27. Op cit 3, Subsection 4.1(2).
28. Op cit 3, Subsection 4(7).
29. Op cit 3, Section 5.
30. Op cit 3, Subsection 5(4).
31. Op cit 3, Subsection 5(2.1).
32. Op cit 3, Subsection 5(3)(b).
33. Op cit 3, Subsection 5(3)(c).
34. Op cit 3, Subsection 5(3.1).
35. Op cit 3, Subsections 6(1), 6(2) and 6.01.
36. Op cit 3, Section 7.
37. Op cit 3, Subsection 6.02.
38. Op cit 3, Subsection 6.03(1).
39. Op cit 3, Subsections 5(3.5)–(3.9) and 6.03(2)–(5).
40. Op cit 3, Subsection 6(3).
41. Op cit 3, Subsections 7(2) to (5).
42. Op cit 3, Section 6.08.
43. *Genentech, Inc v Amgen Canada Inc*, 2018 FC 303, at paragraph 13.
44. Op cit 3, Subsection 6(4).
45. Op cit 3, Subsections 8(1)–(3) and (5).
46. Op cit 3, Subsection 8(4).
47. Op cit 3, Section 8.2.
48. Op cit 3, Section 8.1.
49. Op cit 1, Sections 104–134.
50. *Certificate of Supplementary Protection Regulations (CSP Regulations)*, SOR/2017-165. Government of Canada Justice Laws website. http://

laws-lois.justice.gc.ca/eng/regulations/SOR-2017-165/FullText.html. Accessed 24 April 2018.
51. URL for Health Canada's Guidance Document on the *Certificate of Supplementary Protection Regulations*. Health Canada website. https://www.canada.ca/content/dam/hc-sc/documents/services/drugs-health-products/drug-products/applications-submissions/guidance-documents/csp-guide-cps-ld-sept19-eng.pdf. Accessed 24 April 2018.
52. Op cit 1, Section 116.
53. Op cit 51, at page 13.
54. Op cit 50, Section 2.
55. Op cit 1, Subsections 105(5) and (6).
56. Op cit 51, at pages 13–16.
57. Op cit 1, Subsection 106(2).
58. Op cit 51, at page 17.
59. Op cit 1, Subsection 106(3) and op cit 50, Subsection 6(2).
60. Op cit 1, Subsection 6(1)(b).
61. Op cit 1, Section 110 and op cit 50, Section 11.
62. *Guidance Document [for] Data Protection under C.08.004.1 of the Food and Drug Regulations*. Health Canada website. https://www.canada.ca/content/dam/hc-sc/documents/services/drugs-health-products/drug-products/applications-submissions/guidance-documents/data_donnees_protection-eng.pdf. Accessed 24 April 2018.
63. *Epicept Canada Limited v Canada*, 2010 FC 956; *Teva Canada Limited v Canada*, 2012 FCA 106; *Canada v Celgene Inc*, 2013 FCA 43; *Takeda Canada Inc v Canada*, 2013 FCA 13; *Photocure ASA v Canada*, 2015 FC 959.
64. Op cit 62, at page 5.
65. Op cit 62, at pages 6 and 7.
66. PMPRB website. http://www.pmprb-cepmb.gc.ca/home. Accessed 24 April 2018.
67. Op cit 1, Sections 79 to 103.
68. *Compendium of Policies, Guidelines and Procedures*, last updated February 2017. PMPRB website. http://www.pmprb-cepmb.gc.ca/CMFiles/Compendium_Feb_2017_EN.pdf. Accessed 24 April 2018.
69. Op cit 1, Sections 83–87.
70. Op cit 1, Section 89.
71. Op cit 1, Subsection 79(1).
72. Op cit 68, at page 12.
73. Op cit 1, Subsection 79(1).
74. Op cit 68, at pages 8–9.
75. *ICN Pharmaceuticals, Inc v Canada* [1996] FCJ No 1065 (FCA).
76. *Galderma Canada Inc v Canada*, 2017 FC 1023.
77. Op cit 75.
78. *Shire BioChem Inc v Canada (Attorney General)*, 2007 FC 1316.
79. Op cit 68, at pages 15–16.
80. Op cit 68, at page 9. See also *Celgene Corp v Canada*, 2011 SCC 1.
81. Ibid.
82. Op cit 1, Subsection 85(1).

Chapter 9

Abbreviated New Drug Submissions

Updated by Bhavesh Patel, CChem, Bocar Guisse, MSc and Fraidianie Sevigne

OBJECTIVES

❏ Understand the requirements of Abbreviated New Drug Submissions in Canada.

❏ Understand policies regarding requirements for comparative biostudies.

❏ Learn the differences between New Drug Submissions and Abbreviated New Drug Submissions.

REGULATIONS AND GUIDELINES COVERED IN THIS CHAPTER

❏ *Food and Drugs Act*

❏ *Food and Drug Regulations*

❏ Policy: *Canadian Reference Product* (5 December 1995)

❏ Guidance Document: Use of a Foreign-sourced Reference Product as a Canadian Reference Product (24 November 2017)

❏ Policy: *Interpretation of "Identical Medicinal Ingredient"* (9 July 2003)

❏ Guidance Document: *Comparative Bioavailability Standards: Formulations used for Systemic Effects* (22 May 2012)

❏ Guidance Document: *Conduct and Analysis of Comparative Bioavailability Studies* (22 May 2012)

❏ Guidance Document: *Preparation of Drug Regulatory Activities in the Common Technical Document (CTD) Format* (22 June 2012)

❏ Guidance Document: *Biopharmaceutics Classification System Based Biowaiver* (29 May 2014)

❏ Notice: Clarification of bioanalytical method validation procedures (8 October 2015)

❏ Notice: Policy on Bioequivalence Standards for Highly Variable Drug Products (18 April 2016)

❏ Form: Sponsor Attestation Checklist for Abbreviated New Drug Submissions (ANDS) and Supplements to an Abbreviated New Drug Submission (SANDS) (12 May 2016)

❏ Form: Foreign Review Attestation and Summary of Quality Differences: Subsequent Market Entry Products (Human Drugs) (28 September 2012)

❏ Notice: Submission Filling Requirements—Good Manufacturing Practices (GMP)/Drug Establishment Licenses (DEL (10 February 2017)

Chapter 9

- Notice: Mandatory Requirements for using the Common Electronic Submissions Gateway (CESG) and the Electronic Common Technical Document (eCTD) Format (8 July 2016)
- Notice: Validation rules for regulatory transactions submitted to Health Canada in the electronic Common Technical Document (eCTD) format (27 November 2017)
- Template: Draft Comprehensive Summary—Bioequivalence (CS-BE) (6 May 2004)
- Guidance for Industry: Pharmaceutical Quality of Aqueous Solutions (15 February 2005)
- Guidance Document: Quality (Chemistry and Manufacturing) Guidance: New Drug Submissions (NDSs) and Abbreviated New Drug Submissions (ANDSs) (30 October 2017)
- Notice: Tablet Scoring of Subsequent-entry Pharmaceutical Products (28 May 2017)
- Notice: Publication of the Guidance Document: Certificate of Supplementary Protection Regulations (19 September 2017)
- Guidance Document: Use of Certificates of Suitability as supporting information in Drug Submissions (21 August 2017)
- Guidance Document: Questions and Answers: Plain Language Labelling Regulations (8 September 2016)
- Guidance for Industry: Stability Tests of Existing Drug Substances and Products (1 April 2006)
- Draft Guidance for Industry: Impurities in Existing Drug Substances and Products (6 September 2005)
- Guidance for Industry: Management of Drug Submissions (19 December 2013)
- Guidance Document: Notice of Compliance with Conditions (NOC/c) (16 September 2016)
- Policy: Submissions for Generic Parenteral Drugs (1 March 1990)
- Policy: Submissions for Generic Topical Drugs (24 September 1990)
- Guidance Document: Data Requirements for Safety and Effectiveness of Subsequent Market Entry Steroid Nasal Products for Use in the Treatment of Allergic Rhinitis (19 September 2011)
- Guidance Document: Guidance to Establish Equivalence or Relative Potency of Safety and Efficacy of a Second Entry Short-Acting Beta$_2$-Agonist Metered Dose Inhaler (February 1999)
- Final Guidance Document: Data Requirements for Safety and Effectiveness of Steroid Nasal Products for Use in the Treatment of Allergic Rhinitis for Industry (19 September 2011)
- Guidance for Industry: Pharmaceutical Quality of Inhalation and Nasal Products (1 October 2006)
- Canada Gazette, Part II, Ottawa, Registration SOR/2017-165 1 September 2017 Patent Act, Certificate of Supplementary Protection Regulations

Introduction

Generic products are approved through Abbreviated New Drug Submissions (ANDSs). Products qualifying as generic products are defined in *Food and Drug Regulations'* (*FDR*) Section C.08.002.1(1):

a) a new drug that is the pharmaceutical equivalent of the Canadian reference product (CRP)
b) a new drug that is the bioequivalent with the CRP, based on the pharmaceutical and, where the minister considers it necessary, bioavailability characteristics
c) a new drug with the same route of administration as the CRP
d) a new drug with conditions of use that fall within the CRP's conditions of use

As stated in *FDR* C.08.001.1, "pharmaceutical equivalent" is "a new drug that, in comparison with another drug, contains identical amounts of the identical medicinal ingredients, in comparable dosage forms, but that does not necessarily contain the same non-medicinal ingredients."

Generally, all second-entry or subsequent market entry products qualify for the ANDS format.

In addition to the *FDR*, generic drugs are subject to the *Patented Medicines (Notice of Compliance) Regulations* under the *Patent Act* (see Chapter 8, Patented Medicines (Notice of Compliance) Regulations).

In the early 20th century, the commissioner of patents granted compulsory licences to parties wishing to produce generic drugs in Canada. Inquiries into Canadian drug pricing during the late 1950s resulted in several investigations, ending with an amendment to the *Patent Act* in 1969. At that time, compulsory licences were granted to parties wanting to import generic drugs into Canada. The patent holder was paid a standard 4% royalty. The 1969 amendment allowed Canada's generic drug industry to flourish, and lowered drug prices. Further *Patent Act* amendments came about in the late 1980s and early 1990s. Under these provisions, generic product sponsors can conduct bioequivalence and bioavailability studies before the innovator product patent expires. However, stockpiling generic products before patent expiration is forbidden. These regulations outline patented medicine protection measures and the conditions under which Health Canada will consider a second-entry drug product for review and approval.

In October 2006, data protection under *FDR* Section C.08.004.1 was introduced, allowing the manufacturer of an innovative drug (including pharmaceutical, biological and radiopharmaceutical products) an eight-year marketing exclusivity period (extended an additional six months when information regarding pediatric use is provided). A second entry manufacturer may not file a submission for a copy of that innovative drug during the first six years of that period.

Further, on 21 September 2017, Health Canada provided information regarding implemented Certificates of Supplementary Protection (CSP) for medicinal ingredients. This is part of Canada's Comprehensive Economic and Trade Agreement obligations with the European Union, under which innovators are provided a period of extended market exclusivity to compensate for time lost due to regulatory obligations in obtaining market approval. This protection is a form of *sui generis* exclusivity for up to two years and applies to patents claiming the medicinal ingredient contained in pharmaceuticals, biologics and veterinary drugs.

Canadian Reference Product

FDR Section C.08.001.1 defines "Canadian reference product" in terms of an ANDS filing as:
- (a) "a drug in respect of which a notice of compliance is issued pursuant to section C.08.004 or C.08.004.01 and which is marketed in Canada by the innovator of the drug,
- (b) a drug, acceptable to the Minister, that can be used for the purpose of demonstrating bioequivalence on the basis of pharmaceutical and, where applicable, bioavailability characteristics, where a drug in respect of which a notice of compliance has been issued pursuant to section C.08.004 or C.08.004.01 cannot be used for that purpose because it is no longer marketed in Canada, or
- (c) a drug, acceptable to the Minister, that can be used for the purpose of demonstrating bioequivalence on the basis of pharmaceutical and, where applicable, bioavailability characteristics, in comparison to a drug referred to in paragraph (a)."

Per Health Canada's revised policy under "Use of a foreign sourced referenced product as a Canadian reference product," sponsors can demonstrate pharmaceutical equivalence and bioequivalence with a Canadian Reference Drug under *FDR* C.08.001.1 Paragraph (c). Demonstrating pharmaceutical equivalence and bioequivalence against the Canadian Reference Product ("CRP") is intended to provide evidence the subsequent-entry (generic) product's safety and efficacy profiles will be equivalent to those of the innovative product, for which safety and efficacy have been demonstrated clinically. Under the foreign sourced reference product policy, the sponsor can satisfy criteria for solid oral, immediate-release dosage forms, immediate-release oral suspensions, immediate-release orally inhaled suspensions, immediate-release nasal suspensions and immediate-release orally inhaled solutions that require an in vivo demonstration of bioequivalence and immediate-release orally inhaled dry powders (inhalation powders).

As stated in *FDR* Section C.08.001.1, pharmaceutical equivalence for an ANDS applies to "a new drug that, in comparison with another drug, contains identical amounts of identical medicinal ingredients, in comparable dosage forms, but that does not necessarily contain the same non-medicinal ingredients." The policy, *Interpretation of "Identical Medicinal Ingredients,"* delineates the guiding principles used to determine whether two medicinal ingredients with the same active moiety are considered "identical." ANDS sponsors are encouraged to discuss in advance with Health Canada when the "identicalness" of two active ingredients is in doubt.

FDR Section C.08.004(4) states, "a Notice of Compliance issued in respect of a new drug on the basis of information and material contained in a submission filed pursuant to Section C.08.002.1 shall state the name of the CRP referred to in the submission and shall constitute a declaration of equivalence for that new drug."

Bioequivalence Study Requirements

The Therapeutic Products Directorate (TPD) defines "bioequivalence" as "a high degree of similarity in the bioavailabilities of two pharmaceutical products (of the same galenic form) from the same molar dose that are unlikely to produce clinically relevant differences in therapeutic effects, or adverse reactions, or both."

Two Health Canada guidance documents outline the data requirements and bioequivalence criteria intended to be applied to all comparative bioavailability studies for determining bioequivalence:
- Guidance Document: Comparative Bioavailability Standards: Formulations used for Systemic Effects

- Guidance Document: Conduct and Analysis of Comparative Bioavailability Studies

Guidance Document: Comparative Bioavailability Standards: Formulations used for Systemic Effects outlines the bioequivalence standards and exceptions that require modifications to the standards, including:
- modified-release dosage forms
- drugs with serious toxicity within the normal dosage range
- drugs exhibiting non-linear pharmacokinetics
- drugs with a terminal elimination half-life of more than 24 hours
- drugs with an important time of onset of effect or rate of absorption
- critical dose drugs
- combination products
- drugs with highly variable pharmacokinetics
- drugs with measurable endogenous levels
- drugs for which pharmacodynamic studies are appropriate alternatives to comparative bioavailability studies of oral dosage formulations
- drugs for which urine drug concentration data is used

Guidance Document: Conduct and Analysis of Comparative Bioavailability Studies provides recommendations on study design and conduct, test and reference drug products, bioanalytical methodology validation and statistical data analysis.

While both guidance documents are oriented toward solid oral dosage formulations, the principles and standards described also may be applied, as appropriate, to other oral dosage forms and non-injectable formulations that are intended to deliver drugs to the systemic circulation.

Comparative bioequivalence studies must be summarized and documented in the Health Canada template, "Comprehensive Summary: Bioequivalence (CS-BE)."

ANDS Format and Structure

An ANDS must be submitted in the Common Technical Document (CTD) format outlined in *Guidance Document: Preparation of Drug Regulatory Activities in the Common Technical Document (CTD) Format*. Health Canada is accepting ANDSs in electronic CTD (eCTD) format. Nonclinical information would not be relevant for an ANDS and therefore may be omitted. It is anticipated the majority of ANDSs will require the modules discussed below.

Please note, as of 1 January 2018, the following regulatory activity types, as well as all additional information and subsequent regulatory activities and transactions (per *Guidance Document: Preparation of Drug Regulatory Activities in eCTD Format* Section 1.3) for human drugs, must be filed in eCTD format:
- New Drug Submission (NDS)
- Supplement to a New Drug Submission (SNDS)
- Abbreviated New Drug Submission (ANDS)
- Supplement to an Abbreviated New Drug Submission (SANDS)

Regulatory activities for the following are recommended, but not mandatory, for filing in eCTD format:
- Master Files
- Clinical Trial Applications (eCTD CTA pilot only)
- Drug Identification Number (DIN) Applications and Post-Authorization Division 1 Changes (PDC) for human drugs
- Administrative Licensing Agreement (i.e., NDS, ANDS)
- Non-prescription human drugs regulated under Division 1 of the *Food and Drug Regulations* (i.e., DINA, DINB, DIND, DINF and PDC)
- Labelling only (i.e., NDS, ANDS, SNDS, SANDS)

Please note, since 1 January 2017, the Common Electronic Submissions Gateway (CESG) has been mandatory for all regulatory transactions under 10 GB in size (including first transactions) prepared in the eCTD format.

Module 1: Administrative and Product Information

1.0 Correspondence
1.1 Table of Contents
1.2 Administrative Information
    1.2.1 Application Forms
    1.2.2 Fee Forms
    1.2.3 Certification and Attestation Forms
    This section includes a Submission Certification Form, an ANDS Attestation Checklist, a Foreign Review Attestation (as applicable) and a BSE/TSE Attestation form/certificates of suitability to the European Pharmacopeia (as applicable). The Attestation Checklist and Foreign Review Attestation template for generic drugs are available on the Health Canada website. Notices and/or guidance documents also are available for consultation.
    1.2.4 Intellectual Property Information
    Patent Form V should be completed for subsequent entry drug submissions.
    1.2.5 Compliance and Site Information
    The notice, *Submission Filing Requirements-Good Manufacturing Practices (GMP)/*

Establishment Licences (EL), outlines the requirements for evidence of GMP compliance. Sponsors should submit the applicable GMP documentation to the inspectorate prior to filing an ANDS to ensure all applicable sites listed in the ANDS have a Canadian GMP compliance rating at the time of filing. A list of all applicable manufacturing sites, with confirmation these sites have a GMP compliance rating with HPFBI, should be included in Subsection 1.2.5.5, with DEL information included in Subsection 1.2.5.2.

Good Clinical Practices documentation as applicable is included in Subsection 1.2.5.3.

- 1.2.6 Authorization for Sharing Information
- 1.2.7 International Information
  Foreign reviews for a similar filing may be included in this section.
- 1.2.9 Other Administrative Information
  This section serves as a placeholder for other administrative information.

1.3 Product Information
- 1.3.1 Product Monograph
  Generic product monographs must provide information directly relevant to the new drug's safe and effective use. The new generic drug's conditions of use must fall within the CRP's conditions of use. Any differences between the two monographs should be annotated with supporting data in Module 2. The product monograph also must include the comparative biostudy data summary table(s). Information required in this summary table is specified in Appendix A of Health Canada's *Draft Guidance for Industry: Preparation of Comparative Bioavailability Information for Drug Submissions in the CTD Format.*
- 1.3.2 Inner and Outer Labels
  Inner and outer labels should be provided according to *FDR* Section C.04. (See Chapter 12, Pharmaceutical and Biologics Labelling, Advertising and Promotion, for labelling requirements.)
- 1.3.3 Non-Canadian Labelling
- 1.3.5 Reference Product Labelling
  A copy of the CRP's current monograph is to be included in this section.
- 1.3.6 Certified Product Information Document (CPID)
  The CPID template is available on Health Canada's website and is completed and submitted at time of ANDS filing.

1.4 Health Canada Summaries
- 1.4.2 Comprehensive Summary: Bioequivalence (CS-BE)
  The CS-BE template is available on Health Canada's website. If the CS-BE is completed for studies relying solely on pivotal comparative bioavailability studies to establish safety and efficacy, CTD Modules 2.4–2.7 do not need to be completed.

  Comparative biostudy and CS-BE requirements may be waived if the submission involves only a parenteral solution and the product monograph has been provided along with pharmaceutical equivalence data and formulation characteristics in Module 3 of the submission's chemistry and manufacturing portion. A comparative study may be required for parenterals with complex formulation.

  The CS-BE is a pivotal document in the ANDS review process. It should provide a comprehensive, integrated summary of submission information as it pertains to the product's safety and efficacy comparability with the CRP under the proposed conditions of use. This summary should include the study design's scientific rationale and justification, the parameters assessed and the standards applied. The CS-BE should be cross-referenced to appropriate clinical study reports in Module 5 or, in the case of the drug product's pharmaceutical characteristics, to Module 3.

1.5 Environmental Assessment Statement
Since September 2001, all drug products including active ingredients and excipients have been subject to the *Canadian Environmental Protection Act* (*CEPA*) and the *New Substances Notification Regulations* (*NSNR*). An environmental assessment statement is required for new substances in *F&DA*-regulated products. A New Substances Notification package is submitted to Environment Canada for new ingredients that are not on the Domestic Substances List (DSL).

1.6 Regional Clinical Information
- 1.6.1 Comparative Bioavailability Information
  Documents to be included in this section are specific to the pivotal comparative bioequivalence (BE) studies, such as confirmation of the CRP, biowaiver requests, Certificates of Analysis for the test and reference lots used in the biostudy and the BE data sets arranged as specified in Appendix B of Health Canada's

Draft Guidance for Industry: Preparation of Comparative Bioavailability Information for Drug Submissions in the CTD Format.

Canadian Reference Product Confirmation
A document confirming a CRP was used in the comparative bioavailability study should be provided. For the product administered in the biostudy, this should include a purchase receipt(s), signed confirmation (in writing) that the reference product was purchased in Canada or a photocopy of the product label(s) clearly showing the trade name, product strength, lot number, expiration date and Drug Identification Number (DIN). If the reference product was purchased outside Canada, it must be supported by a justification statement addressing all the criteria outlined in the TPD policy on CRPs.

Waiver Requests
Generally, comparative biostudy results should be provided to support each proposed product and strength's safety and efficacy included in an ANDS. In the absence of such studies, this section should include justification supporting a waiver of this requirement for each product and strength. For example, if there are several proposed product strengths, and comparative bioavailability data have not been submitted for all strengths, scientific justification may address such issues as the kinetic nature (linear compared with nonlinear) and proportionality of the strengths for which a waiver is sought to the strength on which a comparative biostudy was conducted. This scientific justification statement for a waiver will include supporting data (e.g., comparative dissolution data) that should be provided in the relevant CTD submission module(s). For example, comparative dissolution profiles should be provided in Module 3, Section 3.2.P.2 (pharmaceutical development). The waiver request also may include justification to support pharmaceutical equivalence as well as results of comparative physiochemical testing. Health Canada's *Guidance for Industry: Pharmaceutical Quality of Aqueous Solutions* includes test parameter recommendations that should be used for aqueous solutions to establish bioequivalence based on pharmaceutical characteristics.

Certificates of Analysis
This section should provide Certificates of Analysis to verify the potency (as a percentage of the label claim) of both test and reference products. For an eCTD submission, Section 1.6.1 can include a hyperlink to the test product Certificates of Analysis placed in Module 3, Section 3.2.P.5.4.

Module 2: Common Technical Document Summaries
2.1 Overall CTD Table of Contents (Modules 2–5)
2.2 Introduction
2.3 Quality Overall Summary (QOS)
A QOS template is available on Health Canada's website and is completed and submitted at ANDS filing. Alternatively, an ICH CTD QOS can be used so long as all items in the Health Canada template are addressed.
2.4–2.7 Clinical/Nonclinical Overviews and Summaries
If the CS-BE is completed for studies that rely solely on pivotal comparative bioavailability studies to establish safety and efficacy, CTD Modules 2.4–2.7 do not need to be completed.

Module 3: Quality

The information in this section should be presented in accordance with relevant Health Canada guidelines and policies regarding quality, including the guidance documents, *Quality (Chemistry and Manufacturing) Guidance: Quality (Chemistry and Manufacturing) Guidance: New Drug Submissions (NDSs) and Abbreviated New Drug Submissions (ANDSs)* (30 October 2017); *Guidance Document Addendum—Quality (Chemistry and Manufacturing) Guidance: Questions and Answers* (30 October 2017; and *Guidance Document: Use of Certificates of Suitability as supporting information in Drug Submissions* (21 August 2017).

These guidances are intended to aid applicants in providing appropriate information and justifying the product's quality using all the information provided. The required information should be provided in detail in Module 3 and be briefly summarized or cross-referenced in the QOS as appropriate.

Section S Drug Substance
The CTD sections must be presented and discussed in a way to ensure interconnected information is provided appropriately.

Master Files (MFs)
Some information outlined in various sections, including the Section S Drug Substance of the drug submission, may be considered proprietary and may not be available to the NDS or ANDS sponsor. If this is a confidential Master File (MF) submitted directly to Health Canada, it will be held in strict confidence and will be used to support the drug submission only upon receipt of a written letter of authorization (i.e., a letter of access).

Certificates of Suitability to the Monographs of the European Pharmacopoeia (CEPs)
Health Canada encourages sponsors to file CEPs when they are available. An appropriately referenced CEP will expedite the assessment of information related to the detailed synthesis method and impurity control and, in some cases, storage conditions and retest period.

Important consideration should be given to the following dossier aspects:
- drug substance physicochemical and other relevant properties
- each manufacturer's identification and responsibility, including contractors, and each proposed production site or facility involved in manufacturing and testing should be provided
- API starting material and its specifications justification
- identification of potential and actual impurities, including genotoxic impurities
- drug substance controls and testing, with validated analytical procedures
- supportive stability data

Section P Drug Product
The sponsor should provide a description of the drug product, and its composition should be provided.

The Pharmaceutical Development section should contain information on development studies conducted to establish the dosage form, formulation, manufacturing process, container closure system, microbiological attributes and usage instructions are appropriate for the purpose specified in the application. This section should include elements defining the drug product's quality target product profile (QTPP) as it relates to quality, safety and efficacy. Drug product critical quality attributes (CQAs) should be identified.

A dissolution test is an important performance indicating test. Thus, depending on the information level, the dissolution test could be a simple quality control test used to ensure lot-to-lot similarity, or a surrogate for bioequivalence when an *in vitro-in vivo* correlation (IVIVC) is established.

Manufacturing process selection and optimisation should be described, and its critical process parameters, in particular, should be identified and explained.

For sterile processes, the sterilization method (e.g., aseptic vs. terminal) should be explained and justified. Evidence should be provided to confirm that the sterilization process will produce a sterile product with a high degree of reliability and that the drug product's physical and chemical properties as well as its safety will not be affected. The drug product's specification(s) should be provided. Proper justification with validated analytical procedures should be provided.

Generally, a minimum of three batches of each strength should be manufactured to a minimum of pilot scale from each proposed commercial manufacturing site, and the complete analytical results for those batches provided.

As outlined in ICH's Q1A guidance document, stability study results up to 12 months (six months for existing drugs) at regular storage conditions and up to six months at accelerated and intermediate storage conditions will be expected.

Module 4: Nonclinical Study Reports
This module normally is exempt because nonclinical data are not required for subsequent market entry products.

Module 5: Clinical Study Reports
5.1 Table of Contents for Module 5
5.2 Tabular Listing of all Clinical Studies
5.3 Clinical Study Reports
    5.3.1   Reports of Biopharmaceutical Studies
        5.3.1.2   Comparative Bioavailability and Bioequivalence Study Reports
        5.3.1.3   *In vitro-In vivo* Correlation Study Reports
        *5.3.1.4   Reports of Bioanalytical and Analytical Method for Human Studies
    5.3.7   Case Report Forms and Individual Patient Listings
5.4 Literature References

*Bioanalytical or analytical methods for bioavailability and bioequivalence or *in vitro* dissolution studies ordinarily should be provided in the individual clinical study reports. However, where a method is used in multiple studies, the method and its validation should be included only once, in Section 5.3.1.4, and referenced in the appropriate individual clinical study reports.

Clinical study reports of comparative bioavailability and bioequivalence studies should be prepared in accordance with the ICH guideline, *Structure and Content of Clinical Study Reports E3*.

Review Process
Failure to provide a completed Attestation Checklist in ANDS Module 1 will result in the issuance of a Screening Deficiency Notice (SDN). Significant deficiencies noted during ANDS screening will be forwarded to the sponsor in either a request for clarification or an SDN. The sponsor will be required to send its response to a request for clarification within 15 calendar days and to an SDN within 45 days from the date of request.

Once acceptable responses to the requested information have been received, the submission will be accepted for review. **Table 9-1** presents the target performance standards for ANDS reviews.

Other Considerations

Developing Generic Versions of Canadian Products with NOC/c Approvals
An ANDS may be granted a Notice of Compliance with conditions (NOC/c) under the NOC/c policy. As per *Guidance Document: Notice of Compliance with conditions*

Table 9-1. Target Review Times

Type of Submission	Content	First Review		Second Review	
		Screening	Review	Screening Response to NON	Review of Response to NON
ANDS or Response to NOD	• Comp/C&M • C&M/labelling • Published data • Labelling only • Administrative	45 days 45 days 45 days 7 days 45 days	180 days 180 days 300 days 60 days 0	45 days 45 days 45 days 0 0	150 days 150 days 150 days 0 0

NON: Notice of Noncompliance; NOD: Notice of Deficiency
Appendix 3 of Guidance for Industry: Management of Drug Submissions

(NOC/c), a sponsor may file an ANDS with respect to a CRP that has been issued a Notice of Compliance (NOC) under the NOC/c policy, and for which the CRP sponsor has yet to fulfill the conditions outlined in its Letter of Undertaking.

Prior to issuance of the NOC/c for an ANDS, sponsors are to provide undertakings—similar but not necessarily identical to those provided by the CRP sponsor. For subsequent market entry products, minimum undertakings will include: a commitment to closely monitor and provide postmarket safety information regarding the subsequent entry product, and a commitment that the subsequent entry product's labelling, including the Product Monograph and related educational materials, contain adequate information to permit healthcare professionals and patients to understand the NOC/c nature of the approval. As for the CRP, these conditions will be reflected in a request for a Letter of Undertaking (similar to the CRP's Qualifying Notice) and detailed in the Letter of Undertaking for the subsequent market entry product.

Confirmatory studies will not be sought automatically from manufacturers that file ANDSs referencing CRPs issued NOCs pursuant to the NOC/c policy. The need for postmarket conditions, including confirmatory studies and/ or heightened postmarket surveillance, will be determined on a case-by-case basis.

Generic Parenterals

The generic parenteral drug policy, *Submissions for Generic Parenteral Drugs*, outlines the general and special requirements for such products. Parenteral drugs are classified as:
- Category I
  - water-soluble powders for reconstitution (no non-medicinal ingredients)
  - aqueous solutions (no non-medicinal ingredients other than the vehicle)
  - nonaqueous single-solvent solutions (other than oil preparations, no non-medicinal ingredients other than the vehicle)
- Category II
  - lyophilized powders
  - buffered powders
  - aqueous solutions (with non-medicinal ingredients)
  - nonaqueous solutions (other than oil preparations with non-medicinal ingredients)
- Category III
  - oil-soluble preparations involving a single oil
- Category IV
  - suspensions
  - emulsions
  - preparations involving co-solvent systems
  - modified-release preparations
  - special drug classes
  - drugs subject to Schedule D of the *F&DA*

Comparative bioequivalence studies are not required for Category I, II or III products. This policy provides more-detailed requirements to prove pharmaceutical equivalence. *In vivo* and/or *in vitro* animal studies and/or clinical trials are required where pharmaceutical equivalence has not been established. For aqueous solutions, proving the drug product contains identical quantities of a chemically equivalent drug but does not necessarily contain the same non-medicinal ingredients generally is acceptable. The policy's requirements are geared primarily toward providing proof of pharmaceutical equivalence (drug product) and chemical equivalence (drug substance). For Category IV parenteral products, the policy states—because particular considerations apply to these products—requirements will be provided in writing upon request.

Another particularity for parenteral generics is the requirement to perform additional container closure tests such as USP <381> Elastomeric Closures for Injections test. Refer to *Guidance for Industry: Pharmaceutical Quality of Aqueous Solutions* for details on additional tests required (e.g., extractables and leachables, performance tests for metered dose drug delivery, etc.).

For sterile products, terminal steam sterilization, when practical, is considered the method of choice to ensure final drug product sterility. Therefore, scientific justification for selecting any other sterilization method should be provided.

Topical Generics

Similarly, the generic topical drug policy, *Submissions for Generic Topical Drugs*, defines general and special requirements for two dermal topical drug classes applied to achieve localized effects. This policy does not apply to topical generics intended for subdermal or systemic effects.

- Category I—Simple formulation products, such as solutions containing a drug substance in which the solvent does not include non-medicinal ingredients that may affect the drug's penetration or absorption through the skin.
- Category II—Complex formulation products, such as emulsions, suspensions, ointments, pastes, foams, gels, sprays and medical adhesive systems.

Because Category I products usually are simple formulations, they may not require clinical trials. Instead, extensive physicochemical parameter comparison testing versus innovator products may be accepted as sufficient product safety and efficacy evidence. On the other hand, because of Category II formulations' complexity, extensive safety and efficacy evidence through clinical trials (or via surrogate models) must be provided.

Topical semi-solid generics such as transdermal patches require additional functional testing, which may include weight per area of coated patch, adhesion, peel or shear force, mean weight per unit area, *in vitro* drug release and monitoring for crystal growth.

Subsequent Market Entry Nasal and Inhalation Products

Guidance documents provide advice on the types of therapeutic studies required to support subsequent market entry nasal and inhalation products' equivalence to the Canadian reference product.

Nasal and inhalation products require specific efficacy and functional testing, including: consistency of delivered dose (throughout the product's use), particle or droplet size distribution profiles (comparable to the product used in *in vivo* studies, where applicable) and, if applicable for the dosage form, its moisture content, leak rate, microbial limits, preservative assay, sterility and weight loss.

Particle size is particularly important in inhalation dosage form performance for optimum inhalation product delivery to the lungs.

Nasal

Drug sponsors may be exempt from conducting comparative bioavailability, pharmacodynamic and/or clinical studies for subsequent market entry nasal drug products formulated as solutions, since *in vitro* studies may provide sufficient information to support a proposal of equivalence to the CRP. For a nasal solution product to be considered for exemption, a scientific justification for the waiver of such studies must be submitted and found acceptable. On the other hand, for complex nasal product formulations, evidence of comparative safety and efficacy, through well-designed comparative clinical trials with appropriate clinical endpoints, is required to demonstrate equivalence with the Canadian reference product. See *Guidance Document: Data Requirements for Safety and Effectiveness of Subsequent Market Entry Steroid Nasal Products for Use in the Treatment of Allergic Rhinitis*.

Inhalation—Short-Acting ß2-Agonists

Two different types of pharmacodynamic studies, a bronchodilator or bronchoprotection study, are recommended to establish the equivalence of a subsequent market entry, short-acting, $ß_2$-agonist metered dose inhaler (MDI). Either study approach may be used to satisfy the comparative efficacy requirement, provided the comparison is between identical $ß_2$-agonists with similar delivery systems. See *Guidance to Establish Equivalence or Relative Potency of Safety and Efficacy of a Second Entry Short-Acting Beta$_2$-Agonist Metered Dose Inhaler*.

Inhalation—Corticosteroids

A therapeutic equivalence study should be conducted to examine the efficacy of a subsequent market entry inhaled corticosteroid (ICS) product in comparison with a Canadian reference ICS product using a clinically meaningful endpoint. A sensitive and specific airway inflammatory marker is recommended as the primary endpoint. Additionally, a pharmacokinetic study should be carried out to examine the subsequent market entry ICS product's safety in comparison with the Canadian reference ICS product. Systemic blood levels of the active substance should be measured and meet the usual bioequivalence standards for uncomplicated drugs. *Draft Guidance Document: Data Requirements for Safety and Effectiveness of Subsequent Market Entry Inhaled Corticosteroid Products for Use in the Treatment of Asthma* is intended for MDIs and dry powder inhalers (DPIs).

Guidance for Industry: Pharmaceutical Quality of Inhalation and Nasal Products is intended for human medicinal products in which the drug substance is delivered into the lungs or to the nasal mucosa, with the purpose of evoking a local or systemic effect. This guidance document outlines the subsequent market entry product's expected quality aspects.

A submission for a subsequent market entry product that relies on comparative clinical data rather than standard bioequivalence data may be required to be filed as a New Drug Submission (NDS), not as an ANDS.

Summary

- Abbreviated new drug submissions (ANDSs) apply to products that are pharmaceutically equivalent, bioequivalent, given via the same route of administration and sold under the same conditions of use as a Canadian reference product (CRP).
- A CRP is a drug that: has a Notice of Compliance and is marketed in Canada by the innovator; is another drug acceptable to the minister of health, where the Canadian drug is no longer marketed; or is another drug acceptable to the minister, where it can be proven it is the same as the Canadian drug.
- The Notice of Compliance for an ANDS names the Canadian reference product and constitutes a "declaration of equivalence" for the new product. This is important from a provincial perspective for substituting a less expensive generic product for an innovator product.
- ANDSs are submitted in electronic Common Technical Document (eCTD) format and usually are composed of Modules 1, 2 (most often only the QOS), 3 and 5. Module 4 normally is exempt because nonclinical data are not required for subsequent market entry products.

Recommended Reading
Food and Drugs Act and *Food and Drug Regulations*
Patented Medicines (Notice of Compliance) Regulations
Certificate of Supplementary Protection Regulations
Canada-European Union Comprehensive Economic and Trade Agreement (CETA) Regulations

Chapter 10

Nonprescription Drugs

Updated by Kristin Willemsen

OBJECTIVES

❑ Learn the different ways to register a nonprescription drug

❑ Become familiar with some of the key guidance documents and policies pertaining to nonprescription drugs

❑ Understand how nonprescription drugs are regulated—both federally and provincially

❑ Understand the process for switching a product from prescription to nonprescription status

LAWS, REGULATIONS AND GUIDELINES COVERED IN THIS CHAPTER

❑ Food and Drugs Act

❑ Food and Drug Regulations

❑ *Determining Prescription Status for Human and Veterinary Drugs* (December 2013)

❑ *Guideline on Preparation of DIN Submissions* (February 1995)

❑ *Post-Notice of Compliance (NOC) Changes: Quality Document* (October 2016)

❑ *Post-Notice of Compliance (NOC) Changes: Safety and Efficacy Document* (February 2016)

❑ *Guidance Document on Post-Drug Identification Number (DIN) Changes* (December 2013)

❑ *Guidance Document Administrative Processing of Submissions and Applications: Human or Disinfectant drugs* (February 2018)

❑ *Guidance Document—Disinfectant Drugs* (January 2018)

❑ *Guidance Document: Questions and Answers: Plain Language Labelling Regulations for Non-prescription Drugs* (February 2018)

❑ *Guidance Document: Drug Facts Table for Non-prescription Drugs* (June 2017)

❑ *Good Label and Package Practices Guide for Non-prescription Drugs and Natural Health Products* (May 2017)

❑ *Guidance Document: Electronic Canadian Drug Facts Table Technical Standards* (August 2017)

❑ *Guidance for Industry: Management of Drug Submissions* (March 2011)

❑ Various Health Canada Policies

❑ NDSAC Drug Scheduling Factors

Introduction

Self-care comprises the decisions and actions people take everyday to maintain and improve their health. Self-care is the foundation of patient-centered care and often is overlooked as a public health resource. Self-care involves making healthy choices, self-recognizing symptoms, self-monitoring, seeking health professional advice when needed and using medicines responsibly. When Canadians are faced with a minor ailment, the most frequent response is to take a nonprescription medicine to help manage their symptoms and get relief. In Canada, products available without a prescription fall into a number of regulatory classifications—these include nonprescription drugs, natural health products, cosmetics and medical devices. This chapter focuses on nonprescription drugs. Since these products can be obtained without a prescription, they all must meet the same government safety criteria to ensure they can be used safely without a doctor's supervision.

Nonprescription drugs often are referred to as over-the-counter drugs or OTCs. Examples of nonprescription drugs include pain relievers, cold medications, stomach remedies, toothpastes and diaper rash creams. Nonprescription drugs are subject to Part C of the *Food and Drugs Act* (*F&DA*) and *Food and Drug Regulations* (*FDR*) and consequently follow many of the same requirements as prescription drugs, including establishment licensing and Good Manufacturing Practices (GMPs). Most nonprescription drugs are subject to Division 1 of the *FDR* and are considered "old drugs," and correspond to Health Canada's labelling standards and monographs (detailed later in this chapter). *FDR* Division 1 sets out general requirements such as labelling, postmarket changes and allowable colour additives. However, about one-third of nonprescription drugs are regulated as "new drugs" under *FDR* Division 8, as the drug, or combination of drugs (or other ingredients) or conditions of use, has not been sold in Canada for sufficient time and in sufficient quantity to establish safety and effectiveness. New drugs require additional safety and postmarket reporting requirements relative to "old drugs;" they are considered new chemical entities (NCE) and receive a Notice of Compliance (NOC) under Division 8 and are present on the "new drugs list."[1] All prescription-to-nonprescription switches (detailed later in this chapter) are regulated as "new drugs," but combining two "old drugs" or the addition of a new nonmedicinal ingredient may trigger the need to be regulated as "new drugs."

Division 9 is the only *FDR* Part C division that is specific to nonprescription drugs and that contains additional requirements for labelling and dosing of acetaminophen and acetylsalicylic acid products. A number of nonprescription drug guidances and policies that help sponsors navigate the meaning of the *F&DA* and *FDR* are referenced throughout this chapter

Nonprescription Drug Submissions

All nonprescription drugs must go through a formal Health Canada review before they can be marketed. This is in contrast to the US, where a sponsor can attest to an established OTC monograph and go to market without preapproval from the regulatory authority.

In Canada, nonprescription new chemical entities are filed as New Drug Submissions (NDSs) or Abbreviated New Drug Submissions (ANDs), and sponsors must demonstrate that the drug does not meet the criteria for listing on the Prescription Drug List.[2] A successful application will receive a Notice of Compliance (NOC) under Division 8.

The majority of nonprescription drugs are approved under Division 1 and are assigned a Drug Identification Number (DIN) when approved. The process for filing DIN submissions is outlined in Health Canada's *Guideline: Preparation of DIN Submissions*,[3] which includes information needed to assess drug products' safety, efficacy and quality.

There are two main routes for gaining nonprescription drug product approval: attesting to established Category IV Monographs or labelling standards or via a general DIN submission. A sponsor also may wish to provide additional data to support a stronger claim or deviation from the existing Category IV Monograph or labelling standard, in which case a DIN submission would also be filed.

Category IV Monographs

A nonprescription drug Category IV Monograph outlines the permissible conditions of use and labelling requirements, such as dose, intended use, directions for use, warnings, active ingredients and combinations thereof. Category IV Monographs are developed by Health Canada for drugs with a well-characterized safety and efficacy profile under specific conditions of use.[4] A manufacturer may reference a Category IV Monograph in a drug submission when the product and its labelling are consistent with the information in the monograph. As of May 2018, there are eight Category IV Monographs, most of which cover multiple ingredients, including ingredients regulated as natural health products (NHPs) and, thus, these monographs are considered joint OTC and NHP monographs. The following information is required for a Category IV Monograph submission:
- cover letter stating the application is being submitted under the specified Category IV Monograph
- completed Category IV Drug Submission Certification
- submission fee application form and payment; completed Drug Submission Application form (HC-SC 3011)
- proposed Canadian labels and prescribing information or a package insert where applicable
- labels and packages' certification form for nonprescription drugs

- animal tissue form (if applicable)

The Therapeutic Products Directorate (TPD) has a 45-day target for approval of Category IV Monograph submissions per its guidance *Management of Drug Submissions*.

Labelling Standards

A nonprescription drug labelling standard outlines the permissible conditions of use and labelling requirements, such as dose, intended use, directions for use, warnings, active ingredients and combinations thereof. Labelling standards are developed by Health Canada for drugs that have a well-characterized safety and efficacy profile under specific conditions of use.[5] A manufacturer may reference a labelling standard in a drug submission when the product and its labelling are consistent with the information set out in the document. As of May 2018, there were 33 labelling standards, most of which cover multiple ingredients. As a result of the reclassification of many drug ingredients to NHP status, some of these monographs are shared by TPD and the Natural Health Products Directorate (NHPD). The following information is required for a labelling standard submission:
- cover letter stating the application is being submitted under the specified labelling standard
- completed Drug Submission Application form (HC-SC 3011)
- submission fee application form and payment
- proposed Canadian labels and prescribing information or a package insert where applicable
- completed DIN submission certification
- Labels and Packages Certification Form for Nonprescription Drugs
- Animal Tissue Form (if applicable)

TPD has a 45-day target for approval of labelling standard submissions per its guidance *Management of Drug Submissions*.

Disinfectant Drugs

Disinfectant drugs fall within the scope of nonprescription drugs and, as such, also have labelling standards and Category IV Monographs as detailed above.[6] Disinfectant drugs that do not have either labelling standards or Category IV Monographs are filed as new drugs. The guidance document, *Disinfectant Drugs*,[7] last revised in January 2018, details the considerations for DIN submissions for these products.

General DIN Submissions

Health Canada's *Guideline on Preparation of DIN Submissions* describes the requirement for submitting sufficient data to evaluate a drug's safety and efficacy for its intended use. The guideline itself is outdated, as certain sections, such as homeopathic preparations and traditional herbal medicines, now fall under the scope of NHPD, and it contains references to *FDR* Part C, Division 10, which was repealed in 1998. The guideline also is not specific to nonprescription drugs, as certain prescription drugs are captured. Nonetheless, the guideline is still the basis on which to file most nonprescription drug applications, including those Category IV Monographs and labelling standards described above. The guideline describes the information needed for filing DIN applications, as described above, and provides additional considerations for modified release oral dosage forms, solutions for inhalation and ophthalmic preparations.

TPD has a 45-day target for screening and a 180- to 210-day target for approval of these types of DIN submissions per its guidance *Management of Drug Submissions*.

Postmarket Changes

Four guidance documents outline the requirements for changes to marketed nonprescription drug products. If the product received an NOC under Division 8, changes are subject to Health Canada's guidance *Post-Notice of Compliance (NOC) Changes: Safety and Efficacy*[8] or the *Post-Notice of Compliance (NOC) Changes: Quality Document*[9] (depending on the nature of the change). If the product received a DIN under Division 1, changes are subject to TPD's *Guidance Document on Post-Drug Identification Numbers (DIN) Changes*.[10] Both guidance documents provide examples of postmarket changes that either are required to be filed by the *FDR* or are recommended to be filed along with criteria sets and supporting documentation. Depending on whether the sponsor meets the criteria, the change could require either approval prior to implementation or annual notification post-implementation. The target review timeline for changes requiring Health Canada approval is 90–120 days for Division 8 nonprescription drugs and 30 days for Division 1 nonprescription drugs.

The fourth guidance document, *Guidance Document Administrative Processing of Submissions and Applications: Human or Disinfectant Drugs*,[11] and the *Changes in Manufacturer's Name and/or Product Name*[12] policy, pertain to administrative changes, like postmarket changes to the product name or manufacturer name due to mergers and acquisitions. The scope of administrative changes is narrow, and if the change's nature is considered administrative, the target screening is 45 days. However, if a brand-name change is outside the scope of the administrative change guidance and policy, a brand-name assessment could be required to mitigate the risk of confusion with another drug. The brand-name assessment screening criteria and process are outlined in *Guidance Document: Questions and Answers: Plain Language Labelling Regulations for Non-prescription Drugs* Appendix 1 and 2.[13] Postmarket brand-name changes falling outside the administrative route technically are considered new submissions and would require labeling-only submissions to be filed, which can take 60–120 days.

Plain Language Labelling

Since June 2016, all new nonprescription drug applications must be in compliance with the 2014 *FDR* Plain Language Labelling (PLL) amendments. All marketed nonprescription drugs are expected to update labels to be compliant with these new rules by June 2021. The amendments introduced five new requirements to:
- mandate content be presented in plain language and the format not impede comprehension
- review mock ups for new submissions so that industry and Canada can agree on package design
- display Canadian contact information on outer labels using a phone number or website
- perform brand name assessments
- display adequate directions for nonprescription drug use in a table format

Health Canada has developed a number of guidance documents to assist with compliance including:
- *Guidance Document: Drug Facts Table For Non-Prescription Drugs*:[14] This guidance assists in meeting the plain language regulatory requirement by setting out acceptable minimum content for Facts Tables for over 120 nonprescription drug ingredients.
- *Good Label and Package Practices Guide for Non-Prescription Drugs and Natural Health Products*:[15] This guidance sets out the acceptable technical facts table formats that could be applied to different product or packaging types. For example, products attesting to Category IV Monographs can leverage the tailored flexibility approach that enables all point-of-use information in the directions and warning section to be present on an electronic label extension only, due to their lower-risk nature. This guidance also establishes a six-point font minimum for inner and outer labels to meet the regulatory requirement to ensure key information is "clearly and prominently displayed" and describes how graphics could be designed to ensure the format does not impede comprehension.
- *Guidance Document: Electronic Canadian Drug Facts Table Technical Standards*:[16] This guidance describes how electronic label extensions can be developed to help consumers search for and access Facts Table content electronically.
- *Guidance Document: Questions and Answers: Plain Language Labelling Regulations for Non-Prescription Drugs*: This guidance describes how the *PLL Regulations* are administered, what submissions are required or recommended to be filed, and the process for brand-name assessments.

Other Policies Related to Nonprescription Drugs

All Health Canada policies impacting drugs are posted on its website.[17] Policies of particular importance for nonprescription drugs are outlined below.

Absence of Ingredient Statements for Nonprescription Drugs

This policy outlined in the *Guidance Document: Labelling of Pharmaceutical Drugs For Human Use* describes the circumstances under which it is appropriate to declare the absence of both medicinal and nonmedicinal ingredients on nonprescription drug product labels.[18]

Assignment of Drug Identification Numbers for Drug Products in Kits

This policy describes the requirements for combining more than one drug product in the same package. These products commonly are seen in the nonprescription cough and/or cold category.[19]

DIN: A Brand Name Product with Different Fragrances, Flavours or Colours

This policy permits the use of one DIN for products that differ only in fragrance, flavour or colour.[20]

Prescription to Nonprescription Switch

Switching a product from prescription to nonprescription status in Canada used to be a very lengthy process. A regulatory amendment was needed to give a drug prescription status by adding it to *FDR* Schedule F, or to switch its status from prescription to nonprescription by removing it from Schedule F. Depending on their complexity, switches used to take three or more years to approve from the time of filing.

On 20 June 2012, the Government of Canada amended the *F&DA* to give the minister of health certain powers, including the power to establish a list that sets out prescription drugs. *FDR* Schedule F was replaced with the administrative Prescription Drug List. This was an historic and significant change to the Canadian prescription-to-OTC switch process and came into effect 19 December 2013.

The general principles for a switch submission remain unchanged. The process begins via a sponsor's application to Health Canada. If the proposed product currently is approved, and the application's intent is solely to switch its intended use to nonprescription, the application is submitted via a Supplemental New Drug Submission (SNDS). If the proposed product has not been marketed in Canada (i.e., the active ingredient strength is not that of the current prescription product), the application is submitted via an NDS. In the former instance, the application must demonstrate the currently approved prescription product can be used safely as a nonprescription product. The sponsor must provide data that demonstrate the product no longer meets Health Canada's criteria for prescription status, as outlined in the *Guidance Document: Determining Prescription Status for Human and Veterinary Drugs* (see **Appendix 10-1**). When the product has not been marketed in Canada, the application also must include efficacy and quality data.

Health Canada evaluates data from a drug submission to assess a medicinal ingredient's safety, quality and efficacy and whether it should be available by prescription only. Health Canada scientific staff make a recommendation to the existing Health Canada committee of scientific experts to remove a medicinal ingredient from the Prescription Drug List. Following committee endorsement, the following steps occur (in this order):

- Notice of consultation posted to the Health Canada website regarding the minister's intent to remove a medicinal ingredient from the Prescription Drug List, including:
  o notification that Health Canada will undertake a consultation
  o rationale for proposed removal
- 75-day consultation—Health Canada evaluates comments received during the consultation:
  o where the comments raise important questions related to the proposed removal, the proposal is returned to the committee for further consideration
  o where the comments support the proposed removal, the decision is made to revise the Prescription Drug List
- Notice of decision posted to Health Canada website, including:
  o a summary of comments received and Health Canada's response
  o the minister's decision to remove the medicinal ingredient

External stakeholders are informed of removal by email.

The medicinal ingredient is removed from the Prescription Drug List six months after the notice of decision is posted. Although the product is deemed nonprescription from Health Canada's perspective, this new status needs to be validated and further refined by the provinces. This entails applying for nonprescription status with the National Association of Pharmacy Regulatory Authorities (NAPRA), as described in the next section. The product will remain in a prescription classification until this is done. A sponsor may send an application to NAPRA at any point in the switching process, even prior to submitting to Health Canada, and NAPRA will provide a decision that is pending until an NOC is received. A complete graphic of Canada's switch and scheduling process for nonprescription drugs can be found online on Consumer Health Products Canada's website[21] (https://www.chpcanada.ca/advocacy/briefs-submissions/).

Provincial Scheduling of Nonprescription Drugs

As outlined above, Health Canada determines whether a product is available by prescription or nonprescription; however, it is the provinces' responsibility to determine the actual conditions of sale of the product in the nonprescription environment in accordance with Provincial Pharmacy Legislation and Regulation. NAPRA maintains National Drug Schedules that show drug scheduling.[22] Drugs are scheduled using a three-schedule/four-category model.

- Schedule I—products that require a prescription to be dispensed by a pharmacist.
- Schedule II—products that do not require a prescription but require a pharmacist's intervention. These products are not accessible to the public for self-selection and often are referred to as "Behind the Counter" or "BTC" drugs. They have been determined to need a pharmacist's advice and interaction prior to dispensing.
- Schedule III—products available in pharmacies' self-selection areas. These products can be purchased by consumers by self-selection but are located within a specified area in close proximity to a pharmacist, in the event a consumer has a question about the product.
- Unscheduled—products that can be sold in any retail outlet, sometimes referred to as "mass market" drugs.

A drug is assessed using a "cascading" approach against the factors for listing a drug in each given schedule (see **Table 10-1**), beginning with Schedule I. Schedule I factors are similar to the factors Health Canada uses in determining whether a product should be sold by prescription and placed on the Prescription Drug List. If sufficient Schedule I factors pertain to the drug, it will be scheduled as a prescription product. If not, the drug then is assessed against Schedule II factors and subsequently, if warranted, against Schedule III factors. The main difference between Schedule II and III is the degree of pharmacist involvement at the point of sale. If it is determined that the drug does not meet any of the scheduling factors, it is classified as "Unscheduled." Interestingly, even though Health Canada may determine a product is suitable for nonprescription use, NAPRA still may choose to schedule the drug as a prescription product under Schedule I if it feels sufficient Schedule I factors pertain to the drug.

Table 10-1. NAPRA Scheduling Factors

Schedule I Factors	
I-1	The need for the drug is identifiable only by the prescribing practitioner.
I-2	Use of the drug requires adjunctive therapy or evaluation.
I-3	Appropriate use of the drug may produce dependency.
I-4	Serious adverse drug reactions are known to occur or have a recognized potential to occur at normal therapeutic dosage levels.
I-5	There is a narrow margin of safety between the therapeutic and toxic dosages of the drug, either in the general population or in identified subpopulations, or in patients with multiple medical problems.
I-6	Serious drug interactions are known to occur.
I-7	Use of the drug has contributed to, or is likely to contribute to, the development of resistant strains of microorganisms.
I-8	The medicinal ingredient is new or is being used for a new indication that is not amenable to self-treatment, and the consequences of widespread use are not adequately established.
Schedule II Factors	
II-1	The initial need for the drug is identified or confirmed by a regulated health professional.
II-2	Chronic therapy or subsequent re-treatments should be monitored by a pharmacist.
II-3	The drug must be readily available under exceptional circumstances when a prescription is not practical.
II-4	The drug is intended for administration in a healthcare setting or under the direction of a regulated health professional, or is an injectable dosage form and is not otherwise included in Schedule I.
II-5	There is significant potential for misuse or abuse of the drug due to its inherent pharmacological action or chemical properties.
II-6	The selection of the drug requires intervention by a pharmacist: –to confirm that an appropriate self-assessment has been made by the patient; or –for a condition that is new to patient self-assessment; or –for a condition that is generally not amenable to patient self assessment.
II-7	Use of the drug may delay recognition or mask the symptoms of serious disease.
II-8	The drug may cause serious or significant adverse drug reactions or drug interactions that cannot be adequately addressed through product labelling.
II-9	Safe and appropriate use of the drug requires intervention by a pharmacist to reinforce or expand on limited or complex information that appears on product labelling.
II-10	The medicinal ingredient is new or is in a new drug delivery system, for self-medication.
Schedule III Factors	
III-1	Chronic use may delay recognition or mask the symptoms of serious disease.
III-2	The drug is a new ingredient for self-selected self-medication, and the availability of a pharmacist to provide advice can promote appropriate use.
III-3	The drug is used to treat a persistent, chronic or recurring condition, and the availability of the pharmacist to provide advice can promote appropriate use.
III-4	There is potential for misuse or abuse of the drug due to its inherent pharmacological action or chemical properties.
III-5	The availability of a pharmacist to reinforce or expand on product labelling, or where product selection is likely to cause confusion, could contribute to the safe and appropriate use of the drug.

The process for scheduling drugs is as follows. Briefly, a sponsor proposes a desired schedule by submitting an application to NAPRA that addresses the factors the association uses in determining scheduling. The National Drug Scheduling Advisory Committee (NDSAC), a group that advises NAPRA on the scheduling of drugs, reviews the information. The sponsor makes a presentation to NDSAC, and a scheduling verdict is rendered shortly thereafter. The flow charts of the pre-NDSAC review process[23] and post-NDSAC review processes[24] can be found online at NAPRA's website. Applications can be made to determine a drug's initial scheduling in the nonprescription environment—such as for NCEs or switched products—or when a sponsor wishes to change a drug's current scheduling.

All NDSAC review applications must be based on a specific drug rather than a drug product. Submissions should include the following components:

- index

- statement of the requested schedule recommendation
- brief overview of the drug including: conditions for use, safety and efficacy, a description and incidence of adverse reactions and experience with overdose, if relevant
- application of the scheduling factors, with a copy of the appropriate literature citations including literature search parameters (In keeping with the cascading principle of drug scheduling, an application of all schedules' factors should be included to support the scheduling request.)
- proposed product labelling, including labelling standards or monographs prepared for the appropriate directorate (where applicable)
- consumer usage studies' results in a market consistent with the scheduling request regarding compliance and such related issues as reading and comprehension studies of labels and patient information (for nonprescription drugs)
- drug status in other countries
- exposure assessment (market penetration)

When the scheduling request is pursuant to a deregulatory proposal, the applicant provides the committee with a summary of the background information and the Health Canada reviewer panel's evaluation.

NAPRA must receive the submission documents at least 60 days before the scheduled committee meeting.

NAPRA will post a notice of each review or reassessment and particulars of the submission on its website, with an invitation to any party interested in the submission to become an "interested party" and have an opportunity to be heard. Members of the Drug Scheduling External Liaison Group will be specifically notified.

Requests for interested party status must be received by NAPRA no later than 45 days prior to the NDSAC meeting. Once NAPRA has ruled on who will be granted interested party standing, a list of such parties, with contact information, is prepared and forwarded to all such parties, directing them to send any information or materials they wish to file to each party on the list. Any document provided to NDSAC will be on the public record unless the provider requests that it be held confidential and NDSAC agrees to its confidentiality, in which case an abridged version will be made available to the public or, at the least, a claim for the document's confidentiality recorded.

The applicant is entitled to present before the committee. A delegation of up to three representatives may attend on the sponsor's behalf. NDSAC also can request the attendance of any other person believed to have information relevant to the proceeding.

NDSAC's initial recommendation and its reasons are published on the NAPRA website and subsequently forwarded to NAPRA's executive committee within seven days of publication.

Any reassessment request NDSAC deems to be in the public interest must be received in writing within 30 days of the recommendation's posting to the NAPRA website. Since the NAPRA process is public, the sponsor forgoes confidentiality of the Health Canada submission when it decides to start the scheduling process prior to obtaining an NOC for the switch submission.

NAPRA's National Drug Model currently has not been adopted by all provinces; some provinces require a subsequent provincial approval after NAPRA decisions are made, and others do not follow the recommendations at all. An updated status of each province's position can be found on NAPRA's website.[25] For the most part, provinces adopt a structure similar to NAPRA's model regarding the different schedules. The province of Quebec's schedules are called annexes (ranging from 0 to 3) and do bear some similarity to NAPRA's, although the scheduling process is completely independent from NAPRA. A separate application needs to be made to the province of Quebec to obtain a desired scheduling status. Once a switching submission receives an NOC, the drug automatically defaults to Annex 2 in Quebec, which is similar to NAPRA's Schedule II or BTC.

Since NDSAC's establishment, there have been a few cases where a new nonprescription drug or deregulated (prescription-to-OTC switch) drug manufacturer has not requested a national drug scheduling recommendation from NDSAC and, accordingly, a national drug schedule assignment has not been made. In the absence of NDSAC review (initiated by sponsor request) and information to support a specific nonprescription drug status, federally deregulated and newly approved nonprescription drugs will be placed in Schedule I of the national drug scheduling model and identified accordingly.

Summary

- Nonprescription drugs are subject to *F&DA* Part C and the *FDR* and, consequently, follow many of the same requirements as prescription drugs, including establishment licensing and GMPs.
- Nonprescription drugs can be regulated as either "new drugs" under *FDR* Division 8 or "old drugs" under *FDR* Division 1.
- All nonprescription drugs must go through a formal Health Canada review before they can be marketed in Canada.
- There are two main submission routes for gaining approval for nonprescription drug products: attesting to established monographs or labelling standards, or via a submission to obtain a DIN or a DIN and NOC (for new drugs).
- Four guidance documents outline the requirements for changes to marketed nonprescription

drug products: *Post-Notice of Compliance (NOC) Changes: Quality Document, Post-Notice of Compliance (NOC) Changes: Safety and Efficacy Document, Guidance Document on Post-Drug Identification Numbers (DIN) Changes* and *Guidance Document Administrative Processing of Submissions and Applications: Human or Disinfectant Drugs*
- Four guidance documents outline the requirements for Plain Language Labelling: *Guidance Document: Drug Facts Table For Non-Prescription Drugs, Good Label and Package Practices Guide for Non-Prescription Drugs and Natural Health Products, Guidance Document: Electronic Canadian Drug Facts Table Technical Standards* and *Guidance Document: Questions and Answers: Plain Language Labelling Regulations for Non-Prescription Drugs.*
- Health Canada determines whether a product is available by prescription or nonprescription; however, it is the provinces' responsibility to determine the product's actual placement in the nonprescription environment.
- Drugs can be moved from prescription to nonprescription status via the submission of a Supplemental New Drug Submission providing the rationale for the switch and data supporting it.
- Provinces schedule products according to conditions of sale (Schedule 1—prescription required, Schedule 2—under a pharmacist's control, Schedule 3—under the supervision of a pharmacist or unscheduled—without conditions of sale).
- Although there is a harmonized schedule for nonprescription drugs, not all Canadian provinces and territories strictly adhere to it.

References
1. Listing of Drugs Currently Regulated as New Drugs (The New Drugs List). Health Canada website. https://www.canada.ca/en/health-canada/services/drugs-health-products/drug-products/applications-submissions/guidance-documents/listing-drugs-currently-regulated-new-drugs.html. Accessed 28 May 2018.
2. *Guidance Document: Determining Prescription Status for Human and Veterinary Drugs.* Health Canada website. https://www.canada.ca/en/health-canada/services/drugs-health-products/drug-products/prescription-drug-list/guidance-document.html. Accessed 28 May 2018.
3. *Guideline on Preparation of DIN Submissions.* Health Canada website. https://www.canada.ca/en/health-canada/services/drugs-health-products/drug-products/applications-submissions/guidance-documents/preparation-drug-identification-number-submissions.html. Accessed 28 May 2018.
4. Non-prescription Drugs: Category IV Monographs. Health Canada Website https://www.canada.ca/en/health-canada/services/drugs-health-products/drug-products/applications-submissions/guidance-documents/non-prescription-drugs-category-iv-monographs.html. Accessed 28 May 2018.
5. Nonprescription Drugs: Labelling Standards - Drug Product. Health Canada website. https://www.canada.ca/en/health-canada/services/drugs-health-products/drug-products/applications-submissions/guidance-documents/nonprescription-drugs-labelling-standards.html. Accessed 28 May 2018.
6. Disinfectants. Health Canada website https://www.canada.ca/en/health-canada/services/drugs-health-products/drug-products/applications-submissions/guidance-documents/disinfectants.html. Accessed 28 May 2018.
7. *Guidance Document—Disinfectant Drugs.* Health Canada website https://www.canada.ca/en/health-canada/services/drugs-health-products/drug-products/applications-submissions/guidance-documents/disinfectants/disinfectant-drugs.html. Accessed 28 May 2018.
8. Post-Notice of Compliance (NOC) Changes: Safety and Efficacy Document. Health Canada website. https://www.canada.ca/en/health-canada/services/drugs-health-products/drug-products/applications-submissions/guidance-documents/post-notice-compliance-changes/safety-efficacy-document.html. Accessed 28 May 2018.
9. Post-Notice of Compliance (NOC) Changes: Quality Document. Health Canada website. https://www.canada.ca/en/health-canada/services/drugs-health-products/drug-products/applications-submissions/guidance-documents/post-notice-compliance-changes/quality-document.html. Accessed 28 May 2018.
10. *Guidance Document on Post-Drug Identification Number (DIN) Changes.* Health Canada website. https://www.canada.ca/en/health-canada/services/drugs-health-products/drug-products/applications-submissions/guidance-documents/post-drug-identification-number-changes.html. Accessed 28 May 2018.
11. *Guidance Document Administrative Processing of Submissions and Applications: Human or Disinfectant Drugs.* Health Canada website. https://www.canada.ca/en/health-canada/services/drugs-health-products/drug-products/applications-submissions/guidance-documents/guidance-administrative-processing-human-disinfectant-drugs.html. Accessed 28 May 2018.
12. Changes in Manufacturer's Name and/or Product Name. Health Canada website. https://www.canada.ca/en/health-canada/services/drugs-health-products/drug-products/applications-submissions/policies/changes-manufacturer-name-product-name.html. Accessed 28 May 2018.
13. *Guidance Document: Questions and Answers: Plain Language Labelling Regulations for Non-Prescription Drugs.* Health Canada website. https://www.canada.ca/en/health-canada/services/drugs-health-products/drug-products/applications-submissions/guidance-documents/guidance-document-questions-answers-plain-language-labelling-regulations-non-prescription-drugs-contact-lens-disinfectants.html. Accessed 28 May 2018.
14. *Guidance Document: Drug Facts Table For Nonprescription Drugs.* Health Canada website. https://www.canada.ca/en/health-canada/services/drugs-health-products/public-involvement-consultations/natural-health-products/guidance-document-drug-facts-table-non-prescription-drugs.html. Accessed 28 May 2018.
15. Good Label and Package Practices Guide for Non-prescription Drugs and Natural Health Products. Health Canada website. https://www.canada.ca/en/health-canada/services/drugs-health-products/reports-publications/medeffect-canada/good-label-package-practices-guide-non-prescription-drugs-natural-health-products.html. Accessed 28 May 2018.
16. *Guidance Document: Electronic Canadian Drug Facts Table Technical Standards.* Health Canada website. https://www.canada.ca/en/health-canada/services/drugs-health-products/reports-publications/medeffect-canada/guidance-electronic-canadian-drug-fact-table-technical-standards.html. Accessed 28 May 2018.
17. Policies. Health Canada website. https://www.canada.ca/en/health-canada/services/drugs-health-products/drug-products/applications-submissions/policies.html. Accessed 28 May 2018.
18. *Guidance Document: Labelling of Pharmaceutical Drugs For Human Use.* Health Canada website. https://www.canada.ca/en/health-canada/services/drugs-health-products/drug-products/applications-submissions/guidance-documents/labelling-pharmaceutical-drugs-human-use-2014-guidance-document.html. Accessed 28 May 2018.

19. Assignment of Drug Identification Numbers for Drug Products in Kits. Health Canada website. https://www.canada.ca/en/health-canada/services/drugs-health-products/drug-products/applications-submissions/policies/assignment-drug-identification-numbers-drug-products-kits.html. Accessed 28 May 2018.
20. Drug Identification Number: A Brand Name Product with Different Fragrances, Flavours or Colors. Health Canada website. https://www.canada.ca/en/health-canada/services/drugs-health-products/drug-products/applications-submissions/policies/policy-issues-drug-identification-number-brand-name-product-different-fragrances-flavours-colours.html. Accessed 28 May 2018.
21. Canada's Current Process for Switching Prescription Drugs to Nonprescription Status. Consumer Health Products Canada website. https://www.chpcanada.ca/wp-system/uploads/2017/10/process.png. Accessed 28 May 2018.
22. National Drug Schedules. National Association of Pharmacy Regulatory Authorities website. http://napra.ca/national-drug-schedules. Accessed 28 May 2018.
23. Pre-NDSAC meeting procedure. National Association of Pharmacy Regulatory Authorities website. http://napra.ca/sites/default/files/documents/NDSAC_PreMeetingFlowChart_UPDATE_March2018_FINAL.pdf. Accessed 28 May 2018.
24. Post-NDSAC meeting procedure. National Association of Pharmacy Regulatory Authorities website. http://napra.ca/sites/default/files/documents/NDSAC_PostMeetingFlowChart_UPDATE_March2018_FINAL_0.pdf. Accessed 28 May 2018.
25. Implementation of the National Drug Schedules National Association of Pharmacy Regulatory Authorities website. http://napra.ca/implementation-national-drug-schedules . Accessed 28 May 2018.

Chapter 10

Appendix 10-1

Guidance Document: Prescription Status for Guidance Document Human and Veterinary Drugs

Effective Date: 19 December 2013

APPENDIX: LIST OF PRINCIPLES, FACTORS AND EXCEPTIONS

Principle 1:

Supervision by a practitioner is necessary (i) for the diagnosis, treatment, mitigation or prevention of a disease, disorder or abnormal physical state, or its symptoms, in respect of which the drug is recommended for use, or (ii) to monitor a disease, disorder or abnormal physical state, or its symptoms, in respect of which the drug is recommended for use, or to monitor the use of the drug.

Factor 1.1 The drug is used in the treatment of a serious disease not easily diagnosed by the public.
Factor 1.2 The use of the drug may mask other diseases.
Factor 1.3 Practitioner supervision is necessary for treatment and/or monitoring.
Factor 1.4 The use of the drug requires complex or individualized instructions.
Factor 1.5 Practitioner expertise is necessary to administer the drug or oversee the drug's administration.
Factor 1.6 The drug has a narrow margin of safety.
Factor 1.7 At normal therapeutic dosage levels, the drug has potential or is known to cause serious adverse reactions or serious interactions with food or other drugs.
Factor 1.8 The drug has dependence and/or addiction potential.

Principle 2:

The level of uncertainty respecting the drug, its use or its effects justifies supervision by a practitioner.

Factor 2.1 There is limited market experience with the use of the drug.

Principle 3:

Use of the drug can cause harm to human or animal health or a risk to public health and the harm or the risk can be mitigated by a practitioner's supervision.

Factor 3.1 There is potential for harm to public health.
Factor 3.2 There is potential for diversion or abuse leading to harmful non-medical use.

Exceptions:

Exceptions may be made in cases where the health and safety benefit of drug accessibility outweighs the benefits of the prescription requirements.

Chapter 11

Biologics Submission, Approval and Postmarketing

Updated by Marcia Sam and Mahdis Dorkalam, MSc, RHN

OBJECTIVES

❑ Understand how the regulatory process for biologics differs from those for other drugs for human use

❑ Understand biologics' New Drug Submission (NDS) process

❑ Understand the On-Site Evaluation (OSE)

❑ Understand biologics' postapproval requirements

❑ Understand the lot release procedures for higher-risk biologics

---

GUIDELINES COVERED IN THIS CHAPTER

❑ *Food and Drugs Act*

❑ *Food and Drug Regulations*

o Guidance for Sponsors: Lot Release Program for Schedule D (Biologic) Drugs (June 2005)

o Guidance for Industry: Post-Notice of Compliance (NOC) Changes—Quality Guidance (October 2016)

o Guidance for Industry: Preparation of the Quality Information for Drug Submissions in the CTD Format: Biotechnological/ Biological (Biotech) Products (May 2004)

o Guidance for Industry: Preparation of the Quality Information for Drug Submission in the CTD Format: Blood Products (Archived June 2004)

o Guidance for Industry: Preparation of the Quality Information for Drug Submissions in the CTD Format: Vaccines (Archived June 2004)

o Guidance for Industry: Product Monograph (June 2017)

❑ *Guidance Document: Preparation of Drug Regulatory Activities in the Common Technical Document (CTD) Format* (June 2012)

❑ *Guidance Document for Clinical Trial Sponsors: Clinical Trial Applications* (May 2013)

❑ *Guidance for Industry: Management of Drug Submissions* (December 2013)

❑ *Guidance for Industry: Product Monograph— Product Monograph Template - Schedule D* (December 2016)

❑ *Certified Product Information Document (Schedule D Drugs) Template* (December 2016)

Introduction

Biological drugs, more commonly referred to as biologics, although not formally defined within either the *Food and Drugs Act* (*F&DA*) or *Food and Drug Regulations* (*FDR*), are listed on *F&DA* Schedule D, either specifically or within a class and addressed in *FDR* Section C. Generally, they are derived from or through the metabolic activity of living organisms (natural or genetically modified). Schedule D includes individual product names (e.g., insulin), product classes (e.g., immunizing agents), references to particular sources (e.g., "drugs, other than antibiotics, prepared from microorganisms") and methodology (e.g., "drugs obtained by recombinant DNA procedures"). Drugs or biological preparations similar to those listed in Schedule D, for which there are special safety, efficacy and quality concerns, are treated as biologics for regulatory purposes.

Biologics are variable and structurally complex. They typically are manufactured from or through the use of animals or microorganisms. Biologics tend to be labile and sensitive to changes in manufacturing processes. Biological source materials, production cells and their fermentation media can present risks, such as the initial presence of pathogens or the growth of adventitious agents, such as viruses. Consequently, careful attention must be paid to raw material controls, viral or bacterial inactivation or clearance during product purification and testing. Changes to source materials, manufacturing processes, equipment or facilities can result in significant, unexpected changes to the intermediate and/or final product. For biologics, the process defines the product, in that quality cannot be established entirely by testing the material in the final container.

The review process for biologics regulated as new drugs involves several additional layers of oversight. Biologic New Drug Submissions (NDSs) are required to include product-specific facility information that outlines the biologic's method of manufacture in significant detail and provides overall more-detailed chemistry and manufacturing information than submissions for pharmaceutical products. Biologics require an inspection of the manufacturing facility and production process, known as an On-Site Evaluation (OSE), a lot-release program, both pre- and postapproval, and a yearly biologic product report (YBPR) submission to Health Canada. Postapproval changes also are subject to a greater level of scrutiny by Health Canada than pharmaceuticals. This additional monitoring helps ensure the product's purity and quality.

Depending on the biologic type, specific additional requirements may apply. For example, *FDR* Section C.04.019(b)(ii) for whole blood and its components requires the establishment licence number of the distributor referred to in paragraph C.01A.003(b), preceded by the words "Establishment Licence Number," "*Numéro de licence d'établissement*," or an abbreviation thereof, on the outer label.

In addition, Health Canada has provided separate requirements for biosimilars, as these are considered new drugs and are subject to the *F&DA* and *FDR* Part C. The concepts and the scientific and regulatory principles within the existing regulatory frameworks for biologic, pharmaceutical and generic pharmaceutical drugs provide the basis for the biosimilars' regulatory framework. Unlike pharmaceuticals, Health Canada does not consider biosimilars to be generic biologics, and many characteristics associated with the generic pharmaceutical drug authorization process and marketed use do not apply. A biosimilar's authorization is not a declaration of pharmaceutical equivalence, bioequivalence or clinical equivalence to the reference biologic drug.

Biological Drug Product Clinical Trials

All drugs marketed in Canada are subject to the *F&DA* and *FDR*, collectively referred to as the *Food and Drug Act and Regulations*, or *FDAR*. Within Health Canada, the Biologics and Genetic Therapies Directorate (BGTD) is responsible for reviewing and approving all types of drug submissions for biological drug products, including but not limited to Clinical Trial Applications (CTAs) and NDSs.

Clinical trial sponsors must submit a CTA to Health Canada per section C.05.005 prior to using a product not authorized for sale in Canada for use in human clinical trials. This applies to Phase 1–3 clinical trials, including comparative bioavailability trials for biologics. A full CTA must be submitted for bioavailability trials.

If a trial involves a marketed product, where the drug's proposed use is outside the Notice of Compliance (NOC) or Drug Identification Number (DIN) parameters, a CTA is required. Some reasons for postmarketing trials requiring a CTA submission include a different: 1) indication and clinical use, 2) target patient population, 3) route of administration or 4) dosage regimen. It is important to note, if postmarketing trials are conducted within the approved NOC or DIN parameters (C.05.006(2)), a CTA is not required.

With the exception of Phase 4 studies, clinical trial sponsors must submit a CTA to Health Canada for authorization to sell or import a drug for the purpose of a clinical trial. The CTA format, as outlined in Health Canada's *Guidance Document for Clinical Trial Sponsors: Clinical Trial Applications*, is consistent with that used for other types of drug submissions and is based on the format of the International Council on Harmonisation's (ICH) Common Technical Document (CTD). Although the scope of the ICH CTD does not include applications at the clinical research development stage, the CTD's modular format is being extended by Health Canada to CTAs to facilitate the preparation of drug submission information throughout a drug's lifecycle.

Sponsors must conduct all clinical trials, including Phase 4 trials, in accordance with Division 5, including the principles of GCPs, labeling requirements and obtaining Research Ethics Board (REB) approval.

Preclinical Trial Application (CTA) Consultation Meeting

Health Canada invites sponsors to request a pre-CTA consultation meeting. Such consultations may be particularly useful for new active substances or applications that include complex issues that may be new to Health Canada, such as those seen with biologics. The pre-CTA consultation meeting provides an opportunity for the sponsor to present relevant data and discuss concerns and issues regarding drug development. It also gives Health Canada an opportunity to provide guidance on the acceptability of the proposed trial(s).

The process for requesting a pre-CTA consultation meeting is the same for both drugs and biologics, as outlined in *Guidance Document: Clinical Trial Submissions*. One difference for biologics is the pre-CTA Information Package should contain additional quality information, including a list all production site(s) to be used during manufacture.

Clinical Trial Applications

As with pharmaceuticals, biological product clinical trial sponsors must file a CTA prior to initiating the trial. Health Canada's authority to regulate clinical trials stems from *FDAR* Section C.08.005, and clinical trial sponsors are directed to the Clinical Trial Review and Approval policy found on the Health Canada website. This policy aims to define the information BGTD requires from sponsors and to provide information on the evaluation process for the conduct of clinical trials in Canada.

Health Canada's *Guidance Document: Clinical Trial Submissions* and *Guidance Document: Preparation of Drug Regulatory Activities in the Common Technical Document (CTD) Format* and the updated *Guidance Document: Preparation of Regulatory Activities in the "Non-eCTD Electronic-Only" Format* should be referenced for preparing and submitting CTAs to Health Canada. While the Investigational New Drug Submission (INDS) process and reporting criteria are the same for pharmaceutical and biological drugs, three additional pieces of information are required by BGTD:
- Module 1.2.3 Certification and Attestation Forms: additional requirement for a Submission Disclosure Form
- Module 3.2.R.3 Lot Release Documentation: provision to BGTD only
- Module 3.2.R Yearly Biologic Product Report (YBPR): provision to BGTD only

For Module 2 CTD Summaries and Module 3 Quality, Health Canada directs the sponsor to consult the ICH M4Q Guidelines, which can be obtained from the ICH website. With respect to biologicals, there are five Quality Overall Summary (QOS) guidance documents referenced in *Guidance Document: Clinical Trial Submissions* to provide direction for completing the biologic drug submission quality section:
- *Guidance for Industry: Preparation of the Quality Information for Drug Submissions in the CTD* Format: *Biotechnological/Biological (Biotech) Products* (May 2004)
- *Guidance for Industry: Preparation of the Quality Information for Drug Submissions in the CTD Format: Blood Products* (May 2004)
- *Guidance for Industry: Preparation of the Quality Information for Drug Submissions in the CTD Format: Conventional Biotherapeutic Products* (May 2004)
- *Guidance for Industry: Preparation of the Quality Information for Drug Submissions in the CTD Format: Vaccines* (May 2004)
- *Guidance for Sponsors: Lot Release Program for Schedule D (Biologic) Drugs* (June 2005)

For biologics in early development, Module 3 submission is not always necessary if the QOS is detailed and likely is sufficient. For additional questions, the agency may be consulted.

It should be noted, these guidance documents have been archived by Health Canada since June 2013 to be used for reference, research or recordkeeping purposes, with the exception of *Preparation of the Quality Information for Drug Submissions in the CTD Format: Biotechnological/Biological (Biotech) Products: Guidance for Industry* (May 2004). In addition, previously available Health Canada quality templates, such as the Quality Information Summary-Biologicals, or QIS-B template, were superseded by the ICH CTD, and as of June 2013, have been archived on the Health Canada website.

Clinical Trial Application-Amendments (CTA-A) and Clinical Trial Application—Notification (CTA-N)

Clinical Trial Application-Amendments (CTA-As) and Clinical Trial Application-Notification (CTA-N) filing requirements are outlined in *Guidance Document: Clinical Trial Submissions*. For biologics, differences in manufacturing strategies can lead to the production of a novel drug product requiring both nonclinical and clinical data to support its use and are considered beyond the scope of an authorized CTA. In such cases, a new CTA is required. Examples of differences in manufacturing strategies include, but are not limited to:
- change in the drug substance source (e.g., from a fermentation process to transgenic milk)

Table 11-1. Drug Substance (Biologics and Radiopharmaceuticals)

Type of Change		Submission Type
1. Replacement or addition of a manufacturing site, involving:	a. production of the starting material, intermediate, or drug substance	Amendment
	b. testing (e.g., release, stability)	Notification
2. Change in the manufacturing process for the drug substance intermediate, involving:	a. the fermentation process (e.g., scale-up, new bioreactor technology, use of new raw materials of biological origin); or change in the route of synthesis of the radiopharmaceutical drug substance or critical component	Amendment
	b. the purification process (e.g., addition/removal/replacement of a purification step)	Amendment
3. Change in the specifications for the drug substance, involving:	a. deletion or replacement of a test, relaxation of an acceptance criterion or addition of a test for a new impurity	Amendment
	b. addition of a test (other than a test for new impurity) or tightening of an acceptance criterion	Notification
4. Change in the primary container closure system(s) for the storage and shipment of the drug substance, provided the proposed container closure system is at least equivalent to the approved container closure system with respect to its relevant properties, and the change does not concern a sterile drug substance		Notification
5. Change in the shelf life for the drug substance, involving:	a. (i) Extension if the approved shelf life is less than or equal to 18 months	Amendment
	a. (ii) Extension if the approved shelf life is more than 18 months	Notification
	b. Reduction (due to stability concerns)	Amendment

Source: Health Canada website. Guidance Document for Clinical Trial Sponsors: Clinical Trial Applications.

- change in the host cells used to express the same coding sequence
- change in the virus strain used in manufacturing a vaccine
- change in the oncolytic virus strain used in cancer treatment
- change in the immune globulin's animal source (e.g., from rabbit to sheep)

For additional guidance regarding quality change classification, sponsors are encouraged to consult with BGTD.

For a commercially available product used in clinical trials for which a quality change has been made according to the Post-Notice of Compliance (NOC) Changes guidance document, supporting data are not required to support the same change affecting the clinical product. The change can be notified to BGTD with cross-reference to the approved submission filed for the commercial product. If a change made to the commercial product has not yet been approved and is affecting the clinical material, a CTA-A or a CTA-N must be submitted according to the information in **Tables 11-1** and **11-2**. For Level 3 changes made to a biologic or radiopharmaceutical, a CTA-N is not required for the clinical product.

For quality (chemistry and manufacturing) CTA-As, a revised Investigator's Brochure (IB) or an Addendum to the IB describing any new quality information, including supporting data, is required, if applicable. Further, a list of all proposed quality changes from the authorized application should be provided in the cover letter.

It should be noted that Health Canada's administrative seven-day review target for comparative bioavailability trials does not apply to biologics, radiopharmaceuticals and cellular therapies, including Phase I trials using somatic cell therapies, xenografts, gene therapies, prophylactic vaccines or reproductive and genetic technologies.

Lot Release—Clinical Trials

While not a requirement for pharmaceuticals, all investigational biologic drug product lots to be used in a clinical trial are subject to the risk-based lot release requirements outlined in *Guidance for Sponsors: Lot Release Program for Schedule D (Biologic) Drugs* (2005) for both pre- and postmarket stages and before sale in Canada. Of note, Health Canada assignment to a lot-release group starts at the clinical trial stage and occurs throughout the biologic's lifecycle. Release is on a lot-by-lot basis and continues indefinitely. Products are assigned to one of four evaluation groups, each having different levels of regulatory oversight. The criteria used to determine the appropriate evaluation group include, but are not limited to, the product's nature, the target population, the BGTD lot-testing history and the manufacturer's production and testing history.

Group 1 is the preapproval stage and consists of Group 1A (preapproval stage) and Group 1b (consistency testing). Evaluation groups 2–4 apply to biologic products for which an NOC has been issued. Movement through the

Table 11-2. Drug Product (Biologics and Radiopharmaceuticals)

Type of Change		Submission Type
1. Replacement or addition of a drug product manufacturing site, involving:	a. production of a drug product (including primary packaging)	Amendment
	b. secondary packaging	Notification
	c. testing (e.g., release, stability)	Notification
2. Change in the drug product manufacturing process (e.g., scale-up, changes to the formulation process); change from manual synthesis of positron-emitting radiopharmaceutical to use of Automatic Synthesis Unit (ASU) or change in type of ASU		Amendment
3. Deletion of a drug product manufacturer/manufacturing site, primary or secondary packaging site or testing site		Notification
4. Change in the specifications for the drug product, involving:	a. deletion or replacement of a test, relaxation of an acceptance criterion or addition of a test for a new impurity	Amendment
	b. addition of a test (other than a test for new impurity) or tightening of an acceptance criterion	Notification
5. Change in the shelf life for the drug product, involving:	a. (i) Extension - if the approved shelf life is less than or equal to 18 months	Amendment
	a. (ii) Extension - if the approved shelf life is more than 18 months	Notification
	b. Reduction (due to stability concerns)	Amendment
6. Change in the storage conditions for the drug product		Amendment
7. Changes in final product dosage form (e.g., liquid to lyophilized formulation)		Amendment
8. Changes in final product strength		Amendment
9. Change in diluent, involving replacement or addition of a diluent for a lyophilized powder or concentrated solution by a diluent which is commercially available in Canada, is water for injection (WFI) or a salt solution, and after reconstitution, there is no change in the drug product specifications outside of the approved ranges		Notification
10. Change in radiolytic protective agent or antioxidant		Amendment

Source: Health Canada website. Guidance Document for Clinical Trial Sponsors: Clinical Trial Applications.

evaluation groups may be bi-directional and at BGTD's discretion, based on the product indication, nature, production history, inspection history, testing history and postmarket experience.

With the exception of prophylactic vaccines, BGTD requires the CTA sponsor or manufacturer to provide the directorate, before its use in the trial, with the following information via the "Fax-Back" process on the final product and its material bulk product, attesting all specifications have been met:
   a. lot numbers of materials being used during the trial and any Batch Identification Numbers assigned to lots received from elsewhere (i.e., all numbers associated with a particular lot)
   b. lot number(s) and manufacturing source of any associated human-derived excipient (e.g., human albumin)

The sponsor or manufacturer is required to sign a certification stating all testing on the drug substance and any human-derived excipients is complete and within specification. A completed Fax-Back form, including the required certification, should be sent to BGTD. This will be faxed back to the sponsor within 48 hours, providing the CTA has received prior BGTD authorization. If BGTD has not cleared the CTA, the Fax-Back will be held until CTA authorization has been granted. Upon receipt of the Fax-Back form, the sponsor may implement the particular lot's use.

If the sponsor wishes to use a lot that has failed one or more specifications, it must provide the testing protocol, an explanation and the rationale for its use along with the completed Fax-Back form. The lot must not be used until BGTD has released it.

For investigational prophylactic vaccines' lot release for use in an authorized CTA, BGTD will require the submission of testing protocols and/or Certificates of Analysis before it can be used in the trial. BGTD issues a formal release letter for using a prophylactic vaccine lot in a clinical trial. The lot must not be used until BGTD has released it. Additional information with respect to Health Canada's lot release requirements is provided later in this chapter under Lot Release—Postapproval.

Table 11-3. Sample Table of Contents for a Schedule D (Biological) Product Monograph (PM)

Title Page
Recent Major Label Changes (with dates) †
Table of Contents

    Part I: Health Professional Information
        Indications*
            Pediatrics
            Geriatrics
        Contraindications
        Serious Warnings and Precautions Box*
        Dosage and Administration
            Dosing Considerations
            Recommended Dose and Dosage Adjustment
            Administration
            Reconstitution
            Missed Dose
        Overdosage
        Dosage Forms, Strengths, Composition and Packaging
        Description
        Warnings and Precautions*
            Special Populations
                Pregnant Women
                Breastfeeding
                Pediatrics
                Geriatrics
        Adverse Reactions
            Adverse Reaction Overview
            Clinical Trial Adverse Reactions
            Less Common Clinical Trial Adverse Reactions
            Abnormal Laboratory Findings: Hematologic, Clinical Chemistry and other Quantitative Data
            Clinical Trial Adverse Reactions (Pediatrics)
            Post-Market Adverse Reactions
        Drug Interactions
        Action and Clinical Pharmacology*
        Storage, Stability and Disposal
        Special Handling Instructions
    Part II: Scientific Information
        Pharmaceutical Information*
        Clinical Trials*
            Trial Design and Study Demographics
            Study Results
            Comparative Bioavailability Studies
        Microbiology
        Nonclinical Toxicology*
        Supporting Product Monographs (formerly References)
    Patient Medication Information* (formerly Part III: Consumer Information)

† *New section for all product monograph templates to identify latest changes and when they were included into the PM*
* *Section is in standard monograph, but requirements differ for a Schedule D (biological) product monograph – refer to the current template on the Health Canada website for specific headings that are contained within the sections*

Clinical Trial Drug Importation

Additional information is provided in *Guidance Document: Clinical Trial Submissions* for sponsors who wish to import a drug into Canada for a clinical trial. Minor differences between pharmaceuticals and biologics exist, and sponsors are encouraged to consult the guidance and/or BGTD for clarification.

Review and Evaluation Process

Before a biologic can be considered for approval, sufficient scientific evidence must be collected to show it is safe, efficacious and of suitable quality. Biologics differ from other drugs for human use in that they must include, in addition to the information required for other drugs, more detailed chemistry and manufacturing information. This is necessary to help ensure the product's purity and quality, e.g., to help ensure it is not contaminated by an undesired microorganism or another biologic. Detailed information, which is harmonized between pharmaceuticals and biologicals, to be submitted in a NDS includes:

- preclinical studies done *in vitro* (test tube) and *in vivo* (using animals) to assess drug performance, including the extent of any toxic effects
- results of clinical trials (for all drugs) involving humans
- the way the product is manufactured or produced (including quality controls and evidence of consistent manufacture and stability)
- packaging and labelling
- product therapeutic claims
- conditions for use
- potential side effects

Facility Information

As part of the NDS process, biologics manufacturers also must supply product-specific facility information outlining the biologic's method of manufacture in significant detail, since slight variations can result in a different final product. The former *Guidance for Industry: Changes in Product-Specific Facility Information* was superseded by the Post-Notice of Compliance (NOC) Changes documents published by Health Canada in 2009 and subsequently archived in June 2013.

Further, for biological products, an OSE is completed to assess the production process and facility, since these aspects also have a significant impact on product safety and efficacy. The OSE is one of the critical steps in the NDS review process, and a favorable outcome is necessary to achieve marketing authorization.

The OSE is a preapproval inspection of the manufacturing facility that is a process- and product-specific inspection rather than facility-specific. There is some obvious overlap with current Good Manufacturing Practice (CGMP) inspection; however, this is not the OSE's focus. It should be noted, both drug substance and drug product manufacturing facilities are subject to the OSE. The decision to conduct an OSE is based on a number of criteria, including but not limited to:
- experience with the manufacturer
- experience with the manufacturing process
- facility issues identified during review
- laboratory testing problems
- known compliance problems at the facility
- not in production

In the case of blood components, establishments that perform licensable activities in Canada (fabricating, packaging/labeling, testing, distributing, importing or wholesaling) must provide sufficient evidence of the drug's safety and obtain an establishment license.

Since 1 January 1998, all Canadian drug establishments have been required to hold an establishment license to fabricate, package, label, distribute, import, wholesale or test a drug, whether pharmaceutical or biological, and, in the case of biological drugs, licenses are required for bulk process intermediates intended for use in the fabrication of final dosage forms.

Product Labelling

As detailed in Chapter 8, labelling drugs intended for human use is regulated under *FDAR*. General labelling requirements are outlined in *FDR* Section C.01.004, and Health Canada subsequently updated labelling regulations in 2014 to improve readability and enhance patient safety. These were known as the *Plain Language Labelling Regulations* (or PLL requirements). The labelling requirements specific to biological drugs are outlined in *FDR* Part C Division 3 and 4, respectively. Health Canada held a public consultation in July 2011 to improve product labelling materials' readability and include the consumer section of the Product Monograph (PM). Health Canada subsequently revised existing PM guidance documents and issued additional guidelines to assist industry compliance with the new label regulations. Thus, biologics' labelling components are subject to the new guidance documents, and industry is strongly encouraged to ensure draft mock-up labelling materials are generated in consultation with the current *Guidance Document: Labelling of Pharmaceutical Drugs for Human Use, Guidance Document: Questions and Answers: Plain Language Labelling Regulations* and *Post-Notice of Compliance (NOC) Changes: Safety and Efficacy* for changes involving postapproval labelling revisions.

Preparing a Biological Product PM

The PM is an integral part of New Drug, Supplemental New Drug, Abbreviated New Drug and Supplemental Abbreviated New Drug Submissions and Notifiable Changes. A PM is intended to provide the necessary information for the new drug's safe and effective use, and serves as a standard against which all drug promotion and advertising can be compared.

Biological products have certain unique information requirements that do not fall within the scope of the standard PM guidance. Except for the PM sections identified here, the core guidance document released by Health Canada should be used to prepare a biological product monograph as outlined in Health Canada's *Guidance for Industry: Product Monograph*. Sponsors also are directed to the current version of the *Product Monograph Template—Schedule D* on the Health Canada website. For Subsequent Entry Biologics (SEB), there are separate information requirements, and the *Guidance Document: Information and Submission Requirements for Biosimilar Biologic Drugs* should be consulted to ensure that requirements are met.

To assist in developing the PM, the current sample table of contents has been provided in **Table 11-3**, with sections required specifically for biological products as well as those where the information requirements may differ from the standard PM. Additional information on preparing a biological product PM can be found in Health Canada's current version of *Guidance Document: Product Monograph*.

Postmarketing

If Health Canada has determined there is sufficient evidence to support safety, efficacy or quality claims for an NDS or a Supplement to a New Drug Submission (SNDS), the agency will issue an NOC and a DIN for the product, indicating the biologic is approved for sale in Canada.

Biologics then are monitored periodically by being placed on a lot-release schedule tailored to their potential risk, manufacturing, testing and inspection history to date as discussed below.

Lot Release—Postapproval

Since biologic drugs are isolated from, or manufactured using, living organisms, they are inherently more variable than chemically synthesized drugs and require additional regulatory oversight. Biologic drugs are sensitive to changes in the starting materials and manufacturing and, therefore, are difficult to produce and characterize consistently. The Lot Release Program provides a check on biologic drugs to help assure their safety for human use and, as discussed earlier, the risk-based program covers both pre-(e.g., clinical trial stages) and postmarket stages and derives its legislative authority from *FDAR* Section C.04.015.

The Lot Release Program consists of four product categories from full and complete testing through protocol review down to notification and tracking, based on the product's associated degree of risk (see **Table 11-4**). The graduated risk-based approach to testing and oversight allows BGTD to focus ongoing testing on products for which enhanced surveillance is indicated, such as vaccines and blood products.

Products are assigned to one of four evaluation groups based on their risk profiles relative to regulatory inspection, lot testing and manufacturing testing histories. Group 1 pertains to preapproval biologic testing, and Groups 2–4 apply to biologics for which an NOC has been issued.

Group 1 comprises all products under review as a CTA or NDS and, in some cases, as an SNDS. They are assigned to Group 1 in one of two distinct subgroups:

- Group 1A: Clinical trial materials consist of materials associated with authorized CTAs. Sponsors are required to file a Fax-Back form and await a signed response from BGTD prior to using the clinical trial material. For prophylactic vaccines, BGTD issues a formal release letter for the vaccine lot's use in the trial; the testing protocol and, usually, samples are required to be submitted to BGTD.
- Group 1B: Consistency testing is an evaluation group intended for testing materials associated with an NDS or SNDS. Generally, BGTD requires samples from three to five consecutively manufactured lots to ensure manufacturing process consistency. Upon request, consistency lots may be released for sale in Canada following issuance of an NOC. A formal release letter from BGTD is required.

Group 2 (high-risk) products are subject to the most-stringent assessment (referred to as targeted testing) in terms of lot approval timelines and testing schedules; the manufacturer must routinely submit samples and testing protocols to BGTD for testing. The targeted timeframe for BGTD product release is six weeks from the date of receipt of all required information and samples. However, expedited release may be negotiated in exceptional cases if there is appropriate justification.

Group 3 products are tested on a periodic rather than a routine basis. Samples are not routinely submitted to BGTD for targeted testing; instead, BGTD routinely will review testing protocols. At BGTD's discretion, samples may be requested for periodic testing. The target timeframe for BGTD release is two weeks from the date all required information for Group 3 products is received.

Group 2 and 3 products require a formal BGTD release letter before each lot can be sold in Canada.

Group 4 products are low-risk, well-characterized products that do not undergo BGTD sample testing or protocol review. Group 4 biologic manufacturers must notify BGTD via a Fax Back form when a lot is to be sold in Canada. A release letter is not required for sale. At BGTD's discretion, Group 4 products also may be subject to periodic testing.

Assignment to Groups 2–4 is based on:
- product indication (e.g., patient population ages, disease state and health status of those being treated, etc.)
- product nature (e.g., raw material source and control level; manufacturing process complexity, robustness and control level; reliability and complexity of methods to evaluate the drug substance's identity, purity and potency)
- production history (including lot failures, aborted lots and reprocessed lots)
- inspection history
- testing history (including manufacturer-submitted results, BGTD testing results and additional data derived from test protocol review and inspection report exchanges via Mutual Recognition Agreements with foreign agencies)
- postmarket experience

Table 11-4. Summary of Requirements for Evaluation Groups

Evaluation Group Description	GROUP 1A Preapproval Clinical Trials	GROUP 1B Preapproval associated with NDS or S/NDS submissions	GROUP 2 Postapproval products requiring the highest level of assessment	GROUP 3 Postapproval products requiring a moderate level of assessment	GROUP 4 Postapproval products requiring a low level of assessment
Sample Requirements	*Prophylactic Vaccines:* Samples submitted for testing by BGTD *Other Biologics:* No samples required	Samples from three to five consecutively manufactured lots are submitted to BGTD for lot-to-lot consistency testing	Targeted Testing (mandatory submission of samples of all lots to BGTD for testing)	Products in Group 3 are subject to periodic testing	Products in Group 4 are subject to periodic testing. The manufacturer must notify BGTD on an annual basis of lots sold in Canada
Document Requirements	*Prophylactic Vaccines:* Submission of testing protocols and/or CoAs to BGTD for review *Other Biologics:* Sponsors are required to complete and file a Fax-Back form, which must include a rationale if testing specifications have not been met	Submission of testing protocols and/or CoAs to BGTD for review	Submission of testing protocols and or CoAs to BGTD for review	Submission of testing protocols and/or CoAs to BGTD for review	Fax-Back form with lot number of product at time of sale in Canada plus information on HDEs if product contains HDE
Approval Mechanism	*Prophylactic Vaccines:* A written approval in the form of a release letter is required *Other Biologics:* Fax-Back form will be returned by fax to the sponsor	Upon request, lots from which consistency samples were taken may be released for sale in Canada once an NOC is issued. A written approval in the form of a release letter is required for all lots	A written approval for sale in the form of a release letter is required for all lots	A written approval for sale in the form of a release letter is required for all lots	Not Applicable
Target Timeline	Not Applicable	Not Applicable	Six weeks after receipt of all required information and samples. Expedited release may be granted in exceptional cases and upon appropriate justification, such as product shortage	Two weeks after receipt of all required information. If periodic testing samples are requested by BGTD, the target timeline is six weeks	If periodic testing samples are requested by BGTD, the target timeline is six weeks
Reporting Requirements	Not Applicable	Not Applicable	Yearly Biologic Product Report	Yearly Biologic Product Report	Yearly Biologic Product Report

Usually, with the exception of vaccines (which may remain in Group 2 indefinitely), products assigned to Group 2 remain in that group for one year or until five lots have been tested and released, whichever period is longer. At that point, the product may be reassigned into Group 3 or 4, providing there have been consistent and reliable testing outcomes and no manufacturing process changes that might impact product quality. Movement through Groups 1–4 is bi-directional. For example, information obtained from periodic testing may cause the product to be reassigned from Group 3 into Group 2. Information obtained through YBPR review and routine inspection processes also may affect classification.

Regulatory Affairs Professionals Society

In general, the testing and/or protocol review outcome is communicated to the manufacturer via a Release Letter prior to the product's release for sale in Canada. In certain situations, a Fax Back process is used. A Fax Back form is submitted by the manufacturer, attesting all specifications have been met; receipt is acknowledged by BGTD sign-off on the Fax Back form within 48 hours.

BGTD carries out this work throughout the product lifecycle in Canada. Review and testing requirements are reviewed periodically to ensure the appropriate level of scrutiny is applied for each product, in line with its historic profile. Additional information on evaluation groups and factors considered during product assignment to evaluation groups can be found in *Guidance for Sponsors: Lot Release Program for Schedule D (Biologic) Drugs*.

Yearly Biologic Product Report (YBPR)

The YBPR is a report that all biologic drug manufacturers must submit annually in accordance with *Guidance for Sponsors: Lot Release Program for Schedule D (Biologics) Drugs*. The report contains both drug substance and drug product lot production information, including test methods and results, reasons for any recalls and corrective action taken, as well as other pertinent postmarket information.

Health Canada has the authority to request a YBPR, based on *FDR* Section C.01.014.5, C08.007 and/or C.08.008, which require biologic drug manufacturers to provide information annually to Health Canada. *FDR* Section C.04.015 requires manufacturers to provide information supporting lot release as discussed above.

As part of Health Canada's lifecycle approach to biologics' regulation, BGTD uses information from the YBPR to assess ongoing product safety and quality, verify manufacturing process consistency and highlight any trends. In addition, the YBPR is useful for providing regulatory context when only a few lots produced in a facility are released in Canada or when post-NOC changes are filed infrequently. The information also may be used to support a product's assignment into a different lot release evaluation group or justify continuing the current level of oversight.

Specific details on required content are provided in Section 5.1.1 of *Guidance for Sponsors: Lot Release Program for Schedule D (Biologics) Drugs*. The following information should be included in the YPBR:
- both drug substance and drug product lot production information
- drug substance and drug product test method and result information, including trend analysis for stability-indicating methods
- facility information, including foreign regulatory decisions that affect Good Manufacturing Practices (GMP) status
- analysis of Adverse Drug Reaction Reports (Canadian and international) attributable to product quality (postmarket technical complaints)
- all product recalls, including the reason of the recall and a summary of any corrective actions taken
- if changes affecting the Certified Product Information Document (CPID) have been made, an updated CPID

To decrease sponsors' regulatory burden, no Canada-specific format is required. Sponsors may file a report prepared for another competent regulatory authority, such as the US Food and Drug Administration (FDA) or European Medicines Agency (EMA), as long as it contains the Canada-specific information outlined in the guidance document.

An electronic PDF version and paper copy or duplicate paper copies of the report are requested no later than October of each year as an addendum to the Annual Drug Notification Report. However, this submission date is flexible, and sponsors are free to negotiate an alternate yearly filing date (e.g., one that coincides with filing to another regulatory body) by contacting the Regulatory Affairs Division–Centre for Policy and Regulatory Affairs. The YBPR also may be submitted directly to the Regulatory Affairs Division at the contact address listed on the Health Canada website (BGTD_RAD_Enquiries@hc-sc.gc.ca).

The Regulatory Affairs Division will issue:
1. an acknowledgement letter upon YBPR receipt
2. an information request (with a 30-day target) if clarification or additional information is required
3. a final letter to indicate the review is complete and to provide feedback to sponsors, if necessary (e.g., if the CPID was submitted, the CPID cover page with the recent BGTD review completion date is included)

Scientifically justified groupings may be submitted as one YBPR. Questions regarding groupings should be forwarded to the BGTD Regulatory Affairs Division.

A YBPR is required for all biologic drugs regulated by BGTD, whether or not the product is being manufactured or sold. If no lots are manufactured or sold within the reporting year, the sponsor should indicate this in the YBPR.

Summary

Biologic drugs are subject to additional regulatory oversight compared to pharmaceuticals, as they are variable and structurally complex. Also, their source materials, production cells and fermentation media present risks, such as the potential initial presence of pathogens or the growth of adventitious agents, such as viruses. A biologic NDS requires detailed chemistry and manufacturing information submission, with a preapproval OSE for most new products. Biologics also are subject to lot-release requirements and submission of an annual YBPR postapproval. There is additional regulatory oversight of postapproval quality changes.

Recommended Reading

Certified Product Information Document (Schedule D Drugs) Template (May 2004). Health Canada website. http://www.hc-sc.gc.ca/dhp-mps/brgtherap/applic-demande/guides/qualit/prod/tech-doc-biologic/ctd_cpid-dcip_schd-ann-eng.php. Accessed 21 April 2018.

Guidance Document: for Clinical Trial Sponsors: Clinical Trial Applications (May 2013). Health Canada website. http://www.hc-sc.gc.ca/dhp-mps/prodpharma/applic-demande/guide-ld/clini/ctdcta_ctddec-eng.php. Accessed 21 April 2018.

Guidance Document: Preparation of Drug Regulatory Activities in the Common Technical Document (CTD) Format (June 2012). Health Canada website. http://www.hc-sc.gc.ca/dhp-mps/prodpharma/applic-demande/guide-ld/ctd/ctd_prep_nds-eng.php. Accessed 21 April 2018.

Guidance for Industry, Preparation of the Quality Information for Drug Submissions in the CTD Format: Biotechnological/Biological (Biotech) Products (May 2004). Health Canada website. http://www.hc-sc.gc.ca/dhp-mps/brgtherap/applic-demande/guides/qualit/prod/tech-doc-biologic/ctd_biotech-eng.php. Accessed 21 April 2018.

Guidance for Industry: Management of Drug Submissions (December 2013). Health Canada website. http://www.hc-sc.gc.ca/dhp-mps/prodpharma/applic-demande/guide-ld/mgmt-gest/mands_gespd-eng.php. Accessed 21 April 2018.

Guidance Document: Post-Notice of Compliance (NOC) Changes: Quality Document (October 2016). Health Canada website. http://www.hc-sc.gc.ca/dhp-mps/prodpharma/applic-demande/guide-ld/postnoc_change_apresac/noc_pn_quality_ac_sa_qualite-eng.php. Accessed 21 April 2018.

Product Monograph Template - Schedule D (December 2016). Health Canada website: http://www.hc-sc.gc.ca/dhp-mps/prodpharma/applic-demande/guide-ld/monograph/pmappi_mpanni-eng.php. Accessed 21 April 2018.

Guidance Document: Product Monograph (June 2017). Health Canada website. https://www.canada.ca/content/dam/hc-sc/migration/hc-sc/dhp-mps/alt_formats/pdf/prodpharma/applic-demande/guide-ld/monograph/pm-guid-ld-mp-eng.pdf. Accessed 21 April 2018.

Post-Notice of Compliance (NOC) Changes: Framework Document (2011). Health Canada website. https://www.canada.ca/en/health-canada/services/drugs-health-products/drug-products/applications-submissions/guidance-documents/post-notice-compliance-changes/draft-framework-document.html. Accessed 21 April 2018.

Guidance Document: Labelling of Pharmaceutical Drugs for Human Use (2015). Health Canada website. https://www.canada.ca/en/health-canada/services/drugs-health-products/drug-products/applications-submissions/guidance-documents/labelling-pharmaceutical-drugs-human-use-2014-guidance-document.html. Accessed 21 April 2018.

Guidance Document: Questions and Answers: Plain Language Labelling Regulations for Non-prescription Drugs (2018). Health Canada website. https://www.canada.ca/en/health-canada/services/drugs-health-products/drug-products/applications-submissions/guidance-documents/guidance-document-questions-answers-plain-language-labelling-regulations-non-prescription-drugs-contact-lens-disinfectants.html. Accessed 21 April 2018.

Guidance Document: Information and Submission Requirements for Biosimilar Biologic Drugs (2017). Health Canada website. https://www.canada.ca/en/health-canada/services/drugs-health-products/biologics-radiopharmaceuticals-genetic-therapies/applications-submissions/guidance-documents/information-submission-requirements-biosimilar-biologic-drugs-1.html. Accessed 21 April 2018.

Guidance for Sponsors: Lot Release Program for Schedule D (Biologic) Drugs (June 2005). Health Canada website. http://www.hc-sc.gc.ca/dhp-mps/brgtherap/applic-demande/guides/lot/gui_sponsors-dir_promoteurs_lot_program-eng.php. Accessed 21 April 2018.

Chapter 12

Labelling, Advertising and Promotion: Prescription Pharmaceutical Drugs, Biologics and Radiopharmaceuticals

Updated by Marcia Sam, Veronica Yip and Sandra Alderdice

OBJECTIVES

❑ Gain an overview of the legislation and guidelines governing labelling, advertising and promotion of prescription pharmaceutical drugs, biologic drugs and radiopharmaceuticals

❑ Understand the key labelling components of prescription pharmaceutical drugs, biologic drugs and radiopharmaceuticals

LEGISLATION AND GUIDELINES COVERED IN THIS CHAPTER

❑ *Food and Drugs Act (F&DA)*

❑ *Food and Drug Regulations (FDR)*

❑ *Guidance Document: Labelling of Pharmaceutical Drugs for Human Use (2015)*

❑ *Guidance Document: Questions and Answers: Plain Language Labelling Regulations (2015)*

❑ *Guidance Document: Product Monograph (2016)*

❑ *Therapeutic Comparative Advertising Directive and Guidance Document (2005)*

❑ *Guidance Document—Health Canada and Advertising Preclearance Agencies' Roles Related to Health Product Advertising (2010)*

❑ *Guidance Document: Post-Notice of Compliance (NOC) Changes: Framework Document (2011)*

❑ *Policy on The Distinction Between Advertising and Other Activities (2005)*

❑ *Interim Guidance on Fair Balance in Direct-to-Consumer Advertising of Vaccines (2009)*

❑ *PAAB Code of Advertising Acceptance (2017)*

❑ *Guidelines for Consumer Advertising of Health Products (2018)*

Introduction

Health Canada regulates the labelling of drugs for human use under the Canadian *Food and Drugs Act (F&DA)* and *Food and Drug Regulations (FDR)*. A drug's labelling includes not only the container labels but also the Product Monograph (PM) or prescribing information, package insert and the patient medication/consumer information, which are critical product components because they contain important information about a drug for both the healthcare professional and patient or consumer. This chapter discusses the regulations and guidance governing the labelling content, as well as the submission and approval of these labelling components.

Advertising and promotion of drugs and biologics for human use also are regulated under the *F&DA* and *FDR*. Health Canada usually does not play a direct role in reviewing and preclearing advertising or promotional material; instead, such materials are precleared through a voluntary self-regulatory mechanism. The manner in which drug

Chapter 12

promotion and advertising are governed are also discussed in this chapter.

Labelling

The *F&DA* defines the term "label" as "including any legend, word or mark attached to, included in, belonging to or accompanying any food, drug, cosmetic, device or package."[1] The labelling, therefore, includes the labels affixed to the container or packaging of the drug, PM, prescribing information, package insert, fact sheets, patient medication and/or consumer information documents (i.e., patient leaflets), wallet/dosing cards and any document provided on request and setting out supplementary information on the drug's use. The *F&DA* prohibits labelling, selling or advertising a drug or device in a manner that is false, misleading or likely to create an erroneous impression about its quality, efficacy or safety.[2] The *FDR* specify the requirements for labelling content and formatting, and prohibit the sale of a drug not labelled in accordance with the regulations.

Drug Container Labels

Drug labelling requirements are found in *FDR* Part A and Part C, Division 1, 3 and 4. Part A includes the Plain Language Regulatory Provision, which applies to prescription pharmaceutical drugs, biologic drugs and radiopharmaceuticals. Part C Division 1 details provisions for drug closure labelling content, including the location of the information to appear on the labels, noting that a subset within does not apply to Schedule C and D drugs as specified. Divisions 3 and 4 outline additional specific labelling content requirements for Schedule C and D drug closures, respectively. The relevant sections of the regulations should be consulted to ensure all labelling content requirements are met for prescription pharmaceutical and Schedule C and D drugs, as required.

Further guidance on labelling of pharmaceutical drugs for human use is detailed in *Guidance Document: Labelling of Pharmaceutical Drugs for Human Use*.[3] This guidance interprets the regulatory information content requirements for prescription pharmaceutical drugs, including providing direction on further abbreviated labelling requirements for containers that are too small to accommodate the complete requirements for inner labels and those whose design causes their label to be destroyed during use.

Drug container labelling is submitted as part of the DIN application[4] or, in the case of a new drug, in the New Drug Submission (NDS).[5] Pursuant to the 2014 *Regulations Amending the Food and Drug Regulations (Labelling, Packaging and Brand Names of Drugs for Human Use)* for prescription products and those administered or obtained through a healthcare professional (known as the *Plain Language Labelling Regulations*), mock-up labelling materials are reviewed and approved before the Notice of Compliance (NOC) and/or Drug Identification Number (DIN) will be issued.[6] Subsequent labelling changes usually require prior approval; *Post-Notice of Compliance (NOC) Changes: Framework Document*,[7] and associated documents referenced within, and *Guidance Document: Questions and Answers: Plain Language Labelling Regulations* should be consulted for details on the type of submission required.[8] Note, a drug's directions for use must be in both French and English if the drug is available for sale without prescription in an open self-selection area.[9] Provincial regulations impose additional requirements for French and English labelling in some provinces, particularly Quebec.

PM

The PM summarizes a drug product's factual, scientific information. It includes information on the drug's properties, its indications and conditions for use and claims and instructions for use. The PM is intended to provide the information necessary to ensure the drug's safe and effective use. It is devoid of promotional material for the drug. New drugs subject to *FDR* Part C Division 8 are required to have a PM to obtain authorization.

The drug manufacturer develops the PM and submits it as part of an application (i.e., NDS, Supplemental NDS, Abbreviated NDS, Supplemental Abbreviated NDS or Notifiable Change). The PM is approved by Health Canada and is part of the NOC issued for the NDS and authorization for subsequent application changes submitted, such as a new approved indication or dosage form. The PM also provides the basis against which all advertising material should be compared for compliance with the regulations, as discussed later in this chapter.

Health Canada issued guidance on the PM format and content[10] that took effect 1 October 2004. It was subsequently revised in 2014, and most recently on 6 December 2016, which came into effect in June 2017. The current guidance document divides product information into three categories:
- Part I—Health Professional Information
- Part II—Scientific Information
- Part III—Patient Medication Information

Part I (Health Professional Information) provides healthcare professionals with the information required for safe and appropriate medication prescribing, dispensing and administration.

Part II (Scientific Information) contains more in-depth and extensive scientific and research information on the drug, such as clinical trial results and toxicology data.

Part III (Patient Medication Information, previously called Consumer Information) helps the patient (i.e., the general public) understand what the medication is, how it should be used and what side effects to expect. Part III is required for all drugs, regardless of the location of use (e.g., hospital) or method of administration.

Patient Medication Information summarizes the information in Part I in plain language (i.e., layman's language). If a drug has substantially different indications, separate Patient Medication Information sections should be considered and developed for each. Manufacturers may wish to consult with patient groups in developing PM Part III.

The 2014 and 2017 PM guidance documents detail what information should be included and the order in which it should be presented. Health Canada provides PM templates as appendices to the guidance document. The templates for new pharmaceutical products are slightly different from those for subsequent-entry products and for Schedule C or Schedule D products. Also, a standard template has been developed for products approved with a notice of compliance with conditions (NOC/c) in addition to one for biosimilars.

If requested, the sponsor should provide the PM to healthcare professionals. The PM must be available in both English and French. Part I of the PM identifies the information to be provided if a package insert for healthcare professionals is made available with the drug. The information included in PM Part III (Patient Medication Information or Consumer Information) usually is provided as a new drug product's package insert.

Traditionally, the drug manufacturer has been the primary disseminator of the PM and prescribing information to healthcare professionals and consumers. Public interest in increased communication about drugs was one of the factors that led to the current PM format, as a key Health Canada objective was to make the information more useful and accessible to healthcare professionals and consumers, as well as easy to retrieve, and to provide consistency across different drugs and drug classes. Therefore, Health Canada posts PMs on the publicly accessible Drug Product Database website (DPD) and the Drug and Health Product Register.[11]

The PM contains information specific to the drug and also may contain class labelling, applicable to all drugs in the class. With few exceptions (e.g., nonsteroidal anti-inflammatory drugs (NSAIDs) and noncontraceptive estrogen/progestin-containing products), class labelling is not published as such by Health Canada. Manufacturers are expected to assess a class effect and the need to update their PMs with respect to the safety information to be reviewed by Health Canada. Similarly, Health Canada can request an assessment or a class labelling change from market authorization holders.

Generic drug manufacturers are required to create and maintain the safety information in their PMs in alignment with those of the innovators. To facilitate this, Health Canada issues a monthly Product Monograph Brand Safety Update, indicating which safety-related sections of the innovator company's PM have changed.

Biosimilar manufacturers are expected to monitor the postmarket safety profile of both their own products and the reference biologic PMs and modify the biosimilar PMs as appropriate.

Prescribing Information

Prescription products that are not new drugs under the *FDR* (i.e., those subject to Part C, Division 1) have prescribing information rather than a PM.

To create a new prescribing information document where none previously existed, or to revise one, sponsors are encouraged to use the outline for Part I, Health Professional Information of the *Guidance Document: Product Monograph*, where possible.

The package insert for prescribed drug products is usually the prescribing information document and is equivalent to Part I of the new PM format for new drugs. Both these documents are intended for use by a healthcare professional.

Promotion and Advertising

The *F&DA* establishes a general prohibition for advertising content as follows: "No person shall label, package, treat, process, sell or advertise any drug in a manner that is false, misleading or deceptive or is likely to create an erroneous impression regarding its composition, merit or safety."[12] To comply with the *F&DA*, advertising must be consistent with the conditions of sale authorized in the product's NOC and provide a balanced representation of its benefits and risks.

As noted previously, the PM or other labelling associated with the approval for sale serves as the reference against which all promotional materials are assessed. Thus, the *F&DA* restricts advertising to drugs that have been approved for sale in Canada.[13] As discussed below, unlike the US, Canada currently restricts the promotion of prescription drugs and biologics directly to consumers. Only the drug name, price and quantity can be advertised to the general public per the *FDR*.

"Drug advertising" is defined in the *F&DA* as "any representation by any means whatever for the purpose of promoting directly or indirectly the sale or disposal of any food, drug, cosmetic or device."[14] Although Health Canada does not require submission or prior authorization of advertising, it strongly recommends industry submit all advertising materials to independent advertising preclearance agencies that have attested to meeting Health Canada's criteria.

- The Pharmaceutical Advertising Advisory Board (PAAB) reviews and approves health product advertising directed to healthcare professionals.
- Ad Standards and Extreme Reach review and approve nonprescription drug and natural health product advertising directed to consumers. Ad

- Standards also reviews and approves medical device advertising.
- In addition, PAAB and Ad Standards provide advisory opinions on messages directed to consumers for prescription drugs and on educational material discussing a medical condition or disease.

Health Canada works in collaboration with these agencies and has detailed their respective roles in the following policies: *Guidance Document—Health Canada and Advertising Preclearance Agencies' Roles Related to Health Product Advertising* (2010).

PAAB

PAAB was incorporated in 1976 with a multi-stakeholder board of directors. It is an autonomous, multidisciplinary body that provides a mechanism for the independent review and preclearance of health product advertising and promotional materials submitted by market authorization holders and intended to be directed to healthcare professionals. This preclearance system was established as an alternative to government preauthorization of advertising.

PAAB advertising review standards are set out in its *Code of Advertising Acceptance* (the PAAB Code), which conforms to all relevant requirements of the act and regulations and various applicable guidelines and policies.[15]

PAAB's role is to review submitted advertising material and ensure it is consistent with the product's approved labelling before its dissemination. PAAB may request changes to the advertisements and will formally approve them for one year of use. Advertising a drug product before it has received approval from Health Canada (e.g., an NOC) is prohibited. However, to assist manufacturers with timely introduction of new products or indications, PAAB will, at its discretion, pre-review some advertising materials before the NOC is issued. Generally, PAAB considers reviews only when the PM is at "final draft" review process stage with Health Canada; the advertising material will gain final acceptance only upon receipt of an NOC from Health Canada. The PAAB logo appearing directly on an advertising piece indicates to healthcare professionals that PAAB has pre-cleared the content.

The PAAB Code requires adequate product disclosure with promotional materials, often referred to as "fair balance."[16] The required fair balance level of detail is tiered, depending on the advertising claims. Until July 2013, distribution of a summary of prescribing information also was required with promotional materials. This recently has been replaced with a statement and link to the PM on the sponsor's or Health Canada's website.

During the review of an advertisement or an appeal or complaint, PAAB may consult Health Canada's Marketed Health Products Directorate (MHPD) about interpreting the terms of market authorization. Similarly, MHPD sometimes may wish to bring an advertising issue to the attention of PAAB.

Distinction Between Advertising and Other Activities

Health Canada has issued several policies, guidelines and guidance documents to assist manufacturers in interpreting the act and regulations. Some activities may be interpreted as advertising even though they are not intended to be promotional. Health Canada's policy helps distinguish promotional from nonpromotional activities.[17] In general, apart from content, the most important factors considered in making this distinction include the degree of sponsor control over material content and in what context, by whom, how often and how widely the material is distributed.

Educational meetings and subsequently generated reports are examples of activities that might be interpreted as advertising or promotions, depending on, among other things, the manufacturer's role in controlling the meeting's agenda and presentation content or the distribution of meeting proceedings. For example, accredited healthcare professional meetings or continuing medical education (CME) events, organized independently of the sponsor and whose materials are not focused on and do not emphasize a sponsor's products generally are considered nonpromotional and are exempt from PAAB review. However, reports, edited scripts or recorded videos of the proceedings focusing on a specific drug may be considered advertising if they are disseminated by or on behalf of a sponsor after the meeting.[18]

Advertising Restrictions Under an NOC/c

Promoting a drug prior to receiving marketing authorization is not permitted in Canada.[19] Manufacturers should be aware advertising and promotion restrictions apply when an NOC/c has been issued for a product. Health Canada guidance on NOC/cs,[20] as well as the PAAB supplementary guideline on *Advertising Disclosure for Drugs with "Notice of Compliance with Conditions,"*[21] should be consulted for additional information. PAAB requires a statement about the market authorization's conditional nature to appear prominently on the display portion of advertising.

Complaints About Advertising

Anyone having an issue with a promotional piece may file a complaint with either Health Canada or the advertising preclearance agencies, depending on the product's status and the target audience. For details on the review and complaint-handling process, refer to Health Canada's *Guidance Document: Health Canada and Advertising Preclearance Agencies' Roles Related to Health Product Advertising*. When an advertising preclearance agency deems the advertising in question to raise a significant health hazard, it requests

Health Canada to intervene. In addition, Health Canada may become involved in an advertising issue any time it considers a significant health hazard exists.

Since pre-NOC promotion is prohibited, and direct-to-consumer (DTC) advertising is restricted in Canada, they are outside the scope of PAAB's complaint-resolution process. Complaints about these types of alleged infractions should be forwarded directly to Health Canada. Health Canada's current webpage on advertising complaints[22] should be consulted for further details.

DTC Advertising

DTC prescription drug advertising is restricted under the *FDR*. Prescription drug advertising to the general public is restricted to brand name, proper name, common name, price and drug quantity. Health Canada's *Policy on the Distinction Between Advertising and Other Activities* provides additional information on the criteria used to determine whether a material is advertising or information.[23] For example, materials not intended to promote the sale of a particular drug may include disease-specific brochures in which various therapy options are discussed objectively and without undue emphasis on a particular treatment option.

"Help-seeking" messages also may be permitted for the general public if they do not mention or imply a particular drug but do inform consumers therapy is available through consultation with their prescribers.

Summary

- Labelling is regulated in Canada and includes container labels, Product Monograph (PM), package inserts, patient medication and consumer information documents and wallet or dosing cards.
- The PM is divided into three sections: Part I—Health Professional Information, Part II—Scientific Information and Part III—Patient Medication Information/Consumer Information. The PM is the reference against which all promotional materials are assessed.
- Drug advertising is restricted to products approved for sale in Canada, usually authorized by a Notice of Compliance (NOC).
- Prescription drug advertising to the general public is restricted to brand name, proper name, common name, price and drug quantity.
- Currently, three independent advertising preclearance agencies review the bulk of health product advertisements: the Pharmaceutical Advertising Advisory Board, Ad Standards and Extreme Reach.

References

1. *Food and Drugs Act*, Section 2. Government of Canada Justice Laws website. http://laws.justice.gc.ca/eng/acts/F-27/page-1.html. Accessed 27 May 2018.
2. Ibid.
3. *Guidance Document: Labelling of Pharmaceutical Drugs for Human Use* (2015). Health Canada website. https://www.canada.ca/en/health-canada/services/drugs-health-products/drug-products/applications-submissions/guidance-documents/labelling-pharmaceutical-drugs-human-use-2014-guidance-document.html. Accessed 27 May 2018.
4. *Guideline on the Preparation of Drug Identification Number Submissions* (1995). Health Canada website. https://www.canada.ca/en/health-canada/services/drugs-health-products/drug-products/applications-submissions/guidance-documents/preparation-drug-identification-number-submissions.html. Accessed 27 May 2018.
5. *Guidance Document: Preparation of Drug Regulatory Activities in the CTD Format* (2012). Health Canada website. http://www.hc-sc.gc.ca/dhp-mps/prodpharma/applic-demande/guide-ld/ctd/ctd_prep_nds-eng.php. Accessed 21 April 2018.
6. *Guidance Document: Questions and Answers: Plain Language Labelling Regulations* (2016). Health Canada website. https://www.canada.ca/en/health-canada/services/drugs-health-products/drug-products/applications-submissions/guidance-documents/questions-answers-plain-language-labelling-regulations.html. Accessed 21 April 2018.
7. *Post-Notice of Compliance (NOC) Changes: Framework Document* (2011). Health Canada website. https://www.canada.ca/en/health-canada/services/drugs-health-products/drug-products/applications-submissions/guidance-documents/post-notice-compliance-changes/draft-framework-document.html. Accessed 21 April 2018.
8. *Guidance Document: Questions and Answers: Plain Language Labelling Regulations for Non-prescription Drugs.* (2017). Health Canada website. https://www.canada.ca/en/health-canada/services/drugs-health-products/drug-products/applications-submissions/guidance-documents/guidance-document-questions-answers-plain-language-labelling-regulations-non-prescription-drugs-contact-lens-disinfectants.html. Accessed 21 April 2018.
9. Op cit 6.
10. *Guidance Document: Product Monograph* (2017). Health Canada website. https://www.canada.ca/en/health-canada/services/drugs-health-products/drug-products/applications-submissions/guidance-documents/product-monograph/guidance-document-product-monograph.html. Accessed 21 April 2018.
11. The Drug and Health Product Register (2018). Health Canada website. https://hpr-rps.hres.ca/. Accessed 21 April 2018.
12. *Food and Drugs Act*, Section 9. Government of Canada Justice Laws website. http://laws-lois.justice.gc.ca/eng/acts/F-27/. Accessed 21 April 2018.
13. *Food and Drugs Act*, Sections 3 and 9. Government of Canada Justice Laws website. http://laws-lois.justice.gc.ca/eng/acts/F-27/. Accessed 21 April 2018.
14. Op cit 1.
15. PAAB *Code of Advertising Acceptance* (2017). Pharmaceutical Advertising Advisory Board website. http://code.paab.ca/. Accessed 21 April 2018.
16. Ibid, Section 7.
17. *Policy on the Distinction Between Advertising and Other Activities* (2005). Health Canada website. http://www.hc-sc.gc.ca/dhp-mps/advert-publicit/pol/actv_promo_vs_info-eng.php. Accessed 21 April 2018.
18. Op cit 15, Section 1.5.
19. Op cit 1, Section 9(1) and *Food and Drug Regulations*, Section C.08.002. Government of Canada Justice Laws website. http://laws-lois.justice.gc.ca/eng/regulations/C.R.C.,_c._870/page-134.html#docCont. Accessed 21 April 2018.
20. *Guidance Document: Notice of Compliance with Conditions (NOC/c)* (2003). Health Canada website. http://www.hc-sc.gc.ca/dhp-mps/prodpharma/applic-demande/guide-ld/compli-conform/noccg_accd-eng.php. Accessed 21 April 2018.

21. PAAB *Guideline on Advertising Disclosure for Drugs with "Notice of Compliance with Conditions" (NOC/c)*. (2017). PAAB website. http://www.paab.ca/Guidance_on_Advertising_for_Drugs_with_Notice_of_Compliance_with_Conditions_(NOCc)_Feb_2018_(typofix)_docx.pdf. Accessed 21 April 2018.
22. Health Product Advertising Complaints (2018). Health Canada website. https://www.canada.ca/en/health-canada/services/drugs-health-products/regulatory-requirements-advertising/health-product-advertising-complaints.html. Accessed 21 April 2018.
23. Op cit 20.

Chapter 13

electronic Common Technical Document (eCTD)

By Khaled Yahiaoui, MSc, RAC

OBJECTIVES

❑ Gain an overview of the Canadian electronic Common Technical Document (eCTD) for drug regulatory activities

❑ Understand the eCTD submission process and the Canadian electronic regulatory environment

❑ Understand the validation criteria for an eCTD submission

❑ Understand the electronic regulatory requirements governing both submission format and filing

❑ Assist sponsors in demonstrating compliance with the principles of eCTD dossiers submitted to Health Canada

❑ Understand lifecycle management at dossier, regulatory activity and regulatory transaction levels

GUIDANCE DOCUMENTS COVERED IN THIS CHAPTER

❑ *Guidance Document: Preparation of Drug Regulatory Activities in the Electronic Common Technical Document Format* (14 May 2015)

❑ *Guidance Document: Creation of the Canadian Module 1 Backbone* (30 September 2012)

❑ *International Council for Harmonisation Guidelines: Electronic Common Technical Document Specification*—Version 3.2.2 dated 16 July 2008 developed by the ICH M2 Expert Working Group

Introduction

eCTD is the abbreviation for electronic Common Technical Document, the electronic format of the CTD. It is a format used to transfer regulatory documentation and information from sponsors to Health Canada, while considering ease of creation, evaluation, lifecycle management and archiving. Health Canada started accepting regulatory submissions for drugs in eCTD format in 2004. Further, if a sponsor has filed regulatory activities in non-eCTD format already (i.e., paper, non-eCTD Electronic-Only) and then switches to eCTD format, there is no need to refile any previously approved regulatory activities in eCTD format.

To be accepted by Health Canada, an eCTD regulatory transaction must comply with the following guidelines:
- *Guidance Document: Preparation of Drug Regulatory Activities in the Electronic Common Technical Document*
- *Guidance Document: Creation of Canadian Module 1 Backbone*
- *Electronic Common Technical Document Specification*—Version 3.2.2 dated 16 July 2008, developed by the ICH M2 Expert Working Group
- eCTD Validation Criteria developed by Health Canada
- Applicable Health Canada Updates and Notices

Chapter 13

Scope of eCTD

The regulatory activity types and regulatory transactions accepted in eCTD format are constantly and rapidly evolving. Currently, most drug regulatory activities are accepted in eCTD format. This includes, but is not limited to:

- New Drug Submission (NDS)
- Supplement to a New Drug Submission (SNDS)
- Abbreviated New Drug Submission (ANDS)
- Supplement to an Abbreviated New Drug Submission (SANDS)
- Extraordinary Use New Drug Submission (EU NDS)
- Extraordinary Use Supplement to a New Drug Submission (EU SNDS)
- Supplement to a New Drug Submission-Confirmatory (SNDS-C)
- Request for Priority Review Status for NDS or SNDS
- Periodic Safety Update Report—Confirmatory (PSUR-C) or Periodic Benefit Risk Evaluation Report—Confirmatory (PBRER-C)
- Notifiable Change (NC)
- Level III
- Yearly Biologic Product Report (YBPR)
- Pre-Submission Meeting Information
- Application for Drug Identification Number (DINA)
- Application for Drug Identification Number—Biologic (DINB)
- Application for Drug Identification Number—Disinfectant Product (DIND)
- Application for Drug Identification Number—Category IV Product (DINF)
- Post-Authorization Division 1 Change (PDC)
- Post-Authorization Division 1 Change—Biologics (PDC-B)
- Periodic Safety Update Report (PSUR) or Periodic Benefit Risk Evaluation Report (PBRER), when provided to the Marketed Health Products Directorate (MHPD)
- Risk Management Plan (RMP), when provided to MHPD
- Undefined Regulatory Activity (UDRA), such as a DIN Cancellation

As of 1 January 2018, the eCTD format became mandatory for NDS, SNDS, ANDS and SANDS. Nevertheless, Health Canada can consider an exemption from the mandatory eCTD format requirement on a case-by-case basis.

All regulatory transactions related to the regulatory activities listed above must be filed in eCTD format if the regulatory activity was filed in eCTD format. These regulatory transactions include, but are not limited to:

- response to a clarification request
- response to a Screening Deficiency Notice (SDN)
- response to a Notice of Deficiency (NOD)
- response to a Notice of Non-compliance (NON)
- response to Notice of Compliance with Conditions—Qualifying Notice (NOC/c-QN)
- PSUR or PBRER requested during the premarket review process
- RMP requested during the premarket review process by TPD, BGTD or NNHPD
- PSUR requested during the premarket review process by TPD, BGTD or NNHPD
- comments to the Summary Basis of Decision/Notice of Decision
- Second Language Product Monograph (PM)
- Market Notification Form (Drug Notification Form)
- Form IV, including updates, filed in accordance with the *Patented Medicines (Notice of Compliance) Regulations*
- Form V, including updates, filed in accordance with the *Patented Medicines (Notice of Compliance) Regulations*
- documents related to data protection under *Food and Drug Regulations* (*FDR*) Section C.08.004.1
- reconsideration of decisions
- written correspondence related to the *Patented Medicines (Notice of Compliance) Regulations*
- notice of allegation and related materials (i.e., notice of allegation, proof of service, certification of filing date) under the *Patented Medicines (Notice of Compliance) Regulations*
- Consent Letter (Authorization for Sharing Information)
- Consent Letter (Data Protection Information)
- Consent Letter (Patent Information)

For an exhaustive list of regulatory activities and transactions accepted in eCTD format, refer to *Guidance Document: Preparation of Drug Regulatory Activities in the Electronic Common Technical Document Format* Section 1.3 and *Questions and Answers—Regulatory Activities in eCTD Format (question 25)*. In the author's experience, if a regulatory activity or transaction is not listed in Section 1.3 of the guidance document, the regulatory professional is encouraged to communicate with Health Canada via email, ereview@hc-sc.gc.ca, to inquire about its acceptability in eCTD format.

Once a drug product, either a chemical entity or a biologic, is filed in eCTD format, all subsequent regulatory activities and transactions for that product must be filed in eCTD format.

eCTD is the legal format in Canada. Thus, any information or documentation provided to reviewers by email

Figure 13-1. Structure of a Regulatory Transaction in eCTD Format

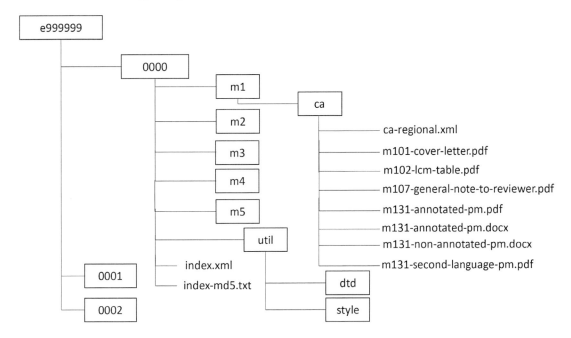

or any other non-eCTD format should be followed by a regulatory transaction in eCTD format.

Structure of a Regulatory Transaction in eCTD Format

Figure 13-1 illustrates regulatory transaction content in eCTD format. The various components are described below.

eCTD Specification

The eCTD specification is the list of criteria that make an electronic regulatory submission technically valid, allowing the transfer of all regulatory activities or transactions to Health Canada electronically. It is based on the CTD's defined content. The specification is programmed in XML (eXtensible Markup Language). In the eCTD format, the XML is called "Document Type Definition" or DTD. Thus, an eCTD is a folder structure containing the submission content in CTD format in addition to the DTD (XML).

eCTD Identifier and Top-Level Folder

The top-level folder contains all other subfolders and their contents. Prior to filing a specific drug product's first regulatory transaction, sponsors must ask Health Canada to assign an eCTD identifier. The name of the top-level folder is the eCTD identifier, which is an "e" for "electronic" followed by six digits (e.g., e999999). The eCTD identifier is unique for a specific drug product. Any subsequent regulatory activity or transaction submitted to Health Canada in eCTD format for the same dossier (drug product) should have the same identifier.

eCTD Sequence

In an eCTD, each regulatory transaction with the health authority is called a "sequence," whether or not the information sent is solicited. A sequence is a four-digit number starting at 0000 for regulatory transactions sent to Health Canada in eCTD format. All files and folders included in the regulatory transaction should be in the sequence number folder.

Sequence numbers are incremental for each new regulatory transaction within the same eCTD dossier (0000, 0001, 0002, etc.), and each transaction has a unique sequence number. Nevertheless, if there is any issue with a sequence once received by Health Canada, the sponsor may be asked to resubmit the regulatory transaction with the same sequence number. In the author's experience, it is recommended the sponsor confirm with Health Canada that the erroneous sequence is deleted from systems prior to filing the corrected one.

Each sequence contains the following files and folders:
- m1 folder
- m2 to m5 folders (if documentation is submitted)
- util folder (contains the DTD)
- index.xml file
- index-md5.txt file (checksum)

Table 13-1. Localization of Main XML Files Within an eCTD Sequence

XML File	Path Within the eCTD Sequence*
Index.xml	e999999/0000
ca-regional.xml	e999999/0000/m1/ca
ca-regional-2-2.xsd ich-ectd-3-2.dtd	e999999/0000/util/dtd

*In this example, "e999999" is the dossier eCTD identifier, and "0000" is the sequence number.

m1 Folder

This contains a folder named "ca." The ca folder contains all Module 1 documents submitted in that sequence in addition to the ca-regional.xml file. The ca folder should not contain any subfolders. This folder's structure and content are defined in *Guidance Document: Creation of the Canadian Module 1 Backbone*. The m1 folder is always present within a sequence, whether or not Module 1 content is submitted.

m2 to m5 Folders

These contain submission content for CTD Modules 2–5. Unlike the m1 folder, folders m2–m5 are present only if content is submitted in those respective modules. Refer to the following guidelines for Modules 2–5's structure and content:

- Guidance Document: Preparation of Drug Regulatory Activities in the Common Technical Document (CTD) Format
- International Council for Harmonisation, *Electronic Common Technical Document Specification*, Version 3.2.2 dated 16 July 2008, developed by the ICH M2 Expert Working Group

util Folder

The util folder does not contain any regulatory documentation. It contains the xml files describing the electronic structure of Canadian Module 1 (ca-regional-2-2.xsd) and ICH Modules 2–5 (ich-ectd-3-2.dtd).

Index File

The index.xml, or xml backbone, is like a container with links to Modules 2–5's documentation. It is based on the xml files present in the util subfolder. The index.xml file is present in all sequences and is considered the equivalent of the table of contents (TOC).

Index-md5 File

Each eCTD sequence contains a mechanism to guarantee the regulatory submission contents' integrity and completeness. The sum of checks, or checksum, is a unique string of letters and numbers generated from the checks.

Table 13-1 summarizes the localization of the main xml files within an eCTD sequence.

eCTD Metadata

To organize and structure the eCTD dossier with its multiple sequences through the drug product lifecycle, the eCTD offers the possibility of tagging multiple CTD sections.

Table 13-2. Canadian eCTD Envelope Elements

Element	Importance	Description
Applicant	Mandatory	Contains the sponsor's name, i.e., the company submitting the regulatory transaction
Product Name	Mandatory	Contains the drug product name
Dossier Identifier	Mandatory	Contains the unique dossier identifier in the format "e999999" assigned by Health Canada
Dossier Type	Mandatory	Contains the type of file (pharmaceutical, biological, Drug Master File) (Selected from a drop-down list)
Regulatory Activity Type	Mandatory	Contains the type of regulatory activity (Selected from a drop-down list)
Regulatory Activity Lead	Mandatory	Determines which group at Health Canada should take responsibility for the review of the regulatory activity supported by this regulatory transaction (Selected from a drop-down list)
Sequence Number	Mandatory	Contains a four-digit number that is the unique identifier for this sequence (regulatory transaction) in the folder. At Health Canada, a subsequent validation will be performed to ensure the number is unique in the record and is greater than any previously filed sequence.
Sequence Description	Mandatory	Contains a description of the sequence (regulatory transaction) according to a series of possibilities described in Table 4 of *Guidance Document: Creation of the Canadian Module 1 Backbone*
Related Sequence Number	Optional	Contains the four-digit sequence number of the first sequence in this regulatory activity

eCTD Envelope

The eCTD envelope allows the sponsor to provide information about the regulatory transaction submitted to Health Canada in a specific sequence. It also describes its relation to any regulatory information previously filed. In addition, it enables Health Canada to efficiently manage and process regulatory activities and transactions received in eCTD format while reducing the risk of errors. **Table 13-2** gives a brief description of the Canadian eCTD envelope. For more information and details about eCTD envelope elements, refer to *Guidance Document: Creation of the Canadian Module 1 Backbone*.

m2–m5 Attributes

eCTD m2–m5 content is organized using attributes. These are elements that define and distinguish repeated sections in the eCTD structure. For instance, each drug substance should have its own 3.2.S section if the drug product is a combination of more than one drug substance. Also, if the same drug substance is supplied by different manufacturers, there will be a 3.2.S section for each manufacturer.

Table 13-3 summarizes the CTD sections necessitating the use of attributes. The attributes are case-sensitive and must not be changed throughout the drug product's lifecycle unless previously discussed and agreed with Health Canada. If there is any modification (even minor) in the attributes' syntax, a new section will be created in Health Canada's submissions viewing system without any change in the sponsor's eCTD publishing and viewing system. Thus, sponsors should be very careful when choosing and managing attributes in eCTD dossiers. For more information about eCTD attributes, refer to *Electronic Common Technical Document Specification*, Version 3.2.2, dated 16 July 2008, developed by the ICH M2 Expert Working Group.

Table 13-3. m2-m5 eCTD Attributes

Module	CTD Section	Attributes
2	2.3.S	Substance Manufacturer
2	2.3.P	Product Name Manufacturer Dosage Form
3	3.2.S	Substance Manufacturer
3	3.2.P	Product Name Manufacturer Dosage Form
3	3.2.P.4	Excipient
5	5.3.5	Indication

Validation of Regulatory Tranactions in eCTD format (eCTD Sequence)

To be accepted by Health Canada, in addition to complying with Health Canada and ICH eCTD guidance documents, the eCTD sequence must pass validation. Two types of validation are performed: electronic validation and structure validation.

Table 13-4. Validation Rule Samples and Their Descriptions and Severities

Category	Rule	Description	Severity
A. General	A01 Empty Folders	Checks the sequence folder structure for any empty folders (folders without any files or subfolders)	Error
B. PDF Analysis	B24 PDF Protection	Finds PDF documents with password protection	Error
C. Referenced Files	C07 Unreferenced Files	Searches for files not referenced in an index file (ICH, regional or STF)	Error
D. XML Analysis	D04 Validate against delivered DTD	Performs XML validation for ICH backbone and regional backbones. Uses the DTD or schema given in the sequence number folder (util/dtd).	Error
F. CA Regional 2.2	F08 Application folder name must match dossier-identifier	The element value for the dossier identifier must match the name of the parent folder of the sequence folder. The dossier identifier must start with the letter "e" or "s"	Error
G. ICH Backbone 3.2	G13 Folder util exists	The util folder must be present.	Error
H. STF 2.2	H05 Study identifier category must not be empty	The value of the study identifier/category element must not be empty.	Warning

Table 13-5. Document Formats Health Canada Expects for Specific Documents

Document	Version	Required Formats
Product Monograph (PM)	Annotated	PDF and Microsoft® Word
	Non-Annotated	Microsoft® Word
	English Pristine	Microsoft® Word
	Second Language	PDF
Certified Product Information Document (CPID)	Annotated	PDF
	Non-Annotated	Microsoft® Word
Quality Overall Summary (QOS)		PDF and Microsoft® Word
Sponsor Attestation Checklist for ANDS		PDF and Microsoft® Word
Responses to Clarification Request, SDN, NON and NOD		PDF and Microsoft® Word
Comprehensive Summary–Bioequivalence (CS-BE)		PDF and Microsoft® Word

Electronic Validation

Health Canada established regulatory transaction validation criteria for eCTDs. These validation rules are revised and posted to assist stakeholders in preparing compliant regulatory transactions in eCTD format. The validation criteria are based on information provided in *Guidance Document: Preparation of Drug Regulatory Activities in Electronic Common Technical Document (eCTD) Format* and specifications for the eCTD regional administrative module (Module1) defined in *Guidance for Industry: Creation of the Canadian Module 1 Backbone (eCTD)* and ICH's *Electronic Common Technical Document Specification* (Version 3.2.2).

Health Canada's validation criteria include seven categories (A, B, C, D, F, G and H). Each category contains several rules and validates a specific aspect, such as PDF Analysis (B), XML Analysis (D) or CA Regional 2.2 (F). Category E was assigned to validate CA Regional 1.0, the xml structure of the old Canadian Module (version 1.0), which no longer is accepted by Health Canada since the newer version (2.2) was issued.

Health Canada validation criteria have three severity levels: error, warning and information. Sponsors are expected to validate their eCTD regulatory transactions using eCTD validation software and to correct any warnings and errors prior to filing them to Health Canada. An electronic validation also generates a report and provides the result for each rule.

Table 13-4 provides some examples of validation rules, their severity and a quick description of what is being validated. For a comprehensive list of Health Canada validation rules, refer to the agency's notice. The latest revision available at the time of writing is *CA eCTD–Profile 4.3*, published 27 November 2017 and accessed 30 March 2018. eCTD validation software vendors use the revised rules to update their tools and then make them available to sponsors to use in validating any eCTD regulatory transaction.

Structure Validation

Once Health Canada receives the eCTD regulatory transaction, an electronic validation is performed. Also, the regulatory transaction is verified from a structure perspective. Even if the transaction passes electronic validation, it could fail structure validation. In this case, Health Canada will reject the sequence and email the sponsor a list of the adjustments to perform in the sequence structure.

Table 13-6. Lifecycle Management Table Template

Sponsor Name:					
Brand Name:					
Dossier Identifier:					
Sequence Number	Date Submitted	Control Number	Related Sequence	Regulatory Activity Type	Sequence Description

Table 13-7. Lifecycle Management Table Example with Three Regulatory Activities and Related Regulatory Transactions

Sponsor Name: MyCompany					
Brand Name: MyDrugProduct					
Dossier Identifier: e111111					
Sequence Number	Date Submitted	Control Number	Related Sequence	Regulatory Activity Type	Sequence Description
0000	12 Dec. 2014	—	—	MPNDS	Presubmission Meeting Request
0001	6 Jan. 2015	123456	0000	MPNDS	Presubmission Meeting Package
0002	24 Feb. 2015	123456	0000	MPNDS	Minutes of Meeting, 10 Feb. 2015
0003	3 Jul. 2015	123654	—	NDS	Initial
0004	8 Jul. 2015	123654	0003	NDS	Response to Processing Clarification Request dated 6 Jul. 2015
0005	3 Dec. 2015	123654	0003	NDS	Response to NOD dated 2 Nov. 2015
0006	14 Jul. 2016	123654	0003	NDS	Response to Clinical Clarification Request dated 6 Jul. 2016
0007	12 Dec. 2016	123654	0003	NDS	Response to Labelling Clarification Request dated 6 Dec. 2016
0008	20 Dec. 2016	123654	0003	NDS	Pristine PM
0009	6 Jan. 2017	123654	0003	NDS	Drug Notification Form
0010	13 Feb. 2017	132456	—	SNDS	Post NOC Change
0011	25 Apr. 2017	132456	0010	SNDS	Response to Quality Clarification Request dated 10 Apr. 2017
0012	4 Aug. 2017	132456	0010	SNDS	Response to Labelling Clarification Request dated 31 Jul. 2017
0013	15 Aug. 2017	132456	0010	SNDS	Pristine PM

Technical Requirements for Regulatory Transactions in eCTD Format

File Formats

Before compiling PDF regulatory documents in the eCTD structure, it is important the documents be formatted properly to ensure they will meet Health Canada's document validation criteria.

Generating the PDF documents from electronic source documents is always recommended. If the source is being scanned, an OCR (Optical Character Recognition) using Adobe Acrobat® should be used to allow selection of PDF document content.

Other file extensions are accepted in eCTD regulatory transactions. Valid file extensions include: .pdf, .doc, .docx, .xls, .xlsx, .wpd, .ppt, .pptx, .xml, .dat, .inf, .txt, .png, .gif, .svg, .wav, .mp3, .mp4, .wmv, .jpg, .jpeg, .tif, .tiff and .bpm.

In addition to PDF format, Health Canada recommends sponsors provide specific documents in other formats (**Table 13-5**).

In the author's experience, communicating with eReview by email (ereview@hc-sc.gc.ca) is recommended if there is any doubt about required formats for other files.

Bookmarking

Most submission content is in PDF format. To facilitate the submission review and navigation, the PDF files must be properly bookmarked and comply with the following Health Canada requirements regarding bookmarking:
- Documents of 10 pages or more should be bookmarked.
- Bookmarks should be equivalent to the document's table of contents and should be organized as such.
- Sections, subsections, tables, figures and appendices should all be bookmarked.
- Too many or too few bookmarks are ineffective.

In the author's experience, bookmarking should be adjusted to the number of pages in the document. A document of 1,000 pages should not be bookmarked at the same level as

Table 13-8. Lifecycle Management of Specific Documents

Document	Operation Attribute
Cover Letter	"New" in all regulatory transactions (all sequences)
LCM Table	"New" in sequence 0000
	"Replace" in sequence 0001 and higher
Forms in Section 1.2 (application form, fee form, etc.)	"New" in the first sequence of a regulatory activity
	"Replace" when correcting an error in response to a Health Canada request
Proposed Product Monograph (for review)	"New" when provided as part of the first sequence of the regulatory activity
	"Replace" when provided in response to a Health Canada request (solicited information)
Pristine Product Monograph	"New" when provided for the first time. All proposed Product Monographs related to that regulatory activity should be deleted.
	"Replace" when provided to replace a previously approved pristine Product Monograph. All proposed Product Monographs related to that regulatory activity should be deleted.

a 10-page document, and sponsors always should keep in mind that the final objective is to facilitate navigation and review of the content.

Hyperlinking
In the eCTD format, there are two types of hyperlinks: intra-document and inter-document links. Hyperlinks should be used when cross-references have been used in the CTD, e.g., from QOS to Module 3, Section 2.4 to Module 4, Section 2.5 or CS-BE to Module 5, etc. Hyperlinks should be provided from the beginning of each regulatory transaction to the end, to facilitate navigation to annotations, associated sections, publications, appendices, tables and figures on different pages. Overusing hyperlinks may delay regulatory transaction processing and potentially confuse the reviewer, so it is important to use them appropriately.

Hyperlinks should be indicated typographically by blue text or a blue box around the text; the RGB color code (0, 0, 255) is recommended. In the author's experience, hyperlinks should be specified as cross-references by explicit citation of the target CTD section (e.g., "Please refer to section 3.2.P.3.2.").

Lifecycle Management and Lifecycle Management Table

In eCTD format, CTD Section 1.0.2 is allocated to the lifecycle management table. This table enables tracking and linking between CTD dossier sequences. The lifecycle management table identifies each sequence by its control number, when applicable, the sequence to which it is related within the same regulatory activity, the regulatory activity type and a brief description of its content and/or purpose. **Table 13-6** shows a lifecycle management table template.

Lifecycle Management at the Dossier Level

All regulatory activities within an eCTD dossier should pertain to the drug product for which the dossier identifier was issued and should be linked by that identifier. An eCTD dossier usually contains multiple regulatory activities, such as the original filing, its preparatory regulatory activities (e.g., presubmission meetings), supplements, etc. As such, it is important for Health Canada to establish each regulatory activity's location within the drug product lifecycle.

Lifecycle Management at the Regulatory Activity Level

At the regulatory activity level, the lifecycle is managed in two different locations: the eCTD envelope and the lifecycle management table.

In the eCTD envelope, the "Related Sequence" field indicates the relationship between the additional information and the initial or subsequent regulatory activity. This field is left empty in the envelope of the first regulatory activity sequence. For additional information, the "Related Sequence" field contains the regulatory activity sequence number to which the information applies. In addition to the eCTD envelope, the lifecycle management table links the eCTD sequences of the same regulatory activity. **Table 13-7** is an example of a lifecycle management table with three regulatory activities and their related sequences.

Lifecycle Management at the Document Level

For eCTD regulatory transactions filed to Health Canada, three operations are possible:
- Operation attribute «New» is used for documents that have no relation to documents previously submitted. It can be used throughout the entire

Figure 13-2. End-to-End Process for Preparing and Filing Regulatory Transactions in eCTD Format

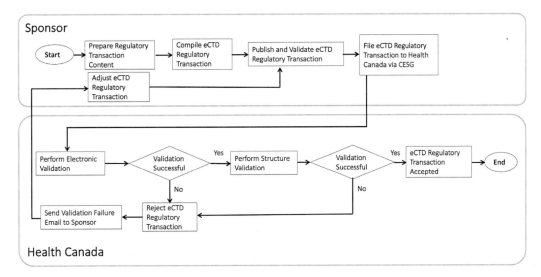

dossier lifecycle. All content files submitted in sequence 0000 are "New."

- Operation attribute «Replace» is used in eCTD sequences 0001 and higher to file a new version of documents already submitted. For example, the operation attribute for the lifecycle management table is "New" in sequence 0000 and "Replace" in subsequent lifecycle sequences (sequence 0001 and higher).
- Operation attribute «Delete» is used for documents in a previous regulatory transaction that no longer should be considered for review. For example, if a submitted regulatory activity is withdrawn, a withdrawal sequence should be submitted, and all documents submitted as "New" in that regulatory activity should be deleted. It is important to ensure the "Delete" operation attribute is used properly and is visible in the index.xml file.

Table 13-8 describes the operation attribute used for specific documents. For complete Module 1 document lifecycle management, refer to Section 3.3.3 of *Guidance Document: Preparation of Drug Submissions in the Electronic Common Technical Document*.

Filing eCTD Regulatory Transactions to Health Canada

Effective 1 January 2017, the use of the Common Electronic Submission Gateway (CESG) for submitting regulatory transactions under 10GB prepared in eCTD format became mandatory. Submissions greater than 10GB should use media. For more information on using media to file regulatory transactions in eCTD format, refer to section 3.2 of *Guidance Document: Preparation of Drug Submissions in the Electronic Common Technical Document*. Once published and validated, the eCTD sequence should be copied into a folder, with the dossier identifier name to which that sequence pertains, and then filed via the CESG. For more information regarding the process of filing eCTD sequences through the CESG, refer to *Frequently Asked Questions—Common Electronic Submission Gateway (CESG FAQ)*. Questions or comments regarding the CESG can be sent by email to: hc_cesg_pcde_sc@hc-sc.gc.ca.

Preparation and Filing Process for Regulatory Transactions in eCTD Format

The end-to-end process of preparing and filing regulatory transactions in eCTD format is described in **Figure 13-2**.

Best Practices

In the author's experience, the following aspects should be considered in preparing a high-quality eCTD regulatory transaction:

- Section 1.0.4 must not contain any data or attachments. Responses must refer to the documents provided in the appropriate CTD sections.
- The proper lifecycle operations are performed on specific documents.
- Document names are short, meaningful and in alignment with their content.
- Node extensions (folders) are used to organize content.
- Submitted eCTD sequences are locked as soon as the CESG acknowledgement is received.

- When a sponsor responds by email to Health Canada, it always is recommended to follow with an eCTD sequence. eCTD is the legal format.
- The presubmission meeting request should be filed in eCTD format as an initial regulatory activity.
- There is currently no standard terminology for attributes (2.3.S, 2.3.P, 3.2.S, 3.2.P, 3.2.P.4, etc.). However, sponsors should choose these attributes carefully, as they cannot be modified during the dossier lifecycle.
- The cover letter must contain neither any scientific information nor answers to questions from the regulatory authority or notes to the evaluator; instead, this information can be provided in the following sections:
  o Scientific information: Modules 2–5
  o Answers to questions: Section 1.0.4
  o General note to the reviewer: Section 1.0.7
  o A note to the reviewer pertaining to a specific section should be provided at the beginning of that section

Summary

- Health Canada started accepting regulatory transactions in eCTD format in 2004. As of 1 January 2018, NDS, SNDS, ANDS and SANDS regulatory transactions are required to be submitted in eCTD format.
- Once a regulatory activity for a drug product is filed in eCTD format, it is not possible to send regulatory transactions for that product in any format except eCTD.
- Prior to filing the first regulatory transaction in eCTD format for a specific drug product, sponsors should request an eCTD identifier (dossier identifier) from Health Canada.
- Each regulatory transaction should be filed as an eCTD sequence. Sequence numbers are incremental for subsequent transactions. All sequences pertaining to the same drug product are linked by the same dossier identifier.
- The eCTD envelope and lifecycle management table describe the relationship between the sequences within the same eCTD dossier.
- Prior to filing to Health Canada, eCTD sequences should be validated from electronic and structure perspectives.
- Granularity is extremely important for proper lifecycle management. Each document lifecycle in the regulatory dossier should be handled carefully, and the correct operation attributes should be used.
- All eCTD regulatory transactions under 10GB should be filed via the CESG.
- The eCTD is all about regulatory content organization and structure. This is accomplished through strict standards and formats.

Recommended Reading
- *Guidance Document: Preparation of Drug Regulatory Activities in the Electronic Common Technical Document Format* (14 May 2015)
- *Guidance Document: Creation of the Canadian Module 1 Backbone* (30 September 2012)
- *International Council for harmonisation Guidelines: Electronic Common Technical Document Specification – Version 3.2.2* (16 July 2008) developed by the ICH M2 Expert Working Group
- *Questions and Answers – Regulatory Activities in eCTD Format* https://www.canada.ca/en/health-canada/services/drugs-health-products/drug-products/applications-submissions/guidance-documents/ectd/questions-answers.html. Accessed 31 March 2018.
- *Frequently Asked Questions – Common Electronic Submission Gateway (CESG FAQ).* https://www.canada.ca/en/health-canada/services/drugs-health-products/drug-products/applications-submissions/guidance-documents/common-electronic-submissions-gateway/frequently-asked-questions.html. Accessed 31 March 2018.
- *Notice – Mandatory Requirements for using the Common Electronic Submissions Gateway (CESG).* https://www.canada.ca/en/health-canada/services/drugs-health-products/drug-products/announcements/notice-mandatory-requirements-using-common-electronic-submissions-gateway.html. Accessed 31 March 2018.

Chapter 14

Product Lifecycle Management Guidance

by Ajay Babu Pazhayattil, Naheed Sayeed-Desta and Queenia Lee

OBJECTIVES

- ❏ Understand the International Council on Harmonisation (ICH) Q8 and Quality by Design (QbD) requirements, developing design space

- ❏ Understand Health Canada and other regulatory body requirements for Product Control Strategy and Established Conditions

- ❏ Understand Health Canada, ICH, Pharmaceutical Inspection Convention and Pharmaceutical Inspection Co-operation Scheme (PIC/S) requirements

- ❏ Understand the product lifecycle concept and its development through the years

- ❏ Understand how guidances are inter-related and how they work in tandem

GUIDANCE DOCUMENTS COVERED IN THIS CHAPTER

- ❏ ICH, *Q8 (R2): Pharmaceutical Development*

- ❏ ICH, *Q9: Quality Risk Management*

- ❏ ICH, *Q10: Pharmaceutical Quality System*

- ❏ ICH, *Q8, Q9 and Q10 Questions & Answers (R4)*

- ❏ ICH, *Q11: Development and Manufacture of Drug Substances (Chemical Entities and Biotechnological/Biological Entities)*

- ❏ ICH, *Q12: Technical and Regulatory Considerations for Pharmaceutical Product Lifecycle Management*

Introduction

A systematic product lifecycle management approach is essential for effective continuous improvement and maintaining an undisrupted drug product supply. This chapter provides an understanding of the current lifecycle-related guidances and how they work in tandem to achieve the desired outcomes regulators expect. The biopharmaceutical industry is eager to utilize these approaches, strategies and tools, as it anticipates adoption of the International Council on Harmonisation's (ICH) Q12 guidance. Therefore, drug manufacturers must thoroughly understand this subject. This harmonized lifecycle management at both the regulatory and technical levels will benefit patients, regulatory authorities and industry alike. The approach promotes innovation and continual biopharmaceutical industry improvement while strengthening quality assurance and improving essential drug products' supply to patients.

The approaches outlined in ICH quality guidances *Q8(R2): Pharmaceutical Development, Q9: Quality Risk Management, Q10: Pharmaceutical Quality System* and *Q11: Development and Manufacture of Drug Substances* provide opportunities for a science- and risk-based approach for development and decision making throughout the product lifecycle. The guidelines are valuable in assessing chemistry, manufacturing and controls (CMC) changes across the product lifecycle. The ICH Q12 guidance will address currently identified technical and regulatory gaps for implementation to help realize past guidance. The guidance will enable more flexible regulatory approaches for postapproval CMC changes.

Applying the ICH Q12 approaches will depend on the product and process knowledge understanding, risk management principles' application and the availability of an effective pharmaceutical quality system. The guidance will provide a background to facilitate postapproval CMC change management in a highly predictive and efficient manner. Implementing programs like continued or ongoing process verification, that increases product and process knowledge, is essential to meeting postapproval change management protocol (PACMP) requirements and reducing regulatory submissions for continuous improvement changes. Continued or ongoing process verification is a commitment for a Quality by Design (QbD) submission per ICH Q8. Effectively implementing the tools and enablers will enhance industry's ability to manage many CMC changes efficiently under the firm's pharmaceutical quality system, with minimal regulatory oversight prior to implementation.

ICH *Q12: Technical and Regulatory Considerations for Pharmaceutical Product Lifecycle Management* will pertain to biopharmaceutical drug substances and drug products, including marketed chemical, biotechnological and biological products and drug-device combination products that meet the definition of a pharmaceutical, biotechnological or biological product. This guidance's tools and enablers do not change the relationship between regulatory assessment and inspection, but necessitate collaboration and communication between assessors and inspectors for implementation.

The Enablers

ICH Q12 recommends tools that enable flexibility in making postapproval changes. It intends to improve regulatory evaluation efficiency, in both review and inspection over the product lifecycle through regulatory dossiers, pharmaceutical quality systems and postaproval change management plans and protocols. The guidance defines established conditions (regulatory commitments), with further reliance on the PQS, implementing PACMPs and flexibility in managing changes to ensure continued drug product supply.

Established conditions are legally binding information (or approved matters) considered necessary to assure product quality. Consequently, any established condition change necessitates a submission to the regulatory authority. A submission's established conditions are either implicit or explicit. Implicit established conditions are elements not specifically proposed by the Marketing Authorization Holder (MAH), but derived from and revised according to regional regulation or guidance related to postapproval changes. Explicit established conditions are specifically identified and proposed by the MAH together with its proposed reporting category as part of a regulatory submission. Multiple approaches are used alone or in combination to identify established conditions for manufacturing processes; these include a parameter-based approach, an enhanced approach or a performance-based approach. A parameter-based approach, in which product development prior to regulatory submission provides a limited understanding of the relationship between inputs and resulting quality attributes, will include a large number of inputs (e.g., process parameters and material attributes) along with outputs (including in-process controls). An enhanced approach, with increased understanding of interaction between inputs and product quality attributes, together with a corresponding control strategy, can lead to established conditions' identification focused on the most important input and output parameters, as appropriate. Applying knowledge from a data-rich environment enables a performance-based approach in which established conditions could be focused primarily on controlling unit operation outputs rather than process inputs (e.g., process parameters and material attributes). Established conditions are defined in the application dossier's quality section (CTD Module 3) and listed in a product-specific lifecycle management strategy document.

Revision to approved established conditions may be required at various lifecycle stages. Options include:
- Submitting a postapproval regulatory submission describing and justifying the proposed revision to the approved established conditions. Justification may include such information as validation data and batch analyses.
- Submitting a postapproval change management protocol in the original application or as part a postapproval submission, detailing established conditions' revisions or reporting categories, and how the change will be justified and reported.
- Utilizing an approved postapproval regulatory commitment.

ICH Q12 introduces utilization of a comparability protocol or postapproval change management protocol. A postapproval change management protocol is a tool that helps in prospective strategic change management, ensuring supply chain reliability. It is expected to accompany the original submission. Subsequent postapproval change management protocol submission and revision would require preapproval. The postapproval change management protocol is a component of postapproval change management strategy. The framework included in the strategy has the established conditions, reporting categories for making changes, any postapproval commitments and all supporting documents in addition to the protocol. A postapproval change management protocol can be applied to specific product changes. It also can be used for lifecycle changes on the product change type. A protocol that applies to multiple products also can be developed. In such cases, uniform risk management, studies and tests should be applied to all products. A postapproval change management protocol is a regulatory tool for improving operational flexibility when postapproval changes are introduced. It is intended to provide predictability and transparency between the firms and agencies. The expectation is the QbD-based product with process characterization and product understanding gathered through the lifecycle benefits the organization during future changes. An effective pharmaceutical quality system, per ICH Q10, and compliance with Health Canada GMPs are necessary to implement ICH Q12. Managing manufacturing changes across the supply chain is an essential part of an effective change management system. This guideline will provide recommendations for robust change management across multiple entities involved in pharmaceutical product manufacture.

ICH has a vision of harmonized quality systems applicable across the product lifecycle, emphasizing an integrated approach to quality risk management and science. The Q12 guidance will realize this vision by encouraging pharmaceutical manufacturers to adopt continual improvement and innovation strategies in the industry. The regulatory expectations for changes are diverse across markets. This guidance aims at harmonizing the expectations across multiple markets, ensuring reliable product supply by safeguarding efficient management of CMC changes, improving manufacturing turnaround and applying risk- and science-based decision making.

Status of ICH Q8, Q9, Q10 and Q11: Implementation in Canada

Health Canada is committed to adopting and implementing ICH guidances and standards as a council member. The ICH council was established in October 2015 as a continuation of the International Conference on Harmonisation. The initiative transforms ICH into a truly cross-national initiative supported by robust and transparent governance. As required by the ICH guidance development process, Health Canada requests comments at Step 2 of the draft process. ICH provides the finalized draft guidance for public comment as part of Step 4. The ICH Steering Committee-endorsed guidance then is adopted by Health Canada to utilize as an official Health Canada guidance document. ICH Q8, Q9, Q10 and Q11 have gone through the aforementioned review and adoption process. The guidance's effective date is determined by Health Canada, based on such factors as collateral guidance and policy work, training aspects, staff restrictions, impact on business processes, need for regulatory amendment, etc. The impact on industry or stakeholders also is a reason for Health Canada to select an appropriate guidance effective date. In exceptional circumstances, Health Canada cannot establish the effective date at the time of adoption and publication. Otherwise, the agency will continue its adoption after the administrative steps have been completed.

Health Canada adopted *ICH Q8(R2): Pharmaceutical Development* on 11 February 2016. Health Canada clarifies that the document should be read in conjunction with the accompanying notice and relevant sections of other applicable Health Canada guidances. Health Canada recognizes the adopted Q8 guidance's scope and subject matter may not be entirely consistent with those of other guidances. When such scenarios arise, the agency confirms the Health Canada-adopted ICH guidance take precedence. ICH *Q9: Quality Risk Management* was adopted by Health Canada on 5 February 2016. The ICH Steering Committee endorsed the final draft of ICH Q9 and recommended its adoption by the EU, Japan and US regulatory bodies. Subsequently, Health Canada endorsed the principles and practices the guidance describes.

ICH *Q10: Pharmaceutical Quality System* was developed by an ICH expert working group and has been subject to consultation by the regulatory parties, in accordance with the ICH process. Health Canada adopted it on 15 February 2016. The document describes a model for an effective quality management system, referred to as the pharmaceutical quality system. In this guidance, the term "pharmaceutical quality system" refers to the ICH Q10 model. ICH Q10 describes one comprehensive model for an effective pharmaceutical quality system based on International Standards Organisation (ISO) quality concepts, includes Health Canada Good Manufacturing Practice (GMP) regulations and complements ICH *Q8 Pharmaceutical Development* and ICH *Q9 Quality Risk Management*. ICH Q10 should be implemented throughout the product lifecycle to facilitate innovation and continual improvement and strengthen the link between pharmaceutical development and manufacturing activities within Canada.

A question and answer (Q&A) document referring to the current ICH Q-IWG working procedure on implementing Q8, Q9 and Q10 was approved by the ICH Steering Committee. Health Canada adopted *Q8, Q9 and Q10 Questions & Answers (R4)* on 5 February 2016. The document's development was based on the realization that harmonizing technical requirements across the ICH regions can only be reached if the various ICH Q guidelines are implemented and interpreted consistently across the regions. On 12 February 2016, Health Canada adopted ICH *Q11: Development and Manufacture of Drug Substances (Chemical Entities and Biotechnological/Biological Entities)*. The guideline describes approaches to developing and understanding the drug substance's manufacturing process, and also provides guidance on what information should be provided in Common Technical Document (CTD) Module 3, Sections 3.2.S.2.2–3.2.S.2.6. It addresses drug substance development and manufacture aspects, including steps designed to reduce impurities. In addition, ICH Q11 provides further clarification on the principles and concepts described in Q8, Q9 and Q10 as they pertain to drug substance development and manufacture.

Harmonization Initiatives Facilitating Product Lifecycle Management

The Pharmaceutical Inspection Co-operation Scheme (PIC/S) is a nonbinding, informal cooperative arrangement between regulatory authorities on Good Manufacturing Practices (GMPs) for medicinal products for human or veterinary use. It is open to any authority having a comparable GMP inspection system. PIC/S aims at harmonising inspection procedures worldwide by developing common standards in the field of GMP and providing inspector training opportunities. It also aims to facilitate cooperation and networking among competent authorities and regional and international organisations, thus increasing mutual confidence. This is reflected in PIC/S' mission, which is to lead the international development, implementation and maintenance of harmonised GMP standards and quality systems of medicinal products' inspectorates. PIC/S was initiated in November 1995.

Canada has been represented in PIC/S by the Health Products and Food Branch Inspectorate (HPFBI) since January 1999. One additional advantage for HPFBI's participation in PIC/S is the acceptance of inspection reports, issued by regulatory authorities that also are part of the scheme, for the purpose of listing foreign sites on importers' establishment licences. The initiative facilitates networking and cooperation, improves mutual confidence, promotes inspections' quality assurance, exchanges GMP information, facilitates cross-training among agencies and improves and harmonizes technical standards, thus contributing to the guidances' global alignment. PIC/S has working relationships with ICH and other industry organizations. Revisions to chapters 1 Pharmaceutical Quality Systems, 2 Personnel, 6 Quality Control and 7 Outsourced Activities of the PIC/S *GMP Guide* were completed in January 2017. The Pharmaceutical Inspection Convention (PIC) was the first body to attempt to achieve mutual recognition of regulatory inspections.

The Parenteral Drug Association (PDA) has recognized the need for a paradigm shift in how changes are regulated, considering the pharmaceutical industry's global nature. PDA's Post-approval Change: Innovation for Availability of Medicines (PAC iAM) initiative focuses on identifying, assessing and addressing barriers to implementing postapproval changes. PDA's Technical Report No. 54 has a comprehensive description of quality risk management elements and tools in line with ICH Q9. PDA and the International Federation of Pharmaceutical Manufacturers and Associations (IFPMA) have highlighted insights into the draft ICH Q12: *Technical and Regulatory Considerations for Pharmaceutical Product Lifecycle Management*, through its practical application workshop on PAC implementation through PDA's PAC iAM task force. More harmonized legislation on postapproval changes across countries would help industry implement postapproval changes more quickly and predictably, while also fostering compliance and ensuring continuous supply of state-of-the-art medicines.

Product Lifecycle Stages

The product lifecycle concept was described in the US Food and Drug Administration's (FDA) August 2002 new initiative for Pharmaceutical Current Good Manufacturing Practices (CGMPs) for the 21st Century. The purpose was to enhance and modernize pharmaceutical manufacturing and product quality regulation. The call was to encourage the early adoption of new technological advances by the pharmaceutical industry to:

- facilitate industry application of modern quality management techniques, including quality system approach implementation to all pharmaceutical production and quality assurance aspects
- encourage risk-based approach to implementation focusing both industry and agency attention on critical areas
- ensure regulatory review, compliance and inspection policies are based on state-of-the-art pharmaceutical science
- enhance FDA drug quality regulatory programs' consistency and coordination, in part by further integrating enhanced quality systems approaches into the agency's business processes and regulatory policies concerning review and inspection activities

Risk-based approaches regarding inspectional scrutiny, use of advanced technologies and articulation of a clearer role of conformance batches in the product lifecycle is part of the approach. Applying knowledge throughout the product lifecycle is a key element.

ICH Q10 demonstrates industry's and Health Canada's support for an effective pharmaceutical quality system to enhance medicines' quality and availability around the world to promote public health. Implementing ICH Q10 throughout the product lifecycle facilitates innovation and continual improvement and strengthens the link between pharmaceutical development and manufacturing activities. ICH Q10 elements should be applied in a manner that is appropriate and proportionate to each product lifecycle stage, recognising the differences among, and the different goals of, each stage. Health Canada GMPs do not explicitly address all product lifecycle stages (e.g., development). The quality system elements and management responsibilities described in this guideline are intended to encourage the use of science- and risk-based approaches at each stage, thereby

promoting continual improvement across the entire product lifecycle. Applying knowledge and quality risk management will enable a company to implement ICH Q10 effectively and successfully. The lifecycle stages are:
- Pharmaceutical development: These activities' goal is to design a product and its manufacturing process to consistently deliver the intended performance and meet patients and healthcare professionals' needs, and regulatory authorities and internal customers' requirements. Approaches to pharmaceutical development are described in ICH Q8.
- Technology transfer: These activities are intended to transfer product and process knowledge between development and manufacturing, and within or between manufacturing sites, to achieve product realisation
- Commercial manufacturing: The goals include achieving product realisation, establishing and maintaining a state of control and facilitating continual improvement.
- Product discontinuation: The aim here is to manage the product lifecycle's terminal stage effectively.

Each stage is interrelated, as is application of ICH Q8 to Q11 throughout the lifecycle stages. ICH Q8 is applied for QbD-based product development. The quality risk management process per ICH Q9 should be utilised to evaluate any proposed changes and risks. The pharmaceutical quality system per ICH Q10 is a required management system to direct and control a pharmaceutical company's quality. An effective monitoring system providing assurance of processes and controls' continued capability to produce commercial product of desired quality and to identify areas for continual improvement is a requirement for both ICH Q8 and Q10.

Lifecycle Change Management: ICH Q12 Implementation Prerequisites

The 'enhanced' QbD approach as described in ICH Q8(R2) is encouraged by Health Canada. Ensuring a process design yields a consistent product is expected when using ICH Q8, Q9 and Q10. All three provide a structured way to define product critical quality attributes, design space, the manufacturing process and the control strategy. This information is used to identify the type and focus of studies to be performed prior to and on initial commercial production batches. As an alternative to traditional process validation, continuous process verifications, per ICH Q8(R2), also can be utilised in process validation protocols for initial commercial production and manufacturing process changes for continual improvement throughout the remainder of the product lifecycle. Like the product itself, process validation also has a lifecycle (process design, process qualification and ongoing process verification).

The Quality Target Product Profile (QTPP) forms the basis of the product development's design. A critical quality attribute (CQA) is a physical, chemical, biological or microbiological property or characteristic that should be within an appropriate limit, range or distribution to ensure desired product quality. CQAs generally are associated with the drug substance, excipients, intermediates (in-process materials) and drug product. The relationship between process inputs (material attributes and process parameters) and CQAs can be described in the design space. Regardless of how a design space is developed, operation within the design space is expected to result in a product meeting the defined quality. The design space is developed based on "Design of Experiments" results, a structured, organized method for determining the relationship among factors affecting a process and that process' output. A control strategy is designed to ensure a product of required quality will be produced consistently. Control strategy includes different types of control the applicant proposes to assure product quality (ICH Q10), such as in-process and end-product testing. Under QbD, the control strategy is derived using a systematic science- and risk-based approach. Testing, monitoring or controlling often is moved earlier in the process and conducted using in-line, on-line or at-line testing.

A risk assessment (ICH Q9) conducted prior to initial commercial validation batches can highlight areas requiring particular focus and data to demonstrate the desired high level of assurance for commercial process robustness. Continual monitoring (continued or ongoing process verification) further demonstrate process consistency's actual level of assurance and provide the basis for continual product improvement. PIC/S *Guide to GMP for Medicinal Products* Annex 15 requires ongoing process verification during the lifecycle, where manufacturers should monitor product quality to ensure a state of control is maintained throughout the product lifecycle and the relevant process trends are evaluated. ICH Q9 quality risk management methodologies can be applied throughout the product lifecycle to maintain a state of process control. With the ICH Q8-based QbD product development process, ICH Q9's quality risk management, science- and risk-based process validation approach and an increasing body of knowledge gained through development and continued process verification, implementing ICH Q12 postapproval change approaches should be seamless. An integrated application of ICH Q8–Q11, as well as process validation lifecycle elements, is required to enable more-flexible regulatory approaches for postapproval CMC changes.

Health Canada Involvement in Lifecycle Guidance Harmonization

Health Canada continues to adopt ICH guidance once routine administrative steps have been completed. The Canada-United States (US) Regulatory Cooperation Council (RCC) was created in February 2011 to better align the two countries' regulatory approaches, where possible. Under the RCC initiative, Health Canada and FDA are conducting joint public consultation meetings on ICH guidelines currently under development. This initiative's aim is to hold public consultation meetings prior to each bi-annual ICH meeting to seek input on current regulatory disharmony areas and where harmonised ICH guidelines would be beneficial. Stakeholder input received through this initiative will be considered in current or future guideline development. Health Canada also intends to use these opportunities to understand drug product regulation areas where Canadian requirements may differ from US regulations better, with a view to minimizing these differences. Meetings will continue to alternate between Canada and the US, with the next meeting (to be hosted by FDA) to occur in spring 2018, prior to the scheduled spring ICH meeting (June 2018 in Kobe, Japan). The ICH Assembly meeting in Montreal, Canada held 31 May–1 June 2017 endorsed the Q12 EWG's work plan.

Summary

- Canadian product and process validation lifecycle requirements are aligned with ICH and PIC/S requirements.
- ICH Q12's proposed postapproval change management strategies are applicable and will be adopted by Health Canada.
- Adoption of ICH Q8-based product development principles; ICH Q9's quality risk management approach, ICH Q10's pharmaceutical quality systems, knowledge management and continued process verification are prerequisites for flexible application of such regulatory strategies as postapproval change management protocols.
- By adopting ICH Q8–11, Health Canada recommends the approaches' integrated use during product development, commercial manufacturing and the submission process.
- The guidances' proposed tools and principles are applicable for all product lifecycle stages.
- The effective application of ICH Q12 regulatory pathways and tools allows industry to apply operational flexibility strategies for postapproval changes while ensuring uninterrupted drug product supply to patients.

Recommended Reading
- Pazhayattil, A.B., Sayeed-Desta, N., Iyer, V., ICH Q12 Post Approval Change Management Protocol: Advantages for Consumers, Regulators and Industry, *Regulatory Focus, RAPS (16 May 2017)*
- Sayeed-Desta, N., Pazhayattil, A.B., Louis, I., Prospects for Post-Approval Change Management, PDA Letter, PDA (*01 June 2018*)

Useful Links
- Notice: Health Canada and US FDA Administration Joint Public Consultation on ICH Harmonization Guidelines for Registration of Pharmaceuticals for Human Use. Government of Canada website. https://www.canada.ca/en/health-canada/services/drugs-health-products/public-involvement-consultations/drug-products/regulatory-cooperation-council-september2017.html. Accessed 20 May 2018.
- ICH Assembly Final Minutes, 31 May and 1 June 2017, Montreal Canada. ICH website. http://www.ich.org/fileadmin/Public_Web_Site/Meetings/Ass_MC_Meetings_Reports/Assembly_report_Montreal_2017.pdf. Accessed 20 May 2018.
- Revised Annex 15 to PIC/S GMP Guide, (13 April 2015). PIC Scheme website. https://picscheme.org/en/news/19/-revised-annex-15-to-pic-s-gmp-guide. Accessed 20 May 2018.
- PIC/S International Co-operation. PIC website. https://www.pic-scheme.org/en/about-international-co-operation. Accessed 20 May 2018.
- Adoption of International Conference on Harmonization of Technical Requirements of Pharmaceuticals for Human Use (ICH) Guidances. Government of Canada website. https://www.canada.ca/en/health-canada/services/drugs-health-products/drug-products/applications-submissions/guidance-documents/international-conference-harmonisation/quality/adoption-international-conference-harmonisation-technical-requirements-registration-pharmaceuticals-human-use-guidance-1.html. Accessed 20 May 2018.
- ICH Quality Guidance. Government of Canada website. https://www.canada.ca/en/health-canada/services/drugs-health-products/drug-products/applications-submissions/guidance-documents/international-conference-harmonisation/quality.html. Accessed 20 May 2018.
- PDA's Post Approval Change Innovation for Availability of Medicines Program (PAC iAM). PDA website. https://www.pda.org/conference/pac-iam/home. Accessed 20 May 2018.

Index

Major discussions of a topic are indicated by page numbers given in **bold** typeface. In each chapter tables and figures are indicated by page number with "t" or "f" and the number of the table or figure following, with the chapter number omitted. In chapter 5, Figure 5-1 on page 54 will appear as 54f1.

A

Abbreviated New Drug Submissions (ANDS)
    See also Canadian Reference Product
    bioequivalence study requirements, 97–98
    CRP for, 97
    eCTD format for, 134
    format and structure of, 98
    generic parenterals, 102–103
    generic topical products, 103
    generic versions of Canadian products, 101–102
    Module 1: administrative/product information, 98–100
        Certificates of Analysis, 100
        CRP confirmation, 100
        waiver requests, 100
    Module 3: quality
        Section P drug product, 101
        Section S Drug Substance, 100–101
    Module 4: nonclinical studies, 101
    Module 5: clinical studies, 101
    nasal and inhalation products, 103–104
    NOC/c approved products, 99–101
    patent obligations, 83
    reference products for, 97
    review process, 101, 102t1
abbreviated new drug submissions (ANDS), CPID for, 98

Access to Cannabis for Medical Purposes Regulations (ACMPR), 9
Active Pharmaceutical Ingredients (APIs)
    in ANDS, 101
    definitions for, 30t1
    finished product importation, 43
    foreign build license, 32
    GMP for, 8t1, 42–43
    importation of, 42
Ad Standards and Extreme Reach, 129
Adulteration Act of 1884, 4
adverse drug reaction (ADR)/events
    bioequivalence studies, 97
    biological product monograph, 120
    biologics yearly report, 124
    causality assessment for, 70, 71–72
    classifications of, 71t1, 74t2
    in clinical trials, 20
    CTA submission and meetings, 20–21
    drug scheduling factors, 110t1, 111, 114
    individual case safety reports, 70–72
    MAH reporting of, 73–75
    mandatory reporting of, 7–9t1, 9
    MHPD analysis of, 4
    NDS under review, 52
    NOC with conditions, 56
    postapproval requirements, 27t4
    postapproval surveillance, 73–76
    reporting of, 7–9t1, 59–60, 70, 74–75
    solicited reports of, 75
    WHO causality criteria, 75
advertising
    complaint handling, 130–131
    DTC advertising, 131

Regulatory Affairs Professionals Society

Index

to healthcare professionals, 129
NDS with NOC, 56
NOC/c restrictions, 130
preclearance agencies for, 131
prohibition of, 129
regulatory framework, 12
Advisement Letters, 62
Alberta, 3
Allard v. Canada, 9
Annual Drug Notification Form (ADNF), 63
annual summary report (ASR), 75–76
appeal/reconsideration procedures
for advertising, 130
NDS decisions, 53
NOC/c, 54
under PM/NOC, 81
priority review status, 54
SCC inspections, 15
assisted conception product regulation, 4
Atlantic region, 3
Attestation Checklist, 101

B

batch certification, 41, 43
benefit-risk profile
assessment for, 12
NOC with conditions, 55
Notifiable Changes and, 60
proposed legislation, 4, 5
reporting changes in, 72, 75–76
in risk management planning, 76
in SBD, 53
bioavailability trials/studies
biologics clinical trials, 116
clinical trials, 70
CTA submissions, 23, 26
for generics, 96–98, 99, 100–101
Health Canada review, 118, 120
nasal products, 103
standards, 97–98
bioequivalence criteria/studies
electronic format for summary, 138t5
generic parenterals, 102
generic requirements, 97–98
biologic drug product submissions
clinical trial applications, 116
clinical trials for, 115
CTA amendments/notifications, 117
CTA changes, 119t2
CTA modifications, 118t1
evaluation group requirement summary, 123t4
labelling, advertising, of, **127–132**
overview, 115, 124–125
postmarketing activities, post-approval lot release, 122

pre-CTA consultation meetings, 116
product monograph contents, 120t3
quality changes in, 24–25t2
responsibilities and activities, 121
review and evaluation
facility information, 121
monograph preparation, 121–122
product labelling, 121
risk-based lot release, 118
On-Site Evaluation (OSE), 115, 118, 121, 125
YBPR for, 124
Biologics and Genetic Therapies Directorate (BGTD)
biologics submissions, 115
clinical trial surveillance, 70–72
expedited reporting to, 72
lot release for biologics, 118–119, 122–124
NDS to, 47
NHP CTA review, 23, 25
responsibilities and activities, 4
YBPR for biologics, 124
biologics source materials
FD&A exclusion, 73
source material risks, 116, 124
study requirements for, 118
Vanessa's Law, 5
biosimilar drugs, 115, 129
blood and blood components
EL number for, 115
regulatory framework, 4
Blood Regulations, 5
Blueprint for Renewal legislation goals, 5
brand names
DTC advertising, 131
intellectual property (IP) protection, 80–81
Look-Alike/Sound-Alike assessment, 5, 50
PLL requirements, 107–108
post-DIN changes, 62
product-line extension, 90
British Columbia, 3
British North America Act, 1

C

Canada Health Protection Act, 5, 8t1
Canada Vigilance Adverse Event Report (AER), 75
See also adverse drug reaction/events
Canada Vigilance Program, 73, 75
Canada-European Union Comprehensive Economic and Trade Agreement (CETA), 80–81, 86
Canadian Environmental Protection Act (CEPA), 13, 51, 99
Canadian Food Inspection Agency Act, 4
Canadian Food Inspection Agency (CFIA), inspections, 2, 2f1, 4, 30–31

Canadian Food Inspection Agency's (CFIA), Food Directorate monitoring of, 2, 4
Canadian Institutes of Health Research, 2f1, 3
Canadian Reference Product (CRP)
    ANDS submissions, 97
    confirmation, 100
    nasal/inhalation products, 103
    with NOC/c, 97
    second person copy of, 81, 83
Cannabis Legalization and Regulation Branch, 2
cannabis legislation, 9–10
carry-forward provisions, 83
causality assessment, 70–72, 73, 75
Cells, Tissues and Organs for Transplant Regulations, 5, 7t1
cells/tissues/organs. *See* biologic source materials
Certificate of Compliance (CoC), 31, 42
Certificate of Supplementary Protection (CSP), **86–89**
    application/co-pending applications, 88
    first authorization for sale, 87
    history of, 9t1
    listing of, 82
    noncompliance proceedings, 88
    patent register listing, 82–83
    PM(NOC) Regulation summary, 89
    priority and conflicts, 88
    product eligibility, 86–87
    register of applications, 88–89
    term and scope of, 86
    timing requirements, 87–88
Certificate of Supplementary Protection (CSP) Regulations, 7t1, 82–83, 86–89, 86–87
Certified Product Information Document (CPID)
    in ANDS, 98
    electronic submission format, 138t5
    in YBPR, 124
Chief Financial Officer Branch, 2
Clinical Trial Application (CTA)
    amendments, 116
    bioavailability trials, 26
    for biologics, 115
    chemistry and manufacturing, 23
    electronic requirements, 26
    notifications, 23, 116
    postapproval requirements, 26
    review process, 23–26
    submission package contents, 21–23, 22t1
Clinical Trial Application-Amendments (CTA-A), 116
Clinical Trial Application—Notification (CTA-N), 116
clinical trials
    definitions for, 71t1
    GCP for, 26
    lot release for biologics, 118
    NNHPD, 70
    periodic reporting, 72–73

    phases of, 20, 28
    postapproval requirements, 26t4
    pre-CTA consultation meetings, 20–21
    published information on, 25
    regulatory framework, 20
    safety information requests during, 72
    special populations in, 5
    surveillance of, 70–72
Clinical Trials Expedited Reporting Summary Form, 72
Common Technical Document (CTD)
    See also electronic Common Technical Document (eCTD)
    ANDS structure and format, 98–101
    biologics submissions, 115
    CTA submissions, 21–23
    human-use pharmaceutical registration, 47
    Module 1 requirements, 48–51
    Module 2: biologics, 116
    Module 3: quality--biologics, 116
    NDS format and content, 47–48, 49t1
Communications and Public Affairs Branch, 2
comparative bioavailability studies. *See* bioavailability trials/studies
Compendium of Policies, Guidelines and Procedures, 90
compliance monitoring and enforcement
    See also Good Manufacturing Practice Regulations
    for ANDS, 98–99
    DEL, 30–31, 30t1
    DEL for GMP compliance, 32
    examples for, 13–14, 14t1
    F&DR requirements for DEL, 33
    GLP requirements, 11–17
    GMP, 31–42, 49–50
    HPFBI inspections for, 12
    MRA and, 30t1
    OECD principles/requirements, 13
    OSE for, 115, 118, 121, 125
    PM(NOC) Regulation, 83
    product labelling, 108, 111, 121, 128
    QMS in, 34–35
    RORB role, 4
    VCU for pricing, 82
Consumer Information. *See* Product Monograph
Controlled Drugs and Substances Act (CDSA), 30–31, 61, 66
Corporate Services Branch, 2
corticosteroids, 103–104
cosmetics
    See also nonprescription drugs
    F&DR framework for, 2, 6t1, 12, 30, 106
    GLP applicability for, 13
    modernization of, 9–10
Council for International Organizations of Medical Sciences (CIOMS), 72–73, 75

Index

current Good Manufacturing Practice (CGMP). *See* Good Manufacturing Practice

D

data protection provisions
    See also intellectual property (IP) protection
    application for, 90, 134
    F&DR framework, 80, 89–90
    guidance documents, 90
    history of, 7t1, 80, 97
    innovative drug, 90–91
    innovative drug exclusivity, 96–97
    intellectual property (IP) protection, **89–90**
    pediatric extension, 91
    product-line extension, 91
    subsequent-entry filing, 48–49
declaration of equivalence, 97, 104
Department of Health Act: *PM(NOC) Regulation* added, 2, 80
Development Safety Update Report (DSUR), 72–73
direct-to-consumer advertising (DTC), 131
discontinuation reporting, 63–64
disinfectant drugs. *See* nonprescription drugs
Drug and Health Product Register, 129
Drug Establishment Licence (DEL), **31–32**
    Acknowledgement of Application Acceptance, 50
    defined, 38t1
    for GMP compliance, 32, 34, 49–50
    MRA for, 31
    for NDS, 49–50
    non-MRA countries, 31–32
    responsibility of holder, 33–34
Drug Identification Number (DIN)
    application, 62–63
    container labelling for, 128
    defined, 46
    inactivation of, 63
    nonprescription drugs, 107
    for nonprescription kits, 108
    for OTC drugs, 4
    parameters for biologics, 115
    post-issue changes, 62
    variations of brand-name product, 108
Drug Notification Form (DNF), 63
Drug Product Database website (DPD), 129
drug scheduling
    advisory committee, 110
    application/review, 110–111
    NAPRA factors, 110t1
    Provincial Pharmacy Legislation and Regulation, 109
    scheduling model for, 109–110
drug shortage reporting, 63–64

E

early working exception *(Patent Act)*, 80
educational material requirements, 56
electronic Common Technical Document (eCTD)
    See also Common Technical Document
    acceptance guidelines for, 133–134
    best practices for, 141–142
    Clarification Request formats, 138t5
    CTA and CTA-A submissions, 26
    document formats, 138t5
    eCTD envelope elements, 136t2
    electronic validation, 138
    exemptions for, 134
    file location in sequence, 136t1
    filing to Health Canada, 141
    lifecycle management
        document level, 140–141, 140t8
        dossier level, 140
        management table, 140
        regulatory activity level, 140
        template, 138t6, 139t7
    m2-m5 attributes, 137t3
    NDS format and content, 47–48
    preparation and filing of, 141–142
    regulatory filing process, 141f2
    regulatory transaction
        identifier/top-level folder, 135
        sequence, 135–137
        specification, 135
    regulatory transaction summary, 135f1
    scope of, 134
    structure validation, 138–139
    technical requirements
        bookmarking, 139–140
        file format, 139
        hyperlinking, 140
    validation of transactions/sequence, 137–138, 137t4
environmental assessment, 49t1, 51, 99
Establishment Licenses (ELs)
    See also Drug Establishment License
    for blood and blood components, 115
    quality management requirements, 34–35
ethics code and values
    Clinical Trial Regulations, 6–7t1
    Research Management and Operations Directorate, 4
evaluation group. *See* Lot Release Program
exclusivity for NCE, 90, 96–97
exemption numbers (EN), 5
expedited reporting, 27, 70–73
    See also adverse drug reaction/event

F

"FAX-Back" process, 119
feed additives, 12–13

Food and Drug Regulations (FDR)
    clinical trial definition and requirements, 20–21
    clinical trial surveillance/reporting, 70–73
    clinical trials, 20, 28
    compliance and enforcement framework, 30–34
    CTA submissions, 21–23
    data protection amendment, 80, 89–90, 97
    F&DA as framework, 30–31
    GCP for clinical trials, 26, 28
    generic product definition, 96
    GMP regulation, 32–34
    import/export, 28
    labelling regulation, 127–128
    lot release for biologics, 124–125
    new drug criteria, 46–47, 74t2
    nonprescription drugs, 30–31, 98, 106
    pharmaceutical/device regulation, 4, 61
    postapproval surveillance, 73–76
    post-NOC changes, 60–62
    product standards, 12
    reference products for, 97
    regulatory definitions by, 30t1, 46
    timeline of, 6–9t1
Food and Drugs Act (F&DA)
    See also Food and Drug Regulations
    Blueprint for Renewal, 5
    drug defined by, 46
    Health Canada regulatory framework, 2
    history of, 4, 6–9t1, 30
    HPFB regulation, 12
    labelling requirements, 61, 127
    marketed health products defined, 73
    nonprescription drugs, 106
    regulatory definitions by, 46
    Schedule D (biologics), 116
    scope of, 30–31

G

generic products
    See also Abbreviated New Drug Submissions
    approval of, 95–104
    biologics, 115
    parenterals, 102
    PM(NOC) Regulation, 96
Good Clinical Practice (GCP)
    clinical trials requirements, 20, 26, 28
    drug lifecycle and, 12
Good Laboratory Practice (GLP)
    compliance requirements, 14t1
    filing requirements
        computerized systems/validation, 15
        facilities, 14
        record retention, 14, 14t1
        studies, 13–14

    framework applicability, 13–14
    implementation of, 12–13
    for nonclinical studies, 11–16
    Notifiable Change requirements, 13
    OECD principles/requirements, 12–13, 16
    SCC GLP Monitoring Authority application, 15
    SCC monitoring for, 11–12
    SCC recognition process application, 15–16
Good Manufacturing Practice (GMP), **32–43**
    Active Pharmaceutical Ingredients, 38t1, 42
    biologics submissions, 121
    clinical trial materials, 28, 41
    compliance for NDS, 49
    compliance regulation, 12
    definitions for, 38t1
    DEL for GMP compliance, 32, 49–50
    drug lifecycle and, 12
    ELs for, 43
    Establishment License (GMP/EL), 14
    foreign site compliance, 31–32
    harmonized batch certification, 41
    inspections, 42–43
    interpretation of regulation, 36–41
    licensable activities and, 33t2
    quality management for drugs, 35–36
    quality management system, 34–36
    regulations, 32–35
        for drugs, 35–36
        interpretation examples, **36–41**
    regulatory framework, 8t1, 33t2
    summary of, 42–43
    veterinary drug products, 41
Good Manufacturing Practice (GMP) Regulations
    See also licensable activities
    Equipment, 32, 36
    Finished Product Testing, 33, 39
    guidance documents for, 33
    Manufacturing Control, 32, 37–38, 38
    Packaging Material Testing, 32–33, 39
    Personnel, 32, 36–37
    Pharmaceutical design/development, 38–39
    Premises, 32, 36
    Quality Control Department, 32, 38
    Raw Material Testing, 32, 37, .37, 38
    Records, 33, 39–40
    Samples, 33, 40
    Sanitation, 32, 37
    Stability, 33, 40
    Sterile Products, 33, 40–41

H

harmonization initiatives
    modernization for, 4–5
    MRA for, 31–32, 34

Index

Hatch-Waxman Act, 81
Health Canada, **1–10**
   See also specific branches and directorates
   advertising criteria and review, 129–130
   CTA for biologics, 115
   directorates, 70
   drug GMP documents, 33
   eCTD identifier/dossier identifier request, 142
   eCTD transaction filing, 141
   ethics code and values, 4
   GLP implementation status, 12–13
   history, 1–2, 4–10
   legislative timeline, 6t1–9t1
   mandated safety changes, 62
   modernization and legislation, 4–5, 13
   monograph postings by, 129
   organization and structure, 2–3, 2f1
   pre-NDS meetings, 47
   regional operations, 3
   responsibilities and activities, 3f2, 12
   transparency initiatives, 5
health product legislation
   See also Food and Drug Regulations
   annual summary reports, 76
   cannabis, 9–10
   framework for, 1
   history of, 4–5, **6–9t1**
   nonprescription drug scheduling, 109
   Provincial Pharmacy Legislation and Regulation, 109
   Research Management and Operations Directorate, 4
   self-care framework, 9–10
health product regulation
   advertising, **127–132**
   ANDS, **95–104**
   biologics submissions, **115–125**
   CTA submissions, **19–26**
   DELs, **31–32**
   eCTD for, **133–142**
   GCP in, **26–28**
   GLP for, **11–17**
   GMP for, **33–41**
   Health Canada, **1–10**
   health product vigilance, **69–76**
   intellectual property protection, **79–93**
   labelling, advertising and promotion, **127–132**
   NDS process, **45–57**
   nonprescription drugs, **105–114**
   PM(NOC) Regulation, **80–86**
   postmarketing/maintenance activities, **59–67**
   prescription (pharmaceutical) drugs, **127–132**
   risk management, **76–77**
health product vigilance
   See also adverse drug reaction/event
   clinical trial surveillance

   directorates for, 70
   periodic reporting, 72
   reporting for, 70–72
   issue-related summary report, 76
   post-approval surveillance, ADR reporting, 73–75
   risk management, 76–77
   summary reports for drugs and NHPs, 75–76
Health Product Vigilance Framework, 70
Health Products and Food Branch (HPFB)
   modernization plans, 9–10
   MOU with SCC, 12, 16
   regional operations, 3
   responsibilities and activities, 3–4, 3f2, 12
Health Products and Food Branch Inspectorate (HPFBI)
   compliance monitoring/enforcement, 30–31
   GLP compliance monitoring, 12–16
   GMP inspections, 42–43
Health Products Compliance Directorate, 34
Health Professional Information, 128
Health Protection Act, 4–5, 8t1
   legislative renewal and, 5
Healthy Environment and Consumer Safety Branch, 2

I

import/export
   of API, 42
   drugs for clinical trials, 27t4, 28
   finished product, 43
   regulatory framework, 12
individual case safety report: causality assessment, 70, 71
informed consent documentation
   in CTA submission, 21, 22t1, 23, 28
   REB review of, 27t4
   written form, 27t4
inhalation and nasal products, 103–104
innovative drug
   data protection provisions, 80, 89–90
   defined, 90–91
   exclusivity for, 96–97
   intellectual property information for, 48, 85
inspections
   biologic products, 116, 119, 121–123
   Canadian Food Inspection Agency (CFIA), 2, 2f1, 4, 30–31
   for Certificate of Compliance (CoC), 31, 42
   for EL issue, 42
   equipment, 36
   GLP compliance, 14
   GMP risk classification assignment, 42–43
   harmonization (PIC/s), 34
   for Mutual Recognition Agreement (MRA), 42
   quality management self-inspections, 35, 38
   RORB functions, 4
   SCC recognition process, 15–16

SOPs in, 40
summary report postings of, 5
intellectual property (IP) protection
   24-month stay, 84–85
   administration of PM(NOC) regulations
      listing patents, 81
      patent eligibility, 81–82
   ANDS and SANDS, 83
   CSP listing, 82–83
   CSP Regulations, 80, 86–89
   data protection, 89–90
   dosage claims, 82
   formulation claims, 82
   infringement actions, 84
   medicinal ingredient claims, 82
   medicinal ingredient use claims, 82
   noninfringement/invalidity, 85
   Notice of Allegation (NOA), 84
   OPML patent list audit, 83
   patent relation to SNDS, 82
   patented medicine price control, 90–92
   regime for, 80
   related rights of action, 85
   remedial actions, 85
   updating of patent information, 83
International Council on Harmonisation (ICH)
   biologics submissions, 115
   Common Technical Document, 47
   eCTD specifications, 136
   GMP for APIs, 42
   GMP harmonization, 34–36
   guidelines for nonclinical studies, 13
   human-use pharmaceutical registration, 47
   pharmacovigilance planning, 76
   safety reporting guidance/DSURs, 72–73
   solicited reports for vigilance, 75
Investigational New Drug Submission (INDS), 117
Investigator's Brochure (IB)
   bioavailability study filing, 29
   chemistry and manufacturing, 118
   in CTA submission, 22t1, 23, 71t1
   record retention, 27t4
issue-related summary report (IRSR), 76

L

labelling standards
   components of, 131
   defined, 128
   drug container, 128
   legal framework, 127
   NDS with NOC, 56
   with NOC/c-QN, 56
   nonprescription labelling, 107–108
   PLL requirements for, 5

language requirements
   nonprescription drugs, 108
   PLL requirements, 5
   provincial requirements, 128
Legal Services, 2
Letter of Undertaking, 55, 56, 102
licensable activities, regulations, 33t2
lifecycle management (eCTD)
   documents, 140–141, 140t8
   dossier, 140
   eCTD template/example, 138t6, 139t7
   management/management table, 140, 142
lifecycle management (product)
   benefit-risk profile, 12, 70
   biologics submissions, 115
   regulatory activities during, 59–67
Look-Alike/Sound- Alike assessment, 5, 50–51
Lot Release Program
   biologics, 122
   clinical trials, 118–119
   consistency testing, 122
   documentation for, 117
   evaluation groups for, 122
   evaluation groups summary, 123t4
   postapproval requirements, 122–124
   requirement summary, 123t4
   risk-based, 118
   vaccines, 119, 122

M

Manitoba-Saskatchewan region, 3
marihuana. *See* cannabis
Marihuana for Medical Purposes Regulations (MMPR), 9
Market Authorization Holder (MAH)
   clinical trial responsibilities and activities, 70–75
   foreign, 73
   issue-related summary reporting, 76
   new safety information from, 77
   summary reports/drugs and natural health products, 75
Marketed Health Products Directorate (MHPD)
   adverse event reporting, 73, 75
   advertisement review, 130
   eCTD documentation, 134
   responsibilities and activities, 4
Master File(s) (MFs), 47, 49–50, 100
Maximum Average Potential Price, 91
medical device regulation, 4, 5, 13
Memorandum of Understanding (MOU), HPFB and SCC, 12, 16
Mutual Acceptance of Data (MAD), 11, 14, 16
mutual joint visit (MJV) peer review team, 16
Mutual Recognition Agreement (MRA)
   batch certification, 41

Index

CoC, 31
  definitions for, 30t1
  inspections for, 42

N

nasal and inhalation products, 103–104
National Association of Pharmacy Regulatory Authorities (NAPRA), 109–111
  drug scheduling, 110t1
National Capital Region, 3
National Drug Schedules, 109
National Drug Scheduling Advisory Committee (NDSAC), 110–111
Natural and Non-prescription Health Products Directorate (NNHPD)
  adverse event reporting form, 72
  clinical trial surveillance, 70–72
  clinical trials, 70
  OTC regulation, 4
  responsibilities and activities, 4
Natural Health Products (NHPs)
  ADR reporting, 27t4, 72–73, 76
  CTA submission review, 23, 25
  GLP requirements, 13
  monographs for, 76
  regulatory framework, 4
  submission format and review of, 28
Natural Health Products Regulations (NHP-UPLAR)
  annual summary report (ASR), 75–76
  clinical trial definition and requirements, 20–21
  clinical trial surveillance, 70
  CTA amendments/changes, 22–23, 28
  exemption numbers, 5
  GCP and GMP, 26, 28
  GCP for clinical trials, 26, 28
  NHP clinical trials, 20–21
  post-approval surveillance, 73–76
NERBY (new evidence required by) date, 32
new chemical entity (NCE), 90
new drug submission (NDS) process
  See also biologics submissions
  adding information during review, 52
  appeal procedures, 53
  biologics, 115
  container labelling for, 128
  CTD structure and content, 48–51, 50
  eCTD format and dossier validation, 51, 134
  finalization of review/DIN issue, 52
  ICH guidance, 47
  NDS review and decisions, 52–53, 53t2
  new drug criteria, 46–47
  Notice of Compliance
    NOC/c, 54–56
    NOC/c-QN, 52–53
  Notice of Deficiency, 52
  Notice of Noncompliance, 53
  patent list and, 81–82
  pre-NDS meetings, 47
  preparation and format for, 47–48, 49t1
  pre-submission meetings for, 47
  priority review application, 54
  procedures for, 51f1
  publication of decisions, 53–54
  review/approval process, 51, 53t2
  screening deficiency notice, 51
  submission fees, 54
  submission types/review process, 51–52
New Substances Notification Regulations (NSNR), 51, 99
NHP-UPLAR. *See Natural Health Products Regulations*
No Objection Letter (NOL), 23, 60
nonclinical laboratory studies. *See* Good Laboratory Practice
nonprescription drugs
  advertising, 129
  DIN assignments for kits, 108
  F&DR framework for, 30–31
  ingredient absence declaration, 108
  labelling standards, 5, 107
  monographs for, 106
  NAPRA application, 109
  nonmedicinal ingredients declaration, 8t1
  plain language labeling, 108
  PLL requirements, 5, 9t1
  postmarket changes, 107–108
  Prescription Drug List criteria and, 106
  product monographs, 106
  provincial scheduling of, 109–111
  self-care framework modernization, 9
  submissions, **106–107**
Northwest Territories, 3
Not Satisfactory Notice (NSN), 23
Notice of Allegation (NOA): patent infringement actions, 83, 83–86
Notice of Authorization (NOA), 23
Notice of Compliance (NOC)
  biologics proposed use, 115
  with conditions, 52f2, 54–56, 130
  generic product development, 101–102
  for NCE, 90
  NOC/c-QN, 52–53
  postapproval changes, 60–62
  postapproval changes with, 60
  product advertising, 131
Notice of Deficiency (NOD), 52, 134
Notifiable Change (NC), 13, 60, 128, 134

O

Office of Patented Medicines and Liaison (OPML), 81

Office of Submissions and Intellectual Property (OSIP), 51
old drug (defined), 47
On-Site Evaluation (OSE), 115, 118, 121, 125
Ontario and Nunavut region, 3
Opioid Response Team (ORT), 2
Organisation for Economic Co-operation (OECD) Convention
    compliance monitoring, 13
    OECD principles/requirements, 11–12, 16
over-the-counter (OTC) products
    See also nonprescription drugs
    regulation of, 4
    switch from prescription, 108–109
    Vanessa's Law, 5

P

patent. *See* intellectual property (IP) protection
Patent Act
    bioequivalence/bioavailability studies, 97
    combinations of ingredients, 88
    co-pending CSP applications, 88
    CSP Regulations, 9t1, 86
    early working exception, 80
    eligible medicinal ingredients, 87, 91
    eligible patents, 87
    generic drugs under, 96–97
    infringement actions/remedies, 85
    intellectual property protection, 80
    invention pertaining to medicine, 91
    patented medicine regulation, 2
    patentee defined, 90–91
    PM(NOC) Regulation added, 7t1
    PMPRB established, 66, 90
    price control amendment, 90, 91–92
    second-person obligations, 83
patent register and patent list, 81
patent submission forms, 64f1–65f1, 66
patent term restoration. *See* Certificate of Supplementary Protection
Patented Medicines (Notice of Compliance) Regulations (PM(NOC))
    appeal procedures, 81
    carry-forward provisions, 83
    claims under
        dosage form, 82
        formulation patent claims, 82
        medicinal ingredient claim, 82
        medicinal ingredient use, 82
    early working exception, 80–84
    first-person obligations, 83
    generic drugs under, 81, 96–97
    generic pharmaceuticals, 80
    Notice of Allegation (NOA), 83–86

OPML Patent List audit, 83
    patent list exemptions under, 83
    Patent Register/ Patent List requirements, 81
    protection by, 66
    second-person obligations, 83–84
Patented Medicines Prices Review Board (PMPRB), 59
    See also Patent Act
    comparator countries for, 92
    functions of, 3, 66
    IP protection, 91
    jurisdiction, 90–91
    Maximum Average Potential Price, 91
    organization and structure, 2f1
    price regulation factors, 91–92
    remedial actions, 92
    responsibilities and activities, 90–92
Patient Medication Information, 128–129
Periodic Benefit-Risk Evaluation Report (PBRER), 76
Periodic Safety Update Report (PSUR), 76
Pest Management Regulatory Agency (PMRA), 2, 12–13
Pharmaceutical Advertising Advisory Board (PAAB), 129–130
pharmaceutical equivalent, 96
Pharmaceutical Inspection Cooperation/Scheme (PIC/S), 34–36
pharmaceutical/biological regulation
    abbreviated NDS, **95–104**
    biologics submissions, 115
    Drug Establishment Licenses, 31
    Good Clinical Practice (GCP), **19–28**
    Good Laboratory Practice (GLP), **11–17**
    Good Manufacturing Practice (GMP), 32
    Health Canada, **1–10**
    health product vigilance/risk management, 69
    intellectual property protection, 79
    new drug submission process, **45–57**
    nonprescription drugs, **105–113**
    postmarketing/maintenance activities, **59–67**
pharmacovigilance. *See* health product vigilance
plain language labeling (PLL)
    brand names, 107–108
    drug container labelling, 128
    nonprescription drugs, 5, 9t1
    Patient Medication Information, 128–129
post-approval activities. *See* postmarketing/maintenance activities
postmarketing/maintenance activities
    ADNF completion, 63
    adverse reaction reporting, 73–75
    Advisement Letters, 62
    DIN application changes, 62–63
    DIN inactivation, 63
    discontinuation reporting, 63–64
    DNF completion, 63

Index

drug shortage reporting, 63–64
NOC/c-QN, 56
patent submission forms, 64–65f1, 66
PMPRB review, 66
post-approval stage definitions, 74t2
post-DIN changes, 62
post-NOC changes, 60–62
in regulatory lifecycle, 59
surveillance, 73
prescribing information. *See* Product Monograph
Prescription Drug List
assessment for, 108–109
criteria for listing, 106
Schedule F replacement by, 5
prescription drugs
advertising of, 131
switch to OTC, 108–109
Vanessa's Law, 5
Priority Review status
appeal/reconsideration procedures, 54
eCTD submission, 134
for NDS, 54, 55, 57
Product Monograph Brand Safety Update, 129
Product Monograph (PM)
biologics, 120t3, 121
Category IV/Monographs, 106–107
components of, 131
Consumer Information, 61, 128–129
eCTD submission, 138t8
electronic format for, 138t5
format for, 128–129
    Health Professional Information, 128
    Patient Medication Information, 128–129
    Scientific Information, 128
for Natural Health Products (NHPs), 106–107
in NDSs, 50
nonprescription drugs, 106–107
Patient Medication Information, 128–129
promotion and advertising, **129–131**
See also advertising
Proprietary or Patent Medicine Act, 4
Protecting Canadians from Unsafe Drugs Act
Advisement Letters, 62
postmarketing mandated safety changes, 62
scope of, 5–9
Provincial Pharmacy Legislation and Regulation, 109
Public Health Agency of Canada (PHAC), 2, 4

Q

quality management system (QMS) framework
in GMP compliance, 34–35
wholesale drugs, 35–36
Quality Overall Summary (QOS)
biologics submissions, 116
electronic format for, 138t5
Quebec region, 3

R

radiopharmaceuticals
CTA modifications, 118t1
CTA requirements, 21
labelling, advertising, of, **127–132**
Recall Policy (POL-0016), 38
regulatory authorities
See also Health Canada
independent agencies, 2–3
Regulatory Decision Summaries (RDSs), 5
regulatory framework
adverse event reporting, 70–71
batch certification/MRA, 41, 42
biosimilar products, 116
clinical trial surveillance, 70
clinical trials, 20
CSP issuance and administration, 80
generic product approval, 95–96
for GLP, 13–14
hierarchy in, 31
IP protection, 80–93
labelling and advertising, 127–128
mandated safety changes, 62
for NDS applications, 56–57
pharmacovigilance, 70, 77
PMPRB functions, 66
post-approval surveillance, 73
quality management, 34, 42
self-care modernization, 9
summary reports/drugs and NHPs, 75–76
timeline, 6–9t1
Regulatory Impact Analysis Statement (RIAS), 81
Regulatory Operations and Regions Branch (RORB), 2f1, 4
research and development (R&D) regulation, 66
Research Ethics Board (REB)
biologics submissions, 116
clinical trial approval, 116–117
clinical trial approvals, 20, 26
in clinical trials, 20
CTA refusals, 22t1, 23, 27t3
expedited reporting to, 70
Research Management and Operations Directorate, 4
Risk Classification of GMP Observations (GUI-0023), 42
risk management plan (RMP)
benefit-risk profile, 76
computerized systems/validation, 15
electronic submission, 134
elements of, 76–77
EU RMP or US REMS for, 51, 76
GMP requirements, 35

natural health products, 76
for NDS, 51
with Notifiable Change, 60
objectives of, 76

S

safety reporting
See also Adverse Drug Reaction
changes in benefit-risk assessment, 72
criteria for, 71
foreign MAH, 70, 73
forms for, 72
individual case safety reports, 70
unsolicited, 73
Schedule F replacement, 5
Schedule I -III products. *See* drug schedules
Schedule IV products, 66
Schedule V products, 66
Scientific Information, 128
Screening Deficiency Notice (SDN), 101
self-care framework
See also nonprescription drugs
legislation, 9t1
modernization of, 9–10
overview, 106
self-care products. *See* cosmetics; nonprescription drugs; natural health products
serious adverse drug reaction. *See* adverse drug reaction/event
serious adverse events (SAEs). *See* adverse drug reaction/event
serious unexpected adverse drug reaction. *See* adverse drug reaction/event
short-acting ß2 agonists, 103
SNDS-confirmatory (SNDS-C)
eCTD for, 134
NOD in, 52
postmarket commitments, 56
solicited reports, 74t2, 75
Sponsor Attestation Checklist for ANDS, 138t5
stability (APIs), 42
standard operating procedures (SOPs)
in foreign site compliance, 32
GMP inspections, 40
post-NOC changes, 61
standardization of GLP requirements, 11–12
Standards Council of Canada Act (SCCA), 12
Standards Council of Canada (SCC)
compliance monitoring and, 11–12
facility requirements for GLP recognition inspections, 15
peer review, 16
MOU with HPFB, 12, 16
responsibilities and activities, 12

Strategic Policy Branch, 2
subsequent entry company (second person), 80
sui generis exclusivity, 97
Summary Basis of Decisions (SBDs), 5
Summary Safety Reviews (SSRs), 5
Supplement to a New Drug Submission (SNDS)
See also Canadian Reference Product
eCTD format for, 134
patent and, 82
supplement to ANDS (SANDS)
eCTD format for, 134
patent obligations, 83

T

Therapeutic Access Strategy, 4–5
Therapeutic Products Directorate (TPD)
bioequivalence definition, 97–98
clinical trial surveillance, 70–72
CSP applications, 88–89
expedited reporting to, 72
NDS to, 47
NHP CTA review, 25
nonprescription labelling, 107
Office of Clinical Trials, 70
PM(NOC) Regulation administration, 81
regulatory scope, 31
responsibilities and activities, 4
three-schedule/four-category model scheduling, 109
transfusion. *See* blood and blood components
transparency initiatives, 5
transplantation products regulatory framework, 4
24-month stay, 84–85

U

Unprocessed Product License Applications. *See Natural Health Products Regulations*
Unprocessed Product License Applications (NHP-UPLAR), 5
Unscheduled products, 109
unsolicited reporting, 73
US Drug Price Competition and Patent Term Restoration Act, 81
US Environmental Protection Agency (EPA), 11
US Food and Drug Administration (FDA), 11
US Risk Evaluation and Mitigation Strategy system (REMS), 76
user fees, 5

V

vaccines
evaluation group 1A, 123t4
lot release of, 119, 123
postapproval surveillance, 73
pricing of, 91

Index

Vanessa's Law, 5–9, 62
veterinary drug products
    CSPs for, 80, 86, 97
        data protection provisions, 89
        first authorization for sale, 87
        GLP requirement implementation, 12–13
        GMP for, 34, 41
        prescription status of, 109, 114
        regulation of, 3, 3f1
        regulatory framework, 4, 12
Veterinary Drugs Directorate (VDD), 4, 81
Vigilance Adverse Reaction Online Database, 75
Voluntary Compliance Undertaking (VCU), 92

W

Western region, 3
World Health Organization (WHO)
    adverse reaction causality criteria, 72, 75
    GLP guidance, 16
    GMP harmonization, 34
    resources from, 16

Y

yearly biologic product report (YBPR), 115, 124
Yukon, 3